Auditing
Theory and Practice

Eighth Edition

TO THE STUDENT

A Study Guide is available through your bookstore. The purpose of the Study Guide is to assist you in studying and reviewing the text material and provide you with a means of self-test by the study of the detailed outline, true-false questions, and other objective questions, completion statements, and exercise. These may be used both in your initial study of the chapter material and in your subsequent review. If the Study Guide is not in stock in your bookstore, ask the bookstore manager to order a copy for yourself.

Auditing
Theory and Practice

Eighth Edition

JERRY R. STRAWSER, Ph.D., CPA
Associate Dean
Arthur Andersen & Co. Professor of Accounting
University of Houston

ROBERT H. STRAWSER, D.B.A., CPA
Arthur Andersen & Co. Professor of Accounting
Texas A&M University

1997

DAME
PUBLICATIONS, INC.
Houston, TX 77074

Artist:	Cindy Romero
Cover Design:	Carol Pickens Amanda Austin
Cover Photo:	© Corel Professional Photos (modified)
Desktop Publishing:	Sheryl New Joseph Marquez III Jan Tiefel
Graphics:	Amanda Austin Joseph Marquez III

© **DAME PUBLICATIONS, INC.—1997**
Houston, TX

All rights reserved. No part of this publication may be reproduced, stored in a retrieval system, or transmitted, in any form or by any means, electronic, mechanical, photocopying, recording, or otherwise, without the prior written permission of the publisher.

ISBN 0-87393-616-7

Library of Congress Catalog No. 96-71819

Printed in the United States of America.

Preface

The eighth edition of *Auditing Theory and Practice* continues the traditions established in previous versions. This edition incorporates accounting and auditing pronouncements issued through the fall of 1996 (through *Statement on Auditing Standards No. 79*). In addition, the proposed guidance provided by two important *Exposure Drafts* ("Consideration of Fraud in a Financial Statement Audit" and "Assembly of Financial Statements for Internal Use Only") is also included. This enables students to have an understanding of two very important issues (and the auditing guidance provided for those issues) that are currently facing the auditing profession.

The eighth edition includes a number of new features. In addition to completely updating the contents of the previous edition for relevant professional pronouncements, this edition includes the following changes:

1. Numerous excerpts from articles in both the business and popular press are included throughout the text to illustrate the application of concepts discussed in the text to "real-world" settings. Some of the periodicals referenced include *The Wall Street Journal*, *Forbes*, and *Business Week*. In addition, numerous excerpts related to internal control weaknesses have been drawn from *The Internal Auditor*. Using excerpts in this fashion provides students with an indication of current issues facing the accounting and auditing profession as well as encourages them to follow this profession through articles appearing in the business and popular press.

2. The discussion of the basic auditing process has been substantially changed to reflect the "audit risk" approach addressed in *Statement on Auditing Standards No. 47*. For each account balance, the relevant text chapter discusses factors affecting the inherent risk and control risk associated with each account balance or class of transactions. In addition, the effect of these levels of inherent risk and control risk on the nature, timing, and extent of tests performed by the auditor are discussed. Both discussions focus on individual assertions affecting the account balance or class of transactions.

3. This text utilized both a "cycle" approach and a "balance sheet" approach in discussing the audit examination. From an internal control standpoint, the focus is on four major operating cycles (the Revenue cycle, the Purchases and Disbursements cycle, the Conversion cycle, and the Investing and Financing cycle); relevant control activities for these cycles are discussed as they affect all of the accounts in those cycles. In substantive testing, the discussion focuses on the individual account balances comprising those operating cycles.

4. The chapters discussing internal control (Chapter 5) and the internal control issues related to various operating cycles (Chapters 10, 12, 14, and 15) have been revised to fully incorporate the

definition of internal control provided by the COSO report (and embraced by *Statement on Auditing Standards No. 78*). In addition, these chapters have been revised as follows:

▶ Summary figures are provided that link the various control activities in each operating cycle to the management assertions addressed by those control activities.

▶ The appendix to these chapters provides a discussion of the computerized processing of transactions affecting each of the operating cycles.

5. The chapters discussing substantive tests (Chapter 6) and substantive tests for the various account balances and classes of transactions (Chapters 11, 13, 14, and 15) have been revised to more closely link the various types of substantive tests performed by the auditor to the management assertions addressed by those tests.

6. The discussion of audit reporting has been simplified by including three chapters on audit reporting. Chapter 17 discusses the auditor's responsibility for reporting on the client's financial statements. Chapter 18 discusses the responsibility for reporting on information accompanying the client's financial statements and also discusses special reports and other reports that are provided based on an audit examination. Finally, in Chapter 19, the nature of and reporting responsibility for attestation and accounting and review service engagements are discussed. This discussion has been significantly expanded from the previous edition, consistent with the greater frequency with which accountants conduct these types of engagements.

◘ Organization of the Contents

The material is divided into five categories:

Part I	(Chapters 1-3)	The Auditing Environment
Part II	(Chapters 4-9)	The Audit Process
Part III	(Chapters 10-16)	Audit Procedures
Part IV	(Chapters 17-19)	Auditor's Communications
Part V	(Chapter 20)	Other Types of Auditing

Part I introduces the audit environment, discusses the Code of Professional Conduct, and summarizes the accountant's legal liability under both common and statutory law. Important highlights in these chapters include an excerpted article in Chapter 1 discussing the auditor's role in the financial reporting process (as illustrated by the recent Phar-Mor, Inc. case). In addition, Chapter 3 begins with a Position Paper authored by the Big Six accounting firms which illustrates the various issues facing auditors in today's litigious environment.

Part II covers the basic audit process. Chapters 4, 5, and 6 focus on the major standards of field work (planning the audit, studying internal control, and gathering sufficient and competent evidential matter). As noted previously, these chapters have been substantially revised to focus on the risk assessment process as demonstrated by the audit risk model provided by *Statement on Auditing Standards No. 47*. Chapters 7 and 8 cover audit sampling through comprehensive illustrations and examples. Finally, Chapter 9 provides a discussion of auditing in a computerized processing environment.

Part III is concerned with the specific audit procedures for various types of accounts. This part discusses the four major operating cycles affecting most companies: (1) the Revenue cycle (Chapters 10 and 11); (2) the Purchases and Disbursements cycle (Chapters 12 and 13); (3) the Conversion cycle (Chapter 14); and, (4) the Investing and Financing cycle (Chapter 15). As noted earlier, these chapters have been extensively revised to accommodate both a "cycle" and "balance sheet" approach to auditing. In addition, figures summarizing the relationship between various control activities and substantive testing procedures to the five management assertions are provided. The discussion of internal control related to the Conversion cycle is a particularly important addition from the previous version of the text. This section concludes with various procedures performed by the auditor in the completion stages of the audit (Chapter 16).

Part IV discusses the auditor's reporting responsibility. Chapter 17 introduces audit reporting and the various types of opinions that can be issued by the auditor on the client's financial statements; this discussion is expanded in Chapter 18 by including the auditor's responsibility for reporting on other information accompanying the financial statements and other types of reports that may be issued in an audit examination. These other reports include special reports, reports on financial statements prepared for use in other countries, reports on interim financial information, letters to underwriters, and reports on condensed financial information and selected data. Finally, Chapter 19 includes an expanded discussion of attestation and accounting and review service engagements and reports. The dedication of an entire chapter to these engagements and reports is consistent with the increased frequency with which these engagements are performed and allows instructors to have maximum flexibility in discussing audit reporting.

The final part of the text (Part V) discusses compliance, internal, and operational auditing and contrasts these types of auditing with financial statement audits. Particular emphasis has been placed on compliance auditing, since this topic has been the subject of recent pronouncements of the AICPA.

Other Special Features

The following features have been retained and enhanced from previous versions of the text:

- ▶ Using learning objectives at the introduction of the chapter to preview the important issues to be discussed in that chapter.
- ▶ Including a glossary of key terms, a summary of major points, and a listing of professional pronouncements at the end of each chapter.
- ▶ Incorporating numerous questions and problems both throughout and at the end of each chapter.

One significant change from the previous versions of this text is the use of "Chapter Checkpoints" throughout the chapter. These checkpoints are short questions that highlight the most important concepts covered in that section of the chapter. The use of these checkpoints should allow students to assess their understanding of the material in each chapter before proceeding to the next section.

Acknowledgements

The authors appreciate the permissions to use materials under copyright. We especially thank the American Institute of Certified Public Accountants for permission to use material from the Uniform CPA Examination as well as from other sources. Throughout the text, constant reference is made to current AICPA pronouncements.

Several individuals have made helpful comments on various portions of the manuscript. These individuals include James C. Flagg, David S. Kerr, and L. Murphy Smith of Texas A & M University;

John Ledbetter and Eric Typpo of the University of Houston; and Roselyn Morris of Southwest Texas State University. A special thanks is given to Timothy Louwers of the University of Houston for the numerous discussions, insights, and comments he has provided with regards to this text and auditing education in general.

Finally, we acknowledge a special thanks to Joseph Marques III, Sheryl New, Cindy Romero, and Jan Tiefel for turning our draft materials into the finished product. Without their valuable assistance, the final output would not have been possible. These individuals made the entire process truly enjoyable and ensured a timely completion of all necessary tasks. Of course, the authors are solely responsible for any shortcomings in the final version.

1997

Jerry R. Strawser
Robert H. Strawser

Table of Contents

Part I

The Auditing Environment

1 The CPA and the Auditing Environment 1-1

THE PURPOSE OF AUDITING. The Definition of Auditing. Why do Audits Occur? Parties Involved in the Audit. THE PUBLIC ACCOUNTING/AUDITING ENVIRONMENT. CPA Firms. Hierarchy within the Firm. Types of Audits. Types of Auditors. Functions Other than Auditing. PROFESSIONAL ORGANIZATIONS OF ACCOUNTANTS. American Institute of Certified Accountants (AICPA). State Societies. Boards of Accountancy. Securities and Exchange Commission. AUDITING STANDARDS. General Standards. Standards of Field Work. Standards of Reporting. Statements on Auditing Standards (SASs). **APPENDIX**. They're Bean Counters, Not Gumshoes. SUMMARY OF KEY POINTS. GLOSSARY. SUMMARY OF PROFESSIONAL PRONOUNCEMENTS. QUESTIONS AND PROBLEMS.

2 The Code of Professional Conduct 2-1

WHY IS A CODE OF CONDUCT IMPORTANT? THE STRUCTURE OF THE CODE OF PROFESSIONAL CONDUCT. Principles. Rules of Conduct. Interpretations and Ethics Rulings. RULES OF CONDUCT. Independence: Rule 101. Integrity and Objectivity: Rule 102. General Standards: Rule 201. Compliance with Standards: Rule 202. Accounting Principles: Rule 203. Confidential Client Information: Rule 301. Contingent Fees: Rule 302. Acts Discreditable: Rule 501. Advertising: Rule 502. Commissions: Rule 503. Form of Organization and Name: Rule 505. ENFORCEMENT OF THE CODE OF CONDUCT. QUALITY CONTROL. Monitoring Quality Control Standards: Peer Reviews. **APPENDIX**. CURRENT INTERPRETATIONS UNDER THE CODE OF PROFESSIONAL CONDUCT. Interpretations of Rule 101: Independence. Interpretations of Rule 102: Integrity and Objectivity. Interpretation of Rule 201: General Standards. Interpretations of Rule 203: Accounting Principles. Interpretations of Rule 301: Confidential Client Information. Interpretation of Rule 302: Contingent Fees. Interpretations of Rule 501: Acts Discreditable. Interpretations of Rule 502: Advertising and Solicitation. Interpretations of Rule 505: Form of Practice and Name. SUMMARY OF KEY POINTS. GLOSSARY. SUMMARY OF PROFESSIONAL PRONOUNCEMENTS. QUESTIONS AND PROBLEMS.

3 Auditors' Legal Liability 3-1

LITIGATION, LIABILITY, AND THE ACCOUNTING PROFESSION. OVERVIEW OF LEGAL LIABILITY. Terminology. COMMON LAW LIABILITY. Liability to Clients and Subrogees. Liability to Third Parties. Significant Court Cases under Common Law. STATUTORY LIABILITY. Securities and Exchange Commission (SEC). Securities Act of 1933. Securities Exchange Act of 1934. Auditor's Liability under the 1933 Act. Auditor's Liability under the 1934 Act. OTHER STATUTORY LIABILITY. LEGAL LIABILITY: WHAT DOES THE FUTURE HOLD? SUMMARY. **APPENDIX A:** Summary of Other Court Cases under Common Law. Liability to Clients and Subrogees. Liability to Third Parties Other than Primary Beneficiaries. **APPENDIX B:** Summary of Other Court Cases under Statutory Law. McKesson & Robbins. National Student Marketing Case. Yale Express Case. Continental Vending Case. Equity Funding Case. Other Cases. SUMMARY OF KEY POINTS. GLOSSARY. SUMMARY OF PROFESSIONAL PRONOUNCEMENTS. QUESTIONS AND PROBLEMS.

Part II
The Audit Process

4 Audit Planning 4-1

OVERVIEW OF THE AUDIT EXAMINATION. Preengagement and Audit Planning. Studying and Evaluating Internal Control. Substantive Testing Procedures. Issuing the Audit Report. PREENGAGEMENT PROCEDURES. Client Contact. Accepting the Engagement. Engagement Letters. AUDIT PLANNING. Obtaining Knowledge about the Client. Responsibility for Financial Statement Misstatements. Determining an Audit Strategy: Materiality, Management Assertions, and Audit Risk. Materiality. Management Assertions. Audit Risk Model. OTHER PLANNING ISSUES. Related Parties and Related-Party Transactions. Using the Work of a Specialist. Internal Audit Function. Performing Preliminary Analytical Procedures. Preparing the Audit Program. SUPERVISION AND STAFFING. ROLE OF PLANNING IN THE AUDIT. **APPENDIX: Proposed Statement on Auditing Standards, Consideration of Fraud in a Financial Statement Audit.** OVERVIEW OF FRAUD. THE AUDITOR'S RESPONSIBILITY FOR FRAUD IN THE FINANCIAL STATEMENT AUDIT. Factors Affecting the Risk of Fraud. Effect of Fraud on Substantive Testing Procedures. Communicating Fraud Discovered during the Engagement. SUMMARY OF KEY POINTS. GLOSSARY. SUMMARY OF PROFESSIONAL PRONOUNCEMENTS. QUESTIONS AND PROBLEMS.

5 Internal Control and the Assessment of Control Risk 5-1

THE AUDIT PROCESS AND AUDIT RISK. OVERVIEW OF INTERNAL CONTROL. Definition of Internal Control. Components of Internal Control. Other Internal Control Considerations. STUDYING INTERNAL CONTROL. Identifying a Preliminary Audit Strategy. Understanding the Components of internal Control. Documenting the Understanding of Internal Control. Making an

Initial Assessment of Control Risk. Obtaining an Additional Reduction in Control Risk. Making a Final Assessment of Control Risk. Documenting Control Risk Assessments. Using the Audit Risk Model to Determine the Necessary Level of Detection Risk. Summary: The Auditor's Study of Internal Control. OTHER ISSUES RELATED TO INTERNAL CONTROL. Communicating Internal Control Deficiencies. Reporting on Internal Control. SUMMARY OF KEY POINTS. GLOSSARY. SUMMARY OF PROFESSIONAL PRONOUNCEMENTS. QUESTIONS AND PROBLEMS.

6 Substantive Testing and Control of Detection Risk 6-1

THE AUDIT PROCESS AND AUDIT RISK. OVERVIEW OF SUBSTANTIVE TESTS. Third Standard of Field Work. Types of Evidence. Qualities of Evidence. Qualities of Evidence: A Summary. General Approaches to Substantive Testing. DETERMINING DETECTION RISK. Factors Affecting Levels of Detection Risk. Detection Risk and Management Assertions. SUBSTANTIVE TESTING PROCEDURES. Physical Observation. Inspecting Documents. Confirmation. Analytical Procedures. Recalculations. Comparisons. Oral Inquiry. Summary: Substantive Testing Procedures. WORKING PAPERS. Types of Workpapers. Interrelationship Among Workpapers. Filing of Workpapers. Ownership and Custody of Workpapers. Workpaper Review. SUMMARY OF KEY POINTS. GLOSSARY. SUMMARY OF PROFESSIONAL PRONOUNCEMENTS. QUESTIONS AND PROBLEMS.

7 Introduction to Sampling and Attribute Sampling 7-1

AUDIT SAMPLING. Sampling Risk versus Nonsampling Risk. Statistical versus Nonstatistical Sampling. Precision and Reliability. Incorporating Statistical Concepts into the Sampling Plan. ATTRIBUTE SAMPLING. Overview of Attribute Sampling. Risks Associated with Attribute Sampling. STEPS IN PERFORMING ATTRIBUTE SAMPLING. Defining the Deviation Conditions. Defining the Population. Determining the Sample Selection Method. Determining Sample Size. Performing the Sampling Plan. Evaluating the Sample Results. OTHER ATTRIBUTE SAMPLING APPLICATIONS. Nonstatistical Sampling. Discovery Sampling. Sequential (Stop-or-Go) Sampling. SUMMARY OF KEY POINTS. GLOSSARY. SUMMARY OF PROFESSIONAL PRONOUNCEMENTS. QUESTIONS AND PROBLEMS.

8 Variables Estimation Sampling 8-1

OVERVIEW OF VARIABLES SAMPLING. Sampling Risks. OVERVIEW: CLASSICAL VARIABLES SAMPLING. Normal Distribution. Standard Deviation. Basic Decision Process in Classical Variables Sampling. CLASSICAL VARIABLES SAMPLING: MEAN-PER-UNIT ESTIMATION. Determining the Audit Objective of the Test. Defining the Population. Choosing an Audit Sampling Technique. Determining Sample Size. Determining the Method of Selecting the Sample. Performing the Sampling Plan. Evaluating the Sample Results. Example: Mean-per-Unit Estimation. OTHER CLASSICAL VARIABLES METHODS: DIFFERENCE AND RATIO ESTIMATION. Difference Estimation. Ratio Estimation. Alternative Approaches to Classical Variables Sampling. Summary: Classical Variables Sampling Methods. PROBABILITY-PROPORTIONAL-TO-SIZE (PPS) SAM-

PLING. Determining Sample Size. Selecting the Sample. Evaluating Sample Results. PPS Sampling versus Classical Variables Sampling. **APPENDIX A:** Controlling Exposure to Sampling Risks. Risk of Incorrect Rejection. Risk of Incorrect Acceptance. **APPENDIX B:** Nonstatistical Sampling. Example: Nonstatistical Sampling. SUMMARY OF KEY POINTS. GLOSSARY. SUMMARY OF PROFESSIONAL PRONOUNCEMENTS. QUESTIONS AND PROBLEMS.

9 Computer Controls and Audit Techniques 9-1

COMPUTERIZED ACCOUNTING SYSTEMS. Batch Processing. Interactive Processing. Batch Processing versus Interactive Processing. Computerized versus Manual Processing. COMPUTER CONTROLS. General Controls. Application Controls. EVALUATING COMPUTER CONTROLS AND ASSESSING CONTROL RISK. General Controls. Application Controls. Service Bureau (Service Organization). ACCESSING DATA MAINTAINED ON CLIENT COMPUTER FILES. SUMMARY OF KEY POINTS. GLOSSARY. SUMMARY OF PROFESSIONAL PRONOUNCEMENTS. QUESTIONS AND PROBLEMS.

Part III

Audit Procedures

10 The Revenue Cycle 10-1

WHAT IS AN OPERATING CYCLE? EVALUATING INTERNAL CONTROL: THE REVENUE CYCLE. Control Environment. Risk Assessment and Control Activities: The Credit Sales Subcycle. Risk Assessment and Control Activities: The Sales Adjustments Subcycle. Risk Assessment and Control Activities: The Cash Receipts Subcycle. Information and Communication. Monitoring. **APPENDIX.** COMPUTERIZED PROCESSING IN THE REVENUE CYCLE. Credit Sales. Cash Receipts and Sales Adjustments. SUMMARY OF KEY POINTS. GLOSSARY. QUESTIONS AND PROBLEMS.

11 The Revenue Cycle: Substantive Tests 11-1

OVERALL AUDIT APPROACH. ACCOUNTS RECEIVABLE. Inherent and Control Risk. Detection Risk. CASH. Inherent and Control Risk. Detection Risk. AUDITING SALES. Tests of the Sales Register (or Sales Journal). Analytical Procedures. Sales Cutoff Tests. SUMMARY OF KEY POINTS. GLOSSARY. SUMMARY OF PROFESSIONAL PRONOUNCEMENTS. QUESTIONS AND PROBLEMS.

12 The Purchases and Disbursements Cycle 12-1

EVALUATING INTERNAL CONTROL: THE PURCHASES AND DISBURSEMENTS CYCLE. Control Environment. Risk Assessment and Control Activities: The Purchases Subcycle. Risk Assessment and Control Activities: The Cash Disbursements Subcycle. Information and Communication. Monitoring. **APPENDIX:** Computerized Processing in the Purchases and Disbursements Cycle. Purchases Subcycle. Cash Disbursements Subcycle. SUMMARY OF KEY POINTS. GLOSSARY. QUESTIONS AND PROBLEMS.

13 The Purchases and Disbursements Cycle: Substantive Tests 13-1

OVERALL AUDIT APPROACH. INVENTORY. Inherent and Control Risk. Detection Risk. ACCOUNTS PAYABLE. Inherent and Control Risk. Detection Risk. ACCRUED PAYABLES AND DEFERRED ASSETS. COST OF GOODS SOLD/PURCHASES. Tests of the Voucher Register (Purchases Journal). Analytical Procedures. Purchase Cutoff Tests. SUMMARY OF KEY POINTS. GLOSSARY. SUMMARY OF PROFESSIONAL PRONOUNCEMENTS. QUESTIONS AND PROBLEMS.

14 The Conversion Cycle 14-1

EVALUATING INTERNAL CONTROL: THE CONVERSION CYCLE. Control Environment. Risk Assessment and Control Activities: The Payroll Subcycle. Risk Assessment and Control Activities: The Production Subcycle. Information and Communication. Monitoring. SUBSTANTIVE TESTS OF INVENTORY BALANCES. SUBSTANTIVE TESTS OF PAYROLL TRANSACTIONS. Inherent and Control Risk for Payroll Transactions. Detection Risk (Substantive Tests) for Payroll Transactions. **APPENDIX:** Computerized Processing in the Conversion Cycle. PAYROLL SUBCYCLE. PRODUCTION SUBCYCLE. SUMMARY OF KEY POINTS. GLOSSARY. QUESTIONS AND PROBLEMS.

15 The Investing and Financing Cycle 15-1

AUDITING THE NEW INVESTING AND FINANCING CYCLE. EVALUATING INTERNAL CONTROL: THE INVESTING AND FINANCE CYCLE. Control Environment. Risk Assessment and Control Activities. Information and Communication. Monitoring. SUBSTANTIVE TESTS: INVESTMENTS. Obtaining or Preparing a Listing of Securities. Verifying Investment Transactions. Inspecting or Confirming Securities. Verifying Market Values. Examining Investment Revenue Accounts. Performing Analytical Procedures. Evaluating Financial Statement Presentation. SUBSTANTIVE TESTS: PROPERTY, PLANT AND EQUIPMENT. Obtaining or Preparing a Listing of PPE. Verifying PPE Transactions. Inspecting PPE and Title to PPE. Examining Subsequent Expenditures. Evaluating the Provision for Depreciation. Performing Analytical Procedures. Evaluating Financial Statement Presentation. SUBSTANTIVE TESTS: NOTES PAYABLE AND LONG-TERM DEBT. Obtaining or Preparing a Listing of IBLS. Verifying IBL Transactions. Inspecting or Confirming IBLS. Recalculating Interest Expense. Searching for Unrecorded Liabilities. Performing Analytical Procedures. Evaluating Financial Statement Presentation. SUBSTANTIVE TESTS: STOCKHOLDER'S

EQUITY ACCOUNTS. Obtaining or Preparing a Schedule of Changes in Stockholders' Equity. Verifying Stockholders' Equity Transactions. Inspecting or Confirming Shares Issued and Outstanding. Verifying Retained Earnings. Performing Analytical Procedures. Evaluating Financial Statement Presentation. SUMMARY OF KEY POINTS. GLOSSARY. SUMMARY OF PROFESSIONAL PRONOUNCEMENTS. QUESTIONS AND PROBLEMS.

16 Completing the Audit Examination 16-1

COMPLETING THE AUDIT. Subsequent Events. Letters of Inquiry. Client Representations. Analytical Procedures. Workpaper Review. Evaluating the Results. THE POSTAUDIT PERIOD. Subsequent Discovery of Facts. Consideration of Omitted Procedures after the Report Date. COMMUNICATIONS WITH THE CLIENT. Communications Related to Internal Control. Other Communications with Audit Committees. Management Letters. SUMMARY OF KEY POINTS. SUMMARY OF PROFESSIONAL PRONOUNCEMENTS. GLOSSARY. QUESTIONS AND PROBLEMS.

Part IV
Auditor's Communications

17 The Auditor's Report 17-1

THE AUDITOR'S REPORT. The Body of the Report. Other Information in the Report. Reporting Standards. Types of Opinions. REASONS FOR DEPARTURE FROM THE WORDING OF THE STANDARD REPORT. Scope Limitations. Division of Responsibility. Lack of Conformity with GAAP. Departure from a Promulgated Principle. Consistency. Uncertainties. Emphasizing a Matter in the Report. Independence. Summary: Departures from the Auditor's Standard Report. COMPARATIVE FINANCIAL STATEMENTS. Comparative Statements not Audited. Comparative Statements Examined by the Same Auditor. Comparative Statements Examined by Another Auditor. Summary: Comparative Reporting. SUMMARY OF KEY POINTS. GLOSSARY. SUMMARY OF PROFESSIONAL PRONOUNCEMENTS. QUESTIONS AND PROBLEMS.

18 Reporting: Other Information and Special Reports 18-1

REPORTING ON INFORMATION PRESENTED WITH THE FINANCIAL STATEMENTS. Other Information Prepared by the Client. Segment Information. Reporting on Required Supplementary Information. Reporting on Information Accompanying the Basic Financial Statements in Auditor-Submitted Documents. Summary: Other Reporting Responsibilities. SPECIAL REPORTS. Basis Other than GAAP. Reports on Specific Elements, Accounts, or Items. Compliance with Contractual Agreements. Financial Presentations Intended to Comply with Contractual or Regulatory Requirements. Prescribed Forms. Summary: Special Reports. OTHER TYPES OF REPORTS ISSUED

IN CONJUNCTION WITH AUDITED FINANCIAL STATEMENTS. Financial Statements Prepared for use in Other Countries. Review of Interim Financial Information. Letters for Underwriters and Other Third Parties. Condensed Financial Statements and Selected Financial Data. SUMMARY OF KEY POINTS. GLOSSARY. SUMMARY OF PROFESSIONAL PRONOUNCEMENTS. QUESTIONS AND PROBLEMS.

19 Other Accountant Engagements and Reports 19-1

ATTESTATION SERVICES. REPORTING ON MANAGEMENT'S ASSERTION ABOUT INTERNAL CONTROL. Management's Assertion about the Effectiveness of the Organization's Internal Control. Management's Assertion about the Effectiveness of a Segment of the Organization's Internal Control. Management's Assertion about the Suitability of the Design of the Organization's Internal Control. Management's Assertion Based on Criteria Specified by a Regulatory Agency. REPORTING ON MANAGEMENT'S ASSERTION ABOUT COMPLIANCE WITH SPECIFIED REQUIREMENTS. PROSPECTIVE FINANCIAL INFORMATION. Types of Prospective Financial Information. Information Provided as Prospective Financial Information. Use of Prospective Financial Information. Engagements Related to Prospective Financial Information. *PRO FORMA* FINANCIAL INFORMATION. ACCOUNTING AND REVIEW SERVICES. Assembly of Financial Statement for Internal Use. Compilation Engagements. Review Engagements. Comparative Reporting Involving Accounting and Review Services. Other Issues Involving Accounting and Review Services. Summary: Accounting and Review Services for Nonpublic Companies. **APPENDIX:** Attestation Standards. SUMMARY OF KEY POINTS. GLOSSARY. SUMMARY OF PROFESSIONAL PRONOUNCEMENTS. QUESTIONS AND PROBLEMS.

Part V

Other Types of Auditing

20 Compliance, Internal, and Operational Auditing 20-1

COMPLIANCE AUDITING. Compliance Auditing in a GAAS Audit. *Government Auditing Standards (The Yellow Book)*. The Single Audit Act. Summary: Compliance Auditing. INTERNAL AUDITING. The Role of Internal Auditing in the Organization. Differences Between Internal Auditing and External Auditing. Code of Ethics. Standards of Internal Auditing. OPERATIONAL AUDITING. Who Performs Operational Audits? Steps in Performing an Operational Audit. SUMMARY: CLASSIFICATIONS OF AUDITING. **APPENDIX.** INTERNAL AUDITING STANDARDS. IIA Standards. SUMMARY OF KEY POINTS. GLOSSARY. SUMMARY OF PROFESSIONAL PRONOUNCEMENTS. QUESTIONS AND PROBLEMS.

Index I-1

I

The Auditing Environment

Learning Objectives

Study of the material in this chapter is designed to achieve several learning objectives. After studying this chapter, you should be able to:

1. Understand the purpose of auditing and identify why audits are performed.
2. Define financial statement audits, compliance audits, and operational audits.
3. List the types of services other than audits that are provided by public accountants and accounting firms.
4. Describe the types of accounting firms and the typical hierarchial structure within a public accounting firm.
5. Define auditing standards and list the ten generally accepted auditing standards.
6. Describe the basic contents of the auditor's report.

1

The CPA and the Auditing Environment

⊙ THE PURPOSE OF AUDITING

To this point in your accounting education, the focus has been on the process of financial accounting. **Financial accounting** is commonly defined as the process of interpreting, classifying, recording, and summarizing financial data. To provide a cursory overview of the financial accounting process, consider the following sequence of events.

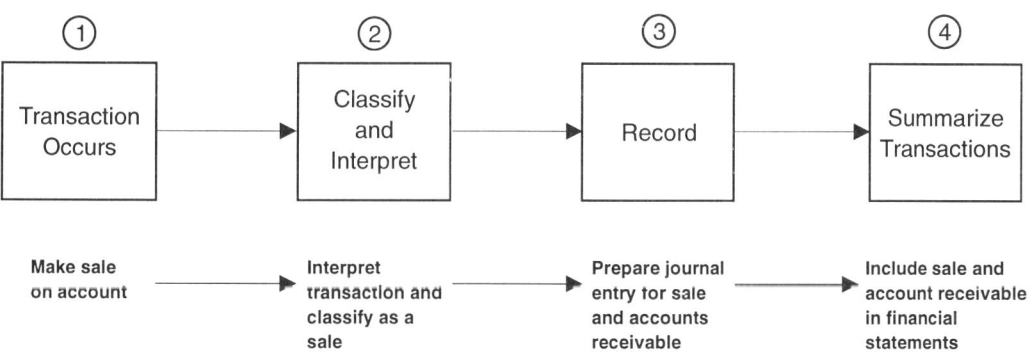

As shown above, the accounting process begins with the occurrence of a transaction or event. In the above illustration, the event represents a sale made on account to one of the entity's customers (Step 1). The entity then interprets this event and determines that a sale has occurred (classification and interpretation) (Step 2). Once the transaction has been interpreted and classified as a sale, the appropriate journal entry is made; this represents the recording element (Step 3). Finally, the information is summarized by including the effects of the journal entry in the entity's financial statements (Step

4). Thus, financial accounting begins with the occurrence of an event or transaction and culminates in the preparation of the entity's financial statements.

Once prepared, the entity's financial statements are used by individuals outside (or external) to the entity for making economic decisions. These users are referred to as **external users** and may include bankers, creditors, and investors. The types of decisions made by these individuals include:

▶ Should I (we) loan money or extend credit to the entity?

▶ Should I (we) invest money in the entity?

What is wrong with the above sequence? The problem lies with who is responsible for preparing the financial statements. **Financial accounting is performed by the entity itself.** Clearly, an incentive exists on the part of the entity to present its financial condition in the best possible light. To illustrate problems that arise from such an incentive, suppose your instructor allowed you to submit your own grade for this course. Would you have an incentive to submit a grade higher than what you actually deserve? More importantly, could other individuals (potential employers, parents, and friends) trust and rely on your grade if you were permitted to submit it to your instructor?

Since the management of the entity is responsible for preparing its own financial statements, users of financial statements have the same dilemma. Because of these problems, a potential lender or investor would be unable to rely on financial statements prepared by management without some form of independent verification. This independent verification is provided in the form of an audit examination.

◻ The Definition of Auditing

The American Accounting Association's Committee on Basic Auditing Concepts has broadly defined **auditing** as:

> "... a systematic process of objectively obtaining and evaluating evidence regarding assertions about economic actions and events to ascertain the degree of correspondence between those assertions and established criteria and communicating the results to interested users."[1]

This definition reveals the following three key aspects related to auditing.

▶ Auditing involves obtaining and evaluating evidence. Evidence is collected by the auditor as he or she evaluates the entity's financial statements.

▶ The evidence gathered by the auditor is used in relation to the second key aspect related to auditing: ascertaining the degree of correspondence between assertions and established criteria. In an audit, the assertions are the financial statements prepared by management; the

---

[1] Joseph A. Silvoso, et al., "Report of the Committee on Basic Auditing Concepts," *The Accounting Review 47* (Supplement 1972), 18.

established criteria are accounting principles (normally, generally accepted accounting principles, or GAAP). Thus, stated another way, the basic purpose of an audit is to determine **whether the entity's financial statements are prepared according to GAAP**.

▶ Finally, the auditor communicates the results of the audit to interested users. This communication is made in the form of an audit report (or opinion). The interested users are third parties, such as stockholders, creditors, and other individuals who make economic decisions regarding the entity.

To briefly illustrate the definition of an audit, assume that an entity is applying for a loan and offers $100,000 of its accounts receivable as collateral. Naturally, the lender is interested in determining whether these accounts receivable are presented in accordance with GAAP. Because of the conflict of interest mentioned earlier, the lender requests an audit of the accounts receivable. The three aspects of the definition of an audit are as follows (see Figure 1-1).

1. In evaluating the accounts receivable, the auditor will gather evidence related to the accounts receivable by confirming (or asking) the customers about the accuracy of the balances.
2. In gathering this evidence, the auditor is verifying that accounts receivable are presented in accordance with GAAP.
3. Finally, the auditor's opinion is used by the lender in making his or her economic decision (should money be loaned to the entity?).

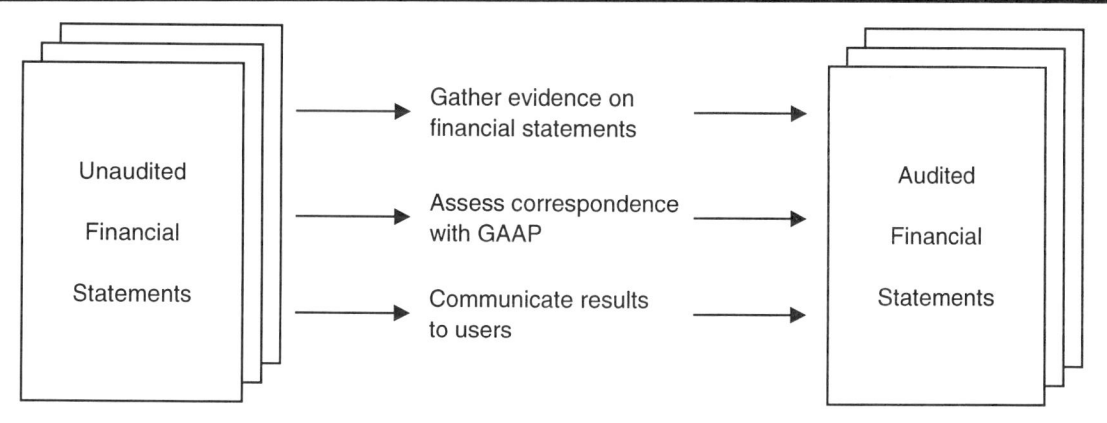

Figure 1-1: *Summary of the Audit Process*

1 / The Purpose of Auditing 1-3

Another term that is used synonymously with auditing is **attestation**. The American Institute of Certified Public Accountants (AICPA) has defined an attest engagement as:

> ... one in which a practitioner is engaged to issue or does issue a written communication that expresses a conclusion about the reliability of a written assertion that is the responsibility of another party.[2]

An audit is an example of an attest engagement, since the auditor issues a written communication (audit opinion) about the reliability of a written assertion (financial statements) that is the responsibility of another party (the entity's management). However, other types of attest engagements exist. These engagements are discussed in more detail later in this text.

◻ Why do Audits Occur?

Audits are performed on the financial statements of two major types of entities. **Public companies** are companies whose securities trade in a public market, either on a stock exchange or in the over-the-counter market. Companies such as Microsoft, McDonald's, Wal-Mart, and Motorola are public companies; their securities trade on stock exchanges such as the New York Stock Exchange, American Stock Exchange, or over-the-counter in the National Association of Securities Dealers Automated Quotations (NASDAQ) market. As discussed in more detail in Chapter 3, public companies must periodically file financial information with the Securities and Exchange Commission (SEC). This information includes financial statements that are audited by an independent accountant. Thus, public companies are required to have their financial statements audited.

Nonpublic companies are companies other than those whose securities trade in a public market. A restaurant owned and operated by a local businessman and the Cleveland Indians baseball team are examples of nonpublic companies. Because these companies do not trade securities in a public market, they are not required to have an independent audit examination. However, in certain cases, users may request an audit. For example, if the restaurant owner asks you to invest in his or her business, you may request audited financial statements for use in your decision. Similarly, if the owner of the Cleveland Indians is attempting to secure a loan to use in operating the baseball team, the creditors may request audited financial statements. Therefore, for nonpublic companies, audits are normally based on user demand.

◻ Parties Involved in the Audit

Three major groups of individuals are involved in the audit process: (1) the entity whose financial statements are being evaluated (the client), (2) the auditor, and (3) third-party users. The relationship among these parties is show below in Figure 1-2.

As shown in Figure 1-2, the auditor examines the financial statements of the entity (or client) to determine whether they are prepared in accordance with GAAP. Upon completing this examination,

---

[2] American Institute of Certified Public Accountants (AICPA), "Attestation Standards," *Statements on Standards for Attestation Engagements No. 1*, (New York: AICPA, 1985, AT 100.01).

the auditor then issues a report on his or her examination that is considered by third-party users in making economic decisions. These decisions involve the entity whose financial statements were examined.

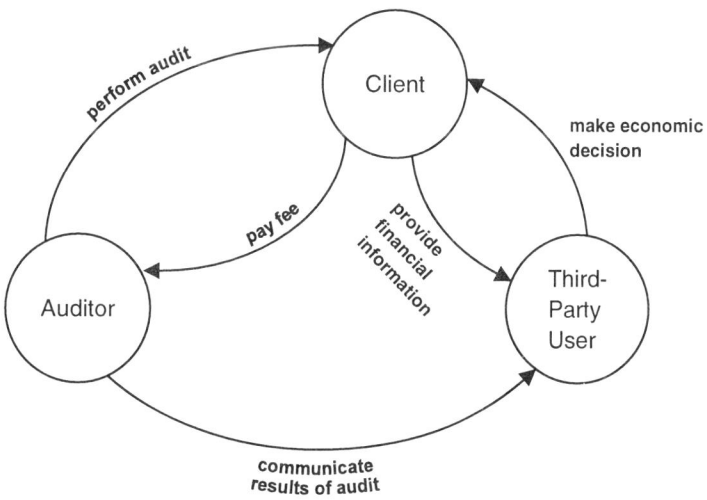

Figure 1-2: *Communication during the Audit*

At this point, it is important to note that performing an audit of the financial statements does not alter the primary communication between the entity and interested users. That is, the entity's management is still responsible for the content and fairness of the financial statements. Also, users still desire financial information (in the form of financial statements) to assist them in making economic decisions involving the entity. The audit function merely adds a secondary line of communication to the financial reporting process.

WHOSE FINANCIAL STATEMENTS ARE THEY, ANYWAY?[3]

The responsibility for the company's financial statements is illustrated by a recent action filed against Deloitte & Touche by the city of Miami, Florida. City officials have charged Deloitte with failing to keep the city informed of its perilous financial condition. Francisco Paredes, a partner with Deloitte, summed up the arguments as follows: "[t]hese are your [city of Miami's] financial statements; the only thing that's our's [Deloitte's] is the opinion."

---

[3] "Miami Declares Fiscal Emergency; Deloitte Dismissed," *The Wall Street Journal* (October 8, 1996), A12.

1 / The Purpose of Auditing

The interrelationships among the client, auditor, and third-party users place the auditor in an unusual position. The auditor's responsibility is to examine the fairness of the client's financial statements. In doing so, the auditor may perform a study of the client's internal controls and provide that client with recommendations allowing them to improve their internal controls. Therefore, the audit examination provides direct benefits to the client. However, the auditor's primary obligation is to third-party users; these users rely on the auditor's opinion in making their economic decisions. Based on this obligation, auditors must act in an objective, unbiased manner toward their clients. Further compounding this situation is the fact that the auditor ordinarily is compensated for his or her services by the client.

The need for an objective attitude on the part of the auditor has resulted in the requirement that prohibits certain relationships between auditors and their clients. For example, auditors are not permitted to own shares of their clients' stock. These types of relationships are related to the auditor's independence and are discussed later in this and other chapters of this text.

CHAPTER CHECKPOINTS

1-1. Discuss the basic financial accounting process. Why does management have a conflict of interest in this process?

1-2. Define the term auditing. Many individuals state that the audit process modifies the basic communication between a company and third-party users. Comment on this statement.

1-3. Who are the primary users of the auditor's report? For what purposes is this report used?

1-4. Define an attest engagement. Is an audit a type of attest engagement?

1-5. What are the two major types of companies that have audits? Why does each type have an audit conducted?

1-6. Who are the three major parties involved in an audit? What are their roles in this process?

THE PUBLIC ACCOUNTING/AUDITING ENVIRONMENT

CPA Firms

Certified Public Accountants (CPAs)[4] conduct their practices as individual practitioners or in firms. CPA firms are generally classified into one of three categories: (1) national firms, (2) regional firms, and (3) local firms.

Until recently, the largest international accounting firms were commonly referred to as the Big Eight. Two mergers reduced this select group of firms from eight to six.[5] The Big Six firms (Arthur Andersen & Co. LLP, Coopers & Lybrand LLP, Deloitte & Touche LLP, Ernst & Young LLP, KPMG Peat Marwick LLP, and Price Waterhouse LLP) have offices throughout the United States and worldwide. The Big Six firms provide audit services to approximately 95 percent of all companies listed on the New York Stock Exchange.[6] In addition to the Big Six, other firms have also attained national stature (e.g., BDO Seidman). National firms generally provide audit, tax, consulting, and a wide array of other services to clients.

Other types of CPA firms have offices in either a few geographic regions or in a single city. These firms are referred to as regional and local firms. Regional and local firms perform audits, although not on as large a scale or for the large clients serviced by national firms. Regional and local firms normally derive a larger proportion of their revenues from non-audit services, such as tax, consulting, and bookkeeping services.

Hierarchy within the Firm

Audit examinations are normally conducted by groups (or teams) of auditors occupying different position levels within the firm. Each of these individuals has certain duties that she or he commonly performs during the course of an audit examination. The following paragraphs identify the various position levels within the firm and describe some of the primary duties of each level.

Partners. In a firm organized as a partnership, the partners own and administer their firm. They maintain the primary contact with clients and have the ultimate responsibility in the audit. Generally, partners review and approve the work of subordinates. In addition, partners perform a high-level review of the engagement to ensure that it complies with professional auditing standards. Only partners may sign the audit report that results from the audit engagement.

Managers and Supervisors. Managers (or supervisors) usually manage the entire scope of several engagements that may be conducted simultaneously. Generally, managers and supervisors prepare, review, and approve drafts of audit reports and other communications. These individuals are also responsible for reviewing the evidence gathered and conclusions reached by senior and staff

---

[4] Because the focus in this text is on auditing, we will use the terms "auditor," "CPA," "accountant," and "public accountant" interchangeably unless specifically noted.

[5] "Arthur Young and Ernst Firm Plan to Merge," *The Wall Street Journal* (May 19, 1989); "Big 8 Merger Makes Waves," *USA Today* (May 23, 1989); and "The New Numbers Game in Accounting," *Business Week* (July 24, 1989).

[6] "Arthur Young and Ernst Firm Plan to Merge," *The Wall Street Journal* (May 19, 1989).

accountants. Along with partners, managers and supervisors review the engagement to ensure that it complies with professional auditing standards.

Senior Accountants. Senior accountants (also known as in-charge accountants) supervise the work and activity of the staff accountants assigned to them on engagements. Senior accountants direct the day-to-day activities of the audit team as they perform their functions at the client's premises. They also draft audit programs, audit reports, and communications to clients (such as listings of deficiencies in internal control). In many instances, seniors will perform or direct staff in performing the review of the client's internal control. In addition, senior accountants undertake certain research projects related to the engagement.

Staff Accountants. Staff accountants (sometimes called junior accountants) participate in engagements under the supervision of more experienced accountants. The primary function performed by staff accountants is to obtain evidence relating to the clients' financial statements. In gathering this evidence, staff accountants prepare detailed analyses (in the form of audit workpapers) that summarize this evidence and their conclusions.

The above discussion illustrates the extensive review of work that normally takes place during the audit. That is, senior accountants review the work of staff accountants, managers review the work of senior accountants and staff accountants, and partners review the work of all subordinate parties (managers, senior accountants, and staff accountants). The nature of the review procedures performed by these parties differs markedly. For example, senior accountants review the work of staff to verify that all necessary procedures were appropriately performed by staff accountants, that staff accountants adequately documented these procedures, and that the conclusions of the staff were consistent with the results of the procedures performed. In contrast, the manager's and partner's review is broader. These individuals review the procedures and conclusions of staff and seniors to determine whether they are appropriate. In addition, managers and partners evaluate the overall effectiveness of the procedures performed in determining whether the client's financial statements are fairly presented according to GAAP. The review of the work of subordinates is discussed in more detail in Chapter 16.

◻ Types of Audits

While the focus of this text is on the independent audit of a company's financial statements (a financial statement audit), other types of audits are performed. These types of audits, as well as the individual(s) performing them, are briefly discussed below.

Operational Audit. An operational audit is performed to determine the extent to which some aspect of an organization's operating activities is functioning effectively and efficiently. In performing an operational audit, an auditor observes and tests various aspects of one or more organization activities. For example, manufacturing companies are interested in determining whether the production process used to manufacture their inventory efficiently utilizes material and labor inputs. Operational audits would assess the performance of the production process, identify opportunities for improving the production process, and develop recommendations for the company to use in improving its production process.

Thus, the company itself is the primary beneficiary of an operational audit; any recommendations and conclusions made by the auditor have the potential to enable the company to improve the efficiency and effectiveness of its operations. Unlike a financial statement audit, the reports and analyses generated by an operational audit are used by individuals internal to the company and do not circulate externally. Operational audits are discussed in greater detail in Chapter 20.

Compliance Audit. Another type of audit conducted on behalf of the organization is a compliance audit. As the name suggests, in a compliance audit, the auditor is determining the extent to which the organization and/or its personnel are performing their duties in a manner consistent with organization policies and procedures. For example, a common organization policy is the requirement that all purchases on account be approved by a purchasing agent or purchasing department. In this case, an audit may be conducted to identify any deviations from this organizational policy.

In addition to determining whether the client is following specified rules and procedures, compliance auditing is also concerned with whether the organization follows the requirements of federal laws, regulations, contracts, and grants. These issues are of particular importance for governmental entities and programs because they are created by laws and regulations. For example, a unique aspect of a governmental agency is that funds received from various sources must be used for specific purposes (*i.e.*, proceeds received from a gasoline tax must be earmarked for future highway improvements or additions). Compliance auditing is discussed in greater detail in Chapter 20.

Types of Auditors

The auditing activities described above are performed by three types of auditors: independent (external) auditors, internal auditors, and governmental auditors. Various characteristics of these auditors are described below

Independent (External) Auditors. Independent auditors are also known as public accountants. **Public accountants** are those individuals or firms who perform audit, tax, consulting, and other types of services for external clients. Most public accountants undertake a certification process to enhance the public's perception of their work and qualifications. These individuals are referred to as Certified Public Accountants (CPAs). An individual designated as a CPA is recognized by at least one state (or the District of Columbia or a United States territory) as possessing a minimum level of competence related to accounting matters. This minimum level of competence is based on a uniform examination prepared and graded nationally by the AICPA. In addition to this level of competence, CPAs must also meet minimum education and experience requirements that vary from state to state.

While independent auditors primarily perform financial statement audits, they can also perform compliance audits. For example, an independent auditor may examine various types of financial information to determine whether a company has violated one or more of its debt covenants.

Internal Auditors. Unlike independent auditors, internal auditors perform services for a single organization for which they are employed on a full-time basis. Internal auditors perform compliance and operational audits for their employing companies. Thus, internal auditors determine: (1) whether the organization and its employees are complying with established policies and procedures, and (2) the efficiency and effectiveness of some aspect of the organization's operating activities. Obviously, because they are employed by the organization for whom their audits are performed, internal auditors lack the degree of independence of external auditors. However, internal audit standards stress the importance of the internal auditor being objective with respect to the function(s) being examined. Internal auditing is discussed in greater detail in Chapter 20.

Governmental Auditors. Governmental auditors fall under the auspices of the General Accounting Office (GAO) and other government agencies. GAO auditors perform all three types of audits (financial statement audits, operational audits, and compliance audits). However, because of the nature of governmental entities, GAO auditors primarily perform compliance audits to evaluate whether a governmental agency's activities are in compliance with federal laws and regulations. Governmental auditing is described in greater detail in Chapter 20.

Certain characteristics related to each of these groups of auditors are summarized in Figure 1-3.

	Auditing Activities Performed	Examples
Independent Auditors	Financial statement audits	Examine financial statements to determine conformity with GAAP
	Compliance audits	Determine whether company is in compliance with its debt covenants
Internal Auditors	Operational audits	Determine the efficiency and effectiveness of some aspect of the organization's operations
	Compliance audits	Determine the degree of compliance with organizational policies
Governmental Auditors	Financial statement audits	Examine financial statements of governmental entities to determine their conformity with appropriate standards
	Operational audits	Determine the efficiency and effectiveness of a governmental entity's operations
	Compliance audits	Determine the degree of compliance with federal laws and regulations

Figure 1-3: *Characteristics of Different Types of Auditors*

◻ Functions Other than Auditing

Tax Services. In 1913, Congress enacted the federal income tax law. Because the tax was based on accounting information, the law placed an added burden on companies to perform these additional accounting responsibilities. However, independent public accountants were well-equipped to assist their clients by virtue of their special knowledge of accounting and of their clients' financial affairs. Today, tax services are an important aspect of the practice of most independent public accountants.

Consulting Services. From the earliest days of the accounting profession, most independent public accountants perceived their responsibility as going beyond the process of audit and tax services. The accountants' position as observers who were both knowledgeable and independent provided them with a unique opportunity to serve as advisers on many matters. Eventually, accountants began providing a vast array of consulting services to their clients. **Consulting services** involve utilizing the accountant's technical skills, education, observation, experiences, and knowledge to provide assistance to clients in a wide range of areas, including:

- reviewing and commenting on a client-prepared business plan
- analyzing an accounting information system
- providing staff and other support services
- developing computer programs or software

Today, consulting services constitute an important portion of the practices of many accounting firms. The expansion of consulting services has reached such a point that public accounting firms earn only about one-half of their total revenues from auditing and accounting services.[7] Large CPA firms have separate consulting departments; in fact, six of the top seven consulting firms in the world are accounting firms or their affiliates.[8] The range of consulting services offered by CPA firms includes such diverse activities as budgeting, systems design and installation, and operations research.

Unaudited Financial Statements. As noted earlier, the SEC requires publicly-held companies to have an audit examination. Currently, no such requirement exists for nonpublic companies not under the SEC's jurisdiction. Nonpublic companies normally have audit examinations only when requested by a specific user (for example, a potential investor, lender, or other creditor). While an audit examination is obviously beneficial to all companies, whether private or public, the cost of an audit may discourage nonpublic companies from voluntarily having an audit examination.

In many cases, CPAs are involved with evaluating a company's financial statements through engagements less comprehensive in scope than an audit. These engagements (often referred to as **limited assurance engagements**) are appealing in that they are less time-consuming (and less costly) than an audit engagement. Three main types of limited assurance engagements are assembly of financial statements, compilations, and reviews. These engagements are discussed in more detail in Chapter 19.

---

[7] "Big Six's Shift to Consulting Accelerates," *The Wall Street Journal* (September 21, 1995), B1, B4.

[8] "Strengthening the Professionalism of the Independent Auditor," *Report to the Public Oversight Board of the SEC Practice Section from the Advisory Panel on Auditor Independence* (September 13, 1994).

Bookkeeping Services (or Write-up work). Some small businesses do not have their own internal accountants. Instead, they rely on a public accountant to periodically do their bookkeeping. The amount of bookkeeping performed by public accountants depends on the accounting expertise of the owners or employees of the business. Sometimes the accounting services are limited to preparing adjusting entries, closing entries, and offering advice on handling unusual transactions. In other cases, the levels of service include preparing journal entries to reflect transactions that have occurred and ultimately preparing the entity's financial statements. This type of service is referred to as bookkeeping services, or write-up work.

Other Services. The wide variety of professional services offered by accounting firms is continually growing. For example, at least one large accounting firm has expanded to provide internal auditing services on a continuous basis to its clients. In addition, accounting firms are beginning to provide investment advice for individuals and other clients.[9] As the following excerpts from the business press note, CPA firms are increasingly moving their services into nontraditional arenas.

Accountants have broadened their audit services by attesting to the voting at the Academy Awards and the drawings of state lotteries. But now the Wilson Sporting Goods Co. unit of Finland's Amer Group Ltd. is using CPAs to prove that amateur golfers can hit Wilson's Ultra golf ball farther than they can hit competitors' golf balls. Wilson says the CPAs certify that Wilson's Ultra outdistances its competitors by an average of 5.7 yards per drive.[10]

In discussing the declining revenues from audit and tax services, Jon Madonna (chairman of KPMG Peat Marwick), made the following observation: "The traditional service revenue is declining...You can't get enough revenue from this stuff [audit and tax engagements] to exist 20 years from today. The only way you can do it is you've got to do new stuff ... So now there are three options. You can deny it. Or you can profitably wind down. Or you can change."[11]

CHAPTER CHECKPOINTS

1-7. What are the responsibilities of the various position levels within a firm?

1-8. Compare and contrast the following types of auditing: financial statement auditing, compliance auditing, and operational auditing. What type of auditors perform each type?

1-9. Discuss the objectives of operational auditing.

1-10. Why are compliance audits particularly relevant for government entities?

1-11. What are the major services usually offered by a public accounting firm?

---

[9] "Big Accounting Firms to Offer Investors Advice," *The Wall Street Journal* (February 9, 1995), C1.

[10] L. Berton, "After This, CPAs May Take Over Instant-Replay Duties for Football," *The Wall Street Journal* (March 9, 1991), B1.

[11] R. Greene and K. Barrett, "Auditing the Accounting Firms," *Financial World* (September 27, 1994), 32.

PROFESSIONAL ORGANIZATIONS OF ACCOUNTANTS

American Institute of Certified Public Accountants (AICPA)

The AICPA is the national professional association of CPAs. The Institute is a voluntary professional association; consequently, not all CPAs are members. However, because of the many services it provides to member CPAs, several CPAs find membership in this organization beneficial.

Headquartered in New York City, the AICPA has a large full-time staff that: (1) provides members with advice on technical matters, (2) performs research, (3) publishes standards relating to accounting and auditing matters, (4) provides a national political lobby for the accounting profession, and (5) administers the national affairs of the accounting profession. The AICPA accomplishes much of its work through committees of members. For example, a board of the AICPA (the Auditing Standards Board) issues Statements on Auditing Standards (SASs) that are authoritative statements on auditing matters. In addition, the AICPA's Quality Control Standards Committee is a senior technical committee that issues authoritative statements on quality control matters relating to CPA firms.

In September 1977, the AICPA established a division within the Institute that firms may join. The division is called the AICPA Division for CPA Firms and consists of two sections: (1) the SEC Practice Section, and (2) the Private Companies Practice Section. Both sections have the objective of improving the quality of accounting and auditing services provided by their member firms.

SEC Practice Section. Any CPA firm auditing the financial statements of companies that fall under the SEC's jurisdiction is required to join the SEC Practice Section. However, membership in this section is open to any CPA firm. Requirements for membership in the SEC Practice Section include:

1. Adhering to quality control standards established by the AICPA.
2. Allowing another CPA or CPA firm to review work performed by the firm every three years. This type of review is knows as **peer review**.
3. Requiring all professional staff to participate in at least 120 hours of continuing professional education every three years.
4. Reporting any disagreements regarding accounting and auditing matters to an independent function within the client (the board of directors or audit committee).
5. Rotating the partner in charge of audits for each SEC client every seven years.
6. Requiring a partner not participating in the audit engagement to review the work performed during that engagement. This review is known as a **"cold"** (or **second-partner**) review.

The SEC Practice Section is governed by the Public Oversight Board. This Board is comprised of five members from such backgrounds as business, education, banking, law, economics, and government. The primary function of the Public Oversight Board is to monitor and evaluate the various regulatory, sanctioning, and other activities of the SEC Practice Section. In particular, the Public Oversight Board is concerned with the fairness and stringency of the peer review process. Recently, the Public

Oversight Board criticized CPAs for being "cheerleaders" for their clients and not acting in the best interests of the accounting profession.[12]

Private Companies Practice Section. Any CPA firm, a majority of whose partners, shareholders, or proprietors that are members of the AICPA may join the Private Companies Practice Section. The firm must apply and agree to abide by the rules for members, many of which are similar in nature to those for the SEC Practice Section. The primary difference between the SEC Practice Section and Private Companies Practice Section is that the Private Companies Practice Section is concerned with firms performing audits for smaller, non-public entities.

State Societies

CPAs in the various states and other jurisdictions have organized State Societies of CPAs. Like the AICPA, these societies are voluntary professional associations. They generally hold monthly meetings and other professional development meetings for their members. The State Societies provide various informational services to members and generally administer the affairs of the accounting profession within each state.

Boards of Accountancy

A Board of Accountancy is the agency of a state or territorial government that is empowered to administer that jurisdiction's accounting law. There are 54 such boards (one in each state, the District of Columbia, and each U.S. territory). As a licensing agency of the state, the board is usually the only body that may issue and revoke CPA certificates and grant licenses to practice. Thus, a Board of Accountancy has much influence over CPAs by permitting and denying individuals the right to practice public accountancy within their jurisdiction.

Securities and Exchange Commission

The Securities and Exchange Commission (SEC) was created by Congress as an independent agency to administer and regulate the sale and trading of securities. The SEC has jurisdiction over the form and content of financial information prepared by companies whose stock is issued or traded in interstate commerce. Therefore, companies whose stock is traded on a national stock exchange or over the counter are subject to SEC regulations. The primary requirement for these companies is that they file periodic financial information (using Form 10-K for annual information and Form 10-Q for interim information) with the SEC. The CPA is affected because the SEC requires this information to be audited (for annual information) or reviewed (for interim information) by an independent accountant.

In addition to reporting on the fairness of the company's financial statements, the auditor also is required to report other matters to the SEC. In some cases, the auditor is required to report irregularities or illegal acts committed by their clients to the SEC. In addition, the termination of any auditor-client relationship must be communicated to the SEC shortly after it occurs. The basic philoso-

---

[12] "Regulators of CPAs Form Panel to Check Work of Auditors," *The Wall Street Journal* (March 25, 1994), A5B.

phy behind reporting these matters to the SEC is that this communication provides the investing public with an opportunity to obtain as much information as possible about publicly-traded companies. Certainly, illegal acts, irregularities, or auditor changes would be of interest to potential investors and other users of financial statements.

CHAPTER CHECKPOINTS

1-12. Are all CPAs required to join both the AICPA and their state society?

1-13. What are the objectives of: (a) the AICPA's SEC Practice Section, and (b) the AICPA's Private Companies Practice Section?

1-14. Who may join the AICPA's SEC Practice Section? What are some of the requirements for membership in this section?

1-15. What is a State Board of Accountancy? Why do these Boards have influence over the practice of accounting in their jurisdictions?

1-16. How is the Securities and Exchange Commission related to the growth of the audit function?

AUDITING STANDARDS

In the early history of public accounting, the quality of audit examinations often varied widely, depending on the skill, understanding, and judgment of the particular auditor involved. At this time, no guidelines (or standards) were available to provide instruction to the auditor. Even at this early stage in its development, the accounting profession quickly recognized that standards for audits were needed.

In response to these needs, a set of ten basic **generally accepted auditing standards** (or GAAS) was issued by the AICPA. GAAS establish the quality of performance of the auditor and the overall objectives to be achieved in a financial statement audit. The ten basic GAAS provide a broad overview of the qualifications of the auditor (general standards), requirements of an audit (standards of field work), and issues addressed in the auditor's report (standards of reporting). These ten GAAS are summarized below.

> **General Standards**
>
> 1. The audit is to be performed by a person or persons having adequate technical training and proficiency as an auditor.
> 2. In all matters relating to the assignment, an independence in mental attitude is to be maintained by the auditor or auditors.
> 3. Due professional care is to be exercised in the performance of the audit and the preparation of the report.
>
> **Standards of Field Work**
>
> 1. The work is to be adequately planned, and assistants, if any, are to be properly supervised.
> 2. A sufficient understanding of the internal control is to be obtained to plan the audit and to determine the nature, timing, and extent of tests to be performed.
> 3. Sufficient, competent evidential matter is to be obtained through inspection, observation, inquiries, and confirmations to afford a reasonable basis for an opinion regarding the financial statements under audit.
>
> **Standards of Reporting**
>
> 1. The report shall state whether the financial statements are presented in accordance with generally accepted accounting principles.
> 2. The report shall identify those circumstances in which such principles have not been consistently observed in the current period in relation to the preceding period.
> 3. Informative disclosures in the financial statements are to be regarded as reasonably adequate unless otherwise stated in the report.
> 4. The report shall either contain an expression of opinion regarding the financial statements, taken as a whole, or an assertion to the effect that an opinion cannot be expressed. When an overall opinion cannot be expressed, the reasons therefor should be stated. In all cases where an auditor's name is associated with financial statements, the report should contain a clear-cut indication of the character of the auditor's work, if any, and the degree of responsibility the auditor is taking.[13]

◻ General Standards

General standards relate to the qualifications of the auditor and the characteristics he or she should possess. General standards require that the auditor: (1) be trained and proficient, (2) be independent in fact and appearance, and (3) exhibit due professional care during the audit. These standards are discussed below.

---

[13] American Institute of Certified Public Accountants (AICPA), *Statement on Auditing Standards No. 1,* "Codification of Auditing Standards and Procedures" (New York: AICPA, 1973, AU 150.02).

1. **The examination is to be performed by a person or persons having adequate technical training and proficiency as an auditor.**

The first general standard is met through education and experience in the field of auditing. CPAs should have education in the field of auditing prior to beginning their professional careers (in the form of university coursework in auditing) as well as throughout their careers. This latter form of education allows CPAs to remain current with regard to recent developments in accounting and auditing; this type of education is referred to as continuing professional education. Once an accountant becomes a CPA, he or she is required to obtain certain levels of continuing professional education in order remain licensed to practice public accounting.

In addition to education, the first general standard requires that CPAs have practical work experience in the field of auditing. This requirement is evidenced by the fact that, in order to become licensed as a CPA, an individual is required to have some level of work experience of an accounting-related nature. The levels and types of work experience vary from state to state.

2. **In all matters relating to the assignment, an independence in mental attitude is to be maintained by the auditor or auditors.**

As noted earlier in this chapter, the primary reason for an audit examination is the conflict of interest that exists between the company's management and its financial statements. Accordingly, it is critical that the auditor also be free of this type of conflict. This type of requirement is known as **independence**.

Auditors must be independent in both fact and appearance. To be independent in fact, auditors must be objective with respect to the client. To be recognized as independent (and be independent in appearance), auditors must have not have certain types of relationships with their clients (such as ownership of the client's stock). Other factors are also important in evaluating whether auditors are independent in appearance. For example, auditors should not have a close relative in an important position within the client they are auditing. The concept of independence is discussed in greater detail in Chapter 2.

3. **Due professional care is to be exercised in the performance of the audit and the preparation of the report.**

Due professional care requires auditors to conduct their examinations with the degree of skill expected of a similar professional. Under the requirements of due professional care, auditors are expected to observe the standards of field work and reporting (discussed in the following sections). In addition, due professional care requires the auditor to critically review the work performed and judgments made at all levels of supervision. Thus, the review of work by individuals at different hierarchial levels in the firm discussed earlier in this chapter is directly associated with the standard of due professional care.

It is important to note that the concept of due professional care does not require auditors to be error-free. Unintentional errors can (and do) occur during audits. However, CPAs may violate the standard of due professional care if they commit acts of negligence, bad faith, or dishonesty. These acts, and the accompanying sanctions that may result, are discussed in more detail in Chapter 3.

Standards of Field Work

The standards of field work relate to the actual procedures performed during various stages of the audit examination. Three major stages of the audit addressed by the standards of field work are audit planning, the study and evaluation of internal control, and gathering evidence.

1. **The work is to be adequately planned, and assistants, if any, are to be properly supervised.**

Audit planning involves developing an overall strategy for the conduct and scope of the audit. While this process is quite detailed, audit planning involves the following basic tasks:

- reviewing records relating to the client
- discussing matters with firm and client personnel
- obtaining knowledge about matters relating to the client's business
- considering the methods used by the client to process information

Audit planning culminates in the preparation of an **audit program**. The audit program details the audit procedures that should be performed to achieve the objectives of the audit examination.

To adequately plan the audit, it is important for the auditor to be appointed by the client as early as possible. Early appointment allows the auditor to spread the work required in an audit over a greater period of time. To place yourself in the auditor's shoes, consider your reaction if your instructor told you that you would have an exam during the next class. Wouldn't you be able to perform better if you had more time to prepare? The auditor is in a similar situation with respect to being appointed by the client.

Supervision is normally performed on a day-to-day basis by senior accountants. In fulfilling their supervisory roles, senior accountants instruct staff, keep informed of significant problems encountered during the audit, review the work of staff accountants, and handle differences of opinion among firm personnel.

Planning and supervision are discussed in more detail in Chapter 4.

2. **A sufficient understanding of the internal control is to be obtained to plan the audit and to determine the nature, timing, and extent of tests to be performed.**

Internal control will be discussed in Chapter 5. Briefly, from the perspective of the auditor, the client's internal control is concerned with the plans and procedures used by the client to ensure that their financial statements are prepared in conformity with GAAP. As noted in Chapter 5, the auditor studies and evaluates internal control to determine the nature, timing, and extent of auditing procedures (referred to as substantive tests) to be performed. At this point, we will introduce a critical relationship between internal control and substantive testing:

> As the client's internal control is more effective in preventing or detecting misstatements, the auditor must perform *less* effective substantive tests (and *vice versa*).

This relationship and the role of internal control in an audit, is discussed later in Chapters 5 and 6.

3. **Sufficient, competent evidential matter is to be obtained through inspection, observation, inquiries, and confirmations to afford a reasonable basis for an opinion regarding the financial statements under audit.**

Evidence serves as the basis for the auditor's opinion on the financial statements. When gathering evidence, the auditor is attempting to determine whether the entity's financial statements are prepared in conformity with GAAP. For example, when auditing an entity's accounts receivable, the primary form of evidence gathered by the auditor is by requesting third-party customers to verify the amounts owed to the client. This type of evidence is referred to as confirmation; the purpose of obtaining this evidence is to determine whether the entity's accounts receivable are recorded in conformity with GAAP. Evidence is discussed in detail in Chapter 6.

CHAPTER CHECKPOINTS

1-17. What are GAAS? List and briefly describe the three categories of GAAS.

1-18. List and briefly describe the three general standards.

1-19. List and briefly describe the three standards of field work.

◻ Standards of Reporting

The four reporting standards provide guidelines for the independent auditor regarding the matters that should be addressed in the audit report. The first standard indicates that the audit report should indicate whether the entity's financial statements are in conformity with GAAP. The second and third standards indicate that unless noted in the auditor's report: (1) accounting principles have been consistently applied from year to year, and (2) disclosures in the financial statements are adequate to present the company's financial information according to GAAP. The final reporting standard indicates that the auditor must issue an opinion on the client's financial statements or, if an opinion cannot be issued, issue a disclaimer of opinion. This last standard allows users to ascertain the degree of responsibility (if any) that the auditor is assuming for the fairness of the client's financial statements. Clearly, a disclaimer of opinion suggests that any auditor association with the client does not imply that the financial statements were prepared in conformity with GAAP.

Figure 1-4 provides an example of an auditor's report (or opinion). Auditors' reports are addressed to the group or individuals that requested them; normally, the stockholders and/or the board of directors. The auditor's report in Figure 1-4 consists of three paragraphs. An introductory paragraph identifies the responsibilities of both the client (ABC Company) and the auditor regarding the financial statements. In the second (scope) paragraph, auditors discuss the scope and purpose of the audit examination. Finally, in the opinion paragraph, auditors provide their conclusion as to the fairness of the client's financial statements. The audit report should be signed by a partner of the CPA firm involved (using the firm name) and dated as of the date the audit field work was completed. Dating the report in this manner allows users to determine the point at which the auditor was in position to render an opinion.

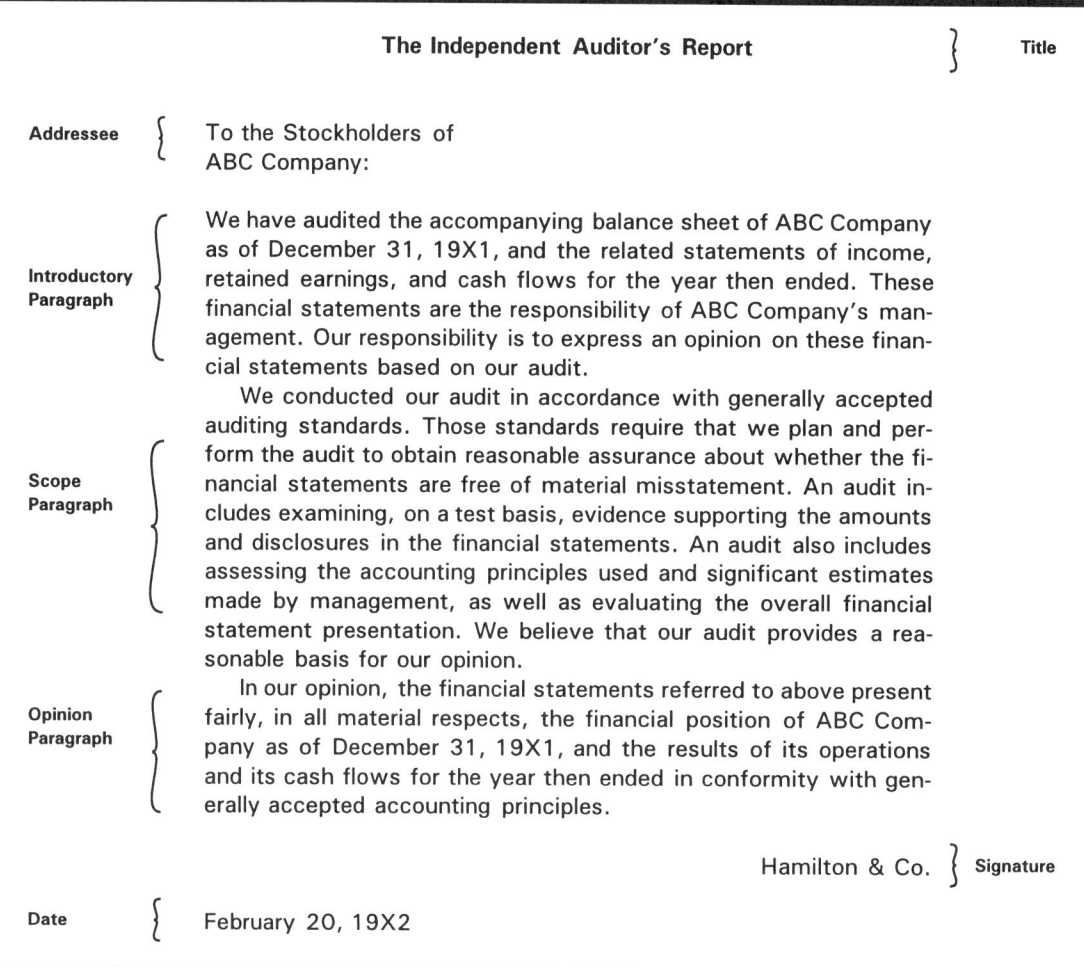

Figure 1-4: *Example of Auditor's Report*

The report shown in Figure 1-4 is an example of an **unqualified**, or "clean," audit opinion. In this case, the auditor's conclusion is that the client's financial statements are presented in conformity with GAAP. In addition, recalling the second and third standards of reporting, the fact that no mention of these issues is made in the audit report indicates that: (1) GAAP have been applied on a consistent basis, and (2) no necessary disclosures have been omitted from the financial statements. In cases where the auditor has certain reservations about the financial statements and/or the scope of the audit examination, a qualified opinion, adverse opinion, or disclaimer of opinion may be issued. In a **qualified opinion**, the auditor expresses certain reservations in the report concerning the scope of the audit and/or the financial statements. When the auditor's reservations are more serious, a disclaimer of opinion or an adverse opinion may be given. In an **adverse opinion**, the auditor's opinion states that the financial statements are not presented fairly in conformity with GAAP. A **disclaimer of opinion** indicates that the auditor cannot issue an opinion on the entity's financial statements because of scope limitations or some other reason (e.g., the auditor is not independent).

The four reporting standards as well as the four major types of opinions are discussed in much greater detail in Chapter 17 of this text.

Statements on Auditing Standards (SASs)

The above section discussed the ten basic GAAS. While these GAAS cover most aspects of the audit examination, they provide broad objectives and are not of sufficient detail to provide auditors with practical guidance for conducting audit examinations. For example, while the second standard of field work indicates that the auditor should study and evaluate the client's internal control, this standard does not provide detailed guidelines on what procedures should be performed by the auditor. As a result, the Auditing Standards Board of the AICPA issues more specific standards based on the overall guidelines provided by the ten GAAS. These more specific standards (known as **Statements on Auditing Standards**, or **SASs**) may cover a specific issue (e.g., internal control or analytical procedures) or represent several more technical issues combined into a single statement (an Omnibus SAS). While SASs represent the minimum level of performance expected of a CPA during an audit examination, in many cases the actual procedures performed by an auditor exceed the requirements of auditing standards.

In some cases, the guidance provided by the SASs is not sufficient to handle all situations that arise in practice. Often, a very technical matter may arise that is related to a particular SAS but is not explicitly covered in that pronouncement. When this occurs, the Auditing Standards Board will issue *Interpretations* to a SAS. Collectively, the guidance provided by SASs as well as Interpretations to those SASs is referred to as **generally accepted auditing standards** (or **GAAS**).

The relationships among the ten basic GAAS, SASs, and Interpretations to the SASs are shown in Figure 1-5.

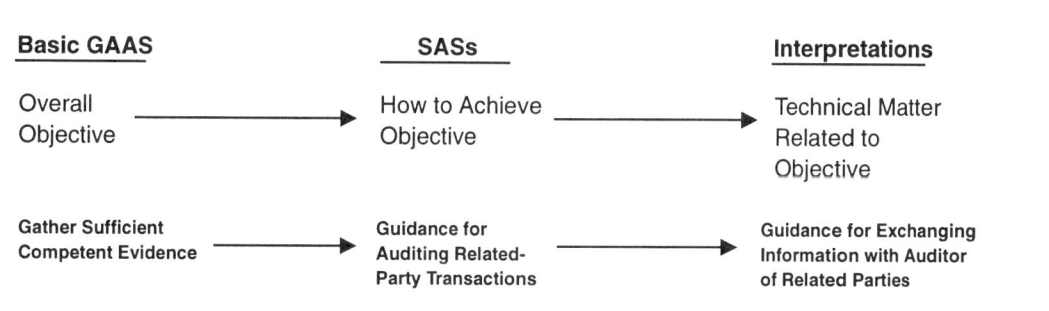

Figure 1-5: *Relationships Among Basic GAAS, SASs, and Interpretations*

It is essential that every auditor have a thorough understanding of GAAS for a number of reasons. First, as shown in Figure 1-4, the scope paragraph of the auditor's report refers directly to GAAS by indicating that the audit was performed in accordance with these standards. Also, as Chapter 2 will show, the lack of compliance with GAAS is a violation of the AICPA's Code of Professional Conduct. Furthermore, *Statement on Auditing Standards (SAS) No. 25* notes that accounting firms themselves must comply with GAAS in conducting an audit practice.[14]

Note that there is a clear distinction between auditing standards and auditing procedures. **Auditing procedures** are specific methods and techniques used by the auditor in the conduct of the examination. For example, when auditing accounts receivable, the auditor will confirm amounts with the client's customers; the confirmation of accounts receivable is an example of an auditing procedure. The audit procedures used will vary according to the particular circumstances of the individual audit examination. In contrast, auditing standards deal with measures of the quality of the auditor's overall performance and the objectives to be attained by the use of the procedures undertaken.

CHAPTER CHECKPOINTS

1-20. List the four standards of reporting.

1-21. What are the three paragraphs of the auditor's standard report? What information is contained in each paragraph?

1-22. Write the auditor's standard report.

1-23. What is the difference between auditing standards and auditing procedures?

1-24. What are *Statements on Auditing Standards* and *Interpretations to Statements on Auditing Standards*?

---

[14] American Institute of Certified Public Accountants (AICPA), *Statement on Auditing Standards No. 25*, "The Relationship of Generally Accepted Auditing Standards to Quality Control Standards" (New York: AICPA, 1979, AU 161).

Appendix

◉ THEY'RE BEAN COUNTERS, NOT GUMSHOES[15]

The following excerpted commentary provides an illustration of the role of the auditor in the financial reporting process and how the auditor's report is used (and misused) by third parties. This excerpt also highlights the fact that the public often has higher expectations for auditors than required under GAAS.

> Soon after Phar-Mor Inc. accused two of its executives in early August of embezzling at least $10 million from the drugstore chain, Chief Executive David S. Shapira made sure no one would mistake him for Harry Truman: He blamed the retailers' outside auditors, Coopers & Lybrand, for failing to detect phony financial ledgers and sued the firm. Never mind that Shapira himself caught on only after receiving a tip.
>
> For the accounting profession, lawsuits such as Phar-Mor's are becoming increasingly common. At investors and taxpayers search for scapegoats in the wake of financial debacles, the Big Six accounting firms have come under siege. Last year, they spent nearly $480 million to defend and settle lawsuits charging them with shoddy accounting work—roughly 9 percent of their domestic audit revenues.
>
> Some of those judgments may be defensible when auditors perform negligently. Yet unfortunately, the public, in its never-ending quest for fail-safe investments, is coming to expect too much from accountants. They aren't, shouldn't be, and really can't be prosecutors looking to root out all fraud and corruption. Their formal role is much more limited: They are hired by management to examine a company's books and records to determine whether management's financial statements abide by generally accepted accounting principles...
>
> Despite these limits to the role ... of accountants, many investors persist in regarding an auditor's unqualified opinion as the equivalent of a Good Housekeeping Seal of Approval against fraud and mismanagement. And sometimes, the courts do likewise. U.S. District Judge Stanley Sporkin, in a case involving former thrift executive Charles H. Keating Jr., struck a responsive chord when he asked "Where were the professionals ... when these clearly improper transactions were being consummated?"

---

[15] Adapted from D. Foust, "They're Bean Counters, Not Gumshoes," *Business Week* (September 14, 1992), 92.

◉ SUMMARY OF KEY POINTS

1. Auditing is a process of gathering evidence to determine whether management assertions are presented in accordance with established criteria. Stated another way, the objective of a financial statement audit is to determine whether the client's financial statements are presented in conformity with generally accepted accounting principles (GAAP).

2. An attestation is a written conclusion provided by an accountant about a written assertion that is the responsibility of another party. In an audit, the CPA provides an opinion (written conclusion) about the client's financial statements (written assertion). These financial statements are the responsibility of the client's management.

3. In addition to audits of financial statements, two other types of audit examinations exist. Compliance audits assess the degree to which the organization and its personnel perform their duties in a manner consistent with organization policies and procedures. Compliance audits also determine the extent to which the organization's operations are conducted in compliance with applicable laws and regulations. In an operational audit, the auditor attempts to provide management with information concerning the efficiency and effectiveness of the organization's operating activities.

4. A major service performed by independent accountants is the audit function. However, independent accountants may also: (1) provide tax services, (2) provide management consulting services, (3) prepare or comment on unaudited financial statements, and (4) provide write-up (bookkeeping) services.

5. The authoritative statements on matters relating to auditing are Statements on Auditing Standards (SASs). These are pronouncements issued by the Auditing Standards Board of the AICPA. SASs may be clarified through the issuance of Interpretations.

6. Auditing standards refer to measures of the quality of the auditor's performance. There are ten basic generally accepted auditing standards (GAAS). These standards are divided into three categories: (1) general standards, (2) standards of field work, and (3) standards of reporting.

7. General standards require that the auditor: (1) have adequate technical training and proficiency, (2) be independent in fact and appearance, and (3) exercise due professional care in performing the examination.

8. The standards of field work relate to actual audit work performed by the CPA and state that: (1) the audit work should be properly planned and any assistants properly supervised; (2) a study and evaluation of internal control should be made; and (3) sufficient, competent evidential matter should be obtained.

9. The standards of reporting deal exclusively with the communication (audit report) issued by the auditor. This report should: (1) state whether the financial statements are presented in conformity with GAAP, (2) indicate any inconsistencies in the application of GAAP, (3) indicate any informative disclosures that are inadequate, and (4) express the auditor's opinion concerning the fairness of the financial statements or contain an assertion that an opinion cannot be expressed.

10. The auditor's report communicates the auditor's opinion concerning the financial statements to the users of those financial statements. This report is addressed to the parties who retained the

auditors (stockholders and/or board of directors). It is dated as of the last date of the CPA's field work and is signed by a partner of the CPA firm.

◉ GLOSSARY

Adverse Opinion. An opinion in which the auditor states that the client's financial statements do not present fairly the financial position, results of operations, and cash flows according to GAAP.

American Institute of Certified Public Accountants (AICPA). A voluntary national professional association of CPAs that provides members with advice on technical matters, performs research on accounting and auditing issues, and provides a national political lobby for the accounting profession.

Attest Engagement. An engagement in which a practitioner is engaged to issue or does issue a written communication that expresses a conclusion about the reliability of a written assertion that is the responsibility of another party.

Auditing. A systematic process of objectively obtaining and evaluating evidence regarding assertions about economic actions and events to ascertain the degree of correspondence between those assertions and established criteria and communicating the results to interested users.

Auditing Procedures. The methods and techniques used by the auditor in the conduct of the audit examination.

Auditing Standards. See Generally Accepted Auditing Standards

Board of Accountancy. The body within each jurisdiction that has the responsibility for administering that jurisdiction's public accounting legislation. Boards of Accountancy may issue and revoke CPA certificates and grant licenses to practice public accountancy in their jurisdictions.

Certified Public Accountant (CPA). An individual who is recognized by at least one state government, the District of Columbia, or a U.S. territory as possessing a minimum level of competence in certain designated areas of accounting.

Compliance Audit. An examination performed by auditors to determine the extent to which the organization and/or its personnel are: (1) performing their duties in a manner consistent with organizational policies and procedures, or (2) complying with applicable laws, regulations, contracts, or grants.

Disclaimer of Opinion. In a disclaimer of opinion, the auditor states that he or she cannot express an opinion on the client's financial statements because of scope limitations or some other reason.

Financial Statement Audit. Performed by an independent CPA, a financial statement audit determines the correspondence between the organization's financial statements and some established criteria (usually GAAP).

Generally Accepted Auditing Standards (GAAS). Authoritative statements regarding the qualifications of the auditor, objectives of the audit examination, and issues mentioned in the auditor's report. GAAS represent measures of the quality of the auditor's performance.

General Standards. General standards require the auditor to be trained and proficient, independent in fact and appearance, and exhibit due professional care during the engagement.

Managers. The level below partners in a CPA firm. They manage the entire scope of several professional engagements that may be conducted simultaneously.

Operational Audit. An audit examination (performed primarily by internal auditors) that provides management with information about the effectiveness and efficiency of the organization's operating activities.

Partners. Owners and administrators of a CPA firm organized as a partnership.

Private Companies Practice Section. A section within the AICPA that firms who do not audit publicly-traded companies may join.

Qualified Opinion. An opinion in which the auditors express certain reservations concerning the scope of the audit and/or the financial statements.

SEC Practice Section. A section within the AICPA that any CPA firm having an interest in SEC practice may join. Firms auditing publicly-traded companies who must file financial information with the SEC are required to join this section.

Senior Accountants (In-Charge Accountants). Individuals occupying the level below manager in a CPA firm. Among other duties, senior accountants supervise the work and activity of the staff accountants assigned to them on field engagements.

Staff Accountants (Junior Accountants). Generally, the entry-level professional accountants in a public accounting firm. The work of staff accountants is supervised by more experienced accountants.

Standards of Field Work. The standards of field work relate to the primary activities performed during the audit. These standards involve planning the audit, studying and evaluating internal control, and gathering sufficient, competent evidence.

Standards of Reporting. The standards of reporting identify the major contents of the auditor's report.

State Societies of CPAs. Voluntary professional associations in the various states and jurisdictions. They hold monthly meetings and other professional development meetings for their members.

Unqualified Opinion. A "clean" opinion which indicates that the auditor concludes that the financial statements present fairly the financial position, results of operations, and cash flows in accordance with GAAP.

◉ SUMMARY OF PROFESSIONAL PRONOUNCEMENTS

Statement on Auditing Standards No. 1, "Codification of Auditing Standards and Procedures" (New York: AICPA, 1972, various sections).

Statement on Auditing Standards No. 22, "Planning and Supervision" (New York: AICPA, 1978, AU 311).

Statement on Auditing Standards No. 25, "The Relationship of Generally Accepted Auditing Standards to Quality Control Standards" (New York: AICPA, 1979, AU 161).

◎ QUESTIONS AND PROBLEMS

1-25. Select the **best** answer for each of the following items:

1. Auditing standards differ from auditing procedures in that procedures relate to:

   a. Measure of performance.
   b. Audit principles.
   c. Acts to be performed.
   d. Audit judgments.

2. Independent auditing can best be described as:

   a. A branch of accounting.
   b. A discipline that attests to the results of accounting and other functional operations and data.
   c. A professional activity that measures and communicates financial and business data.
   d. A regulatory function that prevents the issuance of improper financial information

3. An attestation engagement is one in which a CPA is engaged to:

   a. Issue a written communication expressing a conclusion about the reliability of a written assertion that is the responsibility of another party.
   b. Provide tax advice or prepare a tax return based on financial information the CPA has not audited or reviewed.
   c. Testify as an expert witness in accounting, auditing, or tax matters, given stipulated facts.
   d. Assemble prospective financial statements based on the assumptions of the entity's management without expressing any assurance.

4. The fourth standard of reporting requires an auditor to render a report whenever an auditor's name is associated with financial statements. The overall purpose of the fourth standard of reporting is to require that reports:

   a. State that the examination of financial statements has been conducted in accordance with generally accepted auditing standards.
   b. Indicate the character of the auditor's examination and the degree of responsibility assumed by the auditor
   c. Imply that the auditor is independent in fact as well as in appearance with respect to the financial statements under examination.
   d. Express whether the accounting principles used in preparing the financial statements have been applied consistently in the period under examination.

5. The auditor's report makes reference to the basic financial statements, which are customarily considered to be the balance sheet and the statements of:

   a. Income and cash flows.
   b. Income, changes in retained earnings, and cash flows.
   c. Income, retained earnings, and cash flows.
   d. Income and retained earnings.

6. The first general standard which states, in part, that the examination is to be performed by a person or persons having adequate technical training, requires that an auditor have:

   a. Education and experience in the field of auditing.
   b. Ability in the planning and supervision of the audit work.
   c. Proficiency in business and financial matters.
   d. Knowledge in the area of financial accounting.

7. The first standard of field work, which states that the work is to be adequately planned and assistants, if any, are to be properly supervised, recognizes that:

   a. Early appointment of the auditor is advantageous to the auditor and the client.
   b. Acceptance of an audit engagement after the close of the client's fiscal year is generally not permissible.
   c. Appointment of the auditor subsequent to the physical count of inventory requires a disclaimer of opinion.
   d. Performance of substantial parts of the examination is necessary at interim dates.

8. Which of the following best describes why an independent auditor is asked to express an opinion on the fair presentation of financial statements?

   a. It is difficult to prepare financial statements that fairly present a company's financial position and cash flows and operations without the expertise of an independent auditor.
   b. It is management's responsibility to seek available independent aid in the appraisal of the financial information shown in its financial statements.
   c. The opinion of an independent party is needed because a company may not be objective with respect to its own financial statements.
   d. It is a customary courtesy that all stockholders of a company receive an independent report on management's stewardship in managing the affairs of the business.

9. The third general standard states that due care is to be exercised in the performance of the examination. This standard should be interpreted to mean that a CPA who undertakes an engagement assumes a duty to perform:

   a. With reasonable diligence and without fault or error.
   b. As a professional who will assume responsibility for losses consequent upon error of judgment.
   c. To the satisfaction of the client and third parties who may rely upon it.
   d. As a professional possessing the degree of skill commonly possessed by others in the field.

10. Which of the following is not related to the standards of field work?

    a. Gathering sufficient, competent evidential matter.
    b. Maintaining independence in fact and appearance from the client.
    c. Performing a study and evaluation of internal control.
    d. Planning the audit and supervising any assistants.
    e. All of the above are related to the standards of field work.

11. An audit that attempts to determine whether the organization and its personnel are performing their duties consistent with organization policies and procedures is referred to as a(n):

    a. Compliance audit.
    b. Financial statement audit.
    c. Income tax audit.
    d. Operational audit.
    e. None of the above.

12. Which of the following individuals frequently performs operational audits?

    a. Governmental auditors.
    b. Independent auditors.
    c. Internal auditors.
    d. Both a and c above.
    e. Both a and b above.

13. Which of the following types of activities may be performed by public accountants?

    a. Audits of financial statements.
    b. Compilations and reviews of unaudited financial statements.
    c. Consulting services.
    d. Tax services.
    e. All of the above.

14. Which of the following agencies was created to administer and regulate the interstate sale and trading of securities?

    a. American Institute of Certified Public Accountants.
    b. Financial Accounting Standards Board.
    c. Auditing Standards Board.
    d. Securities and Exchange Commission.
    e. State Boards of Public Accountancy.

15. The primary difference between auditing standards and auditing procedures is that:

    a. Auditing standards relate to specific actions performed during an engagement to gather evidence.
    b. Auditing procedures are based on pronouncements issued by the Auditing Standards Board of the AICPA.
    c. Auditing standards provide a minimum level of performance required of CPAs during an audit engagement.
    d. Auditing procedures do not vary from one audit engagement to another.
    e. None of the above represent differences between auditing standards and auditing procedures.

    (Items 1 through 9 in 1-23; AICPA Adapted)

1-26. CPA J, a staff accountant, is assigned to the audit of EXITS Company. Before the field work was started, CPA J reviewed last year's workpapers. When the field work began, CPA J noted that EXITS Company actually prepares and distributes 15 copies of each purchase order. CPA J feels that there is an unnecessary amount of paperwork. What should CPA J do?

1-27. Comment on each of the following statements made by Nathan, a new staff accountant.

a. It's really not important whether management agrees with my adjusting entries. Because I'm the auditor, they need to adjust their financial statements, or I'll adjust the statements for them.
b. Even though I own a small number of shares of stock in this client, that will not affect my judgment. Therefore, I really don't see any problem with owning the stock.
c. If the client cannot afford an audit, I suggest that we do a compilation or a review engagement. Both of these engagements provide the same level of services as an audit, but at a much lower cost.
d. Our firm would like to join the SEC Practice Section, but we do not currently perform an audit for any clients falling under the jurisdiction of the SEC.

1-28. Evaluate each of the following statements, supporting or refuting the statement by reference to the ten generally accepted auditing standards:

a. In assessing independence, the auditor's true state of mind during the audit is critical. Perceptions of external third parties are relatively unimportant in this regard.
b. During the audit examination, it is important to allow subordinates as much freedom as possible to perform their duties. Accordingly, senior accountants rarely need to communicate with subordinates during the audit examination.
c. If GAAP are not consistently applied by the company, it is up to management to alert users to this fact in the company's financial statements. The auditor should not modify her or his report unless management consents to this modification.
d. Under the concept of due professional care, auditors are not permitted to make errors in judgment, because doing so would represent performance inconsistent with CPAs who are members of the accounting profession.

1-29. How would you reply to the following questions?

a. Because responsible financial reporting seems to be directed principally toward outside stockholders and creditors, to what extent do you suppose generally accepted auditing standards can be relaxed in the case of:

1. A small corporation that has no creditors and is wholly-owned by the chairman of the board, who asks for an audit?
2. A sole proprietorship with no creditors?

b. Because the accountants' report is sometimes referred to as a "certificate," what do you think about changing the wording to: "We hereby certify that the ... [financial statements] ... are accurate, ... etc."?
c. Generally accepted auditing standards state quite clearly that the auditor must disclose any exceptions that are taken to the financial statements. Rather than go through all the difficulties of qualifying the opinion, why doesn't the auditor simply change the statements to reflect an acceptable treatment?

1-30. "An audit by a CPA is essentially negative and contributes to neither the gross national product nor the general well-being of society. The auditor does not create; he or she merely checks what someone else has done." Comment on the statement.

(AICPA Adapted)

1-31. Shown below are a number of independent scenarios encountered by CPAs during audit engagements. For each scenario, indicate which of the ten basic GAAS is most pertinent.

   a. A CPA was not appointed as the auditor for Oriole Company until December 20. Because Oriole Company's fiscal year-end is December 31, the CPA did not have much time to plan and observe Oriole's year-end inventory counts.
   b. Brewer Company changed the depreciation method for its fixed assets from sum-of-the-years' digits to straight-line. The CPA feels that this change is appropriate because it more closely reflects the expiration of benefits associated with the machinery. In addition, Brewer has adequately disclosed this change in the footnotes accompanying their financial statements.
   c. Alister and Mark, CPAs, recently acquired a large number of new audit clients. Because these new clients required additional attention, many of the staff accountants were asked to assume additional responsibility on the audits of Alister and Mark's existing clients. In many cases, staff accountants were actually running the day-to-day activities on the audit engagements.
   d. In the audit of Ranger, Inc.'s accounts receivable, Sierra, CPA was unable to locate addresses for many of Ranger's customers in order to confirm their accounts receivable. Ranger's management informed Sierra that these customers have done business with Ranger for many years and always paid their bills in a timely manner.
   e. The spouse of Emmitt Irvin, a staff accountant for Cowboy CPAs, has just been promoted to Chief Executive Officer of White. White is an audit client of Cowboy CPAs.
   f. Meghan Corporation has correctly implemented *FASB Statement No. 87* in accounting for its defined-benefit pension plans in their balance sheet and income statement. However, because of the complexity of this information, Meghan does not present the required supplementary footnote disclosures called for by this pronouncement.
   g. Randolph and Mortimer, CPAs, are interviewing candidates for a staff accountant (auditor) position. Through unusual circumstances, they have found a potential candidate, Ms. Penelope Fletcher. However, Ms. Fletcher studied engineering in college and has never taken an accounting course in her life.

1-32. Student A says that the primary responsibility for the adequacy of disclosure in the financial statements and footnotes rests with the auditor in charge of the audit field work. Student B says that the partner in charge of the engagement has the primary responsibility. Student C says that the staffperson who drafts the statements and footnotes has the primary responsibility. Student D contends that it is the client's responsibility. Which student is correct?

(AICPA Adapted)

1-33. Feiler, the sole owner of a small hardware business, has been told that the business should have financial statements reported on by an independent CPA. Feiler, having some bookkeeping experience, has personally prepared the company's financial statements and does not understand why such statements should be examined by a CPA. Feiler discussed the matter with Farber, a CPA, and asked Farber to explain why an audit is considered important.

Required:

   a. Describe the objectives of an independent audit.
   b. Identify ways in which an independent audit may be beneficial to Feiler.

(AICPA Adapted)

1-34. Ray, the owner of a small company, asked Holmes, CPA, to conduct an audit of the company's records. Ray told Holmes that an audit is to be completed in time to submit audited financial statements to a bank as part of a loan application. Holmes immediately accepted the engagement and agreed to provide an auditor's report within three weeks. Ray agreed to pay Holmes a fixed fee plus a bonus if the loan was granted.

Holmes hired two accounting students to conduct the audit and spent several hours telling them exactly what to do. Holmes told the students not to spend time reviewing the controls but instead to concentrate on proving the mathematical accuracy of the ledger accounts and on summarizing the data in the accounting records that support Ray's financial statements. The students followed Holmes's instructions and after two weeks gave Holmes the financial statements, which did not include footnotes. Holmes reviewed the statements and prepared an unqualified auditor's report. The report did not refer to generally accepted accounting principles nor to the year-to-year application of such principles.

Required:

Briefly describe each of the generally accepted auditing standards, and indicate how the action(s) of Holmes resulted in a failure to comply with each standard

(AICPA Adapted)

Learning Objectives

Study of the material in this chapter is designed to achieve several learning objectives. After studying this chapter, you should be able to:

1. Describe why establishing and following a Code of Professional Conduct is necessary for a profession.
2. Discuss the general nature of the Rules of Conduct that comprise the AICPA's Code of Professional Conduct.
3. Identify the specific requirements and the accepted and prohibited actions under the Code of Professional Conduct.
4. Tell how the Code of Professional Conduct is enforced and describe some of the problems associated with its enforcement.
5. Define quality control standards and understand how quality control standards provide benefits to CPA firms.

2

The Code of Professional Conduct

◉ WHY IS A CODE OF CONDUCT IMPORTANT?

A **Code of Conduct** is a set of guidelines that describes desirable and undesirable behavior on the part of a group of individuals. Throughout your life, you have either knowingly or unknowingly been subject to various Codes of Conduct. For example, as a college student, your university has a Code of Conduct that indicates behaviors that are expected of its students. In addition, this Code of Conduct also details behaviors that are unacceptable (such as academic dishonesty). Finally, while it may not be formally documented, your professor probably has expectations regarding classroom attendance, homework assignments, and other matters. These expectations are another type of Code of Conduct.

While Codes of Conduct are important for all groups of individuals, the adoption of a Code of Conduct is an important milestone in the professionalization of any occupation. This is particularly true for occupations that serve the general public, like the public accounting profession. For example, recall from the previous chapter that the work of the independent auditor is used by investors and creditors in making economic decisions with respect to a company. For an audit to be useful to investors and creditors, they must be able to trust and rely on the auditor's work. However, what if auditors could own shares of their clients' stock? Clearly, the auditor would have a conflict of interest when examining his or her client's financial statements. This conflict of interest would reduce the trust that could be placed on the auditor's work. It is because of this possibility that the AICPA's Code of Conduct prohibits CPAs from owning direct financial interests (such as shares of stock) in their audit clients.

In addition to occupations that rely on the public's trust, the adoption of a Code of Conduct is also critical for professions that have autonomy in establishing their rules and guidelines. Because the AICPA establishes the standards for performing audits (through the issuance of *Statements on Auditing Standards*) and the requirements for membership in the public accounting profession, it is important that a Code of Conduct is established and enforced. Doing so serves to increase the public's confidence in the accounting profession. For example, the independence requirement of the Code of

Conduct allows third-party users to have confidence that the audit of an entity's financial statements is conducted by a team of unbiased individual(s).

Thus, establishing a Code of Conduct for the public accounting profession is important because this profession:

▶ serves the public and relies on the public's trust

▶ is self-regulated and establishes its own rules and guidelines

◉ THE STRUCTURE OF THE CODE OF PROFESSIONAL CONDUCT

The AICPA, the State Societies of CPAs, and the various Boards of Accountancy have each adopted a **Code of Professional Conduct**.[1] In many instances, the State Societies and the Boards of Accountancy have adopted or at least modeled their own Codes after the AICPA Code. As a result, the discussion in this chapter will be limited to the AICPA's Code of Professional Conduct.

It is important to note that the AICPA's Code of Professional Conduct derives its authority from the Bylaws of the AICPA. That is, membership in the AICPA requires CPAs to adhere to the Code of Professional Conduct. If AICPA members violate one or more Rules of Conduct (discussed in the following section of this chapter), they are subject to various types of disciplinary actions.

The AICPA's Code consists of four primary components: (1) Principles, (2) Rules of Conduct, (3) Interpretations, and (4) Ethics Rulings. These general components are described in the following subsections.

◻ Principles

The first component of the Code is a set of general Principles. These **Principles** represent a broad conceptual framework used to develop the more specific Rules of Conduct and outline the desired characteristics and responsibilities of CPAs. The development of a set of basic Principles recognizes that prior to creating specific rules, it is important for the AICPA to establish ideal standards of conduct. In other words, what characteristics should a CPA possess? In what activities should a CPA engage or not engage? While the Principles themselves are not enforceable (*i.e.*, CPAs cannot be charged with violating a particular Principle), the Rules of Conduct that have emerged from these Principles are enforceable. The six Principles are summarized in Figure 2-1.

◻ Rules of Conduct

The **Rules of Conduct** (or Rules) are specific requirements that govern the performance of CPAs. These Rules delineate minimum standards of conduct and identify activities in which CPAs may or may not be engaged. As noted above, the Rules are developed based on the aspirational guidelines established by the Principles. For example, one of the six Principles established by the AICPA is that the CPA

---

[1] Throughout the remainder of this chapter, the terms "Code of Conduct" and "Code" will be used interchangeably with "Code of Professional Conduct."

Article I: Responsibilities

In carrying out their responsibilities as professionals, members should exercise sensitive professional and moral judgments in all their activities.

Article II: The Public Interest

Members should accept the obligation to act in a way that will serve the public interest, honor the public trust, and demonstrate commitment to professionalism.

Article III: Integrity

To maintain and broaden public confidence, members should perform all professional responsibilities with the highest sense of integrity.

Article IV: Objectivity and Independence

A member should maintain objectivity and be free of conflicts of interest in discharging professional responsibilities. A member in public practice should be independent in fact and appearance when providing auditing and other attestation services.

Article V: Due Care

A member should observe the profession's technical and ethical standards, strive continually to improve competence and the quality of services, and discharge professional responsibility to the best of the member's ability.

Article VI: Scope and Nature of Services

A member in public practice should observe the Principles of the Code of Professional Conduct in determining the scope and nature of services to be provided.

Adapted from the "Code of Professional Conduct," *Professional Standards: Volume II* (New York: AICPA, 1996). Copyright © 1996 by the AICPA.

Figure 2-1: *Principles of the Code of Professional Conduct*

should be independent in fact and appearance when providing auditing or attestation services (see Article IV in Figure 2-1). As a result of this Principle, Rule 101 has been established to prohibit CPAs from having certain financial and managerial interests in a company that is a CPA's client. This relationship is depicted below.

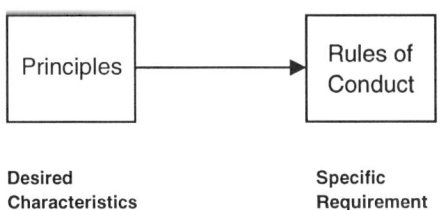

Desired Characteristics   **Specific Requirement**

The Rules of Conduct are enforceable; that is, if a CPA violates a particular Rule, he or she may be formally charged and disciplined by the AICPA, State Societies of CPAs, or State Boards of Accountancy. As noted later in this chapter, disciplinary actions range from a warning given to the CPA to expulsion from the AICPA. Although we will discuss these Rules primarily from the auditor's standpoint, it is important to note that the Rules of Conduct apply to all services (*i.e.*, tax services and consulting services) provided by CPAs to their clients. The only instance where CPAs performing nonattest services are not responsible for a Rule is when that Rule specifically exempts a particular type of service. For example, it is not expected that CPAs performing tax services would be independent with respect to their clients.

The Rules of Conduct are discussed in detail in the next major section of this chapter.

◻ Interpretations and Ethics Rulings

While the Rules of Conduct have been drafted with some degree of specificity, it is simply not possible for every situation encountered in practice to be clearly classified as conforming with a Rule or violating a Rule. An analogy can be drawn between the Rules of Conduct and laws that currently exist in our legal system. To illustrate, while the definition of murder is fairly easy to understand, interpretations are necessary for cases where an individual kills an intruder in his or her home or otherwise acts in self-defense. Similarly, although the concept of independence is not difficult to understand, questions arise as to what constitutes a financial interest or managerial interest in a client. Although direct ownership of shares of stock appears to clearly represent a financial interest (and thus impair the CPA's independence), the status of joint ventures or investments held by the CPA with client officers are not as clear. To clarify the Rules of Conduct, Interpretations and Ethical Rulings are necessary.

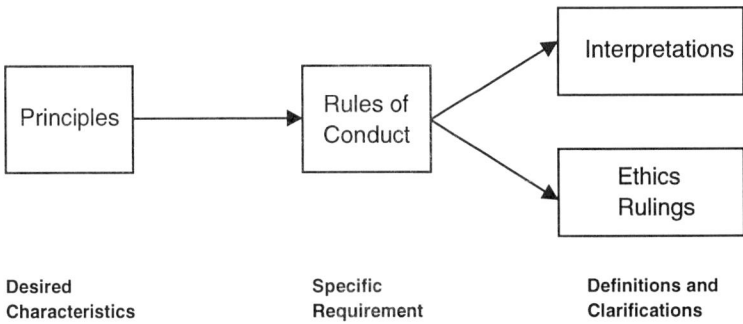

Desired Characteristics   **Specific Requirement**   **Definitions and Clarifications**

Interpretations and **Ethics Rulings** are somewhat similar in nature. Both represent clarifications of existing Rules of Conduct that are adopted by the Professional Ethics Division of the AICPA after exposure of actual situations encountered in practice to State Societies, State Boards of Accountancy, CPAs and CPA firms, and other interested parties. Thus, Interpretations and Ethics Rulings are similar to legal precedents established by courts based on cases coming before those courts. Interpretations and Ethics Rulings represent applications of the Rules of Conduct to actual situations encountered in practice.

The primary difference between Interpretations and Ethics Rulings is the degree of specificity contained in the two components. Interpretations represent relatively general clarifications of Rules or of terms addressed by Rules. In contrast, Ethics Rulings are more specific applications of the Rules to practice. Ethics Rulings are presented in a question/answer format based on very specific situations encountered by CPAs in practice. Consider the following Interpretation and Ruling related to the Independence Rule (Rule 101):

Interpretation: A CPA cannot perform in any capacity equivalent to that of management or a client employee (ET 101.02).

Ethics Ruling: If a CPA accepts the responsibility of cosigning checks for a client, independence would be considered to be impaired (ET 191.005–191.006).

Note that the Interpretation indicates that a CPA cannot perform in any capacity equivalent to a client employee; the Ethics Ruling indicates that the act of cosigning checks is equivalent to performing in a capacity similar to that of a client employee.

The number of Interpretations and Ethics Rulings for each of the Rules of Conduct varies greatly, depending on the nature of the Rule. For example, independence is a controversial topic that is often difficult to define precisely. This Rule is currently clarified through 11 Interpretations and 68 Ethics Rulings. In contrast, the Rule related to confidential client information has been clarified through only one Interpretation and ten Ethics Rulings. Generally, as Rules of Conduct become more precise and less controversial, the number of Interpretations and Rulings related to those Rules decreases.

It is important to note that, like Principles, Interpretations and Ethics Rulings are not enforceable. Therefore, violating an Interpretation or Ethics Ruling does not necessarily expose the CPA to disciplinary action. However, the CPA does have to justify any departure from existing Interpretations and Ethics Rulings. The Interpretations to the Rules of Conduct are summarized in the appendix to this chapter.

CHAPTER CHECKPOINTS

2-1. What is a Code of Conduct? Why is a Code of Conduct necessary for the public accounting profession?

2-2. Do all states follow the AICPA's Code of Professional Conduct?

2-3. Name and define the four components of the current Code of Professional Conduct.

2-4. Distinguish between Ethics Rulings and Interpretations.

RULES OF CONDUCT

As noted earlier, the Rules of Conduct (or Rules) represent minimum standards that must be followed by CPAs. In general, these Rules are applicable to CPAs in "public practice." **Public practice** is defined as any type of professional accounting-related services that are provided to external clients. Therefore, all auditing services are considered to be a form of public practice. In addition to audits, consulting, tax, bookkeeping, and other types of services fall under the umbrella of public practice. In contrast, a CPA in private practice performs services for, and is employed by, a single organization or entity. CPAs in private practice are required to adhere only to Rules 102, 201-203, and 501.

It is important to note that the Rules of Conduct discussed in this section relate to all services performed by CPAs, unless specifically exempted by the Rule itself. Two exceptions currently exist: only CPAs performing audit or other attestation services are responsible for Rules 101 (Independence) and 203 (Accounting Principles). In addition, two other Rules (Rule 302–Contingent Fees and Rule 503–Commissions) are only partially applicable to CPAs performing nonattest services.[2]

The Rules discussed in the following section represent the formal Rules of Conduct approved by the AICPA's membership. Many states follow the AICPA Rules, but some have different requirements for licensing within that state. In addition, many public accounting firms require their employees to comply with stricter standards than those embodied in the AICPA Rules.[3]

Independence: Rule 101

Rule 101 requires that CPAs may perform an attest engagement (including an audit examination) only if the CPA is independent in both fact and in appearance with respect to the client. **Independence in fact** refers to the actual state of mind of the CPA; that is, is the CPA totally unbiased with respect to the client and its financial information? One problem in attempting to identify possible violations of independence in fact is that this condition is only observable to the CPA. That is, only the CPA him- or herself knows whether independence in fact exists.

In contrast, **independence in appearance** refers to whether individuals other than the CPA perceive the CPA to be independent with respect to the client and its financial information. The requirement that CPAs maintain independence in appearance acknowledges that the CPA's opinion on a company's financial statements has little value unless outside parties believe that the CPA is independent. Unlike independence in fact, independence in appearance is determined by the perceptions of external parties, such as third-party users.

To illustrate the difference between independence in fact and independence in appearance, assume that a CPA is performing an audit examination for a publicly-traded company. During the audit, he or she decides to enter into a joint venture with that company's chief financial officer. Although this arrangement may have no impact on the CPA's actions during the audit examination (*i.e.*, the CPA

---

[2] In addition to the Rules of Conduct discussed in this chapter, CPAs performing nonattest services (such as tax and consulting services) are subject to more specialized rules relating to these services. A discussion of these more specialized rules is beyond the scope of this text.

[3] The actual Rules and Interpretations quoted in this section were adapted from American Institute of Certified Public Accountants (AICPA), "Code of Professional Conduct," *Professional Standards: Volume II* (New York: AICPA, 1996). Copyright © 1996 by the AICPA.

is independent in fact), it is likely that third parties would feel that this joint venture compromises the CPA's independence (the CPA would not be perceived as independent in appearance).

Interpretation 101-1 of Rule 101 provides the most detailed guidance on independence. This Interpretation notes that independence is considered to be impaired if:

> A. During the period of a professional engagement or at the time of expressing an opinion, a member or a member's firm:
>
>   1. Had or was committed to acquire any direct or material indirect financial interest in the enterprise.
>   2. Was a trustee of any trust or executor or administrator of any estate if such trust or estate had or was committed to acquire any direct or material indirect financial interest in the enterprise.
>   3. Had any joint, closely-held business investment with the enterprise or with any officer, director or principal stockholders thereof that was material in relation to the member's net worth or to the net worth of the member's firm.
>   4. Had any loan to or from the enterprise or any officer, director, or principal stockholder of the enterprise except as specifically permitted in Interpretation 101-5.
>
> B. During the period covered by the financial statements, during the period of the professional engagement, or at the time of expressing an opinion, a member or a member's firm:
>
>   1. Was connected with the enterprise as a promoter, underwriter, or voting trustee, as a director or officer, or in any capacity equivalent to that of a member of management or of an employee.
>   2. Was a trustee for any pension or profit-sharing trust of the enterprise.

The above Interpretation indicates that two main types of relationships hinder the CPA's independence. The first is a financial relationship between the CPA and the client (part A). According to Interpretation 101-1 the CPA is not permitted to have any direct financial interest with the client. Direct ownership of shares of the client's stock is considered to be a direct financial interest. In addition, the CPA is not permitted to have a *material* indirect financial interest in a client. An example of an indirect financial interest would be owning shares of a mutual fund that invested in the client's stock. Finally, part A of Interpretation 101-1 identifies three other types of financial relationships (serving as a trustee or executor, having material joint business investments with client personnel, and having certain types of loans) that may also impair the CPA's independence.

In addition to financial relationships, managerial (or employment) relationships with the client also impair a CPA's independence (part B). That is, the CPA is not permitted to undertake any activities that are equivalent to the duties of management or of a client employee. As will be discussed later, this proscription does not prevent the CPA from performing consulting services.

Who must be Independent? The first issue in discussing independence is to identify the types of engagements in which CPAs must be independent. It is important that CPAs have independence in any engagements in which their work will be used by third parties in the public domain. Therefore, in any type of attest engagement (including an audit examination), it is imperative for the CPA to be independent in fact and independent in appearance. In contrast, the primary beneficiary of the CPA's work in tax engagements or consulting engagements is the client itself. As a result, CPAs are not required to be independent when performing tax and consulting services. In fact, in providing these types of services, CPAs assume the role of a "client advocate."

Once the types of engagements in which a CPA must be independent have been identified, the next issue is which individuals within a CPA firm must be independent with respect to attest clients. Interpretation 101-9 summarizes the AICPA's basic posture with respect to this issue by defining the phrase "member or a member's firm" as:

1. All partners, proprietors, or shareholders located in any offices of a firm.
2. All individuals with a "managerial position" located in any office of the firm performing a significant portion of the engagement. In most cases, individuals at the rank of audit manager/supervisor and above are considered to hold "managerial positions."
3. All individuals participating in the actual audit engagement.

▶ **Example**

CPA Firm X has offices in Los Angeles and Baltimore, with the Los Angeles office performing the entire audit of Client Y. The following individuals are precluded from having the relationships noted in Interpretation 101-1 with Client Y:

1. Partners in either office of Firm X.
2. Managers and/or supervisors in the Los Angeles office of Firm X.
3. Audit seniors and staff that participate in the audit of Client Y.

Although these relationships are identified by the AICPA, many firms implement even stricter guidance for their own practice. For example, some firms prohibit the relationships specified in Interpretation 101-1 for all of their personnel in any office of the firm.

Family Relationships. If a CPA meets the definition of "member or member's firm," the next question is whether his or her relatives are affected by the relationships summarized in Interpretation 101-1. Interpretation 101-9 identifies three groups of relatives. Spouses and dependent persons are generally prohibited from having the same relationships with clients as CPAs. The exception is that a spouse or dependent person can be employed with an audit or attest client as long as the position does not allow him or her to exert "significant influence" over the operating policies and procedures of the client. Positions of significant influence include promoter, underwriter, voting trustee, general partner, director, Chief Executive Officer, Chief Operating Officer, Chief Financial Officer, and Chief Accounting Officer. In addition, if a spouse or dependent person occupies an "audit-sensitive" position, the member should not participate in the engagement. Audit-sensitive positions include cashier, internal auditor, accounting supervisor, purchasing agent, and inventory warehouse supervisor.

The second group of relatives identified by Interpretation 101-9 is nondependent close relatives. Nondependent close relatives include nondependent children, stepchildren, brothers, sisters, parents, parents-in-law, and their respective spouses. With respect to these relatives, the following relationships are prohibited:

1. A direct financial interest for close relatives of members participating in the engagement. This interest is only prohibited if it is material and the member has knowledge of the investment.
2. Employment of close relatives of members participating in the engagement in positions of "significant influence" or "audit-sensitive" positions.
3. Employment of close relatives of partners and managerial personnel of offices participating in a significant portion of the engagement in a position of "significant influence."

The final group of relatives identified by Interpretation 101-9 is nonclose relatives. These relatives would be any individuals not classified as: (1) spouses and dependent persons, or (2) nondependent close relatives. Relationships between these relatives and clients generally would not inhibit the independence of the member or his or her firm.

> ▶ **Example**
>
> A partner of CPA Firm Z has a nondependent son employed with a potential audit client as a cashier and a wife employed as a chief financial officer. Because the partner meets the definition of "member or member's firm," the partner's spouse impairs the independence of the firm, for the wife's position is one of significant influence.
>
> In contrast, while the son's position is "audit-sensitive", it would not impair the firm's independence as long as the partner does not participate in the audit engagement. According to Interpretation 101-9, the son would be classified as a nondependent close relative.
>
> What if a staff member had a spouse that was employed in a position of significant influence? This would not impair the firm's independence as long as the staff member did not participate in the engagement. Recall that, unless a staff member participates in the engagement, he or she does not meet the definition of "member or member's firm."

In any case, CPAs should carefully evaluate all possible impairments of their independence. Because of the importance of independence, it is generally advisable to conservatively evaluate any potential impairments.

Loans. The AICPA's position on permitting loans to CPAs or CPA firms from their audit clients has recently changed.[4] Prior to 1992, CPAs were permitted to have loans from their clients as long as these loans were made using "normal lending procedures". Normal lending procedures mean that the loan has similar interest rates, repayment schedules, and collateral requirements as other loans made by that institution. However, because of some well-publicized loans (and non-repayments) involving CPAs and their audit clients, the AICPA has recently placed more restrictions on loans made to CPAs.[5]

---

[4] "Accounting Group Restricts Loans Given by Clients," *The Wall Street Journal* (October 1, 1991), A2.

[5] "Cheap Bank Loans for Accountants Come Under Fire," *The Wall Street Journal* (February 27, 1991), B1, B3.

Under the current Code of Professional Conduct, the following types of loans are permitted between clients and CPAs:

1. Automobile loans and lease agreements collateralized by the automobile.
2. Loans of the surrender value under terms of an insurance policy.
3. Borrowings collateralized by cash deposits at the lending institution.
4. Credit card balances and cash advances on checking accounts with an aggregate balance of $5,000 or less.

In addition to the above, any home mortgages, other secured loans, or loans not material to the CPA's net worth can be held if obtained prior to January 1, 1992. These types of loans are referred to as "grandfathered" loans. However, after January 1, 1992, CPAs are not permitted to obtain these types of loans from attest clients.

Bookkeeping/Accounting Services. Another issue related to independence is whether a CPA can perform accounting services and then perform an audit examination for the same client. A question arises about the CPA's independence in these situations because CPAs are auditing their own work. However, in Interpretation 101-3, the AICPA does not consider the CPA's independence impaired when he or she performs accounting or bookkeeping services if the following three conditions are met:

1. The client must accept final responsibility for the financial statements.
2. The CPA must not assume the role of a client employee or management.
3. When financial statements are prepared from books or records the CPA has maintained, she or he must comply with generally accepted auditing standards.

Interestingly, the SEC disagrees with the AICPA on this issue. For SEC clients, CPAs cannot perform bookkeeping/accounting services and audit services. However, most SEC companies have large accounting staffs and do not have the need for an external CPA to perform accounting and bookkeeping services.

Consulting Services. A dramatically-growing function for accounting firms is providing consulting services to clients. As noted in Chapter 1, consulting services involve CPAs providing technical advise and recommendations to their clients on various financial and operating matters. The large revenues provided by consulting services has raised questions about the effect of these services on the CPA's independence in performing attest services. That is, will CPAs be willing to issue unfavorable opinions on the client's financial statements and risk the loss of revenues from both future audit engagements and consulting engagements?

The AICPA has concluded that performing consulting services does not impair a CPA's independence with respect to the audit of a client's financial statements. However, in its deliberations on this matter, the AICPA cautions that the CPA must not assume the role of client management or an employee as she or he renders these services. To enhance perceptions of independence, Big Six firms have started organizing their consulting services apart from the remainder of their practices.[6]

Other Issues Related to Independence. The above issues reflect only a small number of possible influences on the CPA's independence with respect to their clients. Many other issues and influences could be discussed at this point. For example, the AICPA notes that the CPA is not considered to be independent during the current year's audit examination if audit fees from one or more prior year(s) remain unpaid by the client (Interpretation 101-6). In addition, actual or threatened litigation by the client against the auditor would also impair that auditor's independence.

The Appendix summarizes the current Interpretations related to independence. While many of these Interpretations have been discussed throughout this chapter, the reader should refer to the Professional Standards for more information regarding the various issues affecting auditor independence. In addition, it is important to note that a large number of Ethics Rulings provide practitioners with further guidance regarding factors affecting the independence of a CPA.

◘ Integrity and Objectivity: Rule 102

> In the performance of any professional service, a member shall maintain objectivity and integrity, shall be free of conflicts of interest, and shall not knowingly misrepresent facts or subordinate his or her judgment to others.

Rule 102 prohibits the CPA from misrepresenting facts to the client or other third parties (Interpretation 102-1). In addition, under Interpretation 102-2, if CPAs maintain any significant relationships with persons, entities, products, or services that may impair their objectivity with respect to their clients, these relationships should be disclosed to the client or other appropriate parties (such as the employing firm). Finally, under Interpretation 102-4, CPAs are not permitted to subordinate their judgment to others.

---

[6] For example, Arthur Andersen & Co., S.C. is the parent to Arthur Andersen and Andersen Consulting. See R. Greene and K. Barrett, "Auditing the Accounting Firms," *Financial World* (September 27, 1994), 30-55.

CHAPTER CHECKPOINTS

2-5. What portions of the Code of Conduct must be observed by CPAs in private practice? CPAs performing nonattest services?

2-6. Define independence in fact and independence in appearance. Which type of independence is necessary under the Code of Professional Conduct?

2-7. In what types of engagements are CPAs required to maintain independence?

2-8. What individuals in a CPA firm fall under the category of a "member or a member's firm"?

2-9. Can CPAs perform bookkeeping services for clients and retain their independence? Consulting services?

◘ General Standards: Rule 201

A member shall comply with the following standards and with any interpretations thereof by bodies designated by Council:

> **A.** *Professional Competence.* Undertake only those professional services that the member or the member's firm can reasonably expect to be completed with professional competence.
>
> **B.** *Due Professional Care.* Exercise due professional care in the performance of professional services.
>
> **C.** *Planning and Supervision.* Adequately plan and supervise the performance of professional services.
>
> **D.** *Sufficient Relevant Data.* Obtain sufficient relevant data to afford a reasonable basis for conclusions or recommendations in relation to any professional services performed.

Rules 201 B (due professional care), 201 C (planning and supervision) and 201 D (sufficient relevant data) are incorporated in the ten basic GAAS discussed in the previous chapter. The remaining part of this Rule (professional competence) indicates that CPAs should only undertake work for which they are technically qualified. CPAs initially may have, or feel they have, the competence to complete a particular engagement. However, during the course of their engagement they may find that they must do additional research or consultation with others in particular areas. In interpreting Rule 201, the AICPA notes that this is normal and does not signify any lack of competence (Interpretation 201-1).

◘ Compliance with Standards: Rule 202

> A member who performs auditing, review, compilation, management consulting, tax, or other professional services shall comply with standards promulgated by bodies designated by Council.

Rule 202 requires that CPAs comply with the professional standards that apply to the type of engagement they are conducting. As noted in Rule 202, different professional standards apply to various engagements performed by CPAs. Figure 2-2 identifies the various bodies designated by the Council of the AICPA for different types of engagements. Notice from Figure 2-2 that the "body" designated to establish auditing standards is the Auditing Standards Board of the AICPA. Also notice that the "standards" applicable to audits are GAAS (in the form of *Statements on Auditing Standards*). Thus, if a CPA does not comply with *Statements on Auditing Standards* in performing an audit, that CPA has violated Rule 202.

Body	Service Area	Pronouncements
Auditing Standards Board	Audits of financial statements	Statements on Auditing Standards
	Attest engagements	Statements on Standards for Attestation Engagements
Management Consulting Services Committee	Consulting services	Statements on Standards for Consulting Services
Financial Accounting Standards Board	Standards for preparation and presentation of financial statements	Statements on Financial Accounting Standards and Interpretations
Accounting and Review Services Committee	Unaudited financial statements and unaudited information for nonpublic entities	Statements on Standards for Accounting and Review Services
Tax Executive Committee	Tax services	Statements on Responsibilities in Tax Practice

Figure 2-2: *Bodies Designated to Establish Professional Standards*

◻ Accounting Principles: Rule 203

> A member shall not: (1) express an opinion or state affirmatively that the financial statements or other financial data of any entity are presented in conformity with GAAP; or (2) state that or she is not aware of any material modifications that should be made to such statements or data in order for them to be in conformity with GAAP, if such statements or data contain any departure from an accounting principle promulgated by bodies designated by Council to establish such principles that has a material effect on the statements or data taken as whole. If, however, the statements or data contain such a departure and the member can demonstrate that due to unusual circumstances the financial statements or data would otherwise have been misleading, the member can comply with the rule by describing the departure, its approximate effects, if practicable, and the reasons why compliance with the principle would result in a misleading statement.

Rule 203 relates to the role of GAAP during the auditor's examination. In general, Rule 203 notes that the auditor should not issue an unqualified opinion on an entity's financial statements if they are not presented in accordance with GAAP. However, Interpretation 203-1 indicates that in some very unusual circumstances, GAAP will result in misleading financial statements. As will be discussed in Chapter 17, when the application of GAAP results in misleading financial statements, the CPA can issue an unqualified opinion. If a CPA does so, his or her report must be modified to: (1) describe the departure from GAAP, (2) discuss the effects of the departure on the financial statements, and (3) describe why compliance with GAAP would result in misleading financial statements.

CHAPTER CHECKPOINTS

2-10. List and briefly discuss the four general standards under Rule 201.

2-11. What body is designated to establish standards for auditing engagements? What are the standards promulgated by this body?

◻ Confidential Client Information: Rule 301

> A member in public practice shall not disclose any confidential client information without the specific consent of the client. This rule shall not be construed: (1) to relieve a member of his or her professional obligations under Rules 202 and 203; (2) to affect in any way the member's obligations to comply with a validly-issued and enforceable subpoena or summons; (3) to prohibit review of a member's professional practice under AICPA or state CPA society or Board of Accountancy authorization; or (4) to preclude a member from initiating a complaint with, or responding to any inquiry made by, the ethics division or trial board of the Institute or a duly-constituted investigative or disciplinary body of a State CPA Society or Board of Accountancy. Members of any of the bodies identified in (4) above and members involved with professional practice reviews in (3) above shall not use to their own advantage or disclose any member's confidential client information that comes to their attention in carrying out those activities. This prohibition shall not restrict members' exchange of information in connection with the investigative or disciplinary proceedings described in (4) above or the professional practice reviews described in (3) above.

During an audit examination, the CPA acquires a great deal of knowledge about the client and its operations. For example, in gathering evidence during the audit, CPAs have knowledge of the net income earned by their clients before this information is known by the investing public. In addition, CPAs are frequently in position to obtain knowledge of important nonfinancial information (such as trade secrets and other product development matters) with respect to their clients. Rule 301 strictly prohibits disclosure of any confidential client information obtained during the course of an audit examination.

Rule 301 identifies four situations in which CPAs can disclose client information without their consent. First, this rule does not supersede the auditor's responsibility with respect to the client's financial statements under Rules 202 and 203. For example, if a client does not wish to disclose a contingent liability in its footnotes when the disclosure of such a liability is required under GAAP, the auditor must mention this liability in his or her audit report, even without the client's consent. Secondly, Rule 301 does not apply to situations where CPAs may need to reveal information about their clients in a court of law. While society has granted certain professions (e.g., medicine and law) the right of "privileged communication," the accounting profession does not have this right. The final two situations in which client information may be revealed by the CPA relate to peer reviews of the CPA's practice and responding to inquiries of the AICPA, State Societies of CPAs, or State Boards of Accountancy.

Interpretation 301-3 indicates that others may have access to certain client information in cases where a CPA's practice is being reviewed in conjunction with a prospective sale, purchase, or merger. In these cases, Rule 301 does not prohibit the CPA from revealing client information. However, this Interpretation indicates that appropriate precautions should be taken to ensure that the second party does not disclose any information obtained during such a review.

AND THE OSCAR GOES TO ...[7]

A unique example of confidential client information is the role played by Price Waterhouse in tabulating the votes for the winners of the Academy Awards, which are presented every March. One of the partners involved in the tally (Dan Lyle) notes that "while you have that information, you have some thing significant." During their tenure in providing assistance to the Academy of Motion Picture Arts and Sciences, Price Waterhouse partners have withstood many temptations. For example, when Chevy Chase was the emcee, he offered a $1,000 reward for information about the identify of a winner in any category for use in his opening monologue. While Mr. Lyle noted that "I had never seen anyone pull a thousand-dollar bill out of his wallet before," he politely refused Mr. Chase's offer.

---

[7] "Who'll Win the Oscars? Only They Know," *The Wall Street Journal* (March 29, 1993), A10.

◻ Contingent Fees: Rule 302

> A member in public practice shall not:
>
> 1. Perform for a contingent fee any professional services for, or receive such a fee from, a client for whom the member or a member's firm performs:
>   a. An audit or review of a financial statement; or
>   b. A compilation of a financial statement when the member expects, or reasonably might expect, that a third party will use the financial statement and the member's compilation report does not disclose a lack of independence; or,
>   c. An examination of prospective financial information, or,
> 2. Prepare an original or amended tax return or claim for a tax refund for a contingent fee for any client.
>
> ..... Solely for purposes of this rule, fees are not regarded as being contingent if fixed by courts or other public authorities, or in tax matters, if determined based on the results of judicial proceedings or the findings of governmental agencies.
>
> A member's fees may vary depending, for example, on the complexity of services rendered.

A **contingent fee** is any charge for services provided by a CPA that is based on the finding or outcome of that service. For example, if the CPA's fee is dependent on the type of opinion she or he expresses on the client's financial statements, it is fairly obvious that this opinion will be of little value to third parties. Prohibiting contingent fees is one means of not providing CPAs with an incentive to reach a particular conclusion.

Prior to the 1990s, CPAs were not permitted to accept contingent fees for any type of engagement. However, actions by the Federal Trade Commission resulted in the AICPA permitting contingent fees for nonattest engagements. Paragraph (1) of Rule 302 identifies the various types of engagements for which contingent fees are not permitted. Also, Rule 302 notes that CPAs cannot charge a contingent fee for preparing an original or amended tax return or claim for a tax refund.

CHAPTER CHECKPOINTS

2-12. What are some exceptions to the rule regarding confidential client information?

2-13. What is a contingent fee? In what types of engagements are CPAs permitted and not permitted to charge contingent fees to their clients?

◻ Acts Discreditable: Rule 501

Rule 501 prohibits the CPA from committing an act discreditable to the accounting profession. Interpretations of Rule 501 note that the following actions may be considered to be "acts discreditable": (1) retaining client records as a method to enforce payment of fees; (2) discriminating in hiring, promotion, or salary practices; (3) failing to follow standards, procedures, and/or other requirements in an audit of a governmental entity; (4) committing negligence in the preparation of financial statements or other records; (5) failing to follow requirements of regulatory agencies in providing attest or similar services; and (6) soliciting or disclosing CPA Examination questions or answers from the May 1996 exam and beyond without authorization.

◻ Advertising: Rule 502

> A member in public practice shall not seek to obtain clients by advertising or other forms of solicitation in a manner that is false, misleading, or deceptive. Solicitation by the use of coercion, over-reaching, or harassing conduct is prohibited.

For more than 50 years, the AICPA prohibited all forms of advertising. In the mid-1970s, pressures to allow advertising began to appear. These pressures culminated with the United States Supreme Court ruling in *Bates v. State Bar of Arizona* that certain forms of advertising were permissible in the legal profession.[8] Based on this outcome, CPAs questioned the prohibition on advertising in their profession. Eventually, the AICPA moved to permit advertising for CPAs.

Currently, CPAs may advertise in any manner they wish. That is, the CPA may advertise as frequently as she or he desires, using any medium (television, radio, or print). Common characteristics of a CPA firm and its partners that can be included in advertising are listed below. While this list is not intended to be all-inclusive, it does provide an indication of how firms may choose to advertise their services:

1. Firm name, address, and telephone number.
2. Office hours.
3. Any foreign-language expertise.
4. Services offered by the firm and fees charged for those services.
5. Educational and professional attainments by firm members.

The only restriction imposed by Rule 502 is that advertising should not be "false, misleading, or deceptive." Examples of advertising activities identified by Interpretation 502-2 as false, misleading, or deceptive are presented in Figure 2-3.

The second part of Rule 502 relates to solicitation. **Solicitation** refers to the process of actively pursuing clients that are currently served by other CPAs. Like advertising, solicitation was banned for many years. While now permissible, Rule 502 prohibits the use of coercion, over-reaching, or harassing conduct in proposing services to another CPA's clients.

---

[8] *Bates, et al. v. State Bar of Arizona*, 97 S.Ct. 2691 (1977).

1. An activity that would create a false or unjustified expectation of favorable results.
2. An activity that implies the ability to influence any court, tribunal, regulatory agency, or similar body or official.
3. An activity that contains any other representations that would be likely to cause a reasonable person to misunderstand or be deceived.
4. An activity that contains a quote of a fee for services in the current or a future period when the CPA is aware but the potential client is not aware that the fee will likely be substantially increased.

Figure 2-3: *A Partial List of Activities Considered to be False, Misleading, or Deceptive*

CPA FIRMS IN THE PUBLIC EYE

The decreased restrictions on advertising by CPA firms can be readily seen by viewers of major sporting events. For example, professional golfer Loren Roberts sports a visor bearing the name of Ernst & Young as he competes on the Professional Golfers' Association (PGA) tour. Also, Andersen Consulting (the consulting arm of Arthur Andersen & Co., S.C.) sponsors a world "match-play" golf championship. Finally, Coopers & Lybrand was the sixth-heaviest advertiser during Super Bowl XXVII, trailing only such advertising giants as Pepsi-Cola, Anheuser-Busch, Reebok International, Seven-Up, and Nike. Coopers spent a total of $1.7 million for two 30-second spots during the game between the Dallas Cowboys and Buffalo Bills.[9]

---

[9] "Super Bowl '93: The Bodies are Already Piled Up," *Business Week* (January 25, 1993), 65.

◻ Commissions: Rule 503

A. *Prohibited commissions*

A member in public practice shall not for a commission recommend or refer to a client any product or service, or for a commission recommend or refer any product or service to be supplied by a client or receive a commission, when the member or the member's firm also performs for that client

(a) an audit or review of a financial statement; or
(b) a compilation of a financial statement when the member expects, or reasonably might expect, that a third party will use the financial statement and the member's compilation report does not disclose a lack independence; or
(c) an examination of prospective financial information.

B. *Disclosure of permitted commissions*

A member in public practice who is not prohibited by this rule from performing services for or receiving a commission and who is paid or expects to be paid a commission shall disclose that fact to any person or entity to whom the member recommends or refers a product or service to which the commission relates.

C. *Referral fees*

Any member who accepts a referral fee for recommending or referring any service of a CPA to any person or entity or who pays a referral fee to obtain a client shall disclose such acceptance or payment to the client.

During an engagement, CPAs may provide the client with various suggestions regarding the products or services of another entity. For example, clients may ask CPAs to evaluate various computer systems or software packages and make recommendations about these products. Alternatively, CPAs may find themselves in a position to recommend the products or services of their clients to others. If the CPA receives a commission for his or her referral, a potential conflict of interest exists. This situation is depicted below.

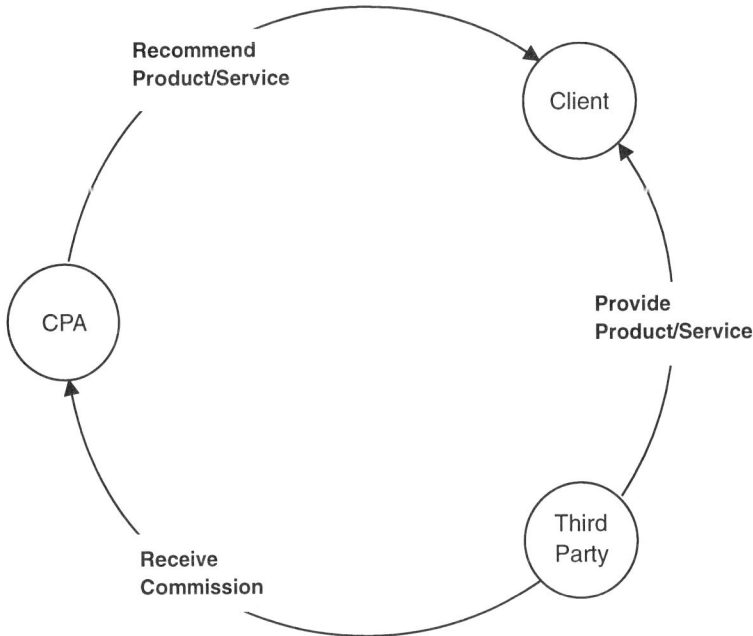

Similar to contingent fees, the portion of the Code relating to commissions has been substantially changed to reflect the consent agreement between the AICPA and the Federal Trade Commission in 1990. Under the revised Code, CPAs are not permitted to accept commissions when certain types of attest engagements are performed for the client.[10] Commissions are acceptable for nonattest clients as long as the CPA discloses the commission to individual(s) to whom products or services are referred. It is important to note that, under previous rules, CPAs were not permitted to accept a commission for referring products or services involving any clients (either attest or nonattest).

In Rule 503, the AICPA has distinguished between commissions (normally related to products and services provided by non-CPAs) and referral fees (relating to the services of a CPA). Under Rule 503, CPAs can accept or pay referral fees for any type of engagement (either attest or nonattest) as long as these fees are disclosed to the client. Previously, all such fees were prohibited.

---

[10] Technically, a compilation engagement (see (b) of part A) is not considered an attest engagement. However, Rule 503 specifically prohibits CPAs from accepting commissions for compilation engagements when the CPA's report does not disclose the lack of independence resulting from the commission.

2-20   I/ The Auditing Environment

Form of Organization and Name: Rule 505

> A member may practice public accounting only in the form of organization permitted by state law or regulation whose characteristics conform to resolutions of Council. A member shall not practice public accounting under a firm name that is misleading. Names of one or more past partners or shareholders may be included in the firm name of a successor partnership or corporation. Also, a partner or shareholder surviving the death or withdrawal of all other partners or shareholders may continue to practice under such name which includes the name of past partners or shareholders for up to two years after becoming a sole practitioner.
>
> A firm may not designate itself as "Members of the American Institute of Certified Public Accountants" unless all of its partners or shareholders are members of the Institute.

In general, the basic idea underlying the guidance for naming a CPA firm is to do so in a manner that does not mislead outside parties. Thus, the firm name should not indicate that the firm is comprised of more than one CPA unless this is the case. Notice from the text of Rule 505 that the sole exception to this Rule is in cases where all but one partner or shareholder withdraws from a partnership. In these cases, the remaining partner can continue to use the partnership name for up to two years.

Another issue related to the name of the CPA firm is indicating specialization. For example, can a CPA use the name "Albert Vaughn, Tax Specialist"? As long as the specialization is not misleading, Rule 505 does not preclude the use of this designation. Also, if the firm name includes the designation "Members of the American Institute of Certified Public Accountants," all shareholders and partners (whether included in the firm name or not) must be members of the AICPA.

> ▶ Example
>
> A CPA firm consists of five partners: A, B, C, D, and E. The firm cannot use the designation "A, B, and C, CPAs" unless A, B, C, D, and E are CPAs. Note that it is irrelevant that D and E are not named in the firm designation.

In addition to the name of practice used by a CPA, Rule 505 also addresses the form of entity under which the CPA may practice. Prior to 1992, CPAs could practice as a proprietorship, partnership, or professional corporation; however, most auditing services were performed by firms organized as partnerships. Two major disadvantages of the partnership form of organization are: (1) creditors may seek recovery against the personal assets of a firm's partners for partnership obligations, and (2) a partner may be held personally liable for all actions of other partners as well as individuals under the supervision of a partner.

To limit the personal liability of their CPAs, firms may practice as a professional corporation. These corporations provide advantages to the CPA in that creditors cannot seek recovery against the personal assets of a partner for firm obligations. However, the rules and liabilities for professional corporations vary widely from state to state; the rules in certain states treat professional corporations like partnerships, while others treat these forms of organization like ordinary corporations.[11] Thus, in some cases, practicing public accounting as a professional corporation provides no real benefit to the CPA. In addition, the income earned by a professional corporation is taxed twice: once as income to the corporation (when earned) and again as income to the shareholders (when distributed).

In response to the increasing number and magnitude of lawsuits facing CPA firms in today's environment, Rule 505 has been modified to allow firms to practice public accounting in any manner permitted by the states in which they operate. Recent cases in New York and Hawaii that recognized the **limited liability partnership (LLP)** form of organization have led to all of the Big Six firms reorganizing from partnerships to LLPs.[12] An LLP is a form of partnership available to certain groups of licensed professionals, such as attorneys, doctors, and accountants. The distinguishing feature of an LLP is that these organizations combine the limited liability feature of corporations with the ease of formation feature of a partnership. Under an LLP, a partner's (owner's) personal assets are only at risk if his or her actions are responsible for the obligation. Figure 2-4 contrasts various characteristics of the partnership, professional corporation, and LLP forms of organization.

	Partnership	Professional Corporation	Limited Liability Partnership
Taxation of Firm Income	Partners	Firm and Partners	Partners
Personal Assets "At Risk" for Actions of Others	Yes	Varies by State	No
Personal Assets "At Risk" for Own Actions	Yes	Varies by State	Yes

Figure 2-4: *Characteristics of Forms at Organizing CPA Firms*

---

[11] G. Gantt and L.D. Pumphrey, "Vicarious Liability in Accounting Corporations," *CPA Journal* (January 1991), 38-41.

[12] "LLP Becomes the Closing of Choice," *The CPA Journal* (October 1994), 8.

> **CHAPTER CHECKPOINTS**
>
> 2-14. List specific actions that are considered to be acts discreditable to the accounting profession.
>
> 2-15. Identify the types of advertising and solicitation in which CPAs are permitted to engage. What are some examples of advertising that are considered to be "false, misleading, or deceptive"?
>
> 2-16. Define commissions and referral fees. In what situations are CPAs permitted to accept commissions and referral fees?
>
> 2-17. List the advantages and disadvantages of organizing a CPA firm as a partnership, professional corporation, and limited liability partnership.

ENFORCEMENT OF THE CODE OF CONDUCT

The AICPA, State Societies of CPAs, and the State Boards of Accountancy each have the authority to enforce their individual Codes of Conduct. In order to standardize the enforcement of the Code of Professional Conduct, many State Societies have become involved in a national ethics enforcement system. Under this arrangement (known as the Joint Ethics Enforcement Program), complaints against a CPA or CPA firm can be referred to either the AICPA or a State Society of CPAs. Based on the nature of the complaint, it is heard by the AICPA Ethics Division, a State Society Ethics Committee, or both. These bodies, in turn, can either rule on the compliant or refer the compliant to a National Joint Trial Board. The following are possible disciplinary actions that can result from violations of the Code of Professional Conduct:

- acquittal
- censure
- suspension of membership in the AICPA or State Society of CPAs (for up to two years)
- termination of membership in the AICPA or State Society of CPAs
- enrollment in continuing education courses and submission of working papers and other engagement information for review

While both the AICPA and State Societies have enforcement power, these two organizations are voluntary professional associations. As a result, the right of a CPA to practice public accounting is not affected by termination of membership in either of these organizations. Therefore, the real power to enforce the Code of Professional Conduct lies with the various State Boards of Accountancy. The State Boards of Accountancy have the power to revoke or suspend the practitioner's CPA license or their right to practice.

In addition to violations of the Code of Professional Conduct, the AICPA's bylaws identify certain actions that result in automatic disciplinary actions. Two examples of actions that result in automatic termination of AICPA membership for CPAs are: (1) conviction of crimes punishable by imprisonment for more than one year, or (2) filing or assisting their clients in filing a false and fraudulent income tax return.

Figure 2-5 provides a sample of violations of the Code of Conduct and disciplinary actions resulting from those violations, as reported in *The CPA Letter* (a periodic publication of the AICPA) and the monthly newsletter of a State Board of Public Accountancy.

Violation	Disciplinary Action
Rule 301 (disclosed client information to a newspaper reporter)	• Six-month suspension of AICPA and State Society membership • Complete seven hours of continuing professional education
Rules 102 and 501 (filed documents which knowingly misrepresented facts)	• Expelled from AICPA and State Society
Rules 101, 202, 203, and 501 (on governmental audit)	• Two-year suspension of AICPA and State Society membership • Complete 87 hours of continuing professional education • Submit all audit, review, and compilation engagements for review prior to issuing reports during two-year period
Committing securities fraud, mail fraud, and obstruction of justice	• Membership terminated
Rule 102, 201(A), 202, and 203 (failed to properly prepare an audit opinion and financial statements)	• Prohibited from performing attest engagements • Complete three-hour college course with a grade of "B" or better • Accept reprimand

Figure 2-5: *Violations of Code of Conduct and Disciplinary Actions*

◉ QUALITY CONTROL

The preceding discussion illustrates the importance of complying with the Code of Professional Conduct. Now, the obvious question arises: How do CPAs and CPA firms make sure their actions do not violate the Code? This is done by establishing firm-wide policies and procedures regarding professional activities. These firm-wide policies and procedures are collectively known as quality control standards.

Quality control standards comprise the methods used by a firm to ensure that their practices are in accordance with professional responsibilities. Effective quality control standards provide CPAs and CPA firms with reasonable assurance of conforming with the Rules of Conduct. Recalling that Rule 202 requires CPAs to comply with the professional standards related to the type of engagement they are performing, quality control standards will also allow CPAs and CPA firms to comply with GAAS. To date, two *Statements of Quality Control Standards* have been issued to provide firms with respect to establishing quality control standards.

In addition to allowing firms to enhance the conformity of their practices with GAAS and the Rules of Conduct, quality control standards help improve the overall efficiency and quality of firm practice. In establishing quality control policies and procedures, a CPA firm should consider the following five categories:[13]

1. **Independence, Integrity, and Objectivity.** Personnel should maintain independence (in fact and in appearance), perform all professional responsibilities with integrity, and maintain objectivity in discharging professional responsibilities.
2. **Personnel Management.** Personnel management encompasses hiring, assigning personnel to engagements, professional development, and advancement activities.
3. **Acceptance and Continuance of Clients and Engagements.** Policies and procedures should be established for deciding whether to accept or continue a client relationship and whether to perform a specific engagement for that client.
4. **Engagement Performance.** Engagement performance encompasses planning, performing, supervising, reviewing, documenting, and communicating the results of each engagement.
5. **Monitoring.** The firm should consider whether the elements of quality control are suitably designed and are being effectively applied.

◘ Monitoring Quality Control Standards: Peer Reviews

Once the quality control standards described above have been established by a CPA firm, it is important that they be monitored on a periodic basis to ensure their effectiveness. The importance of periodic monitoring is evidenced by the AICPA requirement that all member firms participate in an approved practice-monitoring program. According to the AICPA Bylaws, firms must participate in peer review programs administered by the AICPA. The purpose of these programs is to allow CPAs to improve their practice through having their work evaluated by other CPAs.

Peer review covers three major areas: (1) the effectiveness of the firm's quality control standards, (2) the adequacy of the engagements performed by firms and the reports issued on those engagements, and (3) the firm's adherence to requirements for membership in the SEC Practice Section (SECPS) or Private Companies Practice Section (PCPS) (if applicable). Figure 2-6 summarizes the nature of the peer review undergone by CPA firms performing different types of engagements.

---

[13] American Institute of Certified Public Accountants (AICPA), *Statement of Quality Control Standards No. 2*, "System of Quality Control for a CPA Firm's Accounting and Auditing Practice" (New York: AICPA, 1996, QC 20.07).

	Audits/ Examinations	Compilations/ Reviews	Others
Review of Engagements and Reports	On-site	Off-site except for SECPS (on-site)	None
Quality Control Standards	Extensive Review	Limited Review	None
AICPA Section Membership Requirements	Yes, if Applicable	Yes, if Applicable	Yes, if Applicable

Figure 2-6: *Peer Review Requirements for CPA Firms*

As shown in Figure 2-6, the extent of peer review undergone by CPA firms depends upon: (1) their membership in a section of the Division for CPA Firms, and (2) the types of services provided by the CPA firm. Note from Figure 2-6 that all CPA firms performing audits are required to have a review of their quality control policies and procedures. In addition, these firms are required to have an on-site review[14] conducted by a peer review team. In an **on-site review**, the review team evaluates selected audit engagements performed during a particular year. In their evaluation, the review team examines documentation related to these engagements (in the form of audit workpapers) and the reports issued by the firm. Two primary questions are addressed during this review:

▶ Has the CPA's report been prepared in conformity with professional standards?

▶ Does the evidence gathered by the CPA provide a sufficient basis for his or her report?

Further, the CPA firms' quality control standards are evaluated to determine that they meet the criteria of *SQCS No. 1*. Finally, firms that are members of either the SECPS or PCPS are evaluated to determine whether they comply with the membership requirements of those sections.

If firms do not perform audits or examination engagements, but perform accounting and review services (such as compilations and reviews of financial statements), the scope of the peer review is less comprehensive. With the exception of firms belonging to the SECPS, CPA firms performing only accounting and review services are required to have off-site reviews. **Off-site reviews** require firms to submit background information, the client's financial statements, and their report for selected engagements to the peer review team. This information is examined to determine whether the financial statements and the CPA's report on the engagement conform with professional standards. In addition, as the peer review team examines information related to the selected engagements, they evaluate evidence relating to the reviewed firm's quality control standards. However, the scope of this evaluation is less than that of an on-site review. Finally, as with on-site reviews, firms that are mem-

---

[14] On-site reviews are also required for firms performing an examination of prospective financial statements. Similar to an audit, an examination of prospective financial statements is a type of attest engagement. These engagements are discussed in further detail in Chapter 17 of this text.

bers of either the SECPS or PCPS are evaluated to determine whether their practices conform to the membership requirements of those sections.

If firms do not perform audits or accounting and review services, there are generally no peer review requirements. However, as shown in Figure 2-6, firms belonging to the PCPS or SECPS are examined to determine whether they comply with the membership requirements of those sections.

WHAT PROBLEMS CAN BE FOUND BY PEER REVIEW[15]

Through the result of peer reviews, the following common deficiencies have been identified in the nine categories of quality control standards.

- Failure to document the firm's compliance with independence policies
- Failure to document resolution of independence questions
- Failure to document whether necessary consultations occurred
- Little or no continuing professional education in accounting and auditing areas related to the firm's areas of practice
- Failure to document the firm's compliance with client acceptance and continuance policies
- Inadequate or no annual inspection of engagements and of the firm's accounting and auditing policies and procedures

---

CHAPTER CHECKPOINTS

2-18. What parties can prevent individuals from practicing public accountancy because of violations of the Code of Professional Conduct?

2-19. Why should CPA firms establish quality control standards? List the five categories of quality control standards.

2-20. What is a peer review? What are the major areas of a firm's practice or operations covered in a peer review?

2-21. Distinguish between an on-site peer review and an off-site peer review.

---

[15] American Institute of Certified Public Accountants (AICPA), *Quality Control Manual for CPA Firms* (New York: AICPA, 1995).

Appendix

⊙ CURRENT INTERPRETATIONS UNDER THE CODE OF PROFESSIONAL CONDUCT

◘ Interpretations of Rule 101: Independence

101-1: Factors impairing independence of members (see text).

101-2: Former practitioners serving a client do not inhibit independence if:

1. payments to the practitioner for his or her interest in the firm do not create substantial doubt about the firm's ability to continue in existence;
2. the practitioner does not participate in the firm's business or professional activities; and,
3. the practitioner is not provided with office space and other amenities by his or her former firm.

101-3: Accounting services (see text).

101-4: A member can lend his or her name as honorary director or trustee for a not-for-profit organization, as long as the position is honorary and he or she does not participate in board or management functions.

101-5: Loans (see text).

101-6: Either potential or actual litigation brought by the client's management against the auditor may impair independence. Similarly, litigation brought by the auditor against the client's management would also impair independence.

101-7: Deleted.

101-8: If an audit client has an investee/investor relationship with another entity with whom the auditor has a financial or other relationship, the auditor's independence would be impaired with respect to the client when:

1. The member's investment in a nonclient investee is material (assuming that the client-nonclient relationship is not material);
2. The member's investment in a nonclient investor allows the auditor to exercise "significant influence" over the nonclient (assuming that the client-nonclient relationship is not material);
3. The member has any material indirect financial interest in a nonclient investee/investor having a material relationship with a client; and,
4. The member has any direct financial interest in a nonclient investee/investor having a material relationship with the client.

101-9: Definition of Member or Member's Firm and Family Relationships (see text).

101-10: General-purpose financial statements for a governmental entity may consist of financial statements of an oversight entity and one or more other entities (component entities). In the audit of governmental entities, the member must be independent of both the oversight entity and each component entity.

101-11: The member must remain independent in performing attest services. An attest service is one in which the member issues a written communication that expresses a conclusion about the reliability of a written assertion that is the responsibility of another party.

101-12: The existence of a material cooperative arrangement between a member's firm and the client will impair independence. Examples of cooperative arrangements include joint ventures to develop products or services and prime/subcontractor arrangements to provide services or products to a third party.

◻ Interpretations of Rule 102: Integrity and Objectivity

102-1: The member should not knowingly make, or permit or direct others to make, false and misleading entries in an entity's financial statements.

102-2: If a member has some relationship with another entity that could impair his or her objectivity with respect to a client, he or she may consider disclosing this relationship to the client and obtaining the client's consent for continuing this relationship.

102-3: When dealing with his or her employer's external accountant, a member must be candid and not knowingly misrepresent facts or fail to disclose material facts.

102-4: A member cannot knowingly misrepresent facts or subordinate his or her judgment when performing professional services.

102-5: The provisions of Rule 102 apply to members providing educational services (teaching full- or part-time at a university, teaching a continuing education course, or engaging in research or scholarship).

102-6: The provisions of Rule 102 apply to members performing professional services that involve supporting the client's position or otherwise acting as an advocate on behalf of the client (such as tax services, consulting services, or advocating the client's position on accounting or financial reporting issues).

◘ Interpretation of Rule 201: General Standards

201-1: The need for additional research and/or consultation during an engagement does not signify a lack of technical competence.

◘ Interpretations of Rule 203: Accounting Principles

203-1: Misleading departures from GAAP (see text).

203-2: Interpretations issued by the FASB should be considered by the auditor in determining whether a departure from GAAP exists.

203-3: Deleted.

203-4: Rule 203 applies to any communication between the client and its auditor or others regarding the client's financial statements.

◘ Interpretations of Rule 301: Confidential Client Information

301-1: Deleted.

301-2: Deleted.

301-3: A member can allow others to review his or her practice in conjunction with the purchase, sale, or merger of that practice as long as the member takes precautions so that the prospective purchaser does not disclose any information obtained during the review.

◘ Interpretation of Rule 302: Contingent Fees

302-1: CPAs can charge contingent fees in performing certain types of tax services.

◘ Interpretations of Rule 501: Acts Discreditable

501-1: The member should not retain client records after a demand has been made for them. While the member should return workpapers that contain information not reflected in the client's books and records (for example, adjusting, closing, or combining journal entries) to the client upon request, he or she may require that fees due be paid prior to the return of this information.

501-2: Discrimination in hiring, promotion, or salary practices is an act discreditable to the accounting profession.

501-3: Failure to follow required standards or procedures in governmental audits is an act discreditable to the accounting profession.

501-4: Negligence in the preparation of financial statements is an act discreditable to the accounting profession.

501-5: If a member performs attest or other services for governmental bodies, commissions, or other regulatory agencies, he or she should follow the established requirements of those agencies. These requirements are in addition to the requirements of GAAS.

501-6: Soliciting or knowingly disclosing Uniform CPA Examination questions and/or answers from the May 1996 exam and beyond without the written authorization of the AICPA is an act discreditable to the accounting profession.

◘ Interpretations of Rule 502: Advertising and Solicitation

502-1: Deleted.

502-2: False, misleading, or deceptive advertising is prohibited.

502-3: Deleted.

502-4: Deleted.

502-5: If members obtain clients through the efforts of third parties, they should ascertain that all promotional efforts conform to Rule 502.

501-6: Soliciting or knowingly disclosing Uniform CPA Examination questions and/or answers from the May 1996 exam and beyond without the written authorization of the AICPA is an act discreditable to the accounting profession.

◘ Interpretations of Rule 505: Form of Practice and Name

505-1: A member may have a financial interest in a commercial accounting corporation if the member's interest is not material and the member is related to the corporation solely as an investor.

505-2: If members operate a separate business that offers clients the types of services rendered by public accountants, the member must abide by all Rules of Conduct. Members must also abide by these Rules if they hold out to the public as being a CPA or public accountant when offering services traditionally rendered by public accountants.

SUMMARY OF KEY POINTS

1. The most recent Code of Professional Conduct consists of four main components. The first component is a set of Principles that are aspirational in nature. The second part of the Code is a set of rules that must be observed by CPAs in public practice. These rules are known as the Rules of Conduct. While CPAs in public practice must observe all Rules, CPAs not in public practice are only required to observe Rules 102, 201-203, and 501.

2. The final two components of the Code of Professional Conduct are Ethics Rulings and Interpretations. These components represent clarifications and elaborations on the existing Rules of Conduct based on actual situations encountered in practice.

3. Independence is the ability to act with integrity and objectivity. Two types of relationships may hinder a CPA's independence. First, the CPA should not hold a direct or material indirect financial interest in the client. Second, relationships in which the CPA is virtually a part of the client's management or an employee under management's control may hinder a CPA's independence.

4. Rule 201 (general standards) describes four general standards that must be followed by the CPA. CPAs must be technically competent, complete the engagement using due professional care, adequately plan and supervise the engagement, and obtain sufficient, relevant data.

5. Under Rule 202, CPAs are asked to comply with technical standards promulgated by appropriate bodies. Rule 203 requires that CPAs should not state that financial statements are presented in conformity with GAAP if these statements contain a material departure from a promulgated accounting principle. Such a departure is acceptable only if presentation under GAAP is misleading.

6. Two rules reflect the CPA's responsibilities to his or her clients. Rule 301 requires that the CPA should not disclose any confidential information obtained during the engagement except with the client's consent. Rule 302 states that a CPA's fee should not be based on a particular finding or outcome. This latter rule only applies to attest engagements.

7. Rule 501 prohibits a CPA from committing an act discreditable to the accounting profession. Such acts include retention of client records as a method of enforcing payment after the client has requested them or discrimination in hiring, promotion, or salary practices by a CPA firm.

8. Rule 502 permits advertising as long as it is not false, misleading, or deceptive. In addition, this rule prohibits solicitation of clients through the use of coercive, over-reaching, or harassing conduct.

9. According to Rule 503, CPAs cannot accept commissions for referring the products or services of another entity to his or her attest clients. However, commissions can be accepted from nonattest clients, as long as they are properly disclosed. In addition, CPAs can accept or pay fees for referrals of the services of other CPAs if these fees are disclosed to clients.

10. Rule 505 presents guidelines to the CPA concerning the form of practice and firm name. Under Rule 505, a CPA may practice public accounting in the form of a partnership,

proprietorship, professional corporation, or other form permitted by the state in which he or she practices.

11. A CPA firm establishes quality control standards to enhance the quality of its audit work. The five quality control standards suggested by *Statements on Quality Control Standards No. 2* include: (1) independence, integrity, and objectivity; (2) personnel management; (3) acceptance and continuance of clients and engagements; (4) engagement performance; and (5) monitoring.

12. To monitor their quality control standards, AICPA member firms are required to undergo a peer review every three years. The type of review required depends on the nature of services offered by the firm being reviewed.

GLOSSARY

Acts Discreditable. Acts discreditable to the accounting profession include: (1) retaining client records as a method to enforce payment of fees; (2) discriminating in hiring, promotion, or salary practices; (3) failing to following standards, procedures, and/or other requirements in the audit of a governmental entity; (4) committing negligence in the preparation of financial statements or other records; (5) failing to follow the requirements of regulatory agencies in performing attest or similar services; and (6) soliciting or disclosing CPA Examination questions and answers from the May 1996 exam and beyond without authorization.

Code of Professional Conduct. The Code of Professional Conduct consists of Principles, Rules, Interpretations, and Ethics Rulings that define acceptable and unacceptable behaviors for CPAs.

Commissions. Amounts paid or received by CPAs for referring: (1) the products and services of others to a client, or (2) the products or services of a client to others. Under Rule 503, CPAs are not permitted to accept commissions for attest clients. Although these commissions are permitted for nonattest clients, they must be disclosed to the client.

Contingent Fees. Fees that are based on the findings or outcomes of the engagement. CPAs are not permitted to charge contingent fees in attest engagements.

Ethics Rulings. Relatively specific clarifications of existing Rules of Conduct. Ethics Rulings are normally provided in a question/answer format.

Independence. The ability of a CPA to act in an unbiased manner. Under the Code of Professional Conduct, CPAs must be independent both in fact and in appearance.

Interpretations. General clarifications of existing Rules of Conduct based on situations encountered by CPAs in practice.

Off-Site Peer Review. A peer review in which the review team examines the client's financial statements and accountant's reports to determine whether they comply with professional standards. Off-site peer reviews are required if firms perform accounting and review service engagements but not audit engagements.

On-Site Peer Review. A peer review in which the review team: (1) examines engagement workpapers and reports, and (2) conducts a relatively thorough evaluation of the firm's quality control standards. On-site reviews are required for firms that perform audits of historical financial statements or examinations of prospective financial statements.

Peer Review. The review of a firm's practice by other CPAs. Peer reviews evaluate the quality control standards established by CPA firms, the reports issued by firms in their engagements and support for these reports, and the firm's adherence to requirements for section membership.

Public Practice. Any type of professional accounting-related services that are provided to external clients. Audits, consulting, tax, accounting/bookkeeping, and other types of services are examples of public practice.

Quality Control Standards. The methods used by a firm to ensure that their practices are in accordance with professional standards and the Code of Professional Conduct.

Rules of Conduct. Specific requirements that govern the performance of CPAs. Rules of Conduct delineate minimum standards of conduct and identify activities in which CPAs may or may not be engaged.

SUMMARY OF PROFESSIONAL PRONOUNCEMENTS

Statement on Quality Control Standards No. 2, "System of Quality Control for a CPA Firm's Accounting and Auditing Practice" (New York: AICPA, 1996, QC 20).

◉ QUESTIONS AND PROBLEMS

2-22. Select the **best** answer for each of the following items:

1. A CPA accepts an engagement for a professional service without violating the AICPA Code of Professional Conduct if the service involves:

   a. An audit engagement, and the fee is based on a percentage of the client's reported net income.
   b. Tax preparation, and the fee will be based on whether the CPA signs the tax returns prepared.
   c. A litigation matter, and the fee is not known but is to be determined by a district court.
   d. Tax return preparation, and the fee is to be based on the amount of taxes saved, if any.

2. Which of the following statements best describes why the public accounting profession has deemed it essential to promulgate a Code of Conduct and to establish a mechanism for enforcing observance of the Code?

   a. A distinguishing mark of a profession is its acceptance of responsibility to the public.
   b. A prerequisite to success is the establishment of a Code of Conduct that stresses primarily the professional's responsibility to clients and colleagues.
   c. A requirement of most state laws calls for the profession to establish a Code of Conduct.
   d. An essential means of self-protection for the profession is the establishment of flexible standards by the profession.

3. The AICPA Code of Professional Conduct states, in part, that a CPA should maintain integrity and objectivity. Objectivity in the Code refers to a CPA's ability:

   a. To maintain an impartial attitude on all matters that come under the CPA's review.
   b. To independently distinguish between accounting practices that are acceptable and those that are not.
   c. To be unyielding in all matters dealing with auditing procedures.
   d. To independently choose between alternative accounting principles and auditing standards.

4. Which of the following components of the Code of Professional Conduct are considered to be enforceable?

   a. Principles
   b. Rules of Conduct
   c. Interpretations
   d. b and c above
   e. All of the above

5. A CPA's retention of client records as a means of enforcing payment of an overdue audit fee is an action that is:

   a. Considered acceptable by the AICPA Code of Professional Conduct.
   b. Ill-advised because it would impair the CPA's independence with respect to the client.
   c. Considered discreditable to the profession.
   d. A violation of generally accepted auditing standards.

6. In which of the following instances would the accountant have least likely violated the Code of Professional Conduct's requirement for independence?

    a. A CPA has a material investment in an audit client held through a mutual fund.
    b. The partner of a CPA firm has a wife who is employed by an audit client as a Chief Executive Officer.
    c. A CPA has a large, direct investment in the stock of a client for whom tax services are provided.
    d. The husband of a staff accountant assigned to an engagement is employed by an audit client as a cashier.

7. Which of the following categories of quality control standards is concerned with planning and supervising personnel during the examination?

    a. Engagement performance.
    b. Independence, integrity, and objectivity.
    c. Monitoring.
    d. Personnel management.

8. Which of the following would be evaluated by the peer review team during an off-site review?

	Engagement Reports	Quality Control Standards
a.	Yes	Yes
b.	Yes	No
c.	No	Yes
d.	No	No

9. Which of the following situations would most likely represent a violation of the Code of Professional Conduct?

    a. A CPA's fee for a consulting engagement is based on the savings that result from her recommendation.
    b. A CPA's wife owns an immaterial direct financial interest in an audit client.
    c. A CPA firm is named "Jack Jones & Co., CPAs". Jack Jones is a retired partner in the firm.
    d. A CPA receives a fee for referring a former attest client to another CPA. This fee is disclosed to the client.

10. All of the following are considered acts discreditable to the accounting profession except:

    a. Disclosing questions appearing on the Uniform CPA Examination without the authorization of the AICPA.
    b. Retaining a client's records as a method to enforce payment of fees.
    c. Charging an attest client a fee based on the type of opinion issued on the financial statements.
    d. Committing negligence in the preparation of financial statements or records.

2-23. H.T. Smith, CPA, is asked by a prospective client to perform a consulting engagement. Smith, realizing the engagement is beyond her abilities, refers the prospective client to R. Jones, CPA, who performs the engagement. R. Jones sends H.T. Smith 10 percent of the fee in payment for the referral. Comment on this arrangement.

2-24. Joe Tack, CPA, performed tax and bookkeeping services for I.M. Cheap, Inc., for the fiscal year ended December 31, 19X1. Tack billed Cheap, Inc., $8,000 for his services. Cheap feels the fee is too high and refuses to pay anything. Because Tack is holding all of Cheap's journals and ledgers, he informs the president of Cheap, Inc., that he will retain Cheap Inc.'s books until the fee is paid. Comment on this situation.

2-25. J.C. Conman, president of Marginal Corporation, is in need of audited financial statements. He asks Sandra Honest, CPA, to estimate her fees for such an engagement. After a careful evaluation, Honest gives Conman an estimate range. Conman says that the estimate is too high but says he would be happy to pay Honest 4 percent of net income for that year. Comment on this situation.

2-26. I.M. Old, CPA, has a large practice. He is 65 years old and would like to retire. J.C. Young, CPA, is interested in purchasing Old's practice. To determine a fair purchase price, Old lets Young examine all of his records, working papers, and other documentation involving Old's clients. Comment on this situation.

2-27. R.A. Sideline, CPA, decides to render an additional service for her clients by arranging for them to purchase office supplies from a particular company at a reduced price. The supplier gives Sideline 1 percent of all such sales. Comment on this situation.

(AICPA Adapted)

2-28. Indicate whether each of the following situations would result in a violation of the AICPA's Code of Professional Conduct.

a. A sole proprietor (Jerry Jones) names his practice "Jerry Jones & Co., CPAs".
b. Mike Walters, CPA learns that one of his audit clients has earnings much higher than analyst forecasts. Noticing that the client's stock is trading at a low price, he mentions the abnormally high earnings to his uncle, who is considered to be a nonclose relative under the Code of Conduct.
c. Packard-Hewlett, one of Bell CPA's audit clients, has departed from a promulgated accounting principle in preparing its financial statements. Bell agrees with this departure from GAAP, because she feels that the financial statements would be misleading if prepared under GAAP.
d. Kelly, CPA accepts an engagement to audit a manufacturer of high-technology computer components. Kelly initially believes that she has sufficient industry knowledge to complete that engagement in accordance with professional standards. During the engagement, she realizes that she needs to obtain additional knowledge and refers to industry publications and audit guides.
e. Joe Alvarez, CPA is performing tax services for Ready-Fix. During his engagement, Joe comments about how his friends would really be interested in some of the products sold by Ready-Fix. After hearing this comment, Ready-Fix offers to pay Joe two percent of any sales made by Ready-Fix to Joe's friends.
f. Johnson, CPA advertises that he has expertise in providing tax services related to individual estates.
g. Seyl and Company, CPAs perform an audit of the financial statements of Wittenauer, Inc. Wittenauer's financial statements contain material misstatements. However, Seyl and Company did not know of these misstatements nor was their examination considered to be deficient in any manner.

h. CPA J is called into federal district court. The government subpoenas her workpapers for a particular client. J refuses, claiming that she is a professional and therefore has "privileged communication" with that client.

i. Steve Smith, CPA, is moving his office to a new building. He sends a notice to this effect to the local newspaper, which published it.

2-29. An auditor's report was appended to the financial statements of Worthmore, Inc. The statements consisted of a balance sheet, as of November 30, 19X1, and statements of income, retained earnings, and cash flows for the year then ended. The first three paragraphs of the report contained the wording of the standard unqualified report, and an additional paragraph read as follows:

> The wives of two partners of our firm owned a material investment in the outstanding common stock of Worthmore, Inc., during the fiscal year ending November 30, 19X1. The aforementioned individuals disposed of their holdings of Worthmore, Inc. on December 3, 19X1, in a transaction that did not result in a profit or a loss. This information is included in our report in order to comply with certain disclosure requirements of the Code of Professional Conduct of the American Institute of Certified Public Accountants.
>
> Bell & Davis
> Certified Public Accountants

Required:

a. Was the CPA firm of Bell & Davis independent with respect to the fiscal 19X1 examination of Worthmore's financial statement?
b. Do you find Bell & Davis's auditor's report satisfactory?
c. Assume that no members of Bell & Davis or any members of their families held any financial interests in Worthmore, Inc., during 19X1. For each of the following cases, indicate if independence would be lacking on behalf of Bell & Davis. In each case, explain why independence would or would not be lacking.

1. Two directors of Worthmore, Inc., became partners in the CPA firm of Bell & Davis on July 1, 19X1, resigning their directorships on that date.
2. During 19X1, the former controller of Worthmore, now a Bell & Davis partner, was frequently called on for assistance by Worthmore. He made decisions for Worthmore's management regarding fixed asset acquisitions and the company's product marketing mix. In addition, he conducted a computer feasibility study for Worthmore.

(AICPA Adapted)

2-30. Hostetler, CPA, is currently performing the audit examination of Giant Company and has done so for the last five years. In the current year, a disagreement concerning the appropriate form of disclosing a lawsuit brought against Giant Company has arisen. Hostetler believes that this litigation should be disclosed in Giant Company's footnotes as a contingency under FASB Statement No. 5, while Giant feels that such disclosure is unwarranted.

Can Giant use Rule 301 (confidential client information) as a basis for preventing disclosure of the litigation?

2-31. Comment on each of the following potential violations of the AICPA Code of Professional Conduct:

a. A CPA is performing an audit examination for a client. His uncle, with whom the CPA has infrequent contact, has a small investment in the common stock of that client.

b. Thurman, CPA is performing consulting services for Thomas, Inc. In the past, Thurman has always been paid an hourly fee. To increase Thurman's incentives, Thomas has offered to base Thurman's current fee on the amount of cost savings that result from implementing Thurman's recommendations.

c. S.H. Smith, CPA, is building her own office building. She places a sign on the building site that reads: "This is the future home of S. H. Smith, CPA."

d. A CPA is performing the audit examination for a mortgage company that holds the mortgage on that CPA's personal residence. The terms of that mortgage are identical to those offered by another institution at the time the CPA obtained the mortgage.

e. A CPA firm named itself Jones and Company, CPAs. All partners in the firm were CPAs; however, Jones is a former partner no longer affiliated with the firm.

f. CPA J places the following advertisement in the business section of the local newspaper: "Having problems with your independent auditor? Call CPA J at 555-1834 to find out how inexpensive our unqualified opinions are. We have no dissatisfied clients."

g. CPA Alex normally charges his audit clients a fixed fee for any audit services. One of his clients suggested basing Alex's fee on the earnings per share reported for the following year.

h. An audit client refused to disclose a contingent liability that meets criteria for disclosure at year end. This client cited Rule 301 (confidential client information) as the justification for not allowing the CPA to disclose this contingency in his report.

i. A CPA firm included information in its advertising brochures about the types of services offered and the qualification of its personnel.

2-32. During 19X1, your client, Big Corporation, requested that you conduct a feasibility study to advise management of the best way the corporation can utilize electronic data processing equipment and which computer, if any, best meets the corporation's requirements. You are technically competent in this area and accept the engagement. Upon completion of your study the corporation accepts your suggestions and installs the computer and related equipment that you recommended.

Required:

a. Discuss the effect the acceptance of this consulting engagement would have on your independence in expressing an opinion on the financial statements of the Big Corporation.

b. Instead of accepting the engagement, assume that you recommended Ike Mackey, of the CPA firm of Brown and Mackey, who is qualified in specialized services. Upon completion of the engagement, your client requests that Mackey's partner, John Brown, perform services in other areas. Should Brown accept the engagement?

c. A local printer of data processing forms customarily offers a commission for recommending him as supplier. The client is aware of the commission offer and suggests that Mackey accept it. Would it be proper for Mackey to accept the commission with the client's approval?

(AICPA Adapted)

2-33. The Rocky Hill Corporation was formed on October 1, 19X1, and its fiscal year ends on September 30, 19X2. You audited the corporation's opening balance sheet and rendered an unqualified opinion on it.

A month after rendering your opinion, you are offered the position of secretary of the company because of the need for a complete set of officers and for convenience in signing various documents. You will have no financial interest in the company through stock ownership or otherwise, will receive no salary, will not keep the books, and will not have any influence on its financial matters, other than occasional advice on income tax matters and similar advice normally given a client by a CPA.

Assume that you accept the offer but plan to resign the position prior to conducting your annual audit, with the intention of again assuming the office after rendering an opinion on the statements. Can you render an independent opinion on the financial statements?

(AICPA Adapted)

2-34. Tom Jencks, CPA, conducts a public accounting practice. In 19X1, Mr. Jencks and Harold Swann, a non-CPA, organized Electro-Data Corporation to specialize in computerized bookkeeping services. Mr. Jencks and Mr. Swann each supplied 50 percent of Electro-Data's capital, and each holds 50 percent of the capital stock. Mr. Swann is the salaried general manager of Electro-Data. Mr. Jencks is affiliated with the corporation only as a stockholder; he receives no salary and does not participate in day-to-day management. However, he has transferred all of his bookkeeping accounts to the corporation and recommends its services whenever possible.

Required:

Organizing your presentation around Mr. Jencks's involvement with Electro-Data Corporation, discuss the propriety of:

a. A CPA's participation in an enterprise offering computerized bookkeeping services.
b. The use of advertising by an enterprise in which a CPA holds an interest.
c. A CPA's transfer of bookkeeping accounts to a service company.
d. A CPA's recommendation of a particular bookkeeping service company.

(AICPA Adapted)

Learning Objectives

Study of the material in this chapter is designed to achieve several learning objectives. After studying this chapter you should be able to:

1. Describe the source of auditors' liability to clients and third parties.
2. Distinguish between common law liability and statutory liability.
3. Distinguish among the three levels of tort liability (ordinary negligence, gross negligence, and fraud) that may arise during the engagement.
4. Define the auditor's liability to clients and subrogees under common law.
5. Describe the reporting requirements of the Securities Act of 1933 and Securities Exchange Act of 1934.
6. Define the auditor's liability to third-party investors under the Securities Acts.

3

Auditors' Legal Liability

◉ LITIGATION, LIABILITY, AND THE ACCOUNTING PROFESSION

Exposure to legal liability is not unique to the accounting profession. Physicians, dentists, engineers, and other professionals have experienced exposure to litigation for many years. The accounting profession, however, currently faces a major crisis in this important area. The magnitude and extent of this problem is described in a Statement of Position issued by the Big Six accounting firms on August 6, 1992, and distributed to "all of [their] clients, all accounting faculty in the United States and Canada, all United States Senators and Representatives, and officials of interested government agencies." This statement is reproduced below. Although you may not be familiar with some of the terminology used, the statement provides an excellent overview of the issues and problems currently faced by the accounting profession; these will be illustrated and discussed in detail in this chapter.

**THE LIABILITY CRISIS IN THE UNITED STATES:
IMPACT ON THE ACCOUNTING PROFESSION
A STATEMENT OF POSITION**

The tort liability system in the United States is out of control. It is no longer a balanced system that provides reasonable compensation to victims by the responsible parties. Instead, it functions primarily as a risk transfer scheme. Marginally culpable or even innocent defendants too often must agree to coerced settlements in order to avoid the threat of even higher liability, pay judgments totally out of proportion to their degree of fault, and incur substantial legal expenses to defend against unwarranted lawsuits.

continued:

The flaws in the liability system are taking a severe toll on the accounting profession. If these flaws are not corrected and the tort system continues on its present inequitable course, the consequences could prove fatal to accounting firms of all sizes. But a liability system seriously lacking in logic, fairness, and balance is not just the accounting profession's crisis. It is a business crisis and a national crisis.

This position statement describes these matters in more detail, as well as needed reforms that the American Institute of CPAs (AICPA) and the six largest accounting firms are advocating. In seeking these reforms, the firms are not attempting to avoid liability where they are culpable. Rather, the firms seek equitable treatment that will permit them and the public accounting profession to continue to make an important contribution to the U.S economy.

An Epidemic of Litigation

The present liability system has produced an epidemic of litigation that is spreading throughout the accounting profession and the business community. It is threatening the independent audit function and the financial reporting system, the strength of U.S. capital markets, and the competitiveness of U.S. economy.

The principal causes of the accounting profession's liability problems are unwarranted litigation and coerced settlements. The present system makes it both easy and financially rewarding to file claims regardless of the merits of the case. As former SEC Commissioner Philip Lochner recently pointed out in *The Wall Street Journal*, plaintiffs may simply be seeking to recoup losses from a poor investment decision by going after the most convenient "deep pocket"—the auditor.* In too many cases, moreover, claims are filed with the sole intent of taking advantage of the system to force defendants to settle.

The doctrine of joint and several liability makes each defendant fully liable for all assessed damages in a case, regardless of the degree of fault. In practical terms this means that, even with no evidence of culpability, a company's independent auditors are almost certain to be named in any action filed against that company alleging financial fraud for no reason other than the auditors' perceived "deep pockets" or because they are the only potential defendant that is still solvent. A particularly egregious example of the abuses encouraged by joint and several liability is the common practice of plaintiffs' attorneys settling with the prime wrongdoers, who don't have a defense or money, at a fraction of what these parties should pay. The attorneys then pursue the case against the "deep pocket" professionals, who as a result of joint and several liability are exposed for 100 percent of the damages even if found to be only 1 percent at fault.

---

* Philip R. Lochner, Jr., "Black Days for Accounting Firms," *The Wall Street Journal* (May 22, 1992), A10.

continued:

Other elements in the system also act as incentives for unwarranted litigation leading to forced settlements. For example, American judicial rules make no effective provision for recovery of legal costs by prevailing defendants, even if the plaintiff's case is meritless. In addition, judicial restrictions on the types of cases in which punitive damages may be awarded have been significantly relaxed in recent years, making solvent professional and business defendants a prime target. The prospect of having to pay all damages as a consequence of joint and several liability, the high costs of defense, and possible punitive damages are persuasive factors in coercing settlements.

Abusive and unwarranted litigation is a problem not just for the accounting profession, but for business and the economy generally. A small group of attorneys is reaping millions of dollars by bringing in federal securities fraud claims (under SEC Rule 10b-5) against public companies whose only crime has been a fluctuation in their stock price. These attorneys use the threat of enormous legal costs, a lengthy and disruptive discovery process, protracted litigation, and damage to reputation to force large settlements.

The CEO of a high-tech company that has been the target of thirteen specious Rule 10b-5 suits calls these actions "legalized extortion," and their effects go far beyond the "payoffs" demanded. These meritless suits siphon off funds needed for research and development, capital investment, growth, and expansion. They divert management's time, talent, and energy from the principal mission of running the business. They send liability insurance premiums skyrocketing. Ultimately, the direct and indirect costs of these suits are borne by shareholders, along with employees, customers, and all of a company's stakeholders.

Joint and several liability encourages the inclusion of "deep pocket" defendants such as independent accountants, lawyers, directors, and underwriters in these suits in order to increase the prospect and size of settlements. Prohibitive legal costs, the unpredictable outcome of a jury trial, and the risk of being liable for the full damages compel even blameless defendants to race each other to the settlement table. And they do this despite the realization that, to the uninformed public, "agreeing" to settle is seen as an admission of wrongdoing.

A survey by the six largest accounting firms of the cases against them involving 10b-5 claims which were concluded in fiscal year 1991 showed that: (1) the average claim subjecting the accounting firm to joint and several liability was for $85 million; (2) the average settlement by the firm was $2.7 million, suggesting there might have been little or no merit to the original claim against the accountant; yet, (3) the average legal cost per claim was $3.5 million. It is not surprising that an accounting firm would agree to settle a case for less than what it had already spent in legal fees and, therefore, avoid the risk of over twenty times the settlement by a jury that may be hostile to a business with "deep pockets." However, controlling where you did nothing wrong becomes a very expensive strategy for "winning" the liability game.

continued:

Financial Crisis for the Accounting Profession

The financial impact of rampart litigation on the six largest accounting firms has been well-publicized. Numerous headlines and articles resulted from the firms' own disclosure that, in 1991, total expenditures for settling and defending lawsuits were $477 million—9 percent of auditing and accounting revenues in the United States. This figure, a multiple of what other businesses spend on litigation, does not even include indirect costs. It overs only costs of legal services settlements and judgments, and liability insurance premiums minus insurance reimbursements. The 1991 figure represent a substantial increase over the 1990 figure of $404 million of 7.7 percent of audit and accounting revenues. And based on reported settlements through June 30, 1992, there appears to be no end to the continuous upward spiral.

The litigation explosion has affected the entire accounting profession. It has been estimated that there are about $30 billions in damage claims currently facing the profession as a whole. A recent survey by the AICPA indicates that claims against firms other than the six largest rose by two-thirds between 1987 and 1991. Ninety-six percent of those firms having more than 50 CPAs reported an increase in exposure to legal liability. The same group has experienced a 300 percent increase in liability insurance premiums since 1985. Smaller firms must now carry far more coverage, and high deductibles force them to pay even medium-sized claims out-of-pocket. The median amount for deductibles is now $240,000—nearly six times the 1985 median of $42,000. Forty percent of all the firms surveyed are "going bare," largely because liability insurance is simply too expensive.†

For the largest firms, the increase in insurance premiums was dramatically higher than that reported by the smaller firms, coupled with drastically reduced policy limits. Deductibles also have risen dramatically and now exceed $25 million for a first loss. The higher rate of increase in liability insurance for the largest firms generally reflects the larger proportion of audit work for publicly held companies, thereby subjecting them to a greater liability risk.

Impact on Corporate Accountability and Economic Competitiveness

The heavy financial burden placed on accounting firms by runaway litigation affects business and the economy in two major ways: first, through the actual and threatened failure of accounting firms; and, second, through the "survival tactics" firms are forced to employ.

---

† Survey of accounting firms (excluding the six largest), American Institute of Certified Public Accountants, 1992.

continued:

In 1990, Laventhol & Horwath, the seventh-largest firm, collapsed—the largest bankruptcy for a professional organization in U.S. history—necessitating that its former partners agree to pay $48 million to avoid personal bankruptcy. While other factors contributed to the firm's demise, the overriding reason was the weight of its liability burden. According to former CEO Robert Levine, L&H, like other accounting firms, was included as a defendant because of the perception of being a "deep pocket" rather than deficiencies in the performance of its professional responsibilities. "It wasn't the litigation we would lose that was the problem," he asserted. "It was the cost of winning that caused the greatest part of our financial distress."

The consequences of L&H's failure reverberated throughout the capital markets. Audits in process were interrupted. New auditors had to be found, with the inevitable time lag that occurs for start-up. Special rules had to be adopted by the SEC to deal with public companies whose prior-yea financial statements reported on by L&H had to be reissued in connection with public offerings and periodic public filings. Companies whose financial statements were audited by L&H were placed under a cloud through no fault of their own.

Furthermore, the failure undermined confidence in the ability of the profession to carry out its public obligations by creating concerns about the financial viability of other firms. It also created a deep sense of apprehension throughout the accounting profession that has only grown worse. During 1992, another prominent firm, Pannell Kerr Foster, closed or sold about 90 percent of its offices and opted to reorganize its offices as individual professional corporations. *Accounting Today* quoted a former PKF partner who indicated that liability was one of the reasons for this massive restructuring.

The magnitude of the six largest accounting firms' liability-related costs, as well as the size of some highly publicized judgments and settlements, has fueled speculation about their survival. This is not surprising. A grim precedent has been set, and without decisive action the liability crisis will grow worse and the six firms' collective liability burden, enormous as it is, will increase.

This potential long-term threat to the survival of the six firms has serious implications for the independent audit function, the financial reporting system, and the capital markets. As a group, the six largest accounting firms audit all but a handful of the country's largest and most prominent public companies in every category:

494 of the Fortune 500 industrials.
97 of the Fortune 100 fastest-growing companies.
99 of the Fortune 100 largest commercial banks.
92 of the top 100 defense contractors.
195 of the 200 largest insurance companies.

continued:

In each of these categories, at least one of the six firms audits more than 20 percent of the companies. According to figures from *Who Audits America*, the six firms audit 90 percent (4,748 of 5,266) of the publicly-traded companies in the U.S. with annual sales of one million dollars or more.‡

The detrimental effects on auditing, financial reporting, and our capital markets are already very much in evidence. They are a natural consequence of the risky and uncertain practice environment which this litigation epidemic has created not only for the six largest firms, but for the entire accounting profession.

The "Tort Tax"

One obvious effect is what the media have called "the tort tax"—that is, the increased cost of goods and services caused by runaway litigation. To quote SEC Chairman Richard C. Breeden, "Accounting firms, in particular, pay substantial and increasing costs to litigate and settle securities cases. At some point, these increasing litigation costs will increase the cost of audit services and tend to reduce access to our national securities markets."§ If companies must pay higher costs for services provided not only by auditors, but by underwriters, attorneys, and other frequent "deep pocket" defendants, it will be more expensive for them to raise needed capital. Opportunities for investors will be reduced, and U.S. businesses will be placed at a competitive disadvantage vis-a-vis companies in countries with more rational liability systems—virtually every other country in the world.

The Impact of Risk Reduction

The liability burden cannot be measured only in dollars and cents. Other effects are less easy to detect, but are no less costly. For example, groups targeted by frequent litigation now practice risk reduction as a matter of professional survival. Physicians, for instance, are avoiding such fields as gynecology and obstetrics. The result is a scarcity of practitioners in crucial specialties.

Accountants are also practicing risk reduction. The six largest firms are attempting to reduce the threat of litigation by avoiding what are considered high-risk audit clients and even entire industries. High-risk categories include financial institutions, insurance companies, and real estate investment firms. Also considered "high risk" are high-technology and mid-sized companies, and private companies making initial public offerings (IPOs). These companies are a ready target of baseless Rule 10b-5 suits because their stock prices tend to be volatile. Unfortunately, they are also the companies that most need quality professional services, are a key source of innovation and jobs, and play a crucial role in keeping this country competitive.

---

‡ *Who Audits America*, 25th Edition (Data Financial Press:, Menlo Park, CA, June 1991), 393-396.
§ Letter from SEC Chairman Richard C. Breeden to Rep. John D. Dongell (D-MI, Chairman, Committee on Energy and Commerce, U.S. House of Representatives (May 5, 1992).

continued:

Risk avoidance is not confined to only the largest accounting firms. Smaller and medium-sized firms are dropping their public clients or abandoning their audit practices altogether. A recent survey of California CPA firms showed that only 53 percent are willing to undertake audit work. This creates serious problems for smaller companies (and their shareholders) that need viable alternatives to the major firms. Additionally, the survey showed that 32 percent of the reporting CPA firms are discontinuing audits in what they consider as high-risk sectors. Another survey by Johnson & Higgins found that 56 percent of the mid-sized firms surveyed will not do business with clients involved in industries they consider high-risk.

Impact on Professional Recruitment and Morale

Another troubling effect of the litigation explosion on the accounting profession, its clients, and the public is one that cuts across all industries and services. The litigious practice environment is making it increasingly difficult to attract and retain the most qualified individuals at every level. The *Atlantic Monthly* has reported that fewer top business students are choosing to go to public accounting firms to do audit work because, among other things, they perceive it as risky.

It is likely that the most serious impact on recruitment and retention of qualified people is yet to be felt, since widespread media and public attention have only recently begun to focus on the accounting profession's liability plight. Recruiters from the six largest firms report that they are encountering more awareness, more questions, and more apprehension about the liability risk on college campuses across the country. Transforming public accounting from a secure and respected career to one in which becoming a partner carries with it the threat of personal financial ruin is no way to ensure the profession's ability to meet its responsibilities to investors and the public.

Needed Reforms

To restore equity and sanity to the liability system and to provide reasonable assurance that the public accounting profession will be able to continue to meet its public obligations requires substantive reform of both federal and state liability laws.

continued:

Proportionate Liability

While other serious problems must also be addressed, the principal cause of unwarranted litigation against the profession is joint and several liability, which governs the vast majority of actions brought against accountants at the federal and state levels.

In arguing for an end to joint and several liability, the profession is in no way attempting to evade financial responsibility in cases where accountants are culpable. The profession is merely asking for fairness—the replacement of joint and several liability with a proportionate liability standard that assesses damages against each defendant based on that defendant's degree of fault. SEC Chairman Breeden recently acknowledged that joint and several liability can lead to unfair results by forcing marginal defendants to settle even weak claims. He has also expressed support for reducing the coercive "effect of allegations of joint and several liability in cases of relatively remote connection by the party to the principal wrongdoing."*

Proportionate liability will help restore balance and equity to the liability system by discouraging specious suits and giving blameless defendants the incentive to prove their case in court rather than settle. By creating overwhelming pressure on innocent defendants to settle, joint and several liability gives plaintiffs' lawyers a strong incentive to bring as many cases as possible without regard to the relative merits, include as many defendants as possible without regard to their degree of fault, and to settle these cases at a fraction of the alleged damages. Thus victims of real fraud receive no more (on average, 5 to 15 percent of their alleged damages) than so-called professional plaintiffs and speculators trying to recoup investment losses. On the other hand, the lawyers bringing these suits typically receive 30 percent of the settlement plus expenses. If plaintiffs' lawyers were not able to use the threat of joint and several liability to compel innocent defendants to settle meritless cases, they would have to focus all of their efforts on meritorious claims. That, in turn, would result in more appropriate awards for true victims.

Current Reform Efforts

The six largest firms have joined with the AICPA and concerned businesses in calling for federal securities reform to curb unwarranted litigation brought under Rule 10b-5. Proposed remedies include replacing joint and several liability with proportionate liability and requiring that plaintiffs pay a prevailing defendant's legal fees if the court determines that the suit was meritless.

---

* Letter from SEC Chairman Richard C. Breeden to Sen. Terry Sanford (D-NC), June 12, 1992.

concluded:

Curbing baseless Rule 10b-5 actions will, however, ease but not solve the liability problem. Of the total cases pending against the six largest firms in 1991, only 30 percent contained Rule 10b-5 claims. Of that 30 percent, less than 10 percent were exclusively 10b-5 claims.

The greatest liability exposure resides in the states. Reform of state liability laws affecting accountants is of critical importance to the future viability of the profession. The 10b-5 effort, if successful, will certainly serve as an important precedent for further reform. Beyond proportionate liability, reasonable limitation on punitive damages, as well as disincentives to filing meritless claims, ought to be enacted. Reforms could be accomplished either through federal preemption or state-by-state modification of their statutes governing legal liability. The accounting profession will continue to participate in various state liability reform initiatives.

No less important is the need for the accounting profession to remove legislative, regulatory, and professional restrictions on the forms of organization that may be used by accounting firms. Accountants must be free to practice in any form of organization permitted by state law, including limited liability organizations. The accounting profession is not seeking special treatment. Importantly, public accountants only seek to practice in forms of organization that are available to the vast majority of American businesses. Such changes will not relieve culpable individuals of legal responsibility for their own actions, but simply end the current inequity of full personal liability on all partners for all judgments against their firm:s resulting from the actions of others. The six largest firms will continue to aggressively pursue needed state-level liability reform.

The six largest firms are exploring all possible alternatives for reducing the threat that liability poses to their ability to meet their public obligations and to their survival. In this pursuit the firms cannot support any legislative or regulatory proposal that increases the responsibilities of the profession unless these increased responsibilities are accompanied by meaningful and comprehensive liability reform. The firms will support initiatives at both the federal and state levels that will restore balance to the current system of justice.

August 6, 1992

(Signed)

J. Michael Cook	Eugene M. Freedman
Chairman and Chief Executive Officer	Chairman
Deloitte & Touche	Coopers & Lybrand
Ray J. Groves	Jon C. Madonna
Chairman	Chairman and Chief Executive
Ernst & Young	KPMG Peat Marwick
Shaun F. O'Malley	Lawrence A. Weinbach
Chairman and Senior Partner	Managing Partner-Chief Executive
Price Waterhouse	Arthur Andersen & Co., S.C.

OVERVIEW OF LEGAL LIABILITY

During an examination conducted under generally accepted auditing standards (GAAS), the auditor performs various procedures to examine the fairness of the client's financial statements. After doing so, an opinion is expressed concerning the fairness of those financial statements that ultimately will be used by third parties in making various economic decisions with respect to the client. Thus, two groups of individuals are affected by the auditor's examination: **clients** and **third-party users**. Each of these parties can suffer losses as a result of errors, acts, or omissions of auditors. The events that may ultimately result in these losses are briefly summarized in Figure 3-1.

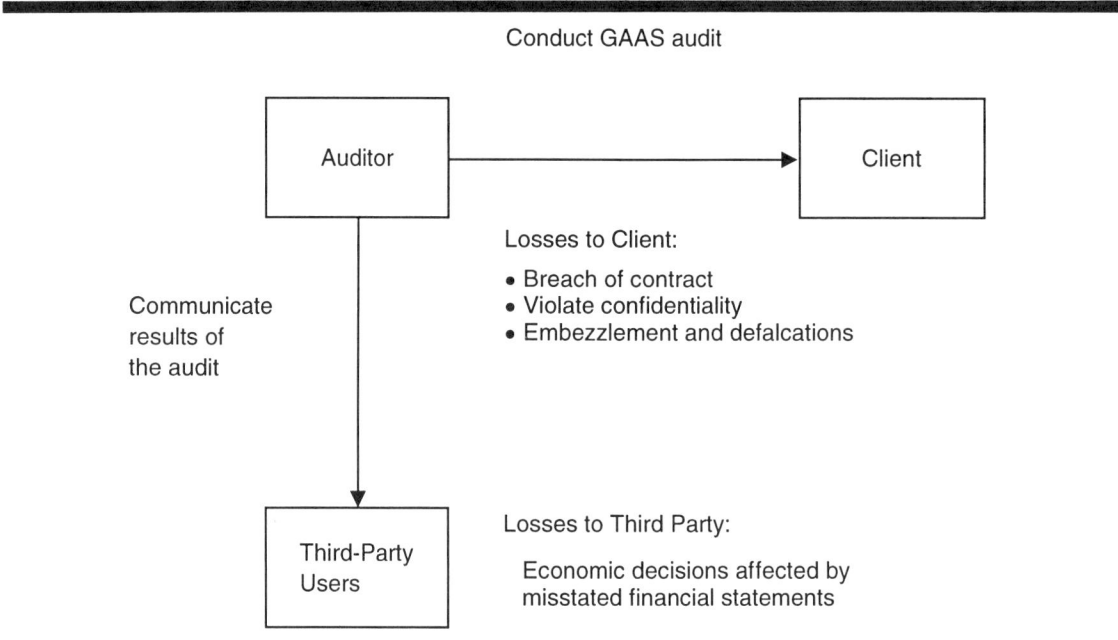

Figure 3-1: *Overview of Auditor Liability to Clients and Third-Party Users*

Clients can suffer three types of losses. First, losses may result from a **breach of contract** between the auditor and the client. Assume that the auditor agrees to complete his or her examination by a specified date in order to allow the client to obtain financing from a third party. If the engagement is not completed by that time and, as a result, alternative sources of financing must be sought, the client may suffer losses in the form of higher costs and/or less favorable terms. In such cases, clients normally attempt to recover these losses from the auditor. In addition, if the client suffers losses because of the auditor's **breach of confidentiality** (as outlined under Rule 301 in the Code of Professional Conduct), the auditor may be sued to recover any losses.

A common source of litigation between clients and auditors results from the auditor's failure to detect client defalcations. A **defalcation** is a scheme conducted by client employees to embezzle or otherwise misappropriate assets. As noted later, the auditor is required to plan the audit to detect errors and irregularities that are material to the financial statements. Although the auditor does not have the formal responsibility of detecting defalcations (a type of irregularity) during the audit, she or he may be held responsible if the audit was conducted in a negligent manner.

Third-party users may suffer losses because of the economic decisions they make based on the auditor's opinion. For example, assume that a lender provides financing to the client. In making the decision to provide financing, the lender relied on the auditor's opinion. Also assume that the client's accounts receivable are later shown to be fictitious and the auditor failed to detect these misstatements because of a substandard examination. If the lender is unable to recover funds loaned to the client, she or he may bring suit against the auditor for losses suffered. Similarly, investors in the securities of the client may bring suit if the price at which they purchased or sold the securities was affected by the auditor's actions.

In today's litigious society, both clients and third parties bring lawsuits against auditors based on their actions, errors, or omissions. Although many of these suits are the result of substandard audit work, it is important to note that many cases largely reflect third-party dissatisfaction. When third parties lend money to or invest money in an entity and financial difficulties of the entity result in losses, lawsuits may be brought against auditors because they are the only potential source of relief, not because of substandard work (the **deep-pockets theory**). In short, auditors may be sued because the entity's financial difficulties make recovery from the client difficult, if not impossible.

In this chapter, we provide an overview of the auditor's liability to both clients and third-party users. Selected actual court cases involving auditors, clients, and third parties are discussed to highlight important aspects of the auditor's liability. The Appendices to this chapter summarize additional court cases that may be of interest to the student attempting to gain a more thorough understanding of the auditor's legal liability.

◻ Terminology

Throughout this chapter, we will use specific terminology to describe the auditor's legal liability to clients and third parties. Some of these terms are defined below:

1. **Breach of contract** is the failure of the auditor to perform the examination in accordance with one or more provisions of the contract. In an audit, an **engagement letter** (discussed later in this chapter) serves as the contract between the auditor and client. Auditors can breach contracts, for example, by failing to complete the audit examination on a timely basis. In addition, because most engagement letters indicate that the audit is to be performed under generally accepted auditing standards (GAAS), the failure of the auditor to perform in accordance with GAAS is also considered a breach of contract.

2. **Privity** refers to a contractual relationship between two parties. Privity involving auditors is generally restricted to their clients (or subrogees, who are individuals acquiring the legal rights of clients). However, in certain cases, the auditor may have privity with third parties who are the ultimate recipients of the auditor's work.

3. **Tort liability** represents a civil wrong other than breach of contract. Tort liability arises when the auditor performs a substandard audit engagement. Three levels of tort liability are ordinary negligence, gross negligence, and fraud.

4. **Ordinary negligence** is a lack of reasonable care in the exercise of a duty. Ordinary negligence occurs when the auditor fails to exercise the standard of due care expected of CPAs when conducting audit examinations. In general, an auditor is considered to have committed ordinary negligence when he or she violates GAAS in the conduct of the audit.

5. **Gross negligence** is a lack of minimum care in the exercise of a duty. Gross negligence is often considered to have occurred when the auditor exhibits reckless disregard with respect to his or her duties. Relatively significant departures from GAAS are examples of gross negligence.

6. **Fraud** is an actual misrepresentation of a material fact known to be false.

The interrelationships among these forms of tort liability are summarized in Figure 3-2. As shown therein, fraud represents intent to deceive and auditor knowledge of the defalcation or misstatement. If the engagement is conducted in a substandard manner but the auditor did not know of the defalcation scheme or misstatement, this behavior would be classified as **ordinary negligence** or **gross negligence**. It is important to note that no detailed descriptions of actions that constitute ordinary negligence and gross negligence exist. It is simply impossible to classify all possible errors, actions, and omissions that can (and, unfortunately, sometimes do) occur during an audit examination. These issues are decided by the court as lawsuits are brought by clients and third parties. In many cases, other CPAs serving as expert witnesses provide their opinions about the severity of the auditor's actions.

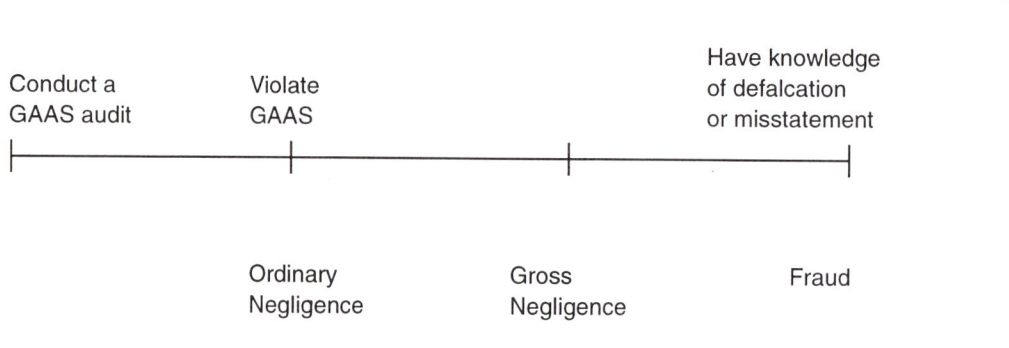

Figure 3-2: *Comparison of Tort Liability*

> ▶ **Example**
>
> Assume that an auditor is examining the financial statements of Tree, Inc. Several employees of Tree are engaging in a defalcation scheme to embezzle Tree's cash receipts from its customers. If the auditor conducts the audit in accordance with GAAS, she or he has not committed any degree of negligence and would not generally be liable to the client. If, however, the auditor slightly departed from GAAS and this departure prevented him or her from uncovering the defalcation scheme, the auditor has committed ordinary negligence. More severe departures from GAAS would be considered gross negligence. Finally, if the auditor knew of the scheme but took no action to prevent or disclose the scheme, the auditor has committed fraud.

In examining auditor liability for torts to clients and third parties, two key questions must be considered. First, what level of misperformance has occurred. That is, did the auditor commit ordinary negligence, gross negligence, or fraud? This question is normally addressed based on the facts of the case and the evaluation of experts (*i.e.*, other auditors) regarding the auditor's performance. The second question is the proper level of duty owed to individuals (clients and third parties). The courts rely on legal precedents under common law and written rules and regulations under statutory law to identify this obligation.

CHAPTER CHECKPOINTS

3-1. For what types of losses may the client bring suit against the auditor? For what types of losses may third parties bring suit against the auditor?

3-2. What is tort liability? What are the three classes of tort liability for which the auditor may be held responsible?

3-3. What is privity? What parties may have privity with the auditor?

COMMON LAW LIABILITY

The auditor is liable to both clients (and subrogees) and third-party users under the common law. **Common law liability** is based on prior legal decisions and not the violation of a written rule or law. The third-party users bringing suit under common law are normally nonshareholders (*e.g.*, lenders, creditors, and other investors). Because common law liability is based on prior legal decisions, the auditor's common law liability differs from one state to another. The rights of shareholders are protected under written laws through the Securities Act of 1933 and Securities Exchange Act of 1934. Therefore, if auditors fail to perform the audit using due care, shareholders may bring suit under statutory law (discussed in the following section). However, it is important to note that shareholders are not precluded from bringing suit under common law. In fact, it may sometimes be more advantageous for them to do so.

Liability to Clients and Subrogees

Clients and subrogees can be treated as one distinct group of individuals for purposes of auditor liability. A **subrogee** is an individual who acquires, by substitution, the rights of the client. To illustrate, assume that the auditor fails to detect a defalcation scheme, and as a result, employees embezzle funds from the client. If the client carries fidelity bonds on these employees, the client will be reimbursed for any embezzlement losses by a bonding (or surety) company. At this point, the surety company is now the party suffering the loss. As a result, the surety company is considered to be a subrogee and can bring suit against the auditor.

The auditor's liability to clients and subrogees can be classified into three categories: (1) breach of contract, (2) violation of confidentiality of client information, and (3) tort liability for failure to conduct the audit with due care. These issues are discussed below.

Breach of Contract. Normally, the auditor has a contractual relationship with the client (known as **privity**). In any case where a contract exists, the auditor can obviously breach some aspect of this contract. Breaches of contract can include failure to perform the audit within a specified period of time and failure to perform certain procedures specified in the contract. In addition, because most audit contracts indicate that the engagement is to be conducted in accordance with GAAS, failure to perform the audit under GAAS can also be considered to be a breach of contract. Thus, if the auditor does not perform the audit in conformity with GAAS, a suit could be brought by a client for either breach of contract or tort liability (as a form of ordinary negligence).

Because of the contractual relationship between the auditor and client, it is recommended that the auditor outline in a letter to the client the various aspects and details of the agreement with the client. This letter is referred to as an **engagement letter** and evidences the auditor's agreement with the client. The letter containing the client's signature should be retained by the auditor. The engagement letter can serve as a contract between the two parties, or a separate contract may be drawn between the parties. Engagement letters are discussed in greater detail in Chapter 4.

The importance of a well-written contract or engagement letter was illustrated in the case of *Maryland Casualty Co. v. Jonathon Cook*.[1] In this case, Jonathon Cook (the auditor) failed to detect an embezzlement of $12,969.15 in his audit of the City of Flint Michigan. Maryland Casualty Company carried a surety bond on the treasurer of the City of Flint and reimbursed the city for its loss, becoming a subrogee. Two important conclusions in the court's decision in this case were:

1. Since Jonathon Cook did not perform the engagement in accordance with the contract (engagement letter), he was found liable.
2. Auditors owe subrogees (in this case, Maryland Casualty Company) the same degree of care owed to clients.

Disclosure of Confidential Information. As discussed in Chapter 2, the auditor owes the client the duty of confidentiality. This responsibility is formally incorporated into the Code of Professional Conduct as Rule 301. In addition to being charged with violating the Code of Conduct, auditors may be held liable for any losses incurred by clients as a result of the disclosure of confidential client information. Because an audit conducted under GAAS obligates the auditor to keep certain information confidential, this type of liability can be considered as a special form of breach of contract.

Consolidata Services, Inc. v. Alexander Grant & Company addresses the auditor's liability for disclosing confidential client information. In this case, the auditors and Consolidata's management determined that Consolidata was insolvent. Against the wishes of Consolidata's management, the CPA firm notified several of Consolidata's customers (who were also clients of that CPA) of Consolidata's impending insolvency. Consolidata then brought suit against the auditor for negligence and breach of contract for breaking an obligation of confidentiality. The court awarded damages to Consolidata based on the CPA firm's breach of contract. In this case, the court found that the CPA firm had an obligation to keep Consolidata's insolvency confidential, despite the fact that this information affected other clients of the CPA.

In 1982, a court decision on a similar issue contradicted the finding in *Consolidata* somewhat. This case, The Fund of *Funds Limited v. Arthur Andersen & Co.*, involved two enterprises (Fund of Funds and King Resources) that were audited by the same key personnel of the CPA firm. Fund of Funds,

---

[1] *Maryland Casualty Co. v. Jonathon Cook*, 35 F. Supp., 160 (E.D. MI, 1940).

a mutual investment company, entered into an agreement with King Resources to purchase oil and gas properties at prices similar to those King Resources charged to its other customers.

During the examination of King Resources, the auditor determined that King was charging higher prices to Fund of Funds than to its other customers. The plaintiff's suit arose from a specific representation made by the CPA firm to Fund of Funds in the engagement letter. This representation stipulated that any irregularities discovered by the CPA firm would be revealed to Fund of Funds. The CPA firm asserted that it was not obligated to inform Fund of Funds of the overcharge and, in fact, it was prohibited from doing so based on the Rules of Conduct of the Code of Professional Conduct.

The court found the auditor liable to Fund of Funds for civil liability under the Securities Exchange Act of 1934. In addition, the CPA firm was also found liable for common law fraud and breach of contract. This liability stemmed from the CPA firm's failure to disclose the excess charges made by King Resources and, therefore, its violation of the specific representation made in the engagement letter.

Tort Liability to Clients and Subrogees. As defined earlier, a **tort** is any civil wrong, other than breach of contract. The primary basis for lawsuits between clients (subrogees) and their auditors is to recover losses resulting from defalcations that were not detected by auditors because of auditors' substandard performance. Auditors have liability to their clients for torts arising from ordinary negligence, gross negligence, and fraud. Recall that violating GAAS in conducting an audit gives rise to claims as a result of ordinary negligence.

To bring suit on the basis of ordinary negligence, the plaintiff must demonstrate that:

1. Injuries were sustained (normally, monetary losses from defalcations by client personnel).
2. The auditor had a legal duty to perform (in most cases, to conduct a GAAS audit).
3. The auditor breached this duty (failed to conduct the audit under GAAS or committed ordinary negligence).
4. The proximate (direct) cause of the injuries was the breach of the legal duty.

Proving the above facts will not necessarily result in a judgment against the auditor. Several defenses are available to the auditor. First, the auditor can attempt to provide evidence that she or he was not negligent. In most cases, if the auditor can show that GAAS were followed during the audit, he or she will not be held liable under ordinary negligence. Other defenses include the **causation defense** (which indicates that the loss was caused by factors other than the auditor's performance and **contributory negligence defense**. The latter defense asserts that the loss was caused, at least in part, by the client. For example, if the client failed to establish key internal controls or organizational policies to prevent employee defalcation schemes, the negligence of the client, not the auditor's performance, may have been responsible for the losses.

Several court cases have affirmed the auditor's responsibility to clients and subrogees for ordinary negligence. For example, in the *Maryland Casualty Company* case discussed earlier in this section, the basis for the suit was ordinary negligence as well as breach of contract. In addition, both *Dantzler*

Lumber & Export Co. v. Columbia Casualty Co.[2] and *Fidelity & Deposit Co. of Maryland v. Atherton*[3] also reaffirm the auditor's responsibility for this level of care.

The above cases clearly indicate that auditors owe clients the duty of conducting the audit examination without ordinary negligence. Under common law, if the auditor is responsible for one level of tort liability, he or she is also liable for more severe levels. That is, auditors also owe their clients the responsibility of conducting the audit without gross negligence or fraud. The only difference in bringing suits under these levels of tort liability is that the client must prove either reckless conduct or intention to deceive on the part of the auditor prior to bringing suit for gross negligence or fraud, respectively.

◻ Liability to Third Parties

In addition to clients, auditors can also be held liable to third parties for their actions, errors, or omissions. Unlike clients, auditors do not generally owe third parties the obligation for breach of contract or disclosure of confidential client information. However, they do owe third parties tort liability. This obligation results from the role of audited financial statements in the decision processes of users. To illustrate, assume that an audit is conducted in a negligent manner and, as a result, the auditor fails to detect material misstatements. If third parties make decisions with respect to the client based on the audited financial statements, these parties may attempt to recover losses resulting from these decisions from the auditor. For example, if money is loaned to a company and that company subsequently defaults on the loan, third parties may be able to recover these losses from the auditor if the auditor's substandard performance resulted in misleading financial statements. The auditor's liability to primary beneficiaries and other third parties is separately discussed.

To bring suit under common law, third parties must prove similar facts as client and subrogees. Recall that these facts are that:

1. Injuries were sustained (normally, monetary losses from economic decisions made by a third party).
2. The auditor had a legal duty to perform the audit with due care (in most cases, to conduct a GAAS audit).
3. The auditor breached this duty (committed ordinary negligence, gross negligence, or fraud).
4. The proximate (direct) cause of the injuries was the breach of the legal duty.

Primary Beneficiaries. Primary beneficiaries are unique third parties in that they may have a contractual relationship with the auditor. Two key characteristics of a primary beneficiary are:

▶ The auditor knows the primary beneficiary by name prior to the audit.

▶ The auditor knows that the primary beneficiary will rely on his or her opinion in making economic decisions regarding the client.

---

[2] *Dantzler Lumber & Export Co. v. Columbia Casualty Co.*, 115 FL 541, 156 So. 116 (1934).

[3] *Fidelity & Deposit Co. of Maryland v. Atherton*, 47 NM 443, 144 P.2d 157 (1943).

Because primary beneficiaries are known to the auditor by name and their reliance is known, the auditor owes primary beneficiaries a similar type of obligation as that owed to clients and subrogees. That is, under tort conduct, auditors may be held liable for ordinary negligence, gross negligence, or fraud. In addition, if a contract exists between the auditor and a primary beneficiary, that contract can be breached. In *CIT v. Glover*, the courts ruled that auditors would be liable for ordinary negligence to third parties who are primary beneficiaries.[4]

Liability to Other Third Parties. A great deal of controversy exists concerning the auditor's liability to third parties who are not primary beneficiaries Opinions rendered by auditors, when exhibited to such parties, can serve as a basis for adverse legal action. These additional third-party groups are usually user groups, such as creditors, investors, or potential investors, who rely on the auditors' opinions as to the fairness of presentation of the financial statements but who are not identified by name to the auditor prior to the audit. Because third parties are not considered to be parties to the audit contract (therefore lacking privity) nor to be the primary benefactors of an audit, they would have little or no basis for a breach of contract action against an auditor.

In the earliest American case involving the auditor's liability to third parties, *Landell v. Lybrand*, it was found that a third-party investor who relied on audited financial statements when making investment decisions could not hold an auditor liable for investment losses even if the auditor was guilty of ordinary negligence in performing the audit in question.[5]

Since *Landell v. Lybrand*, the issue of auditor liability to non-primary beneficiaries has continued to be controversial. Three approaches to determining the auditor's liability to third parties are the *Ultramares, Restatement of Torts*, and foreseeability approaches.

Ultramares. The *Ultramares* approach derives its name from the landmark case of the same name.[6] In this case, the defendant auditors had examined the client firm and certified the financial statements. The auditors prepared thirty-two copies of the financial statements for the client firm, which indicated that the client intended to seek the credit that it needed.

The accounting firm's client had included fictitious balances in the various ledger accounts. The auditors did not uncover the manipulations because they failed to verify the underlying documents that would have exposed the proper balances of the ledger accounts. Actually, the client was near bankruptcy.

The plaintiff creditor made loans to the client; the client went bankrupt, and the creditor charged the auditors with negligent misrepresentations and fraudulent misrepresentations.

The court recognized that the audit was made for the primary benefit of the clients, not the third-party creditor. Thus, the third party was not considered to be a primary beneficiary. In this case, the judge, Justice Cardozo, established certain dimensions for the auditor's liability to these third parties:

---

[4] *CIT Financial Corporation v. Glover*, 224 F.2d 44 (2d Cir. 1955).
[5] *Landell v. Lybrand*, 264 PA 406, 107 A. 783 (1919).
[6] *Ultramares Corp. v. Touche*, 225 NY 170, 174 N.E. 441 (1931).

> The defendants owed to their employer a duty imposed by law to make their certificate without fraud, and a duty growing out of contract to make it with the care and caution proper to their calling.... To creditors and investors to whom the employer exhibited the certificate, the defendants owed a like duty to make it without fraud, since there was notice in the circumstances of its making that the employer did not keep it to himself.... If liability for negligence exists, a thoughtless slip or blunder, the failure to detect a theft or forgery beneath the cover of deceptive entries, may expose accountants to a liability in an indeterminate amount for an indeterminate time to an indeterminate class.[7]

This ruling definitely eliminated the charge of ordinary negligence as an acceptable basis for suit for third parties other than primary beneficiaries. In this same case, Justice Cardozo, recognizing that auditors only express an opinion on financial statements, explicitly established law defining the basis on which auditors could be held liable in third-party suits:

> Even an opinion, especially an opinion by an expert, may be found to be fraudulent if the grounds supporting so flimsy as to lead to the conclusion that there was no genuine belief back of it....
>
> * * * *
>
> Our holding does not emancipate accountants from the consequences of fraud ... negligence or blindness, even when not equivalent to fraud, is none the less evidence to sustain an inference of fraud. At least this is so if the negligence is gross.[8]

This was considered a landmark case, at least in part because of the great stature Justice Cardozo held in the legal profession. The legal theory enunciated by Cardozo made it very difficult for these third parties to win suits against auditors. They could do so only if there was gross negligence or fraud. In such situations, lack of privity is not a valid defense.

The legal principles set forth in the Ultramares case were later upheld in *State Street Trust Co. v. Ernst*.[9] An appeals court indicated that auditors were not liable to third parties for ordinary negligence. However, as noted in the following excerpt, a liability for gross negligence did exist.

> Accountants, however, may be liable to third parties, even where there is lacking deliberate or active fraud. A representation certified as true to the knowledge of the accountants when knowledge there is none, a reckless misstatement, or an opinion based upon grounds so flimsy as to leads to the conclusion that there was no genuine belief in its truth, are all sufficient upon which to base liability. A refusal to see the obvious a failure to investigate the doubtful, if sufficiently gross, may furnish evidence leading to an inference of fraud so as to impose liability for losses suffered by those who rely on the balance sheet. In other words, heedlessness and reckless disregard of consequence may take the place of deliberate intention.[10]

---

[7] *Ibid.*, 444.

[8] *Ibid.*, 447-449.

[9] *State Street Trust Co. v. Ernst*, 278 NY 104, 15 N.E.2d 415 (1938). See Saul Levy, *Accountants' Legal Responsibility* (NY: American Institute of Accountants, 1954), 34-39, for more details of this case.

[10] *Ibid.*, 112

Recently, the *Ultramares* precedent was upheld in New York in *Credit Alliance Corporation and Leasing Services Corporation v. Arthur Andersen & Co.*[11] In this important case, the New York Court of Appeals identified three criteria that must be met in order for parties lacking privity to bring suit against auditors for ordinary negligence:

1. The auditor must be aware that the reports were to be used for a particular purpose.
2. A known party or parties must intend to rely on these reports.
3. Some action on the part of the auditor must link them to this party or parties.

Thus, based on the *Ultramares* precedent and the conclusion in the *State Street* and *Credit Alliance* cases, auditors do not owe nonprimary beneficiaries an obligation for ordinary negligence. However, these parties are owed an obligation for gross negligence and fraud. Using the *Ultramares* precedent and approach, it appears that primary beneficiaries are the only third parties that can bring suit against the auditor for ordinary negligence.

Restatement of Torts. An alternative view of the auditor's liability to nonprimary beneficiary third parties is often referred to as the *Restatement of Torts* approach.[12] Under this principle, the auditor may owe nonprimary beneficiaries an obligation for ordinary negligence. The *Restatement of Torts* approach is illustrated by the ruling in the *Rusch Factors, Inc. v. Levin* case,[13] where Rusch Factors had requested audited financial statements of a corporation seeking a loan. The auditor examined the financial statements, which showed the corporation to be solvent. Actually, the corporation was insolvent. The corporation later submitted the certified financial statements to Rusch Factors and received the loan. The company subsequently went into receivership. Rusch Factors sued the auditor for damages resulting from its reliance on the fraudulent or negligent misrepresentations in the financial statements. The defendant moved for dismissal on the basis of privity of contract. Here, the court said:

> this court holds that an accountant should be liable in negligence for careless financial misrepresentations relied upon by *actually foreseen and limited classes of persons*. According to the plaintiff's complaint in the instant case, *the defendant knew that his certification was to be used for*, and had as its very aim and *the reliance of potential financiers* of the ... corporation ...[14] [Emphasis added.]

This case would seem to indicate that some courts are changing the liability to third parties who are not primary beneficiaries. Once regarded as not being liable to these third parties for ordinary negligence, an auditor can now be held as liable for ordinary negligence *if* they are *informed* of a specific use (the category of user and the type of decision) that is to be made of the certified statements. This liability exists even when he or she does not know the exact identity by name (e.g., *Rusch Factors*) who is to rely on the statements. That is, if the auditor is aware of how his or her work

---

[11] 483 N.E.2d 100 (New York: 1985).

[12] American Law Institute, *Restatement (Second) of Torts*, Section 522 (1977).

[13] *Rusch Factors, Inc. v. Levin*, 284 F. Supp. 85 (D.C.R.I. 1968).

[14] *Ibid.*, 92-93.

will be used, any parties relying on the financial statements in that manner are referred to as **foreseen** third parties and may bring suit against the auditor for ordinary negligence.

Foreseeable Third Parties. A final view of the auditor's liability to nonprimary beneficiaries is the **foreseeability approach**. Under this approach, auditors can be held liable to third parties for ordinary negligence if their use of the auditor's work is **reasonably foreseeable**. While this may seem to mirror the *Restatement of Torts* approach for foreseen third parties, there is a slight difference. Under *Restatement of Torts*, a party is classified as foreseen if the auditor knows (or has a general idea) that the audit work is to be used in a particular fashion. In contrast, the **foreseeable** third-party approach suggests that liability exists when the auditor *should know* that the work *could be used* for a particular purpose. Clearly, the auditor would have liability to a greater number of individuals under the foreseeable approach.

Rosenblum v. Adler[15] illustrates the use of the foreseeability approach in a case involving auditors and nonprimary beneficiaries. In this seminal case, the New Jersey Supreme Court ruled that a CPA firm has a responsibility to any persons who may ultimately rely on its opinion. In this case, the plaintiffs charged that their acquisition of worthless stock was based on their reliance on the audited financial statements of the client, statements that were subsequently discovered to be fraudulent. The plaintiffs brought suit against the auditors on the grounds that the auditors were negligent in their conduct of their examination of these financial statements.

The court denied the auditor's defense that the plaintiffs were not a foreseeable party, noting that: (1) when an auditor issues an opinion on an entity's financial statements, she or he has a duty to any party who is reasonably foreseeable as a recipient of the financial statements; and (2) the situation in which the plaintiffs used and relied upon the audited financial statements was reasonably foreseeable.

Summary: Liability to Nonprimary Beneficiaries. At this point, it may be useful to summarize the auditor's liability for ordinary negligence to third parties who are not primary beneficiaries. Figure 3-3 summarizes the approaches that may be used in identifying auditor liability to nonprimary beneficiaries under common law. As shown therein, all approaches recognize that third parties can bring suit against auditors for acts representing either gross negligence or fraud.

However, the requirements for bringing suit under ordinary negligence vary under these approaches, with Ultramares resulting in the least exposure for auditors and the foreseeability approach the greatest exposure.

Because tort liability to nonprimary beneficiaries is defined under common law, it varies from state to state. Based on one classification of court cases, the Restatement of Torts approach is endorsed as the law in nineteen states (Alabama, California, Florida, Georgia, Iowa, Kentucky, Louisiana, Michigan, Minnesota, Missouri, New Hampshire, North Carolina, North Dakota, Ohio, Rhode Island, Tennessee, Texas, Washington, West Virginia) and the foreseeability approach by three (Mississippi, New Jersey, and Wisconsin).[16] However, it is important to note that the auditor's obligation to these parties is constantly being examined and reexamined. For example, the outcomes of two recent cases in the states of New York[17] and California[18] appear to limit an auditor's liability for negligence solely to their

---

[15] 461 A.2d 138 (NJ 1983).

[16] R.K. Hanson and J.W. Rockness, "Gaining a New Balance in the Courts," *Journal of Accountancy* (August 1994), 40-44.

[17] *Security Pacific Business Credit, Inc. v. Peat Marwick Main & Co.*, 79 NY 2d 695 (1992).

[18] *Bily v. Arthur Young & Co.*, 11 California Reporter 2d 51 (1992).

	Ordinary Negligence	Gross Negligence and Fraud
Ultramares Approach	Not liable unless the parties are known to the auditor	Liable to all parties
Restatement of Tort Approach	Liable to classes of persons whose use of the auditor's work is known (foreseen)	Liable to all parties
Foreseeability Approach	Liable to classes of persons who could reasonably be expected to use the auditor's work	Liable to all parties

Figure 3-3: *Summary of Legal Approaches for Auditor Liability to Nonprimary Beneficiaries*

clients. This development is particularly remarkable in California, whose courts had previously developed a liberal rule of "reasonable foreseeability."[19]

◘ Significant Court Cases under Common Law

Figure 3-4 summarizes some of the more important court cases that have helped to shape the auditor's liability to various parties under common law. It is important to note that the cases discussed to this point are only a small subset of cases that affect the legal liability of auditors to clients, subrogees, and third parties under common law. Additional cases are discussed in Appendix A to this chapter.

---

[19] See B.S. Augenbraun, "Courts in Two States Reaffirm the Requirements of Privity for Accountants' Liability," *The CPA Journal* (July 1993), 44-46 and "California Court Limits Liability of Auditors," *The Wall Street Journal* (August 28, 1992), B1.

Liability to Clients and Subrogees:

Breach of Contract	*Smith v. London Assurance Corporation* *Maryland Casualty Co. v. Jonathan Cook* *Dantzler Lumber & Export Co. v. Columbia Casualty*
Confidentiality	*Consolidata Services, Inc. v. Alexander Grant & Co.* *Fund of Funds Limited v. Arthur Andersen & Co.*
Tort Liability	*Maryland Casualty Co. v. Jonathan Cook* *Dantzler Lumber & Export Co. v. Columbia Casualty* *Fidelity & Deposit Co. of Maryland v. Atherton*

Liability to Primary Beneficiaries:

CIT Financial Corporation v. Glover

Liability to Nonprimary Beneficiaries:

Ultramares Approach	*Ultramares Corporation v. Touche* *State Street Trust Co. v. Ernst* *Credit Alliance Corporation and Leasing Services Corporation v. Arthur Andersen & Co.*
Restatement of Torts Approach	*Rusch Factors, Inc. v. Levin*
Foreseeability Approach	*Rosenblum v. Adler*

Figure 3-4: *Summary of Significant Cases—Common Law*

CHAPTER CHECKPOINTS

3-4. What is common law liability? What parties generally may bring suit against auditors under common law liability?

3-5. Define a subrogee. What is the auditor's liability to clients and subrogees?

3-6. What basic facts must be demonstrated by plaintiffs prior to bringing suit under common law?

3-7. What is a primary beneficiary? What is the auditor's liability to primary beneficiaries?

3-8. Identify and define the three viewpoints with respect to the auditor's liability to third parties who are not primary beneficiaries. Cite any court cases supporting these viewpoints.

◉ STATUTORY LIABILITY

In addition to common law liability, the auditor can also be held liable to third parties as a result of violating federal regulations. These regulations were designed to protect issuers and investors of securities by requiring that issuing companies provide complete information to current and potential investors in the form of financial statements and other necessary disclosures. Because the financial statements are normally required to be audited by an independent CPA, the auditor is exposed to potential liability to parties purchasing and selling securities. The underlying cause of this liability is similar to that for third parties under common law. That is, if users' decisions are based on audited financial statements that contain a material misstatement, the auditor can be held liable if her or his engagement was conducted in a substandard fashion.

The focus in this section is on the auditor's liability under the two Securities and Exchange Commission acts. Because they represent federal regulations, the auditor's liability under the Securities Acts does not vary from state to state. Prior to discussing these acts, a brief introduction to the SEC and its functions is provided.

◘ Securities and Exchange Commission (SEC)

The SEC was created by the Securities and Exchange Act of 1934 to regulate the sale of securities in national markets. With certain exceptions, the SEC has jurisdiction over the form and content of financial information that must be prepared, distributed, and filed by public companies. The SEC operates under the philosophy of **full and fair disclosure**. That is, the basic goal of the SEC is to ensure that both current and potential investors are provided with a complete set of information, both financial and nonfinancial, to use in making investment decisions. The SEC does not attempt to evaluate the merits of a particular security. The financial information that must be provided to investors and filed with the SEC is detailed in Regulations S-X (financial statements and similar schedules) and S-K (financial information other than that in the financial statements). This information includes:

1. Two years of audited balance sheets and three years of audited statements of income and cash flows.
2. A five-year summary of selected financial data (net sales, total assets, income/loss from continuing operations, etc.).
3. Management discussion and analysis of financial condition and results of operations.
4. Three-year information about industry segments, foreign and domestic operations, and export sales.
5. Brief description of the issuer's business.
6. Names of directors and executive officers.

With some exceptions (primarily for smaller companies), any company whose shares are traded in more than one state, registered on a national stock exchange, or traded over-the-counter are subject to the disclosure requirements of the SEC. The traditional events occurring with respect to an issuance of stock are summarized in the following illustration.

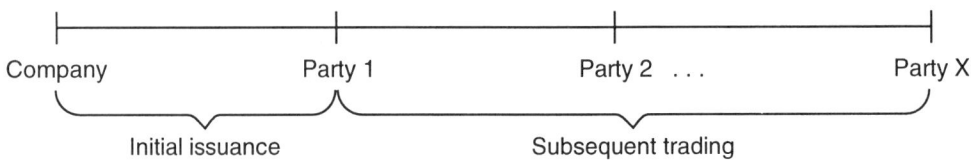

For purposes of disclosure requirements, the SEC distinguishes between the **initial issuance** of an issue of stock to the public and the **subsequent trading** of those shares. The SEC generally has more stringent requirements for initial issuances of stock with respect to: (1) the types of disclosures required of the issuing company, and (2) the level of auditor performance. These requirements are based on the premise that investors require a greater amount of information and assurance about new issuances of stock because less is known about the issuing companies.

The initial issuance of stock to the public is governed by the Securities Act of 1933—that is, when companies issue a class of stock to the public, they are subject to the disclosure and reporting requirements of this act. Once stock has been issued and is exchanged among investors, companies are still required to adhere to SEC disclosure and reporting requirements as long as the stock is registered on a national exchange or traded over-the-counter in interstate commerce. These requirements are specified by the Securities and Exchange Act of 1934. Both acts are discussed below.

◻ Securities Act of 1933

The Securities Act of 1933 (the 1933 Act) requires that initial public offerings (or IPOs) of securities must be registered with the SEC before they may be sold. Offerings restricted to the residents of the state in which the issuing company is organized and doing business are exempt, as are government securities and private sales. A sale is considered private if an entire issue is sold for investment to a limited number of knowledgeable investors and will not be distributed to the public. The SEC has also adopted regulations that exempt certain other sales of securities from registration. (The details of these regulations are beyond the scope of this text.)

The act's two objectives are: (1) to provide investors with information about securities offered for sale to the public, and (2) to prohibit misrepresentation or fraud in the sale of securities. Full and fair disclosure is to be made in a **registration statement**, which is a public document on file at the SEC offices. This registration statement contains both financial and nonfinancial information with respect to the issuing company. Included in this registration statement is a **prospectus** (selling circular), which is the principal source of information for an investor about the securities to be offered for sale.

Registration Process. Making a public offering is a complex task, and registering securities is a major event for most companies. Usually, it requires the joint efforts of at least three professionals: the underwriter, the attorney, and the auditor. The 1933 Act imposes considerable potential liability on these professionals, as well as on company management and directors.

The registration process generally begins with negotiations between the company (and perhaps selling shareholders) and the "lead" underwriter. The auditor's advice may be sought, and early participation of the auditor can be of great assistance.

The auditor's participation in the registration process is an important service to the client. The principal responsibility of the auditor in any SEC filing is to report on the financial statements. The auditor should, however, read the entire filing to ensure that nothing included elsewhere contradicts the audited financial statements. Although the auditor usually does not draft other sections of the filing and does not include them in the scope of the audit report, she or he is frequently asked to assist in the compilation of some of the financial data included in those sections. Accordingly, the auditor should be familiar with the requirements for financial statements and nonfinancial statement information in SEC filings. Although no two filings are exactly alike, the main steps in most filings are similar. They usually occur as follows:

1. The participating parties (client, legal counsel, auditors, and underwriter) attend a preliminary planning meeting. The parties establish a tentative timetable and assign tasks.
2. The auditor completes the examination of the financial statements and those schedules in the filing that are required to be audited.
3. Through its attorneys, the client will file the **preliminary registration statement** with the SEC. This statement is reviewed by the SEC for missing and/or inadequate disclosures.
4. The SEC prepares a **letter of comments** to the issuing company that details any inadequacies in the disclosures provided in the preliminary registration statement.
5. The client amends the preliminary registration statement to correct any deficiencies noted by the SEC during its review. Once complete, the **amended registration statement** is then refiled with the SEC.
6. The auditor performs postaudit procedures to ensure that no material changes have occurred since the completion of the audit. These procedures are not as detailed as those performed in the GAAS audit.
7. A **due diligence** meeting is held between all parties to ensure that they have performed their duties with proper care. Under the 1933 Act, underwriters are required to exercise "due diligence" in verifying the accuracy of any financial information filed with the registration statement. Because the auditor has expertise in this area, he or she is asked to provide a comfort letter to the underwriter This **comfort letter** addresses the following topics.[20]
    a. The independence of the auditor.
    b. An opinion as to whether the audited financial statements comply with accounting requirements of the 1933 Act.
    c. The auditor's conclusion with respect to nonfinancial statement information (such as tables, statistics, and other financial data) presented in the registration statement.
8. The SEC declares the registration statement effective. The parties hold a closing meeting to exchange the securities, and funds. The securities are then sold by the underwriters. On a "best efforts" offering where the underwriter uses its best efforts to sell securities but does not guarantee the sale, securities are sold before the closing.

---

[20] American Institute of Certified Public Accountants (AICPA), *Statement on Auditing Standards No. 76*, "Letters for Underwriters and Certain Other Requesting Parties" (New York: AICPA, 1995, AU 634).

◻ Securities Exchange Act of 1934

The specific purpose of the Securities Exchange Act of 1934 is:

> To provide for the regulation of securities exchanges and of over-the-counter markets operating in interstate and foreign commerce and through the mails to prevent inequitable and unfair practices on such exchanges and markets.[21]

The 1934 Act as amended in 1964 extended the "disclosure" doctrine of investor protection to all securities listed and registered for trading on the national securities exchanges and to equity securities of many companies traded over-the-counter. Thus, the 1934 Act pertains to securities trading instead of to the original distribution of securities. The 1934 Act generally covers periodic reporting requirements for registered companies in reporting to the SEC.

Companies whose stock is listed on a national exchange (with limited exceptions) are subject to the reporting requirements of the 1934 Act. In addition, every company: (1) operating in interstate commerce, (2) with more than $5 million in total assets, and (3) having 500 or more shareholders is subject to the 1934 Act when it first meets these three requirements.

Reporting Requirements under the 1934 Act. Similar to the 1933 Act, the major requirement for companies subject to the provisions of the 1934 Act relates to filing financial information with the SEC and providing information to shareholders. These statements must be audited by an independent accountant; this audit requirement results in the potential exposure of liability to the auditor. In addition, various requirements exist to provide or file information with respect to: (1) shareholder proxy requests, (2) tender offer solicitations, and (3) securities transactions involving insiders (individuals holding more than 10 percent of the registered shares of the corporation and all directors and officers of the corporation). Because most of the auditor's liability stems from her or his involvement with financial information filed with the SEC and provided to shareholders, our focus in this chapter is on the involvement with these financial statements.

Each company must file an annual report to the SEC (which usually includes by reference the financial statements from a company's annual report to shareholders and also includes other data about the company's activities during the year) within ninety days after the end of its fiscal year. Domestic companies file this annual report on Form 10-K. Special industries and special situations may require other forms.

Registered companies are also required to file quarterly reports containing specified financial information on Form 10-Q within forty-five days after each of the first three fiscal quarters. A report need not be filed for the fourth quarter since Form 10-K is filed instead.

Additionally, registered companies must report events such as: (1) changes in control, (2) bankruptcy or receivership, (3) change in independent auditors, (4) acquisition or disposition of assets, and (5) other materially important events on Form 8-K soon after those events occur.

---

[21] Securities Exchange Act of 1934, Public Law 291, 73rd Congress, as amended to August 20, 1964, 1.

> **CHAPTER CHECKPOINTS**
>
> 3-9. What is statutory liability? What parties may bring suit under statutory liability?
>
> 3-10. Briefly describe the purpose and significance of the: (a) Securities Act of 1933, and (b) Securities Exchange Act of 1934.
>
> 3-11. List the main steps in the typical registration filing under the Securities Act of 1933.
>
> 3-12. What type of information is required under Regulation S-X and S-K?

◻ Auditors' Liability under the 1933 Act

As stated earlier, the Securities Act of 1933 requires audited financial statements to be included with the registration statement that must be filed with the Securities and Exchange Commission prior to the offering of certain securities for sale. Section 11 of the Act, "Civil Liabilities on Account of False Registration Statement," is the most important noncriminal section for the auditor. This section imposes responsibility for false or misleading statements or omissions in a registration statement on:

> every accountant, engineer, or appraiser, or any person whose profession gives authority to a statement made by him, who has with his consent been named as having prepared or certified any part of the registration statement....

In order to bring suit, the investor must prove:

1. A loss was suffered in the acquisition of securities through a registration statement.
2. A material false statement or misleading omission was contained in the financial statements.

Importantly, under the 1933 Act, the burden of proof is placed on the auditor. Unlike common law, investors do not need to provide that: (1) they relied on the financial statements, (2) the financial statements were the cause of their loss, or (3) the auditor committed any form of tort liability. Under the 1933 Act, the auditor is liable for ordinary negligence, gross negligence, and fraud.

Once a suit is brought against the auditor, there are two possible defenses. First, the auditor may not be held liable if it can be proven that a reasonable examination has been performed. This is referred to as the **due diligence** defense. The second defense available is known as the **causation** defense. Using this latter defense, if the auditor can prove that something other than the false statement or material omission in the financial statements resulted in the purchaser's loss, liability may be avoided.

Any action brought against the auditor under the 1933 Act must be filed within three years after the securities have been offered to the public and within one year after the discovery of the error or omission has been made.[22] Unless both of these conditions are met, no action can be brought.

As the following excerpt from a recent *The Wall Street Journal* article notes, the high risk associated with audits conducted under the 1933 Act has affected accounting firms' desires to conduct these audits.

> Big accounting firms say they have begun dropping risky audit clients to lower their risk of lawsuits for allegedly faulty audits. New companies, which have a particularly high chance of failure, are affected most, because almost nothing triggers lawsuits against accountants faster than company failures....
>
> To protect his firm against these costs, Mr. [J. Michael] Cook says, Deloitte [& Touche] has begun weeding out audit clients with potential problems and refusing to handle the audit of companies making initial public offerings, or IPOs, because so many of them fail. And all of his competitors among the Big Six are doing likewise. The portion of all IPOs audited by these prestigious firms declined to 75 percent last year from 84 percent in 1992....[23]

BarChris Case. Under the 1933 Act, the auditor is responsible for reporting any significant changes in the financial affairs of the firm offering the securities that occur between the audit date and the effective date of the registration statement.

The courts had never defined what was required in such a review until the case of *Escott v. BarChris Construction Corporation*.[24] Purchasers of the subordinated debentures of BarChris Construction Corporation initiated the action, under Section 11 of the Securities Act of 1933, against any persons signing the registration statement, the underwriters, and the auditors. They charged that the registration statement directly relating to the bond issue contained material false statements and material omissions.

The impact of this case, from a liability standpoint, revolved around the review. The court recognized that the review should not be a complete audit. The auditors had prepared a written program for the review that the court found to be acceptable. This program included: (1) a review of various minutes of meetings, latest interim financial statements, and the more important financial records; and (2) an inquiry into changes in material contracts, significant bad debts, and newly discovered liabilities as well as other investigations. The court indicated that the senior auditor on the audit (who had not yet received his CPA certificate and was on his first assignment as a senior):

---

[22] Securities Act of 1933, Public Law 212, 73d Congress as amended, Section 13.

[23] "Big Accounting Firms Weed Out Risky Clients," *The Wall Street Journal* (June 26, 1995), B1, B6.

[24] *Escott v. BarChris Construction Corporation*, 283 F. Supp. 643 (S.D.N.Y. 1968).

> asked questions, he got answers which he considered satisfactory, and he did nothing to verify them.
>
> * * * * *
>
> There had been a material change for worse in BarChris' financial position. That change was sufficiently serious so that the failure to disclose it made the 1960 figures misleading. [The senior] did not discover it. As results were concerned his ... review was useless.[25]

The final paragraphs of the judge's decision concerning the auditor's liability in this case were probably the first outlining the standards of care the auditor must use in the review:

> Accountants should not be held to a standard higher than that recognized in their profession. I do not do so here. [The senior's] review did not come up to that standard.... Most important of all, he was too easily satisfied with glib answers to his inquires.
>
> This is not to say that he should have made a complete audit. But there were enough danger signals in the material which he did examine to require some further investigation on his part. Generally accepted accounting standards required such further investigation under these circumstances. It is not always sufficient to ask questions.[26]

The auditors were unable to prove that they acted with due diligence in this landmark case. They were found to be liable.

Fraud and Criminal Liability under the 1933 Act. In addition to civil liability, the 1933 Act provides criminal liability for auditors if fraud is involved. Fraud is defined by Section 17 of the 1933 Act as an effort to use any means to defraud a purchaser of securities. Section 24 of the 1933 Act notes that criminal liability (such as fines and imprisonment) may be levied upon auditors who willfully violate a provision of the 1933 Act or willfully cause misleading financial information to be filed with the SEC. In *United States v. Benjamin*[27] and *United States v. White*,[28] auditors were held liable for fraudulent activity under Sections 17 and 24 of the 1933 Act.

---

[25] *Escott v. BarChris Construction Corporation*, 702.

[26] *Ibid.*, 703.

[27] *United States v. Benjamin*, 328 F.2d 854 (2d Cir. 1964).

[28] *United States v. White*, 124 F.2d 181 (2d Cir. 1941).

> **CHAPTER CHECKPOINTS**
>
> **3-13.** Describe the auditor's noncriminal liability under the 1933 Act.
>
> **3-14.** Under the 1933 Act, what party has the burden of proof? What degree of tort liability does the auditor have to investors under the 1933 Act?
>
> **3-15.** What is the significance of the *BarChris* case in determining auditor liability under the 1933 Act?

Auditors' Liability under the 1934 Act

As stated earlier, the 1934 Act requires companies whose securities are traded on the exchanges and certain companies whose shares are traded over-the-counter to file audited financial statements periodically with the SEC. The auditor can be held liable because of the audit and subsequent opinion given on the financial statements. Section 18(a) of the act points out the noncriminal liability of the auditor when it states that:

> Any person who shall make or cause to be made any statement in any application, report, or document filed pursuant to this title ... which ... was made false or misleading with respect to any material fact, shall be liable to any person (not knowing that such statement was false or misleading) who, in reliance upon such statement, shall have purchased or sold a security at a price which was affected by such statement, for damages caused by such reliance, unless the person sued shall prove that he acted in good faith and had no knowledge that such statement was false or misleading.[29]

Because the 1934 Act pertains to the subsequent trading of securities, either the buyer or seller may suffer a loss if the price at which a security is traded is affected by a false or misleading statement in the entity's financial statements. Thus, either party may bring suit under Section 18 of the 1934 Act. To bring suit under the 1934 Act, the purchaser or seller (plaintiff) must prove that:

1. A loss was incurred.
2. The financial statements contained a false or misleading statement.
3. The price of the security was affected by the false or misleading statement.
4. They relied on the financial statements.
5. They were not aware of the false or misleading statement.

---

[29] Securities Exchange Act of 1934, Section 18(a).

Notice that the 1934 Act places the burden of proof on the purchaser or seller of securities, who must prove both reliance and causation.

In attempting to determine the degree of duty owed by the auditor to third parties under the 1934 Act, Rule 10b-5 has played a major role in current cases brought under the 1934 Act.

SECTION 240. 10b-5
EMPLOYMENT OF MANIPULATIVE AND DECEPTIVE DEVICES

It shall be unlawful for any person directly or indirectly by the use of any means or instrumentality of interstate commerce, or of the mails or of any facility of any national securities exchange: (a) to employ any device, scheme, or artifice to defraud; (b) to make any untrue statement of a material fact or omit to state a material fact necessary in order to make the statements made in the light of the circumstances under which they were made, not misleading; or (c) to engage in any act, practice, or course of business which operates or would operate as a fraud or deceit upon any person in connection with the purchase or sale of any security.[30]

Based on a literal reading of the text of the 1934 Act, it appears that the auditor is only liable to third parties for fraud under this act. The *Hochfelder* case (discussed below) concluded that the auditor cannot be held liable when there is a lack of intentional participation. However, under Section 18, the requirement to act in **good faith** has been generally considered to hold the auditor liable for acts of gross negligence. Therefore, under the 1934 Act, the auditor is generally liable for gross negligence and fraud.

Two defenses are available to the auditor under the 1934 Act. The first defense (the so-called **good faith defense**) is merely that the auditor had no knowledge of the misleading statement or was not grossly negligent in the performance of his or her duties. Assuming that this cannot be proved, the auditor can demonstrate that the loss was caused by a factor other than the misleading statement.

Hochfelder Case. Hochfelder (the plaintiffs) brought suit against Ernst & Ernst (now Ernst & Young) for failure to detect a fraud perpetrated by Lester Nay (president of First Securities Company of Chicago). The plaintiffs were investors in an escrow account maintained by Nay. When Nay received deposits from investors, he diverted these deposits for his own use (Nay persuaded investors to make the checks payable to himself or to a designated bank). This fraud was revealed in a suicide note prepared by Nay.

The defrauded customers charged that Nay's scheme violated 10(b) and SEC's Rule 10b-5 and that Ernst & Ernst aided and abetted Nay's fraud by its failure to conduct proper audits of First Securities. More specifically the customers charged that Ernst & Ernst was negligent in failing to use appropriate auditing procedures, thereby not discovering the fraud. The customers expressly stated that they were not accusing Ernst & Ernst of international fraud but, rather, with "inexcusable negligence."[31]

---

[30] Code of Federal Regulations. Title 17—*Commodity and Securities Exchanges*, Section 240, 10b-5.
[31] J. Jay Hampton, "Accountants' Liability—The Significance of Hochfelder," *The Journal of Accountancy* (December 1976), 69.

The question the court faced was whether the wording of Rule 10b-5 limits the auditor's liability to intentional participation (fraud) or includes negligent conduct as well. The district court found for the auditor. On appeal, a federal court of appeals reversed the decision and found for the plaintiffs. When the case was then appealed to the U.S. Supreme Court, the Court found that the auditor could not be held liable *because the auditor did not know of or intentionally participate in the fraud.*

The syllabus to the decision of the U.S. Supreme Court stated in part:

A private cause of action for damages will not lie under §10(b) and Rule 10b-5 in the absence of any allegation of "scienter" (i.e., intent to deceive, manipulate, or defraud on the defendant's part)....

(a) The use of the words "manipulative," "device," and "contrivance" in §10(b) clearly shows that it was intended to proscribe a type of conduct quite different from negligence, and more particularly the use of the word "manipulative"... connotes international or willful conduct designed to deceive or defraud investors by controlling or artificially affecting the price of securities.

(b) The 1934 Act's legislative history also indicates that §10(b) was addressed to practices involving some element of scienter and cannot be read to impose liability for negligent conduct alone.[32]

What Constitutes Scienter? One lingering question after the *Hochfelder* decision is whether gross negligence is equivalent to scienter. While the U.S. Supreme Court's decision in *Hochfelder* did not completely address this issue, the U.S. Circuit Courts of Appeal have generally concluded that reckless conduct is equivalent in nature to scienter.[33] Thus, under the 1934 Act, auditors are held to the standard of gross negligence.

CHAPTER CHECKPOINTS

3-16. What acts are considered to be illegal under the SEC's Rule 10b-5?

3-17. Under the 1934 Act, who has the burden of proof? What degree of tort liability does the auditor have to investors under the 1934 Act?

3-18. Describe the auditor's noncriminal liability under the 1934 Act. What effect did the *Hochfelder* case have in clarifying this liability?

3-19. What is scienter? With respect to auditor's liability, how have the courts interpreted scienter?

---

[32] *Ernst & Ernst v. Hochfelder*, 425 U.S. 185 (1976).

[33] *Sundstrand Corp. v. Sun Chemical Corp.*, 553 F.2d 1033, 1044-45 (7th Cir. 1977) *cert. denied*, 434 U.S. 875 (1977) and *Hollinger v. Titan Capital Corp.*, 914 F.2d 1564 (9th Cir. 1990).

⦿ OTHER STATUTORY LIABILITY

In addition to the Securities Acts of 1933 and 1934, auditors have been subject to litigation from two additional sources connected with the issuance and sale of securities. The **Racketeer Influenced and Corrupt Organization Act (RICO)** was passed by Congress in 1970 as part of the Organized Crime Control Act of 1970. While the intent of the Organized Crime Control Act (and, therefore, RICO) was to reduce the movement of organized crime into the legitimate business world, its provisions unintentionally exposed professionals (such as auditors and attorneys) to additional liability. Under RICO, any persons incurring losses because of certain types of organized crime by an entity engaged in a pattern of racketeering activity could bring civil suits seeking treble damages (*i.e.*, amounts equal to three times actual damages) as well as reimbursement for their litigation costs. The auditor's exposure to potential liability was based on RICO's definition of a "pattern of racketeering activity" as two or more civil or criminal convictions within a ten-year period and the inclusion of fraud in the sale of securities as a type of "organized crime."

U.S. Supreme Court Chief Justice William H. Renquist commented that "[t]he legislative history of the RICO Act strongly suggests that Congress never intended it to be used in ordinary disputes divorced from the influences of organized crime."[34] However, because of the "deep pockets" of CPA firms, over 2,000 lawsuits were filed against auditors and lawyers under the provisions of RICO as of 1992.[35] In 1993, in *Reeves v. Arthur Young*, the U.S. Supreme Court ruled that to be held liable under the provisions of RICO, a party must participate in the operation or management of the enterprise engaging in fraud (the client). Thus, it appears that auditors are not generally subject to the provisions of RICO unless they are directly involved in the fraud.

A second source of lawsuits by investors and other parties against auditors is under **aiding-and-abetting**. Under this theory, professionals such as attorneys, underwriters, and auditors are charged with having an indirect role in filing misleading financial information with the SEC because of their involvement with the client's financial statements. However, in *Central Bank of Denver v. First Interstate Bank of Denver*[36], the U.S. Supreme Court ruled that auditors could not be sued under this provision of Section 10(b) of the Securities and Exchange Act of 1994.

⦿ LEGAL LIABILITY: WHAT DOES THE FUTURE HOLD?

CPA firms continue to experience tremendous exposure to litigation arising from their professional services. In many cases, this exposure does not result from any wrongs committed by auditors but instead the fact that CPA firms are the only parties that have the ability to provide compensation to victims (the "deep pockets" syndrome). Several suggestions for combatting the problem of legal liability are currently being evaluated.

---

[34] W.H. Renquist, "Get RICO Cases Out of My Courtroom," *The Wall Street Journal* (May 19, 1989).

[35] "Limit of Anti-Racketeering Law is Main Issue in High-Court Case," *The Wall Street Journal* (October 13, 1992), B1, B5.

[36] *Central Bank of Denver v. First Interstate Bank of Denver*, 1145 S.Ct. 1439 (1994).

1. **Proportionate liability.** Under the concept of joint and several liability, each defendant is fully liable for all assessed damages, regardless of their relative degree of fault. In contrast, proportionate liability only holds each party liable for damages based on their degree of fault. For example, assume that a $100 million judgment is assessed and a CPA firm is judged to be responsible for half of the damages. Under the concept of joint-and-several liability, the plaintiffs could recover all $100 million from the CPA firm. However, under proportionate liability, the CPA firm would only be responsible for $50 million (one-half of $100 million). Currently, ten states (Alaska, Illinois, Indiana, Kansas, Kentucky, Oklahoma, Tennessee, Utah, Vermont, and Wyoming) have abandoned joint-and-several liability; twenty-five others have adopted limitations on the joint-and-several liability rule.[37]

2. **Limits on punitive damages.** In many cases, the judgments against auditors reflect a high level of punitive damages (damages paid to penalize auditors for substandard performance) in relation to compensatory damages (damages paid to compensate parties for losses actually suffered). Currently, five states (Louisiana, Massachusetts, Nebraska, New Hampshire, and Washington) do not permit punitive awards in auditors' liability cases. In addition, 12 other states limit the amount of punitive damages that can be assessed against auditors, based either on a specific dollar amount (from $100,000 to $350,000) or a multiple of compensatory damages (from one to four times).[38]

3. **Limited liability partnership.** As noted in Chapter 2, CPA firms are now permitted to practice public accounting in any form of organization permitted by the states in which they practice. Recently, the Big Six firms adopted the limited liability partnership form of organization. While this form of organization itself will not affect the firm's exposure to litigation, it does protect the individual partner's personal assets from exposure to loss (unless the partner him- or herself was involved in activities related to litigation). Therefore, the vicarious liability existing under ordinary partnerships is no longer applicable. By the end of 1995, it is anticipated that over 40 states will permit CPAs and CPA firms to practice as a limited liability partnership.[39]

4. **British Rule.** Another proposal for reducing the legal liability faced by CPA firms is adoption of the "British" (or "loser pays") rule. Under this rule, an unsuccessful litigant would be required to pay the legal fees of a successful defendant. Adoption of this rule would reduce a large number of meritless lawsuits brought against auditors. Currently, many of these lawsuits are settled out-of-court not because of auditor liability, but because of the high costs of defending themselves against these lawsuits.[40]

In 1992, Ernst & Young agreed to pay $400 million to settle federal charges related to their audit of four large, failed thrifts. The failure of these thrifts cost the government $6.6 billion.

Ray Groves, the chairman of Ernst & Young, made the following observation: "Although this is a costly settlement, it's the only realistic solution to an endless stream of lawsuits that would have been expensive to defend. Resolving all outstanding and potential government claims relating to failed financial institutions allows Ernst & Young to continue to devote its resources and energy to the business of serving our clients."[41]

---

[37] D.L. Goldwasser, "Is the Storm Ending?," *The CPA Journal* (October 1995), 16-21.

[38] *Ibid.*

[39] *Ibid.*

[40] *Statement of Position*, "The Liability Crisis in the United States: Impact on the Accounting Profession" (August 6, 1992).

[41] "Ernst to Pay $400 Million Over Audit of 4 Big Thrifts," *The Wall Street Journal* (November 24, 1992), A3.

Recent legislative activity has also affected the auditor's liability under both common and statutory law. For example, the U.S. House of Representatives recently overrode President Bill Clinton's veto of the securities litigation reform bill (H.R. 1058). This legislation limits the application of joint-and-several liability to situations where the CPA engaged in fraud. As a result, a system of proportionate liability has been adopted for nonfraud-related behavior, which should reduce the exposure of accounting firms for tortious conduct.

CHAPTER CHECKPOINTS

3-20. How does RICO affect auditor liability?

3-21. Briefly describe how auditor liability arises under the aiding-and-abetting doctrine.

3-22. Distinguish between joint and several liability and proportionate liability.

SUMMARY

Figure 3-5 summarizes various aspects of the auditor's liability to clients, subrogees, and third parties under common law and the 1933 and 1934 Securities Acts. Several points illustrated in this figure bear emphasis. Note that the plaintiff (client, subrogee, or third party) has the burden of proof under common law and the Securities Act of 1934; that is, the plaintiff must show that the auditor committed a breach of duty and this duty was the cause of his or her loss. In contrast, under the 1933 Act, the auditor has the burden of proving that she or he did not breach her or his legal duty. Also, note that the auditor has a high degree of responsibility for performance under common law and the 1933 Act. In both cases, the auditor is liable for ordinary negligence, gross negligence, or fraud. Under the 1934 Act, the auditor is not liable to third parties for ordinary negligence.

	Party(ies) Involved	Burden of Proof	Tort Liability	Auditor Defenses
Common Law	Clients and subrogees Primary beneficiaries Foreseeable third parties Nonforeseeable third parties	P P P P	ON, GN, F ON, GN, F ON, GN, F GN, F	No breach of legal duty Loss was caused by other factors
1933 Act	Purchasers of securities	A	ON, GN, F	Due diligence Loss was caused by other factors
1934 Act	Purchasers or sellers of securities	P	GN, F	Good faith Loss was caused by other factors

P = plaintiff (party bringing suit)
A = auditor
ON = ordinary negligence
GN = gross negligence
F = fraud

Figure 3-5: *Auditor's Legal Responsibility under Common Law and Statutory Liability*

Appendix A
Summary of Other Court Cases Under Common Law

◻ Liability to Clients and Subrogees

Smith v. London Assurance Corporation. *Smith v. London Assurance Corporation* was the initial American court case involving an auditor. It illustrated the auditor's liability for breach of contract with a client. In this case, the client charged that the auditor's failure to detect an embezzlement occurred as a result of a breach of contract on the part of the auditor. The court ruled in favor of the client, noting that: (1) the auditors were skilled professionals, and (2) the contract called for certain auditing procedures that were not performed in the proper manner by the auditor during the examination. The auditor was found liable for the embezzlement losses; the court ruled that he would have uncovered these losses if he had conducted the examination as provided for under terms of the contract.[42]

National Surety Corporation v. Lybrand. In *National Surety Corporation v. Lybrand*,[43] the client brought charges for breach of contract, breach of warranty, negligence, and fraud. A cashier was "kiting" and "lapping" (techniques of misappropriating cash that are described in Chapter 11), and the auditors failed to discover the defalcations. There were late deposits, and bank transfers were made by the cashier to cover a shortage. The auditors never checked the deposit slips against the entries in the accounts, nor did they follow the standard cash audit procedure of checking the balances in all of the banks as of the same day. An appellate court concluded that the auditors' failure to detect the embezzlement amounted to "constructive fraud."

---

[42] *Smith v. London Assurance Corporation*, 109 App. Div. 882, 96 N.Y.S. 820 (1905).
[43] *National Surety Corporation v. Lybrand*, 256 A.D. 226, 236, 9 N.Y.S. 2d 554 563 (1939).

versus Atlas Automobile Finance Corporation. The protection that a contract can
[provid]e was aptly illustrated in the case of *O'Neill v. Atlas Automobile Finance Corporation.*[44] The
[audit]ors sued their client for fees for professional services rendered during July and August 1936. The
[clien]t introduced a counterclaim for damages suffered as a result of defalcations made by their
[boo]kkeeper during prior periods. In reply to the countersuit, the auditors' contention was "that their
[con]tract was for a limited examination, and a financial review of defendant's books, without verifica-
[ti]on."[45] The judgment of the court was in favor of the auditors. In its decision, the court indicated that
the engagement letter established the scope of the engagement and the duties and standard of care
to be exercised by the auditors.

1136 Tenants' Corporation. The *1136 Tenants' Corporation* case is a more recent case dealing with the failure of a CPA firm to have an engagement letter that was clear in every respect.[46] In this important case, a cooperative apartment corporation (1136 Tenants' Corporation) sued a CPA firm (Max Rothenberg & Co.), alleging that the auditors had failed to uncover defalcations of 1136 Tenants' Corporation's funds by the former managing agent for the plaintiff. Max Rothenberg & Co. had been engaged in August 1963 by an officer of the managing agent to perform certain accounting services for the plaintiff for a fee of $600 per year. While the parties never specified that an audit would be performed, Max Rothenberg & Co. were found liable and were required to pay $240,000 to 1136 Tenants' Corporation. Two authors noted that the failure to obtain an engagement letter resulted in the court's finding.[47]

◘ Liability to Third Parties Other than Primary Beneficiaries

In *Rhode Island Hospital Trust National Bank v. Swartz*,[48] the auditor was held liable to a third party for ordinary negligence (the court used the *Rusch Factors* precedent) even though the auditor issued a disclaimer of opinion (discussed in detail in Chapter 17) on the fairness of the presentation of the financial statements. In its decision, the court emphasized the need for the auditor to indicate any reason(s) for disclaiming an opinion on financial statements.

---

[44] *O'Neill v. Atlas Automobile Finance Corporation*, 139 Pa. Super. 346, 11A.2d 782 (1940).

[45] *Ibid.*

[46] *1136 Tenants' Corporation v. Max Rothenberg & Co.*, 36 App. Div. 2d 804, 319 N.Y.S.2d 1007 (1971); 30 N.Y.S.2d 585, 330 N.Y.S.2d 800 (1972). For a synopsis of this case, see *The Journal of Accountancy* (November 1971), 67-73.

[47] C. Chazen and K.L. Solomon, "The Unaudited State of Affairs," *The Journal of Accountancy* (December 1972), 43.

[48] *Rhode Island Hospital Bank v. Swartz*, 455 E.2d 847 (4th Cir. 1972). For the full details of this case, see "Rhode Island Hospital Trust Decision," *The Journal of Accountancy* (April 1973), 63-66.

Appendix B
Summary of Other Court Cases Under Statutory Law

◻ McKesson & Robbins

The *McKesson & Robbins* case was a landmark case in that it led to the development of GAAS and the extensive use of two important auditing procedures. In this case, the auditors failed to discover a material overstatement of inventory and accounts receivable that was the result of recording fictitious transactions. Operating under auditing standards in existence at that time (1940), the auditors did not physically observe client inventories or confirm accounts receivable with third-party customers. The result of this case was the extensive use of observation and confirmation for inventories and accounts receivable, respectively.

◻ National Student Marketing Case

In a case involving National Student Marketing Corporation, two auditors were accused and convicted (in December 1974) of making false and misleading statements in a 1969 proxy statement. The audit partner received a fine of $10,000 and was sentenced to a one-year jail term with all but sixty days suspended. The other party (the audit supervisor) was fined $2,500 and was sentenced to a one-year jail term with all but ten days suspended. The sentences were appealed. The federal appeals court affirmed the conviction of the audit partner, but it reversed the audit supervisor's conviction.[49]

---

[49] "Auditors Sentenced in National Student Marketing Case," *The Journal of Accountancy* (February 1975), 24. For other details of this case, see the March 12, 1970, March 23, 1970, February 4, 1972, January 18, 1974, July 29, 1975, December 6, 1976, January 19, 1977, and May 3, 1977, issues of *The Wall Street Journal*.

◻ Yale Express Case[50]

In this case, the stockholders and creditors of Yale Express Systems, Inc., brought suit against a national CPA firm for issuing an unqualified opinion on Yale's 1963 financial statements. The auditors' opinion was subsequently included in the 10-K report filed with the SEC. In 1964, the CPA firm performed management consulting services for Yale Express. While engaged in this management service work, the CPA firm "discovered that figures in the 1963 annual report were substantially false and misleading."[51] The CPA firm did not report its discovery to the SEC or the public until March 1965. When Yale Express later filed for bankruptcy, a number of shareholders and creditors filed suit against the CPA firm under Section 18(a) of the 1934 Act and Rule 10(b)-5. The CPA firm moved to have certain aspects of the case dismissed. The court refused to dismiss the claim, and the CPA firm paid $650,000 in the settlement.

◻ Continental Vending Case[52]

In one of the more significant cases of the past quarter century, two partners and a manager of a large CPA firm were found guilty of conspiring and adopting a scheme to violate federal criminal statutes as a result of issuing a misleading opinion on financial statements. The auditors were fined, and the convictions were upheld under appeal. Eventually, the auditors received a presidential pardon, and the CPA firm settled the civil suit out of court. However, the fact that three professional auditors had received criminal sentences was (and is) of great concern to the accounting profession.

◻ Equity Funding Case

Another case that received substantial publicity was the Equity Funding Life Insurance Co. case. Of the $53 million settlement in this case, the CPA firms involved were required to pay $39 million.[53] Three of the auditors "after an arduous four-month trial ... were found guilty on multiple criminal counts of securities fraud and of filing falsified financial statements with the Securities and Exchange Commission."[54]

◻ Other Cases

Several recent court decisions have illustrated the auditor's obligations and liabilities under Rule 10b-5. *McLean v. Alexander* involved charges by the plaintiff that the auditor had indications of discrepancies in the accounts receivable of a client and did not investigate these discrepancies further. The plaintiff purchased the stock of the auditor's client, allegedly relying on accounts receivable as a

---

[50] *Fischer v. Kletz*, 266 F. Supp. 180 (1967).

[51] Henry B. Reiling and Russell A. Taussig, "Recent Liability Cases—Implications for Accountants," *The Journal of Accountancy* (September 1970), 50.

[52] *United States v. Simon*, 425 F.2d 796 (1969).

[53] "Equity Funding Suits are Settled for $53 million," *The Wall Street Journal* (January 5, 1977), 4.

[54] "Three Former Equity Funding Auditors Convicted of Fraud, Filing False Data," *The Wall Street Journal* (May 21, 1975), 11.

measure of the business potential of this company. The lower court ruled that the auditor's failure to disclose the indications of these discrepancies in the company's accounts receivable constituted reckless disregard of the truth and therefore liability under Rule 10b-5. This decision was overruled by the appellate court, which found the auditor guilty of negligence, and, therefore, not liable under Rule 10b-5.

In *Howard Sirota v. Solitron Devices, Inc.*, the auditor was accused of reckless behavior in the conduct of the audit of Solitron, a company whose management intentionally overstated profits in order to aid in the acquisition of new companies. A jury found the auditor guilty of reckless behavior in the conduct of the audit. This finding was overturned by the trial judge, who ruled that the auditor could not be held liable under Rule 10b-5 because the auditor, while guilty of reckless behavior, did not have actual knowledge of the misstatement. On appeal, the Court of Appeals ruled that the auditor had knowledge of the fraud and therefore was liable under Rule 10b-5.

In *Ceneco Incorporated v. Seidman & Seidman*, the court found that the auditor's liability to a client may be limited in instances when management fraud occurs. Ceneco's management was involved in a fraud that inflated the value of its inventories. As a result, Ceneco stockholders filed a class-action suit against the company. A new management then charged the auditors with breach of contract, negligence, and fraud with regard to the auditors' failure to detect fraud as specified under Rule 10b-5. The auditors defended their performance, claiming that they acted diligently in examining indications of fraud. In addition, the auditors contended that the actions of Ceneco's management were a valid defense against any possible negligence. The court ruled in favor of the CPA firm, citing that: (1) auditors are not hired to detect fraud; and (2) although auditors must investigate if they suspect fraud, in this instance management made the fraud difficult to detect. Therefore, management's wrongdoing was a valid defense for the CPA firm against the charges brought by Ceneco.

SUMMARY OF KEY POINTS

1. Two sources of liability exist for auditors. Common law liability is based on prior legal judgments; in contrast, statutory liability is based on the auditor's violation of a written rule or law. Auditors may be held liable to clients, subrogees, and nonstockholder third parties under common law. Under statutory law, the auditor is liable to purchasers and sellers of securities.

2. An engagement letter is a written agreement between the auditor and client for the conduct of the audit engagement that serves as a contract between these parties. If the terms of this letter are breached, the auditor may be held liable to clients and subrogees for breach of contract. A special form of breach of contract is the disclosure of confidential client information.

3. Under common law, plaintiffs may bring suit for tort liability (civil wrongs other than breach of contract) if the auditor breached a duty to act, monetary losses were sustained, and the auditor's breach of the duty resulted in the monetary losses.

4. In addition to breach of contract, the auditor can be liable to clients and subrogees for substandard performance if she or he failed to detect client defalcations. Three levels of tort liability exist: ordinary negligence (the lack of reasonable care), gross negligence (the lack of minimum care), and fraud (intent to deceive). Auditors owe clients and subrogees tort liability for ordinary negligence, gross negligence, and/or fraud.

5. In addition to their clients, auditors are also liable to third parties for tort liability. Primary beneficiaries are third parties who are known by name to the auditor and who the auditor knows will rely on his or her work. Based on *CIT v. Glover*, auditors are liable to primary beneficiaries for ordinary negligence, gross negligence, and/or fraud.

6. Three different viewpoints have emerged with respect to the auditor's tort liability to nonprimary beneficiaries under common law. Based on the *Ultramares* case, auditors are only liable to third parties for gross negligence or fraud. The *Restatement of Torts* approach (as evidenced by the *Rusch Factors, Inc. v. Levin* case) suggests that auditors may be held liable for ordinary negligence to actually foreseen third parties. Finally, the findings of the court in *Rosenblum v. Adler* extend the auditor's liability for ordinary negligence to all foreseeable third parties. The auditor's liability to nonprimary beneficiaries is currently evolving and differs markedly from state to state.

7. The Securities and Exchange Commission (SEC) is an independent regulatory agency of the federal government created by the Securities Exchange Act of 1934. The SEC administers federal laws intended to provide investors with information about companies issuing securities so that investors can evaluate the merits of these securities.

8. The Securities Act of 1933 (1933 Act) governs the initial public issuance of securities. Under the 1933 Act, auditors can be held liable if the registration statement through which the securities were offered contains a false statement or misleading omission. The auditor has the burden of proof to show that the engagement was conducted without negligence or that the loss was caused by some other factor. Under the 1933 Act, auditors can be held liable for ordinary negligence, gross negligence, or fraud.

9. The Securities Exchange Act of 1934 (1934 Act) contains periodic reporting requirements for registered companies reporting to the SEC. Under the 1934 Act, any seller may bring suit against the auditor if: (a) the financial statements contain a false statement or misleading omission, (b) the price of the security was affected by the false statement or misleading omission, (c) the purchaser or seller relied on the false statement or misleading omission, and (d) the purchaser or seller did not know of the false statement or misleading omission.

10. Two defenses available to the auditor under the 1934 Act are that he or she acted in good faith (had no knowledge of the false statement or misleading omission) or that some other factor resulted in the loss.

◉ GLOSSARY

Aiding and Abetting. A theory under which lawsuits are brought against auditors by investors and other parties charging that auditors have an indirect role in filing misleading financial information with the SEC.

Breach of Contract. An instance where the auditor does not perform his or her examination in accordance with one or more aspects of the audit contract (or engagement letter). The auditor's liability for breach of contract is generally limited to clients and subrogees.

Causation. An auditor defense asserting that the plaintiff's loss was caused by a factor other than the auditor's performance.

Comfort Letter. A letter written by the auditor and addressed to the underwriter that summarizes the auditor's findings with respect to financial information included in a registration statement submitted to the SEC.

Common Law Liability. A form of auditor liability that is based on prior legal decisions and court cases. Auditors have common law liability to their clients, subrogees, and nonstockholder third parties.

Contributory Negligence. An auditor defense asserting that the client's negligence contributed to the plaintiff's loss.

Defalcations. Schemes used to embezzle funds or otherwise misappropriate assets. The failure of the auditor to detect defalcations is a frequent basis for lawsuits brought against auditors.

Due Diligence Meeting. A meeting conducted near the end of the registration process in which the auditor, client attorney, and underwriter ensure that they have performed their duties properly. "Due diligence" is a common defense for the auditor under the 1933 Act.

Engagement Letter. A letter written by the auditor and addressed to the client that summarizes the major aspects of the audit examination. The primary purpose of the engagement letter is to prevent misunderstandings from arising concerning the degree of responsibility assumed by the auditor. The engagement letter often serves as the audit contract.

Foreseeability. A viewpoint of auditor liability indicating that auditors may be held liable to all individuals who could foreseeably rely on their work. The foreseeability approach is illustrated by the court's decision in the *Rosenblum v. Adler* case.

Fraud. An actual misrepresentation of a material fact known to be false.

Full and Fair Disclosure. The SEC doctrine that investors should be provided with sufficient information on which to base their economic decisions.

Good Faith. A defense available to the auditor under the 1934 Act indicating that the auditor was not aware of any misleading misstatements or material omissions in the financial statements.

Gross Negligence. A lack of minimum care in the exercise of a legal duty. Gross negligence is generally acknowledged to have occurred when the auditor exhibits "reckless disregard" with respect to her or his duties.

Joint and Several Liability. A form of legal liability where a defendant is fully liable for all assessed damages in a case, regardless of that defendant's relative degree of fault.

Ordinary Negligence. A lack of reasonable care in the exercise of a duty. Ordinary negligence occurs when the auditor does not follow generally accepted auditing standards in performing an audit.

Primary Beneficiary. A third party known by name to the auditor who will be the primary recipient of the auditor's report. The auditor may be held liable to primary beneficiaries for ordinary negligence, gross negligence, or fraud.

Privity. A contractual relationship between two parties. In general, the auditor is only in privity with clients or subrogees.

Proportionate Liability. A form of legal liability where a defendant is only liable for damages based upon their relative degree of fault.

Prospectus. A document included in the registration statement that provides information about companies issuing stock to the public through an initial public offering.

Racketeer Influenced and Corrupt Organization Act (RICO). A provision allowing persons to bring suit against accountants based on participation in a pattern of racketeering activity. Under RICO, investors can bring suit for treble damages as well as their litigation costs.

Registration Statement. A public document containing both financial and nonfinancial information that must be filed with the SEC under the 1933 Act. The registration statement contains audited financial statements of the company offering its securities for sale to the public.

Regulation S-K. Contains the disclosure requirements for nonfinancial statement information filed with the SEC.

Regulation S-X. Contains the disclosure requirements for all financial information filed with the SEC.

Restatement of Torts. A legal doctrine holding that auditors should be held liable to foreseen third parties for ordinary negligence, gross negligence, and fraud. The *Rusch Factors v. Levin* case illustrates the *Restatement of Torts* approach.

Scienter. An intent to deceive or mislead. Scienter has eventually been broadened to include reckless behavior, or gross negligence.

Securities Act of 1933. This act specifies the reporting requirements and auditor responsibility for companies making initial public offerings of securities.

Securities Exchange Act of 1934. This act specifies the reporting requirements and auditor responsibility for the subsequent trading of securities. It regulates the national securities exchanges and over-the-counter markets.

Securities Exchange Commission. An independent regulatory agency of the federal government charged with administering laws governing the sale and trading of securities.

Statutory Liability. An auditor's obligation based on written rules or laws. The auditor's statutory liability is based on the Securities Acts.

Subrogee. A party who acquires, by substitution, the legal or other rights of another party.

Tort Liability. A civil wrong committed by the auditor other than breach of contract. Tort liability normally arises when a substandard audit examination has been conducted and can include ordinary negligence, gross negligence, or fraud.

SUMMARY OF PROFESSIONAL PRONOUNCEMENTS

Statement on Auditing Standards No. 76, "Letters to Underwriters and Certain Other Requesting Parties" (New York: AICPA, 1993, AU 634).

QUESTIONS AND PROBLEMS

3-23. Select the **best** answer for each of the following items:

1. The traditional common law rules regarding accountants' liability to third parties for negligence:

    a. Remain substantially unchanged since their inception.
    b. Were more stringent than the rules currently applicable.
    c. Are of relatively minor importance to the accountant.
    d. Have been substantially changed at both the federal and state levels.

2. Gaspard & Devlin, a medium-sized CPA firm, employed Marshall as a staff accountant. Marshall was negligent in auditing several of the firm's clients. Under these circumstances, which of the following statements is true?

    a. Gaspard & Devlin is not liable for Marshall's negligence because CPAs are generally considered to be independent contractors.
    b. Gaspard & Devlin would not be liable for Marshall's negligence if Marshall disobeyed specific instructions in the performance of the audits.
    c. Gaspard & Devlin can recover against its insurer on its malpractice policy even if one of the partners was also negligent in reviewing Marshall's work.
    d. Marshall would have no personal liability for negligence.

3. Which of the following represents an intentional act on the part of the auditor?

    a. Carelessness.
    b. Ordinary negligence.
    c. Fraud.
    d. Gross negligence.

4. Winslow Manufacturing, Inc., sought a $200,000 loan from National Lending Corporation. National Lending insisted that audited financial statements be submitted before it would extend credit. Winslow agreed to this and also agreed to pay the audit fee. An audit was performed by an independent CPA who submitted his report to Winslow to be used solely for the purpose of negotiating a loan from National. National, upon reviewing the audited financial statements, decided in good faith not to extend the credit desired. Certain ratios, which as a matter of policy were used by National in reaching its decision, were deemed too low. Winslow used copies of the audited financial statements to obtain credit elsewhere. It was subsequently learned that the CPA, despite the exercise of reasonable care, had failed to discover a sophisticated embezzlement scheme by Winslow's chief accountant. Under these circumstances, what liability does the CPA have?

    a. The CPA is liable to third parties who extended credit to Winslow based upon the audited financial statements.
    b. The CPA is liable to Winslow to repay the audit fee because credit was not extended by National.
    c. The CPA is liable to Winslow for any losses Winslow suffered as a result of failure to discover the embezzlement.
    d. The CPA is not liable to any of the parties.

5. Martinson is a duly-licensed CPA. One of his clients is suing him for negligence, alleging that he failed to meet generally accepted auditing standards in the current year's audit, thereby failing to discover large thefts of inventory. Under the circumstances:

   a. Martinson is not bound by generally accepted auditing standards unless he is a member of the AICPA.
   b. Martinson's failure to meet generally accepted auditing standards would result in liability.
   c. Generally accepted auditing standards do not currently cover the procedures that must be used in verifying inventory for balance-sheet purposes.
   d. If Martinson failed to meet generally accepted auditing standards, he would undoubtedly be found to have committed the tort of fraud.

6. DMO Enterprises, Inc., engaged the accounting firm of Martin, Seals & Anderson to perform its annual audit. The firm performed the audit in a competent, nonnegligent manner and billed DMO for $16,000, the agreed fee. Shortly after delivery of the audited financial statements, Hightower, the assistant controller, disappeared, taking with him $28,000 of DMO's funds. It was then discovered that Hightower had been engaged in a highly-sophisticated, novel defalcation scheme during the past year. He had previously embezzled $35,000 of DMO funds. DMO has refused to pay the accounting firm's fee and is seeking to recover the $63,000 that was stolen by Hightower. Which of the following is correct?

   a. The accountants can not recover their fee and are liable for $63,000.
   b. The accountants are entitled to collect their fee and are not liable for $63,000.
   c. DMO is entitled to rescind the audit contract and thus is not liable for the $16,000 fee, but it can not recover damages.
   d. DMO is entitled to recover the $28,000 defalcation and is not liable for the $16,000 fee.

7. An investor seeking to recover stock market losses from a CPA firm, based upon an unqualified opinion on financial statements that accompanied a registration statement, must establish that:

   a. There was a false statement or omission of material fact contained in the audited financial statements.
   b. He or she relied upon the financial statements.
   c. The CPA firm did not act in good faith.
   d. The CPA firm would have discovered the false statement or omission if it had exercised due care in its examination.

8. Josephs & Paul is a growing medium-sized partnership of CPAs. One of the firm's major clients is considering offering its stock to the public. This will be the firm's first client to go public. Which of the following is true with respect to this engagement?

   a. If the client is a service corporation, the Securities Act of 1933 will not apply.
   b. If the client is not going to be listed on an organized exchange, the Securities Exchange Act of 1934 will not apply.
   c. The Securities Act of 1933 imposes important additional potential liability on Josephs & Paul.
   d. As long as Josephs & Paul engages exclusively in intrastate business, the federal securities laws will not apply.

9. A CPA is subject to criminal liability if the CPA:

   a. Refuses to turn over the workpapers to the client.
   b. Performs an audit in a negligent manner.
   c. Willfully omits a material fact required to be stated in a registration statement.
   d. Willfully breaches the contract with the client.

10. A third-party purchaser of securities has brought suit based upon the Securities Act of 1933 against a CPA firm. The CPA firm will prevail in the suit brought by the third party even though the CPA firm issued an unqualified opinion on materially incorrect financial statements if:

    a. The CPA firm was unaware of the defects.
    b. The third-party plaintiff had no direct dealings with the CPA firm.
    c. The CPA firm can show that the third-party plaintiff did not rely upon the audited financial statements.
    d. The CPA firm can establish that it was not guilty of actual fraud.

11. The lack of reasonable care during an audit examination is often referred to as:

    a. Breach of contract.
    b. Fraud.
    c. Gross negligence.
    d. Ordinary negligence.
    e. Scienter.

12. Which of the following cases is most closely related to the auditor's liability to primary beneficiaries?

    a. *CIT v. Glover.*
    b. *Maryland Casualty Company.*
    c. *Rosenblum v. Adler.*
    d. *Rusch Factors v. Levin.*
    e. *Ultramares.*

13. To which of the following parties does the auditor have the least obligation for performance according to tort liability?

    a. Clients and subrogees under common law.
    b. Investors under the 1933 Act.
    c. Investors under the 1934 Act.
    d. Primary beneficiaries under common law.
    e. Nonprimary beneficiaries under the Restatement of Torts approach.

14. If a suit is brought against an auditor for ordinary negligence by a primary beneficiary, which of the following would probably be the auditor's best defense?

    a. The auditor did not conduct the audit recklessly.
    b. The auditor was unaware of the matter giving rise to the suit.
    c. The auditor conducted his or her examination in accordance with GAAS.
    d. The auditor was not in privity with the plaintiff.

15. A recent trend in litigation against CPA firms is that they may be held liable for ordinary negligence to:

    a. Nonusers of financial statements.
    b. Foreseen third parties.
    c. Clients and subrogees.
    d. Unforeseen third parties.
    e. All of the above.

16. The auditor's liability stemming from violations of a written rule or law is referred to as:

    a. Breach of contract.
    b. Common law liability.
    c. Ordinary negligence.
    d. Statutory liability.
    e. Tort liability.

17. To bring suit against a CPA for ordinary negligence under common law, the plaintiff must prove all of the following except:

    a. A legal duty must have existed for the CPA to act or not act.
    b. The CPA must have breached her or his legal duty.
    c. The CPA must have acted recklessly or intended to deceive the plaintiff.
    d. Monetary losses must have been sustained by the plaintiff.
    e. The CPA's breach of the legal duty must be the direct cause of the monetary losses.

18. A document that must be filed with the SEC for companies issuing shares of stock to the public in an initial public offering under the 1933 Act is a:

    a. Comfort letter.
    b. Prospectus.
    c. Proxy solicitation.
    d. Registration statement.
    e. Selling circular.

19. Which of the following must be shown by plaintiffs in bringing suit against a CPA for ordinary negligence under the 1933 Act?

    a. The financial statements contained a false statement or misleading omission.
    b. The plaintiff relied on the false statement or misleading omission in the financial statements.
    c. The plaintiff's loss was caused by the false statement or misleading omission in the financial statements.
    d. The CPA was negligent in her or his examination of the financial statements.
    e. All of the above.

20. Which of the following does not represent a difference between the 1933 and 1934 SEC Acts?

   a. The 1933 Act relates to the initial issuance of securities; the 1934 Act relates to the subsequent trading of securities.
   b. Under the 1933 Act, the burden of proof is placed on the accountant; under the 1934 Act, the burden of proof is placed on the investor (or seller) bringing suit.
   c. The BarChris case dealt with legal liability under the 1933 Act; Hochfelder defined the auditor's liability under the 1934 Act.
   d. The auditor is only liable under the 1933 Act if she or he is grossly negligent or fraudulent; under the 1934 Act, the auditor can be held liable for ordinary negligence, gross negligence, or fraud.
   e. Under the 1933 Act, the auditor is liable up to the date the registration statement becomes effective; under the 1934 Act, the auditor is generally liable up to the date on her or his audit report.

   (Items 1 through 10 in 3-23; AICPA Adapted)

3-24. Discuss the auditor's liability under common law, the 1933 Act, and the 1934 Act. Provide your answer in the following general format:

Area of Liability	Parties Involved	Burden of Proof	Tort Liability	Auditor Defenses
Common Law	Clients and subrogees			
	Primary beneficiaries			
	Foreseeable third parties			
	Nonforeseeable third parties			
1933 Act	Purchasers of securities			
1934 Act	Purchasers or sellers of securities			

3-25. Jones, a CPA engaged in practice without any partners or associates, was retained by Abrams to audit his accounts and prepare a report including her professional opinion for submission to a prospective purchaser of Abrams's business. When the field work was about half completed, Jones became seriously ill and was unable to complete the engagement. The prospective buyer lost interest, and the sale of the business fell through.

   Required:

   a. Abrams sues Jones for breach of contract. Does he have a valid right of action for damages? Explain the legal principles involved.
   b. Jones sues Abrams for her fee for the work she was able to complete. Does she have a valid right of action? Explain the legal principles involved.

   (AICPA Adapted)

3-26. Meglow Corporation manufactured ladies' dresses and blouses. Because its cash position was deteriorating, Meglow sought a loan from Busch Factors. Busch had previously extended $25,000 credit to Meglow but refused to lend any additional money without obtaining copies of Meglow's audited financial statements.

   Meglow contacted the CPA firm of Watkins, Winslow & Watkins to perform the audit. In arranging for the examination, Meglow clearly indicated that its purpose was to satisfy Busch Factors about the corporation's sound financial condition and thus to obtain an additional loan of $50,000. Watkins, Winslow & Watkins accepted the engagement, performed the examination in a negligent manner (ordinary negligence), and rendered an unqualified auditor's opinion. If an adequate examination had been performed, the financial statements would have been found to be misleading.

Meglow submitted the audited financial statements to Busch Factors and obtained an additional loan of $35,000. Busch refused to lend more than that amount. After several other factors also refused, Meglow finally was able to persuade Maxwell Department Stores, one of its customers, to lend the additional $15,000. Maxwell relied upon the financial statements examined by Watkins, Winslow & Watkins.

Meglow is now in bankruptcy and Busch seeks to collect from Watkins, Winslow & Watkins the $60,000 it loaned Meglow. Maxwell seeks to recover from Watkins, Winslow & Watkins the $15,000 it loaned Meglow.

Required:

a. Will Busch recover? Explain.
b. Will Maxwell recover? Explain.

(AICPA Adapted)

3-27. Barton and Company have been engaged to examine the financial statements of Mirror Manufacturing Corporation for the year ended September 30, 19X1. Mirror Manufacturing needed additional cash to continue its operations. To raise funds, it agreed to sell its common stock investment in a subsidiary. The buyers insisted upon having the proceeds placed in escrow because of the possibility of a major contingent tax liability. Carter, president of Mirror, explained this to Barton, the partner in charge of the Mirror audit. He indicated that he wished to show the proceeds from the sale of the subsidiary as an unrestricted current account receivable. He stated that in his opinion the government's claim was groundless and that he needed an "uncluttered" balance sheet and a "clean" auditor's opinion to obtain additional working capital. Barton acquiesced in this request. The government's claim proved to be valid, and, pursuant to the agreement with the buyers, the purchase price of the subsidiary was reduced by $450,000. This, coupled with other adverse developments, caused Mirror to become insolvent, with assets to cover only some of its liabilities. Barton and Company is being sued by several of Mirror's creditors who loaned money in reliance upon the financial statements upon which it rendered an unqualified opinion.

Required:

What is the liability, if any, of Barton and Company to the creditors of Mirror Manufacturing? Explain.

(AICPA Adapted)

3-28. Charles Worthington, the founding and senior partner of a successful and respected CPA firm, was a highly competent practitioner who always emphasized high professional standards. One of the policies of the firm was that all reports by members or staff be submitted to Worthington for review.

Recently, Arthur Craft, a junior partner in the firm, received a phone call from Herbert Flack, a close personal friend. Flack informed Craft that he, his family, and some friends were planning to create a corporation to engage in various land development ventures; that various members of the family were currently in a partnership (Flack Ventures) that held some land and other assets; and that the partnership would contribute all of its assets to the new corporation and the corporation would assume the liabilities of the partnership.

Flack asked Craft to prepare a balance sheet of the partnership that he could show to members of his family, who were in the partnership, and to friends to determine whether they might have an interest in joining in the formation and financing of the new corporation. Flack said he had the partnership general ledger in front of him and proceeded to read to Craft the names of the accounts and their balances at the end of the latest month. Craft took the notes he made during the telephone conversation with Flack, classified and organized the data into a conventional balance sheet, and had his secretary type the balance sheet and an accompanying letter on firm stationery. He did not consult Worthington on this matter or submit his work to him for review.

The transmittal letter stated: "We have reviewed the books and records of Flack Ventures, a partnership, and have prepared the attached balance sheet at March 31, 19X1. We did not perform an examination in conformity with generally accepted auditing standards and therefore do not express an opinion on the accompanying balance sheet." The balance sheet was prominently marked "unaudited." Craft signed the letter and instructed his secretary to send it to Flack.

Required:

What legal problems are suggested by these facts? Explain.

(AICPA Adapted)

3-29. Jackson was a junior staff member of an accounting firm. She began the audit of the Bosco Corporation, which manufactured and sold expensive watches. In the middle of the audit, she quit. The accounting firm hired another person to continue the audit of Bosco. Due to the changeover and the time pressure to finish the audit, the firm violated certain generally accepted auditing standards when they did not follow adequate procedures with respect to the physical inventory. Had the proper procedures been used during the examination, they would have discovered that watches worth more than $20,000 were missing. The employee who was stealing the watches was able to steal an additional $30,000 worth before the thefts were discovered six months after the completion of the audit.

Required:

Discuss the legal problems of the accounting firm as a result of the above facts.

(AICPA Adapted)

3-30. The CPA firm of Martinson, Brinks & Sutherland, a partnership, was the auditor for Masco Corporation, a medium-sized wholesaler. Masco leased warehouse facilities and sought financing for leasehold improvements to these facilities. Masco assured its bank that the leasehold improvements would result in a more efficient and profitable operation. Based on these assurances, the bank granted Masco a line of credit.

The loan agreement required annual audited financial statements. Masco submitted its 19X1 audited financial statements to the bank; these showed an operating profit of $75,000, leasehold improvements of $250,000, and a net worth of $350,000. In reliance thereon, the bank loaned Masco $200,000. The audit report, which accompanied the financial statements, disclaimed an opinion because the cost of the leasehold improvements could not be determined from the company's records. The part of the audit report dealing with leasehold improvements reads as follows:

> Additions to fixed assets in 19X1 were found to include principally warehouse improvements. Practically all of this work was done by company employees, and the cost of materials and overhead was paid by Masco. Unfortunately, fully complete detailed cost records were not kept of these leasehold improvements, and no exact determination could be made on the actual cost of said improvements.

In late 19X2, Masco went out of business, at which time it was learned that the claimed leasehold improvements were totally fictitious. The labor expenses charged as leasehold improvements proved to he operating expenses. No item of building material cost had been recorded. No independent investigation of the existence of the leasehold improvements was made by the auditors.

If the $250,000 had not been capitalized, the income statement would have reflected a substantial loss from operations and the net worth would have been correspondingly decreased.

The bank has sustained a loss on its loan to Masco of $200,000 and now seeks to recover damages from the CPA firm, alleging that the accountants negligently audited the financial statements.

Required.

Answer the following, setting forth reasons for any conclusions stated:

a. Will the disclaimer of opinion absolve the CPA firm from liability?
b. Are the individual partners of Martinson, Brinks & Sutherland, who did not take part in the audit, liable?
c. Briefly discuss the development of the common law regarding the liability of CPAs to third parties.

(AICPA Adapted)

3-31. Marcall is a limited partner of Guarcross, a limited partnership, and is suing a CPA firm that was retained by the limited partnership to perform auditing and tax return preparation services. Guarcross was formed for the purpose of investing in a diversified portfolio of risk capital securities. The partnership agreement included the following provisions:

> The initial capital contribution of each limited partner shall not be less than $250,000; no partner may withdraw any part of his or her interest in the partnership, except at the end of any fiscal year upon giving written notice of such intention not less than thirty days prior to the end of such year; the books and records of the partnership shall be audited as of the end of the fiscal year by a certified public accountant designated by the general partners; and proper and complete books of account shall be kept and shall be open to inspection by any of the partners or his or her accredited representative.

Marcall's claim of malpractice against the CPA firm centers on the firm's alleged failure to comment in its audit report on the withdrawal by the general partners of $2,000,000 of their $2,600,000 capital investment based on back-dated notices and the lumping together of the $2,000,000 withdrawals with $49,000 in withdrawals by limited partners so that a reader of the financial statement would not be likely to realize that the two general partners had withdrawn a major portion of their investments.

The CPA firm's contention is that its contract was made with the limited partnership, not its partners. It further contends that since the CPA firm had no privity of contract with the third-party limited partners, the limited partners have no right of action for negligence.

Required:

Discuss the various theories Marcall would rely upon in order to prevail in a lawsuit against the CPA firm.

(AICPA Adapted)

3-32. Farr & Madison, CPAs, audited Glamour, Inc. Their audit was deficient in several respects:

a. Farr & Madison failed to verify properly certain receivables that later proved to be fictitious.
b. With respect to other receivables, although they made a cursory check, they did not detect many accounts that were long overdue and obviously uncollectible.
c. No physical inventory was taken of the securities claimed to be in Glamour's possession, which in fact had been sold. Both the securities and cash received from the sales were listed on the balance sheet as assets.

There is no indication that Farr & Madison actually believed that the financial statements were false. Subsequent creditors, not known to Farr & Madison, are now suing, based upon the deficiencies in the audit described above. Farr & Madison moved to dismiss the lawsuit against it on the basis that the firm did not have actual knowledge of falsity and therefore did not commit fraud.

Required:

May the creditors recover without demonstrating Farr & Madison had actual knowledge of falsity?

(AICPA Adapted)

3-33. The Chriswell Corporation decided to raise additional long-term capital by issuing $3 million of 8 percent subordinated debentures to the public. May, Clark & Company, CPAs, the company's auditor, was engaged to examine the June 30, 19X1, financial statements that were included in the bond registration statement.

May, Clark & Company completed its examination and submitted an unqualified auditor's report dated July 15, 19X1. The registration statement was filed and became effective on September 1, 19X1. Two weeks prior to the effective date, one of the partners of May, Clark & Company called on Chriswell Corporation and had lunch with the financial vice president and the controller. She questioned both officials on the company's operations since June 30 and inquired whether there had been any material changes in the company's financial position since that date. Both officers assured her that everything had proceeded normally and that the financial condition of the company had not changed materially.

Unfortunately, the officers' representation was not true. On July 30, a substantial debtor of the company failed to pay $400,000 due on its account receivable and indicated to Chriswell that it would probably be forced into bankruptcy. This receivable was shown as a collateralized loan on the June 30 financial statements. It was secured by stock of the debtor corporation that had a value in excess of the loan at the time the financial statements were prepared but was virtually worthless at the effective date of the registration statement. This $400,000 account receivable was material to the financial condition of Chriswell Corporation, and the market price of the subordinated debentures decreased by nearly 50 percent after the foregoing facts were disclosed.

The debenture holders of Chriswell are seeking recovery of their loss against all parties connected with the debenture registration.

Required:

Is May, Clark & Company liable to the Chriswell debenture holders? Explain.

(AICPA Adapted)

3-34. Whitlow and Wyatt, CPAs, have been the independent auditors of Interstate Land Development Corporation for several years. During these years, Interstate prepared and filed its own annual income tax returns.

During 19X4, Interstate requested Whitlow and Wyatt to examine all the necessary financial statements of the corporation to be submitted to the Securities and Exchange Commission (SEC) in connection with a multistate public offering of one million shares of Interstate common stock. This public offering came under the provisions of the Securities Act of 1933. The examination was performed carefully, and the financial statements were fairly presented for the respective periods. These financial statements were included in the registration statement filed with the SEC.

While the registration statement was being processed by the SEC, but prior to the effective date, the Internal Revenue Service (IRS) subpoenaed Whitlow and Wyatt to turn over all its workpapers relating to Interstate for years 19X1-19X3. Whitlow and Wyatt initially refused to comply for two reasons. First, Whitlow and Wyatt did not prepare Interstate's tax returns. Second, Whitlow and Wyatt claimed that the workpapers were confidential matters subject to the privileged communications rule. Subsequently, however, Whitlow and Wyatt did relinquish the subpoenaed workpapers.

Upon receiving the subpoena, Wyatt called Dunkirk, the chairman of Interstate's Board of Directors, and asked him about the IRS investigation. Dunkirk responded, "I'm sure the IRS people are on a fishing expedition and that they will not find any material deficiencies."

A few days later, Dunkirk received written confirmation from the IRS that it was contending that Interstate had underpaid its taxes during the period under review. The confirmation revealed that Interstate was being assessed $800,000 including penalties and interest for the three years.

This $800,000 assessment was material relative to the financial statement as of December 31, 19X4. The amount for each year individually exclusive of penalty and interest was not material relative to each respective year.

Required:

a. Discuss the additional liability assumed by Whitlow and Wyatt in connection with this SEC registration engagement.
b. Discuss the implications to Whitlow and Wyatt and its responsibilities with respect to the IRS assessment.
c. Could Whitlow and Wyatt have validly refused to surrender the subpoenaed materials? Explain.

(AICPA Adapted)

3-35. A CPA firm has been named as a defendant in a class action by purchasers of the shares of stock of the Newly Corporation. The offering was a public offering of securities within the meaning of the Securities Act of 1933. The plaintiffs allege that the firm was either negligent or fraudulent in connection with the preparation of the audited financial statements that accompanied the registration statement filed with the SEC. Specifically, they allege that the CPA firm either intentionally disregarded, or failed to exercise reasonable care to discover, material facts that occurred subsequent to January 31, 19X1, the date of the auditor's report. The securities were sold to the public on March 16, 19X1. The plaintiffs have subpoenaed copies of the CPA firm's workpapers. The CPA firm is considering refusing to relinquish the papers, asserting that they contain privileged communication between the CPA firm and its client. The CPA firm will, of course, defend on the merits irrespective of the questions regarding the working papers.

Required:

Answer the following, setting forth reasons for any conclusions stated:

a. Can the CPA firm rightfully refuse to surrender its workpapers?
b. Discuss the liability of the CPA firm in respect to events that occur in the period between the date of the auditor's report and the effective date of the public offering of the securities.

(AICPA Adapted)

3-36. Whitlow & Company is a brokerage firm registered under the Securities Exchange Act of 1934. The act requires such a brokerage firm to file audited financial statements with the SEC annually. Mitchell & Moss, Whitlow's CPAs, performed the annual audit for the year ended December 31, 19X1, and rendered an unqualified opinion, which was filed with the SEC along with Whitlow's financial statements. During 19X1, Charles, the president of Whitlow & Company, engaged in a huge embezzlement scheme that eventually bankrupted the firm. As a result, substantial losses were suffered by customers and shareholders of Whitlow & Company, including Thaxton, who had recently purchased several shares of stock of Whitlow & Company after reviewing the company's 19X2 audit report. Mitchell & Moss's audit was deficient; if they had complied with generally accepted auditing standards, the embezzlement would have been discovered. However, Mitchell & Moss had no knowledge of the embezzlement, nor could their conduct be categorized as reckless.

Required:

Answer the following, setting forth reasons for any conclusions stated:

a. What liability to Thaxton, if any, does Mitchell & Moss have under the Securities Exchange Act of 1934?
b. What theory or theories of liability, if any, are available to Whitlow & Company's customers and shareholders under the common law?

(AICPA Adapted)

3-37. Jackson is a sophisticated investor. As such, she was initially a member of a small group that was going to participate in a private placement of $1 million of common stock of Clarion Corporation. Numerous meetings were held among management and the investor group. Detailed financial and other information was supplied to the participants. Upon the eve of completion of the placement, it was aborted when one major investor withdrew. Clarion then decided to offer $2.5 million of Clarion common stock to the public pursuant to the registration requirements of the Securities Act of 1933. Jackson subscribed to $300,000 of the Clarion public stock offering. Nine months later, Clarion's earnings dropped significantly, and as a result the stock fell 20 percent beneath the offering price. In addition, the Dow Jones Industrial Average was down 10 percent from the time of the offering.

Jackson has sold her shares at a loss of $60,000 and seeks to hold all parties liable who participated in the public offering including Allen, Dunn, and Rose, Clarion's CPA firm. Although the audit was performed in conformity with generally accepted auditing standards, there were some relatively minor irregularities. The financial statements of Clarion Corporation, which were part of the registration statement, contained minor misleading facts. It is believed by Clarion and by Allen, Dunn, and Rose that Jackson's asserted claim is without merit.

Required:

Answer the following, setting forth reasons for any conclusions stated:

a. Assuming Jackson sues under the Securities Act of 1933, what will be the basis of her claim?
b. What are the probable defenses that might be asserted by Allen, Dunn, and Rose in light of these facts?

(AICPA Adapted)

The Audit Process

Learning Objectives

Study of the material in this chapter is designed to achieve several learning objectives. After studying this chapter, you should be able to:

1. Provide an overview of the major steps in an audit examination.
2. Describe the procedures performed by the auditor in the preengagement stages of the audit and understand the objective of those procedures.
3. Define errors, irregularities, and illegal acts and describe the auditor's responsibility for detecting and communicating these occurrences to the client and to individuals other than the client.
4. Define materiality and discuss how the concept of materiality affects the auditor's examination.
5. Define audit risk, inherent risk, control risk, and detection risk and describe how these risks are determined by the auditor.
6. Discuss how the audit risk model is used by the auditor in the engagement.
7. Discuss the remaining procedures that should be performed by the auditor in the planning stages of the audit.
8. Define supervision and identify various elements of supervising the work of assistants.

4

Audit Planning

◉ OVERVIEW OF THE AUDIT EXAMINATION

This section begins our overview of the process by which the auditor examines and reports on the client's financial statements. This and the five chapters that follow provide a discussion of audit planning (Chapter 4), the auditor's study and evaluation of internal control (Chapter 5), the auditor's substantive testing procedures (Chapter 6), the use of statistical sampling in the audit (Chapters 7 and 8), and the effect of computer processing on the auditor's examination (Chapter 9). These concepts are then applied to individual account balances and classes of transactions in the following section of the text (Chapters 10-15).

An overview of the independent auditor's examination is illustrated in Figure 4-1. Each major step in the audit examination is briefly discussed in turn.

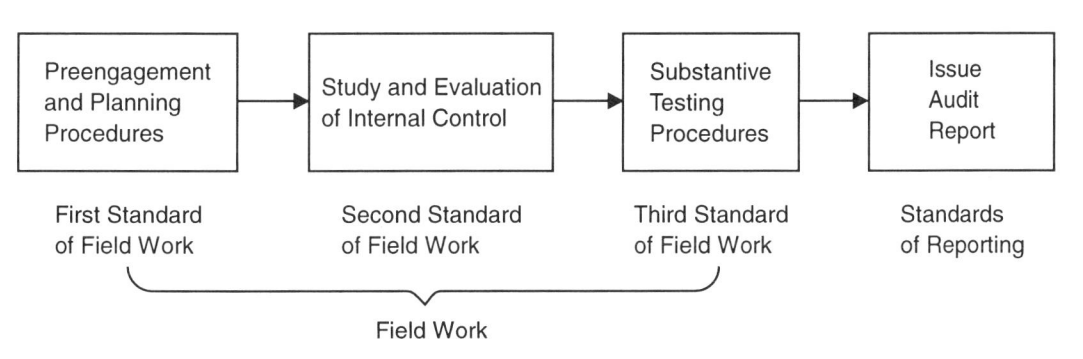

Figure 4-1: *Overview of the Audit Engagement*

4-1

◻ Preengagement and Audit Planning

Prior to accepting and beginning the audit examination, several procedures should be performed by the auditor to evaluate prospective audit clients and consider areas that may require special attention during the audit examination. These procedures may be classified into two categories: preengagement procedures and audit planning procedures. **Preengagement procedures** focus on matters considered by the auditor in deciding whether to accept prospective clients and continue to provide services to existing audit clients.

Once the engagement has been accepted by the auditor, planning procedures are initiated. **Planning procedures** are used to direct the tests performed by the auditor during the engagement. These procedures enable the auditor to identify areas (account balances and classes of transactions) that may require special attention during the examination.

This chapter describes and discusses various procedures performed prior to the acceptance of the audit engagement as well as during the planning stages of the audit.

◻ Studying and Evaluating Internal Control

Once the auditor has accepted the engagement and performed the necessary planning procedures, the next step is to evaluate the entity's internal control. An entity's internal control consists of the policies and procedures implemented by management to ensure that transactions are recorded accurately and that assets are adequately safeguarded. As noted in the second standard of field work, the auditor performs a study and evaluation of an entity's internal control to determine the necessary extent of the auditing procedures to be used. Chapter 5 provides an overview of the auditor's study and evaluation of a client's internal control; Chapters 10, 12, 14, and 15 provide a more specific discussion on the study of internal control related to various types of transactions.

◻ Substantive Testing Procedures

The third standard of field work requires the auditor to gather sufficient, competent evidential matter. This evidence is gathered through the use of substantive testing procedures. The basic purpose of substantive testing procedures is to allow the auditor to determine whether the entity's financial statements are recorded and presented according to generally accepted accounting principles (GAAP). Once an auditor has performed the substantive testing procedures, the auditor may propose adjustments to the client's financial statements, depending on the findings. Chapter 6 discusses substantive testing from a general perspective; Chapters 11, 13, 14, and 15 discuss the substantive tests performed for specific account balances or classes of transactions.

◻ Issuing the Audit Report

The final step in an audit examination is reporting the findings. The auditor's report expresses an opinion as to whether the client's financial statements are prepared and presented according to GAAP. Note that the financial statements and the accompanying footnotes are presentations made by, and are the primary responsibility of, the management of the client, not the auditor. The four reporting standards and the author's standard report were discussed in Chapter 1. Chapters 17 and 18 contain a further discussion of reporting.

> **CHAPTER CHECKPOINTS**
>
> **4-1.** List the major stages in the audit examination.
>
> **4-2.** What is the basic objective of preengagement procedures?
>
> **4-3.** What is the basic objective of planning procedures?

◉ PREENGAGEMENT PROCEDURES

◻ Client Contact

Any auditor-client relationship begins, of necessity, with some form of contact between the auditor and client. While it is not possible to describe all situations that may be encountered in practice, these contacts may be classified into one of two general categories. First, a client that has not previously had its financial statements audited may now be required to have an audit examination. Alternatively, the client may have been audited by another CPA firm. In this case, the auditor may submit a proposal to attempt to obtain the client or otherwise engage in competitive bidding for the opportunity to serve the client. Although this type of behavior may appear to be detrimental to the accounting profession and be inconsistent with the Code of Professional Conduct, Rule 502 indicates that solicitation is permitted as long as it is not false or deceptive and does not involve coercion, overreaching behavior, or harassing conduct.

Some auditor changes are initiated by the client. In many cases, these changes are: (1) the result of client dissatisfaction with the current auditor, or (2) an attempt to obtain a lower fee. In other cases, clients may attempt to change auditors to find support for questionable accounting practices. This latter type of change is of particular concern to the auditing profession and is often referred to as **opinion shopping**. As discussed later in this chapter, GAAS impose certain requirements on the part of both the current and prospective auditor to attempt to reduce incidences of opinion shopping.

In any case, once the client contact has been initiated, the auditor should meet with client personnel to determine various characteristics of the engagement. For many companies, this meeting will involve the **Audit Committee**. An Audit Committee is a group of directors who are neither officers nor employees of the company. Audit committees are required for companies listed on all of the three major U.S. stock exchanges (New York Stock Exchange, American Stock Exchange, and the NASDAQ). The Audit Committee is generally charged with appointing the CPA firm and acting as a liaison between the client and the CPA firm on issues that may arise during the audit examination.

Matters that are commonly discussed with the Audit Committee in the preengagement stage include:

1. The type and scope of services desired by the client.
2. The purpose of the audit examination and potential users of the auditor's report.

3. The number of separate physical locations that will require audit attention.
4. Any deadlines for completion of the audit examination.

It is important to note that under *Statement on Auditing Standards No. 61 (SAS No. 61)*,[1] the independent auditor should continue to communicate with the client's Audit Committee during the various stages of the audit examination. The matters of communication include any significant financial statement adjustments revealed by the auditor's testing procedures and any disagreements that arise between the auditor and management during the examination. In addition, upon the completion of the audit, the auditor reviews the financial statements and the results of the independent audit with the Audit Committee. Communication with the client's Audit Committee is discussed in more detail in Chapter 16.

◘ Accepting the Engagement

At this point, the auditor has identified the nature of services desired by the client, potential users of the audit report, and the desired time frame for the audit. The auditor should now determine whether the technical expertise and manpower exist in the audit firm to complete the audit engagement within the constraints of the desired time frame. It is important to note that *Statement on Quality Control Standards No. 2*[2] indicates that a CPA firm's quality control standards include policies and procedures to decide whether to accept new audit clients and continue to serve existing clients. The primary objective of these policies and procedures is to minimize the possibility that the auditor becomes associated with a client whose management lacks integrity.

In evaluating a new audit client, the auditor should perform the following procedures:

1. Obtain and read financial information relating to the client and its operations. This information includes annual reports and financial information filed with the SEC and other regulatory bodies (including forms 10-K and any registration statements).
2. Make inquiries of third parties who have previous business associations with the client, including the client's attorneys, underwriters, bankers, and predecessor auditor, if applicable (discussed below).
3. Evaluate the firm's independence with respect to the client.
4. Evaluate the firm's ability to adequately staff the engagement.
5. Evaluate whether the appointment would take effect early enough to allow all necessary audit procedures to be performed.
6. Determine whether the engagement would require specialized industry knowledge or other types of expertise (for example, knowledge of computer auditing procedures) and whether this knowledge can be obtained prior to completing the engagement.

---

[1] American Institute of Certified Public Accountants (AICPA), *Statement on Auditing Standards No. 61*, "Communication with Audit Committees" (New York: AICPA, 1988, AU 380).

[2] American Institute of Certified Public Accountants (AICPA), *Statement on Quality Control Standards No. 2*, "System of Quality Control for a CPA Firm's Accounting and Auditing Practice" (New York: AICPA, 1996, QC 20).

It is important to emphasize that these same issues are considered by auditors for existing audit clients. The major difference between the decision to accept a new client and the decision to continue an existing client is that the auditor has much more firsthand knowledge concerning the client and its management in the latter case.

Communications with Predecessor Auditors. As noted above, an important consideration in deciding whether to accept a new audit client is communication with third parties having previous professional associations with that client. A particularly important party in this regard is the auditor who previously performed the examination of the client's financial statements (the predecessor auditor).

When an auditor considers a prospective client whose audit was previously performed by another firm, *Statement on Auditing Standards No. 7 (SAS No. 7)*[3] outlines requirements of both the predecessor and successor auditors. The **predecessor auditor** is the firm that previously provided services to the client and has resigned or been notified that its services have been terminated. The **successor auditor** is the firm that has been approached by the client or invited to make a proposal on the engagement.

Before accepting an engagement, the prospective successor auditor should ask the prospective client to authorize communication with the predecessor auditor. Under Rule 301, this permission must be obtained for the successor auditor's inquiries. Failure to obtain the prospective client's permission should raise serious questions as to whether the potential successor auditor should accept the engagement.

Once permission of the client is obtained, the prospective successor auditor should inquire into matters that may affect acceptance of the engagement. This includes questions regarding: (1) the integrity of management, (2) disagreement(s) with management on accounting or auditing matters, and (3) the reason(s) for the change in auditors. The predecessor auditor should respond fully, except when an unusual circumstance (such as pending litigation) limits a response. Either prior to or after acceptance of the engagement, the successor auditor should review the predecessor's working papers (after obtaining permission of the client and agreement of the predecessor auditor) and make such other inquiries of the predecessor auditor as are needed to obtain evidence for expressing an opinion in an auditor's report. The responsibilities of both the predecessor and successor auditors under *SAS No. 7* are summarized in Figure 4-2.

◻ Engagement Letters

Once the auditor has decided to accept or continue a particular audit examination, she or he normally confirms the understanding of the engagement with the client by the use of an engagement letter. An example of an **engagement letter** appears in Figure 4-3.

Notice that the engagement letter is simply a letter sent by the auditor to the client that summarizes the type and nature of services that are to be provided by the auditor. The client is asked to sign a

---

[3] American Institute of Certified Public Accountants (AICPA), *Statement on Auditing Standards No. 7*, "Communications between Predecessor and Successor Auditors" (New York: AICPA, 1975, AU 315).

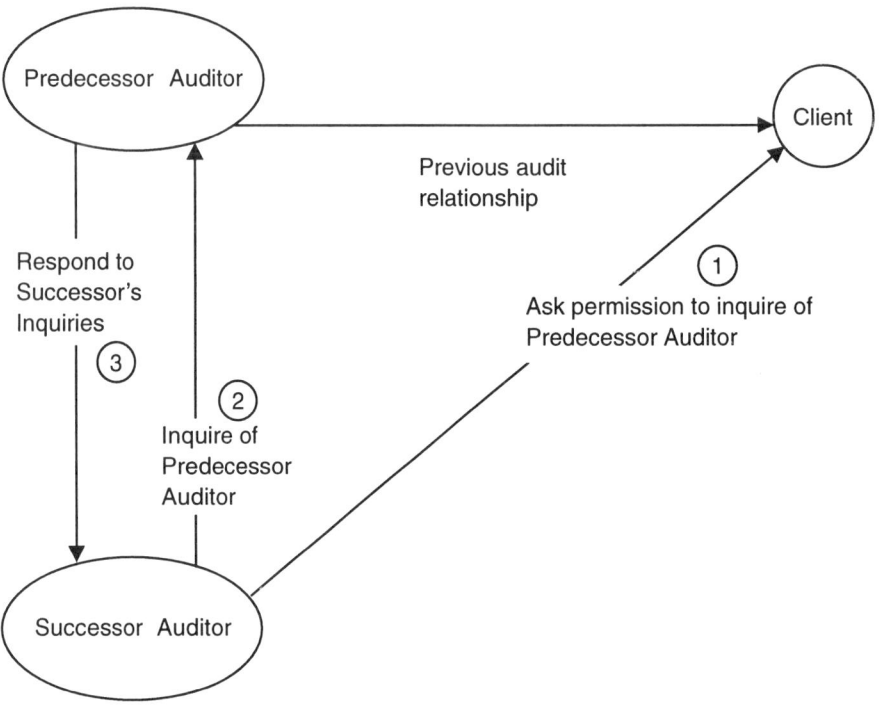

Figure 4-2: *Responsibilities of Predecessor and Successor Auditors under SAS No. 7*

copy of the engagement letter to confirm the client's understanding of the services to be provided by the auditor. Engagement letters include statements that indicate:

1. The audit will be performed in accordance with GAAS.
2. The purpose of an audit examination is to determine whether the financial statements are prepared in conformity with GAAP.
3. The audit may not detect defalcations or other irregularities.
4. Management's responsibility for the financial statements and providing written representations to the auditor.
5. Estimated audit fees and completion dates.

The discussion of auditor liability in Chapter 3 (particularly the *Maryland Casualty Co.* and *O'Neill v. Atlas Automobile Finance Corporation* cases) illustrates the importance of a clearly defined engagement letter. Engagement letters are not required under GAAS; however, most firms use engagement letters for both new and continuing clients. Also, engagement letters are recommended for other types of services (such as compilation engagements, review engagements, and engagements involving prospective financial statements) to clearly delineate the responsibilities assumed by the accountant.

JERRY & JONES, CPAs
1001 Main Street
Baltimore, MD 21820

August 31, 19XX

Mr. Sam Smith, President
Washington Corporation
9 Arbor Lane
Gold Spring, MD 21714

Dear Mr. Smith:

This letter is to confirm our understanding of the arrangements for our audit of the financial statements of Washington Corporation for the year ended December 31, 19XX.

We will audit Washington Corporation's balance sheet at December 31, 19XX, and the related statements of income, retained earnings, and cash flows for the year then ended, for the purpose of expressing an opinion on these statements. Our audit will be in accordance with generally accepted auditing standards, which require that we plan and perform the audit to obtain reasonable assurance that the financial statements are not materially misstated.

Our audit will include examining, on a test basis, evidence supporting the amounts and disclosures in the financial statements. We will also assess the accounting principles used and significant estimates made by management, and evaluate the overall presentation of the financial statements.

An examination directed to the expression of an opinion on the financial statements is not primarily or specifically designed, and cannot be relied upon, to disclose defalcations or other similar irregularities should any exist, although their discovery may result. We will report to you any defalcations or irregularities that are discovered by us during the audit.

We remind you that the preparation of the financial statements, including adequate disclosure, is the responsibility of Washington Company's management. As part of our audit process, we will request from management certain written representations concerning information provided to us in connection with the audit.

Our charge for this work will be at our regular rates. A billing will be rendered at the completion of the engagement.

We are pleased that you have selected us as your independent auditor and look forward to a continuing pleasant relationship with you. Please indicate your agreement with the arrangements discussed in this letter by signing and returning the enclosed copy.

Sincerely,

Accepted by: _____

Date: _____

Jerry & Jones, CPA [Signed]

Figure 4-3: *Sample Engagement Letter*

> **CHAPTER CHECKPOINTS**
>
> 4-4. What is an Audit Committee? What types of matters are commonly discussed by auditors with the clients' Audit Committees?
>
> 4-5. What specific procedures are performed by the auditor in evaluating prospective audit clients?
>
> 4-6. Define predecessor and successor auditors. What type of communications should take place between predecessor and successor auditors?
>
> 4-7. What is an engagement letter? List some of the major contents of engagement letters.

AUDIT PLANNING

The importance of audit planning is acknowledged by its incorporation as the first standard of field work. *SAS No. 1* (AU 310.01) notes that "[t]he work is to be *planned* and assistants, if any, are to be properly supervised" (emphasis added). Audit planning basically consists of all activities performed prior to the auditor's study and evaluation of the client's internal control. In planning the audit, it is important to note that early appointment of the auditor is most advantageous to both the auditor and the client because such appointment allows the audit to be planned more extensively.

The auditor's basic goal in planning the audit is to determine the scope of the audit work that is necessary and ensure that this work can be completed in a timely manner and in conformity with GAAS. Chapter 3 illustrates the potential legal liability that may arise when GAAS are violated during the audit examination. The duties commonly performed by the auditor during the planning stages of the audit examination are discussed below.

Obtaining Knowledge about the Client

During the planning stages of the audit, the auditor should obtain an overall understanding of the client, its industry, operations, and the nature of the client's business. One of the auditor's goals in obtaining such an understanding is to become familiar with the client, its environment, and the economic conditions facing that client.

Statement on Auditing Standards No. 22 (SAS No. 22)[4] identifies the following procedures that can be performed by the auditor in obtaining an understanding of the client and its industry:

1. Reviewing correspondence files, prior-year's workpapers, permanent files, financial statements, and auditor's reports.

---

[4] American Institute of Certified Public Accountants (AICPA), *Statement on Auditing Standards No. 22*, "Planning and Supervision" (New York: AICPA, 1978, AU 311).

2. Inquiring of client management about current developments affecting the entity.
3. Reading the client's current-year financial statements.
4. Considering the impact of recently-issued accounting and auditing pronouncements on the audit examination.
5. Touring client facilities.
6. Reading minutes of meetings of stockholders and the Board of Directors.
7. Considering economic conditions and governmental regulations that may affect the client.
8. Consulting AICPA *Accounting and Auditing Guides*, industry trade publications, and individuals knowledgeable about the client and its industry.

In addition to the client's industry and business, it is also important for the auditor to obtain knowledge about the methods used by the client to process transactions. These methods are referred to as the client's **accounting system**, a concept that will be discussed at length in Chapter 5. According to *SAS No. 22*, a primary consideration for the auditor is the extent to which the client utilizes the computer in processing and recording its transactions. The effect of computerized processing on the auditor's examination is discussed in detail in Chapter 9.

◻ Responsibility for Financial Statement Misstatements

At this point, the auditor has obtained a general understanding of the client and its industry. Now the audit areas that may require special consideration should be identified. Recall from Chapter 1 that the auditor's primary responsibility is to examine the client's financial statements to determine whether they present the financial condition, results of operations, and cash flows in conformity with GAAP. In examining these statements, auditors search for misstatements or omissions in the client's financial statements. *Statement on Auditing Standards No. 53 (SAS No. 53)*[5] identifies two types of misstatements of interest to the auditor: errors and irregularities.

Errors and irregularities can be distinguished by the factors causing their occurrence. **Errors** represent unintentional misstatements or omissions in the client's financial statements. Examples of errors include mathematical mistakes in gathering or processing accounting data or mistakes made in the application of GAAP in recording and summarizing transactions. In contrast, **irregularities** are intentional misstatements or omissions in the client's financial statements. Irregularities include falsification of accounting records or supporting documentation, misrepresentation or intentional omission of transactions or events, and intentional misapplication of accounting principles. An irregularity may present a more favorable impression in the company's financial statements (for example, increasing net income by recording fictitious sales to customers). An irregularity also may be committed by client personnel to hide a defalcation scheme (for example, writing off accounts receivable to conceal embezzlement of cash receipts).

---

[5] American Institute of Certified Public Accountants (AICPA), *Statement on Auditing Standards No. 53*, "The Auditor's Responsibility to Detect and Report Errors and Irregularities" (New York: AICPA, 1988, AU 316).

Currently, a proposed *Statement on Auditing Standards* replaces the term "irregularity" with "fraud" and defines two types of fraud: (1) fraudulent financial reporting, and (2) misappropriation of assets. This proposal is discussed in the Appendix to this chapter.

Responsibility for Detecting Errors and Irregularities. Under GAAS, the auditor is required to plan the audit to provide reasonable assurance of *detecting material errors* and *irregularities*. Although the concept of *materiality* has not yet been addressed, materiality represents an amount that would influence the decisions of users with respect to the client's financial statements—in other words, an amount which would make a difference. Thus, the responsibility for detecting errors and irregularities is limited to those items having a material (large) dollar impact on the client's financial statements.

Notice that the auditor is not expected to detect all material errors and irregularities under GAAS. The concept of reasonable assurance indicates that some uncertainty will normally exist with respect to the auditor's work because not all transactions or balances can normally be examined. Thus, the auditor cannot be certain that all material errors and irregularities have been detected. *SAS No. 53* notes that certain irregularities, particularly those involving forgery and collusion, may be quite difficult to detect even in a properly-designed and executed audit examination. For example, a substantive testing procedure used by the auditor to verify sales made to customers on account is the examination of Invoices prepared for those sales. However, if the Invoices represent a well-developed forgery by sales personnel, the auditor might fail to detect a deliberate overstatement of sales.

In designing the audit to detect material errors and irregularities, the auditor should consider the effects of various factors at both the financial statement level and the account balance level. As noted in Figure 4-4, three main types of characteristics influence the likelihood of errors and irregularities at the financial statement level: (1) management characteristics, (2) operating and industry characteristics, and (3) engagement characteristics. In considering these characteristics, the auditor should look at those factors that would make material misstatements more likely to occur or easier for client personnel to conceal. For example, if management has an aggressive attitude toward financial reporting, revenues may be recognized prior to the proper accounting period. In addition, if the client's profitability is inadequate relative to its industry, client personnel may feel the need to deliberately misstate the financial statements so that they compare more favorably with similar companies in the industry. Each of the conditions shown in Figure 4-4 would suggest a higher probability of material misstatement.

In addition to the considerations outlined in Figure 4-4, the auditor should also consider characteristics of the account balance or class of transactions in determining the possibility of material misstatements. These factors include the complexity of accounting issues, the presence of difficult-to-audit transactions, and the susceptibility of the related assets to theft or other misappropriation. Once both the financial statement characteristics and the account balance or class of transactions characteristics have been identified, the auditor will have an idea of the susceptibility of the account balance to misstatement. This susceptibility is referred to as inherent risk. As noted in a following section, the auditor will use the assessment of inherent risk (along with other information) in determining the nature, timing, and extent of the substantive testing procedures to be used.

Responsibilities if Errors or Irregularities are Detected. If errors and irregularities are detected by the auditor during the examination, the initial issue facing the auditor is whether these errors or irregularities are material with respect to the financial statements. In assessing materiality, the auditor should consider the effect of all discovered errors and irregularities on the financial statements

Management Characteristics

1. Client operating and financing decisions are dominated by a single individual.
2. Management has an unduly aggressive attitude toward financial reporting.
3. Management places undue emphasis on meeting earnings projections.
4. Management's reputation in the business community is poor.

Operating and Industry Characteristics

1. The client is experiencing inadequate profitability relative to other companies in the industry.
2. The client's operating results are highly sensitive to economic factors (such as inflation, interest rates, etc.).
3. The rate of change in the client's industry is rapid.
4. The client's organization is decentralized, without adequate monitoring by upper management.
5. Doubt exists concerning the client's ability to continue in existence.

Engagement Characteristics

1. Many difficult accounting issues or difficult-to-audit transactions exist.
2. Significant related-party transactions occur that are not in the ordinary course of business.
3. Previous audit engagements have noted significant misstatements in the client's financial statements.
4. The client has never been audited, or the auditor is unable to obtain sufficient information from the predecessor auditor.

Source: American Institute of Certified Public Accountants (AICPA), *Statement on Auditing Standards No. 53*, "Errors and Irregularities" (New York: AICPA, 1988, AU 316.10).

Figure 4-4: *Factors Affecting the Possibility of Material Misstatements*

taken as a whole. If the auditor determines that the financial statements are materially misstated, an adjustment to the client's financial statements will be proposed. As noted earlier, under *SAS No. 61*, the auditor is required to communicate all significant adjustments (regardless of whether they arise from errors or from irregularities) to the client's Audit Committee. The actual process used in proposing adjustments to the client's financial statements is discussed in Chapter 16 of this text.

The auditor does not normally communicate immaterial errors to the Audit Committee. In contrast, because of the intentional nature of irregularities, the auditor is generally more concerned about communicating these misstatements to the client. Irregularities may have implications for other areas of the audit because they reveal situations where client employees are in a position to intentionally distort financial statements. When an irregularity is discovered, the auditor should communicate it to an individual at least one level above the individual(s) involved in the irregularity, whether its effect on the financial statements is material or immaterial. In addition, the auditor will normally communicate all irregularities to the client's Audit Committee, unless the Irregularities are deemed to be clearly inconsequential.

While communication of irregularities to individuals external to the entity is normally the responsibility of the client, *SAS No. 53* notes that the auditor may be required to communicate irregularities to:

1. The SEC, when reporting an auditor change on Form 8 K.
2. A predecessor auditor, under the provisions of *SAS No. 7*.
3. A court, in response to a valid subpoena.
4. A funding entity or other agency, if the client receives financial assistance from a federal government agency.

Responsibilities for Illegal Acts. In addition to errors and irregularities, another possible source of financial statement misstatements is from illegal acts committed by clients. **Illegal acts** are client activities that involve violations of laws or governmental regulations by employees acting on behalf of the client. For purposes of auditor responsibilities, the auditor is only responsible for illegal acts committed by employees acting on behalf of the client. The auditor is not responsible for any violations committed by client employees unrelated to business activities.

Statement on Auditing Standards No. 54 (SAS No. 54)[6] notes that the auditor's responsibility for detecting illegal acts is generally similar to that for detecting errors and irregularities under *SAS No. 53*—that is, the auditor is required to plan the audit to detect illegal acts having a direct and material effect on the financial statements. For example, if violating income tax laws would result in materially misstated income tax expense and taxes payable, the auditor is required to plan the audit to detect these misstatements. While illegal acts may also have indirect effects on the financial statements (for example, possible contingent liabilities for fines and penalties if securities laws are violated), the auditor's responsibility is limited to those illegal acts directly affecting the financial statements.

If the auditor finds evidence of a possible illegal act, additional procedures should be employed to investigate the possibility further. In addition, the auditor should consider whether the occurrence of illegal acts affects the reliability that can be placed on management's representations. When the auditor does not feel that management's representations are reliable, an alternative that must be considered is to issue a disclaimer of opinion and withdraw from the audit.

The auditor's responsibility for communicating illegal acts to the client are similar to that for irregularities. That is, the auditor should communicate any illegal act discovered to the client's Audit Committee, unless the effect of the illegal act is clearly inconsequential. Also, like irregularities, the auditor may need to communicate illegal acts to the SEC, successor auditors, governmental agencies, or courts of law in some situations.

Summary: Errors, Irregularities, and Illegal Acts. Figure 4-5 summarizes the auditor's responsibility for detecting and reporting errors, irregularities, and illegal acts. In terms of detecting these actions, the auditor is responsible only for errors, irregularities, and illegal acts having a **material**

---

[6] American Institute of Certified Public Accountants (AICPA), *Statement on Auditing Standards No. 54*, "Illegal Acts by Clients" (New York: AICPA, 1988, AU 317).

effect on the client's financial statements. However, as indicated in Figure 4-5, the auditor's responsibility for communicating these actions to the client differs. Note that the auditor generally only communicates material errors to the client; however, all irregularities and illegal acts are normally communicated. Because these latter types of misstatements represent intentional behavior on the part of the client and its personnel, the auditor has concerns beyond the dollar effect(s) of these actions. This communication should be made to the Audit Committee and individual(s) at least one level above the occurrence of the irregularity or illegal act.

	Responsible for Detecting?		Responsible for Communicating?	
	Material	**Immaterial**	**Material**	**Immaterial**
Errors	Yes	No	Yes[a]	No
Irregularities	Yes	No	Yes[a,b]	Yes[a,b]
Illegal Acts	Yes	No	Yes[a]	Yes[a]

[a]Communication is with the Audit Committee.
[b]Communication is with individual(s) at least one level above the occurrence of the irregularity.

Figure 4-5: *Auditor Responsibility for Detecting and Communicating Errors, Irregularities, and Illegal Acts*

CHAPTER CHECKPOINTS

4-8. What is the primary purpose of planning the audit?

4-9. List some sources of information that allow the auditor to obtain an understanding of the client and its industry.

4-10. Define errors and irregularities.

4-11. What is the auditor's responsibility for detecting errors and irregularities during the audit?

4-12. What is the auditor's responsibility for communicating information about errors and irregularities detected during the audit?

4-13. What are illegal acts? What is the auditor's responsibility for detecting and communicating illegal acts?

◻ Determining an Audit Strategy: Materiality, Management Assertions, and Audit Risk

From the previous discussion, it is evident that the auditor is required to plan the examination so as to detect errors, irregularities, and illegal acts that have a **material** effect on the client's financial statements. The auditor considers three major conceptual issues in planning the audit to detect material misstatements.[7] One of these issues involves establishing materiality levels; that is, at what dollar amount is a misstatement considered to be sufficiently large to affect users' perceptions of the company and its financial condition? Once materiality has been established, the auditor should also consider the different ways in which accounts may contain misstatements. These ways are referred to as management assertions. Finally, the auditor considers information about the susceptibility of the account balance to misstatement and the effectiveness of the client's internal control in preventing and detecting misstatements. This information is used by the auditor to determine the nature, timing, and extent of the substantive tests used. The latter concept is the audit risk model. These issues are discussed below.

◻ Materiality

Prior to devising an audit strategy, the auditor should establish preliminary levels of materiality for use during the audit examination. The concept of materiality recognizes that certain matters are clearly important to investors and other third parties, while others are less important. In an audit setting, materiality is usually defined as the dollar amount of misstatement that would affect the perceptions and decisions of users of financial statements. For example, if accounts receivable recorded at $1,000,000 were misstated by $100, users' perceptions and decisions about a company would not be affected by this misstatement. However, if the amount of the misstatement was $200,000, users' perceptions and decisions may be affected. Thus, it can be stated that the latter ($200,000) misstatement is more likely to be **material** than the former misstatement.

Current professional pronouncements (*Statement on Auditing Standards No. 47*)[8] require the auditor to consider materiality in two stages of the audit examination: prior to conducting the audit examination (in the planning stage) and in evaluating the results of the evidence provided by the substantive testing procedures (in the evaluation stage). In this chapter, the focus is on the role of materiality in the planning stage of the audit; Chapter 16 discusses the role of materiality during the evaluation stage.

How is Materiality Determined? Determining the materiality levels for use in examining a particular account balance is a two-step procedure. First, the auditor should judgmentally determine the materiality level for the financial statements taken as a whole. When establishing materiality levels

---

[7] Throughout the remainder of this text, we use the term misstatement to refer to either an error, irregularity, or illegal act. That is, we do not distinguish between the cause of a material financial statement misstatement because the auditor's responsibility for detecting misstatements is identical for each type.

[8] American Institute of Certified Public Accountants (AICPA), *Statement on Auditing Standards No. 47*, "Audit Risk and Materiality" (New York: AICPA, 1983, AU 312).

on a financial-statement basis, it is important for the auditor to consider the interrelationships that exist between the financial statements. The auditor should establish materiality levels so that materiality is expressed in terms of the smallest amount that would be significant to any one of the financial statements. For example, assume that the auditor decides that misstatements would need to total $100,000 to have a significant effect on users' decisions and perceptions related to a company's net income. Even though misstatements would need to total $300,000 to affect users' decisions and perceptions of the company's balance sheet, the auditor should design the substantive testing procedures using the $100,000 level.

A common method of determining materiality for any given financial statement is to use some percentage of a subtotal on that statement. Establishing materiality levels in this manner recognizes that when an account balance is larger, it must be misstated by a greater amount before users' decisions relating to this statement would be affected. Common guidelines for materiality levels are usually considered to be 5 to 10 percent of net income (for income statement purposes) or 1 percent of total assets (for balance sheet purposes). Thus, the larger a company's net income or total assets, the greater the dollar amount of materiality levels.

SAS No. 47 notes that once the overall materiality levels for planning purposes are determined (as described above), materiality must be considered on an individual account-balance or class-of-transactions level. That is, when planning the audit, the auditor must design substantive tests to detect errors in each account that would be material to the financial statements taken as a whole. In a sense, the auditor "allocates" the financial statement materiality over the affected accounts. When establishing the materiality levels for a particular account, the auditor should consider the relationships between the financial statements taken as a whole and the account in question.

The process by which materiality is determined is illustrated in Figure 4-6. It is important to recognize that this process is highly subjective and requires the exercise of a great deal of judgment by the auditor.

Effect of Planning Materiality on the Audit Examination. Once preliminary materiality levels have been established, the auditor then considers these levels in identifying the scope of the examination. Because the auditor is required to detect misstatements that, either individually or in the aggregate, would have a material effect on the financial statements, those misstatements that would not materially affect the financial statements are normally not a matter of concern.

Assume that the account could contain errors ranging from zero percent of the account balance to 100 percent of the account balance and that the auditor establishes materiality for this account at 15 percent of the balance, or (A). Recall that once a materiality level is established, the auditor considers only components of the account balance or transactions that, either individually or combined, could have some probability of resulting in materially misstated financial statements. As a result, the auditor may need to examine transactions or components involving amounts less than the materiality level (A), because these items could combine to result in materially misstated financial

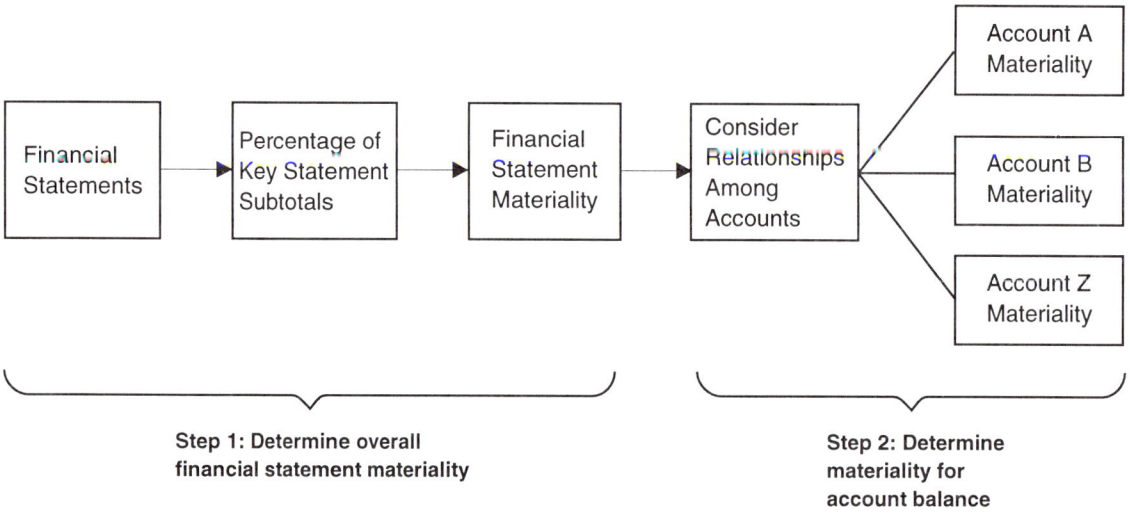

Figure 4-6: *Determining Materiality at the Account Balance Level*

statements. The point where all transactions at that amount or lower would not combine to result in material misstatements is represented by A*.

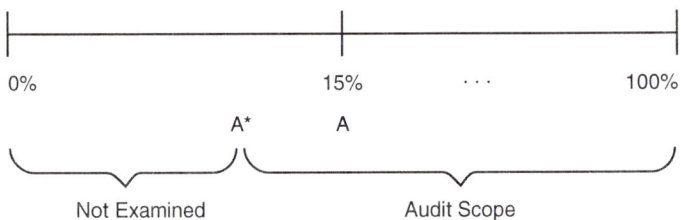

An additional point should be emphasized. If the auditor lowers materiality levels—for example, to a level left of (A) in the above illustration—the number of components or transactions that could result in materially misstated financial statements increases. As a result, the scope of the auditor's examination would also increase. This illustrates the inverse relationship between materiality and the scope of the auditor's examination; as materiality decreases (increases), the scope of the engagement increases (decreases).

> **CHAPTER CHECKPOINTS**
>
> 4-14. What is materiality? In what stages of the engagement should the auditor consider materiality?
>
> 4-15. How does the auditor establish materiality at the financial-statement level and account-balance level during the audit?
>
> 4-16. Describe the inverse relationship between materiality and the scope of the auditor's examination.

◻ Management Assertions

The previous section discussed the concept of materiality and how the materiality levels established by the auditor influence the scope of his or her examination. In planning the audit to detect material misstatements, the auditor should also consider the manner in which the client's financial statements could be materially misstated. For example, if the client reports accounts receivable on its balance sheet of $200,000, the following situations could cause this account balance (and assuming that the misstatements were material, the financial statements) to be misstated:

- Fictitious sales are included in the account balance (the $200,000 of accounts receivable includes sales transactions that did not actually occur)

- Sales are included in the account balance that will ultimately be uncollectible (the client records all sales transactions accurately, but the $200,000 is not the amount of cash that will be received)

- Sales actually made during the current period are not recorded until the following period (the $200,000 does not include all sales transactions that occurred during the year)

- Sales are recorded at incorrect dollar amounts (the $200,000 includes transactions that are recorded at incorrect dollar amounts)

- Failure to disclose that some accounts receivable are pledged as collateral for a loan (the restriction on part of the $200,000 is not mentioned in the footnotes accompanying the financial statements)

Recall from our earlier discussion that the client's management is responsible for preparing the client's financial statements. In preparing these financial statements, management makes several representations (or **assertions**) to the users of those financial statements. The auditor's objective in planning the audit to detect material misstatements is to verify the material assertions affecting the account balances and classes of transactions included in the client's financial statements. The five categories of management assertions suggested by the above situations are classified as:

1. Existence or occurrence
2. Rights and obligations

3. Completeness
4. Valuation or allocation
5. Presentation and disclosure

The relationship between management's assertions, the fairness of the client's financial statements, and the auditor's responsibility for detecting material misstatements is summarized below. These assertions are described briefly in the following subsections.

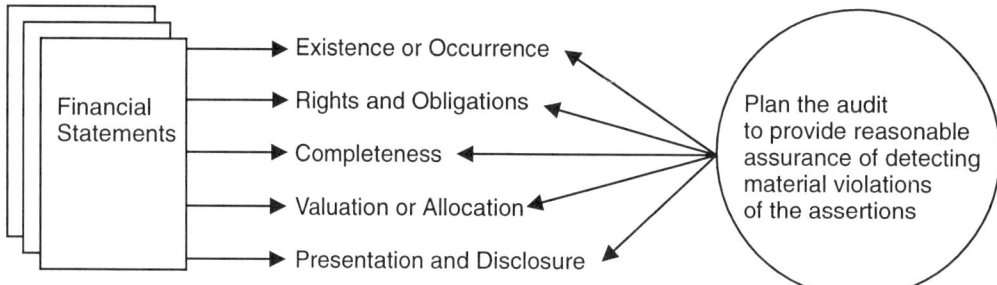

Existence or Occurrence. The existence or occurrence assertion (the EO assertion) deals with whether the assets or liabilities of an entity exist at a given date and whether the recorded transactions have occurred during a given period. For example, under the EO assertion, management is representing that all cash, inventory, marketable securities, and property, plant and equipment shown in a company's balance sheet actually exist. In addition, this assertion also extends to assets and liabilities not having physical substance (such as accounts receivable and accounts payable). For income statement accounts, the EO assertion indicates that all items shown in the income statement reflect transactions that have actually occurred during a given period of time.

The EO assertion means that the client has not recorded fictitious transactions in the accounting records. For example, if management records fictitious sales near year-end in order to increase the company's reported profitability, these fictitious sales would violate the EO assertion. Similarly, by recording sales *prior to* the date of the actual transaction, the company's financial statements would also violate the EO assertion.

From the auditor's standpoint, the EO assertion is of primary concern when examining asset or revenue accounts. Because of the favorable effect(s) of assets and revenues on a company's financial condition and results of operations, the company's management has an incentive to overstate these accounts (or to record fictitious transactions involving these accounts). Therefore, the auditor generally tests for overstatement in examining asset and revenue accounts.

Rights and Obligations. The rights and obligations assertion (the RO assertion) is concerned with whether assets are the rights of the entity and liabilities the obligations of the entity at a given date. It is important to distinguish between the EO assertion and the RO assertion. Assets and liabilities may exist (and meet the criteria for the EO assertion); however, in order to be presented on the company's balance sheet, the entity must own the assets (rights) or owe the liabilities (obligations). Some examples of issues related to the RO assertion are shown below:

▶ Accounts receivable that exist may prove to be uncollectible

- Inventory on the client's premises may be held for sale on consignment or for customer pick-up
- Property, plant and equipment held by the client may be leased from other parties under an operating lease agreement

In each of the above cases, the assets existed (and the related transactions actually occurred), but the assets were not the rights of the company. Thus, while these items meet the criteria for the EO assertion, they do not meet the criteria for the RO assertion.

Completeness. The completeness assertion (the CO assertion) relates to whether all transactions and accounts that should be presented in the financial statements are so included. For example, when management indicates that accounts receivable are recorded at some amount (e.g., $200,000), they are asserting that this amount includes all accounts receivable transactions during the period under examination. Simply stated, management indicates that no transactions have been omitted. In addition, the CO assertion also extends to cases where transactions that occur in a given year are recorded in a later year.

From the auditor's standpoint, the CO assertion is of primary concern when examining liability or expense accounts. Because of the unfavorable effect(s) of liability and expenses on a company's financial condition and results of operations, the company's management may have an incentive to understate these accounts (or fail to record transactions affecting these accounts). Therefore, the auditor generally tests for understatement in examining liability and expense accounts.

Valuation or Allocation. The valuation or allocation assertion (the VA assertion) is concerned with whether asset, liability, revenue, and expense components have been included in the financial statements at the appropriate dollar amounts. The VA assertion involves such issues as:

- Are transactions recorded at the proper dollar amount?
- Are components or accounts shown using the proper valuation methods?
- Are accounting estimates made by management reasonable?
- Have GAAP been properly applied to components or accounts?

To illustrate the VA assertion, consider the property, plant and equipment account. The VA assertion involves determining whether: (1) property transactions occurring during the year are recorded at the proper dollar amounts; (2) property, plant and equipment is shown on the balance sheet at historical cost minus accumulated depreciation; (3) estimates of the salvage value and useful life of property, plant and equipment are reasonable; and (4) transactions related to property, plant and equipment leased from others are properly classified as an operating lease or capital lease. The VA assertion is affected by violations of the above issues.

It is important to clearly distinguish between situations representing violations of the EO and CO assertions and those representing violations of the VA assertion. If fictitious transactions are recorded by the client, two major assertions appear to be affected: the EO assertion (since a transaction that did not occur is included in the financial statements) and the VA assertion (since the transaction is not recorded at the proper dollar amount, which would be zero). A similar argument could be made regarding unrecorded transactions and the CO and VA assertions. For example, if a sales transaction of $60,000 is not recorded by the client, this transaction would be omitted from the account or component (the CO assertion). In addition, the transaction would be recorded at $0 and not at its proper amount, $60,000 (the VA assertion). Unrecorded transactions (fictitious transactions) are generally viewed as relating to the CO (EO) assertion(s) and not the VA assertion. The VA assertion is concerned with instances where an actual transaction has been recorded; however, this transaction (or the account balance related to this transaction) is not recorded or presented according to GAAP.

Presentation and Disclosure. The presentation and disclosure assertion (the PD assertion) is concerned with whether particular components of the financial statements are properly classified, described, and disclosed. Presentation and disclosure relates primarily to the footnote disclosures and classification of items within the financial statements. Some examples of issues relating to the PD assertion are:

- Failure to disclose compensating balance requirements for cash
- Failure to disclose accounts receivable or inventories pledged as collateral
- Failure to classify property, plant and equipment not being used in operations as "other assets"
- Disagreements with management's classification of marketable securities

Figure 4-7 summarizes the five management assertions and indicates situations that may result in violations of these assertions. In addition, examples involving the accounts receivable account are also provided in Figure 4-7.

◘ Audit Risk Model

At this point, the auditor has: (1) identified his or her preliminary materiality levels, and (2) identified the important management assertions affecting the account balance or class of transactions. Recall that the auditor's responsibility under *SAS Nos. 53* and *54* is to plan the audit to provide **reasonable assurance** of detecting misstatements that have a **material** effect on the client's financial statements. Reasonable assurance means that the auditor cannot possibly expect to detect all material misstatements; instead, he or she should perform auditing procedures (substantive tests) to provide a high likelihood of detecting these misstatements. Stated another way, the auditor is required to plan the audit so that the probability that a material misstatement goes undetected is relatively low.

To plan the audit (and develop substantive testing procedures) to detect material misstatements, the auditor considers three main issues:

1. What probability does the auditor wish to attain that a material misstatement goes undetected? As this probability is lowered, the auditor's procedures must be devised to be more effective in detecting misstatements.
2. How likely is it that the account balance or class of transactions contains misstatements? If this likelihood is higher, the auditor's procedures must be devised to be more effective in detecting misstatements.
3. How effective is the client's internal control in preventing or detecting misstatements? If the client's internal control is less effective, the auditor's procedures must be devised to be more effective in detecting misstatements.

Assertion	Violations of Assertion	Example for Accounts Receivable
EO Assertion	Recording fictitious transactions or components	Recording fictitious sales transactions
	Recording components or transactions in a period earlier than when they occurred	Recording sales transactions in an earlier period than when they occurred
RO Assertion	Recording transactions or components at amounts different from the benefits to be received or foregone	Failing to write-off uncollectible accounts receivable or provide an adequate provision for uncollectible accounts
CO Assertion	Failing to record transactions	Failing to record sales transactions
	Recording transactions in a period later than when the transactions occurred	Recording sales transactions in a later period than when they occurred
VA Assertion	Recording transactions at the incorrect dollar amount	Recording sales transactions at the incorrect dollar amount
	Presenting transactions and/or the account balance using incorrect valuation methods	Presenting accounts receivable at other than their net realizable value
	Using inappropriate estimates in recording transactions	Using inappropriate estimates for uncollectible accounts receivable
	Failing to record transactions under GAAP methods	Not Applicable
PD Assertion	Classifying transactions and/or the account balance incorrectly	Classifying receivables from employees and officers as accounts receivable
	Failing to provide adequate disclosures regarding the account balance	Failing to disclose accounts receivable pledged as collateral

Figure 4-7: *Management Assertions and Situations Violating the Assertions*

These three issues form the basis of audit risk and the audit risk model. *Statement on Auditing Standards No. 47 (SAS No. 47)*[9] views audit risk as the combination of three independent events: (1) the risk that a material misstatement occurs in an assertion affecting an account balance or class of

---

[9] American Institute of Certified Public Accountants (AICPA), *Statement on Auditing Standards No. 47*, "Audit Risk and Materiality" (New York: AICPA, 1983, AU 312).

transactions, (2) the risk that this misstatement is not prevented or detected by the client's internal control, and (3) the risk that this misstatement is not detected by the auditor's substantive testing procedures. The following represents the audit risk model illustrated by SAS No. 47:

$$\text{Audit Risk} = \text{Inherent Risk} \times \text{Control Risk} \times \text{Detection Risk}$$

These components and the steps involved with using the audit risk model are discussed in the following subsections.

Audit Risk. As noted above, **audit risk** is the joint combination of three component risks (inherent risk, control risk, and detection risk). The definition of audit risk is based on the eventual outcome that occurs; a material misstatement will occur and not be detected by the auditor. As a result, the auditor issues an unqualified opinion on financial statements that contain a material misstatement. The definition of audit risk provided by SAS No. 47 is:

> **Audit risk** is the risk that the auditor may unknowingly fail to appropriately modify his opinion on financial statements that are materially misstated.[10]

In the planning stages of the audit, the auditor should establish audit risk at acceptable (low) levels. Audit risk can never be zero percent because the auditor can never be assured that every misstatement has been detected; however, the auditor should limit his or her exposure to this risk to low levels. Although no explicit professional guidance is provided in this regard, 5 and 10 percent are commonly-used levels of audit risk. As audit risk is established at lower levels, the probability of a material misstatement being undetected during the audit examination decreases. Therefore, holding other factors constant, for lower levels of audit risk, the auditor must devise more effective substantive tests.

Inherent Risk

> **Inherent risk** is the susceptibility of an assertion to a material misstatement, assuming that there are no related internal control policies or procedures.[11]

The concept of inherent risk recognizes that some account balances or classes of transactions are more susceptible to misstatement than others. For example, accounts like cash are highly susceptible to theft by client personnel. One means used by client personnel to conceal the theft of cash is to either record fictitious journal entries (violating the EO assertion) or fail to record actual journal entries (violating the CO assertion). As a result, the cash account would contain a material misstatement. Therefore, because of its high level of susceptibility to theft, the cash account (and the EO and CO

---

[10] American Institute of Certified Public Accountants (AICPA), *Statement on Auditing Standards No. 47*, "Audit Risk and Materiality" (New York: AICPA, 1983, AU 312.02).

[11] American Institute of Certified Public Accountants (AICPA), *Statement on Auditing Standards No. 47*, "Audit Risk and Materiality" (New York: AICPA, 1983, AU 312.20).

assertions related to the cash account) generally have higher levels of inherent risk than accounts less susceptible to theft, such as property, plant and equipment.

Note that the definition of inherent risk addresses the susceptibility of an account balance or class of transactions to misstatement on an assertion-by-assertion basis. As noted earlier in our discussion of the five management assertions, the EO assertion is ordinarily considered to be of more importance in the examination of assets and revenues. Viewed in another way, assets and revenues ordinarily have higher levels of inherent risk for the EO assertion. Similarly, the assessed level of inherent risk for the CO assertion is generally high for liabilities and expenses.

Inherent risk is normally assessed by the auditor in the planning stages of the audit. In making inherent risk assessments, the auditor considers factors that may affect the risk of misstatement on an overall financial-statement basis as well as factors that relate to specific accounts and assertions. Recall from our earlier discussion that factors related to the risk of misstatement on an overall financial-statement basis can be roughly classified into three categories (see Figure 4-4 for a complete listing):

1. Management Characteristics (*e.g.*, an aggressive attitude toward financial reporting)
2. Operating and Industry Characteristics (*e.g.*, client is experiencing inadequate profitability relative to other companies in its industry)
3. Engagement Characteristics (*e.g.*, difficult accounting issues or difficult-to-audit transactions)

Factors affecting the inherent risk for specific accounts or assertions related to accounts include:

1. The difficulty of the accounting issues related to the account or class of transactions.
2. The susceptibility of items in accounts or classes of transactions to defalcation.
3. The complexity of calculations related to the account or class of transactions.
4. The extent of management judgment related to the account or class of transactions.

For these specific factors, higher levels of inherent risk are normally associated with accounts or classes of transactions characterized by more difficult accounting issues, more susceptible to defalcation, more complex calculations, and a greater extent of management judgment.

Chapters 11, 13, 14, and 15 discuss the levels of inherent risk relating to the assertions associated with various accounts examined by the auditor.

Control risk

> **Control risk** is the risk that a material misstatement that could occur in an assertion will not be prevented or detected on a timely basis by the organization's internal control policies or procedures.[12]

---

[12] American Institute of Certified Public Accountants (AICPA), *Statement on Auditing Standards No. 47*, "Audit Risk and Materiality" (New York: AICPA, 1983, AU 312.20).

Control risk is related to the effectiveness of the client's internal control. Like inherent risk, control risk exists independently of the audit of the financial statements and is assessed using the auditor's professional judgment regarding the perceived effectiveness of the client's internal control in preventing and/or detecting misstatements. As the effectiveness of the organization's internal control increases, the assessed level of control risk should decrease (and *vice versa*).

The auditor's assessment of control risk is discussed in detail in Chapter 5. This assessment is based on the following three major steps:

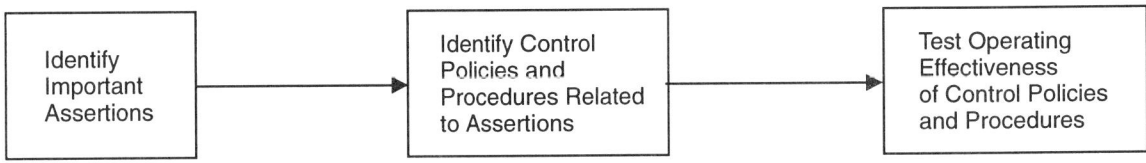

Detection Risk

Detection risk (DR) is the risk that the auditor will not detect a material misstatement that exists in an assertion.[13]

Detection risk relates to the necessary effectiveness of the auditor's substantive tests in detecting material misstatements. Unlike the previous components (inherent risk and control risk), the auditor can control the level of detection risk based on the types of substantive testing procedures performed. The necessary level of detection risk is inversely related to both inherent risk and control risk. For example, as the client's internal control is determined to be more effective in preventing or detecting misstatements (*i.e.*, the control risk is lower), the auditor is able to utilize less effective substantive tests (*i.e.*, higher detection risk). Similarly, the auditor is able to utilize less effective substantive tests (*i.e.*, higher detection risk) if the account balance is less susceptible to misstatement (*i.e.*, lower levels of inherent risk). In contrast, more effective substantive tests (*i.e.*, lower levels of detection risk) are necessary when internal control is less effective in preventing or detecting misstatements (*i.e.*, higher levels of control risk) or the account balance is more susceptible to misstatement (*i.e.*, higher levels of inherent risk).

The auditor controls the necessary level of detection risk through the nature, timing, and extent of his or her substantive tests. The effect of these factors on the level of detection risk is discussed in detail in Chapter 6.

Summary: The Audit Risk Model. A pictorial depiction of the audit risk model is shown in Figure 4-8. The four major steps in using this model (and the stage of the audit in which these steps are performed) are:

---

[13] American Institute of Certified Public Accountants (AICPA), *Statement on Auditing Standards No. 47*, "Audit Risk and Materiality" (New York: AICPA, 1983, AU 312.20).

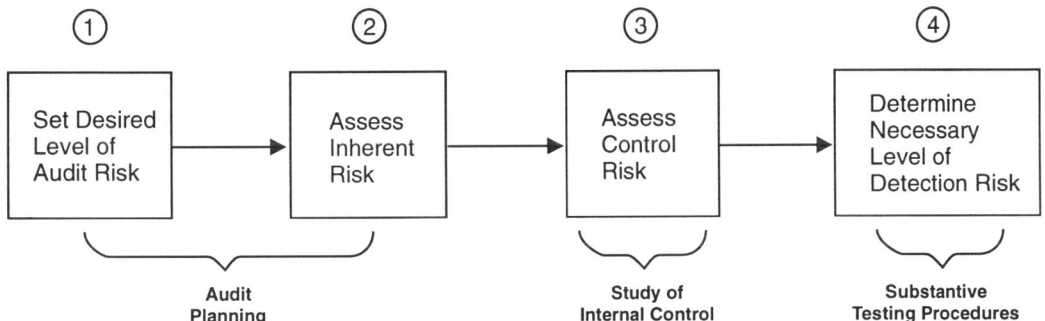

The third and fourth steps in the above process (assessing control risk and determining the necessary level of detection risk) are discussed in more detail in Chapters 5 and 6.

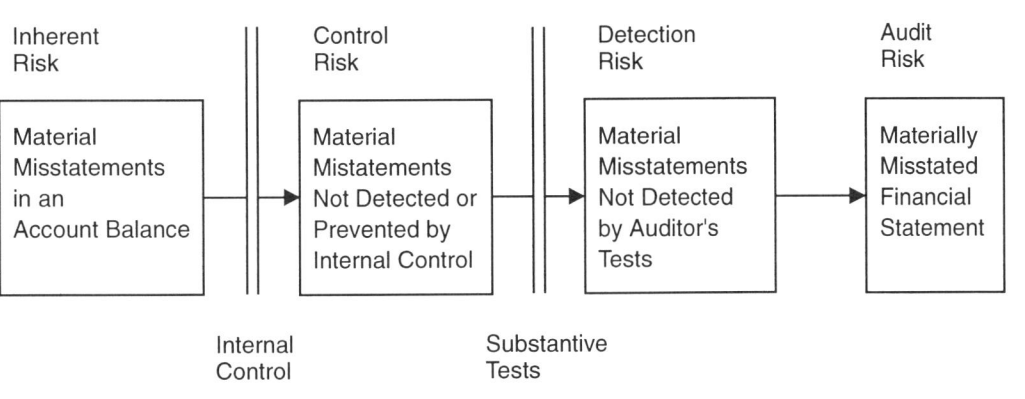

Figure 4-8: *Audit Risk Model*

CHAPTER CHECKPOINTS

4-17. What are the five assertions made by management in preparing its financial statements?

4-18. Which assertion(s) are of particular importance in the examination of assets and revenues? Liabilities and expenses?

4-19. Define audit risk. What is the audit risk model established by *SAS No. 47*?

4-20. Identify and define the components of the audit risk model.

4-21. What are the basic steps involved with the use of the audit risk model?

OTHER PLANNING ISSUES

In addition to the above areas, other factors are considered by the auditor in planning the engagement. These factors include: (1) the existence of related parties and transactions with related parties, (2) the need for a specialist, (3) the work of internal auditors, (4) the use of preliminary analytical procedures, and (5) the development of the audit program. These issues are discussed in the following subsections.

Related Parties and Related-Party Transactions

Related parties are defined by FASB *Statement No. 57* as those parties that can "significantly influence the management or operating policies of [one of] the transacting parties ... and can significantly influence the other to an extent that one or more of the transacting parties might be prevented from fully pursuing its own separate interests."[14] An example of a transaction between related parties would be the sale of inventory or provision of services between two closely-held companies owned by the same individual. Other types of related-party transactions include borrowing or lending money at abnormally high or low interest rates and selling assets for amounts significantly different from their market value.

Related parties include any companies/individuals having one of the following relationships with an enterprise:

1. Officers or shareholders of the enterprise.
2. Affiliates of the enterprise.
3. Entities for which investments are accounted for by the enterprise using the equity method.
4. Members of the immediate families of principal owners of the enterprise and its management.

The auditor's primary concern in identifying related parties is to ensure that: (1) all transactions between related parties are properly disclosed in the footnotes accompanying the financial statements, as required by *FASB Statement No. 57*; and (2) related-party transactions are recorded to reflect the economic substance of the transaction, not the legal form. For example, assume that a company provides an interest-free loan to a related party (such as an officer). Although the legal form of this transaction is a non-interest-bearing loan, the economic substance is that the company is providing a bonus or other form of compensation to the officer. Thus, the auditor should ensure that this transaction is recorded based on the economic substance, with some recognition of the compensation element of the transaction.

To identify related parties, *Statement on Auditing Standards No. 45*[15] notes that the auditor can utilize the following procedures:

---

[14] Financial Accounting Standards Board (FASB), *Statement of Financial Accounting Standards No. 57*, "Related Party Disclosures" (FASB, 1982).

[15] American Institute of Certified Public Accountants (AICPA), *Statement on Auditing Standards No. 45*, "Omnibus Statement on Auditing Standards-1983" (New York: AICPA, 1983, AU 334).

1. Inquire of appropriate management personnel and obtain written representations that all related parties have been disclosed by management to the auditor.
2. Review filings with the SEC and other regulatory agencies.
3. Review stockholder listings to identify principal stockholders
4. Review prior-years' workpapers for names of known related parties.
5. Inquire of predecessor auditors or auditors of related entities.
6. Review material investment transactions during the period to determine whether related-party transactions were created.

For each material related-party transaction identified, the auditor should determine whether the transaction is properly disclosed in the financial statements based on the economic substance of the transaction. In addition, the auditor should verify that any relationships involving other companies for which disclosure is required under *FASB No. 57* have been disclosed, regardless of whether any transactions were undertaken with those parties. These relationships are normally limited to companies for which common ownership or control exists.

An issue of particular concern to the auditor in reviewing the disclosure of related-party transactions is whether the client asserts that the transaction would have taken place regardless of the relationships among the parties. In general, it is very difficult for the auditor to substantiate such a claim. When this assertion is made by the client, the client is responsible for providing some form of evidence to substantiate the occurrence of the transaction. If management cannot do so, the auditor should suggest modification of the disclosure. A refusal on management's part to modify the disclosure should be viewed as a departure from GAAP and may require modification of the auditor's opinion.

◻ Using the Work of a Specialist

Prior to commencing the substantive testing procedures, the auditor should consider whether an outside specialist is needed. *Statement on Auditing Standards No. 73 (SAS No. 73)*[16] notes that specialists may be necessary in the following circumstances:

1. Valuation of works of art and other difficult-to-value inventories (*e.g.*, jewelry, antiques, etc.).
2. Determination of physical quantities (*e.g.*, mineral reserves).
3. Determination of amounts derived by specialized methods (*e.g.*, obligations for future pension and postretirement benefits based on actuarial calculations).
4. Interpretation of legal agreements or regulations (*e.g.*, determining whether legal title is held by the client).

Once it has been determined that the use of a specialist is appropriate, the auditor should investigate the qualifications and professional reputation of the specialist. In doing so, the auditor should inquire of individuals having previous dealings with the specialist and consider any professional certifi-

---

[16] American Institute of Certified Public Accountants (AICPA), *Statement on Auditing Standards No. 73*, "Using the Work of a Specialist" (New York: AICPA, 1994, AU 336).

cations held by the specialist. In addition, because the specialist's work will be relied upon by the auditor in supporting some of the assertions in the client's financial statements, the auditor should also understand the methods and assumptions used by the specialist.

Once the auditor has decided that the specialist's work can be relied on, the findings of the specialist are considered in determining the fairness of the client's financial statements. At this point, two possibilities exist. If the specialist's findings corroborate the information presented in the financial statements, the auditor can issue an unqualified opinion on the financial statements without any reference to either the specialist or the specialist's findings.

Alternatively, the specialist's findings may not be consistent with the information presented in the client's financial statements. In this case, the auditor considers whether these findings are reasonable. Assuming that the findings are reasonable, the auditor will modify the report and refer to the specialist and the specialist's findings. If the auditor believes that these findings are not reasonable, additional procedures should be performed or another specialist engaged. Depending on the results of these procedures, the auditor can issue either an unqualified opinion (with no reference to the specialist) or a qualified or adverse opinion (referring to the specialist and the specialist's findings).

◘ Internal Audit Function

An internal audit function is established by an organization to provide analyses, evaluations, assurances, recommendations, and other information to the client and its management regarding the operations of the organization. An organization's internal audit function is considered to be a key element in its internal control. Because of the activities performed by the internal audit function and their pervasive effect on the organization's internal control, the work of the internal audit function can affect the auditor's examination in a number of ways:

1. Internal auditors review, monitor, and assess the organization's internal control. As a result, the independent auditor may wish to review the work of the internal auditor in obtaining an overall understanding of the client's internal control.

2. In some cases, internal auditors perform procedures that provide evidence concerning the fairness of account balances or classes of transactions (*e.g.*, by confirming accounts receivable with customers). In these cases, the auditor may wish to consider the evidence gathered by the internal audit function in planning the substantive testing procedures to be used in the examination.

3. Internal auditors may also influence the risk of material misstatements at both the financial-statement level and account-balance level. For example, if the internal audit function is extremely active in monitoring the operations of certain geographic locations, the risk of misstatement (inherent risk) at those locations may be assessed at lower levels. Also, the internal auditor may test the operating effectiveness of control policies and procedures for certain accounts and classes of transactions. In these cases, the independent auditor may consider the results of these tests of controls in considering the appropriate level of control risk for that account balance or class of transactions.

Statement on Auditing Standards No. 65 (SAS No. 65) [17] discusses the matters that should be considered by the independent auditor in evaluating whether the work of the internal auditors can be relied upon to some extent in the audit examination. In conjunction with obtaining an overall understanding of the organization's internal control (see Chapter 5), the independent auditor should also determine whether considering the work of the internal audit function would be efficient. In some cases, the work of the internal auditors is either not relevant to the independent auditor's examination or it is not cost-efficient to evaluate the work of internal auditors. When either of these conditions exists, no additional steps should be taken with respect to evaluating the organization's internal audit function.

If the independent auditor believes that the work of the internal audit function is relevant and that considering this work would be efficient, the independent auditor would then assess the competence and objectivity of the internal audit function. **Competence** is assessed by considering factors such as the educational level and professional experience of internal auditors, any professional certifications and continuing education standards, and the quality of reports and recommendations of internal auditors. Although internal auditors cannot be independent of the company, their **objectivity** can be assessed by evaluating the organizational status of the internal audit function and any policies prohibiting the internal audit function from examining the operations of specified areas. In general, internal audit functions are considered to be more objective when they report to a higher-level individual within the organization and are not permitted to examine areas where: (1) relatives are employed in an audit-sensitive position, and (2) internal auditors were recently assigned or are scheduled to be assigned at a later time.

Assuming that the internal audit function is judged to be both competent and objective, the independent auditor should consider the effect of the internal auditors' work on the audit engagement and coordinate his or her work with the work of the internal auditors. It is important to note that responsibility to audit the financial statements can neither be shared nor delegated to the internal auditor. Thus, the independent auditor should evaluate and test the effectiveness of the internal auditors' work by examining the same or similar controls, transactions, or balances examined by the internal audit function. Any significant differences in the results obtained by the two groups of auditors would indicate that less reliance should be placed on the internal auditors' work.

Figure 4-9 summarizes the major issues considered by the independent auditor when determining whether the work of internal auditors can be used during the audit examination.

---

[17] American Institute of Certified Public Accountants (AICPA), *Statement on Auditing Standards No. 65*, "The Auditor's Consideration of the Internal Audit Function in an Audit of Financial Statements" (New York: AICPA, 1990, AU 322).

Step 1:	Obtain an understanding of the internal audit function.	
Step 2:	Consider the relevance and efficiency of considering the work of the internal audit function.	If the work is not relevant or considering the work is not efficient, no further procedures should be performed to evaluate the internal audit function.
Step 3:	Evaluate the competence and objectivity of the internal audit function.	If the internal audit function lacks competence or objectivity, no further procedures should be performed to evaluate the internal audit function.
Step 4:	Consider the effect of the internal auditors' work on the independent auditor's examination.	Consider the materiality of the financial statement amounts, the risk of material misstatement, and the degree of subjectivity involved in evaluating evidence.
Step 5:	Evaluate and test the effectiveness of the internal auditors' work.	If the internal auditors' work does not appear to be properly performed, the reliance on this work should be reduced or eliminated.
Step 6:	Consider reducing the extent of work if internal auditors are competent and objective and their work is effective.	Internal auditors' work may affect (reduce) the extent of the independent auditors' work in the study and evaluation of the internal control or substantive testing stages of the audit.

Figure 4-9: *Issues Considered in Evaluating the Work of Internal Auditors*

◘ Performing Preliminary Analytical Procedures

Statement on Auditing Standards No. 56 (SAS No. 56)[18] requires the auditor to perform analytical procedures in the preliminary stages of the audit examination. *Analytical procedures* consist of evaluations of recorded (unaudited) financial information based on the underlying relationships among financial and nonfinancial data. In performing analytical procedures, the auditor develops some expectation of the proper amount of an account balance and compares this expectation to the recorded (unaudited) balance.

---

[18] American Institute of Certified Public Accountants (AICPA), *Statement on Auditing Standards No. 56*, "Analytical Procedures" (New York: AICPA, 1988, AU 329).

To develop an expectation of a particular account balance, the auditor should consider: (1) financial information for comparable prior periods, (2) anticipated results, (3) relationships between the account balance or class of transactions and other financial information in the same period, (4) information regarding the industry in which the client operates, and (5) relationships between the account balance or class of transactions and nonfinancial information.

For example, in developing an expectation of the balance in accounts receivable, the auditor may use last year's accounts receivable balance as a possible expectation (financial information for prior periods) by adjusting this balance for any known changes occurring during the year. A second possibility is to use the sales account to generate the expectation of accounts receivable. Accounts receivable and sales are closely related because credit sales result in accounts receivable; as a result, auditors expect accounts receivable to approximate some percentage of credit sales made during the period. This is an example of using the relationships between an account balance and other financial information in the same period. In any case, the method used to generate the expectation is a matter of auditor judgment.

When used in the planning stages of the audit examination, analytical procedures: (1) provide the auditor with an understanding of the client's business and events that have occurred since the date of the previous audit, and (2) identify areas that represent specific risks during the audit.

Analytical procedures performed in the planning stages of the audit are often referred to as **attention-directing procedures** because they identify account balances that have significantly changed from one year to another or balances that are significantly different than expected. For example, assume that the auditor expected sales in 19X1 to approximate $2 million; however, based on the client's records, sales were recorded at $5 million. One of two possibilities may account for the difference. First, the client may have significantly expanded its product lines and customer markets, resulting in a greater level of sales during the current year. In this case, the large difference between the expected balance and recorded balance may reveal a significant change in the client's business environment.

Alternatively, the difference could reveal that the client's sales account may contain misstatements (in particular, overstatements of sales). When a large difference is noted, the auditor should investigate the account further to determine whether the difference was the result of: (1) changes in business or economic conditions, or (2) material errors or irregularities in recording transactions. Any accounts where large differences between the recorded balance and the expected balance exist are generally subjected to more extensive subsequent analysis through substantive tests of details and balances.

In some cases, the use of analytical procedures reveals that the difference between the recorded balance and expected balance is small. In these cases, the auditor would not consider it necessary to perform a great amount of additional substantive testing. The general approach used in performing preliminary analytical procedures is depicted below:

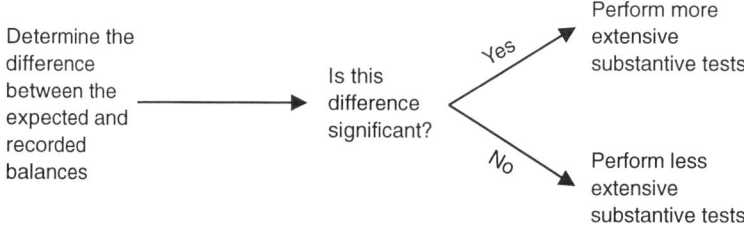

In addition to the planning stage, analytical procedures are also utilized in the substantive testing and final review stages of the audit examination. The use of analytical procedures is discussed in greater detail in Chapter 6.

◘ Preparing the Audit Program

SAS No. 22 notes that the end result of the procedures performed by the auditor in the planning stages of the audit is the preparation of an audit program. An **audit program** is a written set of audit procedures that are to be performed in the engagement. This program is designed or tailored to meet the specific needs of each audit client and is affected by the auditor's planning procedures. For example, if the auditor's use of the audit risk model indicates that the substantive testing procedures should be more effective in detecting material misstatements, the audit program would consist of a greater number of audit procedures or a more effective type of audit procedure. *Statement on Auditing Standards No. 77 (SAS No 77)*[19] requires the use of an audit program in all GAAS audits.

It is important to note that standardized audit programs exist for most types of account balances. These programs are then modified by the auditor for use in a particular engagement by adding or deleting audit procedures as appropriate for that particular client. At this point, the auditor uses the program to guide the study of the client's internal control as well as the tests of account balances (substantive tests).

Figure 4-10 illustrates an excerpted audit program for accounts receivable. As shown therein, the program provides a list of audit procedures that are to be performed in the examination. Other information of interest in the sample audit program shown in Figure 4-10 are the columns that provide a workpaper reference, the date the audit procedures were performed, and the initials of the individual performing the audit procedures. This information is useful when workpapers are reviewed or if any subsequent questions arise concerning the audit procedures performed for a particular account balance. The actual procedures illustrated in this sample audit program are discussed in subsequent chapters of this text.

---

[19] American Institute of Certified Public Accountants (AICPA), *Statement on Auditing Standards No. 77*, "Amendments to *SAS No. 22*, 'Planning and Supervision'...." (New York: AICPA, 1995, AU 311.05).

Procedure	Workpaper Reference	Performed by	Date
1. Obtain an Aged Listing of Accounts Receivable from the client.	A-1	JRS	2-01-X1
2. Confirm a sample of accounts receivable balances with customers.	A-1-A/ A-1-Z	JRS	2-15-X1

3. For any exceptions noted in (2) above:
 	
  a. Examine Sales Invoices and cash receipts to reconcile recorded amounts to confirmed amounts.
  b. Examine subsidiary accounts to ensure that sales and cash receipts are posted in a timely fashion.
	A-1-A/ A-1-Z	JRS	2-17-X1

Figure 4-10: *Sample Audit Program: Accounts Receivable*

CHAPTER CHECKPOINTS

4-22. Define and give examples of related parties.

4-23. When should the auditor consider the use of a specialist in the engagement?

4-24. How can internal auditors influence the independent auditor's examination?

4-25. What are analytical procedures? Name three stages of the audit in which analytical procedures can be used.

4-26. What is an audit program?

◉ SUPERVISION AND STAFFING

Audits are performed by groups of auditors, often referred to as an **audit team**. As noted in Chapter 1, both senior accountants and staff accountants are involved in the day-to-day conduct of the audit. Senior accountants (or in-charge accountants) are responsible for planning the audit, conducting limited tests of internal control and substantive tests, and supervising the day-to-day audit operations. Staff accountants (or assistants) are generally charged with performing most of the evidence-gathering procedures. The fact that a single audit conclusion is expected to be made from the work performed by a number of individuals underlines the need for effective supervision of the assistants' work. Also, the need to coordinate the efforts of a number of individuals to complete the audit on a timely basis emphasizes the need for adequate supervision.

In addition to planning, the first standard of field work also notes that assistants should be properly supervised. **Supervision** involves actions on the part of the senior accountant to ensure that assistants perform in such a manner as to accomplish the objectives of the audit. As noted above, an audit program is an element of supervision, because this program provides assistants with a written set of audit procedures to be performed during the examination. Other elements of supervision include:

1. Instructing assistants about audit procedures to be performed.
2. Keeping assistants informed about any significant accounting or auditing problems encountered during the audit.
3. Reviewing the work performed by assistants to ensure that the audit objectives have been met and that the results are consistent with the overall conclusion presented in the audit report.
4. Considering differences of opinion that arise among firm personnel.

In cases where disagreements exist between personnel regarding accounting and auditing issues that affect the client's financial statements or auditor's report, the senior accountant should attempt to resolve these differences. If this cannot be done, any personnel should have the opportunity to document their disagreement if that person believes it is necessary to be disassociated with the resolution of the matter.

CHAPTER CHECKPOINT

4-27. Define supervision. What are some important elements of supervision?

ROLE OF PLANNING IN THE AUDIT

At this point, the auditor has performed a wide variety of procedures in planning the audit engagement and obtaining an understanding of the type of procedures to be performed. In practice, the results of peer reviews of CPAs and CPA firms have concluded that auditors are often deficient in the planning stages of the audit. Some of these deficiencies are summarized below.

▶ Engagement planning was inadequate or inadequately documented

▶ Audit program was inadequate or missing

▶ Analytical review procedures were inadequately documented

▶ Audit risk and materiality assessments were inadequately considered or inadequately documented[20]

As shown earlier in Figure 4-1, the next steps performed by the auditor in the engagement relate to studying and evaluating the internal control and performing substantive tests. These steps are discussed in the following two chapters.

---

[20] American Institute of Certified Public Accountants (AICPA), *Quality Control Manual for CPA Firms* (New York: AICPA, 1995).

Appendix

Proposed *Statement on Auditing Standards*, Consideration of Fraud in a Financial Statement Audit[21]

The AICPA has issued a proposed *Statement on Auditing Standards* related to the auditor's consideration of fraud in a financial statement audit.[22] This pronouncement would supersede *Statement on Auditing Standards No. 53* by replacing the concept of "irregularities" with that of "fraud." The major provisions of this proposal are discussed in this appendix.

◉ OVERVIEW OF FRAUD

Fraud represents intentional actions of the part of the client or its personnel related to the client's financial statements, assets, or both. Two common types of fraud include fraudulent financial reporting and misappropriation of assets.

Fraudulent financial reporting refers to intentional misstatements or omissions in the financial statements perpetrated by client personnel. Fraudulent financial reporting is usually committed by management in an effort to deceive financial statement users. Actions that are examples of fraudulent financial reporting include:

1. Manipulation, falsification, or alteration of accounting records or supporting documents
2. Misrepresentation or intentional omission of transactions in the financial statements
3. Intentional misapplications of GAAP

---

[21] All Chapter Checkpoints and End of Chapter Items related to the Appendix are marked with an asterisk (*).

[22] American Institute of Certified Public Accountants (AICPA), *Proposed Statement on Auditing Standards*, "Consideration of Fraud in a Financial Statement Audit" (New York: AICPA, May 1, 1996).

Misappropriation of assets refers to instances where the client's employees or third parties engage in a scheme to perpetrate the theft of assets. These actions differ from fraudulent financial reporting in that they are committed by client personnel against the client. Misappropriation of assets can be accomplished through:

1. Embezzling cash receipts
2. Stealing or misusing assets
3. Causing an entity to pay for goods or services not received

It is important to note that both types of fraud have the potential to affect the client's financial statements. While the effect of fraudulent financial reporting appears to be relatively straightforward, the question arises as to how misappropriating client assets affects the financial statements. This effect is through efforts taken on the part of client personnel to conceal their misappropriation. For example, assume that a customer purchases $100 of goods on account and remits $100 in cash for payment on this account. If the employee receiving cash in the mail commits a misappropriation, this could be concealed as follows:

▶ Misappropriate the $100, record the sale to the customer, and prepare a journal entry writing off the receivable as uncollectible.

▶ Misappropriate some amount less than $100 ($50), record the sale to the customer at $50, and prepare a journal entry recording the receipt of cash at $50.

▶ Misappropriate the $100 and do not record the sale of $100.

THE AUDITOR'S RESPONSIBILITY FOR FRAUD IN THE FINANCIAL STATEMENT AUDIT

The auditor's responsibility with respect to fraud parallels that for irregularities identified by *Statement on Auditing Standards No. 53*: to plan the audit to provide reasonable assurance of detecting fraudulent acts that have a **material** effect on the client's financial statements. Thus, as with irregularities, the auditor's concern with fraud is limited to the extent that it influences the fairness of the client's financial statements.

Factors Affecting the Risk of Fraud

In planning the audit to provide reasonable assurance of detecting fraudulent activities having a material effect on the financial statements, the auditor should consider factors that influence the risk of fraudulent activities. The risks of fraud are separately considered for fraudulent financial reporting and misappropriation of assets.

Fraudulent Financial Reporting. For fraudulent financial reporting, risk factors can be classified as relating to management characteristics, industry conditions, and client operating characteristics/financial stability. Some examples of risk factors in each of these three categories are as follows:

Management Characteristics:

1. Management's attitude regarding internal control and financial reporting.
2. The extent to which management's compensation is based on bonuses, stock options, or other incentives related to targeted levels of operating performance.
3. Excessive interest on the part of the company or its management in maintaining or increasing the entity's stock price.
4. Commitments made by the company or its management to analysts, creditors, and other third parties to achieve aggressive or unrealistic forecasts.

Industry Conditions:

1. New accounting or other regulatory requirements that could impair the financial stability or profitability of the company.
2. High degrees of competition in the client's industry resulting in declining profit margins.
3. The extent to which the client's industry is characterized by a general decline or rapid changes.

Operating Characteristics/Financial Stability:

1. Significant pressure to obtain additional capital to remain competitive.
2. Unusually rapid growth or profitability in comparison to the remainder of the industry (this may be the result of fraudulent financial reporting).
3. Inability to generate cash flows from operations while reporting earnings and earnings growth.
4. Unusually high dependence on debt.

The above examples suggest that fraudulent financial reporting is more likely to occur when management has an incentive to report favorable performance, the industry is experiencing difficulty or change, and the client's overall financial performance is declining. In these cases, fraudulent financial reporting may serve as a means of concealing unfavorable current or future financial performance.

Misappropriation of Assets. In planning the audit to detect material instances of misappropriation of assets, the auditor considers three primary factors: (1) the susceptibility of assets to misappropriation, (2) the propensity of employees to commit defalcation, and (3) the extent to which controls have been designed to prevent or detect the misappropriation of assets. Some assets (such as cash) are highly susceptible to theft; therefore, the amount of cash processed by the client will influence the risk of misappropriation of assets. In addition, the auditor should consider the nature of the client's inventories and fixed assets. Companies whose inventory is small in size and high in value or demand are highly susceptible to misappropriation. Similarly, fixed assets that are small in size, highly marketable, and not readily identifiable as being owned by the client may also be highly susceptible to misappropriation.

With respect to the employees' propensity to commit defalcation, the auditor should focus on employees who have access to assets susceptible to misappropriation. These would include employees who process cash and have access to the organization's inventory. In addition, the auditor should consider personal factors that influence the propensity of various individual(s) within the organization to misappropriate assets. Factors that may influence the propensity to commit defalcation include employees who are subject to anticipated future layoffs, dissatisfied with their jobs, and subject to personal financial pressure.

Finally, the extent to which controls have been implemented to prevent or detect misappropriation of assets will influence the risk of this type of fraud. As will be discussed in Chapter 5, one important benefit of internal control is that it may prevent the unauthorized use of the entity's assets. In fact, two of the four control activities are concerned with protecting the company's assets from misappropriation:

1. Physical controls, such as keeping inventory in a secured location and depositing cash receipts in the bank intact and daily.
2. Segregation of duties controls, which require different individual(s) or department(s) to handle various aspects of a transaction (authorization, recording, and custody of the asset).

Segregation of duties controls and physical controls, as well as their effect on the ability of client personnel to misappropriate assets, will be discussed further in Chapter 5.

Other Factors. In addition to the above, matters may come to the auditor's attention during the engagement that affect the risk of fraudulent financial reporting and misappropriation of assets. These matters include discrepancies in the accounting records (such as last-minute adjustments made by the client and unauthorized balances or transactions), conflicting or missing evidential matter (the unavailability of original copies of documents and presence of significant unexplained items on reconciliations), and problematic or unusual relationships between the auditor and client (the client's denial of auditor access to records or facilities and undue time pressure placed on the auditor by the client to resolve complex or contentious issues). As the auditor discovers these matters during the examination, his or her prior assessments of the risk of fraud in the planning stages may need to be revised.

◘ Effect of Fraud on Substantive Testing Procedures

The results of the auditor's consideration of the risk of fraud will affect the planned level of substantive tests to be performed. From an overall standpoint, as the risk of misstatement from fraud is judged to be greater, the auditor will need to vary the nature, timing, and extent of his or her substantive testing procedures to perform more effective substantive tests. The relationship between the effectiveness of the auditor's substantive testing procedures and the nature, timing, and extent of these procedures is discussed further in Chapter 6.

In addition to the general nature, timing, and extent of the auditor's substantive testing procedures, the risk of misstatement from fraud may result in the auditor performing the following procedures specifically related to the possible existence of fraud:

- Visiting locations or performing tests (such as inventory observation) on a surprise basis
- Contacting major customers or suppliers orally in addition to obtaining written confirmation
- Investigating significant and unusual transactions occurring near year-end
- Interviewing personnel involved in areas where a concern about fraud is present

Communicating Fraud Discovered during the Engagement

The auditor's responsibility for communicating fraud discovered during the engagement parallels his or her responsibility with respect to irregularities. That is, these matters should be communicated to the client's Audit Committee unless the matters are clearly inconsequential. In addition, the auditor may be required to communicate instances of discovered fraud to the following parties external to the client:

1. The SEC, when reporting an auditor change on Form 8-K.
2. A predecessor auditor, under the provisions of *SAS No. 7*.
3. A court, in response to a valid summons or subpoena.
4. A funding entity or other agency, if the client receives financial assistance from a federal government agency.

ANATOMY OF A FRAUD[23]

A recent fraud perpetrated by the former President and Co-Chief Executive of Kurzweil Applied Intelligence, Inc. consisted of the following actions:

- Booking revenues from sales made after year-end in the current period.
- Forging customers' signatures on sales papers to create fictitious sales near year-end.
- Forging customers' signatures on confirmations mailed by the auditor to those customers.

These actions were perpetrated to enhance the price received during the initial public offering of Kurzweil stock. The President and Co-Chief Executive of Kurzweil is currently awaiting sentencing on this matter.

---

[23] "Anatomy of a Fraud," *Business Week* (September 16, 1996), 90-94.

SUMMARY OF KEY POINTS

1. The four major steps of the auditor's examination are: (1) performing preengagement procedures and audit planning, (2) studying and evaluating the client's internal control, (3) performing substantive tests, and (4) reporting the findings of the audit.

2. The auditor's preengagement procedures focus on matters considered by the auditor in deciding whether to accept a prospective audit client or continue to provide services to an existing client. In making this decision, the auditor should meet with the Audit Committee, obtain and read financial information relating to the client and its operations, inquire of third parties who have previous business associations with the client, and evaluate the firm's independence and ability to effectively perform the engagement.

3. In deciding whether to accept a prospective audit client, *SAS No. 7* indicates that the successor auditor should make certain inquiries of any predecessor auditor(s). These inquiries relate to such matters as the integrity of the client's management and the reason for the change in auditors. Under *SAS No. 7*, these inquiries cannot be made without the client's permission.

4. Once the auditor has accepted the engagement, an engagement letter should be prepared. An engagement letter is a written communication sent from the auditor to the client that confirms the understanding of both parties about the nature and types of services to be provided during the audit engagement. This letter acts as a type of "contract" between the auditor and client.

5. The primary procedures performed by the auditor in the audit planning stages are: (1) obtaining knowledge about the client; (2) considering the effect of errors, irregularities, and illegal acts on the financial statements; and (3) developing an audit strategy through the use of the audit risk model. The auditor obtains knowledge about the client through inquiries made of client personnel, reviews of correspondence files and other information related to the client, and consideration of economic conditions and other factors affecting the client.

6. *SAS No. 53* distinguishes between two types of financial statement misstatements. Errors are unintentional mistakes made by client personnel in recording or summarizing transactions; in contrast, irregularities are misstatements resulting from intentional actions or omissions involving the client's financial statements. The auditor is responsible for planning the audit to detect errors and irregularities material to the financial statements. *SAS No. 54* provides a similar responsibility for the auditor in detecting illegal acts. An illegal act is any activity that involves violations of laws or governmental regulations by employees acting on behalf of the client.

7. In planning the audit to detect material misstatements, the auditor should consider the possible causes of material misstatements. These causes are represented by the following five assertions made by management in the client's financial statements: (1) all recorded components exist and all recorded transactions actually occurred (the EO assertion); (2) all recorded assets and liabilities are owned and owed by the client (the RO assertion); (3) all transactions that occurred during the period have been recorded (the CO assertion); (4) all components and transactions are included at the appropriate dollar amounts (the VA assertion); and (5) all components are properly classified, described, and disclosed (the PD assertion).

8. In devising an overall audit strategy, the auditor attempts to reduce the likelihood that a material misstatement occurs in an assertion, is not prevented or detected by the client's internal control, and is not detected by the auditor's substantive testing procedures. This likelihood is referred

to as audit risk and represents the probability that the auditor will unknowingly fail to modify his or her opinion on financial statements that are materially misstated.

9. In using the audit risk model, the auditor follows four steps: (1) set the desired level of audit risk (normally, at low levels); (2) based on the susceptibility of the account balance, class of transactions, or assertion affecting the account balance or class of transactions, assess inherent risk; (3) based on the effectiveness of the client's internal control, assess control risk; and (4) based on the audit risk, inherent risk, and control risk, determine the necessary level of detection risk.

10. Other procedures performed by the auditor in the planning stages of the audit include identifying related parties, considering the need for specialists, considering the work of internal auditors, and performing preliminary analytical procedures.

*11. Fraud represents intentional actions on the part of the client or its personnel. The auditor's responsibility for fraud is to plan the audit to provide reasonable assurance of detecting fraudulent actions that have a material effect on the client's financial statements. Two types of fraudulent activities are fraudulent financial reporting and misappropriation of assets.

◉ GLOSSARY

Analytical Procedures. Evaluations of financial information made by a study of relationships among both financial and nonfinancial data. In the planning stages of the audit, analytical procedures are used to gain an understanding of the client's business and transactions occurring since the last audit and identify accounts that may represent specific risks during the audit.

Audit Committee. A group of directors not employed by the client who act as liaison between the auditor and client management.

Audit Risk. The risk that the auditor unknowingly fails to modify his or her opinion on financial statements that are materially misstated. Audit risk can be operationalized as the risk that a material misstatement exists in an assertion, is not prevented or detected by the client's internal control, and is not detected by the auditor's substantive tests.

Control Risk. The risk that a material misstatement that could occur in an assertion will not be prevented or detected by the client's internal control policies or procedures. Control risk is assessed by the auditor based on the effectiveness of the client's internal control.

Detection Risk. The risk that the auditor will not detect a material misstatement that exists in an assertion. Detection risk is influenced by the auditor through the nature, timing, and extent of his or her substantive tests.

Engagement Letter. A letter sent by the auditor to the client that summarizes the nature and type of services that are to be provided by the auditor.

Error. A type of misstatement that represents an unintentional mistake on the part of the client.

*****Fraud.** Intentional actions on the part of the client or its personnel. Fraud includes both fraudulent financial reporting and misappropriation of assets.

*****Fraudulent Financial Reporting.** Intentional misstatements or omissions in the financial statements perpetrated by client personnel. Types of fraudulent financial reporting include: (1) manipulation, falsification, or alteration of accounting records or supporting documents; (2) misrepresentation or intentional omission of transactions in the financial statements; and (3) intentional misapplication of GAAP.

Illegal Act. Misstatements arising from client activities that involve violations of laws or governmental regulations by employees acting on behalf of the client.

Inherent Risk. The susceptibility of an assertion to a material misstatement, assuming that there are no related internal control policies or procedures. This risk is assessed by the auditor based on the susceptibility of an account balance, class of transactions, or assertion related to an account balance or class of transactions to misstatement.

Irregularity. A misstatement arising from an intentional action or omission on the part of the client's personnel.

Materiality. A dollar amount of misstatement that would result in changes in users' decisions or perceptions with respect to the client. Materiality is an important concept because the auditor plans the audit to detect misstatements that are material to the financial statements.

*Misappropriation of Assets. Instances where the client's employees or third parties engage in a scheme to perpetrate the theft of assets. This can be accomplished by embezzling cash receipts, stealing or misusing assets, and causing an entity to pay for goods or services not rendered.

Predecessor Auditor. The auditor who previously provided services to the client and has resigned or been notified that her or his services have been terminated. Under SAS No. 7, the predecessor auditor must respond to inquiries made by a successor auditor if these inquiries are permitted by the client's management.

Preengagement Procedures. These procedures are performed prior to accepting the engagement and allow the auditor to determine whether engagements for prospective clients should be accepted or services to existing clients should be continued.

Related Parties. Parties that can significantly influence the management or operating policies of another party so that the two transacting parties may be prevented from pursuing their own interests. The auditor's primary concerns with respect to related parties are that: (1) all related parties are disclosed by the client; and (2) all related-party transactions are recorded based on the economic substance of the transaction, not the legal form.

Specialist. An individual providing assistance during the audit examination in areas that require specialized knowledge or other types of expertise. Examples of situations where the use of a specialist may be considered necessary include valuation of difficult-to-value inventory items and determination of amounts derived by specialized methods.

Successor Auditor. The auditor who has been approached by the client or invited to make a proposal on the engagement. If permitted by the client, the successor auditor makes inquiries of the predecessor auditor regarding the integrity of management and the reason for change in auditors.

Supervision. In an audit engagement, the senior (or in-charge) accountant is responsible for supervising the work of assistants (or staff accountants). Supervision includes instructing assistants, keeping them informed about significant problems encountered during the audit, reviewing work performed by assistants, and dealing with differences of opinion among firm personnel.

◉ SUMMARY OF PROFESSIONAL PRONOUNCEMENTS

Statement on Auditing Standards No. 1, "Codification of Auditing Standards and Procedures" (New York: AICPA 1973, various sections).

Statement on Auditing Standards No. 7, "Communications Between Predecessor and Successor Auditors" (New York: AICPA, 1975, AU 315).

Statement on Auditing Standards No. 22, "Planning and Supervision" (New York: AICPA, 1978, AU 311).

Statement on Auditing Standards No. 43, "Omnibus Statement on Auditing Standards—1983" (New York: AICPA, 1983, AU 334).

Statement on Auditing Standards No. 47, "Audit Risk and Materiality" (New York: AICPA, 1983, AU 312).

Statement on Auditing Standards No. 50, "Reports on the Application of Accounting Principles" (New York: AICPA, 1986, AU 625).

Statement on Auditing Standards No. 53, "The Auditor's Responsibility to Detect Errors and Irregularities" (New York: AICPA, 1988, AU 316).

Statement on Auditing Standards No. 54, "Illegal Acts by Clients" (New York: AICPA, 1988, AU 317).
Statement on Auditing Standards No. 56, "Analytical Procedures" (New York: AICPA, 1988, AU 329).
Statement on Auditing Standards No. 61, "Communication with Audit Committees" (New York: AICPA, 1988, AU 380).
Statement on Auditing Standards No. 65, "The Auditor's Consideration of the Internal Audit Function in an Audit of Financial Statements" (New York: AICPA, 1991, AU 322).
Statement on Auditing Standards No. 73, "Using the Work of a Specialist" (New York: AICPA, 1994, AU 336).
Statement on Auditing Standards No. 77, "Amendments to SAS No. 22, ..., No. 59, ..., and No. 62 ..." (New York: AICPA, 1995, AU 311.05).
Statement of Quality Control Standards No. 2, "System of Quality Control for a CPA Firm's Accounting and Auditing Practices" (New York: AICPA, 1996, QC 20).
Proposed Statement on Auditing Standards, "Consideration of Fraud in a Financial Statement Audit" (New York: AICPA, May 1, 1996).

QUESTIONS AND PROBLEMS

4-28. Select the **best** answer for each of the following items.

1. Which of the following statements is not true with respect to the communications between predecessor and successor auditors under *SAS No. 7*?

    a. Prior to initiating communication, the successor auditor should request permission of the client to speak with the predecessor.
    b. The predecessor auditor should respond to inquiries of the successor auditor unless it is not practical to do so.
    c. The areas of inquiry by successor auditors should focus on observed weaknesses in the client's internal control.
    d. The successor auditor should generally not accept the engagement if the client does not authorize communication with the predecessor.
    e. All of the above are true.

2. Which of the following represents the order in which these events normally occur during an audit?

    1 = Studying and evaluating internal control.
    2 = Preengagement procedures.
    3 = Substantive testing procedures.
    4 = Planning procedures.
    5 = Reporting.

    a. 2, 4, 3, 1, 5.
    b. 2, 4, 1, 3, 5.
    c. 4, 2, 3, 1, 5.
    d. 4, 2, 1, 3, 5.
    e. None of the above.

3. Which of the following procedures is performed by the auditor in the preengagement stages of the audit?

    a. Establishing preliminary materiality levels.
    b. Identifying internal control policies and procedures that will be relied upon.
    c. Discussing matters of importance with the client's Audit Committee.
    d. Obtaining a list of customer accounts receivable balances for confirmation.
    e. Forming preliminary assessments of inherent risk.

4. The first standard of field work relates to:

    a. The exercise of due professional care during the engagement.
    b. The independence of the auditor.
    c. The auditor's responsibility for studying and evaluating internal control.
    d. The auditor's responsibility for planning the audit and supervising assistants.
    e. The need for the auditor to have technical training and proficiency.

5. An agreement (or contract) between the auditor and client that establishes the scope of the audit is known as a(n):

   a. Engagement letter.
   b. Letter of inquiry.
   c. Management letter.
   d. Management representation letter.
   e. None of the above.

6. Amount(s) that may affect the perceptions of users with respect to the client's financial statements are referred to as:

   a. Audit risk.
   b. Control risk.
   c. Detection risk.
   d. Inherent risk.
   e. Materiality.

7. Holding all other factors constant, which of the following conditions would result in lower levels of detection risk being utilized during a particular audit engagement?

   a. Higher materiality levels established by the auditor.
   b. A higher desired exposure to audit risk.
   c. Account balances that are less susceptible to misstatement.
   d. An internal control that is more effective in preventing and detecting misstatements.
   e. A lower desired exposure to audit risk.

8. Which of the following misstatements would most likely represent an error?

   a. An action committed by a client in violation of federal laws or statutes.
   b. A sale recorded by client personnel based on forged sales documents.
   c. A mathematical mistake in calculating interest revenue earned at year-end.
   d. Accounts receivable written off as uncollectible in order to conceal a defalcation scheme.

9. Which of the following represents the auditor's responsibility for detecting errors during the audit and communicating errors discovered during the audit to client personnel?

   a. The auditor is required to plan the audit to detect both immaterial and material errors, but need only communicate material errors to the client.
   b. The auditor is required to plan the audit to detect material errors, but should communicate both material and immaterial errors to the client.
   c. The auditor is required to plan the audit to detect material errors and is only required to communicate material errors to the client.
   d. The auditor is required to plan the audit to detect both material and immaterial errors and should communicate both material and immaterial errors to the client.

10. Which of the following procedures is least likely to be performed in the planning stages of the audit?

   a. Obtaining knowledge about the client, its industry, and its operations.
   b. Performing preliminary analytical procedures to identify accounts that may require special audit attention.
   c. Obtaining an overall understanding of the client's internal control.
   d. Considering whether the use of a specialist is necessary during the audit.
   e. Determining the extent to which the client utilizes the computer in processing its transactions.

11. Which of the following best indicates the auditor's responsibility for planning the audit to detect irregularities during the audit examination?

	Material	Immaterial
a.	Yes	Yes
b.	No	Yes
c.	Yes	No
d.	No	No

12. Which of the following statements with regard to the auditor's responsibility for illegal acts is not true?

   a. The auditor is required to plan the audit to detect illegal acts having material direct or indirect financial statement effects.
   b. The auditor should communicate all illegal acts discovered during the audit to the client's Audit Committee, unless clearly immaterial.
   c. In evaluating the effect of an illegal act on the client's financial statements, the auditor should consider both the direct and indirect effect(s) of the illegal act.
   d. The auditor is not responsible for illegal acts committed by client employees outside of the scope of client operations.
   e. All of the above are true.

13. Which of the following components of the audit risk model cannot be controlled by the auditor?

   a. Audit risk.
   b. Inherent risk.
   c. Control risk.
   d. (a) and (b) above.
   e. (b) and (c) above.

14. Which of the following characteristics would indicate that the client's financial statements are less likely to contain misstatements?

   a. Client operating and financing decisions are dominated by a single individual.
   b. The rate of change in the client's industry is rapid.
   c. Few difficult accounting issues or difficult-to-audit transactions exist.
   d. The client has never been audited prior to the current engagement.
   e. Management has an unduly aggressive attitude toward financial reporting.

15. Which of the following conditions would yield the most effective level of substantive testing?

	Audit Risk	Inherent Risk	Control Risk
a.	High	High	High
b.	High	Low	Low
c.	Low	High	High
d.	Low	High	Low
e.	Low	Low	Low

16. The risk that the auditor's substantive testing procedures fail to detect a material misstatement is referred to as:

    a. Audit risk.
    b. Control risk.
    c. Detection risk.
    d. Inherent risk.
    e. Sampling risk.

17. Which of the following statements is not true regarding the audit risk model, holding all other factors constant?

    a. The auditor must plan the audit to perform more effective substantive testing procedures to achieve higher levels of audit risk.
    b. The auditor should assess inherent risk at lower levels when the account balance is less susceptible to theft and misappropriation.
    c. A more effective internal control is generally associated with lower levels of control risk.
    d. Higher levels of control risk result in lower levels of audit risk.
    e. All of the above statements are true.

18. When investigating the possibility of related-party transactions, the auditor's primary concern is that:

    a. The client has not entered into any transactions with related parties during the year under audit.
    b. All transactions with related parties were consummated on an "arm's-length" basis.
    c. All transactions with related parties are properly disclosed in the financial statements.
    d. Related-party transactions are recorded based on their legal form.
    e. All sales to related parties are correctly eliminated from total sales reported on the income statement.

19. In which of the following types of audit opinions might the work of a specialist be appropriately referenced:

	Standard	Qualified
a.	Yes	Yes
b.	Yes	No
c.	No	No
d.	No	Yes

20. Preliminary analytical procedures are performed for the primary purpose of:

   a. Ascertaining the effectiveness of the client's internal control.
   b. Identifying areas that may represent specific risks during the audit examination.
   c. Examining whether transactions and components of the account balance have been properly recorded.
   d. Assessing the reasonableness of the overall conclusions reached during the audit.
   e. Determining the desired level of audit risk and associated level of materiality.

4-29. Financial statement misstatements may arise from one of three possible sources: errors, irregularities, and illegal acts.

Required:

a. Define and give examples of errors, irregularities, and illegal acts.
b. Identify the auditor's responsibility during the audit for detecting errors, irregularities, and illegal acts.
c. What is the auditor's responsibility for communicating any errors, irregularities, and illegal acts discovered during the audit to the client? At what level of the client should these items be communicated?
d. Does the auditor have any responsibility for communicating errors, irregularities, and illegal acts to individuals external to the client? If so, to whom?

4-30. Almost, Inc., is currently having its financial statements audited by AM, CPAs, a large regional accounting firm. AM has provided services to Almost for over 10 years. During the current year's audit engagement, the management of Almost, Inc., and the senior accountant for AM (Jane Morning) had a disagreement about the treatment of certain of Almost's lease obligations. While Jane felt that these obligations should be capitalized under the provisions of *FASB Statement No. 13*, Almost refused to capitalize these lease agreements. As Almost has not yet established an Audit Committee, AM decided to withdraw from the audit engagement.

Because of its need to provide audited financial statements to Prism Bank, a potential financier, Almost has contacted the CPA firm of PM, CPAs. PM is currently deciding whether to accept the audit engagement.

Required:

a. What are some procedures that should be performed by PM, CPAs, in deciding to accept this engagement?
b. What is the general procedure that should be followed by PM in discussing matters with AM? What matters should be discussed between these two auditors?
c. Assume that PM requests permission of Almost to contact AM and receives the following response: "I don't think you should speak with them. They were quite upset about being replaced on this audit. There's no telling what they'll say about our engagement." What should PM do?
d. Assume that PM decides to accept the engagement. What matters should they discuss in their engagement letter?
e. Would PM's decision about accepting the engagement be influenced by the presence of an Audit Committee? Why or why not?

4-31. Reynolds, CPA, is beginning his examination of the financial statements of Martin Company. In planning the engagement, Reynolds is considering using the audit risk model.

Required:

a. Define audit risk and the components of the audit risk model. What is the audit risk model identified by *SAS No. 47*?
b. How does the auditor establish the various components of the audit risk model?
c. Identify the four-step procedure used by the auditor in implementing the audit risk model.

4-32. Comment on each of the following statements overheard in the discussion between Jones and Johnson, two beginning staff accountants working on the audit of Easy Company:

a. "After we establish materiality levels at the account-balance level, we have a basic idea of what types of transactions we need to examine. Basically, any transactions for amounts less than that materiality level are not of interest during the audit."
b. "Because a specialist assisted in the valuation of inventory for that jewelry store that we audited last month, we need to be sure to disclose this fact in our audit report. After all, her work agreed with the client's valuation of jewelry."
c. "Because irregularities and illegal acts may reflect a lack of integrity or honesty on the part of the client or its personnel, we have a greater responsibility for detecting these misstatements in planning the audit engagement."
d. "I've requested permission from Easy Company to contact their previous auditor. Because they will not allow this discussion to take place, we aren't permitted to talk to the auditor. It looks like we'll just have to accept the engagement and perform more extensive audit procedures in the planning stages of the examination."

4-33. Ready, CPAs, is performing the audit examination of a new audit client, Later Company. Because Ready has not audited this client in previous years, it is interested in identifying areas that are likely to contain material financial statement misstatements in the current audit.

In preparing for this audit examination, assume that Ready has consulted *SAS No. 53* and identified various characteristics that can result in financial statement misstatements. In addition, Ready has considered applying analytical procedures in the planning stages of the audit examination.

Required:

a. What factors should Ready consider in identifying the overall potential for misstatements in Later's financial statements? Group these factors by category and identify how they would affect the potential for misstatements.
b. Define analytical procedures. What is the purpose of performing analytical procedures in the planning stages of the audit?
c. What are five methods that can be used by the auditor to determine the expected value for use in performing analytical procedures? For each of these methods, give one possible example of how Ready could calculate the expected balance for Later Company's accounts receivable.
d. Once Ready has identified the potential for misstatements for a particular account balance or class of transactions, what procedures are performed prior to determining the nature, timing, and extent of substantive tests to be performed in the audit examination of Later Company?

4-34. The first standard of field work requires that the audit should be planned and assistants, if any, should be properly supervised. An effective tool that aids the auditor in planning the work is an audit program. An audit program represents the culmination of the auditor's planning process.

Required:

a. What is an audit program? What is its purpose?
b. Is an audit program a form of supervision? Why or why not?
c. Identify the elements of proper supervision. Why is supervision such an important part of the audit examination?
d. What steps should be taken if a staff accountant disagrees with the ultimate resolution of an issue that arises during the audit examination?

Learning Objectives

Study of this chapter is designed to achieve several learning objectives. After studying this chapter, you should be able to:

1. Discuss how internal control affects the audit process and the determination of detection risk.
2. Define internal control and identify the three objectives of internal control.
3. List the components of internal control and identify important controls comprising these components.
4. Identify the two major audit approaches and their effect on the auditor's study of internal control.
5. Describe the major steps performed by the auditor in his or her study of internal control.
6. Discuss different types of tests of controls performed by the auditor.
7. Define the terms reportable condition and material weakness and discuss the auditor's responsibility for communicating these items to the client.

5

Internal Control and the Assessment of Control Risk

◉ THE AUDIT PROCESS AND AUDIT RISK

In the preceding chapter, we introduced the audit risk model and indicated that the purpose of using this model is to allow the auditor to determine the nature, timing, and extent of the auditor's substantive testing procedures. The audit risk model is applied to the following assertions affecting the client's account balances and classes of transactions:

- ▶ **Existence or occurrence**: The assets or liabilities of a client exist at a give date and the recorded transactions have occurred during a given period (the EO assertion).

- ▶ **Rights and obligations**: Assets are the rights of the client and liabilities are the obligations of a client at a given date (the RO assertion).

- ▶ **Completeness**: All transactions and accounts that should be presented in the financial statements are included (the CO assertion).

- ▶ **Valuation or allocation**: Asset, liability, revenue, and expense components are included in the financial statements at the appropriate dollar amounts (the VA assertion).

- ▶ **Presentation and disclosure**: Particular components of the financial statements are properly classified, described, and disclosed (the PD assertion).

Recall the four basic steps involved with the use of the audit risk model:

1. The auditor sets audit risk at desired levels. **Audit risk** is the risk that the auditor may unknowingly fail to modify his or her opinion on financial statements that contain a material misstatement. Viewed in another way, audit risk is the risk that a material misstatement may occur in an assertion,

not be prevented or detected by internal control, and not be detected by the auditor's substantive testing procedures.

2. Based on the susceptibility of an assertion in an account balance or class of transactions to material misstatement, the auditor assesses inherent risk. **Inherent risk** is the risk that a material misstatement exists in an assertion assuming that no internal control policies or procedures exist.

3. Based on the effectiveness of internal control, the auditor assesses control risk. **Control risk** is the risk that a material misstatement in an assertion will not be prevented or detected on a timely basis by the organization's internal control policies and procedures.

4. After considering the audit risk, inherent risk, and control risk, the auditor determines the necessary level of detection risk. **Detection risk** is the risk that the auditor's substantive tests will fail to detect a material misstatement in an assertion. The necessary level of detection risk is controlled by the auditor through the nature, timing, and extent of his or her substantive testing procedures.

This four-step procedure (as well as the major stage in the audit in which each of these four steps is performed) is depicted below:

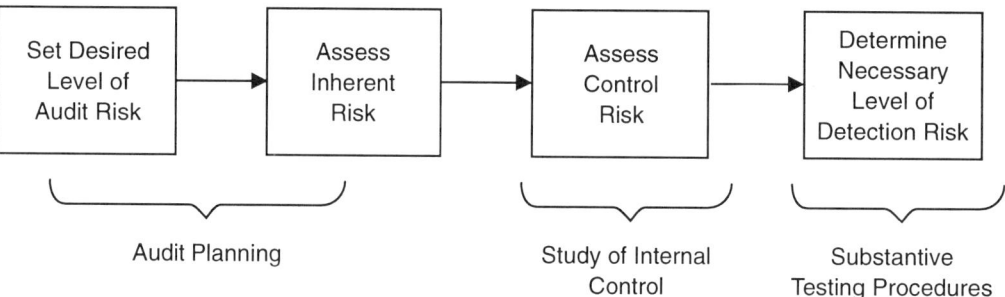

To this point, we have discussed the first two steps in the above process: (1) setting the appropriate level of audit risk, and (2) assessing the appropriate level of inherent risk. In this chapter, we discuss the methods used by the auditor to assess control risk. As noted above, once control risk has been assessed, the auditor can determine the nature, timing, and extent of his or her substantive tests. The auditor's substantive tests are reflected in the necessary level of detection risk, which is the focus of Chapter 6.

◉ OVERVIEW OF INTERNAL CONTROL

◻ Definition of Internal Control

In 1987, the National Commission on Fraudulent Financial Reporting (known as the Treadway Commission) performed an extensive investigation of the financial reporting system used by corporations throughout the United States. As part of their report, the Treadway Commission requested that a common conceptual framework relating to internal control be developed. The result of this recommendation is the study *Internal Control—Integrated Framework* (also known as the COSO report).[1] This report represents the efforts of individuals from the American Institute of Certified Public Accountants, American Accounting Association, Institute of Internal Auditors, Institute of Management Accountants, and Financial Executives Institute to understand, integrate, and reconcile various ideas about what factors constitute effective internal control.

Based on the work of the Treadway Commission, the AICPA recently revised its definition of internal control (formerly known as internal control structure). *Statement on Auditing Standards No. 78*[2] (*SAS No. 78*) defines internal control in the following manner:

> Internal control is a process—effected by an entity's Board of Directors, management, and other personnel—designed to provide reasonable assurance regarding the achievement of objectives in the following categories: (a) reliability of financial reporting, (b) effectiveness and efficiency of operations, and (c) compliance with applicable laws and regulations.

The above definition identifies three objectives of internal control. The first objective relates to the **reliability of financial reporting** (the **financial objective**). An effective internal control enhances the reliability of the financial data provided by the organization's accounting and recording function. These data include both externally-reported financial information (such as transactions comprising the organization's financial statements) and information used for internal decision-making purposes. Several internal control policies established by the organization are designed to enhance the accuracy of the information included in the organization's financial statements, such as:

▶ Sending monthly statements to the organization's customers and following up any discrepancies noted by these customers.

▶ Maintaining perpetual inventory records and periodically reconciling physical inventory on hand to those records.

▶ Reconciling the organization's cash balances to the balance reported on the monthly bank statement.

In addition to external reporting, it is important that the organization have reliable financial data for internal decision-making purposes. Financial information is often useful in many internal decisions, such as product pricing. When management must decide on the price to charge for one of the organization's products, it is imperative that the cost of producing or acquiring that product be accurately communicated throughout the organization. An effective internal control will allow this accurate communication to take place.

---

[1] Committee of Sponsoring Organizations of the Treadway Commission (COSO), *Internal Control—Integrated Framework* (Jersey City, NJ: American Institute of Certified Public Accountants, 1992).

[2] American Institute of Certified Public Accountants (AICPA), *Statement on Auditing Standards No. 78*, "Consideration of Internal Control in a Financial Statement Audit: An Amendment to *SAS No. 55*" (New York: AICPA, 1995, AU 319.06).

The second objective of internal control identified by *SAS No. 78* is to enhance the **effectiveness and efficiency of operations** (the **operating objective**). Internal control policies and procedures related to this objective include:

▶ Monitoring inventory levels to ensure that orders are placed (or production runs are initiated) so that inventory shortages (or stockouts) do not occur.

▶ Keeping assets and documents that provide access to the organization's assets (such as Checks and Shipping Documents) in a secure location.

▶ Comparing the actual cost of producing the organization's inventory to the standard costs to identify inefficiencies in the production process.

The final objective of internal control relates to the organization's **compliance with laws and regulations** (the **compliance objective**). Organizations in all types of industries are required to comply with certain laws and regulations. It is important that organizations closely monitor their compliance with these laws and regulations and, if violations are noted, modify their activities to comply with the appropriate regulations. The following are some examples of compliance with regulations that may be monitored by internal control policies and procedures:

▶ Manufacturers must conduct their operations in conformity with various environmental regulations, such as the Clean Air Act.

▶ Organizations are required to provide their employees with a safe work environment in compliance with the Occupational Safety and Health Act (OSHA).

▶ Governmental entities must observe a large number of laws and regulations in conducting their activities, such as limiting the purposes for which funds can be expended.

It is important to note that the three objectives of internal control are interrelated; that is, certain aspects of an organization's internal control may allow that organization to achieve more than one of these objectives. For example, an effective standard costing system and accurate calculation and reporting of production variances will affect both the financial information reported by the organization as well as its operating effectiveness. Thus, this aspect of internal control may relate to both the financial and operating objectives. Additionally, careful monitoring by the organization to ensure its compliance with laws and regulations will reduce the possibility that fines or other detrimental penalties (closings, shut-downs, etc.) will occur; therefore, controls of this nature may relate to both the operating and compliance objectives of internal control. As will be discussed later, any single aspect of internal control can relate to one or more of the three objectives noted above.

> **CHAPTER CHECKPOINTS**
>
> 5-1. What are the major steps in the use of the audit risk model?
>
> 5-2. Define internal control.
>
> 5-3. What are the primary objectives of internal control? Give some examples of controls that would apply to each objective.

◻ Components of Internal Control

SAS No. 78 identifies the following five components of internal control:

1. Control Environment
2. Risk Assessment
3. Control Activities
4. Information and Communication
5. Monitoring

Figure 5-1 summarizes the relationship between the five components of internal control and the objectives of internal control. This relationship highlights two major points. First, to achieve each objective of internal control, the organization must consider each of the five components. This can be seen by reading down the three columns of the matrix in Figure 5-1. For example, each of the five components of internal control (control environment, risk assessment, control activities, information and communication, and monitoring) allows the organization to prepare and provide reliable financial information (financial objective). Similarly, these components also allow the organization to achieve the operating and compliance objectives of internal control.

Second, when designing each component of internal control, the organization should consider the three objectives of internal control. This is represented by the rows of the matrix in Figure 5-1. For example, in designing the "information and communication" component, management should realize that information is needed to prepare reliable financial information, conduct the operations of the organization efficiently and effectively, and ensure that the organization is adequately complying with applicable laws and regulations.

It is important to note that all three objectives are of concern to the organization as it establishes its internal control. However, recall that the purpose of an audit examination is to determine whether the organization's financial statements are prepared in conformity with GAAP. Therefore, from the auditor's standpoint, the financial objective of internal control is of most importance. In our subsequent discussion of the components of internal control, we will focus on this objective.

	Financial Objective	Operating Objective	Compliance Objective
Control Environment			
Risk Assessment			
Control Activities			
Information and Communication			
Monitoring			

Figure 5-1: *Relationship Between Objectives and Components of Internal Control*

Control Environment

> The **control environment** sets the tone of an organization, influencing the control consciousness of its people. It is the foundation for all other components of internal control, providing discipline and structure.[3]

The initial component of an organization's internal control is the control environment. Simply stated, the control environment consists of a broad set of factors that reflect management's attitude toward internal control. Factors influencing the control environment include:

- ▶ High Levels of Integrity and Ethical Values
- ▶ Commitment to Competence
- ▶ Board of Directors or Audit Committee Participation
- ▶ Management's Philosophy and Operating Style
- ▶ Organizational Structure
- ▶ Assignment of Authority and Responsibility
- ▶ Human Resource Policies and Practices

---

[3] American Institute of Certified Public Accountants (AICPA), *Statement on Auditing Standards No. 78*, "Consideration of Internal Control in a Financial Statement Audit: An Amendment to *SAS No. 55*" (New York: AICPA, 1995, AU 319.06).

High Levels of Integrity and Ethical Values. The integrity and ethical values of the organization's employees are essential components of the control environment, since they affect the design, administration, and monitoring of the remaining components of internal control. Management should set an example for its employees, communicate their expectations to employees through policy standards and codes of conduct, and reduce incentives for employees to engage in dishonest, illegal, or unethical acts. Examples of controls that relate to this component include:

- Written codes of conduct describing acceptable and unacceptable behavior
- Written policies concerning conflicts of interest and standards of ethical behavior

Commitment to Competence. Commitment to competence refers to the ability of the organization's employees to have the knowledge and skills necessary to perform their jobs. Management should carefully consider the levels of competence needed to perform various jobs and how this competence translates into specific job skills and knowledge. In addition, management should take actions (such as rewards and other inducements) to encourage quality performance from their personnel.

Board of Directors or Audit Committee Participation. The purpose of a **Board of Directors** is to provide oversight for the activities of an organization to ensure that the organization is operated in the interests of its shareholders. As noted in Chapter 15, the organization's Board of Directors authorizes important transactions, such as the issuance of stock, purchase of property, plant and equipment, and declaration of dividends. The **audit committee** is a subgroup of the Board of Directors that oversees the organization's accounting and financial reporting practices and serves as a liaison between the auditor and client management.

Factors influencing the effectiveness of the organization's Board of Directors or audit committee include the:

- Independence from management
- Experience and stature of its members
- Extent of its involvement and scrutiny of the organization's activities
- Appropriateness of its actions
- Degree to which difficult questions are raised and pursued with management
- Interaction with internal and external auditors

Management's Philosophy and Operating Style. Each organization has different philosophies regarding the operation of its activities. For example, management may place an extremely high priority on meeting its short-term profit objectives. As a result, management may be more likely to enter into riskier business activities with the objective of earning higher returns. In addition, management's philosophy and operating style may also be reflected in the conservatism with which it selects accounting principles and develops important estimates that affect the organization's financial statements. The auditor should consider issues such as:

- Do the accounting principles selected by management result in higher or lower levels of income?
- Do the estimates established by management reflect a conservative or aggressive position?
- Does management have an aggressive or conservative attitude toward revenue recognition and financial reporting?

An example of how management's philosophy and operating style may affect the organization's operations is shown in the following excerpt:

SHOOT THE MESSENGER[4]

The new CEO at an unnamed financial services company previously held a position in the head office of a finance department. Within a few months, the company started selling currency options to increase profits on its foreign exchange loans. The company's internal auditor was alarmed by the lack of guidelines and controls over exposure to risk with respect to these option contracts. A report and comprehensive action plan was provided to the CEO, who ignored it. The Board of Directors called an emergency meeting and relieved the CEO of his duties after discovering that open option contracts would result in a $12 million loss to the company. The CEO was later replaced by a close colleague who did away with the company's internal audit function six months later.

Organizational Structure. The organization's organizational structure is a critical component for allowing it to plan, control, and direct its operations efficiently and effectively. The organizational structure provides the basis for the responsibility and authority of various individuals and departments within the organization. In evaluating the organizational structure, the auditor should consider issues such as:

- Does a formal organizational chart provide clear lines of authority and reporting relationships?
- Do the lines of authority and reporting relationships allow the organization to meet its goals and objectives?
- Do the lines of authority and reporting relationships allow transactions to be processed and reported in an accurate and timely manner?

Assigning Authority and Responsibility. The authority assigned to various individuals within the organization has a significant effect on the organization's internal control. It is important that individuals understand the objectives of internal control, how their individual actions and jobs

---

[4] "Shoot the Messenger," *Internal Auditor* (April 1996), 78.

contribute to these objectives, and how they will be held accountable. For example, as you will see later in this chapter, to enhance the reliability of its financial statements as well as restrict unauthorized access to its assets, companies should assign the responsibility for: (1) initiating and authorizing transactions, (2) recording transactions, and (3) maintaining custody of assets to different individuals within the organization. This method of assignment is referred to as segregation of duties. Methods of ensuring effective assignment of authority and responsibility within the organization include a set of written policies and procedures and employee job descriptions that detail the specific duties and constraints associated with each position.

Human Resource Policies and Practices. Internal control is only as effective as the individuals who comprise it. As a result, the qualifications of the organization's personnel are an important component of the control environment. Human resource policies should exist related to hiring, orientation, training, evaluating, counseling, promoting, compensating, and disciplining the organization's employees. Examples of control policies related to human resource policies and practices include:

▶ Establishing standards for hiring the most qualified personnel

▶ Providing training to enhance employees' levels of performance and behavior

▶ Considering performance appraisals in decisions related to the advancement and retention of employees

Risk Assessment

> An entity's **risk assessment** for financial reporting purposes is its identification, analysis, and management of risks relevant to the preparation of financial statements that are fairly presented in conformity with generally accepted accounting principles.[5]

Earlier in this chapter, the three objectives of internal control (financial, operations, and compliance) were stated. The risk assessment component of internal control is concerned with how the organization identifies, analyzes, and manages the risks associated with achieving these objectives. In other words, risk assessment is concerned with how the organization attempts to ensure that these objectives are attained.

For purposes of an audit examination, the auditor should focus on the organization's assessment of risks related to the financial reporting objective of internal control. Thus, the auditor is concerned with risks associated with the preparation of financial statements in accordance with GAAP. To

---

[5] American Institute of Certified Public Accountants (AICPA), *Statement on Auditing Standards No. 78*, "Consideration of Internal Control in a Financial Statement Audit: An Amendment to *SAS No. 55*" (New York: AICPA, 1995, AU 319.28).

illustrate, consider the following risks that may affect the organization's recording of purchase transactions.

- Purchase transactions may not be recorded
- Fictitious purchase transactions may be recorded
- Purchase transactions may be recorded at the incorrect dollar amount

Once these risks have been identified, management implements control policies and procedures to reduce the likelihood that they occur. For example, considering the risk that all purchase transactions may not be recorded, the use of prenumbered documents and periodically accounting for the numerical sequence of these documents would be a method of managing this risk. Control policies and procedures of this type are referred to as control activities and are discussed in the following section.

SAS No. 78 notes that the following circumstances may affect the client's risk assessment process by creating new risks or changing the importance of existing risks:

- Changes in the operating environment
- New personnel
- New or revamped information systems
- Rapid growth
- New technology
- New business or product lines
- Corporate restructurings
- Foreign operations
- Accounting pronouncements

It is important to note that management also undertakes the risk assessment process with regard to the operating and compliance objectives of internal control. To illustrate, consider the risks associated with technological changes in the music industry. Prior to 1985, most prerecorded music was sold in the form of long-playing (LP) record albums. However, technological advances have resulted in compact disks (CDs) achieving domination in the market for prerecorded music. In response to these changes, producers expanded their production facilities to produce CDs. Eventually, as the demand for CDs exploded and the demand for LPs dwindled, producers completely reorganized their production capabilities to focus on the production of CDs.

> **CHAPTER CHECKPOINTS**
>
> 5-4. What are the five components of internal control? How do these components relate to the objectives of internal control?
>
> 5-5. What is the control environment?
>
> 5-6. Give examples of components of the control environment.
>
> 5-7. What is risk assessment? What factors may influence the types of risk faced by the organization?
>
> 5-8. How does the process of risk assessment relate to the objectives of internal control?

Control Activities

> **Control activities** are the policies and procedures that help ensure that management directives are carried out. They help ensure that necessary actions are taken to address risks to achieve the entity's objectives.[6]

As noted in the above definition, the primary goal of the control activities is to allow the organization to achieve the operating, financial, and compliance objectives of internal control. Control activities are implemented based on the risks identified in the risk assessment process (see the previous section). To illustrate, assume that an objective identified by the organization is to reduce the losses resulting from uncollectible accounts receivable (an operating objective). In this case, the risks that may prevent the organization from achieving this objective include making sales on account to customers who represent poor credit risks. To address this risk, assume that management implements a control activity that requires a check of all customers' credit histories and formal approval of all sales on account to customers. The role of control activities in the organization's internal control is summarized below:

---

[6] American Institute of Certified Public Accountants (AICPA), *Statement on Auditing Standards No. 78*, "Consideration of Internal Control in a Financial Statement Audit: An Amendment to *SAS No. 55*" (New York: AICPA, 1995, AU 319.32).

As with all components, it is important to note that control activities may relate to more than one of the major objectives of internal control. For example, carefully controlling and recording Credit Memoranda for merchandise returned by customers allows the organization to ensure that all sales returns are recorded, which is primarily related to the financial objective of internal control. In addition, this activity also allows the organization to have an accurate record of its current inventory levels, which is useful in decisions about future purchases of inventory and other inventory control matters. Accordingly, this activity also relates to the operating objective of internal control.

Control activities related to the financial objective of internal control can be classified into four categories: (1) performance review controls, (2) information processing controls, (3) physical controls, and (4) segregation of duties controls. These categories of controls are discussed in the following subsections.

Performance Review Controls. Performance reviews include the following types of evaluations:

▶ Reviewing actual performance versus budgets, forecasts, and prior-period performance

▶ Relating different sets of operating and financial data to one another

Performance reviews generally relate to both the operating and financial objectives of internal control. For example, comparing actual (recorded) sales to budgeted, forecasted, or prior-period sales allows the organization to identify instances where its personnel are performing better or worse than expected. Identifying these areas of operations that may be improved relates to the operating objective of internal control. Alternatively, large differences between actual sales and budgeted, forecasted, or prior-year sales may result from: (1) fictitious transactions being recorded (the EO and RO assertions), (2) actual sales transactions not being recorded (the CO assertion), and/or (3) sales transactions being recorded at the incorrect dollar amount (the VA assertion).[7] To the extent that performance reviews identify misstatements in the financial statements, they also relate to the financial objective of internal control.

Information Processing Controls. Information processing controls are implemented by the organization to verify the accuracy, completeness, and authorization of individual transactions. The primary purpose of these control activities is to ensure that the organization's financial statements are prepared in conformity with GAAP; therefore, these control activities relate primarily to the financial objective of internal control.

SAS No. 78 identifies two broad categories of information processing controls: general controls and application controls. **General controls** are control activities that affect the overall processing of

---

[7] In this section, general relationships between control activities and management assertions are drawn. It is important to note that the assertions related to different control activities may vary slightly from one operating cycle to another. Chapters 10 (for the Revenue cycle), 12 (for the Purchases and Disbursements cycle), 14 (for the Conversion cycle), and 15 (for the Investing and Financing cycle) provide more detailed information about the relationship between control activities and management assertions.

transactions; that is, these control activities affect all (or most) of the transactions processed by the organization. Examples of general controls include controls over:

- Data center operations
- System software acquisition and maintenance
- Access to system hardware and software
- Application system development and maintenance

General controls are discussed in greater detail in Chapter 9 of this text.

In contrast, **application controls** are control activities designed to enhance the processing and recording of individual transactions affecting a specific account balance or class of transactions. Thus, unlike general controls, a different set of application controls will be implemented for the processing of different types of transactions. Three common types of application controls are related to: (1) authorization of transactions, (2) the use of adequate documents and records, and (3) independent checks on performance. An example of these controls, along with the relevant assertion(s) affected by these controls, is shown in Figure 5-2.

Category of Control	Assertion(s) Affected by Control	Examples
Authorization of Transactions	EO RO	▸ Authorization of sales to customers on account ▸ Authorization of purchases made from vendors ▸ Authorization of cash disbursements for purchases ▸ Authorization of write-offs of accounts receivable
Adequate Documents and Records	EO RO CO	▸ Using formal, prenumbered documents
Independent Checks on Performance	VA	▸ Mathematically verifying Sales Invoices ▸ Reconciling bank statements ▸ Sending monthly statements to customers

Figure 5-2: *Application Controls*

The first category of application controls is related to **authorization of transactions**. In an effective internal control, an individual's ability to authorize transactions and activities should be well-documented. As noted in the discussion of the control environment, only specific individuals and/or departments should have the authority to initiate (authorize) transactions. For example, in most companies, the Board of Directors has the responsibility for approving acquisitions of property, plant and equipment over a specified dollar amount. By formally approving transactions in this manner, the likelihood of recording fictitious transactions in the accounts decreases. Therefore, controls that require authorization of transactions relate primarily to the EO and RO assertions.

The use of **adequate documents and records** is the second category of application controls. Companies should use prenumbered, formal documents and records to process and record their transactions. In addition, access to these documents and records should be limited to certain individuals. By using prenumbered documents and accounting for the numerical sequence of these documents, the organization decreases the likelihood that transactions are not recorded (the CO assertion). An example of this is the use of preprinted and prenumbered Shipping Documents. If the organization wants to ensure that all shipments made to customers have been recorded, an employee could be assigned the task of accounting for the numerical sequence of Shipping Documents. Any Shipping Document numbers that are not located in the accounting records can then be investigated by the organization.

In addition to prenumbering, the access to documents and records used to process and record transactions should be restricted to certain personnel. If access is restricted in this manner, it will be more difficult for employees to process fictitious transactions. For example, if access to Shipping Documents is restricted and Shipping Documents are required prior to recording a sale, the ability of employees to process fictitious sales transactions is limited. Thus, these controls also relate to the EO and RO assertions.

The final category of application controls is **independent checks on performance**. This category of controls recognizes that the work of employees should be checked against other sources of information. Controls in this category include:

1. **Comparing External Records to Internal Records** (such as preparing bank reconciliations and using monthly statements to investigate the accuracy of accounts receivable balances).
2. **Comparing Information on a Single Document** (such as comparing quantities on a Vendor's Invoice with quantities received by the organization and mathematically verifying the accuracy of the Invoice).

Because these types of independent checks will identify transactions recorded at the incorrect dollar amounts, they relate to the VA assertion.

It is important to note that all three categories of information processing controls relate to both the financial objective of internal control and the operating objective of internal control. For example, as noted above, proper authorization of transactions reduces the likelihood that fictitious purchases are recorded in the organization's accounting records (the EO and RO assertions). In addition, by authorizing purchases, the organization also reduces the likelihood that purchases are made for unauthorized purposes or from unauthorized vendors; this latter benefit relates to the operating objective of internal control.

Physical Controls. Physical controls are implemented by companies to improve the physical security over their assets. Physical controls reduce the ability of employees to engage in defalcation schemes involving the organization's assets by either: (1) reducing employees' access to the organization's assets, or (2) allowing the organization to identify instances where defalcation schemes have occurred. Common physical controls include:

- Adequate safeguards, such as secured facilities, over access to assets and documents that control the disposition of assets.
- Authorization for access to computer programs and data files.
- Periodic counting and comparison of physical assets with amounts shown on control records (such as cash from over-the-counter sales, inventory, and investments in securities).

Because they protect the organization's assets from theft, physical controls relate to the operating objective of internal control. In addition, because employees may attempt to conceal a theft or defalcation of assets by: (1) recording a fictitious transaction (the EO and RO assertions), or (2) failing to record an actual transaction (the CO assertion), these controls also relate to the financial objective of internal control.

Segregation of Duties Controls. The final type of control activity is segregation of duties. **Segregation of duties** recognizes that certain aspects of a transaction need to be performed by different individuals, departments, and/or functions. For an effective segregation of duties to be maintained, different individuals, departments, and/or functions should be assigned the following responsibilities with respect to a transaction:

- Authorization
- Recording
- Custody of the Related Asset

As an example of segregation of duties, consider the individuals involved in the processing of a organization's cash receipts from its customers. An effective internal control would dictate that different individuals should perform the following duties: (1) authorize write-offs of uncollectible accounts (authorization), (2) receive cash in the mails (custody), and (3) update subsidiary accounts receivable records (recording). If these three functions are performed by one individual, that individual could be in the position to embezzle customer remittances and conceal this embezzlement through fictitious write-offs. Although segregating these duties does not prevent embezzlement from occurring (the three individuals could conspire to embezzle the funds), it does prohibit a single individual from perpetrating such a defalcation.

As with other control activities, segregation of duties is related to both the operating and financial objectives of internal control. Like physical controls, the fact that individuals have less of an ability to commit a defalcation provides benefits to the organization by protecting their assets from theft (the operating objective). In addition, as with physical controls, the reduced ability of organization employees to engage in a defalcation scheme reduces the likelihood that defalcations are concealed through: (1) recording fictitious transactions (the EO and RO assertions), or (2) failing to record actual transactions (the CO assertion). As a result, this control activity also corresponds to the financial objective of internal control.

> **COLLECTING AND LOANING**[8]
>
> The bank's collection manager often assisted customers seeking loans when a loan manager was out of the office. The collection manager approved the loan and forwarded the paperwork to operations for processing. While it appeared that the collection manager was a great "team player," he was, in reality, engaging in a defalcation scheme. The collection manager would approve these loans and divert the receipts by writing off the loans as uncollectible. To escape suspicion, the loans were booked in the names of persons previously denied credit by the bank. This practice allowed the credit manager to embezzle $87,000. If proper segregation of duties had been followed, this scheme would not have been able to be perpetrated.

Control Activities: A Summary. At this point, we have introduced the four major categories of control activities (performance review controls, information processing controls, physical controls, and segregation of duties controls). These control activities will be applied to specific account balances and classes of transactions in the following chapters of this text:

- ▶ Chapter 10: The Revenue Cycle
- ▶ Chapter 12: The Purchases and Disbursements Cycle
- ▶ Chapter 14: The Conversion Cycle
- ▶ Chapter 15: The Investing and Financing Cycle

> **CHAPTER CHECKPOINTS**
>
> **5-9.** What are control activities? How do control activities relate to the risk assessment component of internal control?
>
> **5-10.** Identify and give examples of the four types of control activities.
>
> **5-11.** Distinguish between general controls and application controls. What are the major categories of application controls?
>
> **5-12.** What assertions are affected by the major categories of application controls?
>
> **5-13.** In an effective internal control, which duties related to the processing of a transaction should be segregated?

---

[8] "Collecting and Loaning," *The Internal Auditor* (October 1994), 74.

Information and Communication

> The information system relevant to financial reporting objectives, which includes the accounting system, consists of the methods and records established to record, process, summarize, and report entity transactions (as well as events and conditions) and to maintain accountability for the related assets, liabilities, and equity.[9]
>
> Communication involves providing an understanding of individual roles and responsibilities pertaining to internal control over financial reporting.[10]

The fourth component of internal control identified by the *SAS No. 78* is information and communication. Information must be identified, summarized, and communicated throughout the organization to allow its employees to conduct their responsibilities. Doing so will further allow the organization to achieve its objectives with respect to internal control. For example, manufacturing companies use information about direct materials inventories to prepare their financial statements; this affects the financial reporting objective of internal control. Information about direct materials inventories will also permit management to ensure that sufficient quantities of direct materials inventories are on hand to allow the organization to continue its production without interruption. This latter use of information relates to the operating objective of internal control.

While the traditional focus on information is on internal information (such as financial summaries, production statistics, etc.), it is important to note that external information is also an important consideration. Examples of external information include information on competitors' product development, changes in economic conditions affecting the organization and its products, and changes in the legislative and regulatory environment that affect the organization and its operations. This type of information has the capability to affect the operating and compliance objectives of the organization's internal control. For example, if the stringency of environmental regulations are increased, organizations may need to alter their production processes to ensure that their operations are conducted in compliance with these stricter regulations.

From the auditor's standpoint, the primary concern with respect to the information and communication component is with the **accounting system** (or **information system**). The organization's accounting system includes all methods and records that:

▶ Identify and record all valid transactions

▶ Properly classify transactions

▶ Record transactions at the proper monetary amounts

---

[9] American Institute of Certified Public Accountants (AICPA), *Statement on Auditing Standards No. 78*, "Consideration of Internal Control in a Financial Statement Audit: An Amendment to *SAS No. 55*" (New York: AICPA, 1995, AU 319.34).

[10] American Institute of Certified Public Accountants (AICPA), *Statement on Auditing Standards No. 78*, "Consideration of Internal Control in a Financial Statement Audit: An Amendment to *SAS No. 55*" (New York: AICPA, 1995, AU 319.35).

- Record transactions in the proper accounting period
- Properly present transactions and related disclosures in the financial statements

Thus, the accounting system is concerned with preparing financial statements according to GAAP. To illustrate the operation of an accounting system, consider the methods and records used by a organization to record sales made to its customers on account (credit sales). We will discuss this accounting system in greater detail in Chapter 10; at this point, we merely wish to introduce the concept of an accounting system. As shown in Figure 5-3, the accounting system consists of a four-level hierarchy: (1) document (Sales Invoice), (2) departmental report (Daily Sales Summary), (3) journal or register (Sales Register), and (4) General Ledger. The distinction between each stage of the hierarchy is the level of aggregation (the number of transactions represented). For example, as shown in Figure 5-3:

1. The Sales Invoice represents a single transaction (a sale on account to J. Carr).
2. The Daily Sales Summary summarizes a series of transactions (sales made on 1-1-x1).
3. The Sales Register summarizes information from a number of Daily Sales Summaries (sales from 1-1-x1 through 1-15-x1).
4. The General Ledger entry represents a single total from the Sales Register (sales made from 1-1-x1 through 1-15-x1).

The fourth component of internal control also relates to the communication of information throughout the organization. In an effective internal control, all personnel must understand that internal control responsibilities must be taken seriously. In addition, each individual needs to understand the relevant aspects of the internal control, how his or her position in the organization affects internal control, and how his or her activities relate to the work of other individuals. Without such communication, the control activities established by the organization are unlikely to be effective in achieving the objectives with respect to internal control.

Monitoring

> Monitoring is a process that assesses the quality of internal control performance over time. It involves assessing the design and operation of controls on a timely basis and taking necessary corrective actions.[11]

The final component of internal control identified by the *SAS No. 78* is monitoring. The process of **monitoring** allows management to determine whether the organization's internal control is operating effectively. Two primary methods are used by organizations to conduct their monitoring activities.

---

[11] American Institute of Certified Public Accountants (AICPA), *Statement on Auditing Standards No. 78*, "Consideration of Internal Control in a Financial Statement Audit: An Amendment to *SAS No. 55*" (New York: AICPA, 1995, AU 319.37).

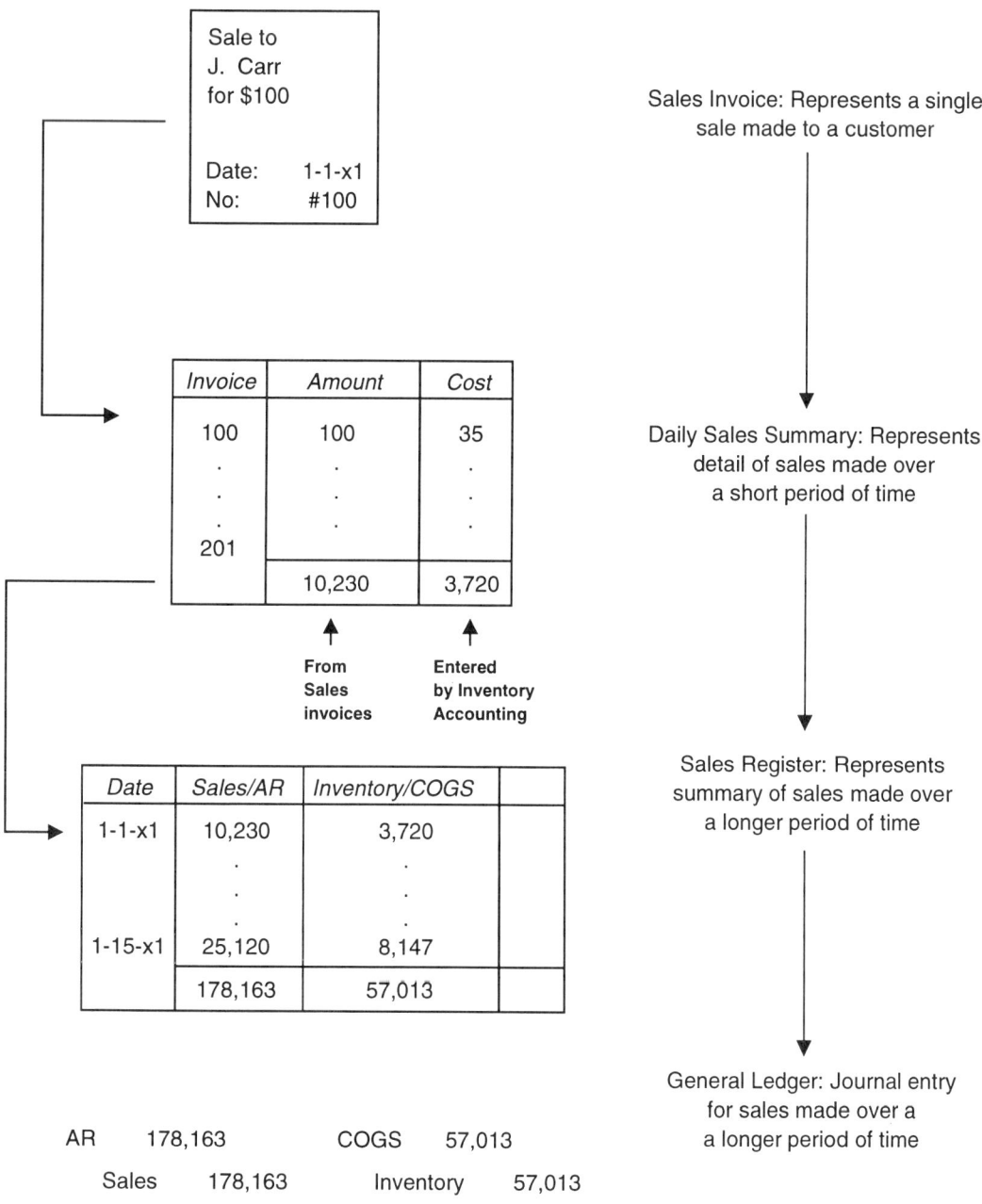

Figure 5-3: *Accounting System for Credit Sales*

Ongoing monitoring activities include regular management and supervisory activities and other routine actions conducted by the organization's employees as part of their ordinary day-to-day operations. For example, when companies mail statements of account to their customers, discrepancies between the statement amounts and the customers' records are occasionally identified. Management identification and follow-up of these discrepancies is an example of an ongoing monitoring activity. The lack of discrepancies noted between customers' payments and information from customers' statements provides the organization with some assurance that sales transactions are being processed accurately. Assuming that the above comparisons reveal only isolated (and minor) differences, management may feel fairly confident that its internal control continues to function effectively.

In addition to ongoing activities it is often useful for organizations to perform a **separate evaluation** of their internal control. These separate evaluations vary in terms of scope and frequency, depending on the significance of the risks and importance of the control activities in reducing the risk. Separate evaluations of internal control may be conducted by both the organization's internal auditors as well as their external auditors. In any instance, separate evaluations focus on how effectively the internal control actually functions. The end result of a separate evaluation of internal control is an identification of deficiencies in internal control and potential areas for improvement.

One particularly important aspect of monitoring internal control is that management should consider corrective actions regarding any deficiencies noted by ongoing monitoring activities or separate evaluations of internal control. Thus, it is important that any observed deficiencies be communicated to the organization. Once detected, deficiencies in internal control should be communicated to the individual who is responsible for the activity involved, since he or she is in position to correct the deficiency. Also, any deficiencies should be communicated to individual(s) at least one level of management above the individual directly responsible for the deficiency. This communication should ensure that the necessary corrections are made. For particularly important deficiencies, many organizations require communication to relatively high levels within the organization, such as the Board of Directors or the audit committee.[12]

Some benefits of monitoring internal controls that are based on actual situations encountered in practice are shown below.

---

[12] *Statement on Auditing Standards No. 60*, "Communication of Internal Control Structure Related Matters Noted in an Audit" (New York: AICPA, AU 325) requires deficiencies in internal control noted during a GAAS audit to be communicated to the client's Board of Directors or audit committee. *SAS No. 60* is discussed later in this chapter.

> As part of a review of bus depot operations, an internal auditor noticed that bus drivers sat in their vehicles while revenue attendants emptied the buses' fare boxes. Wondering why the bus drivers couldn't perform this function under management supervision, the internal auditor recommended eliminating the revenue attendants' positions. The end result is that management is beginning negotiations with the appropriate unions to begin saving an estimated $6.3 million per year.[13]
>
> An internal auditor's review of the purchasing function revealed that suppliers were billing the organization using catalog prices, despite the fact that they had quoted a lower price over the telephone. After informing the Purchasing Manager of this practice, the auditor helped negotiate the return of $100,000 in excess charges and interest. As a result of this finding, changes in control policies were suggested to prevent this from occurring in the future.[14]

CHAPTER CHECKPOINTS

5-14. Define an accounting (information) system. What are the objectives of an accounting (information) system?

5-15. Define and give some examples of monitoring.

◻ Other Internal Control Considerations

Auditor's Responsibility for Internal Control. The auditor's responsibility with respect to the organization's internal control is best summarized by the second standard of field work:

> A sufficient understanding of the internal control is to be obtained to plan the audit and to determine the nature, timing, and extent of tests to be performed.[15]

Thus, the auditor's primary reason for studying internal control is to determine the necessary level of substantive tests. As discussed in this and other chapters, **substantive tests** refer to the procedures performed by the auditor to evaluate whether the organization's financial statements are prepared according to GAAP. Perhaps the most critical relationship in auditing is the inverse relationship

---

[13] "Unproductive Idling," *The Internal Auditor* (April 1993), 70.

[14] "Higher vs. Lower," *The Internal Auditor* (December 1994), 78.

[15] American Institute of Certified Public Accountants (AICPA), *Statement on Auditing Standards No. 1*, "Codification of Auditing Standards and Procedures" (New York: AICPA, 1972, AU 150.02).

between the effectiveness of the client's internal control and the necessary effectiveness of the auditor's substantive tests:

> When the client's internal control is more effective at preventing and/or detecting financial statement misstatements, the auditor's substantive tests can be less effective (and *vice versa*).

The above relationship is consistent with the audit risk model. Stated another way, when control risk is lower (more effective internal control), the auditor is permitted a higher level of detection risk (less effective substantive tests). The inverse relationship between the effectiveness of the client's internal control and the effectiveness of the auditor's substantive tests is depicted below:

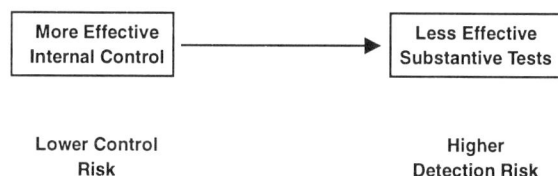

Since the primary purpose of the auditor's examination is to determine whether the organization's financial statements are prepared according to GAAP, the auditor focuses on control policies and procedures related to the financial objective of internal control. However, in some cases, controls related to the operating and compliance objectives have an effect on the procedures performed by the auditor; if so, the auditor would also consider these controls during his or her examination. Some examples of controls of this nature include:

1. Controls over compliance with income tax laws and regulations used to determine the organization's provision for income taxes (compliance objective).
2. Controls over nonfinancial data (such as production statistics) used by the auditor in performing analytical procedures (operating objective).

A secondary reason for the auditor's study of the client's internal control is to provide the client with suggestions to allow them to improve their internal control. Doing so allows the client (organization) to more thoroughly benefit from the auditor's expertise and understanding of internal control. However, this reason is clearly secondary to that of allowing the auditor to determine the nature, timing, and extent of substantive testing procedures.

Management's Responsibility for Internal Control. As noted above, the auditor's responsibility is to examine internal control to determine the nature, timing, and extent of his or her substantive tests. While the auditor may identify deficiencies in internal control and communicate those deficiencies to the organization's management, it is management's responsibility to establish and maintain internal control. This responsibility was initially provided in the Foreign Corrupt Practices Act of 1977 as follows:

> [public companies are required to] devise and maintain a system of internal accounting control sufficient to provide reasonable assurance that—
>
> (i) transactions are executed in accordance with management's general or specific authorization;
>
> (ii) transactions are recorded as necessary (I) to permit preparation of financial statements in conformity with GAAP or any other criteria applicable to such statements, and (II) to maintain accountability for assets;
>
> (iii) access to assets is permitted only in accordance with management's general or specific authorization; and
>
> (iv) the recorded accountability for assets is compared with the existing assets at reasonable intervals and appropriate action is taken with respect to any differences.

Reasonable Assurance. In designing its internal control, management must consider the concept of **reasonable assurance**. Reasonable assurance recognizes that the cost of internal control to an organization should not exceed the benefits provided by that internal control. Management must take these costs and benefits into consideration when evaluating additions or improvements to an existing internal control. For example, while hiring hundreds of employees to mathematically verify Sales Invoices would increase the likelihood that incorrect footings and extensions would be detected, the additional costs of hiring these employees would undoubtedly exceed any benefits associated with their work.

IS INTERNAL CONTROL WORTH THE COST?

A good example of the failure to consider the concept of reasonable assurance can be found by reviewing the experience of a transit authority in its efforts to discourage employee pilferage of office supplies, long-distance services, and other items. This company was so concerned about pilferage that its Board of Directors approved a large budget expenditure to identify cases of theft. The transit authority spent over $500,000 to recover $10,000 of items pilfered.[16]

An unnamed company processed and distributed over 100 computer-generated reports daily. Most of these reports were unnecessary. For example, the company's Production Control Office received four copies of six different reports every day; however, an internal auditor's investigation revealed that the office only reviewed a weekly summary of two of these reports. Therefore, all of the daily reports were unnecessary! Eliminating the daily reports saved $1,000 a year in paper costs, in addition to the savings from increasing the useful life of the equipment used to generate all of this unnecessary paperwork.[17]

---

[16] J.T. Wells, "The Billion Dollar Paper Clip," *The Internal Auditor* (October 1994), 35.

[17] "Unnecessary Reports," *Internal Auditor* (February 1995), 57.

Limitations of Internal Control. SAS No. 78 recognizes that certain limitations exist with respect to any internal control. These limitations include:

- **Human errors or mistakes**: Individuals may misunderstand their responsibilities or make simple errors in conducting their internal-control related duties. For example, individuals verifying the mathematical accuracy of Sales Invoices may fail to detect mistakes because of fatigue, carelessness, or distraction.

- **Collusion between two or more individuals**: While segregation of duties reduces the likelihood that any **one** individual can commit and conceal a defalcation, employees having the responsibilities of authorization, recording, and custody of assets could collaborate (or collude) to commit a defalcation.

- **Management override of internal control**: In some cases, management can circumvent internal controls. For example, assume that a control activity is implemented to only allow the purchase of inventory from certain vendors. Also assume that a clerical employee detects a purchase from an unauthorized vendor and provides the documentation to a person in a higher position of responsibility. That individual may simply submit the purchase for processing, resulting in a circumvention in a control activity.

Example: A Simple Internal Control. In order to illustrate an internal control familiar to most accounting students, consider the policies and procedures implemented by Bijou Theatres over the sale of tickets, process of admitting patrons, and method of handling of cash receipts. Figure 5-4 illustrates several control activities and discusses the objectives of internal control addressed by each activity. Notice that a single control activity can be classified as relating to more than one objective of internal control.

Control Activity	Category	Objectives of Internal Control
The use of prenumbered tickets for patron admission	Information Processing (Adequate Documents and Independent Checks on Performance)	Can determine total amount of cash that should be collected by providing an independent count of the number of patrons (financial). Reduces the likelihood that cash receipts can be stolen by employees without detection (operating).
Different persons should collect cash and authorize admission	Segregation of Duties	Reduces the likelihood that one person authorizes patron admission and has access to cash receipts (operating). Reduces the likelihood that cash receipts and sales will not be recorded to conceal a defalcation scheme (financial).
Cash registers should have "locked-in" totals which are reconciled to cash on hand	Physical Controls Information Processing (Independent Checks on Performance)	Reduces the likelihood that cash receipts can be stolen by employees without detection (operating). Reduces the likelihood that cash receipts and sales will not be recorded to conceal a defalcation scheme (financial).
Cash receipts should be deposited on a daily basis	Physical Controls	Reduces the likelihood that cash receipts can be stolen by employees (operating). Improves the theater's cash management (operating).

Figure 5-4: *A Simple Internal Control: Bijou Theatres*

CHAPTER CHECKPOINTS

5-16. What are the responsibilities of the auditor and management with respect to internal control?

5-17. Define reasonable assurance. How does reasonable assurance affect management's responsibility for internal control?

5-18. What are some inherent limitations of internal control?

STUDYING INTERNAL CONTROL

The auditor's primary reason for studying internal control is to determine the nature, timing, and extent of substantive tests. This is done through the use of the audit risk model. As noted at the beginning of this chapter, the third step in using the audit risk model requires the auditor to assess the level of control risk. **Control risk** is the risk that a material misstatement in an assertion will not be prevented or detected on a timely basis by the client's internal control policies and procedures. Once control risk has been assessed, the auditor can determine the necessary level of detection risk, which represents the nature, timing, and extent of his or her substantive tests. The ultimate determination of control risk and detection risk can be simplified as shown below:

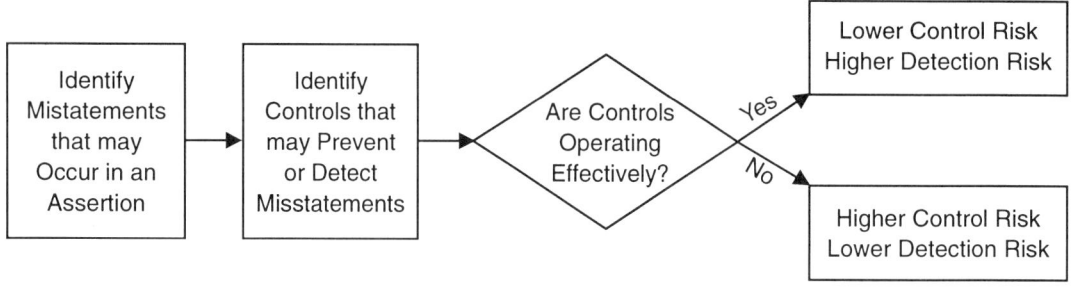

In order to assess control risk and determine detection risk, the auditor must study the client's internal control. This is done through the following eight-step procedure:

1. Identifying a Preliminary Audit Strategy
2. Understanding the Components of Internal Control
3. Documenting the Understanding of Internal Control
4. Making an Initial Assessment of Control Risk
5. Obtaining an Additional Reduction in Control Risk
6. Making a Final Assessment of Control Risk
7. Documenting Control Risk Assessments
8. Using the Audit Risk Model to Determine the Necessary Level of Detection Risk

Figure 5-5 summarizes the eight-step procedure used by the auditor to study internal control and assess control risk. This procedure serves as the focus of the discussion in the remainder of this section.

Identifying a Preliminary Audit Strategy

Prior to obtaining an understanding of the components of internal control, the auditor begins with a preliminary audit strategy in mind. This preliminary audit strategy involves one of two approaches to examining an assertion within an account balance or class of transactions. Under the **substantive approach**, the auditor spends a limited amount of time studying internal control and concentrates his

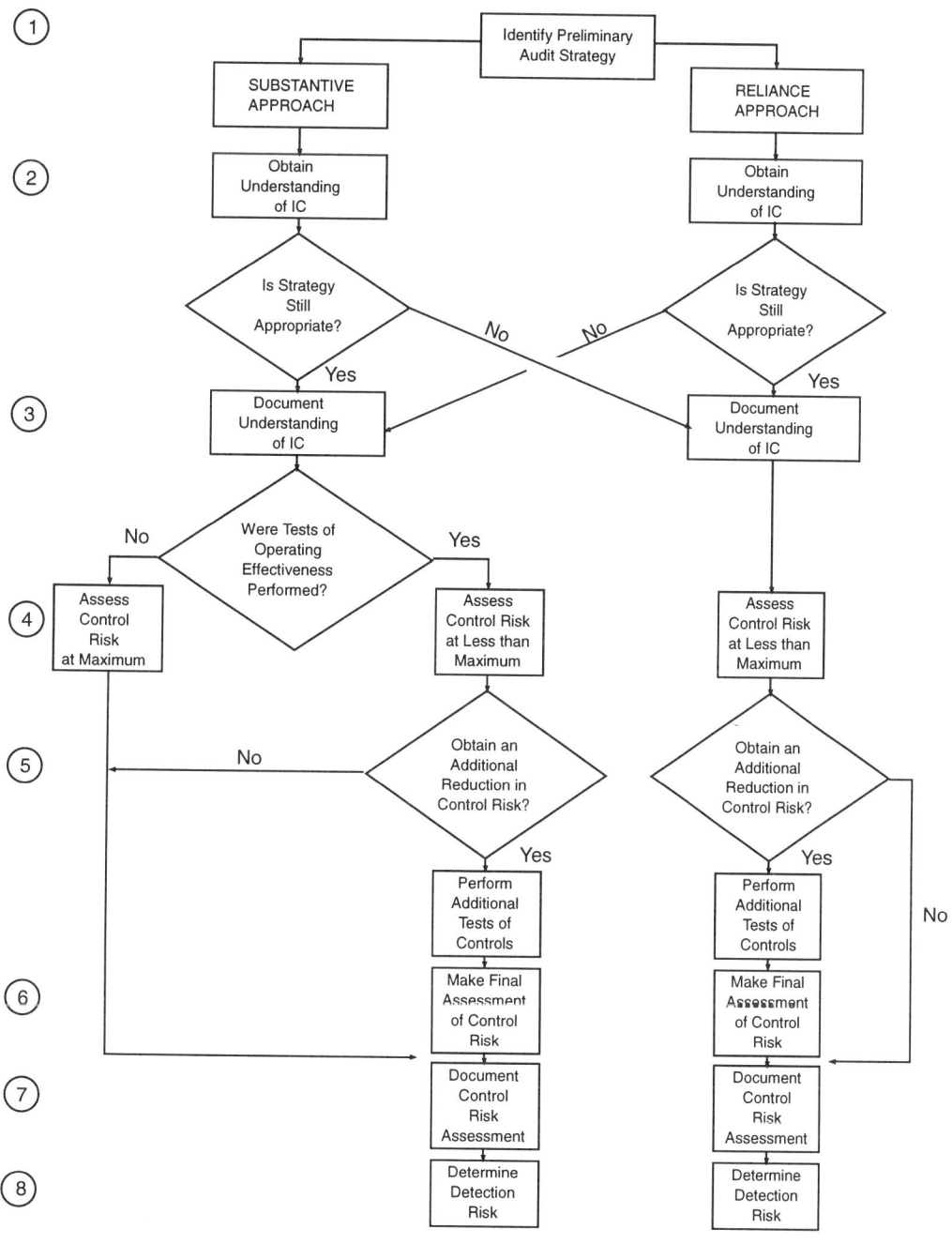

Figure 5-5: *Steps in the Auditor's Study of Internal Control*

or her efforts on substantive tests. In contrast, the **reliance approach** requires greater effort in studying internal control. However, the trade-off is that the auditor spends less time performing substantive tests. The substantive and reliance approaches are summarized below:

	Substantive Approach	Reliance Approach
Study of Internal Control	Less Extensive	More Extensive
Assessment of Control Risk	Maximum or High	Moderate or Low
Substantive Testing	More Extensive	Less Extensive
Level of Detection Risk	Lower	Higher

As shown above, the primary trade-offs in using the above approaches are between auditor effort in studying internal control and performing substantive tests. The substantive approach is used in situations where control risk will be assessed at either the maximum level or at high levels. Assessing control risk at these levels is appropriate in any of the following instances:

▶ Important control policies related to the assertion do not exist

▶ Control policies are not effective in preventing or detecting misstatements related to the assertion

▶ It is not cost-efficient to examine the operating effectiveness of control policies

The auditor's preliminary audit strategy may be based on previous experience with the client, initial discussions with client personnel, or the nature of the account balance being examined. For example, experience of the auditor with the client in previous engagements may have revealed that the client has not implemented control policies to address certain assertions. In other cases, the client may have implemented control policies, but these control policies are not effective in preventing or detecting misstatements related to the assertion. If either situation exists, the auditor may decided to assess control risk at relatively high levels and perform relatively extensive substantive tests (the substantive approach). For new clients, initial discussions with client personnel may reveal conditions of a similar nature, resulting in the auditor utilizing the substantive approach.

The auditor's preliminary audit strategy may also be affected by the nature of the assertion or account balance being examined. For example, consider the auditor's tests with respect to the property, plant and equipment account. This account typically has a small number of transactions; in addition, these transactions are ordinarily for relatively large dollar amounts. As a result, it may be more cost-efficient for the auditor to perform substantive tests and not perform tests of the operating effectiveness of internal control policies. Thus, in this instance, the auditor would utilize the substantive approach.

Finally, the preliminary audit strategy may be affected by the method used by the client to process its information. In situations where the client extensively utilizes electronic means to transmit, process, maintain, or access information, the auditor may not be able to control audit risk by performing effective substantive tests. For example, if information is processed electronically, the potential for improper alteration of information without detection is greater than if information is processed manually. In these cases, the auditor should consider utilizing the reliance approach and reducing the assessments of control risk.[18]

**INTERNAL CONTROL CASE:
WATERWORKS, INC.**

Scott Jordan is establishing a preliminary audit strategy for the assertions related to two different accounts in the audit of WaterWorks, Inc., a company specializing in irrigation systems for commercial and residential customers. These assertions are the EO assertion for accounts receivable and the CO assertion for property, plant and equipment.

Based on previous audits, Scott feels that WaterWorks has established effective internal control over the assertions for both accounts; in fact, Scott feels that WaterWorks may have gone a little "over-board" in setting up its internal control. In devising his audit strategy, Scott's knowledge of Water-Works' business indicates that they have a large number of revenue transactions for varying amounts occurring throughout the year. In contrast, the only transactions affecting property, plant and equipment are purchases of new vehicles and disposals of older vehicles; based on Scott's audit last year, he recalls that their fleet of work vehicles is relatively new.

Because of the large number of transactions in accounts receivable, Scott feels that it may be cost-efficient to study internal control to reduce the level of substantive testing that will be performed. In contrast, few (if any) transactions affecting property, plant and equipment are expected; these transactions will be for larger dollar amounts. As a result, Scott will probably want to examine these transactions as part of his substantive tests. This provides Scott with the following preliminary audit approaches:

Accounts Receivable (EO Assertion):   Reliance Approach
Property, Plant and Equipment (CO Assertion):   Substantive Approach

---

◘ Understanding the Components of Internal Control

Regardless of the preliminary audit strategy selected by the auditor, he or she is required to obtain an understanding of the components of internal control in all GAAS audits. During this step, the auditor gathers information about all five components of internal control: (1) control environment, (2) risk assessment, (3) control activities, (4) information and communication, and (5) monitoring. The auditor's emphasis in gathering this information depends upon his or her basic audit approach. Under the substantive approach, the auditor's understanding will be limited to the components of internal control other than the control activities. In addition, the extent of the auditor's understanding of the control environment, risk assessment, information and communication, and monitoring will be somewhat limited. In contrast, the reliance approach requires the auditor to acquire a more in-depth understanding of all of the components of internal control, including the control activities. In fact,

---

[18] American Institute of Certified Public Accountants (AICPA), *Proposed Statement on Auditing Standards*, "Amendment to *Statement on Auditing Standards No. 31*, 'Evidential Matter'" (New York: AICPA, May 20, 1996).

under the reliance approach, the auditor's focus is obtaining an understanding of the control activities implemented by the client.

Purpose of Understanding. The purpose of obtaining an understanding of the components of internal control is to:

▶ Identify the types of misstatements that may occur

▶ Consider factors that affect the risk of material misstatements

▶ Design substantive tests to detect misstatements

The first issue represents the relative susceptibility of each assertion in an account balance to misstatement (or, inherent risk). As noted throughout this section, the auditor's study of internal control (and assessment of control risk) is done on an assertion-by-assertion basis. This recognizes that some assertions are of greater importance to the auditor than others. For example, when auditing accounts receivable, the auditor's primary concern is that all recorded accounts receivable transactions actually occurred (the EO assertion). This assertion is of greater importance than the CO assertion because of the relative levels of inherent risk associated with the two assertions. That is, if management is intentionally misstating its financial statements, they would be more likely to record fictitious accounts receivable transactions (resulting in additional revenues and assets) then to fail to record actual accounts receivable transactions. In contrast, the opposite would be true with respect to purchases made on account.

Once the assertions (and potential misstatements) have been identified, the auditor should consider what factors affect the risk of material misstatement. In this instance, the auditor identifies specific control policies and procedures that **may be relied upon** to prevent or detect misstatements in those assertions. Notice that the terms "may be relied upon" are emphasized. In obtaining an understanding of the components of internal control, the auditor focuses on the **design** of internal controls (what controls are supposed to be in place?) and whether the controls have been **placed in operation** (is the client using these controls?). However, it is important to remember that just because a control has been designed and placed in operation does not mean that it is operating effectively. In order to rely on internal controls to prevent or detect misstatements, the controls must also be operating effectively. As a result, at this stage, the auditor is only able to identify controls that **may be relied upon** to prevent or detect misstatements. As noted later, tests of the operating effectiveness of internal control policies and procedures provide the auditor with more information about whether these controls can be relied upon in this manner.

Finally, based on the control policies and procedures established by the client, the auditor can identify a planned level of substantive tests. Recall that the auditor's primary objective in studying the client's internal control is to determine the necessary level of detection risk (the nature, timing, and extent of substantive tests). As noted later, the planned level of the auditor's substantive tests may need to be modified by the auditor depending on the operating effectiveness of the client's internal control policies and procedures.

How to Obtain the Understanding. The auditor's understanding of the components of the client's internal control is ordinarily obtained through the following procedures:

1. Previous experience with the client
2. Inquiry of client personnel
3. Inspection of client documents and records
4. Observation of client activities

If the auditor has performed an audit of the client in one or more previous years, he or she will have been required to obtain an understanding of the components of internal control in previous audits. Through this understanding, the auditor will already have a great deal of knowledge regarding the client's internal control policies and procedures. This understanding will have been documented in prior years and can be reviewed by the auditor. In cases such as this, the auditor would focus on major changes in internal control during the most recent year and update any previous documentation to reflect these changes.

Other methods for obtaining an understanding of components of internal control include inquiry of client personnel, inspection of client documents and records, and observation of client activities. For example, consider the process used by the auditor to obtain an understanding of the components of internal control related to the processing of credit sales transactions. Through inquiry, the auditor could learn that formal credit checks are performed before any sales are made to customers on account. If this credit approval involves the formal use of documentation, the auditor could inspect the documents to verify that they are prepared in an appropriate manner. In addition, the auditor could observe client employees performing the credit authorization function to determine that they are not performing other (incompatible) functions.

A common method used by the auditor to obtain an understanding of the components of internal control is a walk-through. A **walk-through** involves identifying one (or a few) specific transactions and following those transactions from their initiation until their ultimate recording in the accounts. As the auditor follows these transactions through the accounting system, he or she identifies important control policies and procedures that have been implemented with respect to these transactions.

Tests of Operating Effectiveness. Although the auditor is most concerned with determining how the client's internal control is designed when obtaining an understanding of the components of internal control, it is important to note that it may be cost-effective to perform tests of the operating effectiveness of the internal control in this stage. This is particularly true if the preliminary audit strategy is the reliance approach. Tests of the operating effectiveness of internal control are referred to as **tests of controls**. Tests of controls provide the auditor with the following information related to the client's control policies and procedures:

- ▶ How are the policies and procedures applied?
- ▶ How consistently are the policies and procedures applied?
- ▶ Who applies the policies and procedures?

If the auditor plans to assess control risk at less than the maximum level, he or she must perform some tests of the operating effectiveness of internal control. Thus, when the auditor's preliminary strategy is the reliance approach, he or she ordinarily performs some limited tests of controls in this stage to provide for control risk assessments at less than the maximum. Tests of controls are discussed in more detail in a later section of this chapter.

Other Issues in Obtaining an Understanding. As the auditor obtains the understanding of the components of the client's internal control, he or she should consider whether the preliminary audit strategy is still appropriate. For example, assume that the auditor's previous experience with the client suggests that effective control policies have been implemented and therefore, the auditor selects the reliance approach as his or her preliminary audit strategy. Also assume that the understanding of the components of the internal control indicates that several control policies and procedures are no longer in place. If so, the auditor may decide to modify the preliminary audit strategy to utilize the substantive approach (or *vice versa*).

In extreme situations, the auditor's understanding of the components of the internal control may raise doubts about management's integrity or the extent and condition of the client's accounting records. If either condition would result in the auditor being unable to obtain sufficient, competent evidence upon which to base an audit opinion, the auditor should withdraw from the engagement.

INTERNAL CONTROL CASE: WATERWORKS, INC.

Because Scott Jordan is conducting his tenth audit of WaterWorks, Inc., he has extensive previous knowledge of their internal control. Based on some limited inquiry of client personnel, inspection of WaterWorks, Inc.'s documents, and observation of their activities, he concludes that WaterWorks has continued to place important control policies in operation and that these policies should be effective in preventing or detecting misstatements. Since his preliminary audit strategy for accounts receivable and property, plant and equipment is based on the nature of the account balances, he decides that these preliminary strategies are still appropriate.

Scott's understanding of the components of WaterWorks' internal control has identified two potential types of misstatements with respect to the two accounts he is examining (accounts receivable and property, plant and equipment):

Property, plant and equipment: The balance in property, plant and equipment may not be reduced for items of property, plant and equipment disposed during the period (the CO assertion)

Accounts receivable: Fictitious sales could be recorded in the accounting records (the EO assertion).

In order to address these potential misstatements, Scott has identified the following control activities:

Property, plant and equipment: Client personnel periodically reconcile items in the property ledger with items located at the client's premises.

Accounts receivable: Sales Invoices are prepared based on a Shipping Document that represents a *bona fide* shipment of inventory.

Because Scott has selected the reliance approach for accounts receivable, he performed some limited tests of controls of the operating effectiveness of this control. In contrast, since Scott utilized the substantive approach for property, plant and equipment, no tests of controls were performed.

CHAPTER CHECKPOINTS

5-19. What are the major steps in the auditor's study of internal control?

5-20. What are the two major preliminary audit strategies that can be used by the auditor? When would each type of strategy be most appropriate?

5-21. What are the objectives of obtaining an understanding of the components of internal control?

5-22. What methods can be used by the auditor to obtain an understanding of the components of internal control?

Documenting the Understanding of Internal Control

Once the auditor has obtained an understanding of the components of internal control (as discussed in the previous step), he or she is required to document the understanding. This documentation is required regardless of whether the reliance or substantive approach is to be utilized. While *SAS No. 55* does not require any specific form of documentation, the type of documentation used by the auditor will be influenced by the size of the client and complexity of its internal control. In general, as the client's size and complexity of internal control increases, the complexity of the auditor's documentation should also increase. By documenting his or her understanding of the components of the internal control, the auditor provides answers to questions such as:

- ▶ How are transactions initiated?
- ▶ What documents are prepared to support transactions?
- ▶ What individuals or departments are involved with processing transactions?
- ▶ What is the ultimate disposition of documents?
- ▶ What types of control policies are implemented for transactions?

In documenting the understanding of internal control, three basic methods may be used, either alone or in combination. These methods are a narrative, an internal control questionnaire, and a flowchart. The **narrative** is a written description of the client's internal control prepared by the auditor. In the narrative, the auditor describes any policies and procedures that exist as well as any weaknesses noted in the client's internal control. Although the narrative may be fairly easy for the auditor to prepare, it is difficult for persons other than the auditor to quickly gain an overall understanding of the organization's internal control by reviewing this description. In addition, narratives are more difficult to interpret for clients having larger, more complex internal controls. However, a narrative may provide an effective supplement for other forms of documentation, especially flowcharts.

As its name implies, the **internal control questionnaire** is a series of questions used by the auditor to evaluate the client's internal control. Standardized internal control questionnaires are prepared which require the auditor to answer specific questions about the client's internal control. The answers to these questions allow the auditor to identify: (1) important control policies that have been implemented by the client (internal control strengths), and (2) important control policies that are not implemented by the client (internal control weaknesses). The primary advantage of using an internal control questionnaire is that pre-established questions help ensure that the auditor does not overlook a particular area or important control policies and procedures related to that area. However, like the narrative description, an internal control questionnaire does not permit persons other than the auditor to quickly gain an overall understanding of the client's internal control.

A third way to document a client's internal control is through the use of **flowcharts**. Flowcharts are schematic drawings using established symbols to illustrate the documents and control policies that exist in an internal control. The primary advantage of using a flowchart to document a client's internal control is that flowcharts allow a person who did not assist in their preparation to obtain a relatively clear understanding of the client's internal control. However, the use of flowcharts does have some disadvantages. In some cases, flowcharts can be relatively difficult and time-consuming to prepare, compared to the narrative and internal control questionnaire. In addition, unlike the internal control questionnaire, flowcharts are prepared "from scratch"; as a result, the auditor may unintentionally forget to document his or her understanding of important control polices and procedures. A summary of important flowcharting symbols is provided in Figure 5-6.

To illustrate the use of these three methods of documentation, assume that the auditor's understanding of components of a portion of his client's internal control revealed the following series of events:

1. The organization receives an order from a customer.
2. If the customer is an existing customer, his or her order is checked against their credit limit. If the customer is a new customer, a general credit check is conducted.
3. If the credit check in (2) is favorable, three copies of a prenumbered Sales Order are prepared. One is sent to the customer, one is sent to the Shipping Department, and one is filed in the Credit Department.
4. If the credit check in (2) is unfavorable, two copies of a notification are prepared. One is sent to the customer and one is filed in the Credit Department.

Figure 5-7 summarizes how the auditor might document this internal control using the three methods discussed above.

**INTERNAL CONTROL CASE:
WATERWORKS, INC.**

Scott Jordan documented his understanding of WaterWorks' internal control over accounts receivable through the use of the flowchart method because of the large number of transactions involved with accounts receivable as well as the complexity of controls related to this area. Internal control over property, plant and equipment was documented through the use of the narrative method, since the processing of these transactions is relatively simple.

◻ Making an Initial Assessment of Control Risk

Once the auditor has gained an understanding of the components of the client's internal control and documented this understanding (through the use of narratives, internal control questionnaires, and/or flowcharts), he or she must now make an initial assessment of control risk. Recall that control risk is the risk that "... a material misstatement that could occur in **an assertion** will not be prevented or detected on a timely basis by the client's internal control policies or procedures" [emphasis added].[19] Thus, if the auditor believes that a client's internal control is relatively effective in preventing and detecting material misstatements, he or she will assess the control risk at a relatively low level. If, on the other hand, internal control is relatively ineffective in preventing and detecting misstatements, he or she will assess control risk at higher levels.

---

[19] American Institute of Certified Public Accountants (AICPA), *Statement on Auditing Standards No. 55*, "Internal Control Structure in a Financial Statement Audit" (New York: AICPA, 1988, AU 319.46).

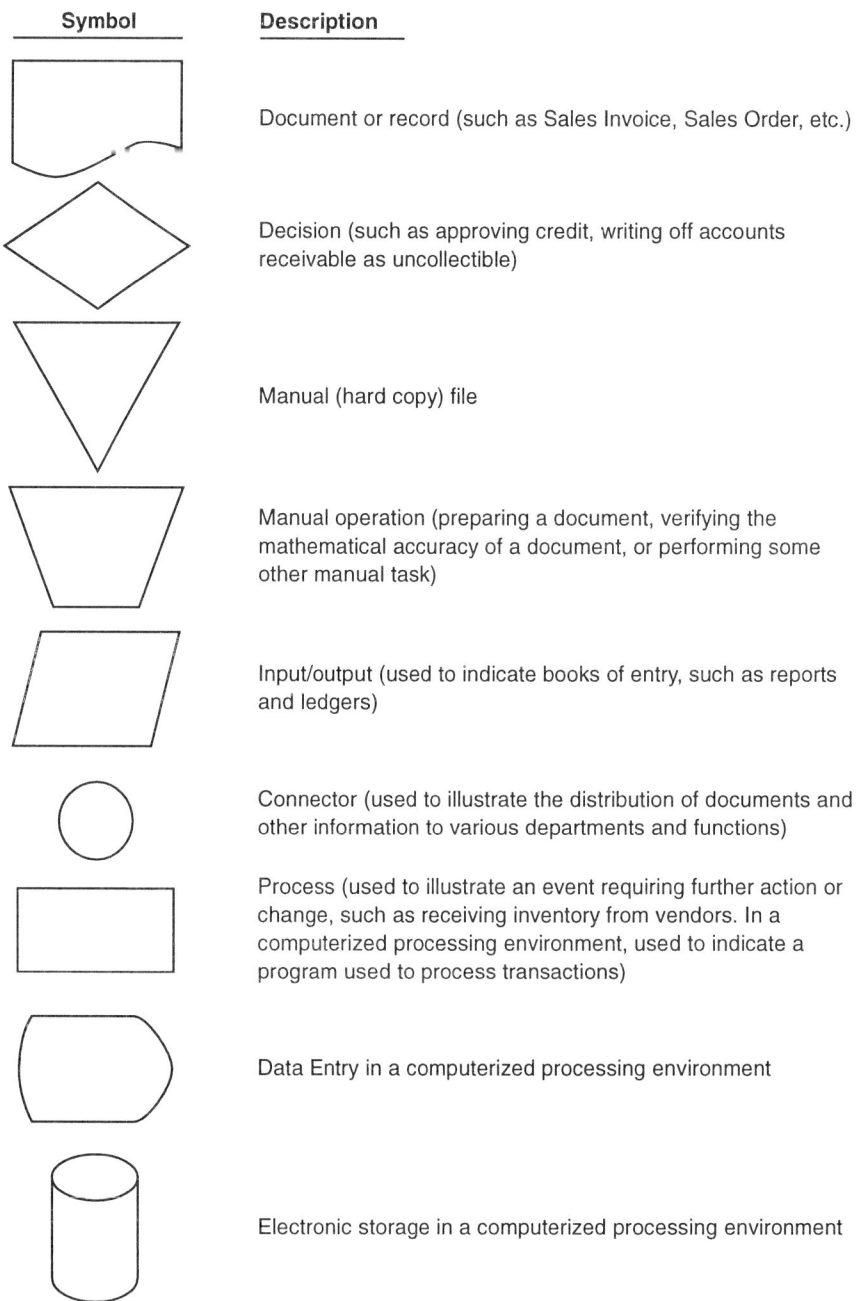

Figure 5-6: *Standard Flowchart Symbols*

NARRATIVE

Upon receipt of an order from a customer, a credit check is performed. If the sale to the customer is approved, three copies of a Sales Order are prepared. Two of the copies are distributed to the customer and the Shipping Department; the third copy is filed in the Credit Department. If the sale to the customer is not approved, two copies of a notification are prepared. These copies are (1) sent to the customer and (2) filed in the Credit Department.

INTERNAL CONTROL QUESTIONNAIRE

Control	Yes	No	N/A	Comments
1. Are credit checks performed prior to making sales on account?	X			Existing customers are checked against credit limits; a general credit check is made for new customers
2. Are prenumbered Sales Orders prepared to evidence authorized sales?	X			Copies are provided to customer, Shipping Department, and kept on file in the Credit Department
3. Are customers whose credit is denied notified of this denial in writing?	X			An additional copy of the notification is filed in the Credit Department

Figure 5-7: *Methods of Documenting Internal Control*

Notice from the definition of control risk that the auditor assesses control risk on an assertion-by-assertion basis; control risk can be assessed separately for each assertion. For example, if the client has effective internal control policies relating to the use of prenumbered documentation to provide evidence of transactions, the auditor would assess control risk for the EO and CO assertions at low levels. In contrast, if that same client does not implement control policies or procedures that affect whether transactions are recorded at the proper dollar amounts, control risk would be assessed at high levels for the VA assertion.

Making an assessment of control risk involves the following three major steps:

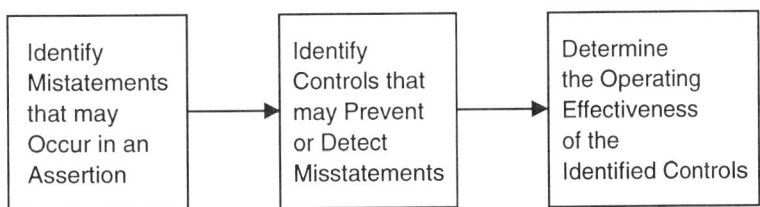

As noted earlier, the first two steps are required to be performed as the auditor obtains an understanding of the components of the client's internal control. In addition, the auditor **may** choose to evaluate the operating effectiveness of controls in this stage of his or her study of internal control.

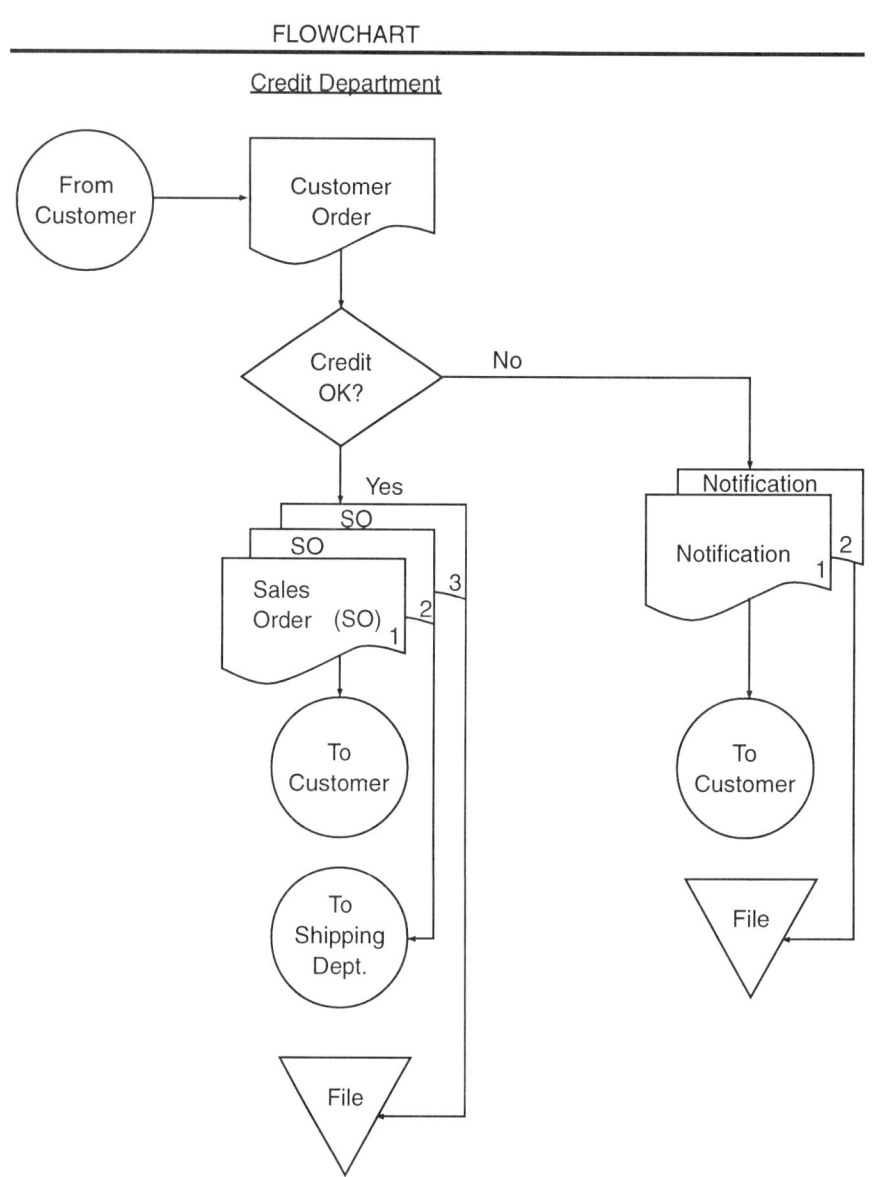

Figure 5-7: *Methods of Documenting Internal Control (continued)*

Alternatively, the operating effectiveness of controls can be evaluated in a later stage of the auditor's study of internal control, as noted in the following section.

For purposes of our discussion, the auditor's initial assessment of control risk can be thought of at one of two levels: the maximum level (100 percent) or less than the maximum level.

Assessing Control Risk at Maximum. Recall that control risk is assessed at the maximum level if one of the following is noted:

1. Important control policies related to the assertion do not exist
2. Control policies are not effective in preventing or detecting misstatements related to the assertion
3. It is not cost-efficient to examine the operating effectiveness of control policies

As shown in Figure 5-5, if the auditor's preliminary audit strategy is the substantive approach and he or she does not perform any tests of the operating effectiveness of internal control, the auditor will assess control risk at the maximum level. Also, while not shown in Figure 5-5, if the auditor initially selects the reliance approach as his or her preliminary audit strategy and tests of the operating effectiveness of internal controls indicate that control policies and procedures are not operating effectively in preventing or detecting misstatements related to the assertion being examined, the auditor may choose to assess control risk at the maximum level.

Assessing Control Risk at Less than the Maximum. To assess control risk at below the maximum level, the auditor is required to:

1. Identify specific control polices and procedures designed to prevent or detect material misstatements in an assertion
2. Perform tests of controls on the operating effectiveness of these control policies and procedures

Recall that the major task in obtaining an understanding of the components of internal control is to identify control policies and procedures that may be relied upon to prevent or detect misstatements. If the auditor performs tests of the operating effectiveness of these policies or procedures during this stage, he or she may form an assessment of control risk at less than the maximum level. While the assessed level of control risk is a matter of audit judgment, control risk is ordinarily assessed at lower levels in cases where: (1) control policies and procedures are operating more effectively, and (2) control policies and procedures have been tested more extensively. As shown in Figure 5-5, control risk could be assessed at less than the maximum level under either the reliance or substantive approach as long as tests of the operating effectiveness of internal control were performed by the auditor.

> **INTERNAL CONTROL CASE:**
> **WATERWORKS, INC.**
>
> Recall that Scott Jordan selected the substantive approach for his examination of property, plant and equipment and the reliance approach for his examination of accounts receivable. His initial assessments of control risk were as follows:
>
> **Property, plant and equipment:** Scott did not perform tests of controls in obtaining an understanding of the components of internal control, since he did not feel that the reliance approach was cost-efficient. As a result, his initial assessment of control risk for the EO assertion for property, plant and equipment was at the maximum level.
>
> **Accounts receivable:** Scott performed relatively extensive tests of controls in obtaining an understanding of the components of internal control over accounts receivable transactions. These tests of controls indicated that the control policies and procedures were operating effectively; in fact, only one instance was noted where a Shipping Document could not be located to support a Sales Invoice. As a result, Scott's initial assessment of control risk for the EO assertion for accounts receivable was at moderate levels.

> **CHAPTER CHECKPOINTS**
>
> 5-23. What are three methods used by auditors to document their understanding of the components of internal control? What are some of the advantages and disadvantages of each method?
>
> 5-24. What are the major steps involved in assessing control risk? During what stage of the auditor's study of internal control would these steps be performed?
>
> 5-25. When would auditors assess control risk at the maximum level? At less than the maximum level?

◻ Obtaining an Additional Reduction in Control Risk

As noted above, the auditor's initial assessment of control risk is based upon information regarding the operating effectiveness of the client's internal control obtained during his or her understanding of the components of internal control. At this point, the auditor will have assessed control risk at either the maximum level (100 percent) or at some level below maximum based on evidence obtained as he or she obtained an understanding of the components of internal control. If the decision is to assess control risk at less than the maximum, the auditor should then consider whether a further reduction in control risk can be obtained. In doing so, the auditor evaluates the following factors:

1. Can sufficient evidence be obtained to justify a reduction in the level of control risk?
2. Is it cost-efficient to perform tests of controls to reduce control risk?

If the answer to either of the above questions is no, the auditor's final assessment of control risk would be identical to the initial assessment of control risk. As shown in Figure 5-5, the auditor would then document his or her assessment of control risk without performing additional tests of controls. If, however, the auditor decides that a further reduction in control risk may be obtained, additional tests of controls to support this level of control risk would be performed. In making the decision about whether to perform additional tests of controls, the auditor considers a trade-off between the time needed to perform additional tests of controls and the time savings resulting from performing less extensive substantive tests, as follows:

- ▶ If the time required to perform additional tests of controls is **less than** the time savings in substantive tests, perform additional tests of controls
- ▶ If the time required to perform additional tests of controls is **greater than** the time savings in substantive tests, do not perform additional tests of controls

Performing additional tests of controls is discussed in the remainder of this section.

Performing Tests of Controls. Earlier, we described the basic steps in assessing control risk as follows:

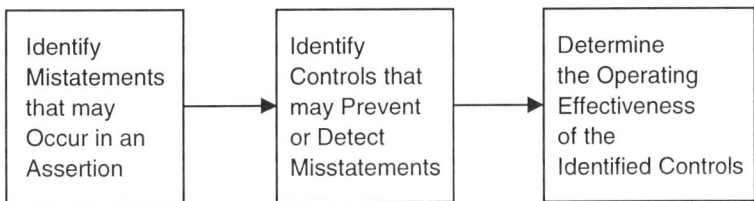

Performing tests of controls is most closely related to determining the operating effectiveness of internal controls. In performing tests of controls, it is important to note that the auditor will only test the operating effectiveness of controls that have been identified that may prevent or detect misstatements. That is, the auditor will only test controls that he or she plans to rely upon. These controls are ordinarily identified as the auditor obtains an understanding of the components of the client's internal control.

To be operating effectively, a control policy or procedure should be implemented consistently throughout a period of time by the person or person(s) who have responsibility for implementing that policy or procedure. For example, assume that the client has placed a control policy in operation that requires sales on account to be authorized by the Credit Manager. As evidence of this authorization, the Credit Manager is required to prepare a document known as a Sales Order. The following situations may represent instances where this control policy is not operating effectively (known as **deviations** or **exceptions**):

1. Sales made on account not authorized through a Sales Order.
2. Sales made on account authorized by a Sales Order prepared by an employee other than the Credit Manager.

Nature of Tests of Controls. Methods of performing tests of controls include: (1) inquiry of client personnel, (2) inspection of client documents and records, (3) observation of client activities, and (4) reperformance of control policies and procedures. These tests are discussed in the following paragraphs.

Inquiry of Client Personnel. Inquiry of client personnel consists of the auditor obtaining oral evidence regarding the functioning of one or more internal control policies or procedures. For example, a common internal control policy is the requirement that invoices received from vendors for purchases made on account are mathematically verified by the Accounts Payable Department prior to being approved for payment. Through inquiry, the auditor can determine that the Accounts Payable Department does indeed verify all invoices in this manner.

One problem with inquiry is that client personnel may not understand the nature of the auditor's inquiries or may understand the nature of the inquiries but intentionally respond in a misleading manner. However, in cases where a control policy or procedure does not leave a documentary trail (such as segregation of duties), the auditor may be limited to utilizing inquiries as evidence of the operating effectiveness of internal controls.

Inspection of Client Documents and Records. In an effective internal control, a trail of documentary evidence exists with respect to many of the necessary control policies and procedures. In the above example, a more reliable form of evidence regarding the operating effectiveness of the control policy that requires the Accounts Payable Department to mathematically verify invoices would be inspecting copies of the Vendor Invoices for initials or some other form of indication that this verification was performed.

Observation of Client Activities. The auditor uses observation to evaluate internal control policies and procedures that do not operate through the preparation of documents or other written forms of evidence. For example, consider the control activity of segregation of duties. In this case, the auditor can examine written job descriptions to determine what functions various individuals should be performing. However, to gather evidence about the actual functioning of this control procedure, the auditor would observe the duties performed by individuals to ascertain that no one individual is performing incompatible duties (custody of asset, recording of the transaction, and/or authorization of the transaction).

Reperformance. In many instances, the most effective way for the auditor to evaluate a control policy or procedure is to actually reperform this policy or procedure. Continuing with our earlier example, assume that the auditor is interested in verifying the operating effectiveness of a control policy that the Accounts Payable Department mathematically verify Vendors' Invoices prior to payment. One method of testing the operating effectiveness of this control is to reperform the mathematical verification. If no problems are noted, the auditor would conclude that the control is operating effectively. In contrast, if the auditor is unable to verify the mathematical accuracy of the Vendors' Invoices, he or she would conclude that the control policy was not operating effectively, since these errors should have been detected by the Accounts Payable Department.

When reperforming controls in the above manner, the auditor may also be gathering evidence regarding the recording of transactions affected by those controls. For example, verifying the mathematical accuracy of Vendors' Invoices would allow the auditor to conclude that these invoices have been recorded at the proper dollar amount. Thus, this type of test can be viewed as a form of substantive test. Tests that provide evidence about the operation of a control policy (test of controls) and fairness of an account balance or class of transactions (substantive tests) are known as **dual-purpose tests**.

Extent of Tests of Controls. Obviously, the auditor cannot possibly examine all occurrences of an internal control policy or procedure. In Chapter 7, the manner in which the auditor determines the number of items to be examined is discussed. Along these lines, *SAS No. 55* notes a basic relationship between the assessment of control risk and the amount of evidence required. For lower assessments of control risk, the auditor must obtain more extensive evidence regarding the operating effectiveness of the internal control. The need to obtain more extensive evidence results in the auditor: (1) examining a larger number of different control policies and procedures, and (2) performing more extensive tests of each control policy and procedure. For higher assessed levels of control risk, the opposite relationships would be noted.

Timing of Tests of Controls. In order to spread their work load more evenly throughout the year, many auditors perform procedures (including tests of controls) prior to year-end. These procedures are known as **interim tests**. Both tests of controls and substantive tests can be performed during an interim period. When tests of controls are conducted during the interim work, additional testing may or may not be done at year-end. In determining whether or not to test the remaining period, *SAS No. 55* suggests that the auditor consider:

1. The significance of the assertion involved.
2. The degree to which the design and operation of those policies and procedures were evaluated.
3. The results of the tests of controls.
4. The length of the remaining period.[20]

In general, the auditor should consider testing the remaining period if: (1) assertions are more significant, (2) the policies and procedures have been evaluated to a lesser extent, (3) the results of tests of controls are less conclusive, and (4) the length of the remaining period is longer.

Example: Tests of Controls. Figure 5-8 illustrates selected sample tests of controls that could be performed for control activities related to credit sales made by a organization to its customers. At this point, you should not concern yourself with the specific control activities and tests of controls performed for credit sales transactions, as these will be the focus of a subsequent chapter. Three important points should be emphasized. First, tests of controls are primarily performed on the control activities identified by *SAS No. 78*. Second, the auditor's tests of controls normally consist of one of four types of procedures: observation, inquiry, reperformance, or inspection of documents and records. Third, more than one type of method could be used to test controls.

---

[20] American Institute of Certified Public Accountants (AICPA), *Statement on Auditing Standards No. 55*, "Internal Control Structure in a Financial Statement Audit" (New York: AICPA, 1988, AU 319.55).

Control Activity	Example	Test of Controls
Performance Reviews	Comparing actual sales activity to budgeted sales activity (by product)	Inspect Reports (Documents) Inquiry
Information Processing (Authorization)	Sales made to customers on account are authorized	Inspect Sales Orders (Documents)
Information Processing (Documents)	Sales are recorded using prenumbered Sales Invoices	Inspect Sales Invoices (Documents)
Information Processing (Independent Checks)	Sales Invoices are mathematically verified by client personnel	Inspect Sales Invoices (Documents) Reperformance
Physical Controls	Inventory is kept in a physically-secure location with restricted access by organization personnel	Observation Inquiry
Segregation of Duties	Duties of authorizing transactions, recording transactions, and maintaining custody of the assets have been properly segregated	Observation Inquiry

Figure 5-8: *Sample Tests of Controls*

INTERNAL CONTROL CASE: WATERWORKS, INC.

Scott Jordan carefully considered his initial control risk assessments for property, plant and equipment (maximum control risk) and accounts receivable (moderate control risk). Because Scott selected the substantive approach for property, plant and equipment and assessed control risk at the maximum level, he did not consider performing additional tests of controls.

In contrast, the large number of accounts receivable transactions offered Scott an opportunity to improve the overall efficiency of his audit. If control risk stayed at moderate levels, Scott would need to send accounts receivable confirmations to approximately 60 of WaterWorks' customers; however, by reducing the assessment of control risk to "low", the number of customer accounts confirmed could be reduced to 25. Scott estimated that this would save him approximately ten hours of substantive tests. To reduce the assessment of control risk from "moderate" to "low", Scott would need to verify Shipping Documents for 50 additional Sales Invoices. Scott felt that doing so would take him approximately two hours. As a result, Scott decided to perform additional tests of controls, since doing so would result in a net savings of eight hours (10 hours − 2 hours = 8 hours).

CHAPTER CHECKPOINTS

5-26. What are tests of controls? When should the auditor perform additional tests of controls?

5-27. What are the four major types of tests of controls? Give an example of each type.

5-28. Define interim tests. List some factors that influence the auditor's decision to test controls during the period between the interim date and year-end.

◻ Making a Final Assessment of Control Risk

As shown in Figure 5-5, once the tests of controls have been performed by the auditor, she or he assesses the level of control risk. The assessment is based on the operating effectiveness of the client's internal control policies and procedures, as determined by the additional tests of controls performed by the auditor. In making this assessment, the auditor considers the following basic relationship:

As the operating effectiveness of the client's control policies and procedures is greater, the auditor should assess control risk at lower levels (and *vice versa*).

In evaluating the operating effectiveness of a control policy or procedure, the auditor compares the frequency with which a control policy is not operating effectively (known as the **deviation rate** or **exception rate**) to some allowable rate. Based on this comparison, the auditor will make an evaluation about the operating effectiveness of internal control and, ultimately, control risk. Based on the additional tests of controls, the auditor's final assessed level of control risk can either be lower, the same, or higher than his or her initial assessment, depending upon the results of the additional tests of controls. This process is discussed further in Chapter 7 of this text.

INTERNAL CONTROL CASE:
WATERWORKS, INC.

Scott Jordan examined the additional Sales Invoices and found Shipping Documents to support all of these Sales Invoices. As a result, his final assessment of control risk for accounts receivable (the EO assertion) was changed from "moderate" to "low."

As noted earlier, because Scott assessed control risk at the "maximum" level for the CO assertion for property, plant and equipment, he did not perform additional tests of controls. Thus, the final assessment of control risk is the same as the initial assessment ("maximum").

◻ Documenting Control Risk Assessments

After evaluating the results of the tests of controls and making the final assessment of control risk, the auditor is required to document his or her control risk assessment. The documentation requirements of *SAS No. 55* are summarized below:

	Document Level of Control Risk?	Document Basis for Assessment?
Assess Control Risk at Maximum Level	Yes	No
Assess Control Risk at Less than Maximum Level	Yes	Yes

As shown above, the auditor is required to document the assessed level of control risk in all cases. However, documentation about the basis for the control risk assessment (*i.e.*, why is control risk assessed at a given level) is only required when control risk is assessed at less than the maximum level. Information that would be documented as part of this latter requirement includes:

▶ The control policies or procedures relied upon by the auditor

▶ The fact that the auditor tested the operating effectiveness of these control policies and procedures.

▶ The results of the auditor's tests of controls

**INTERNAL CONTROL CASE:
WATERWORKS, INC.**

Scott Jordan's final assessments of control risk for property, plant and equipment and accounts receivable were "maximum" and "low", respectively. For property, plant and equipment, Scott documented that control risk was assessed at the maximum level. No explanation as to why control risk was assessed at the maximum level is needed.

For accounts receivable, Scott documented the "low" level of control risk. In addition, he provided the following information in his workpapers:

1. The low level of control risk was based on WaterWorks' use of Shipping Documents in preparing Sales Invoices.

2. Scott examined 84 Sales Invoices and noted only one situation where a Shipping Document could not be located.

◻ Using the Audit Risk Model to Determine the Necessary Level of Detection Risk

Based on the audit risk model introduced in Chapter 4 (and summarized at the beginning of this chapter), the auditor is now able to determine the necessary level of detection risk to limit audit risk to acceptable levels. In the planning stages of the audit, the auditor develops a planned level of substantive tests that are reflected in his or her preliminary audit strategy (either the substantive or reliance approach). In using the audit risk model, the auditor determines whether the assessment of control risk allows him or her to support the planned level of substantive testing. Based on the results of assessing control risk, one of the three following possibilities exists:

1. **Final Control Risk is Less than Planned Control Risk**: The auditor would need to reduce the planned effectiveness of his or her substantive tests.
2. **Final Control Risk is Equal to Planned Control Risk**: The auditor would not modify the planned effectiveness of his or her substantive tests.
3. **Final Control Risk is Greater than Planned Control Risk**: The auditor would need to increase the planned effectiveness of his or her substantive tests.

The above information is consistent with the basic relationship between internal control (control risk) and substantive tests (detection risk) noted earlier: **As internal control is more effective (lower control risk), the auditor can perform less effective substantive tests (higher detection risk).** The planned effectiveness of substantive tests relates to the nature, timing, and extent of substantive tests and will be discussed in more detail in the following chapter.

**INTERNAL CONTROL CASE:
WATERWORKS, INC.**

Scott developed planned substantive tests based on expected control risk assessments of maximum (for property, plant and equipment) and moderate (for accounts receivable). Based on the final assessments of control risk, Scott would modify these planned substantive tests as follows:

Property, plant and equipment: No modification
Accounts Receivable: Reduce the planned effectiveness of substantive tests.

Summary: The Auditor's Study of Internal Control

Figure 5-9 summarizes the major steps in the auditor's study of internal control. In addition, this figure identifies important differences between the use of the substantive and reliance approaches.

OTHER ISSUES RELATED TO INTERNAL CONTROL

Communicating Internal Control Deficiencies

As noted throughout this chapter, the primary reason for the auditor's study and evaluation of internal control is to determine the necessary level of detection risk (the nature, timing, and extent of the auditor's substantive tests). During the study of internal control, the auditor may notice deficiencies in the client's internal control (such as the absence of important control activities). Two major types

Step	Description	Control Risk Assessed at Maximum	Control Risk Assessed at Less than Maximum
1	Identifying a Preliminary Audit Strategy	Substantive Approach	Reliance Approach
2	Obtaining an Understanding of the Components of Internal Control	Focus on four components other than control activities Understand the design of controls and identify controls placed in operation Ordinarily do not perform extensive tests of operating effectiveness	Obtain an understanding of all five components of internal control Understand the design of controls and identify controls placed in operation Ordinarily will perform tests of operating effectiveness
3	Documenting the Understanding of Internal Control	Use narratives, flowcharts, and/or internal control questionnaires	Use narratives, flowcharts, and/or internal control questionnaires
4	Making an Initial Assessment of Control Risk	Assess at maximum	Assess at less than maximum
5	Obtaining an Additional Reduction in Control Risk	Does not apply (it would not be cost-efficient to perform additional tests of controls)	More likely to be cost-efficient to perform additional tests of controls
6	Making a Final Assessment of Control Risk	Does not apply (same as initial assessment of control risk)	Based on the results of additional tests of controls (if performed)
7	Documenting Control Risk Assessments	Document the level of control risk	Document both the level of control risk and the basis for that assessment
8	Using the Audit Risk Model to Determine the Necessary Level of Detection Risk	Lower levels of detection risk (more effective substantive tests)	Higher levels of detection risk (less effective substantive tests)

Figure 5-9: *Major Steps in the Auditor's Study of Internal Control (the Substantive and Reliance Approaches)*

of deficiencies in internal control are identified by *Statement on Auditing Standards No. 60*[21] (*SAS No. 60*). **Reportable conditions** are deficiencies in the design or operation of internal controls that affect the organization's ability to record, process, summarize, and report financial data. A **material weakness** in internal control is a more serious reportable condition that has a high likelihood of resulting in the failure of employees to detect material misstatements as they perform their assigned functions.

In general, the difference between a material weakness and a reportable condition is the severity of the internal control deficiency and its ultimate effect on the fairness of the organization's financial statements. Material weaknesses represent deficiencies that may ultimately result in material financial statement misstatements; reportable conditions do not currently pose this threat. However, it is important to note that a reportable condition may eventually worsen and become a material weakness in a future period. The relative severity of these two internal control deficiencies is illustrated below:

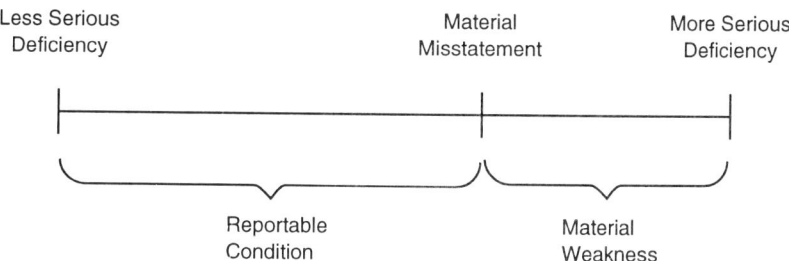

SAS No. 60 requires that all reportable conditions and material weaknesses noted during the audit examination be communicated to the client's audit committee. If the client does not have an audit committee, these deficiencies should be communicated to individuals with a level of authority and responsibility equivalent to an audit committee. This communication of internal control deficiencies may be either oral or written. If deficiencies are communicated to the client orally, *SAS No. 60* notes that the auditor should document this communication in the workpapers.

In most instances, the auditor will communicate internal control deficiencies to the client in writing. When communicated in writing, the auditor will prepare a report to the client that discusses any deficiencies in internal control. The communication of internal control deficiencies are discussed in Chapter 16 of this text.

◻ Reporting on Internal Control

An independent auditor may study an organization's internal control for reasons other than determining the nature, timing, and extent of his or her substantive tests. For example, in some cases, the client may wish to communicate to owners, regulators, creditors, or shareholders that they have established an effective internal control. If this communication is made in the form of a written statement, they may wish to have an auditor issue an opinion on their written statement about the

---

[21] American Institute of Certified Public Accountants (AICPA), *Statement on Auditing Standards No. 60*, "Communication of Internal Control Structure Related Matters Noted in an Audit" (New York: AICPA, 1988, AU 325).

effectiveness of their internal control. If so, the auditor would perform a separate engagement to examine internal control and provide an opinion on the fairness of management's statement about its internal control. This type of engagement is known as reporting on management's "assertion" (or statement) about its internal control and is discussed in further detail in Chapter 19 of this text.

CHAPTER CHECKPOINTS

5-29. What information should be documented by the auditor when control risk is assessed at the maximum level? At less than the maximum level?

5-30. What is the basic relationship between the effectiveness of internal control and the necessary effectiveness of the auditor's substantive tests?

5-31. Define reportable conditions and material weaknesses. What is the auditor's responsibility with respect to communicating these items to the client?

SUMMARY OF KEY POINTS

1. Internal control is a process designed to provide the organization with reasonable assurance of achieving objectives related to the reliability of financial reporting, effectiveness and efficiency of operations, and compliance with applicable laws and regulations. The five major components of internal control are the control environment, risk assessment, control activities, information and communication, and monitoring.

2. The first two components of internal control are the control environment and risk assessment. The control environment reflects the control consciousness of the organization and management's attitude about the importance of internal control. Risk assessment is the process through which risks related to the objectives of internal control are identified, analyzed, and managed.

3. Based on the risk assessment process, the organization establishes control activities (the third component of internal control). Control activities represent the actual internal control policies and procedures implemented to achieve the objectives of internal control. Four major categories of control activities include: (1) performance review controls, (2) information processing controls (both general controls and application controls), (3) physical controls, and (4) segregation of duties controls.

4. The final two components of internal control are information and communication and monitoring. The information and communication component of internal control is concerned with identifying, summarizing, and communicating information throughout the organization to allow its employees to conduct their responsibilities. Monitoring is the process through which the quality of internal control is evaluated by assessing the design and operation of controls and taking any necessary corrective actions to improve the quality of internal control.

5. The primary reason for the auditor's study of internal control is to determine the nature, timing, and extent of substantive tests. The auditor's study of internal control includes the following steps: (1) identifying a preliminary audit strategy, (2) understanding the components of internal control, (3) documenting the understanding of internal control, (4) making an initial assessment of control risk, (5) obtaining an additional reduction in control risk, (6) making a final assessment of control risk, (7) documenting control risk assessments, and (8) using the audit risk model to determine the necessary level of detection risk.

6. In studying internal control, the auditor begins by selecting one of two preliminary audit strategies: the reliance approach or the substantive approach. The auditor then obtains an understanding of the components of internal control and documents this understanding using either narratives, internal control questionnaires, or flowcharts. The purpose of obtaining an understanding of the components of internal control is to: (1) identify potential misstatements that may occur, (2) consider factors that may affect the risk of misstatement, and (3) design substantive tests.

7. Next, the auditor forms an initial assessment of control risk. The initial assessment of control risk is based on the auditor's preliminary audit strategy as well as any tests of operating effectiveness performed as he or she obtains an understanding of the components of internal control. At this point, control risk assessments can be thought of at one of two levels: maximum (or 100 percent) or less than the maximum (less than 100 percent).

8. After making the preliminary assessment of control risk, the auditor considers performing additional tests of controls to obtain a further reduction in control risk. Tests of controls are tests directed toward the operating effectiveness of internal control policies or procedures. The primary types of tests of controls are: (1) inquiry of client personnel, (2) inspection of client documents and records, (3) observation of client activities, and (4) reperformance of control policies and procedures.

9. The remaining steps in the study of internal control are: (1) making a final assessment of control risk, (2) documenting control risk assessments, and (3) using the audit risk model to determine the necessary level of detection risk. The necessary level of detection risk represents the nature, timing, and extent of the auditor's substantive tests.

10. As part of the study of internal control, the auditor may note deficiencies in the client's internal controls. If these deficiencies represent reportable conditions or material weaknesses, they must be communicated to the client's audit committee (or equivalent). This communication can either be oral or written.

GLOSSARY

Accounting System. The accounting system includes all methods and records that: (1) identify and record all valid transactions, (2) properly classify transactions, (3) record transactions at the proper monetary amounts, (4) record transactions in the proper accounting period, and (5) properly present transactions and related disclosures in the financial statements.

Application Controls. Control activities designed to enhance the processing and recording of individual transactions affecting a specific account balance or class of transactions. Three common types of application controls relate to authorization of transactions, the use of adequate documents and records, and independent checks on performance.

Control Activities. The policies and procedures that help ensure that the objectives of internal control are achieved. The four categories of control activities are: (1) performance review controls, (2) information processing controls, (3) physical controls, and (4) segregation of duties controls.

Control Environment. A component of internal control that reflects the control consciousness of the organization and management's attitude about the importance of internal control. The control environment includes such factors as: (1) high levels of integrity and ethical values, (2) commitment to competence, (3) participation of the Board of Directors or audit committee, (4) management's philosophy and operating style, (5) organizational structure, (6) assignment of authority and responsibility, and (7) human resource policies and practices.

Control Risk. The risk that a material misstatement in an assertion will not be prevented or detected on a timely basis by the organization's internal control policies and procedures.

Dual-Purpose Tests. Tests performed by the auditor that provide evidence relating to both the operating effectiveness of an internal control policy or procedure (tests of controls) and the fairness of an account balance or class of transactions (substantive tests).

Flowchart. A schematic drawing using symbols that is prepared by the auditor to document his or her understanding of the components of internal control.

General Controls. Control activities that affect the overall processing of most (or all) of the transactions processed by the organization. Examples of general controls include controls over data center operations, system software acquisition and maintenance, access to system hardware and software, and application system development and maintenance.

Information and Communication. The component of internal control concerned with identifying, summarizing, and communicating information throughout the organization to allow its employees to conduct their responsibilities.

Information Processing Controls. Controls implemented by the organization to verify the accuracy, completeness, and authorization of individual transactions. Two broad categories of information processing controls are general controls and application controls.

Information System. See accounting system.

Interim Tests. Procedures performed by the auditor prior to year-end. Interim tests can be used in performing tests of controls or substantive tests.

Internal Control. A process designed to provide the organization with reasonable assurance of achieving objectives related to the reliability of financial reporting, effectiveness and efficiency of operations, and compliance with applicable laws and regulations.

Internal Control Questionnaire. A series of pre-established questions used by the auditor to document his or her understanding of the components of internal control.

Material Weakness. A deficiency (reportable condition) in internal control so severe that a high likelihood exists that client employees will not detect material misstatements while performing their assigned duties.

Monitoring. The process that assesses the quality of internal control performance over time by assessing the design and operation of controls and taking any necessary corrective actions to improve the quality of internal control.

Narrative. A written description prepared by the auditor to document his or her understanding of the components of internal control.

Performance Review Controls. A type of control activity that evaluates organizational performance by comparing (1) actual performance against budgets, forecasts, and prior-period performance or (2) different sets of operating and financial data to one another.

Reasonable Assurance. A concept that recognizes that the cost of internal control should not exceed the benefits provided by that internal control.

Reliance Approach. A preliminary audit strategy that requires the auditor to make a more extensive study of internal control in return for performing less extensive substantive tests.

Reportable Condition. Deficiencies in the design or operation of internal controls that affect the organization's ability to record, process, summarize, and report financial data.

Risk Assessment. The process of identifying, analyzing, and managing risks related to the objectives of internal control.

Segregation of Duties Controls. These controls recognize that responsibilities related to the authorization of transactions, recording of transactions, and custody of the related assets should be performed by different individuals, functions, and/or departments.

Substantive Approach. A preliminary audit strategy in which the auditor makes a less extensive study of internal control in return for performing more extensive substantive tests.

Tests of Controls. Procedures performed by the auditor to verify the operating effectiveness of selected internal control policies and procedures. Types of tests of controls performed by the auditor include: (1) inquiry of client personnel, (2) inspection of client documents and records, (3) observation of client activities, and (4) reperformance of control policies and procedures.

Walk-Through. A method used to obtain an understanding of the components of internal control in which the auditor follows a transaction from its initiation to its ultimate recording in the accounts.

SUMMARY OF PROFESSIONAL PRONOUNCEMENTS

Statement on Auditing Standards No. 1, "Codification of Auditing Standards and Procedures" (New York: AICPA, 1972, AU 150.02).

Statement on Auditing Standards No. 55, "Consideration of the Internal Control Structure in a Financial Statement Audit" (New York: AICPA, 1988, AU 319).

Statement on Auditing Standards No. 60, "Communication of Internal Control Structure Related Matters Noted in an Audit" (New York: AICPA, 1988, AU 325).

Statement on Auditing Standards No. 78, "Consideration of Internal Control in a Financial Statement Audit: An Amendment to *SAS No. 55*" (New York: AICPA, 1995, AU 319).

Proposed Statement on Auditing Standards, "Amendment to *Statement on Auditing Standards No. 31*, 'Evidential Matter'" (New York: AICPA, May 20, 1996).

QUESTIONS AND PROBLEMS

5-32. Select the **best** answer for each of the following items:

1. When preparing a record of a client's internal control, the independent auditor sometimes uses a systems flowchart, which can best be described as a(n):

   a. Pictorial presentation of the flow of instructions in a client's internal computer system.
   b. Diagram that clearly indicates an organization's internal reporting structure.
   c. Graphic illustration of the flow of operations that is used to replace the auditor's internal control questionnaire
   d. Symbolic representation of a system or series of sequential processes.

2. Effective internal control in a small company that has an insufficient number of employees to permit proper division of responsibilities can best be enhanced by:

   a. Employment of temporary personnel to aid in the separation of duties.
   b. Direct participation by the owner of the business in the recordkeeping activities of the business.
   c. Engaging a CPA to perform monthly "write-up" work.
   d. Delegation of full, clear-cut responsibility to each employee for the functions assigned to each.

3. The independent auditor studies a client's internal control:

   a. For the primary purpose of issuing a management letter, which identifies ways in which the operating effectiveness of the company's internal control may be improved.
   b. Only if she or he intends to rely on the client's internal control to reduce her or his substantive testing.
   c. For the primary purpose of determining the nature, extent, and timing of her or his substantive tests.
   d. For the primary purpose of assisting management in evaluating the performance of its employees.

4. Which of the following factors is not a component of a company's control environment?

   a. Integrity and ethical values of client personnel.
   b. The company's accounting system.
   c. The existence of an audit committee comprised of outside directors.
   d. Management's philosophy and operating style.

5. As a part of understanding the components of internal control, an auditor is **not** required to:

   a. Consider factors that affect the risk of misstatement.
   b. Ascertain whether internal control polices and procedures have been placed in operation.
   c. Identify the types of potential misstatements that can occur.
   d. Obtain knowledge about the operating effectiveness of internal control.

6. In a GAAS audit, the auditor is required to:

   a. Perform tests of controls to evaluate the effectiveness of the entity's accounting system.
   b. Determine whether control activities are suitably designed to prevent or detect material misstatements.
   c. Document the understanding of internal control.
   d. Search for significant deficiencies in internal control.

7. All of the following are benefits an organization realizes from having an effective internal control except for:

   a. Adherence to the organization's prescribed procedures.
   b. Enhanced reliability of financial information for management decision-making.
   c. Improved safeguards over access to the organization's assets.
   d. Increased likelihood that the organization's activities are conducted in compliance with laws and regulations.
   e. All of the above represent benefits of an effective internal control.

8. In which of the following situations would the auditor be most likely to assess control risk at the maximum level?

   a. Control activities related to the assertion of interest appear to be effective in preventing or detecting misstatements.
   b. Performing substantive tests related to the assertion is relatively expensive compared to performing tests of controls.
   c. The client has not implemented important control activities related to the assertion of interest.
   d. The auditor performed limited tests of operating effectiveness of control activities during his or her understanding of the components of internal control.

9. Maintaining perpetual inventory records and periodically comparing physical inventories to those records is an example of which of the following types of control activities?

   a. Information processing controls.
   b. Performance reviews.
   c. Physical controls.
   d. Segregation of duties.

10. _____ is (are) the process of evaluating the quality of internal control over time.

   a. Control activities.
   b. Information processing.
   c. Monitoring.
   d. Risk assessment.

11. Which of the following is **not** considered to be an example of an information processing control under *SAS No. 78?*

   a. Documents and records.
   b. Independent checks.
   c. Proper authorization.
   d. Segregation of duties.
   e. All of the above are examples of information processing controls.

12. Comparing the actual performance of an individual or department to their expected performance (through the use of budgets, forecasts, or prior-period amounts) is an example of a(n):

   a. Control environment.
   b. Monitoring.
   c. Performance review.
   d. Risk assessment.

13. If the auditor decides to assess control risk at the maximum level, he or she would next:

   a. Document his or her understanding of the components of internal control.
   b. Document the assessment of control risk.
   c. Evaluate the need to perform additional tests of controls.
   d. Reevaluate his or her preliminary audit strategy.

14. All of the following are stages in the auditor's study of an organization's internal control except:

   a. Assessing the preliminary level of control risk.
   b. Determining the necessary level of detection risk.
   c. Designing the auditor's substantive testing procedures.
   d. Obtaining an understanding of the components of internal control.
   e. Performing tests of controls.

15. The auditor performs detailed tests of controls on selected internal control policies and procedures:

   a. In the preliminary stages of the audit to provide a measure of management's integrity.
   b. To corroborate the preliminary assessment of control risk.
   c. Only as part of a special engagement separate from the financial statement audit.
   d. Only after the completion of the year under audit.
   e. To determine whether the entity's financial statements are presented in conformity with GAAP.

16. The entity's _____ consists of the methods used to record, classify, summarize, and report the entity's transactions.

   a. accounting system.
   b. control activities.
   c. control environment.
   d. general controls.
   e. monitoring process.

17. Which of the following procedures is generally not used by the auditor in performing tests of controls?

   a. Analytical procedures.
   b. Inquiry.
   c. Observation.
   d. Reperformance.

18. During which of the following stages of the auditor's study and evaluation of internal control would a flowchart be prepared to document the entity's internal control?

   a. Selecting a preliminary audit strategy.
   b. Understanding the components of internal control.
   c. Documenting the understanding of internal control.
   d. Forming a preliminary assessment of control risk.
   e. Performing tests of controls.

19. When the auditor assesses control risk at less than the maximum level, the auditor is required to document the:

	Level of Control Risk	Basis for the Assessment
a.	Yes	Yes
b.	No	Yes
c.	Yes	No
d.	No	No

20. Which of the following deficiencies in internal control is the auditor required to communicate to the client's audit committee (or equivalent)?

	Reportable Conditions	Material Weaknesses
a.	Yes	Yes
b.	No	Yes
c.	Yes	No
d.	No	No

(Items 1 through 6 in 5-32; AICPA Adapted)

5-33. Respond to each of the following statements relating to internal control made by Mr. Knew, a staff accountant on his initial assignment:

   a. "Why should I study internal control? My job is to examine the financial statements for material errors, not provide the client with advice on how to improve its internal control."
   b. "I'm pretty certain that I don't want to rely on internal control during the audit. Thus, I plan to omit all of my planned work in studying internal control."
   c. "I didn't know that internal control affects the financial statements, operating effectiveness, and compliance with laws and regulations! Looks like I'll need to extend my work on internal control to consider all three of these objectives."

d. "The client has separated the responsibilities of authorization, custody, and recording. Therefore, I can be certain that employees are in no position to embezzle funds."
e. "I've noted several internal control deficiencies during my study and evaluation of internal control. However, these deficiencies don't look too serious right now. I guess I don't need to report these to management."
f. "While I'm obtaining an understanding of the components of internal control, I might as well do some tests of controls. I'll need to do these anyway, since I'm auditing the financial statements."
g. "Maybe I should do some additional tests of controls. I don't think it will affect the substantive testing I will need to do, but I'll learn more about the client and its internal control that way."

5-34. Eastern Meat Processing Company buys and processes livestock for sale to supermarkets. In connection with your examination of the company's financial statements, you have prepared the following notes based on your review of procedures:

a. Livestock buyers submit a daily report of their purchases to the Plant Superintendent. This report shows the dates of purchase and expected delivery; the vendor; and the number, weights, and type of livestock purchased. As shipments are received, any available plant employee counts the number of each type received and places a check mark beside this quantity on the buyer's report. When all shipments listed on the report have been received, the report is returned to the buyer.

b. Vendors' Invoices, after a clerical check has been made, are sent to the buyer for approval and returned to the Accounting Department. A disbursement Voucher and a Check for the approved amount are prepared in the Accounting Department. Checks are forwarded to the Treasurer for a signature. The Treasurer's office sends signed Checks directly to the buyer for delivery to the vendor.

c. Livestock carcasses are processed by lots. Each lot is assigned a number. At the end of each day, a tally sheet reporting the lots processed, the number and type of animals in each lot, and the carcass weight is sent to the Accounting Department, where a perpetual inventory record of processed carcasses and their weights is maintained.

d. Processed carcasses are stored in a refrigerated cooler located in a small building adjacent to the employee parking lot. The cooler is locked when the plant is not open, and a company guard is on duty when the employees report for work and leave at the end of their shifts. Supermarket truck drivers wishing to pick up their orders have been instructed to contact someone in the plant if no one is in the cooler.

e. Substantial quantities of by-products are produced and stored, either in the cooler or elsewhere in the plant. By-products are initially accounted for as they are sold. At this time, the Sales Manager prepares a two-part form; one copy serves as authorization to transfer the goods to the customer, and the other becomes the basis for billing the customer.

Required:

For each of the lettered notes (a) through (e) above, state:

a. What the specific internal control objective(s) should be at the stage of the operating cycle described by the note.
b. The control weaknesses in the present procedures, if any, and suggestions for improvement, if any.

(AICPA Adapted)

5-35. Classify each of the following items as to whether they are most closely related to the control environment (CE), risk assessment (RA), control activities (CA), information and communication (IC), or monitoring (MO).

    a. Requiring different employees to record transactions and authorize those transactions.
    b. Establishing a Board of Directors independent from management.
    c. Using journals to summarize similar types of transactions.
    d. Requiring the use of prenumbered, controlled documents to authorize transactions.
    e. Sending monthly statements to customers and following up on any discrepancies noted by these customers.
    f. Preparing summary journal entries to record transactions that have been entered in journals or registers.
    g. Requiring client bank accounts to be reconciled at the end of each month.
    h. Using budgets and performance standards to evaluate employee performance.
    i. Identifying instances where the organization's operations may be subject to laws and regulations.
    j. Developing a corporate code of conduct for employees.
    k. Mathematically verifying Sales Invoices prior to payment.
    l. Ensuring that individuals understand how their roles fit into the organization's internal control.

5-36. Indicate how the auditor could evaluate whether each of the following control policies and procedures is functioning. In your answer, use the following abbreviations: (O) observation, (I) inquiry of client personnel, (IN) inspection of documents and records, and (R) reperformance. More than one test of control can be used for each policy.

    a. Incompatible duties are performed by different client personnel.
    b. Client personnel are reconciling bank statements in a timely fashion.
    c. The client maintains perpetual inventory records and periodically compares physical inventories to those records.
    d. Client personnel verify the mathematical accuracy of Sales Invoices.
    e. The client has billed its customers for all goods shipped.
    f. All purchases made by the client have been properly authorized.
    g. Physical controls over the receipt of cash have been properly implemented.
    h. The performance of manufacturing personnel is evaluated through the use of production standards.

5-37. Indicate which of the following types of control activities are represented by each of the following control policies and procedures. Use the following abbreviations:

    IP(A): Information Processing (Authorization)
    IP(D): Information Processing (Documents and Records)
    IP(I): Information Processing (Independent Checks)
    SD: Segregation of Duties
    PC: Physical Controls
    PR: Performance Reviews

    a. Comparing actual manufacturing costs against performance standards.
    b. Requiring the use of prenumbered, controlled documents to record all transactions.
    c. Depositing cash receipts intact and daily.
    d. Maintaining inventories in a locked, secure location.
    e. Verifying the mathematical accuracy of a Sales Invoice prior to payment.
    f. Comparing perpetual inventory records to physical inventory on hand.

g. Requiring a Purchase Order to be prepared prior to purchasing goods or services.
h. Preparing bank reconciliations upon receipt of the bank statement.
i. Evaluating the report of sales activity by region, division, or product line.
j. Not permitting individuals who receive cash to post receipts to the customers' ledger accounts.
k. Comparing cash received from "over-the-counter" sales to amounts from cash register tapes.

5-38. Dunbar Camera Manufacturing, Inc., is a manufacturer of high-priced precision motion picture cameras for which the specifications of component parts are vital to the manufacturing process. Dunbar buys valuable camera lenses and large quantities of sheet metal and screws. Screws and lenses are ordered by Dunbar and are billed by the vendors on a unit basis. Sheet metal is ordered by Dunbar and billed by the vendors on the basis of weight. The Receiving Clerk is responsible for documenting the quantity and quality of merchandise received.

A preliminary review of the internal control indicates that the following procedures are being followed:

Receiving Report

1. Properly-approved Purchase Orders, which are prenumbered, are filed numerically. The copy sent to the Receiving Clerk is an exact duplicate of the copy sent to the vendor. Receipts of merchandise are recorded on the duplicate copy by the Receiving Clerk.

Sheet Metal

2. The company receives sheet metal by railroad. The railroad independently weighs the sheet metal and reports the weight and date of receipt on a Bill of Lading (Waybill), which accompanies all deliveries. The Receiving Clerk only checks the weight on the Waybill to the Purchase Order.

Screws

3. The Receiving Clerk opens cartons containing screws, then inspects and weighs the contents. The weight is converted to number of units by means of conversion charts. The Receiving Clerk then checks the computed quantity to the Purchase Order.

Camera Lenses

4. Each camera lens is delivered in a separate corrugated carton. Cartons are counted as they are received by the Receiving Clerk, and the number of cartons are checked to Purchase Orders.

Required:

a. Explain why the internal control procedures as they apply individually to Receiving Reports and the receipt of sheet metal, screws, and camera lenses are adequate or inadequate. Do not discuss recommendations for improvements.
b. What financial statement misstatements may arise because of the inadequacies in Dunbar's internal control, and how may they occur?

(AICPA Adapted)

5-39. Bertly Company was organized in 1935. Management has always recognized that a well-designed internal control provides many benefits, including reliable financial records for decision-making and an increased probability of preventing or detecting errors or irregularities. Thus, Bertly has developed an adequate internal control.

Bertly's Internal Audit Department periodically reviews the company's accounting records to determine if the internal control is functioning effectively. The Internal Audit Director believes such reviews are important because inconsistencies or discrepancies can serve as a warning that something is amiss. The seven conditions listed below were detected by Bertly's Internal Audit Staff during a routine examination of the accounting records:

1. Daily bank deposits do not always correspond with cash receipts.
2. Bad checks from customers are consistently approved by the same employee.
3. Physical inventory counts sometimes differ from perpetual inventory records, and there have been alterations to physical counts and perpetual records.
4. There is a high percentage of customer refunds and credits.
5. There is an excessive use of substitute documents because originals are lost or missing.
6. An unexplained and unexpected decrease in Bertley's gross profit percentage has occurred.
7. Many documents are not countersigned.

Required:

For each of the seven conditions detected by Bertly Company's Internal Audit Staff:

a. Describe a possible cause of the condition.
b. Recommend actions to be taken and/or controls to be implemented that would correct the condition.

Use the following format to present your answer:

Condition Number	Possible Cause	Recommended Actions and/or Controls to Correct Condition

(CMA Adapted)

5-40. An auditor is required to obtain a sufficient understanding of each of the components of internal control to plan the audit of the entity's financial statements and to assess control risk for the assertions embodied in the account balance, transaction class, and disclosure components of the financial statements.

Required:

a. Identify the components of an entity's internal control.
b. For what purposes should an auditor's understanding of the internal control components be used in planning an audit?
c. Explain the reasons why an auditor may assess control risk at the maximum level for one or more assertions embodied in an account balance.
d. What must an auditor do to support assessing control risk at less than the maximum level when the auditor has determined that the controls have been placed in operation?

(AICPA Adapted)

5-41. An auditor is required to obtain a sufficient understanding of each of the components of an entity's internal control. This is necessary to plan the audit of the entity's financial statements and assess control risk.

Required:

a. For what purposes should an auditor's understanding of the internal control components be used in planning an audit?
b. What is required for an auditor to assess control risk at below the maximum level?
c. What should an auditor consider when seeking a further reduction in the planned assessed level of control risk?
d. What are an auditor's documentation requirements concerning an entity's internal control and the assessed level of control risk?

(AICPA Adapted)

Learning Objectives

Study of this chapter is designed to achieve several learning objectives. After studying this chapter, you should be able to:

1. Define substantive tests and identify the auditor's objective in performing substantive tests.
2. List and identify the two types of evidence available to the auditor.
3. Describe what is meant by the competence and sufficiency of audit evidence.
4. Identify the two general approaches to substantive testing available to the auditor and indicate when each is most likely to be used.
5. Identify how the nature, timing, and extent of the auditor's substantive testing procedures are affected by the necessary level of detection risk.
6. Identify seven methods of gathering evidence commonly used in the audit examination.
7. Discuss the importance of audit workpapers and identify the major types of workpapers.

6

Substantive Testing and Control of Detection Risk

◉ THE AUDIT PROCESS AND AUDIT RISK

In Chapter 4, we introduced the audit risk model and discussed how this model is used to determine the nature, timing, and extent of the auditor's substantive testing procedures. Recall the four basic steps involved with the use of the audit risk model:

1. The auditor sets audit risk at desired levels. **Audit risk** is the risk that the auditor may unknowingly fail to modify his or her opinion on financial statements that contain a material misstatement. Viewed in another way, audit risk is the risk that a material misstatement may occur in an assertion, not be prevented or detected by internal control, and not be detected by the auditor's substantive testing procedures.

2. Based on the susceptibility of an assertion in an account balance or class of transactions to material misstatement, the auditor assesses inherent risk. **Inherent risk** is the risk that a material misstatement exists in an assertion assuming that no internal control policies or procedures exist.

3. Based on the effectiveness of internal control, the auditor assesses control risk. **Control risk** is the risk that a material misstatement in an assertion will not be prevented or detected on a timely basis by the company's internal control policies and procedures.

4. After considering the audit risk, inherent risk, and control risk, the auditor determines the necessary level of detection risk. **Detection risk** is the risk that the auditor's substantive tests will fail to detect a material misstatement in an assertion. The necessary level of detection risk is controlled by the auditor through the nature, timing, and extent of his or her substantive testing procedures.

This four-step procedure (as well as the major stage in the audit in which each of these four steps is performed) is depicted below:

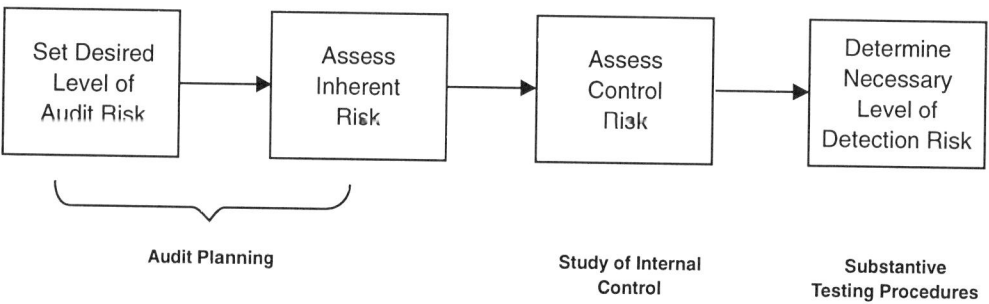

To this point, we have discussed the first three steps in the use of the audit risk model. In this chapter, we discuss the final step: determining the necessary level of detection risk. As you will see, the detection risk component of the audit risk model reflects the nature, timing, and extent of the auditor's substantive tests. Viewed in another way, detection risk provides the auditor with answers to the following types of questions:

▶ What types of substantive tests do I need to perform?

▶ When should I perform substantive tests?

▶ How much substantive testing should I perform?

OVERVIEW OF SUBSTANTIVE TESTS

Third Standard of Field Work

The purpose of the auditor's substantive tests is addressed by the third standard of field work. This standard states that:

> Sufficient, competent evidential matter is to be obtained through inspection, observation, inquiries, and confirmations to afford a reasonable basis for an opinion regarding the financial statements under audit.[1]

As noted in the above standard, the auditor gathers evidence during his or her examination to determine whether the client's financial statements are prepared in conformity with GAAP. Specifically, the auditor gathers evidence regarding the fairness of the account balances and classes

---

[1] American Institute of Certified Public Accountants (AICPA), *Statement on Auditing Standards No. 1*, "Codification of Auditing Standards and Procedures" (New York: AICPA, 1972, AU 150.02).

of transactions included in the client's financial statements. The process of gathering evidence of this nature is referred to as **substantive tests**. These tests draw their name from the fact that the is attempting to "substantiate" the client's account balances.

◘ Types of Evidence

The third standard of field work identifies the need for the auditor to gather "evidential matter." *Statement on Auditing Standards No. 31 (SAS No. 31)*[2] notes that two types of evidential matter (or evidence) support management's financial statements. The first is referred to as the **underlying accounting data**. Underlying accounting data include books of original entry, general and subsidiary ledgers, client-prepared worksheets that support cost allocations, and other accounting records. The important characteristics of underlying accounting data are that they: (1) are prepared by the client's personnel, and (2) represent the end result (or recording) in the processing of transactions. Although the auditor often refers to this information during the conduct of the examination, underlying accounting data are not, by themselves sufficient for the auditor to express an opinion on management's financial statements.

A second type of evidence is referred to as **corroborating information**. Corroborating information consists of documents and other forms of evidence that support (or corroborate) the underlying accounting data. These other forms of evidence include: (1) responses to confirmations sent to third parties by the auditor; and (2) other evidence gathered through auditor observation, inspection, and inquiry. The auditor utilizes corroborating information to verify the fairness of the underlying accounting data; as a result, both types of evidence are considered to be necessary in the examination. The relationship between underlying accounting data and corroborating information is summarized below:

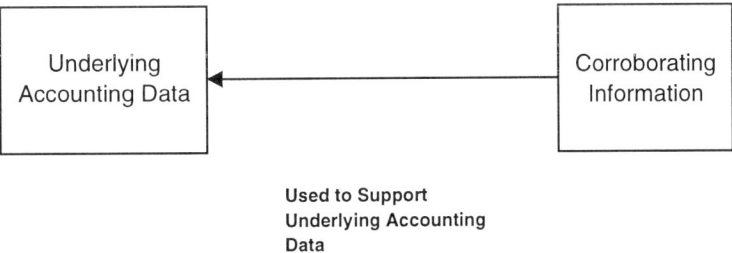

To illustrate, assume that an auditor is examining cash to determine whether the recorded cash balance is presented in conformity with GAAP. By reviewing the client's Trial Balance, Cash Receipts Journal, and Check Register (all forms of underlying accounting data), the auditor could determine the recorded cash balance; however, he or she could not determine whether this balance was fairly stated.

---

[2] American Institute of Certified Public Accountants (AICPA), *Statement on Auditing Standards No. 31*, "Evidential Matter" (New York: AICPA, 1980, AU 326).

To do so, the auditor should examine some corroborating information regarding the client's cash balance, such as:

- The results of counts of cash on hand
- Bank statements received from the client's banks

This chapter discusses various types of corroborating information used in the examination of a client's financial statements.

CHAPTER CHECKPOINTS

6-1. Define detection risk. How is detection risk related to the auditor's substantive tests?

6-2. What is the third standard of field work?

6-3. Identify and define the two major types of evidence. How is each type of evidence used by the auditor?

◻ Qualities of Evidence

The third standard of field work requires the auditor to gather "sufficient, competent evidential matter." Thus, this standard identifies two important qualities of audit evidence: sufficiency and competence.

Sufficiency of Evidence. **Sufficiency of evidence** relates to the *quantity* of evidence gathered by the auditor. That is, for a particular account balance or class of transactions, how many components or transactions involving that account should be examined? It is important to note that the auditor cannot possibly be expected to examine all transactions or components of an account balance and still complete the audit in a timely fashion. Therefore, a major decision faced by the auditor is how much evidence should be gathered. The sufficiency of evidence is related to questions such as the following:

1. How many of the client's bank accounts should be confirmed?
2. How many of the client's accounts receivable balances should be confirmed?
3. How many inventory items should be observed?
4. How many investment transactions should be verified?

Although other factors influence the amount of evidence gathered, an important factor is the effectiveness of the client's internal control. Recall the inverse relationship between the effectiveness of the client's internal control and the necessary effectiveness of the auditor's substantive tests:

If the client's internal control is more effective in preventing or detecting errors, the auditor's substantive testing procedures can be less effective.

In terms of sufficiency, less effective tests mean that the auditor would not be required to gather as much evidence. This issue is explored further in a subsequent section of this chapter.

Competence of Evidence. Competence relates to the *quality* of evidential matter. *SAS No. 31* identifies two aspects of competence: relevance and validity. **Relevance** refers to whether evidence provides the auditor with the information sought by him or her. Recall the five management assertions initially introduced in Chapter 4:

- ▶ Existence or occurrence (the EO assertion)
- ▶ Rights and obligations (the RO assertion)
- ▶ Valuation or allocation (the VA assertion)
- ▶ Completeness (the CO assertion)
- ▶ Presentation and disclosure (the PD assertion)

Assume the auditor is attempting to determine whether a delivery truck that was purchased in the previous year is recorded at the proper dollar amount (the VA assertion). Although actually observing the presence of the delivery truck would allow the auditor to conclude that the truck exists (the EO assertion), this procedure provides little (if any) information concerning the cost of that truck. That is, this evidence is not relevant. A more relevant form of evidence for verifying the VA assertion would be examining the invoice or other record of the cost of the delivery truck.

Validity relates to the reliability of the audit evidence. Although no unequivocal statements can be made, *SAS No. 31* notes the following general rules relating to the validity of audit evidence:

1. Evidence obtained from sources external to the client is more reliable than evidence obtained from the client.
2. Evidence resulting from more effective internal control is more reliable than evidence resulting from less effective internal control.
3. Evidence obtained directly by the auditor is more reliable than evidence obtained indirectly from other sources (either the client or sources external to the client).

Figure 6-1 illustrates the emerging hierarchy of evidence (from most reliable to least reliable) and provides an example of each type of evidence.

It is important to note that evidence may be valid but not relevant, or *vice versa*. To illustrate, if the auditor physically inspects the delivery truck discussed earlier, this is a very reliable (or valid) form of evidence, since it represents a form of evidence obtained directly by the auditor. However, if the auditor is interested in determining whether the truck was recorded at the proper amount, this form of evidence is not relevant. Therefore, both relevance and validity should be considered by the auditor in deciding upon the type of evidence to acquire.

Direct Evidence	▶ Physical Observations by the Auditor
	▶ Calculations Made by the Auditor
Evidence Received Directly From External Sources	▶ Confirmations Received from Banks and Customers
	▶ Bank Statements Received from Banks
Evidence Created by External Sources but Received from the Client	▶ Bank Statements Received from the Client
	▶ Vendor Invoices for Purchases Made by the Client
Evidence Created by the Client	▶ Invoices for Sales Made to Customers
	▶ Cost Allocations and Other Internal Records

Figure 6-1: *Hierarchy of Reliability of Evidence*

◘ Qualities of Evidence: A Summary

Figure 6-2 summarizes the two important qualities of evidence identified by *SAS No. 31*. It is important to note that both characteristics are of importance to the auditor during his or her examination.

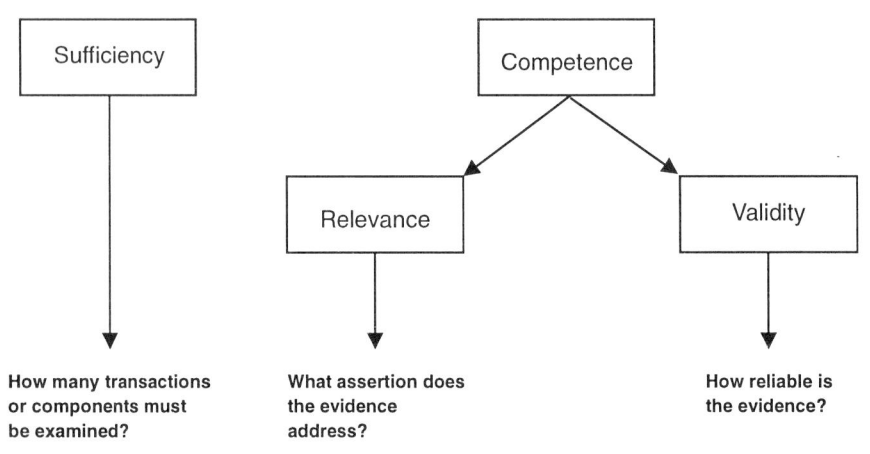

Figure 6-2: *Summary of Qualities of Evidential Matter*

General Approaches to Substantive Testing

Two general approaches are available to the auditor with respect to substantive testing: tests of balances and tests of transactions. Although each method of substantive testing is normally associated with account balances having certain characteristics, they can be used interchangeably in practice. These substantive testing approaches are discussed below.

Test of Balances Approach. Many of the account balances and classes of transactions composing the client's financial statements are the result of numerous transactions that occur during the year. Consider, for example, the cash account. Most large organizations have thousands of individual receipts and disbursements of cash each day. Although some of these transactions may be large in terms of the dollar amount, most individual cash transactions are immaterial to the financial statements taken as a whole. Therefore, transactions affecting the cash account have the following characteristics:

1. A large volume of transactions occur during the year.
2. Many (or most) of the transactions are for relatively small dollar amounts.

Consider the nature of the cash account from another perspective. At the end of a given year, the cash account can be easily decomposed into several identifiable components. Each of these components represents a large number of individual transactions. Decomposition of a typical cash account may yield the following components:

```
Cash on deposit, Account A  . . . . . . . . . . . . . . . . . . . . . .  $   150,126
Cash on deposit, Account B  . . . . . . . . . . . . . . . . . . . . . .       35,000
Cash on deposit, Account C (Payroll)  . . . . . . . . . . . . . . . .      203,126
                    *                                                          *
                    *                                                          *
Cash on deposit, Account X  . . . . . . . . . . . . . . . . . . . . . .       15,620
Cash on hand  . . . . . . . . . . . . . . . . . . . . . . . . . . . . . .        5,230

Ending cash balance  . . . . . . . . . . . . . . . . . . . . . . . . . .   $2,320,100
```

In this instance, it is ordinarily easier for the auditor to use the **test of balances** approach. That is, instead of examining individual transactions that make up the account balance (individual receipts and payments of cash), the auditor investigates components of the account balance. Each of these components represents a subbalance of the particular account of interest. For accounts receivable, the components are individual customer account balances; for inventory, the components are individual inventory items. Note that this method of gathering evidence focuses on the end result (the ending cash balance) rather than the transactions leading to the end result. However, it is also important to point out that when the auditor gathers evidence by verifying these components, the transactions comprising these components are also indirectly verified.

The test of balances approach consists of the following major steps:

1. Identify components of the account balance or class of transactions.
2. Perform substantive testing procedures on a sample of components of the account balance or class of transactions.
3. Form a conclusion about the account balance or class of transactions based on the tests performed in (?)

In general, tests of balances are a more useful substantive testing approach for accounts such as cash because:

▶ The large volume of transactions makes it less cost-efficient for the auditor to verify a large percentage of these transactions.

▶ The small dollar amount of these transactions makes it less likely that any individual transaction will materially affect the financial statements.

Test of Transactions Approach. In contrast to the cash account, many account balances and classes of transactions are comprised of a smaller number of transactions representing relatively large dollar amounts. Examples of these accounts are property, plant and equipment; investments; prepaid assets; bonds payable; and stockholders' equity accounts. From the auditor's standpoint, the characteristics of these accounts encourage testing the individual transactions occurring during the year for the following reasons:

▶ The small volume of transactions makes it cost-efficient for the auditor to verify a large percentage of these transactions.

▶ The large dollar amount of these transactions makes it more likely that any individual transaction will materially affect the financial statements.

In these situations, the auditor will normally verify all (or most) of the transactions occurring during the year. This substantive testing approach is referred to as the **tests of transactions** approach. To illustrate how the ending balances in these accounts are verified, consider the following T-account (assume an account that normally has a debit balance):

Beginning Balance	
Debits to Account	Credits to Account
Ending Balance	

The tests of transactions approach is comprised of three steps:

1. Verify the accuracy of the beginning account balance.
2. Verify the accuracy of the transactions occurring during the year.
3. Based on (1) and (2), form a conclusion about the ending account balance.

In verifying the accuracy of the beginning balance for continuing audit clients, it is important to note that the beginning balance represents last year's ending balance. Therefore, the auditor has already obtained evidence about the accuracy of this balance. If the audit is being performed for a new client or one that has not previously had its financial statements audited, the auditor must perform additional procedures in order to ascertain that the beginning account balance is, in fact, fairly stated.

Once the accuracy of the beginning balance has been verified, the auditor verifies the recording of transactions occurring during the year. This will be done by examining some form of evidence relating to that transaction. For example, if the auditor is attempting to determine that the purchase of a fixed asset has been recorded at the correct dollar amount, the entry in the fixed asset account would be compared with an Invoice or other evidence of the cost of that asset.

At this point, the auditor has verified the accuracy of: (1) the beginning balance, and (2) the transactions occurring during the year. Since the accuracy of most (if not all) of the individual transactions occurring during the year has been verified, the ending balance can be determined through mathematical recalculation. Once recalculated, the auditor should agree the ending balance with the amount shown on the client's Trial Balance.

While the tests of balances approach is generally used for account balances having a small number of transactions with a larger dollar amount per transaction, auditors may perform tests of transactions for other accounts as well. For example, in examining accounts receivable, the primary substantive testing procedure performed by the auditor is to directly confirm a customer's account balance with that customer. This type of substantive test represents a test of balances because the auditor is verifying a component of the client's accounts receivable balance. An alternative to confirming customer account balances is to verify individual transactions (*i.e.*, customer purchases and payments) occurring during the year. In cases where customers fail to respond to the auditor's confirmation request, the auditor must corroborate this information using the tests of transactions approach to verify that customer's outstanding balance.

Figure 6-3 contrasts the test of balances and test of transactions approaches to substantive testing.

	Number of Transactions	Dollar Amount per Transaction	Accounts
Test of Balances	Relatively Large	Relatively Small	Cash Accounts Receivable Inventory Accounts Payable
Test of Transactions	Relatively Small	Relatively Large	Property, Plant and Equipment Investments Notes and Bonds Payable Stockholders' Equity

Figure 6-3: *Alternative Approaches to Substantive Testing*

CHAPTER CHECKPOINTS

6-4. What are the two qualities of evidence identified by the third standard of field work?

6-5. What is the overall hierarchy of evidence in terms of its reliability?

6-6. What are the basic steps involved with using the test of balances approach? Test of transactions approach?

6-7. When would the test of balances and test of transactions approach be used in an audit?

◉ DETERMINING DETECTION RISK

As noted at the beginning of this chapter, the end result of using the audit risk model is determining the necessary level of detection risk. The necessary level of detection risk represents the nature, timing, and extent of the auditor's substantive tests and can be determined using either a mathematical formula or a matrix, as shown below:

Formula Approach: If Audit Risk = Inherent Risk × Control Risk × Detection Risk, then

$$\text{Detection Risk} = \frac{\text{Audit Risk}}{\text{Inherent Risk} \times \text{Control Risk}}$$

Matrix Approach: Using a matrix, the auditor can determine the necessary level of detection risk based on inherent risk and control risk by reading the cells at the intersection of the assessed level of inherent risk and control risk. Assuming a low level of audit risk, a matrix such as the following could be used:

	High Inherent Risk	Moderate Inherent Risk	Low Inherent Risk
Maximum Control Risk	Low Detection Risk	Low to Moderate Detection Risk	Moderate Detection Risk
Moderate Control Risk	Low to Moderate Detection Risk	Moderate Detection Risk	Moderate to High Detection Risk
Low Control Risk	Moderate Detection Risk	Moderate to High Detection Risk	High Detection Risk

To illustrate the use of these approaches, assume that the auditor makes the following assessments:

	Formula	Matrix
Audit Risk	5 percent	Low
Inherent Risk	100 percent	High
Control Risk	40 percent	Moderate

The formula approach would yield a necessary level of detection risk of 12.5 percent, as shown below:

$$\text{Detection Risk} = \frac{\text{Audit Risk}}{\text{Inherent Risk} \times \text{Control Risk}}$$

$$= \frac{0.05}{1.00 \times 0.40}$$

$$= 0.125 \text{ (or 12.5 percent)}$$

Based on: (1) low levels of audit risk; (2) high levels of inherent risk; and (3) moderate levels of control risk, the use of the matrix yields a necessary level of detection risk of "Low to Moderate."

6/ Substantive Testing and Control of Detection Risk

To illustrate the impact of the effectiveness of the client's internal control on the necessary level of detection risk, assume that the auditor decided to obtain a lower assessment of control risk by performing additional tests of controls. For purposes of illustration, assume that additional tests of controls allowed the auditor to reduce his or her assessment of control risk to 10 percent (for the formula approach) or "low" (for the matrix approach). In this case, the revised necessary levels of detection risk would be as follows:

Formula Approach:

$$\text{Detection Risk} = \frac{\text{Audit Risk}}{\text{Inherent Risk} \times \text{Control Risk}}$$

Matrix Approach:

$$= \frac{0.05}{1.00 \times 0.10}$$

$$= 0.50 \text{ (or 50 percent)}$$

These results reveal the inverse relationship between control risk and detection risk. As control risk decreases (*i.e.*, internal control is judged to be more effective), detection risk increases. Since the detection risk is defined as the risk that the auditor's substantive tests will fail to detect a material misstatement in an assertion, higher levels of detection risk indicate that the auditor's substantive testing procedures must be less effective in detecting material financial statement misstatements. This relationship is summarized below:

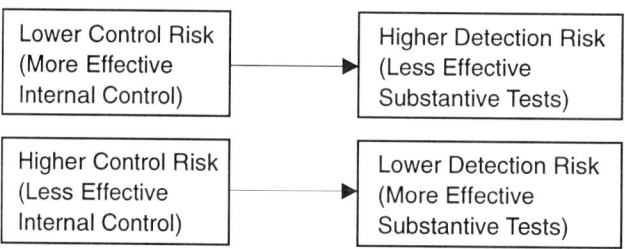

The remaining components of the audit risk model will impact the auditor's substantive testing procedures as shown in Figure 6-4. Each of these effects is provided assuming that all other factors are held constant. For example, if the client's internal control is less effective (higher control risk), the auditor's substantive testing procedures must be more effective, assuming the same levels of inherent risk and audit risk.

Note from Figure 6-4 that more effective substantive tests are necessary when: (1) the desired exposure to audit risk is lower, (2) the account balance is more susceptible to misstatement (higher inherent risk), and (3) the client's internal control is less effective in preventing or detecting misstatements (higher control risk).

Component	Level of Component	Necessary Level of Detection Risk
Audit Risk (AR)	Lower Desired Exposure to AR	More Effective Substantive Tests (Lower DR)
	Higher Desired Exposure to AR	Less Effective Substantive Tests (Higher DR)
Inherent Risk (IR)	Account More Susceptible to Misstatement (Higher IR)	More Effective Substantive Tests (Lower DR)
	Account Less Susceptible to Misstatement (Lower IR)	Less Effective Substantive Tests (Higher DR)
Control Risk (CR)	More Effective Internal Control (Lower CR)	Less Effective Substantive Tests (Higher DR)
	Less Effective Internal Control (Higher CR)	More Effective Substantive Tests (Lower DR)

Figure 6-4: *Effect of Audit Risk Model Components on Overall Effectiveness of Substantive Testing*

CHAPTER CHECKPOINTS

6-8. Determine the necessary level of detection risk in each of the following independent cases using both the formula approach and the matrix approach:

   a. Audit risk = 0.05 (low), Inherent risk = 1.00 (high), Control risk = 1.00 (maximum)
   b. Audit risk = 0.05 (low), Inherent risk = 0.60 (moderate), Control risk = 1.00 (maximum)
   c. Audit risk = 0.05 (low), Inherent risk = 0.60 (moderate), Control risk = 0.50 (moderate)

6-9. How does each component of the audit risk model influence the necessary level of detection risk?

◻ Factors Affecting Levels of Detection Risk

At this point, the auditor has determined the necessary level of detection risk through the use of the audit risk model. This detection risk provides him or her with an indication of the overall necessary effectiveness of his or her substantive tests. The overall effectiveness of the auditor's substantive testing procedures is influenced by three factors: (1) the nature of the substantive testing procedures, (2) the timing of the substantive testing procedures, and (3) the extent of the substantive testing procedures. These dimensions of the effectiveness of substantive testing are discussed below. The effect of these factors on the auditor's substantive tests is summarized in Figure 6-5 and discussed in the following subsections.

	Lower Detection Risk	Higher Detection Risk
Overall Effectiveness of Substantive Tests	More Effective	Less Effective
Nature	More Competent Tests	Less Competent Tests
Timing	More Tests Performed at Year-end	More Tests Performed at Interim
Extent	More Extensive Tests	Less Extensive Tests

Figure 6-5: *Relationship Between Detection Risk and Nature, Timing, and Extent of Substantive Testing*

Nature of Substantive Tests. The nature of the auditor's substantive tests relates to competence of evidence; as noted earlier, the competence dimension represents the quality of evidence obtained by the auditor. Although the auditor would normally prefer to gather the most competent evidence available, the type of evidence required depends on the necessary level of detection risk. When more effective substantive testing procedures are required (lower levels of detection risk), the auditor must utilize more reliable forms of evidence than when less effective substantive testing procedures are required (higher levels of detection risk).

To illustrate how the level of detection risk affects the nature of substantive tests, consider the auditor's verification of the client's year-end Bank Reconciliation (a substantive test discussed in greater detail in Chapter 11). As part of the auditor's verification of the Bank Reconciliation, he or she should obtain a Bank Statement from any banks where the client has cash on deposit. In cases where a lower level of detection risk is necessary, the auditor may request that the client's bank send the statement directly to the auditor (a form of evidence received directly from an external party). In contrast, if the necessary level of detection risk is higher, the auditor may not need to make such a request and instead obtain the Bank Statement from the client (evidence created by an external party but received from the client).

It is important to note that, for some forms of evidence, the level of detection risk will not influence the source (or nature) of the auditor's evidence. For example, in investigating accounts receivable, the auditor will ordinarily obtain confirmations directly from the client's customers, regardless of the necessary levels of detection risk. In addition, when examining inventories, the auditor will ordinarily perform a physical observation of the client's inventory regardless of the necessary level of detection risk.

A final matter related to the nature of substantive tests is its relationship to the cost of gathering evidence. Generally, it is more costly to gather more competent evidence. While the auditor should consider the cost of evidence in determining the nature of his or her substantive tests, *SAS No. 31* notes that cost is not a valid reason for omitting a particular test.

Timing of Substantive Tests. Current professional guidance regarding the timing of substantive testing procedures is provided by *Statement on Auditing Standards No. 45*.[3] Two alternatives exist for the auditor: substantive tests may be performed prior to the end of the year (or at an **interim date**) or at year-end. In general, performing substantive tests at an interim date results in a greater level of detection risk to the auditor than applying procedures at year-end, because events may occur in the period between the interim date and year-end to affect the auditor's conclusions. *SAS No. 45* notes that the overall level of detection risk increases as the length of the intervening period increases; that is, interim testing is associated with higher levels of detection risk. Although performing interim tests provides the auditor with an advantage in that a great deal of work can be "spread out" over longer periods of time, the increased exposure to additional detection risk must be considered in making the decision about the timing of substantive testing procedures.

In deciding whether to perform other types of substantive testing procedures at an interim date, *SAS No. 45* indicates that the auditor should consider the following factors:

▶ The effectiveness of the client's internal control. (As the effectiveness of the internal control increases, the auditor can more reliably perform interim tests.)

▶ The existence of rapidly-changing business conditions. (As conditions change, the auditor cannot perform interim tests with as much reliability.)

In any case, if the auditor decides to perform substantive tests at an interim date, he or she should also perform procedures to test the intervening period. These procedures allow the auditor to evaluate whether the conclusions made in the interim period remain valid. Examples of procedures commonly used to test intervening time periods include: (1) identifying any significant fluctuations occurring between the interim date and year-end, and (2) performing other analytical procedures or substantive tests of details to provide a basis for extending the results from the interim date to year-end. The auditor's tests during the intervening period are summarized below:

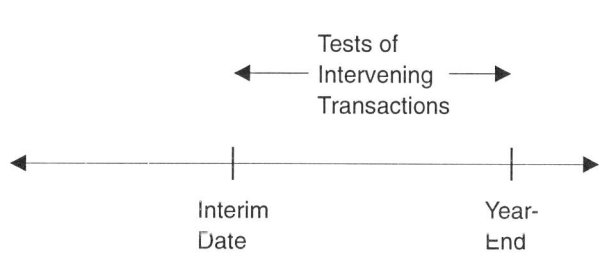

For example, assume that the auditor confirms a customer's accounts receivable balance as of November 10, 19x1; the returned confirmation indicates that $10,000 is owed on the account. Assuming that the customer makes purchases of $6,000 and payments of $12,000 in the period from

---

[3] American Institute of Certified Public Accountants (AICPA), *Statement on Auditing Standards No. 45*, "Omnibus Statement on Auditing Standards—1983" (New York: AICPA, 1983, AU 313).

November 10, 19x1 through December 31, 19x1, the auditor could verify the ending balance of $4,000 as follows:

1. Confirming balance of $10,000 on November 10, 19x1
2. Investigating Sales Invoices or other evidence for purchases of $6,000
3. Investigating Remittance Advices or other evidence for payments of $12,000
4. Mathematically recalculating balance of $4,000 ($10,000 + $6,000 − $12,000 = $4,000)

A proposed pronouncement notes that the auditor should consider the time during which information is available in determining the timing of his or her substantive tests. For example, in a computerized accounting system, electronic evidence may exist at a certain point in time. However, if files are changed and backup files do not exist, the auditor may be unable to examine this evidence at a later date. In these cases, the auditor would ordinarily examine the evidence prior to year-end.[4]

Extent of Substantive Tests. The extent of substantive tests relates to the quantity (or sufficiency) of evidence; in other words, how much evidence must the auditor gather? In terms of substantive tests, sufficiency will be the number of transactions (for tests of transactions) or components (for tests of balances) that must be examined by the auditor. As noted in Figure 6-5, the sufficiency of evidence is inversely related to detection risk. That is, as detection risk decreases (the auditor's substantive testing procedures must be more effective), the auditor must gather more sufficient evidence (perform more extensive substantive testing procedures). Determining the extent of substantive tests is discussed in more detail in Chapter 8 of this text.

◘ Detection Risk and Management Assertions

The above discussion illustrates the methods used by the auditor to determine detection risk. It is important to remember that the auditor controls audit risk on an assertion-by-assertion basis; that is, the audit risk model is separately applied by the auditor to each assertion related to an account balance or class of transactions. Thus, the auditor will also design substantive tests to achieve different levels of detection risk for each assertion. The necessary level of detection risk will ordinarily vary among the assertions affecting an account balance or class of transactions. As first described in Chapter 4 (and introduced earlier in this chapter), these assertions are:

1. Existence or occurrence (the EO assertion)
2. Rights and obligations (the RO assertion)
3. Valuation or allocation (the VA assertion)
4. Completeness (the CO assertion)
5. Presentation and disclosure (the PD assertion)

---

[4] American Institute of Certified Public Accountants (AICPA), *Proposed Statement on Auditing Standards*, "Amendment to *Statement on Auditing Standards No. 31*, 'Evidential Matter'" (New York: AICPA, May 20, 1996).

To illustrate the application of the audit risk model to an account balance or class of transactions, assume that the auditor is examining accounts receivable. As noted later in Chapter 11, because of pressure to meet earnings expectations, companies may: (1) record fictitious sales and accounts receivable, (2) record sales and accounts receivable prior to the point when revenue should be recognized, and/or (3) understate the provision for uncollectible accounts receivable. As a result, high levels of inherent risk are ordinarily associated with the EO and VA assertions for this account. In addition, the potential existence of uncollectible accounts receivable results in moderate levels of inherent risk for the RO assertion. Because of the levels of inherent risk associated with these assertions, the auditor would normally choose to obtain an assessment of control risk at less than the maximum level. As noted in Chapter 5, this is done by performing tests of the operating effectiveness of important control policies and procedures related to the EO, RO, and VA assertions. Once these tests of controls have been performed, the auditor would assess control risk based on the operating effectiveness of the control policies and procedures.

In contrast, for the remaining assertions affecting accounts receivable (the CO and PD assertions), assume that inherent risk is assessed at low levels. In this case, the auditor may decide that it is more efficient to assess control risk at the maximum level and perform relatively effective levels of substantive tests (lower levels of detection risk). If so, the auditor would obtain and document his or her understanding of internal control and proceed directly to substantive testing.

Figure 6-6 illustrates the resultant levels of detection risk for the five management assertions related to accounts receivable. These levels of detection risk were obtained from the matrix shown earlier in this chapter and illustrate that the effectiveness of the auditor's substantive testing procedures may vary across the different assertions affecting the account balance or class of transactions.

	Inherent Risk	Control Risk	Detection Risk
Existence or Occurrence	High	Low	Moderate
Rights and Obligations	Moderate	Low	Moderate to High
Completeness	Low	Maximum	Moderate
Valuation or Allocation	High	Moderate	Low to Moderate
Presentation and Disclosure	Low	Maximum	Moderate

Figure 6-6: *Levels of Detection Risk for Assertions Related to Accounts Receivable*

In this instance, the effectiveness of the substantive tests for the assertions are as follows:

1. VA assertion (highly effective)
2. EO, CO, and PD (moderately effective)
3. RO (less than moderately effective)

Chapter 11 provides a further discussion of the nature, timing, and extent of substantive tests related to accounts receivable. Other chapters illustrate the effect of detection risk on the nature, timing, and extent of substantive tests for cash (Chapter 11), accounts payable (Chapter 13), and inventory (Chapter 13).

CHAPTER CHECKPOINTS

6-10. How does the necessary level of detection risk influence the nature, timing, and extent of substantive tests?

6-11. Would the auditor modify the nature of substantive tests in all cases in response to the necessary level of detection risk?

6-12. What factors should the auditor consider in performing tests at an interim date?

⊙ SUBSTANTIVE TESTING PROCEDURES

At this point, the auditor has determined the necessary level of detection risk for each of the assertions related to the account balance or class of transactions being examined. In order to examine these assertions, the auditor then performs substantive testing procedures. This relationship is depicted below:

The substantive testing procedure(s) selected by the auditor will depend upon both the necessary level of detection risk as well as the assertion(s) being examined. Seven common types of substantive testing procedures can be used by the auditor. These procedures are: (1) physical observation, (2) inspecting documents, (3) confirmation, (4) analytical procedures, (5) recalculation, (6) comparisons, and (7) oral inquiry. These procedures are discussed in the remainder of this section.

Physical Observation

The physical observation of items by the auditor is ordinarily the most reliable form of evidence as to their existence (the EO assertion).[5] The reliability of physical observation is based on the fact that it is a form of evidence obtained directly by the auditor. Items that are normally observed by the auditor include:

- Cash on hand
- Inventory
- Property, plant and equipment
- Investments
- Bonds and notes payable
- Canceled stock certificates

When observing items, it is important that the auditor also consider other matters. For example, when observing inventories, the auditor will consider whether the inventories are still saleable; if not, inventories may need to be written down to reflect a decline in their market value. Similarly, when observing property, plant and equipment, the auditor should consider whether the items can still be used in the company's operations. If not, property, plant and equipment may need to be reclassified as "other assets" on the balance sheet. Thus, in some cases, physical observation may provide the auditor with evidence regarding the PD and VA assertions.

It is important to note that observing an item does not necessarily mean that the client owns or owes the item (the RO assertion). For example, while it may appear that observing inventories on the client's premises indicates that these inventories are owned by the client, they may represent inventories: (1) held on consignment for another party, or (2) already sold to the client's customers and held for customer pick-up. Similarly, property, plant and equipment observed by the auditor may be leased from other companies under operating lease agreements. Thus, for the RO assertion, the auditor would need to examine Vendors' Invoice, title, or some other evidence regarding ownership.

---

[5] In this section, general relationships between substantive testing procedures and management assertions are drawn. It is important to note that the assertions related to different substantive testing procedures varies slightly from account to account. Chapters 11 (for accounts receivable and cash), 13 (for inventories and accounts payable), 14 (for payroll), and 15 (for investments, property, plant and equipment, notes and bonds payable, and stockholders' equity account) provide more detailed information about the relationship between substantive testing procedures and management assertions verified by these procedures.

VERIFYING PHYSICAL EXISTENCE OF ASSETS[6]

A company with a large inventory of movable fixed assets (in the form of welding machines) had difficulty scheduling the physical observation of those assets, because they were located throughout the organization and were continuously moved to other locations as they were needed. However, the auditor discovered that the company had a requirement that these machines be tested and certified every six months by a reputable third-party inspection agency. As a result, the third-party testing was used as verification of the existence of the welding machines.

◘ Inspecting Documents

Documents are the component of the accounting system that are created by the client and external parties upon the initiation of a transaction. Documents provide the auditor with evidence related to the existence of a particular transaction and, in some cases, the proper valuation of such transactions. For example, examining a copy of the client's Sales Invoice for a sale made to a customer can tell the auditor: (1) that a sale to a customer actually occurred (the EO assertion), and (2) the amount at which the transaction should be recorded (the VA assertion). Examples of documents that may be examined by the auditor include:

- ▶ **Sales to Customers:** Sales Invoices
- ▶ **Purchases from Vendors:** Vendor's Invoices
- ▶ **Payments made to Vendors:** Canceled Checks
- ▶ **Write-offs of Accounts Receivable:** Memorandum authorizing write-offs

Reliability of Documentary Evidence. In general, the reliability of any particular document depends on the source of the document and the party who initially receives the document. The four types of documents are listed below in order of reliability (from highest to lowest).

1. Documents created externally and sent directly to the auditor.
2. Documents created externally and retained by the client.
3. Documents created internally that have circulated externally.
4. Documents created internally that have not circulated externally.

Documents created by outside entities and sent directly to that auditor are the most reliable type of evidence, since there is little possibility that client personnel have altered of modified these documents. In certain situations, the auditor will request that third parties send documents directly to them instead of the client. For example, for the audit of cash, clients may instruct their banks to send Bank Statements for periods of time near year-end directly to the auditor. Similarly, the auditor may request

---

[6] "Verifying Physical Existence of Assets," *Internal Auditor* (February 1996), 69-70.

that the client's vendors send their statements directly to them instead of to the client. By making these requests, the auditor will obtain evidence of a higher quality (more competent evidence) that provides a lower level of detection risk.

Documents created externally but held by the client generally are not as reliable a form of evidence as those created externally and sent directly to the auditor. The lower level of reliability results from the possibility that client personnel have altered these documents. Documents of this nature normally include Bank Statements summarizing cash transactions, Vendor's Invoices and Statements for purchases made by the client, and Broker's Advices representing investment transactions.

Most documents created within a client's organization are generally considered to be evidence of a lower quality than those created outside the organization. Internal documents include Sales Invoices, Receiving Reports, Checks, and Deposit Slips. Two factors that may affect the reliability of internal documents are:

1. Documents that circulate outside the client and are reviewed by external parties (for example, canceled Checks and Deposit Slips reviewed by the bank) are more reliable than those not reviewed by external parties.
2. Documents reviewed by one or more employees other than the preparer of the document are more reliable than those not reviewed in this manner.

Methods of Inspecting Documents. When inspecting documents, the auditor can proceed (gather evidence) in one of two directions. In **vouching** to a document, the auditor begins by selecting an item recorded in a particular account (e.g., a debit in a customer's subsidiary account receivable). The auditor then goes backward through the accounting system to find the source document (a Sales Invoice) that supports the entry in the account. Notice that although the auditor can compare the recorded amount of the sale to the amount indicated on the Invoice (the VA assertion), vouching also helps auditors determine whether all recorded transactions are adequately supported by documents. Since documents represent existence that transactions actually took place, this procedure helps the auditor evaluate the EO and RO assertions.

In contrast, when **tracing** is performed, the auditor selects source documents and follows those documents through the accounting system to their ultimate recording in the accounts. As with vouching, the amount on the document can be compared to the recording in the accounts to evaluate the VA assertion. However, tracing also assures the auditor that selected transactions (represented by the source documents) have been recorded. Thus, tracing allows the auditor to evaluate the CO assertion.

The two directions taken by the auditor in the examination of documents are illustrated below. Remember, although both vouching and tracing involve comparison of one or more source document(s) with the accounting records, the assertion(s) of interest to the auditor (the EO and RO assertions versus the CO assertion) will dictate the auditor's approach in inspecting documents.

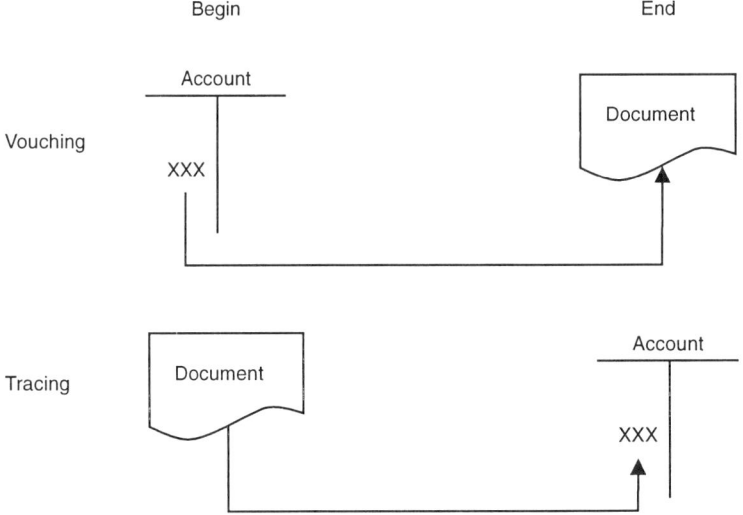

Dual-Purpose Tests. As noted in Chapter 5, the auditor can also inspect documents as part of his or her tests of controls. In some instances, a single procedure may provide the auditor with evidence related to both control risk and detection risk. For example, assume that the auditor is selecting a sample of sales transactions to determine that they were recorded at the proper dollar amount. By mathematically verifying the total of the Sales Invoice and agreeing this total to the amount recorded in the accounting records, the auditor is gathering evidence relating to the VA assertion. However, an important control policy related to the preparation of Sales Invoices is that client personnel verify the mathematical accuracy of Sales Invoices. Mathematically verifying the Sales Invoice also provides the auditor with evidence that the client's control policy was operating effectively. Since this type of evidence serves two purposes, tests of this nature are often referred to as **dual-purpose tests**.

IS IT REAL?

As a result of management fraud perpetuated through the use of photocopied Invoices, an unnamed CPA firm now requires that auditors check the authenticity of documents and accept only original documents as corroborating evidence.[7]

---

[7] *In the Public Interest* (Public Oversight Board, 1993), 28.

> **CHAPTER CHECKPOINTS**
>
> 6-13. List seven types of substantive testing procedures.
>
> 6-14. What types of items can be observed by the auditor? What assertion(s) are ordinarily verified by physical observation?
>
> 6-15. List the order of reliability of documentary evidence.
>
> 6-16. Distinguish between vouching and tracing. What assertion(s) are verified by each method of inspecting documents?

◻ Confirmation

For many types of account balances, one of the most effective methods of gathering evidence is direct communication with third parties. This communication, which is primarily performed by having third parties respond to a written request, is referred to as **confirmation**. Some examples of confirmation include verifying:

Account	Third Party
Cash	Banks
Accounts Receivable	Customers
Inventory	Consignees and Public Warehouses
Property, plant and equipment	Lessees (under operating leases)
Investments	Brokers and Independent Custodians
Accounts Payable	Vendors
Bonds or Notes Payable	Makers, Holders, and Trustees
Stockholders' Equity	Registrar

Statement on Auditing Standards No. 67[8] notes that, to increase the reliability of confirmations, the auditor should maintain control over confirmations at all times. That is, the confirmation should be directly mailed by the auditor to the third parties. In addition, the auditor should request that the third parties return the confirmation directly to him or her. If controlled in this manner, the auditor has received direct external evidence; as noted earlier, this is a highly reliable (competent) form of evidence. By controlling confirmations, the auditor reduces the probability that client personnel have somehow altered responses from third parties.

Confirmations can be designed to address any of the five management assertions; however, they do not address all assertions equally well. For example, in confirming accounts receivable from

---

[8] American Institute of Certified Public Accountants (AICPA), *Statement on Auditing Standards No. 67*, "The Confirmation Process" (New York: AICPA, 1991, AU 330).

customers, if customers indicate that a particular amount is owed to the client, the auditor has obtained evidence that the accounts receivable transactions occurred (the EO assertion). While it may also appear that the auditor has proved that the accounts receivable are the rights of the client (the RO assertion) and that accounts receivable are recorded at the correct dollar amount (the VA assertion), the customer may have no intention of repaying the amount owed to the client. To verify these assertions, the auditor may need to perform additional testing procedures (such as evaluating the adequacy of the client's provision for uncollectible accounts and examining the time period over which certain accounts are outstanding).

In contrast, cash on deposit in the bank is not subject to uncertainty regarding future collection and use. As a result, confirming cash balances with the client's bank allows the auditor to determine whether all recorded cash transactions actually occurred (the EO assertion), recorded cash transactions were the right of the company (the RO assertion), all cash transactions were recorded (the CO assertion), and cash transactions were recorded at the proper dollar amount (the VA assertion).

◻ Analytical Procedures

In Chapter 4, we noted that analytical procedures are used in the planning stages of the audit as an attention-directing procedure. **Analytical procedures** involve comparing the recorded amount of a particular account balance or class of transactions (or a ratio involving an account balance or class of transactions) with an expectation developed by the auditor. Expectations may be developed from the following sources:

1. Financial information for comparable prior period(s).
2. Anticipated results, such as budgets, forecasts, or extrapolations from interim or annual data.
3. Relationships with other financial information within the period.
4. Information regarding the industry in which the client operates.
5. Relationships of the financial information with relevant nonfinancial information.

To illustrate the use of analytical procedures, consider the auditor's examination of rental revenue for the Bates Hotel, an audit client. One obvious expectation of the current rental revenue for the Bates Hotel would be their rental revenue from last year. A second expectation would be determined by examining the rental revenue earned by similar hotels and adjusting these amounts to consider differences between these hotels and the Bates Hotel (such as capacity, room rates, and location). A final expectation could be determined by a rough mathematical calculation. If the Bates Hotel's average room rate was $100 per night, the hotel had 1,000 rooms, and the average occupancy rate was 80 percent, the following expectation of rental revenue for the Bates Hotel could be developed:

$$\text{Expected revenue} = \$100 \times 1{,}000 \text{ rooms} \times 0.80 \text{ rate} \times 365 \text{ days}$$
$$\text{Expected revenue} = \$29{,}200{,}000$$

SAS No. 56[9] notes that analytical procedures may be used in three stages of the audit examination: (1) the planning stages, (2) the substantive testing stages, and (3) the overall review stages. As noted in Chapter 4, the purpose of using analytical procedures in the planning stages of the audit is to allow the auditor to identify unusual or unexpected differences. Any account balances or classes of transactions that have unusual or unexpected differences are then subjected to more extensive substantive testing by the auditor.

Analytical procedures may also be used as substantive testing procedures to gather evidence about the fairness of a particular account balance or class of transactions. SAS No. 56 notes that substantive tests may consist of: (1) analytical procedures, (2) tests of details of transactions and balances, or (3) a combination of these procedures. In this form, analytical procedures are used to develop an expectation of the account balance that is compared to the recorded balance. The observed difference is then compared to some tolerable difference (based on the auditor's judgment of materiality) to determine whether extensive additional investigation of the recorded account balance is necessary. Unlike the planning stages of the audit, the auditor is not required to use analytical procedures during the substantive testing stages of the audit.

Finally, analytical procedures can be used in the overall review stages of the audit. Similar to the planning stages, SAS No. 56 requires the use of analytical procedures in the overall review stages of the audit examination. In the overall review stages, analytical procedures are used to assess the validity of the overall conclusions reached by the auditor, including the opinion on the financial statements taken as a whole. Results of such a review may reveal unusual or unexpected account balances not identified: (1) in the preliminary (planning) stages, or (2) during the audit. If this is the case, additional procedures may be needed before an opinion can be issued on the client's financial statements.

The use of analytical procedures in the three stages of the audit is summarized in Figure 6-7. It is important to note that regardless of the stage of the audit in which these procedures are utilized, the auditor follows a basic three-step procedure:

1. Develop an expectation of the account balance or some ratio involving the account balance.
2. Compare the expectation from (1) above with the recorded account balance or ratio developed from recorded account balances.
3. Investigate any significant differences in (2) above.

Unexpected differences between the expected account balance or ratio and the recorded account balance or ratio revealed by analytical procedures may result from one of three sources: (1) fictitious transactions recorded by the client (the EO and RO assertions), (2) the failure to record all transactions (the CO assertion), or (3) recording transactions at the incorrect dollar amount (the VA assertion). Thus, analytical procedures may correspond to a number of different management assertions.

---

[9] American Institute of Certified Public Accountants (AICPA), *Statement on Auditing Standards No. 56*, "Analytical Procedures" (New York: AICPA, 1988, AU 329).

Stage of the Audit	Required or Optional Use	Purpose of Analytical Procedures
Planning	Required	1. To enhance the auditor's understanding of the client's business and transactions and events occurring since the last audit 2. To identify areas representing specific risks during the audit.
Substantive Testing	Optional	To achieve an audit objective related to a particular assertion
Overall Review	Required	To assess the overall conclusions reached and evaluate the overall financial statement presentation

Figure 6-7: *The Use of Analytical Procedures in the Audit Examination*

CAN ANALYTICAL PROCEDURES BE USED TO SPOT FRAUD?

In the early 1990's, the top officers of Comptronix Corp., a manufacturer of electronics products, engaged in a scheme to inflate sales and profits. The following relationships, which could have been revealed by performing analytical procedures, would have enabled auditors to detect this fraud:

▶ Comptronix' sales grew much faster than its receivables; as a result, Comptronix' ratio of sales to receivables was much different than industry competitors.

▶ Comptronix' ratio of sales to property, plant and equipment was unusually low for companies in their industry.

▶ Given the high level of growth in sales, Comptronix' inventory turnover ratios were unusually low.[10]

---

[10] "Comptronix Fires Its CEO but Keeps Two Other Aides," *The Wall Street Journal* (December 14, 1992).

> **CHAPTER CHECKPOINTS**
>
> 6-17. What is confirmation? Give some examples of items that could be confirmed by the auditor.
>
> 6-18. What are analytical procedures? What are some methods that can be used by the auditor to develop expectations for use in performing analytical procedures?
>
> 6-19. During what stages of the audit can analytical procedures be used? What are the auditor's objectives in using analytical procedures during these stages of the audit?

◻ Recalculations

A form of evidence often utilized by the auditor is performing independent calculations with respect to the account balance under examination. For income statement and balance sheet accounts where the final balances are completely determined by mathematical calculations, performing calculations is often a relatively cost-effective measure of gathering evidence about whether accounts are recorded at the proper dollar amounts (the VA assertion). The following accounts may be verified primarily through recalculation:

- Bad debt expense and allowance for uncollectible accounts
- Depreciation expense and accumulated depreciation
- Interest expense and interest payable
- Warranty expense and the obligation for warranties

In performing calculations, the auditor often must consider the problems introduced with accounting estimates. An **accounting estimate** is an approximation of a financial statement element, item, or account. Examples of accounting estimates include:

1. The provision for bad debt expense and allowance for uncollectible accounts related to accounts receivable.
2. The useful lives and salvage values associated with fixed assets.
3. Expenses and liabilities associated with warranties regarding the number and extent of future customer claims.

Accounting estimates are the responsibility of the client's management. Unlike other items in the financial statements, objective evidence regarding the accuracy of accounting estimates cannot be obtained by the auditor. Under *Statement on Auditing Standards No. 57 (SAS No. 57)*,[11] the auditor should perform the following procedures for accounting estimates:

1. Evaluate whether all accounting estimates that could be material to the financial statements have been developed.
2. Determine that these estimates are reasonable.
3. Determine that all accounting estimates are presented in conformity with GAAP and are adequately disclosed in the financial statements.

In sum, although the auditor cannot absolutely verify the accuracy of accounting estimates, it is the auditor's responsibility under GAAS to evaluate the reasonableness of these estimates and verify that the estimates are properly disclosed in the financial statements.

Comparisons

Comparisons involve agreeing the total amount of an account balance or class of transactions from the client's accounting records (the Trial Balance or General Ledger) to a summary of the transactions or components underlying that account balance or class of transactions. For example, when examining accounts receivable, the auditor will request that the client prepare an Aged Listing of Accounts Receivable. The Aged Listing of Accounts Receivable is a listing of the client's accounts receivable by due date. Upon receipt of this schedule, the auditor will mathematically verify (or "foot") the listing and agree the total to the accounts receivable included in the client's Trial Balance. By performing this procedure, the auditor obtains evidence that the sum of the components of the account balance or class of transactions agree with the total amounts in the client's financial records. Comparisons of this nature provide the auditor with evidence regarding the VA assertion.

Oral Inquiry

In some situations, written documentary evidence is not available to the auditor. This is particularly true with respect to various disclosures required under GAAP for different account balances or classes of transactions. In these cases, the auditor should obtain evidence through inquiry of client personnel. Examples of evidence that may be obtained in this fashion include:

- **Cash:** The existence of compensating balances or other arrangements
- **Accounts Receivable:** Accounts factored, assigned, or pledged as collateral
- **Inventory:** Inventories held on consignment
- **Investments:** Management's intent with respect to holding its investments in marketable securities

---

[11] American Institute of Certified Public Accountants (AICPA), *Statement on Auditing Standards No. 57*, "Auditing Accounting Estimates" (New York: AICPA, 1988, AU 342).

Oral inquiry is most frequently used to verify the PD assertion; that is, the auditor makes inquiries of client personnel to ensure that specific aspects of different account balances are properly disclosed in the client's financial statements or footnotes to the financial statements. In addition, inquiries may provide the auditor with information that affects the recorded value of the account balance. For example, management's intent with respect to its investments in marketable securities affects how unrealized gains or losses in those securities are reported in the financial statements. Therefore, inquiry may also provide assurance related to the VA assertion.

Although client responses to oral inquiries are often very helpful, oral evidence should also be confirmed by other types of evidence. The auditor will corroborate oral evidence received through his or her inquiries by obtaining **written representations** (also known as **management representations** or **client representations**) from the client. Written representations are discussed by *Statement on Auditing Standards No. 19*.[12] These representations cover many topics, including:

1. Stating that management is responsible for the fairness of its financial statements.
2. Acknowledging that all financial records and related data have been made available to the auditor.
3. Corroborating oral representations made by management and its employees to the auditor.

Written representations are described in greater detail in Chapter 16 of this text.

◘ Summary: Substantive Testing Procedures

Figure 6-8 summarizes the substantive testing procedures discussed in this chapter. For each procedure, Figure 6-8 indicates: (1) the relative competence of the substantive testing procedure, (2) the management assertion(s) that are normally verified by the substantive testing procedure, and (3) an example of how each type of substantive testing procedure can be used in the audit of cash.

CHAPTER CHECKPOINTS

6-20. Give some examples of items that can be verified through recalculation.

6-21. What are accounting estimates? What is the auditor's responsibility with respect to accounting estimates?

6-22. Give some examples of information that can be verified through oral inquiries. What assertion(s) are normally verified through the use of oral inquiries?

6-23. What are written representations? How do written representations relate to oral inquiries?

---

[12] American Institute of Certified Public Accountants (AICPA), *Statement on Auditing Standards No. 19*, "Client Representations" (New York: AICPA, 1977, AU 333).

Substantive Test	Competence	Assertion(s)	Example
Physical Observation	Direct Evidence	EO (All Accounts) RO, CO, VA (Some Accounts)	Count cash held by the client
Examining Documents			
a. Tracing	Varies, depending on the source of the document	CO, VA	Trace from Checks returned with the Bank Statement to the client's Bank Reconciliation
b. Vouching	Varies, depending on the source of the document	EO, RO, VA	Vouch from deposits listed on the client's Bank Reconciliation to Deposit Slips returned with the Bank Statement
Confirmation	Evidence Received Directly from External Parties	EO (All Accounts) RO, CO, VA (Some Accounts)	Confirm cash balances on deposit with the client's banks
Analytical Procedures	Direct Evidence	EO, RO, CO, VA	Compare recorded cash balances to budgeted cash balances
Recalculation	Direct Evidence	VA	Mathematically verify the client's Bank Reconciliation
Comparison	Direct Evidence	VA	Compare total from Bank Reconciliation to Schedule of Cash Balances
Oral Inquiry	Evidence Obtained from the Client	PD (All Accounts) VA (Some Accounts)	Inquire about the existence of compensating balances related to cash

Figure 6-8: *Summary of Substantive Testing Procedures*

◉ WORKING PAPERS

Working papers (or **workpapers**) are the primary record of the procedures performed and conclusions reached by the auditor during the engagement. In addition, workpapers assist the auditor the conduct and supervision of the audit. Workpapers may take a variety of forms, such as:

- Audit programs
- Analyses performed by the auditor
- Letters of confirmation or representation
- Copies or abstracts of client documentation
- Schedules or commentaries prepared or obtained by the auditor

The quantity, content, and types of workpapers prepared by the auditor will vary from one engagement to another. Factors affecting the quantity, content, and types of workpapers include:

1. The nature of the engagement (is the engagement an audit of the entire financial statements, an audit of a portion of the financial statements, or an engagement less in scope than an audit?)
2. The nature of the report to be issued by the auditor (is the report an audit report or a report on an engagement less in scope than an audit?)
3. The nature of the financial statements, schedules, or other information on which the auditor is reporting (does the client use GAAP in preparing its financial statements or do they use another comprehensive basis of accounting?)
4. The nature and condition of the client's records
5. The assessed level of control risk (do the workpapers include evidence of performing tests of controls, substantive tests, or both?)
6. The necessary levels of supervision and review in the audit[13]

In any instance, workpapers should provide the auditor with documentation that:

1. The accounting records agree with or reconcile to the client's financial statements.
2. The auditor has observed the standards of field work. These standards (as discussed earlier in Chapter 1) are:
   a. The work has been planned and assistants properly supervised.
   b. A sufficient understanding of internal control has been obtained.
   c. Sufficient, competent evidential matter has been gathered.

◻ Types of Workpapers

Workpapers generally are comprised of the following: (1) Working Trial Balance, (2) Assembly Sheets or Lead Schedules, (3) Audit Schedules, (4) Audit Memoranda and Other Information, and (5) Summaries of Adjusting and Reclassifying Journal Entries.

---

[13] American Institute of Certified Public Accountants (AICPA), *Statement on Auditing Standards No. 41*, "Working Papers" (New York: AICPA, 1982, AU 339).

Working Trial Balance. The Working Trial Balance represents a listing of the ending balance in all of the client's accounts prior to preparing adjusting journal entries. The Working Trial Balance is ordinarily prepared by the client based on the ending balance in their General Ledger accounts and contains the following information:

1. Reference to Assembly Sheets and Lead Schedules for each account.
2. Prior-year's ending balance.
3. Current-year's ending balance.
4. Adjustments/reclassifications.
5. Reference for adjustments/reclassifications.

Once the auditor obtains the Working Trial Balance, he or she foots this balance and agrees the account totals to the client's General Ledger.

Assembly Sheets (or Lead Schedules). Assembly Sheets (or Lead Schedules) summarize the major components of the account balance or class of transactions. For example, consider some of the information that would be included on Assembly Sheets for the following balance-sheet accounts:

- ▶ **Cash:** A summary of cash on deposit in banks and cash on hand
- ▶ **Accounts Receivable:** A listing of amounts owed by the client's customers
- ▶ **Inventory:** A listing of the inventory items held at year-end
- ▶ **Property, plant and equipment:** Major groupings of property, plant and equipment (land, equipment, machinery, and other)

In some instances, the Assembly Sheets are prepared by the client. For example, it is ordinarily easier for the client to prepare a listing of their accounts receivable at year-end. Once the auditor obtains (or prepares) an Assembly Sheet, he or she should perform the following procedures:

1. Verify the mathematical accuracy of the Assembly Sheet.
2. Agree the total of the account balance to the client's Working Trial Balance.

Audit Schedules. Audit schedules are worksheets that provide a detailed analysis of the procedures performed by the auditor during his or her examination. It is on these schedules that the types of substantive tests discussed in this chapter are summarized. A sample Audit Schedule is shown in Figure 6-9.

The significant components of the Audit Schedule are discussed through reference to the numbers appearing on the schedule shown in Figure 6-9.

1. **Heading.** The heading indicates the following major information: (1) the name of the client, (2) a description of the contents of the workpaper, and (3) the date of the financial statements being audited. In this case, the heading identifies that the Audit Schedule illustrates the auditor's procedures for the Bank Reconciliation of Attaya Company. The date of the financial statements being audited is 12-31-x1.

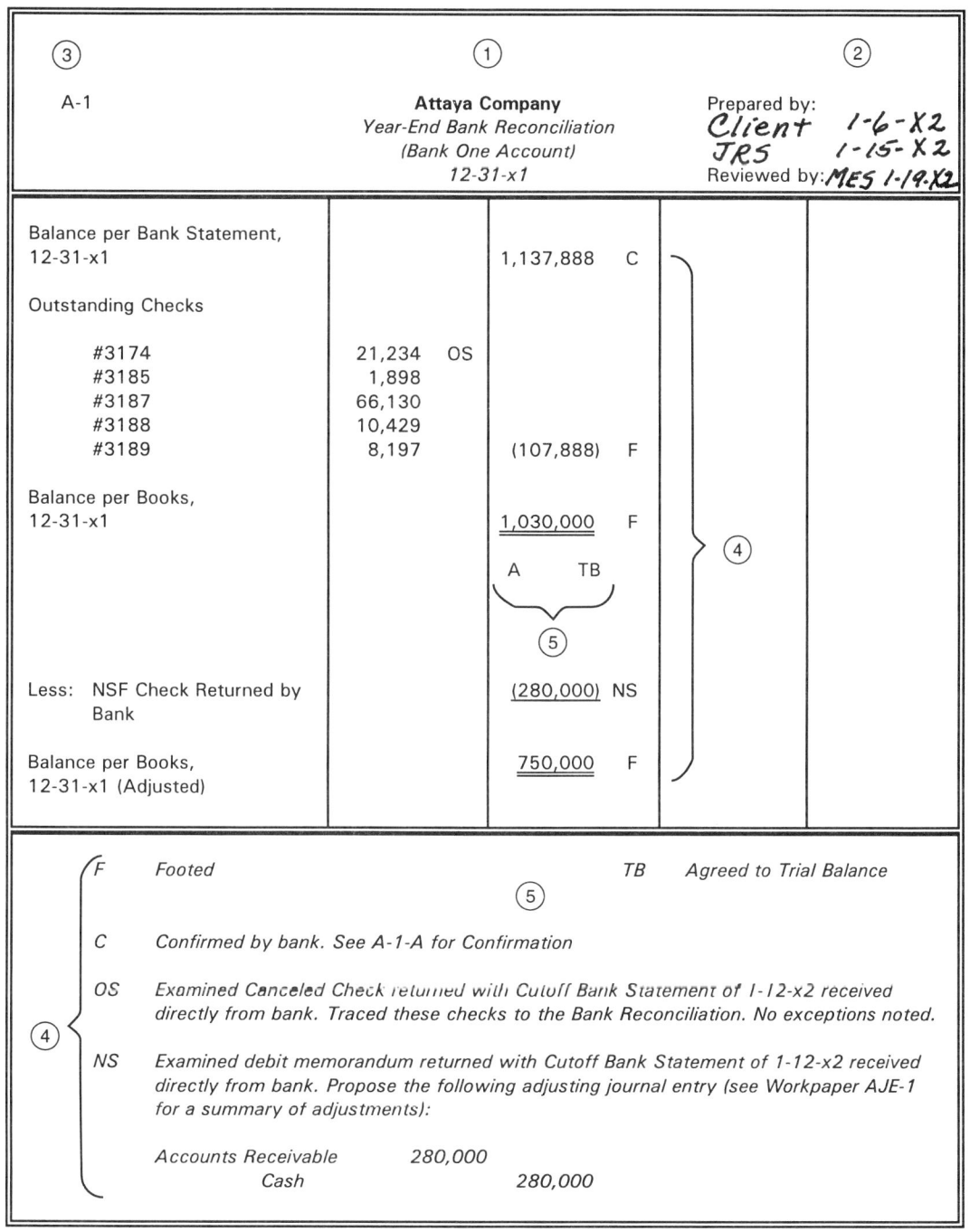

Figure 6-9: Sample Audit Schedule

6/ Substantive Testing and Control of Detection Risk

2. **Initials.** The initials of the individual(s) preparing and reviewing each workpaper should be included on each workpaper so that if necessary these individuals may be identified at a later time. In addition, the date(s) that these individual(s) performed this activity should also be noted.

   For the Audit Schedule in Figure 6-9, the workpaper was prepared by two persons: the client (on 1-6-x2) and "JRS" (on 1-15-x2). This double set of initials indicates that the client prepared the basic Bank Reconciliation and JRS (an auditor) performed analysis on the Bank Reconciliation. The Audit Schedule (and analysis performed by JRS) was reviewed by MES on 1-19-x2.

3. **Numbering.** The Audit Schedules are numbered consecutively for convenience in referring to the procedures performed by the auditor (in this case, A-1).

4. **Tickmarks.** Tickmarks are used by the auditor to describe the audit procedures performed during the examination. The tickmarks are accompanied by a complete discussion of the actual procedures performed. For example, the tickmark "C" in Figure 6-9 indicates that the "Balance per Bank Statement" on the year-end Bank Reconciliation was based on a confirmation received from their bank.

5. **Cross-referencing.** Cross-referencing is an important device used to allow an efficient review of the workpapers. Referring to Figure 6-9, the "TB" and "A" references indicate that the "Balance per Books" is agreed to Attaya Company's Working Trial Balance and an Assembly Sheet numbered "A". In addition, the bank confirmation used to corroborate the "Balance per Bank" can be found at workpaper A-1-A.

Audit Memoranda and Other Information. The fourth type of workpapers are audit memoranda and other information used to support the analyses in the Audit Schedules. As such, these items are normally referenced in the Audit Schedules. These items include copies of:

▶ Confirmations and other documentation

▶ Letters of representation received from the client

▶ Letters from the client's attorneys

▶ Important client documents (Board of Directors' minutes, Bylaws and Articles of Incorporation)

▶ Narrative explanations of audit procedures and findings

An example of information that would appear in this section of the auditor's workpapers from Figure 6-9 is the bank confirmation received from Attaya Company's bank.

Summaries of Adjusting or Reclassifying Journal Entries. As the auditor analyzes the various accounts, items may be found that the auditor believes require adjustment or reclassification. An **adjusting journal entry** is prepared to correct errors or situations where the financial statements are not prepared according to GAAP. **Reclassifying journal entries** are prepared within the auditor's workpapers to reclassify accounts for presentation in the financial statements; however, these entries are not recorded by the client.

The need for adjusting or reclassifying journal entries may be because of a client error or simply to a difference of opinion regarding the accounting treatment to be accorded a particular item. In many instances, the auditor and client may have different approaches to the recording of a transaction.

If the difference is material, the auditor will propose an adjustment to the client. If the client refuses to record a material adjustment, then the auditor may have to consider modifying the opinion.

If the client approves the adjustment, then the auditor will make an adjusting entry on the workpaper related to the account under consideration. The entry will be made on both the Working Trial Balance and a separate summary of adjusting and reclassifying journal entries.

◘ Interrelationship Among Workpapers

The relationship among the various types of workpapers discussed in this section is illustrated in Figure 6-10. The hierarchy of workpapers shown therein is summarized below:

1. The amount of cash shown on the balance sheet is $1,000,000 (Financial Statement).
2. The ending balance in cash (after adjustments) is $1,000,000 (Working Trial Balance).
3. The ending balance in cash (before adjustments) consists of $1,030,000 on deposit in Bank One and $250,000 on deposit in Bank Two (Assembly Sheet).
4. The balance of $1,030,000 in Bank One is verified through the client's Bank Reconciliation (Audit Schedule).
5. The "balance per bank" from the Audit Schedule is confirmed with Bank One (Audit Memoranda and Other Information).
6. The adjusting entries for cash are summarized in a Schedule of Adjusting Entries.

◘ Filing of Workpapers

Workpapers are filed in two principal categories: (1) current files, and (2) permanent files. The **current file** includes information that is only pertinent to the current-year's audit. Information in the current workpaper file is critical to the auditor in supporting his or her opinion on the current-year's financial statements. While current workpapers may be used in the following year as an example of substantive tests to be performed in that year, these workpapers will not be of much importance beyond the current audit. Information ordinarily included in the current file includes:

- ▶ A copy of the current-year's financial statements.
- ▶ All workpapers (Working Trial Balance, Assembly Sheets, Audit Schedules, Audit Memoranda and Other Information, and Summary of Adjusting and Reclassifying Journal Entries) related to the current-year's audit.

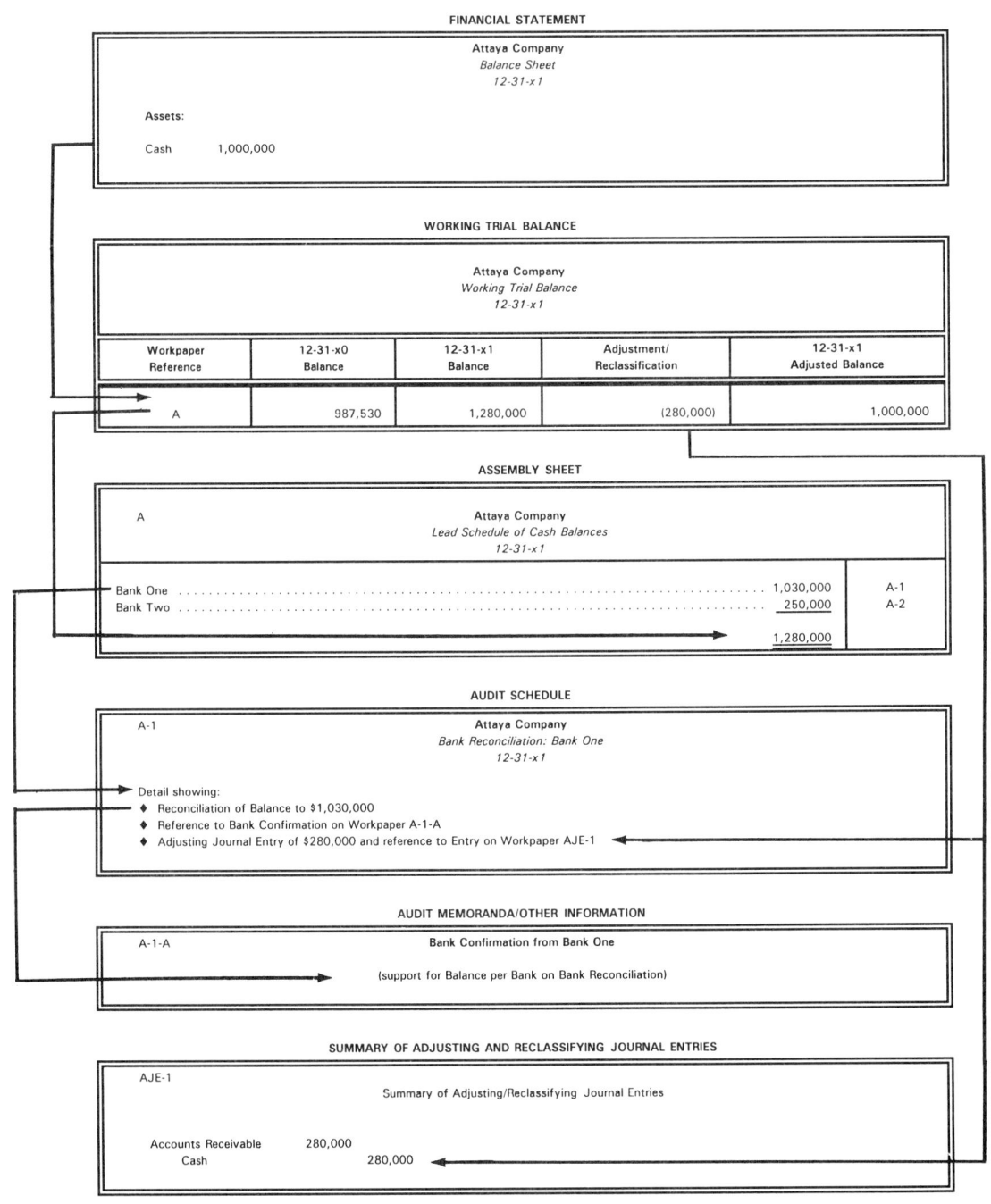

Figure 6-10: *Interrelationship Among Working Papers*

Permanent files normally contain information that the auditor will use on the engagement in both the current and future years. The information that may be included in the permanent file varies, but often includes:

- Notes for future audits.
- The documentation of the client's internal control.
- Copies of letters of recommendation sent to clients.
- Copies of Articles of Incorporation or excerpts therefrom.
- Copies of Bylaws or excerpts therefrom.
- Sample of stock certificates.
- Copies of indenture or loan agreements, with notations as to sections pertinent to the financial statements.
- Computations of retained earnings restrictions under loan agreements.
- Copies of bonus, pension, and profit-sharing plans.
- Copies of important royalty agreements, leases, and other contracts.
- Analyses of capital stock and surplus accounts.
- Depreciation and property-lapsing schedules.
- Certain data relating to reports filed and correspondence with regulatory agencies.
- Client's accounting manuals and charts of accounts.
- Minutes of meetings of stockholders or the Board of Directors.
- Agreements with stock exchanges.
- Registration statements, proxy statements, etc.

Ownership and Custody of Workpapers

Workpapers are the property of the auditor. In some states, laws specifically indicate that the workpapers are owned by the auditor. However, despite this ownership, it is important that the auditor observes the Code of Professional Conduct with respect to workpapers. For example, Rule 301 indicates that the auditor should not disclose client information to others without the client's consent; since workpapers will contain important client information, this information falls under the jurisdiction of Rule 301. Recall that four exceptions to Rule 301 allow the auditor to reveal client information in conjunction with:

1. His or her obligation under Rules 202 and 203 (to present the financial statements according to GAAP).
2. A legal subpoena or summons.
3. A review of his or her professional practice.
4. Responding to inquiries of the AICPA, State Societies of CPAs, or State Boards of Accountancy.

In discussing the custody of workpapers, the auditor should maintain custody of the permanent file for an indefinite period of time, since these workpapers have continuing use throughout as the auditor performs future examinations of the client. The current file should be retained for a sufficient period of time to meet the legal requirements for records retention. While this varies from state to state, most CPA firms keep the current file on its premises for two years and transfer this file to an off-site location in later years.

◻ Workpaper Review

In addition to supporting the auditor's opinion on the financial statements, the workpapers also provide the auditor with a form of supervision by allowing the work performed to be reviewed throughout the firm's hierarchy. The hierarchy of review of workpapers is shown below:

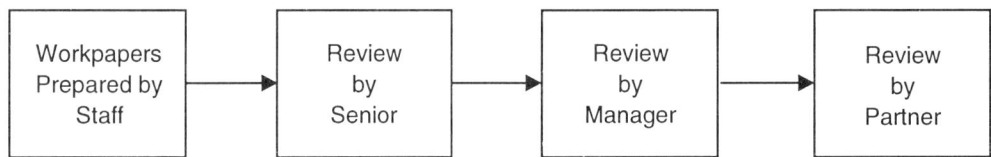

The purpose of these reviews of workpapers is to evaluate the procedures performed, evidence gathered, and conclusions reached by the preparer. In cases where workpapers are initially prepared by the senior, these workpapers are subsequently reviewed by the manager and partner. The review of workpapers at the conclusion of the audit is discussed further in Chapter 16 of this text.

> **CHAPTER CHECKPOINTS**
>
> **6-24.** What are workpapers? What type of documentation should workpapers provide to the auditor?
>
> **6-25.** List and define the major types of workpapers.
>
> **6-26.** What are the major components of Audit Schedules?
>
> **6-27.** Distinguish between workpapers included in the current file and permanent file. Provide examples of items that would be included in each type of file.
>
> **6-28.** Who owns the audit workpapers?

◉ SUMMARY OF KEY POINTS

1. The third standard of field work requires the auditor to obtain sufficient, competent evidential matter before issuing an opinion on the fairness of the client's financial statements. The process of gathering this evidence is referred to as substantive testing.

2. Two important characteristics of evidence are sufficiency and competence. The sufficiency of evidence relates to the quantity of evidence that an auditor needs in a particular circumstance; that is, how many components or transactions of an account balance or class of transactions should be examined? The competence of evidence relates to the quality of evidence. In order to be competent, evidence must be both relevant (relate to the assertion of interest) and valid (be obtained from a reliable source).

3. Two general approaches are available to the auditor in performing substantive tests. Tests of balances are characterized by selecting specific components of the final account balance for verification. In contrast, when using the test of transactions approach, the auditor verifies all (or most) of the transactions affecting a particular account balance during a given period. The substantive testing approach selected by the auditor depends on characteristics of the account being examined, such as the number and dollar amount of transactions affecting this account.

4. The necessary level of detection risk can be determined by the auditor after assessing the levels of audit risk, inherent risk, and control risk. The level of detection risk is related to the nature, timing, and extent of the auditor's substantive tests and is determined on an assertion-by-assertion basis.

5. In order to achieve lower levels of detection risk, the auditor should obtain more reliable evidence (the nature of substantive tests), perform tests at year-end (the timing of substantive tests), and examine a larger number of components of the account balance or class of transactions (the extent of substantive tests).

6. Substantive testing procedures include: (1) physical observation, (2) inspecting documents, (3) confirmations, (4) analytical procedures, (5) computations, (6) comparisons, and (7) oral inquiry.

These procedures are used by the auditor to verify the assertions for account balances and classes of transactions.

7. When inspecting documents, the auditor can proceed in one of two directions. If the auditor vouches from a recorded entry to a document, she or he selects an entry in the account balance and then tries to support this entry by examining the appropriate document. Alternatively, the auditor can trace from a document to an entry in the accounting records.

8. Analytical procedures involve comparing the recorded amount of a particular account balance or class of transactions (or ratio involving an account balance or class of transactions) with an expectation developed by the auditor. Expectations may be developed based on: (1) financial information for comparable prior period(s); (2) anticipated results (such as budgets, forecasts, or extrapolations from interim or annual data); (3) relationships with other financial information within the period; (4) information regarding the industry in which the client operates; and (5) relationships of the financial information with relevant nonfinancial information.

10. Workpapers are records of the procedures performed and conclusions reached by the auditor during the engagement. The major types of workpapers include: (1) Working Trial Balance, (2) Assembly Sheets or Lead Schedules, (3) Audit Schedules, (4) Audit Memoranda and Other Information, and (5) Summaries of Adjusting and Reclassifying Journal Entries.

◉ GLOSSARY

Accounting Data. Books of original entry, general and subsidiary ledgers, and worksheets that are prepared by the client. Accounting data represent the end result of the processing of transactions and are supported by corroborating information.

Accounting Estimates. An approximation of a financial statement element, item, or account. While estimates cannot be determined with certainty, the auditor is required to verify the reasonableness of accounting estimates.

Adjusting Journal Entries. A journal entry prepared to correct errors or situations where the financial statements are not prepared in conformity with GAAP.

Analytical Procedures. A substantive testing procedure that involves comparing the recorded amount of a particular account balance or class of transactions (or ratio involving an account balance or class of transactions) with an expectation developed by the auditor.

Assembly Sheets. Also known as Lead Schedules, these workpapers summarize the major components of the account balance or class of transactions.

Audit Memoranda. Information used to support the analysis performed by the auditor in the Audit Schedules.

Audit Schedules. A type of workpaper that provides a detailed analysis of the procedures performed by the auditor during his or her examination.

Comparison. A form of substantive testing procedure that involves agreeing the total amount of an account balance or class of transactions from the client's accounting records (the Trial Balance or General Ledger) to a summary of the transactions or components underlying that account balance or class of transactions.

Competence of Evidence. A measure of the quality of the evidence gathered by the auditor (or the nature of the auditor's substantive tests). The competence of evidence is related to both the reliability of the source of the evidence (or validity) and the information provided by the evidence (or relevance).

Confirmation. A form of substantive testing procedure in which the auditor obtains evidence directly from third parties external to the client. Confirmations can be used in the audit of cash, accounts receivable, accounts payable, and other accounts.

Corroborating Information. Information that verifies or supports the client's accounting data. This information includes documents, responses to confirmations sent to third parties by the auditor, and other evidence gathered through auditor observation, inspection, and inquiry.

Current File. Workpapers that are only pertinent to the current-year's audit examination. Information in the current file includes a copy of the client's current-year financial statements and all workpapers related to the current-year's audit.

Detection Risk. The risk that the auditor's substantive tests will fail to detect a material misstatement in an assertion. Detection risk is related to the nature, timing, and extent of the auditor's substantive tests.

Dual-Purpose Tests. Tests performed by the auditor that provide evidence relating to both the operating effectiveness of an internal control policy or procedure (tests of controls) and the fairness of an account balance or class of transactions (substantive tests).

Lead Schedule. See Assembly Sheet.

Oral Inquiry. A form of substantive testing procedure that requires the auditor to ask questions of client personnel. These inquiries are usually corroborated by obtaining written representations (see definition).

Permanent File. Workpapers that contain information the auditor will use on the engagement in both the current and future years. Examples of information included in the permanent file are notes for future audits, copies of the client's Articles of Incorporation and Bylaws, and copies of indenture or loan agreements.

Physical Observation. A form of substantive testing procedure in which the auditor inspects a physical item, such as cash; inventory; property, plant and equipment; and, bonds and notes payable.

Recalculation. A form of substantive testing procedure in which the auditor performs independent verification with respect to the account balance under examination.

Reclassifying Journal Entries. Journal entries prepared within the auditor's workpapers to reclassify accounts for presentation in the financial statements.

Relevance. A component of the competence of evidence (see definition) that relates to the financial statement assertion verified by evidence.

Substantive Tests. Tests performed by the auditor to obtain evidence regarding the fairness of the account balances and classes of transactions that make up the company's financial statements. Substantive tests are related to the detection risk component of the audit risk model.

Sufficiency of Evidence. A measure of the quantity of evidence gathered by the auditor (or the extent of the auditor's substantive tests). The sufficiency of evidence is related to the number of components or transactions of an account balance or class of transactions examined by the auditor.

Tests of Balances. A substantive testing approach that focuses on individual components (such as cash on deposit in a particular bank or a particular customer's account receivable balance) of the account balances under examination.

Tests of Transactions. A substantive testing approach that involves verifying individual transactions affecting the account balances during a particular period.

Tickmarks. Symbols or abbreviations that are used by the auditor to describe the audit procedures performed during the examination. Tickmarks are accompanied by a complete description of the actual procedures performed.

Tracing. The process of identifying transactions or items that exist or occur and verifying that these items are recorded. Tracing is performed to provide assurance regarding the CO and VA assertions.

Underlying Accounting Data. See Accounting Data.

Validity. A component of the competence of evidence (see definition) that relates to the reliability of the source of the evidence.

Vouching. The process of obtaining support for recorded items by locating documentation or other evidence related to the item. Vouching is performed to provide assurance regarding the EO, RO, and VA assertions.

Working Trial Balance. A type of workpaper that represents a listing of the ending balance in the client's accounts prior to preparing the adjusting and/or reclassifying journal entries.

Workpapers. The primary record of the procedures performed and conclusions reached by the auditor during the engagement.

Written Representations. Documents that are provided by the client to the auditor that: (1) acknowledge management's responsibility for the financial statements; (2) indicate that all financial records and related data have been made available to the auditor; and (3) corroborate oral inquiries made by client personnel to the auditor.

◉ SUMMARY OF PROFESSIONAL PRONOUNCEMENTS

Statement on Auditing Standards No. 1, "Codification of Auditing Standards and Procedures" (New York: AICPA, 1972, AU 150.02).

Statement on Auditing Standards No. 19, "Client Representations" (New York: AICPA, 1977, AU 333).

Statement on Auditing Standards No. 31, "Evidential Matter" (New York: AICPA, 1980, AU 326).

Statement on Auditing Standards No. 41, "Working Papers" (New York: AICPA, 1982, AU 339).

Statement on Auditing Standards No. 45, "Omnibus Statement on Auditing Standards–1983" (New York: AICPA, 1983, AU 313).

Statement on Auditing Standards No. 56, "Analytical Procedures" (New York: AICPA, 1988, AU 329).

Statement on Auditing Standards No. 57, "Auditing Accounting Estimates" (New York: AICPA, 1988, AU 342).

Statement on Auditing Standards No. 67, "The Confirmation Process" (New York: AICPA, 1991, AU 330).

Proposed Statement on Auditing Standards, "Amendment to *Statement on Auditing Standards No. 31*, 'Evidential Matter'" (New York: AICPA, May 20, 1996).

QUESTIONS AND PROBLEMS

6-29. Select the **best** answer for each of the following items:

1. The following four statements were made in a discussion of audit evidence between two CPAs. Which statement is not valid concerning evidential matter?

    a. "I am seldom convinced beyond all doubt with respect to all aspects of the statements being examined."
    b. "I would not undertake that procedure because at best the results would only be persuasive and I'm looking for convincing evidence."
    c. "I evaluate the degree of risk involved in deciding the kind of evidence I will gather."
    d. "I evaluate the usefulness of the evidence I can obtain against the cost to obtain it."

2. Evidential matter supporting the financial statements consists of the underlying accounting data and all corroborating information available to the auditor. Which of the following is an example of corroborating information?

    a. Minutes of meetings.
    b. General and subsidiary ledgers.
    c. Accounting manuals.
    d. Worksheets supporting cost allocations.

3. From which of the following evidence-gathering procedures would an auditor obtain most assurance concerning the existence of inventories?

    a. Observation of physical inventory counts.
    b. Written inventory representations from management.
    c. Confirmation of inventories in a public warehouse.
    d. Auditor's recalculation of inventory extensions.

4. The permanent section of the auditor's workpapers generally should include:

    a. Time and expense reports.
    b. Names and addresses of all audit staff personnel on the engagement.
    c. A copy of key customer confirmations.
    d. A copy of the engagement letter.

5. Which of the following is not a primary purpose of audit workpapers?

    a. To coordinate the examination.
    b. To assist in preparation of the audit report.
    c. To support the financial statements.
    d. To provide evidence of the audit work performed.

6. To be competent, evidence must be both:

   a. Timely and substantial.
   b. Reliable and documented.
   c. Valid and relevant.
   d. Useful and objective.

7. The auditor performs preliminary analytical review procedures in order to:

   a. Form a preliminary assessment of the client's control risk.
   b. Identify accounts that may contain significant errors.
   c. Assure herself that the integrity of management is as sound as in prior years.
   d. Determine whether a specialist should be engaged to assist in some phase of the examination.
   e. Assess the reliability of the overall conclusions contained in the financial statements.

8. Which of the following types of workpapers contains the majority of information about the tests performed by the auditor?

   a. Assembly Sheets.
   b. Audit Memoranda.
   c. Audit Schedules.
   d. Working Trial Balance.

9. Tests of balances differ from tests of transactions in that:

   a. Tests of transactions are tests of controls, while tests of balances are substantive tests.
   b. Tests of transactions are always performed during the year, while tests of balances are performed only after the end of the year.
   c. Tests of balances are performed to evaluate whether the internal control is operating as planned, while tests of transactions are conducted to determine whether a new engagement should be accepted.
   d. Tests of balances directly evaluate the accuracy of a recorded account balance, while tests of transactions evaluate the component entries that result in recorded balances.
   e. Tests of transactions are normally performed for accounts having a large number of transactions, while tests of balances are performed for accounts having a small number of transactions.

10. The auditor normally employs substantive tests of balances rather than substantive tests of transactions:
    a. Because tests of transactions provide no evidence of the validity of the beginning balance of an account.
    b. Except in testing income statement accounts, which require no evaluation of the beginning balance because they begin each year at zero.
    c. When the ending balances are the results of many immaterial transactions and the component balances can be verified directly with outside parties.
    d. When the prior-year financial statements (*i.e.*, the beginning balances) were audited by another CPA.
    e. None of the above.

11. The reliability (or competence) of evidence:

    a. Is not affected by its source (*i.e.*, from within the company or from outside parties).
    b. Is higher when obtained from independent sources rather than from the client.
    c. Is not affected by the effectiveness of the client's internal control.
    d. Is lower for the auditor's personal knowledge (obtained through such processes as physical examination and observation) than for information obtained indirectly.
    e. Is the only quality of evidence that the auditor needs to consider during his or her examination.

12. Which of the following strategies could not be used by the auditor to reduce the necessary level of detection risk?

    a. Testing a greater number of components or transactions underlying an account balance.
    b. Changing the nature of evidence to obtain externally-generated evidence as opposed to internally-generated evidence.
    c. Modifying the timing of substantive tests to perform tests during the interim period as opposed to year-end.
    d. Utilizing direct as opposed to indirect evidence.

13. The auditor may rely on substantive tests performed at an interim date:

    a. Without performing any compensating or "follow-up" procedures after the end of the year.
    b. In only those accounts whose balances are not expected to change materially before the end of the year.
    c. If the auditor performs other analyses and makes other assessments after the end of the year that indicate that the results of interim testing are still relevant.
    d. Only if general business conditions do not deteriorate before the end of the year.
    e. None of the above.

14. In determining the sufficiency of evidence gathered, the auditor must consider:

    a. The increase in detection risk that results from any increase in the volume of transactions or balances examined.
    b. The inverse relationship between the effectiveness of the auditor's substantive testing procedures and detection risk.
    c. Omitting a test solely because the cost of gathering the evidence is prohibitive.
    d. The competence of the evidence, but not the timing of evidence.
    e. None of the above.

15. In deciding which type of substantive test to perform in evaluating an account balance, the auditor should consider:

    a. The desired effectiveness of the substantive testing procedures to be performed.
    b. The financial statement assertion under consideration.
    c. The nature of the account being examined.
    d. All of the above.
    e. None of the above.

16. The auditor may perform analytical procedures:

    a. Only in the planning phase of the audit.
    b. Throughout the audit process.
    c. Both in planning and reviewing the audit, but not as one of the actual substantive tests.
    d. Only after the completion of field work, to determine whether unexpected relationships exist in the financial statements that cannot be explained with evidence already gathered.
    e. None of the above.

17. Workpapers retained in the auditor's files should demonstrate all of the following except:

    a. Examples of errors and inefficiencies to be avoided in subsequent examinations of the client, in the form of improperly prepared analyses that were superseded.
    b. The extent and results of the study of the internal control.
    c. That the evidence obtained in the audit affords a reasonable basis for an opinion on the financial statements.
    d. The adequacy of the audit planning process and the supervision of assistants on the engagement.
    e. All of the above.

18. The workpapers prepared and retained by the auditor:

    a. May be subpoenaed as evidence in subsequent litigation involving the client.
    b. May be subject to a peer review by CPAs from another firm.
    c. Are the property of the auditor.
    d. Include information for the year under examination as well as that for future audit examinations.
    e. All of the above.

19. Which of the following statements is generally correct about the competence of evidential matter?

    a. To be competent, evidence must be either valid or relevant, but need **not** be both.
    b. Accounting data alone may be considered sufficient, competent evidential matter to issue an unqualified opinion on financial statements.
    c. Competence of evidential matter refers to he amount of corroborative evidence to be obtained.
    d. The auditor's direct personal knowledge, obtained through observation and inspection, is more persuasive than information obtained indirectly from independent outside sources.

20. Comparisons of current financial statement information with information for comparable prior periods are examples of:

    a. Analytical procedures.
    b. Confirmation.
    c. Inspecting documents.
    d. Physical observation.
    e. Recalculation

(Items 1 through 6 in 6-29; AICPA Adapted)

6-30. Janice Smith, CPA, has performed the annual audit of Mean, Inc., for a number of years. In January of 19X1 the Board of Directors of Mean, Inc., decided to change auditors. The president of Mean asked Smith for all of her workpapers for the Mean audits. The president asserts that the workpapers belong to Mean and he wants to give them to the new auditors.

Required:

a. Comment on the president's assertion that the workpapers belong to Mean, Inc.
b. Comment on how the new auditor may gain access to the workpapers.

6-31. I.M. Young is a new staff accountant with Big and Small, a public accounting firm. Young is assigned to his first task: auditing the cash account of a large client. After spending two hours on the task, Young shows the workpapers to the senior in charge of the job. The senior finds that Young made some mistakes and consequently has to start over again. Young asks the senior what should be done with the workpapers that reflect the incorrect work. The senior says: "They are of no value; however, you might as well include them in the workpapers so that someone does not make the same mistake next year."

Required:

Comment on the senior's statement.

6-32. Indicate how each of the following factors influences the effectiveness of the auditor's substantive testing procedures. For each factor, provide a brief explanation.

a. Audit risk.
b. Inherent risk.
c. Control risk.

6-33. In each of the following situations, identify the financial statement assertion of interest to the auditor. Also, provide an example of an evidence-gathering procedure(s) that would be used by the auditor to evaluate that assertion.

a. Accounts payable recorded by a client represent legitimate obligations that are owed to vendors.
b. Inventory recorded in the year-end financial statements actually exists.
c. The amount of cash on deposit at an identified financial institution is fairly stated.
d. The amount of interest expense recorded for notes payable during the year is fairly stated.
e. All purchases of property, plant, and equipment made during the year are recorded.
f. Any minimum balances required by financial institutions as compensating balances are appropriately disclosed in the footnotes accompanying the financial statements.
g. The client actually owned a delivery truck parked on its premises.
h. An increase in marketable equity securities noted during the year represented an actual purchase transaction.
i. The annual provision for depreciation is correctly stated.
j. The totals from the client's Inventory Listing agree with their Trial Balance.

6-34. An important part of every examination of financial statements is the preparation of audit workpapers.

Required:

a. Discuss the relationship of audit workpapers to each of the standards of field work.
b. You are instructing an inexperienced staffperson on her first auditing assignment. She is to examine an account. An analysis of the account has been prepared by the client for inclusion in the audit workpapers. Prepare a list of the comments, commentaries, and notations that she should make or have made on the account analysis to provide an adequate workpaper as evidence of her examination. (Do not include a description of auditing procedures applicable to the account.)

(AICPA Adapted)

6-35. The source of accounting evidence is of primary importance in the CPA's evaluation of its quality. Accounting evidence may be classified according to source. List the classifications of accounting evidence according to source, briefly discussing the effect of the source on the reliability of the evidence.

(AICPA Adapted)

6-36. The preparation of workpapers is an integral part of the CPA's examination of financial statements. On a recurring engagement, a CPA reviews the audit programs and workpapers from the prior examination while planning the current examination to determine their usefulness for the current engagement.

Required:

a. 1. What are the purposes or functions of audit workpapers?
   2. What records may be included in audit workpapers?
b. What factors affect the CPA's judgment as to the type and content of the workpapers for a particular engagement?
c. To comply with generally accepted auditing standards, a CPA includes certain evidence in the workpapers—for example, "evidence that the engagement was planned and work of assistants was supervised and reviewed." What other evidence should a CPA include in audit workpapers to comply with generally accepted auditing standards?
d. How can a CPA make the most effective use of the preceding year's audit programs in a recurring examination?

(AICPA Adapted)

6-37. Analytical procedures are a commonly-used type of substantive testing procedure. *SAS No. 56* recently modified the professional guidance provided to auditors for the use of analytical procedures.

Required:

a. What are analytical procedures? What types of analytical procedures are suggested by *SAS No. 56*?
b. *SAS No. 56* identifies three primary stages of the audit examination during which analytical procedures could be used. What are these stages? According to *SAS No. 56*, is the use of analytical procedures in each of these stages required or discretionary?

c. For each stage identified in (b) above, what is the auditor's objective in using analytical procedures?

6-38. In examining financial statements, an auditor must judge the validity of the audit evidence obtained.

Required:

a. In the course of the examination, the auditor asks many questions of client officers and employees.
   1. Describe the factors that the auditor should consider in evaluating oral evidence provided by client officers and employees.
   2. Discuss the validity and limitations of oral evidence.
b. An auditor's examination may include computation of various balance sheet and operating ratios for comparison to prior years and industry averages. Discuss the validity and limitations of ratio analysis.
c. In connection with the examination of the financial statements of a manufacturing company, an auditor is observing the physical inventory of finished goods, which consist of expensive, highly-complex electronic equipment. Discuss the validity and limitations of the audit evidence provided by this procedure.

(AICPA Adapted)

6-39. Analytical procedures are substantive tests that are extremely useful in the initial audit planning stage.

Required:

a. Explain why analytical procedures are considered substantive tests.
b. Explain how analytical procedures may be useful in the initial audit planning stage.
c. Identify the analytical procedures that one might expect a CPA to utilize during an examination performed in accordance with generally accepted auditing standards.

(AICPA Adapted)

6-40. The purpose of all auditing procedures is to gather sufficient competent evidence for an auditor to form an opinion regarding the financial statements taken as a whole.

Required:

a. In addition to the example below, identify and describe six means or techniques of gathering audit evidence used to evaluate a client's inventory balance.

Technique	Description
Observation	An auditor watches the performance of some function, such as a client's annual inventory count.

b. Identify the five management assertions regarding a client's inventory balance and describe one **different** substantive testing procedure for each assertion. Use the format illustrated below.

Assertion	Substantive Auditing Procedure

(AICPA Adapted)

6-41. Cook, CPA, has been engaged to audit the financial statements of General Department Stores, Inc., a continuing audit client, which is a chain of medium-sized retail stores. General's fiscal year will end on June 30, 19x3, and General's management has asked Cook to issue the auditor's report by August 1, 19x3. Cook will not have sufficient time to perform all of the necessary field work in July 19x3, but will have time to perform most of the field work as of an interim date, April 30, 19x3.

For the accounts to be tested at an interim date, Cook will also perform substantive tests covering the transactions of the final two months of the year. This will be necessary to extend Cook's conclusions to the balance-sheet date.

Required:

a. Describe the factors that Cook should consider before applying principal substantive tests to General's balance sheet accounts at April 30, 19x3.
b. For accounts tested at April 30, 19x3, describe how Cook should design the substantive tests covering the balances as of June 30, 19x3, and the transactions of the final two months of the year.

(AICPA Adapted)

Learning Objectives

Study of this chapter is designed to achieve several learning objectives. After studying this chapter, you should be able to:

1. Define audit sampling and understand why sampling is necessary in the audit examination.
2. Distinguish between statistical sampling and nonstatistical sampling.
3. Make statements about a population using the concepts of precision and reliability.
4. Define attribute sampling and list the basic steps in performing an attribute sampling plan.
5. Identify the two types of sampling risks faced by the auditor in performing an attribute sampling plan.
6. Execute an attribute sampling plan, including determining the necessary sample size, selecting sample items, and evaluating results.

7

Introduction to Sampling and Attribute Sampling

Thus far, we have discussed the need for the auditor to gather evidence during the examination. This evidence is gathered in two general stages of the audit: (1) during tests of controls, when the auditor is studying and evaluating the client's internal control (as discussed in Chapter 5); and (2) as substantive testing procedures are performed, when the auditor is gathering evidence on which to base the opinion (as discussed in Chapter 6). As noted in these and later chapters, in gathering evidence, the auditor examines various controls and transactions and subjects these items to verification.

The large volume of controls and transactions makes it extremely difficult, if not impossible, for the auditor to verify each item occurring during the entire period of the audit examination. If the auditor attempted to do so, audit examinations could not be completed on a timely basis and the cost of the annual audit would be prohibitive for most clients. As a result, the auditor must limit testing procedures to only a subset of the controls and transactions occurring during each year. The need to limit the number of items examined during any given year results in the use of sampling during the audit engagement.

Audit sampling is the focus of this and the following chapter. This chapter introduces the concept of audit sampling and discusses basic terminology related to sampling. In addition, the use of audit sampling in the study and evaluation of the client's internal control is discussed. In the following chapter, the use of audit sampling in the substantive testing stage of the audit examination is illustrated.

AUDIT SAMPLING

Statement on Auditing Standards No. 39 (SAS No. 39) defines audit sampling as follows:

> Audit sampling is the application of an audit procedure to less than 100 percent of the items within an account balance or class of transactions for the purpose of evaluating some characteristic of the (account) balance or class (of transactions).[1]

Thus, in sampling, the auditor is attempting to make some statement about a population of interest based on the examination of only a subset (sample) drawn from that population. For example, if your instructor was interested in determining the average exam grade in your class, the instructor could sum the grades of all students in the class and divide by the total number of students. Because the number of students in the class is generally not too large, such a calculation could be done without a great deal of effort. However, if 10,000 students were enrolled in your class, calculating an average grade would become quite time-consuming. In such a case, the instructor could select a **sample** of 100 students and assume that their grades were similar to those of the 9,900 students not included in the sample of 100. The auditor uses a similar reasoning when employing sampling during the audit examination. For example, if attempting to estimate the extent to which a particular control is actually functioning as intended, the auditor selects a sample of applications of that control and makes an assumption that the remaining applications are similar to those in the sample. Or, if attempting to determine the correct (true) amount of a particular account balance, the auditor examines a sample of transactions or components underlying that account balance and assumes that those not selected are similar in nature to the transactions and components included in the sample.

The important point to remember when discussing audit sampling is that the auditor is attempting to make a statement about some population based on a subset of items composing that population. However, as discussed in the following section, the use of sampling exposes the auditor to certain risks that must be considered and evaluated.

Sampling Risk versus Nonsampling Risk

The preceding discussion suggests a limitation to the use of sampling: the possibility that the sample selected by the auditor may not be representative of the population of interest. For example, if an instructor who wants to estimate the average grade on an exam selects the test scores of students having either the 100 highest grades or 100 lowest grades on that exam, the estimate of the overall class average will be unreasonably high or low, depending on the sample selected. Similarly, if an auditor selects a sample of controls or transactions and components of an account balance that is not representative of the population, the estimates concerning the client's internal control and account balances will be inaccurate. Unfortunately, this limitation exists in all cases where a population is evaluated based on the examination of only a subset of that population.

---

[1] American Institute of Certified Public Accountants (AICPA), *Statement on Auditing Standards No. 39*, "Audit Sampling" (New York: AICPA, 1983, AU 350).

The above type of risk is referred to as **sampling risk** (or **sampling error**). Sampling risk can be defined as the probability that the auditor's decision based on the sample selected differs from the decision that would have been made if the entire population had been examined. Sampling risk occurs because the sample selected by the auditor may not be truly representative of the population it purports to represent. As shown later in this chapter, the use of statistical sampling techniques allows auditors to control their exposure to sampling risk at desired levels.

Selecting a representative sample by itself *does not* ensure that evaluation errors cannot occur. **Nonsampling risk** is caused by factors other than the sample selected by the auditor. For example, assume that the auditor selects a sample that adequately represents the population of interest. Errors could still remain undetected by the auditor because of inadequate or inappropriate auditing procedures. Also, the auditor could fail to identify the errors because of auditor negligence or misperformance.

Careful review of work performed at all levels within the firm and adequate training and supervision should allow accounting firms to reduce nonsampling risk to a relatively low level. Because nonsampling risk is totally unrelated to the auditor's sampling procedures, the focus in this and the following chapter is on how auditors can control and limit their exposure to sampling risk.

Based on the above discussion, when evaluating a sample, the following situations could result in evaluation errors by the auditor:

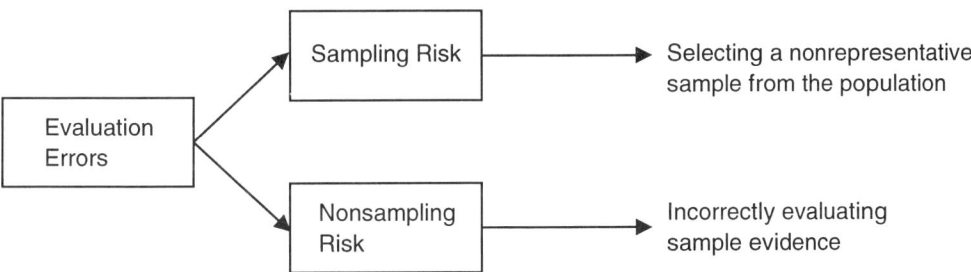

◻ Statistical versus Nonstatistical Sampling

SAS No. 39 identifies two approaches to audit sampling: statistical sampling and nonstatistical sampling. **Statistical sampling** involves the application of a sampling plan by the auditor in order to use the laws of probability to make objective statements about a population of interest. The use of statistical sampling differs from nonstatistical sampling in three important respects:

1. The auditor incorporates the desired exposure to sampling risk in determining the appropriate sample size.
2. The sample is selected in such a manner that every item in the population has some known chance of selection (also known as a **probabilistic selection technique**).
3. The auditor incorporates the desired exposure to sampling risk in evaluating the results of the audit procedures.

Thus, an important benefit provided by statistical sampling is that it allows the auditor to control the exposure to sampling risk through: (1) selecting a sufficient sample size, (2) subjecting each item in the population to selection, and (3) statistically evaluating the sample results.

These requirements may be viewed as disadvantages in some instances, however. In general, statistical sampling plans involve additional training costs to the CPA firm to acquaint its personnel with statistical sampling. Also, statistical sampling plans can be more expensive than nonstatistical plans because of the additional costs associated with sample design and sample selection.

It is important to note that nonstatistical sampling is often employed in practice because of the lower cost of this type of plan. Both approaches require professional judgment on the part of the auditor in planning, performing, and evaluating a sample. In addition, *SAS No. 39* recognizes that either a statistical or nonstatistical approach can provide the auditor with sufficient evidence. Although this and the following chapter focus on statistical sampling applications, nonstatistical methods are also discussed and illustrated.

CHAPTER CHECKPOINTS

7-1. Why do auditors need to sample during their examinations?

7-2. What is audit sampling?

7-3. Distinguish between sampling risk and nonsampling risk. What are the causes of each type of risk?

7-4. Define statistical sampling. What aspects differentiate statistical sampling from nonstatistical sampling? What is the primary benefit of statistical sampling?

7-5. Can the auditor appropriately utilize nonstatistical sampling during the audit?

◻ Precision and Reliability

Because a sample may not truly represent the population of interest, the auditor's conclusions with respect to a sample cannot be exact. Remember, the sample estimate of the true population mean is just one possible estimate of that mean. Although one cannot be certain that the sample estimate equals the population mean (this is never known unless all sampling units in the population have been examined), statistical theory can be used to establish a range of values (referred to as the **precision interval**) that has a certain probability of including the true population mean. Establishing the precision interval allows the auditor to control the exposure to sampling risk at desired levels.

To illustrate the concept of precision, recall the previous example of an instructor wishing to estimate the average grade on an exam. Assume that a sample of 100 students yields an average grade of sixty points. We cannot state with any confidence that the average grade in the population (class of students) is sixty; however, this sample estimate should represent a close approximation of the true population average. Using statistical theory, we can establish a precision interval that has a given probability of including the true population average. This interval is calculated as:

Sample Average ± Precision
(Mean)   (Allowance for Sampling Risk)

It is on the basis of this interval that we can make conclusions with respect to the population of interest.

The **precision** of an estimate (or **allowance for sampling risk**) is a measure of its accuracy—that is, how close the sample estimate is to the true population value. The **reliability** is the probability of achieving a given degree of precision. If we are considering sample means, then the precision interval is that range surrounding the sample estimate that has an x percent (reliability) chance of including the true population mean.

For the classroom example presented earlier, assume that you took a large number of different samples of 100 students. After calculating the average grades of these samples, you determined that 90 percent of the estimates were within ten points of your original sample estimate of sixty. The method of calculating this precision and reliability is illustrated later in this and the following chapter. The precision in this example is ten points, and the corresponding reliability is 90 percent. In this case, we can make two statements relating to the population:

▶ There is a 90 percent probability that the absolute difference between the sample estimate (60 points) and the true population mean is less than or equal to ten points.

▶ There is a 90 percent probability that the true population average is between fifty points (60 points − 10 points) and seventy points (60 points + 10 points).

The previous example also illustrates another important concept related to precision and reliability: these are not independent terms. Precision can only be defined for a specified reliability, and reliability can only be defined for a specified precision. For example, if precision in the above example is changed to fifteen points, the corresponding precision interval widens to between forty-five points and seventy-five points. As a result, the probability that the true population mean falls within this interval increases, because the revised precision interval now includes sample estimates between forty-five and seventy-five points, rather than fifty and seventy points. Note that as the interval widens (increased precision), the corresponding reliability also increases—there is a higher probability that the true population value falls within that interval.

Remember that sampling risk reflects the probability that the sample selected by the auditor will not be representative of the population. As originally noted, there is a 90 percent (reliability) probability that the true population mean lies within the precision interval. However, 10 percent of the time, the true population mean falls outside of this interval (*i.e.*, either greater than 70 points or less than 50 points). When this occurs, the sample was not representative of the population of interest because the sample estimate differed greatly from the true population mean. As a result, the latter probability reflects sampling risk. Therefore, sampling risk may be expressed as the complement of reliability (sampling risk = 1 − reliability).

◘ Incorporating Statistical Concepts into the Sampling Plan

How do auditors use the concepts of precision and reliability to control the exposure to sampling risk? Although this is illustrated in detail in both this and the following chapter, a simple illustration at this point will help clarify this point. Assume that the auditor wishes to determine whether a particular internal control is functioning effectively in preventing and detecting material errors. The auditor decides that a control must be functioning 95 percent of the time in order to rely on it. Therefore, if the control is not functioning 5 percent of the time or more, the auditor cannot rely on this procedure to reduce the nature, timing, and extent of the substantive testing procedures. The latter rate is referred to as the **tolerable rate of occurrence** (or **tolerable deviation rate**). The tolerable deviation rate represents the extent to which a control can deviate in a population without requiring the auditor to change the degree of reliance on the client's internal control.

If no time or cost constraints existed, the auditor could examine all applications of the control and determine whether the deviation rate was greater or less than 5 percent. However, because of time and cost limitations, auditors must base their ultimate decision on a sample drawn from an audit population. To control sampling risk, the auditor constructs a precision interval that has an x percent (reliability) probability of containing the true population deviation rate. In particular, the auditor would like to determine a deviation rate that has a probability of reliability of equaling or exceeding the true population deviation rate. Determining this deviation rate (referred to as the **upper precision limit**) is the focus of this chapter.

At this point, the auditor evaluates internal control based on the upper precision limit. It is important to note that, under the theory of statistical sampling, the true population deviation rate will exceed this upper precision limit (1 − reliability) percent of the time. This probability is equal to sampling risk. The upper precision limit allows the auditor to evaluate the results from a statistical sample while controlling the exposure to sampling risk to a desired level. For example, assume that the auditor's sample results yielded a 3 percent sample deviation rate and an upper precision limit and reliability of 6 percent and 90 percent, respectively. This information is summarized in Figure 7-1.

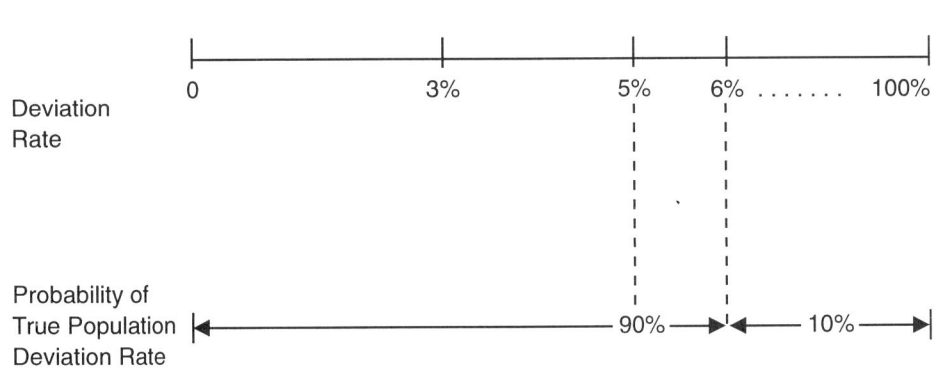

Figure 7-1: *Example: Precision and Reliability*

As indicated in Figure 7-1, the true population deviation rate has a 90 percent (reliability) chance of being less than or equal to 6 percent (the upper precision limit). This reliability measure indicates that the auditor limited the exposure to sampling risk to 10 percent (100 percent − 90 percent). Figure 7-1 also indicates that the probability that the true population deviation rate exceeds the tolerable deviation rate of 5 percent is greater than the desired sampling risk of 10 percent. Therefore, if the auditor decides to rely on this internal control as planned, the exposure to sampling risk is greater than the desired level.

In this case, the precision (or allowance for sampling risk) is equal to the difference between the upper precision limit and the sample estimate. Along with this precision, the reliability allows the auditor to control the probability of obtaining an unrepresentative sample estimate (sampling risk) at given levels. The method of calculating and controlling precision and reliability is discussed in the following section.

CHAPTER CHECKPOINTS

7-6. Define precision and reliability. How are these terms related?

7-7. If a sample estimate of the average score on an auditing test is 70 points, the precision of that estimate is 5 points, and the corresponding reliability is 90 percent, summarize the conclusion that could be made regarding the true population average.

ATTRIBUTE SAMPLING

Overview of Attribute Sampling

Estimation sampling for attributes (**attribute sampling**) should be utilized by the auditor when only one of two possibilities exists in the population under consideration: an attribute either exists (occurs) with respect to a particular item or does not exist (occur) with respect to that item. When using attribute sampling, the auditor's goal is to obtain an estimate of the extent to which the attribute exists in the population. An important occasion to use attribute sampling in auditing is when the auditor's objective is to estimate the entity's degree of compliance, such as in the auditor's study and evaluation of the client's internal control. In this application, deviations from prescribed controls are the attributes of interest to the auditor.

Recall from Chapter 5 the discussion of the auditor's study and evaluation of a client's internal control. As noted in that chapter, the result of this study and evaluation is the auditor's assessment of the risk that the client's internal control fails to detect and/or prevent material financial statement errors (**control risk**). In assessing this risk, the auditor gathers evidence about how well the client's internal control is actually functioning. This evidence is gathered as the auditor performs tests of controls.

The auditor's study and evaluation of the entity's internal control begins with the obtaining of an overall understanding of the internal control. After obtaining this overall understanding, the auditor establishes a preliminary assessment of control risk. This assessment is based upon a judgment about the effectiveness of the client's internal control in preventing and detecting errors and irregularities. If the client's internal control is perceived as being more effective in preventing and detecting financial statement errors, the auditor should assess control risk at lower levels. Conversely, if the internal control is less effective in preventing or detecting financial statement errors, this risk should be assessed at higher levels.

Once this preliminary assessment is made, the auditor performs tests of controls to support the preliminary assessment of control risk. When performing these tests of controls, the auditor employs audit sampling to determine how well the client's internal control is *actually* functioning in preventing errors and irregularities.

When conducting tests of controls, the auditor is interested in determining whether the client's internal control may be relied upon to reduce the nature, timing, and extent of substantive testing procedures. In doing so, the auditor wishes to identify instances where prescribed internal controls are not functioning as intended. These instances are known as **exceptions** or **deviations**. The auditor's objective in examining an entity's internal control is to determine whether the **population deviation rate** (the percentage of items in the population containing a deviation) exceeds the **tolerable deviation rate** (the maximum rate of deviations that the auditor is willing to accept without changing the degree of reliance on the internal control). These terms are also known as the **population rate of occurrence** and **tolerable rate of occurrence**, respectively.

If the population deviation rate exceeds the tolerable deviation rate, the auditor should decide to lessen the reliance on internal control—that is, the assessment of control risk should be increased to a higher level. In such cases, the auditor must correspondingly reduce the necessary level of detection risk to achieve the desired level of audit risk. Reductions in detection risk are made by increasing the effectiveness of the auditor's substantive testing procedures. On the other hand, if the population deviation rate is less than the tolerable deviation rate, the auditor may appropriately rely on internal control as planned.

As noted earlier in this chapter, making conclusions about a population based upon the examination of only a sample drawn from that population exposes the auditor to sampling risk. The sampling risks associated with attribute sampling are discussed in the following section.

◘ Risks Associated with Attribute Sampling

SAS No. 39 identifies two aspects of sampling risks associated with attribute sampling:

> ▶ The **risk of overreliance** (or **risk of assessing control risk too low**) is the risk that the sample supports the planned degree of reliance on the internal control when the true deviation rate would not justify such reliance.

> ▶ The **risk of underreliance** (or **risk of assessing control risk too high**) is the risk that the sample does not support the auditor's planned degree of reliance on the internal control when the true deviation rate supports such reliance.

These risks are illustrated in Figure 7-2. The two rows in the figure represent the auditor's decision based on the results of attribute sampling. Note that the auditor will either: (1) decide to rely on the internal control as planned (row 1), or (2) decide that the internal control cannot be relied upon as planned and perform additional substantive tests (row 2). The two columns in Figure 7-2 represent the auditor's decision that would be made if the entire population were examined. **Sampling risk** is the risk that the auditor's decision based on the sample differs from the decision that would be made if the entire population was examined. Cells b and c of Figure 7-2 represent the risk of overreliance and underreliance, respectively.

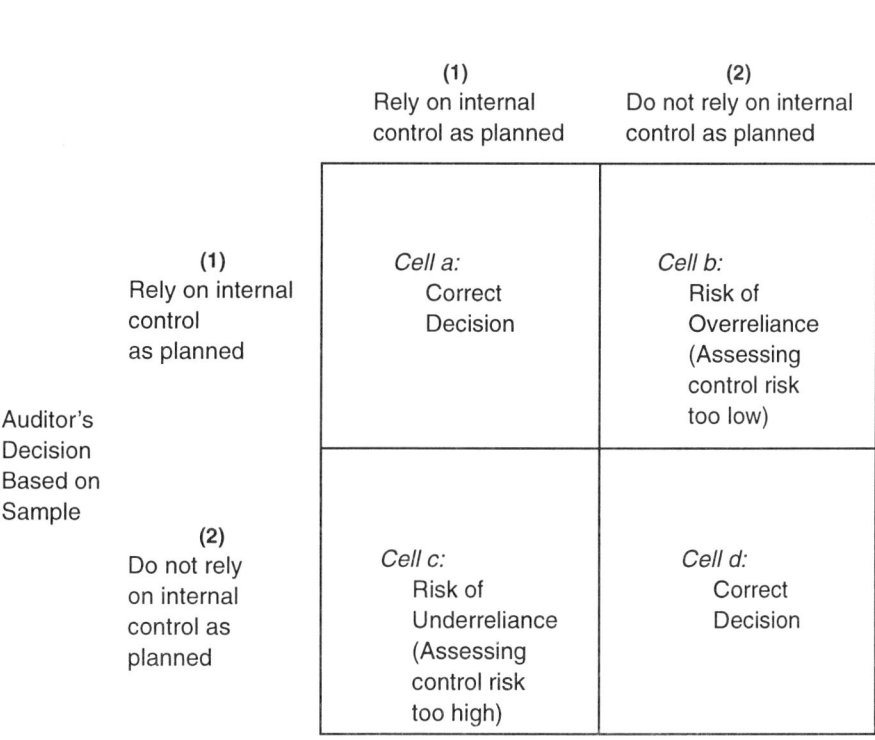

Figure 7-2: *Risks Associated with Attribute Sampling*

Let us now consider the consequences of each of these sampling risks. When the risk of underreliance has been committed, the auditor could have chosen to rely on internal control as planned, but did not. As a result, the auditor will assume internal control is less effective than it really is, resulting in a higher assessment of control risk. Recalling the audit risk model, this higher assessment of control risk will result in a lower assessment of detection risk. Therefore, the ultimate outcome of committing the risk of underreliance is that unnecessary substantive tests will be performed by the auditor. The risk of underreliance is sometimes referred to as creating an **efficiency loss**.

Conversely, if the risk of overreliance is committed, the auditor is assessing control risk at an excessively low level—that is, the auditor feels that internal controls are functioning effectively when, in fact, they are not. As a result, detection risk will be assessed at a high level, resulting in insufficient substantive tests. These insufficient substantive tests may, in turn, prevent the auditor from detecting material financial statement errors. Thus, the risk of overreliance is often referred to as creating an **effectiveness loss**.

Which of these risks is of the most concern to the auditor? Although the auditor obviously wishes to avoid either the risk of overreliance or the risk of underreliance, clearly it is better to perform excessive substantive testing compared to insufficient substantive testing. Therefore, in the sampling plan, the auditor will take steps to control the exposure to the risk of overreliance. In doing so, the auditor is willing to perform the additional substantive tests associated with the risk of underreliance to avoid the highly negative consequences associated with the risk of overreliance.

A final point of interest is how the auditor decides whether to rely on internal control structure as planned. The auditor establishes a rate of deviations in the population that is allowable before the reliance on the internal control is reduced (the **tolerable deviation rate**). Although the auditor could examine the entire population and compare the population deviation rate to the tolerable deviation rate, in most cases a sample will be drawn. The auditor selects a sample, calculates a **sample deviation rate**, and statistically adjusts this sample deviation rate to control for the desired level of the risk of overreliance. This adjusted deviation rate (referred to as the **upper precision limit**) is then compared to the tolerable deviation rate. The procedure used by the auditor in making the decisions reflected in rows 1 and 2 of Figure 7-2 is discussed in detail in the following section.

CHAPTER CHECKPOINTS

7-8. Define attribute sampling. When could attribute sampling be used during the audit examination?

7-9. Define the following terms:

a. Deviation.
b. Population deviation rate.
c. Tolerable deviation rate.
d. Sample deviation rate.

7-10. What are the two sampling risks associated with attribute sampling? What is the ultimate consequence to the auditor of committing each type of sampling risk?

STEPS IN PERFORMING ATTRIBUTE SAMPLING

SAS No. 39 notes that, prior to using attribute sampling, the auditor should: (1) determine that attribute sampling meets his or her audit objectives, and (2) identify the objective of the test. As noted earlier, attribute sampling is considered to be appropriate when the auditor is interested in estimating the rate at which some characteristic occurs in the population, such as in performing tests of controls. The basic objective of attribute sampling plans in an audit setting is to determine whether internal control policies and procedures are functioning as intended. These procedures are generally concerned with the following types of questions:

- Were the appropriate policies and procedures followed by the entity's personnel?
- Were the policies and procedures performed by the appropriate individual?

Once the auditor determines that attribute sampling meets the objectives and identifies the objectives of the test, the following steps are usually performed in executing an attribute sampling plan:[2]

1. Defining the deviation conditions.
2. Defining the population.
3. Determining the method of selecting the sample.
4. Determining the sample size.
5. Performing the sampling plan.
6. Evaluating the results.

Each of these steps is briefly discussed in the following paragraphs.

◻ Defining the Deviation Conditions

Once the auditor determines that attribute sampling will properly meet the audit objective(s), the characteristic to be observed must be defined. In an attribute sampling application, the auditor is examining a population consisting of items falling in one of two categories: (1) the item possesses a given attribute, or (2) the item does not possess that attribute. The auditor is usually looking for instances where an internal control established by the client is not being followed or is not functioning as intended. As noted earlier, such situations are referred to as deviations.

As noted in Chapter 12, an important control is the preparation of a Purchase Order as a means of authorizing purchases on account. If the auditor wishes to ensure that all purchases made by the client are properly authorized according to company policy, a sample of Purchase Orders should be selected. Once selected, the Purchase Order is examined to ensure that some form of authorization (either initials, signature, or other documentation) is present. Thus, the deviation condition is defined as missing authorization. Any instances where such documentation is lacking (or missing) indicate that the control is not functioning as intended. These instances are recorded as deviations by the auditor and will be evaluated in a subsequent step of the sampling plan.

---

[2] See American Institute of Certified Public Accountants (AICPA), *Audit Sampling* (New York: AICPA, 1983).

Defining the Population

Carefully defining the population is critical in any sampling application because the auditor's sample is selected from this population. Therefore, if the population is not correctly defined, the auditor's sample cannot be appropriate for the application in question. For attribute sampling, the population is normally defined as all instances where a given internal control policy or procedure should have been followed by the client or its employees. In the previous example, if the population is defined as all approved Purchase Orders, the auditor is not able to appropriately make a conclusion about the effectiveness of the client's internal control. The reason is that purchases that are not approved by the client are not made available for selection. Instead, the appropriate population of interest in this example is the population of *all* purchases made during the year.

In addition to defining the population, the auditor must also decide on the period to be examined by the tests of controls. If the auditor decides to perform tests of controls up to some interim date prior to year-end, a sample from the population of possible internal control applications occurring prior to that interim date may be selected. However, if it is desired to examine internal control applications throughout the entire year of the audit, the auditor must wait until year-end to select and evaluate these controls. Therefore, by necessity, the auditor's definition of the population must consider when tests of controls are to be performed.

Determining the Sample Selection Method

In selecting an attribute sample, the auditor should use a selection method that allows all items in the population to have some probability of being selected. Such methods are referred to as **probabilistic selection techniques**. Methods commonly used by auditors include unrestricted random sampling, systematic sampling, block sampling, and haphazard sampling. The first two methods are used with statistical sampling applications because they subject all items to selection. Because block sampling and haphazard sampling require the auditor to judgmentally select items for examination, they are normally only utilized with nonstatistical sampling plans.

Unrestricted Random Sampling. Unrestricted random sampling consists of drawing individual items at random from a population so each item has an equal chance of being selected. If a sample item chosen is returned to the population so that it has a chance of being selected again, the method is called sampling with replacement. If the item is not returned, it is called sampling without replacement. Sampling without replacement gives greater sample efficiency (*i.e.*, a smaller sample to achieve the same precision and reliability).

One method for drawing an unrestricted random sample is to use a **random number table** (Figure 7-3 is an example of a random number table). Use of this method will help guard against bias in selection. It has the added advantage that a second, or reviewing, auditor can duplicate the exact sample using the same starting point and route through the table. The digits in most random number tables have been generated by a computer and subjected to statistical tests to ensure randomness. There is approximately an equal number of each of the digits 0 through 9 in these tables.

	Column				
Row	1	2	3	4	5
1	9588	3810	1161	5716	7048
2	6291	3964	9133	8362	7441
3	6766	8404	9939	1648	2143
4	2470	4741	5764	4033	7752
5	7647	4332	2897	8289	4810

Figure 7-3: *Random Number Table Excerpt*

The steps to follow when using a random number table to select an unrestricted random sample are:

1. Find a method of proceeding so that there is agreement between numbers in the random number table and the population items. For example, sometimes an auditor will renumber the elements in the population to agree with the digits in the random number table.
2. Select and record a starting point in a random fashion (for example, pointing to a number on the page).
3. Select and record a route through the table. (It may be sequential.)
4. Record the stopping point.

The auditor should record all random numbers selected and the method of corresponding these numbers with the items selected from the population.

The primary advantages of random sampling are its relative ease in application and the fact that each item in the population has an equal chance of being selected by the auditor. However, a disadvantage associated with random sampling is that if the population is not prenumbered its use becomes somewhat cumbersome. For example, imagine counting through a large population to find the 9,588th item, 6,291st item, etc. Because of this limitation, an alternative method of selection is available that incorporates the advantages of random sampling, yet reduces the time required to physically select the sample items: systematic sampling.

▶ **Example:** *Drawing an Unrestricted Random Sample Using a Table of Random Numbers*

Assume there are approximately 10,000 items in a given population and that the items have been numbered 1 to 10,000. The items to be included in the sample could be selected by starting anywhere in the table. For instance, assume that it is decided to start with the first number in the table (Figure 7-3). The first number is 9,588; thus, the 9,588th item in the population would be selected for inclusion in the sample. If a decision was made to proceed sequentially through the table, the next number in the table would then be used. The next number is 6,291, so the 6,291st item would also be included in the sample. The auditor would continue in this manner until enough items had been selected to meet the sample size requirements. Alternatively, a different route through the table could be selected as long as randomization is preserved (*e.g.*, one would not be permitted to go through the table and select only those numbers starting with a 9 or some similar scheme).

Systematic Sampling. In systematic sampling, beginning sample item(s) are randomly chosen, a fixed number of items skipped, another item selected, and the same fixed number of items skipped. The process is continued throughout the frame (a frame is a listing of a population). The number of items skipped each time is called the **skip interval**.

A skip interval is obtained by dividing the sample size into the number of items in the population. To obtain comparable results from systematic sampling as from unrestricted random sampling, it is absolutely necessary that the frame be arranged in random order with respect to the population characteristic being measured. For example, if accounts receivable amounts are to be tested, systematic sampling might be used, even though the accounts are filed alphabetically—provided the dollar amounts have no relation to the account names.

To employ systematic sampling, the auditor first calculates the skip interval, as above. Once this has been done, the auditor selects a random starting point in the population, which represents the initial selection. Then, a fixed number of items (equal to the skip interval) is bypassed, with the next item being identified for selection. This procedure is repeated until the desired number of items has been selected for examination. To illustrate how systematic sampling is utilized by the auditor, consider the following example:

▶ **Example:** *Systematic Sampling*

Assume that an auditor wishes to select ten invoices for examination from a population of 5,000 invoices. The auditor decides upon a random start of twenty-eight. The appropriate skip interval is 500 (5,000 invoices ÷ 10 items = 500). Therefore, after selecting the 28th invoice, the auditor will then select every 500th invoice, as below:

	Previous Selection		Skip Interval		New Selection
Item 1	—		—		28 (start)
Item 2	28	+	500	=	528
Item 3	528	+	500	=	1028
Item 4	1,028	+	500	=	1528
Item 5	1,528	+	500	=	2028
Item 6	2,028	+	500	=	2528
Item 7	2,528	+	500	=	3028
Item 8	3,028	+	500	=	3528
Item 9	3,528	+	500	=	4028
Item 10	4,028	+	500	=	4528

This example indicates that the auditor would select the 28th, 528th, 1,028th, etc., items in a population. Using systematic sampling when the population is not prenumbered (e.g., a stack of unnumbered purchase orders) is normally more efficient than random sampling. If systematic sampling is used, the auditor could start with the 28th item, "count" through 500 items to item 528, through an additional 500 items to item 1,028, and so forth. Such a procedure is much less time-consuming than having to individually count to each selected item (as is necessary under random sampling).

One limitation of using systematic sampling is that the population should be randomly ordered. If not, the auditor may "skip" a group of items having a unique characteristic, thus biasing the sample.

Block Sampling. In **block sampling**, the auditor selects the necessary number of items by choosing a series of contiguous sampling units. The auditor might select all purchase orders prepared on several specific dates (February 7, September 12, November 10, etc.). Notice that block sampling does not allow as many different time periods to be examined as might random sampling and systematic sampling. A limitation of using block sampling is that the auditor judgmentally selects sample items, and all items are not made available for selection. Consequently, the sample results cannot be statistically projected to the population. Although block sampling can be used with nonstatistical sampling plans, it should always be used cautiously by the auditor.

Haphazard Sampling. A **haphazard sample** consists of items selected without any conscious bias on the part of the auditor. In selecting these items, the auditor does not have any reason or rationale for picking certain items and omitting others. For instance, the auditor could simply choose to select certain purchase orders by "blindly" pulling these orders without giving consideration to the type of purchase, date of purchase, or location in the population. As with block sampling, the results obtained through the use of a haphazard sample cannot be statistically projected to the population. Therefore, its use is limited to nonstatistical sampling applications.

CHAPTER CHECKPOINTS

7-11. List the major steps performed by the auditor in an attribute sampling plan.

7-12. What is the general procedure used by the auditor in performing random sampling? Systematic sampling? What are the advantages and disadvantages of each?

7-13. Define block sampling and haphazard sampling. What is the major drawback associated with each of these methods?

7-14. What is a skip interval? How is it used in attribute sampling?

7-15. For a population of 5,000 cash disbursements, assume that the auditor calculates a sample size of 100 items. What is the skip interval? If a random start of 23 is selected, what numbers would be used to select the first five items from the population?

◻ Determining Sample Size

Factors Affecting Sample Size. The auditor must specify three parameters as integral parts of the sampling plan in order to calculate sample size: (1) the desired reliability level (risk of overreliance), (2) the tolerable deviation rate, and (3) the expected deviation rate. The reliability level should be inversely related to the auditor's desired exposure to the risk of overreliance. Earlier, it was noted that the auditor's exposure to sampling risk was equal to (1 − reliability). Because the auditor controls the exposure to the risk of overreliance, the risk of overreliance can be viewed as (1 − reliability). This subsection discusses the method used by the auditor to specify these parameters.

When establishing the desired exposure to the risk of overreliance, the auditor considers the importance of the internal control being evaluated. The desired exposure to the risk of overreliance should decrease as the importance of the internal control under examination increases. That is, if an internal control is extremely important in terms of its effect on substantive testing, the auditor should attempt to control the risk of overreliance to lower levels. SAS No. 39 notes that in most cases the auditor should establish the risk of overreliance at relatively low levels (such as 5 and 10 percent).

The tolerable deviation rate (or tolerable rate of occurrence) is the maximum rate of deviation the auditor will allow in the specific control being examined without altering the reliance on that control. The tolerable deviation rate is set judgmentally by the auditor. In establishing this rate, the auditor should consider how much reliance is being placed on the particular internal control being examined to reduce the nature, timing, and extent of the substantive testing procedures. The tolerable deviation rate established by the auditor should be inversely related to that reliance. Therefore, if substantial reliance on a particular control is planned, the tolerable rate should be lower because it is more important that the control be functioning effectively (and vice versa). The AICPA *Audit Sampling Guide* suggests the following guidelines for establishing the tolerable deviation rate:

Amount of Planned Reliance	Tolerable Rate
Substantial Reliance	2% to 7%
Moderate Reliance	6% to 12%
Little Reliance	11% to 20%
No Reliance	omit test

Finally, the expected deviation rate reflects the extent of deviations the auditor expects to find in the particular internal control being examined. To establish this rate, the auditor can rely on knowledge obtained in previous audit examinations or evaluate an initial presample of items (sometimes known as a **pilot sample**). It is important to note that the expected deviation rate (or expected rate of occurrence) should be less than the tolerable deviation rate discussed above. If not, there is little need to proceed with the test of controls because the auditor believes that a greater than acceptable rate of deviation exists in the population.

Calculating Sample Size. Once the auditor establishes the level of reliability (risk of overreliance), tolerable deviation rate, and expected deviation rate, the appropriate sample size can be calculated. In doing so, the auditor may utilize AICPA Sampling Tables. Tables reflecting a desired risk of overreliance of 5 percent and 10 percent are reproduced as Tables 7-1 and 7-2, respectively. As implied by our earlier discussion, these sampling tables incorporate three key factors in determining sample sizes:

1. The desired risk of overreliance (reliability).
2. The tolerable deviation rate.
3. The expected deviation rate.

Table 7-1: *Statistical Sample Sizes for Tests of Controls (5 Percent Risk of Overreliance)*

Expected Deviation Rate	Tolerable Deviation Rate										
	2%	3%	4%	5%	6%	7%	8%	9%	10%	15%	20%
0.00%	149	99	74	59	49	42	36	32	29	19	14
.25	236	157	117	93	78	66	58	51	46	30	22
.50	*	157	117	93	78	66	58	51	46	30	22
.75	*	208	117	93	78	66	58	51	46	30	22
1.00	*	*	156	93	78	66	58	51	46	30	22
1.25	*	*	156	124	78	66	58	51	46	30	22
1.50	*	*	192	124	103	66	58	51	46	30	22
1.75	*	*	227	153	103	88	77	51	46	30	22
2.00	*	*	*	181	127	88	77	68	46	30	22
2.25	*	*	*	208	127	88	77	68	61	30	22
2.50	*	*	*	*	150	109	77	68	61	30	22
2.75	*	*	*	*	173	109	95	68	61	30	22
3.00	*	*	*	*	195	129	95	84	61	30	22
3.25	*	*	*	*	*	148	112	84	61	30	22
3.50	*	*	*	*	*	167	112	84	76	40	22
3.75	*	*	*	*	*	185	129	100	76	40	22
4.00	*	*	*	*	*	*	146	100	89	40	22
5.00	*	*	*	*	*	*	*	158	116	40	30
6.00	*	*	*	*	*	*	*	*	179	50	30
7.00	*	*	*	*	*	*	*	*	*	68	37

*Sample size is too large to be cost-effective for most audit applications.

Source: American Institute of Certified Public Accountants (AICPA), *Audit and Accounting Guide*, "Audit Sampling" (New York: AICPA, 1983), 106.

To use the AICPA Tables, the auditor employs the following general procedure:

1. Based on the desired risk of overreliance, select the appropriate sampling table. While Tables 7-1 and 7-2 represent risks of overreliance of 5 percent and 10 percent, respectively, tables are available for other levels of risk.
2. Identify the row pertaining to the auditor's estimate of the expected deviation rate.
3. Identify the column representing the desired tolerable deviation rate.
4. Read the sample size at the junction of the column and row obtained in steps 2 and 3 above.

Table 7-2: *Statistical Sample Sizes for Tests of Controls (10 Percent Risk of Overreliance)*

Expected Deviation Rate	Tolerable Deviation Rate										
	2%	3%	4%	5%	6%	7%	8%	9%	10%	15%	20%
0.00%	114	76	57	45	38	32	28	25	22	15	11
.25	194	129	96	77	64	55	48	42	38	25	18
.50	194	129	96	77	64	55	48	42	38	25	18
.75	265	129	96	77	64	55	48	42	38	25	18
1.00	*	176	96	77	64	55	48	42	38	25	18
1.25	*	221	132	77	64	55	48	42	38	25	18
1.50	*	*	132	105	64	55	48	42	38	25	18
1.75	*	*	166	105	88	55	48	42	38	25	18
2.00	*	*	198	132	88	88	48	42	38	25	18
2.25	*	*	*	132	88	75	65	42	38	25	18
2.50	*	*	*	158	110	75	65	58	38	25	18
2.75	*	*	*	209	132	75	65	58	52	25	18
3.00	*	*	*	*	132	94	65	58	52	25	18
3.25	*	*	*	*	153	194	82	58	52	25	18
3.50	*	*	*	*	194	113	82	73	52	25	18
3.75	*	*	*	*	*	113	98	73	52	25	18
4.00	*	*	*	*	*	131	98	73	65	25	18
5.00	*	*	*	*	*	149	160	115	78	34	18
6.00	*	*	*	*	*	*	*	182	116	43	25
7.00	*	*	*	*	*	*	*	*	199	52	25

*Sample size is too large to be cost-effective for most audit applications.

Source: American Institute of Certified Public Accountants (AICPA), *Audit and Accounting Guide*, "Audit Sampling" (New York: AICPA, 1983), 107.

The resultant sample size is the number of items that the auditor needs to select and examine to control the risk of overreliance at the desired level. For example, if the auditor desires a risk of overreliance of 5 percent and specifies an expected deviation rate and tolerable deviation rate of 2 percent and 8 percent, respectively, the correct sample size would be 77, as highlighted in the following excerpt from Table 7-1:

Expected Deviation Rate	Tolerable Deviation Rate			
	5%	... 7%	8%	9%
2.00	181	88	77	68

Effect of Factors on Sample Size. How do changes in each of the factors affect sample size? The answer to this question can be determined by referring to Table 7-1. For example, as the auditor holds constant the risk of overreliance and the tolerable deviation rate, decreases in the expected deviation rate gradually yield reduced sample sizes. On the other hand, if a greater rate of deviation is expected by the auditor, the auditor must examine a larger number of items in that population. Thus, sample size is directly related to the expected deviation rate. For a tolerable rate of 8 percent and a risk of overreliance of 5 percent, the following sample sizes correspond to various expected deviation rates (from Table 7-1).

Expected Deviation Rate	Sample Size
4.0	146
3.5	112
3.0	95
2.0	77

In contrast, decreases in the tolerable deviation rate result in increased sample sizes, holding all other factors constant, and vice versa. This relationship is inverse and suggests that a larger number of items must be examined when the auditor requires the control to be functioning more effectively. This should not be surprising because lower tolerable rates are associated with more important internal controls. Reading across the row for a 2 percent expected deviation rate in Table 7-1, notice that if the tolerable deviation rate is 10 percent, the appropriate sample size is 46. However, reducing the tolerable deviation rate to 5 percent increases the necessary sample size to 181 items.

As noted earlier, the auditor may reduce the exposure to sampling risk by examining a larger number of items. Therefore, the risk of overreliance has an inverse relationship with sample size. To achieve lower levels of the risk of overreliance, the auditor must examine a larger number of items, and vice versa. Given an expected deviation rate of 1 percent and a tolerable deviation rate of 6 percent, a total of 64 items must be examined if the auditor desires a risk of overreliance of 10 percent (see Table 7-2). However, if the exposure to risk of overreliance is decreased to 5 percent, the appropriate sample size is 78 items (Table 7-1).

Notice that the AICPA Sampling Tables do not incorporate the size of the population in determining sample size. It would seem logical that if a greater number of possible internal control applications existed, the auditor should verify a larger number of these applications (holding all other factors constant). However, the large size of most attribute sampling populations causes the effect of population size to be relatively insignificant. Under statistical theory, populations containing over 5,000 sampling units are treated as though they were infinite. For populations of less than 5,000 units, the size of the population has a minimal effect on sample size.[3] Because most attribute sampling populations are relatively large, the population size is not explicitly considered by the auditor in determining the appropriate sample size.

The effect of these factors on sample size is summarized in Figure 7-4. It is assumed that for each factor, all other relevant factors are held constant. For example, as the tolerable deviation rate decreases, the auditor needs to select a larger sample size, holding the expected deviation rate and the risk of overreliance constant. In contrast, as this factor increases, a smaller sample size is required, again holding all other factors constant.

	Factor Increases	Factor Decreases
Tolerable Deviation Rate	Smaller sample size	Larger sample size
Expected Deviation Rate	Larger sample size	Smaller sample size
Risk of Overreliance	Smaller sample size	Larger sample size

Figure 7-4: *Effect of Factors on Attribute Sample Sizes*

---

[3] For example, the AICPA's "Audit Sampling" calculates the following sample sizes for populations of 500, 1,000, 5,000, and 100,000 sampling units assuming a 5 percent risk of overreliance, 1 percent expected deviation rate, and 5 percent tolerable deviation rate:

Population Size	Sample Size
500	87
1,000	90
5,000	93
100,000	93

This calculation illustrates two basic points. First, once a population reaches a size of 5,000 sampling units, population size has no effect on sample size. In addition, under any circumstances, the size of the population has only a minimal effect on sample size.

CHAPTER CHECKPOINTS

7-16. Briefly describe the procedure used by the auditor to determine the appropriate sample size using sample tables such as those shown in Tables 7-1 and 7-2.

7-17. What factors should the auditor consider in determining sample size? How do each of these factors affect sample size?

7-18. For a risk of overreliance of 5 percent, calculate the sample size using Table 7-1 for each of the following sets of conditions (EDR = expected deviation rate; TDR = tolerable deviation rate).

    a. EDR = 1 percent, TDR = 7 percent.
    b. EDR = 2.5 percent, TDR = 10 percent.
    c. EDR = 3 percent, TDR = 7 percent.

7-19. For the set of conditions shown in Problem 7-18, repeat the calculation using a 10 percent risk of overreliance (Table 7-2). Comparing the results of the two sets of calculations, identify how the risk of overreliance affects sample size.

7-20. Why does the size of the population have such a limited effect on sample size in an attribute sampling plan?

◻ Performing the Sampling Plan

After the auditor has calculated the appropriate sample size and selected a method of drawing the sample, the sampling plan is executed. The sampling plan consists of two major steps. First, the auditor selects sample items from the population of interest based on the sample size calculated in the previous step and the method of selection. When selecting the sample, the auditor simply applies the appropriate selection procedure to the population of interest, as illustrated earlier. The auditor can take several approaches in selecting the sample:

1. Select the sample after year-end, with all items occurring during the year being subject to selection.
2. Select the sample during an interim period, with all items occurring before the interim date and items that are expected to occur after the date being subject to selection. In this case, the items occurring prior to the interim date can be evaluated in the interim period. For items occurring between the interim period and end of the year, the auditor must wait until year-end to verify them.
3. Select the sample during an interim period, with only items occurring before the interim date subject to selection.

If the third approach is chosen by the auditor, transactions occurring between the interim period and the end of the year may not need to be examined. However, in making this decision, the auditor must consider the results of the tests in the interim period, the length of time between the interim date and year-end, and the results of inquiries of client personnel. In general, the auditor is interested in determining whether conditions have substantially changed since the application of procedures in the interim period. If so, additional testing during this period would probably be considered necessary.

Once the auditor has selected the sample items, they are examined to determine whether they represent deviations from expected internal control policies and procedures. For example, if the auditor is interested in ensuring that a sample of purchases has been properly authorized by the client, the selected purchase orders should be examined for appropriate verification (such as signatures, initials, or other form of documentation). In cases where the selected items cannot be located by the auditor (if missing or incomplete), these items should be counted as deviations. At this point, the **sample deviation rate** (or **sample rate of occurrence**) can be calculated by dividing the number of deviations by the sample size. Remember, this rate provides the auditor with only one possible estimate of the true population deviation rate.

◻ Evaluating the Sample Results

Calculating the Upper Precision Limit. After performing the sampling plan, the auditor now has an **estimate** of the population deviation rate (the sample deviation rate). As noted earlier, a limitation associated with making a decision based on the results of a sample is that the sample may not be representative of the population of interest. This possibility is referred to as **sampling risk**. To evaluate the results of the sampling plan, the auditor must determine the precision of the sample deviation rate—that is, how close the sample deviation rate is to the true (but unknown) population deviation rate. Although the auditor cannot observe the population deviation rate unless every item is examined, statistical theory allows certain statements about this rate based on the results of a sample to be made using the concepts of precision and reliability.

In particular, the auditor is interested in obtaining an estimate of the population deviation rate that permits control of the desired exposure to the risk of overreliance. This conservative estimate represents a deviation rate (derived from sample results) that has a probability equal to reliability of equaling or exceeding the true population deviation rate. The resulting deviation rate (the upper precision limit) equals the sample deviation rate plus precision (at the desired reliability level). The statements that can be made about the upper precision limit are summarized in Figure 7-5. In this figure, all probabilities and deviation rates refer to the true population deviation rate.

To illustrate, assume that the auditor calculates a sample deviation rate of 5 percent. In addition, based on a desired reliability level of 95 percent (5 percent risk of overreliance), the precision of the sample is 2 percent. Recall that the precision is the closeness of an estimate to the true population value. Because of the relationship between precision and reliability, it may be stated that 95 percent of all sample means are within 2 percent of the true deviation rate. Therefore, the precision interval in this example can be calculated by taking the sample estimate and adding and subtracting the precision, as below:

$$\begin{aligned} \text{Precision Interval} &= \text{Sample Estimate} \pm \text{Precision} \\ &= 5 \text{ percent} \pm 2 \text{ percent} \\ &= 3 \text{ percent to } 7 \text{ percent} \end{aligned}$$

In attribute sampling, the auditor is interested in determining whether the population deviation rate is *less than* some tolerable deviation rate. The auditor is not concerned with how much less this difference actually is. In the previous example, the auditor is more interested in knowing that there

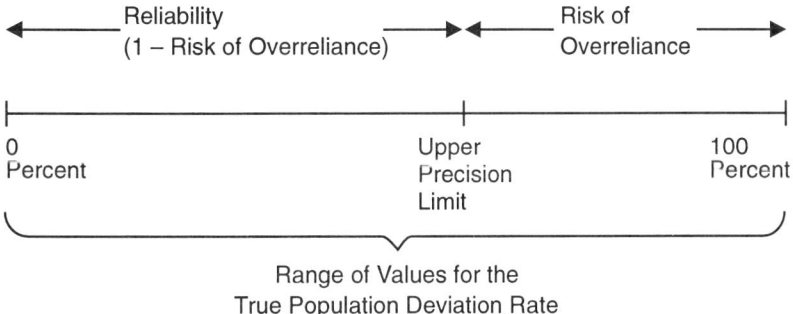

Notes
1. There is a (*1 – risk of overreliance, or reliability*) probability that the upper precision limit equals or exceeds the true population deviation rate.
2. There is a *risk of overreliance* probability that the upper precision limit is less than the true population deviation rate.

Figure 7-5: *Illustration of the Upper Precision Limit*

is an x (reliability) percent probability that the population deviation rate is less than 7 percent (5 percent + precision of 2 percent) than knowing that there is a 95 percent probability that the true population deviation rate is between 3 percent and 7 percent (5 percent + precision of 2 percent). That is, the auditor is not concerned with the probability that the true deviation rate is less than 3 percent.

As a result, an upper precision limit is calculated in such a manner that it has an x (reliability) percent probability of exceeding or equaling the population deviation rate. Conversely, (1 − x) percent of the time (risk of overreliance), the true population deviation rate exceeds the upper precision limit.

The precision can be calculated through the use of formulas. Alternatively, sampling tables are available that directly calculate the upper precision limit based on the desired risk of overreliance and sample deviation rate. Tables for a 5 percent and 10 percent risk of overreliance (95 percent and 90 percent reliability) are presented in Tables 7-3 and 7-4, respectively.

To calculate the upper precision limit using these tables, the auditor follows the following steps:

1. Based on the desired risk of overreliance, select the appropriate sample evaluation table. It is important to note that tables are available for risks of overreliance other than 5 and 10 percent. These particular levels were selected for illustration because they represent commonly-used levels.
2. Locate the row in the sampling table corresponding to the number of items (sample size) examined by the auditor. If the exact sample size does not appear in the sampling table, the auditor should use the highest sample size that does not exceed the actual sample size. This provides a more

conservative measure of the sample deviation rate because decreasing the sample size increases the sample deviation rate.[4]

3. Select the column corresponding to the number of deviations noted by the auditor.
4. Once the row and column from steps 2 and 3 have been identified, read the number in the table at the junction of the row and column. This number represents the **upper precision limit**.

Table 7-3: *Statistical Sample Results Evaluation Table for Tests of Controls (Upper Limits at 5 Percent Risk of Overreliance)*

Sample Size	Actual Number of Deviation Found										
	0	1	2	3	4	5	6	7	8	9	10
25	11.3	17.6	*	*	*	*	*	*	*	*	*
30	9.5	14.9	19.6	*	*	*	*	*	*	*	*
35	8.3	12.9	17.0	*	*	*	*	*	*	*	*
40	7.3	11.4	15.0	18.3	*	*	*	*	*	*	*
45	6.5	10.2	13.4	16.4	19.2	*	*	*	*	*	*
50	5.9	9.2	12.1	14.8	17.4	19.9	*	*	*	*	*
55	5.4	8.4	11.1	13.5	15.9	18.2	*	*	*	*	*
60	4.9	7.7	10.2	12.5	14.7	16.8	18.8	*	*	*	*
65	4.6	7.1	9.4	11.5	13.6	15.5	17.4	19.3	*	*	*
70	4.2	6.6	8.8	10.8	12.6	14.5	16.3	18.0	19.7	*	*
75	4.0	6.2	8.2	10.1	11.8	13.6	15.2	16.9	18.5	20.0	*
80	3.7	5.8	7.7	9.5	11.1	12.7	14.3	15.9	17.4	18.9	*
90	3.3	5.2	6.9	8.4	9.9	11.4	12.8	14.2	15.5	16.8	18.2
100	3.0	4.7	6.2	7.6	9.0	10.3	11.5	12.8	14.0	15.2	16.4
125	2.4	3.8	5.0	6.1	7.2	8.3	9.3	10.3	11.3	12.3	13.2
150	2.0	3.2	4.2	5.1	6.0	6.9	7.8	8.6	9.5	10.3	11.1
200	1.5	2.4	3.2	3.9	4.6	5.2	5.9	6.5	7.2	7.8	8.4

*Over 20 percent.

Note: This table presents upper limits as percentages and assumes a large population.

Source: American Institute of Certified Public Accountants (AICPA), *Audit and Accounting Guide*, "Audit Sampling" (New York: AICPA, 1983), 108.

---

[4] Alternatively, the auditor could utilize more precise tables or interpolate the results. These methods are not commonly used and are beyond the scope of this text.

Table 7-4: *Statistical Sampling Results Evaluation Table for Tests of Controls (Upper Limits at 10 Percent Risk of Overreliance)*

Sample Size	Actual Number of Deviations Found										
	0	1	2	3	4	5	6	7	8	9	10
20	10.9	18.1	*	*	*	*	*				
25	8.8	14.7	19.9	*	*	*	*	*	*	*	*
30	7.4	12.4	16.8	*	*	*	*	*	*	*	*
35	6.4	10.7	14.5	18.1	*	*	*	*	*	*	*
40	5.6	9.4	12.8	16.0	19.0	*	*	*	*	*	*
45	5.0	8.4	11.4	14.3	17.0	19.7	*	*	*	*	*
50	4.6	7.6	10.3	12.9	15.4	17.8	*	*	*	*	*
55	4.1	6.9	9.4	11.8	14.1	16.3	18.4	*	*	*	*
60	3.8	6.4	8.7	10.8	12.9	15.0	16.9	18.9	*	*	*
70	3.3	5.5	7.5	9.3	11.1	12.9	14.6	16.3	17.9	19.6	*
80	2.9	4.8	6.6	8.2	9.8	11.3	12.8	14.3	15.8	17.2	18.6
90	2.6	4.3	5.9	7.3	8.7	10.1	11.5	12.8	14.1	15.4	16.6
100	2.3	3.9	5.3	6.6	7.9	9.1	10.3	11.5	12.7	13.9	15.0
120	2.0	3.3	4.4	5.5	6.6	7.6	8.7	9.7	10.7	11.6	12.6
160	1.5	2.5	3.3	4.2	5.0	5.8	6.5	7.3	8.0	8.8	9.5
200	1.2	2.0	2.7	3.4	4.0	4.6	5.3	5.9	6.5	7.1	7.6

*Over 20 percent.

Note: This table presents upper limits as percentage. This table assumes a large population.

Source: American Institute of Certified Public Accountants (AICPA), *Audit and Accounting Guide*, "Audit Sampling" (New York: AICPA, 1983), 109.

For example, assume that the auditor examined 100 items and found three deviations. A sample deviation rate of 3 percent (3 deviations ÷ 100 items = 3 percent) is calculated. Using Table 7-3 (which controls the risk of overreliance at 5 percent), an upper precision limit of 7.6 percent is identified, as highlighted in the excerpted table below:

Sample Size	Actual Number of Deviations Found		
	1	3	5
100	4.7	7.6	10.3

7 / Introduction to Sampling and Attribute Sampling

In this case, the upper precision limit would be 7.6 percent. This parameter includes the following components:

- An actual sample deviation rate of 3 percent.

- An allowance for sampling risk (precision) of 4.6 percent. This is calculated as the difference between the sample deviation rate and the upper precision limit (7.6 percent − 3 percent = 4.6 percent).

CHAPTER CHECKPOINTS

7-21. In terms of timing, what three approaches are available to the auditor in selecting a sample?

7-22. If the risk of overreliance in a given sampling plan is 5 percent and the upper precision limit is 12 percent, summarize the statement that could be made with respect to the true deviation rate.

Making the Reliance Decision. Based on the previous example, the auditor concludes that there is a 95 percent probability that the true population deviation rate is less than or equal to 7.6 percent (the upper precision limit). Therefore, a 5 percent probability exists that the true population deviation rate is greater than 7.6 percent. Once this limit is calculated, the auditor compares the upper precision limit to the tolerable deviation rate. If the upper precision limit is less than the tolerable deviation rate, the control is relied upon as planned. Note that if the auditor relies on the control, the risk that the population deviation rate is actually greater than the tolerable deviation rate has been controlled to the planned level (5 percent risk of overreliance).

However, if the upper precision limit is greater than the tolerable deviation rate, the auditor should reduce the reliance on the internal control and increase control risk. As noted in Chapter 5, the increase in control risk will ultimately result in more effective substantive testing procedures being performed (in the form of a lower detection risk). The possible outcomes and ultimate actions in an attribute sampling application are summarized as follows:

- Upper precision limit < Tolerable deviation rate: Rely on internal control as planned.

- Upper precision limit > Tolerable deviation rate: Reduce reliance on internal control and increase control risk.

▶ **Example:** *Attribute Sampling*

To illustrate an attribute sampling application, assume that the auditor is interested in determining the effectiveness of internal controls with respect to cash disbursements. In particular, the auditor wishes to determine whether cash disbursements are only made for purchases authorized through the preparation of a Voucher. During the year, the client made a total of 10,000 payments by check. These 10,000 payments represent the population of possible internal controls for cash disbursements.

The auditor defines a deviation condition as an instance where a payment is made without first being approved through the use of a Voucher. Based on the auditor's overall understanding of internal control, internal control has been assessed to be moderately effective in preventing and detecting errors in cash disbursements; as a result, control risk was assessed at moderate levels.

At this point, the auditor has determined the objective of the test, defined the deviation condition, and identified the population of interest. As noted earlier, these are the initial steps in an attribute sampling application. Next, the auditor should determine the method of selecting the sample. For purposes of this example, assume that systematic sampling is used.

The next step in performing an attribute sampling plan is to determine the appropriate sample size. As noted earlier, three factors must be quantified by the auditor: (1) the risk of overreliance, (2) the tolerable deviation rate, and (3) the expected deviation rate. Assume that the auditor established a risk of overreliance of 5 percent and a tolerable deviation rate of 7 percent. Also, based on a sample of items drawn from the population of interest, the auditor estimates the population deviation rate to be 3.5 percent. Using Table 7-1, the appropriate sample size is 167 items (cash disbursements). Therefore, the auditor will select 167 disbursements and determine whether they have been properly approved through a Voucher.

Once the sample size has been established, the auditor now performs the sampling plan. This plan consists of two tasks: (1) selecting the sample from the population, and (2) examining the sample items. Because systematic sampling is used in this example, the auditor selects a random start as the first item and then skips a fixed number of items to select the remaining items. The sampling (skip) interval can be calculated as:

$$\text{Skip Interval} = \frac{\text{Number of Items in Population}}{\text{Sample Size}}$$
$$= \frac{10,000}{167} = 60 \text{ (rounded)}$$

If the random start chosen by the auditor was 15, the auditor would select the 15th item, 75th item (15 + 60 = 75), 135th item (75 + 60 = 135), and so on until 167 items (the desired sample size) are selected. Because cash disbursements are being examined in this example, the auditor would ordinarily select check numbers corresponding to the items in the population.

concluded:

After selecting the sample items from the population, the auditor next examines those items to determine whether they contain deviations. In this case, a deviation occurs when a payment was made without first being authorized through the use of a Voucher. Assume that for the 167 items selected by the auditor, a total of four deviations was noted. The sample deviation rate in this case is 2.4 percent, as shown below:

$$\text{Sample Deviation Rate} = \frac{\text{Number of Deviations}}{\text{Sample Size}}$$

$$= \frac{4}{167}$$

$$= 2.4 \text{ Percent}$$

After calculating the sample deviation rate, the auditor evaluates the sample results. Remember that the 2.4 percent sample deviation rate is only one possible estimate of the true population deviation rate. The auditor wishes to determine the maximum population deviation rate corresponding to the desired risk of overreliance. This rate is referred to as the upper precision limit. Using Table 7-3 with: (1) a desired risk of overreliance of 5 percent; (2) a sample size of 167 items (round down to 150);[5] and (3) 4 deviations, the upper precision limit is 6 percent. As noted earlier, this indicates that there is a 95 percent probability that the true population deviation rate is less than or equal to 6 percent.

Finally, the upper precision limit is compared to the tolerable deviation rate. In this case, because the upper precision limit is 6 percent and the tolerable deviation rate is 7 percent, the auditor would decide to rely on internal control as planned. Control risk would be assessed at the planned level (moderate), and there is no need to increase the planned extent of substantive testing relating to cash disbursements. Upon examining Table 7-3, note that the auditor could have found up to 5 deviations (an upper precision limit of 6.9 percent) before reducing the reliance on internal control.

What would have happened if the upper precision limit was greater than the tolerable deviation rate? In this case, the auditor would decide not to rely on internal control to the extent planned. Control risk would be increased, with a resulting increase in the planned extent of substantive testing procedures.

Although Table 7-3 computes the upper precision limit assuming a 5 percent risk of overreliance, similar tables are available for other levels as well. Recall from our earlier discussion of precision and reliability that as the reliability increases, the precision also increases. That is, as the auditor wants to increase the probability that the true population deviation rate is less than a given upper precision limit, that limit is higher (precision is higher). In turn, higher upper precision limits result in a lower exposure to the risk of overreliance.

---

[5] Using a lower sample size has the effect of increasing the upper precision limit, because the number of deviations are assumed to occur over fewer observations. This provides the auditor with a more conservative measure.

> **CHAPTER CHECKPOINTS**
>
> **7-23.** Describe the procedure used by the auditor to determine the upper precision limit using sampling tables (such as Tables 7-3 and 7-4).
>
> **7-24.** Consider the relationship between the tolerable deviation rate and the upper precision limit. When would the auditor decide to rely on the internal control as planned? When would the auditor choose to reduce the level of reliance on internal control?
>
> **7-25.** Using Tables 7-3 and 7-4, how would each of the following factors affect the upper precision limit calculated by the auditor?
>
>   **a.** Risk of overreliance.
>   **b.** Rate of deviation in the sample.
>
> **7-26.** For each of the following sets of facts, determine the upper precision limit using Tables 7-3 and 7-4 (OR = risk of overreliance; SS = sample size; ND = number of deviations).
>
>   **a.** OR = 5 percent, SS = 60, ND = 5.
>   **b.** OR = 5 percent, SS = 200, ND = 3.
>   **c.** OR = 10 percent, SS = 120, ND = 4.
>
> **7-27.** Why does the upper precision limit exceed the deviation rate calculated by the auditor as a result of the sampling application?

OTHER ATTRIBUTE SAMPLING APPLICATIONS

Nonstatistical Sampling

The major difference between statistical sampling and nonstatistical sampling is that nonstatistical sampling does not explicitly incorporate the auditor's desired exposure to sampling risk in calculating sample size and evaluating the sample results. However, other than this difference, nonstatistical sampling plans are quite similar to statistical plans. To illustrate nonstatistical methods, assume that an auditor establishes the tolerable deviation rate at 8 percent. A sample of items from the population of interest would be chosen. Two key differences between statistical and nonstatistical sampling are:

1. The number of items composing the sample is judgmentally selected by the auditor. Unlike statistical sampling, there is no attempt by the auditor to control exposure to the risk of overreliance.
2. The method of selecting sample items for examination is not required to expose each item in the population to possible selection. Therefore, block sampling and haphazard sampling (discussed earlier in this chapter) are often used in conjunction with nonstatistical sampling applications.

Next, the auditor performs the sampling plan as before. After examining the sample items and noting any deviations, the auditor evaluates the sample results. In this case, if the sample deviation rate was clearly less than 8 percent (say, between 2 percent and 5 percent), the auditor would probably choose to rely on internal control as planned. If the sample deviation rate was clearly greater than 8 percent (e.g., greater than 10 percent), the auditor would reduce the reliance on internal control structure. For sample deviation rates of between 5 percent and 9 percent, the auditor must use professional judgment in making the reliance decision. Although the above levels are only examples, note that the basic criteria for the auditor's decision have not changed. The only difference is that the auditor does not explicitly control the exposure to the risk of overreliance in evaluating the sample results.

◻ Discovery Sampling

Another type of sampling that auditors use in special situations is **discovery sampling**. The objective of discovery sampling is to provide a specified assurance of locating at least one example of an attribute if its rate of occurrence in the population is at or above a specified rate. Discovery sampling is appropriate in situations where, despite the occurrence rate being low, the auditor wants to have a specified chance that the sample selected is large enough that the observation of at least one occurrence may be expected.

Discovery sampling is most frequently used in special-purpose examinations. For example, after dismissing an employee, a company might engage an auditor for a special-purpose examination to determine whether errors (or defalcations) occurred in the employee's work. If the employee approved disbursements up to $2,000 from a special bank account, the auditor might select a sample large enough that if 1 percent or more of the approved disbursements contained irregularities, the auditor would be 95 percent sure of finding at least one example. In such a case, seeing one example of fraudulent action would naturally lead to expanding the investigation.

Table 7-5 allows the auditor to calculate the necessary sample sizes for a discovery sampling application. To illustrate its use, assume that a given population of 8,000 internal control applications exists and this control is believed to be relatively free of deviations (expected deviation rate less than 1 percent). After considering the importance of this control, also assume that the auditor would choose to reduce the reliance on internal control if the deviation rate was 2 percent or less (i.e., the tolerable deviation rate is 2 percent). Because the expected deviation rate is relatively small, it is quite possible that the sampling methods discussed to this point in the text would not yield a large enough sample size to observe any deviations. The ability of discovery sampling to provide the auditor with a desired probability of observing a deviation is one of the primary benefits associated with this type of sampling.

If the auditor wants to have a 90 percent probability of observing a deviation for a control procedure with a 2 percent tolerable deviation rate, Table 7-5 indicates that a sample size of 120 items must be examined. As shown in Table 7-5, this sample would provide a 91 percent chance of observing one deviation. Once the sample is selected, the auditor evaluates the sample items for presence of deviations. If no deviations are found in this sample, the auditor can conclude that a 90 percent probability exists that the population deviation rate is less than 2 percent. If a deviation is noted by the auditor, the most likely step would be to use a traditional statistical sampling approach (as discussed earlier in this chapter) to estimate the upper precision limit.

◻ Sequential (Stop-or-Go) Sampling

The sampling plans discussed thus far have employed a fixed sample size—that is, these plans have evaluated a single sample of *n* items and have made the conclusions based only on the results of that

Table 7-5: *Probability of Discovering at Least One Deviation in a Sample (for Population Sizes of 5,000 – 10,000)*

Sample Size	Tolerable Rate							
	0.1%	0.2%	0.3%	0.4%	0.5%	0.75%	1.0%	2.0%
50	5	10	14	18	33	31	40	64
60	6	11	17	21	38	36	45	70
70	7	13	19	25	43	41	51	76
80	8	15	21	28	48	45	55	80
90	9	17	24	30	52	49	60	84
100	10	18	26	33	56	53	64	87
120	11	21	30	38	62	60	70	91
140	13	25	35	43	51	65	76	94
160	15	28	38	48	55	70	80	96
200	18	33	45	56	64	78	87	98
240	22	39	52	62	70	84	91	99
300	26	46	60	70	78	90	95	99+
340	29	50	65	75	82	93	97	99+
400	34	56	71	81	87	95	98	99+
460	38	61	76	85	91	97	99	99+
500	40	64	79	87	92	98	99	99+
600	46	71	84	92	96	99	99+	99+
700	52	77	89	95	97	99+	99+	99+
800	57	81	92	96	98	99+	99+	99+
900	61	85	94	98	99	99+	99+	99+
1000	65	88	96	99	99	99+	99+	99+
1500	80	96	99	99+	99+	99+	99+	99+
2000	89	99	99+	99+	99+	99+	99+	99+

Note: 99+ indicates a probability of 99.5 percent or greater because probabilities in this table are rounded to the nearest 1 percent.

Source: Adapted from *Audit Sampling* (Cleveland: Ernst & Whinney [Young], 1979), 169.

sample. An alternative is a **sequential** (or **stop-or-go**) sampling plan, in which the auditor evaluates an initial sample in a manner similar to that discussed earlier. In general, this initial sample is smaller than that needed for an attribute sampling plan employing a fixed sample size. Based on the auditor's evaluation of this initial sample, one of three courses of action may be taken:

1. Decide to rely on internal control as planned, based only on the results of the initial sample. In this case, the auditor would not examine any additional items.
2. Decide to reduce the reliance on internal control, based only on the results of the initial sample. Once again, the auditor would not examine any additional items beyond the initial sample.
3. Select one or more additional sample(s) and consider the joint evidence provided by those sample(s) before making a final decision.

Therefore, sequential sampling may require the auditor to examine a sample of internal control applications, evaluate the results, and examine additional applications. The decision made by the auditor is based on the results of the examination at each stage of the process. A partial table used with sequential sampling is shown in Table 7-6. This table contains the reliability level associated with three factors:

1. Sample size.
2. Number of deviations.
3. Tolerable deviation rate.

To illustrate a sequential sampling application, assume that the auditor establishes a tolerable deviation rate of 10 percent and desires exposure to the risk of overreliance of 5 percent. Thus, as noted earlier, the auditor is willing to accept a 5 percent probability that the actual deviation rate is greater than the tolerable deviation rate (10 percent) and still rely on the client's internal control to the extent planned. Also recall that a 5 percent risk of overreliance corresponds to a reliability of 95 percent (1 − 0.05 = 0.95).

If the auditor selects fifty items, Table 7-6 reveals that three possibilities exist, depending on the number of deviations noted. First, if zero or one deviation is found, the probability that the true deviation rate is less than 10 percent is 99.49 and 96.62 percent, respectively. In these cases, the auditor could rely on internal control as planned without examining any additional sample items. In doing so, the risk of overreliance has been controlled at the desired level. However, if more than one deviation is found, the auditor could take one of two courses of action:

▶ Choose to reduce the reliance on internal control without examining any additional sample items. This decision is most likely for lower reliabilities in Table 7-6.

▶ Select additional items to attempt and achieve the desired reliability. If possible, the auditor would rely on internal control as planned. However, if the additional reliability cannot be achieved, the auditor must again choose between reducing the reliance on the client's internal control and selecting additional items.

For example, if two deviations were noted in the sample of 50 items, the auditor's exposure to the risk of overreliance is greater than the desired level of 5 percent (100 percent − 88.83 percent = 11.17 percent). In this case, the auditor could select an additional 20 items (bringing the total sample size up to 70 items). If none of these 20 items contained a deviation, a total of two deviations from a sample of 70 items was noted. Table 7-6 indicates that there is a 97.58 percent probability that the true deviation rate is less than 10 percent. Based on this result, the auditor would decide to rely on internal control as planned. However, if an additional deviation was noted, the auditor could not rely on internal control structure as planned, because the probability that the true deviation rate is less than 10 percent is only 92.88 percent (3 deviations from a sample of 70 items). In this case, the auditor would again choose between reducing his or her reliance on internal control or selecting additional items for examination.

Table 7-6: *Stop-or-Go Attribute Sampling Reliability Levels (Population Size > 2000)*

Sample Size	Number of Deviations	Tolerable Deviation Rate									
		1%	2%	3%	4%	5%	6%	7%	8%	9%	10%
50	0	39.50	63.58	78.19	87.01	92.31	95.47	97.34	98.45	99.10	99.49
	1	8.94	26.42	44.47	59.95	72.06	81.00	87.35	91.73	94.68	96.62
	2	1.38	7.84	18.92	32.33	45.95	58.38	68.92	77.40	83.95	88.83
70	0	50.52	75.69	88.14	94.26	97.24	98.69	99.38	99.71	99.86	99.94
	1	15.53	40.96	62.47	77.51	87.03	92.81	96.10	97.93	98.92	99.45
	2	3.34	16.50	35.08	53.44	68.63	79.87	87.59	92.60	95.72	97.58
	3	0.54	5.19	15.87	30.71	46.61	61.15	73.07	82.10	88.53	92.88
	4	0.07	1.32	5.93	14.85	27.21	41.13	54.77	66.80	76.61	84.12
100	0	63.40	86.74	95.25	98.31	99.41	99.80	99.93	99.98	99.99	100.00
	1	26.42	59.67	80.54	91.28	96.29	98.48	99.40	99.77	99.91	99.97
	2	7.94	32.33	58.02	96.79	88.17	94.34	97.42	98.87	99.52	99.81
	3	1.84	14.10	35.28	57.05	74.22	85.70	92.56	96.33	98.27	99.22
	4	0.34	5.08	18.22	37.11	56.40	72.32	83.68	90.97	95.26	97.63
	5	0.05	1.55	8.08	21.16	38.40	55.93	70.86	82.01	89.55	94.24
	6	0.01	0.41	3.12	10.64	23.40	39.37	55.57	69.68	80.60	88.28
120	0	70.06	91.15	97.41	99.25	99.79	99.94	99.98	100.00	100.00	100.00
	1	33.77	69.46	87.82	95.53	98.45	99.48	99.83	99.95	99.98	100.00
	2	11.96	43.13	70.16	86.28	94.25	97.75	99.17	99.71	99.90	99.97
	3	3.30	22.00	48.67	71.13	85.56	93.40	97.19	98.87	99.60	99.84
	4	0.74	9.38	29.24	52.67	72.18	85.27	92.83	96.75	98.61	99.44
	5	0.14	3.41	15.29	34.83	55.85	73.23	85.23	92.47	96.42	98.40
	6	0.02	1.07	7.03	20.57	39.37	58.50	74.26	85.35	92.26	96.18
	7	*	0.30	2.86	10.90	25.24	43.20	60.81	75.25	85.57	92.16
	8	*	0.07	1.04	5.21	14.74	29.39	46.51	62.85	76.21	100.00
150	0	77.86	95.17	98.96	99.78	99.95	99.99	100.00	100.00	100.00	100.00
	1	44.30	80.39	94.15	98.41	99.60	99.90	99.98	100.00	100.00	100.00
	2	19.05	57.91	83.07	94.16	98.19	99.48	99.86	99.96	99.99	99.99
	3	6.47	35.28	66.16	85.42	94.52	98.14	99.42	99.83	99.95	99.95
	4	1.80	18.30	46.93	72.04	87.44	95.01	98.20	99.40	99.81	99.81
	5	0.42	8.19	29.57	55.76	76.56	89.17	95.52	98.31	99.41	99.44
	6	0.08	3.20	16.60	39.37	62.71	80.16	90.66	96.03	98.45	98.60
	7	0.02	1.11	8.34	25.32	47.72	68.34	83.12	91.94	96.50	96.93
	8	*	0.34	3.78	14.85	33.62	54.84	72.98	85.58	93.04	94.00
	9	*	0.10	1.55	7.97	21.91	41.26	60.93	76.85	87.65	89.40
	10	*	0.02	0.58	3.93	13.22	29.03	48.15	66.16	80.13	7.6

*Less than 0.01.

Note: For space considerations, only reliabilities corresponding to limited number of deviations are provided in Table 7-6.

Source: Adapted from *Audit Sampling* (Cleveland: Ernst & Whinney [Young], 1979), 186-187.

CHAPTER CHECKPOINTS

7-28. Consider the major steps involved in a statistical sampling application. Where are major differences introduced when a nonstatistical sampling plan is chosen?

7-29. Define discovery sampling. When should discovery sampling be used by the auditor?

7-30. Define sequential (stop-or-go) sampling. Describe the basic procedure employed by the auditor for using sequential sampling.

SUMMARY OF KEY POINTS

1. Audit sampling is the application of an audit procedure to less than 100 percent of the items within an account balance or class of transactions for the purpose of evaluating some characteristic of the account balance or class of transactions. Thus, in sampling, the auditor is attempting to make a statement about a population based on examining only a subset of that population (a *sample*).

2. Sampling risk is the probability that the auditor's decision based on the sample differs from the decision that would have been made if the entire population were examined. Sampling risk arises because the sample selected by the auditor is not representative of the population. Nonsampling risk, on the other hand, is caused by factors other than the sample selected by the auditor—for example, performing inadequate auditing procedures, auditor negligence, or auditor misperformance.

3. Statistical sampling uses the laws of probability to make objective statements about a population. The primary benefit of statistical sampling is that it allows the auditor to control the exposure to sampling risk to desired levels. In a statistical sampling application, the auditor incorporates the desired exposure to sampling risk in determining the sample size and evaluating sample results.

4. Precision reflects the closeness of a sample estimate to the true population value; reliability is the probability of achieving a given degree of precision. For example, if precision is 2 percent and reliability is 90 percent, it may be stated that there is a 90 percent probability that the sample estimate is within 2 percent of the true population value. The interval surrounding the sample estimate is referred to as the precision interval.

5. Attribute sampling is employed by the auditor when the population of interest has only one of two possible outcomes: an attribute either exists (occurs) with respect to a particular item or does not exist (occur) with respect to that item. Attribute sampling is commonly used by the auditor in the study and evaluation of internal control.

6. When conducting tests of controls, the auditor must consider both the risk of overreliance and underreliance. The risk of overreliance (or risk of assessing control risk too low) is the risk that the auditor relies on the internal control as planned (based on the sample) when the population deviation rate does not justify reliance. This risk is very critical to the auditor because it decreases the effectiveness of the audit.

7. The risk of underreliance (or risk of assessing control risk too high) is the risk that the auditor reduces the reliance on internal control when the population deviation rate justifies the original level of reliance. When the risk of underreliance occurs, the auditor suffers an efficiency loss because excessive substantive tests will be performed.

8. Steps involved in attribute sampling include: (a) defining the deviation condition, (b) defining the population of interest, (c) determining the method of selecting the sample, and (d) determining the sample size. Factors that affect the sample size include the desired risk of overreliance, tolerable deviation rate, and expected deviation rate.

9. Once the sample has been selected by the auditor, the sample items are examined and classified as possessing or not possessing the attribute (characteristic) of interest. The end

10. The auditor then calculates the upper precision limit, based on the sample size, desired risk of overreliance, and the number of deviations noted in the sample. AICPA sampling tables may be used to assist the auditor in this calculation. If the upper precision limit is less than the tolerable deviation rate, the auditor concludes that the internal control policy or procedure is functioning as intended and assesses the final level of control risk at the preliminary level.

11. If, however, the upper precision limit is greater than the tolerable deviation rate, the auditor is unable to support the planned degree of reliance on internal control. The auditor would then increase the level of control risk and perform more extensive substantive tests.

12. Two other types of attribute sampling applications are discovery sampling and sequential (stop-or-go) sampling. Discovery sampling provides the auditor with a specified probability of observing at least one deviation if such deviations exist at some specified rate in the population. Sequential sampling may provide the auditor with a more efficient sample by initially selecting a smaller sample and basing decisions about whether to examine additional items on the results obtained through the initial sample.

⬤ GLOSSARY

Audit Sampling. The application of an audit procedure to less than 100 percent of the items within an account balance or class of transactions for the purpose of evaluating some characteristics of the account balance or class of transactions.

Block Sampling. A sampling application where the auditor selects a series of contiguous items for examination. Block sampling is not considered appropriate for statistical sampling applications.

Deviation. An instance where a specified internal control policy or procedure is not being followed by the organization as prescribed.

Discovery Sampling. A method of attribute sampling that provides the auditor with a sample size sufficiently large to have a specified probability of observing at least one deviation in the sample, assuming that deviations occur in the population at some specified rate.

Expected Deviation Rate. The rate of deviations expected by the auditor in the population. This parameter is established based on previous experience with the client or a small initial sample (pilot sample) from the current year.

Haphazard Sampling. A method of sample selection where items are not selected in any particular fashion or using any systematic or organized method.

Nonsampling Risk. The probability that the auditor fails to reach the correct conclusion based on factors unrelated to the representativeness of the sample. Nonsampling risk is caused by such factors as inappropriate auditing procedures and auditor negligence or misperformance.

Nonstatistical Sampling. Nonstatistical sampling violates one or more of the tenets of statistical sampling. The use of nonstatistical sampling does not allow the auditor to control the exposure to sampling risk.

Population Deviation Rate. The actual rate of deviation that exists in a population of interest. The auditor's objective in performing attribute sampling is to calculate an estimate of this rate.

Precision. The closeness of a sample estimate to the true (but unknown) population value. Precision is also referred to as the allowance for sampling risk.

Random Sampling. A method of sampling where each item in the population is randomly selected—that is, has an equal probability of selection.

Reliability. The probability that the sample estimate differs from the true population value by an amount less than or equal to precision.

Risk of Overreliance (or Risk of Assessing Control Risk Too Low). The risk that the auditor chooses to rely on internal control as planned (based on the sample) when the population deviation rate does not justify such reliance.

Risk of Underreliance (or Risk of Assessing Control Risk Too High). The risk that the auditor chooses not to rely on internal control as planned when the population deviation rate justifies reliance.

Sampling Risk. Also known as sampling error, sampling risk is the probability that the auditor's decision based on the sample differs from the decision that would have been made if the entire population had been examined. The primary cause of sampling risk is a nonrepresentative sample.

Sequential Sampling. Also known as stop-or-go sampling. This method begins by having the auditor select a relatively small sample. Based on the evidence from this sample, the auditor may choose to rely on internal control as planned, not to rely on internal control as planned, or to select additional items for examination. The procedure is repeated until a definitive conclusion is reached by the auditor. Sequential sampling has the potential to result in the most efficient sample size.

Statistical Sampling. A method of sampling that uses the laws of probability to make objective statements about a population of interest. In a statistical sampling plan, the auditor considers the desired exposure to sampling risk in determining the appropriate sample size and evaluating the sample results. In addition, the auditor also makes every item available for selection. The primary benefit of statistical sampling is that the auditor is able to control the exposure to sampling risk.

Systematic Sampling. A method of random sampling where the initial sample item is randomly selected and a fixed number of items (the skip interval) are bypassed, with the next item selected. The procedure is repeated until the desired number of items have been selected.

Tolerable Deviation Rate. The maximum allowable rate of deviation in the population that can occur without the auditor reducing the reliance on internal control.

Upper Precision Limit. A statistical estimate of the maximum deviation rate in the population. The upper precision limit has a (1 -risk of overreliance) probability of equaling or exceeding the true population deviation rate. Conversely, there is a probability equal to the risk of overreliance that the true population deviation rate exceeds the upper precision limit.

◉ SUMMARY OF PROFESSIONAL PRONOUNCEMENTS

Statement on Auditing Standards No. 39, "Audit Sampling" (New York: AICPA, 1983, AU 350).

QUESTIONS AND PROBLEMS

7-31. Select the **best** answer for each of the following items.

1. Which of the following aspects of a sampling plan does not distinguish statistical sampling from nonstatistical sampling?

    a. The proportion of items in the population that is made available for examination.
    b. The factors considered by the auditor in determining the sample size.
    c. The factors considered by the auditor in evaluating the sample results.
    —d. The need for the auditor to use judgment in exercising the sampling plan.
    e. All of the above distinguish statistical sampling from nonstatistical sampling.

2. Which of the following terms describes the closeness of a sample estimate to the true population value?

    a. Deviation rate.
    —b. Precision.
    c. Reliability.
    d. Risk of overreliance.
    e. None of the above.

3. Which of the following statements best describes the nature of sampling risk?

    a. Sampling risk occurs when the auditor makes a nonintentional error in evaluating sample results.
    b. Sampling risk results from the application of an inappropriate audit procedure in evaluating items selected from the population.
    —c. Sampling risk is caused by the selection of a sample that does not appropriately represent the population.
    d. Sampling risk can be eliminated through the use of probabilistic selection techniques.
    e. None of the above.

4. If a sample estimate is 70, precision is 20, and reliability is 80 percent, which of the following statements would be correct with respect to the true population value?

    a. There is an 80 percent chance that the true population value is less than or equal to 70.
    b. There is a 20 percent chance that the true population value is less than or equal to 70.
    —c. There is an 80 percent chance that the true population value falls between 50 and 90.
    d. There is a 20 percent chance that the true population value falls between 50 and 90.
    e. None of the above.

5. The maximum allowable rate of deviation that can exist in the population without the auditor reducing the reliance on internal control is referred to as the:

   a. Expected deviation rate.
   b. Population deviation rate.
   c. Risk of overreliance.
   d. Risk of underreliance.
   e. Tolerable deviation rate.

6. Which of the following statements is not true with regard to sample selection?

   a. Both random sampling and systematic sampling are appropriately used in statistical sampling applications.
   b. One disadvantage associated with the use of systematic sampling is that the items must be arranged in a nonrandom fashion.
   c. Systematic sampling is normally easier to use than random sampling, especially in populations where the sampling units are not prenumbered.
   d. Both random sampling and systematic sampling expose each item in the population to the possibility of selection.
   e. All of the above are true.

7. A method of sample selection in which the auditor selects a series of contiguous items for examination is referred to as:

   a. Block sampling.
   b. Cluster sampling.
   c. Haphazard sampling.
   d. Nonstatistical sampling.
   e. None of the above.

8. A form of sampling that attempts to estimate the extent to which some characteristic exists in a population is referred to as:

   a. Attribute sampling.
   b. Discovery sampling.
   c. Nonstatistical sampling.
   d. Statistical sampling.
   e. Variables sampling.

9. The risk that the auditor fails to rely on internal control as planned when such reliance is justified is referred to as the risk of _____.

   a. Incorrect acceptance.
   b. Incorrect rejection.
   c. Overreliance.
   d. Underreliance.
   e. None of the above.

Use the following information to answer questions 10–13.

	Decision Based on the Population	
	Rely on ICS as Planned	Reduce Reliance on ICS
Decision Provided by Sample Evidence		
Rely on ICS as Planned	A	B
Reduce Reliance on ICS	C	D

10. Which cell represents the risk of overreliance?

    a. A.
    b. B.
    c. C.
    d. D.
    e. None of the above.

11. Which cell represents the risk of underreliance?

    a. A.
    b. B.
    c. C.
    d. D.
    e. None of the above.

12. Which cell will result in a loss of audit effectiveness because control risk is assessed at an excessively low level?

    a. A.
    b. B.
    c. C.
    d. D.
    e. None of the above.

13. In which cells would the upper precision limit calculated by the auditor exceed the tolerable deviation rate?

    a. A and B.
    b. B and D.
    c. A and C.
    d. C and D.
    e. None of the above.

14. Which of the following factors would normally have the least significant effect on sample size in an attribute sampling application?

    a. Expected deviation rate.
    b. Risk of overreliance.
    c. Size of the population.
    d. Tolerable deviation rate.
    e. None of the above.

7 / Introduction to Sampling and Attribute Sampling

15. Which of the following conditions, holding all other factors constant, would not result in an increased sample size?

    a. A reduction in the risk of overreliance from 10 percent to 5 percent.
    b. An increase in the desired reliability from 90 percent to 95 percent.
    c. An increase in the expected deviation rate from 3 percent to 4 percent.
    –d. An increase in the tolerable deviation rate from 8 percent to 10 percent.
    e. All of the above factors would result in an increased sample size.

16. Which of the following sets of circumstances would result in the highest sample size?

	Tolerable Deviation Rate	Expected Deviation Rate	Risk of Overreliance
a.	High	Low	High
b.	High	High	Low
c.	Low	Low	High
–d.	Low	High	Low
e.	None of the above		

Use Table 7-3 in answering questions 17–20.

Jones, CPA, performed an attribute sampling plan to determine the effectiveness of a key internal control. Based on a desired risk of overreliance of 5 percent and a tolerable deviation rate of 12 percent, Jones selected ninety items and found nine deviations.

17. What is the sample deviation rate?

    a. 5 percent.
    b. 9 percent.
    –c. 10 percent.
    d. 12 percent.
    e. None of the above.

18. What is the upper precision limit?

    a. 5.0 percent.
    b. 9.0 percent.
    c. 10.0 percent.
    –d. 16.8 percent.
    e. None of the above.

19. What is the precision (allowance for sampling risk)?

    a. 5.0 percent.
    –b. 6.8 percent.
    c. 12.0 percent.
    d. 16.8 percent.
    e. None of the above.

20. What is Jones's conclusion with respect to the internal control examined?

   a. Jones should reduce the reliance on internal control, because the allowance for sampling risk is greater than the risk of overreliance.
   b. Jones should not reduce the reliance on internal control, because the sample deviation rate is less than the tolerable deviation rate.
   c. Jones should reduce the reliance on internal control, because the upper precision limit exceeds the tolerable deviation rate.
   d. Jones should not reduce the reliance on internal control, because the allowance for sampling risk is less than the tolerable deviation rate.
   e. None of the above.

21. The allowance for sampling risk is the difference between the _____ and the _____.

   a. Risk of overreliance; sample deviation rate.
   b. Risk of overreliance; upper precision limit.
   c. Sample deviation rate; upper precision limit.
   d. Upper precision limit; tolerable deviation rate.
   e. None of the above.

22. The maximum rate of deviation in the population that statistically controls the auditor's exposure to sampling risk to desired levels is the:

   a. Expected deviation rate.
   b. Sample deviation rate.
   c. Tolerable deviation rate.
   d. Upper precision limit.
   e. None of the above.

23. An attribute sampling method that provides the auditor with a specified probability of observing at least one sample deviation is known as:

   a. Deviation sampling.
   b. Discovery sampling.
   c. Sequential sampling.
   d. Systematic sampling.
   e. Variables sampling.

24. Which of the following statements is not true with respect to the upper precision limit?

   a. The upper precision limit is a statistical estimate of the maximum deviation rate in the population.
   b. The upper precision limit can be decomposed into two elements: the tolerable deviation rate and the allowance for sampling risk.
   c. As the deviation rate in the auditor's sample increases, the upper precision limit would also increase, holding other factors constant.
   d. As the risk of overreliance decreases, the upper precision limit would increase, holding other factors constant.
   e. All of the above statements are true.

25. Assume that you are performing an attribute sampling plan and have selected 200 invoices for examination. Of these, a total of 20 were found to contain deviations from internal control procedures. Based on a 5 percent risk of overreliance, the allowance for sampling risk is determined to be 6 percent. The auditor's tolerable deviation rate is set at 13 percent. Which of the following statements is correct?

   a. The upper precision limit would equal 23 percent (the tolerable deviation rate plus the sample deviation rate).
   b. The auditor would choose to rely on the internal control as planned, because the sample deviation rate is less than the tolerable deviation rate.
   c. The auditor would choose to reduce the reliance on the internal control, because the sample deviation rate plus the allowance for sampling risk exceeds the tolerable deviation rate.
   d. The auditor would choose to rely on the internal control as planned, because the sample deviation rate minus the allowance for sampling risk is less than the tolerable deviation rate.
   e. The auditor would choose to reduce the reliance on the internal control, because the allowance for sampling risk exceeds the desired level of risk of overreliance.

7-32. Jerry, CPA, is performing the audit examination of a charitable organization that makes disbursements to needy families over the holidays. One of Jerry's objectives is to determine the average disbursement made during the year. Because the number of disbursements is quite large, Jerry is looking for an alternative to investigating all disbursements. Someone mentions the possibility of sampling to Jerry. However, he is unaware of this type of analysis.

Required:

   a. Define sampling. Explain to Jerry the differences between statistical sampling and nonstatistical sampling. In this explanation, summarize the advantages and disadvantages of each of these methods.
   b. What is sampling risk (or sampling error)? Contrast sampling risk to nonsampling risk. Tell Jerry how each of these potential problems arises during a sampling application.
   c. Briefly explain to Jerry why a sample cannot tell him the average disbursement with certainty. In doing so, describe the terms precision and reliability.
   d. Assume that you provide Jerry with enough information to begin his sampling application. Suppose Jerry tells you that the average disbursement in his sample is $10, the precision of his sample estimate is $3, and the reliability is 80 percent. Explain to Jerry what this information tells him about the average disbursement.

7-33. Assume that you are examining the internal control of Rypien, Inc. One of the controls you are most concerned about is that Rypien bills its customers for all shipments made during the year. Rypien made 10,000 shipments during the most recent year; because of this large volume of transactions, you are unable to examine all items. Instead, you decide to perform an attribute sampling plan.

Required:

a. Define attribute sampling. Why would attribute sampling be an appropriate sampling choice in this example?
b. List the steps you would follow in performing an attribute sampling plan. Briefly describe each of these steps with respect to Rypien's control procedure.
c. Various factors are considered in determining the appropriate sample size. What are some of these factors? How does the auditor establish them? How do they affect sample size?

7-34. Four common methods exist for selecting samples: random sampling, systematic sampling, block sampling, and haphazard sampling.

a. Define each of these methods of sample selection.
b. For each method, briefly describe how the items would be selected from the population.
c. What are the advantages and disadvantages of each method of selection?
d. Shown below are three possible sampling environments. In each case, identify which method(s) of sample selection would be most appropriate:

1. The population of items is stored in a file cabinet and arranged by date. This population consists of a large number of documents that are not prenumbered. Because most of the larger transactions (in terms of dollar amounts) occurred earlier in the year, the population is arranged in a nonrandom order. It would be extremely difficult, if not impossible, to randomize the population. The auditor does not feel that statistical sampling is necessary in this situation.
2. The population is a series of customer account balances arranged alphabetically on a computer printout of 1,000 pages. Items are not numbered. The auditor is concerned with controlling sampling risk to a low level in this situation.
3. The population consists of all of the checks (prenumbered) written during the year. Because the company's expenditures do not differ substantially throughout the year, the population is randomly ordered in its current fashion. The auditor is concerned with controlling the exposure to sampling risk in performing the sampling plan.

7-35. Alworth, CPA, is performing the financial statement audit of Charger, Inc. In performing this audit, Alworth has determined that she needs to perform tests of controls on the procedures used by Charger to approve purchases made on account. Specifically, Charger's internal control includes the following control procedures: (1) departments requesting purchases should prepare a Purchase Requisition, and (2) these requisitions should be approved by the Purchasing Agent through the preparation of a Purchase Order. Once items purchased by Charger are received, they are recorded in the Voucher Register. Alworth feels that any cases where either of the controls are not functioning raise serious concerns about Charger's internal control.

Required:

a. What would Alworth consider to be a deviation condition in this situation?
b. How should Alworth define the population? For each item selected from the population, what procedure(s) should Alworth perform?
c. Assume that Alworth decided upon a risk of overreliance of 5 percent and a tolerable deviation rate of 4 percent. In addition, based on her previous experience, Alworth expected a deviation rate in the population of 1.25 percent. What sample size should be selected by Alworth?
d. Ignoring your answer to c, assume that Alworth examined 200 items and found eight deviations. What is the sample deviation rate? What is the upper precision limit? What does the upper precision limit tell Alworth?
e. Based on your analysis in d, what is the maximum number of deviations that Alworth could find without reducing her reliance on internal control?
f. In some cases, the sample deviation rate may be less than the tolerable deviation rate, but the auditor can still choose to reduce the level of reliance on internal control. Why?

7-36. Respond to each of the following comments made by Ralph, a new assistant on the audit engagement.

a. "Why should we waste a lot of time picking sample items? Let's just grab some Invoices and check the results. I'm already way over budget in this area."
b. "My senior told me to be sure and evaluate each item carefully. We're really trying to control our exposure to sampling risk in this area."
c. "There were four or five Invoices that I couldn't find. For those, I just picked another item. All of these disbursements are the same anyway."
d. "Who needs to use those sampling tables to determine the correct sample size? Let's just pick fifty items and be done with it. Besides, I can't come up with an exact measure of the tolerable deviation rate."
e. "Our main concern in this audit is controlling our exposure to the risk of underreliance. We need to be very sure that we don't do any extensive substantive testing."

7-37. One of the requirements of employing statistical sampling is that the auditor control the desired exposure to sampling risk in determining the sample size.

Required:

a. What aspect of sampling risk is the greatest concern of the auditor? Why?
b. How does the auditor control exposure to sampling risk in determining sample size?
c. What other factors are considered by the auditor in determining sample size? How are these parameters established by the auditor?

d. How do each of the factors in (c) affect sample size? That is, do increases in these factors result in increased or decreased sample sizes?

e. For the following conditions, determine the appropriate sample size using the sampling tables shown in Tables 7-1 and 7-2 (OR = risk of overreliance; EDR = expected deviation rate; TDR = tolerable deviation rate).

1. OR = 5 percent, EDR = 3.5 percent, TDR = 9 percent.
2. OR = 5 percent, EDR = 0.5 percent, TDR = 6 percent.
3. OR = 5 percent, EDR = 2 percent, TDR = 15 percent.
4. OR = 10 percent, EDR = 3 percent, TDR = 6 percent.
5. OR = 10 percent, EDR = 1.5 percent, TDR = 7 percent.

7-38. Assume that you are examining the cash disbursements of Most, Inc., to determine that these disbursements were properly authorized by Most's personnel. During 19X1, a total of 4,000 disbursements were made. Assume that you established a desired risk of overreliance of 5 percent, a tolerable deviation rate of 5 percent, and an expected deviation rate of 2 percent.

Required:

a. What sample size should be utilized? What factors influenced your decision on the appropriate sample size?

b. How would your sample size have changed if you decided to increase your desired exposure to the risk of overreliance to 10 percent? What does this tell you about the relationship between the risk of overreliance and sample size?

c. How would you select the sample using the following selection techniques:

1. Random sampling.
2. Systematic sampling.

d. For a risk of overreliance of 5 percent and the following number of deviations, determine the upper precision limit. In each case, what is your decision regarding Most's internal control? [(*Hint:* Remember the sample size you calculated in (a) above.)]

1. 5 deviations.
2. 7 deviations.
3. 8 deviations.

e. Repeat (d) using a risk of overreliance of 10 percent. [(*Hint:* Remember the sample size you calculated in (b) above.)]

7-39. Alex Manta, CPA, is performing the audit of Saint, Inc. During the audit, Alex has identified several internal control policies and procedures he wishes to rely upon. With one exception, the number of items in the population was less than 1,000, so Alex has decided to use traditional sampling methods. In all cases, Alex wishes to control his exposure to the risk of overreliance to 5 percent.

The one internal control policy that is somewhat troubling to Alex is examining whether all Customer Orders are authorized by the Credit Department. During 19X1 (the year of Alex's audit examination), more than 10,000 Customer Orders were received. Alex was initially planning to utilize a systematic sampling approach when somebody mentioned the use of sequential (stop-or-go) sampling.

Required:

a. What is sequential sampling? Describe the basic procedure used by the auditor when performing sequential sampling.
b. What is the primary benefit of sequential sampling to the auditor?
c. Assume that Alex initially selects a sample size of 50 and evaluates the sample items. If the tolerable deviation rate is 7 percent, describe Alex's actions if the following number of deviations are found (refer to Table 7-6):

   1. 0.
   2. 1.
   3. 2.

d. Assume that the initial sample in c yielded one deviation. If Alex examined another twenty items and found one more deviation, what action(s) could be taken?
e. Continuing with the above example, assume that Alex selected an additional sample of thirty items and found no deviations. What would Alex's decision be at this point?
(*Hint*: A total of 100 items have now been selected.)

7-40. Terry Albo, CPA, is conducting the audit examination of Beta, Inc. Terry is responsible for auditing cash disbursements. Based on her preliminary assessment of internal control, Terry has decided to assess control risk at 30 percent. In gaining an overall understanding of Beta's internal control, Terry has identified one important control: the requirement that two signatures are present on all checks for amounts over $5,000.

Because of the importance of this control, Terry has decided to assess the tolerable deviation rate at a low level: 4 percent. A pilot sample of twenty items revealed no deviations. Based on this evidence, as well as the results from previous audits, Terry assessed the expected deviation rate at 0.5 percent. After extensive discussions with her supervisor, Terry determined that the appropriate risk of overreliance was 10 percent.

Terry selected 100 disbursements for examination. She did not include the months of January and February in selecting sample items because the associated checks were located in another physical area, which would have required efforts beyond those considered necessary in the circumstances. Once the item numbers were determined through the use of random sampling techniques, Terry attempted to locate the checks. She was able to locate all but five of the checks in her original sample. Undaunted, she substituted five additional checks to reach the necessary sample size of 100 items.

Terry found a total of three deviations in these 100 items and calculated a sample deviation rate of 3 percent. Because Terry's sample size was determined in such a manner as to control the desired risk of overreliance to 10 percent, she then concluded that the control could be relied upon as planned.

Required:

Evaluate Terry's work in the above audit. Include her method of calculating sample size, selecting sample items, and evaluating sample results.

7-41. Harper Hoffman, CPA, is performing tests of controls over an extremely critical internal control policy. This policy is of such importance that the existence of even a few deviations would suggest that relatively extensive substantive tests be performed. Harper is worried because ordinary attribute sampling methods failed to reveal any deviations in the past. The failure to reveal deviations was even noted for samples selected in such a manner as to control Harper's exposure to sampling risks.

A colleague tells Harper Hoffman about discovery sampling. She indicates that this seems to be the perfect situation for using discovery sampling.

Required:

a. What is discovery sampling?
b. Do you agree with Harper's colleague? Why or why not?
c. If the tolerable deviation rate is 2 percent, how many items must be selected by Harper Hoffman to have a 95 percent probability of observing one deviation if the deviation rate is greater than 2 percent? (Refer to Table 7-5.)
d. If no deviations are found in this situation, what would Harper Hoffman conclude with respect to the sample?
e. If one deviation is found, what would Harper Hoffman conclude? (*Hint*: Refer to Table 7-3 and assume that this is an ordinary attribute sampling evaluation.)

Learning Objectives

Study of this chapter is designed to achieve several learning objectives. After studying this chapter, you should be able to:

1. Define variables estimation sampling and identify when variables sampling should be used in an audit.
2. Identify the two types of sampling risks faced by the auditor when performing variables sampling.
3. Define classical variables sampling and identify three approaches to classical variables sampling.
4. Use mean-per-unit estimation to determine the audited value and make conclusions with respect to an account balance.
5. Distinguish between mean-per-unit estimation, difference estimation, and ratio estimation and be able to calculate an audited value under each method.
6. Perform a probability-proportional-to-size sampling application and identify the advantages of using this method of sampling as opposed to classical variables sampling.

8

Variables Estimation Sampling

As noted in the previous chapter, the auditor gathers evidence during two stages of the examination. First, during the study and evaluation of the client's internal control, the auditor performs tests of controls to determine whether internal controls are effective in preventing and detecting financial statement errors. The auditor's use of attribute sampling in examining a client's internal control was the focus of the previous chapter. The second stage of the audit examination during which the auditor gathers evidence is in performing substantive tests of details. During this stage, the auditor uses **variables estimation sampling** to provide a numerical estimate of a population, such as the balance of a particular account.

Because this chapter continues the discussion of the use of sampling during the audit, it is important to have basic knowledge about important concepts related to sampling. These concepts (e.g., statistical versus nonstatistical sampling, precision and reliability, etc.) were introduced in the preceding chapter. Prior to beginning study of this chapter, the student may wish to briefly review the previous chapter, the end-of-chapter summary, and the glossary to become comfortable with its important concepts and terminology.

◉ OVERVIEW OF VARIABLES SAMPLING

The primary purpose of variables sampling during the audit is to provide the auditor with an estimate of the "true" (correct) balance of a given account. The true account balance represents the amount at which the account would be recorded, assuming that the client had not made any recording errors. The auditor's estimate of the true account balance is often referred to as the **audited account balance** (or **audited value**). The audited value is then compared to the client's recorded (unaudited) account balance. The auditor is interested in determining whether the difference between the audited account balance and the recorded account balance exceeds some prespecified level (referred to as **tolerable error**, or **materiality**).

A possible way of determining the audited account balance is to examine each and every transaction or component underlying the account balance. However, as with studying and evaluating the client's internal control, doing so is simply not feasible because of the extensive amount of time and cost involved. Therefore, as with attribute sampling, the auditor estimates this balance based on examining only a sample of transactions and components underlying that account balance.

❏ Sampling Risks

As discussed in the preceding chapter, the use of sampling exposes the auditor to sampling risk. The concept of **sampling risk** acknowledges that the auditor's decision based on a sample drawn from a population may differ from the decision that would be made if the entire population were examined. Recall that sampling risks arise when the sample selected by the auditor is not representative of the population from which it is drawn.

When performing variables sampling, the auditor compares the audited value to the recorded account balance to determine whether the account is materially misstated. Figure 8-1 illustrates the possible outcomes of the auditor's decision. Rows one and two represent the auditor's conclusion based on the results of the variables estimation sampling procedures. Columns one and two represent what the auditor's decision would be if every transaction or component of a particular account balance is examined. Cells *a* and *d* of Figure 8-1 represent instances where the auditor's conclusion based on the sample is identical to the conclusion that would have been made if 100 percent of the population were examined. Conversely, cells *b* and *c* represent sampling risks the auditor is exposed to through the use of variables estimation sampling. These risks are referred to as the **risk of incorrect acceptance** and the **risk of incorrect rejection**.

> The risk of incorrect acceptance is the risk that the sample supports the conclusion that the recorded account balance is not materially misstated when it is materially misstated.
>
> The risk of incorrect rejection is the risk that the sample supports the conclusion that the recorded account balance is materially misstated when it is not materially misstated.

The consequences of the above sampling risks are somewhat similar to those of the sampling risks related to attribute sampling (the **risk of overreliance** and **risk of underreliance**). With the **risk of incorrect rejection**, the auditor chooses not to accept an account balance as correct when the true account balance is not materially misstated. In most cases, when it is initially decided to reject an account balance, the auditor chooses to investigate the account balance further. This additional investigation normally allows the auditor to ultimately reach the correct conclusion that the account is fairly stated. Thus, like the risk of underreliance, this risk generally results in an efficiency loss, because additional audit procedures are performed. Methods of controlling this risk are discussed later in this chapter and in Appendix A.

In contrast, with the **risk of incorrect acceptance**, the auditor accepts the recorded account balance as correct when this balance is materially misstated. Similar to the risk of overreliance, the risk of incorrect acceptance causes an effectiveness loss, because the correct conclusion regarding the account balance is not ultimately reached by the auditor. It is important to note that the risk of incorrect acceptance is similar in nature to the detection risk component of the audit risk model, because both represent the probability that the auditor's substantive testing procedures will fail to

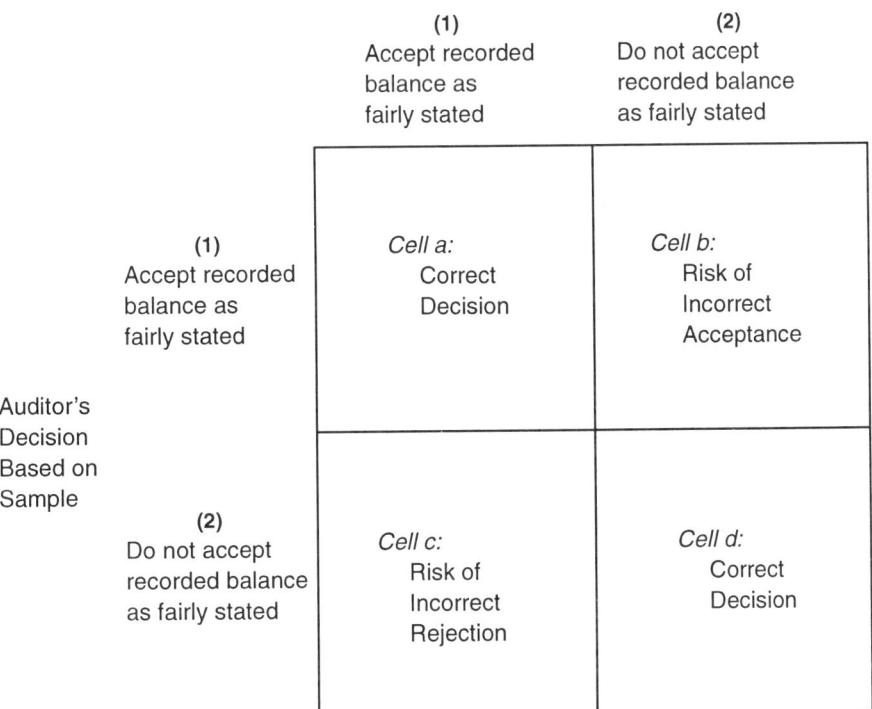

Figure 8-1: *Risks Associated with Variables Sampling*

detect a material error in an account balance. Establishing and controlling this risk is discussed later in this chapter and in Appendix A.

Considering the two sampling risks associated with variables sampling, which should be of the most concern to the auditor? Although the auditor would clearly prefer not to suffer either risk, the risk of incorrect acceptance results in an audit effectiveness loss. Incorrectly accepting a materially misstated account balance may ultimately result in professional liability to the auditor. Thus, the auditor is most concerned with the risk of incorrect acceptance. The risk of incorrect acceptance and risk of incorrect rejection are summarized in Figure 8-2.

As noted in the previous chapter, one of the primary benefits of using statistical sampling is that the auditor's exposure to these sampling risks can be controlled. As before, the auditor considers sampling risks in determining sample size and in evaluating sample results.

Two main approaches to statistical variables sampling are classical variables sampling and probability-proportional-to-size sampling. These approaches are discussed in further detail in the remainder of this chapter. In addition, the use of nonstatistical sampling is also illustrated in Appendix B.

	Auditor Decision	Actual State	Consequences
Risk of Incorrect Acceptance	Account is fairly stated (AB – RB) < TE	Account is not fairly stated (TB – RB) > TE	Make an incorrect conclusion about the account balance
Risk of Incorrect Rejection	Account is not fairly stated (AB – RB) > TE	Account is fairly stated (TB – RB) < TE	Perform additional tests; however, the correct conclusion is usually reached

AB = Audited account balance
TB = True account balance
RB = Recorded account balance
TE = Tolerable error

Figure 8-2: *Risk of Incorrect Acceptance and Incorrect Rejection*

CHAPTER CHECKPOINTS

8-1. What is variables estimation sampling? When is variables sampling used in the audit examination?

8-2. What is the primary purpose of variables sampling? In performing variables sampling, what is the ultimate decision made by the auditor?

8-3. Define each of the two sampling risks associated with the use of variables sampling.

8-4. What is the ultimate consequence of the two sampling risks associated with variables sampling?

◉ OVERVIEW: CLASSICAL VARIABLES SAMPLING

Classical variables sampling approaches use normal distribution theory and the central limit theorem to allow the auditor to make statements and inferences about a population based on a sample from that population. This section provides an overview of classical variables sampling methods. Subsequent sections discuss three approaches to classical variables sampling: (1) mean-per-unit estimation, (2) difference estimation, and (3) ratio estimation.

◻ Normal Distribution

The major concept involved with classical variables sampling is that of the **normal distribution**. As applied to audit sampling, the normal distribution describes the probability that the auditor's sampling procedures will provide various estimates of the true account balance. The auditor uses the normal distribution to determine the probability that the sample estimate will fall within a certain distance (closeness) to the true account balance.

Figure 8-3 illustrates the form of the normal distribution. The curve (known as a **normal curve**, or **bell-shaped curve**) provides the probability that a sample examined by the auditor will yield various audited values. The basic premise of the normal distribution is that if a large number of samples are selected from the same population, the auditor is more likely to form an audited value close to the true account balance than to form an audited value further away from the true account balance.

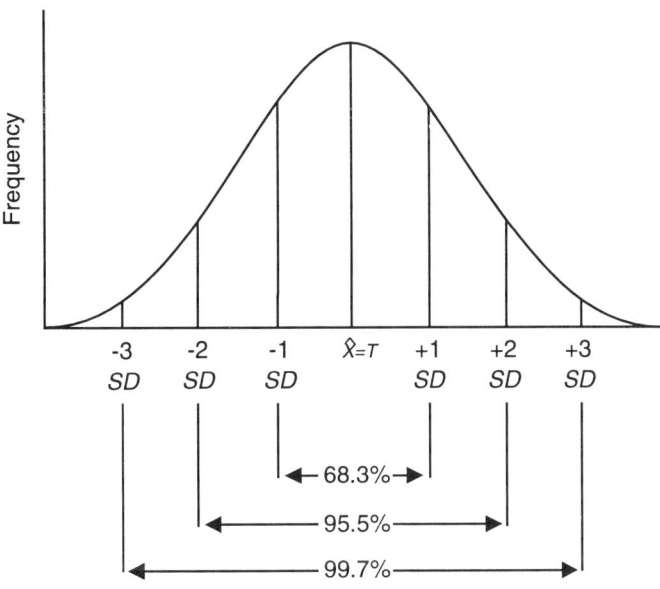

$\hat{X}$ = Audited account balance
T = True account balance
SD = Standard Deviation

Figure 8-3: *Normal Distribution*

As shown in Figure 8-3, the distribution of audited values is centered around the true account balance. That is, if the auditor took an infinite number of samples of a given size and evaluated these samples correctly, the most frequent audited value would equal the true account balance. By making the assumption that the audited values are unbiased (that is, equal to the true account balance), the auditor is able to calculate the probability that the audited value falls within certain limits. For example, under the normal distribution, it is assumed that 68.3 percent of all audited values fall within one standard deviation of the true account balance. Therefore, if 1,000 samples were drawn from a given population, the audited values provided by 683 of these samples (0.683 x 1,000 = 683) would fall within one standard deviation of the true account balance. Also, as implied in Figure 8-3, 95.5 and 99.7 percent of all audited values lie within two and three standard deviations, respectively, of the true account balance.

8/ Variables Estimation Sampling

These relationships can also be expressed in terms of the true account balance. That is, the auditor can conclude that the probability that the true account balance lies within one standard deviation of the audited value is 68.3 percent. Also, the probabilities that the true account balance lies within two and three standard deviations of the audited value are 95.5 percent and 99.7 percent, respectively.

Other statements that can be made based on the normal distribution (see Figure 8-4) are:

1. Because the audited value is assumed to be equally distributed about the true account balance, there is a 34.15 percent (68.3 percent ÷ 2 = 34.15 percent) probability that the true account balance lies between the audited value and the audited value plus one standard deviation. Using the same logic, there is a 34.15 percent probability that the true account balance lies between the audited value and the audited value minus one standard deviation.

2. Given the above analysis, an 84.15 percent probability (34.15 percent + 50 percent = 84.15 percent) exists that the true account balance is less than the audited value plus one standard deviation.

3. There is a 31.70 percent probability (15.85 percent [Figure 8-4] × 2 = 31.70 percent) that the difference between the true account balance and the audited value is greater than one standard deviation (either higher or lower).

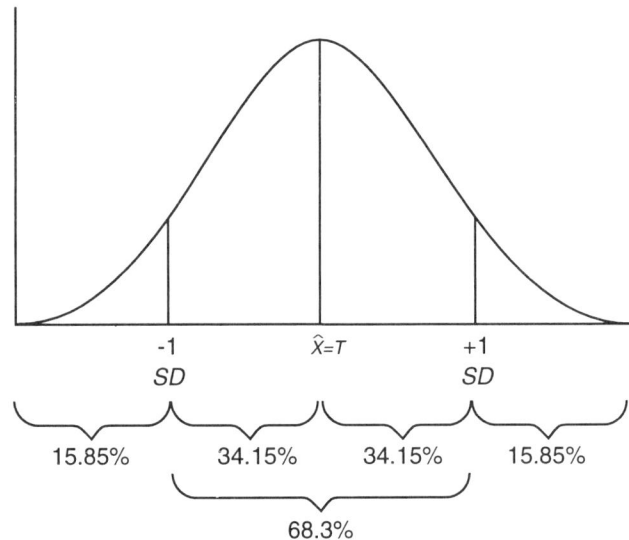

$\hat{X}$ = Audited account balance
T = True account balance
SD = Standard Deviation

Figure 8-4: *Areas of the Normal Distribution*

◻ Standard Deviation

The above discussion expresses various probabilities in terms of a number of standard deviations. The standard deviation is an estimate of the dispersion, or variability, within a population. In other words, the standard deviation of a population is a measure of the extent to which the values of the items in a population differ from that population's mean. The formula for calculating the standard deviation of a sample is:

$$SD = \sqrt{\frac{\sum_{j=1}^{n}(x_j - \bar{x})^2}{n-1}} \qquad (8.1)$$

where

SD = Sample standard deviation
$\bar{x}$ = Mean of the sample
$n - 1$ = Number of items in the sample minus one

▶ **Example:** *Calculating the Standard Deviation of a Sample*

Given: A sample of four items with values of 14, 15, 22, 25.
Solution:

x	$\bar{x}$	$x - \bar{x}$	$(x - \bar{x})^2$
14	19*	−5	25
15	19	−4	16
22	19	3	9
25	19	6	36

$$\sum_{j=1}^{n}(x_j - \bar{x})^2 = 86$$

*The mean of the sample is:

$$\bar{x} = \frac{\sum_{j=1}^{n} x_j}{n}$$

$$\bar{x} = \frac{76}{4} = 19$$

Formula:

$$SD = \sqrt{\frac{\sum_{j=1}^{n}(x_j - \bar{x})^2}{n-1}}$$

$$SD = \sqrt{\frac{86}{3}}$$

$$SD = 5.3 \text{ (rounded)}$$

◻ Basic Decision Process in Classical Variables Sampling

In classical variables sampling, the auditor uses the concepts of precision and reliability introduced in the previous chapter to determine an interval having a specified probability of including the true account balance. Recall that *precision* refers to the closeness of the auditor's sample estimate to the true value and that *reliability* is the probability of achieving that degree of closeness. As used in substantive testing, the precision is the dollar range within which the true account balance is expected to lie, and the reliability is the probability that the dollar range contains the true account balance. Using the concepts of precision and reliability, as well as the normal distribution, the auditor can make specific statements about the true account balance.

To illustrate the auditor's basic decision process in classical variables sampling, assume that the auditor is examining accounts receivable with a recorded balance of $250,000. Also assume that the auditor establishes the desired exposure to the risk of incorrect acceptance and risk of incorrect rejection at 5 percent for both risks. Further, assume that the specified tolerable error is $30,000 and the auditor calculates a precision of $16,300. (The factors considered by the auditor in establishing the desired exposure to the two sampling risks and tolerable error and the calculation of precision are illustrated later.) At this point, the focus is on the auditor's basic decision process. However, it is important to note that these factors consider the number of standard deviations and probabilities of the normal distribution shown in Figure 8-3.

If the auditor calculates an audited balance of $240,000, a precision interval having a *reliability* probability of including the true account balance can be formed. To calculate the precision interval, the auditor would add and subtract the precision from the audited balance. In this case:

$$\begin{aligned} \text{Precision Interval} &= \text{Audited Balance} \pm \text{Precision} \\ &= \$240{,}000 \pm \$16{,}300 \\ &= \$223{,}700 \text{ to } \$256{,}300 \end{aligned}$$

In this case, the auditor would conclude that there is a 95 percent probability (1 − sampling risk) that the true account balance falls within the interval of $223,700 to $256,300.

Given a recorded balance of accounts receivable of $250,000, the auditor would accept the recorded balance as correct, because it falls within the precision interval. In doing so, there is a 5 percent chance (risk of incorrect acceptance) that the difference between the true account balance and the recorded balance was actually greater than $30,000. As described later, the precision used by the auditor statistically controls for the desired exposure to sampling risks.

What would happen if the audited balance yielded a precision interval that did not contain the recorded account balance? For example, if the audited balance were $220,000, the precision interval would be $203,700 ($220,000 − $16,300) to $236,300 ($220,000 + $16,300). Because the recorded account balance does not fall within this interval, the auditor would conclude that the account is materially misstated. In doing so, there is a 5 percent (risk of incorrect rejection) probability that the true account balance did not differ from the recorded account balance by more than $30,000. Thus, in either case, sampling risk has been controlled at the desired levels.

> **CHAPTER CHECKPOINTS**
>
> **8-5.** What is classical variables sampling?
>
> **8-6.** Under the normal distribution, how many sample estimates would be expected to lie within one standard deviation of the true population value? Two standard deviations? Three standard deviations?
>
> **8-7.** Define standard deviation. How does the auditor determine the standard deviation of a population without examining all items in the population? How is the standard deviation related to the amount of variability in the population?
>
> **8-8.** If the auditor estimates the accounts receivable balance at $200,000, with a precision of $10,000 and a reliability of 90 percent, what can be said about the true account balance?
>
> **8-9.** After determining the precision interval, how does the auditor evaluate the fairness of the account balance? What two possible conclusions may be reached?

CLASSICAL VARIABLES SAMPLING: MEAN-PER-UNIT ESTIMATION

Three common approaches to classical variables sampling are **mean-per-unit estimation**, **difference estimation**, and **ratio estimation**. The primary difference in these approaches is the manner of determining the audited value. The AICPA *Audit Sampling Guide*[1] notes the following general procedures for performing a classical variables sampling application:

1. Determine the audit objective of the test.
2. Define the population.
3. Choose an audit sampling technique.
4. Determine the sample size.
5. Determine the method of selecting the sample.
6. Perform the sampling plan.
7. Evaluate sample results.

These steps are discussed in the remainder of this section.

---

[1] American Institute of Certified Public Accountants (AICPA), *Audit Sampling* (New York: AICPA, 1983).

Determining the Audit Objective of the Test

In general, the objective of any variables sampling is to allow the auditor to determine whether the recorded balance of a particular account is fairly stated in conformity with GAAP. "Fairly stated" indicates that the account is not misstated by an amount considered to be material. In making this determination, the auditor will examine a sample of transactions or components underlying the account balance. This examination allows the auditor to form an estimate of the "true" account balance (the audited value). As noted in previous sections of this chapter, the audited value is compared to the recorded account balance to determine whether the latter is materially misstated.

Defining the Population

The **population** represents all of the elements constituting the object of interest (account balance). In variables sampling, the population consists of all transactions and components underlying a particular account balance. The definition of the population is a critical step because the auditor cannot select a representative sample if the population is defined incorrectly.

Along with defining the population, it is also important that the auditor appropriately define the **sampling unit**. Sampling units are the elements that compose the population. For example, if the auditor wishes to estimate the recorded balance of accounts receivable by confirming individual customers' account balances, the sampling unit would be customer account balances and the auditor would select a sample of customer account balances for confirmation. However, if the auditor decided to estimate accounts receivable by examining individual transactions involving accounts receivable, the sampling unit would be Invoices (representing sales) and Remittance Advices (representing collections). In the latter case, the auditor would select a sample of Invoices and Remittance Advices for verification.

Choosing an Audit Sampling Technique

In choosing a sampling technique, the auditor must first decide whether to employ statistical or nonstatistical sampling. Statistical sampling techniques provide an advantage to the auditor in that they allow the auditor to select a sample and evaluate sample results while controlling exposure to sampling risk at desired levels. Although the focus of this chapter is on statistical sampling methods, an illustration of nonstatistical sampling is provided in Appendix B.

Once the auditor has decided to utilize statistical sampling, one of two major categories of variables sampling plans may be selected: **classical variables sampling** or **probability-proportional-to-size (PPS) sampling** (also known as **dollar-unit sampling**). Classical variables sampling uses normal distribution theory to estimate the recorded value of an account balance and is the focus of this section. PPS sampling uses attribute sampling theory to estimate the maximum amount of misstatement in an account balance. PPS sampling is discussed in detail in a subsequent section of this chapter.

Determining Sample Size

A benefit of statistical sampling is that the auditor can determine a sufficiently large sample size to control the desired exposure to sampling risk. In calculating sample size for classical variables sampling, the auditor explicitly incorporates the following six factors:

1. Population size.
2. Population variability.
3. Tolerable error (materiality).
4. Desired risk of incorrect acceptance.
5. Desired risk of incorrect rejection.
6. Planned precision (allowance for sampling risk).

The effect of each of these factors on sample size is discussed below.

Population Size. Step 2 noted the need for the auditor to carefully define the population of interest. In addition to defining this population, it is also important for the auditor to identify the size of the population, as this factor influences both the sample size selected by the auditor and the evaluation of sample results. The size of the population is directly related to sample size—that is, as the population size increases, the auditor should select a larger number of items for examination. Unlike attribute sampling, this factor plays a relatively significant role in the sample size calculation for variables sampling and is explicitly incorporated in the auditor's determination of sample size.

Obviously, the size of the population depends on the auditor's definition of the population. For example, if the auditor wishes to estimate accounts receivable by confirming balances with customers, the population size would be equal to the number of customer balances outstanding at year-end. However, if the auditor examines individual transactions involving accounts receivable, the population size would equal the number of transactions related to accounts receivable during the year. In any case, the auditor should be able to readily determine the size of a given population through reference to the client's accounting records.

Population Variability. Specifying the population variability (or **standard deviation**) is essential for the use of classical variables sampling because the normal curve and its associated probabilities are defined in terms of standard deviations. The standard deviation is a measure of the variability of items within the population; as items vary to a greater extent (*i.e.*, items are less homogeneous), the standard deviation increases.

To estimate the standard deviation, the auditor often relies on past experience with the client. In doing so, it is assumed that the standard deviation in the current year is similar to that for previous years. A second approach for estimating the standard deviation is to take a presample of population items and calculate the standard deviation for them. In either case, formula 8.1 would be used to calculate the standard deviation. The auditor increases sample size as the standard deviation (variability) of the population increases. Therefore, the standard deviation also has a direct relationship with sample size.

Tolerable Error. Tolerable error (also referred to as **materiality**) is the maximum amount by which an account can be in error without the auditor concluding that it is materially misstated. Remember, if it is felt that the account is misstated by an amount less than tolerable error, the auditor concludes that the account balance is fairly stated; in this case, only errors that were actually discovered are corrected. In contrast, if the amount of misstatement is greater than the tolerable error, the auditor proposes an adjustment to correct both: (1) misstatements actually discovered during the audit examination, and (2) the projected effect of undiscovered misstatements on the account balance.

In determining the allowable amount of tolerable error, the auditor relies heavily on professional judgment. However, the tolerable error usually reflects the magnitude of the following financial statement subtotals:

1. The recorded amount of the account examined.
2. The financial statement classification of the account being examined (*e.g.*, assets, liabilities, revenues, expenses).
3. Some measure of client size (total assets, total revenues).
4. Net income.

For example, if the recorded balance of accounts receivable was $2,000,000, the auditor would usually be more willing to accept a $100,000 error as immaterial than if the recorded balance of accounts receivable was $500,000.

The impact of tolerable error on sample size parallels that of the tolerable rate on sample size in attribute sampling. Tolerable error has an inverse relationship with sample size—that is, as the tolerable error increases, the necessary sample size decreases.

Sampling Risks (Risk of Incorrect Acceptance and Risk of Incorrect Rejection).

The risk of incorrect acceptance and risk of incorrect rejection are the two sampling risks associated with variables sampling. The auditor controls the exposure to these risks when: (1) determining the sample size, and (2) evaluating the sample results. As with attribute sampling, both types of sampling risks have inverse relationships with sample size—that is, as the auditor wishes to limit exposure to these risks (lower levels of risk), a larger sample size must be examined. As illustrated below, the risk of incorrect rejection and risk of incorrect acceptance are controlled by adjusting tolerable error. An extensive discussion of how these risks are controlled is beyond the scope of this text, but an illustration of the theoretical method of controlling these risks is presented in Appendix A.

Establishing the Risk of Incorrect Rejection. The risk of incorrect rejection is judgmentally specified by the auditor after considering the cost of additional investigations incurred by incorrectly rejecting a fairly stated account balance. If the auditor decides that additional sampling is not feasible or that the cost of additional sampling is prohibitive, a lower level of this risk (such as 5 percent) should be selected. If additional sampling is thought to be less costly, the auditor may wish to assess this risk at a higher level. However, in most cases, this risk should be maintained at a relatively low level (normally between 5 and 10 percent).

Establishing the Risk of Incorrect Acceptance. Earlier, it was noted that the risk of incorrect acceptance was similar to the detection risk component of the audit risk model. However, because the risk of incorrect acceptance is related solely to substantive tests of details of balances and transactions (tests of details), it is actually only a subset of detection risk. Specifically, detection risk can be decomposed as follows:

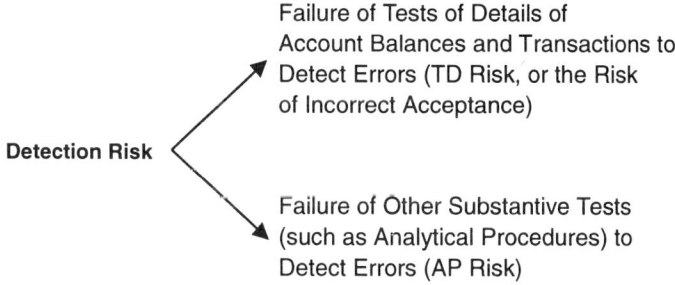

Thus, an expanded audit risk model would be as follows. Note that the only difference between this model and the SAS No. 47[2] version is that detection risk has been replaced by TD risk and AP risk.

Audit Risk = Inherent Risk × Control Risk × AP Risk × TD Risk (8.2)

To determine the appropriate level of the risk of incorrect acceptance, the auditor can "solve" this model for TD risk. The risk of incorrect acceptance is established by the auditor after audit risk, inherent risk, control risk, and the risk associated with other substantive testing procedures are considered. The steps involved with using this model are:

1. Judgmentally establish the desired exposure to audit risk. Normally, the auditor will assess risk at a low level, such as 5 or 10 percent.
2. Based on the susceptibility of the account balance to error, assess inherent risk. Inherent risk is usually assessed at a relatively higher level. In some cases, because of the difficulty of assessing inherent risk, the auditor may use 100 percent.
3. Based on the effectiveness of the client's internal control in preventing and detecting errors, assess control risk. If the internal control is more effective in preventing and/or detecting errors, this risk should be assessed at a lower level (and vice versa).
4. Based on the planned effectiveness of analytical procedures and other substantive tests, assess AP risk.
5. Calculate the necessary level of TD (risk of incorrect acceptance).

Planned Precision. To control sampling risks, the auditor must "adjust" the amount of tolerable error. The "adjusted tolerable error" is referred to as **planned precision**, or the **allowance for sampling risk**. A method of calculating the allowance for sampling risk is to use the following formula, where R(IR) is the reliability factor for the desired risk of incorrect rejection, and R(IA) is the reliability factor for the desired risk of incorrect acceptance:

---

[2] American Institute of Certified Public Accountants (AICPA), *Statement on Auditing Standards No. 47*, "Audit Risk and Materiality in Conducting an Audit" (New York: AICPA, 1983, AU 312).

$$\text{Planned Precision} = \text{Tolerable Error} \times \frac{R(IR)}{R(IR) + R(IA)} \qquad (8.3)$$

The following reliability factors are used by the auditor to control exposure to sampling risk. As illustrated in Appendix A, these coefficients are stated in terms of the number of standard deviations for a given reliability (1 − sampling risk):

Level of Risk	Factor for Risk of Incorrect Rejection	Factor for Risk of Incorrect Acceptance
0.01	2.58	2.33
0.05	1.96	1.65
0.10	1.65	1.29
0.15	1.44	1.04
0.20	1.29	0.85

Alternatively, an AICPA Sampling Table (shown as Table 8-1) has been developed to simplify the above calculation. This table can be used to directly determine the ratio $R(IR) \div [R(IR) + R(IA)]$. To determine the planned precision, the auditor multiplies the tolerable error by the appropriate factor from Table 8-1.

Table 8-1: *Factors to Adjust Tolerable Error for Desired Sampling Risks*

| Risk of Incorrect Acceptance | Risk of Incorrect Rejection | | | |
	.20	.10	.05	.01
.01	.355	.413	.457	.525
.025	.395	.456	.500	.568
.05	.437	.500	.543	.609
.075	.471	.532	.576	.641
.10	.500	.561	.605	.668
.15	.511	.612	.653	.712
.20	.603	.661	.700	.753
.25	.653	.708	.742	.791
.30	.707	.756	.787	.829
.35	.766	.808	.834	.868
.40	.831	.863	.883	.908
.45	.907	.926	.937	.952
.50	1.000	1.000	1.000	1.000

Source: American Institute of Certified Public Accountants (AICPA), *Audit and Accounting Guide*, "Audit Sampling," 115.

As indicated above, the planned precision is derived from tolerable error and the sampling risks. Because both of these factors have inverse relationships to sample size, it is not surprising that the planned precision has an inverse relationship with sample size. That is, as the planned precision increases, the sample size decreases. Once calculated, the planned precision allows the auditor to select a sufficiently large sample to control the exposure to sampling risks to specified levels.

Calculating Sample Size. To calculate the necessary sample size for a classical variables sampling application using mean-per-unit estimation, the auditor uses the following formula:

$$n = \left[\frac{N \times R(IR) \times SD}{PP}\right]^2 \tag{8.4}$$

where

$$
\begin{aligned}
n &= \text{Sample size} \\
N &= \text{Population size} \\
R(IR) &= \text{Reliability coefficient for the risk of incorrect rejection} \\
SD &= \text{Sample standard deviation} \\
PP &= \text{Planned precision}
\end{aligned}
$$

This formula is used for sampling with replacement, wherein, once an item has been selected for examination, it is replaced in the population and is eligible for reselection. In most auditing applications, it is more appropriate for the auditor to use sampling without replacement, wherein an item is not eligible for reselection once it has been selected by the auditor.

To determine the sample size for sampling without replacement, the sample size calculated using the above formula is slightly adjusted:

$$n' = \frac{n}{1 + \frac{n}{N}} \tag{8.5}$$

where

$$
\begin{aligned}
n' &= \text{Sample size using sampling without replacement} \\
n &= \text{Sample size using sampling with replacement} \\
N &= \text{Population size}
\end{aligned}
$$

Summary: The Effect of Factors on Sample Size. Figure 8-5 summarizes how the factors discussed in this section impact sample size.

Factor	Relationship	As Factor	Effect on Sample Size	How Is Factor Determined?
Population Size	Direct	Increases Decreases	Increases Decreases	Reference to accounting records
Population Standard Deviation	Direct	Increases Decreases	Increases Decreases	Estimate from a presample or based on prior audit experience
Tolerable Error	Inverse	Increases Decreases	Decreases Increases	Auditor judgment based on factors related to the account or size of the client
Risk of Incorrect Rejection	Inverse	Increases Decreases	Decreases Increases	Auditor judgment based on the cost of additional testing
Risk of Incorrect Acceptance	Inverse	Increases Decreases	Decreases Increases	Based on audit risk, inherent risk, control risk, and risk associated with other substantive tests
Planned Precision	Inverse	Increases Decreases	Decreases Increases	Adjustment of tolerable error for desired exposure to sampling risks

Figure 8-5: *Effect of Increase (Decrease) in Factors on Sample Size*

CHAPTER CHECKPOINTS

8-10. List the seven steps performed in a classical variables sampling application.

8-11. What are the two major categories of variables sampling plans commonly used by the auditor?

8-12. How is tolerable error established by the auditor? What factors affect the level of tolerable error established by the auditor?

8-13. How does the auditor control exposure to the risk of incorrect acceptance and the risk of incorrect rejection?

8-14. What factors should the auditor consider in establishing exposure to the risk of incorrect rejection?

8-15. What factors should the auditor consider in establishing exposure to the risk of incorrect acceptance?

◻ Determining the Method of Selecting the Sample

Once the auditor has calculated the appropriate sample size, the next step in performing variables sampling is selecting the sample. The previous chapter illustrated four methods of selection that can also be employed in classical variables sampling: unrestricted random sampling, systematic sampling, block sampling, and haphazard sampling. In order to be classified as a statistical sampling plan, the sample must be selected using **probabilistic selection techniques**. Therefore, neither block nor haphazard sampling may be used in conjunction with statistical sampling.

The use of unrestricted random sampling and systematic sampling in variables sampling is quite similar to that discussed earlier for attribute sampling. For example, assume that the auditor is using unrestricted random sampling and the following five random numbers are extracted from a random number table: (1) 1,583, (2) 2,875, (3) 348, (4) 1,295, and (5) 3,002. If the client's population of accounts receivable consists of 3,500 customer accounts, the auditor would select the 1,583rd, 2,875th, etc., accounts for confirmation. Similarly, if systematic sampling is used, the auditor would randomly select the initial sample item (customer account) from the population, skip a fixed number of items (customer accounts), and select the next account. Note that the only difference in selecting a sample under variables sampling and attribute sampling is the definition of the sampling unit.

Effect of Variability on Sample Selection. A difference between an attribute sampling application and a variables sampling application is the effect of population variability on sample size. As shown in the sample size formula, variability (the standard deviation) is explicitly incorporated into the sample size formula. When a population is highly variable (*i.e.*, has a large standard deviation), the resultant sample size tends to be quite large. A technique that may be used to reduce the required sample size is to divide the population into more homogeneous subgroups, or strata. This process is referred to as **stratified sampling**. While an extensive discussion of stratified sampling is beyond the scope of this text,[3] the auditor would follow the following general procedure:

1. Divide the population into *strata*. The general rule is that each item can only belong to one stratum and there must be an identifiable difference that distinguishes the strata from one another. In most cases, this difference represents the dollar amount of the item. For example, accounts receivable might be "stratified" according to the size of the account balance: (1) less than $5,000, (2) $5,001 − $25,000, and (3) more than $25,000.
2. Select a sample of items from each stratum. Because each stratum has a smaller variability than the entire population, the sample sizes would be smaller than if stratification were not used. Different selection methods may be used for each stratum.

The auditor then samples within each stratum. In many cases, he or she examines all items included in the high dollar stratum and selects a sample of items from the remaining strata.

---

[3] See H. Arkin, *Handbook of Sampling for Auditing and Accounting* (New York: McGraw-Hill, 1963), Chapter 10, for a thorough discussion of stratified sampling.

◘ Performing the Sampling Plan

In performing the sampling plan, the auditor first selects items from the population using the sample selection method from the previous step. Once the items have been selected, the auditor performs the appropriate substantive testing procedures to determine the audited amount of the selected items. For example, in examining accounts receivable, the auditor will normally confirm the selected accounts directly with that customer. After receiving the confirmation and investigating any differences between the recorded amount of the customer's account and the amount reported by the customer, the auditor can determine the audited amount for that particular item.

After verifying the selected items in the above manner, the auditor calculates two key components for use in mean-per-unit estimation:

- The mean audited values of the sample items ($\bar{x}$).

- The standard deviation of the audited values of the sample items (SD).

◘ Evaluating the Sample Results

After subjecting the sample items to examination, the auditor knows the mean audited value of the selected items and the standard deviation of these audited values. Once the mean audited value has been calculated, the audited balance is calculated by multiplying the mean audited value per sample item ($\bar{X}$) by the number of items in the population (N):

$$\text{Audited Balance} = \bar{X} \times N \tag{8.6}$$

The achieved precision represents the closeness of the audited balance to the "true" (but unknown) account balance based on: (1) the auditor's desired exposure to the risk of incorrect rejection, and (2) the sample standard deviation (SD). To calculate the achieved precision, the auditor uses the following formula:

$$\text{Achieved Precision} = N \times R(IR) \times \frac{SD}{\sqrt{n}} \tag{8.7}$$

$R(IR)$ represents the reliability coefficient for the auditor's desired exposure to the risk of incorrect acceptance. Formula 8.7 is merely an algebraic manipulation of the sample size formula (8.4) shown earlier. However, a key difference exists: The sample size formula used the *estimated* standard deviation, while formula 8.7 uses the *actual* standard deviation of the sample items.

The auditor now constructs the precision interval by adding and subtracting the achieved precision from the audited balance. This interval allows the auditor to control the exposure to the risk of incorrect acceptance and risk of incorrect rejection to desired levels. If the recorded balance falls within this interval (*i.e.*, the difference between the recorded balance and the audited balance is not greater than precision), the auditor chooses to accept the recorded balance as not materially misstated. If the recorded balance falls outside of this interval, the auditor would conclude that the account balance is materially misstated.

◻ Example: Mean-per-Unit Estimation

In your audit of the Susan Company, you are examining accounts receivable. Assume that Susan's accounts receivable were recorded at $250,000 and were comprised of 2,000 individual customer accounts. The purpose of your examination of accounts receivable is to determine whether the recorded balance of $250,000 is materially misstated. For the purpose of this examination, you establish tolerable error at 10 percent of the recorded balance, or $25,000 ($250,000 × 0.10 = $25,000)

Based on the cost of "oversampling," you establish a desired exposure to the risk of incorrect rejection of 10 percent. In establishing your exposure to the risk of incorrect acceptance, assume the following:

1. Your firm's policy is to restrict overall audit risk to a relatively low level. In this case, overall audit risk has been established at 4 percent.

2. Based on your assessment of accounts receivable, you believe that the account has a high probability of misstatement in the absence of internal control. Therefore, inherent risk (IR) is established at 100 percent.

3. After your study and evaluation of internal control, you conclude that the Susan Company's internal control is relatively ineffective in preventing and detecting financial statement errors. As a result, your final assessment of control risk (CR) is 80 percent.

4. Because you plan on performing only limited substantive tests other than tests of details, you assess the risk that these other substantive testing procedures fail to detect financial statement errors (AP risk) at the maximum level (100 percent).

Using the audit risk model (formula 8.2), we can calculate the **risk of incorrect acceptance (TD risk)** as 5 percent:

$$\text{Audit Risk} = IR \times CR \times AP \times TD \tag{8.2}$$
$$0.04 = 1.00 \times 0.80 \times 1.00 \times TD$$
$$TD = 0.05$$

Therefore, your firm's desired exposure to sampling risks are 10 percent for the risk of incorrect rejection and 5 percent for the risk of incorrect acceptance. From the reliability factors presented earlier in this chapter, these risks correspond to reliability coefficients of 1.65 for both risks.

Finally, before calculating sample size, you need to form an estimate of the population standard deviation. Based on experience from last year's audit, assume a standard deviation of $80.

To calculate the planned precision, tolerable error is adjusted to control for the desired exposure to sampling risk. Using the factor for a 10 percent risk of incorrect rejection and a 5 percent risk of incorrect acceptance from Table 8-1,[4] the planned precision is $12,500:

---

[4] Alternatively, the factor can be calculated as in formula (8.3):

$$\frac{R(IR)}{R(IA) + R(IR)} = \frac{1.65}{(1.65 + 1.65)} = 0.50$$

$$\text{Planned Precision} = \text{Tolerable Error} \times \text{Factor}$$
$$= \$25{,}000 \times 0.50$$
$$= \$12{,}500$$

Once the planned allowance for sampling risk has been calculated, the sample size would be 447,[5] as shown below. Recall that the auditor must determine: (1) the reliability coefficient for the risk of incorrect rejection [$R(IR)$], (2) the population size (N), (3) the estimated standard deviation (SD), and (4) the planned precision (PP) prior to calculating the sample size.

$$n = \left(\frac{2{,}000 \times 1.65 \times 80}{12{,}500} \right)^2 \tag{8.4}$$

$$= 446.05, \text{ or } 447 \text{ items}$$

Based upon examining the 447 accounts, you determine the total audited value to be $53,640. This yields a mean audited value of $120 per item ($53,640 ÷ 447 accounts = $120). Also, you determine that the sample standard deviation is $85. Based on this information, the formulas presented earlier can be used to calculate the audited balance and achieved precision:

$$\text{Audited Balance} = \bar{X} \times N \tag{8.6}$$
$$= \$120 \times 2{,}000$$
$$= \$240{,}000$$

$$\text{Achieved Precision} = N \times R(IR) \times \frac{SD}{\sqrt{n}} \tag{8.7}$$

$$= 2{,}000 \times 1.65 \times \frac{85}{\sqrt{447}}$$

$$= \$13{,}267 \text{ (rounded)}$$

In this case, notice that the achieved precision ($13,267) differs from the planned precision ($12,500). Why? The standard deviation you used to calculate sample size ($80) was different from the actual standard deviation observed during your examination ($85). As a result, using the achieved precision will result in a greater exposure to the risk of incorrect acceptance than desired because the precision interval would be too large. To calculate an adjusted precision, the following formula is used:

---

[5] As noted earlier, sampling without replacement is usually more appropriate in most audit applications. In this example, we assume the use of sampling with replacement to simplify the calculations. To use sampling without replacement, the auditor would adjust the sample size using formula (8.5):

$$n' = \frac{n}{1 + (n \div N)} = \frac{447}{1 + (447 \div 2{,}000)} = 365$$

$$\begin{aligned}\text{Adjusted} \atop \text{Precision} &= {\text{Achieved} \atop \text{Precision}} + \left({\text{Tolerable} \atop \text{Error}}\right)\left[1 - \left[{\text{Achieved} \atop \text{Precision}} \div {\text{Planned} \atop \text{Precision}}\right]\right] \quad (8.8)\\ &= \$13{,}267 + \$25{,}000\ (1 - [\$13{,}267 \div \$12{,}500])\\ &= \$13{,}267 - 1{,}534\\ &= \$11{,}733\end{aligned}$$

The precision interval can now be calculated as the audited balance ± the adjusted precision. In this case, the interval would be:

$$\begin{aligned}\text{Precision Interval} &= \text{Audited Balance} \pm \text{Adjusted Precision}\\ &= \$240{,}000 \pm \$11{,}733\\ &= \$228{,}267 \text{ to } \$251{,}733\end{aligned}$$

Because the recorded balance ($250,000) falls within the precision interval, you would decide to accept this balance as correct. In doing so, you have controlled your exposure to sampling risk at the desired levels (10 percent for risk of incorrect rejection and 5 percent for risk of incorrect acceptance).

CHAPTER CHECKPOINT

8-16. How does the auditor determine the audited value under mean-per-unit estimation?

◉ OTHER CLASSICAL VARIABLES METHODS: DIFFERENCE AND RATIO ESTIMATION

In addition to the mean-per-unit estimation method, there are two other common methods of estimation used with classical variables sampling: difference and ratio estimation. Like mean-per-unit estimation, these methods are categorized as classical variables sampling because they assume that the auditor's sample estimates are normally distributed and centered around the true account balance. The major differences between mean-per-unit estimation and these methods of estimation are:

▶ The measure of population variability used to calculate sample size and achieved precision.

▶ The method of calculating the audited balance.

Once these two differences are considered, the actual mechanics of using difference estimation and ratio estimation are quite similar to mean-per-unit estimation. As a result, the following discussion focuses on how the auditor calculates the audited value.

◘ Difference Estimation

When using difference estimation, the auditor assumes that each sampling unit contains a similar amount of dollar error. Once the auditor has performed the first five steps outlined by the *Audit Sampling Guide* (i.e., determine the objectives of the test, define the population, choose a sampling technique, determine sample size, and select the sample), the auditor examines each selected unit as under mean-per-unit estimation. However, instead of calculating the mean audited value of the items, the auditor calculates an **average difference per item**. The average difference represents the difference between the recorded value and the audited value for the sample items. It is calculated by summing the individual differences and dividing by the sample size.

Using data from the Susan Company example illustrated earlier, assume that instead of using mean-per-unit estimation you are using difference estimation. The primary information of interest is:

$$\text{Recorded accounts receivable} = \$250{,}000$$
$$\text{Number of customer accounts} = 2{,}000$$

The initial modification introduced with the use of difference estimation sampling is that, in calculating sample size, the estimated standard deviation of the differences is substituted for the estimated standard deviation of the mean audited values. For purposes of simplicity, assume that a sample size of 251 items is calculated. After selecting and examining these items, assume that you calculate an average difference ($\bar{d}$) of $-\$10$ per item. That is, on the average, each item had an audited value of $10 less than its recorded value. To estimate the total projected difference (D) in the account, you multiply the average difference per item by the number of items in the population:

$$
\begin{aligned}
D &= N \times \bar{d} \\
&= 2{,}000 \times (-\$10) \\
&= -\$20{,}000
\end{aligned}
\quad (8.9)
$$

Next, the audited balance is calculated by adjusting the recorded account balance by the estimated difference. Because the difference in this example is an overstatement, the recorded account balance is reduced by the amount of the difference to calculate the estimated account balance:

$$
\begin{aligned}
\text{Audited Balance} &= \text{Recorded Account Balance} + D \\
&= \$250{,}000 + (-\$20{,}000) \\
&= \$230{,}000
\end{aligned}
$$

As with mean-per-unit estimation, the final step prior to evaluating sample results is constructing the precision interval. The achieved precision is calculated in almost the same way as under mean-per-unit estimation. The only difference is that you use the standard deviation of the sample differences instead of the standard deviation of the audited values. Once achieved precision is calculated, the precision interval is constructed and your decision about whether the account balance is fairly stated is identical to that illustrated earlier.

◻ Ratio Estimation

The final approach to classical variables sampling is the **ratio estimation method**. The basic assumption underlying the use of ratio estimation is that each dollar of a recorded account balance contains a similar percentage of error. In ratio estimation, the auditor estimates the account balance by multiplying the recorded account balance by the ratio of audited amounts to recorded amounts for items in the sample. As with difference estimation techniques, the auditor must also modify the definition of population variability to reflect the estimation technique used. In this case, the standard deviation of the **ratios of audited value to recorded value** are utilized as a measure of population variability.[6] Similar to difference estimation, the method of calculating the audited balance and the use of a different measure of population variability are the only modifications needed for the mean-per-unit approach illustrated earlier.

To illustrate how the auditor estimates the account balance using ratio estimation, let us continue with the Susan Company example. Assume that you select 400 components of the account balance for examination.[7] These items had a total recorded value of $50,000. Assume that you determine their audited value to be $45,000 (*i.e.*, these items were overstated by $5,000). Your estimate of the account balance is calculated by multiplying the ratio of audited value to recorded value by the recorded value of the population:

$$\text{Audited Balance} = \text{Recorded Account Balance} \times \frac{\text{Sample Audited Value}}{\text{Sample Recorded Value}} \quad (8.10)$$

$$= \$25,000 \times \frac{\$45,000}{\$50,000}$$

$$= \$225,000$$

At this point, you would determine the achieved level of precision and construct the precision interval by adding and subtracting the achieved level of precision from the sample estimate. The standard deviation of the individual ratios is used in lieu of the standard deviation of audited values in making this calculation. As with mean-per-unit and difference estimation, the final step in ratio estimation is identifying whether the recorded value lies within the precision interval.

◻ Alternative Approaches to Classical Variables Sampling

When should each of the estimation techniques illustrated above be used? Although this question relies on the auditor's professional judgment, some guidance is provided in this regard. For example, if the auditor can stratify the sample, difference estimation and ratio estimation usually are not as effective in reducing sample size as mean-per-unit estimation. Also, it is normally easier for the auditor to stratify a sample based on recorded values (mean-per-unit estimation) than it is based on differences (difference estimation) or ratios of audited values to recorded values (ratio estimation). Therefore, if the auditor wishes to stratify the sample to reduce overall sample size, mean-per-unit estimation is usually the best alternative.

A second consideration in selecting a classical variables sampling approach is that, by definition, the difference estimation and ratio estimation methods require differences between audited values and recorded values to calculate the audited value and precision. Evidence suggests that a minimum of 25 to 50 differences are necessary to allow the auditor to accurately estimate the precision in

---

[6] These calculations can become quite complex. See D. M. Roberts, *Statistical Auditing* (New York: AICPA, 1978), 81, for an illustration of this calculation.

[7] Once again, it is important to note that the auditor would use the standard deviation of the ratio of audited values to recorded values in determining sample size.

evaluating the results.[8] As a result, if the auditor does not expect a large number of differences in the population, mean-per-unit estimation should be used.

Despite these advantages of mean-per-unit estimation, it is not always appropriate to use this technique. For example, when the items in the population differ greatly in terms of their audited values, the use of mean-per-unit estimation often results in a relatively extreme audited balance (*i.e.*, an unusually high or low estimate). This occurs because the estimate is driven by the mean audited values of the sample items selected. While stratification allows the auditor to overcome this potential limitation, the use of difference and ratio estimation may be more appropriate in these circumstances.

A final consideration is that, ignoring the above issues, ratio estimation and difference estimation are more efficient than the mean-per-unit approach. In other words, for the same desired exposure to sampling risks, the sample sizes associated with ratio estimation and difference estimation are generally smaller than those used in mean-per-unit estimation. The reduced sample sizes result from the auditor's ability to utilize more information about the population and sampling units (*i.e.*, difference between recorded amounts and audited amounts) in making the evaluation.

◘ Summary: Classical Variables Sampling Methods

The preceding discussion illustrates various alternatives available to the auditor for performing classical variables sampling. Once again, it is critical to emphasize that only two differences exist in these methods: (1) the method of calculating the audited value, and (2) the measure of variability used to calculate sample size and precision. Figure 8-6 summarizes the three classical variables sampling methods and highlights these differences.

CHAPTER CHECKPOINT

8-17. Briefly describe the procedure for estimating the audited value of an account balance using difference estimation and ratio estimation.

◉ PROBABILITY-PROPORTIONAL-TO-SIZE (PPS) SAMPLING

A second major type of variables sampling approach is **probability-proportional-to-size (PPS) sampling**. PPS sampling uses attribute sampling theory to make conclusions about the total misstatement in an account. A unique aspect of PPS sampling is that it defines the sampling unit as an **individual dollar of the account balance**. Thus, larger components and transactions of account balances are more likely to be selected under this method because they contain a greater number of sampling units.

---

[8] American Institute of Certified Public Accountants (AICPA), *Audit and Accounting Guide*, "Audit Sampling" (New York: AICPA, 1983), 91.

	Mean-per-Unit	Difference Estimation	Ratio Estimation
General Assumption	Each item in the population has similar recorded values	Each item in the population has similar amounts of dollar error	Each dollar in the population has similar percentages of error
Sample-Size Formula	$\left(\dfrac{N \times SD \times R(IR)}{Planned\ Precision}\right)^2$	Same as mean-per-unit except that the standard deviation of sample differences is used	Same as mean-per-unit except that the standard deviation of sample ratios is used
Audited Balance	Determine audited amount through tests	Determine audited amount through tests	Determine audited amount through tests
		Determine difference (d) between recorded amount and audited amount	
	Sum audited amounts over sample items to obtain ($\sum x$)	Sum differences (d) over sample items to obtain ($\sum d$)	Sum audited amounts over sample items
	Calculate mean audited amount ($\bar{x}$) by dividing the sum ($\sum x$) by the number of sample items	Calculate the mean difference ($\bar{d}$) by dividing the sum ($\sum d$) by the number of sample items	Calculate ratio (R) of audited amounts to recorded amounts
	Balance = $\bar{x} \times N$	Balance = Recorded Amount $\pm [(\bar{d}) \times N]$	Balance = Recorded Amount $\times (R)$
Precision Formula	$N \times R(IR) \times \dfrac{SD}{\sqrt{n}}$	Same as mean-per-unit except that the standard deviation of sample differences is used	Same as mean-per-unit except that the standard deviation of sample ratios is used
Advantages	Provides more efficient sample sizes when the sample can be stratified	Provides more efficient sample sizes in the absence of stratification	Provides more efficient sample sizes in the absence of stratification
	More appropriate when a small number of differences exist	More appropriate when a large number of differences exist	More appropriate when a large number of differences exist

N = Population size
SD = Standard deviation
$R(IR)$ = Reliability coefficient for the risk of incorrect rejection
n = Sample size

Figure 8-6: *Classical Variables Sampling Methods*

This section illustrates the use of PPS sampling during the audit examination. The major differences in PPS sampling and classical variables sampling are related to: (1) determining the sample size, (2) selecting the sample items, and (3) evaluating results. It is important to note that the first three steps (determining the objective of the test, defining the population, and choosing a sampling technique) are the same as under classical variable sampling. Accordingly, our discussion focuses on these differences through the use of a comprehensive example.

◼ Determining Sample Size

In PPS sampling, sample size is calculated through the use of the following formula:

$$n = \frac{\text{Recorded Balance} \times \text{Reliability Factor}}{[\text{Tolerable Error} - (\text{Expected Error} \times \text{Expansion Factor})]}$$

The **reliability factor** and **expansion factor** are based on the auditor's desired exposure to the risk of incorrect acceptance. Expansion and reliability factors for various levels of the risk of incorrect acceptance are shown in Tables 8-2 and 8-3, respectively. As noted previously with classical variables sampling, this risk has an inverse relationship with sample size—that is, as the risk of incorrect acceptance increases, the necessary sample size decreases. Although this relationship is not obvious from the above formula, examining Tables 8-2 and 8-3 reveals that higher levels of risk are associated with smaller factors. In the above formula, smaller factors will result in a lower sample size, through either a decreased numerator (reliability factor) or increased denominator (expansion factor).

Table 8-2: *Expansion Factors for Expected Errors*

	\multicolumn{8}{c}{Risk of Incorrect Acceptance}
	1%	5%	10%	15%	20%	25%	30%	37%	50%
Factor	1.90	1.60	1.50	1.40	1.30	1.25	1.20	1.15	1.10

Source: American Institute of Certified Public Accountants (AICPA), *Audit and Accounting Guide*, "Audit Sampling" (New York: AICPA, 1983), 118.

Figure 8-7 summarizes the relationships between the remaining factors and sample size in PPS sampling. Note that tolerable error and the recorded balance of the account (population size) have the same relationship with sample size as in classical variables sampling. Two major differences exist between the determination of sample size in classical variables sampling and PPS:

1. In classical variables sampling, both the population variability and risk of incorrect rejection are explicitly incorporated into the determination of sample size; these factors are ignored in PPS.
2. In classical variables sampling, the amount of expected error is not considered in determining sample size. In PPS sampling, this factor is directly related to sample size.

Table 8-3: *Reliability Factors for Errors of Overstatement*

Number of Over-statement Errors	_____ Risk of Incorrect Acceptance _____								
	1%	*5%*	*10%*	*15%*	*20%*	*25%*	*30%*	*37%*	*50%*
0	4.61	3.00	2.30	1.90	1.61	1.39	1.20	1.00	.69
1	6.64	4.74	3.89	3.37	2.99	2.69	2.44	2.15	1.69
2	8.41	6.30	5.32	4.72	4.28	3.92	3.62	3.27	2.69
3	10.05	7.75	6.68	6.01	5.52	5.11	4.76	4.37	3.69
4	11.60	9.15	7.99	7.27	6.72	6.27	5.89	5.46	4.69
5	13.11	10.51	9.27	8.49	7.91	7.42	7.01	6.54	5.69
6	14.57	11.84	10.53	9.70	9.08	8.56	8.11	7.61	6.69
7	16.00	13.15	11.77	10.90	10.23	9.68	9.21	8.68	7.69
8	17.40	14.43	12.99	12.08	11.38	10.80	10.30	9.74	8.69
9	18.78	15.71	14.21	13.25	12.52	11.91	11.39	10.80	9.69
10	20.14	16.96	15.41	14.41	13.65	13.02	12.47	11.86	10.69
11	21.49	18.21	16.60	15.57	14.78	14.12	13.55	12.91	11.69
12	22.82	19.44	17.78	16.71	15.90	15.22	14.62	13.96	12.69
13	24.14	20.67	18.96	17.86	17.01	16.31	15.70	15.01	13.69
14	25.45	21.89	20.13	19.00	18.13	17.40	16.77	16.06	14.69
15	26.74	23.10	21.29	20.13	19.23	18.49	17.83	17.11	15.69
16	28.03	24.30	22.45	21.26	20.34	19.57	18.90	18.16	16.69
17	29.31	25.50	23.61	22.38	21.44	20.65	19.96	19.21	17.69
18	30.58	26.69	24.76	23.50	22.54	21.73	21.02	20.26	18.69
19	31.85	27.88	25.90	24.62	23.63	22.81	22.08	21.31	19.69
20	33.10	29.06	27.05	25.74	24.73	23.88	23.14	22.35	20.69

Source: American Institute of Certified Public Accountants (AICPA), *Audit and Accounting Guide,* "Audit Sampling" (New York: AICPA, 1983), 117.

To illustrate the calculation of sample size, assume that Attaya Company has an accounts receivable balance of $500,000, which represents 400 customer accounts. If the auditor assesses tolerable error at $25,000, expected error at $10,000, and the risk of incorrect acceptance at 5 percent, the sample size would be 167. The expansion and reliability factors are drawn from Tables 8-2 and 8-3, respectively. The auditor normally assumes zero overstatement errors in identifying the reliability factor from Table 8-3.

$$n = \frac{\text{Recorded Balance} \times \text{Reliability Factor}}{[\text{Tolerable Error} - (\text{Expected Error} \times \text{Expansion Factor})]} \qquad (8.11)$$

$$= \frac{\$500{,}000 \times 3.00}{[\$25{,}000 - (10{,}000 - 1.6)]} = 166.67, \text{ or } 167 \text{ items}$$

◻ Selecting the Sample

Once the sample size has been calculated, the auditor then selects the sample. Since PPS sampling defines the sampling unit as a dollar, the auditor will randomly select a number of "dollars" from the

Factor	Relationship	As Factor	Sample Size
Recorded Balance (population size)	Direct	Increases Decreases	Increases Decreases
Risk of Incorrect Acceptance	Inverse	Increases Decreases	Decreases Increases
Tolerable Error	Inverse	Increases Decreases	Decreases Increases
Expected Error	Direct	Increases Decreases	Increases Decreases

Figure 8-7: *Effect of Factors on Sample Size in PPS Sampling*

population. As a particular dollar is identified, the logical item containing that dollar is selected. For example, if the auditor selects the 1,500th dollar of accounts receivable for examination, the auditor will verify the entire balance of the customer's account containing that dollar.

Although the auditor can use unrestricted random sampling to select dollars for examination, a systematic approach is most frequently used. Under this approach, the auditor will perform the following steps:

1. Randomly select a starting point in the population by picking a number between 1 and the sampling interval (discussed below).
2. Skip a fixed number of sampling units (dollars) and select an item for examination.
3. Repeat this procedure until the desired number of items have been selected.

To determine the sampling interval, the auditor divides the recorded balance by the desired sample size. In the Attaya Company example, the sampling interval would equal $2,994 ($500,000 ÷ 167 = $2,994). Therefore, the auditor will select every 2,994th dollar in the population for examination.

Shown below is a partial listing of Attaya Company's accounts receivable. Assuming that the auditor chooses a random start of 180, the first three sample items would be selected as shown below. The auditor would continue with this procedure until the entire sample of 167 items has been selected.

Beginning Dollar	Add: Sampling Interval	Dollar Selected
180	—	180
180	2,994	3,174
3,174	2,994	6,168

Account Number	Recorded Balance	Dollars Contained	Account Selected
1	$ 130	$ 0–$ 130	No
2	$2,100	$ 131–$2,230	Yes
3	$ 800	$2,231–$3,030	No
4	$2,000	$3,031–$5,030	Yes
5	$3,000	5,031–$8,030	Yes
...	...	...	
400	$2,500	$497,501–$500,000	

◻ Evaluating Sample Results

After the sample items have been selected, the auditor will examine accounts receivable through confirmation and other tests described in Chapter 11. Assume the following four overstatement errors are discovered:[9]

Account	Recorded Balance	Audited Balance	Misstatement
33	$2,500	$1,500	$1,000
79	$5,000	$4,600	$ 400
225	$2,000	$1,000	$1,000
350	$1,000	$ 200	$ 800

In evaluating the sample results, the auditor will calculate a maximum error limit. The maximum error limit parallels the upper precision limit used in attribute sampling. The maximum error limit is an estimate that has a (1 − risk of incorrect acceptance) probability of equaling or exceeding the actual error in the account. Stated another way, a (risk of incorrect acceptance) probability exists that the true error in the account exceeds the maximum error limit. By calculating the maximum error limit and comparing it to tolerable error, the auditor controls the exposure to the risk of incorrect acceptance at desired levels.

---

[9] For simplicity, we only illustrate the method used to evaluate overstatements using PPS sampling. This illustration is fairly realistic because PPS is more effective in detecting overstatement errors. For an illustration of how understatement errors are evaluated under PPS sampling, see D.M. Roberts, *Statistical Auditing* (New York: AICPA, 1978), 116-124.

The three components of the maximum error limit are: (1) the projected error, (2) the basic precision, and (3) the incremental allowance. These components are discussed below.

Projected Error. The projected error is determined using the basic assumption that the entire sampling interval contains the same percentage error as the item examined from that interval. For example, consider the misstatement in account number 33. The recorded balance in the account was $2,500; however, examining the customer's account, the auditor believes the correct balance to be $1,500. Thus, a misstatement of $1,000 was noted. Expressed as a percentage of the recorded balance, this is a misstatement of 40 percent (1,000 ÷ 2,500 = 0.40). The projected error assumes that the entire sampling interval from which this item was drawn is misstated by 40 percent. To determine the projected error, simply multiply the percentage misstatement (the **tainting percentage**) by the sampling interval. The tainting percentage is determined by dividing the overstatement by the recorded balance.

The projected error in the Attaya Company example is shown below:

Account	Tainting Percentage	Sampling Interval	Projected Error
33	$1,000 ÷ $2,500 = 0.40	$2,994	$1,198
79	N/A	N/A	400
225	1,000 ÷ 2,000 = 0.50	2,994	1,497
350	800 ÷ 1,000 = 0.80	2,994	2,396
	Total projected error		$5,491

A question that arises in this calculation is why the error in account number 79 was not projected. Recall that the recorded balance of this account was $5,000, an amount greater than the sampling interval. Therefore, there is no need to estimate the amount of error in the sampling interval. Note that the remaining errors were discovered in accounts having recorded balances less than the sampling interval. For these accounts, the amount of error in the interval must be estimated.

Basic Precision. In addition to the projected error, the auditor must also calculate an allowance for sampling risk consisting of two components: basic precision and an incremental allowance. The basic precision is simple to calculate. Basic precision is equal to the sampling interval multiplied by the reliability factor for the risk of incorrect acceptance. Unlike projected errors (discussed above), the basic precision is always calculated, regardless of whether any misstatements are noted in the auditor's sample.

Recalling that the auditor determined a sampling interval of $2,994 and desired exposure to the risk of incorrect acceptance of 5 percent (a reliability factor assuming zero overstatement errors, of 3.0), basic precision would be $8,982, as shown below:

$$\text{Basic Precision} = \$2,994 \times 3.0 = \$8,982$$

Incremental Allowance for Sampling Risk. The final component of the maximum error limit is the incremental allowance for sampling risk. The incremental allowance is determined using the following four-step procedure:

1. For projected errors in sample items with recorded balances less than the sampling interval, rank the projected errors (from highest to lowest).
2. Multiply each of the projected errors by the change in the reliability factors given the occurrence of that error.
3. Sum the product in step 2.
4. Subtract the total projected error determined earlier to obtain the incremental allowance for sampling risk.

Although the theoretical nature of the incremental allowance for sampling risk is difficult to understand, this component considers the possibility that the remainder of the sampling interval may be misstated at a greater rate than the item examined from that interval. Accordingly, because the auditor knows the total misstatement in the sampling interval for account balances greater than the sampling interval, an incremental allowance is not calculated for these accounts.

The calculation of the incremental allowance for the Attaya Company example is shown below. Recall that the auditor established a risk of incorrect acceptance of 5 percent in this example. Therefore, the incremental change would be calculated using the 5 percent column of Table 8-3 for the reliability factors.

Account	Projected Error	×	Incremental Change	=	Adjusted Projected Error
350	$2,396	× 1.74	= (4.74 − 3.00)	=	$4,169
225	$1,497	× 1.56	= (6.30 − 4.74)	=	2,335
33	$1,198	× 1.45	= (6.30 − 6.30)	=	1,737
79	$ 400	×	N/A	=	400
	Adjusted projected error				$8,641
	Less initial projected error				−5,491
	Incremental allowance				$3,150

Once again, it is important to note that an incremental allowance for sampling risk was not calculated for account 79. As before, there is no need to estimate the error in the sampling interval because the recorded balance of this account is greater than the sampling interval.

Making the Decision. At this point, the auditor can calculate the maximum error limit as the sum of the projected error, basic precision, and incremental allowance for sampling risks. From the previous calculations, this error limit would equal $17,623, as shown below:

Projected error	$ 5,491
Basic precision	8,982
Incremental allowance	3,150
Maximum error limit	$17,623

The total allowance for sampling risk is equal to the basic precision plus the incremental allowance, or $12,132 ($8,982 + $3,150 = $12,132). The maximum error limit tells the auditor that there is a 95 percent (1 − risk of incorrect acceptance) probability that the account is misstated by

$17,623 or less. Conversely, there is a 5 percent (risk of incorrect acceptance) probability that the misstatement in the account is greater than $17,623. Comparing the maximum error limit to the tolerable error of $25,000, the auditor would decide to accept Attaya Company's accounts receivable as fairly recorded. In doing so, the auditor has controlled the exposure to the risk of incorrect acceptance to 5 percent.

PPS Sampling versus Classical Variables Sampling

An issue that needs to be addressed is when PPS sampling should be used and when classical variables sampling should be used. The advantages and disadvantages of PPS sampling compared to classical variables sampling are summarized in Figure 8-8. It is important to note that the disadvantages of PPS sampling can be considered as advantages of classical variables sampling, and vice versa.

Advantages

1. Generally easier to use than classical variables sampling.
2. PPS automatically stratifies the population by selecting larger dollar items for examination.
3. The size of a PPS sample is not based on variability (standard deviation), which may be difficult to estimate.
4. If no errors are expected, PPS sampling will usually result in a smaller sample size than classical variables sampling.
5. Compared to classical variables sampling, it is normally easier for the auditor to begin a PPS sampling application before the complete population is available.

Disadvantages

1. Special considerations are required when the auditor anticipates understatements or audit values of less than zero in the account.
2. The selection of zero or negative balances requires special considerations.
3. If errors are detected, PPS sampling may overstate the allowance for sampling risk, resulting in increased exposure to the risk of incorrect rejection.
4. As the expected error in the account increases, the necessary sample size for a PPS sample may exceed that for a classical variable sample.

Figure 8-8: *Advantages and Disadvantages Associated with PPS Sampling*

The AICPA Audit Sampling guide notes that PPS sampling is especially useful for the following accounts and circumstances:

1. Accounts receivable, where unapplied credits are not significant; if unapplied credits are significant, classical variables sampling should be used.
2. Loans receivable.
3. Investment securities.

4. Inventory price tests, where few differences are expected; if many differences are expected, the auditor should use classical variables sampling.
5. Fixed asset additions.

CHAPTER CHECKPOINTS

8-18. What are the primary advantages and disadvantages associated with probability-proportional-to-size (PPS) sampling?

8-19. Why does PPS sampling have the tendency to select the largest dollar items for examination?

8-20. What factors are considered by the auditor in calculating the sampling interval in PPS sampling? How do each of these factors affect sample size?

8-21. Describe how the auditor selects a sample under PPS sampling.

8-22. What is basic precision? What is the incremental allowance for sampling risk? How is each calculated?

8-23. What are three differences that are introduced when the auditor uses nonstatistical sampling in performing variables sampling?

Appendix A

Controlling Exposure to Sampling Risks[10]

◻ Risk of Incorrect Rejection

To illustrate how the auditor's exposure to the risk of incorrect rejection is controlled, assume that the auditor is examining an accounts receivable balance comprised of 1,000 customer accounts. Also assume that the balance is correctly recorded at $250,000. Therefore, the auditor would like the sample estimate to indicate that accounts receivable are fairly stated, because this is the correct decision and does not result in exposure to the risk of incorrect rejection. In controlling the risk of incorrect rejection, the auditor wishes to limit the probability that the audited balance differs materially from the recorded balance.

Figure 8-9 illustrates exposure to the risk of incorrect rejection. If tolerable error equals $30,000, the auditor's sample estimate would signal rejection of the account balance if it is less than $220,000 or greater than $280,000 ($250,000 ± $30,000). Under normal distribution theory, the auditor's estimate of the account balance is centered around the true account balance. However, it is possible for the auditor to observe extremely high or low estimates. If the difference between the recorded account balance and the true account balance is less than $30,000 (as in this example), we attempt to control the probability of observing an extreme sample estimate to prespecified levels (the risk of incorrect rejection).

To control the exposure to this risk, the auditor establishes a level of precision such that the probability of concluding that the account balance is misstated is limited to the desired exposure to the risk of incorrect rejection. This level of precision statistically adjusts the tolerable error to control sampling risk. Normal distribution theory indicates that 95.5 percent of the sample estimates fall within two standard deviations of the true account balance. Therefore, only 4.5 percent of all estimates (100 percent − 95.5 percent = 4.5 percent) differ from the true account balance by more than two standard deviations. As a result, if the auditor sets the risk of incorrect rejection equal to 4.5 percent,

---

[10] All Chapter Checkpoints and End of Chapter Items related to the Appendix are marked with an asterisk (*).

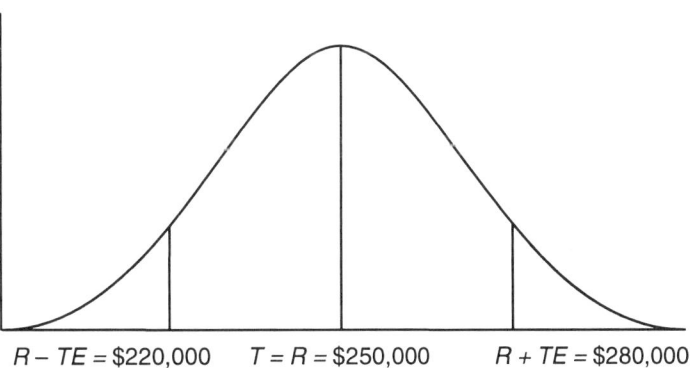

R − TE = $220,000   T = R = $250,000   R + TE = $280,000

T = True account balance
R = Recorded account balance
TE = Tolerable error ($30,000)
The shaded area represents exposure to the risk of incorrect rejection.

Figure 8-9: *Illustration of Risk of Incorrect Rejection*

precision would equal two standard deviations. Note that the risk of incorrect rejection is equal to (1 − reliability).

The number of standard deviations for reliabilities of 68.3 percent, 95.5 percent, and 99.7 percent from the normal curve were shown earlier. It is useful for the auditor to have measures of reliability relating to more operational levels of risk (such as 1 percent, 5 percent, 10 percent, etc.), however. These measures can be extracted from a normal distribution table. Reliability coefficients (number of standard deviations) associated with frequently used levels of risk of incorrect rejection are shown below. Note that the coefficient for a 5 percent risk of incorrect rejection (1.96) approximates two standard deviations, which has a reliability of 95.5 percent (risk of incorrect rejection of 4.5 percent).

Reliability	Risk of Incorrect Rejection	Reliability Coefficients
0.99	0.01	2.58
0.95	0.05	1.96
0.90	0.10	1.65
0.85	0.15	1.44
0.80	0.20	1.29

Therefore, to control exposure to the risk of incorrect rejection at a level of 5 percent, precision should equal 1.96 standard deviations.

◻ Risk of Incorrect Acceptance

Consider the above example and now assume that the true account balance differs from the recorded account balance by a material amount. When this occurs, the auditor would like the recorded account balance to fall outside of the precision interval (audited balance ± precision) so that his or her decision would be to conclude that the account balance is materially misstated. This is the desired outcome because it represents a correct decision and does not expose the auditor to sampling risk in the form of the risk of incorrect acceptance. In this case, the auditor controls the exposure to this risk by establishing a level of precision such that the probability of the audited balance not differing materially from the recorded account balance is limited.

For example, assume that the true balance of the client's accounts receivable is $200,000 and tolerable error is $30,000. Also, assume that this balance is recorded at $250,000. Because the difference between the recorded balance and the true account balance ($250,000 − $200,000 = $50,000) exceeds tolerable error ($30,000), the auditor should not accept the account balance as correct. Also remember from normal distribution theory that the distribution of sample estimates is centered around the true account balance. These facts are depicted in Figure 8-10.

As shown in Figure 8-10, the most frequent sample estimate of the account balance is assumed to be the true account balance ($200,000). Note that most samples drawn would correctly allow the auditor to conclude that the account balance is materially misstated. However, the possibility exists that the sample may yield a relatively extreme audited balance, which could lead the auditor to believe that the account balance is not materially misstated. This possibility is represented by the shaded area of the normal curve in Figure 8-10, which includes any audited balance greater than $220,000.

Notice from the shaded area of Figure 8-10 that the risk of incorrect acceptance is concerned with limiting the possibility that the audited balance is either greater than (if the account is overstated) or less than (if the account is understated) a certain amount. Therefore, unlike the risk of incorrect rejection, we are not interested in controlling the area occurring in both tails of the distribution. In the example depicted in Figure 8-10, extremely low audited balances will still result in the correct decision to reject the account balance. The reliability coefficients for frequently used levels of risk of incorrect acceptance are shown below.

Reliability	Risk of Incorrect Acceptance	Reliability Coefficient
0.99	0.01	2.33
0.95	0.05	1.65
0.90	0.10	1.29
0.85	0.15	1.04
0.80	0.20	0.85

Therefore, to control exposure to the risk of incorrect acceptance at a level of 5 percent, precision should equal 1.65 standard deviations.

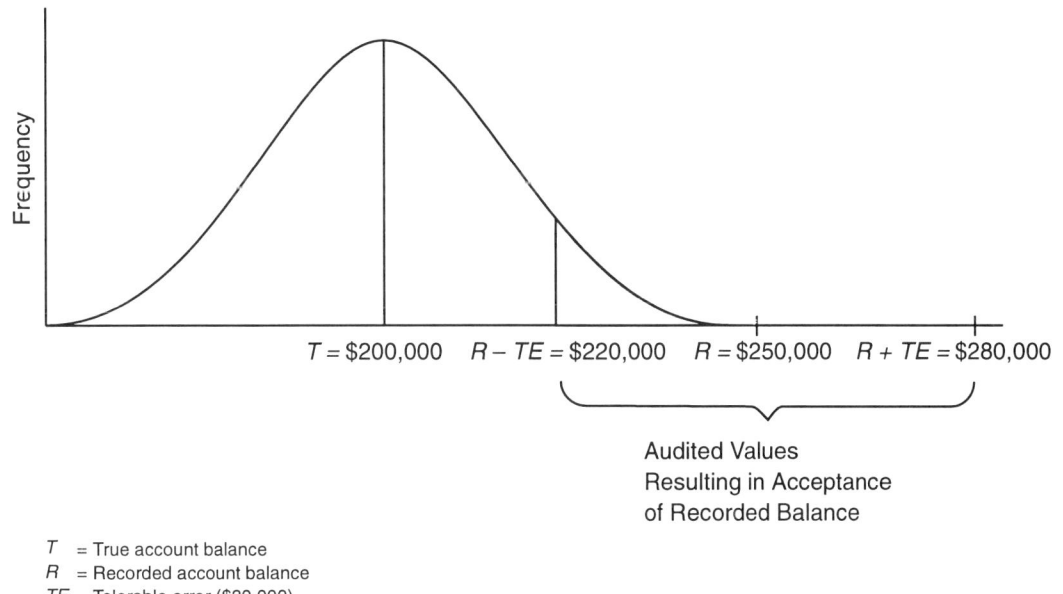

T = True account balance
R = Recorded account balance
TE = Tolerable error ($30,000)
The shaded area represents exposure to the risk of incorrect rejection.

Figure 8-10: *Illustration of Risk of Incorrect Acceptance*

Appendix B

Nonstatistical Sampling

To this point, the discussion has focused on the use of statistical sampling methods. However, it is important to recognize that current professional guidance does not require the use of statistical sampling. In some cases, the auditor may find it more efficient to use nonstatistical sampling. The three main differences between statistical sampling and nonstatistical sampling are:

1. Statistical sampling methods determine sample size in such a manner as to control the auditor's exposure to sampling risk.
2. Statistical sampling methods require the auditor to use probabilistic selection techniques—that is, the auditor must randomly select sample items for examination and subject every item to possible selection.
3. Statistical sampling methods mathematically evaluate the sample results so that the auditor's exposure to sampling risk is controlled.

Although nonstatistical sampling methods are normally easier to apply, they do not allow the auditor to control exposure to sampling risk. This feature is perhaps the largest drawback to the use of nonstatistical sampling.

◻ Example: Nonstatistical Sampling

Assume that you are examining the accounts receivable of Bonilla Company as of December 31, 19X1. On that date, the recorded balance consists of 900 customer accounts with a total balance of $3,700,000. Bonilla's accounts receivable can be classified into the following dollar categories:

Dollar Amount	Number of Accounts	Total Dollar Value
0 – $65,000	889	$2,912,593
Over $65,000	11	787,407
	900	$3,700,000

A major difference in a nonstatistical sampling application is that the auditor does not mathematically incorporate the desired exposure to sampling risk in determining the sample size. However, exposure to sampling risk should be considered. Theoretically, as the auditor wishes to control sampling risk at a lower level, a larger sample size should be selected, and vice versa. Similarly, the auditor should consider the size of the population, tolerable error, and expected error. A method of considering these factors is using the following formula:

$$\frac{\text{Recorded Balance}}{\text{Tolerable Error}} \times \text{Assurance Factor} = \text{Sample Size}$$

The assurance factor is based on the expected error in the account and the degree of audit assurance required from the substantive tests. Figure 8-11 is provided to determine the assurance factor:[11]

Desired Degree of Audit Assurance	Little or No Expected Error	Some Expected Error
Substantial	3	6
Moderate	2.3	4
Little	1.5	3

Figure 8-11: *Determining the Assurance Factor in a Nonstatistical Sampling Application*

Thus, if you assess tolerable error at $185,000, require a substantial level of audit assurance, and expect some error, you would calculate a sample size of 120, as shown below:

$$\text{Sample Size} = \frac{\$3,700,000}{\$185,000} \times 6 = 120$$

Using professional judgment, you decide to examine all items greater than $65,000. Thus, your sample would consist of the 11 items with recorded balances greater than $65,000 and 109 of the accounts recorded at less than $65,000. In a nonstatistical sampling plan, the auditor is permitted to use a judgmental sampling procedure of this nature. After conducting audit tests, you calculate the following results:

Stratum	Number of Accounts	Recorded Value of the Stratum	Recorded Value of Sample	Audited Value of Sample
1	109	$2,912,593	$ 791,577	$ 814,388
2	11	787,407	787,407	789,700
			$1,578,984	$11,604,088

---

[11] American Institute of Certified Public Accountants (AICPA), *Audit Sampling* (New York: AICPA, 1983), 59.

The results of the sample indicate an understatement of $25,104 ($1,601,088 − $1,578,984). To estimate the audited value for the account, you can use a form of the ratio method:

$$\text{Stratum 1:} \quad \frac{\$814,388}{\$791,577} \times \$2,912,593 = \$2,996,526$$

$$\text{Stratum 2:} \quad \frac{\$789,700}{\$787,407} \times \$787,407 = \underline{\$\ 789,700}$$
$$\$3,786,226$$

The difference between the recorded account balance ($3,700,000) and the audited balance ($3,786,226) is $86,226, which is less than the tolerable error ($185,000). Based on this evidence, you may conclude that the risk that the account is misstated by an amount greater than tolerable is small and accept the account balance. Note that you do not establish a level of achieved precision to control your exposure to sampling risk in evaluating the sample results. The failure to consider the exposure to sampling risk in evaluating the sample results represents the final difference between nonstatistical sampling and statistical sampling.

CHAPTER CHECKPOINT

*8-24. What factors does the auditor normally consider in determining the sample size when using nonstatistical sampling? How does each factor affect sample size?

◉ SUMMARY OF KEY POINTS

1. The second stage of the audit where evidence is gathered is in performing substantive tests of details. When performing tests of details, the auditor uses variables estimation sampling to provide a numerical estimate of a population, such as the balance in a particular account. The primary goal of variables sampling is to allow the auditor to determine whether the difference between the recorded account balance and "true" account balance is greater than an amount considered to be material (tolerable error).

2. Similar to attribute sampling, the use of variables sampling poses two types of sampling risk to the auditor. The risk of incorrect rejection is the probability that the auditor incorrectly rejects a fairly stated account balance. Like the risk of underreliance, this risk represents an efficiency loss to the auditor because additional tests will normally be performed.

3. In contrast, the risk of incorrect acceptance results when the auditor incorrectly accepts a materially misstated account balance. This risk is similar in nature to the risk of overreliance, as it results in an effectiveness loss to the auditor. Controlling exposure to this risk is of more concern to the auditor because the correct conclusion regarding the account balance is normally not reached.

4. Classical variables sampling uses normal distribution theory and the central limit theorem to allow the auditor to make statements and inferences about a population based on a sample drawn from that population. Three approaches to using classical variables sampling are: (1) mean-per-unit estimation, (2) difference estimation, and (3) ratio estimation. These approaches differ primarily with respect to the method used to determine the audited value (estimate of the true account balance).

5. Factors considered by the auditor in determining the sample size for a classical variables sampling application are: (1) the size of the population, (2) the population variability, (3) the tolerable error, (4) the risk of incorrect acceptance, (5) the risk of incorrect rejection, and (6) the planned precision (or allowance for sampling risk).

6. After the auditor selects the sample, the audited value and achieved precision are calculated. Under mean-per-unit estimation, the audited value is equal to the average audited value of the items examined multiplied by the number of items in the population. The auditor then forms a precision interval by adding and subtracting the achieved precision from the audited value.

7. Once the precision interval has been established, the auditor evaluates the sample results. If the recorded account balance falls within the precision interval, the auditor concludes that this balance is fairly stated. If, however, the precision interval does not include the recorded balance, the auditor would conclude that the account balance is not fairly stated. In either case, the auditor's desired exposure to the risk of incorrect acceptance and risk of incorrect rejection has been controlled.

8. Two other common methods of classical variables sampling are difference estimation and ratio estimation. These methods differ from mean-per-unit estimation in two ways: (1) the method of calculating the audited value, and (2) the measure of population variability used to determine sample size and achieved precision.

9. A second major classification of variables sampling plans is probability-proportional-to-size (PPS) sampling. PPS sampling is unique in that it defines a sampling unit as individual dollars composing an account balance. PPS sampling has the tendency to select large components and transactions for examination; as a result, this method is particularly beneficial when overstatement errors are expected.

10. In PPS sampling, the auditor calculates a maximum error limit. This maximum error limit consists of three components: (1) the projected error, (2) the basic precision, and (3) the incremental allowance for sampling risk.

11. If the maximum error limit is less than tolerable error, the auditor concludes that the account balance is fairly stated. In contrast, if the maximum error limit is greater than tolerable error, the conclusion would be that the account balance is misstated by a material amount.

*12. In variables sampling, nonstatistical sampling plans may also be used. These plans differ from statistical sampling plans in the determination of sample size, selection of sample items, and evaluation of sample results.

GLOSSARY

Many of the terms that are used in this chapter were introduced in Chapter 7. The student may wish to review the glossary for that chapter while studying Chapter 8.

Achieved Precision. The level of precision used to evaluate the auditor's sample results. The achieved precision differs from planned precision in that it uses the actual variability observed in the auditor's sample.

Allowance for Sampling Risk. See Planned Precision.

Audited Account Balance (Audited Value). The auditor's estimate of the true account balance based on the variables sampling procedures.

Basic Precision. A portion of the total allowance for sampling risk in a PPS sample. The basic precision is calculated by multiplying the sampling interval by the reliability factor for the auditor's desired level of risk of incorrect acceptance.

Classical Variables Sampling. An approach to variables sampling that uses normal distribution theory and the central limit theorem to allow the auditor to make statements and inferences about a population based on a sample drawn from that population.

Difference Estimation. A method of classical variables sampling that calculates an average difference of audited values from recorded values to estimate the total audited value.

Incremental Allowance for Sampling Risk. Along with basic precision, this is a component of the allowance for sampling risk for PPS sampling. It is calculated by multiplying the projected error(s) by the incremental change in reliability factors resulting from the occurrence of those error(s).

Maximum Error Limit. An estimate of the amount of misstatement in PPS sampling. The maximum error limit is composed of the projected error, basic precision, and incremental allowance for sampling risk. The maximum error limit has a (1 − risk of incorrect acceptance) probability of equaling or exceeding the actual error in the account balance.

Mean-per-Unit Estimation. A method of classical variables sampling that calculates the audited value by determining a mean audited value per sample item.

Nonstatistical Sampling. A type of sampling plan that does not control the auditor's exposure to sampling risk in determining the sample size and evaluating the sample results.

Normal Distribution. A concept that describes the probability that the auditor's sample will provide various estimates of the true account balance. The frequency of any interval of this curve can be determined by knowing the sample estimate and the standard deviation.

Planned Precision. Used to calculate sample size, planned precision represents the tolerable error adjusted for the auditor's desired exposure to the risk of incorrect acceptance and risk of incorrect rejection. This term is also known as the allowance for sampling risk.

Probability-Proportional-to-Size (PPS) Sampling. PPS sampling is the second major type of variables sampling approach. PPS sampling uses attribute theory to estimate the total misstatement in an account balance. This method defines the sampling unit as an individual dollar of an account balance, resulting in a tendency to select larger items for examination.

Projected Error. Projected error is calculated by multiplying the sampling interval by the tainting percentage. This component of the maximum error limit assumes that the entire sampling interval is misstated to the same degree as the sample item examined.

Ratio Estimation. A method of classical variables sampling that estimates the audited value based on the ratio of audited balances to recorded balances.

Risk of Incorrect Acceptance. The probability that the sample results indicate that the account balance is fairly stated when, in fact, it is materially misstated. The risk of incorrect acceptance results in an effectiveness loss to the auditor.

Risk of Incorrect Rejection. The probability that the sample results indicate that the account balance is materially misstated when, in fact, it is fairly stated. This risk represents an efficiency loss to the auditor because additional tests will normally be performed.

Standard Deviation. A measure of the variability of a population. The standard deviation has a direct relationship with sample size in classical variables sampling.

Stratified Sampling. A method of reducing sample sizes by subdividing a population into more homogeneous subgroups, or strata.

Tainting Percentage. The percentage misstatement in a sample item for a PPS sample. This percentage is multiplied by the sampling interval to determine the projected error.

Tolerable Error. Also known as materiality, tolerable error is the amount by which an account balance can be misstated without the auditor concluding that the account is materially misstated.

True Account Balance. The amount at which an account would be recorded, assuming that no errors were made by the client in recording transactions. The auditor's purpose in performing variables sampling is to form an estimate of the true account balance.

Variables Estimation Sampling. A form of sampling used to provide a numerical estimate of a population, such as the true balance of an account. Variables estimation sampling is used by the auditor when performing substantive tests.

◉ SUMMARY OF PROFESSIONAL PRONOUNCEMENTS

Statement on Auditing Standards No. 47, "Audit Risk and Materiality in Conducting an Audit" (New York: AICPA, 1983, AU 312).

QUESTIONS AND PROBLEMS

8-25. Select the **best** answer for each of the following items:

1. Which of the following is normally used to provide a numerical estimate of a population?

   a. Attribute sampling.
   b. Discovery sampling.
   c. Numerical sampling.
   d. Variables sampling.

2. The risk that the auditor's sample indicates that the account balance is fairly stated when, in fact, it is materially misstated is referred to as the:

   a. Risk of incorrect acceptance.
   b. Risk of incorrect rejection.
   c. Risk of overreliance.
   d. Risk of underreliance.

3. Which of the following sampling risks in a variables sampling plan results in an efficiency loss to the auditor?

   a. Risk of incorrect acceptance.
   b. Risk of incorrect rejection.
   c. Risk of overreliance.
   d. Risk of underreliance

4. Which of the following is not a classical variables sampling approach?

   a. Difference estimation.
   b. Mean-per-unit estimation.
   c. Probability-proportional-to-size estimation.
   d. Ratio estimation.
   e. All of the above are classical variables sampling approaches.

5. An estimate of the variability in a population that underlies the use of classical variables sampling is referred to as the:

   a. Normal distribution.
   b. Precision.
   c. Standard deviation.
   d. Tolerable error.

6. Which of the following terms is not true in completing the following statement: As the _____ increases, the sample size _____.

   a. Risk of incorrect acceptance; decreases.
   b. Tolerable error; decreases.
   c. Standard deviation; increases.
   d. Planned precision; increases.
   e. Population size; increases.

7. Which of the following represents the dollar error that can exist in an account without the auditor concluding that the account balance is materially misstated?

   a. Precision.
   b. Reliability.
   c. Standard deviation.
   d. Tolerable rate.
   e. Tolerable error.

8. When the auditor commits the risk of incorrect acceptance, which of the following statements is not true?

   a. The true account balance is not materially misstated.
   b. The estimate of the audited value suggests that the difference between the recorded account balance and the true account balance is less than tolerable error.
   c. The auditor suffers an effectiveness loss.
   d. The true account balance is materially misstated.

9. Assume that the auditor is performing variables sampling for accounts receivable recorded at $220,000. The auditor calculates an audited value of $300,000. If the achieved precision is $40,000, which of the following statements is true?

   a. The auditor should reject the account balance because the audited value of $300,000 is equal to the true account balance.
   b. The auditor should accept the account balance as correct because it is less than the audited value plus precision.
   c. The auditor should reject the account balance because it differs from the audited value by an amount greater than precision.
   d. The auditor cannot make a determination based on the above information.

10. Which of the following is least likely to be considered by the auditor in establishing the desired exposure to the risk of incorrect acceptance?

    a. The desired level of audit risk.
    b. The cost associated with performing additional testing procedures.
    c. The effectiveness of the client's internal control.
    d. The planned effectiveness of other substantive testing procedures.
    e. The susceptibility of the account balance to misstatement.

11. In which of the following instances is the true account balance not materially misstated?

	Risk of Incorrect Acceptance	Risk of Incorrect Rejection
a.	No	No
b.	Yes	No
c.	No	Yes
d.	Yes	Yes

Use the following information to answer questions 12–14:

Recorded account balance $500,000
Number of accounts in population 10,000
Recorded balance of accounts sampled $100,000
Audited balance of accounts sampled $150,000
Number of accounts sampled 2,500
Standard deviation of mean audited values .... $ 75
Reliability coefficient for the risk of incorrect
  rejection (5 percent) 1.96

12. What is the estimated audited value under mean-per-unit estimation?

   a. $100,000.
   b. $500,000.
   c. $600,000.
   d. $750,000.

13. What is the estimated audited value under ratio estimation?

   a. $100,000.
   b. $500,000.
   c. $600,000.
   d. $750,000.

14. What is the achieved precision under mean-per-unit estimation?

   a. $ 588
   b. $ 7,350
   c. $14,700
   d. $29,400

15. Which of the following sets of conditions would yield the largest sample size under classical variable sampling?

	Standard Deviation	Risk of Incorrect Acceptance	Tolerable Error
a.	High	High	High
b.	Low	Low	High
c.	High	Low	Low
d.	Low	High	Low

16. Which of the following is not considered to be an advantage of using probability-proportional-to-size (PPS) sampling?

    a. PPS sampling has the tendency to select larger dollar items for examination
    b. PPS sampling normally results in a more efficient sample size than classical variables sampling when the number of expected errors is low.
    c. The auditor is not required to form an estimate of the population variability to determine sample size under PPS sampling.
    d. PPS sampling is relatively effective in detecting understatements in accounts compared to classical variables sampling.
    e. All of the above are advantages associated with the use of PPS sampling.

17. Which of the following factors is not inversely related to sample size in PPS sampling?

    a. Tolerable error.
    b. Expected error.
    c. Risk of incorrect acceptance.
    d. a and b above.
    e. All of the above.

18. Which of the following is included in the maximum error limit as determined under PPS sampling?

	Projected Error	Basic Precision
a.	Yes	Yes
b.	Yes	No
c.	No	Yes
d.	No	No

Use the following information to answer questions 19 and 20:

Ace is auditing the accounts receivable of Deuce using PPS sampling. Deuce's accounts receivable are recorded at $100,000. Ace establishes his exposure to the risk of incorrect acceptance at 10 percent and tolerable error at $20,000. Using these estimates, Ace calculates a sampling interval of $4,000. After performing the necessary substantive tests of details, Ace finds the following two misstatements:

Recorded Amount	Audited Amount
$3,000	$1,500
$2,000	$ 500

19. What is the total projected error?

    a. $3,000.
    b. $3,500.
    c. $4,500.
    d. $5,000.
    e. None of the above.

8/ **Variables Estimation Sampling**

20. Which of the following statements is not true?

    a. The actual error discovered in the account is $3,000.
    b. The basic precision of $9,200 would be calculated regardless of whether any errors are detected.
    c. The incremental allowance for sampling risk is $7,470.
    d. Because the maximum error limit of $16,670 is less than the tolerable error of $20,000, the auditor should decide to accept the account balance as correct.
    e. All of the above statements are true

*21. Which of the following statements is not true with respect to the use of nonstatistical sampling?

    a. The auditor may stratify the population when using nonstatistical sampling.
    b. The auditor must use her or his judgment in evaluating the results of the sample.
    c. In making a decision regarding the fairness of the account balance, the auditor compares the estimate of the error in the account balance with a tolerable error.
    d. The auditor controls exposure to sampling risk in determining sample size but not in evaluating sample results.
    e. All of the above statements are true.

*22. In a nonstatistical sampling application, the auditor may do all of the following except:

    a. Stratify the population into more homogeneous subunits.
    b. Estimate the audited value of the account using a modified form of the ratio method.
    c. Judgmentally determine the sample size and select the sample items.
    d. Judgmentally evaluate the sample results by comparing the estimated error to the tolerable error.
    e. All of the above statements are true.

8-26. How do each of the following factors affect sample size in classical variables sampling? For each, indicate whether the factor is inversely related to sample size (I), directly related to sample size (D), or unrelated to sample size (U). Note: An inverse relationship means that as the factor increases (decreases), sample size decreases (increases).

    a. Population size.
    b. Expected error.
    c. Tolerable error.
    d. Risk of incorrect rejection.
    e. Risk of incorrect acceptance.
    f. Planned precision (allowance for sampling risk).
    g. Population variability.

8-27. For each of the following cases, determine the level of planned precision (allowance for sampling risk). In all cases, TE = tolerable error, IA = risk of incorrect acceptance, and IR = risk of incorrect rejection.

    a. $TE = \$100,000$, $IA = 5$ percent, $IR = 10$ percent
    b. $TE = \$80,000$, $IA = 10$ percent, $IR = 10$ percent
    c. $TE = \$80,000$, $IA = 10$ percent, $IR = 5$ percent

8-28. For each of the following cases, determine the appropriate sample size. In all cases, N = population size, IR = risk of incorrect rejection, IA = risk of incorrect acceptance, TE = tolerable error, and SD = estimated sample standard deviation.

a. N = 2,000, IR = 10 percent, IA = 5 percent, TE = $200,000, SD = $500
b. N = 5,000, IR = 10 percent, IA = 10 percent, TE = $60,000, SD = $200
c. N = 5,000, IR = 10 percent, IA = 10 percent, TE = $60,000, SD = $50

8-29. In a mean-per-unit sampling application, assume that the auditor calculated a planned level of precision of $10,000 (based on a tolerable error of $20,000). Using this planned level of precision, along with the population size of 1,000 items, risk of incorrect rejection of 5 percent, and estimated sample standard deviation of $51, the auditor calculated a sample size of 100 customer accounts. The auditor's examination revealed an average balance of $1,000 per account and a standard deviation of $65 per account.

a. What is the auditor's estimate of the audited account balance?
b. What is the level of achieved precision? Is there a need to calculate an adjusted level of precision? Why?
c. After considering b above, what is the precision interval that should be used by the auditor to evaluate the fairness of the account balance?

8-30. Calculate the sampling interval and sample size in each of the following cases (TE = tolerable error, IA = risk of incorrect acceptance, EE = expected error, RB = recorded balance.)

a. TE = $100,000, IA = 5 percent, EE = $25,000, RB = $2,500,000
b. TE = $ 60,000, IA = 10 percent, EE = $ 6,087, RB = $ 690,000
c. TE = $ 5,000, IA = 5 percent, EE = $ 1,000, RB = $ 700,000

8-31. If the auditor calculates a sampling interval of $30,000, determine the projected error if the following errors are discovered in a PPS sampling application:

	Recorded Amount	Audited Amount
a.	$20,000	$10,000
b.	$ 5,000	$ 1,000
c.	$40,000	$35,000

8-32. Comment on each of the following statements overheard in a discussion between Joe Dumb and Mary Smart, two staff accountants.

a. "Who cares whether we use mean-per-unit estimation, difference estimation, or ratio estimation? The results will end up about the same anyway. Let's just pick a method and start working."
b. "I think we should use PPS sampling. There are a lot of errors in this account, and we need to make sure that we examine larger dollar items."
c. "Because the population we're examining has a great deal of variability, we should consider classifying the items into strata and using a stratified sampling approach. This will substantially reduce the sample size of our PPS samples."

d. "We really need to control the risk of incorrect rejection at a low level. Although incorrect acceptance is also important, we don't want the audit to go too far over budget. If we have too much exposure to the risk of incorrect rejection, we may end up doing too much testing."

8-33. One of the major decisions that should be made by the auditor is whether to use statistical or nonstatistical sampling in performing variables sampling. Also, the auditor has several choices between different types of statistical sampling methods.

Required:

a. Distinguish between statistical and nonstatistical sampling. What are the advantages and disadvantages of each approach? (You may wish to briefly refer to the introduction in the previous chapter and to Appendix B of this chapter in answering this question.)
b. Briefly define classical variables sampling and probability-proportional-to-size (PPS) sampling. What are the advantages and disadvantages of PPS sampling compared to classical variables sampling? When is each likely to be used?
c. What are the three approaches to classical variables sampling? What are the basic steps used in each approach to determine the audited value?
d. When should each of the approaches to classical variables sampling be used?
e. What are the major differences between the three approaches to classical variables sampling identified in (c) above?

8-34. Shown below are data related to the audit of China Corp.'s accounts receivable:

Recorded balance	$1,000,000
Population size	10,000 accounts
Desired risk of incorrect acceptance	10 percent
Desired risk of incorrect rejection	20 percent
Tolerable error	$ 50,000
Estimated standard deviation of audited amounts	$ 80
Estimated standard deviation of differences	$ 40

Required:

a. Using both mean-per-unit estimation and difference estimation, determine the: (1) level of planned precision, and (2) necessary sample size.
b. Ignore your answer to part (2) of item (a) regarding sample size. If the average audited value for a sample of 1,600 accounts was $90 and the standard deviation $90, what would be the precision interval? What would the auditor's conclusion be with respect to the account balance?
c. Ignore your answer to part (2) of item (a) regarding sample size. If the average audited value for a sample of 1,600 accounts was $102 and the standard deviation $70, what would be the precision interval? What would the auditor's conclusion be with respect to the account balance?
d. Ignore your answer to part (2) of item (a) regarding sample size. Assume that the auditor examined 2,000 accounts with a recorded balance of $300,000. After performing the appropriate auditing procedures, the auditor determines that the correct (audited) balance should be $350,000. What is the audited value using: (1) difference estimation, and (2) ratio estimation?

8-35. Sox Stanford, CPA, is performing a classical variables sampling plan. Sox is evaluating an inventory balance that is recorded at $300,000 and consists of 100 different items.

Using Sox's estimates of the population variability, tolerable error, and desired exposure to sampling risks, assume that Sox has determined a sample size of 30 items. The sample items were selected from the population; the total recorded amount of these accounts was $150,000. Based on the substantive tests performed by Sox, the audited amount of these items was $180,000.

Required:

a. What is the audited value calculated by Sox of the account balance using mean-per-unit estimation, difference estimation, and ratio estimation?
b. What is an explanation for the large differences between the audited values provided by these methods?
c. Provide Sox with some advice as to when he should use the various approaches to classical variables sampling.
d. If the standard deviations for the audited value and differences were $6,000 and $400, respectively, what precision interval would be calculated by Sox? (Assume a risk of incorrect acceptance of 5 percent and risk of incorrect rejection of 10 percent.)

8-36. Joel Buschbaum is performing the examination of PFW's accounts receivable. The accounts receivable were recorded at $1,500,000 and consisted of 1,000 customer accounts. For each of the following eases, calculate Joel's estimate of the audited value using: (1) mean-per-unit estimation, (2) difference estimation, and (3) ratio estimation. (RB = recorded balance of sampled accounts, n = sample size, AV = audited value of sampled accounts.)

a. RB = $900,000, n = 900, AV = $1,000,000
b. RB = $300,000, n = 300, AV = $330,000
c. RB = $500,000, n = 500, AV = $450,000
d. RB = $750,000, n = 400, AV = $900,000

8-37. Alex Jones, CPA, is using PPS sampling to examine Alto Company's accounts receivable.

Alex calculates a sample size of 100 items based on the tolerable error of $100,000, expected error of $10,000, and risk of incorrect acceptance of 5 percent. The recorded balance of Alto's accounts receivable is $2,800,000.

Required:

a. How do each of the above factors affect sample size? Verify Alex's calculation of a sample size of 100 items.
b. What is the sampling interval? Calculate the sampling interval that should be used by Alex in the audit of Alto's accounts receivable.
c. Briefly describe the procedure that Alex should use in selecting the sample if a systematic sampling approach is used.

d. If Alex found the following errors, calculate the projected errors

Account Number	Recorded Amount	Audited Amount
6	$15,000	$10,000
23	$20,000	$18,000
07	$45,000	$40,000

e. Given the errors noted in (d) above, calculate the basic precision and incremental allowance for sampling risk.

f. What is the maximum error limit? What would Alex Jones's conclusion be with respect to this account balance?

8-38. Clint White is performing the audit of Brooks, Inc., and has decided to use probability-proportional-to-size (PPS) sampling. Brooks's accounts receivable are recorded at $150,000. Clint has calculated a sample size of 30 based on a risk of incorrect acceptance of 10 percent and sent accounts receivable confirmations to these 30 customers. The following misstatements were observed in these accounts:

Account Number	Recorded Amount	Audited Amount
3	$2,500	$2,000
8	$1,000	0
16	$3,000	$1,000
22	$6,000	$4,000
29	$4,000	$3,000

Required:

a. What sampling interval was used by Clint White in this engagement?
b. What is the total projected error?
c. Calculate the basic precision and incremental allowance for sampling risk. What is the total allowance for sampling risk?
d. What is the maximum error limit?
e. If the tolerable error is $30,000, what would Clint White's conclusion be with respect to Brooks's accounts receivable?

Learning Objectives

Study of this chapter is designed to achieve several learning objectives. After studying this chapter, you should be able to:

1. Describe how computerized accounting systems differ from manual systems.
2. Identify various computer controls, including general controls and application controls.
3. Understand how computerized processing systems influence the auditor's study of internal control.
4. Discuss how the auditor uses test data, parallel simulations, and integrated test facilities to evaluate computer controls.
5. Define generalized audit software and list tasks that can be performed by generalized audit software.

9

Computer Controls and Audit Techniques

Throughout this text, we illustrate and describe the auditor's examination under the assumption that the client uses a manual accounting system to record and process its transactions. Although this discussion provides a solid overview of the nature of the auditor's tests of controls and substantive testing procedures, it ignores one important factor. Most companies utilize the computer to some extent in recording and processing their transactions. It is important to note that the use of the computer *does not* change the basic objectives and procedures relating to the auditor's examination. However, it does require certain additional considerations on the part of the auditor during an examination. The role of the computer during the audit examination is perhaps best summarized by *Statement on Auditing Standards No. 48 (SAS No. 48)*, which states, in part:

> The auditor should consider the methods the entity uses to process accounting information in planning the audit because such methods influence the design of the accounting system and the nature of the internal accounting procedures.[1]

This chapter provides a brief overview of how the client's use of the computer affects the auditor's examination. Systems in which a computer is used in recording and processing transactions are often referred to as **computer systems** or **electronic data processing (EDP) systems**. The chapter first introduces the client's use of the computer in processing transactions and contrasts a computerized accounting system with a manual accounting system. Next, controls that are commonly implemented

---

[1] American Institute of Certified Public Accountants (AICPA), *Statement on Auditing Standards No. 48*, "The Effects of Computer Processing on the Examination of Financial Statements" (New York: AICPA, 1984, AU 311.09).

in a computerized accounting system are discussed, followed by the methods used by auditors to test the effectiveness of those controls. Finally, the use of audit techniques designed to take advantage of the speed and accuracy of the computer are described.

COMPUTERIZED ACCOUNTING SYSTEMS

Batch Processing

In this chapter, we discuss how the entity's use of the computer to process its transactions affects the independent auditor's examination. **Batch processing** is characterized by an environment in which a series of like transactions is accumulated and processed simultaneously by the computer. One example of the kind of transactions normally handled by an entity using batch processing are the payroll transactions. For most entities utilizing computer processing, payroll is performed for all employees at a single time (*i.e.*, the end of the pay period). Thus, the use of batch processing for payroll is appropriate.

To illustrate how the computer can be used to process payroll transactions, Figure 9-1 contrasts a simple batch (computer) processing of payroll transactions with the manual processing of those same transactions. For purposes of simplicity, the computation of payroll taxes and other nonwage expenses is not considered in Figure 9-1.

As shown in Figure 9-1, both systems begin with a source document: employee Time Sheets. These Time Sheets will contain such information as the employee's name, number, and hours worked during the current pay period (both regular hours and overtime hours). Once the Time Sheets have been collected, the individual performing the payroll function in a manual accounting system obtains the employee's Personnel Master File. The Personnel Master File contains permanent information about the employee, such as his or her: (1) wage rate, and (2) withholding information (number of allowances and any additional withholdings requested).

Using the wage rate obtained from the employee's Personnel Master File and the number of hours worked from the Time Sheet, the individual performing the payroll function can calculate gross pay. Note that gross pay consists of amounts for both regular hours and overtime hours worked. Based on the amount of gross pay and the withholding information contained in the employee's Personnel Master File, the amount withheld from each employee's check can be determined. The difference between gross pay and total withholdings is the employee's net pay. After this procedure is repeated for each employee, a Payroll Register is prepared. The Payroll Register is a summary of the payroll data (gross pay, withholdings, net pay, and so forth) for each employee.

Contrast this series of procedures with those performed in a computerized accounting system.[2] Once the series of like transactions (employee Time Sheets) is collected in the batch processing system depicted in Figure 9-1, they are entered into the computer system and a transaction file is created. A **transaction file** consists of records that are temporary and reflect activity (in this case, hours worked)

---

[2] The manual and computerized accounting systems for payroll have been greatly simplified in Figure 9-1 to focus on differences between these systems. A more thorough discussion of these systems can be found in Chapter 14.

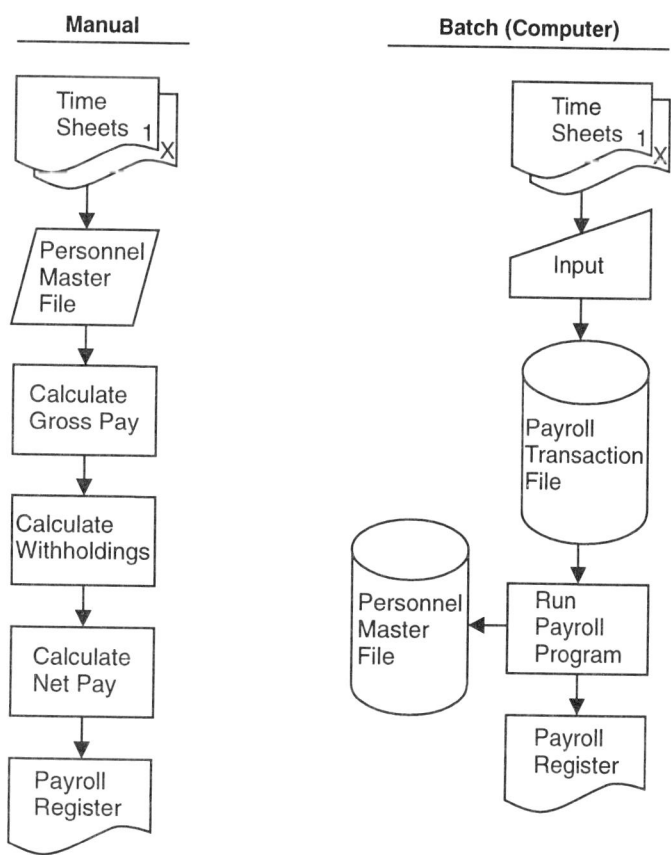

Figure 9-1: *Manual versus Computer Processing of Transactions*

over a specified period of time. In the payroll application discussed in this section, the transaction file will often resemble the information displayed below:

Employee Name	Employee Number	Regular Hours	Overtime Hours
Employee A	111-11-1111	40.0	10.0
Employee B	222-22-2222	39.0	0.0
.	.	.	.
.	.	.	.
.	.	.	.
Employee Z	999-99-9999	35.0	0.0

9/ Computer Controls and Audit Techniques

The Payroll Transaction File shown above contains the employee's name, identification number, and hours worked (both regular hours and overtime hours). Thus, it represents a summary of activity for the current pay period. Once this file has been created, payroll may be prepared using a Payroll Program. In a computer environment, the Payroll Program run begins with the transaction file created above and uses information contained in the Personnel Master File to compute gross pay, total withholdings, and net pay as in the manual system. In contrast to the transaction file, the **Personnel Master File** contains information of a more permanent nature (e.g., employee's name, number, wage rate, number of withholding allowances, and so forth). Note that this information parallels that contained in the employee's personnel file.

The relevant information in the master file is accessed by the Payroll Program through the use of an identifying field (or key field) in the transaction and master files. One example of an identifying field is the employee number. Consider the following sample master file for the computer system depicted in Figure 9-1:

Employee Name	Employee Number	No. of Withholding Allowances	Other Withholding	Regular Wage Rate	OT Wage Rate
Employee A	111-11-1111	2	0.00	10.50	15.75
Employee B	222-22-2222	1	15.00	11.00	16.50
.	.	.	.	.	.
.	.	.	.	.	.
.	.	.	.	.	.
Employee Z	999-99-9999	3	25.00	11.00	24.00

Based on the employee number in the Payroll Transaction File, the computer program will access the appropriate information in the Personnel Master File. For Employee A, the program will compute gross pay by multiplying the regular hours worked (40.0) by the regular wage rate ($10.50) and the overtime hours worked (10.0) by the overtime wage rate ($15.75). Using the number of withholding allowances (2) and the amount of other withholdings ($0.00), the program computes the total amount of withholdings from Employee A's pay. These withholdings are deducted from gross pay to obtain net pay. As in the manual system, the end product of the processing of payroll transactions is the Payroll Register.

◻ Interactive Processing

The above discussion illustrates the use of a batch computer system. The distinguishing feature of a batch system is that a series of similar transactions (e.g., payroll transactions) are collected and processed simultaneously. A second major type of system is an **interactive**, or **on-line**, **real time** (**OLRT**), system. An interactive system is characterized by processing transactions on a one-by-one basis as they occur. A common example of an interactive computerized processing system is the system used by airlines to process travel requests. As each request is received, the airline examines its records to determine the availability of seating. Then, as a customer reserves a seat for a particular flight, the airline's records are updated. Note that customer requests are not collected and processed simultaneously.

To illustrate the use of an interactive computer system, consider the differences between a manual and an EDP system for processing credit sales. While the manual accounting system for processing credit sales is discussed in extensive detail in Chapter 10, we will highlight a few key elements of this system for comparative purposes. These elements are summarized in Figure 9-2.[3]

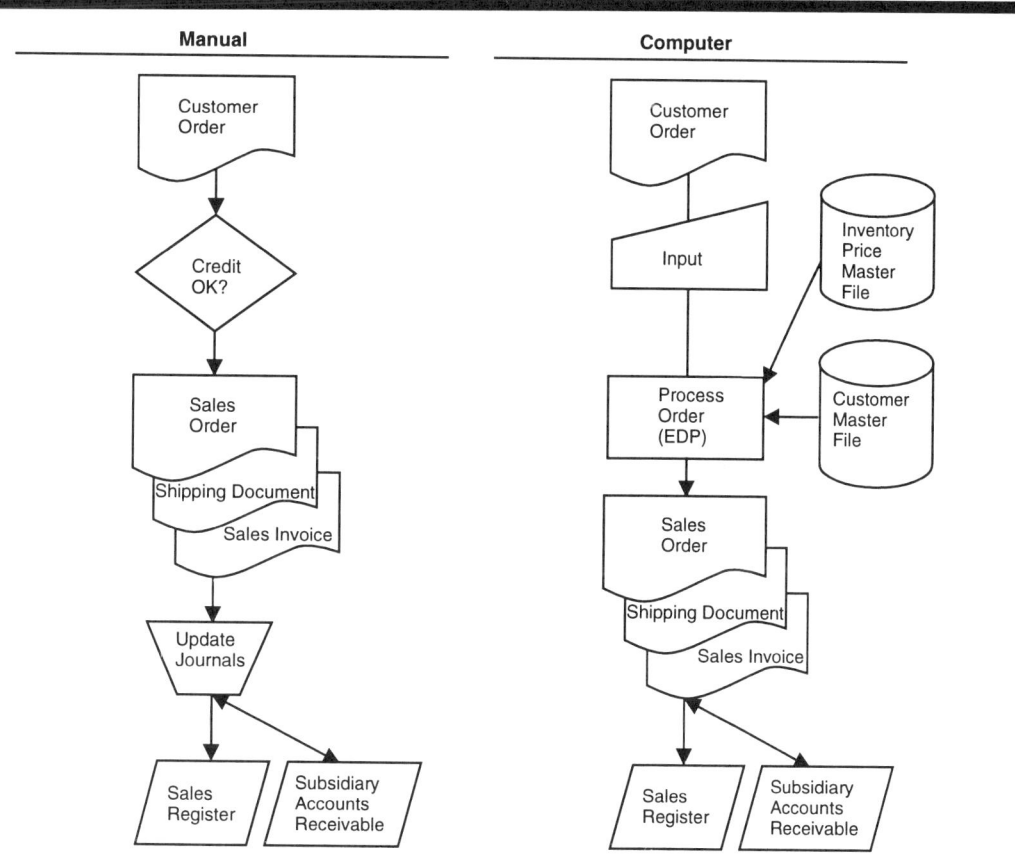

Figure 9-2: *Manual versus Interactive Processing of Transactions*

In the manual system illustrated in Figure 9-2, when customer orders are received by telephone, a "hard-copy" **Customer Order** is prepared by the Order Department. This order acknowledges that a customer has requested the purchase of inventory from the company. Next, client personnel determine that the customer is approved and has not exceeded his or her credit limit. Assuming that

---

[3] The manual and EDP systems depicted in Figure 9-2 are highly simplified to focus on differences associated with these two types of systems. Chapter 10 provides a more detailed depiction of these systems.

no problems are noted, a **Sales Order** is now prepared. The Sales Order serves as an authorization to sell merchandise to a customer on account. Once the Sales Order is prepared, the company will send the goods to the customer and bill the customer for these goods, preparing a **Shipping Document** and **Sales Invoice**. For simplicity, the detailed steps leading up to preparation of these documents are omitted in this discussion: they are described in more detail in Chapter 10.

Two journals (or registers) are updated for the sale on account: the Sales Register (to reflect the sale) and the subsidiary accounts receivable (to reflect the increase in a customer's account balance). These journals/registers are updated manually using information obtained from copies of the Sales Order and Sales Invoice.

An **interactive computer system** combines many of the above steps. When Customer Orders are received, the customer's account number and quantity and types of items are entered directly into the computer terminal. Note that a manual copy of the Sales Order is not prepared in an EDP system. After customer information is entered, the Customer Master File is accessed to determine that: (1) the order has been received from an established customer, and (2) the customer's credit limit is not exceeded by the purchase. This step, while performed by the computer, parallels the credit check performed by client personnel in the manual accounting system.

Assuming that no problems are noted in verifying the customer's credit, inventory prices from the Inventory Price Master File are used along with the quantity of items ordered to prepare a Sales Invoice. The quantities ordered serve as the basis for preparing a Shipping Document. Once this document has been prepared, a "hold" is placed on the inventory, reserving the items ordered for the customer. Using information from the Inventory Price Master File (the sales price and cost of items) and transaction file (quantities ordered and customer account number), the Sales Register and subsidiary accounts receivable records are simultaneously updated to reflect the sale made to the customer. Although these documents and records are all created and updated in a manual system, the records are updated instantaneously when an EDP system is utilized.

◻ Batch Processing versus Interactive Processing

The major difference between batch and interactive processing systems is that the time interval between the occurrence of a transaction and the processing of that transaction is eliminated in an interactive system. This difference has implications for companies in their ability to prevent and detect processing errors. For example, in batch systems, transactions can be examined and key totals (referred to as **control totals**) can be calculated prior to the input of those transactions. As described later in this chapter, these totals can be compared to computer-generated totals to identify whether any errors occurred during the input stage. The importance of data entry (input) in computer systems makes controls relating to the ability of client personnel to access computer files (such as passwords or other security codes) and accurately input data extremely critical.

> **CHAPTER CHECKPOINTS**
>
> 9-1. Define EDP systems. How does the client's use of an EDP system affect the overall objectives of the audit examination?
>
> 9-2. Define batch processing. What is an example of a type of transaction that would be processed using a batch processing system?
>
> 9-3. Distinguish between transaction files and master files.
>
> 9-4. Define interactive processing. What is an example of a type of transaction that would be processed using an interactive processing system?
>
> 9-5. What is the major difference between batch and interactive processing systems?

◻ Computerized versus Manual Processing

The above discussion either identifies or implies several important differences between the computerized (either batch or interactive) and manual processing of transactions. These differences are briefly discussed below.

Existence of the Transaction Trail. One difference involved with using a computer in processing transactions is that many of the steps performed in a manual system are eliminated entirely or performed by the computer. The result is that the "trail" of documentary evidence from the initiation of a transaction to its ultimate recording either does not exist or exists only for a short time. For example, in an EDP system, information from source documents must be transcribed and entered in machine-readable form. In some cases, the actual source documents are not maintained by client personnel once the appropriate information has been entered into the computer system.

Alternatively, in an interactive computer environment, employees may enter data directly into the computer system, eliminating the preparation of source documents commonly used in a manual accounting system. Recall that in an interactive computer system client personnel usually enter Customer Orders directly into the computer and process orders without preparing a hard copy of a Sales Order. Differences of this nature affect the auditor's examination, as they may impede her or his ability to inspect documentary or other evidence relating to certain classes of transactions.

Frequency and Type of Processing Errors. A typical feature of a manual accounting system is that the client's employees are heavily involved in all aspects of processing the related transactions. Human involvement implies a higher frequency of errors than that associated with a computerized accounting system. To illustrate, the various calculations involved with the payroll system described earlier introduce several potential mathematical errors (e.g., miscalculating gross pay or withholdings). In a manual system, these errors would occur at random points and result from factors such as employee fatigue. In contrast, an EDP system processes each transaction uniformly. As a result, any calculation error(s) are identical across all transactions. For example, if the computer program contains an error (such as adding withholdings to gross pay to calculate net pay), all transactions are affected in the same manner.

This characteristic of an EDP system indicates that auditors only need to test once for each potential type of processing error. That is, if the auditor tests the logic of the computer program used to process payroll transactions, she or he can be confident that all transactions have been processed in the same manner. In a manual system, the auditor must be aware of the possibility that random errors have entered the accounting system. In general, the possibility of random errors will increase the number of transactions that need to be examined by the auditor to ensure that a representative sample has been selected.

A second major difference related to the type and frequency of errors in an EDP system is the need to enter input data into computer-readable form. For the payroll example, a transaction file containing payroll information must be created from the source documents (Time Sheets). Similarly, the interactive system used to process sales on account requires personnel to enter customer information into a transaction file. Obviously, the need to input data into the computer system introduces an additional type of error that does not have a counterpart in the manual system: errors associated with keypunching (or inputting) data.

To reduce the rate of these errors, companies normally implement **input controls** into the logic of their computer programs. (These controls will be discussed in a subsequent section of this chapter.) The auditor's study and evaluation of internal control in a computerized accounting environment will include extensive tests of the operating effectiveness of these input controls. Similar tests are not necessary in a manual accounting environment because there is no need to input data into machine-readable form (and thus establish and maintain input controls).

Centralized Processing of Transactions. A third major difference introduced when a computer is used is that transactions are centrally processed by the Computer (or EDP) Department. One problem with centralized processing is that many incompatible functions are often combined. For example, recall from Chapter 5 that effective segregation of duties involves separating the: (1) authorization of a transaction, (2) recording of a transaction, and (3) custody of the related asset. In a computer environment, the recording function is often "shared" between User Departments and the Computer Department. To reduce the possibility that incompatible functions are combined in a computerized accounting system, companies usually establish segregation of duties both: (1) between User Departments and the EDP Department, and (2) within the EDP department. This segregation of duties is often considered the most important control instituted in a computerized accounting environment and is described later in this chapter.

Alteration of Data or Files. A final difference related to an EDP system is that permanent data can often be altered without detection through normal inspection by the client. In the payroll example discussed above, the master file information will normally be maintained as long "strings" of numbers. If this information is somehow altered, it may be impossible for employees to detect the modification without extensive investigation. This introduces the possibility that unauthorized access to this information may lead to irregularities being perpetrated and not being detected for a long time. Also, in an interactive system, the inability to visually verify changes to master files may result in the client inadvertently failing to update its Inventory Master Files to reflect increased sales prices. This may result in the use of outdated sales prices and, eventually, lost sales revenue.

In response to these problems, the auditor will undertake additional precautions to ensure the validity and reliability of any permanent information maintained in computer master files. Procedures performed in this regard include verifying all authorized changes to master file information and periodically reconciling master file information maintained in machine-readable form to hard (paper) copies of that information.

Summary: EDP versus Manual Processing. The differences introduced when the computer is used in processing transactions are summarized in Figure 9-3. In addition, the effect of these differences on the auditor's examination are also noted.

	Difference	Effect on Audit Examination
1.	Transaction trails exist for shorter periods of time.	Auditors may have limited ability to examine some forms of documentary evidence.
2.	Errors in an EDP system are uniform across all transactions.	Auditors can restrict their tests to one transaction or occurrence of a potential error.
3.	Input errors are unique to EDP systems.	Auditors must test the operating effectiveness of controls designed to prevent and detect input errors.
4.	Transactions are processed centrally by an EDP department in a computerized system.	Auditors should examine the operations of the EDP department to verify the appropriate segregation of duties.
5.	Permanent information is easier to alter without being detected in an EDP environment.	Auditors should periodically verify the accuracy of permanent information in an EDP environment.

Figure 9-3: *Differences in EDP and Manual Processing*

The following excerpt illustrates a difference in the nature of manual and computerized processing.

> After implementing a computerized system for accounts payable, Niagara Mowhawk Power Corporation of New York reduced the number of its accounts payable personnel from 24 to 12. However, an unanticipated result of doing so was overpaying its vendors by hundreds of thousands of dollars because of mistakes that would have been detected by human workers. For example, Niagara paid $10,680 twice to a maintenance company because two Purchase Orders with slightly different numbers were issued for the same service. Richard Shaffer, director of Niagara's internal operations, noted that "a payables clerk with long experience would have spotted the error. A computer only spots an error if it's programmed specifically to catch the exact mistake."[4]

---

[4] "Many Firms Cut Staff in Accounts Payable and Pay a Steep Price," *The Wall Street Journal* (September 3, 1996), A1, A6.

> **CHAPTER CHECKPOINTS**
>
> 9-6. List five major types of differences between computerized and manual processing.
>
> 9-7. What are the primary differences in the types of errors that occur in computerized and manual processing systems?
>
> 9-8. What types of segregation of duties are normally implemented in a computerized accounting system?

COMPUTER CONTROLS

The use of the computer in an accounting system does not change the objectives or essential characteristics of internal control discussed in Chapter 5. Both manual and computerized accounting systems are comprised of attributes and procedures designed to achieve the objectives. In manual systems, control objectives are achieved through manual procedures and segregation of functions. In computerized systems, however, many procedures previously performed manually are performed within computer programs and systems software. Furthermore, because accounting data and transactions are processed centrally, various accounting functions become centralized. The elimination of manual procedures and centralization of functions increases the opportunity for errors and irregularities, unless compensating controls are implemented. These compensating controls are known as **computer controls**. Some computer controls are programmed procedures within computer programs and systems software. Others are manual procedures, such as the use of control totals and review of output, often referred to as computer controls because they are related to the use of the computer in the accounting system.

SAS No. 48[5] identifies two major categories of controls in a computerized accounting environment: general controls and application controls. An overview of these controls is provided in Figure 9-4. These controls are discussed in detail in the following sections.

General Controls

SAS No. 48 notes that **general controls** are those computer controls relating to all applications and uses of the computer. These controls are not unique to any one application and are intended to reduce the possibility of errors and irregularities that may affect a number of accounts and classes of transactions. The five categories of general controls are discussed below.

Organization of the Computer Department. The use of a computer affects the basic organization of most businesses. In accounting systems where a computer is not used, the processing

---

[5] American Institute of Certified Public Accountants (AICPA), *Statement on Auditing Standards No. 48*, "The Effects of Computer Processing on the Examination of Financial Statements" (New York: AICPA, 1984).

General Controls

1. Organization of the Computer Department.
2. Application development and maintenance controls.
3. Hardware controls.
4. Access to computer equipment, data files, and programs.
5. Data or procedural controls.

Application Controls

1. Input controls.
2. Processing controls.
3. Output controls.
4. Controls over master file information.

Figure 9-4: *Computer Controls Identified by SAS No. 48*

of data relating to a particular business function, such as sales, is normally centralized within one department under one department head. In computerized accounting systems, the responsibility is shared with the Computer Department, which processes and usually maintains custody of the information on computer files. The Computer Department will usually share this responsibility with several different departments, known as **User Departments**, that utilize its processing services. Thus, although most accounting information will be processed centrally, the responsibility for processing is decentralized, and both the Computer and User Departments must develop and maintain computer controls.

This shared responsibility for processing transactions makes the organizational location of the Computer Department critical. In describing the location of the Computer Department within the organization, it is important to emphasize that the Computer Department should not be under the direct influence of any single User Department. Otherwise, the user may have authority to circumvent established controls. Organizational independence of the data processing function from the User Departments creates a framework within which user controls may be performed in addition to data processing controls.

In addition to the organizational position of the Computer Department, certain functions should be separated within the Computer Department. Figure 9-5 illustrates a sample organizational plan for a Computer Department. As shown therein, three main functions should be organizationally separate within the Computer Department: **applications and programming**, **operations**, and **data control**. The basic responsibilities of these functions, along with those of the Steering Committee and EDP Manager, are briefly identified below.

Steering Committee. The Steering Committee should be composed of a senior executive from each functional area of the organization that is affected by data processing. The EDP Manager should be

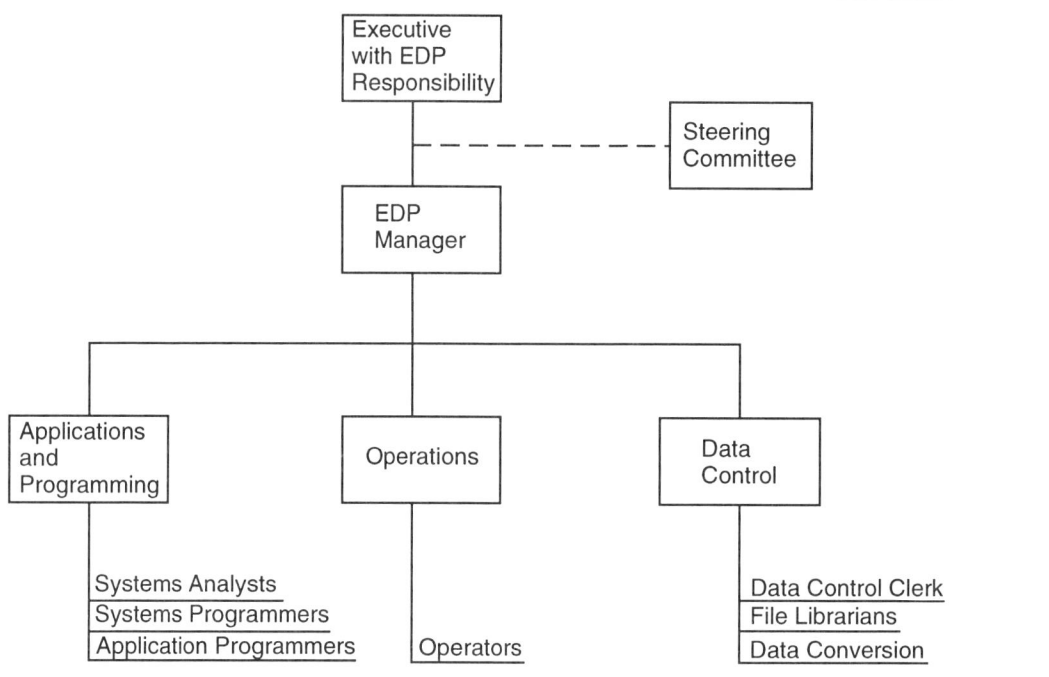

Figure 9-5: *Basic Organizational Structure of a Computer Department*

on the Steering Committee. If the organization has an Internal Audit Department, it is advisable that a representative of that department be a member of the committee. The purpose of the Steering Committee is to:

1. Review, evaluate, and approve planned computer systems and applications.
2. Evaluate and monitor progress in developing the computer systems and applications.
3. Evaluate and approve proposals concerning the acquisition of EDP equipment and facilities.

EDP Manager. The manager of the Computer Department directs the overall operation of the department. The manager should report to a top executive of the company, such as the Controller, Financial Vice-President, or Information Systems Vice-President. The EDP Manager is responsible for providing managerial guidance to the systems and programming, operations, and data control staffs, and for developing standards, policies, priorities, and short- and long-range plans for the department.

Applications and Programming. This function consists of Systems Analysts, Systems Programmers, and Application Programmers. Systems Analysts are responsible for evaluating and designing new or improved computer systems. Systems Programmers maintain the software that controls the hardware and the application programs. Application Programmers prepare, test, and update the application programs required to accomplish user objectives. They prepare program flowcharts in accordance with the specifications provided by the Systems Analysts and then code the required programs in source languages. The programs are then tested using test data, which consist of genuine or dummy records and transactions.

Computer Operations. Computer Operators are responsible for running the computer and executing jobs in accordance with operator instructions and a job schedule. In most cases, the Operations Manager or Supervisor will prepare the job schedule, although this may be done by the EDP Manager in smaller installations. The operators execute jobs via a computer console, which enables them to communicate with the computer's operating system.

Data Control. Data Control is responsible for controlling the timely receipt of data for computer processing and the distribution of computer output to User Departments. In addition, the function usually includes the conversion (keypunching) of data into machine-readable form (in a batch system) and the maintenance of a computer file library. When output is received, the Data Control Group reconciles it to the input, reviews it for accuracy, and supervises its distribution to users.

Application Development and Maintenance Controls.

Application development includes the activities of the Systems Analysts and Programmers, who develop computer systems and applications. Good system and application development requires documentation, management and user review and approval procedures, technical review and approval, rigorous testing, and involvement of the internal and external auditors. Without these, applications may result in inaccurate recordkeeping.

During the process of developing systems and applications, the following types of documentation are usually prepared:

1. **System and application program flowcharts and narratives**, which describe the purpose of the programs and show the sequence of logical operations they perform and the flow of data through the system.

2. **Record and file layouts**, which identify the size and relative location of accounting data stored in each record and the combination of record types within a given file.

3. **Operator instructions**, which guide the computer operators in selecting the files used by the program, handling program halt and error conditions, and providing instructions to the computer's operating system.

4. **Program listings**, which contain the complete program in source code, as well as any changes to the original program listing.

5. **Test data**, including a description of the testing, the data used to verify the accuracy of the application programs, and the results of testing.

6. **Application approval and change sheets**, which evidence approval of the application programs and changes to them, test data, and results from testing program changes.

Documentation is important because it is frequently the best source of information on control features within computer programs. Therefore, the review of computer controls may depend, in part, on adequate documentation. Furthermore, a lack of proper documentation can make the installation dependent on the individuals who prepared the programs, because they would be the only persons capable of maintaining them.

Often, after a system is implemented, it becomes necessary to make changes to the various programs. The process of requesting, approving, testing, and implementing the changes is known as program maintenance. Changes to application programs should be requested and approved in writing and subjected to testing before final implementation. Documentation should be updated to reflect the changes.

Hardware Controls. Computer manufacturers build features into their equipment that will detect and sometimes correct machine-based errors. Most of these features operate on the principle of adding an extra element to a machine process or data code to detect any error that can occur. The following are the more common hardware controls:

1. **Parity Check.** The computer processes data in groups of binary digits (bits) of "1" and "0," which denote alphabetic and numeric characters. An extra, or parity, bit is added to bring the sum of the "1" bits to an even (even parity check) or odd (odd parity check) number, depending on the computer equipment. The parity check is employed while data is being moved to ensure that the number of bits remains constant.
2. **Valid Character Check.** Established patterns are used to identify and accept valid bit combinations for input and output devices. If nonconforming combinations are detected, an error condition is created.
3. **Echo Check.** A remote terminal transmits a signal to the main computer. Before accepting the information it is returned to the sending terminal to verify that the information has been properly transmitted.

Access to Computer Equipment, Data Files, and Programs. Computer data files and programs cannot be altered without the use of computer equipment. Therefore, controlling access to computer equipment is an extremely important control consideration. One of the basic objectives of internal control (safeguarding assets) stresses that access to assets should be permitted only in accordance with management's authorization. In EDP environments, assets take the form of the accounting information (data) on computer files, the computer programs, and the computer equipment itself.

In general, only operations personnel should be allowed in the computer area. There are several methods of restricting access. These may include the use of a locked door to which only authorized personnel have keys or the use of sliding doors that have cipher locks or require magnetic cards. Proper segregation of duties helps to enforce access controls. Programmers, for example, should not be allowed to operate the computer, and operators should not be allowed to program or have access to program documentation.

Control over access to data files is important because it helps ensure that the correct file is used in an application and that files are restricted to authorized users. These controls should be established over both transaction files and master files. Master files are particularly important because errors in master file data can cause errors in the processing of transactions against the master file.

Other control techniques that may be used are passwords, special software librarian packages, and job accounting. It is becoming increasingly popular to establish security systems over files so that the user of the file must not only know its name, but also a security code or password. In controlling access to program libraries, passwords are commonly used in conjunction with special software; this prevents unauthorized attempts to change programs. Job accounting, which provides an audit trail of machine activity in the form of reports of jobs run on the computer, can be used to identify unauthorized execution of programs or use of program libraries.

Data or Procedural Controls. The importance of computer data dictates that all important files and programs be "backed up" to reduce potential losses from accidental erasure or intentional vandalism. In maintaining back-up copies of files and programs, the copies should normally be stored in a separate physical location from the duplicates (often referred to as **off-site storage**). It is not uncommon for these programs and files to be stored in fire-proof locations, to prevent total loss of information in case of fire. A popular method of backing up files is maintaining older generations of files to re-create any that are lost and/or destroyed. One method is known as the **grandfather-father-son** principle of file retention.

The grandfather-father-son principle of file retention is illustrated in Figure 9-6. The basic notion underlying this retention system is that files may be re-created if they are lost or destroyed. For example, suppose that after Master File 2 has been updated, the updated master file (Master File 3) is destroyed. As long as both Master File 2 and Transaction File 2 have been saved, Master File 3 can be re-created by a second updating run. In most cases, it is advisable to save a third "generation" of file (Master File 1 and Transaction File 1) in the event that Master File 2 becomes lost or destroyed.

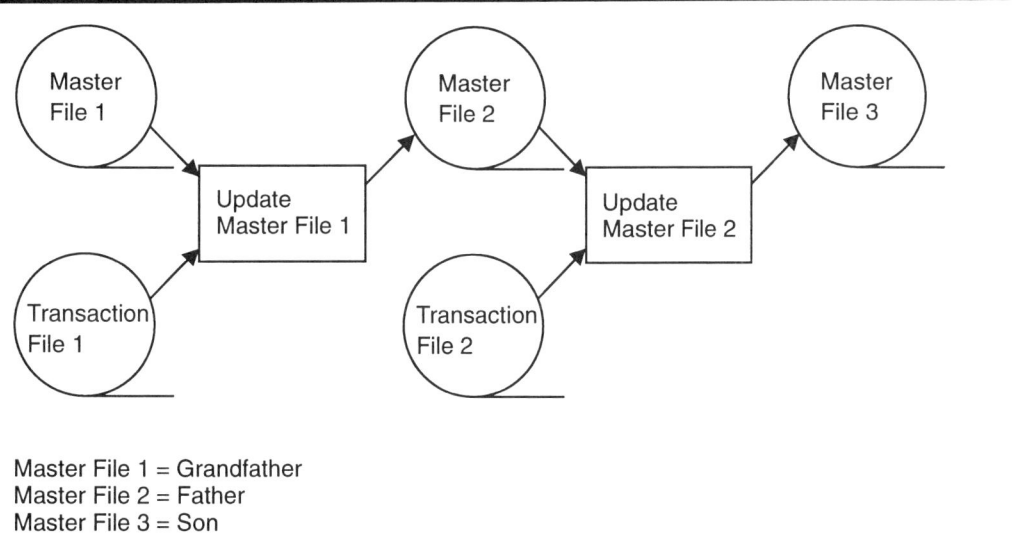

Master File 1 = Grandfather
Master File 2 = Father
Master File 3 = Son

Figure 9-6: *Grandfather-Father-Son File Retention*

Data controls also include policies and procedures implemented to allow files and programs to be readily identified by computer department personnel for easy use. External and internal labels should also be used. Operators can check an external label, affixed to magnetic tape and disk files, to see if it is the correct file. There are no specific requirements about how much information should be on the label. Internal labels, such as header labels containing information that identifies the file, can be checked by the operating system or application programs to help ensure that the correct file is used. Many installations also use another internal label, known as a **trailer label**. This is a record at the end of a file that contains control information, such as the number of records on the file and total dollar amounts.

WHERE ARE THE GENERAL CONTROLS?

Discussed below are examples of missing or inadequate general controls in practice.

▶ Internal auditors noticed that a computer system could not "lock out" users who repeatedly tried to access the system with an invalid password. Management decided not to produce a report of invalid password entries because they felt that producing this report would tie up the system for too long. A thorough investigation by internal auditors identified five employees who were attempting to hack into the system; now, the company produces and reviews a report of invalid password entries on a daily basis.[6]

▶ While walking through the office after the close of business, an internal auditor noticed that several of the computer terminals were active. Inquiry of management indicated that these terminals were allowed to remain active because of the extensive time required to log on and off the system throughout the day. The next day, the auditor noticed that these same terminals were active and had not been logged off overnight. The auditor recommended that an automatic log off be implemented when terminals were inactive for over 30 minutes.[7]

▶ A company was selling several of its used magnetic tapes after deciding to discontinue its data processing operations. The internal auditor suggested that these tapes be erased prior to being sold, because they contained some sensitive client data. At first, the company refused, stating that the tapes could not be read by others. After repeated requests, the tapes were erased prior to sale. It was a good thing—the high bidder for the tapes was a recently-terminated company programmer who knew how to read them.[8]

▶ A Computer Programmer who had access to certain unauthorized files programmed a bank's interest calculation to take five cents in interest from each customer's account over $500. The programmer was able to defalcate over $2,000 using this scheme before he was caught and terminated.[9]

▶ The auditor of a bank found that passwords were not assigned to individuals, but to departments; in addition, all employees in a particular department used the same password. Despite the fact that employees are routinely transferred from one department to another, passwords had not been changed in over two years. Ten employees who had been transferred had knowledge of passwords that would allow them to manipulate assets on loan applications and conceal this manipulation. Now, the company assigns passwords to individuals and changes these passwords upon the transfer of employees.[10]

---

[6] "Hacking Into the System," *Internal Auditor* (August 1996), 69.
[7] "It Pays to Alter One's Schedule," *Internal Auditor* (August 1996), 65.
[8] "Who Has the Mag Tapes Now?," *Internal Auditor* (April 1993), 69.
[9] "Salami Slices," *Internal Auditor* (October 1994), 69.
[10] "Change Those Passwords," *Internal Auditor* (October 1993), 73.

> **CHAPTER CHECKPOINTS**
>
> 9-9. Define general controls. What are the major categories of general controls?
>
> 9-10. What functions should ordinarily be separated in the Computer Department?
>
> 9-11. List the major duties of the following functions or individuals.
>
>   a. Steering Committee.
>   b. EDP Manager.
>   c. Applications and Programming.
>   d. Computer Operations.
>   e. Data Control.
>
> 9-12. What are hardware controls? List some examples of hardware controls.
>
> 9-13. Over what elements in a computerized accounting system should access controls be established?
>
> 9-14. What is the grandfather-father-son principle of file retention?

☐ Application Controls

The Computer Department performs specific tasks for users through computer applications, which are a group of related computer programs and data files designed to accomplish the accounting objectives of User Departments, such as generating Sales Invoices. Any computer application, even the most complex, can be viewed in terms of the accounting information it processes. In fact, regardless of the type of data processed or the kind of equipment used, all data processing usually involves these three basic functions:

1. **Input Function.** The acceptance of information (source data) from other parts of the system.
2. **Processing Function.** The calculation of data or generation of new data.
3. **Output Function.** The return of information (data on output reports, documents, transaction files, or terminals) to other parts of the accounting system.

In any application of the computer, several critical points exist where controls are necessary. First, when inputting data upon receipt of a Customer Order, it is important that controls are established to ensure the accuracy and validity of the input. For example, in the interactive computerized system over sales discussed at the beginning of this chapter, controls should identify instances where customer numbers have been improperly entered by client personnel as the data are input. Next, assuming that data are properly input, the logic of the computer program should be periodically checked to determine that these programs are properly processing transactions. Finally, controls should exist to ensure that output is examined for reasonableness by the data control group and that master file information is periodically examined for accuracy. Controls of this nature are referred to as application controls because they relate to particular uses of the computer in processing transactions. These controls are discussed in detail below.

Input Controls. Input controls are designed to provide reasonable assurance that information accepted from other areas of the accounting system is complete, accurate, and authorized. Different types of input controls include check digits, control totals, validity checks, and error correction routines.

Check Digits. A **check digit** is a number that is algorithmically calculated based on a particular numerical record (such as an employee's identification number). After the check digit is calculated, it is appended to the numerical record from which it originates. As the numerical record (original record with the check digit appended) is entered, the computer program will recalculate the check digit, based on the contents of the original numerical record. If the check digit appended to the record differs from the computer's calculation, an error message is transmitted. Check digits help ensure the accurate entry of numerical records.

▶ **Example:** *Check Digits*

To illustrate the calculation of a check digit, consider the use of the "Modulus 11 Prime Number Method."[11] Assume that a new customer has ordered merchandise and has been approved to establish an account. If that customer is assigned account number 1234, a check digit can be calculated as follows:

Account Number	1		2		3		4		
Prime Number	1		3		5		7		
Product	1	+	6	+	15	+	28	=	50
Multiple of 11 exceeding product									(55)
Check Digit									5

This customer will be assigned an account number of 12345. The last digit appended to the original account number is the check digit. When the customer number is input by client personnel, a computer routine will verify the proper calculation of the check digit. Any cases where a check digit does not match the account number associated with that check digit indicates that an input error has occurred.

Control Totals. A second type of input control is the use of control totals. Three examples of control totals are **record counts, batch totals**, and **hash totals**. When using record counts, the number of records (transactions) is counted prior to input. After the records have been input, the computer will indicate the number of records it has received. Therefore, record counts will enable the person inputting data to ensure that: (1) all records have been input, and (2) no record has been input more

---

[11] See J. G. Burch, Jr., F. R. Strater, Jr., and G. Grudniski, *Information Systems: Theory and Practice* (Santa Barbara, CA: Hamilton Publishing, 1979), 181.

than once. Note that record counts do not ensure the accurate input of records; they merely allow the person inputting data to verify that the correct number of records has been input.

A means of verifying that the records have been input accurately is through the use of batch totals and hash totals. The use of these controls requires the person inputting the data to calculate the total of numeric fields being input prior to keypunching the data. After the records have been input, the computer will also calculate the totals for the numeric fields. The person inputting the records then compares the computer's totals with the manual totals to determine that records have been correctly input. **Batch totals** represent totals that have significance (e.g., the number of hours worked and total pay). **Hash totals**, on the other hand, represent totals of numeric fields that are not of any interest, such as social security numbers or employee identification numbers.

The use of control totals is illustrated in Figure 9-7. When using control totals, it is important to remember that these are totals that are manually determined by User Departments prior to input. Once data are input, the computer program recalculates these totals. They are then compared with the manually-calculated totals, with any differences representing input error. The only difference between batch totals and hash totals is that the former represents a total of some significance.

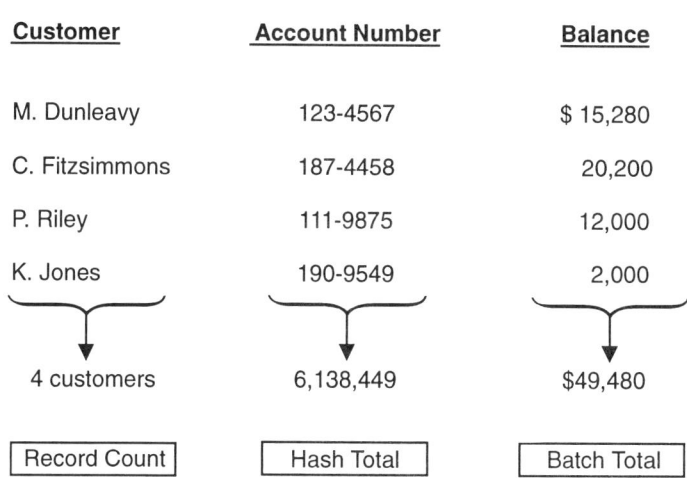

Figure 9-7: *Illustration of Control Totals*

Limits or Reasonableness Tests. **Limits** or **reasonableness tests** compare the input data to some preestablished criteria to identify possible input errors. These controls normally identify input errors by specifying levels that are extremely high or low. For example, a common reasonableness test for a payroll application is that hours worked cannot exceed some total (e.g., greater than 80 per week). For input fields having a fixed size (e.g., all customer numbers are five characters long), limits or reasonableness tests can also be used to identify instances where an improper number of characters has been entered. In any case, like other input controls, the major purpose of limits or reasonableness tests is to ensure that data input or received from other departments are accurate and complete.

Validity Checks. When utilized as an input control, validity checks evaluate the input field to determine the appropriateness of its size and format. Some examples of common validity checks include checking the input fields for:

- Inappropriate characters (*i.e.*, a numeric character in an alphabetic field).
- The correct number of characters (*i.e.*, entering five characters in a nine-character field).
- Proper data format (*i.e.*, ensuring that dashes or other characters are entered in the appropriate field).

Error Correction Routines. A final type of input control relates to the procedures established by the organization for handling input errors. While this may seem beyond the scope of input controls at first, the policies and procedures implemented for error correction will ultimately ensure that all errors have been corrected and that input is therefore accurate and complete. Although interactive computer applications will identify errors as the transactions are processed, batch systems can handle errors by: (1) rejecting the entire batch, (2) rejecting only erroneous transactions within the batch, or (3) processing all transactions and identifying erroneous transactions using a suspense account or code.

Effective internal control over input errors dictates that, regardless of the method used to handle errors, responsibility should be fixed for error correction and timely resubmission. Any identified errors should be returned to user departments for correction and resubmission.

Figure 9-8 summarizes the input controls described in this section and provides some examples of controls commonly implemented in computerized processing systems.

Check Digits	Mathematical digit appended to a numeric field (*e.g.*, appending a digit to a customer's account number).
Record Counts	Manual total of the number of records prior to input.
Batch Totals	Total gross pay, total hours worked, total accounts receivable balances.
Hash Totals	Total of employee numbers, total of department numbers.
Limits or Reasonableness Tests	Hours worked > 90 per week.
Validity Checks	Hours worked contains only numeric characters.
Error Correction	Procedures to handle input errors and allow for immediate correction and resubmission.

Figure 9-8: *Sample Input Controls*

> **UNCERTAIN PENSIONS**[12]
>
> The lack of input controls resulted in input errors in the computerized processing of pension payments for an unnamed company. As an example, pension checks totalling $28,000 were mailed to a pensioner who had been deceased for over five years. By having an input control that identified employee numbers for invalid (or deceased) pension participants, these checks would not have been issued in error.

Processing Controls. Processing controls are designed to provide reasonable assurance that accounting information calculated or generated by the application is accurate. Because the generation or calculation of new data is often done in a manner that is difficult for the user to verify, there are often minimal manual controls in this area. When manual controls are present, they generally consist of someone performing tests over a limited number of items that have been calculated or generated, such as a review for reasonableness, manual recalculation of detail items, and manual recalculation of totals.

In some cases, programmed checks may be performed over calculated items, but because they are usually subject to the same application development criteria as the original calculation, they do not provide the independence found in manual tests performed by the user. Furthermore, they can be difficult to identify and test to determine entity compliance. In general, programmed checks are similar to edits performed over input data. Typical checks include:

1. Verifying the proper format (numeric, significant digits).
2. Verifying the range or sign of resulting values (positive, negative, zero balance).
3. Matching data to a set of allowable entries.
4. Performing limits and reasonableness tests.
5. Recalculating transactions or components using alternative methods.

Output Controls. Output controls are designed to provide reasonable assurance that accounting information returned to other parts of the system is complete and accurate. Output can include printed reports, documents, special forms, and transaction (temporary) files. Obviously, the completeness and accuracy of output cannot be verified unless the physical output item is properly distributed to users. The Data Control Group should have responsibility for distributing the output to the appropriate users and should maintain a routing or distribution schedule.

Prior to distribution of output to User Departments, the Data Control Group should review the computer output for reasonableness. Although complete recalculation is normally not considered necessary, data control may consider performing the following procedures:

---

[12] "Uncertain Pensions," *Internal Auditor* (June 1994), 76.

▶ Recalculate selected items and compare to results from computer output.

▶ Visually scan output for reasonableness, format, and completeness.

In distributing output, the client should take appropriate steps to ensure that output is only distributed to those departments and personnel that are authorized to receive the related information.

MANUALLY FOOT THE TRIAL BALANCE?[13]

Auditors should be careful to place too much reliance on computer processing. After footing the general ledger, the auditor noted a $300,000 discrepancy between his total and the client's computer listing. A detailed examination of the program code revealed the following line of code: "IF CODE = RINKY DINK, THEN ..." This line of program code triggered six $50,000 payments to the company's Treasurer, who was acting in collusion with the Data Processing Manager to commit a defalcation involving payroll.

Master File Information. As previously mentioned, there are two basic types of computer files: transactions files and master files.

The audit significance of master files is that many amounts later calculated or generated by the application depend upon the data contained in the master file. The accuracy of invoice amounts, for example, depends upon the accuracy of the unit sales price for each part number stored in the Inventory Master File. Therefore, master file controls are designed to provide reasonable assurance that the data stored in master files remain authorized, accurate, and complete.

To ensure that the data on master files remain authorized, accurate, and complete, User Departments generally obtain periodic reports containing the contents of the master file. An aged trial balance of accounts receivable or a listing of current customers, for example, may be used to ensure that customer information on the Customer Master File is authorized, accurate, and complete. Alternatively, User Departments may obtain a listing of all changes to the master file. Another important control is balancing the number of records and dollar amounts contained on the file to other accounting records. Where separate generations, or versions, of the file are maintained, there should be procedures to verify that the correct version is used in processing transactions. Computer Department verification consists of adequate library procedures and internal and external file label checking. User verification of the correct file version consists of a detailed examination of application output and periodic review of master file contents.

---

[13] "Manually Foot the Trial Balance?," *Internal Auditor* (June 1994), 78.

> **CHAPTER CHECKPOINTS**
>
> 9-15. Define application controls. What are the major categories of application controls?
>
> 9-16. Define the following:
>
>   a. Check digit.
>   b. Record count.
>   c. Batch total.
>   d. Hash total.
>
> 9-17. What are limits or reasonableness tests? Give some examples of limits or reasonableness tests.
>
> 9-18. List some typical programmed checks used to verify the accurate processing of data.
>
> 9-19. List output controls commonly implemented in the computerized processing of data.

EVALUATING COMPUTER CONTROLS AND ASSESSING CONTROL RISK

As noted throughout our discussion in this chapter, the client's use of the computer in processing its transactions introduces additional considerations to the auditor beyond those in a manual system. The computer and the corresponding programs used by the client to process and record transactions become an important component of that client's internal control. Accordingly, the auditor must study and evaluate computer controls to determine the extent to which they are functioning in preventing and/or detecting errors. The auditor's responsibility for studying and evaluating these computer controls is similar to his or her responsibility for the manual control policies and procedures described in Chapter 5.

The basic steps followed by the auditor in evaluating computer controls is similar to that performed in a manual system, the only difference being that the computer controls implemented by the client must also be considered. First, the auditor will obtain an **overall understanding** of the client's internal control (including any relevant computer controls). During this step, the auditor attempts to understand the flow of transactions through the accounting system, determines the extent of computer involvement in the accounting applications, and identifies whether general and application controls appear to provide a basis for reliance. Recall that the auditor is attempting to obtain an understanding of how the organization's internal control (including computer controls) is supposed to work. In accomplishing this objective, key computer controls (both general controls and application controls) that the auditor wishes to rely on are identified.

Next, the auditor forms a **preliminary assessment of control risk**. As in a manual accounting system, the preliminary assessment of control risk represents the auditor's initial conclusion about the effectiveness of the organization's internal control. The only difference in a computer environment is that the general and application controls implemented by the client over its computer processing are considered by the auditor in making an evaluation. As with a manual system, the auditor can choose to assess control risk at the maximum level and perform extensive substantive tests.

Assuming that control risk is assessed at less than the maximum, the auditor now considers whether an **additional reduction in control risk** can be obtained. If so, tests of controls are performed on those control policies and procedures the auditor intends to rely upon. In a computerized accounting environment, the control policies and procedures will include both manual controls (implemented in User Departments) and computer controls (implemented in the EDP Department). Tests of computer controls are discussed in detail later in this section. In a computer environment, the auditor will test both general and application controls to determine their operating effectiveness. Once completed, the auditor will **reassess control risk** based on the evidence provided by the tests of controls.

It is important to emphasize that the study and evaluation of the client's internal control in an EDP environment parallels that in a manual accounting environment. There is, however, one important exception: the auditor must consider, identify, and test control policies and procedures related to the computerized processing of transactions. The operating effectiveness of these controls will, in turn, affect assessments of control risk. Consider the following possible outcomes of the auditor's study and evaluation of general and application controls.

Type of Computer Control	Possible Outcome of Computer Controls Reviews			
	1	2	3	4
General controls	Strong	Strong	Weak	Weak
Application controls	Strong	Weak	Strong	Weak

The auditor's possible response to each of these four outcomes is summarized below. In all cases, assume that manual control policies and procedures are functioning effectively in preventing and/or detecting errors.

1. Both general and application controls provide a basis for reliance. In this case, the auditor would assess control risk for computer controls at lower levels and restrict the extent of the substantive tests.

2. In this case, while general controls provide a basis for reliance, application programs may not allow control objectives to be accomplished. The auditor would normally attempt to identify compensating application controls (*e.g.*, thorough reconciliation of output by the Data Control Group may compensate for inadequate input controls). If effective compensating controls are not identified, control risk would be assessed at a moderate to high level and more extensive substantive testing would be considered necessary.

3. Application controls appear to be effective in preventing and/or detecting errors in the EDP processing of transactions. However, personnel within the Computer Department may have incompatible functions, or general controls (such as access, documentation, or data and procedural controls) may be absent or missing. Because of the importance of general controls, the auditor would normally assess control risk at a higher level than in case 2 and perform extensive substantive testing.

4. Because of weak or missing general and application controls, little or no reliance can be placed on computer processing. In this case, the auditor would most likely choose to assess control risk at close to the maximum level and perform very extensive substantive tests.

Figure 9-9 summarizes the major differences introduced for the auditor in the study and evaluation of internal control in an EDP environment. The methods used by the auditor to test computer controls are described in the following section.

1.	Obtain an overall understanding of internal control.	Consider the extent to which the computer is used to process transactions. Determine whether general and application controls appear to provide a basis for reliance. Identify key general or application controls that may be relied upon in reducing control risk.
2.	Form preliminary assessment of control risk.	Consider the design of computer controls in forming the assessment.
3.	Tests of controls.	Perform tests of the operating effectiveness of computer controls to determine if they are functioning as intended.
4.	Reassessment of control risk.	Based on the results of tests of controls (which include computer controls), assess control risk.

Figure 9-9: *Procedures Required in Study and Evaluation of Internal in an EDP Environment*

◻ General Controls

In testing general controls, the auditor relies primarily on inquiry of client personnel, observation of activities, and inspection. The five general controls and the methods commonly used by the auditor to test these controls are summarized below:

1. The **segregation of duties**: (1) between the EDP Department and User Departments, and (2) within the EDP department can be observed by the auditor to determine that the incompatible functions identified earlier are performed by different individuals or departments. In addition, the auditor should also inquire of client personnel and inspect organization charts to obtain assurance about the extent to which these functions are organizationally separate.

2. **Documentation of programs and systems** can be visually inspected by the auditor. Information examined by the auditor will normally include record and file layouts, operator instructions, programs listings, and authorizations for program changes and modifications. In examining this information, the auditor should ensure that all changes and modifications to existing programs are approved by appropriate personnel.

3. The auditor will normally verify the existence of **hardware controls** by reference to computer manuals and other forms of evidence regarding the client's computer hardware.

4. **Access controls** and **data and procedural controls** are normally subject to observation by the auditor. For access controls, the auditor observes client efforts to restrict physical access to both

computer hardware and computer software. These efforts include the use of locked equipment rooms, computer logs, identification badges, and other devices. These controls can also be tested by the auditor by attempting to gain access to computer hardware or software. For example, the auditor can attempt to log on to the system to verify that authorized passwords are required for user access. In examining data or procedural controls, the auditor verifies the use of back-up files and other types of file protection devices.

◻ Application Controls

Unlike general controls, application controls are not normally observable by the auditor without verifying the actual processing of client transactions by the computer and related programs. When evaluating the client's application controls, the auditor can use one of two approaches. In one approach, the auditor selects a sample of source documents, manually processes the transactions, and then compares the results of the manual processing with the output generated by the client's computer processing. This approach is referred to as **auditing around the computer**, because the actual programs, input controls, and processing associated with the specific application are not examined by the auditor. To illustrate, in auditing around the computer, the auditor may perform the following procedures:

1. Select a sample of employee Time Sheets.
2. Manually calculate the gross and net pay of the sample employees by referring to payroll information maintained in their Personnel Files.
3. Compare the manually calculated payroll information to the output generated by the client's computer program.

The distinguishing feature of auditing around the computer is that the auditor does not obtain any direct evidence of the effectiveness of application controls. Basically, the auditor is assuming that if the results of computer processing agree with those of manual processing, application controls are functioning to allow transactions to be processed and recorded accurately. Auditing around the computer is generally used for smaller computer applications when the costs of examining the computer processing of transactions outweigh the benefits of doing so.

In contrast, when **auditing through the computer**, the auditor will examine the actual computer controls implemented by the client and test the logic of the programs used to process transactions. Auditing through the computer is generally more cost-effective when the computer plays a major role in the processing of transactions. In these cases, manually verifying a large number of transactions would be prohibitive. Because computers process each transaction identically, the auditor only tests the processing for each type of transaction once. Several approaches to auditing through the computer are described below. These approaches are often referred to collectively as **computer-assisted audit techniques** (CAATs).

Test Data (Test Deck). **Test data** consist of a set of fictitious entries, or inputs, that are processed through the client's computer system under the control of the auditor. These inputs are also processed manually by the auditor and compared to the results obtained through the use of the client's computer system. The use of test data is illustrated below:

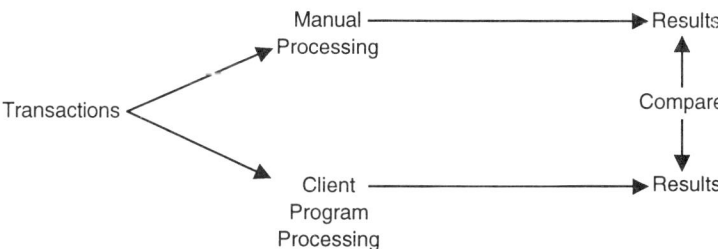

In using test data, the auditor is generally interested in determining that valid transactions are processed correctly, and that invalid transactions are detected by the programmed controls.

When utilizing test data, the auditor should include both valid and invalid conditions (exceptions) for each of the input controls examined. Because the computer handles each transaction identically, only one exception of each type needs to be included in the test data. Some possible exceptions that should be included by the auditor are:

1. Inaccurate check digits (self-checking digits).
2. Invalid account numbers or employee numbers.
3. Data not meeting specified criteria for the field of interest (*e.g.*, entering a 3 in the data field for gender if 1 = male and 2 = female).
4. Data representing unreasonable amounts (*e.g.*, 200 hours worked per week).

Prior to testing the client's computer system, the auditor should prepare a listing of all exceptions that should be identified by the client's input controls. This listing is then compared to the actual exceptions identified by the computer program, providing an indication of the effectiveness with which the input controls are functioning to prevent erroneous input.

In addition to verifying the operating effectiveness of input controls, the auditor also examines the accuracy of the client's computer program in processing transactions. For example, in a payroll application, the auditor manually processes the fictitious transactions (employee payroll transactions) prior to processing these transactions through the client's computer system. Then, after processing through the computer, the auditor compares the manually-determined results to those obtained through computer processing. Any differences suggest possible errors in the client's computer program and should be investigated further by the auditor.

Although very effective for testing programmed controls, the use of test data has some shortcomings. A significant disadvantage is that it tests only preconceived situations and may include the same oversights as exist in the program documentation. The tests may lack objectivity because they are directed toward documented controls only.

Another disadvantage of the use of test data is that the auditor must be certain that the client program being tested (the application program) is the program actually used by the client in routine processing. Finally, because the auditor normally uses fictitious data in processing test data, those fictitious data must be prevented from becoming a part of the client's actual data files.

Parallel Simulation. A second method used to test client computer programs is **parallel simulation**, in which the auditor creates a software program that parallels the logic and processing used by the client's computer program. Either actual or fictitious data are then processed through both the auditor's and client's computer programs, with the results of the processing compared. The parallel simulation technique allows the auditor to determine the accuracy of processing through the client's programs. This technique is illustrated below:

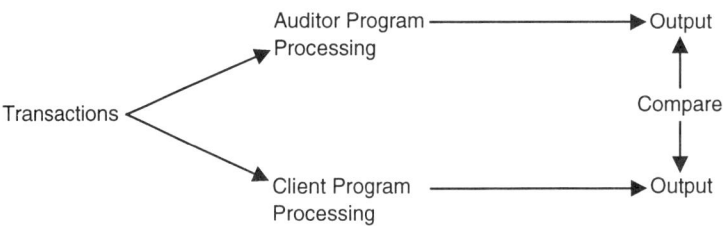

Compared to test data, the major advantage of the parallel simulation technique is that it allows the auditor to process a larger number of transactions. However, parallel simulation requires creation of computer programs, which is often a time-consuming process. In many cases, the auditor can utilize developed programs on a number of different audit engagements, making the preparation of these programs cost-effective. When utilizing fictitious transactions, the auditor will include exceptions representing invalid transactions to test the client's input controls.

Integrated Test Facility (ITF). An **integrated test facility (ITF)** is similar in nature to a test deck, except that the test data is commingled with actual (live) data. Under the ITF, a dummy entity (for example, fictitious customer, employee, or store) is created with the test transactions all relating to that entity. As with test data, the auditor should include a number of exceptions to test the client's input controls. In addition, the transactions related to the ITF are manually processed prior to their input. The results of this manual processing are then compared to those for computer processing, with any exceptions noted and investigated by the auditor. After processing, care should be taken to ensure that the fictitious data is "backed out" of (removed from) the client's accounting system.

The advantage of this approach is that it tests the entire system—the manual procedures as well as the programmed procedures. In addition, when using an ITF, the auditor ordinarily introduces fictitious data for the dummy entity throughout the entire period. This is in contrast to the use of test data, which introduce data at a single point in time. This characteristic of an ITF closely approaches the application of continuous auditing procedures. Finally, unlike test data, when using an ITF, fictitious data is processed concurrently with live (actual) client data, which increases the probability that fictitious data is handled in the same manner as actual client data.

Its chief disadvantage is that it requires considerable time to set up and execute. Also, like the test data, care must be exercised to remove fictitious data from the client's actual data records.

Specialized Programs and Other Techniques. Other computer-assisted audit techniques include the review of program logic, the use of time-sharing, the utility programs, and tagging. By reviewing program logic, the auditor can enhance his or her understanding of a particular program and identify any changes that have occurred during the audit period. Many major time-sharing vendors have libraries of programs that can be helpful to auditors, such as programs for statistical sampling and analytical procedures. Auditors may use utility programs to print all or part of a computer file or to support an audit software application by sorting records or creating a test file. In addition, internal auditors frequently use embedded audit modules, which are sections of program code that perform audit functions and are incorporated into regular application programs. This technique is most efficient when developed during the design of new applications.

Tagging is a process in which certain transactions are tagged (specifically marked or highlighted) by the auditor at the time of their input. The auditor can then obtain a computer trail of all of the steps that are used to process these transactions. Tagging allows the auditor to "view" transactions at intermediate steps during the computer processing and to examine the manner in which these transactions were processed by the computer system.

◻ Service Bureau (Service Organization)

Potential internal control problems arise when a client organization receives certain services from other organizations (service bureaus or service organizations). This situation is specifically addressed by *Statement on Auditing Standards No. 70 (SAS No. 70)*.[14] Services provided by a service organization to a client organization may include: (1) executing client transactions and maintaining accountability for the related transactions, (2) recording client transactions and processing related data, and (3) combinations of these services.

Client organizations may encounter internal control issues in situations involving service organizations, because transactions affecting the client's financial statements are processed through an accounting system physically and operationally removed from the client organization. In certain situations, the control activities necessary for the client to achieve the objectives of internal control are located at the service organization. This separation of the client organization and service organization often makes auditor examination and/or evaluation of these control activities more difficult.

When a client organization utilizes services provided by another organization, the client's auditor (known as the **user auditor**) must evaluate the reliance that can be placed on service organization controls. In order to evaluate control activities that exist at an organization physically separate from the client organization, the user auditor can either: (1) apply appropriate tests of controls at the service organization, or (2) obtain a report from an auditor associated with the service organization (the **service auditor**).

The type of report obtained by the user auditor depends on his or her assessment of control risk. Two basic types of reports can be provided by a service auditor: (1) a report on internal control policies and procedures **placed in operation** at the service organization, and (2) a report on the **operating effectiveness** of internal control policies and procedures at the service organization. The user auditor's decision about the type of report to request is summarized below.

---

[14] American Institute of Certified Public Accountants (AICPA), *Statement on Auditing Standards No. 70*, "Reports on the Processing of Transactions by Service Organizations" (New York: AICPA, 1992, AU 324).

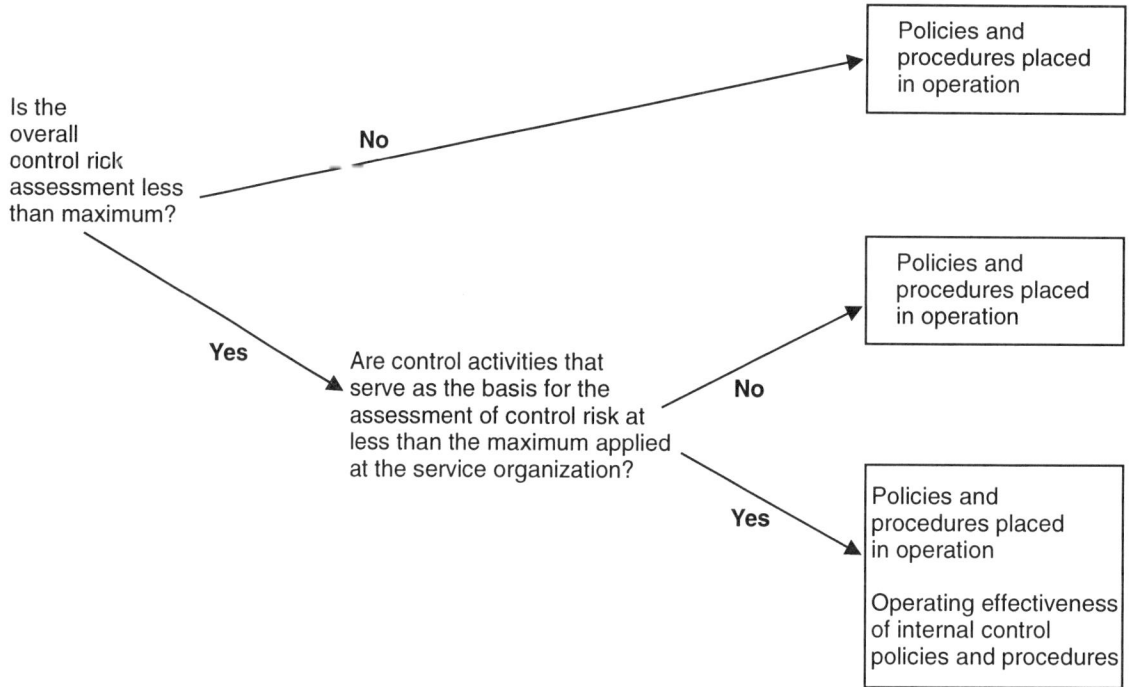

In sum, the user auditor should only obtain a report on the policies and procedures placed in operation unless: (1) he or she decides to assess control risk at less than the maximum level, and (2) important control activities are applied at the service organization. If both of these conditions exist the user auditor should obtain a report on the policies and procedures placed in operation *and* a report on the operating effectiveness of internal control structure policies and procedures.

Policies and Procedures Placed in Operation. When issuing a report on the policies and procedures placed in operation at a service organization, the service auditor should begin by obtaining a description of the internal control policies and procedures that affect the user organization's processing of transactions. The service auditor should then gather evidence about whether these policies and procedures are placed in operation. This evidence may be obtained through past experience with the service organization, inquiry of service organization personnel, inspection of documentary evidence at the service organization, and observation of service organization activities. It is important to note that the service auditor is simply interested in determining whether these internal control structure policies and procedures have been placed in operation; no evidence is gathered regarding the operating effectiveness of these policies and procedures.

The service auditor's report on internal control policies and procedures placed in operation at a service organization includes three main components:

▶ A description of the service organization's policies and procedures that may be relevant to a user organization's internal control.

- An opinion on whether the description of the service organization's policies and procedures is fairly presented.

- An opinion on whether the service organization's policies and procedures are designed to provide reasonable assurance of achieving the objectives of internal control at the service organization.

Note that the above report does *not* express an opinion or mention the operating effectiveness of the service organization's internal control structure.

Operating Effectiveness of Policies and Procedures. As noted above when the user auditor assesses control risk at less than the maximum level and when this assessment is based on internal control policies and procedures applied at a service organization, he or she needs to obtain a report on the operating effectiveness of these policies and procedures. Normally, the service auditor prepares an expanded report that includes: (1) the information in the report on policies and procedures placed in operation (discussed in the preceding subsection), (2) a description of the tests of controls performed by the service auditor, and (3) an opinion on the operating effectiveness of the internal control policies and procedures. The primary difference between this engagement (and report) is that the service auditor specifically tests the operating effectiveness of the identified internal control policies and procedures and issues an opinion on the operating effectiveness of these policies and procedures.

In any case, if the independent auditor is unable to achieve the audit objectives regarding the study and evaluation of internal control because of the client's use of a service organization, *SAS No. 70* suggests that a qualified opinion or a disclaimer of opinion on the financial statements because of a scope limitation, whichever is appropriate, should be issued.

> **CHAPTER CHECKPOINTS**
>
> **9-20.** How is the auditor's study and evaluation of internal control affected by the client's use of computerized processing systems?
>
> **9-21.** What methods are used by the auditor to test the operating effectiveness of general controls?
>
> **9-22.** Distinguish between auditing around the computer and auditing through the computer. When would each type of approach be used?
>
> **9-23.** Briefly discuss how each of the following would be used to evaluate the client's internal control over computerized processing:
>
>   a. Test data.
>   b. Parallel simulation.
>   c. Integrated Test Facility.
>
> **9-24.** What issues are introduced when a client uses a service organization to assist in the processing of its transactions?
>
> **9-25.** What are the two types of reports that may be obtained by the user auditor regarding control activities implemented at a service organization? In what situations would each of these reports be obtained?

◉ ACCESSING DATA MAINTAINED ON CLIENT COMPUTER FILES

To this point, we have described how the client's use of the computer in processing transactions influences the auditor's examination. As noted in the preceding section, the auditor must expand his or her study and evaluation of the client's internal control to include computer controls. Another potential impact of computer processing on the audit examination is the fact that client data files are maintained in machine-readable form. This provides the auditor with an opportunity to utilize the computer in performing tests of controls or substantive tests. In doing so, the auditor can take advantage of the speed and accuracy of the computer in performing tasks that were performed manually in a non-EDP environment.

A generalized audit software (GAS) package is a computer program or group of programs that can perform certain data processing functions, such as reading computer files, performing calculations, printing reports, and selecting desired records. It is the most widely-used computer-assisted audit technique for tests of controls and substantive testing.

Auditors frequently use GAS to perform the following six audit tasks:

1. Examine records for the existence of specified criteria.
2. Test calculations and make computations.
3. Compare data obtained through other audit procedures with client records.
4. Compare data on separate files.
5. Select and print audit samples.
6. Summarize or resequence data.

Each of these tasks is discussed separately in the following paragraphs.

The auditor may use GAS to examine client records for the existence of specified criteria. In these instances, GAS may be instructed to scan records in a file and print a listing of all records that conform or depart from some specified criteria. For example, GAS might be used to scan and examine payroll files for terminated employees (based on these employees' numbers).

GAS may also be used by the auditor to determine the mathematical accuracy of client-prepared calculations and computations. For example, the auditor may wish to use GAS to recalculate depreciation on fixed assets, foot client schedules, etc., rather than manually recalculating these amounts. Using GAS in these applications also allows the auditor to utilize the speed and accuracy of the computer.

A third way in which the auditor can use GAS is in the comparison of data obtained through audit procedures with client records. In this instance, the data obtained through auditing procedures must first be converted into machine-readable data. These machine-readable data are then compared to other machine-readable data (client records). (The time and effort required by the auditor to convert this data to machine-readable form is a major disadvantage of using GAS to perform this comparison.) By using GAS in this manner, the auditor might compare client records of accounts receivable to amounts confirmed with third parties to determine whether any differences exist.

Another task GAS can perform is the comparison of data on two separate data files. This task would assure the auditor that data on one file (personnel records) actually agrees with identical information on another file (payroll detail). In addition, if data files from a prior period are maintained by the client, the auditor might perform analytical procedures by having GAS compare balances and list differences by account balance.

A fifth task GAS can perform is the selection and printing of statistical samples. GAS can select statistical samples using a variety of sampling methods (random, systematic, stratified PPS, etc.) and print the confirmations to be sent to third parties. This task may be used to select samples of accounts receivable balances for confirmation, inventory items for physical observation, and individual fixed assets for vouching. In addition, GAS may be used (as discussed earlier) to statistically analyze the results of examining a sample of items.

Finally, GAS can be used to summarize and resequence data. Examples of this application include: (1) resequencing Check, Sales Invoice, Remittance Advice, and other prenumbered document numbers to facilitate the identification of missing documents; and (2) resequencing inventory items by location to facilitate physical observation.

To illustrate one use of GAS, consider the sample inventory listing presented in Part A of Figure 9-10. This listing represents the inventory held by a small grocery store and is shown in alphabetical order by product. In observing the client's inventory, the auditor could rely on this listing in its current form; however, because inventory is normally located throughout a grocery store based on the type of product involved (e.g., cereal, pet food), the auditor would be required to repeatedly search through this list in performing and recording test counts. A more convenient listing of the client's inventory would be based on aisle location. The auditor can use generalized audit software to rearrange the inventory listing shown in Part A of Figure 9-10 by physical aisle location, as shown in Part B of the figure.

Part A

Product	Quantity		Aisle	Item No.
Cat food	13	cases	13B	104–456
Checks cereal	8	boxes	5B	230–109
Diet cola	5	liters	1A	309–725
Dog food	10	cases	13B	102–456
Klean tissue	15	boxes	4B	111–222
Milk	10	gallons	3A	220–204
Wheato cereal	11	boxes	5B	230–145
Yogurt	5	cartons	3A	230–410

Part B

Product	Quantity		Aisle	Item No.
Diet cola	5	liters	1A	309–725
Milk	10	gallons	3A	220–204
Yogurt	5	cartons	3A	230–410
Klean tissue	15	boxes	4B	111–222
Checks cereal	8	boxes	5B	230–109
Wheato cereal	11	boxes	5B	230–145
Cat food	13	cases	13B	104–456
Dog food	10	cases	13B	102–456

Figure 9-10: *Illustration of the Use of Generalized Audit Software*

Figure 9-11 summarizes a number of other uses of generalized audit software. From the examples listed in the figure, it is apparent that generalized audit software is used to access client information maintained in machine-readable format. In doing so, the auditor is using the speed and accuracy of the computer to perform tasks usually performed manually.

1.	Examine records for the existence of specified criteria.	Review accounts receivable balances for amounts in excess of credit limits.
		Review inventory files for unusually large amounts.
		Review cash disbursements files for payments made subsequent to year-end.
		Review payroll files for terminated employees.
2.	Test calculations and make computations.	Recalculate net pay for employees.
		Recalculate interest income and interest expense.
3.	Compare data obtained through auditing procedures with client records.	Compare, by account number, the balances for customer accounts receivable with confirmed balances.
		Compare, by inventory item number, the quantity of inventory observed via test counts with recorded quantities.
4.	Compare data on separate files.	Perform analytical procedures on sales by comparing sales records and accounts receivable records.
		Perform analytical procedures by comparing current records to records from the previous year.
5.	Select and print audit samples.	Select and print accounts receivable confirmations.
		Select inventory items for test counts.
		Select fixed assets for physical observation.
6.	Summarize or resequence data.	Resequence inventory items by location to facilitate test counts.
		Resequence accounts receivable by due date to perform an aging of accounts.

Figure 9-11: *Uses of Generalized Audit Software*

QUICK AS 1-2-3[15]

By sorting a construction contractor's cost records using a floppy diskette and a popular spreadsheet application, an internal auditor noticed a total of $21,000 of duplicate payments made by his company to the contractor. When presented with the findings, the contractor refunded the duplicate payments.

CHAPTER CHECKPOINTS

9-26. What is generalized audit software?

9-27. What are some of the major tasks that can be performed by generalized audit software?

◉ SUMMARY OF KEY POINTS

1. Data processing is the collection, processing, and distribution of information to achieve a desired result. When a computer performs the data processing procedures, the system is an electronic data processing (EDP) system.

2. When a client uses a computer to process its transactions, certain differences should be considered by the auditor: (1) transaction trails exist for shorter periods of time, (2) errors in a computer environment are uniform across transactions, (3) there is a possibility of input errors, (4) transactions are processed centrally by an EDP Department, and (5) permanent information is easier to alter without detection.

3. Computer controls are organized into two categories: general controls and application controls. General controls are accounting controls in computerized systems that relate to all computer applications. Included among general controls are: (1) the organization of the computer department; (2) application development and maintenance; (3) hardware controls; (4) access to computer equipment, data files, and programs; and (5) data or procedural controls.

4. Application controls are the procedures of a specific computer application designed to control the processing of specific accounting transactions and data. These controls perform specific tasks for individual User Departments. Application controls include: (1) input controls, (2) processing controls, (3) output controls, and (4) master file controls.

5. Input controls are designed to determine whether information accepted by the application from other parts of the accounting system is authorized, accurate, and complete. A record count is one example of an input control. This control consists of manually counting the number of documents and comparing this information with detailed information accumulated by the

---

[15] "Quick as 1-2-3," *Internal Auditor* (February 1995), 59.

program. Other input controls include check digits, batch totals, hash totals, limits or reasonableness tests, and validity checks.

6. Processing controls are designed to determine that accounting information calculated or generated by the application is accurate. Types of processing controls include: (1) reviews for reasonableness, (2) verification of the sign or range of resulting values, (3) manual recalculation of totals, and (4) recalculation of totals using alternate methods.

7. Output controls are designed to provide reasonable assurance that accounting information returned to other parts of the system is complete and accurate. These controls include distribution of the output to appropriate User Departments and examination of the output for reasonableness.

8. In the study and evaluation of a client's internal control when the client uses a computer in processing transactions, the basic procedures described in a manual system are still applicable. The only differences are that the auditor should gain an understanding of computer controls, identify possible computer controls that will help prevent or detect financial statement misstatements, and test the operating effectiveness of computer controls that the auditor wishes to rely on.

9. Two approaches available to the auditor are auditing around the computer or through the computer. When auditing around the computer, the auditor does not consider the programs and logic used to process transactions. In contrast, the computer programs are tested and evaluated when the auditor audits through the computer. Two methods of auditing through the computer are parallel simulation and test data.

10. Parallel simulation processes the client's transactions through both the client's computer program and the auditor's computer program. The results of processing of the two programs are compared and any differences are examined.

11. Test data represent a set of transactions created by the auditor. These transactions are manually processed, and this processing is compared to the computer processing of these transactions.

12. Generalized audit software (GAS) is frequently used by the auditor to perform the following audit tasks: (1) examine records for the existence of specified criteria; (2) test calculations and make computations; (3) compare data obtained through other audit procedures with client records; (4) compare data on separate files; (5) select and print audit samples; and (6) summarize or resequence data.

GLOSSARY

Application Controls. Accounting controls relating to the processing of specific types of transactions in a computerized environment.

Auditing "Around" the Computer. When auditing around the computer, the auditor examines source documents, manually calculates the expected results, and compares those results with those of the computer processing. No attempt is made to examine the logic of computer programs used by the client.

Auditing "Through" the Computer. When auditing through the computer, the auditor examines the program logic and processing of the client's computer system.

Batch Processing. A method of computer processing in which a series of like transactions is collected and processed simultaneously.

Batch Total. The sum of a set of items that is used to check the accuracy of input of a particular batch of records. A batch total represents the total of a set of items that would be added (such as hours worked).

Check Digit. A digit associated with a numeric field for the purpose of checking for errors in inputting that field.

Computer-Assisted Audit Techniques (CAAT). The tools and techniques, such as test data, parallel simulations, and an integrated test facility, used by auditors to audit through the computer.

EDP Systems. An acronym for electronic data processing, these are systems in which the client uses the computer to record, summarize, and/or process transactions.

General Controls. Accounting controls in computerized systems that relate to all computer applications.

Generalized Audit Software. A computer program or group of programs that can perform certain data processing functions, such as reading computer files, performing calculations, printing reports, and selecting desired records. It is the most widely-used computer-assisted audit technique for tests of controls and substantive testing.

Grandfather-Father-Son. A method of file retention that allows any updated files to be re-created from previous generations of those files.

Hardware Controls. Computer controls that are "built into" the computer. These controls verify the proper transmission of data from terminal to the mainframe.

Hash Total. A control total created by the addition of numbers that usually would not be added (for example, the addition of a list of part numbers).

Input Controls. Input controls are designed to detect errors made as the data is input into the computer system. Some examples of input controls include check digits, validity checks, and the use of control totals.

Integrated Test Facility (ITF). A computer-assisted audit technique in which a dummy entity is created (e.g., a fictitious customer, employee, or store) through which test transactions are processed with regular transactions to verify the client's processing of those transactions.

Interactive Processing. In an interactive processing system, each transaction is processed as it is received. This is also referred to as on-line real-time processing.

Limits or Reasonableness Tests. Input controls which compare items to some established criteria to identify potential errors.

Master File. A file containing relatively permanent data that is periodically updated to reflect the effect of transactions occurring during the period.

Output Controls. Controls designed to provide reasonable assurance that accounting information is accurate and complete. Output controls include review by the Data Control Group and limitations on the distribution of output.

Parallel Simulation. The creation of a program by the auditor to perform functions essentially equivalent to those of the client's programs.

Processing Controls. These controls are employed by the client to detect errors made in the processing of transactions. Common processing controls include verifying the proper data format, the range or sign of resulting values, and the reasonableness of results.

Record Count. An input control that is used to ensure that: (1) all transactions (records) have been entered by the keypuncher, and (2) no transactions (records) have been entered more than once by the keypuncher.

Service Auditor. An individual who furnishes the independent auditor with a report on a service organization's internal control.

Service Organization. An organization that provides certain services (such as executing client transactions, maintaining the related accountability for these transactions, recording client transactions, and processing data related to client transactions) for the client organization.

Tagging. A process in which certain transactions are "marked" by the auditor at the time of input in order to view these transactions during intermediate processing.

Test Data. A technique to test programmed procedures and controls. Test data represent a set of transactions created by the auditor. These transactions are processed against the client's application programs, and the actual results are compared to expected results.

Transaction File. A file containing detailed records of temporary data representing events that occurred during a specific period of time.

User Auditor. The auditor of a client who utilizes a service organization in processing transactions.

Validity Check. Input controls that evaluate the input field to determine the appropriateness of its size and format.

◉ SUMMARY OF PROFESSIONAL PRONOUNCEMENTS

Statement on Auditing Standards No. 48, "The Effects of Computer Processing on the Examination of Financial Statements" (New York: AICPA, 1984, AU 311).

Statement on Auditing Standards No. 70, "Reports on the Processing of Transactions by Service Organizations" (New York: AICPA, 1992, AU 324).

QUESTIONS AND PROBLEMS

9-28. Select the **best** answer for each of the following items:

1. The primary purpose of generalized audit software is to allow the auditor to:

   a. Use the client's employees to perform routine audit checks of the electronic data processing records that otherwise would be done by the auditor's staff accountants.
   b. Test the logic of computer programs used in the client's electronic data processing systems.
   c. Select larger samples from the client's electronic data processing records than would otherwise be selected without the generalized program.
   – d. Independently process client electronic data processing records.

2. Where computers are used, the effectiveness of internal control depends, in part, upon whether the organizational structure includes any incompatible combinations. Such a combination would exist when there is no separation of the duties between:

   a. Documentation librarian and manager of programming.
   –b. Programmer and console operator.
   c. Systems analyst and programmer.
   d. Processing control clerk and keypunch operator.

3. An auditor can use generalized audit software to verify the accuracy of:

   a. Data processing controls.
   b. Accounting estimates.
   –c. Totals and subtotals.
   d. Account classifications.

4. Which of the following best describes a fundamental control weakness often associated with EDP systems?

   a. EDP equipment is more subject to systems error than manual processing is subject to human error.
   b. EDP equipment processes and records similar transactions in a similar manner.
   c. EDP procedures for detection of invalid and unusual transactions are less effective than manual control procedures.
   –d. Functions that would normally be separated in a manual system are combined in the EDP system.

5. Which of the following employees normally would be assigned the operating responsibility for designing an EDP installation, including flowcharts of data processing routines?

   a. Computer Programmer.
   b. Data Processing Manager.
   –c. Systems Analyst.
   d. Internal Auditor.

6. If calculated on numeric fields prior to input, which of the following would be considered a hash total?

   a. Total hours worked.
   b. Total inventory quantities.
   c. Total accounts receivable outstanding over 90 days.
   d. Total employee numbers.

7. Which of the following would reduce the effectiveness of internal control in an EDP system?

   a. The Computer Librarian maintains custody of computer program instructions and detailed listings.
   b. Computer Operators have access to operator instructions and detailed program listings.
   c. The Data Control Group is solely responsible for the distribution of all computer output.
   d. Computer Programmers write and debug programs that perform routines designed by the Systems Analyst.

8. Which of the following would ordinarily not be considered a general control in an EDP environment?

   a. The use of documentation in computer programs.
   b. Planned policies and procedures for file back-up and recovery.
   c. Segregation of duties between Systems Analysts and the Data Control Group.
   d. The use of check digits to ensure accurate computer input.
   e. The existence of hardware controls to ensure the accurate transmission of data.

9. The two main groups of computer controls are known as:

   a. Input controls and output controls.
   b. General controls and input controls.
   c. General controls and application controls.
   d. General controls and output controls.
   e. Application controls and input controls.

10. Which of the following pairings of controls and type of control is not correct?

    a. Hardware controls/general.
    b. Limits or reasonableness tests/application.
    c. Segregation of duties/application.
    d. Examining output for reasonableness/application.
    e. All of the above pairings are correct.

11. A form of computer processing in which data is entered and processed immediately is often referred to as _____ processing.

    a. Active.
    b. Batch.
    c. Distributed data.
    d. Immediate.
    e. Interactive.

12. An input control used to ensure that all transactions have been entered by the keypuncher and no transactions have been entered more than one time is a (n):

    a. Batch total.
    b. File control.
    c. Hash total.
    d. Record count.
    e. Source code.

13. Which of the following is not a procedure that could be performed by generalized audit software?

    a. Scanning a computer file for missing check numbers.
    b. Verifying that incompatible duties were properly segregated in an EDP environment.
    c. Recalculating an accrual for interest expense for notes payable owed by the client.
    d. Resequencing an inventory listing to arrange information according to the physical location of the inventory.
    e. All of the above duties could be performed by generalized audit software.

14. The primary difference between batch processing and interactive processing is that:

    a. Input controls are more critical in an interactive computer environment.
    b. It is considered more important that the results of batch processing be reviewed compared to interactive processing.
    c. The shorter time prior to processing in an interactive environment makes the use of input controls (such as control totals) more difficult.
    d. When used in an interactive mode, the computer system simultaneously processes a series of similar transactions.
    e. None of the above statements represent differences between batch processing and interactive processing.

15. A method of auditing where the auditor focuses on the inputs and outputs of the computer processing of transactions is referred to as:

    a. Computer auditing.
    b. EDP auditing.
    c. Manual auditing.
    d. Auditing "through" the computer.
    e. Auditing "around" the computer.

    (Items 1 through 7 in 9-28; AICPA Adapted)

9-29. The Large Corporation has a large number of small customers accounts. A customer file is kept on disk storage. For each customer, the file contains customer name, address, credit limit, and account balance. The auditor wishes to test this file to determine whether credit limits are being exceeded. Assuming that computer time is available, what is the best procedure for the auditor to follow?

(AICPA Adapted)

9-30. Payroll operations for Burns Corporation are processed on a tape-oriented computer. Burns's procedures include:

　　a.　The Personnel Department does the following:

　　　　1.　Places new employees on the payroll.
　　　　2.　Assigns each new employee a permanent employee number.
　　　　3.　Initiates appropriate action for employee terminations or transfers.

　　b.　Timekeepers keep a daily record of the hours worked in each department.
　　c.　The Payroll Department keeps the deduction authorizations for all employees.
　　d.　Some employees have their checks mailed to their homes.
　　e.　The EDP Department prepares the entire payroll. It automatically pays each employee for a 40-hour week unless it is notified otherwise. The department also prepares the Checks and the withholding stubs accompanying the Checks.

Required:

Given these circumstances, discuss some of the controls that might be used to prevent: (a) overpayment, and (b) payment of nonexistent employees.

9-31. In converting an hourly payroll from a manual to a computer system, the rate file was established from rates received from the Payroll Department. Each rate combined the employee's base rate with a cost-of-living hourly bonus factor of $0.25. The program was written to pick up the combined rate from the file and add $0.25 before extending rate times hours worked. As a result, each employee was paid $0.50 in cost-of-living instead of the approved $0.25. What procedures might have detected this programming error?

9-32. Your company plans to have all payrolls processed by a local bank. At the end of each pay period, the company will give the bank a list of employees and the hours they worked during the period. Using the Master Rate File, the bank will calculate the net pay and deposit the net pay directly to each employee's bank account. The bank will send the company a withholding stub for each employee and will prepare the Payroll Register, the quarterly and annual tax reports, and the annual W-2 statements. Identify several questions that might be asked regarding the company-bank relationship.

9-33. In auditing in an EDP environment, the auditor must consider controls implemented by the client over the computer processing of its transactions.

Required:

　　a.　Distinguish between general and application controls. Provide examples of each type.
　　b.　How does the auditor examine general controls?
　　c.　How does the auditor examine application controls?

9-34. George Beemster, CPA, is examining the financial statements of the Louisville Sales Corporation, which recently installed an off-line electronic computer. The following comments have been extracted from Beemster's notes on computer operations and the processing and control of Shipping Notices and Customer Invoices:

a. To minimize inconvenience, Louisville converted without change its existing data processing system, which utilized tabulating equipment. The computer company supervised the conversion and has provided training to all Computer Department employees (except keypunch operators) in systems design, operations, and programming.
b. Each computer run is assigned to a specific employee, who is responsible for making program changes, running the program, and answering questions. This procedure has the advantage of eliminating the need for records of computer operations because each employee is responsible for his or her own computer runs.
c. At least one Computer Department employee remains in the computer room during office hours, and only Computer Department employees have keys to the computer room.
d. System documentation consists of those materials furnished by the computer company (a set of record formats and program listings). These and the tape library are kept in a corner of the Computer Department.
e. The company considered the desirability of programmed controls but decided to retain the manual controls from its existing system.
f. Company products are shipped directly from public warehouses, which forward Shipping Notices to General Accounting, where a billing clerk enters the price of the item and accounts for the numerical sequence of Shipping Notices from each warehouse. The billing clerk also prepares daily adding machine tapes (control tape) of the units shipped and the unit prices.
g. Shipping Notices and control tapes are forwarded to the Computer Department for keypunching and processing. Extensions are made on the computer. Output consists of Invoices (in six copies) and a daily Sales Register. The daily Sales Register shows the aggregate totals of units shipped and unit prices, which the Computer Operator compares to the control tapes.
h. All copies of the Invoice are returned to the billing clerk. The clerk mails three copies to the customer, forwards one copy to the warehouse, maintains one copy in a numerical file, and retains one copy in an open invoice file that serves as a detail accounts receivable record.

Required:

Describe weaknesses in internal control over information and data flows and the procedures for processing Shipping Notices and Customer Invoices. Recommend improvements in these controls and processing procedures.

(AICPA Adapted)

9-35. Talbert Corporation hired an independent Computer Programmer to develop a simplified payroll application for its newly-purchased computer. The programmer developed an on-line database micro computer system that minimized the level of knowledge required by the operator. It was based upon typing answers to input cues that appeared on the terminal's viewing screen, examples of which follow:

a. Access routine:

1. Operator access number to payroll file?
2. Are there new employees?

b. New employees routine:

   1. Employee name?
   2. Employee number?
   3. Social security number?
   4. Rate per hour?
   5. Single or married?
   6. Number of dependents?
   7. Account distribution?

c. Current payroll routine:

   1. Employee number?
   2. Regular hours worked?
   3. Overtime hours worked?
   4. Total employees this payroll period?

The independent auditor is attempting to verify that certain input validation (edit) checks exist to ensure that errors resulting from omissions, invalid entries, or other inaccuracies will be detected during the typing of answers to the input cues.

Required:

Identify the various types of input validation (edit) checks the independent auditor would expect to find in the EDP system. Describe the assurances provided by each identified validation check. Do not discuss the review and evaluation of these controls.

(AICPA Adapted)

9-36. Johnson, CPA, was engaged to examine the financial statements of Horizon Incorporated, which has its own computer installation. During the preliminary review, Johnson found that Horizon lacked proper segregation of the programming and operating functions. As a result, Johnson intensified the study and evaluation of the internal control surrounding the computer and concluded that the existing compensating general controls provided reasonable assurance that the objectives of the internal control were being met.

Required:

a. In a properly-functioning EDP environment, how is the separation of the programming and operating functions achieved?
b. What are the compensating general controls that Johnson most likely found? Do not discuss hardware and application controls.

(AICPA Adapted)

9-37. Examine the flowchart that follows and answer these questions. Indicate the flowchart step that relates to each question.

a. Is input to the EDP department precontrolled?
b. Is the Invoice File verified?
c. Who receives the output from the EDP department?
d. Is input edited manually? By computer?
e. What is the disposition of the Payment Transaction tape?

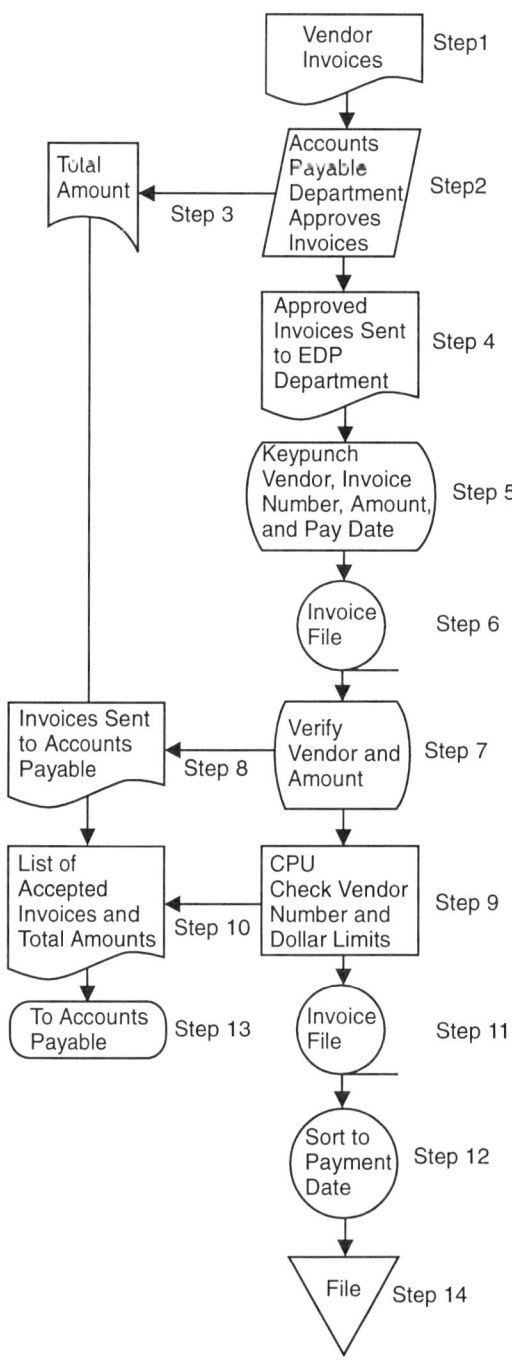

Flowchart for Accounts Payable

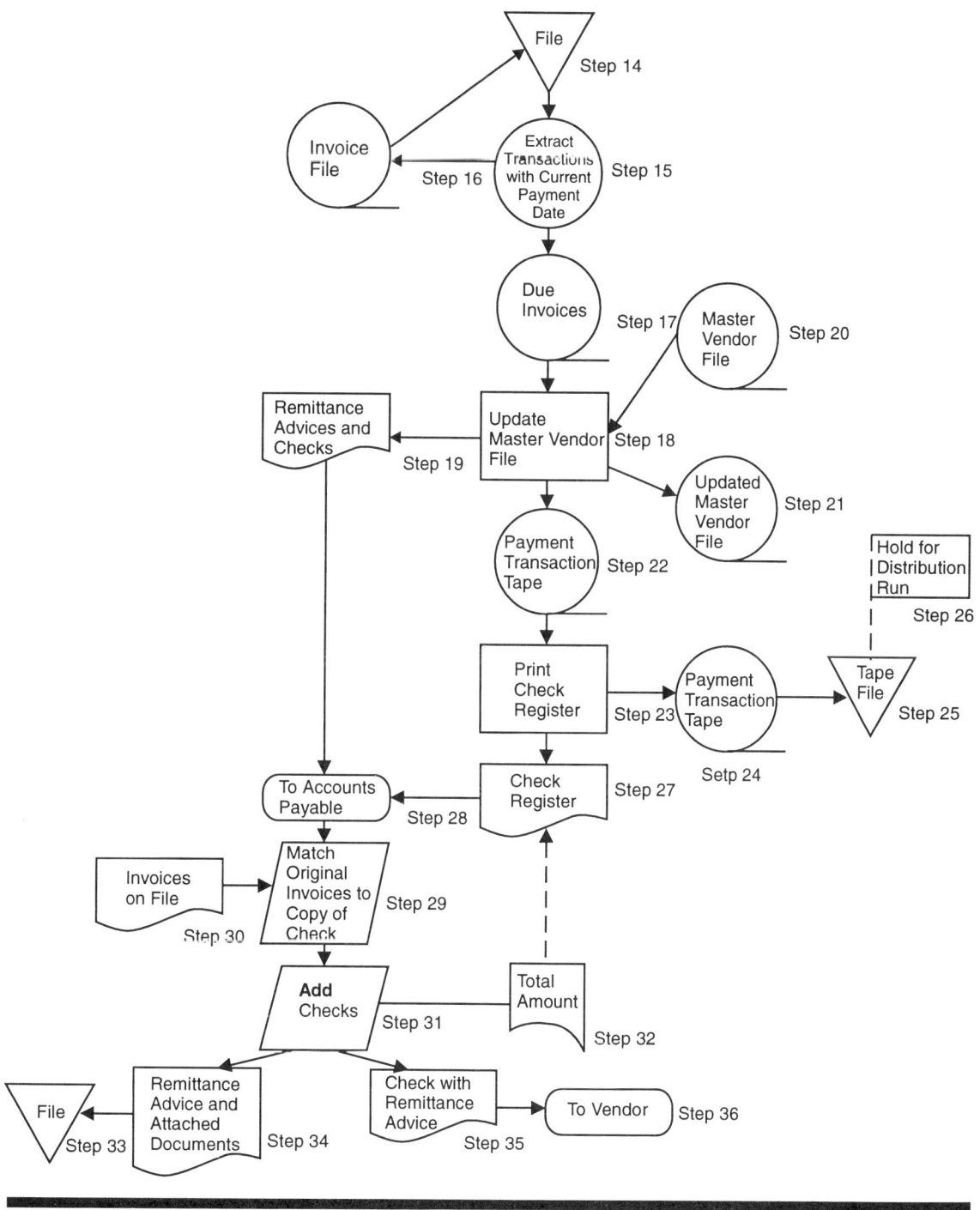

Flowchart: *concluded*

9-38. Discuss control weaknesses in the following four organizations.

Organization A

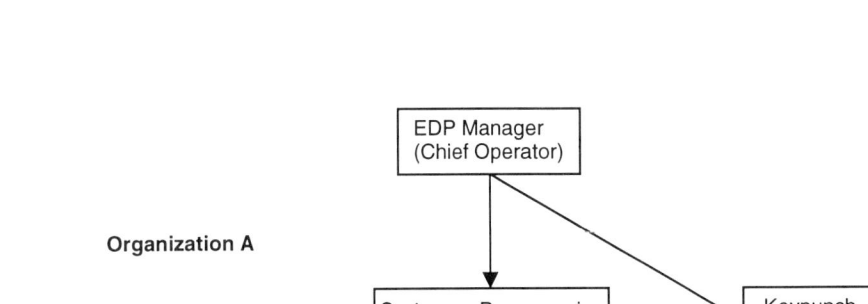

Organization B

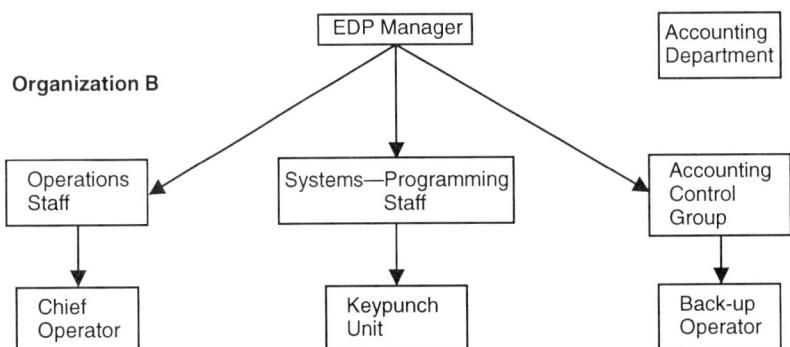

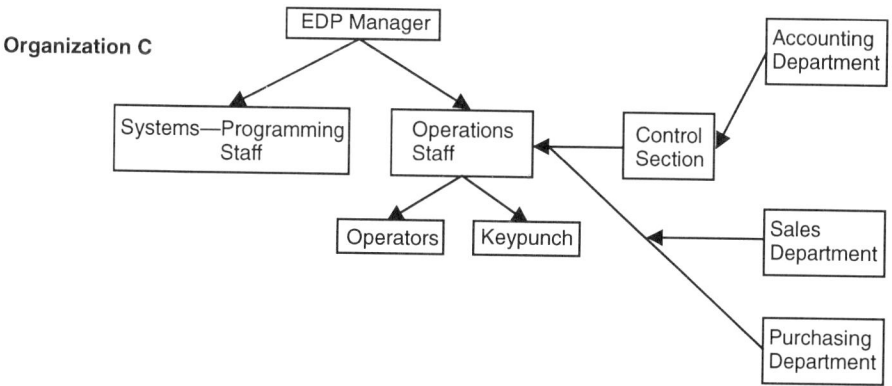

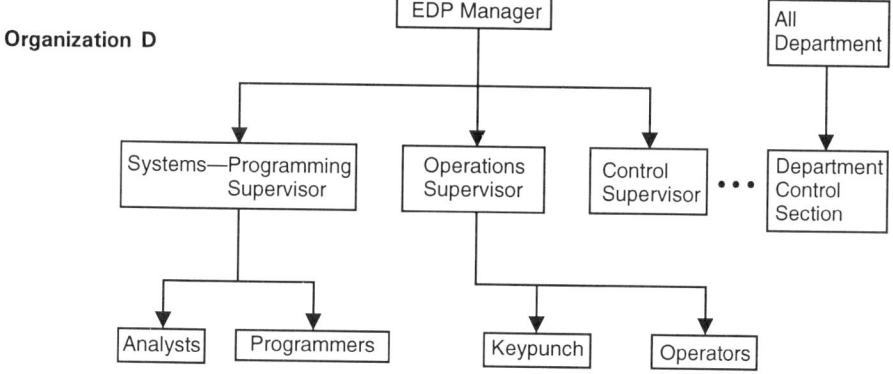

9/ Computer Controls and Audit Techniques

9-39. CPAs may audit "around" or "through" computers in the examination of the financial statements of clients which utilize computers to process accounting data.

Required:

a. Describe the auditing approach referred to as auditing "around" the computer.
b. Under what conditions does the CPA decide to audit "through" the computer instead of "around" the computer?
c. How can the CPA become satisfied that the computer program tapes presented are actually being used by the client to process its accounting data?

(AICPA Adapted)

9-40. Respond to each of the following statements made by Douglas Bracket, a staff accountant working on his initial assignment for a client that utilizes the computer to a significant extent:

a. "The use of the computer really doesn't change the objectives of the audit that I'm performing. Therefore, I'm not too concerned about how the computer processes transactions."
b. "I really can't evaluate the computer controls for this client because they use a service bureau to process transactions. As a result, I will need to assess control risk at the maximum level for this client."
c. "Because master file information does not change frequently, it isn't too important that we evaluate this information for accuracy. There shouldn't be too many errors in the data."
d. "The client should implement control totals (such as record counts) to detect improper inputting of data. With the large volume of transactions they process, keypunching errors involving account numbers are quite frequent."

III

Auditing Procedures

Learning Objectives

Study of this chapter is designed to achieve several learning objectives. After studying this chapter, you should be able to:

1. Define an operating cycle and discuss the basic characteristics of operating cycles.
2. Identify the major types of transactions occurring in the Revenue cycle.
3. List the primary accounts and documents associated with transaction processing in the Revenue cycle.
4. Illustrate how the five major components of internal control exist within the Revenue cycle.
5. Identify specific control activities established within the Revenue cycle.
6. Discuss methods used by the auditor to test control activities in the Revenue cycle.

10

The Revenue Cycle

◉ WHAT IS AN OPERATING CYCLE?

An **operating cycle** consists of the procedures performed, policies followed, and documents created by an organization and its employees from the initiation of a transaction until its ultimate recording in the accounting records. Operating cycles are unique and vary depending upon the type of transaction under consideration. Viewed from another perspective, an operating cycle represents the answer to the following question: What happens when a certain type of transaction occurs? To illustrate, consider some basic procedures that you may follow when you receive your monthly credit card statements in the mail. A sample of these procedures is shown in Figure 10-1.

1. Receive Credit Card Statement in the Mail
2. Verify that Charges Appearing on Credit Card Statement Represent Actual Purchases
3. Verify the Mathematical Accuracy of Credit Card Statement
4. Reconcile Balance on Credit Card Statement to Balance Maintained in Your Records
5. Write Check for Amount of Balance to be Repaid
6. Record Check in your Records
7. Mail Check to Credit Card Company

Figure 10-1: *Common Procedures Used in Recording Credit Card Transactions*

Figure 10-1 illustrates a few basic characteristics of operating cycles. First, operating cycles relate to certain type(s) of recurring transaction(s): in this case, repayments of credit card balances. Establishing a separate cycle for each type of transaction allows all of the procedures to be applied to each transaction. For example, the set of procedures noted in Figure 10-1 could just as easily be applied to statements received from VISA, American Express, or Diner's Club. In addition, with some simple modifications, these procedures are applicable to other cash payments you make on a recurring basis (such as utilities bills, cable bills, rent bills, and mortgage repayments).

Second, operating cycles involve the creation of documentary evidence (or source documents). The documentary evidence created in Figure 10-1 is the Check and any documentation used in recording that Check (such as the Check Log or a Cash Disbursements Journal). Documentation is important, because it represents the initial form of evidence available relating to a transaction. For example, if you wanted to determine the amount you paid on last month's credit card statement, you would refer to the canceled Check representing that month's payment. Alternatively, if you wanted to verify one of the purchases appearing on your Credit Card Statement, you would locate the Charge Slip received from the vendor for that purchase.

Finally, operating cycles require individuals within the organization to apply procedures to achieve certain objectives of internal control. For example, checking the charges listed on the Credit Card Statement will allow you to be sure that your account has not been charged for purchases you did not make. Also, reconciling the balance shown on the Credit Card Statement with your records will ensure that the records you have maintained are accurate. These are both objectives of internal control. Thus, operating cycles include procedures applied by the organization to achieve the objectives of internal control.

Recalling the basic steps in an audit, the auditor has two basic objectives with respect to operating cycles. First, he or she evaluates the operating cycles to determine the effectiveness of the internal control over the transaction(s) affected by that cycle. To illustrate, if your "accounts payable" over credit card transactions were examined, the auditor would verify the extent to which you performed such procedures as: (1) verifying charges appearing on Credit Card Statements, (2) verifying the mathematical accuracy of Credit Card Statements, and (3) reconciling the balance from Credit Card Statements to your records. Second, the auditor would perform substantive tests involving the "accounts payable." Substantive tests would include verifying recorded accounts payable directly with vendors through confirmation.

The following six chapters discuss four major operating cycles that are applicable to most types of businesses. These cycles (and the related chapters) are:

- ▶ Revenue Cycle (Chapters 10 and 11)

- ▶ Purchases and Disbursements Cycle (Chapters 12 and 13)

- ▶ Conversion Cycle (Chapter 14)

- ▶ Investing and Financing Cycle (Chapter 15)

◉ EVALUATING INTERNAL CONTROL: THE REVENUE CYCLE

The Revenue cycle consists of three major types of transactions: (1) credit sales transactions, (2) sales adjustment transactions, and (3) cash receipts transactions. These types of transactions represent the primary subcycles of the Revenue cycle and are summarized in Figure 10-2.

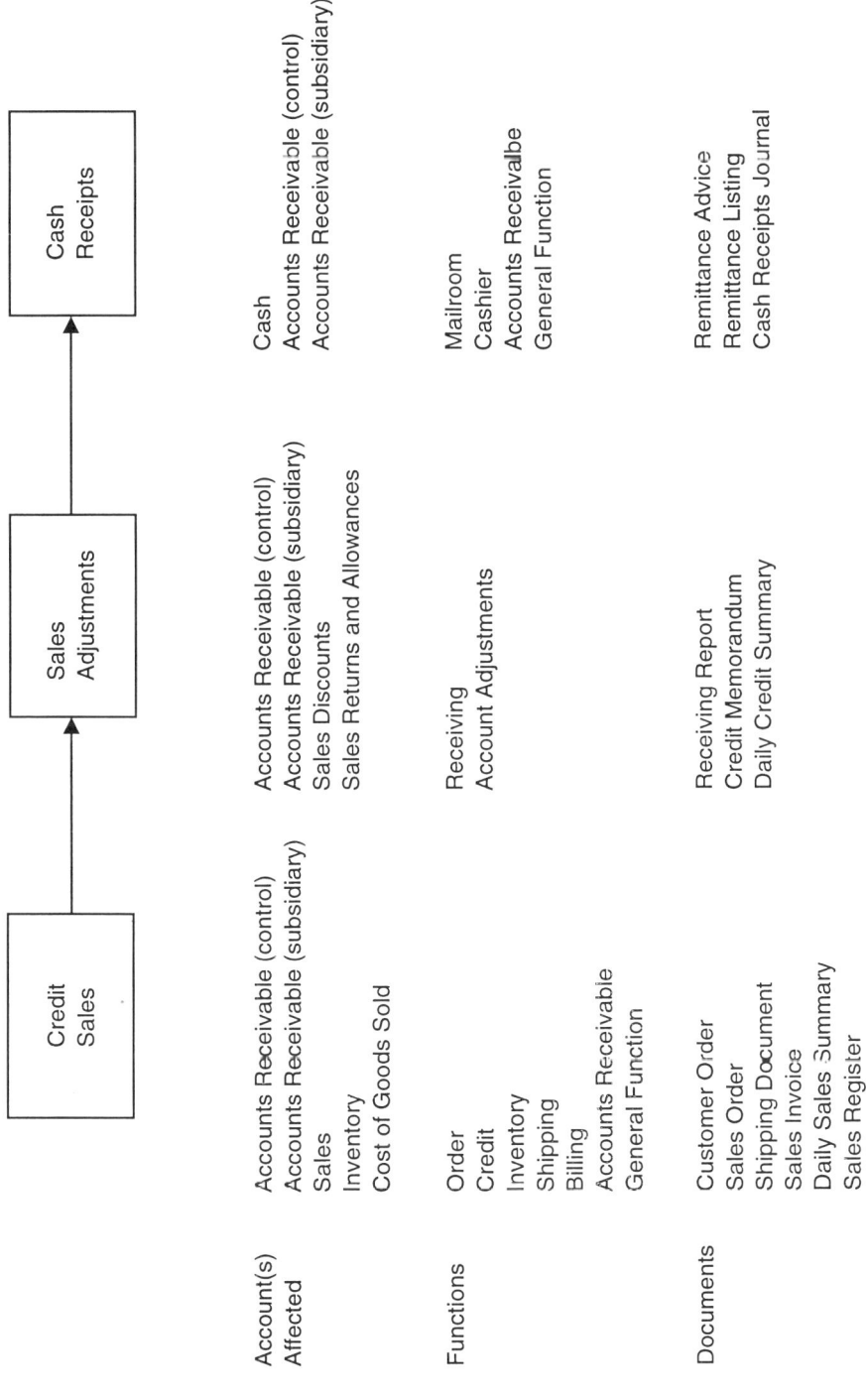

Figure 10-2: *Overview of Subcycles in the Revenue Cycle*

In studying internal control over the Revenue cycle, the auditor considers the five components of internal control identified earlier in Chapter 5. These components are shown below and are discussed in the remainder of this chapter:

1. Control Environment
2. Risk Assessment
3. Control Activities
4. Information and Communication
5. Monitoring

◻ Control Environment

As noted in Chapter 5, the **control environment** is the component of internal control that is established on an overall basis within the organization. The control environment represents the foundation for all other components of internal control, since it reflects the overall control consciousness of the organization and its employees. During the examination, the auditor normally considers the effectiveness of the organization's control environment on a company-wide basis. That is, if an effective control environment exists, this will reflect favorably on the effectiveness of the internal control of each of the operating cycles. In contrast, if the control environment is judged to be ineffective, this will negatively impact the auditor's evaluation of internal control in each of the operating cycles.

Recall that the control environment includes factors such as: (1) integrity and ethical values, (2) commitment to competence, (3) the existence of a Board of Directors and Audit Committee, (4) management's philosophy and operating style, (5) the organizational structure, (6) assignment of authority and responsibility, and (7) human resource policies and practices. During his or her examination of the Revenue cycle, the auditor will evaluate certain areas of the control environment as they relate to the activities within this cycle. For example, the following factors may reflect management's philosophy and operating style as it relates to Revenue cycle transactions:

1. Does management place undue emphasis on meeting revenue targets? (if YES, higher control risk)
2. Does management have an aggressive attitude toward revenue recognition? (if YES, higher control risk)
3. Do estimates of uncollectible accounts represent optimistic assumptions regarding the collection of sales made to customers? (if YES, higher control risk)
4. Do accounting principles regarding inventory flows (FIFO, LIFO, or average) represent a conservative or aggressive selection of accounting principles? (if AGGRESSIVE, higher control risk)
5. Are employees who handle cash receipts bonded against losses from theft? (if NO, higher control risk)

> **CHAPTER CHECKPOINTS**
>
> **10-1.** What is an operating cycle? What are the basic characteristics of all operating cycles?
>
> **10-2.** Name the four operating cycles applicable to most types of businesses.
>
> **10-3.** What are the three major types of transactions in the Revenue cycle?
>
> **10-4.** What is the control environment? What are the major factors that comprise the control environment?

▢ Risk Assessment and Control Activities: The Credit Sales Subcycle

The second and third components of internal control are risk assessment and control activities. As noted earlier in Chapter 5, these components are interrelated. **Risk assessment** is the process through which the organization identifies, analyzes, and manages risks related to the objectives of internal control. Once these risks have been identified, **control activities** are then implemented to address them and reduce the probability that the risks occur. For example, one of the risks associated with your checking account is that you will not record all Checks you have written. In response to this risk, you insist that your banks provide you with prenumbered Checks. To ensure that all Checks you write are recorded, you can periodically scan your Check Register to search for missing check numbers. In this case, the use of prenumbered Checks and periodically accounting for the numerical sequence of Checks is an example of a control activity, as shown below:

Risk Assessment	Control Activities
Risk that should be avoided	Procedures that will assist in avoiding risk
Failure to record all checks written	**Use of prenumbered Checks and accounting for the sequence of Checks written**

Recall from Chapter 5 that the three objectives of internal control are to enhance the:

▶ Reliability of the company's financial information, including the financial statements (the financial objective)

▶ Company's compliance with applicable laws and regulations (the compliance objective)

▶ Effectiveness and efficiency of the company's operations (the operating objective)

While the auditor's focus is on the first of these objectives (the reliability of financial information), many control activities pertain to more than one objective. For example, the process of formally approving customers' credit may initially appear to relate to the operating objective of internal control, since this control activity reduces the company's losses resulting from uncollectible accounts receivable. However, as shown later in this chapter, this activity also reduces the probability that fictitious sales transactions are recorded by client personnel (the financial objective).

The initial subcycle comprising the Revenue cycle relates to credit sales (or sales made to customers on account). Figure 10-3 provides an overview of the major events, functions, and documents included within the Credit Sales subcycle. This figure serves as the basis for the discussion in the remainder of this section.

Information Processing Controls. Information processing controls are implemented by companies to ensure the accuracy, completeness, and authorization of transactions. Thus, these controls correspond closely to the five management assertions introduced earlier in this text:

1. Existence or occurrence (EO)
2. Rights and obligations (RO)
3. Completeness (CO)
4. Valuation or allocation (VA)
5. Presentation and disclosure (PD)

Transaction processing in the Credit Sales subcycle involves the following departments/functions: (1) Order, (2) Credit, (3) Inventory/Warehouse, (4) Billing, and (5) General Function. Common information processing controls in the Credit Sales subcycle are discussed in the remainder of this section.

Order/Credit Departments. The Credit Sales subcycle begins upon receipt of the customer's order. This order may be received in person, over the phone, in the mail, by facsimile, or by any other means. The Order Department prepares a **Customer Order**, which is an internal document summarizing information related to the customer (such as name, account number, address, telephone number) and his or her order (items ordered, quantity, etc.). As shown in Figure 10-3, two copies of the Customer Order are prepared. One copy is filed in the Order Department and the remaining copy is sent to the Credit Department.

Once the Customer Order has been prepared, the Credit Department should use formal procedures and documentation to grant credit to its customers (IP #1 in Figure 10-3). If the customer previously has an account established with the organization, the order should be evaluated to ensure that the customer's established credit limit is not exceeded. If the customer has not previously established an account with the organization, a review of that customer's credit history is in order. Once credit has been approved, the Credit Department prepares a **Sales Order** (or an **"Approved" Sales Order**) to indicate that the sale to the customer has been authorized. If credit is not approved, the Credit Department should notify the Order Department, who then communicates the credit denial to the customer.

Approval of credit in this manner accomplishes two major objectives of internal control. First, evaluating customers' credit helps reduce the probability that the company will incur losses as a result of uncollectible accounts receivable. This benefit is related to the operating objective of internal control. Second, from a recording perspective, the use of formal documentation and procedures for granting credit reduce the probability that: (1) fictitious sales transactions are recorded in the financial statements (EO assertion), and (2) sales will not be collectible by the company (RO assertion). In addition, the use of prenumbered documents allows the company to verify that all transactions are recorded (CO assertion). These three assertions are ordinarily addressed by the use of formal documents for all transactions throughout the various operating cycles. In addition, for the Credit Sales subcycle, if customers' credit is carefully checked, sales will initially be recorded at the net realizable value (VA assertion).[1]

Inventory/Shipping Departments. After credit approval, copies of the approved Sales Order are sent to the Warehouse (or Inventory Department). Based on the Sales Order, the Inventory Department releases the inventory to the Shipping Department so that it can be sent to the customers. It is important that inventory is only released for sales evidenced by a Sales Order (PC #1 in Figure 10-3). This is an important physical control that is discussed later in this section.

The primary function of the Shipping Department is to deliver the merchandise to customers. To ensure that goods are only shipped to approved customers, the Shipping Department should not deliver merchandise unless a Sales Order has been received. Once the inventory has been obtained from the Warehouse, a **Shipping Document** is prepared (IP #2 in Figure 10-3). This document (or **Bill of Lading**) is a record of the item(s) sent by the Shipping Department to the customer and serves as a control if the inventory becomes lost or stolen during transit. Thus, the preparation of Shipping Documents relates to the operating objective of internal control, since it reduces the likelihood of losses related to inventory. In addition, as with Sales Orders, the use of formal documentation reduces the likelihood that fictitious transactions are recorded in the accounting records (EO assertion) and that actual transactions are not recorded (CO assertion).

Ordinarily, recording fictitious transactions influences both the EO and RO assertions. However, for credit sales transactions, it is important to recognize that the related asset (accounts receivable) is not a "right" of the company until it is collected from the customer. Thus, the use of formal documentation other than Sales Orders (which evaluate the creditworthiness of customers) in the Credit Sales subcycle provides only limited assurance with respect to the RO assertion.

An additional control activity in the Shipping Department is agreeing quantities from the Sales Order to the physical quantities shipped to the customer (IP #3 in Figure 10-3). These quantities should then be compared to those on the Shipping Document. This control achieves the following two objectives:

1. If quantities shipped to the customer agree with the Sales Order, the company will not incur costs related to the shipment of inaccurate quantities (costs of additional shipments of goods or accounting for merchandise returned by customers).
2. If quantities shipped to the customer agree with those on the Shipping Document, the company will invoice its customers for the proper quantity of items.

Both of these controls relate to the operating objective of internal control, since they reduce costs involved with shipping inventory and the probability of unbilled sales. In addition, incorrect quantities on a Shipping Document will ultimately result in recording sales transactions at the incorrect dollar amount. As a result, this latter control also relates to the financial objective of internal control (the VA assertion).

---

[1] It is important to note that the EO and CO assertions are classified separately from the VA assertion in this and other chapters. That is, if an internal control policy or procedure prevents companies from recording fictitious transactions, that procedure is classified as affecting the EO assertion. While recording fictitious transactions would result in materially misstated account balances, these possibilities are not classified as relating to the VA assertion. The VA assertion is involved when a transaction has actually occurred and been recorded, but has been recorded at the incorrect dollar amount.

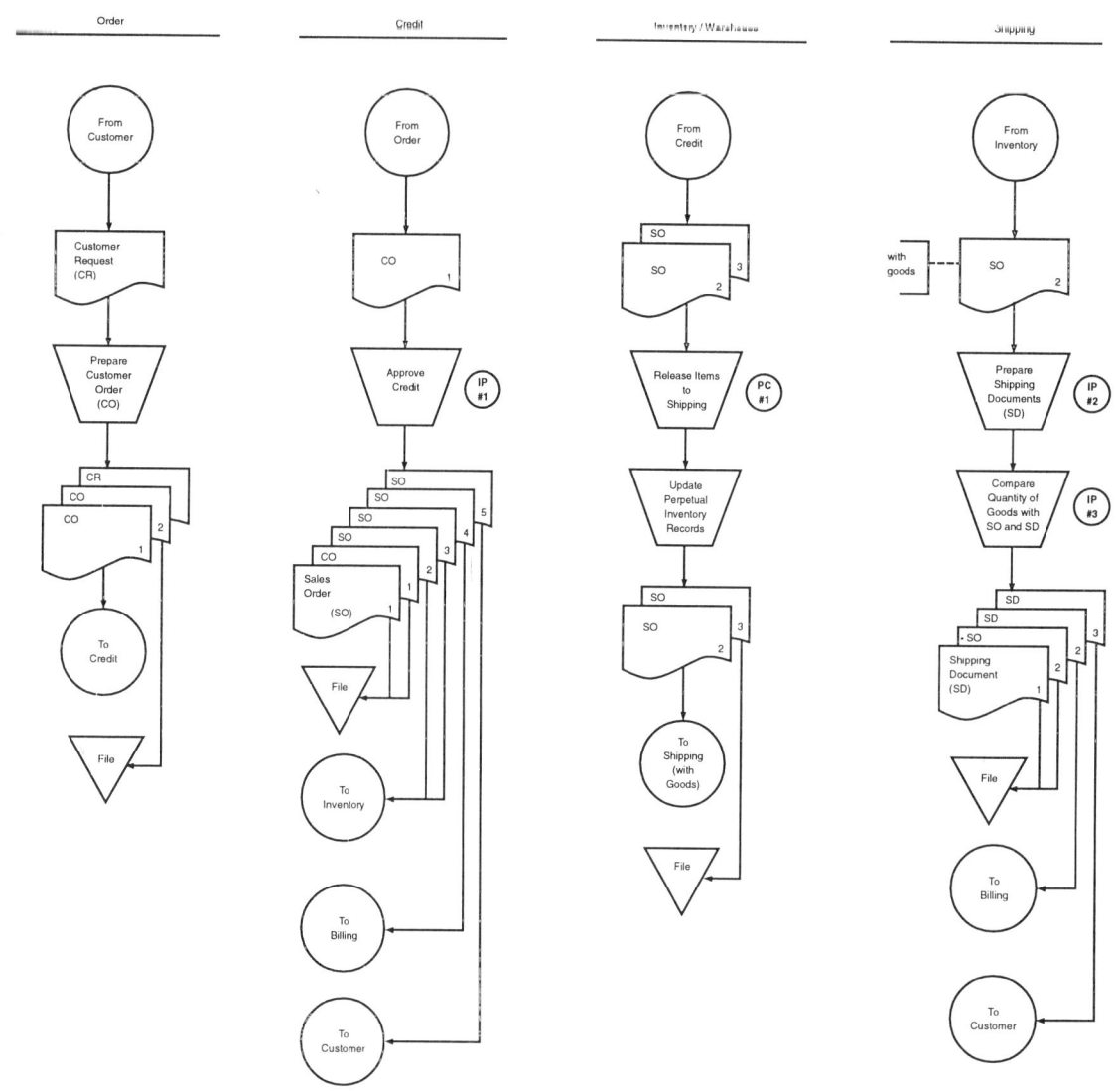

Figure 10-3: *Overview of the Credit Sales Cycle*

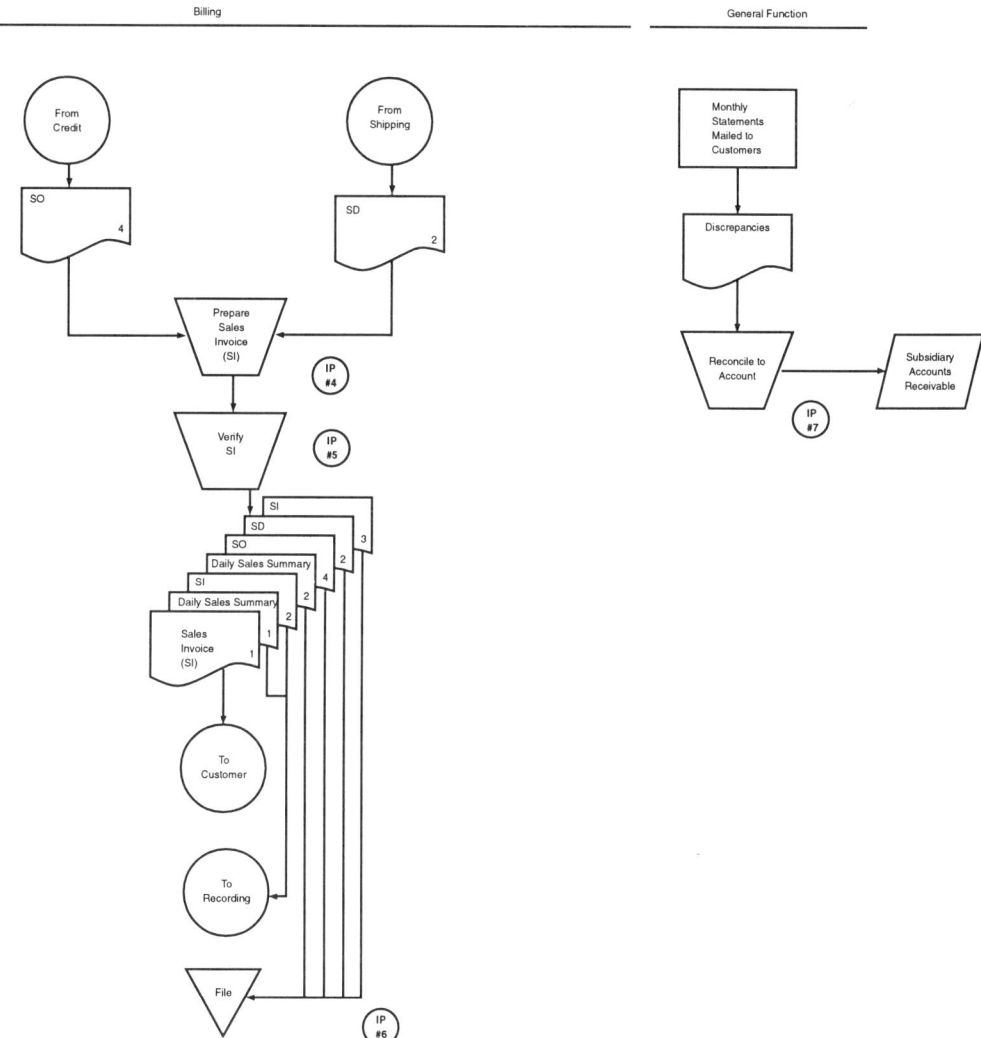

Figure 10-3: *continued*

10 / The Revenue Cycle

While not explicitly shown in Figure 10-3, it is important that the company's method of shipping inventory to its customers allow it to comply with any applicable laws and regulations. This is particularly true in cases where shipments are made across states or countries. In addition, for inventory that may cause environmental damage if mishandled during shipment, companies should take additional precautions in ensuring careful delivery of products. These controls are related to the compliance objective of internal control. The recent Exxon Valdez incident shows the importance of carefully delivering products to their ultimate destination.[2]

Billing Department. Based on copies of the Sales Order and Shipping Document, Billing prepares three copies of a **Sales Invoice** (IP #4 in Figure 10-3). As with the use of other formal documents in the Credit Sales subcycle, this control activity relates to the EO and CO assertions. Once prepared, information from the Sales Invoice is included in a **Daily Sales Summary**. The Daily Sales Summary represents a detailed listing of the total sales made over a specified period of time (normally, a day or a week, depending on the size and volume of the company's sales).

An important control related to the preparation of Sales Invoices is verification of information on these documents by client personnel (IP #5 in Figure 10-3). By verifying information on Sales Invoices, the probability that sales are recorded at incorrect dollar amounts is minimized (the VA assertion). The information on Sales Invoices is verified as follows:

- ▶ Prices are compared to approved price listings
- ▶ Quantities are compared to information from Shipping Documents
- ▶ Extensions and footings are mathematically verified

Notice that the Billing Department maintains a copy of all relevant documentation for credit sales transactions (Sales Order, Shipping Document, and Sales Invoice). One major concern of the company is that invoices should be sent for all shipments made to its customers. By accounting for the numerical sequence of Shipping Documents and determining that a corresponding Sales Invoice has been prepared, the company can identify any sales that have been shipped but not invoiced. Since the failure to invoice a sale would result in this sale being unrecorded, matching Shipping Documents to Sales Invoices in this manner addresses the CO assertion (IP #6 in Figure 10-3).

In some cases, organizations make a large number of frequent sales to their customers. As an alternative to invoicing these customers for each individual sale, the sales made to those customers may be accumulated over a period of time (such as a month) with one invoice or statement sent at the end of that month. It is important to note that the basic control activities discussed above still apply in this situation. The primary difference is that more than one Shipping Document may need to be used in verifying quantities appearing on the Sales Invoices.

General Function. The General Function consists of individuals who do not have other responsibilities within the Credit Sales subcycle. These individuals perform various types of reconciliations within a subcycle. An important control activity is mailing monthly statements to customers and accounting

---

[2] Exxon Corporation was assessed compensatory damages of $286.8 million and punitive damages of $5 billion resulting from damages caused by the 1989 Exxon *Valdez* Oil spill in Prince William Sound Alaska. See "Jury Decides Exxon Must Pay $286.8 Million," *The Wall Street Journal* (August 12, 1994), A3, A5; and "Exxon is Told to Pay $5 Billion for Valdez Spill," *The Wall Street Journal* (September 19, 1994), A3.

for any discrepancies reported by customers (IP #7 in Figure 10-3).[3] In addition to facilitating the receipt of payment, the use of monthly statements provides an external check on the accuracy of the client's accounting records. Through the use of monthly statements, the company may identify: (1) unrecorded sales (CO assertion), (2) fictitious sales recorded in their accounting records (EO assertion), (3) sales or payments posted to the incorrect customer's accounts, and/or (4) sales recorded at incorrect dollar amounts (VA assertion). In addition to observing the use of monthly statements, the auditor should also investigate procedures used by management to follow up customers' exceptions to these statements.

Segregation of Duties Controls. In Chapter 5, segregation of duties was identified as one of the major types of control activities. **Segregation of duties** requires different individuals or departments to handle the various aspects of a transaction. For effective internal control, three aspects of a particular type of transaction are normally separated (or segregated). These aspects (and the segregation of duties reflected in Figure 10-3) are as follows:

▶ Authorization: Credit Department

▶ Custody: Inventory and Shipping Departments

▶ Recording: Accounts Receivable (subsidiary) and General Accounting (control)

The primary benefit provided by segregation of duties is that individual(s) are not provided with an opportunity to commit a defalcation and conceal that defalcation by having incompatible responsibilities. By reducing the opportunity to engage in theft or a defalcation scheme, segregation of duties relates to the operating objective of internal control. In addition, since defalcations of assets can be concealed by recording fictitious transactions (EO assertion) or failing to record actual transactions (CO assertion), this control activity also relates to the financial objective of internal control. Ordinarily, segregation of duties will also relate to the RO assertion; however, unlike other subcycles, recording fictitious transactions in the Credit Sales subcycle does not affect the RO assertion.

Physical Controls. Physical controls encompass the physical security of assets and documents that authorize the disposition of those assets. The primary asset in the Credit Sales subcycle over which physical controls must be established is inventory. As shown in Figure 10-3, physical controls over inventory begin with the release of inventory to the Shipping Department (PC #1 in Figure 10-3). The Inventory Department/Warehouse should only release inventory to the Shipping Department upon the receipt of an approved Sales Order. In addition to the above control activity, three other physical controls related to inventory include:

1. Restricting access to inventories by keeping them in a secured, locked location
2. Keeping documents providing access to inventory (Sales Orders) in a secured location

---

[3] This control activity also affects the Sales Adjustments and Cash Receipts subcycles, since they relate to the accuracy of subsidiary accounts receivable. These subcycles are discussed later in this chapter.

3. Maintaining perpetual inventory records and periodically comparing physical quantities to those records (discussed in more detail in Chapter 12, The Purchases and Disbursements Cycle)

Physical controls over assets (such as inventory) relate to both the operating and financial objectives of internal control. From an operating standpoint, physical controls reduce the possibility that losses will be incurred as a result of theft or some other defalcation scheme. From a financial standpoint, since physical controls reduce the opportunity for the theft or defalcation of assets, the probability that fictitious transactions are recorded in the accounting records (EO assertion) or actual transactions are intentionally not recorded (CO assertion) to conceal theft or defalcation of assets is also reduced. (Recall that the RO assertion is not affected by recording fictitious sales transactions).

Performance Review Controls. Performance reviews involve management review and analysis of data by comparing these data to: (1) data from prior years, and/or (2) budgeted or forecasted data. In the Credit Sales subcycle, management would review and analyze current year sales data by comparing these data to those from prior periods or forecasts. Sales data may be compared on an overall basis, by salesperson, or by product. Reviews of this nature may be useful in identifying both favorable and unfavorable performance for company products and/or salespersons. Identifying potential areas for improvement through the use of performance reviews corresponds to the operating objective of internal control.

While large variations revealed by performance reviews may be the result of substandard or exceptional performance, another possibility is that they may be caused by:

- Fictitious transactions being recorded (EO assertion)
- Actual transactions not being recorded (CO assertion)
- Transactions being recorded at the incorrect dollar amount (VA assertion)

Thus, performance reviews also correspond to the financial objective of internal control.

Summary of Control Activities: The Credit Sales Cycle. Figure 10-4 summarizes the major control activities in the Credit Sales subcycle. Included in this description are the relevant objectives of these control activities, methods that can be used by the auditor to test the operating effectiveness of these control activities (tests of controls), and the financial statement assertions addressed by these control activities.

> **CHAPTER CHECKPOINTS**
>
> **10-5.** What is a Sales Order? What information should ordinarily be included on the Sales Order?
>
> **10-6.** Prior to shipping items to customers, what actions should the Shipping function take to ensure that the quantity of goods shipped is accurate?
>
> **10-7.** What procedures should be performed to verify the accuracy of Sales Invoices prepared by the organization? What assertion(s) are affected by this verification?
>
> **10-8.** What comparison(s) are performed by the General Function in the Credit Sales subcycle.
>
> **10-9.** List some physical controls implemented in the Credit Sales subcycle.

◻ Risk Assessment and Control Activities: The Sales Adjustments Subcycle

The second subcycle in the Revenue cycle relates to recording sales adjustment transactions. Sales adjustment transactions result from one of three events: (1) sales returns, (2) sales allowances, and (3) uncollectible accounts. Transaction processing in the Sales Adjustment subcycle involves the following departments:

- ▶ Receiving
- ▶ Account Adjustments

Information Processing Controls. Figure 10-5 summarizes the major events in processing sales adjustment transactions. As shown therein, the Account Adjustments Department initiates approval for sales adjustment transactions based on a **Receiving Report** evidencing returned goods (sales returns) (PC #2 in Figure 10-5) or an **Adjustment Request** for an allowance or write-off of a particular account (sales allowances or uncollectible accounts). For sales allowances and write-offs, the responsible employee should investigate the request for adjustment to determine its legitimacy. In particular, before approving write-offs of accounts receivable, this individual should examine evidence indicating that a reasonable effort has been made to collect the accounts. The approval of sales adjustment transactions is the first important control in the Sales Adjustments subcycle.

Once the sales adjustment transaction has been approved, a **Credit Memorandum** is prepared (IP #8 in Figure 10-5). Once prepared, these Credit Memoranda are summarized in a **Daily Credit Summary**. Copies of the Credit Memoranda and Daily Credit Summary are forwarded to General Accounting for recording purposes.

As with the Credit Sales subcycle, the use of formal, prenumbered documents addresses both the operating and financial objectives of internal control. From an operating standpoint, the use of formal documentation reduces the likelihood that individuals can record fictitious sales adjustment transactions as part of a defalcation scheme. Relatedly, by requiring the use of a formal document (the Credit Memorandum), only actual sales adjustment transactions will be recorded (EO and RO assertions). Also, by accounting for the numerical sequence of these Credit Memoranda, the company can determine whether any sales adjustment transactions have not been recorded (CO assertion).

Ref.	Control Activity	Objective(s) of Control Activity	Auditor Test(s) of Control Activity	EO	RO*	CO	VA	PD
						Assertions		
IP 1	Prenumbered Sales Orders should be prepared and approved for all customers	O: Reduces losses resulting from uncollectible accounts receivable F: Reduces the likelihood that: (1) fictitious sales transactions will be recorded, (2) actual sales transactions will not be recorded, and (3) sales transactions will be recorded at the incorrect dollar amount (realizable value)	Inspect the use of prenumbered Sales Orders Inquire about credit-granting process	x	x	x	x	
IP 2	Prenumbered Shipping Documents should be prepared for all shipments of goods	O: Reduces losses resulting from theft or misappropriation of goods during delivery F: Reduces the likelihood that: (1) fictitious sales transactions will be recorded, and (2) actual sales transactions will not be recorded	Inspect the use of prenumbered Shipping Documents	x		x		
IP 3	Quantities shipped to customers should be compared to quantities on: (1) Sales Orders, and (2) Shipping Documents	O: Reduces costs of making additional shipments of goods or accounting for returned merchandise not ordered O: Reduces losses from failing to bill customers for all items shipped F: Reduces the likelihood that sales transactions will be recorded based on incorrect quantities	Inspect Sales Orders and Shipping Documents for evidence of comparison				x	
IP 4	Prenumbered Sales Invoices should be prepared for all shipments	F: Reduces the likelihood that: (1) fictitious sales transactions will be recorded, and (2) actual sales transactions will not be recorded	Inspect the use of prenumbered Sales Invoices	x		x		
IP 5	Prices, quantities, and extensions and footings on Sales Invoices should be verified	O: Reduces losses caused by underinvoicing customers for sales F: Reduces the likelihood that sales transactions will be recorded at the incorrect dollar amount	Inspect Sales Invoices for evidence of verification For a sample of Sales Invoices, reperform verifications				x	
IP 6	Shipping Documents should be periodically compared to Sales Invoices	O: Reduces losses from failing to invoice all shipments made to customers F: Reduces the likelihood that actual sales transactions will not be recorded	Inspect Shipping Documents for reference to Sales Invoices For a sample of Shipping Documents, identify the related Sales Invoice			x		

Figure 10-4: *Major Control Activities: Credit Sales Subcycle*

Ref	Control	Objectives of Control Activity	Tests	EO	RO	CO	VA	PD
IP 7	Monthly statements should be sent to customers, with any discrepancies followed up by client personnel	F: Reduces the likelihood that: (1) fictitious sales transactions will be recorded, (2) actual sales transactions will not be recorded, and (3) sales transactions will be recorded at the incorrect dollar amount	Observe the use of monthly statements and follow-up procedures	x		x		x
SD	Appropriate segregation of duties should be established and maintained in the Credit Sales subcycle	O: Reduces losses from defalcation schemes resulting from the ability of employees to participate in incompatible functions F: Reduces the likelihood that: (1) fictitious sales transactions will be recorded, and (2) actual sales transactions will not be recorded	Observe segregation of duties Inquire about segregation of duties	x		x		
PC 1	Inventory should not release items to the Shipping Department without an approved Sales Order	O: Reduces losses resulting from defalcation schemes involving inventory F: Reduces the likelihood that: (1) fictitious sales transactions will be recorded, and (2) actual sales transactions will not be recorded	Observe the release of inventory to the Shipping Department Inspect Sales Orders for indication of release of inventory to the Shipping Department	x		x		
PC	Physical controls should be established over inventories	O: Reduces losses resulting from theft or defalcation of inventories F: Reduces the likelihood that: (1) fictitious sales transactions will be recorded, and (2) actual sales transactions will not be recorded	Observe/inspect physical controls over inventories Inquire of management about physical controls over inventories	x		x		
PR	Performance reviews should compare actual sales data to expected data	O: Allows opportunities for identifying areas of operations that may be improved F: Large variations in performance reviews may result from: (1) fictitious sales transactions, (2) actual sales transactions not recorded, or (3) sales transactions recorded at the incorrect dollar amount	Inquire of management about performance reviews	x		x		x

Note:

Reference
IP = Information Processing Control
SD = Segregation of Duties Control
PC = Physical Control
PR = Performance Review Control

Objectives of Control Activity
O = Operating Objective
F = Financial Objective

Assertions
EO = Existence or occurrence
RO = Rights and obligations
CO = Completeness
VA = Valuation or allocation
PD = Presentation and disclosure

* As discussed in the text, the RO assertion is generally not affected by controls in the Credit Sales subcycle

Figure 10-4: *continued*

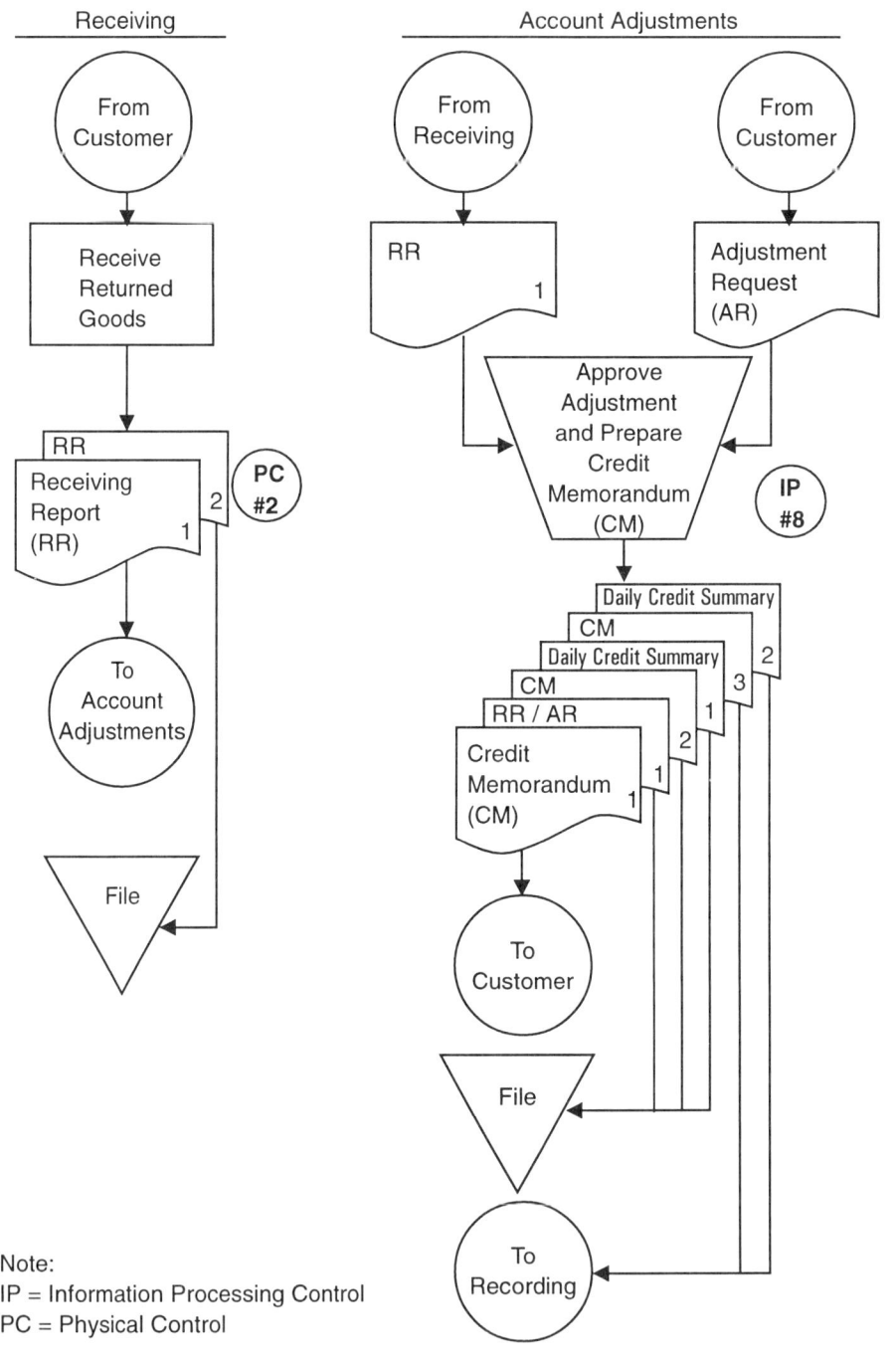

Figure 10-5: *Overview of the Sales Adjustments Subcycle*

Segregation of Duties. An important aspect of the approval process for sales adjustment transactions is the individual (or department) having final approval for sales adjustment transactions should not have any responsibilities in the Credit Sales subcycle or Cash Receipts subcycle. The segregation of duties in the Sales Adjustments subcycle (as reflected in Figure 10-5) is shown below:

- Authorization: Account Adjustments
- Custody: Receiving
- Recording: Accounts Receivable (subsidiary) and General Accounting (control)

As with the Credit Sales subcycle, segregation of duties addresses both the operating and financial objectives of internal control. By reducing the opportunity to engage in theft or a defalcation scheme, segregation of duties relates to the operating objective of internal control. From a financial standpoint, segregation of duties prevents situations where the theft or defalcation of an asset can occur and be concealed by recording fictitious transactions (EO and RO assertions) or intentionally failing to record an actual transaction (CO assertion).

Physical Controls. Physical controls over the Sales Adjustments subcycle are related to inventory returned by customers. An important control activity is the preparation of a Receiving Report evidencing goods returned by customers (PC #2 in Figure 10-5). This control relates to both the operating and financial objective of internal control. From an operating standpoint, preparing a Receiving Report reduces the likelihood that thefts of inventory will occur and go unnoticed. As with other physical controls, by reducing the opportunity for the theft or defalcation of assets, the company also reduces the likelihood that: (1) fictitious transactions are recorded in the accounting records (EO and RO assertion), and (2) actual transactions will intentionally not be recorded (CO assertion) as part of a defalcation scheme. In addition, by recording the quantity of items returned, the company reduces the likelihood that sales adjustments are based on the incorrect quantity of goods (VA assertion).

In addition to the use of Receiving Reports, access to Credit Memoranda should be restricted to reduce the likelihood that these documents are processed as part of a defalcation scheme.

Performance Review Controls. As with the Credit Sales subcycle, performance reviews in the Sales Adjustment subcycle involve management review and analysis of sales adjustments data for the current period and comparison of this information to forecasted sales adjustments or sales adjustments in prior periods. Identifying cases where sales adjustments are much greater than anticipated may reveal customer dissatisfaction with the company's products; the opportunity for improvement provided by these performance reviews corresponds to the operating objective of internal control. In addition, as with the Credit Sales subcycle, performance reviews also correspond to the financial objective of internal control (EO, RO[4], CO, and VA assertions).

---

[4] Unlike transactions in the Credit Sales subcycle, recording fictitious transactions in the Cash Receipts subcycle also affects the RO assertion.

> **DECEITFUL REFUNDS**[5]
>
> One company's policy was to send confirmation letters to a sample of customers who had received refunds to ensure that these refunds were received on a timely basis. On one occasion, two confirmation letters were returned as undeliverable. Upon further review, both refunds were processed by the same employee and were for relatively large dollar amounts. Investigating the original refund request revealed that the handwriting on these requests was identical, despite the fact that these requests were purportedly received from two different customers. When questioned, the employee who processed these refunds admitted to embezzling over $25,000 using this refund scam.

Summary of Control Activities: The Sales Adjustments Subcycle. Figure 10-6 summarizes the major control activities in the Sales Adjustments subcycle. Included in this description are the relevant objectives of these control activities, methods that can be used by the auditor to test the operating effectiveness of these control activities (tests of controls), and the financial statement assertions addressed by these control activities.

---

[5] "Deceitful Refunds," *Internal Auditor* (October 1993), 73.

Ref.	Control Activity	Objective(s) of Control Activity	Auditor Test(s) of Control Activity	Assertions				
				EO	RO	CO	VA	PD
IP 8	All sales adjustment transactions should be approved using prenumbered Credit Memoranda	O: Reduces losses from sales adjustment transactions recorded as part of a defalcation scheme F: Reduces the likelihood that: (1) fictitious sales adjustment transactions will be recorded, and (2) actual sales adjustment transactions will not be recorded	Inspect the use of prenumbered Credit Memoranda	x	x	x		
SD	Appropriate segregation of duties should be established and maintained in the Sales Adjustments subcycle	O: Reduces losses from defalcation schemes resulting from the ability of employees to participate in incompatible functions F: Reduces the likelihood that: (1) fictitious sales adjustment transactions will be recorded, and (2) actual sales adjustment transactions will not be recorded	Observe segregation of duties Inquire about segregation of duties	x	x	x		
PC 2	Prenumbered Receiving Reports should be prepared upon the return of merchandise	O: Reduces the likelihood that theft of inventory will go unnoticed F: Reduces the likelihood that: (1) fictitious sales adjustment transactions will be recorded, (2) actual sales adjustment transactions will not be recorded, and (3) sales adjustment transactions will be recorded based on the incorrect quantity of goods	Inspect the use of prenumbered Receiving Reports	x	x	x	x	
PR	Performance reviews should compare actual sales adjustment data to expected data	O: Allows opportunities for identifying customer dissatisfaction with products F: Large variations in performance reviews may result from: (1) fictitious sales adjustment transactions, (2) actual sales adjustment transactions not recorded, or (3) sales adjustment transactions recorded at the incorrect dollar amount	Inquire of management about performance reviews	x	x	x	x	

Note:

Reference
IP = Information Processing Control
SD = Segregation of Duties Control
PC = Physical Control
PR = Performance Review Control

Objectives of Control Activity
O = Operating Objective
F = Financial Objective

Assertions
EO = Existence or occurrence
RO = Rights and obligations
CO = Completeness
VA = Valuation or allocation
PD = Presentation and disclosure

Figure 10-6: *Major Control Activities: Sales Adjustments Subcycle*

> **CHAPTER CHECKPOINTS**
>
> **10-10.** What document should be used to authorize credits to customers' accounts for sales returns and allowances?
>
> **10-11.** What department should have final approval for sales adjustment transactions?
>
> **10-12.** As a result of performance reviews, what factor may be the cause of a larger number of sales adjustment transactions than anticipated?

◻ Risk Assessment and Control Activities: The Cash Receipts Subcycle

The final subcycle in the Revenue cycle is the Cash Receipts subcycle. The following departments/functions are involved in processing transactions in the Cash Receipts subcycle:

1. Mailroom
2. Cashier
3. General Function

Information Processing Controls. *Mailroom* Figure 10-7 provides an overview of the procedures typically used to account for cash received from customers in the mail. The series of events illustrated in Figure 10-7 begins with the company's receipt of payment from its customers. When remitting cash via the mails, customers should enclose both the payment (preferably in the form of a Check) and a **Remittance Advice**. The Remittance Advice is a "stub" that was originally part of the bill (invoice) sent to the customer. The Remittance Advice serves as evidence of the amount actually paid by the customer. If a customer fails to include a Remittance Advice, one should be prepared by the individual receiving the payment. Both the Check and the Remittance Advice should contain: (1) the customer's name, (2) the customer's account number, and (3) the amount of payment. To discourage theft, customers should be encouraged to pay only by Check and to make the Check payable in the company's name.

Immediately upon receipt in the mailroom, two important control activities are implemented. First, Checks should be restrictively endorsed ("for deposit only") by client personnel (PC #3 in Figure 10-7). The second control activity implemented in the mailroom is preparing a listing of all cash received (known as a **Remittance Listing**) (IP #9 in Figure 10-7). The Remittance Listing should include the date, customer's name, customer's account number, and amount of payment. The preparation of the Remittance Listing addresses both the operating and financial objectives of internal control. From an operating standpoint, the Remittance Listing discourages subsequent theft of cash receipts. If a Remittance Listing is prepared immediately upon the receipt of cash, any attempt to misappropriate either the customer's Check or Remittance Advice can be detected by examining the Remittance Listing.

The preparation of a Remittance Listing is also related to the financial objective of internal control. As noted later, the Remittance Listing will be used in the recording process for cash receipts transactions. Requiring cash receipts to be included on a Remittance Listing prior to recording increases the likelihood that only legitimate cash receipts transactions are recorded (EO and RO

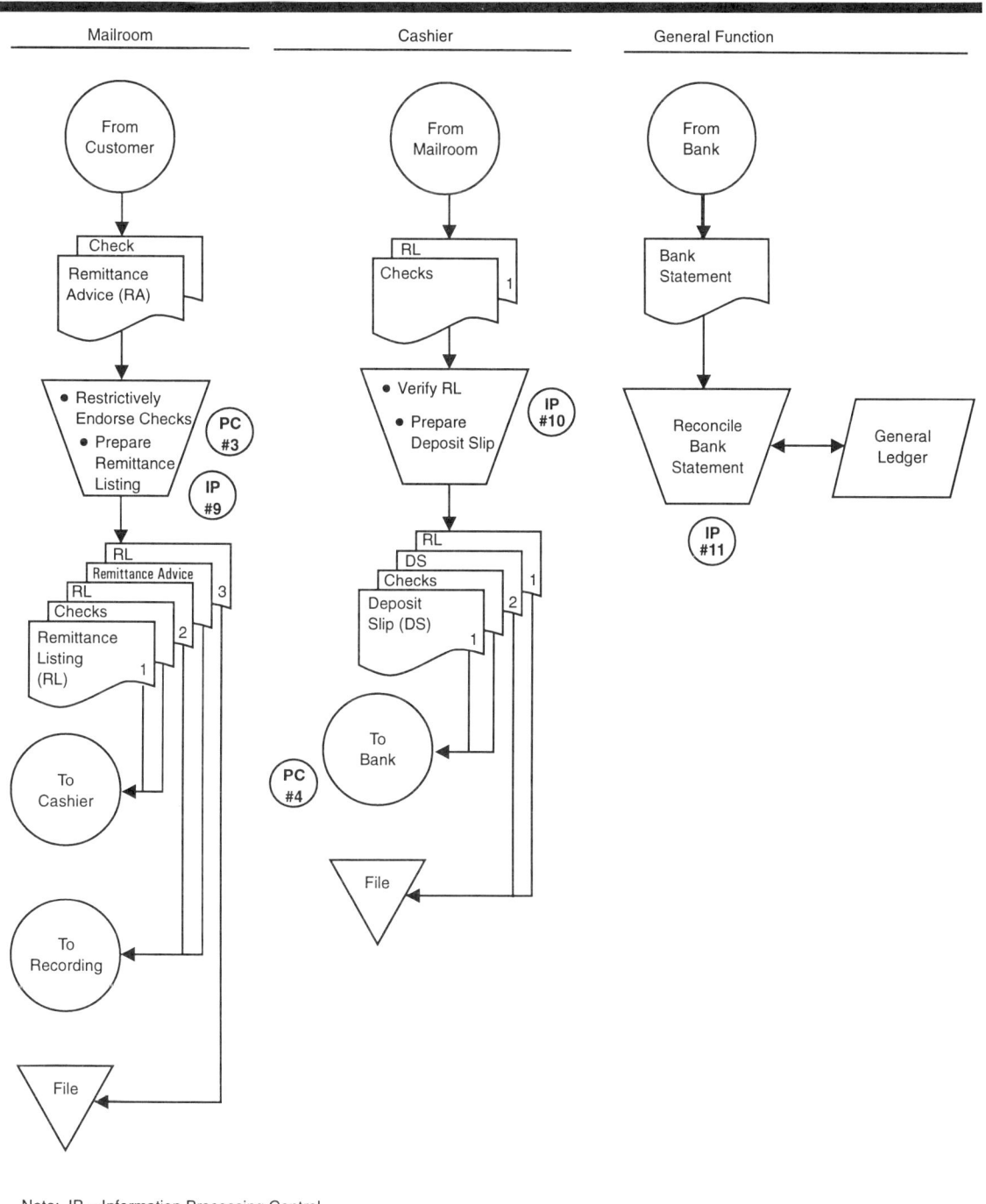

Figure 10-7: *Overview of the Cash Receipts Subcycle*

assertions). Also, accounting for the numerical sequence of all prenumbered Remittance Listings allows the company to verify that all cash receipts have been recorded (CO assertion).

Once the Remittance Listing is prepared, the Checks and a copy of the Remittance Listing are forwarded to the Cashier. The Remittance Advices and another copy of the Remittance Listing are forwarded to General Accounting for use in the recording process.

Cashier. After receiving the Checks (which should be restrictively endorsed) and Remittance Listing from the Mailroom, the Cashier verifies the accuracy of the Remittance Listing (IP #10 in Figure 10-7). This verification consists of the following procedures:

▶ Compare Checks to the Remittance Listing to determine that: (1) all cash receipts have been included on the Remittance Listing (CO assertion), and (2) only legitimate cash receipts are included on the Remittance Listing (EO and RO assertions)

▶ Establish the mathematical accuracy of the Remittance Listing (VA assertion)

Once the Remittance Listing has been verified in the above manner, the Cashier prepares the **Daily Deposit Slip**. Effective internal control over cash receipts dictates that all cash receipts should be deposited intact and daily in the company's bank (PC #4 in Figure 10-7). Depositing **intact** means that *all* cash received from customers should be deposited in the company's bank account; that is, cash should not be maintained on the company's premises. Depositing cash **daily** means that these deposits should be made each day, not weekly or monthly. Depositing cash receipts intact and daily is a physical control that is discussed later in this section.

General Function. The final control activity over cash receipts is performed by an individual or department who has no other recordkeeping responsibilities with respect to cash. This control involves reconciling the bank statements to the cash records maintained by the company (IP #11 in Figure 10-7). By reconciling bank statements, the company determines that: (1) all cash transactions have been recorded (CO assertion), (2) recorded cash transactions actually occurred and are the rights of the company (EO and RO assertions), and (3) cash transactions have been recorded at the proper dollar amount (VA assertion).

Other Cash Receipts. In addition to cash received from customers through the mails (as shown in Figure 10-7), most companies have other types of cash receipts. In particular, many organizations receive cash at the point of sale for sales made to customers. While cash receipts at the point of sale are normally not material in amount, internal control over these receipts is quite important.

For cash sales, it is critical that strict accountability exists at the point of sale to prevent skimming (employee embezzlement of cash without recording the sale). Cash registers or other mechanical devices commonly have "locked-in" totals that accumulate the total sales recorded by a particular cashier, allowing the cash on hand to be reconciled with that employee's recording of cash receipts. Therefore, an important control is to take steps to ensure that employees are recording ("ringing up") all sales made to customers. Many businesses require cashiers to provide receipts to their customers or award a prize or bonus to customers if they are not given a receipt. These actions provide employees with an incentive to record all sales and enhance the accountability for cash sales.

Once obtained, cash receipts at the point of sale are handled in much the same manner as cash received through the mail. While not shown in Figure 10-7, a Cash Summary for these receipts is prepared which is similar in nature to the **Remittance Listing**. One copy of the Cash Summary is forwarded to General Accounting for recording. The cash receipts, along with a second copy of the

Cash Summary, are forwarded to the Cashier and, along with Checks received in the mail, should be deposited in the company's bank account intact and daily.

TRUTH IN DETAIL[6]

An internal auditor for a regional retailer noticed that one store had consistently experienced cash shortages during the most recent year. This retailer had a control policy that all entries into the cash register required specific sign-on numbers that were recorded on the detail cash summary tapes. A detailed investigation of the register tapes for a two-month period revealed ten instances where a replacement Checker had signed on to a register (when the assigned Checker was on break) and rang "no sale" to open the cash register. After being confronted with this fact, the replacement Checker admitted stealing about $6,000 after ringing "no sale" transactions during the assigned Checkers' breaks. As a result, Store Managers were alerted to review detail cash summary tapes for replacement Checkers when they experienced cash shortages.

Segregation of Duties Controls. The segregation of duties in the Cash Receipts subcycle (as reflected in Figure 10-7) is shown below:

▶ Authorization: None

▶ Custody: Mailroom and Cashier

▶ Recording: Accounts Receivable (subsidiary) and General Accounting (control)

As with the other subcycles in the Revenue cycle, the primary motive for establishing segregation of duties is to prevent situations where the theft or defalcation of an asset can occur and be concealed by employees having incompatible responsibilities. Thus, this control activity relates to both the operating and financial (EO, RO, and CO assertions) objectives of internal control.

Physical Controls. The primary consideration in establishing physical controls over cash receipts is to reduce the likelihood that these receipts can be stolen or misappropriated by company employees. Although safeguarding access to the company's assets is always important, access to cash is considered to be particularly critical because cash is highly susceptible to theft for the following reasons:

1. Cash is not readily identifiable. That is, it is difficult (if not impossible) to distinguish cash (in the form of currently) held by an employee from cash held by the client.
2. Cash is easy to conceal. It is much easier for an employee to conceal cash on his or her person than to attempt to conceal a more bulky asset (such as a machine or inventory).

---

[6] "Truth in Detail", *Internal Auditor* (August 1994), 73.

3. Cash is highly liquid. Embezzling cash provides an immediate source of funds to an employee. Conversely, if inventory or some other asset is stolen, it must be sold to a third party before funds are available.

Two important physical controls over cash are shown in Figure 10-7.

▶ Restrictive endorsement of checks upon receipt (PC #3)
▶ Deposit of cash receipts intact and daily (PC #4)

As with all physical controls, by reducing the opportunity for the theft or defalcation of assets, the company also reduces the likelihood that: (1) fictitious transactions are recorded in the accounting records (EO and RO assertions), and (2) actual transactions will intentionally not be recorded (CO assertion). Thus, these control activities relate to the financial objective of internal control.

Physical controls also correspond to the operating objective of internal control. Restrictive endorsement of checks and deposit of cash receipts intact and daily reduce the likelihood of losses from the theft or defalcation of cash. An additional advantage of depositing receipts daily is that it permits the company to make use of the receipts sooner and allows them to earn interest on deposited amounts for a longer period of time.

Performance Review Controls. Performance reviews in the Cash Receipts subcycle would include management review and analysis of cash receipts data for the current period and comparison of this information to forecasted cash receipts or cash receipts in prior periods. Identifying cases where cash receipts are less than expected may reveal dissatisfaction with the company's products or situations where credit is granted to customers with a marginal credit standing. The opportunity for improvement provided by these performance reviews corresponds to the operating objective of internal control. In addition, as with the other subcycles discussed in this chapter, performance reviews also correspond to the financial objective of internal control (EO, RO, CO, and VA assertions). However, recall that performance reviews are **detective** in nature; that is, they would only reveal misstatements after they have been introduced in the accounting records.

Summary of Control Activities: The Cash Receipts Subcycle. Figure 10-8 summarizes the major control activities in the Cash Receipts subcycle. Included in this description are the relevant objectives of these control activities, methods that can be used by the auditor to test the operating effectiveness of these control activities (tests of controls), and the financial statement assertions addressed by these control activities.

> **CHAPTER CHECKPOINTS**
>
> 10-13. Name two control activities implemented in the Mailroom over cash receipts.
>
> 10-14. For effective internal control, how frequently should the organization's cash be deposited in its bank accounts?
>
> 10-15. What controls should be implemented by the organization to handle and account for cash received at the point of sale?
>
> 10-16. Why are physical controls over cash so important?

◻ Information and Communication

The auditor's primary concern related to the information and communication component of internal control is the accounting system used by the client to record revenue/receipts transactions. As noted in Chapter 5, the **accounting system** represents the series of documents, journals, and ledgers used by the client to record its transactions. Figure 10-9 provides an overview of the accounting systems used to record transactions in the Credit Sales, Cash Receipts, and Sales Adjustments subcycles.

Figure 10-9 reveals that a four-tiered hierarchy forms the basis for accounting systems. Using the Credit Sales subcycle as an illustration, the initial source of evidence regarding a transaction is a **document** (in this case, Sales Invoice). The documents relating to a particular type of transaction are then summarized in a **departmental summary**. In this case, the Daily Sales Summary is prepared to summarize sales transactions. Totals from the departmental summary are then posted to the appropriate **journal** or **ledger**; in this case, totals from the Daily Sales Summary are posted to the Sales Register (or Sales Journal). Finally, totals from the journal or ledger are entered into the **General Ledger** in the form of a journal entry.

The above recording process involves four basic control activities shown below. It is important to note that these control activities relate to all three subcycles in the Revenue cycle and address the following assertions:

▶ Using formal documentation in the recording process (EO and RO assertions)

▶ Using prenumbered documents in the recording process, with periodic accounting for the numerical sequence of these documents (CO assertion)

▶ Agreeing control totals from basic documents to the departmental summaries and totals posted to the subsidiary accounts (VA assertion)

▶ Agreeing totals from the departmental summaries to the appropriate journal or ledger (VA assertion)

Ref.	Control Activity	Objective(s) of Control Activity	Auditor Test(s) of Control Activity	EO	RO	CO	VA	PD
IP 9	Prenumbered Remittance Listings should be prepared in Mailroom after opening mail	O: Reduces losses resulting from theft or defalcations involving cash F: Reduces the likelihood that: (1) fictitious cash receipts transactions will be recorded, and (2) actual cash receipts transactions will not be recorded	Inspect the use of prenumbered Remittance Listings prepared by Mailroom personnel	x	x	x		
IP 10	The accuracy of the Remittance Listing should be verified by the Cashier	F: Reduces the likelihood that: (1) fictitious transactions will be recorded, (2) actual cash receipts transactions will not be recorded, and (3) cash receipts transactions will be recorded at the incorrect dollar amount	Inspect documentary evidence of the verification on the Remittance Listing	x	x	x		
IP 11	Personnel independent of cash receipts processing should prepare monthly Bank Reconciliations	F: Reduces the likelihood that: (1) fictitious transactions will be recorded, (2) actual cash receipts transactions will not be recorded, and (3) cash receipts transactions will be recorded at the incorrect dollar amount	Inspect Bank Reconciliations prepared by client personnel Reperform Bank Reconciliations	x	x	x	x	
SD	Appropriate segregation of duties should be established and maintained in the Cash Receipts subcycle	O: Reduces losses from defalcation schemes resulting from the ability of employees to participate in incompatible functions F: Reduces the likelihood that: (1) fictitious cash receipts transactions will be recorded, and (2) actual cash receipts transactions will not be recorded	Observe segregation of duties Inquire about segregation of duties	x	x	x		
PC 3	Checks should be restrictively endorsed by Mailroom personnel upon opening the mail	O: Reduces losses resulting from theft or defalcations involving cash F: Reduces the likelihood that: (1) fictitious transactions will be recorded, and (2) actual cash receipts transactions will not be recorded	Inquire about restrictive endorsement of checks Observe Mailroom personnel restrictively endorsing checks	x	x	x		
PC 4	Cash receipts should be deposited intact and daily	O: Reduces losses resulting from theft or defalcations involving cash O: Increases interest or other return received on deposit of cash F: Reduces the likelihood that: (1) fictitious transactions will be recorded, and (2) actual cash receipts transactions will not be recorded	Compare detail from a sample of Deposit Slips to information from Remittance Listings	x	x	x		

Figure 10-8: *Major Control Activities: Cash Receipts Subcycle*

			Objective			Assertion				
					EO	RO	CO	VA	PD
PC 4	Cash receipts should be deposited intact and daily	O: Reduces losses resulting from theft or defalcations involving cash O: Increases interest or other return received on deposit of cash F: Reduces the likelihood that: (1) fictitious transactions will be recorded, and (2) actual cash receipts transactions will not be recorded	Compare detail from a sample of Deposit Slips to information from Remittance Listings		×	×	×		
PR	Performance reviews should compare actual cash receipts data to expected data	O: Allows opportunities for identifying areas of operations that may be improved F: Large variations in performance reviews may result from: (1) fictitious cash receipts transactions, (2) actual cash receipts transactions not recorded, or (3) cash receipts transactions recorded at the incorrect dollar amount	Inquire of management about performance reviews		×	×	×	×	

Note:

Reference

IP = Information Processing Control
SD = Segregation of Duties Control
PC = Physical Control
PR = Performance Review Control

Objectives of Control Activity

O = Operating Objective
F = Financial Objective

Assertions

EO = Existence or occurrence
RO = Rights and obligations
CO = Completeness
VA = Valuation or allocation
PD = Presentation and disclosure

Figure 10-8: *continued*

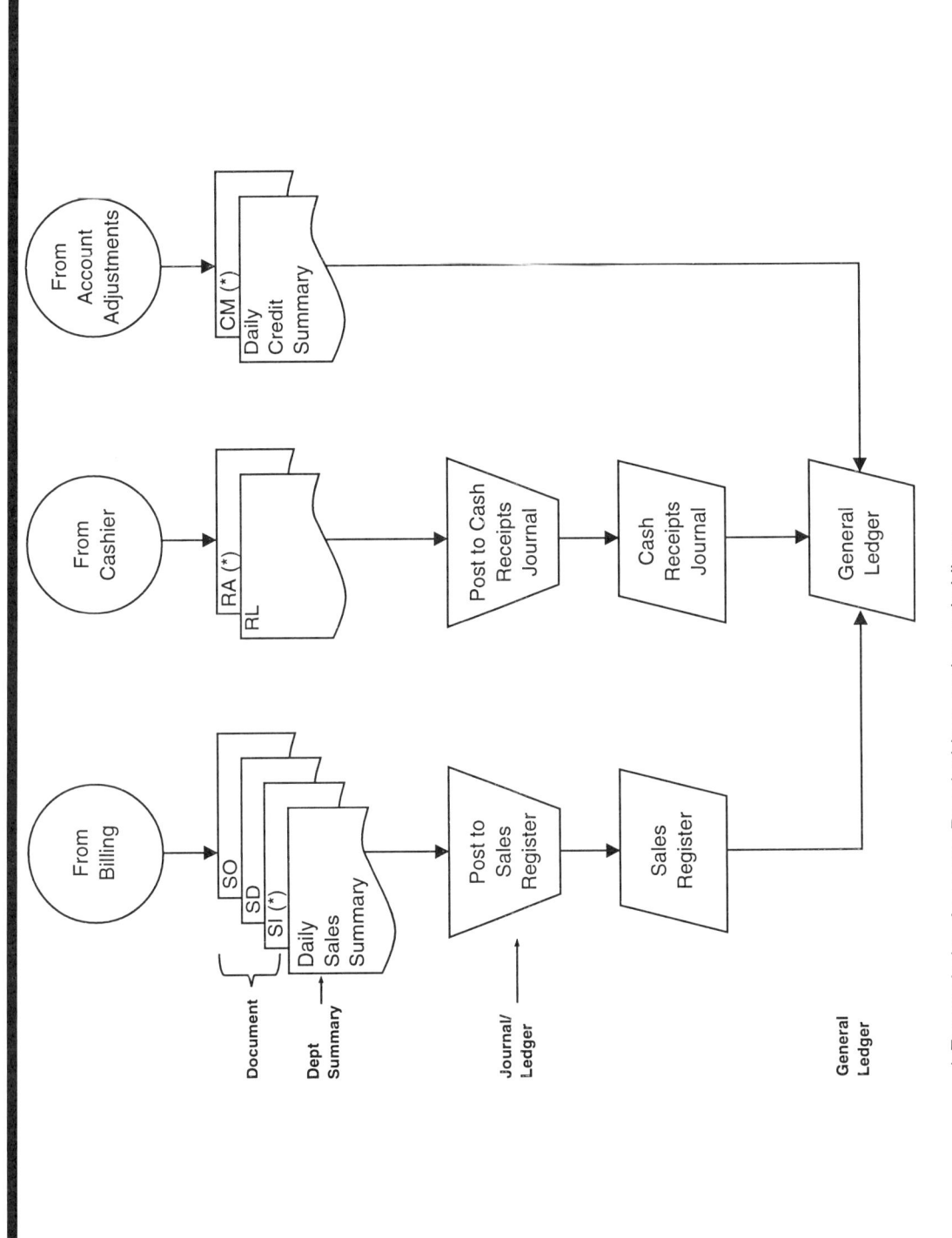

Figure 10-9: *Information and Communication: The Revenue Cycle*

Credit Sales Subcycle

1. The documentation package consisting of the Daily Sales Summary, Sales Order, and Sales Invoice is sent from the Billing Department to Inventory Accounting. After examining Sales Invoices, Inventory Accounting determines the cost of inventory sold to the customer and enters this information on the Daily Sales Summary. This will be used to record the total cost of goods sold associated with the items sold to customers.

2. The documentation package is then forwarded to General Accounting, who uses the Daily Sales Summary to update the Sales Register and make the general ledger journal entries. Two major entries are made at this point:

Accounts Receivable	XXX	
Sales		XXX
Cost of Goods Sold	XXX	
Inventory		XXX

3. Sales Invoices are forwarded to Accounts Receivable Accounting, who updates the customer's subsidiary accounts receivable records.

Sales Adjustments Subcycle

1. Based on totals from the Daily Credit Summary, the following journal entries are made:

Sales Returns/Allowances	XXX	
Accounts Receivable		XXX
Inventory	XXX	
Cost of Goods Sold		XXX
Allowance for Bad Debts	XXX	
Accounts Receivable		XXX

2. Credit Memoranda are forwarded to Accounts Receivable Accounting, who updates the subsidiary customer accounts to reflect the sales adjustment transaction.

Cash Receipts Subcycle

1. One copy of the Remittance Listing is sent from the Mailroom to General Accounting, along with the related Remittance Advices. In addition, Cash Summaries are sent from the company's operating personnel to General Accounting. Remittance Listings and Cash Summaries are used to update the Cash Receipts Journal and make the general ledger journal entry, as follows:

Cash	XXX	
Accounts Receivable		XXX
Sales		XXX (for cash sales)

2. The Remittance Advices are forwarded to Accounts Receivable Accounting, who then updates the customer's subsidiary accounts receivable records.

◻ Monitoring

The final component of internal control is monitoring. As discussed in Chapter 5, **monitoring** is the process of evaluating whether the organization's internal control is operating effectively. Like the control environment, monitoring is normally assessed on a company-wide basis throughout the overall organization. For example, the existence of a competent internal audit function that periodically evaluates the effectiveness of the organization's internal control would be viewed positively by the external auditor during his or her study and evaluation of internal control.

Two examples of on-going monitoring activities in the Revenue cycle are management examination and follow-up of:

▶ Excessive sales returns or allowances that may indicate customer dissatisfaction with product quality

▶ Discrepancies reported from statements sent to the company's customers regarding their accounts receivable balances

In addition to on-going monitoring activities, separate evaluations of internal control over Revenue cycle transactions may be conducted by: (1) internal auditors, (2) other external auditors, or (3) the same external auditor in the prior year. The auditor should consider any deficiencies identified during these separate evaluations of internal control as well as actions taken by management to correct these deficiencies.

CHAPTER CHECKPOINTS

10-17. What are the four major elements of the recording process for Revenue cycle transactions? How are each of the four elements of the recording process used in recording credit sales transactions? Cash receipts transactions?

10-18. What is monitoring? Give some examples of how monitoring exists within the Revenue cycle.

Appendix

◉ COMPUTERIZED PROCESSING IN THE REVENUE CYCLE[7]

In the text of the chapter, our discussion assumed that companies processed Revenue Cycle transactions manually. In practice, most companies extensively utilize computerized processing. In Chapter 9, we provide a general discussion of the effect of computer/electronic data processing (or EDP processing) on the auditor's examination. This appendix applies some of the general concepts discussed in Chapter 9 on computerized processing to the Revenue Cycle introduced in this chapter.

Figure 10-10 provides an overview of computerized processing of transactions in the Credit Sales subcycle. In order to focus on differences between the manual processing discussed in the text of this chapter and computerized processing, many of the detailed control activities and the ultimate disposition of the documents are not shown in Figure 10-10. In reviewing this figure, two important points should be kept in mind:

1. Computerized processing environments utilize the same documents, journals, and ledgers as manual processing environments.
2. Many of the control activities associated with manual processing environments also exist in computerized processing environments.

◻ Credit Sales

Credit Department. As in the manual processing environment, the Credit Sales subcycle begins with the receipt of an order from a customer. A Customer Order is prepared and forwarded to the Credit Department, who inputs the customer's name, items ordered, and quantities ordered into a **Daily Sales Order Transaction File** (Step 1 in Figure 10-10). Prior to input, the following control totals are calculated by Credit Department personnel.

▶ Total number of sales transactions (record counts)

▶ Total quantities of items ordered (batch totals)

---

[7] All Chapter Checkpoints and End of Chapter Items related to the Appendix are marked with an asterisk (*).

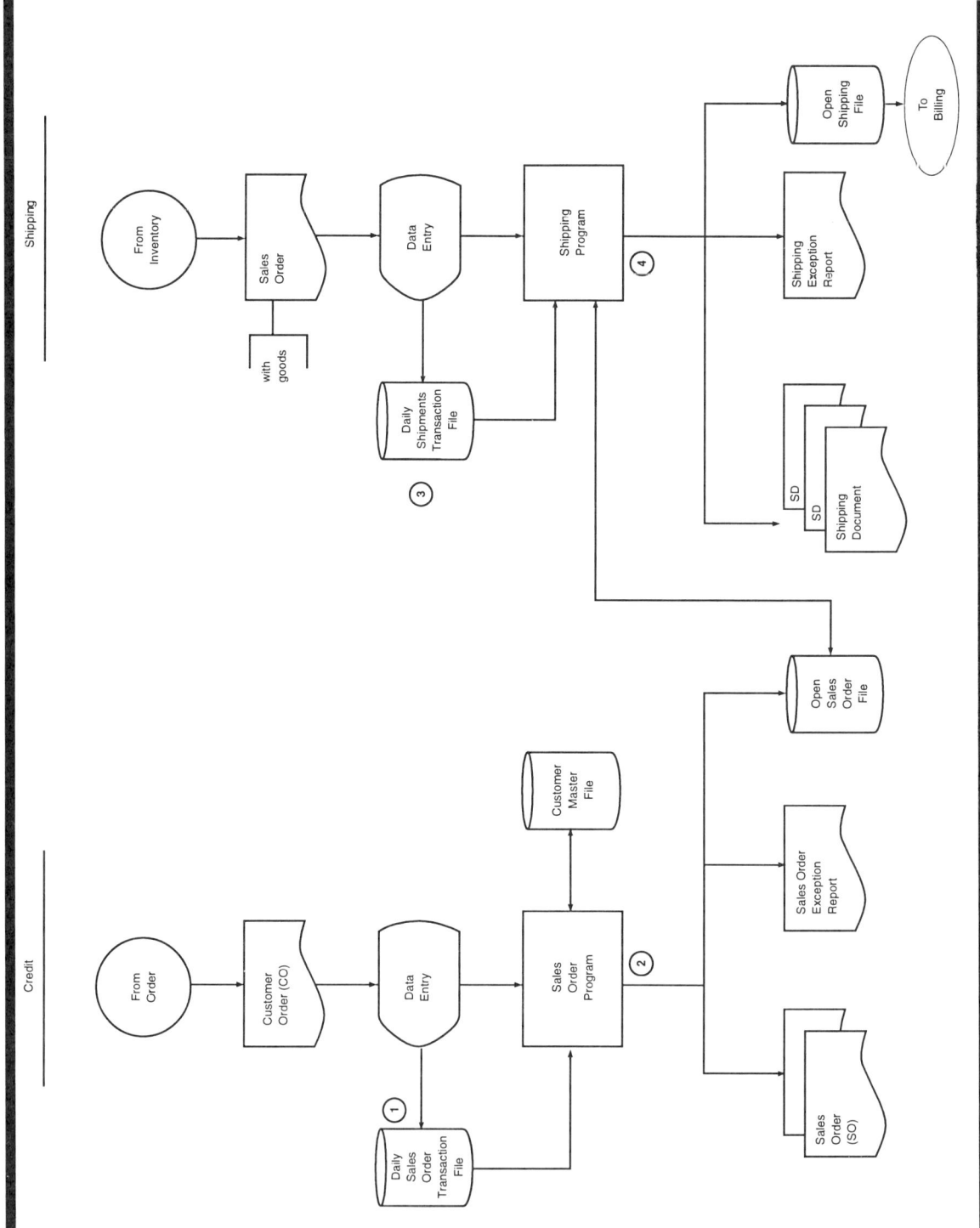

Figure 10-10 Computerized Processing: Credit Sales Subcycle

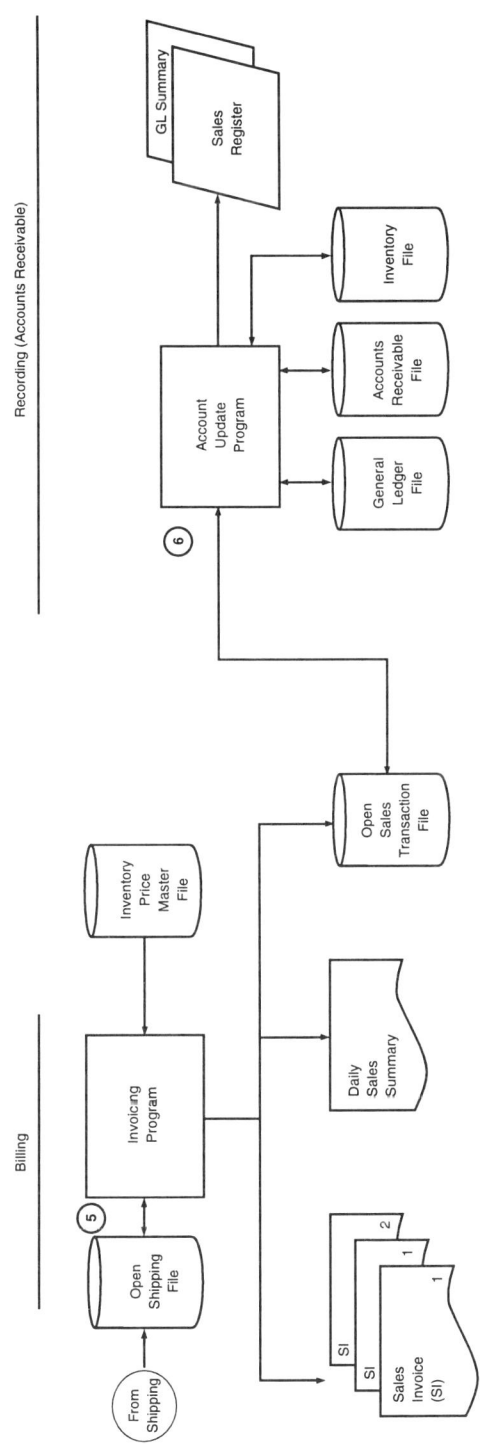

Figure 10-10: *continued*

Recall that the purpose of **control totals** is to allow the organization to enhance the accuracy of its input. The use of control totals involves taking manual totals of the number of records (record counts), numerical fields having a logical total (batch totals), or numerical fields having illogical totals (hash totals) prior to input. These manual totals are then compared to totals generated by the computer program after the transactions have been input. Through control totals, any errors made in inputting transactions can be readily identified.

The **Sales Order Program** then accesses the **Customer Master File** to verify that the customer appears on an authorized customer listing and that the purchase will not exceed that customer's credit limits (Step 2 in Figure 10-10). If the sale is approved by the Sales Order Program, multiple copies of a Sales Order are prepared and the transaction is added to the **Open Sales Order File**. The Open Sales Order File represents all approved sales that have not been shipped to the customer.

In cases where the sale is not approved by the Sales Order Program, the relevant information is summarized on a **Sales Order Exception Report**. Transactions appearing on the Sales Order Exception Report may represent sales to customers who are not authorized to purchase on account from the company. In these cases, company personnel should investigate these individuals' credit history and consider including them on the approved customer listing. Alternatively, these transactions may reflect instances where authorized customers have exceeded their credit limits. In any case, it is important for management to periodically review transactions appearing on the Sales Order Exception Report.

Shipping Department. After approval of the sale (through preparation of the Sales Order), the Inventory Department (or Warehouse) is provided with a copy of the Sales Order. The Inventory Department then releases the appropriate items to the Shipping Department, along with a copy of the Sales Order. While not shown in Figure 10-10, recall that the Shipping Department should count the goods received from the Inventory Department and compare this count to the quantities on the Sales Order. Shipping then enters the customer's account number, Sales Order number, and inventory quantities into a **Daily Shipments Transaction File** (Step 3 in Figure 10-10). As with the Sales Order Program, control totals will be taken to ensure the accuracy of data input. Common control totals include:

- number of shipping transactions (record count)
- total of customer account numbers and Sales Order numbers (hash totals)
- total quantities shipped (batch total)

The **Shipping Program** is then used to compare quantities shipped (from the Daily Shipments Transaction File) to quantities ordered (from the Open Sales Order File). This program yields three types of outputs (Step 4 in Figure 10-10). When quantities from the Daily Shipments Transaction File agree with those from the Open Sales Order File, Shipping Documents and an Open Shipping Order File are created. The **Open Shipping Order File** represents all sales transactions that have been shipped to customers by the company. The two-directional arrow connecting the Open Sales Order File to the Shipping Program indicates that, once a sale has been shipped, the transaction is transferred from the Open Sales Order File to the Open Shipping File.

The third type of output represents transactions where the quantity shipped differs from the quantity ordered. These transactions are written to a **Shipping Exception Report** that should be routinely followed-up by management. In some cases, differences between quantities shipped and quantities ordered may reflect items ordered by customers that are out of stock (backordered items). For these types of transactions, the company would normally ship items on hand and send the backordered items when they are available. In other instances, transactions on this exception report represent honest mistakes on the part of Inventory Department personnel or shipments attempted as part of a defalcation scheme.

Billing Department. After the Open Shipping File has been created, this file is used (along with the **Inventory Price Master File**) to run the **Invoicing Program** (Step 5 in Figure 10-10). As shown in Figure 10-10, the Invoicing Program results in the preparation of Sales Invoices, a Daily Sales Summary, and an **Open Sales Transaction File**. Prior to mailing the Sales Invoice to customers, two important control activities to verify the accuracy of this invoice (not shown in Figure 10-10) should be performed by the Billing Department:

▶ compare information among the Sales Invoice, Sales Order, and Shipping Document

▶ verify the mathematical accuracy of the Sales Invoice

The Open Sales Transaction File is then used to update the accounting records (Step 6 in Figure 10-10). This updating occurs through an **Account Update Program** that accesses the General Ledger File, Accounts Receivable File, and Inventory File. The two-way arrows in Figure 10-10 indicate that the beginning balances in the ledger accounts (General Ledger File), subsidiary accounts receivable accounts (Accounts Receivable File), and inventory item accounts (Inventory File) are accessed for use by the Account Update Program (arrow leading from files to the program). After running the program against the Open Sales Transaction File, the balances are updated and overwritten into the appropriate files (arrows leading from the program to the files). The Account Update Program then prepares a copy of the Sales Register, which represents all of the transactions from the Open Sales Transaction File.

Figure 10-11 summarizes the primary elements of computerized processing in the Credit Sales Subcycle. As shown therein, the inputs represent items from two types of files: a daily transaction file and a file from a previous application. After the program is run, the input file from the previous application is updated to reflect any transactions involving items in that file. For example, the Open Sales Order File is used as an input in the Shipping Program to process shipments of goods to customers. Once items from a particular Shipping Document have been sent, the related transactions are deleted from the Open Sales Order File, since the sale is no longer "open" (*i.e.*, the goods have been shipped to the customer).

Referring to Figure 10-11, computerized processing provides three primary types of outputs: documents, exception or other summary reports, and updated computer files. For example, referring to the Sales Order Program, the outputs of this program are Sales Orders, a Sales Order Exception Report, an Open Sales Order File, and an updated Customer Master File. This Open Sales Order File will contain all undelivered sales existing prior to the Sales Order Program as well as any new sales processed by the Sales Order Program.

Function	Inputs	Processing	Outputs
Credit Authorization	Daily Sales Order Transaction File Customer Master File	Sales Order Program (Access Customer Master File by Customer Number)	Sales Orders Sales Order Exception Report Open Sales Order File Updated Customer Master File
Shipping	Open Sales Order File Daily Shipments Transaction File	Shipping Program (Access Open Sales Order File by Sales Order Number)	Shipping Documents Shipping Exception Report Open Shipping File Updated Open Sales Order File
Billing	Open Shipping File Inventory Price Master File	Invoicing Program (Access Open Shipping File on Periodic Basis)	Sales Invoices Daily Sales Summary Open Sales Transaction File Updated Open Shipping File
Recording/ Accounts Receivable	Open Sales Transaction File General Ledger File Accounts Receivable File Inventory File	Account Update Program (Access Open Sales Transaction File on Periodic Basis)	Sales Register General Ledger Summary Updated General Ledger File Updated Accounts Receivable File Updated Open Sales Transaction File Updated Inventory File

Figure 10-11: *Elements of Computerized Processing: Credit Sales Subcycle*

◘ Cash Receipts and Sales Adjustments

Figure 10-12 provides an overview of computerized processing of transactions in the Cash Receipts and Sales Adjustments subcycles. The computerized processing in these subcycles is fairly similar and consists of the following major steps:

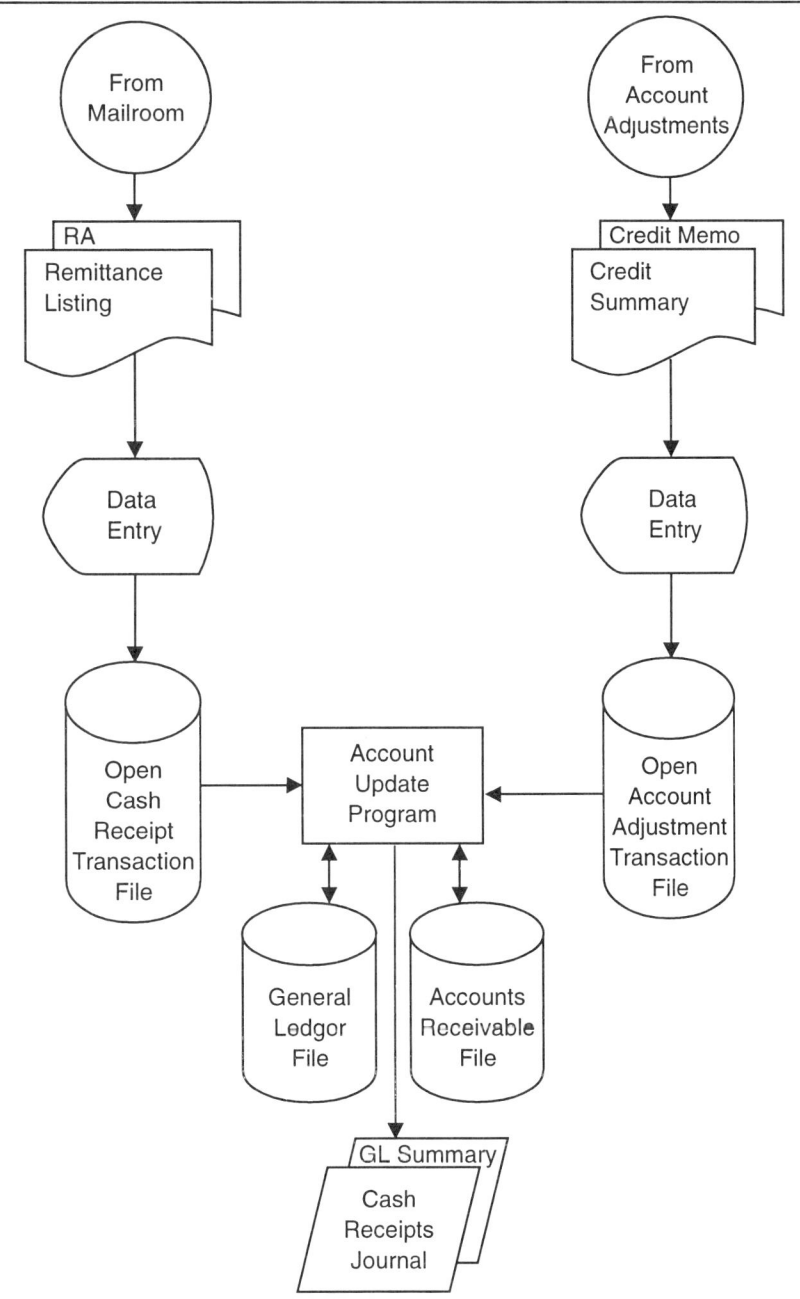

Figure 10-12: *Computerized Processing: Cash Receipts and Sales Adjustments Subcycles*

1. Both processes begin with the receipt of the appropriate documentation from other functions. For cash receipts, a copy of the Remittance Listing and Remittance Advice is received from the Mailroom. For account adjustment transactions, a copy of the Credit Memorandum and Credit Summary is received from Account Adjustments.

2. Data from the source documents (Remittance Advices and Credit Memoranda) are input into a transaction file (the **Open Cash Receipts Transaction File** and **Open Account Adjustment Transaction File**). Prior to input, several control totals are determined, such as:

   ▶ number of transactions entered (record count)

   ▶ total of customer account numbers (hash total)

   ▶ total dollar amount of cash receipts or account adjustments (batch total)

3. Both transaction files are run against the **Account Update Program**. The Account Update Program updates the General Ledger File and Accounts Receivable File for cash receipts and account adjustment transactions. This program then prepares copies of the General Ledger Summary and Cash Receipts Journal.

Once again, while Figure 10-12 focuses on elements involved with the computerized processing of transactions, it is important to note that many of the manual control activities discussed earlier in Figures 10-6 and 10-8 are still applicable. For example, upon receipt of cash from customers in the mail, the mailroom should prepare a Remittance Listing and restrictively endorse all Checks received. Later, these Checks should be deposited in the company's bank account intact and daily. For the Account Adjustments Subcycle, Account Adjustments should approve the sales return, sales discount, or sales allowance prior to preparing the Credit Memorandum.

Figure 10-13 summarizes the primary elements of computerized processing in the Cash Receipts and Account Adjustments Subcycles.

Function	Inputs	Processing	Outputs
Recording/Accounts Receivable (Cash Receipts Subcycle)	Open Cash Receipts Transaction File General Ledger File Accounts Receivable File	Account Update Program (Access Open Cash Receipts Transaction File on Periodic Basis)	General Ledger Summary Cash Receipts Journal Updated General Ledger File Updated Accounts Receivable File
Recording/Accounts Receivable (Sales Adjustments Subcycle)	Open Account Adjustment Transaction File General Ledger File Accounts Receivable File	Account Update Program (Access Open Account Adjustment Transaction File on Periodic Basis)	General Ledger Summary Updated General Ledger File Updated Accounts Receivable File

Figure 10-13: *Elements of Computerized Processing: Cash Receipts and Sales Adjustments Subcycles*

CHAPTER CHECKPOINTS

*10-19. How does the Sales Order Program verify authorization of sales to the organization's customers?

*10-20. What are the primary outputs of the Shipping Program?

*10-21. How does the Invoicing Program ensure that customers are invoiced for all shipments made to customers?

*10-22. How are customer account balances updated for credit sales and cash receipts transactions in a computerized processing environment?

SUMMARY OF KEY POINTS

1. An operating cycle consists of the procedures performed, policies followed, and documents created by an organization and its employees from the initiation of a transaction until its ultimate recording in the accounting records. Separate operating cycles exist for each of the major types of transactions for an organization.

2. The Revenue cycle consists of three major types of transactions: (1) credit sales transactions (the Credit Sales subcycle), (2) cash receipts transactions (the Cash Receipts subcycle), and (3) sales adjustment transactions (the Sales Adjustments subcycle).

3. The Credit Sales subcycle begins with the receipt of an order from a customer. This order is summarized by the Order Department through the preparation of a Customer Order. Once the Customer Order has been prepared, the Credit Department should use formal procedures to grant credit to its customers. If credit is approved, a Sales Order is prepared by the Credit Department.

4. After credit approval, the Shipping Department obtains the ordered items from Inventory. A Shipping Document is prepared which acts as a record of the item(s) sent by the Shipping Department to the organization's customers. Once goods have been sent to customers, the Billing Department prepares a Sales Invoice. The Sales Invoice is the bill sent from the organization to its customers. All sales made by the organization for a specified period of time (normally, a day) are summarized in the Daily Sales Summary.

5. The Sales Adjustments subcycle is concerned with transactions resulting from sales returns, sales allowances, and uncollectible accounts. The most important control activity in this subcycle is that the individual approving the sales adjustment transaction have no other responsibilities in either the Credit Sales or Cash Receipts subcycles. Sales adjustment transactions are approved through the preparation of a Credit Memorandum.

6. The Cash Receipts subcycle begins with the receipt of payment and a Remittance Advice from the organization's customers. Immediately upon receipt in the Mailroom, the organization should: (1) restrictively endorse all Checks received from customers, and (2) prepare a listing of all cash received (a Remittance Listing).

7. Once the Remittance Listing has been prepared, a copy of this document and the Checks are forwarded to the Cashier. The Cashier compares the Checks to the Remittance Listing and verifies the mathematical accuracy of the Remittance Listing. Then, the Cashier prepares the Deposit Slip. Effective internal control dictates that all cash receipts be deposited in the company's bank accounts intact and daily.

*8. In a computerized accounting environment, transactions in the Credit Sales subcycle are processed using four major programs: (1) the Sales Order Program, (2) the Shipping Program, (3) the Invoicing Program, and (4) the Account Update Program. Transactions in the Cash Receipts and Sales Adjustments subcycles are processed using the Account Update Program.

◼ GLOSSARY

*Account Update Program. A program used in a computerized processing environment to update the accounting records for credit sales, cash receipts, and sales adjustment transactions.

Accounting System. The series of documents, journals, and ledgers used by the organization to record its transactions. The accounting system represents the information and communication component of internal control.

Adjustment Request. A request received from the organization's customers for an adjustment to their account resulting from a sales discount, sales allowance, or an uncollectible account.

Cash Receipts Journal. Journal used by the organization to summarize cash received from its customers. Totals from the Cash Receipts Journal serve as the basis for the journal entry for cash receipts transactions.

Control Activities. Components of internal control that are implemented by the organization to address various risks and reduce the likelihood that these risks occur.

Control Environment. The overall level of control consciousness that exists within an organization. The control environment includes such factors as: (1) integrity and ethical values, (2) commitment to competence, (3) the existence of a Board of Directors and Audit Committee, (4) management's philosophy and operating style, (5) the organizational structure, (6) assignment of authority and responsibility, and (7) human resource policies and practices.

Credit Memorandum. A document prepared to authorize credit to a customer's account for sales returns or allowances.

Credit Sales Subcycle. The component of the Revenue cycle concerned with the sale of goods or services to the organization's customers.

Customer Order. A document prepared by the Order Department which summarizes information about a customer's request to purchase items on account. This document is later forwarded to the Credit Department for approval.

Customer Request. A request received from a customer to purchase items from the organization on account.

Daily Credit Summary. Prepared by the Account Adjustments Department, this report summarizes the sales adjustments activity for a limited period of time (normally, a day).

Daily Sales Summary. Prepared by the Billing Department, this report summarizes the sales activity over a limited period of time (normally, a day).

*****Invoicing Program.** A program used in a computerized processing environment to prepare: (1) Sales Invoices, (2) the Daily Sales Summary, and (3) an Open Sales Transaction File.

Monitoring. The process through which the company's internal control is assessed over time.

Operating Cycle. The procedures performed, policies followed, and documents created by an organization and its employees from the initiation of a transaction until its ultimate recording in the accounting records.

Remittance Advice. Received from customers along with their payments, the Remittance Advice indicates the amount paid by a customer on his or her account.

Remittance Listing. A listing of all cash received through the mails from the organization's customers.

Revenue Cycle. The operating cycle that relates to the revenue-generating activities of the organization. The Revenue cycle includes credit sales transactions, cash receipts transactions, and sales adjustments transactions.

Risk Assessment. The process through which the organization identifies, analyzes, and manages risks related to the objectives of internal control. Once these risks have been identified, control activities are implemented to address these risks and reduce the probability that they occur.

Sales Invoice. The document used by the organization to bill its customers for sales.

Sales Order. A document prepared by the Credit Department to authorize sales to a customer on account.

*****Sales Order Program.** A program used in a computerized processing environment to verify the credit worthiness of customers and prepare: (1) Sales Orders, (2) a Sales Order Exception Report, and (3) the Open Sales Order File.

Sales Register. Journal used by the organization to summarize sales made to customers on account. Totals from the Sales Register normally serve as the basis for the journal entry for sales transactions.

Shipping Document (or Bill of Lading). A document providing evidence of the quantity of goods shipped to customers. In addition to protecting goods while they are in transit, the Shipping Document is used by the organization to ensure that it bills customers for all goods shipped.

*****Shipping Program.** A program used in a computerized processing environment to prepare: (1) Shipping Documents, (2) a Shipping Exception Report, and (3) the Open Shipments File. This program also updates the Open Sales Order File.

QUESTIONS AND PROBLEMS

10-23. Select the **best** answer for each of the following items:

1. Internal control over cash receipts is weakened when an employee who receives customer mail receipts also:

    a. Prepares initial cash receipts records.
    b. Records credits to individual accounts receivable.
    c. Prepares bank deposit slips for all mail receipts.
    d. Maintains a petty cash fund.

2. Which of the following would the auditor consider to be an incompatible operation if the Cashier receives remittances from the Mailroom?

    a. The Cashier posts the receipts to the accounts receivable subsidiary ledger cards.
    b. The Cashier makes the daily deposit at a local bank.
    c. The Cashier prepares the daily deposit.
    d. The Cashier endorses the Checks.

3. Proper authorization procedures in the Revenue cycle usually provide for the approval of bad debt write-offs by an employee in which of the following departments?

    a. Treasurer.
    b. Sales.
    c. Billing.
    d. Accounts Receivable.

4. Sound internal control procedures dictate that defective merchandise returned by customers should be presented initially to the:

    a. Sales Clerk.
    b. Purchasing Clerk.
    c. Receiving Clerk.
    d. Inventory Control Clerk.

5. Immediately upon the receipt of cash, a responsible employee should:

    a. Record the amount in the Cash Receipts Journal.
    b. Prepare a Remittance Listing.
    c. Update the subsidiary accounts receivable records.
    d. Prepare a Deposit Slip in triplicate.

6. An entity with a large volume of customer remittances by mail could most likely reduce the risk of employee misappropriation of cash by using:

   a. Employee fidelity bonds.
   b. Independently prepared mailroom prelists.
   c. Daily Check Summaries.
   d. A bank lockbox system.

7. Which of the following internal control procedures most likely would assure the auditor that all billed sales are correctly posted to the accounts receivable ledger?

   a. Daily Sales Summaries are compared to daily postings to the accounts receivable ledger.
   b. Each Sales Invoice is supported by a prenumbered Shipping Document.
   c. The accounts receivable ledger is reconciled daily to the control account in the general ledger.
   d. Each shipment on credit is supported by a prenumbered Sales Invoice.

8. Upon receipt of customers' Checks in the mailroom, a responsible employee should prepare a Remittance Listing that is forwarded to the Cashier. A copy of the listing should be sent to the:

   a. Internal auditor to investigate the listing for unusual transactions.
   b. Treasurer to compare the listing with the monthly bank statement.
   c. Accounts Receivable Bookkeeper to update the subsidiary accounts receivable records.
   d. Entity's bank to compare the listing with the Cashier's Deposit Slip.

9. Which of the following procedures would most likely not be an internal control procedure designed to reduce the risk of errors in the billing process?

   a. Comparing control totals for Shipping Documents with corresponding totals for Sales Invoices.
   b. Using computer programmed controls on the pricing and mathematical accuracy of Sales Invoices.
   c. Matching Shipping Documents with approved Sales Orders before Invoice preparation.
   d. Reconciling the control totals for Sales Invoices with the accounts receivable subsidiary ledger.

10. Which of the following controls would most likely help ensure that all credit sales transactions of an entity are recorded?

    a. The Billing Department Supervisor sends copies of approved Sales Orders to the Credit Department for comparison to authorized credit limits and current customer account balances.
    b. The Accounting Department Supervisor independently reconciles the accounts receivable subsidiary ledger to the accounts receivable control account on a monthly basis.
    c. The Accounting Department Supervisor controls the mailing of monthly statements to customers and investigates any differences reported by customers.
    d. The Billing Department Supervisor matches prenumbered Shipping Documents with entries in the Sales Register.

11. An auditor would most likely review an entity's periodic accounting for the numerical sequence of Shipping Documents and Invoices to support management's financial statement assertion of:

    a. Existence or occurrence.
    b. Rights and obligations.
    c. Valuation or allocation.
    d. Completeness.

12. Alpha Company uses its Sales Invoices for posting perpetual inventory records. Inadequate internal controls over the invoicing function allow goods to be shipped that are not invoiced. The inadequate controls should cause a(n):

    a. Understatement of revenues, receivables, and inventory.
    b. Overstatement of revenues and receivables and an understatement of inventory.
    c. Understatement of revenues and receivables and an overstatement of inventory.
    d. Overstatement of revenues, receivables, and inventory.

13. Tracing Bills of Lading to Sales Invoices provides evidence that:

    a. Shipments to customers were recorded as sales.
    b. Recorded sales were shipped.
    c. Invoiced sales were shipped.
    d. Shipments to customers were invoiced.

14. Which of the following is not a factor creating the special need for physical controls over cash?

    a. Cash is not readily identifiable.
    b. Cash has value to a potential embezzler.
    c. Cash is highly liquid.
    d. Cash is easy to conceal.
    e. All of the above create a special need for physical controls over cash.

15. The Remittance Listing of cash receipts should be prepared by:

    a. The Accounts Receivable Clerk responsible for posting payments to customers' accounts.
    b. The Cashier responsible for preparing the bank deposit.
    c. The General Ledger Accountant responsible for making entries for cash receipts to cash, accounts receivable control, and other credits.
    d. A Mailroom employee upon the opening of the mail.
    e. The Credit Department, once approval for the sale has been made.

16. Comparing the details of a bank Deposit Slip with Remittance Advices allows the auditor to:

    a. Discover lapping that has occurred with that day's deposit.
    b. Determine that deposits of cash receipts are timely and intact.
    c. Observe the segregation of access to cash receipts and cash disbursements.
    d. Discover instances of kiting perpetrated by client employees.
    e. Determine that the allowance for doubtful accounts is reasonably stated.

17. Which of the following departments should not have any recording responsibility for sales on account under an effective internal control?

    a. Accounts receivable.
    b. Billing.
    c. Credit.
    d. General Ledger.
    e. All of the above have recording responsibility for sales on account.

18. A _____ should be prepared by the _____ Department to authorize sale on account to a particular customer.

    a. Customer Order; Credit
    b. Sales Order; Credit
    c. Shipping Document; Shipping
    d. Sales Invoice; Billing
    e. Sales Order; Accounts Receivable

19. The auditor can verify that all recorded sales have been properly authorized by client personnel by:

    a. Vouching recorded sales to Vendor Invoices.
    b. Evaluating the adequacy of the client's allowance for doubtful accounts.
    c. Obtaining an aged listing of accounts receivable.
    d. Vouching recorded sales to Shipping Documents.
    e. Vouching recorded sales to Sales Orders.

20. The auditor normally tests entries in the Sales Register by vouching to underlying documents:

    a. Because the existence or occurrence assertion is generally of more concern than the completeness assertion.
    b. To determine that all shipments of merchandise have been invoiced.
    c. To determine that Sales Register totals are properly posted to the General Ledger.
    d. To determine the arithmetic accuracy of the accounts receivable aging.
    e. Because of the importance of ensuring that all sales transactions have been recorded.

21. By selecting a sample of Shipping Documents and identifying the associated Sales Invoice, the auditor has determined that:

    a. All recorded sales have been shipped to the customers.
    b. All write-offs of accounts receivable have been properly authorized.
    c. All Invoices represent bona fide sales made to customers.
    d. All shipments to customers have been invoiced.
    e. Mathematical extensions on invoices are accurate.

22. In accounting for the numerical sequence of prenumbered Sales Invoices, the auditor attempts to verify that:

   a. All shipments of goods have been recorded.
   b. All sales made to customers have been recorded.
   c. All shipments made to customers have been invoiced.
   d. Individual Sales Invoices are recorded at the appropriate amounts.
   e. The duties of preparing Sales Invoices and having custody of the Inventory have been properly segregated.

23. Using the following key, what is the correct order of preparation of the following documents in the Credit Sales subcycle?

   1 = Shipping Document.
   2 = Sales Order.
   3 = Sales Invoice.
   4 = Customer Order.

   a. 1, 2, 3, 4.
   b. 2, 4, 3, 1.
   c. 4, 2, 3, 1.
   d. 4, 2, 1, 3.
   e. 2, 4, 1, 3.

   (Items 1 through 13 in 10-23; AICPA Adapted)

10-24. For each of the following subcycles, indicate the: (1) account(s) that are affected; (2) the function(s) that are involved in transaction processing; and (3) the documents, journals, and ledgers that are created.

   a. Credit Sales subcycle
   b. Sales Adjustments subcycle
   c. Cash Receipts subcycle

10-25. What are the duties of the six major Departments involved with the Credit Sales subcycle?

10-26. List and describe the major documents created in the Credit Sales subcycle.

10-27. Comment on each of the following statements made by Deion Aikman, an employee at one of your firm's clients.

   a. "I don't know why we waste our time checking customer credit. We ought to sell to anyone who is wiling to buy from us. We just can't afford to turn away any customers."
   b. "There's too long of a delay in sending goods to our customers. What we ought to do is to send the items to Shipping as soon as we get the order. We can worry about approval later."
   c. "Why should we look at the Sales Orders when preparing Invoices? It's not important what the customer ordered; the important thing is what we delivered to the customer."
   d. "Since the Billing Department is so involved with our accounts receivable, they should investigate customer responses to monthly statements and perform reconciliations involving accounts receivable."

10-28. What are the duties of the major Departments involved with the Cash Receipts subcycle?

10-29. List and describe the major documents created in the Cash Receipts subcycle.

10-30. For each of the following control activities over cash receipts, indicate an example of how the auditor could test the operating effectiveness of that control procedure.

  a. Prenumbered Remittance Listings should be prepared in the Mailroom after opening mail.
  b. The accuracy of the Remittance Listing should be verified by the Cashier.
  c. Personnel independent of cash receipts processing should prepare monthly Bank Reconciliations.
  d. Appropriate segregation of duties should be established and maintained in the Cash Receipts subcycle.
  e. Checks should be restrictively endorsed by Mailroom personnel upon opening the mail.
  f. Cash receipts should be deposited intact and daily.
  g. Performance reviews should compare actual cash receipts data to expected data.

*10-31. List the major steps in the computerized processing of transactions in the Credit Sales, Cash Receipts, and Sales Adjustments subcycles.

*10-32. Briefly describe the contents of the following computerized processing files:

  a. Daily Sales Order Transaction File.
  b. Customer Master File.
  c. Open Sales Order File.
  d. Daily Shipments Transaction File.
  e. Open Shipping File.
  f. Open Sales Transaction File.
  g. Open Cash Receipts Transaction File.
  h. Open Account Adjustment Transaction File.

10-33. Jerome Paper Company engaged you to review its internal control. Jerome does not prelist cash receipts before they are recorded and has other weaknesses in processing collections of trade receivables, the company's largest asset. In discussing the matter with the controller, you find she is chiefly interested in economy when she assigns duties to the fifteen office personnel. She feels the main considerations are that the work should be done by people who are most familiar with it, capable of doing it, and available when it has to be done.

The controller says she has excellent control over trade receivables, because receivables are pledged as security for a continually-renewable bank loan and the bank sends out positive confirmation requests occasionally, based on a list of pledged receivables furnished by the company each week (letters asking customers to confirm the amounts listed on the books as owed to the company). You learn that the bank's internal auditor is satisfied if she gets an acceptable response on 70 percent of her requests.

Required:

  a. Explain how prelisting of cash receipts strengthens internal control over cash.
  b. Assume that an employee handles cash receipts from trade customers before they are recorded. List the duties that the employee should not perform in order to withhold from him the opportunity to conceal embezzlement of cash receipts.

(AICPA Adapted)

10-34. The customer billing and collection functions of the Robinson Company, a small paint manufacturer, are attended to by a Receptionist, an Accounts Receivable Clerk, and a Cashier who also serves as a secretary. The company's paint products are sold to wholesalers and retail stores.

The following describes all of the procedures performed by the employees of the Robinson Company pertaining to customer billings and collections:

a. The mail is opened by the Receptionist, who gives the customers' Purchase Orders to the Accounts Receivable Clerk. Fifteen to twenty orders are received each day. Under instructions to expedite the shipment of orders, the Accounts Receivable Clerk at once prepares a five-copy Sales Invoice form, which is distributed as follows:

1. Copy No. 1 is the customer billing copy and is held by the Accounts Receivable Clerk until notice of shipment is received.
2. Copy No. 2 is the Accounts Receivable Department copy and is held for ultimate posting of the accounts receivable records.
3. Copies Nos. 3 and 4 are sent to the Shipping Department.
4. Copy No. 5 is sent to the Storeroom (Inventory Department) as authority for release of the goods to the Shipping Department.

b. After the paint ordered has been moved from the storeroom to the Shipping Department, the Shipping Department prepares the Bills of Lading and labels the cartons. Sales Invoice Copy No. 4 is inserted in a carton as a packing slip. After the trucker has picked up the shipment, the customer's copy of the Bill of Lading and Copy No. 3, on which are noted any undershipments, are returned to the Accounts Receivable Clerk. The company does not "back order" in the event of undershipments; customers are expected to reorder the merchandise. The Robinson Company's copy of the Bill of Lading is filed by the Shipping Department.

c. When Copy No. 3 and the customer's copy of the Bill of Lading are received by the Accounts Receivable Clerk, Copy Nos. 1 and 2 are completed by numbering them and inserting quantities shipped, unit prices, extensions, discounts, and totals. The Accounts Receivable Clerk then mails Copy No. 1 and the copy of the Bill of Lading to the customer. Copy Nos. 2 and 3 are stapled together.

d. The individual accounts receivable ledger cards are posted by the Accounts Receivable Clerk by a bookkeeping machine procedure whereby the Sales Register is prepared as a carbon copy of the postings. Postings are made from Copy No. 2, which is then filed, along with staple-attached Copy No. 3, in numerical order. Each month, the General Ledger Clerk summarizes the Sales Register for posting to the General Ledger accounts.

e. Since the Robinson Company is short of cash, the deposit of receipts is also expedited. The Receptionist turns over all mail receipts and related correspondence to the Accounts Receivable Clerk who examines the Checks and determines that the accompanying Vouchers (Remittance Advices) or correspondence contain enough detail to permit posting of the accounts. The Accounts Receivable Clerk then endorses the Checks and gives them to the Cashier, who prepares the daily deposit. No currency is received in the mail, and no paint is sold over the counter at the factory.

f. The Accounts Receivable Clerk uses the Vouchers or correspondence that accompanied the Checks to post the accounts receivable ledger cards. The bookkeeping machine prepares a Cash Receipts Register as a carbon copy of the postings. Monthly, the General Ledger Clerk summarizes the Cash Receipts Register for posting to the General Ledger accounts. The Accounts Receivable Clerk also corresponds with customers about unauthorized deductions for discounts, freight or advertising allowances, returns, and so on, and prepares the appropriate Credit Memos. Disputed items of large amount are turned over to the Sales Manager for settlement. Each month, the Accounts Receivable Clerk prepares a trial balance of the open accounts receivable and compares the resultant total with the general ledger control account for accounts receivable.

Required:

Discuss the internal control weaknesses in the Robinson Company's procedures related to customer billings and remittances and the accounting for these transactions. In your discussion, in addition to identifying the weaknesses, explain what could happen as a result of each weakness.

(AICPA Adapted)

10-35. Charting, Inc., a new audit client of yours, processes its sales and cash receipts in the following manner:

   a. **Payment on account.** The mail is opened each morning by a Mail Clerk in the Sales Department. The Mail Clerk prepares a Remittance Advice (showing customer and amount paid) if one is not received. The Checks and Remittance Advices are then forwarded to the Sales Department supervisor, who reviews each Check and forwards the Checks and Remittance Advices to the Accounting Department supervisor.

   The Accounting Department supervisor, who also functions as Credit Manager in approving new credit and all credit limits, reviews all Checks for payments on past-due accounts and then forwards all the Checks and Remittance Advices to the Accounts Receivable Clerk, who arranges the Remittance Advices in alphabetical order. The Remittance Advices are posted directly to the accounts receivable ledger cards. The Checks are endorsed by stamp and totaled. The total is posted to the Cash Receipts Journal. The Remittance Advices are filed chronologically.

   After receiving the cash from the previous day's cash sales, the Accounts Receivable Clerk prepares the daily Deposit Slip in triplicate. The third copy of the deposit slip is filed by date, and the original and the second copy accompany the bank deposit.

   b. **Sales.** Sales Clerks prepare Sales Invoices in triplicate. The original and second copy are presented to the Cashier. The third copy is retained by the Sales Clerk in the Sales Book. When the sale is for cash, the customer pays the Sales Clerk, who presents the money to the Cashier with the Invoice copies.

   A credit sale is approved by the Cashier from an approved credit list after the Sales Clerk prepares the three-part invoice. After receiving the cash or approving the invoice, the Cashier validates the original copy of the Sales Invoice and gives it to the customer. At the end of each day, the Cashier recaps the sales and cash received and forwards the cash and the second copy of all Sales Invoices to the Accounts Receivable Clerk.

   The Accounts Receivable Clerk balances the cash received with cash Sales Invoices and prepares a Daily Sales Summary. The credit Sales Invoices are posted to the accounts receivable ledger, and then all Invoices are sent to the Inventory Control Clerk in the Sales Department for posting to the Inventory control cards. After posting, the Inventory Control Clerk files all Invoices numerically. The Accounts Receivable Clerk posts the Daily Sales Summary to the Cash Receipts Journal and Sales Journal (Sales Register) and files the Sales Summaries by date.

   The cash from cash sales is combined with the cash received on account to compose the daily bank deposit.

   c. **Bank deposits.** The bank validates the Deposit Slip and returns the second copy to the Accounting Department, where it is filed by date by the Accounts Receivable Clerk.

   Monthly bank statements are reconciled promptly by the Accounting Department Supervisor and filed by date.

Required:

Prepare a flowchart of the existing system of sales and cash receipts.

(AICPA Adapted)

10-36. Taylor, CPA, has been engaged to audit the financial statements of Johnson's Coat Outlet, Inc., a medium-sized mail-order retail store that sells a wide variety of coats to the public.

Required:

Prepare the "Shipments" section of Taylor's internal control questionnaire. Each question should elicit either a yes or no response. Use the following format:

Question	Yes	No

(AICPA Adapted)

10-37. The flowchart below depicts part of a client's Revenue Cycle. Some of the flowchart symbols are labeled to indicate control procedures and records. For each symbol numbered 1 through 13, select one response from the answer lists below. Each response in the lists may be selected once or **not** at all.

Answer Lists
Operations and Control Procedures

- A. Enter shipping data
- B. Verify agreement of Sales Order and Shipping Document
- C. Write-off accounts receivable
- D. To Warehouse and Shipping Department
- E. Authorize account receivable write-off
- F. Prepare aged trial balance
- G. To Sales Department
- H. Release goods for shipment
- I. To Accounts Receivable Department
- J. Enter price data
- K. Determine that customer exists
- L. Match customer Purchase Order with Sales Order
- M. Perform customer credit check
- N. Prepare Sales Journal
- O. Prepare Sales Invoice

Documents, Journals, Ledgers, and Files

- P. Shipping Document
- Q. General Ledger Master File
- R. General Journal
- S. Master Price File
- T. Sales Journal
- U. Sales Invoice
- V. Cash Receipts Journal
- W. Uncollectible Accounts File
- X. Shipping File
- Y. Aged Trial Balance
- Z. Open Order File

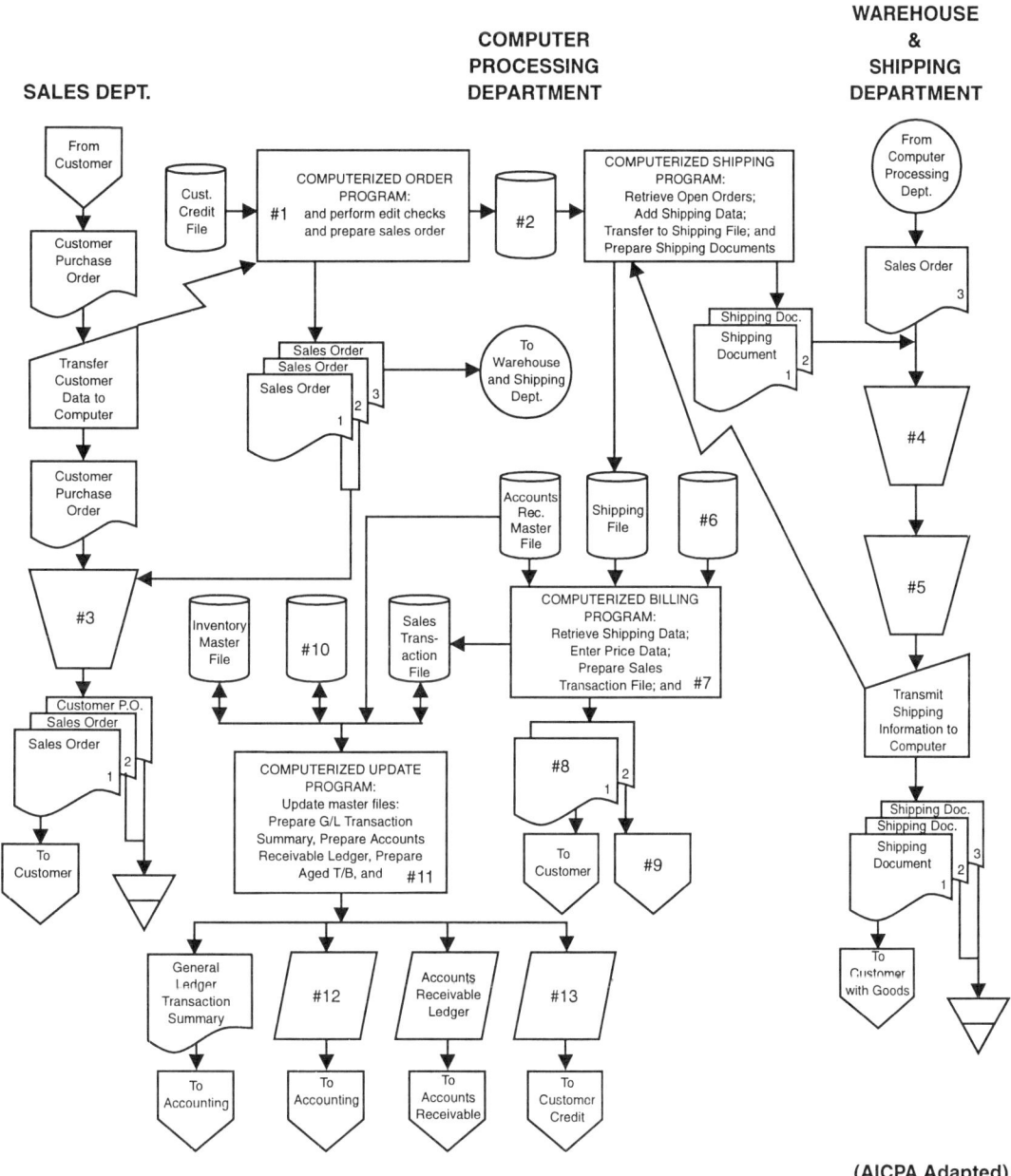

10 / The Revenue Cycle

10-51

10-38. A CPA's audit workpapers include the narrative description below of the cash receipts and billing portions of the internal control of Parktown Medical Center, Inc. Parktown is a small health care provider that is owned by a publicly-held corporation. It employs seven salaried physicians, ten nurses, three support staff in a common laboratory, and three clerical workers. The clerical workers perform such tasks as reception, correspondence, cash receipts, billing, and appointment scheduling and are adequately bonded. They are referred to in the narrative as "Office Manager," "Clerk #1," and "Clerk #2."

Narrative

Most patients pay for services by cash or check at the time services are rendered. Credit is not approved by the clerical staff. The physician who is to perform the respective services approves credit based on an interview. When credit is approved, the physician files a memo with the Billing Clerk (Clerk #2) to set up the receivable from data generated by the physician.

The services physician prepares a Charges Slip that is given to Clerk #1 for pricing and preparation of the patient's bill. Clerk #1 transmits a copy of the bill to Clerk #2 for preparation of the revenue summary and for posting in the accounts receivable subsidiary ledger.

The cash receipts functions are performed by Clerk #1, who receives cash and checks directly from patients and gives each patient a prenumbered cash receipt. Clerk #1 opens the mail and immediately stamps all checks "for deposit only" and lists cash and checks for deposit. The cash and checks are deposited daily by the Office Manager. The list of cash and checks together with the related remittance advices are forwarded by Clerk #1 to Clerk #2. Clerk #1 also serves as receptionist and performs general correspondence duties.

Clerk #2 prepares and sends monthly statements to patients with unpaid balances. Clerk #2 also prepares the Cash Receipts Journal and is responsible for the accounts receivable subsidiary ledger. No other clerical employee is permitted access to the accounts receivable subsidiary ledger. Uncollectible accounts are written off by Clerk #2 only after the communicates the write-off approval to the Office Manager. The Office Manager then issues a write-off memo that Clerk #2 processes.

The Office Manager supervises the clerks, issues write-off memos, schedules appointments for the doctors, makes bank deposits, reconciles bank statements, and performs general correspondence duties.

Additional services are performed monthly by a local accountant who posts summaries prepared by the clerks to the general ledger, prepares income statements, and files the appropriate payroll forms and tax returns. The accountant reports directly to the parent corporation.

Required:

Based only on the information in the narrative, describe the reportable conditions and one resulting misstatement that could occur and not be preventable or detected by Parktown's internal control concerning the cash receipts and billing function. Do **not** describe how to correct the reportable conditions and potential misstatements. Use the format illustrated below.

Reportable Condition	Potential Misstatement
There is no control to verify that fees are billed at authorized rates and terms.	Accounts receivable could be overstated and uncollectible accounts understated because of the lack of controls.

(AICPA Adapted)

10-39. An auditor's workpapers include the narrative description below of the cash receipts and billing portions of the internal control of Rural Building Supplies, Inc. Rural is a single-store retailer that sells a variety of tools, garden supplies, lumber, small appliances, and electrical fixtures to the public, although about half of Rural's sales are to construction contractors on account. Rural employs 12 salaried sales associates, a credit manager, three full-time clerical workers, and several part-time cash register clerks and assistant bookkeepers. The full-time clerical workers perform such tasks as cash receipts, billing, and accounting and are adequately bonded. They are referred to in the narrative as "Accounts Receivable Supervisor," "Cashier," and "Bookkeeper."

Narrative

Retail customers pay for merchandise by cash or credit card at cash registers when merchandise is purchased. A contractor may purchase merchandise on account if approved by the Credit Manager based only on the manager's familiarity with the contractor's reputation. After credit is approved, the Sales Associate files a prenumbered charge form with the Accounts Receivable (A/R) Supervisor to set up the receivable.

The A/R Supervisor independently verifies the pricing and other details on the charge form by reference to a management-authorized price list, corrects any errors, prepares the invoice, and supervises a part-time employee who mails the invoice to the contractor. The A/R Supervisor electronically posts the details of the invoice in the A/R subsidiary ledger; simultaneously, the transaction's details are transmitted to the Bookkeeper. The A/R supervisor also prepares a monthly computer-generated A/R subsidiary ledger without a reconciliation with the A/R control account and a monthly report of overdue accounts.

The cash receipts functions are performed by the Cashier who also supervises the cash register clerks. The Cashier opens the mail, compares each check with the enclosed remittance advice, stamps each check "for deposit only" and lists checks for deposit. The Cashier then gives the remittance advices to the Bookkeeper for recording. The Cashier deposits the checks daily separate from the daily deposit of cash register receipts. The Cashier retains the verified deposit slips to assist in reconciling the monthly bank statements, but forwards to the Bookkeeper a copy of the daily register summary. The Cashier does not have access to the journals or ledgers.

The Bookkeeper receives the details of transactions from the A/R Supervisor and the Cashier for journalizing and posting to the General Ledger. After recording the Remittance Advices received from the Cashier, the Bookkeeper electronically transmits the remittance information to the A/R Supervisor for subsidiary ledger updating. The Bookkeeper authorizes the A/R Supervisor to write off accounts as uncollectible when six months have passed since the initial overdue notice was sent. At this time, the Credit Manager is notified by the Bookkeeper not to grant additional credit to that contractor.

Required:

Based only on the information in the narrative, describe the internal control weaknesses in Rural's internal control concerning the cash receipts and billing functions. Organize the weaknesses by employee job functions: Credit Manager, A/R Supervisor, Cashier, and Bookkeeper. Do not describe how to correct the weaknesses.

(AICPA Adapted)

10-40. The flowchart on the next page depicts the activities relating to the Shipping, Billing, and collecting processes used by Smallco Lumber, Inc.

Required:

Identify weaknesses in internal control relating to the activities of:

a. Warehouse Clerk
b. Bookkeeper #1
c. Bookkeeper #2
d. Collection Clerk

(AICPA Adapted)

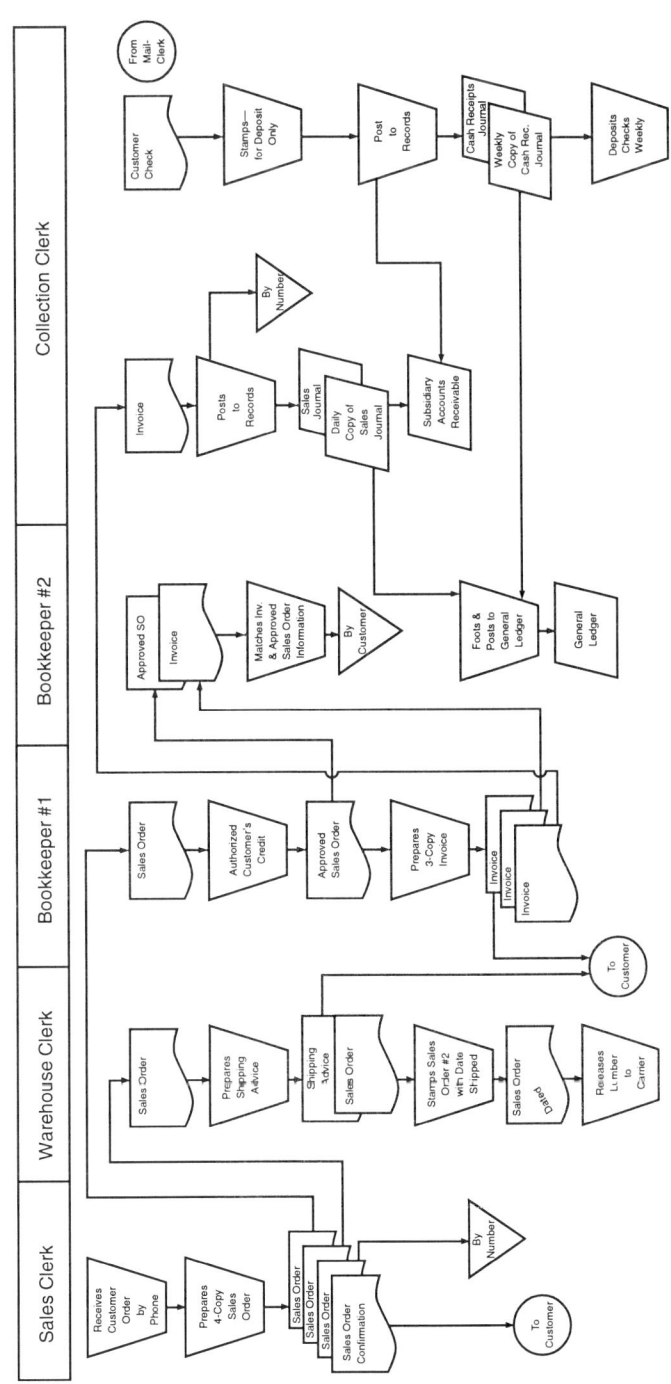

Learning Objectives

Study of this chapter is designed to achieve several learning objectives. After studying this chapter, you should be able to:

1. Discuss the overall audit approach used in the examination of accounts in the Revenue cycle.
2. Identify assertions having relatively high levels of inherent risk in the accounts receivable and cash accounts.
3. Explain how the nature, timing, and extent of the auditor's substantive tests over accounts receivable and cash is affected by the necessary level of detection risk.
4. List important substantive testing procedures used in the auditor's examination of accounts receivable, cash, and sales.
5. Identify the assertions addressed by various substantive tests performed for accounts receivable, cash, and sales.

11

The Revenue Cycle: Substantive Tests

In the previous chapter, we provided a discussion of important aspects of internal control in the Revenue cycle. This chapter moves to the next major stage of the audit examination for this cycle: substantive testing.

OVERALL AUDIT APPROACH

In Chapter 4 ("Audit Planning"), the audit risk model was introduced. As noted therein, this model allows the auditor to control audit risk to desired levels. Audit risk is defined as the risk that the auditor issues an unmodified opinion on financial statements that contain a material misstatement. This would occur when a material misstatement occurs, is not prevented or detected by the client's internal control, and is not detected by the auditor's substantive testing procedures. Recall the basic four-step approach for using the audit risk model.

1. Set audit risk at desired levels (normally, low).
2. Based on the nature of the account balance or class of transactions, assess inherent risk.
3. After studying internal control, assess control risk.
4. Based on the level of audit risk, inherent risk, and control risk, determine detection risk.

Recall from Chapter 4 that the components of the audit risk model are assessed on an assertion-by-assertion basis. This assessment recognizes that the certain assertions assume an increased level of importance and are of greater interest to the auditor than others. For example, as noted in Chapter 6, because of the tendency to overstate assets and revenues, the EO assertion is relatively important in the audit of assets and revenues (such as sales and accounts receivable, the focus of the Revenue cycle). Stated another way, the **inherent risk** associated with the EO assertion for the Revenue cycle is normally high.

After considering the inherent risk associated with the five assertions, the auditor then considers important control activities implemented by the client over these assertions. In particular, the auditor focuses on assertions having relatively high levels of inherent risk. Once these control activities have been identified, the auditor tests the operating effectiveness of these control activities; that is, are they implemented by the client? After performing tests of controls, the auditor has some indication of whether these control activities are being applied as prescribed. At this point, he or she can assess the appropriate level of control risk.

To illustrate the overall audit approach, assume that the auditor is examining accounts receivable. The following steps would be performed:

1. **Identify Assertions Having High Inherent Risk:** As noted above, for accounts receivable, the inherent risk associated with the EO assertion is relatively high.

2. **Consider Important Control Activities Implemented over these Assertions:** The use of formal documentation (such as Shipping Documents and Sales Invoices) to record transactions reduces the likelihood that fictitious sales transactions are recorded (the EO assertion).

3. **Test the Operating Effectiveness of Identified Control Activities:** The auditor would inspect the use of Shipping Documents and Sales Invoices for processing sales transactions.

4. **Assess Control Risk:** Based on the operating effectiveness of identified control activities, the auditor would assess control risk.

Once control risk is assessed, the auditor then considers the level of audit risk, inherent risk, and control risk in setting the appropriate level of detection risk. Recall that **detection risk** is the risk that the auditor's substantive testing procedures fail to detect material misstatements in the financial statements. Using a matrix such as the one below (which assumes that the auditor wishes to control overall audit risk to a low level), the appropriate level of detection risk can be determined by finding the intersection of the row (representing inherent risk) and column (representing control risk).

	Maximum Control Risk	Moderate Control Risk	Low Control Risk
High Inherent Risk	Low Detection Risk	Low to Moderate Detection Risk	Moderate Detection Risk
Moderate Inherent Risk	Low to Moderate Detection Risk	Moderate Detection Risk	Moderate to High Detection Risk
Low Inherent Risk	Moderate Detection Risk	Moderate to High Detection Risk	High Detection Risk

To illustrate, if the auditor is examining accounts receivable, a high level of inherent risk is normally associated with the EO assertion. Assume that the auditor's tests of controls reveal that internal control over accounts receivable transactions (related to the EO assertion) is relatively effective; as a result, the auditor assesses control risk at low levels. This would provide the auditor with a moderate level of detection risk. In contrast, if control activities were not considered to be effective in preventing misstatements related to the EO assertion, the auditor may choose to assess control risk at the maximum level. In this case, the necessary level of detection risk would be low. As noted previously, the level of detection risk and the effectiveness of the auditor's substantive tests have an inverse relationship; that is, lower levels of detection risk imply more effective substantive testing procedures (and *vice versa*).

CHAPTER CHECKPOINTS

11-1. Define audit risk. What are the four basic steps in using the audit risk model?

11-2. What is the basic relationship between the necessary level of detection risk and the effectiveness of the auditor's substantive testing procedures?

ACCOUNTS RECEIVABLE

Inherent and Control Risk

In assessing inherent risk over accounts receivable transactions, the auditor considers the susceptibility of accounts receivable to misstatement. Two important considerations affecting accounts receivable in this regard are:

1. Management may feel undue pressure to meet earnings expectations placed on them by the company. This pressure may result in recording fictitious sales transactions (or recording sales transactions prior to the point at which the revenue should be recognized). Both of these possibilities correspond to the EO assertion.

2. Under GAAP, accounts receivable are presented in the balance sheet at their net realizable value. Because of the uncertainty surrounding the collectibility of accounts receivable, the client must establish a provision for uncollectible accounts receivable. From management's standpoint, the provision for accounts receivable reduces earnings; as a result, they may have a tendency to understate the provision for uncollectible accounts (and overstate accounts receivable and net income). Thus, the VA assertion is also of importance to the auditor.

As noted above, the auditor should identify and test important control activities implemented to address these assertions. For example, the use of formal documentation (such as Shipping Documents and Sales Invoices) to record transactions reduces the likelihood that fictitious sales transactions are recorded (the EO assertion). Mathematically verifying Sales Invoices and using monthly statements (and following up discrepancies noted by customers) are control activities that correspond to the VA assertion. Based on the results of the auditor's tests of these control activities, he or she then assesses control risk for the related assertion.

At this point, the auditor can use the assessments of inherent risk and control risk to determine the appropriate level of detection risk. This can be done using a matrix similar to that shown earlier in the previous section.

◻ Detection Risk

The accounts receivable account is normally comprised of a large number of transactions consisting of relatively small dollar amounts per transaction. Therefore, while some dual-purpose tests of transactions may have been used by the auditor during the study and evaluation of internal control, the auditor normally employs the **tests of balances** approach in examining accounts receivable. Recall the three basic steps used in this approach:

1. Identify individual components of the final account balance.
2. Select a sample of these components for verification.
3. Verify the components using some form of evidence-gathering procedure.

As indicated below, components of the final accounts receivable balance are individual customers' accounts.

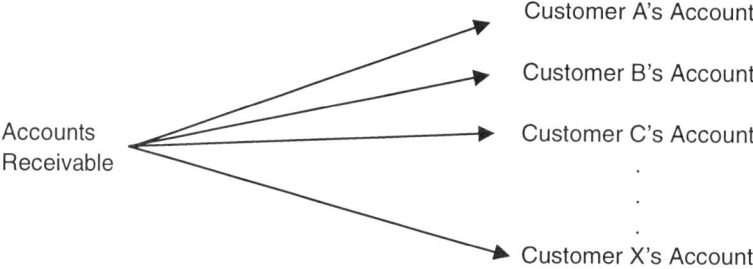

In verifying the customers' balances, the auditor will primarily rely on confirmation of these balances directly with the customer. Once the level of detection risk has been determined, the auditor considers this in designing the nature, timing, and extent of his or her confirmations, as shown in Figure 11-1.

	Lower Detection Risk	Higher Detection Risk
Nature	Rely More Heavily on Positive Confirmation	Rely More Heavily on Negative Confirmation
Timing	Confirm Accounts at Year-end	Confirm Accounts During Interim Period
Extent	Confirm a Larger Number of Accounts	Confirm a Smaller Number of Accounts

Figure 11-1: *Effect of Detection Risk on Auditor's Substantive Tests for Accounts Receivable*

Figure 11-2 summarizes the primary substantive tests performed by the auditor with respect to accounts receivable. These procedures are discussed in the remainder of this section.

Procedure	Classification	Assertion(s)				
		EO	RO	CO	VA	PD
1. Obtain an Aged Listing of Accounts Receivable from the client (Figure 11-3). Foot and cross-foot the Aged Listing and agree totals to the client's Trial Balance.	Recalculation Comparison				x	
2. Confirm a sample of accounts receivable with customers	Confirmation	x	x		x	
3. Evaluate the client's provision for uncollectible accounts receivable (Figure 11-6).						
a. Agree beginning balance to prior-year workpapers	Comparison				x	
b. Recalculate current-year provision for uncollectible accounts	Recalculation			x	x	
c. Vouch current-year write-offs of accounts receivable to documentation	Inspect Documents	x			x	
d. Foot analysis and agree total to the client's Trial Balance	Recalculation Comparison			x	x	
4. Perform analytical procedures for accounts receivable	Analytical Procedures	x	x	x	x	
5. Evaluate the overall presentation of accounts receivable in the financial statements						
a. Review disclosures related to accounts receivable	Inspect Documents					x
b. Inquire about whether accounts receivable are pledged as collateral	Inquiry					x
c. Inquire about whether accounts receivable have been factored, transferred, or assigned	Inquiry			x		x

Figure 11-2: *Major Substantive Tests: Accounts Receivable*

CHAPTER CHECKPOINTS

11-3. For which assertion(s) is the level of inherent risk over accounts receivable transactions relatively high?

11-4. What is the test of balances approach? List the major steps in performing the test of balances approach.

11-5. How does the necessary level of detection risk affect the nature, timing, and extent of the auditor's substantive tests over accounts receivable?

Obtaining an Aged Listing of Accounts Receivable. An Aged Listing of Accounts Receivable is useful in allowing the auditor to evaluate the adequacy of the allowance for uncollectible accounts. An example of an Aged Listing of Accounts Receivable is shown in Figure 11-3. Notice that this schedule lists all accounts receivable, with the total balance in accounts receivable agreed to the amount shown in Meghan's Office Products' Trial Balance (note the "TB" tickmark in Figure 11-3). By footing the Aged Listing and agreeing the total to the Trial Balance, the auditor is obtaining evidence regarding the VA assertion.

In addition to listing the total accounts receivable, the Aged Listing classifies each customer's account by the time period that the receivable has been outstanding. In Figure 11-3, three categories are used for this purpose: (1) 0-60 days, (2) 61-90 days, and (3) over 90 days. Obviously, as the time period that a receivable is outstanding increases, companies are less likely to actually collect that receivable. Therefore, if a greater percentage of the accounts receivable are overdue for relatively long periods of time, the allowance for uncollectible accounts should be higher. In evaluating the adequacy of the allowance for uncollectible accounts, the auditor can compare the percentages of each classification of accounts receivable to those from previous years. This is a type of analytical procedure that is discussed later in this section.

Confirming Accounts Receivable. In gathering evidence about the fairness of selected customers' accounts receivable balances, the auditor would obviously prefer to utilize the most reliable form of evidence possible. As noted in Chapter 6, direct observation by the auditor normally provides the most reliable form of evidence. However, unlike cash (which can be counted), the auditor cannot observe an account receivable. For accounts receivable, the most reliable form of evidence available is direct confirmation with external parties (customers). Thus, accounts receivable conformation constitutes the majority of the substantive tests involving accounts receivable.

Statement on Auditing Standards No. 67[1] notes that confirmation of accounts receivable is considered to be a generally accepted auditing procedure. The fact that confirmation provides the auditor with a highly reliable form of evidence indicates that this procedure should be performed in most GAAS audits. The auditor should request confirmations for accounts receivable unless one or more of the following conditions exist:

1. Accounts receivable are immaterial to the financial statements.
2. The use of confirmations would be ineffective, based on prior audit experience.
3. The combined assessments of inherent risk and control risk are low, resulting in the need to perform less effective substantive testing procedures.

Methods of Confirmation. Accounts receivable may be confirmed by the use of three methods. A **positive confirmation request** requires the debtor to reply directly to the auditor, stating whether the balance as indicated on the request is correct or, if it is incorrect, indicating the correct balance and any possible explanation of the difference. The distinguishing feature of a positive confirmation request is that a response is required in all instances. Figure 11-4 provides an example of a positive confirmation request.

---

[1] American Institute of Certified Public Accountants (AICPA), *Statement on Auditing Standards No. 67*, "The Confirmation Process" (New York: AICPA, 1991, AU 330).

B-1	Meghan's Office Products Accounts Receivable 12-31-x3		Prepared by: Client 1-3-X4 JRS 1-20-X4 Reviewed by: MES 2-1-X4

Customer Name	Balance 12-31-x3	0 - 60 Days	61 - 90 Days	Over 90 Days
Roberts Company	90,502 Ⓒ	71,169	19,333	
Sampson Steel	10,100 Ⓝ	10,100		
Susan Electric	1,221 ②			1,221 ②
Archer & Sons	87,105 ③	74,129	12,976	
Bird, McHale, and Jones	90,124 Ⓒ	87,498	2,626	
Orbach Supply	161,201 ①	161,201		
*	*	*	*	*
*	*	*	*	*
*	*	*	*	*
Johnson, Inc.	120,135 Ⓒ	120,135	0	0
	2,467,193 ⒸⒻ	1,875,067	518,109	74,017
	Ⓕ ⓉⒷ	Ⓕ	Ⓕ	Ⓕ

Percentage of 19x3 Total		76.0%	21.0%	3.0%
19x2 Percentages		74.7%	20.2%	5.1%

Ⓕ   Footed   ⓉⒷ Agreed to Trial Balance

ⒸⒻ   Cross-Footed

Ⓒ   Positively confirmed account with customer (See B-1-A through B-1-ZZ for returned confirmations). No exceptions to recorded amount noted.

Ⓝ   Sent negative confirmation, which was not returned by customer.

①   Customer returned confirmation indicating no balance was due. Further investigation revealed a payment in transit at 12-31-x3 for the full amount. Account appears to be correctly recorded at year-end.

②   Returned negative confirmation, indicating disagreement with amount. Based on review of customer's file, the following adjusting entry is proposed (see Workpaper AJE-1 for a summary of adjustments):

       Allowance for Doubtful Accounts   1,221
              Accounts Receivable   1,221

③   Customer did not respond to positive confirmation. Vouched balance to Sales Invoice. Account appears to be correctly recorded at year-end.

Figure 11-3: *Aged Listing of Accounts Receivable*

January 3, 19X4

Roberts Company
2503 Woodward Avenue
Detroit, Michigan 66001

Gentlemen:

Our auditors are making an examination of our financial statements and wish to obtain direct confirmation of the correctness of the amount owed us as of the date indicated. Please compare the balance shown below with your records, noting details of any exceptions on the reverse side. Then sign this letter in the space provided and return it directly to our auditors, ABC, CPAs. A reply envelope that requires no postage is enclosed for your convenience.

This is not a request for payment, and remittances should not be made to our auditors.

Very Truly Yours,

EZ Green
Credit Manager
Meghan's Office Products

Audit Date: 12/31/X3

Balance: $90,502

ABC CPAs:

____   The balance shown above is correct at 12/31/X3

____   The balance shown above is not correct at 12/31/X3 (Provide details on the reverse side of this form)

Signed _____

Please return this confirmation to ABC, CPAs in the enclosed reply envelope

Figure 11-4: *Positive Confirmation Request*

With a **negative confirmation request**, the debtor is asked to respond to the auditor only if the balance as stated on the request is not in agreement with the debtor's records. When negative requests are used, the request may be attached in the form of a sticker to the company's regular statement to the customer or it may be a special form or business reply card enclosed with the statement. Figure 11-5 is an example of a negative confirmation request.

PLEASE EXAMINE THIS STATEMENT CAREFULLY

If it does not agree with your records, report any differences to our auditors ABC, CPAs. If no differences are reported to them, this statement will be considered correct. This is not a request for payment, and remittances should not be made to our auditors. A reply envelope that requires no postage is enclosed for your convenience.

Figure 11-5: *Negative Confirmation Request*

SAS No. 67 identifies a third type of confirmation: a blank confirmation. A **blank confirmation request** is similar to a positive confirmation request, except that the amounts are omitted and the respondent is asked to provide these amounts to the auditor. This form is considered to be more reliable than a positive confirmation request because the respondent cannot merely sign the confirmation without careful scrutiny. However, the effort required by the respondent results in a relatively low response rate for blank confirmation requests. Therefore, auditors generally restrict their use of confirmations during the audit to either the positive or negative form.

Shown below is a summary of various factors that influence the type of accounts receivable confirmation requests utilized by the auditor. Ordinarily, the auditor will use some combination of positive and negative confirmations; in general, positive confirmation request will be sent to customers with larger account balances and accounts that are more likely to be in dispute (because of the age of the account balance). However, if internal control related to the EO assertion is relatively weak (higher levels of control risk), the auditor will rely more heavily on positive confirmation requests.

	Positive Confirmation	Negative Confirmation
Internal Control	Relatively Weak (Higher Control Risk)	Relatively Strong (Lower Control Risk)
Dollar Amount of Accounts	Larger Accounts	Smaller Accounts
Nature of Accounts	Accounts that may be in Dispute	Accounts that are not likely to be in Dispute
Attention Paid to Negative Confirmation	Inadequate Attention paid to Negative Confirmations	Adequate Attention paid to Negative Confirmations

In concluding our discussion of positive and negative confirmation requests, it is important to note the advantages and disadvantages associated with each form. That is, positive confirmations provide more reliable evidence because a response will be requested regardless of whether the recorded balance is correct or incorrect. However, these confirmations require greater effort on the part of the auditor because nonresponses must be investigated further. Conversely, negative confirmations require less effort on the part of the auditor; if no response is received from the customer, the balance is assumed to be correct. A problem associated with this assumption is that the conclusion may be inaccurate (*i.e.*, the customer may owe a greater balance than the amount recorded but does not respond for fear of the account balance being increased).

Timing of Confirmations. Accounts may be confirmed either at year-end or at an interim date prior to year-end. By selecting a date prior to year-end, the auditor has more time to obtain replies from customers. This reduces the need to perform alternative procedures for nonrespondents and provides the auditor with more time to investigate exceptions reported by customers. However, if the client's internal control is deemed to be relatively weak (higher levels of control risk), it may be necessary to confirm receivables at year-end (see Figure 11-1). If confirmation procedures are performed at an interim date, the auditor should evaluate the changes in the account between the interim date and year-end. In most cases, the auditor would simply review the changes in the balance for reasonableness. However, if the customer's balance changes markedly during this intervening period, the auditor may need to examine specific transactions occurring during this period. The nature of the auditor's work during the intervening period is shown below.

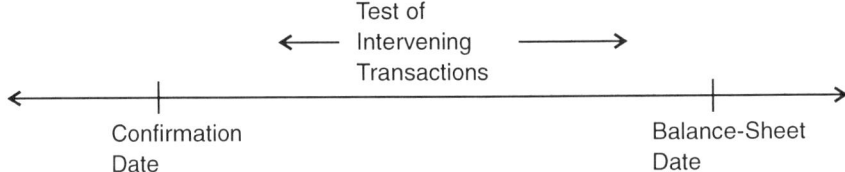

Extent of Confirmations. The extent of confirmations refers to the number of customers' whose balances are confirmed by the auditor. The necessary extent of confirmation procedures is largely influenced by the auditor's evaluation of the client's internal control (see Figure 11-1). However, other factors, such as the nature of the account, the dollar amount of the account, and number of accounts, also influence the number of accounts selected for confirmation. For example, if a substantial portion of the client's sales is made to a very small number of customers, positive confirmation requests would be mailed to all of these customers. In other cases, the auditor may wish to increase the number of accounts confirmed to include accounts with large balances, past-due accounts, very active or inactive accounts, accounts with credit balances, accounts that have been written off or turned over to an agency for collection, and any other accounts of an unusual nature that do not fall within the sample originally selected.

Sending Confirmation Requests. To ensure that all statements or requests will either reach their proper destination or be returned to the auditor by the post office, the auditor must mail out the confirmation requests in envelopes that bear the auditor's (not the client's) return address. In addition, the auditor should maintain control over the statements or requests from the time they are prepared until their deposit in the mail. If the auditor fails to maintain this control, any employee could hide irregularities by removing statements with incorrect balances, altering balances to cover the manipulation of accounts, or mailing statements to fictitious addresses or to an accomplice. If the client's employees assist the auditor by preparing confirmations, stuffing envelopes, and performing other tasks related to the confirmation requests, the auditor must ascertain by personal supervision, observation, and testing that all statements are properly prepared and that none of the statements have been withdrawn or altered before mailing.

Evaluating Confirmation Results. When confirmations are returned by customers, the auditor evaluates the responses to determine whether the balance is fairly recorded. For positive confirmations, the auditor will agree the amount indicated by the customer with the balance recorded in the Aged Listing of Accounts Receivable obtained from the client. As noted in Figure 11-3, the tickmark "C" indicates that the account balance has been verified by a positive confirmation request returned by the customer. These confirmations should be retained by the auditor for inclusion in the workpapers because they represent the evidence obtained regarding each customer's account balance. Also note in Figure 11-3 that the tickmark "N" indicates that: (1) a negative confirmation request was sent to the customer, and (2) the request was not returned to the auditor. As discussed earlier, a nonresponse to a negative confirmation request provides evidence (although less reliable than a positive confirmation) that the customer's account balance was fairly stated. A final observation from Figure 11-3 is that the auditor typically uses positive confirmation requests to verify larger balances and negative confirmation requests to verify smaller balances, as suggested in our earlier discussion.

Exceptions to Confirmation Requests. Exceptions are differences between the client's recorded balances and the balances confirmed by the customers. Many differences result because of normal business reasons, such as shipments or customer payments in transit, unrecorded credits or allowances, disputes between the client and customer, or clerical errors. Other differences could indicate accounts that have been manipulated or are fictitious. All reported exceptions must be investigated by the auditor. If the exceptions are immaterial in amount or do not indicate serious weaknesses, the auditor may request that a responsible employee of the client investigate them. However, the auditor must maintain control over the returned confirmations and must become satisfied as to the reasons given for the exceptions.

In cases where exceptions are noted, the relevant information and any conclusions of the auditor's investigation should be included in the workpapers. To illustrate, tickmarks "1" and "2" in Figure 11-3 describe exceptions noted by the auditor during the examination of accounts receivable. As described therein, the receivable from Orbach Supply was noted as incorrect by the customer because of a payment that was in transit at the time of confirmation. Because the payment was received after year-end, the balance recorded at 12-31-X3 appears to be appropriate. On the other hand, the receivable from Susan Electric Company that is over 90 days past due is currently in dispute; therefore, an adjustment may be necessary. This situation should be investigated further with Meghan's Office Products' credit manager, with the ultimate resolution presented in the workpapers.

Alternative Procedures. The auditor must perform alternative procedures to substantiate the balances of any customers who fail to respond to positive confirmation requests. Such procedures may include examining sales and collections made after the confirmation date by inspecting the appropriate documentation to determine whether these transactions relate to the period under audit. For example, Figure 11-3 (tickmark "3") indicates that Archer & Sons did not return the positive confirmation request mailed by the auditor. After subsequent confirmation efforts, the auditor must perform other procedures. In this case, the Sales Invoices related to the Archer & Sons account were examined and reflected the total amount of the receivable. Although this provides the auditor with some evidence regarding the fairness of the receivable, the auditor should be alert for the possibility that this account may be fictitious or uncollectible.

If customers fail to return negative accounts receivable confirmation requests, the auditor is not required to perform alternative procedures; instead, the account balance is assumed to be correctly stated. This assumption reduces the amount of work that the auditor does, but it may also lead to an incorrect conclusion regarding the account balance. These advantages and disadvantages are the basic trade-offs between using the positive and negative forms of accounts receivable confirmation requests.

Summary: Accounts Receivable Confirmations Confirming accounts receivable with customers provides the auditor with a high quality of evidence; since these confirmations are returned directly to the auditor, this represents external evidence. When customers return a positive confirmation request without exception (or fail to return a negative confirmation request), they agree that the recorded balance represents a legitimate transaction. Viewed in another light, customers are corroborating that the sales transaction(s) actually took place (the EO assertion).

While confirming an account without exception does not guarantee its ultimate collectibility, this procedure may provide some (albeit limited) evidence that the amount will ultimately be collected. Thus, to a lesser extent, accounts receivable confirmations also address the RO and VA assertions.

CHAPTER CHECKPOINTS

11-6. What is an Aged Listing of Accounts Receivable? What information is ordinarily included in this Listing?

11-7. Define the following forms of accounts receivable confirmation requests:

  a. Positive confirmation request
  b. Negative confirmation request
  c. Blank confirmation request

11-8. In what situations would the auditor ordinarily rely on positive confirmation requests? Negative confirmation requests?

11-9. In what circumstances would the auditor be able to confirm accounts receivable at an interim date? In these cases, what additional procedures must be performed?

11-10. What are exceptions to confirmation requests? How are these handled by the auditor?

11-11. What are the primary assertion(s) addressed by accounts receivable confirmations?

Evaluating the Provision for Uncollectible Accounts Receivable. To be presented in conformity with GAAP, accounts receivable should be included in the financial statements at their estimated net realizable value. Thus, the auditor must not only become satisfied that the gross amount of the accounts receivable is fairly stated, but that an adequate provision has been made for uncollectible receivables. In reviewing the collectibility of accounts receivable and evaluating the adequacy of the allowance for uncollectible accounts, the auditor will refer to various client records and to other information.

Figure 11-6 illustrates a workpaper prepared to evaluate the reasonableness of Meghan's Office Products' bad debt expense for 19X3 as well as the allowance for uncollectible accounts as of December 31, 19X3. Several points should be highlighted:

| B-2 | Meghan's Office Products
Allowance for Uncollectible Accounts
12-31-x3 | Prepared by: JRS 1·19·X4
Reviewed by: MES 1·23·X4 |

Balance, 1-1-x3		115,000	✓
Add: 19x3 provision		63,360	Ⓣⓑ Ⓡ
Less: Write-offs during 19x3		(55,000)	①
Balance, 12-31-x3		123,360	Ⓣⓑ
Less: AJE (See B-1, Figure 11-3)		(1,221)	
Adjusted Balance, 12-31-x3		122,139	Ⓕ

Ⓕ   Footed

✓   Agreed to Prior-Year's Workpapers

Ⓣⓑ   Agreed to Trial Balance

①   Investigated authorization and documentation for write-offs during 19x3. Write-offs appear to be reasonable.

Ⓡ   Recalculated based on two percent of total credit sales during 19x3 (0.02 x $3,168,000 = $63,360)

<u>Amount based on Aging of Accounts Receivable:</u>

0 - 60 Days:	1,875,067	x 0.04	=	75,003
61 - 90 Days:	518,109	x 0.08	=	41,449
Over 90 Days:	(74,017 - 1,221)	x 0.15	=	10,919
				127,371

Based on the above aging, recorded amount appears reasonable.

Figure 11-6: *Allowance for Uncollectible Accounts*

1. The allowance for uncollectible accounts cannot be verified with any certainty because this amount represents an estimate made by management. As noted in *Statement on Auditing Standards No.*

57,[2] the auditor evaluates the reasonableness of this estimate, based on past conditions or similar companies in the client's industry.

2. Accounts written off as uncollectible are examined by the auditor to determine that these write-offs were properly authorized by client personnel. In addition, the customer's credit files are investigated to determine that efforts were indeed made to collect any receivables written off (tickmark "1").

3. After the above procedures are performed, the bad debt expense for the current period can be recalculated (tickmark "R"). The allowance for uncollectible accounts and bad debt expense are then agreed to the Trial Balance ("TB" reference).

Since GAAP require accounts receivable to be presented in the balance sheet at net realizable value, evaluating the adequacy of the allowance for uncollectible accounts relates to the VA assertion. In addition, since these procedures provide the auditor with evidence regarding the ultimate collectibility of the accounts receivable, they also address the RO assertion.

IS THE RESERVE HIGH ENOUGH?

MiniScribe Corp., a now-defunct manufacturer of computer disk drives, attempted to conceal a worsening financial condition from their investors by establishing an apparently optimistic allowance for uncollectible accounts receivable. In 1985, total accounts receivable were $15.6 million; MiniScribe established an allowance of $752,000 for uncollectible accounts receivable. In 1986, MiniScribe's accounts receivable more than doubled to $40 million. However, the allowance was actually **reduced** to $736,000.[3]

Performing Analytical Procedures. As discussed in Chapters 4 and 6, **analytical procedures** consist of auditor evaluations of recorded (unaudited) financial information based on the underlying relationships among financial and nonfinancial data. When performing analytical procedures, the auditor compares recorded amounts and ratios derived from recorded amounts to expectations of these amounts or ratios. These expectations can be based on industry data or client data from one or more prior year(s). Any significant departures of recorded amounts or ratios from expected amounts or ratios may signal the presence of a financial statement misstatement.

An analytical procedure commonly used by auditors is comparing the recorded (unaudited) balance in accounts receivable and the allowance for uncollectible accounts to: (1) the balance of these accounts for previous years, and/or (2) the budgeted or forecasted balance of these accounts. For example, in Figure 11-6, the auditor compares the balance in the allowance for uncollectible accounts to an expectation based on the Aged Listing of Accounts Receivable. In addition, the following ratios involving the accounts receivable and other related accounts may be calculated and compared to expectations through the use of analytical procedures.

---

[2] American Institute of Certified Public Accountants (AICPA), *Statement on Auditing Standards No. 57*, "Auditing Accounting Estimates" (New York: AICPA, 1988, AU 342).

[3] "How MiniScribe Got Its Auditor's Blessing on Questionable Sales," *The Wall Street Journal* (May 14, 1992), A1.

- Ratio of accounts receivable to total assets (or sales)
- Accounts receivable turnover ratio (net sales ÷ accounts receivable)
- Ratio of allowance for uncollectible accounts to accounts receivable
- Ratio of bad debt expense to sales
- Ratio of specific classes of accounts receivable (by due date) to total accounts receivable (see Figure 11-3)

Analytical procedures are used by the auditor in his or her examination of accounts receivable to verify the reasonableness of recorded amounts. As with the use of analytical procedures for other accounts, these procedures may assist the auditor in identifying fictitious transactions that have been recorded in the accounting records (the EO assertion), unrecorded transactions (the CO assertion), and transactions recorded at the incorrect dollar amount (the VA assertion). In addition, analytical procedures can also be used to evaluate the reasonableness of the client's provision for uncollectible accounts receivable, which addresses the RO and VA assertions.

Evaluating Financial Statement Presentation. In evaluating the financial statement presentation of accounts receivable, the auditor should inquire about any accounts receivable pledged as collateral or accounts receivable that have been factored, transferred, or assigned. If any of these conditions exist, the relevant information should be disclosed in the footnotes accompanying the financial statements. Therefore, this procedure provides the auditor with assurance regarding the PD assertion. In addition, certain types of transfer arrangements may require the client to relinquish the rights to the receivables; as a result, inquiries of this nature also relate to the RO assertion. Finally, the auditor should review the financial statement disclosures related to accounts receivable. This procedure also relates to the PD assertion.

CHAPTER CHECKPOINTS

11-12. What procedures are performed by the auditor during his or her evaluation of the provision for uncollectible accounts receivable?

11-13. List some ratios examined by the auditor during his or her analytical procedures for accounts receivable.

11-14. What should be considered by the auditor in evaluating the financial statement presentation of accounts receivable?

CASH

Inherent and Control Risk

Two distinguishing features of the cash account affect the inherent risk associated with the five management assertions:

1. Cash is highly susceptible to theft or misappropriation. If employees are in position to misappropriate cash receipts, they may attempt to conceal this theft by failing to record the relevant transactions (the CO assertion). Defalcations involving cash disbursements may result in disbursements being recorded for fictitious transactions (the EO assertion). Therefore, relatively high levels of inherent risk exist for both the EO and CO assertions.

2. Because cash transactions are recorded twice (once by the client and once by the client's bank), errors in processing cash transactions should be readily determinable. Thus, the inherent risk related to the VA assertion is ordinarily low.

The auditor should identify and test important control activities implemented to address these important assertions related to cash. In particular, one important control activity related to cash is the preparation of monthly bank reconciliations by an individual having no other responsibilities with respect to cash. In addition, the auditor should also investigate the presence of physical controls over cash (such as depositing cash receipts intact and daily, securing access to checks and signature plates, and preparing Remittance Listings upon the receipt of cash). Based on the results of the auditor's tests of controls, he or she then assesses control risk.

At this point, the auditor can use the assessments of inherent risk and control risk to determine the appropriate level of detection risk. This can be done using a matrix similar to that shown earlier in this chapter.

Detection Risk

Like accounts receivable (discussed in the preceding section), the cash account is characterized by a large number of transactions consisting of relatively small dollar amounts per transaction. Therefore, the auditor normally employs the **tests of balances** approach in examining cash. This approach requires the auditor to verify a sample of components of the account balance (although the auditor normally will verify all but the smallest components of the client's cash balance). With cash, these components will be cash on hand (including petty cash) and cash on deposit, as shown below.

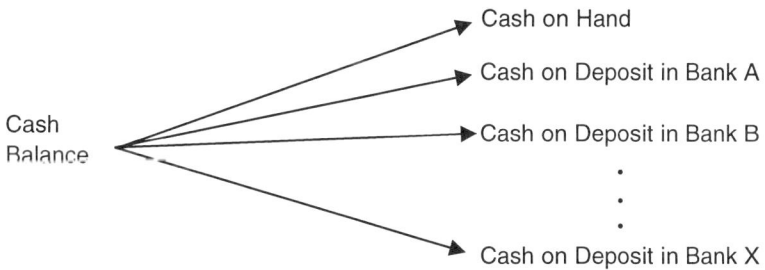

Because of the relative ease in performing substantive tests for cash, the level of detection risk determined by the auditor does not have a significant impact on his or her substantive testing procedures. In general, the auditor performs similar procedures for cash regardless of the necessary level of detection risk. Because cash is normally held by a small number of banks, the level of detection risk will not have a substantial effect on the timing or extent of the auditor's substantive testing procedures. However, in cases where the necessary level of detection risk for cash is judged to be lower, the auditor should perform tests of the client's recording of cash receipts and disbursements transactions through a Proof of Cash. In addition, if control risk is high (resulting in the need for lower levels of detection risk), the auditor may wish to perform procedures to detect the possible existence of lapping. Both the preparation of a Proof of Cash and procedures to detect lapping are discussed later in this chapter. Figure 11-7 summarizes the effect of the necessary level of detection risk on the auditor's substantive tests for cash.

	Lower Detection Risk	Higher Detection Risk
Nature	Prepare a Proof of Cash	Do not Prepare a Proof of Cash
	Perform tests to detect lapping	Do not perform tests to detect lapping
Timing	No effect, since tests are performed at year-end	No effect, since tests are performed at year-end
Extent	No effect, since Confirmations are usually sent to all banks	No effect, since Confirmations are usually sent to all banks

Figure 11-7: *Effect of Detection Risk on Auditor's Substantive Tests for Cash*

Figure 11-8 summarizes the primary substantive tests performed by the auditor with respect to cash.

Procedure	Classification	Assertion(s)				
		EO	RO	CO	VA	PD
1. Obtain a Lead Schedule of Cash Balances from the client (Figure 11-9). Foot the Lead Schedule and agree totals to the client's Trial Balance	Recalculation Comparison				x	
2. Obtain (or prepare) a year-end Bank Reconciliation for each bank account held by the client (Figure 11-10).						
a. Confirm the "balance per bank" directly with the bank (Figure 11-11)	Confirmation	x	x	x	x	x
b. Verify reconciling items by obtaining a subsequent Bank Statement	Inspect Documents					
1. Trace outstanding checks returned with the Bank Statement to the client's year-end Bank Reconciliation				x	x	
2. Vouch deposits-in-transit from the client's year-end Bank Reconciliation to Deposit Slips returned with the Bank Statement		x	x		x	
3. Agree other reconciling items from the Bank Statement to the client's year-end Bank Reconciliation		x	x	x	x	
c. Verify the mathematical accuracy of the Bank Reconciliation and agree the balance per books to the Lead Schedule of Cash Balances	Recalculation Comparison				x	
3. Prepare a Schedule of Interbank Transfers for activity occurring near year-end (Figure 11-12)	Inspect Documents	x	x	x		
4. Perform analytical procedures for cash	Analytical Procedures	x	x	x	x	
5. If control risk is relatively high, prepare a Proof of Cash (Figure 11-13)	Inspect Documents Recalculation	x	x	x	x	
6. If control risk is relatively high, perform tests to detect lapping	Inspect Documents			x		
7. Perform counts of cash on hand	Observation	x	x	x	x	
8. Evaluate the overall presentation of cash in the financial statements						
a. Review disclosures related to cash	Inspect Documents					x
b. Inquire about restrictions on the use of cash	Inquiry					x
c. Consider information received during the confirmation of cash with banks regarding compensating balances	Confirmation					x

Figure 11-8: *Major Substantive Tests: Cash*

> **CHAPTER CHECKPOINTS**
>
> **11-15.** For which assertion(s) is the level of inherent risk over cash transactions relatively high?
>
> **11-16.** How does the assessed level of detection risk affect the nature, timing, and extent of the auditor's substantive tests for cash?

Obtaining a Lead Schedule of Cash Balances. The auditor begins his or her examination of cash by obtaining a **Lead Schedule of Cash Balances**. This schedule is simply a listing of the major components of the client's cash account. Upon receipt by the auditor, the Lead Schedule should be footed and agreed to the client's Trial Balance (the VA assertion).

A sample Lead Schedule is shown in Figure 11-9. As shown therein, the cash balance of Meghan's Office Products consists of the following components:

1. Cash on hand of $1,000
2. Cash on deposit in First National Bank ($563,575 and $10,000 in the regular and payroll accounts, respectively)
3. Cash on deposit in Second National Bank ($256,648)

The references "A-1-1" through "A-1-4" in Figure 11-9 refer to workpapers that illustrate the auditor's detailed substantive tests with respect to these components. These substantive tests are discussed in the remainder of this section.

Verifying the Bank Reconciliation. The majority of the auditor's substantive tests for cash are performed on the client's year-end Bank Reconciliation. This reconciliation can be obtained from the client or prepared by the auditor. A sample Bank Reconciliation is shown in Figure 11-10. Examining Figure 11-10 reveals that three primary types of procedures are performed with respect to this Bank Reconciliation:

1. Confirming year-end balances directly with the bank.
2. Verifying reconciling items (outstanding checks, deposits-in-transit, etc.)
3. Mathematically verifying the accuracy of the Bank Reconciliation.

Confirming Bank Balances. A Standard Bank Confirmation Inquiry (see Figure 11-11) should be mailed to each bank in which the client had a deposit or from which it borrowed funds or had other business during the current year. Whenever practicable, these confirmation requests should be mailed to the banks a few days before the balance-sheet date. As with accounts receivable confirmations (discussed earlier in this chapter), these confirmations should be maintained under control of the auditor from the time they are mailed until their return directly to the auditor.

In Figure 11-11, the information that is required to be included on the request prior to mailing is circled: the date signed by authorized signer, the authorized signature of the client officer making the request (usually an authorized check signer), the bank name and address, the date as of which information is requested, and the bank account name and number. In this case, the bank confirmation

A-1	Meghan's Office Products Lead Schedule of Cash Balances 12-31-x3	Prepared by: *Client* Reviewed by: *MES 1-21-X4*

Component	Balance	Reference
Cash on Hand	1,000	A-1-1
First National Bank (Regular)	563,575	A-1-2
First National Bank (Payroll)	10,000	A-1-3
Second National Bank	256,648	A-1-4
	831,223	
	(F) (TB)	

(F) Footed

(TB) Agreed to Trial Balance

Figure 11-9: *Lead Schedule of Cash Balance*

indicates that balances of $669,935 and $13,000 existed in Meghan's Office Products' regular and payroll accounts, respectively, at year-end. This information will be used by the auditor to reconcile the bank records to those maintained in the accounting records. As shown in Figure 11-10, the "C" tickmark indicates that balance per Bank Statement from the Bank Reconciliation has been agreed to the Confirmation received from the bank.

Note that, in addition to the balances maintained in the client's bank accounts, the Bank Confirmation shown in Figure 11-11 also requests information concerning the client's indebtedness to the financial institution. Referring to the Bank Confirmation, Meghan's Office Products has a mortgage obligation to First National Bank of $350,000 as of December 31, 19X3. To obtain as much information about liabilities as possible, confirmations are sent to all financial institutions with whom the client has done business, regardless of whether the client maintains a year-end cash balance in that institution. In addition to confirming bank balances and direct obligations, the auditor also sends separate confirmations to banks to identify such matters as contingent liabilities, compensating cash balance requirements, and lines of credit.

Bank Confirmations provide the auditor with evidence about the year-end balance in the client's cash accounts. The ability to reconcile bank balances to client balances indicates that all recorded cash transactions actually occurred (the EO assertion), are the rights of the client (the RO assertion), and have been recorded at the proper dollar amount (the VA assertion). In addition, reconciling bank balances to client balances also indicates that all transactions were recorded (the CO assertion).

A-1-2	**Meghan's Office Products** *Year-End Bank Reconciliation* *(First National Regular Account)* *12-31-x3*	Prepared by: Client 1-10-X4 SAS 1-25-X4 Reviewed by: MES 1-28-X4

Balance per Bank Statement, 12-31-x3	669,935	Ⓒ
Deposit-in-Transit	1,528	①
Outstanding Checks		
#3174 21,234 ②		
#3185 1,898		
#3187 66,130		
#3188 10,429		
#3189 8,197	(107,888)	Ⓕ
Balance per Books, 12-31-x3	563,575	Ⓕ
	Ⓐ-1 ⓉⒷ	
Less: NSF Check Returned by Bank	(12,136)	③
Balance per Books, 12-31-x3 (Adjusted)	551,439	Ⓕ

Ⓕ Footed   ⓉⒷ Agreed to Trial Balance

Ⓒ Confirmed by bank. See A-1-2-A for Confirmation (Figure 11-11)

① Vouched to Deposit Slip returned with Cutoff Bank Statement of 1-12-x4 received directly from bank. Examined amount and verified reconciling status of item. Amount appears to be properly classified.

② Examined Canceled Check returned with Cutoff Bank Statement of 1-12-x4 received directly from bank. Traced these checks to the Bank Reconciliation. No exceptions noted.

③ Examined debit memorandum returned with Cutoff Bank Statement of 1-12-x4 received directly from bank. Propose the following adjusting journal entry (see Workpaper AJE-1 for a summary of adjustments):

   Accounts Receivable   12,136
       Cash   12,136

Figure 11-10: *Year-End Bank Reconciliation*

A-1-2-A

**STANDARD FORM TO CONFIRM ACCOUNT
BALANCE INFORMATION WITH FINANCIAL INSTITUTIONS**

Meghan's Office Products
CUSTOMER NAME

We have provided to our accountants the following information as of the close of business on <u>December 31, 19X3</u>, regarding our deposit and loan balances. Please confirm the accuracy of the information, noting any exceptions to the information provided. If the balances have been left blank, please complete this form by furnishing the balance in the appropriate space below.* Although we do not request nor expect you to conduct a comprehensive, detailed search of your records, if during the process of completing this

Financial Institution Name and Address:
First National Bank
PO Box 514
Alton, MN 13486

1. At the close of business on the date listed above, our records indicated the following deposit balance(s):

ACCOUNT NAME	ACCOUNT NO.	INTEREST RATE	BALANCE*
Regular Account	1524-6832	2.5 %	669,935
Payroll Account	1524-6833	2.5 %	13,000

A-1-2

2. We were directly liable to the financial institution for loans at the close of business on the date listed above as follows:

ACCOUNT NO./ DESCRIPTION	BALANCE*	DATE DUE	INTEREST RATE	DATE THROUGH WHICH INTEREST IS PAID	DESCRIPTION OF COLLATERAL
Mortgage	350,000	monthly	8.75%	12-31-x3	Property

Jack Johnson
(Customer's Authorized Signature)

December 28, 19x3
(Date)

The information presented above by the customer is in agreement with our records. Although we have not conducted a comprehensive, detailed search of our records, no other deposit or loan accounts have come to our attention except as noted below.

Olivia Jones
(Financial Institution Authorized Signature)

January 2, 19x4
(Date)

<u>Senior Vice-President</u>
(Title)

EXCEPTIONS AND/OR COMMENTS

Please return this form directly to our accountants:

AB CPAs
12155 Pollard Place
Minneapolis, MN 25698

*Ordinarily, balances are intentionally left blank if they are not available at the time the form is prepared.

Approved 1990 by American Bankers Association, American Institute of Certified Public Accountants and Bank Administration Institute. Additional forms available from: AICPA - Order Department, P O Box 1003, NY, NY 10108-1003

Figure 11-11: *Standard Bank Confirmation Inquiry*

Finally, obtaining information regarding compensating balances and other restrictions on the use of cash allows the auditor to determine that all arrangements of this nature are properly disclosed in the financial statements (the PD assertion).

Verifying Reconciling Items. Once the balance per bank has been verified through confirmation, the next step in the auditor's examination of the client's year-end Bank Reconciliation is to verify reconciling items appearing on the Bank Reconciliation. Depending upon the timing of the auditor's examination of cash, the auditor would utilize the following month's Bank Statement or a Cutoff Bank Statement for this purpose. A **Cutoff Bank Statement** is a statement showing cash transactions and providing normal enclosures (canceled Checks, Deposit Slips, other Bank Memoranda) for a specified number of days (normally 10 or 15 days) following the year-end. Regardless of whether a Cutoff Bank Statement is requested or the following month's Bank Statement is used, the auditor should obtain this statement directly from the bank.

To verify reconciling items appearing on the client's year-end Bank Reconciliation, the auditor examines enclosures included with the Cutoff Bank Statement. For outstanding checks, it is important that the auditor concentrate on whether the outstanding check listing is complete (*i.e.*, all outstanding checks have been recorded, or the CO assertion). Therefore, the auditor should trace from canceled Checks returned with the Bank Statement to the checks listed on the client's Bank Reconciliation. This procedure is evidenced by tickmark "2" in Figure 11-10. As he or she examines the amount of the outstanding checks, the auditor should verify their status as reconciling items (were the checks written prior to year-end but cleared by the bank after year-end?). In addition to ensuring that all outstanding checks have been included in the Bank Reconciliation, this procedure also allows the auditor to determine whether these checks have been recorded at the proper dollar amount (the VA assertion). If any large checks remain outstanding at the cutoff date, the auditor should investigate these items further to determine why they have not yet cleared the bank.

IS IT REAL?[4]

When conducting a review of the company's Bank Reconciliations, an internal auditor noticed that some checks were slightly different in color than others. Closer scrutiny revealed that these checks all had the same serial number, were payable to the same person, but were cashed at different banks. Further investigation allowed the auditor to determine that a former employee had stolen a check and, through available technology, made copies of that check to attempt a defalcation.

Conversely, in verifying deposits-in-transit, the auditor is concerned that all recorded deposits-in-transit are legitimate (the EO and RO assertions). Therefore, all recorded deposits-in-transit are vouched from the Bank Reconciliation to the Deposit Slip enclosed with the Bank Statement. Once again, the auditor should verify the amount of the deposit-in-transit as well as examine the date of the deposit slip and date of cancellation by the bank to determine that this item was in transit at year-end (see tickmark "1" in Figure 11-10). Similar to outstanding checks, this procedure also allows the auditor to determine that deposits-in-transit have been recorded at the proper dollar amount (the VA assertion). If other reconciling items (service charges, note collected by the bank, etc.) are included in the client's

---

[4] "Is It Real?," *Internal Auditor* (June 1994), 77.

year-end Bank Reconciliation, these items should also be verified through reference to the Bank Statement.

Mathematically Verifying the Accuracy of the Bank Reconciliation. Once the bank balances and reconciling items have been examined in the above manner, the auditor verifies the mathematical accuracy of the year-end Bank Reconciliation and agrees the book balances for cash to the Lead Schedule of Cash Balances. The cross-referencing between workpapers is illustrated in both the Bank Reconciliation (Figure 11-10) and the Lead Schedule. For example, the "A-1" reference on the Bank Reconciliation (Figure 11-10) indicates that these amounts agree with the Lead Schedule; similarly, the "A-1-2" reference on the Lead Schedule (Figure 11-9) indicates agreement with the Bank Reconciliation. Agreeing the balance per books on the year-end Bank Reconciliation to the Lead Schedule for Cash Balances addresses the VA assertion.

CHAPTER CHECKPOINTS

11-17. What information is included in a Lead Schedule of Cash Balances?

11-18. What are the major steps performed by the auditor in verifying the client's year-end Bank Reconciliation?

11-19. What information is obtained by the auditor using the Standard Bank Confirmation Inquiry?

11-20. Why would the auditor send a Standard Bank Confirmation Inquiry to banks with whom the client has no year-end cash balance?

11-21. What is a Cutoff Bank Statement? How is it used by the auditor in verifying the client's year-end Bank Reconciliation?

Preparing a Schedule of Interbank Transfers. If companies maintain cash in more than one bank account, transfers of cash among accounts may be necessary. For example, Meghan's Office Products will periodically transfer funds from its regular account to its payroll account to provide sufficient funds for the payment of payroll checks. In other situations, transfers between banks may be done in such a manner as to conceal a cash shortage or intentionally overstate cash at year-end. This type of irregularity is known as **kiting**, and is perpetrated by recording the transfer of cash to the receiving account in an earlier period than the transfer of cash from the disbursing account.

Kiting can be detected through the preparation of a Schedule of Interbank Transfers. This schedule should include all transfers of funds between bank accounts for a few business days both before and after the balance-sheet date. The Schedule of Interbank Transfers lists the date of withdrawal according to the books and according to the bank, as well as the date of deposit according to the books and the bank. Figure 11-12 illustrates a Schedule of Interbank Transfers prepared for transfers between the bank accounts held by Meghan's Office Products.

A-2	Meghan's Office Products Schedule of Interbank Transfers 12-31-x3				Prepared by: SAS 1-10-X4 Reviewed by: MES 1-11-X4	
		Receipt Recorded		Disbursement Recorded		
Description		Books	Bank	Books	Bank	
Check #3188 (from First National Regular Account to First National Payroll Account for $10,429)		12/31/x3 ①	1/2/x4	12/31/x3	1/4/x4	
Check #3182 (from First National Regular Account to Second National Account for $8,128)		12/31/x3 ②	1/2/x4	1/3/x4	1/4/x4	

① Examined Year-End Bank Reconciliations and found item listed as a Deposit-in-Transit (on First National — Payroll Account) and Outstanding Check (on First National — Regular Account). Check cleared First National — Regular Account during the following period. Amount appears to be appropriately recorded.

② Examined Year-End Bank Reconciliations and found item listed as a Deposit-in-Transit (on Second National Account) but could not find item listed as an Outstanding Check (on First National — Regular Account). Further review disclosed that the transfer was incorrectly credited to Miscellaneous Revenue. Propose the following adjustment (see Workpaper AJE-1 for a summary of adjustments):

Miscellaneous Revenue   8,128
    Cash—Second National Bank   8,128

Figure 11-12: *Schedule of Interbank Transfers*

In reviewing the Schedule of Interbank Transfers, two situations suggest the possible presence of kiting:

1. Bank entries dated earlier than book entries.
2. Receipts on the books dated earlier than disbursements on the books.

Two interbank transfers are shown in Figure 11-12. The first transfer (between the regular and payroll accounts in First National Bank) appears to be recorded correctly. Notice that both the disbursement and receipt of the transferred funds are recorded in the same period on the client's records; in addition, this transfer is processed by the bank in the *following period*. As indicated by tickmark "1", the auditor should determine that this transfer is included as an outstanding check in the year-end Bank Reconciliation for the First National Bank (Regular) account and as a deposit-in-transit in the year-end Bank Reconciliation for the First National Bank (Payroll) account. Inclusion as a reconciling item is appropriate, since the transaction is recorded by the client's records prior to it being processed by the bank.

The second transfer (for $8,128 between the regular account of First National Bank and the account at Second National Bank) represents a potential instance of kiting. Notice that the receipt of cash in Second National Bank is recorded in the books prior to year-end; however, the corresponding disbursement is not recorded in the client's records until *after* year-end. If this transfer is found to represent an instance of kiting, an adjustment should be made to the cash account to ensure that it is properly stated at year-end. In this case, because the initial journal entry erroneously recognized miscellaneous revenue upon the transfer of funds, the adjustment would reduce both cash and miscellaneous revenue.

Preparing a Schedule of Interbank Transfers allows the auditor to verify that both the receipt and disbursement of cash from the client's bank accounts are recorded in the proper period. As noted above, kiting may be accomplished by recording the: (1) receipt of cash prior to the actual date of the transaction (the EO and RO assertions), and/or (2) disbursement of cash after the actual date of the transaction (the CO assertion).

INTERBANK TRANSFERS INCREASE PROFITS

College Bound, Inc., was a small Florida company that provided services to prepare high-school students for their future university education (such as providing study hints, selecting extracurricular activities, and selecting a university). To mask their poor financial performance, College Bound concocted revenues by transferring money among its bank accounts. A subsequent investigation by the Securities and Exchange Commission found that these transfers inflated College Bounds' revenues by $8.9 in 1990 (or 489 percent).[5]

Performing Analytical Procedures. Analytical procedures are used by the auditor in his or her examination of cash to verify the reasonableness of recorded amounts. Common analytical procedures would involve comparing the recorded balance of cash or the ratio of cash to total assets to: (1) amounts from prior year(s), and/or (2) budgeted or forecasted amounts. As with the use of analytical procedures for other accounts, these procedures may assist the auditor in identifying fictitious transactions that have been recorded in the accounting records (the EO and RO assertions), unrecorded transactions (the CO assertion), and transactions recorded at the incorrect dollar amount (the VA assertion).

Preparing a Proof of Cash. As noted in the introduction to this section, cash is examined using the test of balances approach. The procedures discussed to this point reflect this approach. However, when the client's internal control over cash is weak and the auditor is required to establish a low level of detection risk, the assurances provided by the substantive tests described above may not be sufficient. In such cases, the auditor may wish to examine individual transactions affecting the cash

---

[5] "How 2 Florida Firms Fooled Stockholders, Auditors, and the SEC," *The Wall Street Journal* (July 8, 1992), A4.

account (*i.e.*, receipts and disbursements). A four-column **Proof of Cash** is often prepared in these situations.

A sample Proof of Cash is illustrated in Figure 11-13. Notice that, for a particular test month, the Proof of Cash reconciles the beginning cash balance, cash receipts, cash disbursements, and ending cash balance from the bank's records (obtained from the Bank Statement) to the same totals from the client's records obtained from the General Ledger, Cash Receipts Journal, and Check Register (or Cash Disbursements Journal).

```
A-3                    Meghan's Office Products
                         October Proof of Cash              Prepared by:
                    First National Bank (Regular Account)    SAS 1-5-X4
                              12-31-x3                      Reviewed by:
                                                             MES 1-10-X4
```

	Balance 9-30-x3	October Receipts	October Disbursements	Balance 10-31-x3
Balance per Bank Statement	651,176 (B)	1,421,117 (B)	1,565,571 (B)	506,722 (B) (CF)
Deposits-in-Transit 10-1-x3	23,714 (1)	(23,714) (1)		
Outstanding Checks				
10-1-x3	(211,584) (2)		(211,584) (2)	
10-31-x3	0	0	210,207 (2)	(210,207) (2)
Balance per Books	463,306	1,397,403	1,564,194	296,515 (CF)
	(X) (F)	(X) (F)	(X) (F)	(X) (F)

(F) Footed

(CF) Cross-Footed

(B) Agreed to Bank Statement

(X) Agreed to totals from Client's General Ledger, Cash Receipts Journal, and Cash Disbursements Journal.

(1) Vouched to Bank Statement received by client on 10-31-x3.

(2) Total per Outstanding Check Listing on Workpaper A-3-A. Agreed individual amounts to Checks returned with following month's Bank Statement received by client.

Figure 11-13: *Proof of Cash*

A Proof of Cash does not attempt to determine a "true" cash balance, instead, it is a reconciliation of the records maintained by the client and the bank. To illustrate the mechanics for preparing the Proof of Cash, consider the total outstanding checks as of 9-30-X3 ($211,584). Because these checks have not yet cleared the bank as of 9-30-X3, the bank balance on that date does not reflect these disbursements. However, in determining the balance per books, these checks have been subtracted by the client. Therefore, to reconcile the bank and book balances, the outstanding checks must be subtracted from the balance per bank.

These outstanding checks will normally clear the bank in the following month (October). Considering only the impact of these checks, the disbursements shown by the bank during October will exceed book disbursements because these checks were recorded as cash disbursements by the client in the previous month (September). Therefore, to reconcile the October disbursements per bank with the October disbursements per books, the $211,584 of outstanding checks must be subtracted from the balance per bank. Using similar logic, you should be able to verify the remaining reconciling items in Figure 11-13. As noted in our discussion of Bank Reconciliations, the auditor should verify all reconciling items and mathematically verify the reconciliations in the Proof of Cash. Like verifying Bank Reconciliations, the Proof of Cash provides the auditor with evidence regarding the EO, RO, CO, and VA assertions.

Performing Tests to Detect Lapping. In cases where an appropriate segregation of duties does not exist, client employees may have access to cash receipts as well as the responsibility of updating the customers' subsidiary accounts receivable records. Employees having these incompatible responsibilities are in a position to commit defalcations by engaging in a scheme known as lapping. **Lapping** occurs when an employee embezzles cash remitted by a customer and "covers" this theft with subsequent receipts from other customers. Later, this shortage is then covered with receipts remitted from still other customers.

To illustrate the process of lapping, consider the following series of cash receipts and recordings. Assume that Customer A remits a $500 payment on his account, which is subsequently embezzled by a client employee. Since the cash is embezzled, no entry is made to update Customer A's account to reflect his payment; however, unless Customer A's account is eventually updated, the customer's inquiry will reveal the defalcation. To prevent this from occurring, the employee applies $500 of Customer B's remittance to credit Customer A's account. Now, Customer B's account is misstated, so the receipts from a third customer's account (Customer C) are credited to Customer B's account, and so on.

	Receive	Record
Customer A	$ 500	None (embezzlement)
Customer B	1,000	$ 500 to Customer A $ 500 to Customer B
Customer C	2,000	$ 500 to Customer B $1,500 to Customer C

The auditor investigates the possibility of lapping by comparing details of the Deposit Slips with details of the Cash Receipts Journal. This procedure is done to ensure that all cash receipts are recorded (the CO assertion).

Counting Cash on Hand. In most cases, the cash held by clients is relatively immaterial in amount. Cash on hand includes petty cash funds, change funds, and undeposited receipts from one or more prior day(s). In planning cash counts, the auditor should take action to ensure that cash funds and other negotiable assets (such as investments in securities) already counted cannot be subsequently substituted for those yet to be counted in an attempt to conceal a shortage or intentionally overstate total assets. This is done by:

1. Assembling all funds and negotiable assets at a central location for simultaneous counting.
2. Using several auditors to count the cash funds and negotiable assets at separate locations at the same time.
3. Sealing or separating each fund once it has been counted and making sure that each seal is unbroken until the count is complete.

It should be emphasized that the auditor must always be careful to avoid making cash counts in a manner that may result in him or her being accused or suspected of causing a shortage. Cash counts should always be made in the presence of the client employee responsible for the funds. If this employee is called away before the count is completed, the auditor should terminate the count and return the cash to the employee. If the auditor wishes to resume the same count at a later time, the fund should be sealed before returning it to the custodian. The auditor should be certain that the seal is unbroken when the count is resumed. The auditor should obtain a signed receipt (in ink) from the custodian of the fund after the count has been completed. This receipt is an acknowledgment of the accuracy of the count and the return of the fund intact to the custodian.

In some instances, companies may have a one-day lag in depositing their cash receipts. That is, the cash received on December 31, 19x3 may not be deposited until the following business day (January 1 or 2, 19x4). If cash on hand includes undeposited cash receipts from the prior day, the auditor should trace the undeposited receipts to both the Cash Receipts Journal and to the Bank Statement for the following period to determine that these receipts were deposited intact and daily.

Counting cash provides the auditor with assurance that the cash exists (the EO assertion) and is owned by the client (the RO assertion). In addition, comparing cash counts to the Lead Schedule of Cash Balances allows the auditor to determine that all cash transactions are recorded (the CO assertion). Finally, by counting cash, the auditor can also verify that cash on hand is recorded at the proper dollar amount (the VA assertion).

SURPRISE CASH COUNTS[6]

An internal auditor's cash count revealed a shortage of $60 in a fund containing $700. While apparently minimal, a further investigation revealed that the employee had embezzled over $7,500 in the prior month. The employee was able to perpetrate this scheme because cash counts had been abandoned by the internal audit staff because they were perceived as not being cost-beneficial.

---

[6] "Surprise Cash Counts," *Internal Auditor* (April 1993), 69.

Evaluating Financial Statement Presentation. In evaluating the presentation of cash in the financial statements, the auditor should inquire about any compensating balance arrangements or other restrictions on the client's cash balances. A **compensating balance** is a minimum amount of cash that must be maintained by the client in its bank account as a form of collateral for a loan received from the bank. Compensating balances and restrictions on cash must be disclosed in the footnotes accompanying the client's financial statements. In addition, cash held for specified future purposes (such as the retirement of debt) should be classified as either a short-term or long-term investment, depending upon the duration of the restriction.

The auditor obtains evidence about compensating balance and other restrictions on cash by reviewing the client's disclosures related to cash, inquiring of management, and considering the results of confirmations received from the client's banks. These procedures relate to the PD assertion.

CHAPTER CHECKPOINTS

11-22. What is kiting? How can possible acts of kiting be identified by the auditor?

11-23. What is a Proof of Cash? When would a Proof of Cash be prepared by the auditor?

11-24. What is lapping? How can the auditor detect instances of lapping?

11-25. Why is it important for the auditor to count cash and all other negotiable assets simultaneously?

11-26. What is a compensating balance? How can the auditor identify compensating balance requirements?

◻ AUDITING SALES

Earlier in this chapter, we discussed the audit of accounts receivable. As the auditor verifies the client's accounts receivable through confirmation and other procedures, he or she is also verifying the sales related to those accounts receivable. In addition to the audit procedures performed with respect to accounts receivable, three other types of procedures are performed for sales: tests of the Sales Register (or Sales Journal), analytical procedures, and sales cutoff tests. These procedures are discussed in the remainder of this section.

◻ Tests of the Sales Register (or Sales Journal)

While confirming accounts receivable provides the auditor with evidence regarding an aggregate number of transactions, this procedure does not ordinarily allow the auditor to verify individual transactions. To examine the recording of individual sales transactions, the auditor will perform tests of transactions recorded in the client's Sales Register (or Sales Journal). While this procedure may not seem to be necessary, given the confirmation of accounts receivable, the auditor ordinarily performs tests of the Sales Register on at least a limited basis. These tests include the following:

1. Scanning entries in the Sales Register for large and unusual transactions. Sales recorded at excessively high dollar amounts (for example, ten times the next highest sale) may represent a careless mathematical mistake in processing Sales Invoices. This procedure provides evidence regarding the VA assertion.
2. Tracing from documentation representing actual sales made by the client (the Shipping Document) to recordings in the Sales Register. By selecting a sample of Shipping Documents, the auditor has identified a number of transactions that actually occurred. By comparing these transactions with entries in the Sales Register, the auditor can determine that: (1) the transaction was recorded (the CO assertion), and (2) the transaction was recorded at the proper dollar amount (the VA assertion).
3. Vouching selected entries in the Sales Register to Shipping Documents. This test is performed to ensure that selected entries in the Sales Register are supported by Shipping Documents. By comparing the entries to the documentation, the auditor can determine that: (1) the transaction actually occurred (the EO assertion), and (2) the transaction was recorded at the proper dollar amount (the VA assertion).

The extent of the auditor's tests of the Sales Register is highly dependent upon the necessary level of detection risk. As the auditor needs to restrict detection risk to lower levels (*i.e.*, perform more effective substantive tests), the extent of these procedures increases (and *vice versa*). It is important to note that some tests of the Sales Register may be performed by the auditor during his or her test of control activities as part of the study and evaluation of internal control.

◻ Analytical Procedures

As noted earlier in this chapter, the auditor's analytical procedures for accounts receivable include comparisons using several ratios that involve sales. In addition to these analytical procedures, the auditor will ordinarily compare the recorded sales in the current period with: (1) budgeted or forecasted sales, and/or (2) the level of sales from one or more prior periods. As with other accounts, significant fluctuations revealed by analytical procedures may reflect the recording of fictitious sales transactions (the EO and RO assertions), the failure to record actual sales transactions (the CO assertion), or sales transactions recorded at the incorrect dollar amount (the VA assertion).

◻ Sales Cutoff Tests

One important objective in the auditor's examination of sales is that transactions occurring near year-end are recorded in the proper accounting period. As noted in our discussion of the Credit Sales subcycle (see Chapter 10), sales to customers involve two entries: (1) the sale (and corresponding increase in accounts receivable), and (2) the reduction of inventory (and corresponding increase in cost of goods sold). Improperly including or excluding sales transactions occurring near year-end can have a substantial impact on the sales and accounts receivable amounts shown in the client's financial statements.

To verify that sales are recorded in the proper period, the auditor performs **sales cutoff tests**. The basic premise underlying these tests is that prenumbered documents can provide some evidence concerning the period in which a transaction took place. In performing sales cutoff tests, the auditor examines sales transactions occurring near year-end (normally, a few days prior to and a few days following year-end) to verify that these transactions are recorded in the correct period. Once the auditor identifies the Shipping Document number representing the last sale made in the year under audit, sales cutoff tests are relatively straightforward.

To illustrate, assume that the auditor has identified Shipping Document #4580 as the last sale made by the client in the year under audit. In performing sales cutoff tests, the auditor notes that Shipping Document #s 4575-4590 occur within a few days of year-end. The auditor would examine each of the sales represented by Shipping Document #s 4575-4590 to determine that:

▶ All sales represented by Shipping Documents 4575-4580 (inclusive) are recorded at year-end (the CO assertion)

▶ No sales represented by Shipping Documents 4581-4590 are recorded at year-end (the EO assertions)

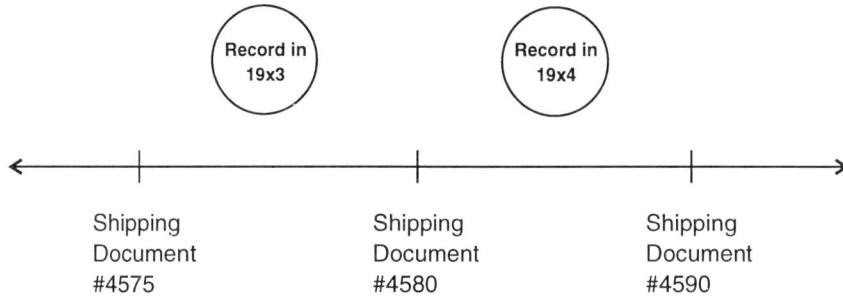

It is important to remember that sales should be recorded when legal title passes from the seller (the client) to the buyer. If the terms of the shipment are F.O.B. (Free on Board) Shipping Point, title passes when the goods are shipped. In this case, the date of the Shipping Document can be reliably used to determine the appropriate recording date. If the terms are F.O.B. Destination, title to the goods does not pass to the buyer until the goods are received by the buyer at their place of business. In these cases, the delivery time should be estimated and added to the date on the Shipping Document to determine the approximate date on which the sale should be recorded.

SALES MANIPULATIONS[7]

MiniScribe Corp., a now-defunct manufacturer of computer disk drives, engaged in several questionable practices to inflate its sales. These practices included:

▶ Creating documentation and shipping disk drives to customers who did not place orders. When the disk drives were later returned by the customers, MiniScribe did not reduce sales to reflect the returned merchandise.

▶ Shipping bricks to its distributors in packaging that was used for its disk drives and recording these shipments as sales of disk drives. The weight of the boxes and markings on the packaging gave the appearance that the shipment was for a sale of disk drives.

▶ Recording $16 million of sales on December 29, 1986 and dating these sales December 28, 1986 (the fiscal year-end). Paul Regan (a forensic accountant) notes that "unusual transactions at or near year-end should trigger extended audit procedures."

CHAPTER CHECKPOINTS

11-27. What are sales cutoff tests? How are these tests performed by the auditor?

11-28. What assertions are verified by performing sales cutoff tests?

◉ SUMMARY OF KEY POINTS

1. The basic steps in using the audit risk model are: (1) set audit risk at desired levels (usually, low); (2) assess inherent risk based on the susceptibility of the account balance to misstatement; (3) assess control risk based on the effectiveness of the client's internal control; and (4) determine detection risk based on prior assessments of audit risk, inherent risk, and control risk. Detection risk represents the nature, timing, and extent of the auditor's substantive testing procedures.

2. In examining accounts receivable and cash, the auditor utilizes the test of balances approach. Under this approach, the auditor identifies components of the account balance or class of transactions under examination. He or she then selects a sample of these components and performs some form of evidence-gathering procedure to verify these components. The test of balances approach is ordinarily used when an account balance is characterized by a large number of transactions for smaller dollar amounts.

---

[7] "How MiniScribe Got Its Auditor's Blessing on Questionable Sales," *The Wall Street Journal* (May 14, 1992), A1, A5.

3. The auditor's examination of accounts receivable begins by obtaining an Aged Listing of Accounts Receivable. The Aged Listing summarizes the client's accounts receivable by due date and is used by the auditor to verify the adequacy of the client's allowance for doubtful accounts.

4. The primary substantive testing procedure related to accounts receivable is the confirmation of accounts receivable. Per *SAS No. 67*, the auditor's confirmation of accounts receivable is a generally accepted auditing procedure. If it is impractical or impossible for the auditor to confirm accounts receivable, she or he must be satisfied as to the reasonableness of the receivables using alternative procedures.

5. Accounts receivable may be confirmed using either the positive request method or the negative request method. With the positive request method, the debtor is asked to respond as to the correctness of his or her account balance, whether the balance shown on the confirmation is correct or incorrect. The negative request method only requires a response from the customer if the amount shown on the confirmation is incorrect.

6. Other important substantive tests performed over accounts receivable include: (1) evaluating the provision for uncollectible accounts receivable, (2) performing analytical procedures, and (3) evaluating the overall financial statement presentation of accounts receivable.

7. The primary substantive test performed in the examination of cash is verifying the client's year-end Bank Reconciliation. The auditor performs the following procedures in this verification: (1) confirming the bank balance directly with the client's bank, (2) verifying reconciling items (such as outstanding checks and deposits-in-transit) returned with a subsequent Bank Statement, and (3) verifying the mathematical accuracy of the Bank Reconciliation.

8. Two methods that may be used to misappropriate cash are kiting and lapping. Kiting involves including an amount of cash in two or more bank accounts simultaneously to cover a theft or shortage of cash. Kiting may be detected by the auditor through the preparation of a Schedule of Interbank Transfers. Lapping occurs when client employees misappropriate cash receipts from customers and cover the theft with receipts from subsequent collections received from other customers. Lapping maybe detected by comparing the details of the cash receipts records to Deposit Slips.

9. Other important substantive tests performed by the auditor in his or her examination of cash include: (1) performing analytical procedures for cash, (2) preparing a Proof of Cash, (3) counting cash maintained by the client on hand, and (4) evaluating the overall financial statement presentation of cash.

10. Much of the auditor's work with respect to sales is done during the audit of accounts receivable. In examining sales, the auditor will perform tests of the Sales Register, analytical procedures, and sales cutoff tests. The purpose of sales cutoff tests is to determine that sales made near the end of the year are recorded in the proper accounting period.

GLOSSARY

Aged Listing of Accounts Receivable. A summary of the client's accounts receivable classified based upon the length of time that amounts have been outstanding. An Aged Listing of Accounts Receivable is used by the auditor to evaluate the adequacy of the allowance for doubtful accounts.

Blank Confirmation Request. A form of accounts receivable confirmation that omits the balance owed by a particular customer and requests the customer to provide the balance. This is the most reliable form of confirmation, but the extensive effort required by the customer often results in a higher number of nonrespondents.

Cutoff Bank Statement. A Bank Statement received by the auditor from the client's bank that covers a specified period of time immediately after year-end. A Cutoff Bank Statement includes paid checks and other customary enclosures and is used to verify the reconciling items appearing on the year-end Bank Reconciliation.

Kiting. A method used by client employees to cover a theft or cash shortage. Kiting involves simultaneously including an amount of cash in two or more bank accounts by recording the transfer of cash to the "receiving" bank prior to recording the transfer from the "disbursing" bank.

Lapping. A method of misappropriating cash by embezzling receipts from customers and covering the shortage with subsequent collections received from other customers. Lapping occurs when inadequate segregation of duties involving cash receipts are established.

Negative Confirmation Request. A form of confirmation request where the customer is asked to reply only if the balance as stated on the request is not correct.

Positive Confirmation Request. A form of confirmation request in which the customer is asked to respond regardless of whether the balance as stated on the request is correct or incorrect.

Proof of Cash. The auditor prepares a Proof of Cash to reconcile bank and accounting records of the beginning cash balance, cash receipts, cash disbursements, and ending cash balance for a selected month. A Proof of Cash is normally prepared in cases where the client's internal control over cash is considered to be weak.

Sales Cutoff Test. Tests applied by the auditor to determine whether sales made near year-end are recorded in the proper accounting period. Sales cutoff tests involve identifying the Shipping Document number representing the last sale made in the year under examination.

Schedule of Interbank Transfers. A summary of all activity (deposits and/or withdrawals) involving two or more banks where the client has funds on deposit. The Schedule of Interbank Transfers is used by the auditor to detect instances of kiting.

Standard Bank Confirmation Inquiry (SBCI). A form mailed by the auditor to each bank with whom the client has a balance or from whom it had borrowed funds or had other business during the current year. The SBCI requests information about cash balances on deposit as well as any direct or contingent liabilities owed by the client.

SUMMARY OF PROFESSIONAL PRONOUNCEMENTS

Statement on Auditing Standards No. 57, "Auditing Accounting Estimates" (New York: AICPA, 1988, AU 342).
Statement on Auditing Standards No. 67, "The Confirmation Process" (New York: AICPA, 1991, AU 330).

QUESTIONS AND PROBLEMS

11-29. Select the **best** answer for each of the following items

1. The Cashier of Safir Company covered a shortage in the cash working fund with cash obtained on December 31 from a local bank by cashing but not recording a check drawn on the company's out of town bank. How would the auditor discover this manipulation?

   a. Confirming all December 31 bank balances.
   b. Counting the cash working fund at the close of business on December 31.
   c. Preparing independent Bank Reconciliations as of December 31.
   d. Investigating items returned with the Cutoff Bank Statements.

2. Which of the following would be the best protection for a company that wishes to prevent the lapping of cash receipts from accounts receivable?

   a. Segregate duties so the Bookkeeper in charge of the General Ledger has no access to incoming mail.
   b. Segregate duties so no employee has access to both Checks from customers and currency from daily cash receipts.
   c. Have customers send payments directly to the company's depository bank.
   d. Request that customers' payment checks be made payable to the company and addressed to the treasurer.

3. The use of the positive (as opposed to the negative) form of receivables confirmation is indicated when:

   a. Internal control over accounts receivable is considered to be effective.
   b. There is reason to believe that a substantial number of accounts may be in dispute.
   c. A large number of small balances are involved.
   d. There is reason to believe a significant portion of the requests will be answered.

4. It is sometimes impracticable or impossible for an auditor to use normal accounts receivable confirmation procedures. In such situations, the best alternative procedure the auditor might resort to would be:

   a. Examining subsequent receipts of year-end accounts receivable.
   b. Reviewing accounts receivable aging schedules prepared at the balance-sheet date and at a subsequent date.
   c. Requesting that management increase the allowance for uncollectible accounts by an amount equal to some percentage of the balance in those accounts that cannot be confirmed.
   d. Performing analytical procedures of accounts receivable and sales on a year-to-year basis.

5. Cooper, CPA, is auditing the financial statements of a small rural municipality. The receivable balances represent residents' delinquent real estate taxes. The internal control at the municipality is weak. To determine the existence of the accounts receivable balances at the balance-sheet date, Cooper would most likely:

   a. Send positive confirmation requests.
   b. Send negative confirmation requests.
   c. Examine evidence of subsequent cash receipts.
   d. Inspect the internal records such as copies of the tax invoices that were mailed to the residents.

6. An auditor ordinarily sends a standard confirmation request to all banks with which the client has done business during the year under audit, regardless of the year-end balance. A purpose of this procedure is to:

   a. Provide the data necessary to prepare a Proof of Cash.
   b. Request a Cutoff Bank Statement and related Checks be sent to the auditor.
   c. Detect kiting activities that may otherwise not be discovered.
   d. Seek information about contingent liabilities and security agreements.

7. Which of the following procedures would an auditor most likely perform for year-end accounts receivable confirmations when the auditor **did not** receive replies to second requests?

   a. Review the Cash Receipts Journal for the month prior to the year-end.
   b. Intensify the study of internal control concerning the Revenue cycle.
   c. Increase the assessed level of detection risk for the existence assertion.
   d. Inspect the shipping records documenting the merchandise sold to the debtors.

8. An auditor's purpose in reviewing credit ratings of customers with delinquent accounts receivable most likely is to obtain evidence concerning management's assertions about:

   a. Presentation and disclosure.
   b. Existence or occurrence.
   c. Rights and obligations.
   d. Valuation or allocation.

9. An Aged Listing of Accounts Receivable is usually used by the auditor to:

   a. Verify the validity of recorded receivables.
   b. Ensure that all accounts are promptly credited.
   c. Evaluate the results of tests of controls.
   d. Evaluate the provision for bad debt expense.

10. An auditor should trace bank transfers for the last part of the audit period and first part of the subsequent period to detect whether:

    a. The Cash Receipts Journal was held open for a few days after year-end.
    b. The last Checks recorded before the year-end were actually mailed by the year-end.
    c. Cash balances were overstated because of kiting.
    d. Any unusual payments to or receipts from related parties occurred.

11. Which of the following most likely would be detected by an auditor's review of a client's sales cut-off?

    a. Shipments lacking Sales Invoices and Shipping Documents.
    b. Excessive write-offs of accounts receivable.
    c. Unrecorded sales at year-end.
    d. Lapping of year-end accounts receivable.

12. Which of the following substantive tests would not provide the auditor with evidence regarding the valuation or allocation assertion for cash?

    a. Confirming cash balances with the client's bank.
    b. Inquiring about compensating balance arrangements with banks.
    c. Agreeing the total of cash on the Lead Schedule of Cash Balances with the Trial Balance.
    d. Verifying the accuracy of the client's year-end Bank Reconciliation.
    e. Counting cash held by the client on hand.

13. If customers fail to respond to positive accounts receivable confirmations, the auditor can verify sales to customers by examining _____ and payments made by customers by examining _____.

    a. Sales Orders; Canceled Checks.
    b. Customer Orders; Canceled Checks.
    c. Sales Invoices; Remittance Advices.
    d. Shipping Documents; Remittance Advices.
    e. Sales Invoices; Canceled Checks.

14. If internal control over cash is more effective, the auditor would vary the nature, timing, and extent of substantive tests by:

    a. Confirming cash balances with banks as of year-end, as opposed to at an interim date.
    b. Confirming a larger number of cash balances.
    c. Confirming cash balances using a negative request method.
    d. Preparing a four-column Proof of Cash.
    e. None of the above.

15. Substantive testing of cash is normally done by performing tests of balances (as opposed to tests of transactions) because:

    a. Cash is highly susceptible to theft and misappropriation.
    b. Cash balances are generally the result of a voluminous number of transactions, each of which is relatively small in amount.
    c. Cash is a balance sheet account as opposed to an income statement account.
    d. Information about the activity in a cash account can be obtained from sources (such as banks) independent of the company.
    e. All of the above.

16. Which of the following statements is not true with respect to the differences between positive and negative confirmations?

    a. Positive confirmations generally require more effort on the part of the auditor.
    b. Negative confirmations are used when the client's internal control over accounts receivable transactions is relatively effective.
    c. Negative confirmations may provide the auditor with incorrect conclusions if customers disregard the confirmation.
    d. Positive confirmations are generally preferred for receivable balances having higher dollar amounts.
    e. All of the above statements are true.

17. The Lead Schedule of Cash Balances:

    a. Summarizes the components of cash for the client.
    b. Allows the auditor to review interbank transfers near year-end to determine whether kiting has occurred.
    c. Provides independent evidence of the client's year-end cash balances according to bank records.
    d. Reconciles the client's records of activity and balances for cash to the records of the corresponding bank.
    e. Includes bank information and reconciling items for a short period of time after year-end.

18. Standard Bank Confirmation Inquiries should be mailed:

    a. To each bank with which the client had business during the year.
    b. By the auditor, to ensure that they are not altered prior to mailing.
    c. With a return envelope, so that the financial institution responds directly to the auditor.
    d. Under the auditor's direct control to financial institutions.
    e. All of the above

19. A document used by the auditor to evaluate the appropriateness of the reconciling items included in a client's Bank Reconciliation is a(n):

    a. Cutoff Bank Statement.
    b. Proof of cash.
    c. Remittance Listing.
    d. Schedule of Interbank Transfers.
    e. Standard Bank Confirmation Inquiry.

20. The purpose of performing sales cutoff tests is to allow the auditor to ensure that:

    a. All sales have been properly authorized by the company.
    b. Sales are recorded at the proper dollar amount.
    c. Sales are recorded in the proper accounting period.
    d. Sales (and the related accounts receivable) will ultimately be collectible by the client.

21. Which of the following procedures would ordinarily not be performed in verifying the client's year-end Bank Reconciliations?

    a. Observing cash on deposit at year-end.
    b. Verifying reconciling items by obtaining a Cutoff Bank Statement.
    c. Verifying the mathematical accuracy of the Bank Reconciliation.
    d. Confirming cash on deposit with banks.
    e. All of the above would be performed in verifying the company's year-end Bank Reconciliation.

22. Which of the following management assertion(s) is least likely to be addressed by the confirmation of accounts receivable?

    a. Completeness.
    b. Existence or occurrence.
    c. Rights and obligations.
    d. Valuation or allocation.

23. Which of the following substantive testing procedures ordinarily provides the auditor with the best evidence regarding the collectibility of accounts receivable?

    a. Inquiring of management regarding overdue accounts.
    b. Preparing an Aged Listing of Accounts Receivable.
    c. Confirming selected accounts receivable with customers.
    d. Performing analytical procedures regarding the accounts receivable balances.

24. In performing sales cutoff tests, the auditor obtains evidence about the proper period in which a sale should be recorded by identifying the last _____ issued during the year.

    a. Bank Confirmation.
    b. Canceled Check.
    c. Sales Invoice.
    d. Shipping Document.

25. Kiting can best be detected through the preparation of a(n):

    a. Bank Reconciliation.
    b. Outstanding Check Listing.
    c. Proof of Cash.
    d. Schedule of Interbank Transfers.

    (Items 1 through 11 in 11-29; AICPA Adapted)

11-30. For each of the following substantive tests, indicate the management assertion(s) that are proven by the auditor. Each test may be associated with more than one assertion.

    a. Confirming cash balances with the bank.
    b. Mathematically verifying the client's outstanding check listing.
    c. Vouching from the Bank Reconciliation to deposits-in-transit returned with the Cutoff Bank Statement.
    d. Counting cash maintained on hand by the client.

e. Inquiring of client personnel regarding the need for compensating balances and other restrictions on the use of cash.
f. Tracing from Checks returned with the Cutoff Bank Statement to the outstanding check listing accompanying the client's Bank Reconciliations.
g. Preparing a Schedule of Interbank Transfers.

11-31. When you arrive at your client's office on January 11, 19X2, to begin the 19X1 audit, you discover the client had been drawing Checks as the creditors' Invoices became due but not necessarily mailing them. Because of a working capital shortage, some Checks may have been held for two or three weeks.

The client informs you that unmailed Checks totaling $27,600 were on hand at December 31, 19X1. He states these December-dated Checks had been entered in the Cash Disbursements Book and charged to the respective creditors' accounts in December because the Checks were prenumbered. Heavy collections permitted him to mail the Checks before your arrival.

The client wants to adjust the cash balance and accounts payable at December 31 by $27,600 because the cash account had a credit balance. He objects to submitting to his bank your audit report showing an overdraft of cash.

Required:

a. Submit a detailed audit program indicating the procedures you would use to satisfy yourself of the accuracy of the cash balance on the client's statements.
b. Discuss the propriety of reversing the indicated amount of outstanding checks.

(AICPA Adapted)

11-32. Your client, who sells products to customers on account, has several bank accounts. A reconciliation of one of these accounts as of the balance-sheet date appears as follows:

Balance per bank, December 31, 19X1	$5,000
Add: Deposit-in-transit	1,000
Total	$6,000
Less: Outstanding Checks	(50)
Balance per books, December 31, 19X1	$5,950

The book balance of $5,950 is shown as cash on the balance sheet. As to the $1,000 shown as a deposit-in-transit, you are to:

a. Briefly describe the major possibilities of fraud or error in these circumstances.
b. List the audit procedures that, if followed in a regular annual audit, would help to verify the deposit-in-transit. Explain fully how these procedures would help to verify the deposit-in-transit and detect possible fraud or error.

(AICPA Adapted)

11-33. In connection with your audit of the ABC Company at December 31, 19X1, you were given a Bank Reconciliation by a company employee, which shows:

Balance per bank	$15,267
Deposits-in-transit	18,928
Total	$34,195
Checks outstanding	(21,378)
Balance per books	$12,817

As part of your verification you obtain the Bank Statement and canceled Checks from the bank on January 15, 19X2. Checks issued from January 1 to January 15, 19X2, per the books, were $11,241. Checks returned by the bank on January 15 amounted to $29,219. Of the checks outstanding December 31, $4,800 were not returned by the bank with the January 15 statement, and of those issued per the books on January 19X2, $3,600 were not returned.

Required:

a. Prepare a schedule showing the above data in proper form.
b. Suggest possible explanations for the condition existing here and state what your action would be in each case, including any necessary journal entry.

(AICPA Adapted)

11-34. A surprise count of the Y Company's imprest petty cash fund, carried on the books at $5,000, was made on November 10, 19X1.

The company acts as agent for an express company in the issuance and sale of money orders. Blank money orders are held by the Cashier for issuance upon payments of the designated amounts by employees. Settlement with the express company is made weekly with its representative who calls at the Y Company office. At that time he collects for orders issued, accounts for unissued orders, and leaves additional blank, serially-numbered money orders.

The count of the items presented by the Cashier as composing the fund was as follows:

Currency (bills and coin)		$2,200
Cashed checks		500
Vouchers (made out in pencil and signed by recipient)		740
N.S.F. checks (dated June 10 and 15, 19X1)		260
Copy of petty cash receipt vouchers:		
Return of expense advance	$200	
Sale of money orders (#C1015-1021)	100	
Total		300
Blank money orders-claimed to have been purchased for $100 each from the Express Company (#C1022-1027)		600

At the time of the count, there was also on hand the following:

Unissued money orders #C1028-1037.
Unclaimed wage envelopes (sealed and amounts not shown).

The following day the custodian of the fund produced vouchers aggregating $400 and explained that these vouchers had been temporarily misplaced the previous day. They were for wage advances to employees.

Required:

a. Show the proper composition of the fund at November 10, 19X1.
b. State the audit procedures necessary for the verification of the items in the fund.

(AICPA Adapted)

11-35. One audit procedure that can be used to detect kiting at year-end is the reconciliation of all bank activity with the books (for all bank accounts) for the period just before and just after the year-end. Certain detailed comparisons can be avoided if this reconciliation is accomplished in summary form.

a. Using the data that follows, devise a good workpaper form to achieve the above-stated objective and reconcile the bank balances at the three dates shown and the bank activity for the period December 1, 19X1, to January 12, 19X2. (Your workpapers must include a "proof of cash transactions" but need not show the corrected balances or totals).
b. For each item on the workpapers, show by appropriate symbols all audit procedures you would take in completing your audit.
c. Prepare journal entries needed as a result of your work.

ACB Corporation	11/30/X1	12/31/X1	1/12/X2
Balance per Bank Statement	$27,324.08	$20,383.89	$29,514.84
Balance per cash book and general ledger	21,214.95	16,689.86	—
Outstanding checks	7,324.13	8,231.12	3,172.50
Deposits-in-transit	2,200.00	3,750.00	1,625.00

	Period 12/1/X1 – 12/31/X1	Period 1/21/X2 – 1/12/X2
Receipts per cash book	$88,546.50	$21,473.26
Credits per Bank Statement	86,324.00	24,372.10
Disbursements per cash book	93,071.59	9,980.03
Charges per Bank Statement	93,264.19	15,241.15

The client obtained Bank Statements for November 30 and December 31, 19X1, and reconciled the balances. You obtained the statements of 1/12/X2 directly and obtained the necessary confirmations. You have found that there are no errors in addition or subtraction in the books. The following information was obtained:

1. Bank service charges of $11.50 were charged on the 11/30/X1 statement and recorded in the cash disbursements on 12/5/X1. Charges of $13.25 were charged on the 12/31/X1 statement and recorded in the cash disbursements on 1/6/X2.
2. A check (#28890) for $22.48 cleared the bank in December at $122.48. This was found in proving the Bank Statement. The bank made the correction on January 8.
3. A note of $1,000 sent to the bank for collection on 11/15/X1 was collected and credited to the account on 11/28/X1 net of a collection fee, $3.50. The note was recorded in the cash receipts on 12/10/X1. The collection fee was then entered as a disbursement.

4. The client records returned checks in red (as a negative amount) in the cash receipts book. The following checks were returned by the bank.

Customer	Amount	Date Returned	Date Recorded	Date Redeposited
A Black	$327.50	12/6/X1	*	12/8/X1
C. Denny	673.84	12/27/X1	1/3/X2	1/15/X2

*No entries made in either receipts or disbursement books for this item.

5. Two payroll checks totaling $215.75 for employees' vacations were drawn on January 3 and cleared the bank January 8. These were not entered on the books because semimonthly payroll summaries (from payroll disbursement records) are entered in the disbursements on days 15 and 31 only.

(AICPA Adapted)

11-36. Toyco, a retail toy chain, honors two bank credit cards and makes daily deposits of Credit Card Sales Slips in two credit card bank accounts (Bank A and Bank B). Each day, Toyco batches its Credit Card Sales Slips, bank Deposit Slips, and authorized sales return documents, and prepares these data for processing by its electronic data processing department. Each week, detailed computer printouts of the General Ledger credit card cash accounts are prepared. Credit card banks have been instructed to make an automatic weekly transfer of cash to Toyco's general bank account. The credit card banks charge-back deposits that include sales to holders of stolen or expired cards.

The auditor conducting the examination of the 19X1 Toyco financial statements has obtained the following copies of the detailed General Ledger cash account printouts, a summary of the Bank Statements, and the Bank Reconciliations, all for the week ended December 31, 19X1.

TOYCO
Detailed General Ledger Credit Card
Cash Account Printouts, for the
Week Ended December 31, 19X1

	Bank A Dr. or (Cr.)	Bank B Dr. or (Cr.)
Beginning balance:		
December 24, 19X1	$ 12,100	$ 4,200
Deposits:		
December 21, 19X1	2,500	5,000
December 28, 19X1	3,000	7,000
December 29, 19X1	0	5,400
December 30, 19X1	1,900	4,000
December 31, 19X1	2,200	6,000
Cash transfer:		
December 27, 19X1	(10,700)	0
Charge-backs:		
Expired cards	(300)	(1,600)
Invalid deposits (physically deposited in wrong account)	(1,400)	(1,000)
Redeposit of invalid deposits	1,000	1,400
Sales returns for week ending December 31, 19X1	(600)	(1,200)
Ending balance:		
December 31, 19X1	$ 9,700	$ 29,200

TOYCO
*Summary of the Bank Statements for the
Week Ended December 31, 19X1*

	Bank A (Charges)	or	Bank B *Credits*
Beginning balance:			
December 24, 19X1	$ 10,000		$ 0
Deposits dated:			
December 24, 19X1	2,100		4,200
December 21, 19X1	2,500		5,000
December 28, 19X1	3,000		7,000
December 29, 19X1	2,000		5,500
December 30, 19X1	1,900		4,000
Cash transfers to general bank account:			
December 27, 19X1	(10,700)		0
December 31, 19X1	0		(22,600)
Charge-backs:			
Stolen cards	(100)		0
Expired cards	(300)		(1,600)
Invalid deposits	(1,400)		(1,000)
Bank service charges	0		(500)
Bank charge (unexplained)	(400)		0
Ending balance:			
December 31, 19X1	$ 8,600		$ 0

TOYCO
*Bank Reconciliations for the Week
Ended December 31, 19X1*

Code No.		Bank A Add	or	Bank B (Deduct)
1.	Balance per Bank Statement—December 31, 19X1	$ 8,600		$ 0
2.	Deposits in transit—December 31, 19X1	2,200		6,000
3.	Redeposit of invalid deposits (physically deposited in wrong account)	1,000		1,400
4.	Difference in deposits of December 29, 19X1	(2,000)		(100)
5.	Unexplained bank charge	400		0
6.	Bank cash transfer not yet recorded	0		22,600
7.	Bank service charges	0		500
8.	Charge-backs not recorded—Stolen cards	100		0
9.	Sales returns recorded but not reported to the bank	(600)		(1,200)
10.	Balance per general ledger—December 31, 19X1	$ 9,700		$ 29,200

Required:

Based on a review of the December 31, 19X1, bank reconciliations and the related information available in the printouts and the summary of Bank Statements, describe what action(s) the auditor should take to obtain audit satisfaction for each item on the Bank Reconciliations.

Assume that all amounts are material and all computations are accurate.

Organize your answer sheet as follows using the appropriate code number for each item on the bank reconciliations:

Code No.	Action(s) to Be Taken by the Auditor to Obtain Audit Satisfaction
1.	

(AICPA Adapted)

11-37. The client-prepared bank reconciliation is being examined by Kautz, CPA, during an examination of the financial statements of Cynthia Company:

CYNTHIA COMPANY
Bank Reconciliation
Village Bank Account 2
December 31, 19X1

Balance per bank (a)		$18,375.91
Deposits in transit (b)		
12/30	$1,471.10	
12/31	2,840.69	4,311.79
Subtotal		$22,687.70
Outstanding Checks (c)		
837	6,000.00	
1941	671.80	
1966	320.00	
1984	1,855.42	
1985	3,621.22	
1987	2,576.89	
1991	4,420.88	(19,466.21)
Subtotal		3,221.49
NSF check returned 12/29 (d)		200.00
Bank charges		5.50
Error Check No. 1932		148.10
Customer note collected by the bank ($2,750 plus $275 interest) (e)		(3,025.00)
Balance per books (f)		$ 550.09

Required:

Indicate one or more audit procedures that should be performed by Kautz in gathering evidence in support of each of the items (a) through (f) above.

(AICPA Adapted)

11-38. Indicate one or more procedures that can be performed by the auditor to verify that:

   a. The total from the Aged Listing of Accounts Receivable is mathematically correct and agrees with the Trial Balance.
   b. Sales made to customers actually occurred.
   c. The client's annual provision for bad debts is reasonable.
   d. Accounts receivable pledged as collateral, factored, transferred, or assigned have been properly disclosed in the footnotes accompanying the financial statements.
   e. Customer accounts are recorded at the proper dollar amount.
   f. Sales occurring near the end of the year are recorded in the proper accounting period.

11-39. You have examined the financial statements of the Heft Company for several years. The internal control for accounts receivable is very satisfactory. The Heft Company is on a calendar-year basis. An interim audit, which included confirmation of the accounts receivable, was performed at August 31 and indicated that the accounting for receivables was very reliable.

   The company's sales are principally to manufacturing concerns. There are about 1,500 active trade accounts receivable, of which about 35 percent in number represent 65 percent of the total dollar amount. The accounts receivable are maintained alphabetically in five subledgers, which are controlled by one General Ledger Accountant.

   Sales are posted in the subledgers by an operation that simultaneously produces: (1) the customer's ledger card and monthly statement, and (2) the Sales Journal. All cash receipts are in the form of Checks and are simultaneously posted to: (1) the customer's ledger card and his or her monthly statement, and (2) the Cash Receipts Journal. Information for posting cash receipts is obtained from the Remittance Advice portions of the Checks. The bookkeeping machine operator compares the Remittance Advices with the list of Checks that was prepared by another person when the mail was received.

   Summary totals are produced monthly by the bookkeeping machine operations for posting to the appropriate general ledger accounts, such as cash, sales, accounts receivable, and so on. Aged Trial Balances by subledgers are prepared monthly.

   Sales returns and allowances and bad debt write-offs are summarized periodically and recorded by standard journal entries. Supporting documents for these journal entries are available. The usual documents arising from billing, shipping, and receiving also are available.

   Required:

   Prepare in detail the audit program for the Heft Company for the year-end examination of the trade accounts receivable. Do not give the program for the interim audit.

   (AICPA Adapted)

11-40. You are engaged in an audit as of December 31 of a medium-sized manufacturing company, it has between 300 and 400 open trade accounts receivable. As a part of the interim work, you decide on October 10 to select approximately 100 customers' accounts for positive confirmations as of September 30. You obtain an Aged Trial Balance of the Accounts Receivable as of September 30 and agree the balances of the open accounts to the Trial Balance from the subsidiary ledgers. In addition, you test the aging, foot the Trial Balance, and agree the total with the accounts receivable control account in the General Ledger. Also, detailed tests of the Sales and Cash Receipts Journals are made for the month of September.

Required:

a. Enumerate the types of accounts you would want to include in your selection of accounts to be confirmed.
b. Assuming that the client is preparing an Aged Trial Balance of Accounts Receivable as of December 31, outline the additional audit steps that should be undertaken in support of the amounts shown as accounts receivable.

(AICPA Adapted)

Learning Objectives

Study of this chapter is designed to achieve several learning objectives. After studying this chapter, you should be able to:

1. Identify the major accounts affected by the Purchases and Disbursements cycle.
2. List the major documents created during the Purchases and Disbursements cycle.
3. Understand the two major types of transactions occurring in the Purchases and Disbursements cycle.
4. Illustrate how the five major components of internal control exist within the Purchases and Disbursements cycle.
5. Understand the primary risks within the Purchases and Disbursements cycle and identify specific control activities designed to address these risks.
6. Discuss methods used by the auditor to test control activities in the Purchases and Disbursements cycle.

12

The Purchases and Disbursements Cycle

◉ EVALUATING INTERNAL CONTROL: THE PURCHASES AND DISBURSEMENTS CYCLE

The primary revenue-generating activity for a large number of organizations is the sale of products to customers. These types of companies can be roughly classified into one of two categories. Retailers (such as Wal-Mart, Sears, and Toys R Us) purchase inventory from suppliers in "ready-to-sell" (or final) form. Other types of companies (such as Nike, General Motors, and Exxon) actually produce or manufacture their own inventory and are referred to as manufacturers. Despite the fact that manufacturers actually produce their own inventory, they begin their process by purchasing direct material inputs (a form of inventory) from their suppliers. Therefore, any company whose revenues result from the sale of inventory must purchase items from outside suppliers.

An important aspect of the overall internal control for both retailers and manufacturers are control activities associated with the purchase of inventory. These control activities are part of the **Purchases and Disbursements cycle**. The Purchases and Disbursements cycle consists of two major types of transactions: (1) purchases made on account, and (2) cash disbursements for purchases made on account and other expenses. These types of transactions represent the two subcycles of the Purchases and Disbursements cycle and are summarized in Figure 12-1.

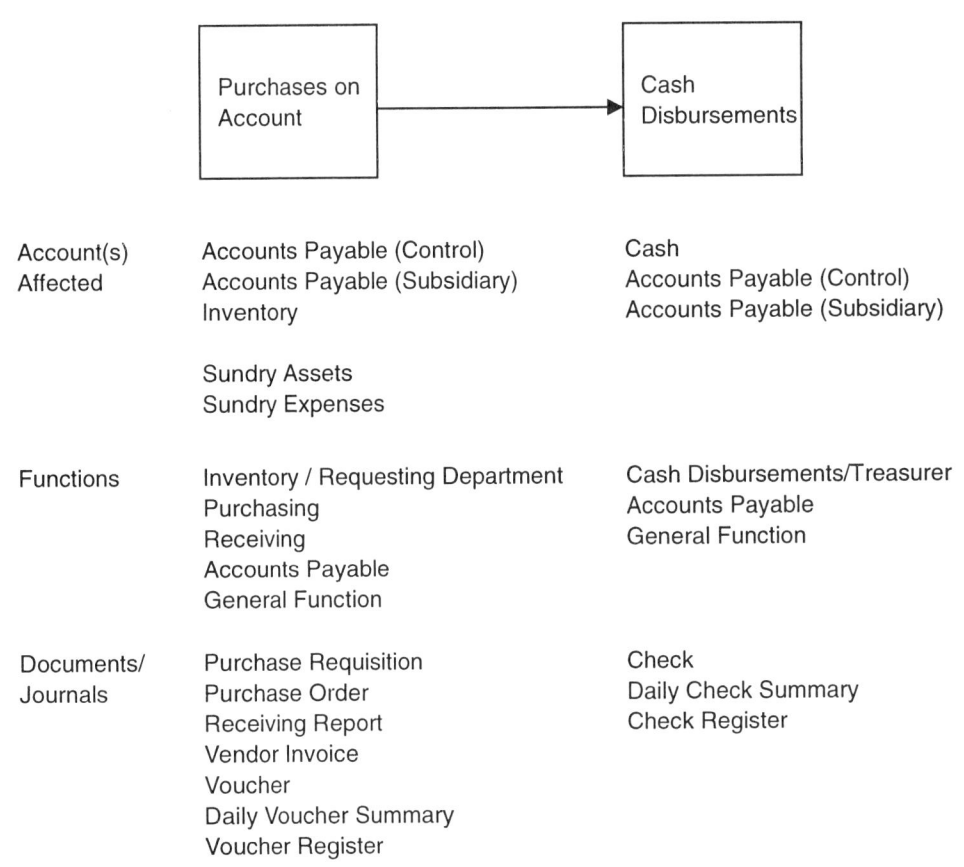

Figure 12-1: *Overview of Subcycles in the Purchases and Disbursements Cycle*

◻ Control Environment

As noted in previous chapters, the control environment is a component of internal control that is established on an overall basis within the organization. Recall that the control environment includes factors such as: (1) integrity and ethical values, (2) commitment to competence, (3) the existence of a Board of Directors and Audit Committee, (4) management's philosophy and operating style, (5) the organizational structure, (6) assignment of authority and responsibility, and (7) human resource policies and practices. During his or her examination of the Purchases and Disbursements cycle, the auditor will evaluate these areas of the control environment as they relate to the activities within this cycle.

> **CHAPTER CHECKPOINTS**
>
> **12-1.** Distinguish between the two types of companies that sell inventory as their primary revenue-generating activity.
>
> **12-2.** What are the two major types of transactions that occur in the Purchases and Disbursements cycle?
>
> **12-3.** How does the control environment affect the auditor's assessment of internal control in the Purchases and Disbursements cycle?

❏ Risk Assessment and Control Activities: The Purchases Subcycle

The first subcycle within the Purchases and Disbursements cycle is the Purchases subcycle. Figure 12-2 provides an overview of the major events, functions, and documents included within the Purchases subcycle. The process depicted in Figure 12-2 ordinarily relates to the purchase of direct materials inventory by a manufacturing company or the purchase of finished goods inventory by a retailer. However, many of these same control activities are also important in the purchase of such items as office equipment, supplies (a form of inventory), and fixed assets. Chapter 15 provides a discussion of the control activities applicable to purchases of assets other than inventory.

Information Processing Controls. The Purchases subcycle involves the following major departments/functions:

- ▶ Requesting Department (Inventory Department/Warehouse)
- ▶ Purchasing Department
- ▶ Receiving Department
- ▶ Accounts Payable Department
- ▶ General Function

Requesting Department (Inventory Department/Warehouse). An important concern of any company is ensuring that adequate levels of inventory are maintained. For a manufacturing company, inadequate direct materials inventories may disrupt production activities and result in losses because of downtime and idle workers. For retailers, inadequate finished goods inventories may result in opportunity costs in the form of lost sales as well as customer dissatisfaction when a desired item is not available. Conversely, maintaining excessive levels of inventory results in an opportunity cost, since funds invested in inventory are not available for alternative uses. Thus, prior to placing orders for inventory, an important control activity is the process through which the organization monitors its inventory balances to ensure that sufficient inventory is maintained on hand. This control activity relates to the operating objective of internal control, as it attempts to minimize the costs associated with maintaining inventories.

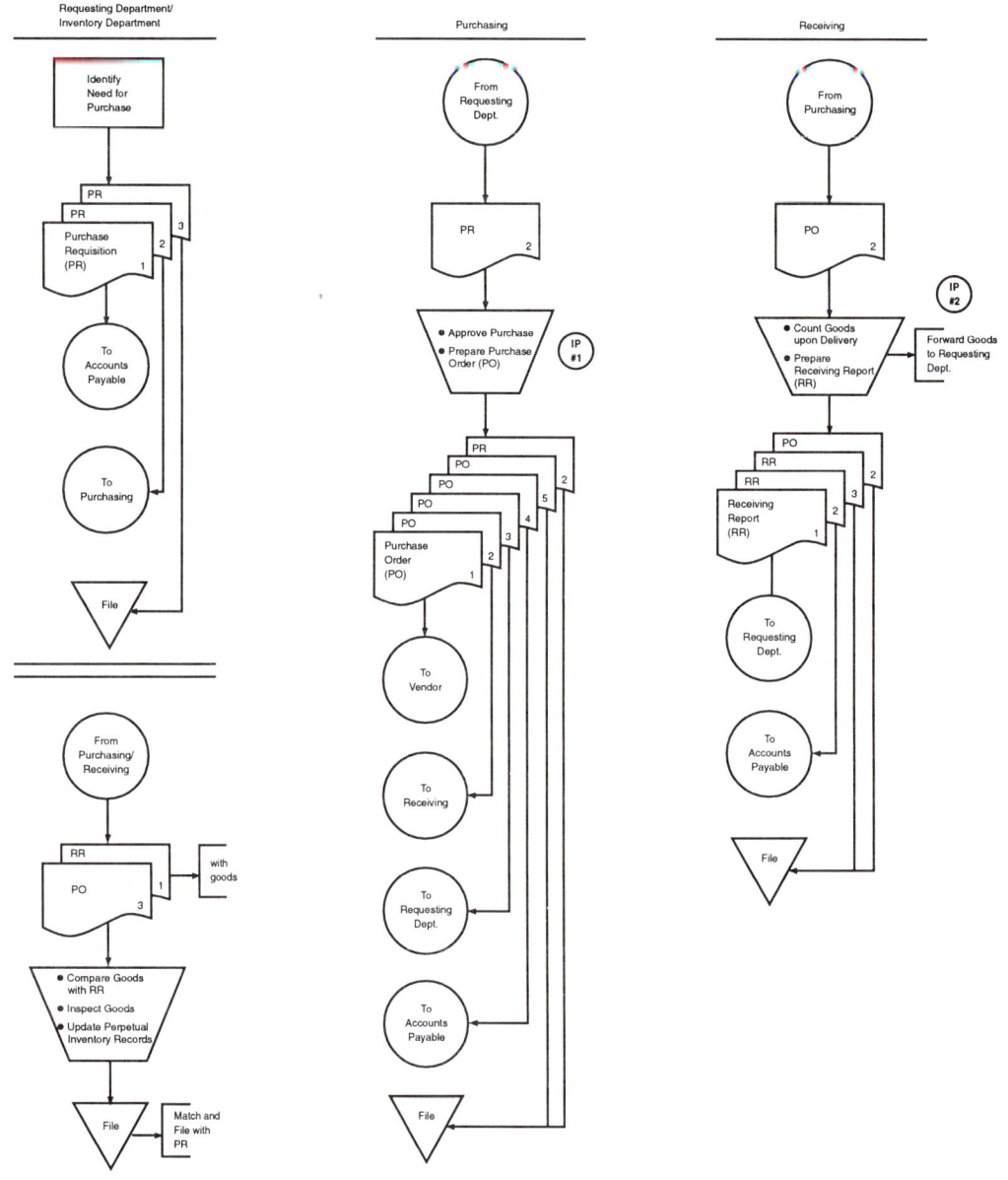

Figure 12-2: *Overview of the Purchases Subcycle*

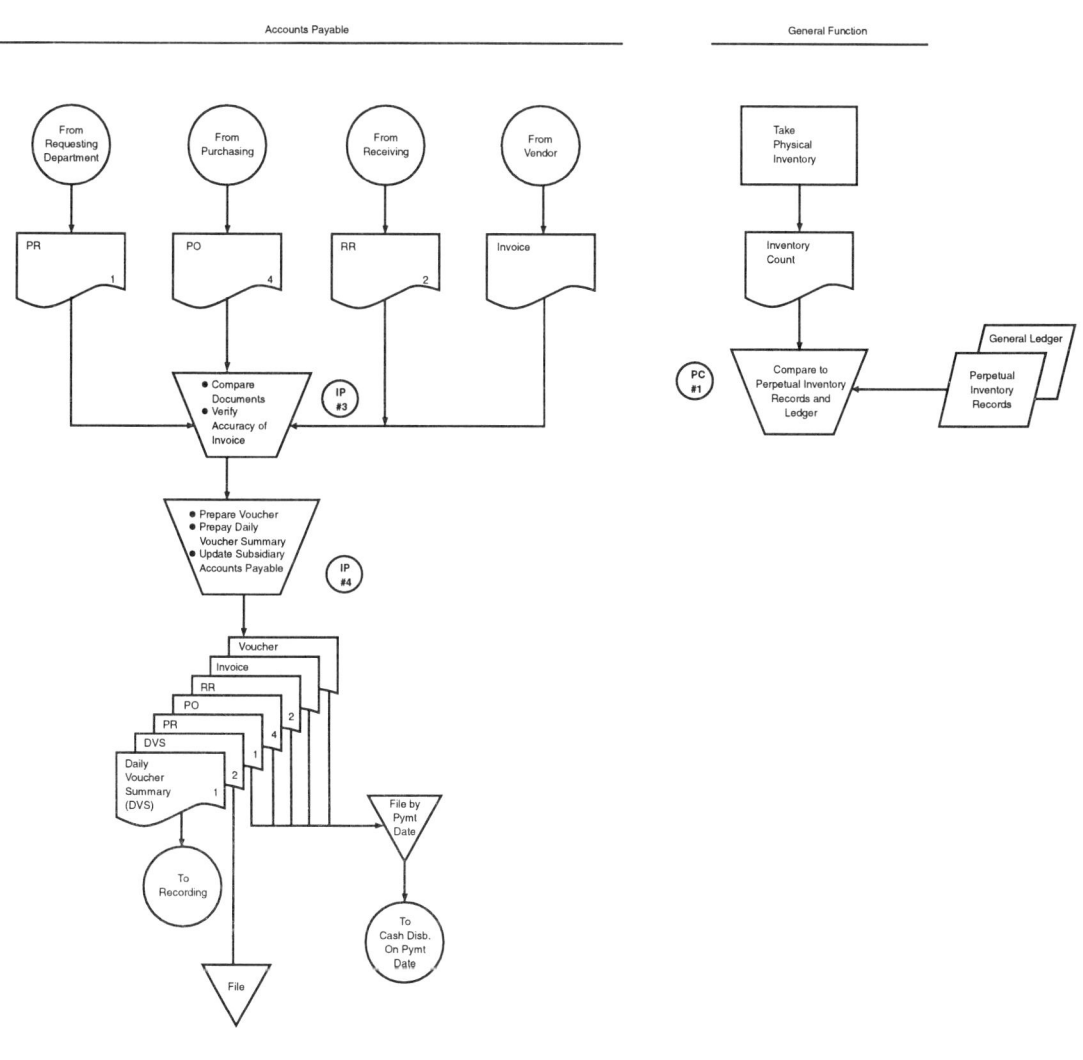

Figure 12-2: *continued*

12 / The Purchases and Disbursements Cycle

When the stock of inventory held by the company becomes low, the Requesting Department (in this case, the Inventory Department or Warehouse) prepares a Purchase Requisition. The **Purchase Requisition** acts as a request from one department (the Requesting Department) to the Purchasing Department that specific item(s) and quantities of inventory be ordered.

Purchasing Department. Once prepared, a copy of the Purchase Requisition is sent to the Purchasing Department. The Purchasing Department then selects a vendor and approves the request for the purchase. In certain cases, competitive bids will be solicited to allow the organization to receive the best possible price for its inventory. Upon approval, a **Purchase Order** is prepared and sent to the vendor (IP #1 in Figure 12-2). Additional copies of the Purchase Order are sent to: (1) the Requesting Department, (2) the Receiving Department, and (3) Accounts Payable. A final copy of the Purchase Order (along with the related Purchase Requisition) is filed by the Purchasing Department.

Approving purchases in the above manner accomplishes two major objectives of internal control. First, only making purchases from approved vendors increases the likelihood that the items will be delivered on a timely basis and will be of adequate quality. In addition, this control activity also ensures that all purchases processed by the organization are for legitimate business purposes. Finally, the process of soliciting bids for certain items will allow the organization to receive the best price for inventory. In these ways, the control activities in the Purchasing Function relate to the operating objective of internal control.

Second, from a recording perspective, using formal documents to authorize transactions reduces the likelihood that fictitious purchase transactions are recorded (EO and RO assertions). Also, by using prenumbered documents and accounting for the numerical sequence of these documents, the company can determine that all transactions have been recorded (CO assertion).

In many cases, purchases of inventories are made through established vendors on a fairly regular basis. For example, many companies order items on a weekly (or even daily) basis from the same vendors. Formalized authorization policies may not be necessary in these situations, since the organization has previously done business with these vendors. In addition, the logistics of obtaining approval for frequent, small dollar purchases may violate the reasonable assurance criterion of internal control; that is, the costs of the control activity may exceed the benefits. In these instances, organizations often permit the inventory warehouse to order goods directly from the supplier without intermediate approval by the Purchasing Department. In other cases, approval by the Purchasing Department may only by sought for purchases over some specified dollar amount.

WHO ENDORSED THE CHECK?[1]

An unnamed company did not have formal procedures for authorizing vendors. A review of Checks revealed three Checks written to what appeared to be the same vendor, but the vendor's name was spelled differently on each check. A closer examination of these checks indicated that the vendor's name on these three checks was slightly different from that of a vendor who actively did business with the company. Examining the reverse side of the checks indicated that they were endorsed by the same company employee.

In this instance, a company employee had set up a fictitious company and sent invoices to that company for payment. The name used by this employee was intentionally similar to that of an established vendor to attempt and conceal the defalcation scheme. A thorough investigation uncovered checks totalling over $60,000 mailed to the fictitious company.

TECHNOLOGY AND THE PURCHASING FUNCTION

DuPont Co. has discontinued the use of Purchase Orders with about five percent of its suppliers. These vendors are linked electronically with DuPont's inventory system; when inventory quantities are running low, an order is automatically triggered by the system. Director of materials and logistics Thomas F. Holmes notes that "when you do it electronically, you simplify the process."[2]

Strawbridge & Clothier, a Philadelphia retailer, has been discontinuing relationships with its vendors that are not part of their computerized point-of-sale system. As noted by Corporate Vice-President Thomas S. Rittenhouse "they couldn't compete."[3]

CHAPTER CHECKPOINTS

12-4. What document is normally prepared by the Requesting Department when it wishes to purchase item(s) from a vendor?

12-5. Briefly describe the process through which purchases are authorized in an effective internal control.

12-6. Must purchases be formally approved by companies in all circumstances? Why or why not?

Receiving Department. Once the purchase has been approved (as noted above), a copy of the Purchase Order is sent to the vendor. The vendor then processes this Purchase Order in much the

---

[1] "Who Endorsed the Check?," *Internal Auditor* (December 1993), 75.
[2] "The Technology Payoff," *Business Week* (June 14, 1993), 58-59.
[3] "The Technology Payoff," *Business Week* (June 14, 1993), 64.

same way as discussed in Chapter 10 (Credit Sales subcycle). The end result of this processing is the vendor's decision to make the sale to the organization and deliver the items. The receipt of these items by the organization is the next major step in the Purchases subcycle.

Upon receipt of the item(s) from the vendor, a **Receiving Report** is prepared (IP #2 in Figure 12-2). The Receiving Report lists the quantity, description, and item number (if known) of all items received from the vendor. A Receiving Report may take one of two forms. This document could be prepared from "scratch"; that is, as goods are delivered, a listing of the quantity, description, and item number can be manually recorded. Alternatively, the Receiving Report could be prepared from a copy of the Purchase Order with the quantities omitted (a "blind" copy of the Purchase Order). In any case, to ensure accuracy in its preparation, the Receiving Report should not be a "checked off" copy of the Purchase Order. Copies of the Receiving Report are forwarded to the Accounts Payable Department and the Requesting Department.

The preparation of Receiving Reports assists in achieving two important objectives of internal control. First, as noted later, quantities from the Receiving Report will be compared to those on the Purchase Order and Vendor's Invoice. This comparison allows the organization to determine that it is not being billed for items it did not order (Purchase Order) or receive (Receiving Report). Protecting the organization's assets in this manner relates to the operating objective of internal control.

Second, Receiving Reports are the initial evidence that a purchase on account has occurred. Therefore, requiring a Receiving Report to be prepared upon delivery of the goods relates to the EO and RO assertions. In addition, by using prenumbered Receiving Reports and accounting for the numerical sequence of Receiving Reports, the company can determine that all purchases have been recorded (CO assertion).

When items are delivered to a central delivery point (such as a general receiving platform or dock), they are sent to the inventory warehouse. Upon receipt of these goods, the warehouse personnel should inspect the goods to determine that they are of appropriate quality. The inspection of goods in this manner is associated with the operating objective of internal control.

TECHNOLOGY AND THE RECEIVING FUNCTION

Kroger Co. (a large chain of grocery retailers) has recently automated their Receiving Function. Prior to the automation, Kroger employees manually counted incoming items, verified that goods received were ordered, checked invoices, and forwarded these invoices to accounting. Now, goods are scanned with a handheld computer programmed with the agreed-upon quantities, prices, and amounts. These and other enhancements have reduced over Kroger's annual operating costs by over $142 million.[4]

Accounts Payable Department. In conjunction with the receipt of the items, an Invoice is sent from the vendor to Accounts Payable. Upon receipt of the Invoice, Accounts Payable should compare the information contained on the Purchase Requisition (received from the Requesting Department), Purchase Order (received from Purchasing), and Receiving Report (received from the Receiving

---

[4] "Cash Flow Joe," *Forbes* (June 6, 1994), 47.

Department) with that on the Invoice. Once it has been determined that the organization is only billed for the appropriate items, the arithmetic accuracy of the Invoice should be checked (IP #3 in Figure 12-2).

The above control activities serve two purposes. First, because comparisons of this nature would reduce the likelihood that the organization pays for items it did not request, order, and/or receive, these control activities relate to the operating objective of internal control. Second, as related to the financial objective, the above comparisons allow the organization to:

▶ Record the purchase at the correct dollar amount (VA assertion).

▶ Determine that purchased items were actually received (EO and RO assertions).

Once the organization has determined the accuracy of the invoice, payment is authorized through preparation of a **Voucher**. The Voucher designates payment of a certain amount to a certain vendor by a certain date. Through the approval process, the Voucher formally recognizes that the organization has a liability for a purchase that has occurred (IP #4 in Figure 12-2). As with other documents, the use of formal, prenumbered documents addresses the EO, RO, and CO assertions. In addition, Vouchers should indicate the manner in which the dollar amount of the Invoice is distributed over the various financial statement accounts (the PD assertion).

In preparing Vouchers, Accounts Payable personnel should also determine *when* a particular Invoice should be paid. In order to maximize the organization's return on its cash, early payment of invoices should be considered if doing so will allow the organization to receive a cash discount. This cash discount should be compared to the return that would be earned by the organization through the alternative use of its funds (for example, interest earned by having funds on deposit in a bank account). In this respect, the preparation of Vouchers also corresponds to the operating objective of internal control.

INEFFICIENT DISBURSEMENT CYCLE[5]

An internal auditor found that checks were being printed for Invoices that were received and entered into the computerized accounting system on the previous day. Almost none of these Invoices were due upon receipt. A more detailed analysis of the activity in the prior year revealed that Invoices were being paid over fifteen days early, resulting in lost interest income of over $212,000.

General Function. The general function consists of individuals who do not have other responsibilities within the Purchases subcycle. As shown in Figure 12-2, periodic physical inventory counts should be made by appropriate personnel and compared to the company's perpetual inventory records (PC #1 in Figure 12-2). This is a physical control that is discussed in a later subsection.

Purchase of Other Assets or Services. The depiction of the Purchases subcycle (in Figure 12-2) relates to purchases of inventory. If the purchase is for other types of assets (such as office equipment, supplies, or fixed assets), most of the same control activities would apply. If the purchase relates to

---

[5] "Inefficient Disbursement Cycle," *Internal Auditor* (February 1995), 57.

some form of service received by the organization, the primary difference is that a physical asset is not received. Upon receipt of an Invoice for services, Accounts Payable would verify that the invoiced services were approved and properly performed. This verification could be in the form of formal documentation received by Accounts Payable or through communication with the department or individual receiving the services. Once this verification has been received, the control process proceeds as in Figure 12-2.

Segregation of Duties Controls. Segregation of duties requires different individuals or departments to handle the various aspects of a transaction. For effective internal control, the following three aspects of a particular type of transaction are normally separated (or segregated).

- Authorization: Purchasing
- Custody: Receiving and the Requesting Department
- Recording: Accounts Payable (subsidiary) and General Accounting (control)

As with the Revenue cycle, establishing segregation of duties reduces the likelihood that individuals can engage in a theft or defalcation scheme and conceal their actions by preparing fictitious journal entries or intentionally not recording actual transactions. Therefore, segregation of duties affects the EO, RO, and CO assertions. In addition, since an appropriate segregation of duties reduces the likelihood that theft or defalcation can occur, this control activity also relates to the operating objective of internal control.

Physical Controls. The primary asset in the Purchases subcycle over which physical controls must be established is inventory. As shown in Figure 12-2, the General Function should periodically compare physical quantities of inventory to perpetual inventory records (PC #1 in Figure 12-2). In addition to these comparisons, other elements of internal control related to physical controls over inventory include:

- Preparing a Receiving Report upon the initial receipt of inventory (IP #2 in Figure 12-2)
- Counting inventory and verifying these counts upon the delivery of inventory to the Inventory Department/Warehouse
- Restricting access to inventories by keeping them in a secured, locked location

Since physical controls reduce the opportunity for theft and defalcation, they are similar in nature to segregation of duties controls. Thus, they relate to both the operating and financial (EO, RO, and CO assertions) objectives of internal control.

Performance Review Controls. Performance reviews involve management review and analysis of actual data for the current period and comparison of these data to forecasted or budgeted information. Large variations between actual purchases and forecasted or budgeted purchases may result from: (1) decisions to increase the inventories held by the company, or (2) purchases made in larger quantities to receive bulk (or quantity) discounts. To the extent that investigating these variations allow the company to minimize the costs associated with maintaining their inventories or reduce the prices paid for their inventories, performance reviews of this nature correspond to the operating objective of internal control. In addition, if large variations result from financial statement misstatements, performance review controls also relate to the financial objective of internal control (EO, RO, CO, and VA assertions).

Summary of Control Activities: The Purchases Subcycle. Figure 12-3 summarizes the major control activities in the Purchases subcycle. Included in this description are the relevant objectives of these control activities, methods that can be used by the auditor to test the effectiveness of these control activities, as well as any financial statement assertions addressed by these control activities.

CHAPTER CHECKPOINTS

12-7. In what two basic formats could a Receiving Report be prepared? What information should ordinarily be included in a Receiving Report?

12-8. Prior to authorizing payment of an invoice, what basic control activities should be performed by the Accounts Payable Department?

12-9. How does the preparation of a Voucher address the objectives of internal control?

12-10. What reconciliation is performed regarding the Purchases subcycle?

12-11. Briefly indicate how the appropriate functional duties are segregated in the Purchases subcycle.

◻ Risk Assessment and Control Activities: The Cash Disbursements Subcycle

The Purchases subcycle discussed in the preceding section concludes with the preparation of a Voucher, which authorizes payment of a Vendor's Invoice by a certain date. On the designated date, all documentation related to a given purchase (Purchase Requisition, Purchase Order, Receiving Report, Vendor's Invoice, and Voucher) is forwarded to the Cash Disbursements Department for processing and preparation of the check. This information is often referred to as a "Voucher Package" and signifies the need for a cash disbursement. Figure 12-4 summarizes the important steps in the Cash Disbursements subcycle.

The Cash Disbursements subcycle involves the following major functions:

- ▶ Cash Disbursements Department/Treasurer
- ▶ Accounts Payable Department
- ▶ General Function

Ref.	Control Activity	Objective(s) of Control Activity	Auditor Test(s) of Control Activity	Assertions				
				EO	RO	CO	VA	PD
IP 1	Purchases should be authorized through the preparation of a prenumbered Purchase Order	O: Reduces the likelihood that goods are of substandard quality and are not delivered on a timely basis O: Reduces the likelihood that purchases will be made from unauthorized vendors or for unauthorized purposes F: Reduces the likelihood that: (1) fictitious purchase transactions will be recorded, and (2) actual purchase transactions will not be recorded	Inspect the use of prenumbered Purchase Orders	x	x	x		
IP 2	Upon receipt of goods ordered from vendors, a prenumbered Receiving Report should be prepared	O: Reduces the likelihood of losses from being billed (and paying) for items not delivered by vendors F: Reduces the likelihood that: (1) fictitious purchase transactions will be recorded, and (2) actual purchase transactions will not be recorded	Inspect the use of prenumbered Receiving Reports	x	x	x		
IP 3	Prices, quantities, and extensions and footings on Vendors' Invoices should be verified	O: Reduces losses from payments of inaccurate invoices F: Reduces the likelihood that: (1) fictitious purchase transactions will be recorded, and (2) purchase transactions will be recorded at the incorrect dollar amount	Inspect documentary evidence of verification For a sample of Vendors' Invoices, reperform verification	x	x		x	
IP 4	Prenumbered Vouchers should be prepared to authorize payment for purchases made on account	O: The use of Vouchers ensures that payment will be made on a timely basis F: Reduces the likelihood that: (1) fictitious purchase transactions will be recorded, (2) actual purchase transactions will not be recorded, and (3) purchase transactions will be distributed incorrectly across the accounts	Inspect the use of prenumbered Vouchers	x	x	x		x

Figure 12-3: *Major Control Activities: Purchases Subcycle*

Reference	Control Activity	Objective		EO	RO	CO	VA	PD
SD	Appropriate segregation of duties should be established and maintained in the Purchases sub-cycle	O:	Reduces losses from defalcation schemes resulting from the ability of employees to participate in incompatible functions					
		F:	Reduces the likelihood that (1) fictitious purchase transactions will be recorded and (2) actual purchase transactions will not be recorded	Observe segregation of duties Inquire about segregation of duties	x	x	x		
PC 1	Physical inventories should be periodically compared to perpetual inventory records, with any differences investigated by management	O:	Reduces losses from theft or misappropriation of inventories					
		F:	Reduces the likelihood that (1) fictitious purchase transactions will be recorded and (2) actual purchase transactions will not be recorded	Inspect evidence of comparison of physical inventories to perpetual inventory records	x	x	x		
PC	Physical controls should be established over inventories	O:	Reduces losses from the theft or misappropriation of inventories					
		F:	Reduces the likelihood that (1) fictitious purchase transactions will be recorded and (2) actual purchase transactions will not be recorded	Observe/inspect physical controls over inventories Inquire of management about physical controls over inventories	x	x	x		
PR	Performance reviews should compare actual purchases data to forecasted or budgeted data	O:	Allows opportunities for improving inventory management and/or purchasing practices					
		F:	Large variations in performance reviews may result from (1) fictitious purchase transactions, (2) actual purchase transactions not recorded, or (3) purchase transactions recorded at the incorrect dollar amount	Inquire of management about performance reviews	x	x	x		x

Note:

Reference
IP = Information Processing Control
SD = Segregation of Duties Control
PC = Physical Control
PR = Performance Review Control

Objectives of Control Activity
O = Operating Objective
F = Financial Objective

Assertions
EO = Existence or occurrence
RO = Rights and obligations
CO = Completeness
VA = Valuation or allocation
PD = Presentation and disclosure

Figure 12-3: *continued*

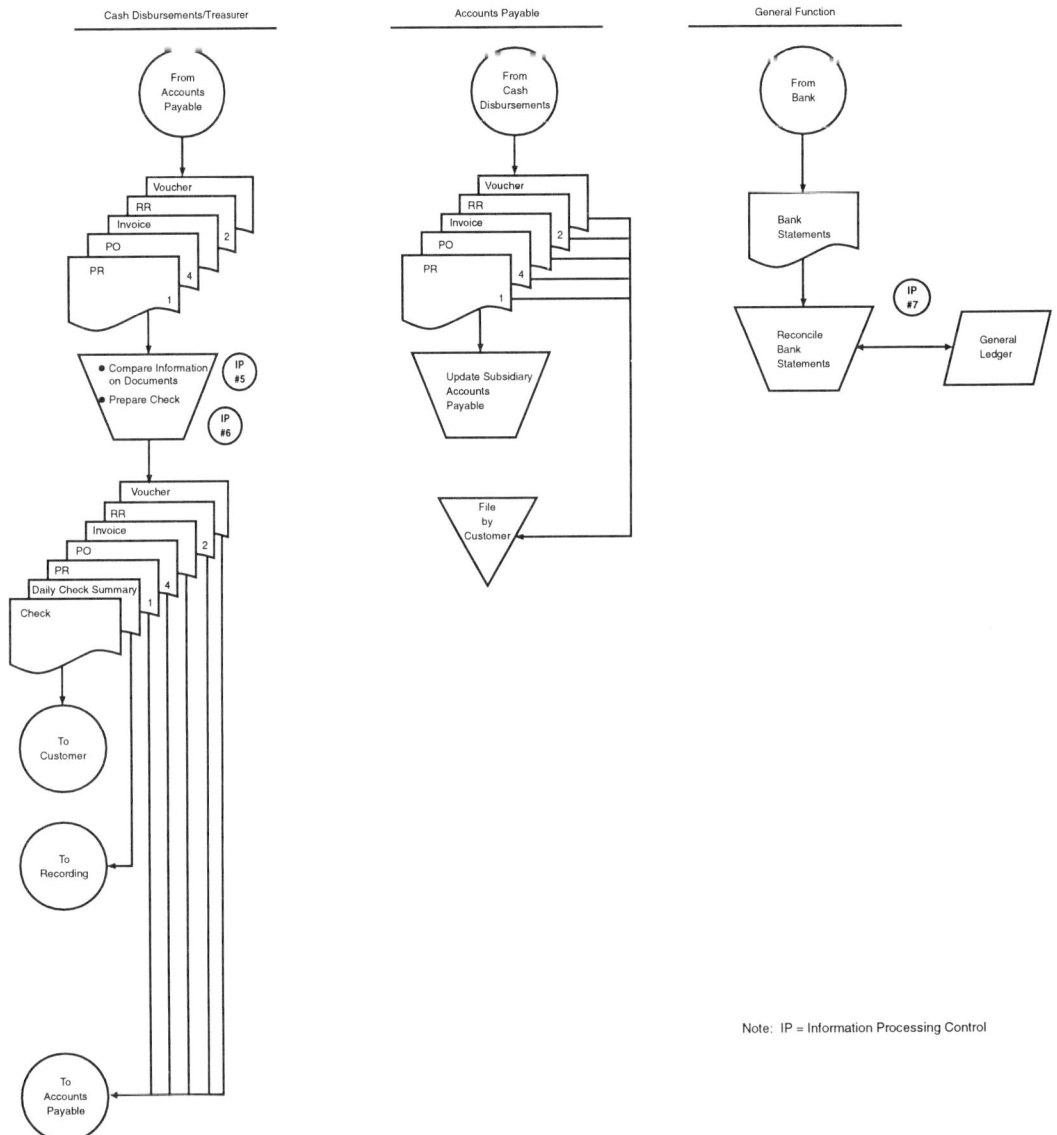

Figure 12-4: *Overview of the Cash Disbursements Subcycle*

Information Processing Controls. *Cash Disbursements Department/Treasurer.* Upon receipt of the Voucher Package, Cash Disbursements performs a final review of the Voucher and the supporting documents (IP #5 in Figure 12-4). This review will take the same form as that performed in Accounts Payable and consists of the following steps:

- ▶ Quantities on the Vendor's Invoice will be compared against quantities from the Receiving Report and Purchase Order

- ▶ The mathematical accuracy of the Vendor's Invoice will be verified

- ▶ Relevant information (vendor's name, payment due date, amount) will be compared from the Vendor's Invoice to the Voucher

The above comparisons serve much the same purpose as those made by Accounts Payable. These comparisons relate to the operating objective of internal control, since they reduce the likelihood that payment will be made for goods or services not received by the company. They also relate to the financial objective of internal control, since checks will be prepared (and recorded) at the proper dollar amount (VA assertion).

INVOICE COMPARISONS CAN SAVE MONEY!

In paying Vendor Invoices, companies should be aware of certain freight billing practices that may result in duplicate payment for freight charges. Under these practices, freight is billed as a line item on a Vendor's Invoice which also includes the items ordered by the company. Then, a subsequent Invoice is received for the freight charges. Since the Invoice numbers and amounts are different, a duplicate payment can result. Periodic review of freight payments sorted by Purchase Order number can detect these duplicate payments.[6]

Internal auditors noted office personnel approving Invoices for payments for printing services received from a number of vendors. These Invoices were approved with a signature stamp without comparing the amounts on the Invoices to the terms of the contract. Based on a sample of comparisons of these Invoices to contract terms, a total of $150,000 of overcharges were revealed. The internal auditors recommended comparing Invoice charges to contract terms prior to approving Invoices for payment.[7]

Once the above comparisons are made, a Check will be prepared by Cash Disbursements (IP #6 in Figure 12-4). These Checks should be prenumbered, with the numerical sequence of Checks periodically accounted for by company employees. As with other subcycles, the use of formal, prenumbered documents addresses the EO, RO, and CO assertions. In addition, the use of Checks provides the company with a record of payments made to vendors in the event that a dispute arises; this corresponds to the operating objective of internal control.

---

[6] "Duplicate Payments," *Internal Auditor* (December 1995), 35.

[7] "Comparison Pays Off," *Internal Auditor* (August 1994), 72.

Once Checks are prepared, they are signed by designated officers or employees of the organization in Cash Disbursements (normally, the Treasurer). Checks can be signed manually or through the use of stamped signatures (known as signature plates). If signature plates are used, care must be taken to restrict employee access to the signature plates. Many companies follow the practice of requiring Checks for dollar amounts greater than some specified level to be signed by: (1) a high-ranking official of the company, or (2) more than one individual. In cases such as these, Cash Disbursements would deliver the Check to the appropriate individual(s) for their signature(s). After signing, the Check should be mailed or given directly to the payee by the signer or an employee operating under the direct control of the signer. This is a physical control that is discussed in a subsequent subsection.

Accounts Payable Department. After the Check has been signed and mailed, the Voucher Package is returned to the Accounts Payable Department. Accounts Payable will use the Voucher Package (marked "paid") to update the subsidiary accounts payable to reflect payment.

General Function. Like cash receipts (see Chapter 10), the final information processing control over cash disbursements involves reconciling the bank statements to the cash records maintained by the company (IP #7 in Figure 12-4). By reconciling bank statements, the company determines that: (1) all cash disbursements transactions have been recorded (CO assertion), (2) recorded cash disbursements actually occurred and are made for obligations of the company (EO and RO assertions), and (3) cash disbursements transactions have been recorded at the proper dollar amount (VA assertion). This activity should be performed by an individual or Department who has no other recordkeeping responsibilities with respect to cash.

Segregation of Duties. As with all operating cycles, an important control activity in the Cash Disbursements subcycle is segregation of various duties within the subcycle. The segregation of duties is accomplished in the Cash Disbursements subcycle as follows (see Figure 12-4).

- ▶ Authorization: Accounts Payable
- ▶ Custody: Cash Disbursements
- ▶ Recording: Accounts Payable (subsidiary) and General Accounting (control)

Similar to the Purchases subcycle, segregation of duties relates to both the operating and financial (EO, RO, and CO assertions) objectives of internal control.

Physical Controls. As with cash receipts (see the Cash Receipts subcycle in Chapter 10), it is critical that companies establish effective physical controls over cash and documents that control access to cash (such as Checks). Several important physical controls over cash include:

- ▶ Making Checks payable to the vendor, not to "cash" or "bearer."
- ▶ Using mechanical check protectors or some other means to imprint the amount of the Check and prevent subsequent alteration.
- ▶ Canceling the Voucher Package (or marking it as "paid") to prevent duplicate repayment.

- ▶ Mailing Checks to the payee immediately after signing.
- ▶ Restricting access to Checks by keeping them in a secured, locked location.

While most of the above controls are fairly self-explanatory, one control activity deserves some additional elaboration. Checks should never be returned to any employee who has participated in the check-processing routine. This prevents an individual from retrieving a Check representing a fictitious payment as part of a defalcation scheme.

GOOD PUBLIC RELATIONS[8]

An unnamed company returned Checks to its salespersons for personal delivery to vendors. The rationale for this practice was that hand-delivery of checks was viewed as good "public relations" for the company. Later, the internal auditors uncovered theft of over $430,000 through Checks written to nonexistent vendors and diverted to the salepersons' bank accounts. As a result of this discovery, the company immediately discontinued the practice of hand-delivering Checks.

As with other physical controls, the above controls relate to both the operating and financial (EO, RO, and CO assertions) objectives of internal control.

Performance Reviews. Because cash disbursement transactions are dependent upon purchases, performance reviews are relatively limited in nature. Thus, these reviews do not have a significant influence on the internal control over cash disbursements transactions.

Summary of Control Activities: The Cash Disbursements Subcycle. Figure 12-5 summarizes the important control activities in the Cash Disbursements subcycle. As with the Purchases subcycle, the objectives, tests of controls, and financial statement assertions affected by these control activities are also included in Figure 12-5.

CHAPTER CHECKPOINTS

12-12. What are the primary control activities performed in the review of the Voucher Package by Cash Disbursements?

12-13. Why should checks be mailed to the payee immediately after being signed?

12-14. List some important physical controls over cash disbursement transactions.

---

[8] "Good Public Relations," *Internal Auditor* (October 1993), 76.

Ref.	Control Activity	Objective(s) of Control Activity		Auditor Test(s) of Control Activity	Assertions					
					EO	RO	CO	VA	PD
IP 5	Cash Disbursements should compare information on documents in the Voucher Package prior to preparing the Check	O:	Reduces losses from payments made for goods or services not received or ordered	Inspect documentary evidence of comparison of documents in Voucher Package				x	
		F:	Reduces the likelihood that payments will be recorded at the incorrect dollar amount						
IP 6	Payments should be made using prenumbered Checks	O:	Provides company with a record of amount paid for purchase of goods or services	Inspect the use of prenumbered Checks	x	x	x		
		F:	Reduces the likelihood that: (1) fictitious payments will be recorded, and (2) actual payments will not be recorded						
IP 7	Personnel independent of Cash Disbursements should prepare monthly Bank Reconciliations	F:	Reduces the likelihood that: (1) fictitious cash disbursements transactions will be recorded, (2) actual cash disbursements transactions will not be recorded, and (3) cash disbursements transactions will be recorded at the incorrect dollar amount	Inspect Bank Reconciliations prepared by client personnel Reperform Bank Reconciliations	x	x	x	x	
SD	Appropriate segregation of duties should be established and maintained in the Cash Disbursements cycle	O:	Reduces losses from defalcation schemes resulting from the ability of employees to participate in incompatible functions	Observe segregation of duties Inquire about segregation of duties	x	x	x		
		F:	Reduces the likelihood that: (1) fictitious cash disbursements transactions will be recorded, and (2) actual cash disbursement transactions will not be recorded						
PC	Physical controls should be established over cash	O:	Reduces losses from theft or defalcation of cash	Observe/inspect physical controls over cash Inquire of management about physical controls over cash	x	x	x		
		F:	Reduces the likelihood that: (1) fictitious cash disbursements transactions will be recorded, and (2) actual cash disbursement transactions will not be recorded						

Note:

Reference

IP = Information Processing Control
SD = Segregation of Duties Control
PC = Physical Control

Objectives of Control Activity

O = Operating Objective
F = Financial Objective

Assertions

EO = Existence or occurrence
RO = Rights and obligations
CO = Completeness
A = Valuation or allocation
PD = Presentation and disclosure

Figure 12-5: *Major Control Activities: Cash Disbursements Subcycle*

◻ Information and Communication

As noted in Chapter 5, the accounting system is the primary element of the information and communication component of internal control. The accounting system represents the series of documents, journals, and ledgers used by the organization to record its transactions. Based on the preceding discussion, Figure 12-6 provides an overview of the accounting systems used to record transactions in the Purchases and Cash Disbursements subcycles. Notice that accounting systems form a four-level basis for recording transactions, as shown below:

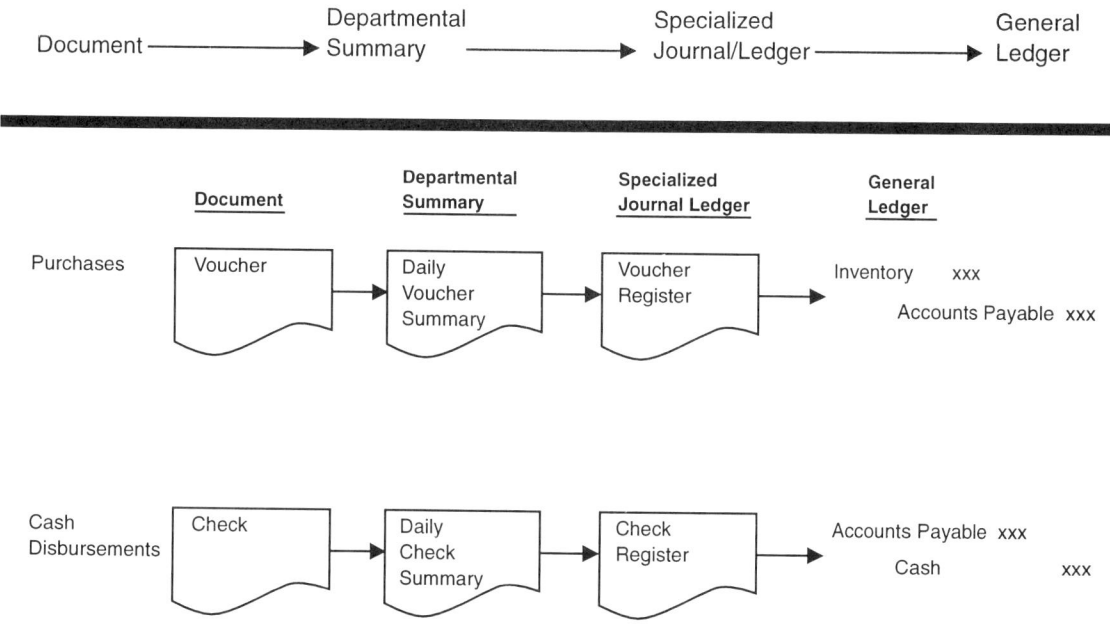

Figure 12-6: *Accounting System for Recording Purchases/Cash Disbursements Transactions*

The above recording process involves four basic control activities shown below. It is important to note that these control activities relate to both subcycles in the Purchases and Disbursements cycle and address the following assertions:

▶ Using formal documentation in the recording process (EO and RO assertions)

▶ Using prenumbered documents in the recording process, with periodic accounting for the numerical sequence of these documents (CO assertion)

▶ Agreeing control totals from basic documents to the departmental summaries and totals posted to the subsidiary accounts (VA assertion)

▶ Agreeing totals from the departmental summaries to the appropriate journal or ledger (VA assertion)

Purchases Subcycle

1. As shown in Figure 12-2, in the process of preparing Vouchers, the Accounts Payable Department updates subsidiary accounts payable based on the Vendor's Invoice.

2. Invoices are summarized in a Daily Voucher Summary. This Daily Voucher Summary is forwarded to General Accounting to update the Voucher Register (or Purchases Journal) and record the general ledger journal entry, as follows:

Inventory/Purchases/		
Sundry Asset or Expense	XXX	
Accounts Payable		XXX

Cash Disbursements Subcycle

1. As shown in Figure 12-4, the Cash Disbursements function summarizes its checks in the form of a Daily Check Summary. The Daily Check Summary is then forwarded to General Accounting to update the Check Register (or Cash Disbursements Journal) and make a general ledger journal entry as follows:

Accounts Payable	XXX	
Cash		XXX

2. The canceled Voucher Package is returned to the Accounts Payable Department. This function updates the subsidiary Accounts Payable to reflect payment made on those accounts.

◘ Monitoring

The final component of internal control is monitoring. **Monitoring** is the process of evaluating whether the organization's internal control is operating effectively. Like the control environment, monitoring is normally assessed on a company-wide basis throughout the organization. For example, the existence of a competent internal audit function that periodically evaluates the effectiveness of the organization's internal control would be viewed positively by the external auditor during his or her study and evaluation of internal control.

Monitoring can occur on an on-going basis or as a separate evaluation of internal control. Examining Invoices or Statements received from vendors and following up on any discrepancies between those Invoices or Statements and recorded accounts payable is an example of an on-going monitoring activity. Separate evaluations of internal control over Purchases and Disbursements cycle transactions may be conducted by: (1) internal auditors, (2) other external auditors, or (3) the same external auditor in a prior year. The auditor should evaluate any deficiencies identified during these separate evaluations of internal control as well as management's corrective action taken in response to these deficiencies.

> **CHAPTER CHECKPOINTS**
>
> **12-15.** What are the major elements used in the recording process for purchase transactions? Cash disbursements transactions?
>
> **12-16.** Provide some examples of how monitoring is accomplished in the Purchases and Disbursements cycle.

Appendix

Computerized Processing in the Purchases and Disbursements Cycle[9]

In the text of the chapter, our discussion assumed that companies processed purchases and cash disbursements transactions manually. In practice, most companies extensively utilize computerized processing. In Chapter 9, we provide a general discussion of the effect of computer/electronic data processing (or EDP processing) on the auditor's examination. This appendix applies some of the general concepts discussed in Chapter 9 on computerized processing to the Purchases and Disbursements cycle introduced in this chapter.

◘ Purchases Subcycle

Figure 12-7 provides an overview of computerized processing of transactions in the Purchases subcycle. In order to focus on differences between the manual processing discussed in the text of this chapter and computerized processing, many of the detailed control activities and the ultimate disposition of the documents are not shown in Figure 12-7. In reviewing this information, two important points should be kept in mind:

1. Computerized processing environments utilize the same documents, journals, and ledgers as manual processing environments.
2. Many of the control activities associated with manual processing environments also exist in computerized processing environments.

Purchasing Department. Once the Requesting Department has identified a need for a purchase and prepares a Purchase Requisition, the Purchasing Department identifies the appropriate vendor, as in the manual processing system. Alternatively, for some purchases, the vendor may have been identified by the Requesting Department. The vendor number, along with important information from the Purchase Requisition (the identity and quantities of items requested) are then entered into a **Daily**

---

[9] All Chapter Checkpoints and End of Chapter Items related to the Appendix are marked with an asterisk (*).

Order Transaction File (Step 1 in Figure 12-7). Prior to entering this information into the transaction file, control totals such as the following are determined:

- ▶ Total number of purchase transactions (record counts)
- ▶ Total sum of vendor numbers and item numbers (hash totals)
- ▶ Total quantities of items ordered (batch totals)

Once Purchasing has determined that the above data have been accurately and completely input, they are run against the **Purchase Order Program** (Step 2 in Figure 12-7). The Purchase Order Program accesses the Vendor Master File and determines that the purchase is being made from an authorized vendor. This comparison replaces the manual authorization procedures illustrated in Figure 12-2.

In cases where a purchase is requested from an unauthorized vendor, that transaction is included in a **Purchasing Exception Report**. The Purchasing Exception Report represents purchases that have been requested from vendors not currently authorized by the company. Items appearing on the Purchasing Exception Report may represent legitimate purchases from vendors that need to be added to the Vendor Master File. Alternatively, these items may represent unauthorized purchases occurring as part of some defalcation scheme.

As shown in Figure 12-7, the outputs of the Purchase Order Program are copies of the copies of the Purchase Order, the Purchasing Exception Report, and an updated version of the **Open Purchase Order File**. The Open Purchase Order File represents all purchases made from authorized vendors that have not been received.

Receiving Department. Upon receipt of the goods from the vendor, the Receiving Department identifies the relevant Purchase Order number (usually provided by the vendor on the Shipping Document), counts the items, and enters these counts into a **Daily Receiving Transaction File** (Step 3 in Figure 12-7). As with purchases on account, control totals such as the following are determined:

- ▶ Total number of receiving transactions (record counts)
- ▶ Total sum of Purchase Order numbers and inventory item numbers (hash totals)
- ▶ Total quantities of items received (batch totals)

Once the accuracy of the transaction file has been verified, this information is run against the **Receiving Program** (Step 4 in Figure 12-7). Using the Purchase Order number, the Receiving Program matches the quantity of items received (by item number) against the quantities ordered from the Open Order File. Any discrepancies between quantities received and quantities ordered (both overages and shortages) are included in a **Receiving Exception Report**. Management should periodically review the Receiving Exception Report to determine whether these items represent: (1) backordered items that will be delivered in the future, or (2) overages or shortages of items representing erroneous deliveries.

The two-directional arrow from the Open Order File to the Receiving Program illustrates the updating process that occurs in a computerized processing environment. The arrow leading from the Open Order File to the Receiving Program indicates that information regarding quantities of items

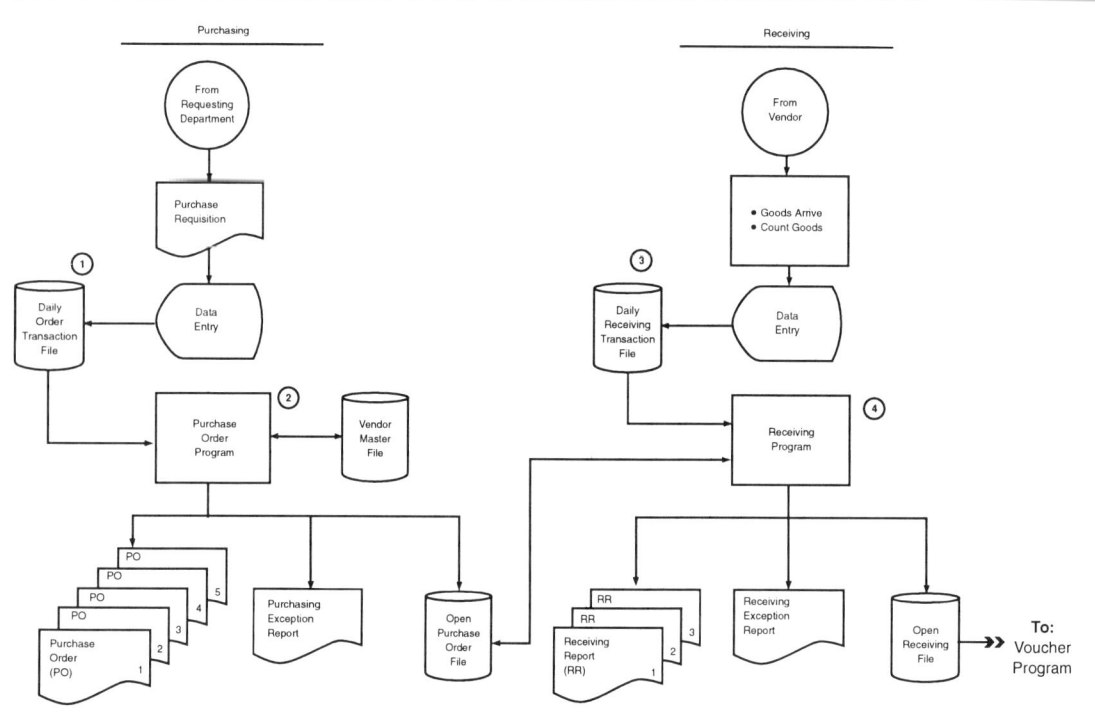

Figure 12-7: *Computerized Processing: The Purchases Subcycle*

ordered is accessed by the Receiving Program to ensure that all items received were actually ordered (and *vice versa*). The arrow leading back from the Receiving Program to the Open Order File reflects the deletion of a purchase transaction from this file once the goods have been received from the vendor. Thus, at any given moment, the transactions in the Open Order File represent all purchases that have not been received by the company.

As shown in Figure 12-7, the outputs of the Receiving Program are copies of the Receiving Report, the Receiving Exception Report, and the **Open Receiving File**. As in the manual processing system depicted in Figure 12-2, a copy of the Receiving Report is compared to the Purchase Order (not shown in Figure 12-7) and filed in the Receiving Department. The Open Receiving File represents all receipts of goods that have yet to be approved for payment. As discussed in the following subsection, the Open Receiving File will be used to verify that the company is only billed for items actually received from vendors.

Accounts Payable Department. Upon receipt of the Invoice from the vendor, two important control activities are performed, as in the manual processing system discussed in the text of the chapter. First, quantities from the Purchase Requisition, Purchase Order, Receiving Report, and Vendor's Invoice are compared to ensure that the company is only being billed for items requested (Purchase Requisition), ordered (Purchase Order), and received (Receiving Report). Second, the arithmetical accuracy of the Vendor's Invoice is examined. Once these control activities have been performed, relevant data from the Vendor's Invoice is entered into a **Daily Invoice Transaction File**

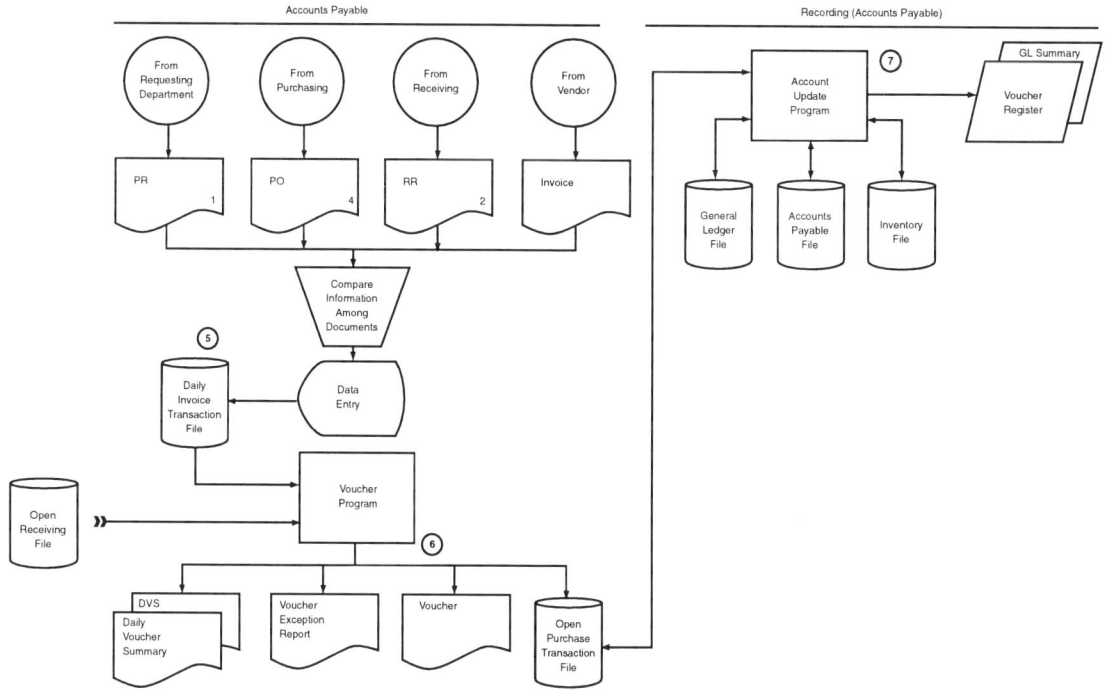

Figure 12-7: *Continued*

(Step 5 in Figure 12-7). Important control totals used to ensure accurate input of transactions include the following:

- ▶ Total number of invoice transactions (record counts)
- ▶ Total sum of Receiving Report numbers (hash totals)
- ▶ Total dollar amount of purchases (batch totals)

Once the accuracy of the transaction file has been verified, this information is run against the **Voucher Program** (Step 6 in Figure 12-7). Using the Receiving Report number, the voucher program accesses the Open Receiving File and matches the quantity of items from the Vendor's Invoice to those from the Receiving Report. Any discrepancies in quantities received from quantities invoiced (both overages and shortages) are included in a **Voucher Exception Report**. As with the Receiving Exception Report, management should periodically review the Voucher Exception Report to determine whether these differences represent: (1) backordered items that will be delivered in the future, or (2) overages or shortages of items representing erroneous invoicing. The outputs of the Voucher Program are copies of the Daily Voucher Summary, Voucher Exception Report, Voucher, and the **Open Purchase Transaction File**.

The Open Purchase Transaction File is then used to update the accounting records (Step 7 in Figure 12-7). This updating occurs through an **Account Update Program** that accesses the General Ledger File, Accounts Payable File, and Inventory File. The two-way arrows in Figure 12-7 indicate that the beginning balances in the ledger accounts (General Ledger File), subsidiary accounts payable accounts (Accounts Payable File), and inventory item accounts (Inventory File) are accessed for use by the Account Update Program (arrow leading from files to the program). After running the program against the Open Purchase Transaction File, the balances are updated and overwritten into the appropriate files (arrows leading from the program to the files). The Account Update Program then prepares a copy of the Voucher Register, which represents all of the transactions from the Open Purchase Transaction File, and General Ledger Summary.

Summary. Figure 12-8 summarizes the primary elements of computerized processing in the Purchases subcycle. As shown therein, the inputs represent items from two types of files: a daily transaction file and a file from a previous application. After the program is run, the input file from the previous application is updated to reflect any transactions involving items in that file. For example, the Open Order File is used as an input in the Receiving Program to process receiving transactions. Once items from a particular Purchase Order have been received, the related transactions are deleted from the Open Order File. These transactions are deleted, since the purchase is no longer "open" (*i.e.*, the goods have been received from the vendor).

Referring to Figure 12-8, computerized processing provides three primary types of outputs: documents, exception or other summary reports, and updated computer files. For example, referring to the Purchase Order Program, the outputs of this program are Purchase Orders, a Purchasing Exception Report, an Open Order File, and an Updated Vendor Master File.

◻ Cash Disbursements Subcycle

Figure 12-9 provides an overview of computerized processing in the Cash Disbursements subcycle. Cash disbursements transactions are initiated when a voucher is due for payment. On a given day, the Accounts Payable Department collects all Vouchers that are to be paid and inputs the related data into a **Daily Cash Disbursements Transaction File** (Step 1 in Figure 12-9). Using the Voucher number, the Cash Disbursements Program accesses the Open Purchase Transaction File (Step 2 in Figure 12-9) and prepares a copy of a Check as well as the Daily Check Summary. The Check is forwarded to the Cash Disbursements/Treasurer function, who reviews the supporting documentation in the Voucher Package and signs the check. As in a manual processing environment, the Voucher Package should be canceled (or marked as "paid") and the Check should be immediately mailed to the payee upon signing. Any unmatched transactions are written to a **Cash Disbursements Exception Report**. These transactions may represent fictitious requests for payment or vouchers that have been paid and are re-submitted for payment (either intentionally or unintentionally).

All cash disbursements transactions that are matched to the Open Purchase Transaction File are written to an **Open Cash Disbursements Transaction File**. At this point, the Open Cash Disbursements Transaction File is run against the **Account Update Program** to update both the general ledger accounts and subsidiary accounts payable to reflect the cash disbursement (Step 3 in Figure 12-9). After updating, the Check Register and General Ledger Summary are prepared. As in a manual system, the Check Register reflects all cash disbursements made by the company for a specified period of time.

Function	Inputs	Processing	Outputs
Purchasing	Daily Order Transaction File Vendor Master File	Purchase Order Program (Access Vendor Master File by Vendor Number)	Purchase Orders Purchasing Exception Report Open Purchase Order File Updated Vendor Master File
Receiving	Open Purchase Order File Daily Receiving Transaction File	Receiving Program (Access Open Order File by Purchase Order Number)	Receiving Reports Receiving Exception Report Open Receiving File Updated Open Purchase Order File
Accounts Payable	Open Receiving File Daily Invoice Transaction File	Voucher Program (Access Open Receiving File by Receiving Report Number)	Daily Voucher Summary Voucher Exception Report Voucher Open Purchase Transaction File Updated Open Receiving File
Recording/Accounts Payable (Purchases Subcycle)	Open Purchase Transaction File General Ledger File Accounts Payable File Inventory File	Account Update Program (Access Open Purchase Transaction File on Periodic Basis)	Voucher Register Updated General Ledger File Updated Accounts Payable File Updated Inventory File

Figure 12-8: *Elements of Computerized Processing: Purchases Subcycle*

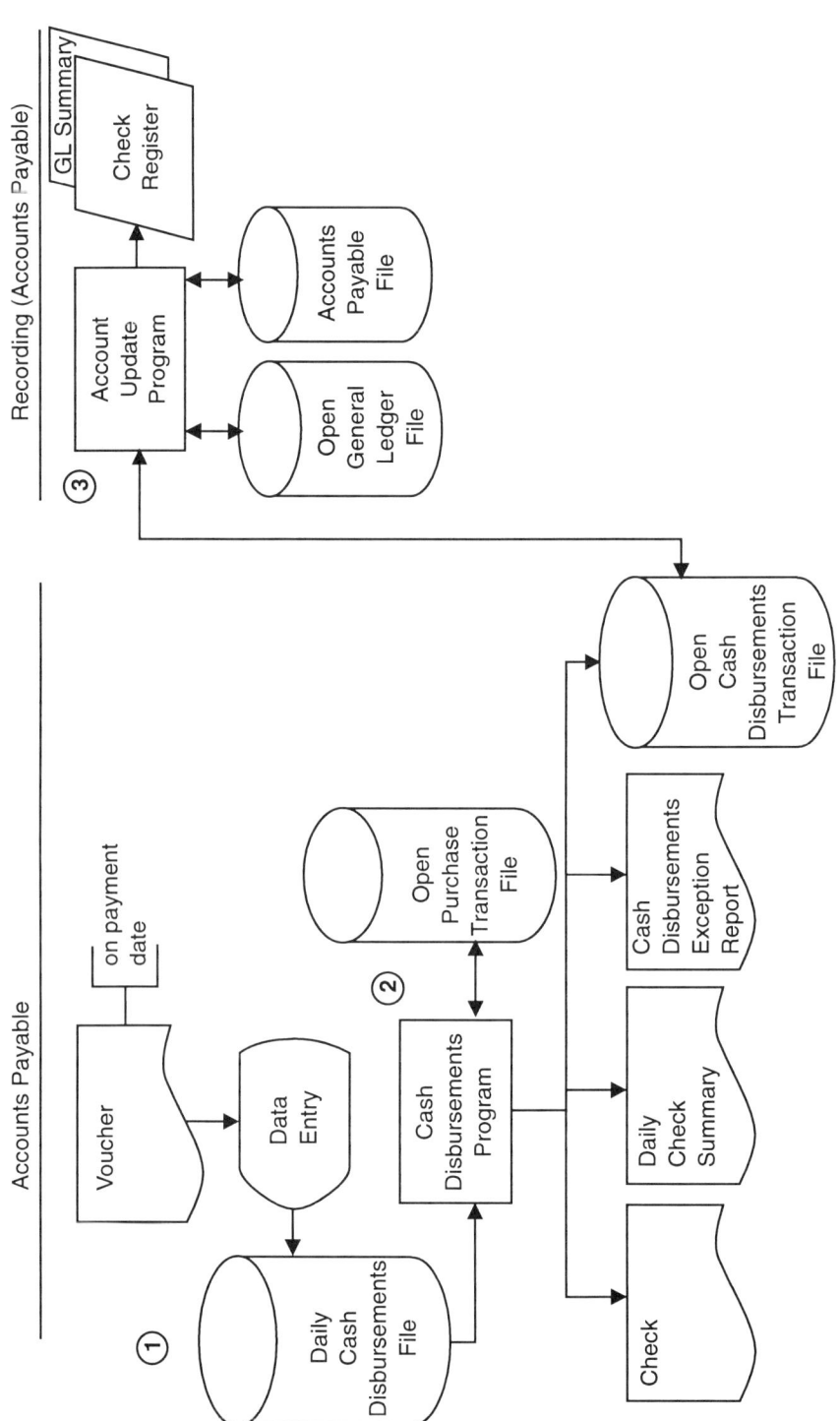

Figure 12-9 *Computerized Processing: The Cash Disbursements Subcycle*

The major elements in computerized processing over cash disbursements transactions are summarized in Figure 12-10.

Function	Inputs	Processing	Outputs
Cash Disbursements	Open Purchase Transaction File Daily Cash Disbursements Transaction File	Cash Disbursements Program (Access Open Purchase Transaction File by Voucher Number)	Checks Cash Disbursements Exception Report Daily Check Summary Open Cash Disbursements Transaction File
Recording/ Accounts Payable (Cash Disbursements Subcycle)	Open Cash Disbursements Transaction File General Ledger File Accounts Payable File	Account Update Program (Access Open Cash Disbursements Transaction File on a Periodic Basis)	Check Register General Ledger Summary Updated General Ledger File Updated Accounts Payable File

Figure 12-10: *Elements of Computerized Processing: Cash Disbursements Subcycle*

CHAPTER CHECKPOINTS

*12-17. What are the outputs of the Purchase Order Program?

*12-18. How is the Open Purchase Order File updated through the Receiving Program?

*12-19. Describe the process used by the Voucher Program to verify that all items invoiced were actually received by the company.

*12-20. What types of transactions may appear on a Cash Disbursements Exception Report?

◉ SUMMARY OF KEY POINTS

1. The Purchases and Disbursements cycle consists of two major types of transactions: (1) purchases made on account, and (2) cash disbursements for purchases made on account and other expenses.

2. The Purchases subcycle begins with the preparation of a Purchase Requisition by the department requesting the purchase of goods or services (the Requesting Department). This Purchase Requisition is forwarded to the Purchasing Department for approval. After approval,

the Purchasing Department prepares a Purchase Order. The use of formal Purchase Orders reduces the likelihood that fictitious purchase transactions are processed by the organization (the EO assertion).

3. Upon delivery of the goods by the vendor, the company prepares a Receiving Report. The Receiving Report includes the quantity, description, and item number of the goods received. Like the Purchase Order, preparing formal Receiving Reports reduces the likelihood that fictitious purchase transactions are recorded (the EO assertion).

4. When the Vendor Invoice is received, personnel in Accounts Payable agree the information among the Purchase Requisition, Purchase Order, Receiving Report, and Vendor Invoice. In addition, the mathematical accuracy of the Vendor Invoice is verified. Once these comparisons have been made, a Voucher is prepared. The Voucher is a document that formally authorizes payment for a purchase made on account as of a particular date.

5. The Cash Disbursements subcycle begins with the receipt of the Voucher Package from Accounts Payable. After reviewing the documents included in the Voucher Package, Cash Disbursements prepares a Check. Effective internal control dictates that Checks should be prenumbered, with the numerical sequence periodically accounted for by company employees.

6. Other important controls in the Cash Disbursements subcycle include: (1) canceling the Voucher Package after payment, (2) mailing Checks to payees immediately after payment, and (3) using authorized signatures on Checks.

7. The recording process for transactions in the Purchases subcycle utilizes Vouchers, the Daily Voucher Summary, and the Voucher Register. Cash Disbursements transactions are recorded through the use of Checks, a Daily Check Summary, and the Check Register.

*8. In a computerized accounting environment, transactions in the Purchases subcycle are processed using four major types of computerized programs: (1) the Purchase Order Program, (2) the Receiving Program, (3) the Voucher Program, and (4) the Account Update Program. Transactions in the Cash Disbursements subcycle are processed using the Cash Disbursements Program and Account Update Program.

GLOSSARY

***Account Update Program.** A program used in a computerized processing environment to update the accounting records for purchases on account and cash disbursements transactions.

Check. The document that represents the organization's payment to vendors for purchases made on account.

Check Register (or Cash Disbursements Journal). Journal used by the organization to summarize all cash disbursements transactions. Totals from the Check Register normally serve as the basis for the journal entry for cash disbursements transactions.

Daily Check Summary. Prepared in Cash Disbursements, this summary represents a listing of all cash disbursements made over a specified period of time (normally, a day).

Daily Voucher Summary. Prepared by the Accounts Payable Department, this summary represents a listing of all vouchers approved for payment over a specified period of time (normally, a day).

Purchase Order. A document prepared by the Purchasing Department authorizing the purchase of goods or services. The Purchase Order is based on a Purchase Requisition received from the Requesting Department.

Purchase Order Program. A program used in a computerized processing environment to approve purchases on account and prepare: (1) Purchase Orders, (2) a Purchasing Exception Report, and (3) the Open Order File.

Purchase Requisition. A document prepared by a department requesting the purchase of goods or services. This document is forwarded to the Purchasing Department for approval of the purchase.

Purchases and Disbursements cycle. The operating cycle which includes transactions related to (1) the purchase of inventory or other goods or services on account and (2) the subsequent payment for purchases made on account.

Receiving Program. A program used in a computerized processing environment to record the items received and prepare: (1) Receiving Reports, (2) a Receiving Exception Report, and (3) the Open Receiving File.

Receiving Report. A summary of the quantities of goods received from a vendor for purchases made on account.

Vendor Invoice. The request for payment sent to the company by a vendor for a purchase made on account.

Voucher. A document which authorizes the payment of a Vendor Invoice by a certain date.

Voucher Package. The documentation (including the Purchase Requisition, Purchase Order, Receiving Report, Vendor Invoice, and Voucher) related to a particular purchase made on account.

Voucher Program. A program used in a computerized processing environment to verify Vendor Invoices and prepare (1) Vouchers, (2) a Voucher Exception Report, (3) Daily Voucher Summaries, and (4) the Open Purchase Transaction File.

Voucher Register (or Purchases Journal). Journal used by the organization to summarize all purchases made on account. Totals from the Voucher Register normally serve as the basis for the journal entry for purchase transactions.

QUESTIONS AND PROBLEMS

12-21. Select the **best** answer for each of the following items:

1. When verifying debits to the perpetual inventory records of a nonmanufacturing company, an auditor would be most interested in examining a sample of purchase:

   a. Approvals.
   b. Requisitions.
   c. Invoices.
   d. Orders.

2. To best ascertain that a company has properly included merchandise that it owns in its ending inventory, the auditor should review and test the:

   a. Terms of the open Purchase Orders.
   b. Purchase cutoff procedures.
   c. Contractual commitments made by the Purchasing Department.
   d. Vendor Invoices received on or around year-end.

3. An effective internal control measure that protects against the preparation of improper or inaccurate disbursements would be to require that all Checks be:

   a. Signed by an officer after necessary supporting evidence has been examined.
   b. Reviewed by the Treasurer before mailing.
   c. Sequentially numbered and accounted for by internal auditors.
   d. Perforated or otherwise effectively canceled when they are returned with the bank statements.

4. Mailing Checks and Remittance Advices should be controlled by the employee who:

   a. Approves the Vouchers for payment.
   b. Matches the Receiving Reports, Purchase Orders, and Vendors' Invoices.
   c. Maintains possession of the mechanical check-signing device.
   d. Signs the Checks last.

5. For effective internal control, the Accounts Payable Department generally should:

   a. Obliterate the quantity ordered on the Receiving Department copy of the Purchase Order.
   b. Establish the agreement of the Vendor's Invoice with the Receiving Report and Purchase Order.
   c. Stamp, perforate, or otherwise cancel supporting documentation after payment is mailed.
   d. Ascertain that each requisition is approved as to price, quantity, and quality by an authorized employee.

6. The authority to accept incoming goods in Receiving should be based on a(n):

   a. Vendor's Invoice.
   b. Materials Requisition.
   c. Bill of Lading.
   d. Approved Purchase Order.

7. Which of the following control activities is **not** usually performed in the Cash Disbursements Department?

   a. Verifying the accuracy of Checks and Vouchers.
   b. Controlling the mailing of Checks to vendors.
   c. Approving Vendors' Invoices for payment.
   d. Canceling the Voucher Package when paid.

8. In a well-designed internal control, employees in the same department most likely would approve Purchase Orders and also:

   a. Reconcile the open Invoice file.
   b. Inspect goods upon receipt.
   c. Authorize requisitions of goods.
   d. Negotiate terms with vendors.

9. In a properly designed internal control, the same employee most likely would match Vendors' Invoices with Receiving Reports and also:

   a. Post the detailed accounts payable records.
   b. Recompute the calculations on Vendors' Invoices.
   c. Reconcile the accounts payable ledger.
   d. Cancel Vendors' Invoices after payment.

10. While of the following control activities most likely would be used to maintain accurate inventory records?

    a. Perpetual inventory records are periodically compared with the current cost of individual inventory items.
    b. A just-in-time inventory ordering system keeps inventory levels to a desired minimum.
    c. Purchase Requisitions, Receiving Reports, and Purchase Orders are independently matched before payment is approved.
    d. Periodic inventory counts are used to adjust the perpetual inventory records.

11. Which of the following internal control procedures is not usually performed in the Accounts Payable Department?

    a. Matching the Vendor's Invoice with the related Receiving Report.
    b. Approving Vouchers for payment by having an authorized employee sign the Vouchers.
    c. Indicating the asset and expense accounts to be debited.
    d. Accounting for unused prenumbered Purchase Orders and Receiving Reports.

12. Which of the following control activities most likely addresses the completeness assertion for inventory?

    a. Work-in-process account is periodically reconciled with subsidiary records.
    b. Employees responsible for custody of finished goods do not perform the Receiving function.
    c. Receiving Reports are prenumbered and periodically reconciled.
    d. There is a separation of duties between Payroll Department and Inventory Accounting personnel.

13. Which of the following control activities would be most effective in assuring that recorded purchases are free of material errors?

    a. The Receiving Department compares the quantity ordered on Purchase Orders with the quantity received on Receiving Reports.
    b. Vendors' invoices are compared with Purchase Orders by an employee who is independent of the Receiving Department.
    c. Receiving Reports require the signature of the individual who authorized the purchase.
    d. Purchase Orders, Receiving Reports, and Vendors' Invoices are independently matched in preparing Vouchers.

14. Which of the following control activities most likely would most likely be included in an internal control questionnaire concerning the completeness assertion for purchases?

    a. Is an authorized Purchase Order required before the Receiving Department can accept a shipment or the Accounts Payable Department can record a Voucher?
    b. Are Purchase Requisitions prenumbered and independently matched with Vendors' Invoices?
    c. Is the unpaid Voucher File periodically reconciled with inventory records by an employee who does not have access to Purchase Requisitions?
    d. Are Purchase Orders, Receiving Reports, and Vouchers prenumbered and periodically accounted for?

15. In assessing control risk for purchases, an auditor vouches a sample of entries in the Voucher Register to the supporting documents. Which assertion would this test of controls most likely support?

    a. Completeness.
    b. Existence or occurrence.
    c. Presentation and disclosure.
    d. Rights and obligations.

16. Which of the following is the most effective control activity to detect Vouchers that were prepared for the payment of goods that were not received?

    a. Count goods upon receipt in the storeroom.
    b. Match the Purchase Order, Receiving Report, and Vendor's Invoice for each Voucher in the Accounts Payable Department.
    c. Compare goods received with goods requisitioned in the Receiving Department.
    d. Verify Vouchers for accuracy and approval in internal audit department.

17. An entity's internal control requires for every check request that there must be an approved Voucher, supported by a prenumbered Purchase Order and a prenumbered Receiving Report. To determine whether Checks are being issued for unauthorized expenditures, an auditor most likely would select items for testing from the population of:

    a. Purchase Orders.
    b. Canceled Checks.
    c. Receiving Reports.
    d. Approved Vouchers.

18. Which of the following documents is prepared to provide evidence that inventory has been received from vendors?

    a. Purchase Order.
    b. Purchase Requisition.
    c. Receiving Report.
    d. Voucher.
    e. Vendor's Invoice.

19. The auditor obtains evidence that all recorded purchases are valid by _____ from the _____ to the _____

    a. vouching; Voucher Register; Vendor's Invoice.
    b. tracing; Voucher Register; Vendor's Invoice.
    c. vouching; Vendor's Invoice; Voucher Register.
    d. tracing; Vendor's Invoice; Voucher Register.
    e. None of the above.

20. Which of the following documents is prepared by the Vouchers Payable Department to authorize payment of a purchase made on account?

    a. Purchase Order.
    b. Purchase Requisition.
    c. Receiving Report.
    d. Sales Order.
    e. Voucher.

21. The use of prenumbered Purchase Orders and Vouchers enhances internal control over purchases of inventory by:

    a. Ensuring authorization over transactions by appropriate client personnel.
    b. Ensuring that transactions that actually occur are recorded by the client.
    c. Providing adequate segregation of duties with respect to inventory.
    d. (a) and (b) above.
    e. All of the above.

22. Signed Checks from the Cash Disbursements function should be:

    a. Returned to the Accounts Payable Department for validation.
    b. Forwarded to a General Ledger clerk for comparison with the Check Register.
    c. Mailed to the payee immediately after signing.
    d. Held with the related Voucher until the designated mailing date.
    e. Restrictively endorsed prior to being deposited in the company's bank account.

23. The purpose of canceling paid Vouchers by stamping, marking, or perforating these Vouchers is to:

    a. Facilitate filing in the Accounts Payable Department.
    b. Prevent accidental repayment of the Voucher by Cash Disbursements.
    c. Enable the auditor to select a sample of paid items from a clearly-identified population.
    d. Provide assurance that all disbursements made by the client have been recorded.
    e. Ensure that all cash disbursements are properly authorized.

                                          (Items 1 through 17 in 12-21; AICPA Adapted)

12-22. What are the duties of the five major Departments involved with the Purchases subcycle?

12-23. List and describe the major documents created in the Purchases subcycle.

12-24. For each of the following control activities in the Purchases subcycle, indicate which management assertion(s) are addressed by that control activity.

    a. Purchases should be authorized through the preparation of a prenumbered Purchase Order.
    b. Upon receipt of goods ordered from vendors, a prenumbered Receiving Report should be prepared.
    c. Prices, quantities, and extensions and footings on Vendors' Invoices should be verified.
    d. Prenumbered Vouchers should be prepared to authorize payment for purchases made on account.
    e. Appropriate segregation of duties should be established and maintained in the Purchases subcycle.
    f. Physical inventories should be periodically compared to perpetual inventory records, with any differences investigated by management.
    g. Physical controls should be established over inventories.
    h. Performance reviews should compare actual purchases data to forecasted or budgeted data.

12-25. What are the duties of the major Departments involved with the Cash Disbursements subcycle?

12-26. List and describe the major documents created in the Cash Disbursements subcycle.

12-27. For each of the following control activities over cash disbursements transactions, provide an example of how the auditor could test the operating effectiveness of that control activity.

    a. Cash Disbursements should compare information on documents in the Voucher Package prior to preparing the Check.
    b. Payment should be made using prenumbered Checks.
    c. Personnel independent of Cash Disbursements should prepare monthly Bank Reconciliations.
    d. Appropriate segregation of duties should be established and maintained in the Cash Disbursements subcycle.
    e. Physical controls should be established over cash.

*12-28. List the major steps in the computerized processing of transactions in the Purchases and Cash Disbursements subcycles.

*12-29. Briefly describe the contents of the following computerized processing files:

a. Daily Order Transaction File
b. Open Purchase Order File
c. Daily Receiving Transaction File
d. Open Receiving File
e. Daily Invoice Transaction File
f. Open Purchase Transaction File
g. Daily Cash Disbursements Transaction File
h. Open Cash Disbursements File

12-30. William Green recently acquired the controlling financial interest of Importers and Wholesalers, Inc., importers and distributors of cutlery. In his review of the duties of employees, Green became aware of loose practices in the signing of Checks and the operation of the petty cash fund.

You have been engaged as the company's CPA, and Green's first request is that you suggest a system of sound practices for the signing of Checks and the operation of the petty cash fund. Green prefers not to acquire a check-signing machine.

In addition to Green, who is the company President, the company has 20 employees, including four corporate officers. About 200 Checks are drawn each month. The petty cash fund has a working balance of about $200, and about $500 is expended from the fund each month

Required:

Prepare a letter to Green containing your recommendations for good control activities for:

a. Signing Checks. (Green is unwilling to be drawn into routine check-signing duties. Assume that you decide to recommend two signatures on each Check.)
b. Operation of the petty cash fund. (Where the effect of the control activity is not evident, give the reason for the activity.)

(AICPA Adapted)

12-31. Franklin, a CPA, has been engaged to audit the financial statements of University Books, Inc. University Books maintains a large revolving cash fund exclusively for the purpose of buying used books from students for cash. The cash fund is active all year because the nearby university offers a large variety of courses with varying starting and completion dates throughout the year.
Receipts are prepared for each purchase, and reimbursement Vouchers are periodically submitted.

Required:

Construct a internal control questionnaire to be used in the evaluation of the internal control of University Books's buying segment's revolving cash fund. The internal control questionnaire should elicit a yes or no response. Do not discuss the internal controls over books that are purchased.

(AICPA Adapted)

12-32. The accounting and control procedures relating to purchases of materials by the Branden Company, a medium-sized concern that manufactures special machinery to order, have been described by your junior accountant in the following terms:

▸ After approval by Manufacturing Department Foremen, Material Purchase Requisitions are forwarded to the Purchasing Department Supervisor, who distributes such Requisitions to the several employees under his control. The latter employees prepare prenumbered Purchase Orders in triplicate, account for all numbers, and send the original Purchase Order to the vendor. One copy of the Purchase Order is sent to the Receiving Department, where it is used as a Receiving Report. The other copy is filed in the Purchasing Department.

▸ When the materials are received, they are moved directly to the storeroom and issued to the foremen on informal requests. The Receiving Department sends a Receiving Report (with its copy of the Purchase Order attached) to the Purchasing Department and sends copies of the Receiving Report to the Storeroom and to the Accounting Department.

▸ Vendors' Invoices for material purchases, received in duplicate in the Mailroom, are sent to the Purchasing Department and directed to the employee who placed the related order. The employee then compares the Invoice with the copy of the Purchase Order on file in the Purchasing Department for price and terms, and compares the Invoice quantity with the quantity received as reported by the Receiving Department on its copy of the Purchase Order. The Purchasing Department employee also checks discounts, footings, and extensions, and initials the Invoice to indicate approval for payment. The Invoice is then sent to the Voucher section of the Accounting Department, where it is coded for account distribution, assigned a Voucher number, entered in the Voucher Register, and filed according to payment date.

▸ On payment dates, prenumbered Checks are requisitioned by the Voucher Section (Accounts Payable Department) from the Cashier and prepared except for signature. After the Checks are prepared, they are returned to the Cashier, who puts them through a check-signing machine, accounts for the sequence of numbers, and passes them to the Cash Disbursements bookkeeper for entry in the Cash Disbursements books. The Cash Disbursements bookkeeper then returns the checks to the Voucher section, which then notes payment dates in the Voucher Register, places the Checks in envelopes, and sends them to the mailroom. The Vouchers are then filed in numerical sequence. At the end of each month, one of the Voucher clerks prepares an adding machine tape of unpaid items in the Voucher Register, compares the total with the General Ledger balance, and investigates any difference disclosed by such comparison.

Required:

Discuss the weaknesses, if any, in the internal control of Branden's purchasing and subsequent procedures, and suggest supplementary or revised procedures for remedying each weakness with regard to:

a. Requisition of materials.
b. Receipt and storage of materials.
c. Functions of the Purchasing Department.
d. Functions of the Accounting Department.

(AICPA Adapted)

12-33. Green, CPA, has been engaged to audit the financial statements of Star Manufacturing, Inc. Star is a medium-sized entity that produces a wide variety of household goods. All acquisitions of materials are processed through the Purchasing, Receiving, Accounts Payable, and Treasury functions.

Required:

Prepare the "Purchases" segment of the internal control questionnaire to be used in the consideration of Star's internal control. Each question should elicit either a yes or no response.

12-34. The flowchart on the following page depicts the activities relating to the Purchasing, Receiving, and Accounts Payable Departments of Model Company, Inc.

Required:

Based only on the flowchart, describe the internal control procedures (strengths) that most likely would provide reasonable assurance that specific internal control objectives for the financial statement assertions regarding purchases and accounts payable will be achieved. Do **not** describe weaknesses in internal control.

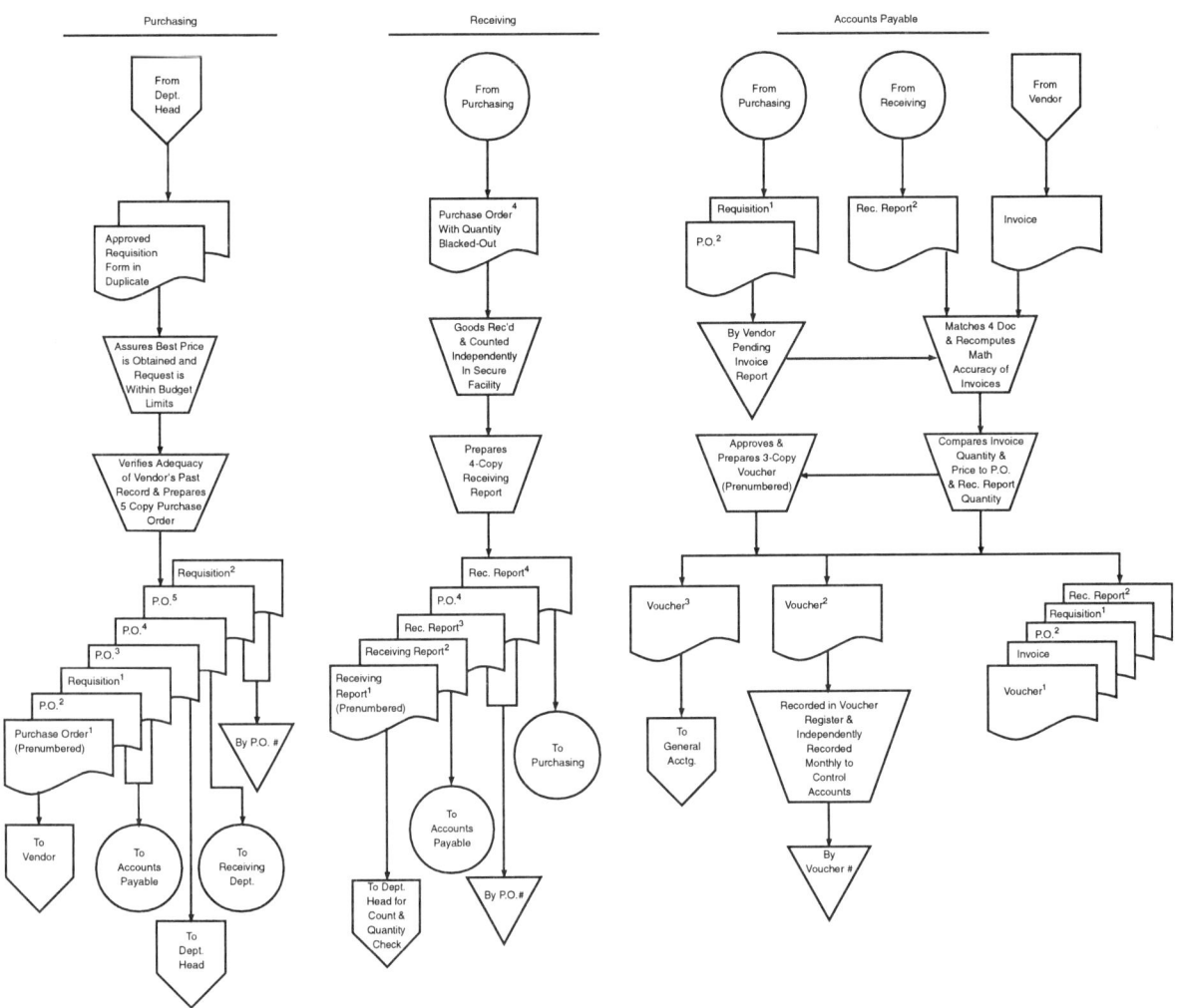

Flowchart

12-40

III / Audit Procedures

Learning Objectives

Study of this chapter is designed to achieve several learning objectives. After studying this chapter, you should be able to:

1. Discuss the overall audit approach used in the examination of accounts in the Purchases and Disbursements cycle.
2. Identify assertions having relatively high levels of inherent risk in the inventory and accounts payable accounts.
3. Explain how the nature, timing, and extent of the auditor's substantive tests over inventory and accounts payable is affected by the necessary level of detection risk.
4. List important substantive testing procedures used in the auditor's examination of inventory, accounts payable, and purchases/cost of goods sold.
5. Identify the assertions addressed by various substantive tests performed for inventory, accounts payable, and purchases/cost of goods sold.

13

The Purchases and Disbursements Cycle: Substantive Tests

In the previous chapter, we discussed internal control in the Purchases and Disbursements cycle. This chapter moves to the next major stage of the audit examination for this cycle: substantive testing.

OVERALL AUDIT APPROACH

The overall audit approach used in the examination of accounts in the Purchases and Disbursements cycle is similar to that for the Revenue cycle (discussed in Chapter 11). Consider the basic nature of the major accounts affected by the Purchases and Disbursements cycle: inventory, accounts payable, and accrued payables. The activity in these accounts can be described as follows:

- ▶ These accounts have a large number of transactions during the year
- ▶ The transactions in these accounts are for relatively small dollar amounts per transaction

Recall that the auditor utilizes the **test of balances** approach for accounts of this nature. Under the test of balances approach, the auditor identifies components of the final account balance and selects a sample of these components for examination. As with substantive tests for the Revenue cycle, the basic steps in determining the necessary level of substantive tests correspond to the audit risk model, as follows:

1. Set audit risk at desired levels (normally, low).
2. Based on the nature of the account balance or class of transactions, assess inherent risk.
3. After studying internal control, assess control risk.
4. Based on the level of audit risk, inherent risk, and control risk, determine detection risk.

The necessary level of detection risk reflects the nature, timing, and extent of the auditor's substantive tests. This issue serves as the focus of the remainder of this chapter.

INVENTORY

Inherent and Control Risk

In assessing inherent risk over inventory transactions, the auditor considers the susceptibility of these transactions to misstatement. Several important considerations affecting inventories in this regard are:

1. Inventories are a current asset and have an important impact on the operating results of the organization. Transactions occurring near year-end can have a particularly substantial effect on the assets and earnings reported by the organization. As a result, the auditor should be concerned that: (1) all inventory transactions (purchases and sales) that occur during the year are recorded, and (2) no fictitious inventory transactions are recorded. These concerns correspond to the CO and EO assertions, respectively.
2. Under GAAP, inventories must be reported at the lower of their cost or market value. If the market value of inventories declines below their cost, a write-down must be recorded which has the effect of reducing both assets and net income. This is related to the VA assertion.

As with the Revenue cycle accounts discussed in Chapter 11, the auditor should identify and test important control activities implemented to address these assertions. For example, the use of formal documentation to record transactions (such as Receiving Reports and Vouchers) reduces the likelihood that fictitious sales transactions are recorded (the EO assertion). In addition, by accounting for the numerical sequence of Receiving Reports, the client can ensure that all purchases of inventory are recorded (the CO assertion). Based on the results of the auditor's tests of controls, he or she then assesses control risk.

At this point, the auditor can use the assessments of inherent risk and control risk to determine the appropriate level of detection risk, using a matrix similar to that shown earlier in this text.

Detection Risk

In performing substantive tests for inventory, the auditor selects a sample of the components of the inventory balance for examination. The components of a typical client's inventory balance are illustrated below:

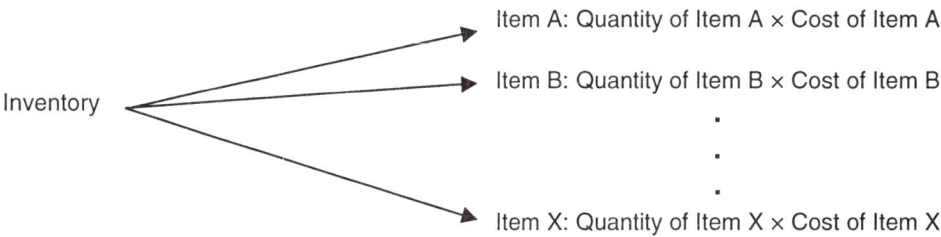

Unlike the examination of accounts receivable and cash, the auditor cannot verify the components of the inventory balance with a single procedure. Recall that, for accounts receivable and cash, the auditor could confirm the entire balance with the client's customers (for accounts receivable) or banks (for cash). For inventory balances, the auditor must verify both the quantity of items on hand as well as the price of those items. The quantity and price of inventory are verified in the following manner:

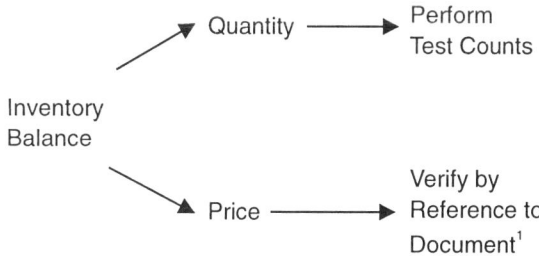

After the auditor has identified the necessary level of detection risk, he or she can determine the nature, timing, and extent of substantive tests for inventory. The effect of detection risk on the test counts and price tests performed by the auditor are summarized in Figure 13-1.

	Lower Detection Risk	Higher Detection Risk
Nature	No Effect on Test Counts	No Effect on Test Counts
	No Effect on Price Tests	No Effect on Price Tests
Timing	Perform Test Counts at Year-End	Perform Test Counts During Interim Period
	No Effect on Price Tests	No Effect on Price Tests
Extent	Perform a Larger Number of Test Counts	Perform a Smaller Number of Test Counts
	Perform a Larger Number of Price Tests	Perform a Smaller Number of Price Tests

Figure 13-1: *Effect of Detection Risk on Auditor's Substantive Tests for Inventories*

---

[1] In this chapter, our focus is on auditing the inventories held by a merchandising company. The distinguishing feature of a merchandising company is that these companies purchase their inventories in saleable form from suppliers. Thus, a Vendor's Invoice will be used by the auditor to verify the price of purchased inventories. In contrast, manufacturing companies produce their own inventories using raw material inputs; the total cost of these inventories includes the cost of raw materials, direct labor, and manufacturing overhead required to produce the inventory. The examination of inventories for manufacturing companies is discussed in Chapter 14 (The Conversion Cycle).

Figure 13-2 summarizes the primary substantive tests performed by the auditor with respect to inventory and the assertions addressed by these tests. These procedures are discussed in the remainder of this section.

Procedure	Classification	Assertion(s)				
		EO	RO	CO	VA	PD
1. Obtain an Inventory Listing from the client (Figure 13-3)						
a. Verify the quantity by price extension on the Inventory Listing	Recalculation				x	
b. Foot the Inventory Listing and agree totals to the client's Trial Balance	Recalculation Comparison				x	
2. Observe the client's physical inventory counts						
a. Make and record test counts for selected items (Figure 13-4)	Observation	x			x	
b. Agree test counts to quantities in Inventory Listing	Comparison			x	x	
3. Confirm inventories held at external locations	Confirmation	x	x		x	
4. Perform price tests for selected inventory items (Figure 13-5)	Inspect Documents				x	
5. Perform analytical procedures for inventories	Analytical Procedures	x	x	x	x	
6. Examine evidence related to inventories on consignment	Inspect documents Inquiry Observation		x	x		
7. Evaluate the need for a write-down to reduce inventory to the lower of cost or market value	Recalculation				x	
8. Evaluate the overall presentation of inventories in the financial statements						
a. Review disclosures related to inventories	Inspect Documents					x
b. Inquire about whether inventories are pledged as collateral	Inquiry					x
c. Inquire about whether the client has entered into material purchase commitments for inventories	Inquiry					x

Figure 13-2: *Major Substantive Tests: Inventories*

> **CHAPTER CHECKPOINTS**
>
> **13-1.** For which assertion(s) is the level of inherent risk for inventory transactions relatively high?
>
> **13-2.** What are the two major types of substantive tests performed by the auditor for inventories?
>
> **13-3.** How does the necessary level of detection risk affect the nature, timing, and extent of the auditor's substantive tests for inventory?

Obtaining an Inventory Listing. The Inventory Listing is normally prepared by the client and contains the following information:

1. The inventory tag number (used in making and agreeing test counts of the client's inventory).
2. A description of the item.
3. The quantities on hand at year-end.
4. The cost used to value ending inventory.
5. The total cost of inventory, both by item and in total.

A sample inventory listing is illustrated in Figure 13-3. Prior to performing any test counts or price tests of items included in this listing, the auditor will mathematically verify the quantity by price extension (tickmark "M" in Figure 13-3) and foot the totals on the Inventory Listing (tickmark "F" in Figure 13-3). Then, these totals are agreed to the client's Trial Balance (tickmark "TB" in Figure 13-3). These procedures correspond to the VA assertion.

Observing Physical Inventory Counts. *Statement on Auditing Standards No. 1*[2] (*SAS No. 1*) indicates that the observation of physical inventory counts is a generally accepted auditing procedure. It is important to note that the auditor is not required to perform the entire physical inventory; instead, he or she observes the year-end counts made by the client or the client's inventory-taking service. If it is impracticable or impossible for the auditor to observe the physical inventory count at year-end, he or she must apply alternative procedures. *SAS No. 1* (AU 331.12) identifies the following types of alternative procedures that must be performed when the auditor is unable to observe the client's year-end physical inventory:

- ▶ Make or observe physical counts of inventory after year-end
- ▶ Test the transactions occurring between the year-end and the auditor's counts
- ▶ Review the records of the client's year-end inventory counts

---

[2] American Institute of Certified Public Accountants (AICPA), *Statement on Auditing Standards No. 1*, "Codification of Auditing Standards and Procedures" (New York: AICPA, 1972, AU 331).

C-1	Meghan's Office Products *Inventory Listing* 12-31-x3			Prepared by: Client 1-3-X4 JRS 1-6-X4 Reviewed by: MES 1-14-X4	
No.	**Description**	**Item Tag No.**	**Quantity (C-1-A)**	**Price (C-1-B)**	**Total**
100-11	Disposable Pens	100	45 cartons	29.47	1,326 Ⓜ
100-12	Rollerball Pen Refills	101	20 cartons	35.00	700
*	*	*	*	*	*
*	*	*	*	*	*
*	*	*	*	*	*
400-19	Bond Paper (20 #)	154	10 boxes	55.00	550
400-20	Bond Paper (10 #)	155	5 boxes	47.50	238
400-21	Bond Paper (20 #), color	156	5 boxes	57.50	288
500-11	Computer Drives	157	100	200.00	20,000
500-12	Laser Printers	158	35	489.60	17,136
500-13	Computer Diskettes	159	250 boxes	7.50	1,875
*	*	*	*	*	*
*	*	*	*	*	*
*	*	*	*	*	*
700-10	Word Processing Software	193	10	60.00	600
					256,789
					Ⓕ ⓉⒷ

Ⓕ Footed

ⓉⒷ Agreed to Trial Balance

Ⓜ Recalculated Quantity by Price Extension. No exceptions noted.

Figure 13-3: *Inventory Listing*

Planning the Inventory Observation. As a part of the procedures used to examine inventories, the auditor should review a copy of the client's inventory instructions prior to the actual counts. Complete instructions would normally address the following topics:

1. Dates and times of the physical inventory.
2. Names of the employees responsible for supervising the physical inventory.
3. Plans for arranging and segregating inventory items.
4. Methods of handling items received and shipped during the physical inventory.
5. The use of prenumbered, inventory tags for identifying items that have been counted.
6. Methods of measuring inventory other than by quantity (such as weight or volume).
7. Plans for determining quantities held at outside locations.
8. The need for a specialist to assist in inventory valuation.

The need for a specialist deserves some additional discussion. Under the provisions of *SAS No. 73*[3], specialists may be useful in determining both the valuation of inventories as well as the physical characteristics of inventories. Using specialists in the examination of inventory would be more relevant for specialized or difficult-to-value inventories, such as minerals, pharmaceutical products, and jewelry. In cases where the auditor decides the use of a specialist is necessary, the auditor should obtain and document an understanding of the nature of the work to be performed by the specialist. As noted previously in Chapter 4, unless the auditor's opinion is modified because of the specialist's findings, the auditor will not reference the specialist's procedures or findings in his or her report.

Observing the Physical Inventory. The primary purpose of the auditor's inventory observation is to determine the effectiveness of the client's physical inventory procedures. This effectiveness is important, since the quantities determined by the client's physical inventory serve as the basis for the valuation of inventory on the balance sheet. During the auditor's observation of the client's physical inventory, the auditor should:

- ▶ Make and record test counts of selected items. As noted earlier in Figure 13-1, the extent of these test counts depends upon the necessary level of detection risk. These test counts will be compared to the inventory counts made by the client or its inventory-taking service. Eventually, these test counts will be compared to information contained in the client's Inventory Listing.

- ▶ Examine the use of prenumbered inventory tags by the client or the client's inventory-taking service to record counts. These tags are placed on stacks of inventory after they are counted. The use of inventory tags helps reduce the possibility that items are not counted or are unintentionally counted twice.

---

[3] American Institute of Certified Public Accountants (AICPA), *Statement on Auditing Standards No. 73*, "Using the Work of a Specialist" (New York: AICPA, 1994, AU 336).

- ▶ Watch for apparently unsalable, damaged, slow-moving, and obsolete items. These items may help the auditor identify inventory whose market value is less than its cost. As noted earlier, GAAP requires inventory to be presented at the lower of cost or market.

- ▶ Be alert for inventory held by the client on consignment and ensure that this inventory is not included in the final counts.

In observing physical inventories, the auditor should be aware of methods used by companies to intentionally overstate inventories. For example, stacks of inventory can be arranged in such a manner that empty spaces exist between stacks of boxes containing inventory. This provides the appearance of having solid rows of inventory when this is not the case ("hollow squares"). In addition, companies may overstate inventory by placing empty boxes at the top of an inventory stack and counting those boxes as containing a full complement of items. Occasionally, the auditor may request that boxes be opened or moved, although such requests are normally made on a limited basis.

STOP, LOOK, AND BEHOLD[4]

An unnamed retail company requested its internal auditors to assist in observing the physical inventory at several of the company's locations. Upon arrival at one of the locations, the internal auditor noticed a tarpaulin-covered object just outside of the rear door. His curiosity aroused, the auditor looked underneath the tarpaulin and found some very expensive items of store merchandise. Further investigation revealed that the store manager was removing merchandise from the retail floor and hiding the merchandise under the tarpaulin until he could remove it later.

Timing of Physical Observation. In cases where the client utilizes a perpetual inventory system and internal control over inventory transactions is effective, the auditor may observe physical inventories prior to year-end. As noted earlier in Figure 13-1, the ability to observe physical inventory prior to year-end is normally limited to situations where the client maintains perpetual inventory records and higher levels of detection risk are necessary. In these cases, the auditor should perform tests of transactions occurring between the time of the physical inventory and the balance-sheet date, such as:

1. Testing individual transactions occurring during this period.
2. Comparing gross profit margins of the current period with those of prior periods.

The basic premise behind the interim observation of physical inventories is shown below:

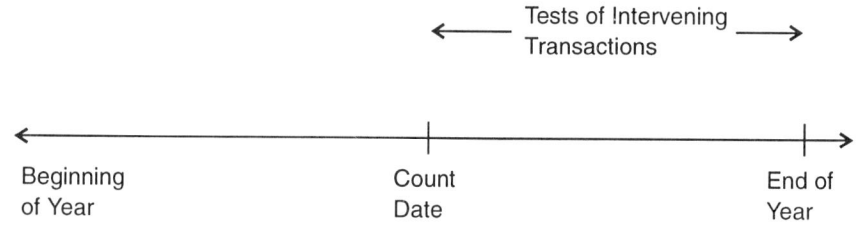

---

[4] "Stop, Look, and Behold," *Internal Auditor* (February 1996), 71.

Agreeing Test Counts to the Inventory Listing. During the observation of the client's physical inventory, the auditor will make test counts and record these test counts in the workpapers. A sample workpaper for recording test counts is shown in Figure 13-4. These test counts should then be agreed to the client's Inventory Listing. This test is made to determine that the quantities included on the Inventory Listing accurately represent the physical quantities on hand at the date the inventory was taken.

C-1-A

Meghan's Office Products
Inventory Test Counts
12-31-x3

Prepared by: JRS 1-4-X4
Reviewed by: MES 1-10-X4

Inventory		Counts		Difference
Tag No.	Item No.	Client	Auditor	
100	100-11	45 cartons ✓	44 cartons	1 carton ①
154	400-19	10 boxes ✓	10 boxes	
157	500-11	100 ✓	90	10 ②
158	500-12	35 ✓	35	

✓ Agreed to client's Inventory Listing (Workpaper C-1, Figure 13-3)

① Carton subsequently located in another area of the warehouse. No adjustment deemed necessary.

② Difference represents 10 computer drives that had been sold to customers and were awaiting customer pick-up. Examined sales agreement and noted that legal title to the computer drives has passed to the customer. Propose the following adjustment to reduce inventory and recognize cost of goods sold for $2,000 (10 drives x $200 cost per drive):

Cost of Goods Sold   2,000
　　Inventory　　　　　　　　2,000

See Workpaper AJE-1 for a summary of adjustments.

Figure 13-4: *Workpaper for Inventory Test Counts*

Refer to the auditor's test count workpaper (Figure 13-4) and the client's Inventory Listing (Figure 13-3). The "✓" tickmark shown in Figure 13-4 indicates that the client counts agree with the quantities in the client's Inventory Listing. The auditor's counts are then recorded and compared to those from the client's Inventory Listing. At this time, any discrepancies should be accounted for, with the disposition noted in the workpapers. For example, note that the auditor counted 44 cartons of the item 100-11 (disposable pens); the client's count revealed 45 cartons. The auditor should investigate this difference further to see whether it resulted from inventory in transit at the time of the count or an error in the counting process. As shown in Figure 13-4, the difference in the count of pens resulted from a carton of pens that was placed in another area of the warehouse. In this case, no adjustment is considered necessary. However, the difference relating to the ten computer drives (item 500-11) resulted from the erroneous inclusion of computer drives that had already been sold to customers. This difference would result in an adjustment of $2,000 to the client's inventory balance (as shown in Figure 13-4).

In some situations, the auditor will not be able to identify individual Tag Numbers in the client's final Inventory Listing. For example, instead of having a single Tag Number represent the entire quantity of a particular inventory item (as in the Meghan's Office Products example shown in Figure 13-3), assume that Meghan's inventory of 100-11 pens was located in six areas of the warehouse and, accordingly, was represented by six Tag Numbers. Also assume that the Inventory Listing only provided the total quantity on hand without reference to individual Tag Numbers comprising that total. In this case, the auditor should examine some documentation of the compilation of the tags and agree the resultant total to the client's Inventory Listing. To illustrate, if the 45 cartons of 100-11 pens were represented by tags 100-105 and the auditor performed test counts of tags 100, 103, and 105, the procedure used to agree this test count to the Inventory Listing is shown below:

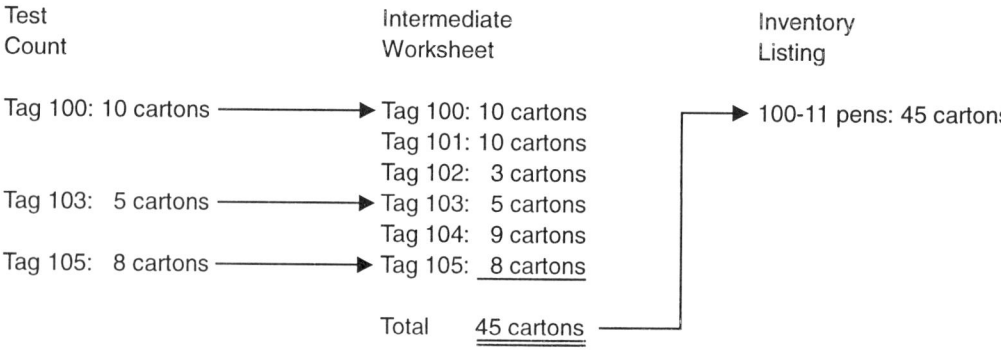

In some cases, the auditor's test counts unintentionally exclude items having a large dollar value on the balance sheet. In these cases, it may be necessary for the auditor to make special tests of these items to determine their existence at the date of the physical count. These tests could include subsequent count of the quantities on hand and reconciling these counts to quantities shown on the Inventory Listing by examining documents representing purchases (Receiving Reports and Vendors' Invoices) and sales (Shipping Documents and Sales Invoices) of inventory after year-end.

Inventory Observation Memorandum. At the conclusion of the inventory observation and tests, the auditor should prepare a memorandum that briefly and accurately describes the work done and the conclusions reached in his or her observation. A typical memorandum would include information concerning:

1. Location, time of visit, and department covered.
2. Whether the client's employees followed the inventory instructions. Any deviations should be noted, as well as the corrective actions that were taken.
3. Comments concerning the client's "housekeeping." (Were the inventory items neatly arranged, and so on?)
4. Procedures followed in observing and test counting and the degree of accuracy indicated by test counts.
5. Notations of any unusual items or conditions observed, such as obsolete or slow-moving inventory, damaged merchandise, consigned inventory, and inventory movement that occurred during the taking of the physical inventory, should be made.
6. Description of the procedures used by the client to obtain accurate shipping and receiving cutoffs and information obtained for future testing of the information.
7. A conclusion, based on the results of tests and observations, as to whether the recorded quantities reasonably represent the quantities actually on hand at that time.

Assertions. Observing the physical inventory and making test counts relate primarily to the EO assertion, since the auditor is verifying the presence of items held by the client at year-end. In addition, agreeing test counts to the Inventory Listing prepared by the client will also verify that those items are included in the inventory on hand at year-end, consistent with the CO assertion. Finally, since the recorded value of inventory is affected by the proper determination of quantities, both procedures provide the auditor with evidence for the VA assertion.

While the existence of inventory would also appear to provide evidence that the inventory is owned by the client (the RO assertion), inventory on hand at year-end (and counted by the auditor) could be held on consignment or have already been sold to customers. Thus, the observation of physical quantities does not necessarily relate to the RO assertion.

INVENTORY MANIPULATIONS[5]

Inventory manipulations can be a convenient mechanism for increasing profits and improving balance sheets. Some recent examples of cases involving inventory are summarized below:

- Laribee Wire Manufacturing Co. is a New York company that manufactures copper wire products. Laribee recorded inventories on its books at $2.20 per pound when Laribee was selling this wire for only $1.70 to $1.75 per pound. In addition, shipments between plants were recorded as inventory located at both plants. The inflation of inventory was so severe that Laribee would have needed three times the capacity of its warehouse space to house its recorded inventory. Laribee's inventory fraud added $5.5 million to its 1989 net income.

- Phar-Mor, Inc., a deep-discount drugstore chain, engaged in a well-publicized inventory fraud in the 1990s. This inventory fraud was based on two types of manipulations: (1) Phar-Mor created fictitious inventories and used these fictitious inventories to overstate assets, and (2) Phar-Mor intentionally did not reduce their inventories for items sold to customers. They were able to engage in these manipulations because their auditors only examined inventory at five of Phar-Mor's locations. Interestingly, the auditors notified Phar-Mor in advance of which locations would be examined. Corporate Partners, L.P., who filed suit against Phar-Mor's auditors, noted that "Phar-Mor made its fraudulent adjustments to the inventory records of the vast majority of other stores that it knew in advance that [its auditors] would not review..."

CHAPTER CHECKPOINTS

13-4. What information is normally included on the client's Inventory Listing?

13-5. What alternative procedures should be performed if the auditor cannot observe the client's year-end physical inventory?

13-6. What should the auditor do during his or her observation of the client's physical inventory?

13-7. In what instances could the auditor observe the physical inventory prior to year-end? What additional procedures should be performed if he or she does so?

13-8. What information should be included by the auditor in an Inventory Observation Memorandum?

13-9. What assertions are normally verified by observing the physical inventory and making test counts? By agreeing test counts into the Inventory Listing?

---

[5] "Inventory Chicanery Tempts More Firms, Fools More Auditors," *The Wall Street Journal* (December 14, 1992), A1, A4.

Confirming Inventory Held at External Locations. *SAS No. 43*[6] (in amending *SAS No. 1*) suggests that the auditor confirm inventory held at external locations (either in a public warehouse or at another location). These confirmations are sent to the warehouseman or, in case of inventory on consignment, the consignee. If a significant amount of inventory is held on consignment, the auditor should also consider applying one or more of the following procedures in addition to the confirmation:

1. Test the client's procedures for evaluating the warehouseman's performance.
2. Obtain an independent accountant's report on the control activities implemented at the warehouse.
3. Observe physical counts of the goods at the warehouse, if practicable and reasonable.
4. Confirm details of any warehouse inventory receipts pledged as collateral.

Similar to the physical observation of inventories, confirming inventory held at external locations relates to the EO and VA assertions. In addition, since the warehouseman's confirmation indicates that the inventory is owned by the client, this procedure also provides assurance regarding the RO assertion.

Performing Price Tests. Once the auditor has verified the quantities of physical inventories on hand at year-end, either through observation or confirmation with an external party, the next step in the examination of inventory is to verify the prices used by the client to cost its ending inventory. In making this determination, the auditor considers both the cost flow assumption (*i.e.*, LIFO, FIFO, or average) as well as documentary evidence supporting that price.

In order to test the prices of purchased inventories, the auditor refers to Vendor Invoices. In examining Vendor Invoices, the following should be kept in mind:

▶ The auditor should consider the client's cost flow assumption. For example, if the client values its inventory using FIFO, the auditor should identify a recent invoice, since inventory on hand under FIFO would represent relatively recent purchases.

▶ The total price (or cost) of inventory includes the purchase price as well as any charges for freight, insurance, etc.

▶ The lack of current invoices for inventory items may indicate that the item is obsolete, slow-moving, or unsalable.

Figure 13-5 provides an example of a workpaper used to summarize price tests performed by the auditor during the examination of inventory. As shown therein, the primary source of evidence obtained by the auditor is through reference to a Vendor's Invoice corresponding to the purchase of that inventory item (see tickmark "1" in Figure 13-5). For example, consider the price tests for item 100-11 (disposable pens). Under a FIFO cost flow, the ending inventory would consist of the most recent forty-five cartons of pens purchased, as follows:

---

[6] American Institute of Certified Public Accountants (AICPA), *Statement on Auditing Standards No. 43*, "Omnibus Statement on Auditing Standards" (New York: AICPA, 1982, AU 331.14).

C-1-B		Meghan's Office Products Inventory Price Test 12-31-x3			Prepared by: JRS 1-4-X4 Reviewed by: MES 1-10-X4	
Item		Date	Document	Quantity	Price	Average Price
No.	Description					
100-11	Disposable Pens	8-31-x3	VO 1289 ①	30 cartons	31.00	
		9-15-x3	VO 1415	20 cartons	28.50	
		12-15-x3	VO 3210	5 cartons	27.20	29.47 Ⓡ
400-20	Bond Paper (10 #)	12-1-x3	VO 2867	5 boxes	47.50	47.50
500-12	Laser Printers	11-15-x3	VO 2678	7	480.00	
		12-15-x3	VO 3249	28	492.00	489.60

① Examined Vendor's Invoice in Voucher Package, verifying date, quantity and price. No exceptions noted.

Ⓡ Based on FIFO cost flows, determined average price for most recent purchases of items. Agreed average price to price used in Inventory Listing (Workpaper C-1, Figure 13-3). No exceptions noted.

Figure 13-5: *Workpaper for Inventory Price Tests*

1. Five cartons purchased on December 15, 19x3
2. Twenty cartons purchased on September 15, 19x3
3. Twenty of the thirty cartons purchased on August 31, 19x3

Based on the above purchases, an average price per carton can be determined and agreed to the client's Inventory Listing. A similar method is used to determine the price of the 400-20 bond paper and 500-12 laser printers. As with the disposable pens, the average price of the ending inventory should be agreed to the client's Inventory Listing.

Although the price test for a client that purchases its inventory from vendors (merchandising companies) is relatively straightforward, some additional complexities are introduced when the client manufactures its inventory. These complexities arise from the fact that the price of inventory cannot be verified through reference to a single Vendor's Invoice. Instead, the price of inventory reflects all of the production costs (raw materials, direct labor, and overhead) incurred in manufacturing the item. It is important to note that, with the exception of materials (which are normally purchased from external vendors), the auditor is examining internal records in performing price tests for manufacturing companies' inventories. Of course, the reliability of internal evidence is normally considered inferior to that obtained from external parties.

When selecting items for price tests, the auditor normally focuses on items having a higher dollar value (similar to test counts described earlier in this chapter). However, it is usually desirable to include a representative group of items of a lesser dollar amount as part of the price tests. In addition, any items having a high dollar value that are subject to wide or rapid price fluctuations should be included in the auditor's price tests, if possible.

Inventory price tests are concerned with verifying that inventory is recorded at the proper dollar amount. Accordingly, this procedure provides the auditor with support for the VA assertion.

Performing Analytical Procedures. Analytical procedures are used by the auditor in his or her examination of inventories to verify the reasonableness of recorded amounts. As with the use of analytical procedures for other accounts, these procedures may assist the auditor in identifying fictitious transactions that have been recorded in the accounting records (the EO and RO assertions), unrecorded transactions (the CO assertion), and transactions recorded at the incorrect dollar amount (the VA assertion).

An analytical procedure commonly used by auditors is comparing the recorded (unaudited) balance in inventory to: (1) the balance of inventory for previous years, and/or (2) the budgeted or forecasted balance of inventory. In addition, the following ratios involving the inventory or other related accounts may be calculated and compared to expectations through the use of analytical procedures.

- Ratio of inventory to total assets (or cost of goods sold)
- Inventory turnover ratio (cost of goods sold ÷ inventory)
- Gross profit percentage (gross profit ÷ sales)

Examining Consigned Inventories. During the physical observation of inventories, the auditor may have noted evidence of inventories held by the client on consignment. Consignment arrangements are situations where one party (the consignor) transfers inventory to another party (the consignee). The consignee attempts to sell the inventory on behalf of the consignor and is provided with a percentage of the proceeds for its efforts. Inventories held by the client on consignment should not be included in their year-end inventory balances. In contrast, if the client has inventory consigned out to external parties, those quantities should be included in the client's year-end inventory balance.

In examining consigned inventories, the auditor should inquire of management about consignments, examine consignment agreements, and/or confirm inventory held by others on behalf of the client. Examining inventories held on consignment provides assurance related to two assertions. First, by verifying that inventories held by the client on consignment for others are excluded from the Inventory Listing, the auditor is ensuring that all recorded inventory is owned by the client (the RO assertion). Second, by verifying inventories held by others on behalf of the client on consignment, the auditor determines that all inventories owned by the client are included in the Inventory Listing (the CO assertion).

Determining the Lower of Cost or Market. Under GAAP, inventories are presented in the balance sheet at the lower of cost or market. Therefore, in addition to evaluating the historical cost of inventory (as described above), the auditor must also determine the market value of inventory to decide whether an unrealized loss has occurred and a write-down is considered necessary. The following may provide the auditor with evidence regarding the need for potential write-downs of inventory:

▸ Obsolete, damaged, or slow-moving inventory noted during the observation of physical inventory.

▸ Inquiry of management regarding obsolete, damaged, or slow-moving inventory.

▸ A lack of recent purchases of inventory noted during price tests.

Once the auditor has identified the need for potential write-downs in the above fashion, he or she should recalculate the amount of the write-down (if any) and determine its reasonableness. The auditor's recalculation may be based on recent purchases and sales of the items. Alternatively, if inventory items are commodities having quoted prices, the auditor may make reference to published quotations included in financial and trade publications. In either case, extreme care should be taken for inventory items that are subject to declining prices or rapid market fluctuations.

For manufacturing companies, the determination of market value is slightly more complex. For these companies, market value may equal:

1. The replacement cost of the inventory item.
2. The selling price of the item minus costs to complete and sell the item.
3. The selling price of the item minus: (a) costs to complete and sell the item, and (b) a normal profit margin.[7]

In these instances, the auditor may verify selling prices through references to the client's price list, contracts, catalogs, or recent Sales Invoices. The costs to complete and sell items are normally estimated by the auditor based on previous experience with the client.

Verifying the need (and amount) of write-downs to inventories to present them at the lower of cost or market is related to the VA assertion.

---

[7] American Institute of Certified Public Accountants (AICPA), Committee on Accounting Procedure, "Restatement and Revision of Accounting Research Bulletins," *Accounting Research Bulletin No. 43* (New York: AICPA, 1953).

> ### IS INVENTORY OBSOLETE?[8]
>
> An example of an apparently small provision for obsolete inventory can be illustrated by MiniScribe Corp., a now-defunct manufacturer of computer disk drives. Accounting for obsolete inventory and declines in the market value of inventory can have a significant effect on net income; this issue is of particular importance in industries characterized by technological changes, like the computer industry. In 1985, MiniScribe had a reserve of $4.05 million for obsolete inventory; this reserve was based, in part, on its sales of $114 million that year. Interestingly, in 1986, sales increased by 62 percent to $185 million. However, MiniScribe **reduced** its allowance for obsolete inventory by almost 43 percent, to $2.78 million.

Evaluating Financial Statement Presentation. GAAP require a relatively extensive set of disclosures with regard to inventories. For example, the existence of purchase commitments for inventory or instances where inventories are pledged as collateral are required to be disclosed by the client. The auditor will ordinarily inquire of management about these situations. In addition, the auditor should review the financial statement disclosures related to inventories. These disclosures will normally include information about the cost flow assumption utilized for inventories as well as the general composition of the client's inventory. As with other accounts, inquiries of management and reviews related to supplemental footnote disclosures address the PD assertion.

> ### CHAPTER CHECKPOINTS
>
> **13-10.** What factors should the auditor consider in performing price tests for inventory?
>
> **13-11.** What form of documentation should be used by the auditor to verify the price of purchased inventory? Manufactured inventory?
>
> **13-12.** How does the auditor verify consigned inventories? For what assertions do these procedures provide evidence?
>
> **13-13.** What are possible sources of information about the need for a write-down of inventory? How would the auditor determine the proper amount of the write-down?

---

[8] "How MiniScribe Got Its Auditor's Blessing on Questionable Sales," *The Wall Street Journal* (May 14, 1992), A1.

ACCOUNTS PAYABLE

Inherent and Control Risk

To this point, we have discussed substantive tests related to asset accounts in both this chapter (inventory) and Chapter 11 (accounts receivable and cash). In recalling the factors affecting the inherent risk associated with these accounts, consider the effect of assets (and the corresponding revenues) on users' perceptions of a company's financial condition. In general, users would have more favorable perceptions of a company's financial condition as their assets and revenues increased. Accordingly, when examining asset and revenue accounts, the auditor is primarily concerned with the EO assertion. Some of the more important substantive tests discussed for these accounts were related to this assertion:

- ▶ Accounts Receivable: Confirming accounts with customers
- ▶ Cash: Confirming balances with banks
- ▶ Inventory: Observing physical inventories and making test counts

In contrast, accounts payable represent a liability (or obligation) of the company. Unlike assets, users' perceptions of a company's financial condition would be enhanced if the recorded amount of liabilities (and the corresponding expenses) were lower. Thus, an incentive exists on the part of management to **understate** (or **omit**) liabilities. This incentive results in an audit strategy designed to identify unrecorded or underrecorded liabilities, which corresponds to the CO assertion (have all liabilities and transactions involving liabilities been recorded?). Stated another way, the inherent risk associated with accounts payable transactions is relatively high for the CO assertion.

Given the high level of inherent risk for accounts payable transactions, the auditor focuses on control activities implemented within the Purchases and Disbursements cycle to address the CO assertion. For example, the use of prenumbered Vouchers and accounting for the numerical sequence of these Vouchers provides the client with reasonable assurance that all purchases are recorded (the CO assertion). The auditor then performs tests of controls to determine the operating effectiveness of these control activities. For example, the auditor would inspect the use of prenumbered Vouchers and obtain evidence (by inspecting documents, inquiring of client personnel, or observing client activities) that client personnel account for the numerical sequence of Vouchers. Based on the results of the auditor's tests of controls, he or she then assesses control risk. As with other control activities, higher (lower) levels of control risk correspond to less (more) effective internal control.

At this point, the auditor uses the assessments of inherent risk and control risk to determine the appropriate level of detection risk. This can be done using a matrix similar to that shown earlier in Chapter 11.

Detection Risk

Similar to the inventory account, accounts payable are characterized by a large number of transactions having relatively small dollar amounts per transaction. Thus, the auditor utilizes the tests of balances approach when examining this account. Under this approach, the auditor identifies components of the ending accounts payable balance and verifies a sample of these components. A typical accounts payable balance can be decomposed into components as shown below:

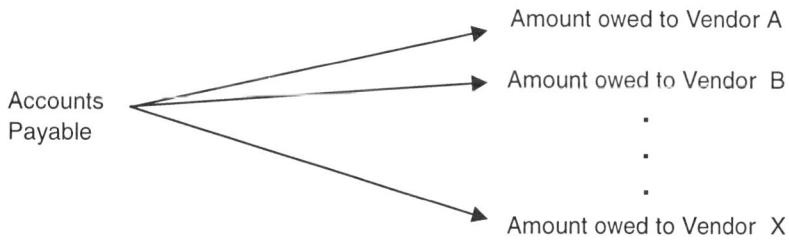

After the auditor has identified the necessary level of detection risk, he or she can determine the nature, timing, and extent of substantive tests for accounts payable. As noted earlier, given the high level of inherent risk associated with the CO assertion for accounts payable, the auditor's primary substantive testing procedure involves searching for unrecorded accounts payable. The effect of detection risk on the auditor's search for unrecorded accounts payable are summarized in Figure 13-6.

	Lower Detection Risk	Higher Detection Risk
Nature	Auditor must rely on External Evidence (Confirmations and Statements Received from the Vendors)	Auditor may rely on Internal Evidence (Vendors' Statements Received from the Client)
Timing	No Effect on Timing (Must be Performed after Year-End)	No Effect on Timing (Must be Performed After Year-End)
Extent	Perform a More Extensive Search for Unrecorded Liabilities	Perform a Less Extensive Search for Unrecorded Liabilities

Figure 13-6: *Effect of Detection Risk on Auditor's Substantive Tests for Accounts Payable*

Figure 13-7 summarizes the primary substantive tests performed by the auditor with respect to accounts payable. These procedures are discussed in the remainder of this section.

Procedure	Classification	Assertion(s)				
		EO	RO	CO	VA	PD
1. Obtain a Listing of Accounts Payable from the Client (Figure 13-8)						
a. Foot the Listing of Accounts Payable and agree totals to the client's Trial Balance	Recalculation Comparison				x	
b. Scan the Listing of Accounts Payable for inappropriate items	Inspect Documents					x
2. Verify the amount of selected accounts payable	Confirmation Inspect Documents	x	x		x	
3. Perform a search for unrecorded accounts payable (Figure 13-10)	Confirmation Inspect Documents			x		
4. Perform analytical procedures for accounts payable	Analytical Procedures	x	x	x	x	
5. Evaluate the overall presentation of accounts payable in the financial statements						
a. Review disclosures related to accounts payable	Inspect Documents					x
b. Inquire about inclusion of inappropriate items in accounts payable	Inquiry					x

Figure 13-7: *Major Substantive Tests: Accounts Payable*

CHAPTER CHECKPOINTS

13-14. How does the examination of liabilities and expenses differ from the examination of assets and revenues?

13-15. What is the auditor's primary substantive test with respect to accounts payable? How does the level of detection risk affect the nature, timing, and extent of this test?

Obtaining a Listing of Accounts Payable. The auditor normally begins the test of accounts payable by obtaining a Listing of Accounts Payable as of the balance-sheet date from the client. A sample Listing of Accounts Payable is shown in Figure 13-8. Prior to verifying the balances shown on this listing, the auditor mathematically verifies the total of the listing (as shown by tickmark "F") and agrees the total to the client's Trial Balance (tickmark "TB"). These procedures relate to the VA assertion.

Prior to examining the accuracy of individual accounts payable balances, the auditor will normally scan the listing to determine that all items are properly classified as accounts payable. Items that may be mistakenly included on the Listing of Accounts Payable include accounts with affiliates; amounts

D-1	Meghan's Office Products Accounts Payable 12-31-x3		Prepared by: SAS 1-15-X4 Reviewed by: MES 1-22-X4
Vendor	**Account #**		**Balance**
Consolidatum Paper Company	110		13,208 ①
Computer Graphics	121		22,869 ⊥
Conroe Water Systems	237		11,680 ②
Houston Electric	238		45,000 ①
*	*		*
*	*		*
*	*		*
Whiz Office Products	115		12,120 ⊥
			178,924
			Ⓕ ⓉⒷ

Ⓕ Footed

ⓉⒷ Agreed to Trial Balance

① Agreed to copies of statement received from vendor. See D-1-A through D-1-RR for copies of statements. No exceptions noted.

② Amount per Vendor Statement recorded at $22,000. Difference relates to payment not received by vendor as of 12-31-x3, as follows:

Recorded Amount	11,680
Payment (Check #3122)	10,320
Amount per Vendor Statement	22,000

Since Check #3122 was dated 12-29-x3, amount appears to be properly recorded at year-end.

Figure 13-8: *Listing of Accounts Payable*

payable to officers, shareholders, or directors; wages payable; and deferred taxes payable. In most cases, a simple review of the Listing of Accounts Payable will reveal accounts of this nature. In addition, special attention should be paid to debit balances (which may need to be reclassified as assets) or past-due accounts payable. Any accounts that are past due may signify payables that are in dispute; for these accounts, the recorded balance may differ significantly from the actual balance. Reviewing the appropriateness of components of the Listing of Accounts Payable in this manner corresponds to the PD assertion.

Verifying Selected Accounts Payable. Once the auditor verifies the mathematical accuracy of the client's Listing of Accounts Payable and scans this listing for inappropriate items, he or she verifies important components of the year-end balance in accounts payable. The most common source of the amount owed by clients to vendors at year-end is a statement prepared by the vendor. In recalling the hierarchy of audit evidence from Chapter 6, it is important to point out that these statements are created by an external party (the vendor). As a result, Vendors' Statements are a more competent form of evidence than internally-created Vouchers and other forms of documentation. The auditor will confirm accounts payable balances with vendors by requesting that the year-end statement be sent directly to the auditor. A sample request for a statement of account is shown in Figure 13-9. The number of accounts confirmed in this manner by the editor will depend upon the necessary level of detection risk; as lower levels of detection risk are necessary, the auditor will confirm a larger number of balances (and *vice versa*).

Once the Vendors' Statements are received, the auditor compares the balance on the year-end statement with the amount included in the Listing of Accounts Payable. The auditor should note the agreement of information received from the vendor with the Listing of Accounts Payable (see tickmark "1" in Figure 13-8). In many cases, differences between recorded amounts and balances from Vendors' Statements will occur. These differences often represent items recorded by the client but not yet processed by the vendor (e.g., a payment made on account). In other cases, the differences could relate to items processed by the vendor that are not recorded by the client. The latter differences might include errors in processing made by the vendor or items that (either intentionally or inadvertently) were not recorded by the client.

The auditor should reconcile any differences noted between the Listing of Accounts Payable and the Vendors' Statements. The auditor tests these differences by tracing payments in transit to the cash disbursements records, examining correspondence and other supporting documents for debit memos that have not been processed by the vendor, and obtaining explanations for any other differences.

Refer again to the Listing of Accounts Payable presented in Figure 13-8. The payable to Conroe Water Systems was recorded by Meghan's Office Products at $11,680; in contrast, the statement received from Conroe Water Systems indicated that the amount owed on that date was $22,000. In this case, the difference of $10,320 ($22,000 - $11,680 = $10,320) represents a payment made by Meghan's Office Products that was not processed by Conroe Water Systems at year-end. As noted in tickmark "2" in Figure 13-8, because the payment was made prior to year-end, the recorded amount correctly reflects the payable owed to Conroe Water Systems at 12-31-X3.

Verifying the recorded accounts payable provides the auditor with assurance that the accounts exist (the EO assertion) and are true obligations of the client (the RO assertion). In addition, by comparing the amount from the Vendors' Statement to the Listing of Accounts Payable and accounting for any differences, the auditor is also ascertaining that accounts payable are recorded at the proper dollar amount. Thus, this procedure also provides assurance regarding the VA assertion.

REQUEST FOR STATEMENT OF ACCOUNT

AllStar Products
105 Main Street
Los Angeles, CA 90012

Gentlemen:

Our auditors are making an examination of our financial statements and wish to obtain a complete statement of our account with you as of the date shown below. Please furnish them with details of our indebtedness to you on open account, notes, acceptances, loans, or contracts. If these accounts are secured, please state the nature of any asset(s) pledged as collateral.

Your prompt rely is requested. Please mail the statement in the enclosed reply envelope directly to our auditors.

Very truly yours,

Timothy Dockery
Accounts Payable Supervisor
Meghan's Office Products

Statement requested as of <u>December 31, 19x3</u>

Figure 13-9: *Request for Statement of Account*

CHAPTER CHECKPOINTS

13-16. What procedures are ordinarily performed by the auditor with respect to the client's Listing of Accounts Payable? What assertions are verified by these procedures?

13-17. What methods can be used by the auditor to verify recorded accounts payable? What is the relative quality of the evidence provided by each of these methods?

13-18. What types of procedures should be performed by the auditor if differences between Vendors' Statements and recorded accounts payable are noted?

Searching for Unrecorded Liabilities. As noted at the beginning of this section, the audit of accounts payable differs from that of assets in that the CO assertion (*i.e.*, all accounts and transactions have been recorded) is of primary importance. Unfortunately, comparing recorded account balances to information obtained from Vendors' Statements provides little (if any) assurance concerning this assertion. To obtain information of this nature, the auditor performs a series of different tests to search for omitted (unrecorded) liabilities. These tests include the following:

1. Examine documentation for purchases made near year-end.
2. Obtain confirmations (or request statements) from vendors with whom the client normally does business.
3. Examine cash disbursements occurring shortly after year-end.

One method of searching for unrecorded liabilities is by examining all documentation (Receiving Reports, Vouchers, Vendor Invoices, etc.) for purchases made both a few days before and a few days after year-end. Normally, the auditor focuses on purchases for larger dollar amounts. In doing so, his or her objective is to ensure that all purchases are recorded in the proper accounting period. Once purchases have been identified, the auditor traces from the documentation related to that purchase to the Voucher Register and, ultimately, the posting in the Subsidiary Accounts Payable. For example, assume that a purchase from a particular vendor was received on December 31, 19x3 and billed by the vendor on January 5, 19x4. In this case, the purchase (and related account payable) should be recorded in 19x3.

A second method of searching for unrecorded liabilities is sending confirmations to vendors with whom the client normally does business. It is important to distinguish these confirmations from those discussed in the previous section. In the previous section, the auditor's objective was to verify that recorded accounts payable balances: (1) existed and were an obligation of the client, and (2) were stated at the proper dollar amount. For these purposes, the auditor would ordinarily focus on larger balances because of materiality considerations.

In contrast, if clients are intentionally not recording accounts payable transactions, the accounts payable balances will be understated (or zero). Therefore, when evaluating the CO assertion, the auditor should focus on smaller (or unrecorded) balances. In searching for unrecorded liabilities, the auditor will send a request for account to the following types of vendors:

▶ Vendors with whom the client has done business in the past

▶ Vendors with small (or zero) recorded balances

▶ Vendors whose account includes a larger number of transactions

A final procedure in the auditor's search for unrecorded liabilities is examining cash disbursements occurring shortly after year-end. Similar to inspecting documentation for purchases made near year-end, the auditor focuses on larger disbursements. While the client may not record a liability, this does not relieve their obligation to pay the liability; most accounts payable owed by the client at year-end will need to be paid shortly after year-end. The purpose of this procedure is to ensure that, if payments made shortly after year-end relate to goods or services received in the preceding year, the related accounts payable is recorded by the client.

As noted in Figure 13-6, the nature and extent of the auditor's search for unrecorded liabilities is influenced by the necessary level of detection risk. If the auditor is required to achieve lower levels of detection risk, he or she should perform a more extensive search for unrecorded liabilities. A more extensive search for unrecorded liabilities would involve examining documentation for a longer period of time both before and after year-end and requesting a greater number of confirmations of accounts payable. In addition, when lower levels of detection risk are required, the auditor should rely more heavily on confirmations (as opposed to internal documentation) in his or her search for unrecorded liabilities. In many cases, given the superiority of external forms of evidence (such as confirmation) as well as the fact that clients may obstruct the auditor from viewing documentation related to liabilities they are intentionally not recording, auditors will rely on confirmations in all situations.

A Schedule of Unrecorded Liabilities noted by the auditor during the examination should be prepared for inclusion in the workpapers. This schedule should indicate the name of the vendor, the date of the invoice, the date goods or services were received, the amount, and the account to be charged. In addition, any necessary adjustments to the financial statements for unrecorded liabilities should be included in this schedule. A Schedule of Unrecorded Liabilities is shown in Figure 13-10.

Performing Analytical Procedures. Like other accounts, analytical procedures are used by the auditor in his or her examination of accounts payable to verify the reasonableness of recorded amounts. Therefore, these procedures may assist the auditor in identifying fictitious transactions that have been recorded in the accounting records (the EO and RO assertions) and transactions recorded at the incorrect dollar amount (the VA assertion). Of particular importance in the examination of accounts payable, instances where the recorded amount of accounts payable are significantly *lower* than expected may indicate unrecorded accounts payable (the CO assertion).

As with other accounts, a common analytical procedure used in the examination of accounts payable is comparing the recorded balance of accounts payable (or expense associated with the accounts payable) to: (1) balances in these accounts from the prior year, or (2) budgeted or forecasted balances. In addition, the ratio of accounts payable to total liabilities or purchases can be compared to expectations through the use of analytical procedures.

Evaluating Financial Statement Presentation. The disclosures required by GAAP for accounts payable are relatively straightforward. In evaluating the PD assertion, the auditor should review these disclosures and determine that they conform with GAAP. In addition, the auditor will inquire of management to ensure that the following types of items are excluded from accounts payable:

- Accounts with affiliates, officers, shareholders, or directors
- Wages payable and deferred taxes payable
- Accounts with debit balances

D-2		Meghan's Office Products Schedule of Unrecorded Liabilities 12-31-x3		Prepared by: SAS 1-22-X4 Reviewed by: MES 1-26-X4

Document No.	Vendor	Date	Description	Amount
VO 3780	Premium Writing Instruments	12-29-x3	Purchase of writing supplies shipped FOB shipping point on 12-29-x3	1,600 ①
VO 3802	Marco's Maintenance	1-15-x4	Receipt for maintenance services from 12-15-x3 to 1-15-x4	3,600 ②

Note: Examined all Vouchers related to Receiving Reports dated from 12-27-x3 through 1-15-x4. Also examined all checks written from 1-1-x4 through 1-16-x4. No items were related to 19x3 activity with the exception of those listed above.

① Examined Vendor's Invoice and determined that item related to 19x3 activity. Propose the following adjustment (see Workpaper AJE-1 for a summary of adjustments):

    Inventory   1,600
        Accounts Payable   1,600

② Examined Vendor's Invoice and determined that a portion of the service related to 19x3 activity. Since one-half of these services related to 19x3, allocated one-half of the cost to 19x3, as follows (see Workpaper AJE-1 for a summary of adjustments):

    Maintenance Expense   1,800
        Maintenance Payable   1,800

Figure 13-10: *Workpaper for Schedule of Unrecorded Liabilities*

> **CHAPTER CHECKPOINTS**
>
> **13-19.** What procedures can be performed by the auditor in his or her search for unrecorded liabilities?
>
> **13-20.** What are some analytical procedures commonly performed for accounts payable? What result from applying analytical procedures would suggest the presence of unrecorded accounts payable?
>
> **13-21.** What types of items should ordinarily be excluded from a company's accounts payable?

ACCRUED PAYABLES AND DEFERRED ASSETS

In addition to inventory and accounts payable, two other types of balance sheet accounts exist in the Purchases and Disbursements cycle: accrued payables and deferred assets. Accrued payables are those liabilities that have been incurred for which invoices normally are not received from vendors. Examples of typical accrued payables are liabilities resulting from wages, income taxes, commissions, guarantees and warranties, and interest. Deferred assets represent assets that arise from prepayments made by the client for services to be received in the future, as rent and insurance.

Accruals and deferrals are not normally significant in amount. Therefore, the auditor will spend a limited amount of effort in this area. For both accruals and deferrals, the auditor will examine documentation related to the item and recalculate the ending balance. For example, if a client paid $120,000 for a one-year lease on October 1, 19x3, the auditor would examine the lease agreement and recalculate the allocation of the $120,000 between prepaid rent and rent expense at year-end. These procedures correspond to the EO, RO, and VA assertions. In addition, the auditor may perform analytical procedures by comparing the balances in accrual, deferral, and expense accounts to balances from prior years or budgeted or forecasted balances. As with other accounts, analytical procedures address the EO, RO, CO, and VA assertions.

An additional issue is introduced with respect to accruals. As with accounts payable, the auditor should conduct a search for unrecorded accrued liabilities (the CO assertion). Since these liabilities do not result from purchases made by the client (and are not invoiced), the auditor must use other methods to identify unrecorded accruals. Some methods used for this purpose include:

1. Many accrued liabilities are revealed by the auditor's investigation of other account balances or classes of transactions. For example, the existence of notes or bonds payable should alert the auditor about the need for an accrual of interest at year-end. In addition, if the auditor becomes aware of pension or profit-sharing plans, an accrued liability for the associated benefits should be expected as well.

2. Previous experience with the client (or the client's industry) often reveals the existence of accrued liabilities. For example, an accrual for income taxes is common for companies earning income that is subject to taxation. Also, if employees are paid on dates other than month-end, a liability for wage expense should be expected by the auditor.

3. Similar to accounts payable, cash disbursements made shortly after year end for interest, wages, bonuses, and dividends should be reviewed to determine whether they were related to liabilities that existed in the prior year.
4. As noted above, analytical procedures involving the accrual, deferral, and expense accounts may reveal the existence of unrecorded accruals. This possibility would exist when the current provision for the accrual is significantly less than the expected provision.

COST OF GOODS SOLD/PURCHASES

During his or her examination of inventories and accounts payable, the auditor has also obtained a degree of evidence regarding cost of goods sold and purchases. If the necessary level of detection risk related to these accounts is high, the auditor would normally do limited additional procedures with respect to cost of goods sold and purchases. However, in most cases, some limited tests of cost of goods sold and purchases are performed. These procedures are discussed in the remainder of this section.

Tests of the Voucher Register (Purchases Journal)

Similar to tests involving the Sales Register (discussed in Chapter 11), the auditor may perform tests of transactions recorded in the Voucher Register (or Purchases Journal). As with the tests involving the Sales Register, the scope of these tests is relatively limited unless low levels of detection risk are considered necessary. In addition, as with tests involving the Sales Register, these tests can be performed during the auditor's test of controls or as part of his or her substantive tests. These tests (and the related assertions verified through these tests) are:

1. Scanning entries in the Voucher Register for large and unusual amounts (the VA assertion)
2. Tracing from documentation representing actual purchases made by the client (the Voucher Package) to a recording in the Voucher Register (the CO and VA assertions)
3. Vouching selected entries in the Voucher Register to documentation representing actual purchases made by the client (the EO, RO, and VA assertions)

Analytical Procedures

As noted earlier in this chapter, the auditor's analytical procedures for inventory and accounts payable include several ratios that involve cost of goods sold and/or purchases. In addition to these analytical procedures, the auditor will ordinarily compare the recorded purchases or cost of goods sold in the current period with budgeted or forecasted amounts or amounts from one or more prior periods. As with other accounts, significant fluctuations revealed by analytical procedures may reflect the recording of fictitious transactions (the EO and RO assertions), the failure to record actual transactions (the CO assertion), or transactions recorded at the incorrect dollar amount (the VA assertion).

◘ Purchase Cutoff Tests

The corollary to sales cutoff tests (discussed in Chapter 11) are **purchase cutoff tests**. The primary purpose of purchase cutoff tests is to determine that all purchases made during the period (and all inventory owned by the client) are recorded in that period. Like sales cutoff tests, the basic premise underlying purchase cutoff tests is that prenumbered documents provide evidence concerning the period in which a transaction took place. In performing purchase cutoff tests, the auditor examines purchase transactions occurring near year-end (normally, a few days prior to and a few days following year-end) to verify that these transactions are recorded in the correct period. Once the auditor identifies the Receiving Report representing the last receipt of inventory in the year under audit, purchase cutoff tests are relatively straightforward. In general, as with sales cutoff tests, any Receiving Reports with a lower number than this document relate to the year under audit; any Receiving Reports with a higher number than this document correspond to the following year.

It is important to remember that purchases should be recorded when legal title passes from the seller to the buyer (the client). Thus, the terms of the shipment [Free on Board (F.O.B.) Shipping Point or F.O.B. Destination] need to be considered in the auditor's purchase cutoff tests. In particular, if the terms of the shipment are F.O.B. Shipping Point, the title to the goods (and ownership of the inventory) passes to the purchaser when the shipment is sent from the vendor. In these cases, the auditor should estimate the date of shipment based on the date of receipt by the client and the normal delivery time. Purchase cutoff tests provide the auditor with evidence that: (1) all purchases of inventory made during the year are recorded (the CO assertion), and (2) all recorded purchases of inventory occurred in the year under audit and are the property of the client (the EO and RO assertions).

CHAPTER CHECKPOINTS

13-22. Define accrued payables and deferred assets. Give some examples of each.

13-23. What are the basic audit procedures used to examine accrued payables and deferred assets?

13-24. List some procedures used by the auditor to search for unrecorded accrued payables.

13-25. What are purchase cutoff tests? What assertions are verified by performing these tests?

◉ SUMMARY OF KEY POINTS

1. In examining the two primary accounts associated with the Purchases and Disbursements cycle (inventory and accounts payable), the auditor utilizes the test of balances approach. Under this approach, the auditor identifies components of the account balance or class of transactions under examination. He or she then selects a sample of these components and performs some form of evidence-gathering procedure to verify these components. The test of balances approach

is ordinarily used when an account balance is characterized by a large number of transactions for smaller dollar amounts.

2. One of the auditor's primary substantive testing procedures related to inventory is observing the client's year-end physical inventory. Per *SAS No. 1*, the observation of inventory is a generally accepted auditing procedure. During the observation of inventory, the auditor should: (1) make and record test counts; (2) examine the use of prenumbered inventory tags; (3) watch for apparently unsalable, damaged, slow-moving, and obsolete inventory items; and (4) inquire about inventories held on consignment. The test counts made by the auditor will ultimately be agreed to quantities included in the client's Inventory Listing.

3. In addition to making test counts, the auditor also performs price tests with respect to inventory. For selected items, the auditor should verify the price shown on the client's Inventory Listing with some form of documentation (such as a Vendor's Invoice or internal cost records). When performing price tests, the auditor must also consider the client's cost flow assumption.

4. Other important substantive tests performed over inventory include: (1) confirming inventory held at external locations, (2) performing analytical procedures, (3) examining consigned inventories, (4) determining the lower of cost or market for inventories, and (5) evaluating the overall financial statement presentation of inventory.

5. Because accounts payable are a liability, an incentive exists for management to understate or omit accounts payable transactions. As a result, the auditor's primary concern in examining accounts payable is with evaluating the CO assertion. This is done by performing a search for unrecorded liabilities, the primary focus of the auditor's substantive tests of accounts payable.

6. The auditor begins his or her examination of accounts payable by obtaining a Listing of Accounts Payable from the client. A sample of recorded account balances is evaluated by examining statements received from the client's vendors. Any differences between the balances reported by the vendors and those on the Listing of Accounts Payable should be evaluated further by the auditor.

7. In searching for unrecorded liabilities, the auditor should: (1) examine documentation for purchases made near year-end, (2) obtain confirmations (or request statements) from vendors with whom the client ordinarily does business, and (3) examine cash disbursements occurring shortly after year-end. Any unrecorded liabilities detected through these procedures should be summarized in a Schedule of Unrecorded Liabilities.

8. In auditing accrued payables and deferred assets, the auditor ordinarily examines documentation relating to these items and recalculates the ending balance. Similar to the examination of accounts payable, the auditor should also evaluate the possible existence of unrecorded accrued liabilities (and unrecorded expenses).

9. Much of the auditor's work with respect to cost of goods sold and purchases is done during the audit of inventory. In examining these accounts, the auditor will perform tests of the Voucher Register, analytical procedures, and purchase cutoff tests. The purpose of purchase cutoff tests is to determine that purchases made near the end of the year are recorded in the proper accounting period.

GLOSSARY

Accrued Payables. Liabilities incurred by the client for which invoices normally are not received. Examples of accrued payables include wages payable, income taxes payable, commissions payable, guarantees and warranties payable, and interest payable.

Deferred Assets. Assets that arise from prepayments made by the client for services to be received in the future. Examples of deferred assets include prepaid rent and prepaid insurance.

Inventory Listing. A listing of quantities and costs of inventory held by the client at year-end. The Inventory Listing is the focus of the auditor's substantive testing procedures and is normally prepared by the client.

Listing of Accounts Payable. A summary (prepared by the client) of all amounts owed to vendors at year-end. The auditor uses this listing to select accounts payable for examination.

Observation of Physical Inventory. A generally accepted auditing procedure in which the auditor observes the client's physical inventory counts. During the inventory observation, the auditor should: (1) make and record test counts; (2) examine the use of prenumbered inventory tags; (3) watch for apparently unsalable, damaged, slow-moving, and obsolete items; and (4) inquire about inventories held on consignment.

Price Test. An audit procedure in which the auditor attempts to determine that the prices used to cost ending are appropriate, given the cost flow assumption used by the client. In performing price tests, the auditor compares prices from the Inventory Listing to some form of documentation of the cost of the inventory.

Purchase Cutoff Tests. Tests applied by the auditor to determine whether purchases made near year-end are recorded in the proper accounting period. Purchase cutoff tests involve identifying the Receiving Report number representing the last purchase made in the year under examination.

Schedule of Unrecorded Liabilities. A listing of all items revealed by the auditor's search for unrecorded liabilities.

Search for Unrecorded Liabilities. Procedures performed by the auditor to determine whether any unrecorded accounts payable exist at year-end. These procedures include: (1) examining documentation for purchases made near year-end, (2) obtaining confirmations (or requesting statements) from vendors with whom the client ordinarily does business, and (3) examining cash disbursements occurring shortly after year-end.

Test Counts. Counts of inventory quantities made by the auditor during the observation of the client's physical inventory. These test counts are ultimately agreed to quantities in the client's Inventory Listing.

SUMMARY OF PROFESSIONAL PRONOUNCEMENTS

Statement on Auditing Standards No. 1, "Codification of Auditing Standards and Procedures" (New York: AICPA, 1972, AU 331).

Statement on Auditing Standards No. 43, "Omnibus Statement on Auditing Standards" (New York: AICPA, 1982, AU 331.14).

Statement on Auditing Standards No. 73, "Using the Work of a Specialist" (New York: AICPA, 1994, AU 336).

QUESTIONS AND PROBLEMS

13-26. Select the **best** answer for each of the following items:

1. Which of the following is the best audit procedure for the discovery of damaged merchandise in a client's ending inventory?

   a. Compare the physical quantities of slow-moving items with corresponding quantities from the prior year.
   b. Observe merchandise and raw materials during the client's physical inventory.
   c. Review management's inventory representation letter for accuracy.
   d. Test overall fairness of inventory values by comparing the company's turnover ratio with the industry average.

2. Under which of the following circumstances would it be advisable for the auditor to confirm accounts payable with creditors?

   a. Internal control over accounts payable is adequate, and there is sufficient evidence on hand to minimize the risk of a material misstatement.
   b. Confirmation response is expected to be favorable, and accounts payable balances are of immaterial amounts.
   c. Creditor statements are **not** available, and internal control over accounts payable is unsatisfactory.
   d. The majority of accounts payable balances are with associated companies.

3. Which of the following is the most reliable audit procedure for determining the existence of unrecorded liabilities?

   a. Examine confirmation requests returned by creditors whose accounts appear on a Trial Balance of Accounts Payable.
   b. Examine unusual relationships between monthly accounts payable balances and recorded purchases.
   c. Examine a sample of Invoices dated a few days prior to and subsequent to year-end to ascertain whether they have been properly recorded.
   d. Examine a sample of cash disbursements in the period subsequent to year-end.

4. To best ascertain that a company has properly included merchandise that it owns in its ending inventory, the auditor should review and test the:

   a. Terms of the open Purchase Orders.
   b. Purchase cutoff procedures.
   c. Contractual commitments made by the Purchasing Department.
   d. Vendor Invoices received on or around year-end.

5. The primary objective of a CPA's observation of a client's physical inventory count is to:

   a. Discover whether a client has counted a particular inventory item or group of items.
   b. Obtain direct knowledge that the inventory exists and has been properly counted.
   c. Provide an appraisal of the quality of the merchandise on hand on the day of the physical count.
   d. Allow the auditor to supervise the conduct of the count so as to obtain assurance that Inventory quantities are reasonably accurate.

6. An auditor will usually agree the details of the test counts made during the observation of the physical inventory to the client's Inventory Listing. This audit procedure is undertaken to provide evidence that items physically present and observed by the auditor at the time of the physical inventory count are:

   a. Owned by the client.
   b. Not obsolete
   c. Physically present at the time of the preparation of the final Inventory Listing.
   d. Included in the final Inventory Listing.

7. Periodic or cycle counts of inventory are made at various times during the year rather than a single inventory count at year-end. Which of the following is necessary if the auditor plans to observe inventories at interim dates?

   a. Complete recounts by independent inventory teams are performed.
   b. Perpetual inventory records are maintained.
   c. Unit cost records are integrated with production accounting records.
   d. Inventory balances are rarely at low levels.

8. A client maintains perpetual inventory records in both quantities and dollars. If the assessed level of control risk is high, an auditor would probably:

   a. Increase the extent of tests of controls of the Purchases and Disbursements cycle.
   b. Request the client to schedule the physical inventory count at the end of the year.
   c. Insist that the client perform physical counts of inventory items several times during the year.
   d. Apply gross profit tests to ascertain the reasonableness of the physical counts.

9. When auditing merchandise inventory at year-end, the auditor performs a purchase cutoff test to obtain evidence that:

   a. All goods purchased before year-end are received before the physical inventory count.
   b. No goods held on consignment for customers are included in the inventory balance.
   c. No goods observed during the physical count are pledged or sold.
   d. All goods owned at year-end are included in the inventory balance.

10. The reason that making test counts of inventory does not necessarily provide the auditor with evidence regarding the rights and obligation assertion is that:

    a. The cost of the items may exceed their market value, necessitating an inventory write-down.
    b. Items on the client's premises may be held on consignment.
    c. Items owned by the client may be held by an external party, such as a public warehouse or consignee.
    d. The ending value of the inventory may not be consistent with the client's inventory cost flow assumption.

11. Liabilities that are not normally evidenced by Vendor's Invoices or other form of documentation are known as:

    a. Accounts payable.
    b. Accrued payables.
    c. Contingent liabilities.
    d. Short-term liabilities.

12. Making test counts of items recorded on a client's Inventory Listing provides the auditor with the greatest assurance regarding which assertion?

    a. Completeness.
    b. Existence or occurrence.
    c. Rights and obligations.
    d. Presentation and disclosure.
    e. Segregation of duties.

13. The auditor reviews the client's shipping and receiving procedures in connection with his or her examination of inventory:

    a. To determine that sales and purchases of inventory are properly authorized.
    b. To evaluate whether transactions are recorded in the proper period.
    c. When both functions occur in the same physical location.
    d. To determine that all goods on consignment are properly included in inventory.
    e. To evaluate the reasonableness of the cost flow assumption selected by the client.

14. If the auditor is unable to observe ending inventories due to unusual circumstances as of the balance-sheet date, the auditor would:

    a. Withdraw from the audit engagement.
    b. Issue either a qualified opinion or disclaimer of opinion, depending on the severity of the scope limitation.
    c. Issue a qualified or adverse opinion because of the failure of the financial statements to be prepared in conformity with GAAP.
    d. Attempt to satisfy him- or herself as to inventory quantities through the use of alternative procedures.
    e. Issue a disclaimer of opinion because of the existence of a severe uncertainty.

15. Which of the following would not be performed by the auditor during the observation of the client's physical inventory?

    a. Evaluating inventory for slow-moving or obsolete items.
    b. Observing the client's shipping and receiving cutoff procedures.
    c. Examining Vendor's Invoices or other forms of evidence for valuation of inventory.
    d. Making test counts and recording these test counts in the workpapers.
    e. All of the above would be performed during the auditor's observation of the client's physical inventory.

16. In which manner would the necessary level of detection risk **least** likely affect the auditor's search for unrecorded liabilities?

    a. Lower levels of detection risk would require the auditor to conduct a more extensive search for unrecorded liabilities.
    b. Lower levels of detection risk would require the auditor to examine subsequent cash disbursements for a longer period of time after year-end.
    c. Lower levels of detection risk would require the auditor to obtain evidence from external parties.
    d. Lower levels of detection risk would require the auditor to perform tests after year-end, as opposed to during an interim period.

17. Which of the following procedures would be the least effective in identifying unrecorded accounts payable?

    a. Tracing from unpaid Vouchers and Invoices to the recording in the accounting records.
    b. Examining Receiving Reports representing purchases made near year-end.
    c. Examining cash disbursements made shortly after year-end.
    d. Sending confirmations to vendors selected from the client's Listing of Accounts Payable.
    e. Reviewing Invoices received from vendors shortly after year-end.

18. Which of the following is the primary reason that accounts payable confirmations are less effective than accounts receivable confirmations?

    a. Vendors are less likely to respond to confirmations than customers.
    b. Accounts receivable normally represent a larger balance sheet total than accounts payable.
    c. Accounts receivable normally have a greater income statement effect than accounts payable.
    d. It is usually easier for the client to accumulate data related to accounts receivable than accounts payable.
    e. The auditor's objective in examining accounts receivable is more consistent with confirming these amounts.

19. As opposed to assets, the assertion of greatest interest in the auditor's examination of liabilities is the _____ assertion.

    a. Completeness
    b. Existence or occurrence
    c. Presentation and disclosure
    d. Rights and obligations
    e. Valuation or allocation

20. Which of the following conditions would ordinarily not provide the auditor with evidence regarding the need for potential write-downs of inventory:

   a. Obsolete, damaged, or slow-moving inventory noted during the observation of physical inventory.
   b. Relatively large quantities of inventory on hand at year-end.
   c. A lack of recent purchases of inventory noted during the auditor's price tests.
   d. Inventory subject to highly fluctuations because of technological obsolescence.

   (Items 1 through 9 in 13-26; AICPA Adapted)

13-27. Identify substantive tests that could be used by the auditor to verify each of the following issues related to the inventory account.

   a. The extensions (per item) on the client's Inventory Listing are accurate.
   b. Any provision for obsolescence or decline in the market value of inventories is reasonable.
   c. Inventory quantities observed by the auditor during her test counts are included in the client's Inventory Listing.
   d. The prices used by the client to cost its ending inventory are appropriate.
   e. The client's overall inventory balance and ratios involving inventory are reasonable in light of prior years and current-year expectations.
   f. All inventory owned at year-end is included in the client's Inventory Listing.
   g. Inventories included on the client's Inventory Listing that are held in a public warehouse exist and are the property of the client.
   h. No inventory on the client's premises at year-end has been sold or is being held on consignment.

13-28. Identify substantive tests that could be used by the auditor to verify each of the following issues related to accounts payable, accrued payables, and deferred assets.

   a. Totals from the client's Listing of Accounts Payable agree to the client's Trial Balance.
   b. No unrecorded accounts payable exist at year-end.
   c. Items recorded in the Voucher Register represent *bona fide* transactions.
   d. The balances in prepaid rent and rent expense at year-end are accurate.
   e. Recorded accounts payable are presented at the proper amount.
   f. No unrecorded accrued liabilities exist at year-end.
   g. The total balance in accounts payable agrees with the total of the individual vendor accounts.
   h. The accrued liability for wages payable is properly stated at year-end. The client's employees are paid on the 15th of each month, and the client has a calendar year-end.

13-29. On January 10, 19X2, you were engaged to make an examination of the financial statements of Kahl Equipment Corporation for the year ended December 31, 19X1. Kahl has sold trucks and truck parts and accessories for many years, but it has never had a financial statement audit. Kahl maintains good perpetual records for all inventories and takes a complete physical inventory each December 31.

The parts inventory account includes the $2,500 cost of obsolete parts. Kahl's executives acknowledge that these parts have been worthless for several years, but they have continued to carry the cost as an asset. The amount of $2,500 is material in relation to 19X1 net income and year-end inventories, but not material in relation to total assets or capital at December 31, 19X1.

Required:

a. List the procedures you would add to your inventory audit program for new trucks because you did not observe the physical inventory taken by Kahl Equipment Corporation as of December 31, 19X1.
b. Should the $2,500 of obsolete parts be carried in inventory as an asset? Discuss.

(AICPA Adapted)

13-30. Late in December 19X1, your CPA firm accepted an audit engagement at Rich Jewelers, Inc., a corporation that deals largely in diamonds. The corporation has retail jewelry stores in several Eastern cities and a diamond wholesale store in New York City. The wholesale store also sets the diamonds in rings and in other quality jewelry. The retail stores place orders for diamond jewelry with the wholesale store in New York City. A buyer employed by the wholesale store purchases diamonds in the New York diamond market, and the wholesale store then fills orders from the retail stores and from independent customers and maintains a substantial inventory of diamonds. The corporation values its inventory by the specific identification cost method

Assume that at the inventory date you are satisfied that Rich Jewelers, Inc., has no items left by customers for repair or sale on consignment and that no inventory owned by the corporation is in the possession of outsiders.

Required:

a. Discuss the problems the auditors should anticipate in planning for the observation of the physical inventory on this engagement because of the:

   1. Difficult locations of inventories.
   2. Nature of the inventory.

b. 1. Explain how your audit program for this inventory would be different from that used for most other inventories.
   2. Prepare an audit program for the verification of the corporation's diamond and diamond jewelry inventories, identifying any steps that you would apply only to the retail stores or to the wholesale store.

c. Assume that a shipment of diamond rings was in transit by corporate messenger from the wholesale store to a retail store on the inventory date. What additional audit steps would you take to satisfy yourself as to the gems that were in transit from the wholesale store on the inventory date?

(AICPA Adapted)

13-31. The observation of the client's physical inventory is an important aspect of a CPA's examination of financial statements.

Required:

a. What are the general objectives or purposes of the CPA's observation of the physical inventory? (Do not discuss the procedures or techniques involved in making the observation.)
b. For what purposes does the CPA make and record test counts of inventory quantities during the observation of the physical inventory? Discuss.
c. A number of companies employ outside service companies that specialize in counting, pricing, extending, and footing inventories. These service companies usually furnish a certificate attesting to the value of the inventory.

Assuming that the service company took the inventory on the balance sheet date:

1. How much reliance, if any, can the CPA place on the inventory certificate of outside specialists? Discuss.
2. What effect, if any, would the inventory certificate of outside specialists have upon the type of report the CPA would render? Discuss.
3. What reference, if any, would the CPA make to the certificate of outside specialists in the standard audit report?

(AICPA Adapted)

13-32. Coil steel constitutes one-half of the inventory of the Metal Fabricating Company. At the beginning of the year, the company installed a system to control coil steel inventory.

The coil steel is stored within the plant in a special storage area. When coils are received, a two-part tag is prepared. The tag is prenumbered; each part provides for entry of supplier's name, Receiving Report number, date received, coil weight, and description. Both parts of the tag are prepared at the time the material is received and weighed and the Receiving Report prepared. The "A" part of the tag is attached to the coil, and the "B" part of the tag is sent to the Stock Records Department (Inventory Department) with the Receiving Report. The Stock Records Department files the tags numerically by coil width and gauge. The Stock Records Department also maintains perpetual stock cards on each width and gauge by total weight; in a sense, the cards are a control record for the tags. No Material Requisitions are used by the plant, but as coils are placed into production, the "A" part of the tag is removed from the coil and sent to Stock Records as support of the Production Report, which is the basis of entries on the perpetual inventory cards.

When the "A" part of the tag is received by the Stock Records Department, it is matched with the "B" part of the tag and the "A" part is destroyed. The "B" part is stamped with the date of use, is processed, and is retained in a consumed file by width and gauge. The coils are neatly stacked and arranged, and all tags are visible.

The balance of the inventory is examined by standard procedures, and you are satisfied that it is fairly stated.

Physical inventories are taken on a cyclical basis throughout the year. About one-twelfth of the coil steel inventories are taken each month. The coil steel control account and the perpetual stock cards are adjusted as counts are made. Internal control of inventories is good in all respects.

In previous years, the client had taken a complete physical inventory of coil steel at the end of the year (the client's fiscal year ends December 31), but none is to be taken this year. You are engaged for the current audit in September and performed the audit of the financial statements last year.

Required:

Assuming that you decide to undertake some preliminary audit work before December 31, prepare programs for:

a. The verification of coil steel quantities previously inventoried during the current year.
b. Observation of physical inventories to be taken in subsequent months.

(AICPA Adapted)

13-33. Line-Rite Manufacturing Company, Inc., is a moderate-sized company that manufactures equipment for use in laying pipelines. The company has prospered in the past, gradually expanding to its present size. Recognizing a need to develop new products, if its growth is to continue, the company created an engineering research and development section. During 19X1, at a cost of $70,000, this section designed, patented, and successfully tested a new machine that greatly accelerates the laying of small-sized lines.

To adequately finance the manufacture, promotion, and sale of this new product, it has become necessary to expand the company's plant and to enlarge inventories. Required financing to accomplish this has resulted in the company engaging you in April 19X1 to examine its financial statements as of September 30, 19X1, the end of the current fiscal year. This is the company's initial audit.

In the course of your preliminary audit work, you obtain the following information:

1. The nature of the inventory and related manufacturing processes do not lend themselves well to taking a complete physical inventory at year-end or at any other given date. The company has an inventory team that counts all inventory items on a cyclical basis throughout the year. Perpetual inventory records, maintained by the Accounting Department, are adjusted to reflect the quantities on hand as determined by these counts. At year-end, an Inventory Summary is prepared from the perpetual inventory records. The quantities in this summary are subsequently valued in developing the final inventory balances.

2. The company carries a substantial parts inventory, which is used to service equipment sold to customers. Certain parts also are used in current production. The company considers any part to be obsolete only if it shows no usage or sales activity for two consecutive years. A full reserve is taken for these parts; at present, this reserve totals $10,000.

Your tests indicate that obsolescence in inventories might approximate $50,000. As part of your audit, you must deal with each of the foregoing matters.

Required:

a. With respect to inventories, define the overall problem involved in this first audit.
b. Outline a program for testing inventory quantities.
c. Enumerate and discuss the principal problems involved in inventory obsolescence for the company, assuming the amount involved was significant with respect to the company's financial statements.

(AICPA Adapted)

13-34. A processor of frozen foods carries an inventory of finished products consisting of 50 different types of items valued at approximately $2 million. About $750,000 of this value represents stock produced by the company and billed to customers prior to the audit date. This stock is being held for the customers at a monthly rental charge until they request shipment and is not separated from the company's inventory.

The company maintains separate perpetual ledgers at the plant office for both stock owned and stock being held for customers. The cost department also maintains a perpetual record of stock owned. The above perpetual records reflect quantities only.

The company does not take a complete physical inventory at any time during the year, because the temperature in the cold storage facilities is too low to allow one to spend more than fifteen minutes inside at a time. It is not considered practical to move items outside or to defreeze the cold storage facilities for the purpose of taking a physical inventory. Due to these circumstances, it is impractical to test count quantities to the extent of completely verifying specific items. The company considers as its inventory valuation at year-end the aggregate of the quantities reflected by the perpetual record of stock owned that is maintained at the plant office, priced at the lower of cost or market.

Required:

a. What are the two principal problems facing the auditor in the audit of the inventory? Discuss briefly.

b. Outline the audit steps that you would take to enable you to render an unqualified opinion with respect to the inventory. (You may omit consideration of a verification of unit prices and clerical accuracy.)

13-35. Describe the audit procedures that would generally be followed in establishing the propriety of the recorded liability for federal income taxes of an established corporation that you are auditing for the first time. Consideration should be given to the status of (a) the liability for prior years and (b) the liability arising from the current year's income.

(AICPA Adapted)

13-36. You were in the final stages of your examination of the financial statements of Ozine Corporation for the year ended December 31, 19X1, when you were consulted by the corporation's President, who believes there is no point to your examining the 19X2 Voucher Register and testing data in support of 19X2 entries. He stated that: (a) bills pertaining to 19X1 that were received too late to be included in the December Voucher Register were recorded by journal entry as of the year-end by the corporation, (b) the internal auditor made tests after the year-end, and (c) he would furnish you with a letter certifying that there were no unrecorded liabilities.

Required:

a. Should a CPA's test for unrecorded liabilities be affected by the fact that the client made a journal entry to record 19X1 bills that were received later? Explain.

b. Should a CPA's test for unrecorded liabilities be affected by the fact that a letter is obtained in which a responsible management official certifies that to the best of his or her knowledge all liabilities have been recorded? Explain.

c. Should a CPA's test for unrecorded liabilities be eliminated or reduced because of the internal audit test? Explain.

d. Assume that the corporation, which handled some government contracts, had no internal auditor but that an auditor for a federal agency spent three weeks auditing the records and was just completing her work at this time. How would the CPA's unrecorded liability test be affected by the work of the auditor for a federal agency?

e. What sources in addition to the 19X2 Voucher Register should the CPA consider to locate possible unrecorded liabilities?

(AICPA Adapted)

13-37. The Moss Company manufactures household appliances that are sold through independent franchised retail dealers. The electric motors in the appliances are guaranteed for five years from the date of sale of the appliances to the consumer. Under the guarantee, defective motors are replaced by the dealers without charge.

Inventories of replacement motors are kept in the dealers' stores and are carried at cost in Moss Company's records. When the dealer replaces a defective motor, he notifies the factory and returns the defective motor to the factory for reconditioning. After the defective motor is received by the factory, the dealer's account is credited with an agreed fee for the replacement service.

When the appliance is brought to the dealer after the guarantee period has elapsed, the dealer charges the owner for installing the new motor. The dealer notifies the factory of the installation and returns the replaced motor for reconditioning. The motor installed is then charged to the dealer's account at a price in excess of its inventory value. In this instance, to encourage the return of replaced motors, the dealer's account is credited with a nominal value far the returned motor.

Dealers submit quarterly inventory reports of the motors on hand. The reports are later verified by Factory Salesmen. Dealers are billed for inventory shortages determined by comparison of the dealers' inventory reports and the factory's perpetual records of the dealers' inventories. The dealers order additional motors as they need them. One motor is used for all appliances in a given year, but the motors are changed in basic design each model year.

The Moss Company has established an account, "Estimated Liability for Product Guarantees," in connection with the guarantees. An amount representing the estimated guarantee cost prorated per sales unit is credited to the "Estimated Liability" account for each appliance sold and the debit is charged to a provision account. The "Estimated Liability" account is debited for the service fees credited to the dealers' accounts and for the inventory cost of the motors installed under the guarantees.

The Engineering Department keeps statistical records of the number of units of each model sold in each year and the replacements that were made. The effect of improvements in design and construction is under continuous study by the Engineering Department, and the estimated guarantee cost per unit is adjusted annually on the basis of experience and improvements in design. Experience shows that, for a given motor model, the number of guarantees made good varies widely from year to year during the guarantee period, but the total number of guarantees to be made good can be reliably predicted.

Required:

a. Prepare an audit program to satisfy yourself as to the propriety of the transactions recorded in the Estimated Liability for Product Guarantees account for the year ended December 31, 19X1.
b. Prepare the worksheet format that would be used to test the adequacy of the balance of the Estimated Liability for Product Guarantees account. The worksheet column headings should describe clearly the data to be inserted in the columns.

(AICPA Adapted)

13-38. Arthur, CPA, is auditing the RCT Manufacturing Company as of February 28, 19X2. One of Arthur's initial procedures is to make overall checks of the client's financial data by reviewing significant ratios and trends so that he has a better understanding of the business and can determine where to concentrate his audit efforts.

The financial statements prepared by the client with audited 19X1 figures and preliminary 19X2 figures are presented here in condensed form.

RCT Manufacturing Company
Condensed Balance Sheets
February 28, 19X2 and 19X1

Assets	19X2	19X1
Cash	$ 12,000	$ 15,000
Accounts receivable, net	93,000	50,000
Inventory	72,000	67,000
Other current assets	5,000	6,000
Plant and equipment, net of depreciation	60,000	80,000
	$ 242,000	$ 218,000

Liabilities and Equities		
Accounts payable	$ 38,000	$ 41,000
Federal income tax payable	30,000	14,400
Long-term liabilities	20,000	40,000
Common stock	70,000	70,000
Retained earnings	84,000	52,600
	$ 242,000	$ 218,000

RCT Manufacturing Company
Condensed Income Statements
Years Ended February 28, 19X2 and 19X1

	19X2	19X1
Net sales	$1,684,000	$1,250,000
Cost of goods sold	927,000	710,000
Gross margin on sales	$ 757,000	$ 540,000
Selling and administrative expenses	682,000	504,000
Income before federal income taxes	$ 75,000	$ 36,000
Net income tax expense	30,000	14,400
Net income	$ 45,000	$ 21,600

Additional information:

a. The company has only an insignificant amount of cash sales.
b. The end of year figures are comparable to the average for each respective year.

Required:

For each year, compute the current ratio. Based on the ratio, identify and discuss audit procedures that should be included in Arthur's audit of accounts payable.

(AICPA Adapted)

13-39. Mincin, CPA, is the auditor of the Raleigh Corporation. Mincin is considering the audit work to be performed in the accounts payable area for the current year's engagement.

The prior year's workpapers show that confirmation requests were mailed to 100 of Raleigh's 1,000 suppliers. The selected suppliers were based on Mincin's sample, which was designed to select accounts with large dollar balances. A substantial number of hours were spent by Raleigh and Mincin resolving relatively minor differences between the confirmation replies and Raleigh's accounting records. Alternate audit procedures were used for those suppliers who did not respond to the confirmation requests.

Required:

a. Identify the audit objectives for accounts payable that Mincin must consider in determining the audit procedures to be used.
b. Identify situations in which Mincin should use accounts payable confirmations and discuss whether Mincin is required to use them.
c. Discuss why the use of large dollar balances as the basis for selecting accounts payable for confirmation might not be the most efficient approach, and indicate what more efficient procedures could be followed when selecting accounts payable for confirmation.

(AICPA Adapted)

13-40. Taylor, CPA, is engaged in the audit of Rex Wholesaling for the year ended December 31, 19X1. Taylor performed a proper study of the internal control relating to the purchasing, receiving, trade accounts payable, and cash disbursement cycles and has decided not to proceed with tests of controls. Based upon analytical procedures Taylor believes that the trade accounts payable balance on the balance sheet as of December 31, 19X1 may be understated.

Taylor requested and obtained a client-prepared Listing of Accounts Payable which contained the total amount owed to each vendor.

Required:

What additional substantive audit procedures should Taylor apply in examining the trade accounts payable?

(AICPA Adapted)

Learning Objectives

Study of this chapter is designed to achieve several learning objectives. After studying this chapter, you should be able to:

1. Identify the major accounts and documents existing in the Conversion cycle.
2. Illustrate how the five components of internal control are implemented in the Conversion cycle.
3. Identify specific control activities designed by companies to address financial statement assertions in the Conversion cycle.
4. Discuss the method used by companies to record transactions in the Conversion cycle.
5. Determine how auditors test control activities in the Conversion cycle.
6. Discuss the types of substantive tests performed by auditors on payroll transactions.

14

The Conversion Cycle

◉ EVALUATING INTERNAL CONTROL: THE CONVERSION CYCLE

An important area of operations for companies who produce (or manufacture) their own inventories is the Conversion cycle. The **Conversion cycle** involves the span of activities which occur from the organization's decision to produce inventory until the completion of the production process and subsequent movement of inventory to the Inventory Department (or Warehouse). The sequence of activities that take place in the Conversion cycle is summarized below in Figure 14-1.

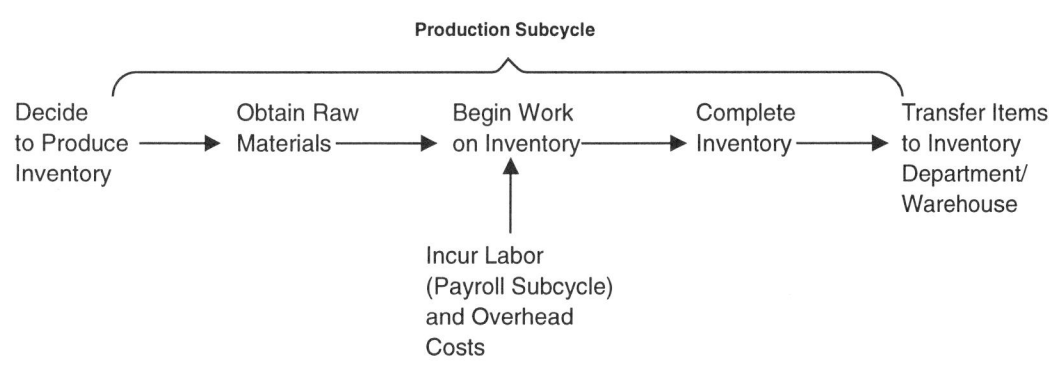

Figure 14-1: *Major Activities in the Conversion Cycle*

Figure 14-2 summarizes the two major subcycles of the Conversion cycle (the Payroll subcycle and the Production subcycle). Included in Figure 14-2 are the accounts, functions, and documents related to each of these subcycles.

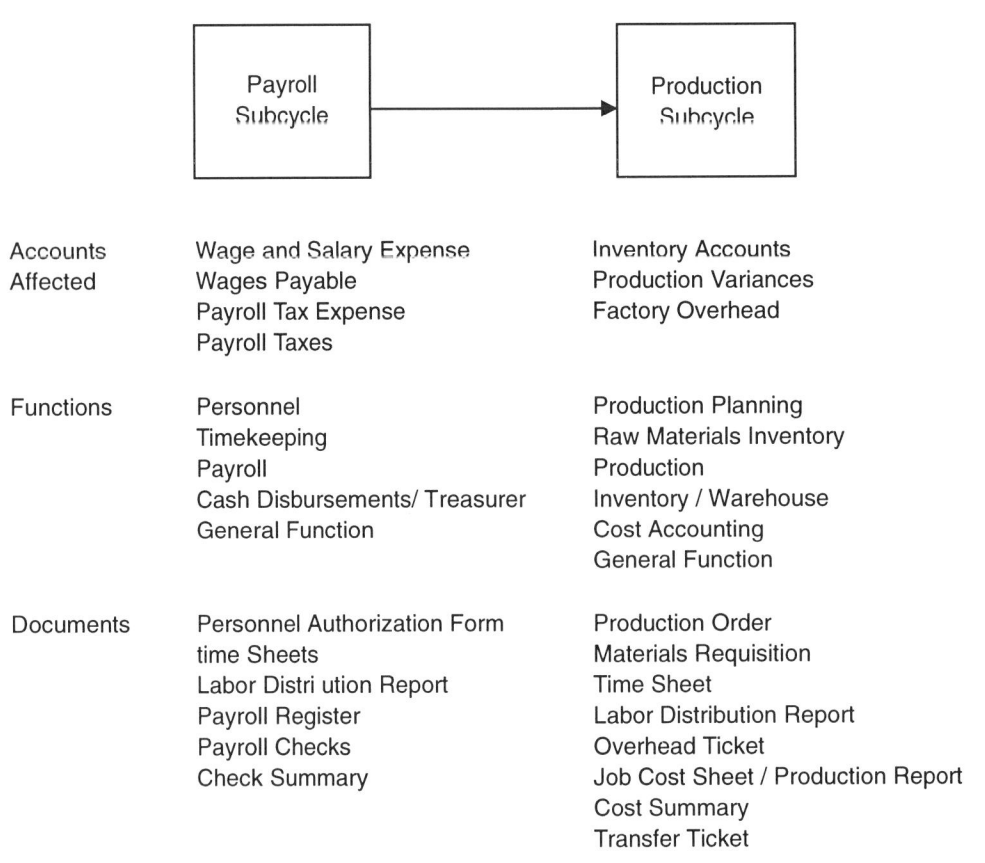

Figure 14-2: *Overview of the Conversion Cycle*

◻ Control Environment

As noted in previous chapters, the control environment is a component of internal control that is established on an overall basis within the organization. Therefore, the auditor ordinarily evaluates the control environment on an organization-wide basis and not strictly as part of any single operating cycle.

In evaluating the control environment over the Conversion cycle, the auditor would consider factors such as: (1) integrity and ethical values, (2) commitment to competence, (3) the existence of a Board of Directors and Audit Committee, (4) management's philosophy and operating style, (5) the organization structure, (6) assignment of authority and responsibility, and (7) human resource policies and practices.

Specifically related to the Conversion cycle, when considering management's philosophy and operating style, the auditor evaluates whether management takes excessive risks with respect to production and inventory decisions. Risks of this nature may include:

1. Authorizing a large number of "rush" production jobs
2. Purchasing materials from less well-known vendors to receive discounts
3. Overscheduling production resources (materials, labor, and production facilities), which may lead to tight production deadlines
4. Failing to maintain and/or replace production equipment, which may lead to breakdowns of this equipment and idle production (or downtime)

CHAPTER CHECKPOINTS

14-1. What are the major activities in the Conversion cycle?

14-2. What are the two subcycles that exist within the Conversion cycle? List the major departments/functions operating within each subcycle.

14-3. List some specific risks that relate to management's philosophy and operating style in the Conversion cycle.

◻ Risk Assessment and Control Activities: The Payroll Subcycle

Figure 14-3 summarizes the major events, functions, and documents included within the Payroll subcycle. As shown therein, five departments are involved in processing transactions in the Payroll subcycle:

1. Personnel Department
2. Timekeeping Department
3. Payroll Department
4. Cash Disbursements Department /Treasurer
5. General Function

The primary responsibilities of these departments are discussed in the remainder of this section.

Information Processing Controls

Personnel Department. The Payroll subcycle begins with the Personnel Department's receipt of a **Personnel Authorization Form** from the department hiring (for new employees) or employing (for existing employees) a particular individual (IP #1 in Figure 14-3). Personnel Authorization Forms are used to: (1) add new employees to the payroll; (2) modify payroll information (such as wage rates,

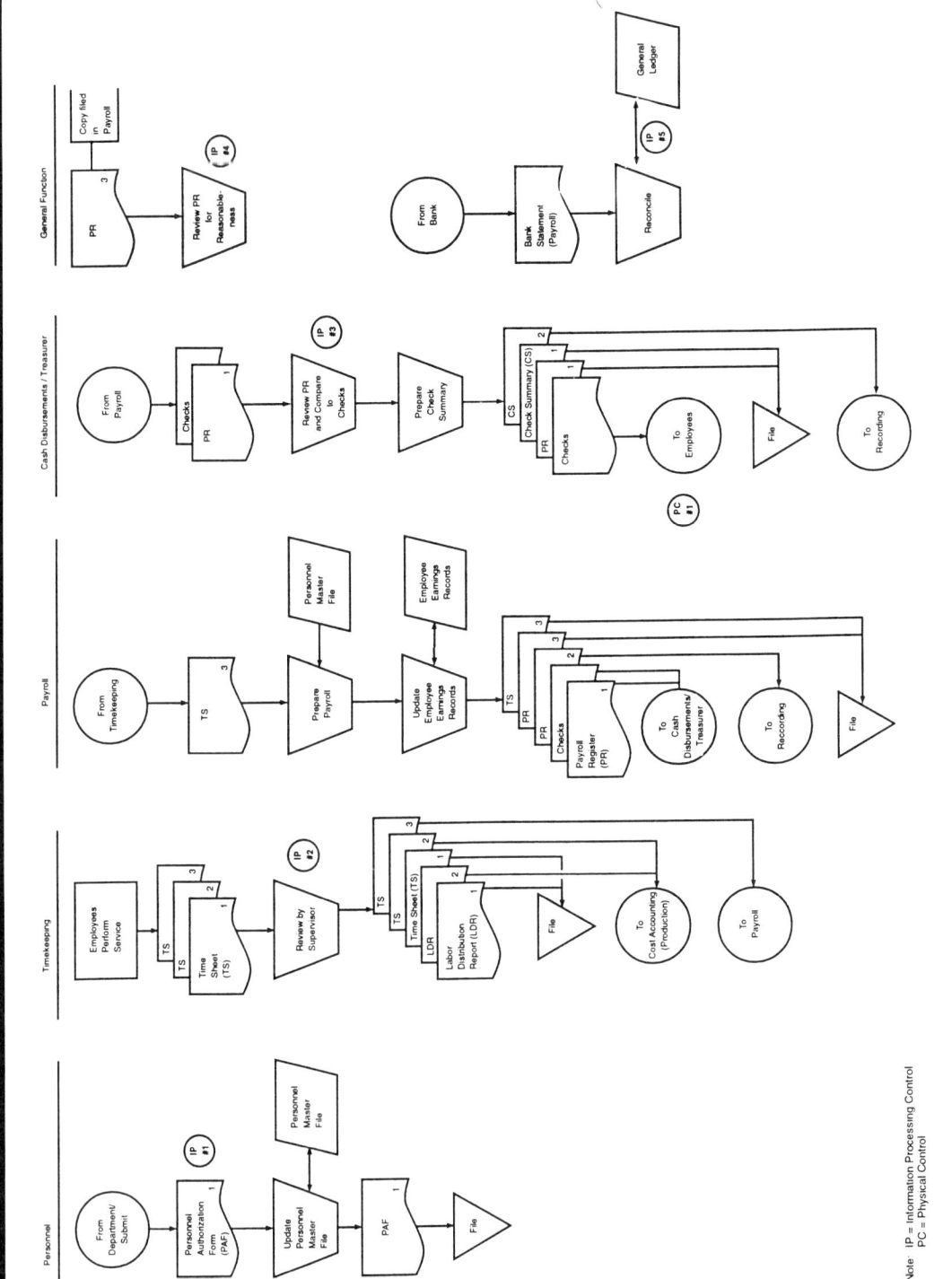

Figure 14-3: *Major Control Activities: The Payroll Subcycle*

deduction information, etc.) for existing employees; and (3) delete terminated employees from the payroll. The following information is generally included on Personnel Authorization Forms:

- Employee Names and Numbers
- Department or Subunit
- Wage Rate
- Deduction Information
- Supervisor Authorization

Once the Personnel Authorization Form has been received from a particular department, Personnel should update the Personnel Master Files to reflect the new information. The use of Personnel Authorization Forms reduces the likelihood that payroll-related payments are made to: (1) fictitious employees added to the payroll as part of a defalcation scheme, and (2) employees no longer affiliated with the company. Therefore, this control activity relates to the operating objective of internal control, since it prohibits the defalcation of assets in this manner.

In addition, the use of Personnel Authorization Forms also relates to the financial objective of internal control, since payments will: (1) only be made to employees who actually perform services for the organization (EO assertion), and (2) represent obligations of the company (RO assertion). In addition, accurately processing changes in wage rates and/or deduction information for existing employees will ensure that employees are paid (and payroll is recorded) at the proper dollar amount (VA assertion).[1]

While not shown in Figure 14-3, it is important that companies establish policies to comply with various federal and state laws regarding employment activities. For example, companies should establish hiring, promotion, and retention policies consistent with Equal Employment Opportunity Commission (EEOC) legislation and the Americans with Disabilities Act (ADA). Policies of this nature are related to the compliance objective of internal control.

Timekeeping Department. As employees perform services for the organization, they maintain a record of their time worked on **Time Sheets**. Time Sheets indicate the hours worked by a particular employee over a given time period (normally, one week). Depending upon the employee's status (hourly or salaried), Time Sheets may require employees to allocate their total hours worked based on the time spent performing various tasks. For factory employees involved with the production of inventory, employees classify their hours worked based on the production jobs (production runs) and type of services performed (direct labor or indirect labor). At the end of the designated time period, supervisory personnel will authorize the distribution of hours worked across production jobs and types of services (IP #2 in Figure 14-3). In some cases, factory employees are required to use a time clock

---

[1] Normally, the use of prenumbered documents also relates to the CO assertion. The "self-policing" nature of the payroll account suggests that employees will alert the company if they do not receive paychecks. In addition, defalcations involving payroll are perpetrated by recording fictitious transactions (EO and RO assertions) and not failing to record actual transactions (CO assertion). As a result, the CO assertion is ordinarily not considered to be an important assertion in the examination of payroll.

to record their arrival and departure from work. If so, the total hours recorded on Time Sheets will be reconciled to the totals from time clock records.

Verifying the accuracy of hours worked on Time Sheets and the distribution of those hours relates to both the operating and financial objectives of internal control. From an operating standpoint, this control activity reduces the likelihood that losses will be incurred by companies if employees record excessive hours in an effort to receive additional compensation. Also, as noted later in our discussion of the Production subcycle, ensuring accurate totals of hours worked will allow the organization to accurately identify the total costs associated with a particular production run. This information is essential in allowing the organization to establish prices for its products to earn a desired level of profit.

From a financial standpoint, verifying the total hours worked by employees allows the organization to ascertain that employees are paid (and transactions are recorded) for the correct number of hours worked (VA assertion). In addition, the supervisory review of Time Sheets may reveal instances where Time Sheets are submitted for fictitious or terminated employees (EO and RO assertions).

In addition to verifying total hours worked, supervisory personnel will also verify the distribution of hours worked over different production jobs and different types of activities. This verification ensures that labor costs are appropriately classified across different types of inventory (work-in-process and finished goods inventory) as well as different types of product costs (direct labor and overhead). Thus, this control activity also corresponds to the PD assertion. Two copies of a **Labor Distribution Report** are prepared to summarize the distribution of direct labor hours across different production jobs and types of activities.

As shown in Figure 14-3, copies of the Time Sheets are: (1) filed (by date) in Timekeeping, (2) forwarded to the Cost Accounting Department along with a copy of the Labor Distribution Report (Production subcycle), and (3) forwarded to the Payroll Department.

Payroll Department. Based on information from the employee's Personnel File (wage or salary rate, deduction information) and Time Sheet (hours worked), the Payroll Department can compute gross and net payroll information. This information is summarized in a **Payroll Register**, which serves as a record of payroll data for each employee. The following information is ordinarily included in the Payroll Register.

1. Employee Name and Number
2. Wage Rate or Salary Rate
3. Hours Worked (for Hourly Employees)
4. Gross Pay
5. Employee Deductions (FICA, State and Federal Income Tax Withholdings)
6. Net Pay
7. Employer Payroll Expenses (FICA, Unemployment Taxes)

As shown in Figure 14-3, three copies of the Payroll Register are prepared and distributed in the following manner:

- ▶ Copy 1 is forwarded to the Cash Disbursements/Treasurer function, along with **Payroll Checks** (also prepared in Payroll).

- ▶ Copy 2 is used to record expenses and liabilities related to the current period's payroll.

- ▶ Copy 3 is filed by date in the Payroll Department, along with the Time Sheets.

Along with preparing the Payroll Register, the relevant information for each employee is accumulated in that employee's **Earnings Record**. The Earnings Record provides a cumulative total of gross pay, deductions, and net pay for each employee during the year.

While not shown in Figure 14-3, an important control activity involving the Payroll Function relates to the payment of payroll taxes. Payroll taxes include: (1) the amounts withheld from employees' pay for FICA and federal and state income taxes, and (2) the employer's (company's) share of FICA and federal and state unemployment taxes. The organization should ensure that these amounts are properly withheld from their employees' pay and remitted to the proper authorities on a timely basis to avoid penalties and interest payments. Thus, this control activity is related to the operating and compliance objectives of internal control.

CHAPTER CHECKPOINTS

14-4. What is a Personnel Authorization Form? How does this document relate to the objectives of internal control?

14-5. What information is ordinarily included in the Time Sheets completed by employees? How are these Time Sheets reviewed by supervisory personnel?

14-6. What information is necessary for the Payroll Department to process and prepare the payroll?

14-7. What information is included in the Payroll Register? How are the copies of the Payroll Register distributed throughout the organization?

Cash Disbursements Department/Treasurer. As shown in Figure 14-3, a copy of the Payroll Register and the Payroll Checks are sent from the Payroll Department to the Cash Disbursements Department. Cash Disbursements (or the Treasurer) should compare the amount and names from the Payroll Checks to the Payroll Register prior to signing the checks (IP #3 in Figure 14-3). This comparison is similar to that performed for checks made payable to vendors for purchases on account (see the Purchases and Disbursements cycle in Chapter 12). Comparing information from the Payroll Register to Payroll Checks relates to the financial objective of internal control, since checks will be prepared (and recorded) at the proper dollar amount (VA assertion). Once this comparison has been performed, a **Check Summary** is prepared that lists the individual Payroll Checks and the total amount paid. A copy of the Check Summary will be used to record the disbursement for payroll along with a reduction of the corresponding liability, similar to other cash disbursements transactions (see Chapter 12).

Once Payroll Checks have been compared in the above manner, they are signed by designated officers or employees of the organization in Cash Disbursements (normally, the Treasurer). As with Checks prepared to vendors, Payroll Checks can be signed manually or through the use of stamped signatures (known as signature plates). If signature plates are used, care must be taken to restrict employee access to the signature plates.

After Payroll Checks have been signed, these Checks should be either mailed or distributed to employees. As discussed in a later subsection, physical controls should be implemented over Payroll Checks to address both the operating and financial objectives of internal control.

General Function. Two important control activities are performed by the General Function. One advantage associated with payroll is that it is a "self-policing" account. That is, employees will generally inform the organization if their pay is incorrectly calculated (particularly if their pay is lower than the true amount!). While recalculation of the entire Payroll Register is too time-consuming to be practical for most organizations, an important control activity requires an employee not involved in the payroll preparation process to review the Payroll Register for reasonableness (IP #4 in Figure 14-3). Doing so reduces the likelihood that payroll will be recorded at the incorrect dollar amount, which corresponds to the VA assertion. In addition, a review of the Payroll Register may uncover payroll transactions for fictitious or terminated employees (EO and RO assertions).

Finally, most companies operate their payroll activities through a separate (imprest) bank account. Similar to other subcycles discussed in previous chapters (such as Cash Receipts in Chapter 10 and Cash Disbursements in Chapter 12), the General Function should reconcile bank statements to the cash records maintained by the company (IP #5 in Figure 14-3). As with previous bank reconciliations, this control activity allows the company to determine that: (1) all cash transactions have been recorded (CO assertion), (2) recorded cash transactions actually occurred and are the rights of the company (EO and RO assertions), and (3) cash transactions have been recorded at the proper dollar amount (VA assertion).

Segregation of Duties Controls. The segregation of duties in the Payroll subcycle (as reflected in Figure 14-3) are summarized below.

- ▶ Authorization: Hiring Department and Personnel Department
- ▶ Custody: Cash Disbursements/Treasurer
- ▶ Recording: Payroll and General Accounting

As in other subcycles discussed throughout this text, segregation of duties reduces the opportunity for the theft or defalcation of assets. Thus, these controls relate to the operating objective of internal control. In addition, from a financial standpoint, this control activity reduces the likelihood that fictitious transactions are recorded in the accounting records (EO and RO assertions) in an effort to conceal the theft or defalcation of assets. (Recall from footnote 1 that defalcation schemes cannot be perpetrated in payroll by failing to record transactions, the CO assertion).

Physical Controls. The primary concern with respect to physical control over assets in the Payroll subcycle involves Payroll Checks (PC #1 in Figure 14-3). While the introduction of direct deposit of

Payroll Checks into employees' personal bank accounts has made the distribution of Payroll Checks fairly routine, four important control activities related to Payroll Checks are:

1. Payroll Checks and signature plates used to sign Payroll Checks should be kept in a secure location with restricted access.
2. Payroll Checks should be distributed by a person or persons not involved in processing or recording payroll.
3. Payroll Checks should be distributed only to employees who present proper identification.
4. Unclaimed Payroll Checks should be stored in a secure location in the Treasurer's office.

Physical controls over Payroll Checks relate to both the operating and financial objectives of internal control. From an operating standpoint, these controls reduce the likelihood of losses resulting from preparing Payroll Checks to fictitious or terminated employees as part of a defalcation scheme. From a financial perspective, these control activities ensure that all Payroll Checks (and, thus, recorded payroll transactions) only reflect payments made for services actually rendered to the organization (EO and RO assertions).

Performance Review Controls. Recall that performance reviews involve management's comparison of current year data to: (1) data from prior years, or (2) budgeted or forecasted data for the current year. The use of performance reviews in the Payroll subcycle is rather limited, since any large variations in payroll-related expenses are identified through determining production variances. This type of performance review is discussed in the following section.

PAYROLL DEFALCATIONS

An internal auditor for an unnamed university noticed something peculiar when he reviewed canceled scholarship checks issued to students: these checks had the second endorsement of the Chairperson or Secretary of an academic department. While the auditor was told that this endorsement was done to ease check-cashing at local banks and to avoid having the student pay a check-cashing fee, in actuality these checks were issued to students who were not enrolled at the university or eligible for scholarships. Once issued, they were then cashed by the university employees whose endorsement appeared on the checks. The students later confirmed the defalcation by noting that the endorsements on the scholarship checks were not their own.[2]

A payroll assistant for an unnamed company was responsible for keying payroll hours from Time Sheets into a computerized payroll file with no review or balancing performed on the assistant's work. In addition, this assistant was also responsible for receiving, sorting, and distributing payroll checks. This company employed a large number of part-time student interns who had frequent periods of inactivity. The incompatible duties allowed the assistant to enter fictitious hours for the interns during their periods of inactivity and intercept the Paychecks in the interns' absence. The assistant was able to embezzle $40,000 before the defalcation scheme was detected.[3]

Summary of Control Activities: The Payroll Subcycle. Figure 14-4 summarizes the various control activities included in the Payroll subcycle. Included in this summary are the relevant objectives of these control activities, methods that can be used by the auditor to test the operating effectiveness of these control activities (tests of controls), and the financial statement assertions addressed by these control activities.

CHAPTER CHECKPOINTS

14-8. When is the Check Summary prepared? How is this summary used in the recording process?

14-9. What are some of the controls that should be observed in distributing Payroll Checks to employees? How do these control relate to the objectives of internal control?

14-10. What two types of comparisons are performed by the General Function in the Payroll subcycle?

14-11. How are the appropriate segregation of duties maintained in the Payroll subcycle?

---

[2] "Payroll Defalcation," *Internal Auditor* (June 1993), 72.

[3] Courtenay Thompson, "Endorsement Review," *Internal Auditor* (April 1993), 60.

◻ Risk Assessment and Control Activities: The Production Subcycle

The basic production process (the Production subcycle) involves the following six departments:

1. Production Planning Department
2. Raw Materials Inventory Department
3. Production Department
4. Inventory Department/Warehouse
5. Cost Accounting Department
6. General Function

Figure 14-5 provides an overview of the major events, functions, and documents included within the Production subcycle. Also included in Figure 14-5 are many of the control activities that are implemented within the Production subcycle. The information in Figure 14-5 is discussed in more detail below.

Information Processing Controls

Production Planning Department. The Production subcycle begins with the company's decision to begin a production run. For companies that produce inventory made to customer specifications, that decision begins with the receipt of a customer order. For other companies, this decision is initiated by anticipated customer demand and current inventory levels. An important control activity related to the production decision is that all production of inventory is properly authorized. This is ordinarily accomplished through the preparation of a **Production Order** (IP #6 in Figure 14-5). The Production Order is a document that describes the quantity and type of inventory to be produced. In addition, the Production Order will include a particular job number assigned by the company to allow the organization to accumulate production costs with that job.

Once the production run has been approved (through the preparation of a Production Order), the Production Planning Department also prepares a **Materials Requisition**. The Materials Requisition is a summary of the types and quantities of raw materials needed for a given Production Order. These quantities are ordinarily based on production standards established by the company. Copies of the Materials Requisition are sent to the Production Department and Raw Materials Inventory Department (or Raw Materials Warehouse).

The authorization of production through the preparation of Production Orders and Materials Requisitions relates to both the operating and financial objectives of internal control. From an operating standpoint, authorization of production is important to ensure that the organization maintains adequate quantities of inventory for sale to its customers. However, care should also be taken so that excessive quantities of inventory are not held by the company. Recall from our discussion in Chapter 12 (The Purchases and Disbursements Cycle) that excessive inventories result in an opportunity cost to the organization, since funds invested in inventories could be used to earn a return from being invested in other areas.

The use of Production Orders and Materials Requisitions also addresses the financial objective of internal control. As with transactions in other subcycles, the use of formal documents to authorize transactions reduces the likelihood that employees attempt to conceal defalcation of assets by: (1) recording fictitious transactions (EO assertion), or (2) not recording legitimate transactions (CO asser-

Ref.	Control Activity		Objective(s) of Control Activity	Auditor Test(s) of Control Activity	Assertions				
					EO	RO	CO	VA	PD
IP 1	Personnel Authorization Forms should be used to authorize personnel-related transactions	O:	Reduces losses from payments made to fictitious or terminated employees	Inspect the use of Personnel Authorization Forms	x	x		x	
		F:	Reduces the likelihood that payroll transactions will be recorded: (1) for fictitious or terminated employees, or (2) using inaccurate wage rates and/or deduction information						
IP 2	Supervisory personnel should review Time Sheets and verify the distribution of hours worked on various jobs	O:	Reduces losses resulting from payments made to: (1) employees recording excessive hours worked, and (2) fictitious or terminated employees	Inspect Time Sheets for indications of authorization by supervisory personnel	x	x		x	x
		O:	Reduces losses from failing to consider total production costs in billing customer for inventory						
		F:	Reduces the likelihood that: (1) payroll transactions will be recorded for fictitious or terminated employees, (2) payroll transactions will be recorded based on an incorrect number of hours worked, and (3) labor costs will be incorrectly classified						
IP 3	Cash Disbursements/Treasurer should review the Payroll Register and compare it to the Payroll Checks	F:	Reduces the likelihood that payroll transactions will be recorded at incorrect dollar amounts	Inspect Payroll Register for evidence of review and comparison				x	
IP 4	The General Function should review the Payroll Register for reasonableness	O:	Reduces losses from payments made to fictitious or terminated employees.	Inspect Payroll Register for evidence of review	x	x		x	
		F:	Reduces the likelihood that payroll transactions: (1) will be recorded at incorrect dollar amounts, and (2) will be recorded for fictitious or terminated employees						
IP 5	Personnel independent of payroll processing should prepare monthly Bank Reconciliations	F:	Reduces the likelihood that: (1) payroll disbursement transactions will be recorded at the incorrect dollar amount, (2) fictitious payroll disbursement transactions will be recorded, and (3) payroll disbursement transactions will not be recorded	Inspect Bank Reconciliations prepared by client personnel Reperform Bank Reconciliations	x	x	x	x	
SD	Appropriate segregation of duties should be established and maintained in the Payroll subcycle	O:	Reduces losses from defalcation schemes resulting from the ability of employees to participate in incompatible functions	Observe segregation of duties Inquire about segregation of duties	x	x			
		F:	Reduces the likelihood that payroll transactions will be recorded for fictitious or terminated employees						

Figure 14-4: *Major Control Activities: The Payroll Subcycle*

Reference	Objectives of Control Activity	Control Activities	Assertions				
			EO	RO	CO	VA	PD
PC1	O: Reduces losses from preparing Payroll Checks to fictitious or terminated employees F: Reduces the likelihood that payroll transactions will be recorded for services not received by the company	Physical controls should be established over Payroll Checks and the distribution of Payroll Checks	Observe/inspect physical controls over Payroll Checks Observe the distribution of Payroll Checks Inquire about the procedures used to distribute Payroll Checks	x		x		

Note:

Reference

IP = Information Processing Control
SD = Segregation of Duties Control
PC = Physical Control

Objectives of Control Activity

O = Operating Objective
F = Financial Objective

Assertions

EO = Existence or occurrence
RO = Rights and obligations
CO = Completeness
VA = Valuation or allocation
PD = Presentation and disclosure

* As discussed in the text, the CO assertion is generally not of concern in the Payroll subcycle

Figure 14-4 *continued*

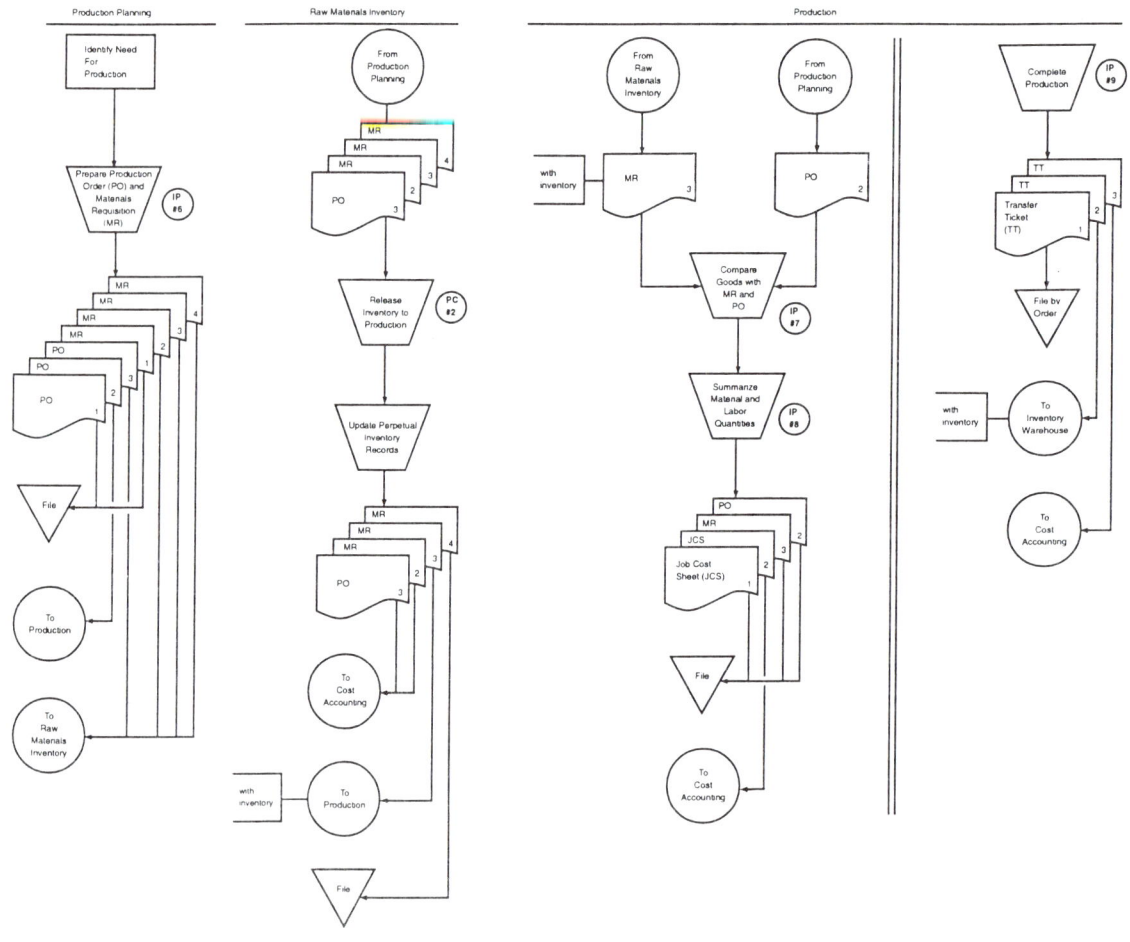

Figure 14-5: *Major Control Activities: The Production Sybcycle*

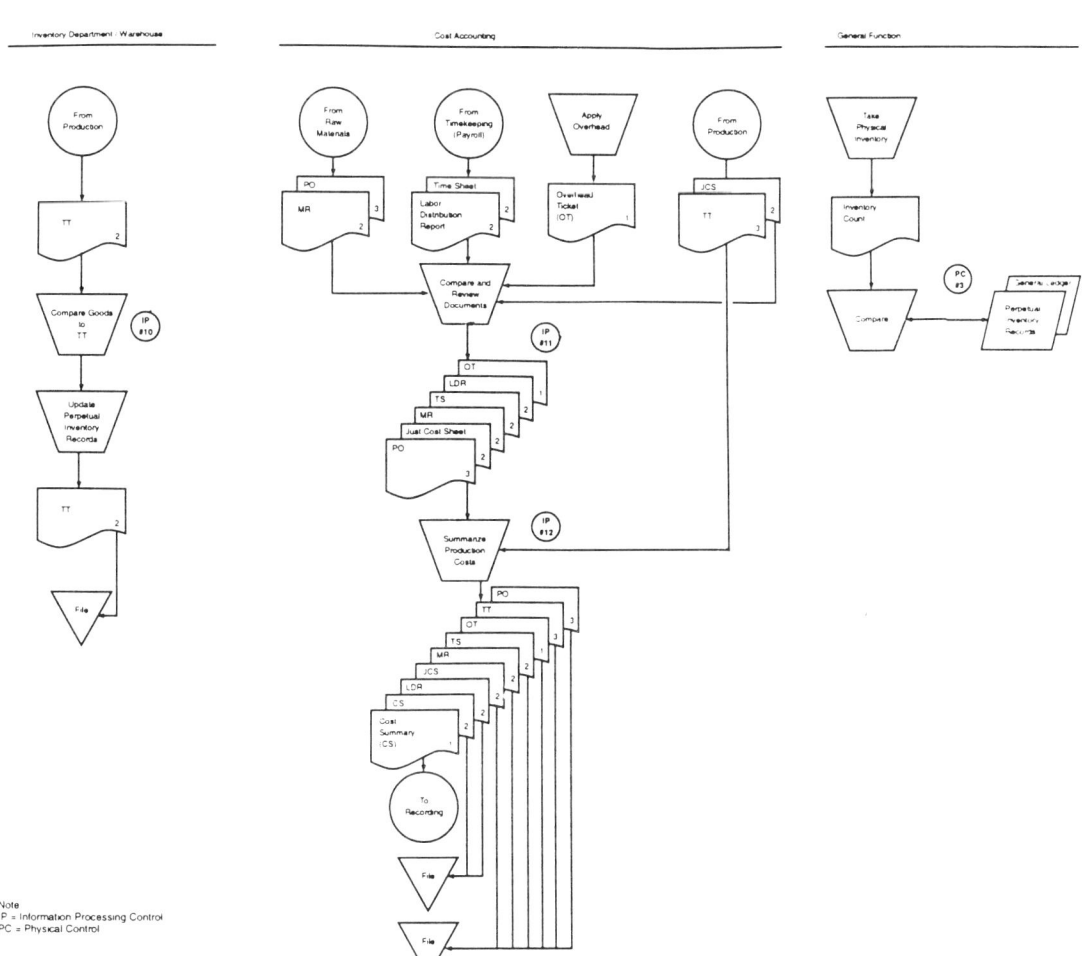

Figure 14-5: *continued*

14 / The Conversion Cycle

tion).[4] Also, the use of prenumbered documents and timely accounting for the numerical sequence of these documents will allow the organization to identify any transactions that were not recorded on an unintentional basis (CO assertion).

Raw Materials Inventory Department. Based on the Materials Requisition, the Raw Materials Inventory Department issues the appropriate materials to the Production Department (PC #2 in Figure 14-5). This control activity is a physical control and is discussed in a later subsection. Upon release of raw materials inventory to Production, the Raw Materials Inventory Department should sign or initial copies of the Materials Requisition and update its perpetual inventory records. The three copies of the Materials Requisition are distributed as follows:

- ▶ Copy filed (by date) in the Raw Materials Inventory Department
- ▶ Copy provided to the Production Department (along with the items)
- ▶ Copy forwarded to Cost Accounting (along with the Production Order) to record the transfer of costs from raw materials inventory to work-in-process inventory

An important control related to the Raw Materials Inventory Department not shown in Figure 14-5 is ensuring that sufficient quantities of raw materials inventory are maintained to allow production to continue without interruption. Recall the trade-offs between maintaining insufficient inventories (losses caused by downtimes or idle production facilities) and excessive inventories (opportunity costs of funds invested in inventories). As noted in our discussion of the Production Planning Function, an important control activity is that the organization carefully monitor its inventory balances (including raw materials inventory).

Production Department. The production process ordinarily begins with the receipt of raw materials inventory from the Raw Materials Inventory Department. As shown in Figure 14-5, the Production Department should inspect and count the raw materials inventory upon receipt. These counts are then compared to information on the Production Order (received from the Production Planning Department) and Materials Requisition (received from the Raw Materials Inventory Department) (IP #7 in Figure 14-5). This control activity parallels the receipt of inventory ordered from external vendors in the Purchases and Disbursements cycle (see Chapter 12). The count and inspection of goods in this manner is associated with the operating objective of internal control, since it reduces the likelihood of losses associated with the theft or defalcation of raw materials inventories during their transfer from Raw Materials Inventory to Production. In addition, by verifying quantities of raw materials inventory, the Production Department can ensure that transfers of raw materials inventory are recorded at the proper quantities (VA assertion). Thus, this control activity also relates to the financial objective of internal control.

---

[4] In previous subcycles, the use of formalized documents also influenced the RO assertion, since recording a fictitious transaction (EO assertion) gave rise to an asset or liability that was not the right or the obligation of the company (RO assertion). However, recording fictitious production transactions results in transferring inventory from one classification (*e.g.*, raw materials inventory) to another (*e.g.*, work-in-process inventory). Thus, on an overall basis, the RO assertion is not of particular importance in the Production subcycle.

As production continues, the organization accumulates the: (1) total quantities of direct materials used, and (2) total direct labor hours worked on a particular production job. These quantities are accumulated using a **Job Cost Sheet** (for companies producing small quantities of heterogenous items in a job-order cost system) or a **Production Report** (for companies producing large quantities of homogenous items in a process cost system) (IP #8 in Figure 14-5). Regardless of whether companies record production costs at actual or standard costs, it is important that the costs of production are accurately recorded. One copy of the Job Cost Sheet/Production Report is filed (by order) in the Production Department. The second copy of this document is forwarded to the Cost Accounting Department, who applies overhead costs to each job and determines the total production cost associated with each job (as represented by the Job Cost Sheet).[5]

The use of formal documentation to record the actual quantities of direct materials and direct labor required to manufacture a given production order addresses the operating objective of internal control, since it allows the organization to identify the total costs associated with a particular production run. This information is essential in allowing the organization to establish prices for its products to allow it to earn a desired level of profit. In addition, information about the quantities of direct materials and direct labor also allows the organization to calculate production variances to identify areas of inefficiency in the production process. From a financial standpoint, like other documents in the Production subcycle, the use of formalized, prenumbered documents also addresses the EO and CO assertions.

When inventory is completed, the items are transferred to the Inventory Department (or Warehouse). Effective internal control dictates that the organization prepare formal documentation to evidence the transfer of goods. The document prepared in this circumstance is a **Transfer Ticket** (IP #9 in Figure 14-5). The Transfer Ticket serves as a record of the goods completed in the Production Department and later transferred to the Inventory Department (or Warehouse). As shown in Figure 14-5, copies of the Transfer Ticket are distributed as follows:

- ▶ Copy filed in the Production Department (by order)
- ▶ Copy provided to the Inventory Department/Warehouse (along with items)
- ▶ Copy forwarded to Cost Accounting to transfer costs from work-in-process inventory to finished goods inventory

The Transfer Ticket somewhat parallels the Materials Requisition prepared for the transfer of raw materials to production. Like Materials Requisitions, Transfer Tickets serve as a control if inventory becomes lost or stolen during transfer. Thus, the preparation of Transfer Tickets relates to the operating objective of internal control, since it reduces the likelihood of losses caused by the theft or defalcation of inventory. In addition, like other documentation discussed in the Production subcycle, the use of formal documentation reduces the likelihood that fictitious transactions are recorded in the accounting records (EO assertion) or actual transactions are not recorded, either intentionally or unintentionally (CO assertion).

---

[5] Under a true standard costing system, the costs of production are based on standard costs and quantities. However, information regarding actual costs and quantities is important, as this information allows production variances (which are eventually used to adjust the standard costs recorded by the company) to be accurately determined.

One other control activity related to the organization's production process that is not reflected in Figure 14-5 relates to monitoring the organization's production process and products to ensure that they comply with any applicable federal regulations. For example, some production processes result in the emission of pollutants or other type of contaminants into the environment. While this is normally beyond the scope of a financial statement audit, instances of environmental contamination may ultimately expose the company to future liabilities. Thus, monitoring the production process for this purpose relates to the compliance and operating objectives of internal control.

CHAPTER CHECKPOINTS

14-12. What document(s) are prepared in Production Planning upon the authorization of production? What is the purpose of each document?

14-13. How does the use of a Materials Requisition address the financial objective of internal control?

14-14. What control activities are performed within the Production Department?

14-15. What document should be prepared to record transfers of inventory to the Inventory Department/Warehouse upon its completion?

Inventory Department/Warehouse. Upon receipt of the finished goods inventory and Transfer Ticket from the Production Department, the Inventory Department/Warehouse should inspect and count the inventory. These counts are then compared to information on the Transfer Ticket (IP #10 in Figure 14-5), similar to the comparison performed in the Production Department for the transfer of raw materials inventory. As with the transfer of raw materials inventory, this control activity relates to both the operating and financial (specifically, the VA assertion) objectives of internal control. Once the items have been transferred, the Inventory Department/Warehouse updates its perpetual inventory records to record the receipt of inventory.

Cost Accounting Department. The Cost Accounting Department is responsible for accumulating production costs with individual jobs (or production runs) and distributing those costs over the appropriate balance sheet and income statement accounts. Upon receipt of the Job Cost Sheet from the Production Department, Cost Accounting applies overhead to the production job using the appropriate basis (e.g., direct labor hours, direct labor costs, raw materials costs) and the predetermined overhead rate. The overhead costs applied to production are recorded on both the Job Cost Sheet and an **Overhead Ticket**. Then, information on the Job Cost Sheet is compared as follows (see IP #11 in Figure 14-5).

- The quantity of raw materials is compared to the Materials Requisition (which is received from Raw Materials Inventory).

- The quantity of direct labor hours is compared to **Time Sheets and Labor Distribution Reports** (which are received from the Timekeeping Department from the Payroll subcycle).

- Applied overhead costs applied are compared to the Overhead Ticket.

Comparing the information from the Job Cost Sheet to supporting documentation addresses both the financial and operating objectives of internal control. As noted previously for Production Orders, the use of formal documentation to authorize and record transactions reduces the likelihood that employees attempt to conceal defalcation of assets by: (1) recording fictitious transactions (EO assertion), or (2) not recording legitimate transactions (CO assertion). In addition, verifying the quantities of raw materials, direct labor hours, and applied overhead costs relates to the VA assertion.[6] Finally, by ascertaining that production costs are correctly distributed across production jobs (and categories of inventory), this comparison also addresses the PD assertion.

The comparisons made in IP #11 also correspond to the operating objective of internal control, since they allow the organization to identify the total costs associated with a particular production run. This information is essential in allowing the organization to establish prices for its products to allow it to earn a desired level of profit. In addition, verifying information about the quantities of direct materials and direct labor also allows the organization to calculate production variances to identify areas of inefficiency in the production process.

Once the production costs have been accumulated with inventory in the above manner, the total production costs for a given period of time will be summarized in a **Cost Summary** (IP #12 in Figure 14-5). In addition, any costs associated with goods completed during the period (as evidenced by a Transfer Ticket) will also be included in the Cost Summary. A copy of the Cost Summary is forwarded to General Accounting. Since this summary will be used to distribute the production costs incurred by a company over the various balance sheet accounts, this control ensures that production costs are accurately recorded (VA assertion) and properly classified across the various accounts (PD assertion).

General Function. Figure 14-5 reveals that the General Function should periodically make physical inventory counts and reconcile these counts to the company's perpetual inventory records (PC #3 in Figure 14-5). This control activity is discussed in more detail later in this section.

Segregation of Duties Controls. The segregation of duties in the Production subcycle (as reflected in Figure 14-5) are summarized below.

- Authorization: Production Planning
- Custody: Raw Materials Inventory Department, Production Department, and Inventory Warehouse
- Recording: Cost Accounting and General Accounting

As in other subcycles discussed throughout this text, segregation of duties reduces the opportunity for the theft or defalcation of assets. Thus, from a financial standpoint, this control activity reduces the likelihood that fictitious transactions are recorded in the accounting records (EO assertion) or actual transactions are intentionally not recorded (CO assertion). (Recall that the RO assertion is unaffected by recording fictitious production transactions).

---

[6] While this comparison does not affect the initial recording in a standard costing system, it does impact the determination of production variances and the eventual adjustment of the accounting records to reflect actual (not standard) costs of production. Therefore, to the extent that it allows production variances to be accurately calculated, this control activity affects the VA assertion.

Physical Controls. The primary asset in the Production subcycle over which physical controls must be established is inventory. As shown in Figure 14-5, physical controls over inventory begin with the release of raw materials inventory to production (PC #2 in Figure 14-5). This control is similar in nature to the release of inventory to the Shipping Department in the Revenue Cycle (see Chapter 10). Recall that this control activity relates to two objectives of internal control. First, requiring a Materials Requisition prior to the release of raw materials inventory reduces the possibility that inventory is released for unauthorized purposes as part of a defalcation scheme (the operating objective of internal control). Second, as with Production Orders, the use of formal documents to authorize production transactions also relates to the EO and CO assertions (the financial objective of internal control).

A second physical control illustrated in Figure 14-5 is the reconciliation of physical inventory counts to perpetual inventory records by the General Function. This reconciliation is similar in nature to that established in the Purchases and Disbursements cycle (see Chapter 12) but is performed for all classes of inventory (raw materials, work-in-process, and finished goods).[7] As before, this control activity reduces the likelihood that: (1) fictitious production transactions are recorded (EO assertion), and (2) actual production transactions are not recorded (CO assertion).

Three other important control activities that relate to physical controls over inventory include:

1. Restricting access to inventories by keeping them in a secured, locked location
2. Keeping documents (Production Orders, Materials Requisitions, Transfer Tickets) that provide access to inventories in a secured location
3. Using Transfer Tickets to record the movement of inventory as it passes through various stages of the production process (IP #9 in Figure 14-5)

As in other subcycles discussed throughout this text, physical controls reduce the opportunity for the theft or defalcation of assets. Thus, these controls relate to the operating objective of internal control. From a financial standpoint, this control activity reduces the likelihood that fictitious transactions are recorded in the accounting records (EO assertion) or actual transactions are intentionally not recorded (CO assertion). (Recall that the RO assertion is unaffected by recording fictitious production transactions).

Performance Review Controls. The final category of control activity is performance reviews. In a manufacturing environment, the primary method used to evaluate performance is establishing manufacturing standards for materials, labor, and overhead costs. The variance of actual manufacturing costs from these standards should be periodically reviewed, with any large variances (both favorable and unfavorable) followed up by management. This review may uncover the presence of fictitious transactions (EO assertion), unrecorded transactions (CO assertion), or transactions recorded at the incorrect dollar amount (VA assertion).

In addition to examining large production variances, it is also important that the performance standards themselves be periodically reviewed to ensure their reasonableness.

---

[7] Technically, performing this control activity for the company's finished goods inventories would fall under the Purchases and Disbursements cycle. However, since it is unlikely that companies would perform reconciliations of physical inventories for some classes of inventory and not others, it is also mentioned in our discussion in this chapter.

Summary of Control Activities: The Production Subcycle. Figure 14-6 summarizes the various control activities included in the Production subcycle. Included in this summary are the relevant objectives of these control activities, methods that can be used by the auditor to test the operating effectiveness of these control activities (tests of controls), and the financial statement assertions addressed by these control activities.

CHAPTER CHECKPOINTS

14-16. What documents are used by Cost Accounting to accumulate production costs with inventory jobs? What is the source of each of these documents?

14-17. What is a Cost Summary? How does this document relate to the financial objective of internal control?

14-18. What control activit(ies) should be performed by the General Function in the Production subcycle?

14-19. Briefly describe the segregation of duties in the Production subcycle. How does this segregation of duties affect the financial objective of internal control?

14-20. List some important physical controls in the Production subcycle. How do these controls affect the financial objective of internal control?

14-21. How are performance reviews utilized in the Production subcycle? How do these reviews affect the financial objective of internal control?

◻ Information and Communication

As noted in our discussion of previous operating cycles, the auditor's primary concern with respect to the information and communication component of internal control is the company's **accounting system**. Figure 14-7 summarizes the documentation used to record transactions in the Conversion cycle.[8]

Most organizations utilize standard costing systems in recording their Conversion cycle transactions. Under standard costing systems, the costs associated with manufacturing inventory (raw materials, direct labor, and overhead costs) are initially recorded at the expected (or standard) costs of production and not actual costs. The actual production costs are then recorded as they are incurred; at this point, any differences between the standard costs and actual costs represent production variances that are eventually closed to cost of goods sold (if they are not material) or apportioned between work-in-process inventory, finished goods inventory, and cost of goods sold (if the variances are material).

---

[8] Our discussion of the accounting system focuses on recording the aggregate standard and actual production costs. Recording production costs on a job-by-job basis would be performed by Cost Accounting and is beyond the scope of this text.

Ref.	Control Activity	Objective(s) of Control Activity	Auditor Test(s) of Control Activity	EO	RO	CO	VA	PD
IP 6	Production runs should be authorized through the preparation of prenumbered Production Orders and Materials Requisitions	O: Reduces losses from having excessive inventory or inadequate inventory F: Reduces the likelihood that: (1) fictitious production transactions will be recorded, and (2) actual production transactions will not be recorded	Inspect the use of prenumbered Production Orders and Materials Requisitions	x		x		
IP 7	Production should inspect and count raw materials inventory and compare counts to the Production Order and Materials Requisition	O: Reduces losses resulting from theft or misappropriation of raw materials inventories F: Reduces the likelihood that transfers of raw materials inventory will be recorded at the incorrect quantities	Inspect copies of the Materials Requisition for evidence of comparison				x	
IP 8	Production should summarize materials and labor quantities on Job Cost Sheets (or Production Reports)	O: Reduces losses from failing to consider total production costs in billing customer for inventory O: Allows the organization to calculate production variances for use in identifying areas of inefficiency F: Reduces the likelihood that: (1) fictitious production transactions will be recorded, and (2) actual production transactions will not be recorded	Inspect the use of Job Cost Sheets or Production Reports	x		x		
IP 9	Transfer of items to the Inventory Department/Warehouse should be evidenced by a prenumbered Transfer Ticket	O: Reduces losses from the theft or misappropriation of inventories F: Reduces the likelihood that: (1) fictitious transfers of inventory will be recorded, and (2) actual transfers of inventory will not be recorded	Inspect the use of prenumbered Transfer Tickets	x		x		
IP 10	Upon transfer of items, the Inventory Warehouse should inspect and count goods and compare quantities to the Transfer Ticket	O: Reduces losses from the theft or misappropriation of inventories F: Reduces the likelihood that transfers of inventory will be recorded at incorrect quantities	Inspect copies of the Transfer Ticket for evidence of comparison				x	

Figure 14-6: *Major Control Activities: The Production Subcycle*

Code	Control		Description	Test					
IP 11	Cost Accounting compares and reviews documentation related to production	O:	Reduces losses from failing to consider total production costs in billing customer for inventory	Inspect Job Cost Sheets and supporting documents for evidence of comparison	X				X	X
		O:	Allows the organization to calculate production variances for use in identifying areas of inefficiency							
		F:	Reduces the likelihood that: (1) fictitious production transactions will be recorded, (2) actual production transactions will not be recorded, (3) production transactions will be recorded at incorrect dollar amounts, and (4) production costs will be associated with the incorrect job							
IP 12	Cost Accounting summarizes production costs using a Cost Summary	F:	Reduces the likelihood that production costs will be recorded at incorrect dollar amounts and in incorrect accounts	Inspect use of Cost Summaries					X	X
SD	Appropriate segregation of duties should be established and maintained in the Production subcycle	O:	Reduces losses from having the ability to participate in incompatible functions	Observe segregation of duties	X	X				
		F:	Reduces the likelihood that: (1) fictitious production transactions will be recorded, and (2) actual production transactions will not be recorded	Inquire about segregation of duties						
PC 2	Raw Materials Inventory should not release raw materials to the Production Department without a Materials Requisition	O:	Reduces losses resulting from defalcation schemes involving unauthorized production transactions	Observe the release of inventory to the Production Department	X	X				
		F:	Reduces the likelihood that: (1) fictitious transfers of inventory will be recorded, and (2) actual transfers of inventory will not be recorded	Inspect Materials Requisitions for indication of release of inventory to the Production Department						
PC 3	Physical inventories should be periodically compared to perpetual inventory records, with any differences investigated by management	O:	Reduces losses from theft or misappropriation of inventories	Inspect evidence of comparison of physical inventories to perpetual inventory records	X	X				
		F:	Reduces the likelihood that: (1) fictitious production transactions will be recorded, and (2) actual production transactions will not be recorded							
PC	Physical controls should be established over inventories	O:	Reduces losses from theft of inventories	Observe/inspect physical controls over inventories	X	X				
		F:	Reduces the likelihood that: (1) fictitious production transactions will be recorded, and (2) actual production transactions will not be recorded	Inquire of management about physical controls over inventories						
PR	Through performance reviews, analyze variances of actual production costs from standard production costs	O:	Allows inefficiencies in the production process to be identified and corrected	Inspect documentary evidence of performance reviews	X	X			X	X
		F:	Large variances may result from: (1) the recording of fictitious production transactions, (2) the failure to record all production transactions, or (3) recording production transactions at the incorrect dollar amounts	Inquire about performance reviews						

Figure 14-6 *continued*

Note:

Reference

IP = Information Processing Control
SD = Segregation of Duties Control
PC = Physical Control
PR = Performance Review Control

Objectives of Control Activity

O = Operating Objective
F = Financial Objective

Assertions

EO = Existence or occurrence
RO = Rights and obligations
CO = Completeness
VA = Valuation or allocation
PD = Presentation and disclosure

* As discussed in the text, the RO assertion is generally not of concern in the Production subcycle

Figure 14-6: *continued*

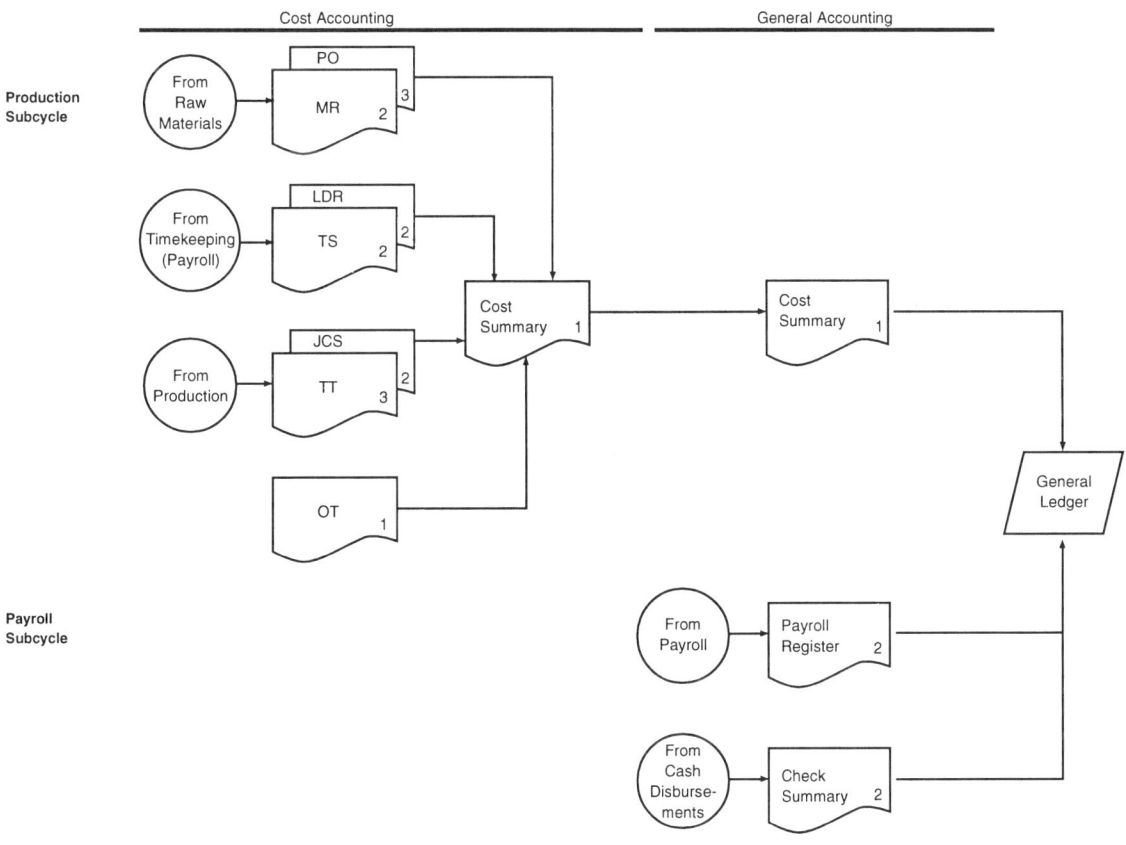

Figure 14-7: *Information and Communication: The Conversion Cycle*

The following steps summarize the recording process for the Conversion subcycle.

1. After verifying the information contained in the Job Cost Sheets received from the Production Department, Cost Accounting summarizes the total production costs in a Cost Summary. Using this summary, the following journal entries would be made ("S" denotes standard costs):

Work-in-Process Inventory	XXX (S)	
Raw Materials Inventory		XXX (S)
Wages Payable		XXX (S)
Overhead Applied		XXX (S)
Finished Goods Inventory	XXX (S)	
Work-in-Process Inventory		XXX (S)

2. As actual production costs are incurred, they are recorded in the accounting records using the appropriate documentation. As these costs differ from standard costs, production variances are recorded to reflect these differences. Using the Materials Requisitions to determine the quantity of raw materials actually used, the following entry would be made for raw materials costs ("S" denotes standard costs and "A" denotes actual costs):

Raw Materials Inventory	XXX (S)	
Production Variances	XXX	
Production Variances		XXX
Raw Materials Inventory		XXX (A)

Using the Payroll Register to record actual direct labor costs, the following entry would be made:

Wage and Salary Expense	XXX (A)	
Payroll Tax Expense[9]	XXX (A)	
Wages Payable	XXX (S)	
Production Variances	XXX	
Production Variances		XXX
Payroll Taxes Payable		XXX (A)
Wages Payable		XXX (A)

Finally, actual overhead costs (for indirect labor, depreciation, and utilities expenses associated with production) are summarized as follows:

Overhead Applied	XXX (S)	
Production Variances	XXX	
Production Variances		XXX
Miscellaneous Credits		XXX (A)

In each of the above entries, the initial credit for standard production costs is offset and the actual production costs are recorded. Any differences between these two amounts is recorded in the production variance account(s).

---

[9] These payroll taxes include the company's share of FICA, company's payroll taxes for federal and state unemployment taxes, and the amounts withheld from the employees' pay for FICA and federal income taxes. In most standard costing systems, payroll taxes are included as part of the standard direct labor costs.

The accounting system depicted above includes the following control activities (some of these have been addressed in our discussion of the subcycles:

- Using prenumbered documents and periodically accounting for the numerical sequence of these documents (CO assertion)
- Using formalized documentation for all entries (EO and VA assertions)
- Agreeing detailed documentation to departmental summaries (EO, CO, and VA assertions)
- Reconciling totals from departmental summaries to postings in journals and ledgers (VA and PD assertions)

◻ Monitoring

The final component of internal control is monitoring. **Monitoring** involves the evaluation of the effectiveness of internal controls on either an ongoing basis or as a separate evaluation of internal control. Three examples of ongoing monitoring activities in the Conversion cycle are management examination and follow-up regarding:

1. Customers' complaints regarding product quality
2. Large variances between actual and standard production costs
3. Discrepancies reported by employees regarding their Payroll Checks

In addition to these ongoing monitoring activities, separate evaluations of internal control over Conversion cycle transactions may be conducted by: (1) the company's internal auditors, (2) other external auditors, or (3) the same external auditor in prior years. In his or her consideration of internal control, the auditor should evaluate any deficiencies reported during these separate evaluations as well as any corrective actions taken by management. In addition to previous examinations of internal control by internal and external auditors, the auditor should consider any communications between the company and governmental agencies regarding problems with the reporting and payment of payroll taxes.

CHAPTER CHECKPOINTS

14-22. What are the major documents and departmental summaries used to record transactions in the Conversion cycle?

14-23. List some of the major monitoring activities that take place in the Conversion cycle.

◉ SUBSTANTIVE TESTS OF INVENTORY BALANCES

The auditor's substantive tests of inventory balances were previously discussed in Chapter 13 (The Purchases and Disbursements Cycle: Substantive Tests). It is important to note that these tests generally apply to both purchased inventory (as discussed in Chapter 13) and manufactured inventory (as discussed in this chapter).

To illustrate, recall that an important substantive test in the auditor's examination of inventory is observation of physical inventories. As noted in Chapter 13, observation of physical inventories primarily provides the auditor with assurance regarding the EO assertion. In the Conversion cycle, the auditor would examine control activities to determine the extent to which these activities reduce levels of control risk for the EO assertion. As shown in Figure 14-6, these control activities would include:

▶ The use of appropriate documentation, such as Production Orders (IP #6), Job Cost Sheets (IP #8), and Transfer Tickets (IP #9)

▶ Comparisons and reviews of production documentation (IP #11)

▶ Periodic comparison of physical inventories and perpetual inventory records (PC #3)

▶ Physical controls over inventories

▶ Appropriate segregation of duties over production transactions

▶ Analysis of production variances through performance reviews

After examining these control activities, the auditor would determine the nature, timing, and extent of his or her substantive tests. Figure 14-8 summarizes how different levels of control risk would affect the auditor's observation of physical inventory counts.

	Higher Control Risk (Lower Detection Risk)	Lower Control Risk (Higher Detection Risk)
Nature	No effect on test counts	No effect on test counts
Timing	Perform test counts at year-end	Perform test counts during the interim period
Extent	Perform and record a larger number of test counts	Perform and record a smaller number of test counts

Figure 14-8: *Effect of Internal Control on Inventory Observation Procedures*

One additional complication introduced when considering the inventory held by a manufacturing company is that inventory is in different stages of completion. To ensure that the inventory is properly presented in the company's financial statements and footnotes accompanying the financial statements, the auditor should evaluate the allocation of total inventory costs across the three major categories of inventory (raw materials inventory, work-in-process inventory, and finished goods inventory). This test provides the auditor with assurance about the PD assertion.

◉ SUBSTANTIVE TESTS OF PAYROLL TRANSACTIONS

◻ Inherent and Control Risk for Payroll Transactions

As noted previously in this chapter, payroll is a "self-policing" account, since employees will ordinarily notify the company if their payroll information is inaccurate. However, the fact that payroll involves cash (a highly liquid asset) introduces some concerns with respect to the recording of payroll transactions. In considering inherent risk over payroll transactions, the auditor has three primary concerns with respect to payroll. These concerns are that payroll-related payments are:

1. Processed and prepared for fictitious employees (EO assertion).
2. Processed using wage rates higher than those authorized (VA assertion).
3. Processed for hours not worked by employees (EO assertion).

Therefore, the inherent risk for the EO and VA assertions is considered to be relatively high. In response to this high level of inherent risk, the auditor ordinarily examines control activities implemented to reduce the risk related to these assertions. As discussed earlier in this chapter, important control activities related to the EO and VA assertions include (see Figure 14-4):

▶ Formal documentation for hiring employees and changing payroll information (IP #1)

▶ Formal documentation for recording attendance data (*e.g.*, hours worked) and supervisory approval of attendance data (IP #2)

▶ Implementing physical controls over the distribution of paychecks and handling of unclaimed paychecks (PC #1)

Based on the auditor's assessment of control risk, he or she determines the appropriate level of detection risk, which represents the nature, timing, and extent of substantive tests. While the primary tests performed by the auditor for payroll transactions are analytical procedures involving payroll expense amounts, some detailed tests of payroll may be considered necessary, particularly when control risk over payroll is high. The effect of control risk on the auditor's substantive tests over payroll transactions is summarized in Figure 14-9.

	Higher Control Risk (Lower Detection Risk)	Lower Control Risk (Higher Detection Risk)
Nature	Perform payroll tests designed to identify fictitious employees included in the payroll	Do not perform payroll tests designed to identify fictitious employees included in the payroll (or perform these tests on a limited basis)
Timing	No effect on timing of payroll tests	No effect on timing of payroll tests
Extent	Perform more extensive detailed tests of payroll	Perform less extensive detailed tests of payroll

Figure 14-9: *Effect of Internal Control on Substantive Tests of Payroll*

◻ Detection Risk (Substantive Tests) for Payroll Transactions

Figure 14-10 summarizes the major substantive tests over payroll transactions. The major categories of substantive tests shown in Figure 14-10 are discussed in the remainder of this section.

Testing the Payroll Register. In cases where internal control over payroll transactions is relatively ineffective (that is, high levels of control risk), the auditor will perform relatively extensive tests of the Payroll Register. However, some tests of this nature are ordinarily performed in most audits. Figure 14-11 illustrates a sample workpaper that summarizes some of the more common tests performed on information contained in the Payroll Register. The auditor begins by selecting a sample of employees and verifying their payroll information for a specified period. The basic tests reflected in Figure 14-11 are summarized below.

1. For hours worked, the auditor verifies information from the Payroll Register with approved Time Sheets. This procedure is illustrated by the tickmark "N" in Figure 14-11. Note that, for salaried employees, no verification of hours worked is necessary.

2. Information on the employees' pay rate is corroborated by examining the Personnel Authorization Forms contained in the employees' personnel files. This test is summarized in tickmark "✗".

3. Based on the hours worked and pay rates, the auditor recalculates the employees' gross pay. For salaried employees, the auditor merely agrees the employees' gross pay to a contract or other salary agreement contained in their personnel files (see tickmark "1").

4. Based on the gross pay, number of exemptions claimed by employees, and statutory FICA rates, the auditor recalculates employee withholdings (see tickmarks "2" and "3" in Figure 14-11). Any other withholdings (for retirement savings and other purposes) can also be verified through reference to information contained in the employees' personnel files.

5. Finally, net pay can be calculated as gross pay minus withholdings. The Payroll Register is then footed (tickmark "F") and cross-footed (tickmark "CF").

Procedure	Classification	Assertion(s)				
		EO	RO	CO	VA	PD
1. Obtain a copy of the Payroll Register from the client. For a sample of entries in the Payroll Register:						
a. Verify information for hours worked to approved Time Sheets	Inspect Documents	x	x		x	
b. Verify information for pay rates to approved Personnel Authorization Forms	Inspect Documents				x	
c. Recalculate gross pay, deductions, and net pay	Recalculation				x	
2. Perform analytical procedures over payroll expense amounts and accrued payrolls	Analytical Procedures	x	x	x	x	
3. Recalculate payroll accruals at year-end	Recalculation				x	
4. Verify officers' compensation	Inspect Documents	x	x	x	x	x
5. Perform other payroll tests designed to identify fictitious employees	Inspect Documents Observation	x	x			

Figure 14-10: *Major Substantive Tests: Payroll Transactions*

By verifying hours worked, the auditor obtains assurance that entries in the Payroll Register represent actual hours worked by employees. In addition, this procedure would provide the auditor with assurance that payroll transactions were not processed for fictitious employees as part of a defalcation scheme (EO and RO assertions). In addition, by verifying that employees are paid for the correct number of hours worked, the auditor has also gathered evidence that payroll transactions are recorded at the proper dollar amount (VA assertion). Verifying the pay rate (Step 1(b) in Figure 14-10) and recalculating gross pay, withholdings, and net pay (Step 1(c) in Figure 14-10) primarily allow the auditor to determine that payroll transactions are recorded at the proper dollar amount (VA assertion).

Performing Analytical Procedures. Analytical procedures performed on payroll balances normally compare the current year's payroll expense to: (1) the prior year's payroll expense, and (2) budgeted payroll expense. In addition, the auditor should use analytical procedures to evaluate the reasonableness of accruals for payroll liabilities at year-end. Large differences revealed by analytical procedures may represent fictitious transactions that have been recorded in the accounting records (EO and RO assertions), unrecorded transactions (CO assertion), and transactions recorded at the incorrect dollar amount (VA assertion).

Recalculating Payroll Accruals. Unless companies pay their employees at the end of each month, a liability for wages and salaries earned (but not paid) will exist at the end of the year. Also, accruals for payroll-related items such as commissions, vacation pay, bonuses, and stock-based compensation may also be made, depending upon the companies' compensation structure. The auditor should independently verify management's calculation of these items. This test provides evidence with respect to the VA assertion.

Prepared by: JRS 1-15-X4
Reviewed by: MES 1-19-X4

Payroll Test
Meghan's Office Products
12-31-x3

Employee Name	Employee Number	Hours Worked	Pay Rate	Gross Pay	Federal Withholding	FICA Withholding	Net Pay
A. Hale	112-91-6724	40.0 ①	20.00 ②	800 ⓡ	81 ③	42 ④	677 Ⓒ︎Ⓕ
H. Maurice	234-11-6835	36.0	25.00	900	52	30	818
B. Fishkin	459-03-0320	40.0	26.00	1,040	68	38	934
J. Meghan	886-27-1283	N/A	N/A	1,720 Ⓢ	161	51	1,508
.		.	.	.	.	.	.
.		.	.	.	.	.	.
G. Pasewark	156-94-2395	35.0 ①	14.00 ②	490 ⓡ	58	39	393
				272,800	37,163	19,474	216,163
				Ⓕ	Ⓕ	Ⓕ	ⓅⓇ

③ Recalculated deductions through verification of withholding tables and signed W-4 forms. No exceptions noted.

④ Recalculated based on statutory rate. No exceptions noted.

Ⓕ Footed
Ⓒ︎Ⓕ Cross-Footed
ⓅⓇ Agreed to posting in Payroll Register.
① Compared hours worked to those recorded on Time Ticket. No exceptions noted.
② Vouched to wage rate contained in employee's Personnel File. No exceptions noted.
ⓡ Recalculated based on hours worked and wage rate. No exceptions noted.
Ⓢ Employee is salaried. Vouched gross pay to contract contained in employee's Personnel File.

Figure 14-11: Workpaper for Tests of Payroll

Verifying Officers' Compensation. As part of the tests of the Payroll Register, we noted that the auditor should select a sample of employees and verify their payroll data. Apart from this test, the auditor should verify the level of compensation paid to officers of the company through reference to authorization by the Board of Directors or other written source (e.g., contracts). Officers' compensation is particularly important from an audit standpoint because it is usually a relatively large expense. In addition, publicly-traded companies must disclose their officers' compensation in 10-K reports filed with the SEC. These tests provide evidence that the compensation is paid to a *bona fide* employee (EO and RO assertions), is recorded at the proper dollar amount (VA assertion), and is properly disclosed in the financial statements and footnotes accompanying the financial statements (PD assertion). In addition, by reviewing the Board of Directors' authorization and contracts, the auditor can ensure that all compensation paid to officers is recorded (CO assertion).

Performing Other Payroll Tests. When internal control over payroll is ineffective, the auditor ordinarily performs various tests to investigate the possibility that fictitious employees have been added to the payroll as part of an employee defalcation scheme. These tests include:

- Vouching employee names and numbers from the Payroll Register to information in the personnel files
- Tracing recent terminations to the Payroll Register
- Examining endorsements of canceled Payroll Checks
- Observing the distribution of Payroll Checks

Because the purpose of these tests is to detect the existence of fictitious employees on the payroll, they provide the auditor assurance with respect to the EO and RO assertions.

CHAPTER CHECKPOINTS

14-24. What additional consideration(s) are necessary in the audit of a manufacturing company's inventory balance compared to the audit of a retail company's inventory balance?

14-25. What are the primary assertion(s) of concern to the auditor in his or her examination of payroll transactions? How does the effectiveness of the company's control activities related to these assertions influence the auditor's substantive testing procedures?

14-26. List some of the procedures performed by the auditor during his or her tests of the Payroll Register.

14-27. What types of "other" payroll tests can be performed to determine the possible existence of payments to fictitious employees?

Appendix

Computerized Processing in the Conversion Cycle[10]

◉ PAYROLL SUBCYCLE

Figure 14-12 provides an overview of computerized processing of transactions in the Payroll subcycle. As in previous chapters, to focus on differences between the manual processing discussed in the text of this chapter and computerized processing, many of the detailed control activities and the ultimate disposition of the documents are not shown in Figure 14-12. In reviewing this figure, two important points should be remembered:

1. Computerized processing environments utilize the same documents, journals, and ledgers as manual processing environments.
2. Many of the control activities associated with manual processing environments also exist in computerized processing environments.

Prior to preparing payroll in a computerized processing environment, the personnel records should be updated to reflect any personnel-related changes (adding employees to the payroll, removing employees from the payroll, or changing information for employees on the payroll). As in the manual processing system described in the text of the chapter, these changes are evidenced by Personnel Authorization Forms prepared by a department or subunit within the company. In a computerized system, information from Personnel Authorization Forms is entered into a **Personnel Changes File** (Step 1 in Figure 14-12). Prior to input, the following control totals may be determined:

▶ Total number of employee change records (record count)

---

[10] All Chapter Checkpoints and End of Chapter Items related to the Appendix are marked with an asterisk (*).

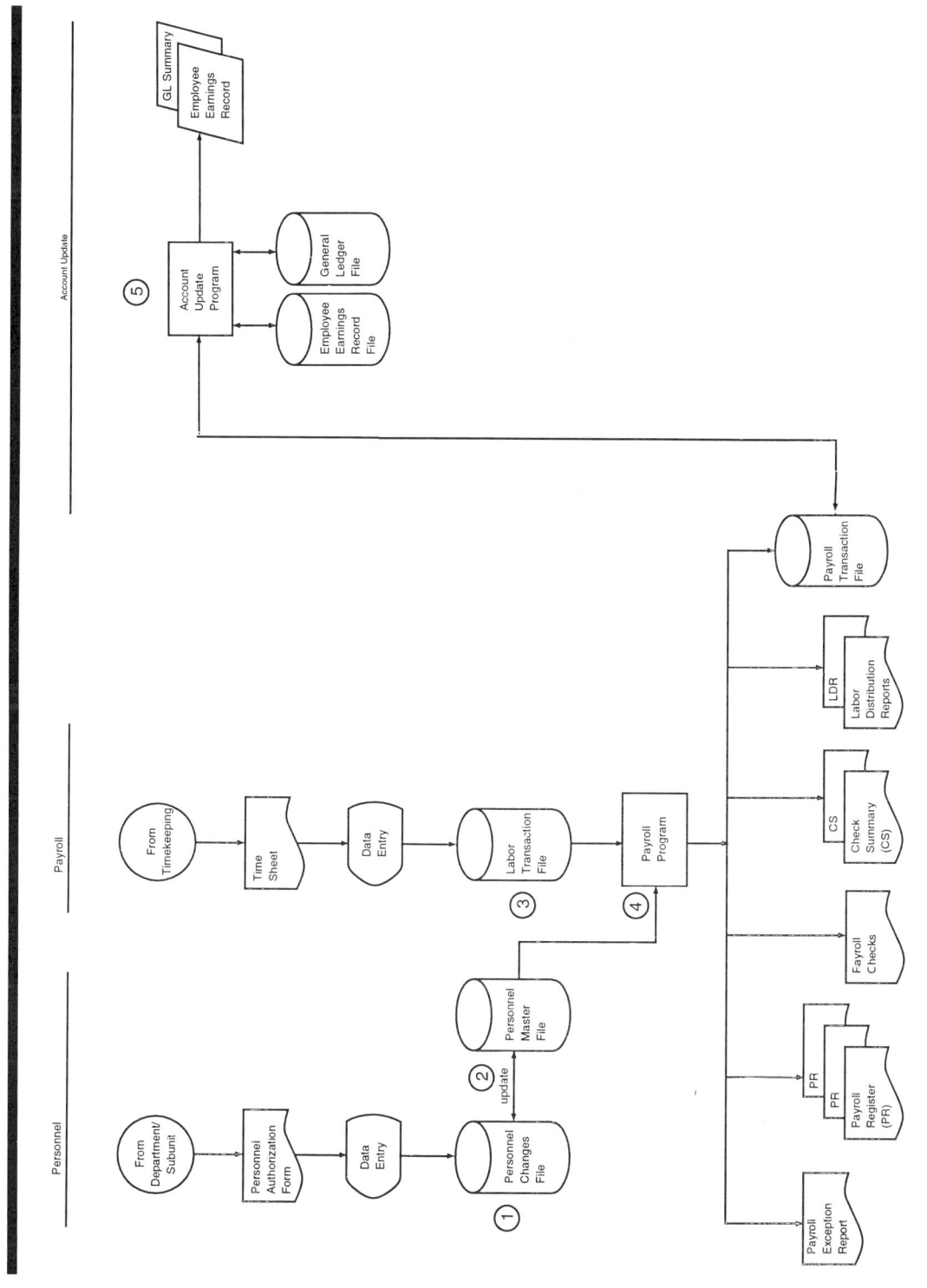

Figure 14-12: *Computerized Processing: The Payroll Subcycle*

14 / The Conversion Cycle

- Sum of employee numbers (hash totals)
- Sum of pay rates and deduction information (batch totals)

These changes are used to update the **Personnel Master File** (Step 2 in Figure 14-12) prior to payroll processing.

Once personnel records have been updated, the company processes its payroll at the end of its pay period. As in the manual processing system described in the chapter, employees record their hours worked and distribute these hours worked over various production and other activities using Time Sheets, which are approved by their supervisor. Once this information has been approved, relevant information (employee number, total hours worked, and hours worked by production job and activity) is entered into a **Labor Transaction File** (Step 3 in Figure 14-12). The Labor Transaction File represents a summary of the labor activity over a specified period of time. The following control totals are normally determined prior to input:

- Total number of employee labor records (record count)
- Sum of employee numbers (hash totals)
- Sum of total hours worked (batch totals)

Once the Labor Transaction File has been created, the **Payroll Program** accesses the Personnel Master File. Important information in the Personnel Master File includes the employees' pay rate and deduction information. Using this information, along with the hours worked from the Labor Transaction File, the Payroll Program calculates the employees' gross pay, total payroll-related deductions and net pay; in addition, the employers' share of payroll-related deductions and payroll taxes are determined (Step 4 in Figure 14-12). The documents/files that are created by the Payroll Program are as follows:

- Payroll Register
- Payroll Checks
- Check Summary
- Labor Distribution Report
- Payroll Exception Report
- Payroll Transaction File

The first four documents noted above are identical to those prepared in the manual processing system discussed in the text of the chapter and are used in a similar manner. The fifth document (Payroll Exception Report) is a listing of all employees having incomplete records in the Payroll Master File; these exceptions may represent situations where a Time Sheet was submitted for a fictitious or terminated employee. The **Payroll Transaction File** includes important payroll information on an employee-by-employee basis. This file is used to update both the employee earnings records and the accounting records (through the **Account Update Program**) (Step 5 in Figure 14-12).

Figure 14-13 summarizes the primary elements of computerized processing in the Payroll subcycle.

Function	Inputs	Processing	Outputs
Personnel	Personnel Changes File Personnel Master File	Updating (Access Personnel Master File by Employee Number)	Updated Personnel Master File
Payroll	Personnel Master File Labor Transaction File	Payroll Program (Access Personnel Master File by Employee Number)	Payroll Register Payroll Checks Check Summary Labor Distribution Report Payroll Exception Report Payroll Transaction File
Account Update	Payroll Transaction File General Ledger File Employee Earnings Record File	Account Update Program (Access Payroll Transaction File on Periodic Basis)	General Ledger Summary Updated General Ledger File Employee Earnings Records Updated Employee Earnings Record File

Figure 14-13: *Elements of Computerized Processing: Payroll Subcycle*

PRODUCTION SUBCYCLE

An overview of computerized processing in the Production subcycle is presented in Figure 14-14. As in the manual processing system discussed in the text of this chapter, the Production subcycle begins with the decision to authorize a production run. At this point, the quantities of inventory to be manufactured are input into a **Production Order Transaction File** (Step 1 in Figure 14-14). Prior to input, the following control totals are calculated by the Production Planning Department:

▶ Total number of production transactions (record count)

▶ Total quantities of inventory (batch totals)

▶ Total of inventory item numbers (hash totals)

Once the Production Order Transaction File has been created, the **Production Order Program** accesses the **Production Standards Master File** to determine the standard production inputs (raw materials, direct labor, and overhead) needed for that Production Order (Step 2 in Figure 14-14).

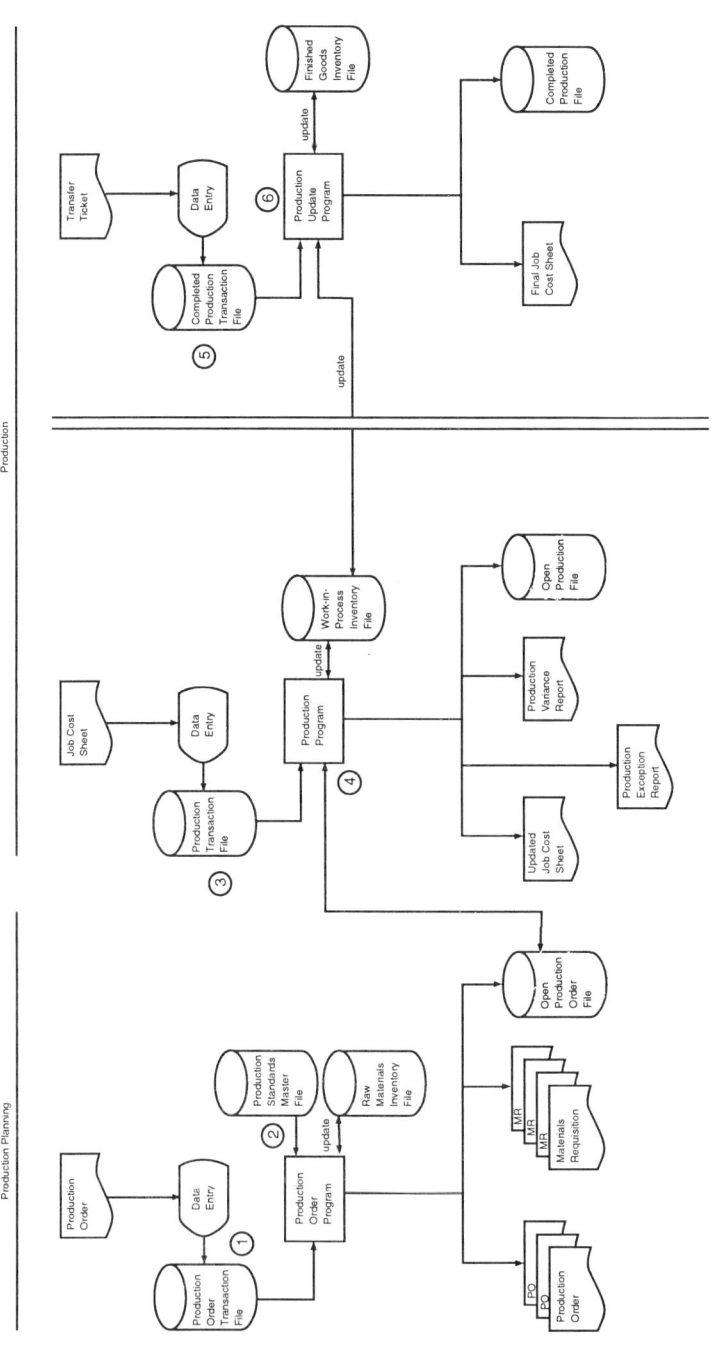

Figure 14-14: *Computerized Processing: The Production Subcycle*

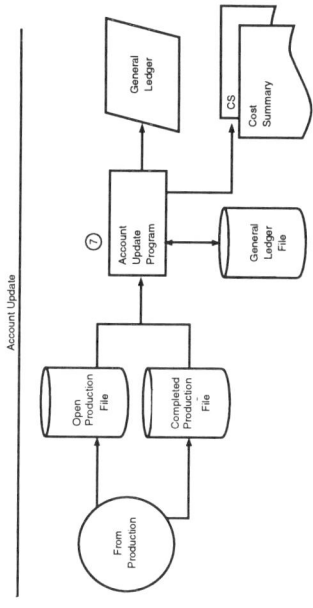

Figure 14-14: *continued*

Based on the quantities of inventory to be produced (from the Production Order Transaction File) and the standard inputs required for that production (from the Production Standards Master File), this program then prepares copies of the Production Order and Materials Requisition. In addition, a **Production Order File** is created which includes information about the standard costs necessary for a given production run (or job). Finally, the Raw Materials Inventory File is updated to reflect the inventory that will be transferred to the Production Department.

As production begins, the actual raw materials and direct labor quantities are accumulated with production jobs using Job Cost Sheets. As materials and labor are used in production, the relevant information from Job Cost Sheets is input to the **Production Transaction File** (Step 3 in Figure 14-14). The **Production Program** then accesses both the Production Transaction File and the Production Order File to create Updated Job Cost Sheets, a Production Exception Report, a Production Variance Report, and a **Production File** (Step 4 in Figure 14-14). The Production File summarizes the costs incurred in the Production Department over a specified period of time on a job-by-job basis. In addition, the Production Program updates the **Work-in-Process Inventory File** for production over a period of time.

Upon completion of production, a Transfer Ticket is prepared, as in the manual processing system described earlier in the chapter. Information from these Transfer Tickets is entered into a **Completed Production Transaction File** (Step 5 in Figure 14-14). Prior to input, the following control totals may be determined:

- Number of completed production orders (record count)
- Sum of inventory quantities completed (batch total)
- Sum of inventory item numbers (hash totals)

The Completed Production Transaction File represents all production orders on which production has been completed. This file is used along with the Work-in-Process Inventory File to run the **Production Update Program** (Step 6 in Figure 14-14). The Production Update Program "transfers" the completed production from the Work-in-Process Inventory File to the Finished Goods Inventory File; in doing so, the following documents and files are created/updated:

- Final Job Cost Sheets
- An Updated Work-in-Process Inventory File
- An Updated Finished Goods Inventory File
- A Completed Production File

Finally, the **Account Update Program** uses both the Production File and the Completed Production File are used to update the General Ledger File and prepare a General Ledger Summary (Step 7 in Figure 14-14). In addition, this program prepares copies of the Cost Summary.

Figure 14-15 summarizes the primary elements of computerized processing in the Production subcycle.

Function	Inputs	Processing	Outputs
Production Planning	Production Order Transaction File Production Standards Master File Raw Materials Inventory File	Production Order Program (Access Production Standards Master File by Item Number)	Production Order Materials Requisition Open Production Order File Updated Raw Materials Inventory File
Production (in Process)	Open Production Order File Production Transaction File Work-in-Process Inventory File	Production Program (Access Production Order File by Job Number)	Updated Job Cost Sheet Production Exception Report Production Variance Report Updated Work-in-Process Inventory File Open Production File
Production (Completion)	Completed Production Transaction File Work-in-Process Inventory File Finished Goods Inventory File	Production Update Program (Access Work-in-Process Inventory File by Job Number)	Final Job Cost Sheet Completed Production File Updated Work-in-Process Inventory File Updated Finished Goods Inventory File
Account Update	Open Production File Completed Production File General Ledger File	Account Update Program (Access Production and Completed Production Files on a Periodic Basis)	General Ledger Summary Cost Summary Updated General Ledger File

Figure 14-15: *Elements of Computerized Processing: Production Subcycle*

> **CHAPTER CHECKPOINTS**
>
> *14-28. How are changes in payroll-related information processed in a computerized system?
>
> *14-29. What are the outputs of the Payroll Program?
>
> *14-30. How are production costs accumulated with inventory in a computerized processing system?

◉ SUMMARY OF KEY POINTS

1. The Conversion cycle involves the span of activities which occur from the organization's decision to produce inventory until the completion of the production process and subsequent movement of the inventory to the Inventory Department (or Warehouse). The Conversion cycle consists of the Payroll subcycle and the Production subcycle.

2. The Payroll subcycle includes important control activities to ensure that: (1) all personnel-related changes are authorized through Personnel Authorization Forms, (2) all hours worked (recorded on Time Sheets) are reviewed and approved by supervisory personnel, and (3) Payroll Checks are accurately prepared and distributed only to persons actually employed by the company.

3. The Production subcycle begins with approval of a production transaction (or production run). This approval occurs in the Production Planning Department and is evidenced by preparation of a Production Order and a Materials Requisition. The Materials Requisition is subsequently used to transfer raw materials from the Raw Materials Inventory Department to the Production Department.

4. As inventory is being produced, raw materials quantities and direct labor hours are accumulated with inventory through the use of Job Cost Sheets or Production Reports. A copy of the Job Cost Sheet is forwarded to Cost Accounting to allow overhead costs to be applied to production and to summarize production costs. When production has been completed, a Transfer Ticket is prepared and used to document the movement of inventory through the organization. The completed inventory items (along with a copy of the Transfer Ticket) are forwarded from the Production Department to the Inventory Department (or Warehouse).

5. The function of the Cost Accounting Department is to accumulate the total costs of producing inventory with the items and to distribute the total production costs across the organization's various balance sheet and income statement accounts. Using documentation received from various departments throughout the organization (such as the Production Order, Materials Requisition, Time Sheets, and Labor Distribution Reports), the Cost Accounting Department prepares a Cost Summary. The Cost Summary is then used to record production transactions in the accounting records.

6. A distinguishing characteristic of a manufacturing company's inventory balances is that three different inventory accounts exist (raw materials inventory, work-in-process inventory, and finished goods inventory). In addition to other substantive tests performed for the company's

inventory balances, the auditor should evaluate the allocation of total inventory costs across these three major categories.

7. In auditing payroll transactions, the primary assertions of interest to the auditor are the EO and VA assertions. If internal control over payroll transactions is relatively ineffective, the auditor should perform extensive tests of the Payroll Register. These tests include verifying hours worked, pay rates, gross pay, deductions, and net pay for a sample of employees. Other substantive tests performed by the auditor over payroll transactions include: (1) analytical procedures, (2) recalculation of payroll accruals, (3) verification of officers' compensation, and (4) other tests to investigate the possibility that fictitious employees have been added to the payroll.

*8. In a computerized processing environment over Payroll subcycle transactions, programs are used to: (1) update the personnel records, and (2) process the payroll and prepare Payroll Checks. For Production subcycle transactions, computerized programs are used to: (1) authorize the release of materials to production, (2) accumulate production costs with inventory, and (3) transfer the costs of completed items from work-in-process inventory to finished goods inventory.

GLOSSARY

***Account Update Program.** A program used in a computerized processing environment to update the accounting records for payroll and production transactions.

Check Summary. A summary prepared by Cash Disbursements listing all payroll checks and the total amount of those checks.

Conversion Cycle. An operating cycle that involves the span of activities which occur from the organization's decision to produce inventory until the completion of the production process and subsequent movement of inventory to the Inventory Department (or Warehouse).

Cost Summary. A summary prepared by Cost Accounting which distributes the total production costs over the various balance sheet and income statement accounts.

Earnings Record. A cumulative record of the gross pay, deductions, and net pay for each employee during the year.

Job Cost Sheet. A document used to accumulate the different production costs (raw materials, direct labor, and manufacturing overhead) associated with a particular production job (or run). Job Cost Sheets are most appropriate when the organization utilizes a job-order cost system.

Labor Distribution Report. A report prepared in Timekeeping that summarizes the total hours worked by employees during a pay period and allocates those hours over the various production jobs.

Materials Requisition. A document prepared in Production Planning that authorizes the release of raw materials inventory to the Production Department. The Materials Requisition is used to record the standard raw materials cost associated with a particular production job (or run).

Overhead Ticket. A document used by Cost Accounting to apply overhead to the various production jobs (or runs).

Payroll Check. A document that is used to compensate employees for services provided to the organization.

***Payroll Program.** A program used in a computerized processing environment to process payroll and prepare the: (1) Payroll Register, (2) Payroll Checks, (3) Check Summary, (4) Labor Distribution Report, (5) Payroll Exception Report, and (6) Payroll Transaction File.

Payroll Register. Prepared in the Payroll Department, this document represents an employee-by-employee summary of important payroll information.

Payroll Subcycle. The component of the Conversion cycle concerned with recording hours worked by employees and compensating them for those hours worked.

Personnel Authorization Form. A document used to authorize payroll-related changes, such as adding new employees to the payroll, deleting terminated employees from the payroll, and modifying payroll-related information (such as wage rates and deduction information) for existing employees.

Production Order. A document prepared in Production Planning that authorizes the production of a particular job (or production run).

__Production Order Program.__ A program used in a computerized processing environment to authorize production and prepare Production Orders and Materials Requisitions.

__Production Program.__ A program used in a computerized processing environment to accumulate raw materials quantities and direct labor hours with production. This program prepares the: (1) Updated Job Cost Sheet, (2) Production Variance Report, (3) Production Exception Report, and (4) Open Production File.

Production Report. A document used to accumulate the different production costs (raw materials, direct labor, and manufacturing overhead) associated with a particular production job (or run). Production Reports are most appropriate when the organization utilizes a process costing system.

Production Subcycle. The component of the Conversion cycle involved with the production (or manufacture) of the organization's inventory.

__Production Update Program.__ A program used in a computerized processing environment to record the completion of production and prepare Final Job Cost Sheets and a Completed Production File.

Time Sheets. Prepared by employees and reviewed by supervisory personnel, Time Sheets allocate an employee's hours worked over the various production jobs served by that employee.

Transfer Ticket. The Transfer Ticket serves as a record of the finished goods transferred from the Production Department to the Inventory Department (or Warehouse). This document is used to record the transfer of goods from work-in-process inventory to finished goods inventory.

QUESTIONS AND PROBLEMS

14-31. Select the **best** answer for each of the following items:

1. The purpose of segregating the duties of hiring personnel and distributing payroll checks is to separate the:

    a. Operational responsibility from the recordkeeping responsibility
    b. Responsibilities of recording a transaction at its origin from the ultimate posting in the general ledger.
    c. Authorization of transactions from the custody of related assets.
    d. Human resources function from the controllership function.

2. Independent internal verification of inventory occurs when employees who:

    a. Issue raw materials obtain Material Requisitions for each issue and prepare daily totals of materials issued.
    b. Compare records of goods on hand with physical quantities do **not** maintain the records or have custody of the inventory.
    c. Obtain receipts for the transfer of completed work to finished goods prepare a completed Production Report.
    d. Are independent of issuing Production Orders update records from completed Job Cost Sheets and Production Reports on a timely basis.

3. Tracing selected items from the Payroll Register to employee Time Sheets that have been approved by supervisory personnel provides evidence that:

    a. Internal controls relating to payroll disbursements were operating effectively.
    b. Payroll checks were signed by an appropriate officer independent of the payroll preparation process.
    c. Only bona fide employees worked and their pay was properly computed.
    d. Employees worked the number of hours for which their pay was computed.

4. The objectives of internal control for the Production subcycle are to provide reasonable assurance that transactions are properly executed and recorded, and that:

    a. Independent internal verification of activity reports is established.
    b. Transfers to finished goods are documented by a completed Transfer Ticket and a quality control report.
    c. Production Orders are prenumbered and signed by a supervisor.
    d. Custody of work-in-process and of finished goods is properly maintained.

5. Effective control activities over the payroll function may include:

   a. Reconciliation of totals on Time Sheets with job reports by employees responsible for those specific jobs.
   b. Verification of agreement of Time Sheets with employee clock cards by a Payroll Department employee.
   c. Preparation of payroll transaction journal entries by an employee who reports to the supervisor of the Personnel Department.
   d. Custody of rate authorization records by the supervisor of the Payroll Department.

6. Which of the following procedures would ordinarily be considered a weakness in an entity's internal control over payroll?

   a. A voucher for the amount of the payroll is prepared in the General Accounting Department based on the Payroll Department's Payroll Register.
   b. Payroll Checks are prepared by the Payroll Department and signed by the Treasurer.
   c. The employee who distributes Payroll Checks returns unclaimed Payroll Checks to the Payroll Department.
   d. The Personnel Department sends employees' termination notices to the Payroll Department.

7. Which of the following departments most likely would approve changes in pay rates and deductions from employee salaries?

   a. Personnel.
   b. Treasurer.
   c. Controller.
   d. Payroll.

8. An auditor would most likely assess control risk at the maximum if the Payroll Department supervisor is responsible for:

   a. Examining Personnel Authorization Forms for new employees.
   b. Comparing Payroll Registers with original batch transmission data.
   c. Authorizing payroll rate changes for all employees.
   d. Hiring all subordinate Payroll Department employees.

9. Which of the following controls would most likely prevent direct labor hours from being charged to manufacturing overhead?

   a. Periodic independent counts of work-in-process for comparison to recorded amounts.
   b. Comparison of daily journal entries with approved Production Orders.
   c. Use of Time Sheets to record actual labor worked on Production Orders.
   d. Reconciliation of work-in-process inventory with periodic cost budgets.

10. An auditor's test of controls over the issuance of raw materials to production would most likely include:

    a. Reconciling raw materials and work-in-process perpetual inventory records to general ledger balances.
    b. Inquiring of the custodian about the procedures followed when defective materials are received from vendors.
    c. Observing that raw materials are stored in secure areas and that storeroom security is supervised by a responsible individual.
    d. Examining Materials Requisitions for an indication of the proper release of materials to production.

11. It would be appropriate for the Payroll Department to be responsible for which of the following functions?

    a. Approval of employee time records.
    b. Maintenance of records of employment, discharges, and pay increases.
    c. Preparation of periodic governmental reports as to employees' earnings and withholding taxes.
    d. Distribution of Paychecks to employees.

12. A surprise observation by an auditor of a client's regular distribution of Payroll Checks is primarily designed to satisfy the auditor that:

    a. All unclaimed payroll checks are properly returned to the Treasurer.
    b. The paymaster is not involved in the distribution of Payroll Checks.
    c. All employees have in their possession proper employee identification.
    d. Names on the company payroll are those of bona fide employees currently on the job.

13. For physical controls in the Payroll subcycle, which department should be responsible for:

	Distribution of Paychecks	Custody of Unclaimed Paychecks
a.	Treasurer	Treasurer
b.	Payroll	Treasurer
c.	Treasurer	Payroll
d.	Payroll	Payroll

14. Which of the following control activities most likely addresses the completeness assertion for inventory?

    a. The work-in-process account is periodically reconciled with subsidiary records.
    b. Supervisory personnel review the allocation of hours worked recorded on Time Sheets to the various production jobs.
    c. Transfer Tickets are prenumbered and periodically accounted for.
    d. The Production Department reconciles the physical quantity of raw materials received with Materials Requisitions.

15. Which of the following control activities most likely addresses the existence or occurrence assertion for production transactions?

    a. Subsidiary ledgers are periodically reconciled with inventory control accounts.
    b. Production costs are summarized through the use of a Cost Summary.
    c. Perpetual inventory records are independently compared with goods on hand.
    d. Personnel periodically account for the numerical sequence of prenumbered Materials Requisitions.

16. To determine that employees actually worked the hours for which they were paid, the auditor would:

    a. Compare hours worked from the Payroll Register to approved Time Sheets.
    b. Examine the employees' personnel files to verify the appropriate wage rates and withholding information.
    c. Observe the distribution of Payroll Checks to employees.
    d. Recalculate the payroll for selected employees.
    e. Scan the Payroll Register for terminated or fictitious employees.

17. For effective internal control over Payroll subcycle transactions, which of the following documents should be used to allocate employees' hours worked across various production jobs?

    a. Labor Distribution Report
    b. Payroll Register
    c. Personnel Authorization Form
    d. Time Sheet

18. Which of the following tests of controls would provide the auditor with some assurance that the company uses accurate wage rates in its payroll calculations?

    a. Inspecting bank reconciliations of the payroll account prepared by company personnel.
    b. Verifying that the Time Sheets completed by employees have been approved by supervisory personnel.
    c. Inspecting the use of Personnel Authorization Forms to authorize personnel-related matters.
    d. Inspecting the Payroll Register for evidence that this information is compared to Payroll Checks.

19. Which of the following control activities is implemented to reduce the likelihood that production costs are misclassified?

    a. The use of prenumbered Production Orders to authorize production of inventory.
    b. Physical controls used to restrict employees' access to inventory.
    c. The use of Materials Requisitions and Transfer Tickets to reduce losses resulting from the theft or defalcation of inventories.
    d. The use of Cost Summaries to summarize production costs.

20. In performing detailed tests involving the Payroll Register, the employees' deduction and wage rate information should be vouched to the:

   a. Employees' personnel files
   b. General ledger journal entry
   c. Labor Distribution Report
   d. Time Sheets completed by that employee

   (Items 1 through 12 in 14-31; AICPA Adapted)

14-32. For the Payroll subcycle:

   a. List the major duties of the departments and functions involved with this subcycle.
   b. List and describe the major documents created in this subcycle.

14-33. For each of the following control activities in the Payroll subcycle, indicate which management assertion(s) are affected by that control activity:

   a. Personnel Authorization Forms should be used to authorize personnel-related transactions.
   b. Supervisory personnel should review Time Sheets and verify the distribution of hours worked on various jobs.
   c. Cash Disbursements/Treasurer should review the Payroll Register and compare it to the Payroll Checks.
   d. The General Function should review the Payroll Register for reasonableness.
   e. Personnel independent of payroll processing should prepare monthly Bank Reconciliations.
   f. Appropriate segregation of duties should be established and maintained in the Payroll subcycle.
   g. Adequate physical controls should be maintained over Payroll Checks.

14-34. For each of the following objectives of internal control over Payroll subcycle transactions, indicate the control activit(ies) that address that objective.

   a. Individuals do not have the ability to participate in incompatible functions involving a particular type of transaction.
   b. Employees have actually worked the number of hours for which they are to be paid.
   c. Significant processing errors (e.g., paying an employee ten times the amount for which he or she is entitled) do not occur in the Payroll subcycle.
   d. The wage rates and deduction information used in processing payroll are accurate.
   e. Payroll disbursement transactions are recorded properly.

14-35. For the Production subcycle:

   a. List the major duties of the departments and functions involved with this subcycle.
   b. List and describe the major documents created in this subcycle.

14-36. For each of the following, list a test of control that could be performed by the auditor to verify the operating effectiveness of that control activity.

a. Direct materials quantities recorded on Job Cost Sheets represent quantities actually used in the production process.
b. Completed inventory items received by the Inventory Department/Warehouse were compared to information on Transfer Tickets.
c. The appropriate segregation of duties has been established and maintained in the Production subcycle.
d. Performance reviews evaluate the variance of actual production costs from standard production costs.
e. Materials are only released from the Raw Materials Inventory Department for authorized production runs.
f. Labor costs accumulated with inventory represent hours worked in the production process.
g. Production costs are appropriately allocated across the various production jobs and financial statement accounts.
h. Inventories are kept in secured, locked areas.
i. All production runs have been authorized by the company.
j. Physical inventories should be periodically compared to perpetual inventory records, with any differences investigated by management.

14-37. Butler, CPA, has been engaged to audit the financial statements of Young Computer Outlets, Inc., a new client. Young is a privately-owned chain of retail stores that sells a variety of computer software and video products. Young uses an in-house Payroll Department at its corporate headquarters to compute payroll data, and to prepare and distribute Payroll Checks for its 300 salaried employees.

Butler is preparing an internal control questionnaire to assist in obtaining an understanding of Young's internal control and in assessing control risk.

Required:

Prepare a "Payroll" segment of Butler's internal control questionnaire that would assist in obtaining an understanding of Young's internal control and in assessing control risk.

Use the format in the following example:

Question	Yes	No

Are Payroll Checks prenumbered and accounted for?

14-38. Give one example of a substantive testing procedure that can be performed by the auditor to verify each of the following matters related to a client's payroll transactions.

a. Wage rates used to calculate payroll are appropriate.
b. The FICA taxes withheld from employees' pay are correctly stated.
c. The total payroll expense recognized during a month is appropriate.
d. Recently-terminated employees are not included in the current month's payroll calculation.
e. Only authorized, bona fide employees are included in the payroll register.
f. The withholdings from each employee's Payroll Check are correctly calculated.
g. Employees actually worked the hours for which they were paid.
h. Paychecks are not being made to fictitious individuals or individuals not employed by the client.

14-39. One of the auditor's primary means of verifying payroll transactions is by a detailed payroll test. You are making an annual examination of the Joplin Company, a medium-sized manufacturing company. You have selected a number of hourly employees for a detailed payroll test. The following worksheet outline has been prepared:

Column Number	Column Heading
1	Employee Number
2	Employee Name
3	Job Classification
	Hours worked:
4	Straight Time
5	Premium Time
6	Hourly Rate
7	Gross Earnings
	Deductions:
8	FICA Withheld
9	Federal Income Taxes Withheld
10	Union Dues
11	Hospitalization
12	Amount of Check
13	Check and Check Number
14	Account Number Charged
15	Description of Account

Required:

a. Using the column numbers above as a reference, state the principal way(s) that the information in each column would be verified.

b. In addition to the payroll test, the auditor employs a number of other audit procedures in the verification of payroll transactions. List some additional procedures that may be employed.

(AICPA Adapted)

14-40. The Generous Loan Company has 100 branch loan offices. Each office has a manager and four or five subordinates who are employed by the manager. Branch managers prepare the weekly payroll, including their own salaries, and pay employees from cash on hand. The employee signs the Payroll Sheet signifying receipt of her or his salary. Hours worked by hourly personnel are inserted in the Payroll Sheet from Time Cards prepared by the employees and approved by the manager.

The weekly Payroll Sheets are sent to the home office along with other accounting statements and reports. The home office compiles employee earnings records and prepares all federal and state salary reports from the weekly payroll sheets.

Salaries are established by home office job evaluation schedules. Salary adjustments, promotions, and transfers of full-time employees are approved by a home office salary committee, based upon the recommendations of branch managers and area supervisors. Branch managers advise the salary committee of new full-time employees and terminations. Part-time and temporary employees are hired without referral to the salary committee.

Required:

a. Based upon your review of the payroll system, how might funds for payroll be diverted?
b. Prepare a payroll audit program to be used in the home office to audit the branch office payrolls of the Generous Loan Company.

(AICPA Adapted)

14-41. James, who was engaged to examine the financial statements of Talbert Corporation, is about to audit payroll. Talbert uses a computer service center to process weekly payroll as follows:

Each Monday, Talbert's Payroll Clerk inserts data in appropriate spaces on the preprinted service center-prepared input form and sends it to the service center via messenger. The service center extracts new permanent data from the input form and updates master files. The weekly payroll data are then processed. The weekly Payroll Register and Payroll Checks are printed and delivered by messenger to Talbert on Thursday.

Part of the sample selected for audit by James includes the following input form and Payroll Register:

Talbert Corporation payroll input: Week ending Friday, November 23, 19X1

	Employee Data—Permanent File			Current Week's Payroll Data				
				Hours		Special Deductions		
Name	Social Security	E-4 Information	Hourly Rate	Reg	OT	Bonds	Union	Other
A. Bell	999-99-9991	M-1	10.00	35	5	18.75		
B. Carr	999-99-9992	M-2	10.00	35	4			
C. Dawn	999-99-9993	S-1	10.00	35	6	18.85	4.00	
D. Ellis	999-99-9994	S-1	10.00	35	2		4.00	50.00
E. Frank	999-99-9995	M-4	10.00	35	1		4.00	
F. Gillis	999-99-9996	M-4	10.00	35			4.00	
G. Hugh	999-99-9997	M-1	7.00	35	2	18.85	4.00	
H. Jones	999-99-9998	M-2	7.00	35			4.00	25.00
I. King	999-99-9999	S-1	7.00	35	4		4.00	
New Employee:								
J. Smith	999-99-9990	M-3	7.00	35				

Talbert Corporation Payroll Register: November 23, 19X1

Employee	Social Security	Hours		Payroll			Taxes Withheld				Net Pay	Check No.
		Reg.	OT	Regular	OT	Gross Payroll	FICA	Fed.	State	Other Withheld		
A. Bell	999-99-9991	35	5	350.00	75.00	425.00	26.05	76.00	27.40	18.75	276.80	1499
B. Carr	999-99-9992	35	4	350.00	60.00	410.00	25.13	65.00	23.60		296.27	1500
C. Dawn	999-99-9993	35	6	350.00	90.00	440.00	26.97	100.90	28.60	22.75	260.78	1501
D. Ellis	999-99-9994	35	2	350.00	30.00	380.00	23.29	80.50	21.70	54.00	200.51	1502
E. Frank	999-99-9995	35	1	350.00	15.00	365.00	22.37	43.50	15.90	4.00	279.23	1503
F. Gillis	999-99-9996	35		350.00		350.00	21.46	41.40	15.00	4.00	268.14	1504
G. Hugh	999-99-9997	35	2	245.00	21.00	266.00	16.31	34.80	10.90	22.75	181.24	1505
H. Jones	999-99-9998	35		245.00		245.00	15.02	26.40	8.70	29.00	165.88	1506
I. King	999-99-9999	35	4	245.00	42.00	287.00	17.59	49.40	12.20	4.00	203.81	1507
J. Smith	999-99-9990	35		245.00		245.00	15.02	23.00	7.80		199.18	1508
Totals		350	24	3,080.00	333.00	3,413.00	209.21	540.90	171.80	159.25	2,331.84	

Required:

a. Describe how James should verify the information in the payroll input form shown above.

b. Describe (but do not perform) the procedures that James should follow in the examination of the November 23, 19X1, Payroll Register shown above.

(AICPA Adapted)

Learning Objectives

Study of this chapter is designed to achieve several learning objectives. After studying this chapter, you should be able to:

1. Identify the major transactions and accounts in the Investing and Financing cycle.
2. Discuss major differences between the nature of transactions in the Investing and Financing cycle and other operating cycles.
3. Understand differences between the test of transactions approach and the test of balances approach to substantive testing.
4. Identify important control activities in the Investing and Financing cycle.
5. Identify factors that affect the inherent risk associated with the following accounts: investments; property, plant and equipment; long-term debt and notes payable; and, stockholders' equity.
6. List substantive testing procedures that should be performed for the following accounts: investments; property, plant and equipment; long-term debt and notes payable; and, stockholders' equity.

15

The Investing and Financing Cycle

The final operating cycle relevant to most companies is the **Investing and Financing cycle**. As its name implies, this cycle relates to two types of transactions: investing transactions (what does the company do with its excess funds?) and financing transactions (other than operations, how does the company obtain its funds?). This chapter focuses on four major groups of accounts involved with investing and financing transactions:

▶ Investments

▶ Property, Plant and Equipment

▶ Notes Payable and Long-Term Debt

▶ Stockholders' Equity

These accounts, along with the related transactions and documents, are summarized in Figure 15-1. As shown in Figure 15-1, all transactions affecting accounts in the Investing and Financing cycle are authorized by the Board of Directors; as discussed later in this chapter, the **Board of Directors' Minutes** will become an important form of evidence for the auditor. In addition, notice that transactions affecting the accounts in the Investing and Financing cycle involve the either the receipt or payment of cash; as a result, the auditor will examine the Cash Receipts Journal and Check Register during his or her examination of these accounts.

◉ AUDITING THE INVESTING AND FINANCING CYCLE

Prior to discussing the specific issues and procedures associated with the Investing and Financing cycle, it is important to identify the major difference between this cycle and the operating cycles

	Authorization	Purchase/Issuance	Disposal/Retirement
Investments	Board of Directors' Minutes	Broker's Advice	Broker's Advice
		Check Register	Cash Receipts Journal
Property, Plant and Equipment	Board of Directors' Minutes	Vendor's Invoice	Property Lapsing Schedule
		Internal Cost Records	Cash Receipts Journal
		Capital Lease Agreement	
		Check Register	
Notes Payable and Long-Term Debt	Board of Directors' Minutes	Confirmation from Debtholders	Confirmation from Debtholders
		Cash Receipts Journal	Check Register
Stockholders' Equity	Board of Directors' Minutes	Confirmation from Registrar	Confirmation from Registrar
		Cash Receipts Journal	Check Register

Figure 15-1: *Documents in the Investing and Financing Cycle*

discussed in Chapters 10-11 (the Revenue cycle), 12-13 (the Purchases and Disbursements cycle), and 14 (the Conversion cycle). The cycles discussed in the preceding chapters are ordinarily characterized by a large number of transactions of relatively small dollar amounts per transaction. To illustrate, consider Revenue cycle transactions for a mail-order retailer such as Land's End. Land's End makes numerous sales to customers and receives numerous payments on their accounts receivable every day. Although some of these transactions are for large dollar amounts, the great majority involve relatively small amounts. Similarly, Land's End and other companies also have a larger number of transactions related to the Purchases and Disbursements cycle (purchases of inventory and payments for inventory and other expenses) and the Conversion cycle (production of inventory and payment to employees). Like Revenue cycle transactions, these individual transactions are for relatively small dollar amounts.

In contrast, transactions related to the Investing and Financing cycle occur less frequently. Also, the dollar amounts associated with an individual transaction are normally larger than those for accounts affected by the other operating cycles. To illustrate, Land's End may occasionally need to replace its production equipment (or enter into a capital lease involving production equipment). However, these types of transactions would occur sporadically during the year. In addition, when these transactions do occur, the dollar amounts involved are relatively large.

The frequency and dollar magnitude of transactions associated with the Investing and Financing cycle result in two changes to the basic audit approach. Recall that two different substantive testing approaches may be employed by the auditor—the test of balances approach and the test of transactions approach. To this point, our focus has been on the test of balances approach because of the nature of the operating cycles discussed in Chapters 10-14. When using the **test of balances** approach, the auditor identifies individual components of the account balance at year-end and selects a sample of these components for examination. For example, in our discussion of substantive tests for Revenue cycle accounts (see Chapter 11), when verifying accounts receivable, the auditor ordinarily selects a sample of customer accounts and directly confirms these accounts with the customer.

The test of balances approach is normally used for operating cycles having a large number of transactions for relatively small dollar amounts per transaction. These characteristics are commonly associated with accounts affected by the Revenue, Purchases and Disbursements, and Conversion cycles (accounts receivable, cash, accounts payable, and inventory).

Because of the nature of the transactions discussed in the Investing and Financing cycle, the test of transactions approach is used. Shown below is a sample T-account used to illustrate the test of transactions approach:

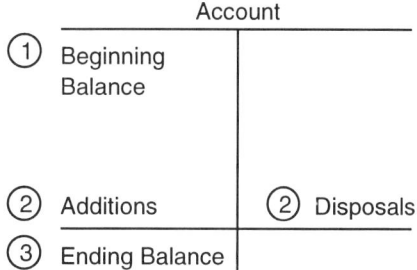

The auditor uses a three-step approach in the **test of transactions** approach. First, because the beginning balance represents last period's ending balance, it has already been verified through a previous audit examination. The auditor simply agrees the beginning balance to the prior-year workpapers. Next, the auditor verifies the changes in the account balance occurring during the year under audit. As the name of the approach implies, these changes will represent individual transactions (*i.e.*, purchases and/or disposals). Because these accounts are generally comprised of only a small number of transactions, doing so is a relatively cost-efficient method of gathering evidence. In addition, the fact that these transactions involve larger dollar amounts increases their importance to the auditor. Finally, by recalculating the ending balance (beginning balance plus additions minus disposals), the auditor can verify that the year-end balance in the account is stated in conformity with GAAP.

A second major difference in the auditor's examination of the accounts related to the Investing and Financing cycle concerns the role of internal control. Given that most changes (transactions) in the account during the year are examined, studying and evaluating internal control will normally not provide the auditor with a substantial reduction in the extent of his or her substantive tests. In most cases, the auditor will employ only limited tests of controls and perform more extensive substantive tests. These tests of controls will focus on authorization of transactions involving the related account balances and classes of transactions. Because of the large dollar amounts and long-term implications associated with these accounts, it is critical that all transactions (both purchases/additions and disposals/reductions) be properly authorized by management.

The two major differences in the auditor's examination of account balances and classes of transactions associated with the Investing and Financing cycle are summarized in Figure 15-2.

	Investing and Financing Cycle	Other Cycles	Reasons for Differences
Internal Control	Limited study and evaluation of internal control	More extensive study and evaluation of internal control	Internal control will not allow the auditor to reduce substantive testing to a great extent in the Investing and Financing cycle
Substantive Tests	Perform tests of all (or most) transactions occurring during the year	Perform tests of a sample of components of the account balance	Fewer transactions exist, making it more cost-efficient to examine all (or most) of them
			Transactions are for larger dollar amounts, making it more desirable to examine all (or most) of them

Figure 15-2: *Audit Approach for the Investing and Financing Cycle*

CHAPTER CHECKPOINTS

15-1. What are the four primary accounts affected by the Investing and Financing cycle?

15-2. Distinguish between the test of transactions and test of balances approaches to substantive testing. For which types of accounts would each approach be used?

15-3. How does the auditor's examination of the accounts affected by the Investing and Financing cycle differ from his or her examination of accounts in other cycles (such as the Revenue cycle)?

◉ EVALUATING INTERNAL CONTROL: THE INVESTING AND FINANCING CYCLE

The Investing and Financing cycle is concerned with transactions related to four primary balance sheet accounts: investments; property, plant and equipment; notes payable and long-term debt; and, stockholders' equity. As noted above, given the small number of transactions affecting these accounts, the auditor ordinarily utilizes the test of transactions approach with respect to this cycle. The test of transactions approach is characterized by the following mix of tests:

▶ Less extensive tests of control activities (tests of controls)

▶ More extensive substantive tests

Thus, the auditor does not usually spend a great deal of time and effort in evaluating internal control over Investing and Financing cycle transactions. However, regardless of the reliance to be placed on internal control, the auditor must obtain an understanding of the five components of internal control to plan the audit. As noted in previous chapters, these five components are the control environment, risk assessment, control activities, information and communication, and monitoring.

◻ Control Environment

As with previous cycles, the control environment reflects the control consciousness of the organization and its employees and is normally assessed by the auditor on an overall basis. Recall that the control environment includes such factors as: (1) integrity and ethical values, (2) commitment to competence, (3) the existence of a board of directors and audit committee, (4) management's philosophy and operating style, (5) the organizational structure, (6) assignment of authority and responsibility, and (7) human resource policies and practices. Unlike other cycles, most of the activities in the Investing and Financing cycle occur at very high levels in the organization, such as upper management and the Board of Directors. Therefore, the auditor's assessment of the control environment as it relates to the Investing and Financing cycle should focus on these individual(s).

One particular matter that reflects management's philosophy and operating style related to the Investing and Financing cycle is management's propensity to assume risks in their investing and financing transactions. For example, is management willing to assume higher risk in selecting investment opportunities? Is management willing to assume higher risk in establishing debt agreements, by using variable interest rates or some other form of derivative? If so, the auditor would normally assess control risk at higher levels.

◻ Risk Assessment and Control Activities

Because of the limited number of transactions affecting accounts in the Investing and Financing cycle, as well as the limited number of persons involved with these transactions, the auditor's consideration of risk assessment and control activities is less extensive than that for other cycles discussed to this point in the text. Some of the more important control activities considered by the auditor are summarized below.

Information Processing. The primary information processing control relates to the authorization of transactions. Authorization of Investing and Financing cycle transactions is of particular importance because these transactions:

- ▶ Involve larger dollar amounts
- ▶ Have longer-term implications for the company

Because of these characteristics, the authorization for transactions in the Investing and Financing cycle should be performed at a relatively high level in the organization. In most cases, Investing and Financing cycle transactions are approved by the client's Board of Directors. When transactions are authorized by the Board of Directors, evidence regarding the transaction initially appears in the **Board of Directors' Minutes**, which serves as a form of documentation that can be examined by the auditor.

As with other cycles, the formal authorization of transactions by the Board of Directors (and existence of formal documentation in the form of Board of Directors' Minutes) reduces the likelihood that fictitious transactions are recorded in the accounts (the EO and RO assertions). In addition, the formal authorization of all transactions in the Investing and Financing cycle increases the likelihood that these transactions will be recorded (the CO assertion). The effect of the Board of Directors' Minutes on these assertions is summarized below:

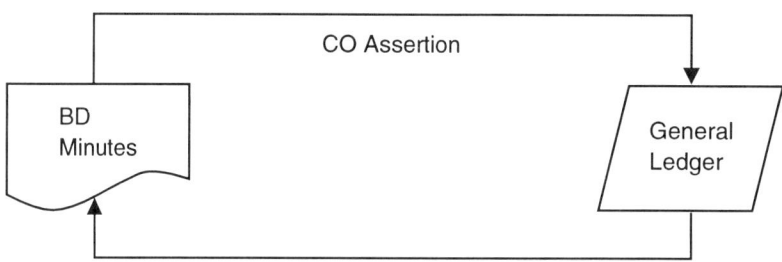

Segregation of Duties. As with the other cycles discussed in the text, companies should establish appropriate segregation of duties over Investing and Financing cycle transactions. This segregation of duties is summarized below:

- Authorization: Board of Directors
- Recording: General Accounting
- Custody: Separate Department or Independent Custodian (for Investments in Securities)

Like other cycles discussed in this text, the primary benefit provided by segregation of duties is that individual(s) are not provided with an opportunity to commit a defalcation and conceal that defalcation by having incompatible responsibilities. By reducing the opportunity to engage in theft or a defalcation scheme, segregation of duties relates to the operating objective of internal control. In addition, since defalcations of assets can be concealed by recording fictitious transactions (the EO and RO assertions) or failing to record actual transactions (the CO assertion), this control activity also relates to the financial objective of internal control.

Physical Controls. With the exception of cash, investments in marketable securities are the most liquid asset held by a company and, therefore, the most attractive asset in terms of employee theft or defalcation. As a result, three important physical controls are normally implemented over marketable securities:

1. Marketable securities should be made in the client's name
2. Marketable securities should be held by an independent custodian or in a secure location (such as a safe-deposit box). If held in a safe-deposit box, access to the contents of the box should require the presence of more than one employee.
3. Marketable securities should be periodically counted and compared to detail records.

As with other subcycles discussed throughout this text, physical controls relate to both the operating and financial objectives of internal control. From an operating standpoint, these controls reduce the possibility that losses will be incurred as a result of theft or some other defalcation scheme. From a financial standpoint, since physical controls reduce the opportunity for the theft or defalcation of assets, the probability that fictitious transactions are recorded in the accounting records (the EO and RO assertions) or actual transactions are intentionally not recorded (the CO assertion) to conceal theft or defalcation of assets is also reduced.

The remaining accounts in the Investing and Financing cycle (property, plant and equipment; notes payable and long-term debt; and, stockholders' equity) do not ordinarily present employees with much of an opportunity for theft or defalcation. Therefore, physical controls over these accounts are normally not implemented. However, cash is received upon the sale of property, plant and equipment or securities or the issuance of notes payable, long-term debt, or common stock. An important physical control over the cash proceeds received from Investing and Financing cycle transactions is that they are deposited intact and daily in the client's bank account.

Performance Reviews. Performance reviews involve management review and analysis of data by comparing these data to: (1) data from prior years, and/or (2) budgeted or forecasted data. In the Investing and Financing cycle, the following amounts are evaluated through the use of performance reviews.

▶ Returns earned by the organization's investments are compared to organizational guidelines

▶ Expenditures for property, plant and equipment are compared to amounts drawn from capital budgets

As with performance reviews performed in other subcycles, significant differences revealed by the above comparisons may highlight potential areas for organizational improvement. Identifying potential areas for improvement through the use of performance reviews corresponds to the operating objective of internal control. However, these differences may also be the result of: (1) fictitious transactions being recorded (the EO and RO assertions), (2) actual transactions not being recorded (the CO assertion), and (3) transactions being recorded at the incorrect dollar amount (the VA assertion). Thus, performance reviews also correspond to the financial objective of internal control.

Information and Communication

Because of the relatively small number of transactions occurring in the Investing and Financing cycle, the accounting system used in recording these transactions is relatively simple. An overview of the basic accounting system used for Investing and Financing cycle transactions is summarized in Figure 15-3.

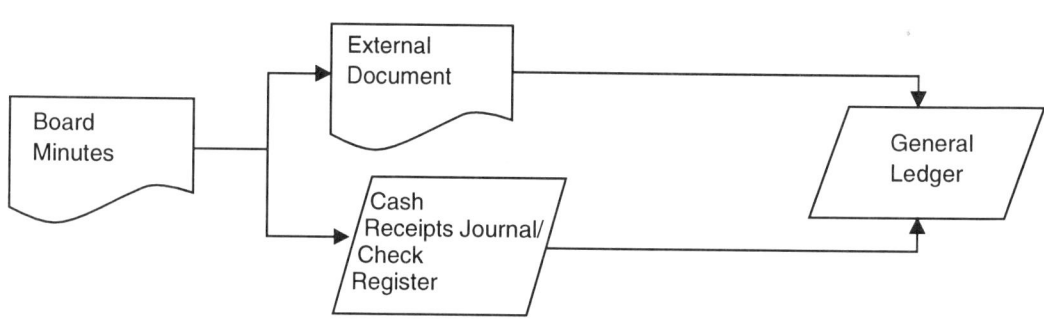

Figure 15-3: *Accounting System for Investing and Financing Transaction*

The accounting system depicted in Figure 15-3 reflects three levels of documentation. The first level of documentation represents the authorization for entering into the transaction itself. As noted earlier in Figure 15-1, most of these transactions are authorized by the client's Board of Directors; as a result, their initial approval can be found in the Board of Directors' Minutes.

The second level of documentation involves evidence of the transaction itself. Two types of documentation are normally created upon the completion of a transaction. First, documentation is ordinarily received from external parties involved with the transaction (e.g., a Vendor's Invoice for property, plant and equipment purchased from external parties or a confirmation from the Registrar for issuances of capital stock). Second, transactions in the Investing and Financing cycle result in either the receipt or payment of cash. Therefore, cash receipts and disbursements records also serve as a form of documentation for the transaction.

The final level of documentation represents the recording of the transaction. Transactions in the Investing and Financing cycle are normally recorded in both the general ledger as well as a detail listing (or subsidiary records).

Monitoring

Monitoring does not play a large role in the internal control over Investing and Financing cycle transactions, since transactions in this cycle do not involve external parties on a day-to-day basis. Two examples of on-going monitoring activities that may require management attention are:

1. Communication from lenders regarding missed or delayed repayments
2. Communication from shareholders regarding dividend payments not received or dividend payments for incorrect amounts

In addition to on-going monitoring activities, separate evaluations of internal control over Investing and Financing cycle transactions may be conducted by: (1) internal auditors, (2) other external auditors, or (3) the same external auditor in a prior year. The auditor should consider any deficiencies identified during these separate evaluations of internal control as well as actions taken by management to correct these deficiencies.

CHAPTER CHECKPOINTS

15-4. How does the authorization of transactions by the Board of Directors affect the financial statement assertions for transactions in the Investing and Financing cycle?

15-5. List some physical controls that should be established over marketable securities.

15-6. What two types of documentation are created when Investing and Financing cycle transactions occur? Provide an example for transactions affecting each of the four accounts in the Investing and Financing cycle.

◉ SUBSTANTIVE TESTS: INVESTMENTS

Most of the investments held by companies are in the form of marketable securities (either debt or equity securities) of other entities. In *Statement of Financial Accounting Standards No. 115*[1] *(SFAS 115)*, the FASB requires marketable securities to be shown on the balance sheet at either amortized cost or market value, depending on the securities' classification. According to SFAS 115, marketable securities should be classified into one of three categories, depending upon management's intent with respect to the securities. **Held-to-maturity securities** are debt securities (*i.e.*, investments in bonds and other debt instruments) that management has the positive intent and ability to hold until maturity. Held-to-maturity securities are shown on the balance sheet at cost adjusted for any unamortized premium or discount. In contrast, marketable securities that are classified as trading securities and available-for-sale securities are carried on the balance sheet at market value. **Trading securities** are securities that are purchased primarily for short-term appreciation; these securities are normally held for relatively short periods of time. **Available-for-sale securities** are investments not classified as either held-to-maturity securities or trading securities; these investments are normally held by management for longer periods of time than trading securities. It is important to note that the classification of

---

[1] Financial Accounting Standards Board (FASB), *Statement of Financial Accounting Standards No. 115*, "Accounting for Certain Investments in Debt and Equity Securities" (Norwalk, CT: FASB, 1993).

marketable securities is based on management's intent with respect to the Investment; therefore, management ultimately decides upon the category into which its marketable securities are classified.

In general, the following discussion regarding the audit of investments pertains to situations where the client owns less than 20 percent of the outstanding stock of another company and does not exert significant influence over that company. For situations where: (1) the client holds from 20 to 50 percent of the outstanding stock and is able to exert significant influence over the investee; or (2) the client has unconsolidated subsidiaries, the independent auditor needs to make sure the provisions of *APB Opinion No. 18* have been applied.[2] In situations where the client owns a controlling interest (more than 50 percent) of a company, the independent auditor needs to be satisfied that *APB Opinions 16 and 17* have been applied.[3] Further discussion of the latter two situations is beyond the scope of this text.[4]

In establishing an overall audit approach over investment transactions, the auditor's primary concerns from an inherent risk standpoint are as follows:

1. Marketable securities are highly susceptible to theft. Therefore, the possibility exists that client employees may attempt to conceal the theft or defalcation of securities by: (1) recording fictitious transactions for the sale of marketable securities (the EO and RO assertions), or (2) intentionally failing to record purchases of marketable securities (the CO assertion).
2. Management's classification of marketable securities can have significant affects on both total assets as well as net income. Therefore, this classification is related to both the VA and PD assertion.

As noted throughout this text, after considering inherent risk, the auditor can rely on: (1) tests of controls (control risk), (2) substantive tests (detection risk), or (3) some combination of these tests to control audit risk at acceptable levels. Because of the low volume of transactions affecting investments, it is ordinarily more cost-efficient to use a substantive testing approach for investments. Figure 15-4 summarizes some of the major procedures performed by the auditor in his or her examination of investments.

◻ Obtaining or Preparing a Listing of Securities

The auditor should obtain or prepare a Listing of Securities that includes information regarding the name of the issuer and description of the security; serial numbers; number of shares owned at year-end; market price per share; and, total market price. This Listing should summarize the securities by major classification (as established by SFAS 115). Figure 15-5 is an example of a Listing of Marketable Securities prepared by the client for use during the audit.

---

[2] Accounting Principles Board (APB), *Opinion of the Accounting Principles Board No. 18*, "The Equity Method of Accounting for Investments in Common Stock" (New York: AICPA, 1971).

[3] Accounting Principles Board (APB), *Opinion of the Accounting Principles Board No. 16*, "Business Combinations" (New York: AICPA, 1970); *Opinion of the Accounting Principles Board No. 17*, "Intangible Assets" (New York: AICPA, 1970).

[4] The issues surrounding the preparation of consolidated financial statements are currently being considered by the FASB in two Discussion Memoranda: "Consolidation Policy and Procedures" (Norwalk, CT: FASB, 1991) and "New Basis Accounting" (Norwalk, CT: FASB, 1991).

Procedure	Classification	Assertion(s)				
		EO	RO	CO	VA	PD
1. Obtain or prepare a Listing of Securities and Investments owned by the client (Figure 15-5)						
a. Agree beginning balances from Listing to prior-year workpapers	Comparison				x	
b. Foot and cross-foot Listing and agree total to the client's Trial Balance	Recalculation Comparison				x	
2. Verify investment transactions occurring during the year						
a. Vouch transactions occurring during the year to appropriate documentation	Inspect Documents	x			x	
b. Trace from authorization in the Board of Directors' Minutes to Listing	Inspect Documents			x		
3. Inspect or confirm securities held at year-end						
a. Inspect and count securities held by client	Observation	x	x	x	x	
b. Confirm securities held by an external custodian	Confirmation	x	x	x	x	
4. Verify the market value of securities at year-end	Inspect Documents Recalculation				x	
5. Examine investment revenue accounts						
a. Verify dividend revenue from equity securities through reference to published sources or cash receipts information	Inspect Documents				x	
b. Recalculate interest revenue from debt securities	Recalculation				x	
6. Perform analytical procedures for investment and investment revenue accounts	Analytical Procedures	x	x	x	x	x
7. Evaluate the overall presentation of investment accounts in the financial statements						
a. Inquire of management about their intent (and classification) with respect to investments and inspect written evidence about management's intent	Inquiry Inspect Documents				x	x
b. Inquire about whether securities are pledged as collateral	Inquiry					x
c. Review disclosures related to investments	Inspect Documents					x

Figure 15-4: *Major Substantive Tests: Investments*

As noted by the "√" tickmark in Figure 15-5, the auditor should agree the beginning balance in the investment accounts to prior-year workpapers. In addition, the schedule should be footed and crossfooted (depicted by the "F" and "CF" tickmarks in Figure 15-5). Finally, all important subtotals should be agreed with the client's Trial Balance ("TB" tickmark). Since these procedures are used to verify the accuracy of the totals that eventually appear on the client's Trial Balance, they correspond to the VA assertion.

E-1

Meghan's Office Products
Investments
12-31-x3

Prepared by: Client 1-2-X4
Reviewed by: BWS 1-6-X4
MES 1-12-X4

Investee	Certificate Number	Shares Owned (12-31-x3)	1-1-x3 Balance	Purchases	Disposals	12-31-x3 Balance	Market Price 12-31-x3 Per Share	Market Price 12-31-x3 Total
LMG Corporation	IA 1234	1,000 ①	100,000		11,500 Ⓢ	100,000	15	115,000
SAS Company	AM 1670	500 ②	23,000			11,500	20	10,000
JRS Company	JJ 1212	2,000 ①	0	90,000 Ⓟ	0	90,000	55	110,000
			123,000 Ⓕ	90,000 Ⓕ	11,500 Ⓕ	201,500 ⒸⒻ		235,000 ⒻⓂ
								ⒻⓉⒷ

Ⓕ Footed
ⒸⒻ Cross-Footed
Ⓣ⒝ Agreed to Trial Balance
✓ Agreed to Prior-Year's Workpapers
① Examined securities and agreed issuer, number of shares, and certificate number. No exceptions noted.
② Confirmed issuer, number of shares, and certificate number with external custodian. No exceptions noted.
Ⓟ Vouched purchase and agreed number of shares and cost with Broker's Advice. Examined Board of Directors' Minutes for authorization.
Ⓢ Vouched sale to Broker's Advice and agreed cash receipts of $20,000 to the Cash Receipts Journal. Examined Board of Directors' Minutes for authorization. See Workpaper R-1 for disposition of $8,500 gain ($20,000 - $11,500).
Ⓜ Agreed with year-end market values in *The Wall Street Journal* and recalculated total market value.

Note: Ending Fair Value Over Basis ($235,000 - $201,500)   33,500
       Balance in Allowance Account   (21,200)
       Additional Adjustment Required   12,300

       AJE: Allowance for
             Market Adjustment   12,300
                 Unrealized Gain
                 in Investment   12,300

       See Workpaper AJE-1 for a summary of adjustments

Figure 15-5: *Listing of Marketable Securities*

◻ Verifying Investment Transactions

Under the test of transactions approach, the auditor should verify all (or most) of the investment transactions occurring during the year. For purchases of marketable securities, the auditor examines a Broker's Advice. The **Broker's Advice** is a document similar to an invoice or statement. Three key items of information may be obtained from the Broker's Advice: (1) the name of the issuing company, (2) the number of shares purchased, and (3) the total cost. Remember that the cost of marketable securities should also include any brokers' commissions incurred in making the purchase. Information from the Broker's Advice is then agreed to the information contained on the Listing of Securities. For all purchases, the auditor should vouch the purchase to the authorization in the Board of Directors' Minutes to determine that the purchase was appropriately authorized by the client. Tickmark "P" in Figure 15-5 illustrates these audit procedures.

A similar approach is used by the auditor to investigate sales of marketable securities. That is, the auditor examines the Broker's Advice to determine the number of shares sold and the cash proceeds from the sale. In addition, the proceeds received from the sale of marketable securities can be verified through reference to the Cash Receipts Journal. Information about the selling price of the securities is important because it is used to recalculate the gain or loss on sale of marketable securities. Tickmark "S" provides a summary of the procedures performed to verify sales of marketable securities. Note that, as with purchases, the auditor should vouch sales of marketable securities to Board of Directors' Minutes to verify that they have been properly authorized. Also, tickmark "S" reveals that the gain or loss on the sale of securities has been recalculated and agreed to workpaper R-1 (not illustrated).

In sum, two basic procedures are performed to verify investment transactions occurring during the year.

1. By inspecting the Broker's Advice and Board of Directors' Minutes, the auditor obtains evidence that the transactions actually occurred (the EO assertion).

2. By verifying both the number of shares purchased or sold (through the Broker's Advice) as well as the price at which the shares were purchased or sold (through the Broker's Advice or internal cash records), the auditor obtains assurance that transactions have been recorded at the proper dollar amount (the VA assertion).

The above procedures are used to verify *recorded* investment transactions. In some cases, in order to alleviate a shortage of cash, companies may need to sell marketable securities and incur losses on the sale of these investments. In these situations, the company may intentionally fail to record the sale to avoid recognizing the loss associated with the sale. Thus, the auditor should be aware of the possibility of *unrecorded* investment transactions. Since investment transactions are authorized by the client's Board of Directors, the auditor should read the Board of Directors' Minutes for any indication that purchases or sales of investments were authorized. Based on this information, the auditor can trace from the authorization to the Listing of Securities to determine that all sales have been recorded (the CO assertion).

◻ Inspecting or Confirming Securities

For securities owned by the client at year-end, the auditor should inspect the securities on hand and confirm any securities held by an outside custodian. The auditor should inspect the securities on hand in the presence of the client's representative and obtain a signed receipt for their return to the custodian. If securities are held in more than one location, arrangements should be made to count securities at all locations at the same time to avoid the possibility of client personnel transferring securities from one location to another in an attempt to cover up theft or unauthorized use. In addition, the security count is ordinarily scheduled at the same time as the count of cash and other liquid assets (see Chapter 11) to reduce the likelihood that securities could be sold in an effort to "double count" liquid assets.

If securities are held by others for the account of the client, then the auditor should request confirmation of the securities as of the balance-sheet date. Like confirmations of accounts receivable and cash (see Chapter 11), the request for confirmation should be mailed by the auditor and should include instructions to mail the reply directly to the auditor.

Tickmarks "1" and "2" in Figure 15-5 summarize the inspection or confirmation of securities. As noted in the workpaper, the auditor should agree the name of the issuer, number of shares, and certificate number from the physical asset (security) to the information provided on the security listing. In addition, the auditor should verify that the securities are made in the client's name and not the bearer or some other party. For debt securities, the maturity date and interest rate are also verified. Special care should be taken by the auditor with regard to verifying that the security numbers on the listing agree with those noted during the physical examination or determined through confirmation with external custodians. Differences in the certificate numbers may reflect unauthorized or unrecorded securities transactions during that year in which common stock or bonds were sold and later replaced with different securities of the same issuer.

Inspecting securities or confirming securities held by external custodians primarily provides the auditor with evidence that the securities exist (the EO assertion) and are owned by the client (the RO assertion). In addition, since some types of marketable securities are recorded at market value, the number of shares directly influences the amount presented on the balance sheet. Thus, this procedure also corresponds to the VA assertion. Finally, if the number of shares counted or confirms differs from the client's records, this difference may be due to unrecorded securities transactions (the CO assertion).

If securities are inspected at any time other than the balance-sheet date, the auditor should account for any transactions that occurred in the intervening period. If, however, the securities are in a safe-deposit box, a letter from the safe-deposit company attesting to nonentry to the box during the interim period may eliminate the need to account for intervening transactions.

◻ Verifying Market Values

As noted at the beginning of this section, *SFAS No. 115* requires some marketable securities to be carried at market value. Therefore, the auditor must determine the market value at the end of the year, normally through reference to published sources (e.g., *The Wall Street Journal*). If the securities held by the client are not actively traded, the auditor may need to obtain market quotations from brokers. Once the market value of the securities has been determined, the total market value can be calculated by multiplying the number of shares by the market price per share (tickmark "M" in Figure 15-5).

Once the market value of the securities has been verified, the auditor should determine if changes in market value during the year have been accounted for in accordance with SFAS 115. For available-for-sale securities, any changes in market value are reported as a separate component of shareholders' equity until realized upon the sale of the security. In contrast, changes in the market value of trading securities are reported in net income in the period of the change. Since held-to-maturity securities are accounted for at amortized cost, changes in the market value of these securities are not reflected in the organization's financial statements. As shown in Figure 15-5, the disposition of unrealized holding gains or losses on marketable securities is summarized in workpaper AJE-1 (not illustrated).

An additional factor that should be considered by the auditor in verifying the market value of marketable securities is whether decreases in market value represent a temporary decline or a permanent impairment. In making this determination, the auditor should consider the following factors:

- The extent to which declines in market values relate to the specific investment, industry, or geographic area versus declines in the overall market
- Whether the client has the ability to hold the investment for a sufficient period of time to allow for recovery in market value
- The extent of time over which the decline has existed[5]

Since changes in market value affect both the amounts presented on the balance sheet (for marketable securities and changes in the market value of available-for-sale securities) and income statement (for changes in the market value of trading securities), this procedure affects the VA assertion.

Examining Investment Revenue Accounts

In addition to examining the balances in the investment accounts, the income derived from those investments should also be verified by the auditor. Income from investments includes both interest revenue (from debt securities) and dividend revenue (from equity securities). Interest revenue is recalculated by the auditor based on the principal amount of the securities and the interest rate; as noted previously, this information is verified by the auditor in his or her examination or confirmation of securities. Dividend revenue can be verified by reference to such sources as *Moody's* and *Standard & Poor's*. In addition, since both interest revenue and dividend revenue eventually result in the receipt of cash by the client, the auditor can also compare recorded dividend and interest revenue to cash receipts records. Procedures involved with verifying the interest and dividend revenue are primarily concerned with the VA assertion.

Performing Analytical Procedures

Analytical procedures can be used by the auditor in his or her examination of investments to verify the reasonableness of recorded amounts. As with the use of analytical procedures for other accounts, these procedures may assist the auditor in identifying fictitious transactions that have been recorded in the accounting records (the EO and RO assertions), unrecorded transactions (the CO assertion), and transactions recorded at the incorrect dollar amount (the VA assertion). In addition, by using analytical procedures to verify the reasonableness of various classes of marketable securities (e.g., trading securities and available-for-sale securities), the auditor may uncover instances where investments are misclas-

---

[5] American Institute of Certified Public Accountants (AICPA), *Proposed Statement on Auditing Standards*, "Investments in Debt and Equity Securities" (New York: AICPA, May 29, 1996).

sified by the client (the PD assertion). An analytical procedure commonly used by auditors is comparing the recorded (unaudited) balance in investments to: (1) the balance of investments for previous years, and/or (2) the budgeted or forecasted balance of investments. In addition, the following ratios involving the investment and other related accounts may be calculated and compared to expectations through the use of analytical procedures.

- Ratio of total investments to total assets
- Ratio of specific classes of investments to total investments
- Ratio of investment income to total investments

Evaluating Financial Statement Presentation

A central issue in evaluating the presentation of investments in the financial statements is considering the classification of marketable securities. Since management intent is the primary criterion for classification of securities, the auditor should inquire of management regarding their intent and evaluate whether management's classification is reasonable. In addition, the auditor should examine written evidence to provide further evidence of the reasonableness of management's classification, such as:

- Written records of investment strategies
- Written instructions to the client's portfolio managers
- Minutes of meetings of the Board of Directors or Investment Committee

For available-for-sale and held-to-maturity securities, the auditor should evaluate the appropriateness of classification in the balance sheet as a current or long-term asset (trading securities are always classified as a current asset). Because classification of securities affects both the overall financial statement presentation as well as the disposition of changes in market values across the financial statements, this procedure is related to both the VA and PD assertions.

In addition to the classification of investments, the auditor should also inquire about any securities being pledged as collateral for loans or other debts. If securities are pledged in this fashion, this information should be disclosed in the footnotes accompanying the financial statements. Therefore, this procedure provides the auditor with assurance regarding the PD assertion.

Finally, the auditor should review the financial statement disclosures required by *SFAS 115*. These disclosures include matters regarding the valuation of investments as well as disclosures regarding changes in market values during the period covered by the financial statements. Reviewing the adequacy of disclosures relates to the PD assertion.

> **CHAPTER CHECKPOINTS**
>
> **15-7.** Identify and define the three major categories into which investments in marketable securities can be classified.
>
> **15-8.** What type of information is normally included in the Listing of Securities?
>
> **15-9.** Describe the procedures used by the auditor to verify:
>
>   **a.** Purchases of investments
>   **b.** Disposals of investments
>
> **15-10.** Why should the auditor agree certificate numbers from the Listing of Securities with those on the actual certificates?
>
> **15-11.** What is the primary procedure used by the auditor in verifying interest revenue? Dividend revenue?
>
> **15-12.** What is the auditor's primary concern with respect to the presentation of information about investments in the financial statements? How does he or she investigate this matter?

SUBSTANTIVE TESTS: PROPERTY, PLANT AND EQUIPMENT

Property, plant and equipment (PPE) represents fixed assets that are used by the client in its revenue-generating activities. These assets should be clearly distinguished from assets of a similar nature that are held for speculative purposes and will be sold upon an increase in market value. For example, a plot of land held by a company for future plant expansion is classified as PPE. If this same tract of land is being held for sale, the asset would be classified as an investment.

In establishing an audit approach for PPE, inherent risk is normally low for all assertions. These assets are normally not highly susceptible to theft; in addition, accounting issues relating to PPE are relatively straightforward. However, the auditor should consider company-specific circumstances in establishing the appropriate level of inherent risk. To illustrate:

▶ If companies frequently dispose of items of PPE, they may inadvertently fail to remove the cost (and accumulated depreciation) of the disposed items from the accounting records. If so, the inherent risk associated with the EO assertion may need to be increased.

▶ If a large number of expenditures are made for PPE after its acquisition, the difficulty in classifying these expenditures as capital or revenue expenditures may result in higher levels of inherent risk with respect to the VA and PD assertions.

Like the audit of investments, the relatively small number of transactions affecting PPE ordinarily results in the auditor performing a substantive audit. However, for companies having a larger number of transactions, the auditor may choose to test important control activities and reduce the extent of substantive tests involving PPE. The major substantive tests over PPE are summarized in Figure 15-6 and are discussed in the remainder of this section.

◘ Obtaining or Preparing a Listing of PPE

Figure 15-7 is a sample workpaper (Listing of PPE) used by the auditor in his or her examination of PPE transactions. The basic approach taken by the auditor is similar to that for the audit of investments. That is, beginning balances in both PPE accounts as well as the accumulated depreciation account should be agreed to the prior-year workpapers. In addition, the schedule should be footed and crossfooted (depicted by the "F" and "CF" tickmarks in Figure 15-7). Since these procedures are used to verify the accuracy of the totals that eventually appear on the client's Trial Balance, they correspond to the VA assertion.

◘ Verifying PPE Transactions

Under the test of transactions approach, the auditor will verify all (or most) transactions involving PPE during the year. In cases where a large number of transactions occur during the year, the auditor may reduce the extent of his or her substantive tests based on the effectiveness of the client's internal control over PPE. As shown in tickmark "P" in Figure 15-7, the procedures performed in testing additions include:

1. Verify the cost of the item through reference to the Vendor's Invoice (if the asset is purchased), Internal Cost Records (if constructed by the client), or Capital Lease Agreement (if leased). In doing so, the auditor should recall that the cost of an asset includes all costs necessary to acquire the asset and place that asset in use. Therefore, any freight charges, handling charges, and installation costs should be verified by the auditor, as these costs should be capitalized.

2. Vouch from the addition of the asset to authorization by the Board of Directors. For the purchase of fixed assets involving smaller amounts (such as office furniture), the auditor should verify authorization by the Purchasing Department through reference to a Purchase Order.

In testing disposals of PPE (see tickmark "S" in Figure 15-7), the auditor would:

1. Determine whether the disposal was properly authorized (by reference to the Board of Directors' Minutes or Property Lapsing Schedules).
2. Determine whether the asset account has been relieved of the amount pertaining to the assets disposed.
3. Substantiate the proceeds of the disposal through reference to cash receipts records.
4. Determine whether gains or losses on the disposals of assets are recorded properly. If the client uses different methods of depreciation for tax and book purposes, the computation of both tax and book gain or loss should be tested.
5. Ascertain whether assets acquired in trade-ins have been recorded correctly.

The above procedures for verifying purchases and disposals of PPE provide auditor with assurance that the transactions involving PPE actually occurred (the EO assertion). In addition, by comparing the recorded amount with the documentation, the auditor can verify that purchases and disposals of PPE are recorded at the correct dollar amount (the VA assertion).

Procedure	Classification	Assertion(s)				
		EO	RO	CO	VA	PD
1. Obtain or prepare a Listing of PPE held during the year under audit (Figure 15-7)						
a. Agree beginning balances from Listing to prior-year workpapers	Comparison				x	
b. Foot and cross-foot Listing and agree total to the client's Trial Balance	Recalculation Comparison				x	
2. Verify PPE transactions occurring during the year						
a. Vouch transactions occurring during the year to appropriate documentation	Inspect Documents	x			x	
b. Trace from evidence of disposals of PPE to Listing	Inspect Documents			x		
3. Inspect assets and title for selected items of PPE	Observation	x		x	x	x
	Inspect Documents	x	x			
	Confirmation	x	x			
4. Examine subsequent expenditures recorded in the repairs and maintenance expense account						
a. Vouch transactions to appropriate documentation	Inspect documents				x	x
b. Inquire of management about policies for classifying expenditures	Inquiry				x	x
5. Evaluate the provision for depreciation (Figure 15-7)						
a. Evaluate the reasonableness of salvage values, useful lives, and depreciation methods	Inspect Documents Inquiry				x	
b. Recalculate the provision for depreciation	Recalculation				x	
6. Perform analytical procedures for PPE and depreciation accounts	Analytical Procedures	x	x	x	x	
7. Evaluate the overall presentation of PPE in the financial statements						
a. Inquire of management about assets pledged as collateral	Inquiry				x	x
b. Inquire of management about impairment of PPE and determine whether write-downs for impairment are necessary	Inquiry					x
c. Review disclosures related to PPE and depreciation accounts	Inspect Documents					x
d. Review lease agreements	Inspect Documents			x		x

Figure 15-6: *Major Substantive Tests: PPE*

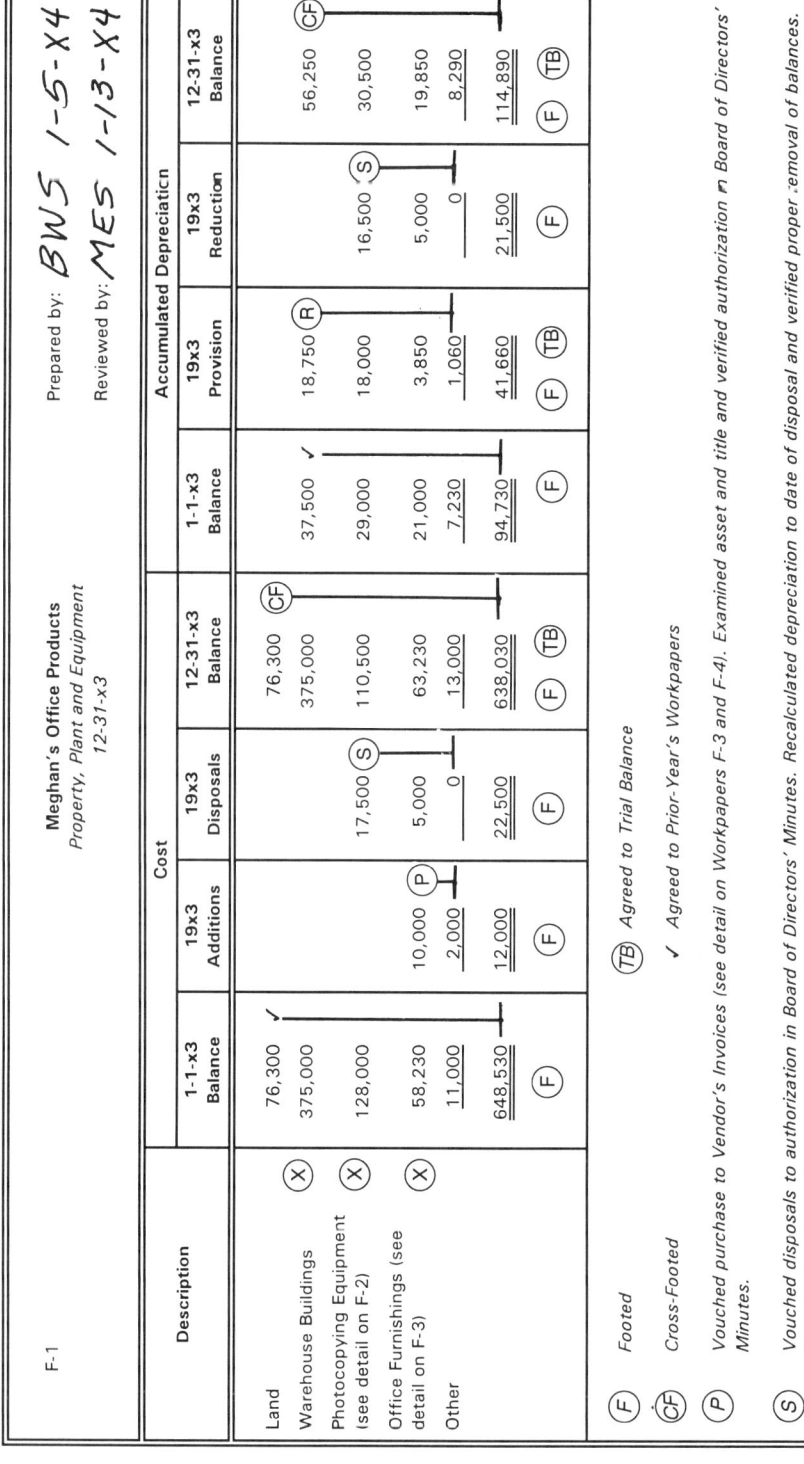

Figure 15-7: *Listing of Property, Plant and Equipment*

In addition to verifying *recorded* PPE transactions, the auditor should also be aware of the possibility that PPE transactions are not recorded. In particular, the auditor should investigate the possibility of unrecorded disposals of PPE. One characteristic of disposals of PPE is that these transactions often result in losses being recognized, especially when PPE is disposed prior to the end of its useful life. As a result, the possibility exists that companies may intentionally fail to record disposals of PPE (the CO assertion). To examine this assertion, the auditor normally examines various sources of information in search of unrecorded disposals. The following are some sources of information available to the auditor about possible disposals of PPE.

▶ Property Lapsing Schedules contained in the permanent workpapers.

▶ Authorization of disposals contained in the Board of Directors' Minutes.

▶ Cash receipts records reflecting proceeds received from the disposal of PPE.

▶ Changes in property tax and insurance records relating to PPE.

DON'T DEPRECIATE WHAT YOU DON'T HAVE[6]

An internal auditor's review noted that PPE previously sold by an unnamed company was still included on the company's records at a historical cost of $1,615,000 and a net book value of $956,000. Because of the failure to remove these assets from the accounting records, depreciation expense was overstated and retained earnings understated by $303,000 over a five-year period. As a result of this error, this company has now established a policy to prepare formal documentation to write off disposed equipment in their financial records.

◻ Inspecting PPE and Title to PPE

In addition to examining changes in the PPE accounts for the year under audit, the auditor should also determine that recorded assets actually exist and are owned by the client. At a minimum, the auditor should inspect (through observation of the assets themselves) any major additions of PPE during the current year. However, the auditor does not need to examine individual items of property, plant, and equipment in every case, since these assets are normally not vulnerable to theft or fraud. Tickmark "X" in Figure 15-7 illustrates the application of this procedure. Observation of PPE in this fashion relates to the EO assertion. While observation of PPE is primarily related to the EO assertion, other assertions may be affected as follows:

▶ As the auditor observes items of PPE, he or she should consider whether the items have continuing utility in the client's operations; if not, they may need to be reclassified as Investments or Other Assets (the VA and PD assertions).

---

[6] "Don't Depreciate What You Don't Have," *Internal Auditor* (October 1995), 55.

▶ As the auditor observes PPE, he or she should note any instances of: (1) assets held by the client not included in the Listing of PPE, or (2) assets that are included in the Listing of PPE but are not observed. These situations would represent cases where purchases and disposals of PPE are not recorded (the CO assertion).

Although inspecting an asset proves its existence, it does not allow legal ownership to be determined. To verify legal ownership of the asset, the auditor must examine such evidence as a deed, title, insurance policy, lease agreement (if applicable) and property tax bills. Assets owned by the client but held by third parties under operating lease agreements may be confirmed with the third-party lessees. Verifying the ownership of PPE provides the auditor with assurance regarding the EO and RO assertions.

◻ Examining Subsequent Expenditures

Certain expenditures, such as those that increase the useful life of PPE or result in an asset that has improved capabilities (e.g., adding a collating tray to an existing photocopier) are referred to as **capital expenditures**. These expenditures must be capitalized to the cost of the asset and depreciated over their useful life or the life of the asset, whichever is shorter. In contrast, expenditures which do not increase the useful life or capabilities of PPE are referred to as **revenue expenditures**. In general, revenue expenditures occur more frequently and are for lower dollar amounts than capital expenditures.

The auditor's primary concern in the examination of PPE is that capital expenditures are not incorrectly charged as revenue expenditures. Accordingly, the auditor will vouch from entries in repairs and maintenance expense to invoices, work orders, and other documents for support of the transaction. Because many companies have written policies for classifying expenditures subsequent to acquisition based on the nature of the item and/or dollar amount of the expenditure, the auditor should evaluate the classifications to determine the consistency with written policy. In addition, the auditor should inquire of the client about any policies with respect to classification of subsequent expenditures. Since these procedures will identify transactions that have been incorrectly recorded and classified, this procedure affects the VA and PD assertions.

◻ Evaluating the Provision for Depreciation

The primary purpose of evaluating the provision for depreciation is to verify that depreciation expense (and accumulated depreciation) are recorded at the proper dollar amount (the VA assertion). Prior to verifying the adequacy of the provision for depreciation, the auditor should consider whether the methods used by the client to determine salvage values, useful lives, and depreciation policies are reasonable and consistently applied. After these factors have been evaluated, the auditor should recalculate the current provision for depreciation (tickmark "R" in Figure 15-7). Once the depreciation expense has been recalculated in the above manner, the auditor should foot the total depreciation expense and accumulated depreciation and agree these totals to the client's Trial Balance.

◘ Performing Analytical Procedures

Analytical procedures can be used by the auditor in his or her examination of PPE to verify the reasonableness of recorded amounts. As with the use of analytical procedures for other accounts, these procedures may assist the auditor in identifying fictitious transactions that have been recorded in the accounting records (the EO and RO assertions), unrecorded transactions (the CO assertion), and transactions recorded at the incorrect dollar amount (the VA assertion). An analytical procedure commonly used by auditors is comparing the recorded (unaudited) balance in PPE and depreciation expense to: (1) the balances in these accounts for previous years, and/or (2) the budgeted or forecasted balances in these accounts. In addition, the following ratios may be calculated and compared to expectations by the auditor through the use of analytical procedures:

- Ratio of PPE to total assets
- Ratio of depreciation expense to PPE
- Ratio of repairs and maintenance expense to net income
- Asset turnover ratio (net sales ÷ total or average PPE)
- Return on assets (net income ÷ total or average PPE)

◘ Evaluating Financial Statement Presentation

Earlier, it was noted that the auditor should verify the recorded amount of leased assets through reference to the capital lease agreement. In addition to this procedure, the auditor should ascertain that leases are properly classified as operating leases (no asset or liability recorded on the balance sheet) and capital leases (asset and liability recorded on the balance sheet). In particular, because capital lease agreements result in companies recognizing both a liability as well as depreciation expense related to the leased asset, the auditor is concerned with ensuring that leases classified as operating leases **do not** meet the criteria for capitalization. Examining lease agreements in this fashion allows the auditor to determine that all PPE "owned" by the client is recorded in the accounts (the CO assertion) and that disclosures related to PPE are adequate (the PD assertion).

In evaluating the PD assertion, the auditor should also inquire of management about PPE pledged as collateral and review the footnote disclosures provided for PPE and related accounts. Some important disclosures include: depreciation expense, the balances of major classes of depreciable assets, accumulated depreciation (either by asset or in total), and a general description of the depreciation methods used with respect to major classes of assets.

A final issue related to the presentation of PPE in the financial statements is recognizing reductions in PPE when impairment (or loss in utility or value) occurs. *Statement of Financial Accounting Standards No. 121*[7] *(SFAS No. 121)* requires companies to evaluate their long-lived assets (such as

---

[7] Financial Accounting Standards Board (FASB), *Statement of Financial Accounting Standards No. 121*, "Accounting for the Impairment of Long-Lived Assets and for Long-Lived Assets to be Disposed Of" (Norwalk, CT: FASB, 1995).

PPE) for impairment and recognize a loss in the period in which impairment is noted. While an extensive discussion of *SFAS 121* is beyond the scope of this text, the auditor should inquire of management about potential impairment of PPE and determine that any necessary write-downs are taken. Since impairment affects both the supplemental footnote disclosures as well as the amounts recognized in the balance sheet, this procedure corresponds to both the VA and PD assertions.

CHAPTER CHECKPOINTS

15-13. What assertion(s) are addressed by agreeing beginning balances on the listing of PPE to the prior year's workpapers?

15-14. Describe the procedures used by the auditor to verify:

a. Purchases of PPE
b. Disposals of PPE

15-15. Why might companies wish to intentionally fail to record disposals of PPE? How does the auditor search for unrecorded disposals of PPE?

15-16. Distinguish between capital expenditures and revenue expenditures. What is the auditor's primary concern with respect to the recording of subsequent expenditures for PPE? How is this matter verified by the auditor?

15-17. What additional issues are introduced when companies lease PPE from third parties?

◉ SUBSTANTIVE TESTS: NOTES PAYABLE AND LONG-TERM DEBT

Notes payable and long-term debt (or bonds payable) may be either a current or a noncurrent liability, depending on the maturity date. Because these liabilities normally obligate the company issuing them to pay interest, they are often referred to as **interest-bearing liabilities** (IBLs). In establishing an audit approach for IBLs, inherent risk is normally low for all but the CO assertion. As with other liabilities, management has an incentive to intentionally fail to record issuances of notes payable and long-term debt. Therefore, to control audit risk to a reasonably low level, the auditor must obtain assurance related to the CO assertion through tests of controls and/or substantive tests. Like other transactions in the Investing and Financing cycle, the low frequency of transactions involving IBLs suggest that a substantive audit approach (the test of transactions) will be conducted. Figure 15-8 summarizes the major substantive tests performed by the auditor over IBLs.

◘ Obtaining or Preparing a Listing of IBLS

Figure 15-9 is a sample workpaper used by the auditor in his or her examination of IBLs. The basic approach taken by the auditor is similar to that for the audit of investments and PPE. That is, beginning balances in both the IBL accounts as well as the interest payable account should be agreed to the

Procedure	Classification	Assertion(s)				
		EO	RO	CO	VA	PD
1. Obtain or prepare a Listing of IBLs (Figure 15-9)						
a. Agree beginning balances from Listing to prior-year workpapers	Comparison				x	
b. Foot and cross-foot Listing and agree total to the client's Trial Balance	Recalculation Comparison				x	
2. Vouch IBL transactions occurring during the year to appropriate documentation	Inspect Documents Confirmation	x	x		x	
3. Inspect debt instruments or confirm debt with third parties						
a. Agree principal amount, maturity date, and interest rate with information in the listing of IBLs	Observation Confirmation	x	x		x	
b. Identify portion of debt maturing during the current year (if any) and/or any debt covenants	Observation Confirmation				x	x
4. Recalculate the provision for interest expense (Figure 15-9)	Recalculation				x	
5. Investigate the possibility of unrecorded issuances of IBLs.						
a. Send confirmations to all banks the client has done business with in the past.	Confirmation			x		
b. Trace from authorizations in the Board of Directors' Minutes to recordings.	Inspect Documents			x		
c. Examine large cash receipts during the year.	Inspect Documents			x		
6. Perform analytical procedures for liability and interest accounts	Analytical Procedures	x	x	x	x	
7. Evaluate the overall presentation of IBLs and interest accounts in the financial statements						
a. Inquire of management about debt covenants	Inquiry					x
b. Inquire of management about contingent liabilities	Inquiry			x		x
c. Review disclosures related to liability and interest accounts	Inspect Documents					x

Figure 15-8: *Major Substantive Tests: IBLs*

prior-year workpapers. In addition, the schedule should be footed and crossfooted (depicted by the "F" and "CF" tickmarks in Figure 15-9). Since these procedures are used to verify the accuracy of the totals that eventually appear on the client's Trial Balance, they correspond to the VA assertion.

G-1

Meghan's Office Products
Interest-Bearing Liabilities
12-31-x3

Prepared by: BSS 1-11-X4
Reviewed by: MES 1-22-X4

Description	Liability				Interest Payable			
	1-1-x3 Balance	19x3 Additions	19x3 Retirements	12-31-x3 Balance	1-1-x3 Balance	19x3 Provision	19x3 Payments	12-31-x3 Balance
10% note payable to First Bank, due $10,000 per year, final payment due 12-31-x6	40,000 ✓		10,000 Ⓟ	30,000 ⒸⒻ	0	4,000 Ⓡ	4,000 Ⓧ	0 ⒸⒻ
12% note payable to Jones Factor, issued 10-1-x3, due 10-1-x7	0	100,000 Ⓘ	0	100,000	0	3,000	0	3,000 Ⓡ
	40,000	100,000	10,000	130,000 ⓉⒷ	0	7,000 ⓉⒷ	4,000	3,000
	Ⓕ	Ⓕ	Ⓕ	Ⓕ	Ⓕ	Ⓕ	Ⓕ	ⒻⓉⒷ

Ⓕ *Footed*

ⒸⒻ *Cross-Footed*

Ⓒ *Confirmed with holder and agreed principal amount, maturity dates, and interest rate.*

Ⓘ *Agreed principal amount, maturity date, and interest rate to confirmation received from holder. Vouched to Board of Directors' Minutes to verify authorization.*

Ⓟ *Examined canceled Check to verify disbursement and agreed amount to the maturity of the note.*

Ⓧ *Examined canceled Check to verify disbursement.*

ⓉⒷ *Agreed to Trial Balance*

✓ *Agreed to Prior-Year's Workpapers*

Ⓡ *Interest Expense:*
$40,000 × 0.10 × 1 year = 4,000
$100,000 × 0.12 × 3/12 year = 3,000

Interest Payable:
$100,000 × 0.12 × 3/12 year = 3,000

Figure 15-9: *Listing of Interest-Bearing Liabilities*

◻ Verifying IBL Transactions

Because of the small number of transactions affecting IBLs, as well as the important implications of these transactions, the auditor ordinarily verifies all transactions occurring during the year under audit. These transactions include both issuances and retirements of IBLs. As shown in tickmark "I" in Figure 15-9, the procedures performed in testing issuances of IBLs include:

1. Vouching the recorded amount of the liability to the face amount of the instrument or a confirmation received from the holder of the instrument. If this the face amount is equal to the cash received, no premium or discount is recorded by the client. However, if the cash received differs from the face amount of the liability, a premium or discount must be established and amortized to interest expense over the life of the obligation.
2. Vouching the issuance to authorization in the Board of Directors' Minutes.

The auditor verifies retirements of IBLs (tickmark "P" in Figure 15-9) as follows:

1. Vouching the reduction in the liability to cash disbursement records and other evidence of the retirement (such as canceled notes or bonds).
2. Vouching the reduction in the liability to authorization in the Board of Directors' Minutes.

As with PPE transactions, these procedures allow the auditor to verify that: (1) recorded transactions actually occurred (the EO assertion), and (2) transactions are recorded at the proper dollar amount (the VA assertion). In addition, since all liability transactions entered into by the client are true obligations of that client, these procedures also pertain to the RO assertion.

◻ Inspecting or Confirming IBLS

The auditor confirms IBLs with the holder or trustee in order to obtain evidence that these liabilities exist and are obligations of the client. In obtaining these confirmations, the auditor will request that the party corroborate the principal amount, date of issuance, maturity date, and interest rate. Alternatively, the auditor can examine the actual debt agreements and agree the pertinent information from the debt agreement to the Listing of IBLs. This procedure is illustrated by tickmark "C" in Figure 15-9. Note that, in addition to the EO and RO assertions, verifying the principal amount provides the auditor with evidence regarding the VA assertion.

In addition to the above information, the auditor should identify: (1) the portion of the obligations (if any) that mature during the subsequent year, and (2) the existence of any debt covenants related to the obligation. Under GAAP, any portion of the obligation that matures during the coming year should be reclassified as a short-term liability (normally, in an account such as "current portion of long-term debt"); thus, this procedure relates to the VA and PD assertions. As short-term liabilities are often included in several important ratios of interest to users (for example, the current ratio), balance sheet classification of IBLs is an important consideration. In addition, the existence of any covenants related to the client's IBLs (such as maintaining a minimum debt-to-equity ratio or sinking-fund requirements) should be disclosed in the footnotes accompanying the financial statements (the PD assertion).

◻ Recalculating Interest Expense

In verifying whether the accrual of interest (and determination of interest expense) is accurate, the auditor normally recalculates these amounts as shown by tickmark "R" in Figure 15-9. Although not illustrated in Figure 15-9, if the issuance of the IBL initially resulted in a premium or discount, the auditor should also recalculate the amortization of that premium or discount, as this amortization affects the amount of interest expense recognized by the client. This purpose of recalculating interest expense is to verify the accuracy of recorded amounts (the VA assertion).

◻ Searching for Unrecorded Liabilities

As with accounts payable, the auditor's primary concern with respect to IBLs is the CO assertion (that is, have all IBLs been recorded?). In searching for unrecorded IBLs, the auditor can perform the following procedures.

1. Send confirmations to all banks that the client has done business with in the current year and in the recent past.
2. Read the Board of Directors' Minutes for meetings occurring during the previous year and trace any authorized issuances of IBLs to a recording in the accounts.
3. Examine the source of all large receipts of cash occurring during the year. One source of large receipts of cash is the issuance of IBLs.

Recall from our discussion in Chapter 11 that, as part of the examination of cash, the auditor normally sends a confirmation to all banks that the client does business with, regardless of whether the client maintains cash balances in those banks. While Chapter 11 focused on confirming cash balances, these confirmations may also serve as a method of identifying unrecorded IBLs.

◻ Performing Analytical Procedures

In performing analytical procedures, the auditor may compare the recorded (unaudited) balances in the IBL and interest expense accounts to: (1) the balances in these accounts from prior years, and/or (2) the budgeted or forecasted balances in these accounts. Also, three important ratios used by the auditor in performing analytical procedures are:

- ▶ The debt-to-equity ratio (total debt ÷ total equity)
- ▶ The times interest earned ratio (operating income before taxes and interest ÷ interest expense)
- ▶ The ratio of interest expense to total debt

As with other accounts, analytical procedures may assist the auditor in identifying fictitious transactions that have been recorded in the accounting records (the EO and RO assertions), unrecorded transactions (the CO assertion), and transactions recorded at the incorrect dollar amount (the VA assertion).

◘ Evaluating Financial Statement Presentation

Three important issues regarding the presentation and disclosure (the PD assertion) of IBLs should be discussed with the client's management. First, the auditor should inquire about any debt covenants related to the client's IBLs. These debt covenants must be disclosed by the client; in addition, any violations of debt covenants often require accelerated payment of the related obligation (and, thus, reclassification of long term liabilities to short-term liabilities).

Second, the auditor should inquire about whether the client may be contingently liable because of the endorsement of notes or guarantee of indebtedness of another party. A **contingent liability** is defined by *Statement of Financial Accounting Standards No. 5*[8] *(SFAS 5)* as a loss (and liability) that may need to be recognized when one or more future events occurs or fails to occur. For example, if Company X guarantees the debt of Company Y, it will be required to repay that obligation upon the default by Company Y. Based on the guidance provided by *SFAS 5*, this contingency may be required to be recognized as a balance sheet liability or disclosed in the footnotes, depending on the likelihood and estimability of the potential loss. In addition to the PD assertion, the possible existence of a contingent liability (and the need to record a loss and liability in the financial statements) also affects the CO assertion.

Finally, the auditor should review the disclosures related to IBLs to verify that they are complete and consistent with GAAP. Important disclosures include interest rates, maturity dates, debt covenants, call provisions, and conversion provisions. In addition, *Statement of Financial Accounting Standards No. 47*[9] *(SFAS 47)* requires disclosures of the aggregate amount and sinking fund requirements (if any) for all long-term debt for each of the five years following the balance-sheet date. In addition, the explosion of new types of instruments used by companies to finance their activities has resulted in more extensive disclosures of potential liabilities. For example, *Statement of Financial Accounting Standards No. 105*[10] requires relatively extensive disclosures regarding different risks associated with various types of financial instruments. A more extensive discussion of these instruments and the required disclosures is beyond the scope of this text.

NEW FINANCIAL INSTRUMENTS[11]

A Rip Van Winkle who fell asleep in 1979 and just woke up would hardly recognize today's financial landscape ... Arthur Andersen & Company has kept a list of new financial products since 1986; it now totals more than 600.

---

[8] Financial Accounting Standards Board (FASB), *Statement of Financial Accounting Standards No. 5*, "Accounting for Contingencies" (Norwalk, CT: FASB, 1975).

[9] Financial Accounting Standards Board (FASB), *Statement of Financial Accounting Standards No. 47*, "Disclosure of Long-Term Obligations" (Norwalk, CT: FASB, 1981).

[10] Financial Accounting Standards Board (FASB), *Statement of Financial Accounting Standards No. 105*, "Disclosure of Information about Financial Instruments with Off-Balance-Sheet Risk and Financial Instruments with Concentrations of Credit Risk" (Norwalk, CT: FASB, 1990).

[11] "Is Financial Product Explosion Perilous for Investors?," *The Wall Street Journal* (December 21, 1989), C1.

> **CHAPTER CHECKPOINTS**
>
> **15-18.** What assertion(s) have relatively high levels of inherent risk in the auditor's examination of IBLs?
>
> **15-19.** Describe the procedures used by the auditor to verify:
>
>   a. Issuances of IBLs
>   b. Retirements of IBLs
>
> **15-20.** Why would the auditor send confirmations to financial institutions with whom clients have done business in the past if no cash is currently maintained on deposit at those institutions?
>
> **15-21.** What types of analytical procedures can be used by the auditor in his or her examination of IBLs? What assertions are addressed by these analytical procedures?
>
> **15-22.** What is a loss contingency? How does the auditor examine the possible existence of loss contingencies?

◉ SUBSTANTIVE TESTS: STOCKHOLDERS' EQUITY ACCOUNTS

Two factors affecting the overall audit approach for stockholders' equity accounts are the level of inherent risk and level of control risk. The accounting issues involved with stockholders' equity accounts are relatively straightforward. Therefore, inherent risk is normally low for all assertions. In some instances, if the client issues its stock in the form of a pooling of interests or has complex convertible securities or stock options, inherent risk for the VA and PD assertions may be assessed at higher levels.

With respect to control risk, the relatively small number of transactions affecting stockholders' equity normally results in assessment of control risk at maximum levels and extensive substantive tests (lower detection risk). One distinguishing feature of stockholders' equity accounts is that transactions are usually handled by external parties, as follows:

▶ **Registrar:** Issues stock

▶ **Transfer Agent:** Maintains records of stock and handles stock transfers

▶ **Payment Agency:** Handles payment of dividends to shareholders

In cases where external parties are involved with stockholders' equity transactions, the auditor can assess control risk at lower levels. Like other transactions in the Investing and Financing cycle, the low frequency of transactions involving stockholders' equity accounts suggest that a substantive audit approach (the test of transactions) will be conducted. Figure 15-10 summarizes the major substantive tests performed by the auditor over stockholders' equity transactions.

Procedure	Classification	Assertion(s)				
		EO	RO	CO	VA	PD
1. Obtain or prepare a Schedule of Changes in Stockholders' Equity (Figure 15-11)						
a. Agree beginning balances from Schedule to prior-year workpapers	Comparison				x	
b. Foot and cross-foot Schedule and agree total to the client's Trial Balance	Recalculation Comparison				x	
2. Vouch stockholders' equity transactions occurring during the year to appropriate documentation	Inspect Documents	x	x		x	
3. Inspect Stockholders' Ledger or confirm shares issued and outstanding with Registrar	Observation Confirmation	x	x	x		
4. Obtain or prepare an analysis of the Retained Earnings account (Figure 15-11)						
a. Agree beginning balances from analysis to prior-year workpapers	Comparison				x	
b. Agree net income (or loss) from analysis to detailed workpapers for operations	Comparison				x	
c. Vouch dividends to Board of Directors' minutes and verify dividends declared	Inspect Documents Recalculation	x	x		x	
d. Foot the analysis and agree the total to the client's Trial Balance	Recalculation Comparison				x	
5. Perform analytical procedures for stockholders' equity accounts	Analytical Procedures	x	x	x	x	
6. Evaluate the overall presentation of stockholders' equity accounts in the financial statements						
a. Review Articles of Incorporation	Inspect Documents					x
b. Inquire of management about stockholders' equity items	Inquiry					x
c. Review disclosures related to stockholders' equity accounts	Inspect Documents					x

Figure 15-10: *Major Substantive Tests: Stockholders' Equity Accounts*

◻ Obtaining or Preparing a Schedule of Changes in Stockholders' Equity

Figure 15-11 is a sample workpaper used by the auditor in his or her examination of stockholders' equity transactions. The basic approach taken by the auditor is similar to that for the audit of other accounts in the Investing and Financing cycle. That is, beginning balances in the stockholders' equity accounts should be agreed to the prior-year workpapers. In addition, the schedule should be footed and crossfooted (depicted by the "F" and "CF" tickmarks in Figure 15-11). Since these procedures are used to verify the accuracy of the totals that eventually appear on the client's Trial Balance, they correspond to the VA assertion.

H-1	Meghan's Office Products Stockholders' Equity 12-31-x3	Prepared by: BSS 1-10-X4 Reviewed by: MES 1-17-X4

Account	1-1-x3 Balance	19x3 Additions	19x3 Reductions	12-31-x3 Balance	
Common Stock, $10 par	100,000 ✓	20,000 (I)		120,000 (CF)	
Additional Paid-in Capital	57,290	8,320		65,610	
Total Contributed Capital	157,290	28,320		185,610	
	(F)	(F)		(F) (TB)	
Retained Earnings	798,163 ✓	198,724 (NI)	25,000 (D)	971,887 (CF) (TB)	

(F) Footed (TB) Agreed to Trial Balance
(CF) Cross-Footed ✓ Agreed to Prior-Year's Workpapers
(I) Vouched issuance of stock to Board of Directors' Minutes to verify authorization. Verified number of shares issued with outside Registrar and agreed proceeds to Cash Receipts Journal. Recalculated distribution between Common Stock and Additional Paid-in-Capital accounts.
(NI) Agreed to Workpapers for operations. See R-1 through R-38 for a summary of audit procedures and conclusions.
(D) Vouched to authorization in Board of Directors' Minutes and recalculated amount of dividend.

Figure 15-11: *Schedule of Changes in Stockholders' Equity*

◻ Verifying Stockholders' Equity Transactions

As with other accounts in the Investing and Financing cycle, the auditor will examine all (or most) of the transactions affecting stockholders' equity during the year. For issuances of stock during the year (see tickmark "I" in Figure 15-11), the auditor first vouches the issuance to the Board of Directors'

Minutes to determine that they were properly authorized by the client. In doing so, the auditor is also able to identify the number of shares issued during the year. The auditor then verifies the cash received upon issuance of the stock through reference to cash receipts records. At this point, the distribution of proceeds between the capital stock account and paid-in capital is recalculated as follows:

▶ **Capital stock:** Number of shares issued multiplied by par value.

▶ **Paid-in capital:** Difference between the par value of shares issued and the total cash proceeds.

For repurchases or retirements of capital stock, the auditor should vouch from the entry reflecting the repurchase to the Board of Directors' Minutes to verify that all repurchases were properly authorized. If shares repurchased by the client are held in the treasury, the auditor would ordinarily inspect these shares. To verify that all transactions involving repurchases of capital stock are accounted for correctly, the auditor agrees the cash paid for the repurchase to the client's cash disbursements records. The distribution of the cash paid to repurchase stock over specific balance sheet accounts is dependent upon the method used by the client to account for its treasury stock (either the cost method or the par value method). Discussion of these two methods is beyond the scope of this text, but the auditor should verify the appropriateness of the entry used to account for these transactions.

For capital stock transactions, examining authorization by the Board of Directors relates to the EO and RO assertions. By verifying the amount of cash received (for issuances) or paid (for repurchases) as well as the allocation of cash between the capital stock and paid-in capital accounts, the auditor is verifying the VA assertion.

BEWARE OF THE "SHELL" GAME

One method of "going public" that companies have used to bilk investors is by merging a fledgling concern into an existing shell corporation. While this method is popular with entrepreneurs because they can save months of work and hundreds of thousands of dollars by avoiding a formal underwriting agreement, investors can suffer. For example, Victor Incendy gave creditors of his corporation (Cascade International) stock in a new cosmetic company. At the same time, Mr. Incendy created and began secretly selling more than six million shares of unauthorized stock. Once it became apparent that the cosmetic company's financial results were largely fictitious, the shares of Cascade International became worthless and the corporation filed for bankruptcy.[12]

◘ Inspecting or Confirming Shares Issued and Outstanding

If the client utilizes a Registrar and Transfer Agent to handle its issuances and recordkeeping, the auditor will confirm the number of shares issued and outstanding at year-end. By comparing this information to the shares issued and outstanding at the beginning of the year, the auditor can

---

[12] "How 2 Florida Firms Fooled Stockholders, Auditors, and the SEC," *The Wall Street Journal* (July 8, 1992), A1.

determine any changes in the number of shares resulting from issuances and repurchases. If the client does not utilize a Registrar or Transfer Agent, the auditor will examine the Stockholders' Ledger to determine the number of shares issued and outstanding.

Confirming shares with the registrar and inspecting the Stockholders' Ledger provide the auditor with assurance that recorded transactions actually occurred (the EO and RO assertions). In addition, this procedure may allow the auditor to detect unrecorded issuances or repurchases of stock (the CO assertion).

◘ Verifying Retained Earnings

In examining retained earnings, the auditor focuses on changes in the retained earnings account in the year of the examination. Figure 15-11 (shown previously) illustrates a sample workpaper used for this analysis. As shown therein, the components of retained earnings are audited as follows:

▶ Beginning balance: Agreed to prior-year workpapers (tickmark "✓" in Figure 15-11).

▶ Net income (loss): Agreed to workpapers related to the examination of operations (revenue and expense accounts) (tickmark "NI" in Figure 15-11).

▶ Dividends declared: Vouched to authorization in the Board of Directors' Minutes and recalculated (tickmark "D" in Figure 15-11).

Once these components are verified, the auditor merely proves the arithmetic accuracy of the retained earnings account by footing the analysis.

The above audit procedures are primarily related to the VA assertion, as they verify the accuracy of the recorded retained earnings balance. In addition to this assertion, vouching dividends declared to the Board of Directors' Minutes provides the auditor with assurance that dividends were declared (the EO assertion) and are an obligation of the client (the RO assertion).

If the client declares a **stock dividend**, the auditor is not able to verify the amount through a single document reflecting payment of that dividend. Instead, he or she must recalculate the charge to retained earnings. This charge will be for the par value of shares issued (for "large" stock dividends) or the market value of shares issued (for "small" stock dividends).[13] After this charge has been recalculated, the auditor should verify that the capital stock account (and paid-in capital, if applicable) have been properly increased to reflect the dividend.

◘ Performing Analytical Procedures

Like the other accounts discussed in this chapter, the auditor may compare the recorded (unaudited) balances in the stockholders' equity accounts to: (1) the balances in these accounts from prior years, and/or (2) the budgeted or forecasted balances in these accounts. Also, three important ratios used by the auditor in performing analytical procedures for stockholders' equity accounts are:

---

[13] American Institute of Certified Public Accountants (AICPA), *Accounting Research Bulletin No. 43*, "Restatement and Revision of *Accounting Research Bulletins 1-42*" (Chapter 7, Section B), indicates that any stock dividend less than 20 to 25 percent of the outstanding shares prior to the declaration of that dividend is considered to be a small stock dividend.

- The ratio of total equity to total assets
- The dividend payout ratio (cash dividends ÷ net income)
- Earnings per share

As with other accounts, analytical procedures may assist the auditor in identifying fictitious transactions that have been recorded in the accounting records (the EO and RO assertions), unrecorded transactions (the CO assertion), and transactions recorded at the incorrect dollar amount (the VA assertion).

◻ Evaluating Financial Statement Presentation

GAAP require relatively extensive disclosures regarding stockholders' equity accounts. In addition to information about the number of shares issued and outstanding, other disclosures include information related to:

- Preferred stock (dividends in arrears, liquidation preferences, conversion and callability features, and redeemable preferred stock)
- Appropriations of retained earnings
- Stock rights, warrants, and options

These disclosures should be evaluated by reading the articles of incorporation, reviewing the disclosures prepared by the client, and inquiring of management. By performing these procedures, the auditor obtains assurance regarding the PD assertion.

CHAPTER CHECKPOINTS

15-23. How are external parties involved in the processing and recording of stockholders' equity transactions? How does this affect inherent risk and/or control risk?

15-24. Describe the procedures used by the auditor to verify:

   a. Issuances of stock
   b. Repurchases of stock

15-25. How does the auditor obtain evidence about the number of shares of the client's stock issued and outstanding? What assertions does verifying this information prove?

15-26. What are the primary procedures performed by the auditor in verifying the retained earnings account?

15-27. What are the auditor's primary sources of information about stock options, warrants, and rights? What is the primary matter of concern to the auditor in examining this information?

◉ SUMMARY OF KEY POINTS

1. The Investing and Financing cycle is the final operating cycle affecting most companies. This cycle involves transactions for the following accounts: (1) investments; (2) property, plant and equipment; (3) notes payable and long-term debt; and (4) stockholders' equity.

2. The accounts affected by the Investing and Financing cycle are characterized by a small number of transactions occurring for relatively high dollar amounts per transaction. Therefore, the auditor ordinarily examines these accounts using the test of transactions approach. Under the test of transactions approach, the auditor performs only limited tests of controls. Instead, the auditor performs relatively extensive substantive testing procedures.

3. The primary control activity of interest in the Investing and Financing cycle is that transactions are ordinarily approved at high levels within the organization (usually, the Board of Directors). If this practice is followed, the Board of Directors' Minutes will contain evidence of transactions in the Investing and Financing cycle.

4. Important procedures performed by the auditor in the examination of investments include: (1) verifying investment transactions, (2) inspecting or confirming securities owned at year-end, (3) verifying market values, (4) examining investment revenue accounts, (5) performing analytical procedures, and (6) evaluating the overall financial statement presentation of investments.

5. The primary audit procedures performed in the examination of PPE are: (1) verifying PPE transactions, (2) inspecting PPE and title to PPE, (3) examining subsequent expenditures related to PPE, (4) evaluating the provision for depreciation, (5) performing analytical procedures, and (6) evaluating the financial statement presentation of PPE.

6. In examining interest-bearing liabilities (IBLs), the auditor is primarily concerned with the CO assertion. Important audit procedures performed in the examination of IBLs include: (1) verifying notes payable and long-term debt transactions, (2) inspecting or confirming IBLs, (3) recalculating interest expense, (4) searching for unrecorded liabilities, (5) performing analytical procedures, and (5) evaluating the financial statement presentation of IBL and interest accounts.

7. Stockholders' equity accounts are unique in that outside parties are involved in the processing and recording of transactions. The primary audit procedures performed in the examination of stockholders' equity include: (1) verifying stockholders' equity transactions, (2) inspecting the stockholders' ledger or confirming shares issued and outstanding with outside parties, (3) verifying retained earnings, (4) performing analytical procedures, and (5) evaluating the financial statement presentation of stockholders' equity accounts.

◉ GLOSSARY

Available-for-Sale Securities. Marketable securities that are not classified as trading securities or held-to-maturity securities. Ordinarily, the company's management intends to hold these securities for relatively long periods of time. These securities are carried on the financial statements at market value.

Board of Directors' Minutes. This documentation reflects matters discussed at meetings of the client's Board of Directors. Because transactions involving: (1) investments; (2) property, plant and equipment; (3) notes payable and long-term debt; and (4) stockholders equity account are authorized by the client's Board of Directors, this is a valuable source of evidence that all related transactions are properly authorized by the client.

Broker's Advice. A statement (or other form of documentation) received from a broker that provides evidence concerning purchases and sales of marketable securities. This document is frequently used by the auditor to examine transactions in marketable securities occurring during the year.

Dividend Payment Agency. An outside party used by companies to prepare and mail dividend checks to that company's shareholders.

Held-to-Maturity Securities. Marketable securities that the organization has both the intent and ability to hold until the securities mature. These securities are carried on the financial statements at amortized cost.

Loss Contingency. A condition or set of circumstances that may result in a loss when one or more future events occur or fail to occur. Loss contingencies must be recognized as a balance sheet liability if they are probable and estimable. These contingencies must be disclosed in the footnotes accompanying the financial statements if they are at least reasonably possible.

Registrar. An outside party used by companies to record issuances and retirements of that company's capital stock.

Repairs and Maintenance. Expenditures for property, plant and equipment made after the acquisition of the related items that represent revenue expenditures. The auditor should ascertain that all of these items are properly charged to expense when incurred.

Tests of Transactions. The audit approach used to examine accounts having a small number of transactions for relatively large dollar amounts. Under this approach, the auditor verifies all (or most) of the transactions affecting an account balance during the year.

Trading Securities. Marketable securities the organization intends to hold for short periods of time. These securities are carried on the financial statements at market value.

Transfer Agent. An outside party used by companies to maintain the records of the stock and handle stock transfers.

SUMMARY OF PROFESSIONAL PRONOUNCEMENTS

Proposed Statement on Auditing Standards, "Investment in Debt and Equity Securities" (New York: AICPA, 1996).

QUESTIONS AND PROBLEMS

15-28. Select the **best** answer for each of the following items:

1. Which of the following audit procedures would be least effective for detecting contingent liabilities?

   a. Abstracting the Board of Directors' Minutes.
   b. Reviewing the bank confirmation letters.
   c. Examining confirmation letters from customers.
   d. Confirming pending legal matters with the corporate attorney.

2. The auditor's program for the examination of long-term debt should include steps that require the:

   a. Verification of the existence of the bondholders.
   b. Examination of any bond trust indenture.
   c. Inspection of the accounts payable subsidiary ledger.
   d. Investigation of credits to the bond interest income account.

3. If a company employs a Capital Stock Registrar and/or Transfer Agent, the Registrar or Agent, or both, should be requested to confirm directly to the auditor the number of shares of each class of stock:

   a. Surrendered and canceled during the year.
   b. Authorized at the balance-sheet date.
   c. Issued and outstanding at the balance-sheet date.
   d. Authorized, issued, and outstanding during the year.

4. An audit program for the examination of the retained earnings account should include a step that requires verification of the:

   a. Gain or loss resulting from disposition of treasury shares.
   b. Market value used to charge retained earnings to account for a two-for-one stock split.
   c. Authorization for both cash and stock dividends.
   d. Approval of the adjustment to the beginning balance as a result of a writedown of an account receivable.

5. Where no independent stock Transfer Agents are employed and the corporation issues its own stock and maintains stock records, canceled stock certificates should:

   a. Be defaced to prevent reissuance and attached to their corresponding stubs.
   b. Not be defaced, but segregated from other stock certificates and retained in a canceled certificates file.
   c. Be destroyed to prevent fraudulent reissuance.
   d. Be defaced and sent to the secretary of state.

6. All corporate capital stock transactions should ultimately be vouched to the:

   a. Board of Directors' Minutes.
   b. Cash Receipts Journal.
   c. Cash Disbursements Journal.
   d. Numbered Stock Certificates.

7. A loss contingency should be accrued as a liability when the contingency is:

	Estimable	Reasonably Possible
a.	Yes	No
b.	No	No
c.	No	Yes
d.	Yes	Yes

8. In order to avoid the misappropriation of company-owned securities, which of the following is the *best* course of action that can be taken by the management of a company with a large portfolio of securities?

   a. Require that one trustworthy and bonded employee be responsible for access to the safekeeping area where securities are kept.
   b. Require that employees who enter and leave the safekeeping area sign and record in a log the exact reason for their access.
   c. Require that employees involved in the safekeeping function maintain a subsidiary control ledger for securities on a current basis.
   d. Require that the safekeeping function for securities be assigned to a bank that will act as a custodial agent.

9. In violation of company policy, the Jefferson City Company erroneously capitalized the cost of painting its warehouse. The CPA examining Jefferson City's financial statements most likely would learn of this by:

   a. Reviewing the listing of construction work orders for the year.
   b. Discussing capitalization policies with the company controller.
   c. Observing, during a physical inventory observation, that the warehouse had been painted.
   d. Examining in detail a sample of construction work orders.

10. Which of the following is a customary audit procedure for the verification of the legal ownership of real property?

    a. Examination of correspondence with the corporate counsel concerning acquisition matters.
    b. Examination of ownership documents registered and on file at a public hall of records.
    c. Examination of corporate minutes and resolutions concerning the approval to acquire property, plant and equipment.
    d. Examination of deeds and title guaranty policies on hand.

15/ The Investing and Financing Cycle

11. Which of the following audit procedures would be least likely to lead the auditor to find unrecorded fixed asset disposals?

    a. Examination of insurance policies.
    b. Review of repairs and maintenance expense.
    c. Review of property tax files.
    d. Scanning of invoices for fixed asset additions.

12. In confirming with an outside agent, such as a financial institution, that the agent is holding investment securities in the client's name, an auditor most likely gathers evidence in support of management's financial statement assertions of existence or occurrence and:

    a. Liquidity.
    b. Rights and obligations.
    c. Completeness.
    d. Presentation and disclosure.

13. In auditing long-term bonds payable, an auditor would most likely:

    a. Perform analytical procedures on the bond premium and discount accounts.
    b. Examine documentation of assets purchased with bond proceeds for liens.
    c. Compare interest expense with the bond payable amount for reasonableness.
    d. Confirm the existence of individual bondholders at year-end.

14. Which of the following assertions is generally not verified when the auditor confirms notes payable with a financial institution?

    a. Existence or occurrence.
    b. Presentation and disclosure.
    c. Rights and obligations.
    d. Valuation or allocation.
    e. All of the above assertions are verified when confirming notes payable with a financial institution.

15. To determine that all transactions related to interest-bearing liabilities have been recorded, the auditor would most likely:

    a. Trace from authorization in the Board of Directors' Minutes to the recording in the accounting records.
    b. Recalculate the provision for interest expense.
    c. Confirm interest-bearing liabilities with third parties.
    d. Inspect copies of interest-bearing liabilities maintained by the client.
    e. Vouch entries in the interest-bearing liability accounts to authorization in the Board of Directors' Minutes.

16. To verify that all dividends declared by the client have been properly authorized, the auditor should:

    a. Agree the amount of dividends with a confirmation received from the Dividend Payment Agency.
    b. Scan the Board of Directors' Minutes and trace any authorizations of dividends to recording in the accounts.
    c. Vouch recorded dividends to information in the Board of Directors' Minutes.
    d. Agree the amount of dividends with cash disbursements records.
    e. Observe the mailing of dividend checks to shareholders.

17. Requiring marketable securities to be made in the company name, not in the name of one or more individual(s), is a control activity related to:

    a. Information Processing.
    b. Physical Controls.
    c. Performance Reviews.
    d. Segregation of Duties.

18. To test whether all marketable securities transactions have been recorded by the client, the auditor would most likely:

    a. Verify dividend revenues through an external source, such as *Moody's*.
    b. Verify recorded purchases and sales of marketable securities through reference to the Board of Directors' Minutes.
    c. Review the client's recalculation of the market value of marketable securities.
    d. Scan the Board of Directors' Minutes for evidence of marketable securities transactions.
    e. Physically inspect marketable securities held by the client at year-end.

19. Which of the following is **not** true with respect to the use of the test of transactions and test of balances approach to substantive testing?

    a. The test of transactions approach is normally used for accounts having a relatively small number of transactions occurring during the year.
    b. The test of balances approach requires the auditor to identify individual components of the final account balance.
    c. The test of balances approach is generally used when transactions of large dollar amounts exist.
    d. The test of transactions approach relies on previous audit examinations in verifying the beginning account balances.
    e. The test of transactions approach requires the auditor to examine a large number (perhaps all) of the transactions occurring during a given year.

20. Physical inspection of items of property, plant and equipment would primarily provide the auditor with evidence regarding the assertion of:

    a. Completeness.
    b. Existence or occurrence.
    c. Presentation and disclosure.
    d. Rights and obligations.
    e. Valuation or allocation.

21. Why is the completeness assertion more important for disposals of property, plant, and equipment (PPE) than for marketable securities?

    a. Companies are more likely to dispose of PPE than marketable securities.
    b. The gains and losses related to the disposal of PPE and marketable securities are shown in different sections of the income statement.
    c. Companies are more likely to suffer a loss on the disposal of PPE than marketable securities.
    d. The income resulting from disposals of PPE and marketable securities has different implications for income tax purposes.
    e. The cash received from disposals of PPE is usually less than that received upon disposal of marketable securities.

22. The auditor's approach in examining Investing and Financing cycle accounts (such as property, plant and equipment) differs from the approach in examining Revenue cycle accounts (such as accounts receivable) because:

    a. The assets in the first group are more significant to the balance sheet because of their longer useful lives.
    b. The assets in the first group are more difficult to physically observe.
    c. The relative infrequency of transactions in the first group of assets facilitates the use of the test of transactions approach.
    d. The assets in the first group normally comprise a high percentage of the total assets reported on the company's balance sheet.
    e. The auditor is more concerned with the assertion of completeness when examining assets in the first group.

23. To determine the propriety of classification of marketable equity securities, the auditor would most likely:

    a. Inquire of management about its intent in holding the securities.
    b. Vouch current year purchases of marketable securities to Broker's Advices.
    c. Perform analytical procedures by computing the ratio of total marketable equity securities to stockholders' equity.
    d. Confirm the details of portfolio accounts with the client's independent securities broker.
    e. Physically inspect marketable securities held by the client.

24. In order to determine that acquisitions of property, plant and equipment (PPE) are recorded at the proper amounts, the auditor should:

    a. Observe the physical existence of items of PPE.
    b. Compare the recorded amount of the purchase to the Vendor's Invoice.
    c. Inspect the title to items of PPE acquired during the year.
    d. Recalculate the provision for depreciation of PPE.
    e. Review the Board of Directors' Minutes to determine that all acquisitions of PPE have been properly authorized.

25. Which of the following types of information and processing control activities are generally considered to be the most important with respect to PPE transactions?

   a. Authorization of transactions.
   b. Documents and records.
   c. Independent checks.
   d. Physical controls.
   e. Segregation of duties.

   (Items 1 through 13 in 15-28; AICPA Adapted)

15-29. For each of the following questions relating to stockholders' equity accounts, give an example of procedure(s) that would be applied by the auditor.

   a. Are issuances of capital stock properly authorized?
   b. Are dividends declared by the client actually recorded?
   c. Is all information related to stock warrants, options, and rights properly disclosed?
   d. Are issuances of capital stock properly recorded?
   e. Do recorded retirements or repurchases of capital stock represent legitimate transactions that actually occurred?
   f. Are the beginning balances of capital stock and additional paid-in capital accounts correct?
   g. Do issuances of capital stock result in outstanding shares issued exceeding authorized shares?

15-30. You were engaged on May 1, 19X2, by a committee of stockholders to perform a special audit as of December 31, 19X1, of the stockholders' equity of the Major Corporation, whose stock is actively-traded on a stock exchange. The group of stockholders who engaged you believes that the information contained in the stockholders' equity section of the published annual report for the year ended December 31, 19X1, is not correct. If your examination confirms their suspicions, they intend to use the report in a proxy fight.

Management agrees to permit your audit but refuses to permit any direct confirmation with stockholders. To secure cooperation in the audit, the committee of stockholders has agreed to this limitation and you have been instructed to limit your audit in this respect. You have also been instructed to exclude the audit of revenue and expense accounts for the year.

Required:

   a. Prepare a general audit program for the usual examination of the stockholders' equity section of a corporation's balance sheet, assuming no limitation on the scope of your examination. Exclude the audit of revenue and expense accounts.
   b. Describe any special auditing procedures you would undertake in view of the limitations and other special circumstances of your examination of the Major Corporation's stockholders' equity accounts.

   (AICPA Adapted)

15-31. You are a CPA engaged in an examination of the financial statements of Pate Corporation for the year ended December 31, 19X1. The financial statements and records of Pate Corporation have not been audited by a CPA in prior years.

The stockholders' equity section of Pate Corporation's balance sheet of December 31, 19X1, follows:

Stockholders' Equity

Capital stock—10,000 shares of $10 par value authorized; 5,000 shares issued and outstanding	$ 50,000
Capital contributed in excess of par value of capital stock	32,580
Retained earnings	47,320
Total Stockholders' Equity	$129,900

Pate Corporation was founded in 19XX. The corporation has 10 stockholders and serves as its own Registrar and Transfer Agent. There are no capital stock subscription contracts in effect.

Required:

a. Prepare the detailed audit program for the examination of the three accounts comprising the stockholders' equity section of Pate Corporation's balance sheet. (Do not include in the audit program the verification of the results of the current year's operations.)

b. After every other figure on the balance sheet has been audited by the CPA, it might appear that the retained earnings figure is a balancing figure and requires no further verification. Why does the CPA verify retained earnings as she does other figures on the balance sheet? Discuss.

(AICPA Adapted)

15-32. A manufacturing company whose records you are auditing has $1 million of buildings and $3 million of machinery on its books. During the year you are covering in your audit, additions amounted to $100,000 for buildings and $500,000 for machinery. All additions were made through construction orders controlled by a Construction Work-in-Progress account, which had a balance of $20,000 at the close of last year and $55,000 at the close of this year. Some of the additions were purchased, and a number were constructed by the company. State in detail the audit procedures you would follow in verification of the fixed asset additions during the year. Assume that your firm made the audit for the prior year.

(AICPA Adapted)

15-33. Terra Land Development Corporation is a closely-held family corporation engaged in the business of purchasing large tracts of land, subdividing the tracts, and installing paved streets and utilities. The corporation does not construct buildings for the buyers of the land and does not have any affiliated construction companies. Undeveloped land is usually leased for farming until the corporation is ready to begin developing it.

The corporation finances its land acquisitions by mortgagees; the mortgagees required audited financial statements. This is your first audit of the company, and you have now begun the examination of the financial statements for the year ended December 31, 19X1.

Your preliminary review of the accounts has indicated that the corporation would have had a highly profitable year, except that the president and vice-president, his son, were reimbursed for exceptionally large travel and entertainment expenses.

Required:

The corporation has three tracts of land in various stages of development. List the audit procedures to be employed in the verification of the physical existence and title to the corporation's three landholdings.

(AICPA Adapted)

15-34. In connection with a recurring examination of the financial statements of the Louis Manufacturing Company for the year ended December 31, 19X1, you have been assigned the audit of the Manufacturing Equipment, Manufacturing Equipment-Accumulated Depreciation, and Repairs to Manufacturing Equipment accounts. Your review of Louis's policies and procedures has disclosed the following pertinent information:

1. The Manufacturing Equipment account includes the net invoice price plus related freight and installation costs for all of the equipment in Louis's manufacturing plant.
2. The Manufacturing Equipment and Accumulated Depreciation accounts are supported by a subsidiary ledger, which shows the cost and accumulated depreciation for each piece of equipment.
3. An annual budget for capital expenditures of $1,000 or more is prepared by the Budget Committee and approved by the Board of Directors. Capital expenditures over $1,000, which are not included in this budget, must be approved by the Board of Directors, and variations of 20 percent or more must be explained to the board. Approval by the supervisor of Production is required for capital expenditures under $1,000.
4. Company employees handle installation, removal, repair, and rebuilding of the machinery. Work orders are prepared for these activities and are subject to the same budgetary control as other expenditures. Work orders are not required for external expenditures.

Required:

a. Cite the major objectives of your audit of the Manufacturing Equipment, Manufacturing Equipment—Accumulated Depreciation, and Repairs to Manufacturing Equipment accounts. Do not include in this listing the auditing procedures designed to accomplish these objectives.
b. Prepare the portion of your audit program applicable to the review of 19X1 additions to the Manufacturing Equipment account.

(AICPA Adapted)

15-35. While auditing an urban bus company in a city with a population of 50,000, you encounter the following situation:

a. You have checked an authorization for the purchase of five engines to replace the engines in five buses.
b. The cost of the old engines was removed from the property account and that of the new engines was properly capitalized. The work was done in the company garage.
c. You find no credits for salvage or for the sale of any scrap metal at any time during the year. You have been in the garage and did not see the old engines.
d. The accountant is also Treasurer and Office Manager. He is an authorized check signer and has access to all cash receipts. Upon inquiry, he says he does not recall the sale of the old engines nor of any scrap metal.

Required:

Assuming that the engines were sold as scrap, outline all steps that this fact would cause you to take in connection with your audit. Also mention steps beyond those related directly to this one item.

(AICPA Adapted)

15-36. The Irving Manufacturing Company uses a system of shop orders in its plant. This system includes a series of orders for construction and installation of fixed assets, another series for retirement of assets, and a third series for maintenance work. There are "standing order" numbers for minor repetitive maintenance items and special orders for unusual or major maintenance items.

In connection with a regular annual audit of the Irving Manufacturing Company, prepare a program for work to be done on the maintenance orders. Assume that there appears to be reasonable internal control in the company. Prepare the program to avoid doing any more work than is necessary to meet acceptable auditing standards. Explain the purpose or objective of each of your proposed steps.

(AICPA Adapted)

15-37. As a result of highly profitable operations over a number of years, Eastern Manufacturing Corporation accumulated a substantial temporary investment portfolio. In her examination of the financial statements for the year ended December 31, 19X1, the following information came to the attention of the corporation's CPA:

1. The manufacturing operations of the corporation resulted in an operating loss for the year.
2. In 19X1, the corporation placed the securities making up the temporary investment portfolio with a financial institution, which serves as custodian of the securities. Formerly, the securities were kept in the corporation's safe-deposit box in the local bank.
3. On December 22, 19X1, the corporation sold and then repurchased on the same day a number of securities that had appreciated greatly in value. Management stated that the purpose of the sale and repurchases was to establish a higher cost and book value for the securities and to avoid the reporting of a loss for the year.

Required:

a. List the objectives of the CPA's examination of the Temporary Investment account.
b. Under what conditions would the CPA accept a confirmation of securities on hand from the custodian in lieu of inspecting and counting the securities herself?
c. What disclosure, if any, of the sale and repurchase of the securities would the CPA recommend for the financial statements? If the client accepts the CPA's recommendations for disclosure, what effect, if any, would the sale and repurchase have upon the CPA's opinion on the financial statements? Discuss.

(AICPA Adapted)

15-38. You are in charge of the audit of the financial statements of the Demot Corporation for the year ended December 31, 19X1. The corporation has had the policy of investing its surplus funds in temporary investments. Its stock and bond certificates are kept in a safe-deposit box in a local bank. Only the President or the Treasurer of the corporation has access to the box.

You were unable to obtain access to the safe-deposit box on December 31 because neither the President nor the Treasurer was available. Arrangements were made for your assistant to accompany the Treasurer to the bank on January 11 to examine the securities. Your assistant has never examined securities that were being kept in a safe-deposit box and requires instructions. She should be able to inspect all securities on hand in an hour.

Required:

a. List the instructions that you would give your assistant regarding the examination of the stock and bond certificates kept in the safe-deposit box. Include in your instructions the details of the securities to be examined and the reasons for examining these details.

b. When she resumed from the bank, your assistant reported that the Treasurer had entered the box on January 4. The treasurer stated that he had removed an old photograph of the corporation's original building. The photograph was loaned to the local chamber of commerce for display purposes. List the additional audit procedures that are required because of the Treasurer's action.

(AICPA Adapted)

15-39. In connection with his examination of the financial statements of Belasco Chemicals, Inc., Kenneth Mack, CPA, is considering the necessity of inspecting securities on the balance-sheet date, May 31, 19X1, or at some other date. The securities held by Belasco include negotiable bearer bonds, which are kept in a safe in the Treasurer's office, and miscellaneous stocks and bonds kept in a safe-deposit box at Merchants' Bank. Both the negotiable bearer bonds and the miscellaneous stocks and bonds are material to proper presentation of Belasco's financial position.

Required:

a. What are the factors that Mack should consider in determining the necessity for inspecting these securities on May 31, 19X1, as opposed to other dates?

b. Assume that Mack plans to send a member of his staff to Belasco's offices and to Merchants' Bank on May 31, 19X1, to make the security inspection. What instructions should he give to this staff member as to the conduct of the inspection and the evidence to be included in the audit workpapers? (Note: Do not discuss the valuation of securities, the income from securities, or the examination of information contained in the books and records of the company.)

c. Assume that Mack finds it impracticable to send a member of his staff to Belasco's offices and to Merchants' Bank on May 31, 19X1. What alternative procedures may he employ to assure himself that the company had physical possession of its securities on May 31, 19X1, if the securities are inspected: (1) May 28, 19X1? (2) June 5, 19X1?

(AICPA Adapted)

15-40. Pierce, an independent auditor, was engaged to examine the financial statements of Mayfair Construction Inc. for the year ended December 31, 19X1. Mayfair's financial statements reflect a substantial amount of mobile construction equipment used in the firm's operations. The equipment is accounted for in a subsidiary ledger. Pierce performed a study and evaluation of internal control and found it satisfactory.

Required:

Identify the substantive audit procedures that Pierce should utilize in examining mobile construction equipment and related depreciation in Mayfair's financial statements.

(AICPA Adapted)

Learning Objectives

Study of this chapter is designed to achieve several learning objectives. After studying this chapter, you should be able to:

1. List the major steps involved with completing the audit examination.
2. Define subsequent events and identify two different types of subsequent events.
3. List the typical contents of a letter of inquiry received from the client's attorney.
4. Discuss the contents of the representation letter obtained from the client's management.
5. Describe the working paper review that occurs during an audit engagement.
6. Describe the nature and purpose(s) of management letters.
7. Identify the types of subjects that are appropriate for inclusion in management letters.

16

Completing the Audit Examination

◉ COMPLETING THE AUDIT

The previous five chapters discussed the auditor's study of internal control (Chapters 10, 12, 14, and 15) and substantive testing procedures (Chapters 11, 13, 14, and 15). As shown below, these tasks are the second and third major steps in an audit examination, respectively.

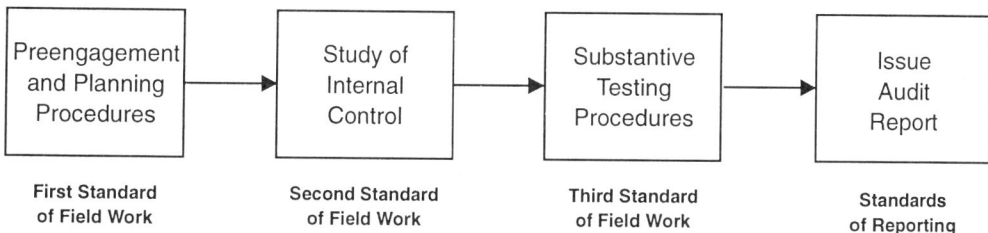

At this point, it appears that the auditor is ready to issue his or her report on the client's financial statements. However, prior to doing so, some "wrap-up" procedures are required. These procedures are ordinarily performed concurrent with or after the bulk of the substantive testing procedures and are discussed in detail in this chapter.

◘ Subsequent Events

The auditor's report on the client's financial statements includes an opinion on their financial position, results of operations, and cash flows as of the date of those financial statements. Certain events and transactions occurring after the date of the financial statements may have an important impact on the financial statements and therefore require extension of the audit into the subsequent period. In certain instances, these events may require changes in the financial statements or in the footnotes accompanying the financial statements.

A **subsequent event** is defined as any event occurring between the balance-sheet date and the issuance of the client's financial statements (and auditor's opinion on the financial statements). Thus, as the name suggests, a subsequent event occurs **after the end of the year**, as shown below:

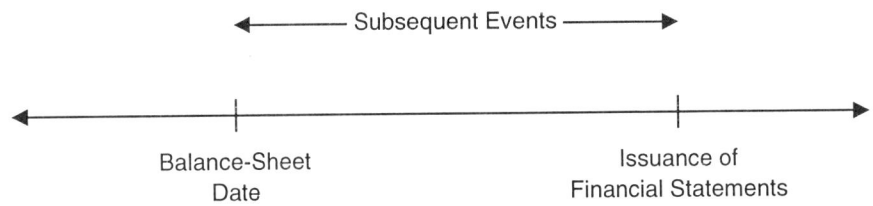

Initially, it appears that subsequent events would not be of concern to the current year's audit, since these events occur after year-end. However, the financial statements may need to reflect the effect of subsequent events, since they often have a material impact on the fairness of the financial statements issued by the client. Stated another way, even though subsequent events did not exist at year-end, the financial statements issued by the client would be misleading without inclusion of the subsequent events.

Types of Subsequent Events. There are two types of subsequent events that should be considered by the auditor:

1. **Events that provide additional information about conditions that existed at the balance-sheet date** In this case, the condition to which the subsequent event relates exists at the balance-sheet date and is recorded in the financial statements. The subsequent event merely provides the auditor with additional information related to the condition (and recorded amount of the asset or liability). For example, assume that on December 31, 19x1, Mike Company is being sued by one of its customers because one of its products caused injury to a customer and an estimated liability has been recorded. If the case is settled prior to the issuance of the client's financial statements, the financial statements should be adjusted to reflect the more current information related to the subsequent event.

    In this instance, since the condition existed at the balance-sheet date and was already included in the financial statements, the financial statements would require **adjustment** because of the subsequent event. Examples of this type of subsequent event (known as a **Type I subsequent event**) are shown below. The important characteristic of a Type I subsequent event is that the event relates to an item recorded in the financial statements at year-end.

    ▶ Realization of assets recorded at year-end at amounts different than recognized in the balance sheet.

    ▶ Settlement of liabilities recorded at year-end at amounts different than recognized in the balance sheet.

2. **Events arising after the balance-sheet date** These subsequent events relate to conditions that arose after the balance-sheet date; that is, as of year-end, no mention of these conditions was included in the client's financial statements or footnotes accompanying the financial state-

ments. Examples of this type of subsequent event (known as a **Type II subsequent event**) include:

▶ Sale of a bond or capital stock issue

▶ Purchase of a business or entity

▶ Settlement of litigation, when the event giving rise to the claim took place after year-end

▶ Loss of plant or inventories as a result of fire or flood

▶ Losses on receivables resulting from conditions arising after year-end

Because these conditions did not exist at the balance-sheet date, they are not recorded in the financial statements. Accordingly, these subsequent events would not require financial statement adjustment. In order to prevent the financial statements from being misleading, these events should be disclosed in the financial statements (normally, in the footnotes accompanying the financial statements). When the effect of this type of subsequent event is particularly material, the client may supplement the historical financial statements by preparing *pro forma* ("as if") financial statements. **Pro forma** financial statements are financial statements that are prepared assuming the occurrence of the subsequent event as of the balance-sheet date. If the effect of this subsequent event is particularly significant, the auditor may refer to the subsequent event in his or her report on the client's financial statements.

These two types of subsequent events are summarized below.

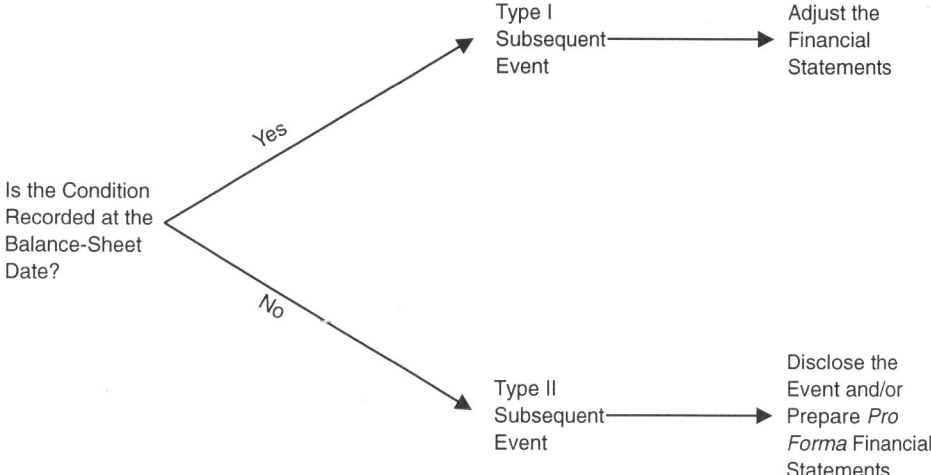

In some instances, classification of a subsequent event as Type I or Type II is not quite as clear. For example, if a customer's account receivable included in the year-end balance is deemed to be uncollectible in the subsequent period, the auditor should consider *when* the collection of the accounts receivable became questionable. For example, if the failure to collect the receivable was because of the customer's deteriorating financial condition (which existed at year-end but was not known to the auditor), it would be classified as a Type I subsequent event and the financial statements should be adjusted to reflect the uncollectibility of the account receivable. If, however, the failure to collect the receivable resulted from an event that occurred after year-end (such as a catastrophe loss), the subsequent event would be classified as a Type II subsequent event. In this latter instance, the company would disclose the event in the footnotes accompanying the financial statements.

Search for Subsequent Events. Prior to issuing his or her opinion on the financial statements, the auditor should search for the occurrence of subsequent events. Such a search may include the following steps (see *SAS No. 1*, AU 560.12):

1. Examine cutoff Bank Statements and enclosures returned with these Bank Statements.
2. Review collections of accounts receivable.
3. Review credit memoranda issued for sales returns and allowances to determine that there is no important time lag in issuing the credits.
4. Scan the Cash Receipts Journal for evidence of proceeds of loans or significant sales of productive assets.
5. Scan the Check Register for unusual payments and payment of liabilities not recorded as of the balance-sheet date.
6. Review corporate minutes and inquire about matters covered at meetings for which minutes are not yet available.
7. Review the client's interim financial statements and compare them to the financial statements being reported upon.
8. Obtain management's representation concerning possible subsequent events (discussed later in this chapter).
9. Inquire of client's legal counsel about matters concerning litigation, claims, and assessments (discussed later in this chapter).

It is important to note that many of these steps would be performed in the auditor's substantive tests of account balances and classes of transactions. For example, during the examination of cash, the auditor would obtain cutoff Bank Statements from the banks with whom the client does business. In addition, the auditor would scan the Check Register for unusual payments during his or her search for unrecorded liabilities. The auditor's primary objective in searching for subsequent events is to identify significant, material events that affect the fairness of the client's financial statements.

> **CHAPTER CHECKPOINTS**
>
> **16-1.** Define a subsequent event. What are the two major types of subsequent events?
>
> **16-2.** How should the client treat the two types of subsequent events?
>
> **16-3.** List procedures ordinarily performed by the auditor in searching for subsequent events.

◻ Letters of Inquiry

Chapter 13 discussed the auditor's search for unrecorded liabilities. One particularly significant liability involves litigation, claims, or assessments against the client at year-end. *Statement on Auditing Standards No. 12 (SAS No. 12)*[1] summarizes the auditor's responsibility with respect to identifying litigation, claims, and assessments against the client at year-end.

The auditor's examination of litigation, claims, and assessments (LCA) involves a two-step procedure. First, the auditor should perform the following procedures to identify potential liabilities:

▶ Inquire and discuss potential LCA with management

▶ Obtain a listing of LCA from management

▶ Examine documentation related to LCA (such as correspondence and invoices from attorneys)

▶ Obtain written assurance from management as to the existence of LCA

▶ Read Board of Directors' Minutes, contracts, loan agreements, and other relevant documentation to identify potential LCA

▶ Obtain information about guarantees from Bank Confirmations

It is important to note that the client's management is the auditor's primary source of information with respect to LCA. However, this information has limited reliability because it was obtained from internal sources. Thus, the auditor will request a **letter of inquiry** from the client's attorney(s). The letter of inquiry includes a listing (prepared by management) of the LCA at year-end and requests the following information related to items included in management's list of LCA:

1. A description of the nature of the matter, progress of the case to date, and any action the client plans on taking.

---

[1] American Institute of Certified Public Accountants (AICPA), *Statement on Auditing Standards No. 12*, "Inquiry of a Client's Lawyer Concerning Litigation, Claims, and Assessments" (New York: AICPA, 1976, AU 337).

2. An evaluation of the likelihood of an unfavorable outcome and an estimate of the amount or range of potential loss.
3. Any LCA omitted from management's list.

The responsibilities of the auditor, management, and client's attorneys with respect to litigation, claims, and assessments (LCA) are summarized below. As shown below, the process of obtaining a letter of inquiry is as follows:

1. The auditor requests a letter of inquiry.
2. The client's management provides a listing of LCA to their attorneys.
3. The attorneys' comments on management's listing of LCA in a direct response to the auditor.

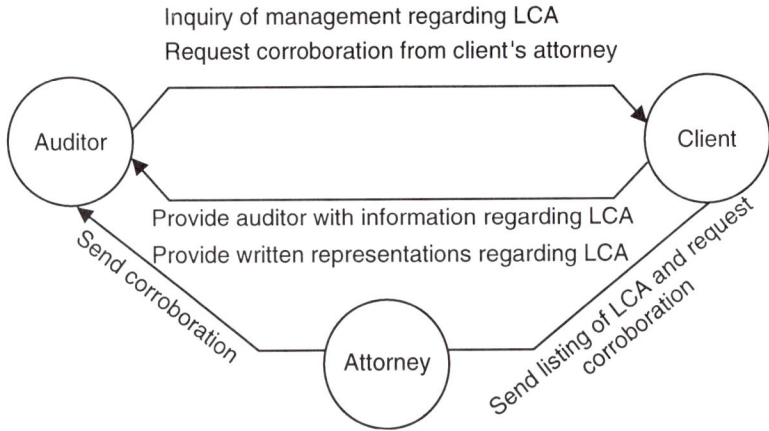

▢ Client Representations[2]

Earlier in Chapter 6, we identified oral inquiry as a type of substantive testing procedure. One limitation associated with oral inquiry is that, at a later date, some dispute may arise regarding the nature of these inquiries. In order to prevent this from occurring, as well as reduce misunderstandings between the auditor and client, the auditor will obtain **client representations** (also known as **written representations** or **management representations**) from the client. These representations are usually provided in the form of a letter addressed to the auditor from the client.

Figure 16-1 summarizes some of the major topics covered by client representations. As shown therein, in addition to confirming the auditor's oral inquiries, client representations: (1) provide the client's officials with an opportunity to consider whether all important matters have been disclosed to the auditor, and (2) act as a reminder to management of its primary responsibility for the fairness of presentation of the financial statements. However, the representations do not in any way relieve the auditor of the responsibility to follow GAAS.

---

[2] This section is based on American Institute of Certified Public Accountants (AICPA), *Statement on Auditing Standards No. 19*, "Client Representations" (New York: AICPA, 1977, AU 333).

1. Management acknowledgment of its responsibility for the fair presentation of the financial statements.
2. The availability of all financial records and any related data.
3. The completeness and availability of all minutes of meetings of stockholders, directors, and committees of directors.
4. The nonexistence of errors or unrecorded transactions in the financial statements.
5. Information concerning:
   a. Subsequent events.
   b. Noncompliance with contracts that may affect the financial statements.
   c. Losses from sales commitments.
   d. Obligations to repurchase assets that were previously sold.
   e. Related-party transactions.
   f. The reduction of excess or obsolete inventories to net realizable value.
   g. Irregularities involving the client's management or employees.
   h. Communications that the client received from regulatory agencies relating to noncompliance with, or deficiencies in, financial reporting practices.
6. The client's plans or intentions that may affect the carrying value or classification of assets or liabilities.
7. The disclosure of compensating balances or other arrangements involving restrictions on cash balances and disclosure of line-of-credit or similar arrangements.
8. The losses from purchase commitments for inventory quantities in excess of requirements or at prices in excess of market.
9. Violations or possible violations of laws or regulations whose effects should be considered for disclosure in the financial statements or as a basis for recording a loss contingency.
10. Other liabilities and gain or loss contingencies that are required to be accrued or disclosed by *Statement of Financial Accounting Standards No. 5*.
11. Unasserted claims or assessments that the client's lawyer has advised are probable of assertion and must be disclosed in accordance with *Statement of Financial Accounting Standards No. 5*.
12. Capital stock repurchase options or agreements or capital stock reserved for options, warrants, conversions, or other requirements.
13. Unaudited replacement cost information and interim financial information included in audited financial statements.
14. Other matters that the auditor may determine, based on the circumstances of the engagement, should be included in written representations from management.

Figure 16-1: *Possible Topics Covered by Client Representations*

Client representations are normally prepared by the auditor and signed by the client's management (ordinarily, the Chief Executive Officer and/or Chief Financial Officer). Once received, client representations become an integral part of the auditor's workpapers. The representations should be dated as of the last day of field work (the date of the auditor's report). Such a date reflects the auditor's concern with events that might occur through the date of the report that may require adjustment or disclosure in the financial statements.

Failure of the client to provide the auditor with representations results in a scope limitation that precludes the issuance of an unqualified opinion. In addition, if the client refuses to provide representations to the auditor, the auditor should consider his or her ability to rely on oral evidence and other information provided by the client during the audit. The exact type of opinion issued by the auditor in these situations is discussed further in Chapter 17 of this text.

CHAPTER CHECKPOINTS

16-4. What type of audit procedures may reveal the possible existence of litigation, claims, and assessments?

16-5. What role do the client and attorney play in the auditor's examination of litigation, claims, and assessments?

16-6. What information is normally included in a letter of inquiry related to litigation, claims, and assessments?

16-7. Define client representations. What topics are normally included in client representations?

16-8. Who is responsible for signing client representations? What date is used for client representations?

16-9. How does the failure of the client to provide the auditor with representations affect the audit engagement?

▢ Analytical Procedures

Analytical procedures were introduced in Chapters 4 and 6 and discussed in more detail in Chapters 11, 13, 14, and 15. As noted in these chapters, **analytical procedures** involve comparing the recorded amount of a particular account balance or class of transactions (or a ratio involving an account balance or class of transactions) with an expectation developed by the auditor.

SAS No. 56[3] notes that analytical procedures may be used in three stages of the audit examination: (1) the planning stages, (2) the substantive testing stages, and (3) the overall review stages. In the overall review stages, analytical procedures are used to assess the validity of the overall conclusions reached by the auditor, including the opinion on the financial statements taken as a whole. Results of such a review may reveal unusual or unexpected account balances not identified in the preliminary (planning) stages or during the audit. If this is the case, additional procedures may be needed before an opinion can be issued on the client's financial statements. When used in the final review stages, it is important that the auditor consider any adjusting or reclassifying entries made by the client in evaluating the reasonableness of the client's account balances or classes of transactions.

---

[3] American Institute of Certified Public Accountants (AICPA), *Statement on Auditing Standards No. 56*, "Analytical Procedures" (New York: AICPA, 1988, AU 329).

◘ Workpaper Review

Earlier, in Chapter 6, we discussed audit workpapers. Recall from that discussion that audit workpapers are the primary record of the procedures performed and conclusions reached by the auditor during the engagement. The review of audit workpapers assists in achieving part of the first standard of field work, which states that:

> The work is to be adequately planned and assistants, if any, are to be properly supervised.[4]

The hierarchy of review of workpapers is shown below:

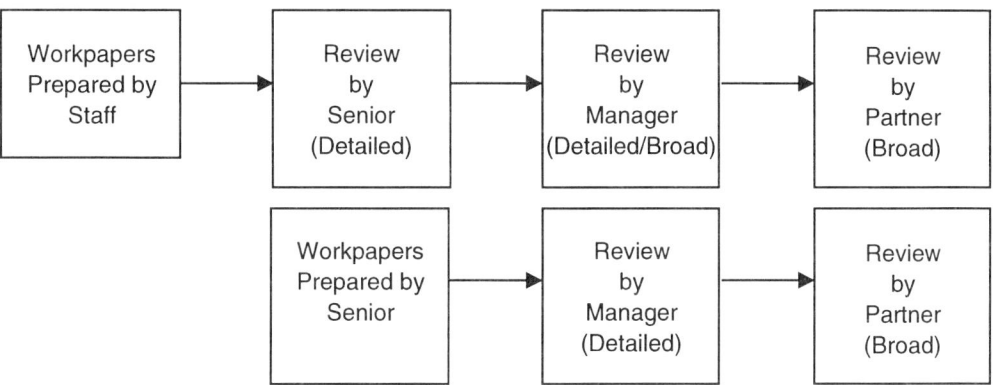

As shown above, senior accountants (for workpapers prepared by staff accountants) and audit managers (for workpapers prepared by senior accountants) will perform a detailed review of workpapers. A detailed review includes some of the following major types of activities:

1. Determine that the workpapers are appropriately initialed and dated by the individual(s) preparing the workpaper.
2. Verify the accuracy of selected calculations and analyses appearing on workpapers.
3. Ensure that steps in the audit program are properly "signed off" by individuals performing those steps.
4. Verify that references from one workpaper to another are appropriate.
5. Read the tickmark explanations and verify the overall reasonableness of the conclusions appearing on the workpaper.

---

[4] American Institute of Certified Public Accountants (AICPA), *Statement on Auditing Standards No. 1,* "Codification of Auditing Standards and Procedures" (New York: AICPA, 1972, AU 310.01).

In contrast, a broad workpaper review (performed by the audit partner-in-charge of the engagement and/or audit manager) focuses on the overall scope of the audit examination. This review addresses broader issues relating to the scope of the audit examination. such as:

1. Has the audit examination been completed in accordance with the terms enumerated in the engagement letter?
2. Has the firm complied with generally accepted auditing standards during the examination?
3. Do the workpapers contain a conclusion as to the fair presentation of each account examined?
4. Have the firm's quality control policies and procedures been achieved?
5. Have all significant accounting and auditing issues encountered during the engagement been properly resolved?
6. Are the conclusions reached on the workpaper consistent with the overall report to be issued on the client's financial statements?

In addition to the partner-in-charge of the engagement, many firms have a partner who is not associated with a particular engagement perform an additional review of the workpapers. This partner's review, referred to as a **second-partner review** or **cold review**, is similar to that performed by the partners in charge of the audit engagement. The basic rationale for having a second partner review is to have someone who is less familiar with the engagement and client become involved in the workpaper review process. Second partner reviews are required for the audits of all SEC registrants.

◘ Evaluating the Results

As the auditor performs the various substantive tests discussed throughout this text, he or she may identify situations where the audited balance differs from the recorded balance. These differences suggest the possibility that the client's financial statements are not presented in conformity with GAAP. In making this assessment, *SAS No. 47*[5] notes that the auditor should consider the **aggregate error** (or **likely error**) contained in a particular account. This likely error includes both: (1) errors specifically identified during the audit examination that were not corrected by the client (**known errors**), and (2) the amount of known errors projected to the account balance or class of transactions (**projected errors**).

Once the amount of likely error has been determined, it is evaluated using a predetermined materiality threshold. The following decisions would be made:

▶ **If Likely Error > Materiality:** Propose an adjustment based on the known errors and projected errors.

Assuming that client management agrees with the proposed adjustment, there is no effect on the auditor's report. If, however, the client refuses to adjust the financial statements, a

---

[5] American Institute of Certified Public Accountants (AICPA), *Statement on Auditing Standards No. 47*, "Audit Risk and Materiality in Conducting an Audit" (New York: AICPA, 1983, AU 312).

qualified or adverse opinion on the financial statements is issued. Audit opinions and audit reporting are discussed in detail in Chapters 17 and 18.

▶ **If Likely Error < Materiality:** Propose an adjustment based on the known error. The projected error should be summarized in another workpaper to ensure that potential adjustments in the current year do not result in material misstatements of the financial statements in future years.

When the likely error does not cause the financial statements to be materially misstated but is uncorrected by the client, the auditor must also evaluate exposure to audit risk. As the likely error becomes closer to the materiality threshold, the risk that the financial statements are materially misstated (audit risk) also increases. According to *SAS No. 47*, if the exposure to audit risk is judged to be relatively unacceptable, the auditor should either: (1) perform additional substantive testing procedures, or (2) obtain satisfaction that the client has adjusted the financial statements so that audit risk has been reduced to acceptable levels.

The auditor's procedures for evaluating the fairness of the account balances are summarized in Figure 16-2.

CHAPTER CHECKPOINTS

16-10. During which stages of the audit can analytical procedures be used by the auditor? What is the purpose of using analytical procedures in the final review stages?

16-11. Describe the nature of a detailed and broad workpaper reviews. Who performs each type of review?

16-12. What is a second-partner (or cold) workpaper review?

16-13. What are the components of likely error?

16-14. How does the auditor evaluate the likely error in issuing his or her opinion on the client's financial statements?

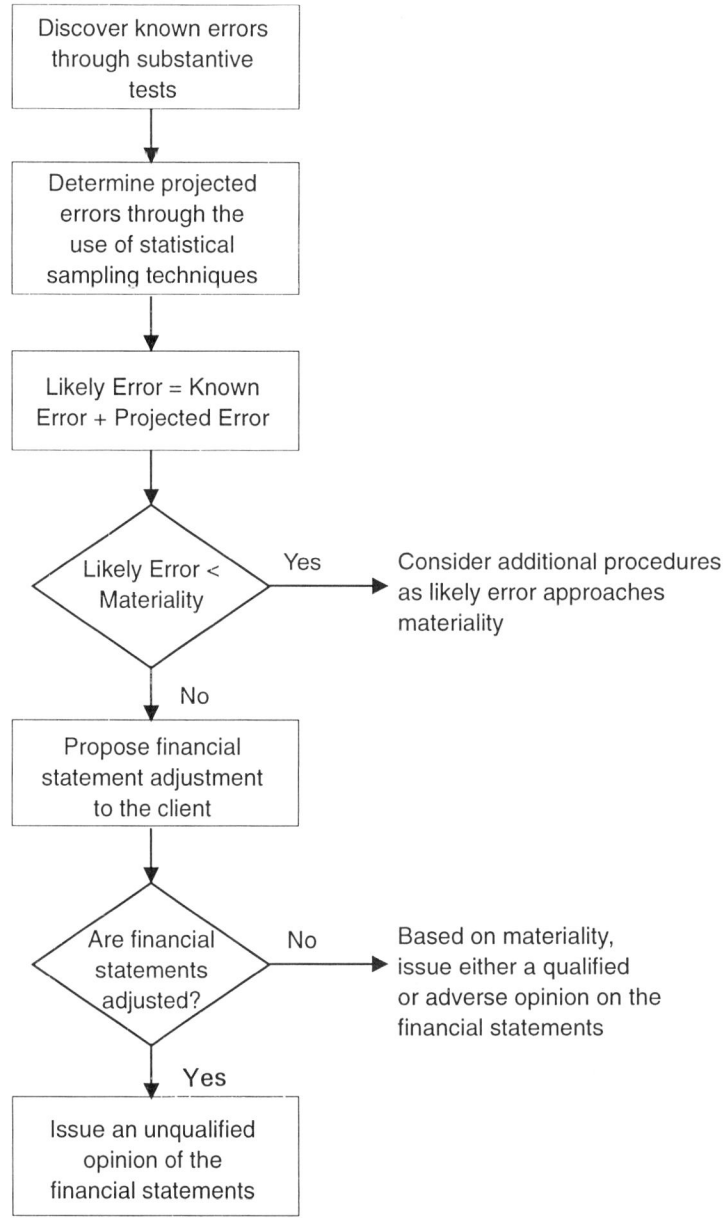

Figure 16-2: *Methodology for Evaluating Audit Errors*

THE POSTAUDIT PERIOD

Subsequent Discovery of Facts

In certain instances, the auditor will learn of events after he or she has completed the field work of a particular client. The auditor's actions will depend upon many factors; however, initially, the overriding issue is the point in time when the auditor learns of the event in question. For purposes of illustration, assume the following key dates in the audit of Jordan Company by Bull, CPAs:

- December 31, 19x1: Balance-sheet date
- March 3, 19x2: Last day of field work
- March 14, 19x2: Issuance of financial statements and report

These dates (and the related time periods) are summarized below:

Event Discovered Prior to the Last Day of Field Work. If the auditor discovers the event or facts prior to the last day of field work, he or she should evaluate the client's handling of the event (*i.e.*, adjustment of the financial statements or footnote disclosure). This situation is represented by time period A in the timeline. Since the date of the auditor's report is the last day of field work, no additional responsibility is assumed for these events beyond that assumed for the remainder of the financial statements.

Event Discovered after the Last Day of Field Work, but Prior to Issuance of Report. In other instances, the auditor may learn of events or facts after the last day of field work but prior to the issuance of his or her report (time period B). In this case, the client can still adjust the financial statements or disclose the event, since the financial statements have yet to be issued. The auditor should evaluate the event in question and determine whether the client has handled the adjustment or disclosure of the event properly.

This type of situation presents the auditor with a dilemma. Assume that the auditor learns of a subsequent event on March 8, 19x2 and examines the client's method of handling this event on March 10, 19x2. Because audit procedures were performed after the original last day of field work (March 3, 19x2), it would be misleading to date the audit report March 3, 19x2. One alternative is to date the audit report March 10, 19x2 to reflect the fact that audit procedures were performed through that date. The problem with this approach is that the auditor is now taking responsibility for all events occurring through March 10, 19x2, despite the fact that his or her work since March 3 has been limited to one single event.

To limit liability for events occurring after the last day of field work, the auditor can **dual-date** his or her report. When a report is dual-dated, it contains two dates: one relating to the subsequent event (the date through which the auditor has examined the event) and one for the remainder of the financial statements (the last day of field work). Dual-dating a report limits the auditor's liability for subsequent events beyond the last day of field work to the specific event referred to in the report. An example of dual-dating for the above situation is shown below:

"March 3, 19x2, except for the event discussed in Note A, dated March 10, 19x2."

Event Discovered after Issuance of the Report. Finally, consider timeperiod C in the above timeline. In general, once the audit report and the financial statements have been issued, the auditor does not have any remaining responsibility for performing audit procedures to identify additional facts that existed at the report date. However, in some situations, the auditor becomes aware of facts that affected the financial statements at the time of their issuance. For example, assume that after the issuance of the financial statements and auditor's report, the auditor learns that a customer's deteriorating financial condition resulted in accounts receivable being materially overstated. In this case, the auditor would request that the client disclose the discovered facts and their impact on both the financial statements and auditor's report to persons currently relying on the financial statements if the following conditions existed:

1. The facts existed at the report date.
2. The information is reliable.
3. Persons are currently relying on or likely to rely on the financial statements and would find this information important.
4. The auditor's report would have been affected if the information had been known to the auditor at the date of the report.

If the client refuses to make these disclosures, the auditor should take steps to prevent future reliance on his or her report. These procedures are outlined in detail in *SAS No. 1* (AU 561.09). They generally require the auditor to notify the client, regulatory bodies (such as the Securities and Exchange Commission), and third parties that the report should no longer be relied upon.

Note in all of the above instances that the event or facts *existed at the date of the auditor's report*. In general, the auditor does not have responsibility for events occurring after the report date (last day of field work). One exception to this general rule is that the auditor is liable for events occurring up to the registration statement date under the Securities Act of 1933.

Figure 16-3 summarizes the auditor's responsibilities with respect to the postaudit period.

◻ Consideration of Omitted Procedures after the Report Date

As discussed in Chapter 2, member firms of the AICPA must have their practices periodically evaluated under a peer review program. A **peer review** represents the examination and evaluation of a CPA firm's work by other CPAs (or another CPA firm). Peer reviews may reveal audit procedures that were omitted by the auditor during her or his examination but were later considered to be necessary to

Date Event or Facts Discovered	Auditor Responsibilities
Prior to Last Day of Field Work	Consider how event should be treated Evaluate client's treatment of the event
After Last Day of Field Work but Prior to Issuance of the Report and Financial Statements	Consider how event should be treated Evaluate client's treatment of the event Dual-date the audit report
After Issuance of the Report and Financial Statements	If applicable, request that the client disclose event to persons relying on the financial statements If client refuses to disclose event, notify the client, SEC, and third parties that the auditor's report can no longer be relied upon

Figure 16-3: *Auditor's Responsibilities in the Postaudit Period*

support the auditor's opinion on the financial statements. These situations are addressed by *Statement on Auditing Standards No. 46 (SAS No. 46)*.[6]

When the auditor becomes aware of a potential omitted procedure, the following questions should be asked:

1. Does the omitted procedure affect the auditor's ability to support his or her opinion on the financial statements?
2. Are persons currently relying on or likely to rely on his or her audit report?

If either of the above situations do not exist, the auditor is under no obligation to perform the omitted procedure or any alternative procedures. From a practical standpoint, if the procedure is not likely to affect the auditor's opinion or persons are not relying on the auditor's report, there is little need to perform the omitted procedure or any procedures compensating for the omitted procedure.

On the other hand, if the answer to the above questions are yes, the auditor should attempt to apply the omitted procedure or alternative procedures. If the results of these procedures do not affect the auditor's conclusion as expressed in the previously-issued opinion on the financial statements, the

---

[6] American Institute of Certified Public Accountants (AICPA), *Statement on Auditing Standards No. 46*, "Consideration of Omitted Procedures After the Report Date" (New York: AICPA, 1983, AU 390).

auditor has no further responsibility. However, if these procedures suggest that the previously-issued opinion is no longer appropriate, the auditor should notify the client, regulatory bodies (such as the Securities and Exchange Commission), and third parties that the previous report should no longer be relied upon.

CHAPTER CHECKPOINTS

16-15. How would the auditor react to the discovery of an event that existed at the report date if the event were discovered:

a. Prior to the last day of field work?
b. After the last day of field work, but prior to the issuance of the report?
c. After the issuance of the report?

16-16. What is dual-dating? When the auditor dual-dates his or her report, what responsibility is being assumed for subsequent events?

16-17. What should the auditor do if the client refuses to disclose a event discovered after the issuance of the audit report to persons relying on the financial statements?

16-18. Describe the procedures undertaken if the auditor becomes aware of a potential omitted procedure.

◉ COMMUNICATIONS WITH THE CLIENT

As noted in Chapter 1, the primary communication made by the auditor is his or her opinion on whether the financial statements are presented in conformity with GAAP. However, either during the audit or at the conclusion of the audit, the auditor will also prepare various types of communications to the client. These communications are discussed in this section.

◻ Communications Related to Internal Control

As noted in Chapter 5, the auditor's primary responsibility for studying the client's internal control is to determine the nature, timing, and extent of his or her substantive tests. As a result, the auditor's work with respect to internal control is conducted with this objective in mind. However, as the auditor studies internal control, he or she may become aware of possible area(s) in which the client can improve its internal control. Therefore, a desirable by-product of the auditor's study of internal control is the ability to provide the client with recommendations for improving its internal control.

It is important to emphasize that communicating internal control deficiencies is clearly a secondary purpose of studying the client's internal control. The auditor is under no requirement under GAAS to identify internal control deficiencies. However, once these deficiencies have been identified by the auditor, GAAS require him or her to communicate these deficiencies to the client.

Statement on Auditing Standards No. 60 (SAS No. 60)[7] requires the auditor to communicate two primary types of deficiencies in internal control to the client. These deficiencies are shown below:

- ▶ **Reportable conditions** are matters coming to the auditor's attention that represent significant deficiencies in the design or operation of internal control that can adversely affect the organization's ability to record, process, summarize, and report financial data.

- ▶ **Material weaknesses** are reportable conditions in which the design or operation of the internal control may result in material financial statement misstatements that may not be detected by employees in the normal course of performing their assigned functions.

The primary difference between a material weakness and a reportable condition is the severity of the internal control deficiency and its ultimate effect on the fairness of the organization's financial statements. Material weaknesses represent deficiencies that may ultimately result in material financial statement misstatements; reportable conditions do not currently pose this threat. However, it is important to note that a reportable condition may eventually worsen and become a material weakness in a future period.

A sample report on a reportable condition is shown in Figure 16-4.[8]

Some important issues related to the auditor's communication of internal control deficiencies are summarized below:

1. The communication should be made to the client's audit committee. As noted earlier in Chapter 4, the **Audit Committee** is a subgroup of the client's Board of Directors that serves as a liaison between the auditor and client. If the client has not established an Audit Committee, the communication should be made to individuals with a level of authority and responsibility equivalent to that of an Audit Committee (such as the Board of Directors, Board of Trustees, or owner of an owner-managed organization).

2. While the communication should preferably be in writing, the auditor may choose to communicate internal control deficiencies orally. If oral communication is chosen, the auditor should document his or her communication of internal control deficiencies in the audit workpapers.

3. Because of the need for timely communications, the auditor may choose to communicate reportable conditions and material weaknesses either as they are discovered or at the conclusion of the audit examination.

4. Because of the limited assurance provided by the auditor's study of internal control with respect to the discovery of reportable conditions and material weaknesses, a communication indicating that no reportable conditions or material weaknesses were discovered should not be issued. Such a communication might provide a false sense of comfort to the client regarding its internal control.

---

[7] American Institute of Certified Public Accountants (AICPA), *Statement on Auditing Standards No. 60*, "Communication of Internal Control Related Matters Noted in an Audit" (New York: AICPA, 1988, AU 325).

[8] American Institute of Certified Public Accountants (AICPA), *Statement on Auditing Standards No. 60*, "Communication of Internal Control Related Matters Noted in an Audit" (New York: AICPA, 1988, AU 325.12). While *SAS No. 60* uses the term "internal control structure" in its reports, we use "internal control" to be consistent with the guidance of *SAS No. 78*.

To: The Audit Committee of Vandalay Industries

In planning and performing our audit of the financial statements of Vandalay Industries for the year ended December 31, 19x2, we considered its internal control in order to determine our auditing procedures for the purpose of expressing our opinion on the financial statements and not to provide assurance on the internal control. However, we noted certain matters involving the internal control and its operation that we consider to be reportable conditions under standards established by the American Institute of Certified Public Accountants. Reportable conditions involve matters coming to our attention relating to significant deficiencies in the design or operation of the internal control that, in our judgment, could adversely affect Vandalay Industries' ability to record, process, summarize, and report financial data consistent with the assertions of management in the financial statements.

Vandalay Industries has not established appropriate segregation of duties over its cash receipts function. Specifically, a single employee has the responsibility for posting cash receipts to the subsidiary accounts receivable records and depositing cash receipts in the company's bank accounts.

A material weakness is a reportable condition in which the design or operation of one or more of the internal control elements does not reduce to a relatively low level the risk that errors or irregularities in amounts that would be material to the financial statements being audited may occur and not be detected within a timely period by employees in the normal course of performing their assigned functions.

Our consideration of the internal control would not necessarily disclose all matters in the internal control that might be reportable conditions and, accordingly, would not necessarily disclose all reportable conditions that are also considered to be material weaknesses as defined above. However, none of the reportable conditions described above is believed to be a material weakness.

This report is intended solely for the information and use of the audit committee, management, and others within the organization.

Figure 16-4: *Sample Communication of Internal Control Deficiencies*

Figure 16-5 provides examples of possible reportable conditions identified by *SAS No. 60*.

◘ Other Communications with Audit Committees

In addition to communicating internal control deficiencies, the auditor has an obligation under GAAS to communicate various other matters to the client's Audit Committee (or equivalent). According to *Statement on Auditing Standards No. 61 (SAS No. 61)*[9], the following matters should be communicated to the client's Audit Committee:

---

[9] American Institute of Certified Public Accountants (AICPA), *Statement on Auditing Standards No. 61*, "Communication with Audit Committees" (New York: AICPA, 1988, AU 380).

- Inadequate overall design of internal control
- Absence of overall segregation of duties
- Absence of reviews and approvals of transactions
- Inadequate procedures for assessing and applying accounting principles
- Inadequate provisions for safeguarding assets
- Absence of other control techniques considered appropriate for the type and level of transaction activity
- Evidence that a system fails to provide complete and accurate output consistent with objectives and current needs because of design flaws
- Failure of identified controls to prevent or detect misstatements
- Failure to provide complete and accurate output because of the misapplication of control activities
- Intentional override of internal control by those in authority
- Failure to perform tasks that are part of internal control
- Willful wrongdoing by employees or management
- Manipulation, falsification, or alteration of accounting records or supporting documents
- Intentional misapplication of accounting principles
- Misrepresentations by client personnel to the auditor
- Lack of qualifications and training of employees of management
- Absence of control consciousness within the organization
- Failure to follow up and correct previously identified internal control deficiencies
- Significant or extensive undisclosed related-party transactions
- Undue bias or lack of objectivity by those responsible for accounting decisions

Figure 16-5: *Examples of Possible Reportable Conditions*

1. The auditor's responsibility under GAAS.
2. The initial selection of and changes in significant accounting policies and their application.
3. Management judgments and accounting estimates.
4. Significant adjustments to the financial statements arising from the audit.
5. The auditor's responsibility for other information in documents containing audited financial statements, such as Management's Discussion and Analysis.
6. Disagreements with management regarding the application of accounting principles and the basis for management's estimates.
7. The auditor's views about matters that were the subject of consultation with other accountants.
8. Issues discussed with management in connection with the selection or retention of the auditor.
9. Any serious difficulties encountered with management in connection with performing the audit.

This last item deserves additional discussion. As part of the liaison role of the Audit Committee, it should be able to assist the auditor in resolving difficulties encountered during the audit. Resolving these difficulties will enable the audit to be completed in a timely fashion. Difficulties of this nature include:

- ▶ Unreasonable delays by management in permitting the beginning of the audit or providing necessary information to the auditor
- ▶ An unrealistic timetable established by management for the completion of the audit
- ▶ The unavailability of client personnel
- ▶ The failure of client personnel to provide client-prepared schedules on a timely basis

Similar to the auditor's communication of internal control deficiencies, the communication of these matters to the Audit Committee can either be oral or written; if oral, the communication should be documented in the auditor's workpapers. In addition, like deficiencies in internal control, these matters can be communicated as they occur or at the completion of the audit.

◻ Management Letters

As noted above, GAAS require auditors to communicate deficiencies in their client's internal control to management. In addition to knowledge about internal control, the auditor also obtains a great deal of knowledge about the client, its business, and method of operations during the audit examination. The extensive knowledge of the auditor about his or her clients, as well as the auditor's overall business knowledge, give auditors a unique opportunity to provide their clients with recommendations for improving some aspect of their operations. The proper forum for communicating these recommendations is a management letter.

Management letters contain suggestions and recommendations for improving procedures, operations, and controls in areas within the auditor's competence in accounting, auditing, tax, and consulting services matters. While not required under GAAS, management letters are an important communication for many reasons. A management letter demonstrates in a very tangible manner the CPA's continuing interest in the client's welfare and also contributes to the quality of the CPA's services in the following ways:

1. In bringing attention to matters of merit that were noted in the performance of the audit procedures, it adds a constructive dimension to the CPA's services.
2. Recommendations for improvement are an integral part of the services offered by auditors, and most clients generally expect to obtain benefits beyond the attest function from their independent accountants.
3. Prosperous, financially-sound clients are the lifeblood of an auditor's continued growth. Ideas that contribute to the improvement of clients' operations or financial position serve to strengthen the auditor's relations with them. In addition, such ideas also provide a source for new services provided to the client.

Although the auditor can make suggestions orally, a timely and well-written letter has several important advantages. It provides the client's executives with the auditor's carefully prepared analysis of the particular situation and recommendations for action. It can be referred to when necessary and passed along for action without the danger of distortion, which is always possible in spoken communications. It is a record of what was said and a reminder of the services rendered by the auditor.

Issues Related to Management Letters. Several important issues related to management letters are discussed below.

Timeliness. Prompt submission of the management letter to the client is important. A client will rarely be favorably impressed with recommendations that are not made on a timely basis. A management letter ordinarily should be issued for each audit client shortly after the conclusion of the field work. In many instances, it also may be desirable to issue a letter upon the completion of interim audit procedures, because this is often the time when attention will be devoted specifically to the study of internal control. Frequently, more than one letter may be issued in connection with a single examination.

Planning. Planning for the management letter should always be an integral part of planning the audit engagement. The audit program should include appropriate steps for gathering information and preparing the letter. Steps such as the following may be appropriate:

1. During the field work, the auditor should be alert for client procedures and internal controls that may be improved. Specific situations, suitably documented, should be accumulated in writing in a separate management letter file as they are encountered.
2. The auditor should note action taken on recommendations provided in the prior year's management letter.

Follow-up. Previous management letters should be filed for reference and subsequent follow-up by the auditor. They represent a valuable history of service and experience with the client. During the course of the audit examination, the auditor should determine the action taken on all important matters discussed in the prior year's management letter. The auditor should note in the workpapers any action taken or why action was not taken on comments made in previous management letters. If no action was taken on an important recommendation, the auditor may wish to repeat the comment. This reminds management and the Audit Committee that a problem situation still exists (which management and/or the Audit Committee may otherwise assume was corrected).

Preparing the Letter. The primary consideration in preparing the management letter is to be familiar with the intended audience's background. The reader's background should be considered as the letter is written. Throughout the letter, the auditor should describe facts and recommendations in terms that the reader will understand; the auditor should offer reasons or advantages that the reader will recognize as valid. A reader with an accounting background may accept a suggestion to hire an internal auditor, because the auditor indicates it will improve internal controls and procedures. Although a CPA might understand the real benefits inferred, a business executive wants the benefits described in understandable terms, as in the following example:

> The salary, expenses, and clerical back-up costs for one experienced internal auditor performing frequent audits of equipment construction materials at job sites might produce time and cost savings as well as "insurance-type" benefits. The internal auditor could suggest improved procedures to provide management with better information in a more timely fashion and to reduce accounting costs. That person could also perform certain audit tasks which may, if coordinated with our work, reduce our audit time and provide a savings in terms of audit costs.

Making Recommendations. In certain situations, bringing the problem to management's attention is the real service of the letter. To say that "negotiable securities are kept in an unlocked file cabinet" alerts management to a problem they should recognize must be corrected promptly. In other situations, the problem is obvious to management but the solution is not. The auditor's service then consists of proposing practical suggestions for solving the problem. Consider the following example:

> The company had a substantial book-to-physical-inventory loss last year. We understand that the causes are not yet known. Accordingly, we recommend that you review all procedures designed to safeguard inventory and correct any weaknesses, take an interim physical inventory during the current fiscal year to determine if shortages are still occurring, and also stress the importance to the receiving clerks of verifying the quantity and condition of goods as they are received.

An unnecessarily critical description of the problem can set a negative tone and anger the reader or others whose work is being criticized. Frequently, a situation can be described more effectively in terms of potential for improvement. Which of the following presentations of the same situation would you prefer to receive in a letter if you were a client?

> The EDP system is not adequately documented because the manager has a lack of experience. Errors can escape detection, personnel training is likely to be inadequate, and it is difficult for an outsider to check what is being done.

or

> In the past, there has been little documentation in the EDP Department. Now the department processes more data, prepares more reports, and employs more people than ever before, and further documentation could improve daily operations. Insufficient EDP documentation of the required type can jeopardize otherwise acceptable federal income tax deductions.
>
> Documentation of EDP procedures and programs reduces errors by clarifying tasks, helps detect errors that do occur, and is valuable in training new operators. It can also assure continuity and avoid confusion should key employees leave the company. We recommend the following kinds of documentation for your most vital programs and their related operating procedures....

The difference in tone of these two remarks is staggering. The first example has a negative tone and is especially likely to anger the EDP manager. In addition, no specific recommendations are provided. In contrast, the second example focuses on potential improvements for the problem and not the problem itself.

In making recommendations, it is important to provide detail of both the expected costs of the recommendations as well as the benefits of these recommendations. For example, if the auditor suggests adding personnel or requiring additional forms of documentation, an estimate of the costs should be made and compared to the potential benefits. Recognizing the costs helps to assure practical and imaginative recommendations. In providing estimated costs and benefits, the auditor should be as specific as possible. For example, consider the following two presentations of a recommendation for a client to arrange to have customer payments mailed to a lockbox.

> While a lockbox will result in an additional expenditure of $5,000 annually, this expenditure will improve control over customers' payments as well as speed the flow of cash receipts into your bank account.

or

> We recommend that you consider using a lockbox for customer remittances. Cash would be credited to or be available for use in your commercial account an average of two days sooner. In 19X1, a two-day speed-up would have freed $138,000 for business use. The method provides strong internal control over cash receipts by completely separating handling and accounting functions. Customers are instructed to send their payments to a post office box to which only your commercial bank has access. Your bank account is immediately credited for the day's receipts, and the account balance can be obtained daily by telephone. The bank sends your accounting department copies of all Checks, Remittance Advices, and correspondence the following day. Service charges by the bank of $5,000 per year for this additional service should be more than offset by the earnings of funds freed and reductions in clerical costs.

Processing the Letter. Before sending the letter, each situation included in the letter should be discussed with an appropriate representative of the client (e.g., one having knowledge of and responsibility for the area under discussion). Such discussions may help to determine whether the recommendations are practicable and also may lessen the chance of possible misrepresentation and resentment from executives concerned with the area under discussion.

In larger CPA firms, it also may be helpful to have consulting services and tax personnel review the supporting documents and the letter itself. This is especially desirable if these specialists are familiar with the client's affairs and have been involved with any of the areas pertaining to the recommendations in the letter.

A typed draft of the letter should be discussed in person with the recipient and other client executives appropriate in the circumstances. In most instances, a draft of the letter should be reviewed with the chief accounting officer of the client before its issuance. This will eliminate the element of surprise from the letter and may avoid embarrassment from making comments about items on which the auditor has not been fully informed.

CHAPTER CHECKPOINTS

16-19. Define reportable conditions and material weaknesses. What is the auditor's responsibility with respect to detecting these deficiencies? What is the auditor's responsibility with respect to communicating these deficiencies to the client?

16-20. In what ways can the auditor communicate deficiencies in internal control to the client?

16-21. What is an Audit Committee? What matters should be communicated by the auditor to the Audit Committee?

16-22. What are management letters? How do management letters contribute to the quality of the CPA's services?

16-23. How should the auditor plan for the management letter during the audit examination?

16-24. What factors should be considered by the auditor in processing the management letter?

SUMMARY OF KEY POINTS

1. A subsequent event is an event occurring after the balance-sheet date but prior to the issuance of the audit report and financial statements. If subsequent events provide additional information about conditions that existed at the balance-sheet date, appropriate adjustments should be made in the financial statements. If the subsequent event relates to a matter arising after the balance-sheet date, the event should be disclosed in the financial statements. Alternatively, *pro forma* financial statements may be prepared to reflect the effects of the subsequent event.

2. Procedures commonly used to search for subsequent events include: (1) examining cutoff Bank Statements; (2) reviewing the collection of accounts receivable; (3) reviewing credit memoranda issued for sales returns and allowances; (4) scanning the Cash Receipts Journal and Check Register; (5) reviewing corporate minutes and the client's interim financial statements; (6) obtaining management's representations concerning possible subsequent events; and (7) inquiring of the client's legal counsel about litigation, claims, and assessments.

3. The auditor should inquire of the client's management concerning litigation, claims, and assessments, since the client's management is the auditor's primary source of information with respect to this information. However, the auditor will also request a letter of inquiry from the client's attorney regarding the litigation, claims, and assessments identified by management. This letter of inquiry serves as corroborating evidence regarding litigation, claims, and assessments.

4. Client representations contain written corroboration of oral statements made to the auditor by client personnel during the examination. Client representations provide the client's officials with an opportunity to consider whether all important matters have been disclosed to the auditor and also act as a reminder to management of its primary responsibility for the fairness of presentation of the financial statements.

5. In evaluating the results of an examination, the auditor should compare the amount of aggregate error (or likely error) to the predetermined materiality threshold. Likely error includes both errors specifically identified during the audit (known errors) as well as the projected effect of known errors on the account balance or class of transactions (projected errors). If the amount of likely error exceeds the tolerable error (or materiality), the auditor should propose an adjustment to the account balance or class of transactions.

6. The auditor's reaction to events discovered after the last day of field work depends upon when the events are discovered. If events are discovered after the last day of field work but prior to the issuance of the financial statements (and auditor's report), the auditor should investigate the client's treatment of the event and dual-date his or her report. If the event is discovered after the issuance of the financial statements, the auditor should consider requesting the client to disclose the event (and its effect on the financial statements and auditor's report) to persons relying on the financial statements. If the client refuses to do so, the auditor should take steps to prevent future reliance on his or her report.

7. If the auditor discovers that a necessary audit procedure was not performed (was omitted) during an examination, he or she should consider whether the omitted procedure is likely to affect his or her ability to support the previously-issued opinion. If so, the auditor should attempt to apply the omitted procedure or apply alternative procedures in order to provide a satisfactory basis for the opinion.

8. Two types of deficiencies in internal control that must be communicated to clients are reportable conditions and material weaknesses. Reportable conditions are deficiencies in internal control that may adversely affect the client's ability to accurately record, process, summarize, and report financial data. Material weaknesses are a serious form of reportable condition that may result in material financial statement misstatements not being detected by employees in the normal course of performing their assigned functions.

9. Management letters contain a written correspondence from the auditor to an official of the client. This letter contains suggestions and recommendations for improving procedures, operations, and controls relating to accounting, auditing, tax, and consulting services matters. These letters demonstrate the CPA's continuing interest in the client's welfare and contribute to the quality of the CPA's services.

◉ SUMMARY OF PROFESSIONAL PRONOUNCEMENTS

Statement on Auditing Standards No. 1, "Codification of Auditing Standards and Procedures" (New York: AICPA, 1972, AU 310.01).

Statement on Auditing Standards No. 12, "Inquiry of a Client's Lawyer Concerning Litigation, Claims, and Assessments" (New York: AICPA, 1976, AU 337).

Statement on Auditing Standards No. 19, "Client Representations" (New York: AICPA, 1977, AU 333).

Statement on Auditing Standards No. 46, "Consideration of Omitted Procedures After the Report Date" (New York: AICPA, 1983, AU 390).

Statement on Auditing Standards No. 47, "Audit Risk and Materiality in Conducting an Audit" (New York: AICPA, 1983, AU 312).

Statement on Auditing Standards No. 56, "Analytical Procedures" (New York: AICPA, 1988, AU 329).

Statement on Auditing Standards No. 60, "Communication of Internal Control Related Matters Noted in an Audit" (New York: AICPA, 1988, AU 325).

Statement on Auditing Standards No. 61, "Communication with Audit Committees" (New York: AICPA, 1988, AU 380).

◉ GLOSSARY

Analytical Procedures. A type of substantive test performed by the auditor that involves comparing the recorded amount of an account balance or class of transactions (or a ratio involving an account balance or class of transactions) with an expectation developed by the auditor.

Audit Committee. The subgroup of the client's Board of Directors that serves as a liaison between the auditor and client.

Client Representations. Information provided by client's management to the auditor that: (1) acknowledge the primary responsibility for the financial statements, (2) indicate that all information and records have been made available to the auditor, and (3) confirm information provided orally to the auditor during the examination.

Dual-Date. When auditors learn of a subsequent event after the completion of the field work but prior to the issuance of their report, they will often dual-date the audit report. A report that is dual-dated limits the auditor's responsibility beyond the last day of field work to a specific subsequent event.

Known Error. The portion of aggregate error that relates to errors specifically identified by the auditor during an examination that are uncorrected by the client.

Letter of Inquiry. A letter from the client's management to their attorney requesting that the attorney corroborate information furnished by management regarding litigation, claims, and assessments to the auditor.

Likely Error. The sum of: (1) errors specifically identified during the audit examination (known errors), and (2) the amount of errors actually discovered during the audit projected to the account balance or class of transactions (projected errors).

Management Letter. A letter addressed by the auditor to the Board of Directors (or its audit committee), to the Chief Executive Officer, or to any official designated as an appropriate recipient. Management letters contain recommendations related to accounting, auditing, tax, and consulting services matters.

Material Weakness. A reportable condition that may result in material financial statement misstatements that will not be detected by employees in the normal course of performing their assigned functions.

Omitted Procedure. An audit procedure that was not performed during the examination but was subsequently considered to have been necessary to support the auditor's opinion.

Projected Error. The component of likely error that is determined by projecting known errors to the total value of the account balance or class of transactions.

Reportable Condition. A deficiency in internal control that affects the organization's ability to record, process, summarize, and report financial data.

Second-Partner Review. Also known as a cold review, this is a review of workpapers by a partner not associated with a particular audit engagement. Second-partner reviews are required for the audits of all SEC registrants.

Subsequent Discovery of Facts. A situation where the auditor discovers events or conditions that existed at the date of his or her report subsequent to the last day of field work.

Subsequent Events. Any event occurring between the balance-sheet date and the issuance of the client's financial statements. These events result in adjustment to or disclosure in the financial statements.

QUESTIONS AND PROBLEMS

16-25. Select the **best** answer for each of the following items:

1. A written communication of reportable conditions relating to an entity's internal control observed during an audit of financial statements should include a:

   a. Restriction on the distribution of the report.
   b. Description of tests performed to search for material weaknesses.
   c. Statement of compliance with applicable laws and regulations.
   d. Paragraph describing management's evaluation of the effectiveness of internal control.

2. Ajax Company's auditor concludes that the omission of an audit procedure considered necessary at the time of the prior examination impairs the auditor's ability to support the previously-expressed unqualified opinion. If the auditor believes there are stockholders currently relying on the opinion, he or she should:

   a. Notify the stockholders currently relying on the previously-expressed opinion that they should not do so.
   b. Advise management to disclose this development in its next interim report to the stockholders.
   c. Advise management to revise the financial statements with full disclosure of the auditor's inability to support the unqualified opinion.
   d. Undertake to apply the omitted procedure or alternate procedures that would provide a satisfactory basis for the opinion.

3. Soon after Boyd's audit report was issued, Boyd learned of certain related-party transactions that occurred during the year under audit. These transactions were not disclosed in the notes to the financial statements. Boyd should:

   a. Plan to audit the transactions during the next engagement.
   b. Recall all copies of the audited financial statements.
   c. Determine whether the lack of disclosure would affect the auditor's report.
   d. Ask the client to disclose the transactions in subsequent interim statements.

4. Reportable conditions are matters that come to an auditor's attention that should be communicated to an entity's audit committee because they represent:

   a. Disclosures of information that significantly contradict the auditor's going-concern assumption.
   b. Material irregularities or illegal acts perpetrated by high-level management.
   c. Significant deficiencies in the design or operation of internal control.
   d. Manipulation or falsification of accounting records or documents from which financial statements are prepared.

5. An auditor's communication of internal control related matters noted in an audit usually should be addressed to the:

   a. Audit Committee.
   b. Director of Internal Auditing.
   c. Chief Financial Officer.
   d. Chief Executive Officer.

6. Which of the following types of subsequent events would most likely require adjustment to financial statements dated December 31, 19x1?

   a. The effects of litigation which was initiated early in January 19x2.
   b. A decline in the market value of marketable securities that occurred during 19x2.
   c. A loss from uncollectible accounts receivable that resulted from a customer's further deteriorating financial condition that existed at year-end but was unknown to the auditor.
   d. A purchase of property, plant and equipment in March 19x2.

7. A CPA has received an attorney's letter in which no significant disagreements with the client's assessments of contingent liabilities were noted. The resignation of the client's lawyer shortly after receipt of the letter should alert the auditor that:

   a. Undisclosed unasserted claims may have arisen.
   b. The attorney was unable to form a conclusion with respect to the significance of litigation, claims, and assessments.
   c. The auditor must begin a completely new examination of contingent liabilities.
   d. An adverse opinion will be necessary.

8. Which of the following would most likely qualify as a subsequent event and require examination by the auditor?

   a. Unanticipated sales made by the client on account immediately after year-end.
   b. The disposal of an asset prior to the end of its useful life.
   c. A stock or bond issuance occurring prior to the last day of field work.
   d. Notification following the issuance of the financial statements from a major customer of her or his inability to pay accounts receivable.
   e. All of the above would qualify as subsequent events.

9. Which of the following parties is the auditor's primary source of evidence with respect to litigation, claims, and assessments?

   a. The predecessor auditor.
   b. The client's management.
   c. The client's attorney.
   d. The client's internal audit staff.

10. The primary purpose of a letter of inquiry sent to the client's attorney is to provide the auditor with:

    a. An estimate of the possible dollar amounts of any losses.
    b. A determination as to the point in time when litigation will ultimately be resolved.
    c. Information that corroborates inquiries provided by the client to the auditor.
    d. Evidence regarding all potential unrecorded liabilities.
    e. A basis for deciding upon the proper method of disclosing loss contingencies that exist at year-end.

11. Assume that the auditor discovers about an event after the issuance of the client's financial statements. If the event existed at the date of the auditor's report and persons are still relying on the client's financial statements, the auditor most likely would:

    a. Issue a disclaimer of opinion.
    b. Request that the client inform persons known to be relying on the financial statements and auditor's report.
    c. Examine the event in question and reissue the audit report bearing a dual-date.
    d. Disclose the event by preparing *pro forma* financial statements.

12. The purpose of analytical procedures applied in the final review stages of the audit is to:

    a. Evaluate the validity of the overall conclusions reached by the auditor.
    b. Identify changes that have occurred during the current year.
    c. Search for the possible existence of subsequent events.
    d. Gather evidence on specific management assertions related to an account balance or class of transactions.

13. A subsequent event is defined as any event occurring between the _____ and the _____.

    a. Balance-sheet date; date the financial statements are issued
    b. Balance-sheet date; last day of field work
    c. Last day of field work; date the financial statements are issued.
    d. None of the above.

14. The primary purpose of the client's representation letter is to:

    a. Confirm the understanding between the auditor and client regarding the scope of the audit examination.
    b. Communicate any material weaknesses in internal control noted by the auditor during the examination.
    c. Summarize any areas of disagreement between the auditor and client during the examination.
    d. Acknowledge the client's responsibility for the financial statements.
    e. Provide the client with a summary of hours worked during the most recent audit engagement.

15. Which of the following is not required under generally accepted auditing standards?

    a. A study and evaluation of the client's internal control.
    b. A report issued by the auditor indicating the degree of responsibility he or she is taking with respect to the financial statements.
    c. A written communication of any internal control deficiencies noted during the audit examination
    d. Permission from the client prior to initiating communication with a predecessor auditor.
    e. All of the above are required under generally accepted auditing standards.

16. Which of the following parties would not be an appropriate addressee for a management letter?

    a. The client's Board of Directors or Audit Committee.
    b. Operating personnel employed by the client.
    c. A third-party user, such as a loan officer or financial analyst.
    d. The Chief Executive Officer of the client.
    e. All of the above would be considered appropriate addressees.

17. Which of the following should be included in the amount that is compared to tolerable error (materiality) to determine whether the client's financial statements are materially misstated:

	Known Error	Projected Error
a.	No	No
b.	Yes	No
c.	No	Yes
d.	Yes	Yes

18. A communication between the auditor and client that contains suggestions and recommendations for improving procedures, operations, and controls is referred to as a(n):

    a. Client representation letter.
    b. Engagement letter.
    c. Management letter.
    d. Material weakness letter.
    e. Reportable condition letter.

19. A significant deficiency in the client's internal control structure that does not currently pose the threat of resulting in materially misstated financial statements is referred to as a(n):

    a. Material weakness.
    b. Internal control deficiency.
    c. Management letter.
    d. Reportable condition.
    e. None of the above.

20. The management letter should:

   a. Be delivered to the client on a timely basis.
   b. Be considered by the auditor in planning the scope of the engagement.
   c. Be discussed with client personnel prior to delivery to management.
   d. Contain suggestions for improving weaknesses identified during the auditor's study and evaluation of internal control.
   e. All of the above.

(Items 1 through 6 in 16-25; AICPA Adapted)

16-26. *Statements on Auditing Standards No. 12 and No. 19* identify two types of communications that should be requested by the auditor near the end of the examination: letters of inquiry to the client's attorney and letters of representation from clients.

Required:

a. Briefly describe each of these two types of communications. What is the primary purpose of each?
b. List several matters that are addressed in the letter of inquiry to the client's attorney.
c. List several matters that are addressed in the client representations.

16-27. In addition to examining financial statement transactions occurring during the previous year, the auditor is also responsible for identifying subsequent events occurring during the current year.

Required:

a. Define and provide examples of subsequent events. What are the two main types of subsequent events that may be identified by the auditor?
b. What procedures can be used by the auditor to identify subsequent events?
c. What is the cutoff date for the auditor's responsibility with respect to subsequent events?
d. What actions are likely to be taken by the auditor for subsequent events identified during the following time periods (assume in all cases that the event existed as of the last day of field work):

   1. Prior to the last day of field work.
   2. After the last day of field work but prior to the issuance of the financial statements.
   3. After the issuance of the financial statements.

16-28. Windek, a CPA, is nearing the completion of an examination of the financial statements of Jubilee, Inc., for the year ended December 31, 19X1. Windek is currently concerned with ascertaining the occurrence of subsequent events that may require adjustment or disclosure essential to a fair presentation in conformity with generally accepted accounting principles.

Required:

a. Briefly explain what is meant by the phrase subsequent event.
b. How do those subsequent events that require financial statement adjustment differ from those that require financial statement disclosure?
c. What procedures should be performed in order to ascertain the occurrence of subsequent events?

(AICPA Adapted)

16-29. During the course of an audit conducted in accordance with generally accepted auditing standards, an auditor may become aware of matters relating to the client's internal control that may be of interest to the client's audit committee or to individuals with an equivalent level of authority and responsibility, such as the Board of Directors, the Board of Trustees, or the owner in an owner-managed enterprise.

Required:

a. What are meant by the terms "reportable conditions" and "material weaknesses"?
b. What are an auditor's responsibilities in identifying and reporting these matters?

(AICPA Adapted)

16-30. Green, CPA, is auditing the financial statements of Taylor Corporation for the year ended December 31, 19x8. Green plans to complete the field work and sign the auditor's report on May 10, 19x9. Green is concerned about events and transactions occurring after December 31, 19x8 that may affect the 19x8 financial statements.

Required:

a. What are the general types of subsequent events that require Green's consideration and evaluation?
b. What are the auditing procedures Green should consider performing to gather evidence concerning subsequent events?

(AICPA Adapted)

16-31. Below are selected statistics that relate to the ABC Company:

ABC Company

	Year Ended December 31			Industry Average
	19X2	19X1	19X0	(19X1)
Financial Position Relationships				
Current assets to current liabilities	2.5	2.2	2.3	2.0
Acid-test, quick assets to current liabilities	1.1	0.9	1.0	---
Operating Relationships				
Net income per share of common stock	$13.10	$ 7.89	$ 4.87	---
Number of days sales in receivables (accounts receivable to average daily sales)	24.9	26.8	29.3	---
Merchandise turnover (cost of sales to average inventory)	8.9	8.3	7.2	8.2
Gross profit to sales	10.3%	9.5%	9.1%	---
Net income to sales	2.2%	1.7%	1.3%	1.3%

Required:

Prepare formal comments on the financial statistics of ABC Company that could be included in a management letter that relates to the following topics:

a. Current assets to current liabilities. (ABC Company has a long-term debt covenant that requires a minimum ratio of 1.5:1.)
b. Net income per share of common stock.
c. Number of days sales in receivables.
d. Gross profit and net income to sales (sales in 19X2 increased by 30 percent).

16-32. Read the following management letter, which is designed to be issued to the partners of the law firm of Smart & Dumb. Keep in mind these questions and note your specific comments:

- Is each topic presented effectively? Why?
- Is the letter organized effectively? Why?
- Could the writing be significantly improved? How?
- Would you delete any topics? Which ones?
- What are the letter's strong points? Why?
- Do you believe you need more information to evaluate its effectiveness? If so, what information do you need and why is it necessary?

J. Jones, CPA
April 12, 19X1

To: The Partners of Smart & Dumb

Gentlemen:

In connection with our examination of the balance sheet of Smart & Dumb as of December 31, 19X0, we reviewed the accounting procedures and systems of internal control employed by the Partnership. We found no material weaknesses in internal control. However, the attached comments and suggestions for improvements therein are submitted for your consideration. They were derived from our examination of the records, general observations, and discussions with various partners and employees.

We wish to express our appreciation for the cooperation and courtesy extended to us by your partners and employees. We would be pleased to discuss any of these matters with you further and to assist in their implementation if you so desire.

Very truly yours,

J. Jones, CPA

Cash Receipts

Cash receipts are manually and separately posted to the Cash Receipts Journal and detail Accounts Receivable Ledger Cards. Pending further evaluation as to the desirability of mechanizing the entire accounting system, we recommend that a pegboard system, which would eliminate this double posting, be implemented as an immediate time-saving device.

To facilitate the daily posting of cash receipts and avoid incorrect postings, we recommend that unidentified receipts be posted initially to a suspense account. A listing of these unmatched receipts could be periodically circulated to the partners for proper identification. Requesting that clients return a copy of the Invoice, or a detachable portion thereof, with their remittances would probably reduce the number of unidentified receipts.

Cash Disbursements

Approved Invoices should be recorded by use of a pegboard system that would simultaneously prepare the Checks. Upon issuance of the Checks, all supporting detail for the disbursement should be defaced to preclude the potential reuse thereof. Signed Checks should be mailed and bank accounts should be reconciled by individuals not connected with the preparation and recording of the respective disbursements.

Petty Cash

To improve internal control over petty cash, each disbursement should be evidenced by a prenumbered Petty Cash Voucher. Applicable supporting detail should be attached thereto, and, upon reimbursement, the Voucher and supporting detail should be defaced to prevent potential reuse.

The Petty Cash Custodian is frequently interrupted in performing her accounting duties to make change for the vending machines. Consideration should be given to maintaining a small change fund at the switchboard, possibly on an honor basis, for this purpose.

Accounts Receivable

Sixty-four accounts receivable confirmation requests were returned by the post office due to bad addresses, and 48 clients reported various differences in their account balances. These latter items were either satisfactorily resolved or were written off as uncollectible. Our review of the accounts and discussion thereof with the respective partners resulted in the write-off of accounts aggregating approximately $80,000 and the recording of allowances for additional doubtful accounts aggregating $40,000. We suggest that additional efforts be made to periodically furnish each partner with a listing of past-due accounts so that appropriate follow-up can be initiated on a timely basis.

A pegboard system, which would provide simultaneous posting of the Revenue Journal and detail Accounts Receivable Ledger Cards, should be instituted.

As a result of the additional effort expended, a reasonably accurate billing cutoff was achieved as of December 31, 19X0. Similar efforts should be made at future fiscal year-ends and particularly at dates of admission, withdrawal, or retirement of partners, when cash payments are required to be calculated on the accrual basis net worth of the firm. However, accurate billing cutoffs are not essential at interim month-ends; and to expedite the monthly closings, we suggest that the established 20th of the following-month cutoff date be strictly adhered to at these times.

Charges Reimbursable from Clients

Although it was impractical to make a complete reconciliation of this account as of December 31, 19X0, our review of these charges resulted in a write-off of approximately $18,000 to adjust this account to a reasonable estimate of charges recoverable from clients as of December 31, 19X0. To ensure that all items are billed or that approved write-offs are recorded for unbilled items, the detail of this account, which consists of various charge slips in the billing folders, should be periodically reconciled to the general ledger control account.

Luncheon Club Billings

A time saving may be achieved by requesting that the Luncheon Club bill each attorney separately or group charge slips by attorney. Each attorney's secretary could then segregate the charge slips and furnish the accounting department with the aggregate personal amount (to be deducted from the monthly dividend) and detail billing memos for amounts chargeable to clients.

Telephone Charges

Switchboard and accounting personnel spend approximately 40 hours each month checking telephone charges and investigating unidentified calls. Consideration should be given to charging unidentified calls, which we were informed were large in number but minor in aggregate amount, to office expense. This policy could be instituted after emphasizing to the staff the importance of placing toll calls through the switchboard, where detail charge slips would be prepared, or obtaining time and charges on calls made after office hours. The telephone company could be requested to review the overall effectiveness of the present phone system.

Duties of Accounting Manager

The Accounting Manager currently spends approximately three hours each day performing duties that could apparently be handled by an Office Clerk. These duties include: (1) changing light bulbs; (2) making bank deposits; (3) ordering, checking, unpacking, and distributing supplies; (4) dealing with taxicab companies and the Highway Express Agency, Inc.; (5) post office errands; (6) personal errands; and (7) obtaining signatures on Checks. An Office Clerk (perhaps a college student on a part-time basis) could be hired at a much lower wage rate to handle these miscellaneous jobs, thereby enabling the accounting manager to devote full time to accounting matters.

Partners' Dividends

Cash receipts on the day of calculation are currently included in the computation of the partners' monthly dividends. To facilitate the orderly preparation of these dividends, consideration should be given to including cash receipts only through the previous day.

Mechanization of Accounting System

As previously mentioned, implementation of pegboard systems should provide immediate time savings in several areas at a nominal cost. However, we believe that further consideration could be given to the desirability of utilizing a personal computer to further reduce clerical time and provide additional management information on a more timely basis.

Time and Billing Controls

We recommend that further consideration be given to improving and standardizing time control and billing procedures. Procedures could be established to:

1. Ensure that all chargeable time is billed.
2. Facilitate more timely billing.
3. Provide comparison of actual fees billed with fees at standard billing rates.
4. Provide an inventory of jobs in process, including appropriate detail of unbilled charges.
5. Provide, if desired, a summary of time devoted to clients, administration, civic activities, professional societies, or other categories.
6. Provide a summary of billings by partner.
7. Ease the work load on attorneys' secretaries.

If it is decided to mechanize the accounting system, as mentioned in the preceding section, a time control and billing system would be an ideal application.

16-33. This question consists of 15 items pertaining to possible deficiencies in an auditor's communication of internal control related matters noted in an audit.

Land & Hale, CPAs, are auditing the financial statements of Stone Co., a nonpublic entity, for the year ended December 31, 19x3. Land, the engagement supervisor, anticipates expressing an unqualified opinion on May 20, 19x4. Wood, an assistant on the engagement, drafted the auditor's communication of internal control related matters that Land plans to send to Stone's Board of Directors with the May 20th auditor's report. Land reviewed Wood's draft and indicated in the *Supervisor's Review Notes* that there were deficiencies in Wood's draft.

Independent Auditor's Report
To the Board of Directors of Stone Company:

In planning and performing our audit of the financial statements of Stone, Co. for the year ended December 31, 19x3, we considered its internal control in order to determine our auditing procedures for the purpose of expressing our opinion on the financial statements and to provide assurance on the internal control. However, we noted certain matters involving the internal control and its operations that we consider to be reportable conditions under standards established by the American Institute of Certified Public Accountants. Reportable conditions involve matters coming to our attention relating to significant deficiencies in the design or operation of the internal control that, in our judgment, could adversely affect the organization's ability to record, process, summarize, and report financial data consistent with our assessment of control risk.

We noted that deficiencies in the internal control design included inadequate provisions for the guarding of assets, especially concerning cash receipts and inventory stored at remote locations. Additionally, we noted failures in the operation of the internal control. Reconciliations of subsidiary ledgers to control accounts were not timely prepared and senior employees in authority intentionally overrode the internal control concerning cash payments to the detriment of the overall objectives of the structure.

A material weakness is not necessarily a reportable condition, but is a design defect in which the internal control elements do not reduce to a relatively low level the risk that errors or irregularities in amounts that would be material in relation to the financial statements being audited may occur and not be detected by the auditor during the audit.

Our consideration of the internal control would not necessarily disclose all matters in the internal control that might be reportable conditions and, accordingly, would not necessarily disclose all reportable conditions that are also considered to be material weaknesses as defined above. However, none of the reportable conditions described above is believed to be a material weakness.

This report is intended solely for the information and use of the Board of Directors of Stone Co. Accordingly, it is not intended to be distributed to stockholders, management, or those who are not responsible for these matters.

Land & Hale, CPAs

May 4, 19x4

Required:

Items 1 through 15 represent the deficiencies noted by Land. For each deficiency, indicate whether Land is correct "C" or incorrect "I" in the criticism of Wood's draft. If you answer "I," provide a brief explanation.

Items to be Answered:

Supervisor's Review Notes

In the 1st paragraph

1. There should be **no** reference to "our audit of the financial statements."

2. The report should indicate that providing assurance is **not** the purpose of our consideration of the internal control.

3. The reference to "our assessment of control risk" as the end of the paragraph should have been a reference to "the assertions of management in the financial statements."

4. There should be a reference to "conformity with generally accepted accounting principles."

In the 2nd paragraph

5. There should be **no** reference to deficiencies because such reference is inconsistent with the expression of an unqualified opinion on the financial statements.

6. When deficiencies (reportable conditions) are noted, the report should include a description of the assessed level of control risk.

In the 3rd paragraph

7. The definition of "material weakness" is incorrect. A material weakness is a reportable condition.

8. The report should indicate that the auditor assume **no** responsibility for errors or irregularities resulting from the deficiencies (reportable conditions) identified in the report.

9. The report should refer to detection by the entity's employees at the end of the paragraph, **not** detection by the auditor.

In the 4th paragraph

10. The report should indicate that our consideration of the internal control expected to disclose a reportable conditions.

11. It is inappropriate to state that "none of the reportable conditions... is believed to be a material weakness."

In the final paragraph

12. The restriction on the reports's distribution is inappropriate because management ordinarily would receive the report.

13. The report should indicate that the financial statement audit resulted in an unqualified opinion.

14. The report should indicate that the auditor is **not** responsible to update the report for events or circumstances occurring after the date of the report.

Dating the Report

15. The report may **not** be dated before the auditor's report on the financial statements.

IV

Auditor's Communications

Learning Objectives

Study of the material in this chapter is designed to achieve several learning objectives. After studying this chapter, you should be able to:

1. Describe the nature and form of the auditor's standard report.
2. Define an unqualified opinion, a qualified opinion, an adverse opinion, and a disclaimer of opinion.
3. Identify situations in which each of the above types of opinions should be used.
4. Describe various modifications to the standard audit report.
5. Discuss how presenting financial statements in comparative form affects the auditor's reporting responsibility.

17

The Auditor's Report

In previous chapters, we have summarized the major steps in the audit examination as well as their relationship to the ten generally accepted auditing standards (GAAS). These steps, and the related GAAS, are shown below:

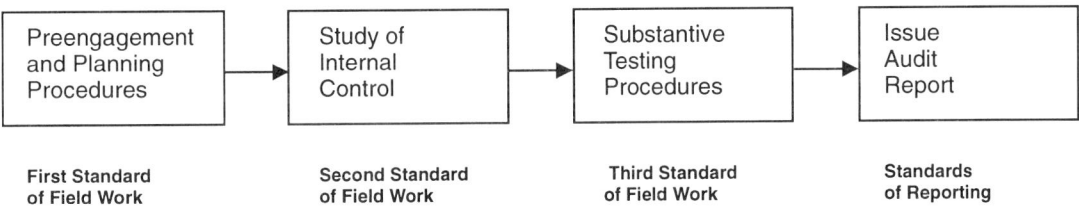

Preengagement and Planning Procedures	Study of Internal Control	Substantive Testing Procedures	Issue Audit Report
First Standard of Field Work	**Second Standard of Field Work**	**Third Standard of Field Work**	**Standards of Reporting**

The previous chapters in this text have focused on the auditor's study of internal control (Chapters 10, 12, 14, and 15) and the auditor's substantive tests and other procedures (Chapters 11, 13, 14, 15, and 16). In this chapter, our focus is on the end product of the auditor's examination: the audit report. The audit report is the most important form of communication used by the auditor. It must clearly and concisely communicate the nature of the auditor's examination and the degree of responsibility taken by the auditor. The report may be a standard report or a departure from a standard report.

Recall from the discussion in Chapter 1 that four standards of reporting must be considered by the auditor as the audit report is prepared. These reporting standards serve as a framework for the auditor's report and are shown below:

1. The report shall state whether the financial statements are presented in accordance with generally accepted accounting principles (GAAP).
2. Unless otherwise stated in the report, accounting principles have been consistently observed in the current period in relation to the preceding period.
3. Informative disclosures in the financial statements are to be regarded as reasonably adequate unless otherwise stated in the report.

4. The report shall either contain an expression of opinion regarding the financial statements taken as a whole or an assertion to the effect that an opinion cannot be expressed. When an overall opinion cannot be expressed, the reasons should be stated. In all cases where an auditor's name is associated with financial statements, the report should contain a clear-cut indication of the character of the auditor's examination, if any, and the degree of responsibility assumed.

Because the auditor's report summarizes the auditor's conclusions regarding whether the client's financial statements are prepared in conformity with GAAP, it is an extremely important communication. This chapter describes the auditor's report for engagements conducted in accordance with GAAS. Chapter 18 extends our discussion of reporting to illustrate: (1) the auditor's responsibility for reporting on information presented along with the financial statements, (2) "special reports" based on an audit examination, and (3) other types of reports issued for companies having audited financial statements.

THE AUDITOR'S REPORT

When the auditor has formed an opinion (on the basis of an audit examination conducted in accordance with GAAS) that the financial statements present fairly the financial position, results of operations, and cash flows in conformity with GAAP on a consistent basis, the auditor should issue what is known as the standard report. This report is shown in Figure 17-1.

The Body of the Report

The report presented in Figure 17-1 consists of three paragraphs. The **introductory paragraph** identifies the financial statements examined by the auditor and defines the responsibility of both the client's management and the independent auditor in the financial reporting process. Note that the fairness of the financial statements is the responsibility of the client's management and not the independent auditor.

The second paragraph of the auditor's report is the **scope paragraph**, which discusses the nature of an audit examination and includes the purpose of an audit examination—namely, to "obtain reasonable assurance about whether the financial statements are free of material misstatement." It also notes that the audit was conducted using GAAS.

The final paragraph of the standard report is known as the **opinion paragraph**. This paragraph states the auditor's conclusion as to whether the entity's financial statements are presented in conformity with GAAP.

Other Information in the Report

In addition to the body of the report, a few other items shown in Figure 17-1 need to be discussed.

1. Unless the auditor is not independent with respect to the entity under audit, the report should contain the word **independent** in its title.
2. The auditor's report should be addressed to individuals within the company who engaged the auditor (the stockholders, Audit Committee, or Board of Directors).
3. The auditor's report should be dated as of the last day of field work.

Independent Auditor's Report

To: The Board of Directors of X Company

We have audited the accompanying balance sheet of X Company as of December 31, 19X1, and the related statements of income, retained earnings, and cash flows for the year then ended. These financial statements are the responsibility of X Company's management. Our responsibility is to express an opinion on these financial statements based on our audit.

We conducted our audit in accordance with generally accepted auditing standards. Those standards require that we plan and perform the audit to obtain reasonable assurance about whether the financial statements are free of material misstatement. An audit includes examining, on a test basis, evidence supporting the amounts and disclosures in the financial statements. An audit also includes assessing the accounting principles used and significant estimates made by management, as well as evaluating the overall financial statement presentation. We believe that our audit provides a reasonable basis for our opinion.

In our opinion, the financial statements referred to above present fairly, in all material respects, the financial position of X Company as of December 31, 19X1, and the results of its operations and its cash flows for the year then ended in conformity with generally accepted accounting principles.

Hamilton & Co.

February 20, 19X2

Source: American Institute of Certified Public Accountants (AICPA), *Statement on Auditing Standards No. 58*, "Reports on Audited Financial Statements" (New York: AICPA, 1988, AU 508).

Figure 17-1: *The Standard Audit Report*

The date of the audit report merits some additional discussion. Recall that the auditor is responsible for all events occurring between the date of the financial statements and the final day of the field work. For example, assume that additional information became available to the auditor on January 15 concerning a lawsuit that was pending at year-end. As noted in Chapter 16, the auditor should request that the client update its financial statements to reflect this additional information. In cases where the auditor becomes aware of a subsequent event prior to issuing the report but after the final day of field work, the report may be dual-dated to limit liability for other subsequent events.

> **CHAPTER CHECKPOINTS**
>
> **17-1.** List the four standards of reporting.
>
> **17-2.** What information is included in the introductory paragraph of the auditor's standard report?
>
> **17-3.** What information is included in the scope paragraph of the auditor's standard report?
>
> **17-4.** What information is included in the opinion paragraph of the auditor's standard report?
>
> **17-5.** To whom should the auditor's report be addressed?
>
> **17-6.** What date should be used in the auditor's report?
>
> **17-7.** What is meant by dual-dating the audit report? Why would the auditor choose to dual-date the report?

◻ Reporting Standards

The four reporting standards presented earlier in this chapter are incorporated (either explicitly or implicitly) in the auditor's standard report. Notice that the opinion paragraph presents the auditor's conclusion about the conformity of the financial statements with GAAP. This conclusion relates to the first and fourth standards of reporting. In this case, the auditor is able to express an opinion on the entity's financial statements. If the auditor is unable to do so (because of reasons discussed later in this chapter), a disclaimer of opinion should be issued.

The second and third standards of reporting indicate that: (1) the financial statements contain adequate informative disclosures; and (2) accounting principles are consistently observed, unless the auditor mentions these items in her or his report. In Figure 17-1, the lack of any mention of these issues indicates that there are no departures. The modifications made to the auditor's report when departures exist in these and other areas are the focus of this chapter.

One aspect of the fourth standard of reporting that deserves additional attention is when an accountant is associated with, but does not audit or provide other forms of assurance on, the client's financial statements. *Statement on Auditing Standards No. 26* (*SAS No. 26*)[1] notes that the auditor is associated with financial statements when:

---

[1] American Institute of Certified Public Accountants (AICPA), *Statement on Auditing Standards No. 26*, "Association with Financial Statements" (New York: AICPA, 1979, AU 504).

- ▶ The auditor consents to the use of his or her name in a written communication containing the financial statements.
- ▶ The auditor submits financial statements that he or she has prepared or assisted in preparing.

When an auditor is associated with financial statements but does not audit or provide other forms of assurance on them, a disclaimer of opinion must be issued. This disclaimer helps to ensure that users do not mistakenly believe that the auditor is assuming any responsibility for the fairness of the financial statements. The following form of report is suggested by *SAS No. 26*:

> The accompanying balance sheet of X Company as of December 31, 19X1, and the related statements of income, retained earnings, and cash flows for the year ended were not audited by us and, accordingly, we do not express an opinion on them.
>
> [Signature and date]

◻ Types of Opinions

Unqualified Opinion. An unqualified opinion states that the financial statements are presented fairly in conformity with GAAP. The standard report, discussed in the previous section of this chapter, is one example of an unqualified opinion. However, in other instances, this standard report may be modified without affecting the unqualified opinion issued on the financial statements.

Qualified Opinion. A qualified opinion is issued when the financial statements present the entity's financial position, results of operations, and cash flows in conformity with GAAP *except for* the matter of the qualification. Qualified opinions are issued, in some cases, when: (1) a scope limitation, or (2) a departure from GAAP exists.

Adverse Opinion. When issuing an adverse opinion, the auditor concludes that the financial statements *do not* present the entity's financial position, results of operations, and cash flows in conformity with GAAP. This type of opinion is only issued when the financial statements contain very material departures from GAAP.

Disclaimer of Opinion. A disclaimer of opinion is issued when the auditor is unable to form an opinion on an entity's financial statements. A disclaimer may be issued in cases when: (1) the auditor is not independent with respect to the entity under audit, (2) a material scope limitation exists, or (3) a significant uncertainty exists.

> **CHAPTER CHECKPOINTS**
>
> 17-8. When is the auditor considered to be associated with financial statements? What type of report should be issued when the auditor is associated with, but did not audit, a client's financial statements?
>
> 17-9. Define the following types of audit opinions: unqualified, qualified, adverse, and disclaimer.
>
> 17-10. When could a qualified, adverse, or disclaimer of opinion be issued?

◉ REASONS FOR DEPARTURE FROM THE WORDING OF THE STANDARD REPORT

SAS No. 58 suggests seven principal reasons why an independent auditor may depart from the wording of the standard report. These are:

1. Limitations on the scope of the auditor's examination.
2. Division of responsibility.
3. Lack of conformity with GAAP.
4. A departure from an accounting principle set by the body designated to establish such principles.
5. Lack of consistency.
6. Uncertainties.
7. Emphasizing a matter.

◘ Scope Limitations[2]

SAS No. 58 notes that the auditor must be able to perform the auditing procedures considered necessary in order to issue an unqualified opinion. The extent of the auditing procedures must enable the auditor to conduct the examination in accordance with GAAS. In some cases, however, this will not be possible. These cases are referred to as **scope limitations**. Examples of scope limitations include:

---

[2] Throughout the remainder of this chapter, the sample reports illustrated have been adapted from *Statement on Auditing Standards No. 58*, "Reports on Audited Financial Statements" (New York: AICPA, 1988, AU 508).

- ▶ Failure to observe the client's ending inventories, because of client requests or a late appointment of the auditor by the client.
- ▶ Failure to confirm the client's accounts receivable, because of client requests or missing or incomplete customer records.
- ▶ Failure to obtain audited financial statements for an investee for which the client accounts using the equity method.
- ▶ Other situations where inadequate accounting records exist.

It is important to note that scope limitations may either be client-imposed (refusal to make records available to the auditor or refusal to allow the auditor to perform certain procedures) or circumstance-imposed (inability to observe year-end inventory because of late appointment of the auditor or incomplete client records). In general, the auditor should have more serious reservations when scope limitations are client-imposed.

The effect of scope limitations on the auditor's report depends on: (1) the availability of alternative auditing procedures, and (2) the importance of the procedures affected by the scope limitation. Figure 17-2 illustrates the possible reporting actions for the auditor when one or more scope limitation(s) exists. As shown in Figure 17-2, the first issue the auditor must address is whether alternative procedures may be performed to compensate for the scope limitation. Note that, if possible, the auditor should perform these alternative procedures. Assuming that no departures from GAAP are discovered, the auditor may issue the standard report without reference to the omission of the restricted procedures or the use of the alternative procedures.

If, however, it is not possible to perform alternative procedures, the auditor must either disclaim an opinion on the financial statements or issue a qualified opinion. If the restriction on his or her examination is relatively significant, a disclaimer should be issued. *SAS No. 58* notes that if the potential effects of an omitted procedure relates to many financial statement components, the scope limitation is more likely to be significant than if only a few components are involved. In addition, disclaimers of opinion are normally more appropriate when the scope limitation is client-imposed, as opposed to circumstance-opposed. For example, if management refuses to provide the auditor with client representations, the auditor would issue a disclaimer of opinion.

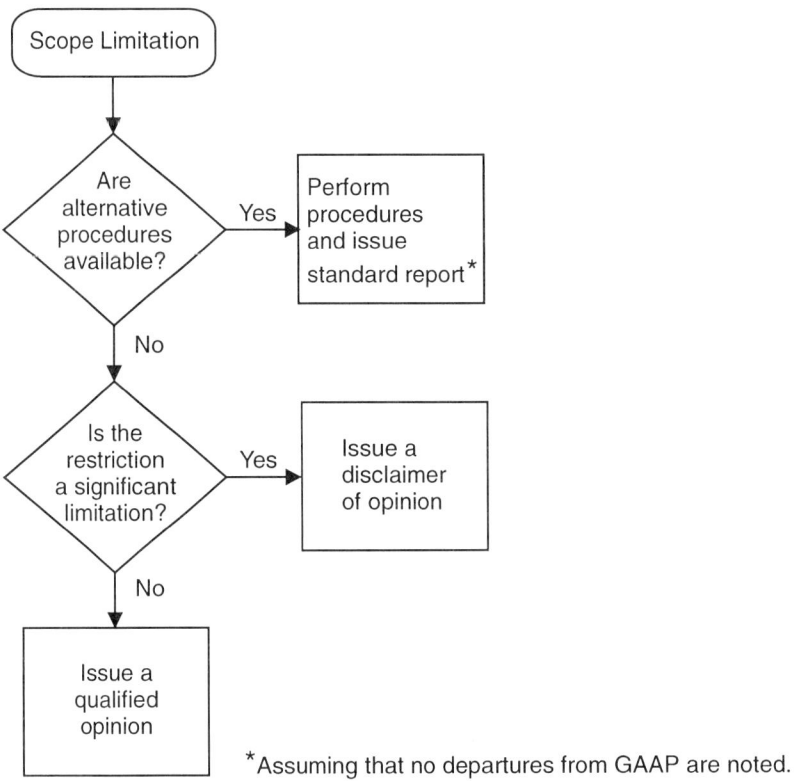

Figure 17-2: *Scope Limitations and Auditor Reporting Actions*

Shown below is an example of a qualified opinion issued as a result of a scope limitation. For both this and the remaining reports illustrated in this chapter, departures from the wording of the standard report are shown in boldface type.

> **SAMPLE AUDITOR'S REPORT**
> **SCOPE LIMITATION (QUALIFIED OPINION)**
>
> **Independent Auditor's Report**
>
> [Same introductory paragraph as the standard report]
>
> **Except as discussed in the following paragraph,** we conducted our audit in accordance with generally accepted auditing standards. Those standards require that we plan and perform the audit to obtain reasonable assurance about whether the financial statements are free of material misstatement. An audit includes examining, on a test basis, evidence supporting the amounts and disclosures in the financial statements. Ah audit also includes assessing the accounting principles used and significant estimates made by management, as well as evaluating the overall financial statement presentation. We believe that our audit provides a reasonable basis for our opinion.
>
> **We were unable to obtain audited financial statements supporting the company's investment in a foreign affiliate stated at $1,700,000 at December 31, 19X1, or its equity in earnings of that affiliate of $500,000, which is included in net income for the year then ended as described in Note X to the financial statements; nor were we able to satisfy ourselves as to the carrying value of the investment in the foreign affiliate or the equity in its earnings by other auditing procedures.**
>
> In our opinion, **except for the effects of such adjustments if any, as might have been determined to be necessary had we been able to examine evidence regarding the foreign affiliate investment and earnings,** the financial statements referred to in the first paragraph above present fairly, in all material respects, the financial position of X Company as of December 31, 19X1, and the results of its operations and its cash flows for the year then ended in conformity with generally accepted accounting principles.

Note that an explanatory paragraph (the third paragraph of the report) discusses both the scope limitation as well as the dollar effects of the limitation. The scope limitation is referred to in both the scope and opinion paragraphs. It should be emphasized that, as illustrated in the opinion paragraph, the auditor's opinion is qualified because of the potential effects of the scope limitation on the fairness of the financial statements and not because of the auditor's failure to perform a specific auditing procedure(s). This is illustrated by the following phrase:

> "...except for the effects of such adjustments, if any, as might have been determined to be necessary had we been able to examine evidence regarding the foreign affiliate investment and earnings..."

An example of a disclaimer of opinion issued as a result of a scope limitation is shown below:

SAMPLE AUDITOR'S REPORT
SCOPE LIMITATION (DISCLAIMER)

Independent Auditor's Report

We were **engaged to audit** the accompanying balance sheet of X Company as of December 31, 19X1 and the related statement of income, retained earnings, and cash flows for the year then ended. These financial statements are the responsibility of the Company's management.

[*Scope paragraph of standard report should be omitted*]

The company did not make a count of its physical Inventory in 19X1, stated in the accompanying financial statements at $21 million as of December 31, 19X1. Further, evidence supporting the cost of property and equipment acquired prior to December 31, 19X1, is no longer available. The Company's records do not permit the application of other auditing procedures to inventories or property and equipment.

Since the company did not take physical inventories and we were not able to apply other auditing procedures to satisfy ourselves as to inventory quantities and the cost of property and equipment, the scope of our work was not sufficient to enable us to express, and we do not express, an opinion on these financial statements.

Once again, notice that an explanatory paragraph discusses both the scope limitation and the dollar amounts related to the limitation. However, as shown in the opinion paragraph, the auditor disclaims an opinion on the financial statements. In addition, the phrase "[w]e have audited" in the introductory paragraph is changed to "[w]e were engaged to audit." This change reflects the inability of the auditor to perform an examination according to GAAS as a result of a material scope limitation. The auditor would more likely issue a disclaimer when the scope limitation is client-imposed.

◘ Division of Responsibility

In some cases, part of an examination will be conducted by another independent auditor. For example, consider an audit of a client having two offices, one in New York and the other in Tokyo. Although an international CPA firm is likely to have offices in both cities, a smaller CPA firm may not, making it very costly for them (or an affiliated office) to conduct an examination of activities at the Tokyo office. In these cases, an alternative is for the auditor to contract with another CPA firm to perform some of the work. The auditor examining the majority of the financial statements is referred to as the **principal auditor**; the CPA examining the remainder is normally known as the **other auditor**. This type of situation is referred to as a **division of responsibility.**

Prior to engaging the other auditor, the principal auditor should consider the professionalism and competence of the other auditor. In addition, the principal auditor should also obtain representations from the other auditor that auditor is independent with respect to the entity under examination.

Referring to Other Auditors. The first decision required when other auditors are involved is whether the principal auditor will refer to the work of the other auditor in his or her report. One alternative is to decide to assume responsibility for the work of the other auditor. In these cases, *SAS No. 1* (AU 543.12) indicates that the principal auditor should:

a. Visit the other auditor and discuss the audit procedures followed and results thereof.
b. Review the audit programs of the other auditor. In some cases, it may be appropriate to issue instructions to the other auditor as to the scope of his or her audit work.
c. Review the workpapers of the other auditor, including his or her evaluation of internal control and conclusions as to other significant aspects of the engagement.

If the principal auditor performs the above procedures and determines that no departures from GAAP or other problems exist, the standard report should be issued. No reference to the work of the other auditor will be contained in this report.

If the principal auditor has instead decided to refer to the work of the other auditor, the next decision is whether the principal auditor will **name** the other auditor. That is, when indicating that other auditors performed part of the examination, the principal auditor may either anonymously refer to other auditors or refer to an auditor (or CPA firm) by name. In order to refer to the other auditor by name, the principal auditor must: (1) obtain the permission of the other auditor, and (2) present the report of the other auditor.

Figure 17-3 summarizes the decisions made by the principal auditor when other auditors are involved. As discussed above, these decisions are whether: (1) to refer to the work of the other auditors, and (2) to name the other auditors.

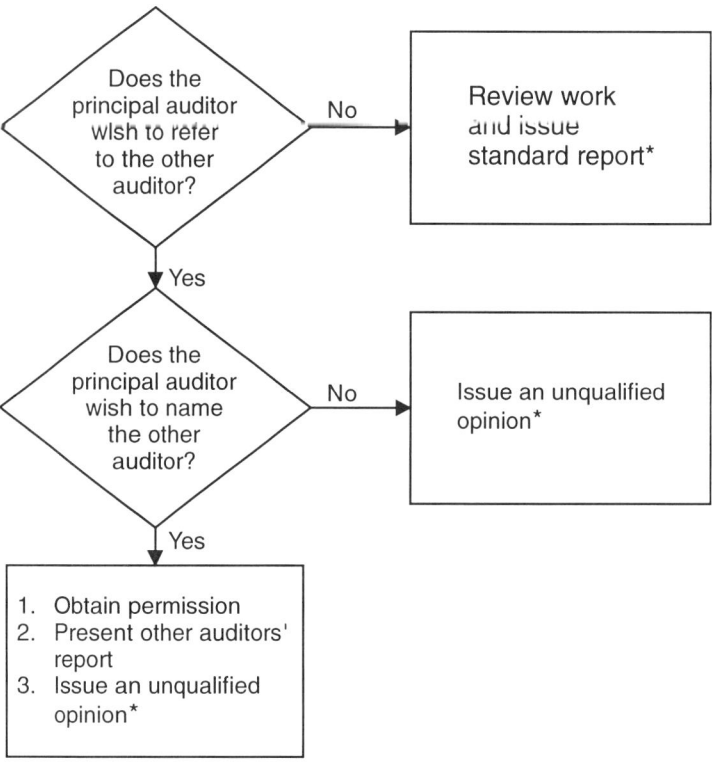

*Assuming that no departures are noted.

Figure 17-3: *Reporting Actions Involving Other Auditors*

In most cases, the principal auditor will merely decide to refer to (and not name) the other auditor. If so, the following major modifications are made to the audit report:

1. The introductory paragraph is revised to indicate that other auditors were responsible for part of the examination. This revision indicates the magnitude (in dollars and/or percentages) of the financial statement items examined by the other auditor. In addition, the introductory paragraph indicates that the principal auditor's opinion on these amounts is based solely on the report of the other auditors.

2. The final sentence of the scope paragraph is revised to indicate that the report of other auditors helps provide a basis for the principal auditor's opinion.

3. The opinion paragraph is modified to indicate that the principal auditor's opinion is based, in part, on the report of the other auditors.

Despite these extensive report revisions, the opinion issued by the principal auditor is still unqualified. Notice that these modifications are intended to alert readers that other auditors participated in the examination and their work served as part of the basis for the principal auditor's opinion. The report is illustrated below.

SAMPLE AUDITOR'S REPORT
OTHER AUDITORS (REFERENCE IN REPORT)

Independent Auditor's Report

We have audited the consolidated balance sheet of X Company as of December 31, 19X1, and the related consolidated statements of income, retained earnings, and cash flows for the year then ended. These financial statements are the responsibility of X Company's management. Our responsibility is to express an opinion on these financial statements based on our audit. **We did not audit the financial statements of YZ Company, a wholly-owned subsidiary, which statements reflect total assets of $2.2 million as of December 31, 19X1, and total revenues of $800,000 for the year then ended. Those statements were audited by other auditors whose report has been furnished to us, and our opinion, insofar as it relates to the amounts included for YZ Company, is based solely on the report of the other auditors.**

We conducted our audit in accordance with generally accepted auditing standards. Those standards require that we plan and perform the audit to obtain reasonable assurance about whether the financial statements are free of material misstatement. An audit includes examining, on a test basis, evidence supporting the amounts and disclosures in the financial statements. An audit also includes assessing the accounting principles used and significant estimates made by management, as well as evaluating the overall financial statement presentation. We believe that our audit **and the report of other auditors** provides a reasonable basis for our opinion.

In our opinion, **based on our audit and the report of other auditors**, the financial statements referred to above present fairly, in all material respects, the financial position of X Company as of December 31, 19X1, and the results of its operations and its cash flows for the year then ended in conformity with generally accepted accounting principles.

Inability to Rely on the Work of Other Auditors. The above reports were prepared under the assumption that the principal auditor could appropriately rely on the work of other auditors. In certain cases, information may come to the principal auditor's attention that may restrict the ability to rely on the work of the other auditor. For example, assume that during the conduct of the audit engagement, the other auditor determines that she or he is not independent with respect to the entity under examination. If this discovery is made during the later stages of the audit, sufficient time may not exist to allow another auditor to be engaged.

When the principal auditor determines that the work of the other auditor cannot be relied upon, a scope limitation exists. Recall from the previous subsection that the reporting alternatives for a scope limitation are as follows:

1. The standard report is issued if alternative procedures are applied and no departures are discovered. Thus, if the principal auditor can become satisfied as to the fairness of the portion of the financial statements that were to be examined by the other auditor, a standard report can be issued.

2. If alternative procedures cannot be applied but the scope limitation is not considered to be extremely significant, a qualified opinion is issued. This opinion contains an explanatory paragraph prior to the opinion paragraph.
3. If alternative procedures cannot be applied and the scope limitation is considered to be significant, a disclaimer of opinion should be issued.

Therefore, for a scope limitation arising because of the inability of the principal auditor to rely on the work of other auditors, the type of opinion issued will depend on: (1) the importance of the components that were to have been examined by the other auditor, and (2) the ability of the principal auditor to apply alternative procedures to examine these components.

CHAPTER CHECKPOINTS

17-11. For what reasons should an independent auditor depart from the wording of the auditor's standard report?

17-12. What is a scope limitation? How may a scope limitation affect the report issued by the auditor?

17-13. How should the auditor's report be modified if alternative procedures are performed when a scope limitation exists?

17-14. Under what circumstances may the principal auditor be willing to assume responsibility for the work of another auditor? How does this affect the auditor's report?

17-15. Assuming that the principal auditor decides not to assume responsibility for the work of the other auditor, how is the principal auditor's report modified?

◻ Lack of Conformity with GAAP

When an auditor issues an unqualified opinion on a client's financial statements, it indicates that the statements present the client's financial position, results of operations, and cash flows in accordance with GAAP. In some cases, the auditor may discover that the client's financial statements contain a departure from GAAP. When this occurs, the auditor will ordinarily propose an adjustment to the client's financial statements that, if recorded, will present their financial position, results of operations, and cash flows in conformity with GAAP. Assuming that the adjustment is recorded by the client, the standard report may be appropriately issued by the auditor.

In some cases, the client will not record the adjustment proposed by the auditor. The opinion issued in these instances depends on the dollar effect of the departure from GAAP on the entity's financial statements, as shown below.

SAS No. 58 notes that, in addition to the relative dollar magnitude of the departure from GAAP, qualitative factors should also be considered when evaluating the materiality of a departure from GAAP. For example, a misstatement of the same relative dollar magnitude in the inventory account for a manufacturing company will usually be of greater materiality than a similar misstatement for a service entity, because the inventory account constitutes a large percentage of the assets for the manufacturing company. If the auditor determines that a qualified or an adverse opinion is appropriate, he or she should include an explanatory paragraph that discusses: (1) the reasons for that conclusion; and (2) the effect of the departure on the client's financial position, results of operations, and cash flows.

An example of an auditor's report where the opinion is qualified because of the use of an accounting principle that departs from GAAP is shown below:

**SAMPLE AUDITOR'S REPORT
DEPARTURE FROM GAAP (QUALIFIED OPINION)**

Independent Auditor's Report

[*Same introductory and scope paragraphs as the standard report*]

The Company has excluded, from property and debt in the accompanying balance sheets, certain lease obligations that, in our opinion, should be capitalized in order to conform with generally accepted accounting principles. If these lease obligations were capitalized, property would be increased by $3 million, long-term debt by $2.7 million, and retained earnings by $600,000, as of December 31, 19X1. Additionally, net income would be increased (decreased) by $120,000 and earnings per share would be increased (decreased) by $0.10 for the year then ended.

In our opinion, **except for the effects of not capitalizing certain lease obligations as discussed in the preceding paragraph,** the financial statements referred to above present fairly, in all material respects, the financial position of X Company as of December 31, 19X1, and the results of its operations and its cash flows for the year then ended in conformity with generally accepted accounting principles.

If the effects of this departure are highly material, an adverse opinion would be appropriate. The adverse opinion issued for this particular departure from GAAP is shown below:

SAMPLE AUDITOR'S REPORT
DEPARTURE FROM GAAP (ADVERSE OPINION)

Independent Auditor's Report

[*Same introductory and scope paragraphs as the standard report*]

As discussed in Note X to the financial statements, the Company carries its property, plant, and equipment accounts at appraisal values and provides depreciation on the basis of such values. Further, the Company provides for income taxes with respect to differences between financial reporting income and taxable income arising because of the use, for income tax purposes, of the installment method of reporting gross profit from certain types of sales. Generally accepted accounting principles require that property, plant, and equipment be stated at an amount not in excess of cost, reduced by based on such amount, and that deferred income taxes be provided.

Because of the departures from generally accepted accounting principles identified above, as of December 31, 19X1, inventories have been increased $1.8 million by inclusion in manufacturing overhead of depreciation in excess of that based on cost; property, plant, and equipment, less accumulated depreciation, is carried at $9 million in excess of an amount based on the cost to the Company; and deferred income taxes of $3 million have not been recorded, resulting in an increase of $1.8 million in retained earnings and in appraisal surplus of $1 million. For the year ended December 31, 19X1, cost of goods sold has increased $1.2 million because of the effects of the depreciation accounting referred to above and deferred income taxes of $3 million have not been provided, resulting in an increase in net income of $1.8 million.

In our opinion, **because of the effects of the matters discussed in the preceding paragraphs, the financial statements referred to above do not present fairly,** in conformity with generally accepted accounting principles, the financial position of X Company as of December 31, 19X1, or the results of its operations or its cash flows for the year then ended.

Notice that, with the exception of the wording in the opinion paragraph, the two reports are almost identical. Both reports provide an explanatory paragraph that: (1) states the reason for the modification of the auditor's report, and (2) discusses the dollar effects of the departure from GAAP. Reading the opinion paragraph clearly allows the distinction between the two opinions to be observed. In the qualified opinion, the misstatements are not so large that the financial statements, taken as a whole, are materially misstated. This opinion notes that "except for the effects of ... the financial statements referred to above present fairly ..." Conversely, an adverse opinion states that "because of the effects of ... the financial statements referred to above *do not* [emphasis added] present fairly ..." Thus, the relative materiality of the departure from GAAP is clearly acknowledged by the auditor in the opinion paragraph of the report.

Inadequate Disclosures. In addition to departing from one or more generally accepted accounting principles, a second type of nonconformity with GAAP is the failure of a client to disclose information necessary for fair presentation of their financial position, results of operations, and cash flows. For example, the client may not wish to record a contingent liability that must be recorded under GAAP. As with all departures from GAAP, the type of opinion issued depends on the relative materiality of the effects of the departure from GAAP. *Statement on Auditing Standards No. 32 (SAS No. 32)*[3] notes that, as required by the third reporting standard, the effects of the item that is not discussed should be provided by the auditor in the report.

Shown below are the necessary modifications to the standard report when the auditor's opinion is qualified because of the failure to adequately disclose all appropriate financial information.

**SAMPLE AUDITOR'S REPORT
INADEQUATE DISCLOSURE (QUALIFIED OPINION)**

Independent Auditor's Report

[*Same introductory and scope paragraphs as the standard report*]

The Company's financial statements do not disclose [*describe the nature of the omitted disclosures***]. In our opinion, disclosure of this information is required by generally accepted accounting principles.**

In our opinion, **except for the omission of the information discussed in the preceding paragraph, ...**

Accounting Changes. A final type of departure from GAAP exists when a company makes certain changes in its accounting principles from one year to the next. According to *SAS No. 58*, three types of changes may result in departures from GAAP:

1. A change to an accounting principle when the newly adopted accounting principle is not a generally accepted accounting principle.
2. A change in which the method of accounting for the change does not conform with GAAP.
3. A change that has not been "reasonably justified" by management.

As before, the relative magnitude of the departure from GAAP on the entity's financial position, results of operations, and cash flows will indicate the type of opinion that should be issued. Shown below is an example of the auditor's report that should be issued when an accounting change results in a departure from GAAP that causes the auditor to qualify an opinion.

---

[3] American Institute of Certified Public Accountants (AICPA), *Statement on Auditing Standards No. 32*, "Adequacy of Disclosure in Financial Statements" (New York: AICPA, 1980, AU 431).

> **SAMPLE AUDITOR'S REPORT**
> **CHANGE IN ACCOUNTING PRINCIPLE (QUALIFIED OPINION)**
>
> **Independent Auditor's Report**
>
> [*Same introductory and scope paragraphs as the standard report*]
>
> **As disclosed in Note X to the financial statements, the Company adopted in 19X1, the first-in, first-out method of accounting for its inventories, whereas it previously used the last-in, first-out method. Although use of the first-in, first-out method is in conformity with generally accepted accounting principles, in our opinion the Company has not provided reasonable justification for making this change as required by generally accepted accounting principles.**
>
> In our opinion, **except for the change in accounting principle discussed in the preceding paragraph,** the financial statements referred to above present fairly, in all material respects, the financial position of X Company as of December 31, 19X1, and the results of its operations and its cash flows for the years then ended in conformity with generally accepted accounting principles.

If the materiality of either the inadequate disclosure or accounting change indicates that an adverse opinion should be issued, the form of the report is similar to the adverse opinion discussed earlier that relates to the departure from GAAP.

It is important to note that the above report is issued when a change in accounting principles causes a departure from GAAP. In cases where a change in accounting principle is made by the client, is accounted for correctly, and is justified, the auditor would issue an unqualified opinion. This type of accounting change is discussed in a subsequent section of this chapter.

◻ Departure from a Promulgated Principle

In Chapter 2, Rule 203 of the Code of Professional Conduct was discussed. This rule indicates that, in certain instances, unusual circumstances may require clients to depart from a promulgated accounting principle in order to prevent financial statements from being misleading. This should be clearly distinguished from a general departure from GAAP. In the former case, the auditor agrees that accounting for a specific type of transaction under GAAP would render the financial statements misleading. Because of this fact, the most appropriate treatment for the client would be to depart from the promulgated accounting principle.

SAS No. 58 suggests that if the auditor believes that such unusual circumstances are present, an unqualified opinion can be given unless there is some other reason to modify the audit report. However, the departure and its effects must be described in a separate paragraph. This separate paragraph can be placed either before or following the opinion paragraph.

◻ Consistency

As discussed in the second standard of reporting, the auditor does not address the issue of consistent application of accounting principles in a report unless a departure is noted. However, if a change in accounting principles or in the application of accounting principles has been made in the current period, the auditor must indicate to the users relying on the report that the financial statements presented are not comparable because of different accounting methods. Changes that affect consistency include:

- A change in accounting principle that is different from one previously used for reporting purposes (*i.e.*, a change from the FIFO method of accounting for inventories to LIFO).
- A change in reporting entity where the overall entity is unchanged but the method of reporting on individual units does change (*i.e.*, changing the method of accounting for a subsidiary from the equity method to preparing consolidated financial statements).
- A change in an accounting principle that is not GAAP to one that is GAAP.
- A change in an accounting principle that is inseparable from a change in accounting method.

It is important to note that changes in accounting estimates (the useful lives for fixed assets) and corrections of errors do not affect consistency.

Assuming that: (1) the newly-adopted principle is in conformity with GAAP; (2) the method of accounting for the change does not depart from GAAP; and (3) the auditor believes that management is justified in making the change, the auditor may issue an unqualified opinion. This opinion will include an explanatory paragraph after the opinion paragraph that refers the reader to a footnote discussing the change. An example of this paragraph is shown below.

SAMPLE EXPLANATORY PARAGRAPH
CONSISTENCY

As discussed in Note X to the financial statements, the Company changed its method of computing depreciation in 19X1.

◻ Uncertainties

In some cases, the auditor may encounter situations where the effect of certain events on the client's financial position, results of operations, and cash flows cannot be reasonably estimated. These situations are referred to as **uncertainties**. Examples of uncertainties include the possible effects of litigation or income tax assessments on the entity's financial statements. *Statement of Financial Accounting Standards No. 5*, "Accounting for Contingencies,"[4] notes that the financial statements must reflect management's estimates about these types of events. One problem facing the auditor in these situations is that the amount of adjustment necessary to allow the financial statements to be presented in conformity with GAAP may not be readily determinable. The auditor's primary concern is that the

---

[4] Financial Accounting Standards Board (FASB), *Statement of Financial Accounting Standards No. 5*, "Accounting for Contingencies" (Stamford, CT: Financial Accounting Standards Board, 1975).

effect of a possible loss resulting from one or more uncertainties is appropriately disclosed in the entity's financial statements.

The auditor's reporting responsibility on financial statements affected by uncertainties has recently changed. Under the provisions of *Statement on Auditing Standards No. 79 (SAS No. 79)*[5], the auditor *may* add an explanatory paragraph to the auditor's report in cases where uncertainties exist. However, unlike previous guidance provided to the auditor regarding uncertainties, he or she is under no obligation to do so. The explanation for the revised guidance is that, since the client is required to disclose uncertainties in order for the financial statements to be presented in conformity with GAAP, the auditor's disclosure of these same items in his or her report is redundant.

Other possible effect(s) of uncertainties on the auditor's opinion are summarized below:

▶ If the auditor is unable to obtain sufficient evidence to support management's assertions about uncertainties, a scope limitation exists. In these cases, the auditor may qualify or disclaim an opinion.

▶ If the auditor concludes that the uncertainty is inadequately disclosed, is accounted for using inappropriate accounting principles, or represents an unreasonable estimate, this is a type of GAAP departure. Accordingly, a qualified or adverse opinion is appropriate, depending upon the magnitude of the departure.

▶ If the uncertainty is of such a magnitude as to not allow the auditor to form an opinion on the fairness of the financial statements, a disclaimer of opinion may be issued.

Questions about Continued Existence. In certain situations, the auditor may become aware of the possibility that the client may not be able to continue in existence in the future. According to the provisions of *Statement on Auditing Standards No. 59*,[6] the independent auditor is required to consider whether conditions and events discovered during the audit examination may affect the entity's ability to continue in existence. When such conditions or events have raised a question about continued existence, the auditor should:

1. Gather evidence related to the identified conditions or events.
2. Based on the evidence obtained in (1) above, assess whether substantial doubt exists about the entity's ability to continue in existence.
3. Consider whether disclosures about the possibility of noncontinued existence are adequate.
4. Consider modifying the report.

If it is concluded that substantial doubt exists about the entity's ability to continue in existence, the auditor should modify the report. Although an unqualified opinion is still appropriate, the following explanatory paragraph should be added to the report following the opinion paragraph:

---

[5] American Institute of Certified Public Accountants (AICPA), *Statement on Auditing Standards No. 79*, "Amendment to *Statement on Auditing Standards No. 58*, 'Reports on Audited Financial Statements'" (New York: AICPA, 1995, AU 508).

[6] American Institute of Certified Public Accountants, *Statement on Auditing Standards No. 59*, "The Auditor's Consideration of an Entity's Ability lo Continue in Existence" (New York: AICPA, 1988, AU 341).

> **SAMPLE EXPLANATORY PARAGRAPH**
> **GOING-CONCERN UNCERTAINTY**
>
> The accompanying financial statements have been prepared assuming that the Company will continue as a going concern. As discussed in Note X to the financial statements, the Company has suffered recurring losses from operations and has a net capital deficiency that raise substantial doubt about the entity's ability to continue as a going concern. Management's plans in regard to these matters are also described in Note X. The financial statements do not include any adjustments that might result from the outcome of this uncertainty.

Statement on Auditing Standards No. 77 (SAS No.77)[7] precludes the use of conditional language (*i.e.*, "if the company continues to suffer recurring losses") when issuing a going-concern modification.

◻ Emphasizing a Matter in the Report

In some cases, it may be concluded that the financial statements are presented according to GAAP; however, there may be some matter that the auditor wishes to emphasize in the audit opinion. For example, the auditor may wish to inform report users that a subsidiary was acquired during the current year, making comparison of this year's financial position and results of operations with those of prior years less meaningful. In these cases, the auditor adds an explanatory paragraph describing the matter to be emphasized. An unqualified opinion is still issued by the auditor.

◻ Independence

As stated earlier, *SAS No. 58* mentions seven reasons why an independent auditor might be required to depart from the wording of the standard report. An additional reason calling for a departure is where the auditor is not independent. Under the Code of Professional Conduct discussed in Chapter 2, you may wonder why an auditor would accept an engagement to audit a client for which he or she is not independent. Ordinarily, this would only occur when the lack of independence was discovered after the acceptance of the engagement but prior to the issuance of a report. In these cases, the auditor should issue a disclaimer of opinion and specifically state that he or she is not independent with respect to the client.

---

[7] American Institute of Certified Public Accountants (AICPA), *Statement on Auditing Standards No. 77*, "Amendments to *Statements on Auditing Standards No. 22*, 'Planning and Supervision,' *No. 59*, 'The Auditor's Consideration of an Entity: Ability to Continue as a Going Concern; and *No. 62*, 'Special Reports'" (New York: AICPA, 1995, AU 341.13).

◘ Summary: Departures from the Auditor's Standard Report

Figures 17-4 and 17-5 summarize the types of audit reports issued and the necessary modifications to the standard report for the conditions discussed in the preceding section.

CHAPTER CHECKPOINTS

17-16. What are the reporting options available when a departure from GAAP exists? What does the auditor consider in deciding which type of report to issue?

17-17. How is the auditor's report different for departures from GAAP when the auditor believes that GAAP would be misleading?

17-18. What type of opinion would be issued when GAAP are not consistently applied from one period to another? How is the auditor's standard report modified in this instance?

17-19. What is the auditor's responsibility for considering the ability of the client to continue in existence in the future? How do questions about continued existence affect the audit report?

◘ COMPARATIVE FINANCIAL STATEMENTS[8]

In each of the examples provided in the preceding section, it was assumed that the auditor was reporting on the financial statements of a single period. Public companies registered with the Securities and Exchange Commission under the 1933 and 1934 Acts must provide financial information for a number of years in comparative form. In addition, for nonpublic companies, users frequently request financial information for more than a single period in making their decisions. As a result, the auditor is confronted with the need to express an opinion (or disclaim an opinion, if an audit engagement was not performed) on the financial statements of all years presented. Recall from the guidance of *SAS No. 26* that the auditor must explicitly express or disclaim an opinion when his or her name is associated with financial statements. The auditor is considered to be associated with financial statements when he or she has audited the financial statements of **any year presented in comparative form**. The failure to simply not mention the comparative financial statements is not sufficient, as users may incorrectly assume that the auditor's report covers all years presented.

Assume that the auditor performs an examination of Bull Company's financial statements for the year ending December 31, 19X3. Also, assume that Bull Company presents financial statements for 19X2 in comparative form. Three general possibilities arise with respect to these comparative financial statements. These possibilities are shown below and are discussed in the remainder of this section:

---

[8] The reports in this section are based on *Statement on Auditing Standards No. 58*, "Reports on Audited Financial Statements" (New York: AICPA, 1988, AU 508).

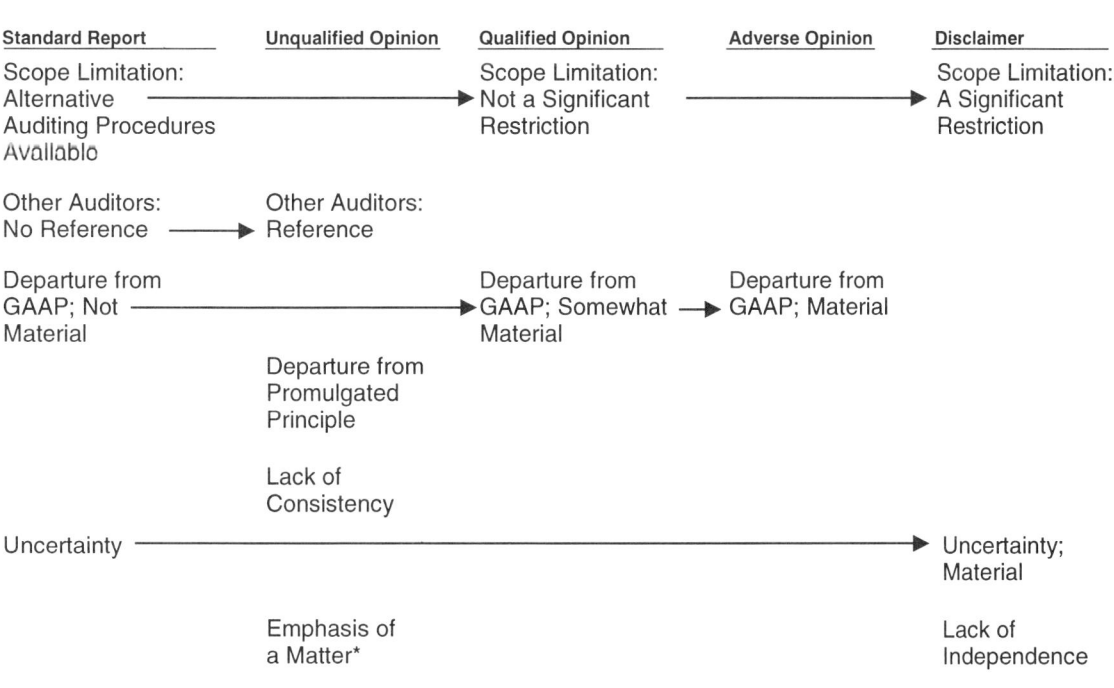

Figure 17-4: *Opinions Issued by the Auditor*

Departure	Introductory Paragraph	Scope Paragraph	Opinion Paragraph	Explanatory Paragraph
Scope Limitation (Qualified)	No Change	Modified	Modified	Prior to opinion
Scope Limitation (Unqualified)	Modified	Omitted	Disclaimer	Prior to opinion
Other Auditors (Unqualified)	Modified	Modified	Modified	None
Departure from GAAP (Qualified)	No Change	No Change	Modified	Prior to opinion
Departure from GAAP (Adverse)	No Change	No Change	Modified	Prior to opinion
Justified Departure from GAAP (Unqualified)	No Change	No Change	No Change	Prior to or following opinion
Consistency (Unqualified)	No Change	No Change	No Change	Following opinion
Uncertainty (Unqualified)	No Change	No Change	No Change	Optional
Empasizing a Matter (Unqualified)	No Change	No Change	No Change	Prior to or following opinion

Figure 17-5: *Departures from the Auditor's Standard Report*

1. The financial statements of 19X2 were not audited.
2. The financial statements of 19X2 were audited by the same auditor.
3. The financial statements of 19X2 were audited by another auditor.

◻ Comparative Statements not Audited[9]

In cases where comparative financial statements are unaudited, the auditor should explicitly disclaim an opinion on these financial statements. *SAS No. 26* refers to this situation as the accountant being "associated" with financial statements. While issuing an opinion on only the year(s) examined may seem to be sufficient, users may incorrectly assume that all information presented has been audited. As a result, the auditor should disclaim an opinion on any years that were not audited.

In our example, assume that the auditor determined that the standard report is appropriate for the 19X3 financial statements of Bull Company. However, because Bull Company is presenting 19X2 financial statements in comparative form, an opinion (or disclaimer of opinion) must be provided on both years. Given that the 19X2 statements were unaudited, a disclaimer should be issued on that year. The auditor's report is as follows:

**SAMPLE AUDITOR'S REPORT
COMPARATIVE FINANCIAL STATEMENTS:
PRIOR YEAR UNAUDITED**

Independent Auditor's Report

[*Standard introductory paragraph for 19X3*]

[*Standard scope paragraph*]

The accompanying balance sheet of Bull Company as of December 31, 19X2, and the related statement of income and retained earnings and cash flows for the year then ended were not audited by us and, accordingly, we do not express an opinion on them.

[*Standard opinion paragraph for 19X3*]

Two other issues with regard to the above scenario should be emphasized. First, the introductory paragraph should indicate that the auditor has examined the financial statements for Bull Company only as of December 31, 19X3. Because 19X2 was not examined, it would be inappropriate to indicate that these statements were audited. Similarly, the opinion paragraph should only express an unqualified opinion on Bull Company's 19X3 financial statements.

---

[9] The reports in this section are based on *Statement on Auditing Standards No. 58*, "Reports on Audited Financial Statements" (New York: AICPA, 1988, AU 508).

◘ Comparative Statements Examined by the Same Auditor

In cases where a **continuing audit** occurs (*i.e.*, each year's examination was performed by the same CPA firm), the opinion issued by the auditor on financial statements from one or more prior periods should be incorporated in the current audit report. *SAS No. 58* notes that the auditor should not merely reissue the opinion from previous years; instead, the auditor should consider whether previously-issued opinions are still appropriate. This process is referred to as **updating the opinion**.

Same Opinion in All Years. When the same opinion (whether unqualified, qualified, adverse, or disclaimer) is appropriate for all years presented, the report is a slight modification of the reports issued on a single period's financial statements. A standard, unqualified opinion on Bull Company's 19X2 and 19X3 financial statements is shown below:

SAMPLE AUDITOR'S REPORT
STANDARD REPORT ON COMPARATIVE FINANCIAL STATEMENTS

Independent Auditor's Report

We have audited the accompanying balance sheets of Bull Company as of December 31, 19X3 and 19X2, and the related statements of income, retained earnings, and cash flows for the years then ended. These financial statements are the responsibility of Bull Company's management. Our responsibility is to express an opinion on these financial statements based on our audit.

We conducted our audits in accordance with generally accepted auditing standards. Those standards require that we plan and perform the audits to obtain reasonable assurance about whether the financial statements are free of material misstatement. An audit includes examining, on a test basis, evidence supporting the amounts and disclosures in the financial statements. An audit also includes assessing the accounting principles used and significant estimates made by management, as well as evaluating the overall financial statement presentation. We believe that our audits provides a reasonable basis for our opinion.

In our opinion, the financial statements referred to above present fairly, in all material respects, the financial position of Bull Company as of December 31, 19X3 and 19X2, and the results of its operations and its cash flows for the years then ended in conformity with generally accepted accounting principles.

Source: American Institute of Certified Public Accountants (AICPA), *Statement on Auditing Standards No. 58*, "Reports on Audited Financial Statements" (New York: AICPA, 1988, AU 508).

The primary differences in this report and the report on a single period's financial statements are:

▶ The introductory paragraph has been modified to indicate that the financial statements of more than one year were audited.

- The opinion paragraph has been modified to express an opinion on more than one year's financial statements.
- The report has been modified throughout to use the plural form (*i.e.*, balance sheets, "We conducted our audits").

Different Opinions. *SAS No. 58* permits different kinds of opinions for the different years for which statements are shown in comparative form. As for the reports in the preceding section dealing with a single period's financial statements, the auditor should explain all substantive reasons for departures from an unqualified opinion in an explanatory paragraph.

Assume that the auditor has examined the financial statements of Bull Company for 19X3 and 19X2. In 19X2, a standard report was issued, while in 19X3, Bull Company incorrectly classified certain lease obligations. Based on the magnitude of this departure from GAAP, the auditor concludes that a qualified opinion is appropriate for the 19X3 financial statements. The modifications to the standard audit report are shown below:

**SAMPLE AUDITOR'S REPORT
COMPARATIVE FINANCIAL STATEMENTS:
DIFFERENT OPINION IN COMPARATIVE YEAR**

Independent Auditor's Report

[*Same introductory and scope paragraphs as the standard report*]

The Company has excluded, from property and debt in the accompanying 19X3 balance sheet, certain lease obligations that were entered into in 19X3 which, in our opinion, should be capitalized in order to conform with generally accepted accounting principles. If these lease obligations were capitalized, property would be increased by $ _____ , long-term debt by $ _____ and retained earnings by $ _____ , as of December 31, 19X3, and net income and earnings per share would be increased (decreased) by $ _____ and $ _____ , respectively, for the year then ended.

In our opinion, **except for the effects on the 19X3 financial statements of not capitalizing certain lease obligations as described in the preceding paragraph,** the financial statements referred to above present fairly, in all material respects, the financial position of Bull Company as of December 31, 19X3 and 19X2, and the results of its operations and its cash flows for the years then ended in conformity with generally accepted accounting principles.

In reading the auditor's opinion expressed in the above report, the opinion paragraph indicates that the financial statements are presented according to GAAP, with the exception of the failure to capitalize lease obligations in 19X3. Essentially, this report represents an unqualified opinion on the 19X2 financial statements and a qualified opinion on the 19X3 statements.

Differing Update Report. In the process of updating a report from a prior period, the auditor should consider anything that may affect the financial statements of that Period. *SAS No. 58* notes that:

> An **updated** report on prior-period financial statements should be distinguished from a **reissuance** of a previous report ... since in issuing an updated report the continuing auditor considers information that he has become aware of during his examination of the current-period financial statements ... and because an updated report is issued in conjunction with the auditor's report on the current-period financial statements.:

When a previous opinion is no longer appropriate, the auditor should add an explanatory paragraph that: (1) indicates the date and type of opinion expressed in the previous year, (2) describes the reason(s) that the previous opinion is no longer appropriate, and (3) states that the present opinion is different from the opinion expressed in a previous report.

If the auditor originally issued an adverse opinion on X Company's 19X2 financial statements but these statements were corrected and restated in 19X3, the following report would be appropriate:

SAMPLE AUDITOR'S REPORT
COMPARATIVE FINANCIAL STATEMENTS:
DIFFERING UPDATE REPORT

Independent Auditor's Report

[Same introductory and scope paragraphs as: the standard report]

In our report dated March 1, 19X3, we expressed an opinion that the 19X2 financial statements did not fairly present financial position, results of operations, and cash flows in conformity with generally accepted accounting principles because of two departures from such principles: (1) the Company carried its property, plant, and equipment at appraisal values and provided for depreciation on the basis of such values, and (2) the Company did not provide for deferred income taxes with respect to differences between income for financial reporting purposes and taxable income. As described in Note X, the Company has changed its method of accounting for these items and restated its 19X2 financial statements to conform with; generally accepted accounting principles. Accordingly, our present opinion on the 19X2 financial statements, as presented herein, is different from that expressed in our previous report.

In our opinion, the financial statements referred to above present fairly, in all material respects, the financial position of Bull Company as of December 31, 19X3 and 19X2, and the results of its operations and its cash flows for the years then ended in conformity with generally accepted accounting principles.

◻ Comparative Statements Examined by Another Auditor

In contrast to the above situations, assume that the 19X2 financial statements of Bull Company were audited by another CPA firm. If another auditor examined comparative statements presented with the current year's statements, two options are available. First, the current auditor could request the predecessor auditor to reissue a report on the prior year's statements. Alternatively, the current auditor could modify the report to disclose: (1) that the comparative statements were examined by another auditor, and (2) the opinion issued on those statements. These alternatives are discussed below.

Reissuance of a Previous Report. *SAS No. 58* notes that a predecessor auditor may reissue a report on statements of a prior period at the request of a former client. When reissuing his or her report, the auditor does not perform extensive procedures to consider whether the previously-issued opinion is still appropriate. *SAS No. 58* indicates that the following procedures are performed prior to reissuing a report:

1. Reading the current financial statements.
2. Comparing the prior-period financial statements that the predecessor reported on with the financial statements for that same year to be presented for comparative purposes.
3. Obtaining a letter from the current auditor that comments on whether the current audit revealed anything that might have a material effect on the financial statements reported on by the predecessor auditor.

If the predecessor auditor becomes aware of something occurring subsequent to the issuance of the report that affects that report, the predecessor auditor should make such inquiries and perform such procedures as are needed. The predecessor auditor should then decide if the report need be changed.

Assuming that the predecessor agrees to reissue his or her report, the comparative financial statements would be accompanied by two audit reports. In this instance, these reports would be:

▶ A report on the 19X2 financial statements reissued by the predecessor auditor.

▶ A report on the 19X3 financial statements issued by the current auditor.

Predecessor's Report not Presented. In cases where the predecessor auditor's report is not presented, the successor auditor should indicate: (1) that the financial statements of one or more prior years were audited by another auditor, (2) the date of the predecessor auditor's report, and (3) the type of opinion issued by the predecessor auditor. If the predecessor auditor issued a report other than the standard report, the successor auditor should provide the reasons for the predecessor's departure in the report.

If the 19X2 financial statements of Bull Company were audited by a predecessor auditor who issued an unqualified opinion on those statements, the following report would be appropriate:

SAMPLE AUDITOR'S REPORT
COMPARATIVE FINANCIAL STATEMENTS:
PREDECESSOR AUDITOR'S REPORT NOT PRESENTED

Independent Auditor's Report

We have audited the balance sheet of Bull Company as of December 31, 19X3, and the related statements of income, retained earnings, and cash flows for the year then ended. These financial statements are the responsibility of Bull Company's management. Our responsibility is to express an opinion on these financial statements based on our audit. **The financial statements of Bull Company as of December 31, 19X2, were audited by other auditors whose report dated March 31, 19X3 expressed an unqualified opinion on those statements.**

[Same scope paragraph as the standard report]

In our opinion, the financial statements referred to above present fairly, in all material respects, the financial position of Bull Company as of December 31, 19X3, and the results of its operations and its cash flows for the year then ended in conformity with generally accepted accounting principles.

Certain aspects of the above report should be emphasized:

1. The initial sentence of the introductory paragraph indicates that only the 19X3 financial statements of X Company were examined by the current auditor.
2. The introductory paragraph has been modified to disclose that the 19X2 financial statements were examined by other auditors, who expressed an unqualified opinion on those statements. In addition, the date of their report is mentioned.
3. The opinion paragraph expresses an unqualified opinion only on the 19X3 statements (the statements examined by the current auditor).

◘ Summary: Comparative Reporting

Figure 17-6 summarizes the various possible actions related to reporting on comparative financial statements.

Comparative Statements Unaudited	Disclaim an opinion on comparative financial statements.
Comparative Statements Audited by Current Auditor	
1. Same opinion in all years.	Report on all years presented.
2. Different opinions in one or more years.	Report on all years presented.
3. Differing update report.	Report on all years presented, and modify current report to indicate that a previous opinion has been changed.
Comparative Statements Audited by Predecessor Auditor	
1. Predecessor agrees to reissue his or her report.	Report on current financial statements, and present predecessor's report.
2. Predecessor does not agree to reissue his or her report.	Report on current financial statements, and indicate predecessor's opinion on the comparative statements.

Figure 17-6: *Summary of Comparative Reporting Actions*

CHAPTER CHECKPOINTS

17-20. In an audit of comparative financial statements, how should the auditor report on unaudited financial statements of one or more prior years?

17-21. Can the auditor subsequently revise an opinion issued in a previous year on comparative financial statements? If so, how is this done?

17-22. What are the two options available to the auditor for reporting on comparative financial statements examined by a predecessor auditor?

SUMMARY OF KEY POINTS

1. The four standards of reporting indicate that the auditor's report should: (1) state whether the financial statements are prepared according to GAAP, (2) indicate any instances where GAAP has not been consistently applied, (3) indicate any informative disclosures in the financial statements that are inadequate, and (4) express an opinion on the financial statements or contain an assertion that an opinion cannot be expressed.

2. The standard audit report contains three paragraphs. The introductory paragraph identifies the financial statements examined by the auditor and defines the responsibility of both the client's management and the auditor in the financial reporting process. Next, the scope paragraph discusses the nature of an audit examination. Finally, the opinion paragraph states the auditor's conclusion about whether the entity's financial statements are presented in conformity with GAAP.

3. A scope limitation occurs when the auditor cannot perform one or more desired audit procedures. A scope limitation results in a qualified opinion or a disclaimer of opinion, depending on the importance of the omitted procedure to the auditor's ability to form an opinion on the financial statements.

4. In some instances, part of the audit examination may be performed by other auditors. If the principal auditor references the other auditor in his or her report, the principal auditor's report should refer to the other auditor in the introductory, scope, and opinion paragraphs. The other auditor cannot be named unless: (1) permission has been obtained from the other auditor, and (2) the other auditor's report is presented. Unless the principal auditor cannot rely on the work of the other auditors, an unqualified opinion is still rendered.

5. If financial statements are not presented in conformity with GAAP, the auditor should issue an unqualified, qualified, or adverse opinion, depending on the materiality of the departure.

6. If the financial statements contain a departure from a promulgated principle, the auditor may issue an unqualified opinion if the financial statements are misleading as prepared under GAAP. In this situation, the auditor must describe the departure from a promulgated principle and its effects in a separate paragraph.

7. The auditor must modify the standard report for consistency exceptions. Most changes resulting in a consistency exception are from GAAP methods to other GAAP methods. In these cases, an explanatory paragraph is appended to the auditor's standard report.

8. When companies present financial statements in comparative form, the auditor must express an opinion (or disclaim an opinion) on all years presented. In a situation where the same auditor has examined all years presented, the auditor's report may: (1) express the same opinion for all years presented, (2) express different opinions for one or more years, or (3) contain a different opinion on comparative financial statements than that previously issued by the auditor.

9. If a predecessor auditor examined comparative financial statements, the current auditor can request that the predecessor reissue the report. If the predecessor auditor does not agree to do so, the current auditor should indicate the type of opinion given by the predecessor auditor on comparative financial statements in the current audit report.

GLOSSARY

Adverse Opinion. An opinion in which the auditors state that the financial statements do not present fairly the financial position, results of operations, and cash flows.

Comparative Financial Statements. Financial statements of one or more prior years presented along with the current year's financial statements. The auditor's report on current financial statements must explicitly indicate the degree of responsibility assumed for comparative financial statements, if any.

Disclaimer of Opinion. When the auditors state that they cannot give an opinion because of scope limitations or some other reason.

Introductory Paragraph. This paragraph discusses the responsibilities of management and the auditor in the financial reporting process.

Opinion Paragraph. The paragraph of the auditor's report that gives the auditor's opinion as to the fairness of the presentation of the financial statements.

Principal Auditor. A principal auditor is the auditor examining the majority of the client's financial statements. This auditor may engage other auditors to assist in the examination.

Qualified Opinion. An opinion in which the auditors express certain reservations concerning the scope of the audit and/or the fairness of the financial statements.

Reissuing an Opinion. Providing copies of a previously-issued audit opinion while taking limited measures to ascertain that the opinion is still appropriate.

Scope Limitation. A scope limitation represents a case where the auditor is unable to perform all of the procedures considered necessary in the circumstances. Scope limitations normally result in the issuance of qualified opinions or disclaimers of opinion.

Scope Paragraph. The paragraph of the auditor's report that describes the scope of the examination.

Standard Opinion. A form of unqualified opinion in which the auditor does not modify the report to discuss any unique matters encountered during the audit.

Unqualified Opinion. A "clean" opinion, meaning that the auditor believes that the financial statements present fairly the financial position, results of operations, and cash flows. An unqualified opinion can either be the standard opinion or the standard opinion modified to discuss some unique matter encountered during the audit.

Updating an Opinion. Expressing an opinion on financial statements from a previous year after giving consideration to whether that opinion is still appropriate.

SUMMARY OF PROFESSIONAL PRONOUNCEMENTS

Statement on Auditing Standards No. 1, "Codification of Auditing Standards and Procedures" (New York: AICPA, 1972, AU 543).

Statement on Auditing Standards No. 26, "Association with Financial Statements" (New York: AICPA, 1979, AU 504).

Statement on Auditing Standards No. 32, "Adequacy of Disclosure of Financial Statements" (New York: AICPA, 1980, AU 431).

Statement on Auditing Standards No. 58, "Reports on Audited Financial Statements" (New York: AICPA, 1988, AU 508).

Statement on Auditing Standards No. 59, "The Auditor's Consideration of an Entity's Ability to Continue in Existence" (New York: AICPA, 1988, AU 341).

Statement on Auditing Standards No. 79, "Amendment to *Statement on Auditing Standards No. 58*, 'Reports on Audited Financial Statements'" (New York: AICPA, 1995, AU 508).

QUESTIONS AND PROBLEMS

17-23. Select the **best** answer for each of the following items:

1. In which of the following circumstances would an auditor be required to issue a qualified report with a separate explanatory paragraph?

   a. The auditor satisfactorily performed alternative accounts receivable procedures because scope limitations prevented performance of normal procedures.
   b. The financial statements reflect the effects of a change in accounting principles from one period to the next.
   c. The company's financial statements deviate from generally accepted accounting principles.
   d. The financial statements of a significant subsidiary were examined by another auditor, and reference to the other auditor's report is to be made in the principal auditor's report.

2. The annual report of a publicly-held company presents the prior-year's financial statements, which are clearly marked "unaudited," in comparative form with current-year audited financial statements. The auditor's report should:

   a. Express an opinion on the audited financial statements and contain a separate paragraph describing the responsibility assumed for the financial statements of the prior period.
   b. Disclaim an opinion on the unaudited financial statements and express an opinion on the current-year's financial statements.
   c. State that the unaudited financial statements are presented solely for comparative purposes and express an opinion only on the current-year's financial statements.
   d. Withdraw from the engagement.

3. When an adverse opinion is expressed, the opinion paragraph should include a direct reference to:

   a. A footnote to the financial statements that discusses the basis for the opinion.
   b. The scope paragraph that discusses the basis for the opinion rendered.
   c. A separate paragraph that discusses the basis for the opinion rendered.
   d. The consistency or lack of consistency in the application of generally accepted accounting principles.

4. An auditor need *not* mention consistency in the audit report if:

   a. The client has acquired another company through a "pooling of interest."
   b. Accounting principles are consistently observed.
   c. This is the first year the client has had an audit.
   d. Comparative financial statements are issued.

5. Jones, CPA, is the principal auditor who is auditing the consolidated financial statements of her client. Jones plans to refer to another CPA's examination of the financial statements of a subsidiary company but does not wish to present the other CPA's audit report. Both Jones's and the other CPA's audit reports have noted no exceptions to generally accepted accounting principles. Under these circumstances, the opinion paragraph of Jones's consolidated audit report should express:

   a. An unqualified opinion.
   b. A "subject to" opinion.
   c. An "except for" opinion.
   d. A standard opinion.

6. A limitation on the scope of the auditor's examination sufficient to preclude an unqualified opinion will always result when management:

   a. Engages an auditor after the year-end physical inventory count.
   b. Refuses to furnish a representation letter.
   c. Knows that direct confirmation of accounts receivable with debtors is not feasible.
   d. Engages an auditor to examine only the balance sheet.

7. An auditor is confronted with an exception considered sufficiently material to warrant some deviation from the standard unqualified auditor's report. If the exception relates to a departure from generally accepted accounting principles, the auditor must decide between expressing a(n):

   a. Adverse opinion and an unqualified opinion.
   b. Adverse opinion and a qualified opinion.
   c. Adverse opinion and a disclaimer of opinion.
   d. Disclaimer of opinion and a qualified opinion.

8. The principal auditor is satisfied with the independence and professional reputation of the other auditor, who has audited a subsidiary, but wants to indicate the division of responsibility. The principal auditor should modify:

   a. The introductory paragraph of the report.
   b. The introductory and opinion paragraphs of the report.
   c. The introductory and scope paragraphs of the report.
   d. The introductory, scope, and opinion paragraphs of the report.
   e. The report should not be modified because the auditor is satisfied with the other auditor's professional reputation.

9. How are the auditor's and management's responsibilities defined in the introductory paragraph of the audit report?

	Auditor Responsibility	Management Responsibility
a.	Explicitly	Explicitly
b.	Implicitly	Explicitly
c.	Explicitly	Implicitly
d.	Implicitly	Implicitly

10. Which of the following topics is not addressed in the scope paragraph of the auditor's standard report?

   a. The fact that the audit examination was conducted in accordance with generally accepted auditing standards.
   b. The financial statements examined by the auditor and the year(s) examined.
   c. A general description of an audit examination.
   d. A statement that an audit provides a reasonable basis for the auditor's opinion.
   e. All of the above are addressed in the scope paragraph of the auditor's standard report.

11. If one or more comparative statements were examined by a predecessor auditor and her or his report is not presented, the successor auditor should:

   a. Disclaim an opinion on the comparative financial statements.
   b. Issue an opinion only on the current period-financial statements, without any mention of the opinion issued by the predecessor auditor.
   c. Indicate the type of opinion issued by the predecessor auditor if the opinion is other than unqualified.
   d. Indicate the type of opinion issued by the predecessor auditor in the introductory paragraph of the current audit report, regardless of the type of opinion issued.
   e. Indicate the type of opinion issued by the predecessor auditor in the opinion paragraph of the current audit report, regardless of the type of opinion issued.

12. Assume that the auditor is examining the financial statements of Jones Company as of December 31, 19x3. He was appointed for this engagement after the balance-sheet date (on January 3, 19x4) and completed his field work on March 13, 19x4. However, because of a delay, the auditor's report was not delivered to Jones Company until March 28, 19x4. What date should be used for the audit report?

   a. December 31, 19x3.
   b. January 3, 19x4.
   c. March 13, 19x4.
   d. March 28, 19x4.

13. In which of the following reporting situations would a qualified opinion not be an option for the auditor?

   a. A departure from GAAP exists, the effect of which has a material effect on the client's financial statements.
   b. The client changes the accounting principles used in preparing the financial statements; the auditor does not agree that this change is appropriate.
   c. Some uncertainty exists as to the client's ability to continue in existence in the future.
   d. The auditor cannot perform alternative procedures to compensate for a scope limitation.
   e. Qualified opinions could be issued in all of the above cases.

14. When a scope limitation exists and the auditor cannot perform alternative procedures, which of the paragraphs of the standard report are modified if a qualified opinion is issued?

	Scope	Introductory
a.	Yes	Yes
b.	Yes	No
c.	No	Yes
d.	No	No

15. If the auditor is associated with financial statements but has not audited those statements, he or she should issue a(n):

   a. Adverse opinion.
   b. Disclaimer of opinion.
   c. Modified opinion.
   d. Qualified opinion.
   e. Unqualified opinion.

(Items 1 through 7 in 17-23; AICPA Adapted)

17-24. CPA X, who practices in Philadelphia, has a client located in Philadelphia. The client has a large division in Georgia. Because CPA X does not have an office in Georgia, he has another firm, ABC, do the audit of the division in Georgia. ABC, in fact, does considerable correspondent work for CPA X in the Southeast. Due to the long and close relationship between CPA X and ABC, X decides not to make reference to ABC in the audit report. Because X will make no reference to ABC, should X perform any additional procedures?

17-25. Balsam Corporation is engaged in a hazardous trade and cannot obtain insurance coverage from any source. A material portion of the corporation's assets could be destroyed by a serious accident. The corporation has an excellent safety record and has never suffered a catastrophe. Assume that the audit examination was made in accordance with generally accepted auditing standards, that generally accepted accounting principles were applied on a consistent basis, and that disclosure was adequate.

Required:

What type of opinion should be rendered?

(AICPA Adapted)

17-26. When the auditor reports on financial statements presented in comparative form, certain responsibilities exist for both the current financial statements and financial statements from prior periods. Assume that Jake Jones examined the financial statements of Centro Company for 19X3. Also assume that Centro is presenting financial statements for 19X1 and 19X2 in comparative form. Indicate how Jake would report on the comparative financial statements in each of the following independent scenarios. It is not necessary to draft the audit report.

   a. Jake examined the financial statements for all three years and issued unqualified opinions in all years.
   b. Jake examined the financial statements for all three years. In 19X2, Jake issued a qualified opinion because of a GAAP departure. Because Centro has changed its method of accounting and adjusted its financial statements, Jake now feels that an unqualified opinion on the 19X2 financial statements is merited.

c. The financial statements for 19X1 and 19X2 were not examined by either Jake or any other CPA.
d. The financial statements for 19X1 and 19X2 were examined by Molson, CPAs. Molson allows Jake to present their report along with the comparative financial statements.
e. The financial statements for 19X1 and 19X2 were examined by Molson, CPAs. Molson refuses to allow Jake to present their report along with the comparative financial statements.

17-27. In each of the following situations, indicate: (1) the type of opinion(s) that may be issued by the auditor, and (2) the paragraphs of the standard audit report that would require modification. If more than one opinion can be issued in a situation, indicate the paragraphs that would be modified for each type of opinion.

a. The auditor is unable to confirm accounts receivable with customers. However, because of detailed billing and cash receipts records, the customers' balances can be evaluated through reliable means.
b. Other CPAs are involved in the audit examination, and the principal auditor decides to rely on the work of the other CPAs.
c. The client uses appraised values (and not historical costs) to record property, plant, and equipment in its balance sheet.
d. The client has changed its method of inventory valuation from LIFO to FIFO; the auditor concurs with the change.
e. The auditor is unable to observe the client's annual inventory and cannot perform alternative procedures because perpetual inventory records are not maintained.
f. The client has changed its method of accounting for long-term construction contracts from completed contract to percentage of completion. Although the auditor concurs with the change, the client did not account for the effect(s) of the change in accordance with GAAP.
g. The auditor would like to emphasize that the composition of the client's Board of Directors has changed significantly from the previous year.

17-28. Stanford, CPA, is examining the financial statements of Sox, Inc., for the year ended December 31, 19X2. This engagement was completed on March 1, 19X3. Because Sox has a small subsidiary located overseas, Stanford engaged Nikita, CPA, to examine the financial position and operating results of this subsidiary. Nikita examined the subsidiary and determined that an unqualified opinion was appropriate. After inquiring of Nikita's professional reputation and independence, Stanford decided to rely on Nikita's audit. Nikita refused to allow his report to be presented along with Sox's financial statements.

During the examination, Stanford noticed that Sox changed its method of depreciation from the previous year. This change (from straight-line to 150 percent declining balance) was presented in footnote 15 to Sox's financial statements. Stanford concurred with Sox's decision to change depreciation methods. No other unusual circumstances were noted during Stanford's audit. Stanford also examined the 19X1 financial statements of Sox. Stanford issued a qualified opinion on those statements because of the inability to examine the overseas subsidiary in that year. Stanford feels that this opinion is still appropriate for 19X1. Sox is presenting its financial statements in comparative form.

Required:

Prepare a draft of the audit report that should be issued by Stanford.

17-29. Shown below is an audit report prepared by Nanook, Bogey, and Bailey, CPAs, on the financial statements of Dog-Gone, Inc. They completed the audit examination on March 3, 19X4, and submitted their report to Dog-Gone, Inc., on April 15, 19X4. List any deficiencies in this report.

To: President of Dog-Gone, Inc.

We have audited the accompanying balance sheet of Dog-Gone, Inc., as of December 31, 19X3, and the related statements of income, retained earnings, and cash flows for the year then ended. These financial statements are the responsibility of Dog-gone, Inc.'s management.

We did not audit Cat Co., a wholly-owned subsidiary of Dog-Gone, Inc. This subsidiary was examined by Jones, CPA, who did not provide a report for its examination.

Generally accepted auditing standards require that we plan and perform the audit to provide reasonable assurance about whether the financial statements are free of material misstatement. An audit includes examining, on a test basis, evidence supporting the amounts and disclosures in the financial statements. An audit also includes assessing the accounting principles used and significant estimates made by management, as well as evaluating the overall financial statement presentation. We believe that our audit provides a reasonable basis for our opinion.

In our opinion, except for the fact that we did not examine Cat Co.'s financial statements and the failure of Dog-Gone, Inc., to capitalize certain lease obligations, the financial statements referred to above present fairly, in all material respects, the financial position of Dog-Gone, Inc., as of December 31, 19X3 and 19X2, and the results of its operations and its cash flows for the year then ended in conformity with generally accepted accounting principles. These principles were applied on a basis consistent with that of the preceding year.

Nanook, Bogey, and Bailey, CPAs (Signed)
December 31, 19X3

17-30. The auditor's report must contain an expression of opinion or a statement to the effect that an opinion cannot be expressed. Four types of opinions that meet these requirements are generally known as:

1. An unqualified opinion.
2. A qualified opinion.
3. An adverse opinion.
4. A disclaimer of opinion.

Required:

For each of the following situations, indicate the type of opinion you would render. Unless there is an implication to the contrary in the situation as stated, you may assume that the examination was made in accordance with generally accepted auditing standards, that the financial statements present fairly the financial position, results of operations, and cash flows in conformity with generally accepted accounting principles applied on a consistent basis, and that the statements include adequate informative disclosure necessary not to be misleading.

a. During the course of the examination, the CPA suspects that a material amount of the assets of the client, Ash Corporation, have been misappropriated through fraud. The corporation refuses to allow the auditor to expand the scope of the examination sufficiently to confirm these suspicions.
b. Dogwood Corporation owns properties that have substantially appreciated in value since the date of purchase. The properties were appraised and are reported in the balance sheet at the appraised values with full disclosure. The CPA believes that the values reported in the balance sheet are reasonable.
c. Subsequent to the close of Holly Corporation's fiscal year, a major debtor was declared bankrupt due to a rapid series of events. The debtor had confirmed the full amount due to Holly Corporation at the balance-sheet date. Because the account was good at the balance-sheet date, Holly Corporation refuses to disclose any information in relation to this subsequent event. The CPA believes that all accounts were stated fairly at the balance-sheet date.

(AICPA Adapted)

17-31. At the beginning of your examination of the financial statements of the Efel Insurance Company, the president of the company requested that in the interest of efficiency you coordinate your audit procedures with the audit being conducted by the state insurance examiners for the same fiscal year. The state examiners audited the asset accounts of the company while you audited the accounts for liabilities, stockholders' equity, income, and expenses. In addition, you obtained confirmations of the accounts receivable and were satisfied with the results of your audit tests. Although you had no supervisory control over the state examiners, they allowed you to review and prepare extracts from their work papers and report. After reviewing the state examiners' work papers and report to your complete satisfaction, you are now preparing your standard report.

Required:

What effect, if any, would the above circumstances have on your auditor's standard report? Discuss.

(AICPA Adapted)

17-32. Following are the financial statements of the Young Manufacturing Corporation and the auditor's report of its examination for the year ended January 31, 19X1. The examination was conducted by John Smith, an individual practitioner, who has examined the corporation's financial statements and reported on them for many years.

Young Manufacturing Corporation
Statements of Condition
January 31, 19X1 and 19X0

Assets	19X1	19X0
Current assets:		
Cash	$ 43,822	$ 51,862
Accounts receivable–pledged–less allowances for doubtful accounts of $3,800 in 19X1 and $3,000 in 19X0 (see note)	65,298	46,922
Inventories, pledged–at average cost, not in excess of replacement cost	148,910	118,264
Other current assets	6,280	5,192
Total current assets	$264,310	$222,240
Fixed assets:		
Land–at cost	$ 38,900	$ 62,300
Buildings–at cost, less accumulated depreciation of $50,800 in 19X1 and $53,400 in 19X0	174,400	150,200
Machinery and equipment–at cost, less accumulated depreciation of $30,500 in 19X1 and $25,640 in 19X0	98,540	78,560
Total fixed assets	$311,840	$291,060
Total assets	$576,150	$513,300

Liabilities and Stockholders' Equity	19X1	19X0
Current liabilities:		
Accounts payable	$ 27,926	$ 48,161
Other liabilities	68,743	64,513
Current portion of long-term mortgage payable	3,600	3,600
Income taxes payable	46,840	30,866
Total current liabilities	$147,109	$147,140
Long-term liabilities:		
Mortgage payable	90,400	94,000
Total liabilities	$237,509	$241,140
Stockholders' equity:		
Capital stock, par value $100, 1,000 shares authorized, issued and outstanding	$100,000	$100,000
Retained liabilities and earnings	238,641	172,160
Total liabilities and stockholders' equity	$576,150	$513,300

Note: I did not confirm the balances of the accounts receivable but satisfied myself by other auditing procedures that the balances were correct.

Young Manufacturing Corporation
Income Statements
For the Years Ended January 31, 19X1, and 19X0

	19X1	19X0
Income:		
Sales	$884,932	$682,131
Other income	3,872	2,851
Total	$888,804	$684,982
Costs and expenses:		
Cost of goods sold	$463,570	$353,842
Selling expenses	241,698	201,986
Administrative expenses	72,154	66,582
Provision for income taxes	45,876	19,940
Other expenses	12,582	13,649
Total	$835,880	$655,999
Net income	$ 52,924	$ 28,983

Mr. Paul Young, President
Young Manufacturing Corporation

We have audited the accompanying balance sheet of Young Manufacturing Corporation as of December 31, 19X1 and 19X0, and the related statements of income, retained earnings, and cash flows for the years then ended.

We conducted our audits in accordance with generally accepted auditing standards. These standards require that we plan and perform the audit to provide reasonable assurance about whether the financial statements are free of material misstatement. An audit includes examining, on a test basis, evidence supporting the amounts and disclosures in the financial statements.

In our opinion, except for the fact that we did not confirm Young Manufacturing Corporation's accounts receivable, the financial statements referred to above present fairly, in all material respects, the financial position of Young Manufacturing Corporation as of December 31, 19X1 and 19X0, and the results of its operations and its cash flows for the year then ended in conformity with generally accepted accounting principles.

(Signed) John Smith
March 31, 19X2

Required:

List and discuss the deficiencies of the auditor's report prepared by John Smith. Your discussion should include justifications that the matters you cited are deficiencies. (Do not check the addition of the statements. Assume that the addition is correct.)

(AICPA Adapted)

17-33. The president's salary has been increased substantially over the prior year by action of the Board of Directors. Her present salary is much greater than salaries paid to presidents of companies of comparable size and is clearly excessive. You determine that the method of computing the president's salary was changed for the year under audit. In prior years, the president's salary was consistently based on sales. In the latest year, however, her salary was based on net income before income taxes. The Claren Corporation is in a cyclical industry and would have had an extremely profitable year except that the increase in the president's salary siphoned off much of the income that would have accrued to the stockholders. The president is a substantial stockholder.

Required:

a. Discuss your responsibility for disclosing this situation.
b. Discuss the effect, if any, that the situation has upon your auditor's opinion as to
   1. The fairness of the presentation of the financial statements.
   2. The consistency of the application of accounting principles.

(AICPA Adapted)

17-34. About two years ago, you were engaged to conduct an annual audit of Pierson Company. This was shortly after the majority stockholders assumed control of the company and discharged the president and several other corporate officers. A new president canceled a wholesaler's contract to distribute Pierson Company products. The wholesaler is a Pierson Company minority stockholder and was one of the discharged officers. Shortly after you commenced your initial audit, several lawsuits were filed against Pierson Company by the wholesaler. Pierson Company filed counter-suits.

None of the suits have been decided. The principal litigation is over the canceled contract, and the other suits are claims against the company for salary, bonus, and pension fund contributions. Pierson Company is the plaintiff in suits totaling approximately $300,000 and defendant in suits totaling approximately $2 million. Both amounts are material in relation to net income and total assets. Pierson's legal counsel believes the outcome of the suits is uncertain and that all of the suits are likely to be "tied up in court" for an extended time.

You were instructed by the Board of Directors each year to issue an audit report only if it contained an unqualified opinion. Pierson Company refuses to provide for an unfavorable settlement in the financial statements because legal counsel advised the Board of Directors that such a provision in the financial statements could be used against Pierson by the opposition in court. The pending litigation was fully disclosed in a footnote to the financial statements, however.

You did not issue a report on the completion of your audit one year ago and you have now completed your second annual audit. The scope of your audits was not restricted in any way and you would render unqualified opinions if there were no pending litigations. You have attended all meetings of the stockholders and the directors and answered all questions directed to you at these meetings. You were promptly paid for all work completed to the current date. The Board of Directors of Pierson Company invited you to deliver to them an audit report containing an unqualified opinion or to attend the annual meeting of the stockholders one week hence to answer questions concerning the results of your audit if you are unwilling to render an unqualified opinion.

Required:

a. Discuss the issues raised by the fact that the auditor attended the stockholders' and directors' meetings and answered various questions. Do not consider the propriety of the failure to issue a written audit report.
b. Should a CPA issue the audit report promptly after completing the examination? Why?

c. 1. What kind of auditor's opinion would you render on Pierson Company's financial statements for the year just ended? Why? (You need not write an auditor's opinion.)
2. Write the explanatory paragraph that you would indicate in your auditor's report for Pierson Company's financial statements for the year just ended.

(AICPA Adapted)

17-35. The following draft of an auditor's report has been submitted for review:

To: Eric Jones, Chief Accountant
Sunshine Manufacturing Company

We have audited the balance sheet of the Sunshine Manufacturing Company for the year ended August 31, 19X1, and the related statements of income, retained earnings, and cash flows. These financial statements are the responsibility of Sunshine Manufacturing Company's management. Our responsibility is to issue an opinion on these financial statements based on our audit.

Except for the fact that we did not count the buyers' cash working fund (per your instructions), we conducted our audits in accordance with generally accepted auditing standards. These standards require that we plan and perform the audit to provide reasonable assurance about whether the financial statements are free of material misstatement. An audit includes examining, on a test basis, evidence supporting the amounts and disclosures in the financial statements. An audit also includes assessing the accounting principles used and significant estimates made by management, as well as evaluating the overall financial statement presentation.

In our opinion, subject to the limitation on our examination discussed above, the accompanying balance sheet and statements of income, earned surplus, and cash flows present fairly, in all material respects, the financial position of the Sunshine Manufacturing Company at August 31, 19X1, and the results of its operations and cash flows for the year then ended.

Frank George & Company
August 31, 19X1

It has been determined that:

1. Except for the omission of the count of the buyers' cash working fund, there were no scope restrictions placed in the auditor's examination.
2. The Sunshine Manufacturing Company has been in continuous operation since for a number of years, but its financial statements have not previously been audited.

Required:

a. Assuming that Frank George & Company was able to perform alternative auditing procedures to satisfactorily substantiate the buyers' cash working fund and purchases through the fund, identify and discuss the deficiencies in the auditor's report.

b. Assuming that Frank George & Company was unable to satisfactorily substantiate the buyers' cash working fund and purchases through the fund by alternative auditing procedures, discuss the appropriateness of the opinion qualification proposed by Frank George & Company's report.

c. Discuss the potential consequences to the CPA of issuing a substandard report or failing to adhere in the examination to generally accepted auditing standards.

(AICPA Adapted)

17-36. Charles Burke, CPA, has completed field work for his examination of the Williams Corporation for the year ended December 31, 19X1, and now is in the process of determining whether to modify his report. Presented below are two independent, unrelated situations that have arisen.

Situation I

In September 19X1, a lawsuit was filed against Williams to have the court order it to install pollution control equipment in one of its older plants. Williams's legal counsel has informed Burke that it is not possible to forecast the outcome of this litigation; however, Williams's management has informed Burke that the cost of the pollution control equipment is not economically feasible and that the plant will be closed if the case is lost. In addition, Burke has been told by management that the plant and its production equipment would have only minimal resale values and that the production that would be lost could not be recovered at other plants.

Situation II

During 19X1, Williams purchased a franchise amounting to 20 percent of its assets for the exclusive right to produce and sell a newly-patented product in the northeastern United States. There has been no production in marketable quantities of the product anywhere to date. Neither the franchisor nor any franchisee has conducted any market research with respect to the product.

Required:

In deciding the reporting modification, if any, Burke should consider the following:

- Relative magnitude.
- Uncertainty of outcome.
- Likelihood of error.
- Expertise of the auditor.
- Pervasive impact on the financial statements.
- Inherent importance of the item.

Discuss Burke's reporting decision for each situation in terms of the above and other appropriate considerations. Assume each situation is adequately disclosed in the notes to the financial statements. Each situation should be considered independently. In discussing each situation, ignore the other. It is not necessary for you to decide the type of report that should be issued.

(AICPA Adapted)

17-37. Presented below is an independent auditor's report. The corporation being reported on is profit-oriented and publishes general-purpose financial statements for distribution to owners, creditors, potential investors, and the general public. The report contains deficiencies.

Auditor's Report

We have audited the consolidated balance sheet of Belasco Corporation and subsidiaries as of December 31, 19X1, and the related consolidated statements of income and retained earnings and cash flows for the year then ended. We did not examine the financial statements of Seidel Company, a major consolidated subsidiary. These statements were examined by other auditors whose report thereon has been furnished to us, and our opinion expressed herein, insofar as it relates to Seidel Company, is based solely upon the report of the other auditors.

We conducted our audit in accordance with generally accepted auditing standards. These standards require that we plan and perform the audit to provide reasonable assurance about whether the financial statements are free of material misstatement. An audit includes examining, on a test basis, evidence supporting the amounts and disclosures in the financial statements. An audit also includes assessing the accounting principles used and significant estimates made by management, as well as evaluating the overall financial statement presentation. We believe that our audit provides a reasonable basis for our opinion.

In our opinion, except for the report of the other auditors, the accompanying consolidated balance sheet and consolidated statements of income and retained earnings and cash flows present fairly the financial position of Belasco Corporation and subsidiaries at December 31, 19X1, and the results of its operations and the cash flows for the year then ended, in conformity with generally accepted accounting principles applied on a basis consistent with that of the preceding year.

Required:

Describe the reporting deficiencies of the auditor's report, explain the reasons therefor, and briefly discuss how the report should be corrected. Do not discuss the addressee, signatures, and date. Also, do not rewrite the auditor's report.

(AICPA Adapted)

17-38. Nancy Miller, CPA, has completed field work for her examination of the financial statements of Nickles Manufacturers, Inc., for the year ended March 31, 19X1, and is now preparing her auditor's report. Presented below are two independent, unrelated assumptions concerning this examination:

Assumption 1

The CPA was engaged on April 15, 19X1, to examine the financial statements for the year ended March 31, 19X1, and was not present to observe the taking of the physical inventory on March 31, 19X1. Her alternative procedures included examination of shipping and receiving documents with regard to transactions during the year under review as well as transactions since the year-end; extensive review of the inventory-count sheets; and discussion of the physical inventory procedures with responsible company personnel. She has also satisfied herself as to inventory valuation and consistency in valuation method. Inventory quantities are determined solely by means of physical count. (Note: Assume that the CPA is properly relying upon the examination of another auditor with respect to the beginning inventory.)

Assumption 2

As of April 1, 19X1, Nickles has an unused balance of $1,378,000 of federal income tax net operating loss carryover that will expire at the end of the company's fiscal years as follows: $432,000 in 19X2, $870,000 in 19X3, and $76,000 in 19X4. Nickles's management expects that the company will have enough taxable income to use the loss carryover before it expires.

Required:

For each assumption described above, discuss:

a. In detail, the appropriate disclosures, if any, in the financial statements and accompanying footnotes.
b. The effect, if any, on the auditor's standard report. For this requirement, assume that Nickles makes the appropriate disclosures, if any, recommended in (a).

Note: Complete your discussion of both (a) and (b) of each assumption before beginning discussion of the next assumption. In considering each independent assumption, assume that the other situation did not occur.

(AICPA Adapted)

17-39. Roscoe, CPA, has completed the examination of the financial statements of Excelsior Corporation as of and for the year ended December 31, 19X1. Roscoe also examined and reported on the Excelsior financial statements for the prior year. Roscoe drafted the following report for 19X1:

> March 15, 19X2
>
> We have examined the balance sheet and statements of income and retained earnings of Excelsior Corporation as of December 31, 19X1. Our examination was made in accordance with generally accepted accounting standards and accordingly included such tests of the accounting records as we considered necessary in the circumstances.
>
> In our opinion, the above-mentioned financial statements are accurately prepared and fairly presented in accordance with generally accepted accounting principles in effect at December 31, 19X1.
>
> Roscoe, CPA
> (signed)

Other information:

a. Excelsior is presenting comparative financial statements.
b. Excelsior does not wish to present a statement of cash flows for either year.
c. During 19X1, Excelsior changed its method of accounting for long-term construction contracts and properly reflected the effect of the change in the current-year's financial statements and restated the prior-year's statements. Roscoe is satisfied with Excelsior's justification for making the change. (The change was discussed in a footnote to the financial statements.)
d. Roscoe was unable to perform normal accounts receivable confirmation procedures, but alternative procedures were used to satisfy Roscoe as to the validity of the receivables.
e. Excelsior Corporation is the defendant in a litigation, the outcome of which is highly uncertain. If the case is settled in favor of the plaintiff, Excelsior will be required to pay a substantial amount of cash, which might require the sale of certain fixed assets. The litigation and the possible effects have been properly disclosed in a footnote to the financial statements.
f. Excelsior issued debentures on January 31, 19X0, in the amount of $10 million. The funds obtained from the issuance were used to finance the expansion of plant facilities. The debenture agreement restricts the payment of future cash dividends to earnings after December 31, 19X5. (Excelsior declined to disclose this essential data in the footnotes to the financial statements.)

Required:

Consider all facts given and rewrite the auditor's report in acceptable and complete format incorporating any necessary departures from the standard report.

Do not discuss the draft of Roscoe's report but identify and explain any items included in "*Other Information*" that need not be part of the auditor's report.

(AICPA Adapted)

17-40. The following report was drafted by an audit assistant at the completion of an audit engagement and was submitted to the audit partner for review. The auditor has reviewed matters thoroughly and has properly concluded that the scope limitation was not client-imposed and was not sufficiently material to warrant a disclaimer of opinion, although a qualified opinion was appropriate.

Independent Auditor's Report

To: Carl Corporation Controller

We have audited the accompanying financial statements of Carl Corporation as of December 31, 19X3. These statements are the responsibility of the company's management. Our responsibility is to express an opinion on these statements based on our audit.

We conducted our audit in accordance with generally accepted auditing standards. These standards require that we plan and perform the audit to provide reasonable assurance about whether the financial statements are free of material misstatement. An audit includes examining, on a test basis, evidence supporting the amounts and disclosures in the financial statements. An audit also includes assessing the accounting principles used and significant estimates made by management, as well as evaluating the overall financial statement presentation. We believe that our audit provides a reasonable basis for our opinion.

On January 15, 19X2, the company issued debentures in the amount of $1,000,000 for the purpose of financing plant expansion. As indicated in note 6 to the financial statements, the debenture agreement restricts the payment of future cash dividends to earnings after December 31, 19X1.

The company's unconsolidated foreign subsidiary did not close down production during the year under examination for physical inventory purposes and took no physical inventory during the year. We made extensive tests of book inventory figures for accuracy of calculation and reasonableness of pricing. We did not make physical tests of inventory quantities. Because of this, we are unable to express an unqualified opinion on the financial statements taken as a whole. However:

Except for the scope limitation regarding inventory, in our opinion the accompanying balance sheet presents, in all material respects, the financial position of Carl Corporation at December 31, 19X1, subject to the effect of the inventory on the carrying value of the investment. The accompanying statements of income and of retained earnings present the income and expenses and the result of transactions affecting retained earnings in accordance with generally accepted accounting principles.

December 31, 19X1

Pate & Co., CPAs

Required:

Identify all of the deficiencies in the above draft of the proposed report.

(AICPA Adapted)

17-41. The following auditor's report was drafted by an assistant at the completion of an audit engagement of Cramdon, Inc., and was submitted to the partner for review. The partner has examined matters thoroughly and has properly concluded that the opinion on the 19X1 financial report should be modified only for the change in the method for computing sales. Also, due to an uncertainty, an unqualified opinion was issued on the 19X0 financial statements, which are included for comparative purposes. The 19X0 auditor's report was dated March 3, 19X1. In 19X1, the litigation against Cramdon, which was the cause of the 19X0 opinion, was resolved in favor of Cramdon.

> **Board of Directors of Cramdon, Inc.:**
>
> We have examined the financial statements that are the representations of Cramdon, Inc., incorporated herein by reference, for the years ended December 31, 19X1 and 19X0. These statements are the responsibility of the company's management. Our responsibility is to express an opinion on these statements based on our audit.
>
> We conducted our audit in accordance with generally accepted auditing standards. These standards require that we plan and perform the audit to provide reasonable assurance about whether the financial statements are free of material misstatement. An audit includes examining, on a test basis, evidence supporting the amounts and disclosures in the financial statements. An audit also includes assessing the accounting principles used and significant estimates made by management, as well as evaluating the overall financial statement presentation. We believe that our audit provides a reasonable basis for our opinion.
>
> As discussed in Note 7 to the financial statements, our previous opinion on the 19X0 financial statements was other than unqualified pending the out-come of litigation. Due to our attorney's meritorious defense in this litigation, our opinion on these financial statements is different from that expressed in our previous report.
>
> In our opinion, based upon the preceding, the accompanying financial statements referred to above present fairly the financial position, results of operations, and cash flows for the period ended December 31, 19X1, in conformity with generally accepted accounting principles consistently applied, except for the change in the method of computing sales as described in Note 14 to the financial statements.
>
> CPA
> March 5, 19X2

Required:

Identify the deficiencies contained in the auditor's report as drafted by the audit assistant in the (a) introductory paragraph, (b) scope paragraph, (c) explanatory paragraph, and (d) opinion paragraph. Rewriting the auditor's report is not an acceptable solution.

(AICPA Adapted)

17-42. The CPA firm of May & Marty has audited the consolidated financial statements of BGI Corporation. May & Marty performed the examination of the parent company and all subsidiaries except for BGI-Western Corporation, which was audited by the CPA firm of Dey & Dee. BGI-Western constituted approximately 10 percent of the consolidated assets and 6 percent of the consolidated revenue.

Dey & Dee issued an unqualified opinion on the financial statements of BGI-Western. May & Marty will be issuing an unqualified opinion on the consolidated financial statements of BGI.

Required:

a. What procedures should May & Marty consider performing with respect to Dey & Dee's examination of BGI-Western's financial statements that will be appropriate, whether or not reference is to be made to the other auditors?

b. Describe the various circumstances under which May & Marty could take responsibility for the work of Dey & Dee and make no reference to Dey & Dee's examination of BGI-Western in May & Marty's auditor's report on the consolidated financial statements of BGI.

(AICPA Adapted)

17-43. Listed below are five independent case situations in which the dollar amounts are material. The facts in each case situation will have to be analyzed and interpreted to determine which type of audit opinion (i.e., unqualified, qualified, disclaimer, or adverse) would be given by each company's external auditor.

Case 1

Raygun Inc. manufactures space-age toys and has just added a new product based on a popular science fiction movie. Special equipment was purchased to manufacture the new product, and it will not be useful for making any future products. Due to the uncertainty of long-term future sales, Raygun has decided to expense the cost of the equipment during the year of purchase, even though all other equipment is depreciated over a period of not less than five years.

Case 2

Groco Company, a plant nursery, adopted a new accounting policy of deferring the recognition of labor, fertilizer, and other costs directly associated with growing seedling trees until the trees are sold—a period of two to three years. In the past, these costs have been expensed in the year incurred. The effect of the changes is to increase net income 20 percent over that which would have resulted if the change had not been made.

Case 3

Carniove Farms Inc. has engaged the local CPA firm of Lilly & Co. to audit its financial statements of March 31, 19X1. The CPA firm was not contacted about performing the audit until April 6, 19X1. Carniove Farms did not take a physical inventory on March 31, 19X0, or March 31, 19X1, and Lilly & Co. is not able to verify the inventory book amounts. Evidence supporting the cost of a material amount of property and equipment acquired prior to March 31, 19X0, is no longer available. Also, there is a large receivable from the U. S. government under a program to keep land out of corn production and thereby reduce the corn surplus. The U.S. government refuses to confirm this receivable, but the CPA firm is satisfied that the receivable is correct.

Case 4
MPT Industries is the defendant in a lawsuit alleging infringement of certain patent rights. The plaintiff is suing for royalties from the patent rights and for punitive damages. MPT has filed a counter-suit, and preliminary hearings on both actions are in progress. MPT's president and legal counsel believe that the company has a good chance of prevailing, but the outcome of the lawsuits cannot be determined with any degree of certainty. Although a potentially material adverse effect on MPT's financial statements could be experienced, no provision for any resulting liability has been made.

Case 5
Conglomo Corp., a large multidivision company, has a Canadian subsidiary, Kanucko, whose financial statements reflect total assets and revenues constituting 21 percent and 24 percent, respectively, of the consolidated totals. Kanucko was audited by a firm of Canadian Chartered Accountants that is unrelated to Vann & Company, the CPA firm that audits Conglomo. Vann & Company has reviewed the unqualified report and work papers of the Canadian Chartered Accountant. The Canadian firm has an excellent reputation and the work papers and procedures employed by it are in order.

Required:

For each of the five case situations, complete the following steps:

1. Indicate what type of audit opinion (*i.e.*, unqualified, qualified, disclaimer, or adverse) should be given by the external auditor of the company involved.
2. Explain why the selected type of opinion is appropriate for the situation presented.

(CMA Adapted)

Learning Objectives

Study of this chapter is designed to achieve several learning objectives. After studying this chapter, you should be able to:

1. Discuss the auditor's responsibility for reporting and examining information presented along with the financial statements.
2. List the types of "special reports" identified by *Statement on Auditing Standards No. 62* and discuss situations in which these reports would be appropriate.
3. Identify the contents of reports issued on financial statements prepared using a comprehensive basis of accounting other than GAAP.
4. Discuss the general contents of other types of reports issued when an audit examination is performed on company's historical financial statements.

18

Reporting: Other Information and Special Reports

The preceding chapter introduced the contents of the auditor's report on historical financial statements and discussed modifications to this report for accounting and auditing issues encountered during the engagement. This chapter continues this discussion and focuses on three major issues: (1) the auditor's responsibility for information presented along with the historical financial statements; (2) "special reports" issued on financial statements or elements, accounts, and items of financial statements; and (3) other types of reports issued in conjunction with an audit examination.

◉ REPORTING ON INFORMATION PRESENTED WITH THE FINANCIAL STATEMENTS

To this point, we have discussed the auditor's reporting responsibility for the client's financial statements (both the current-period financial statements as well as any prior-period financial statements presented in comparative form). It is important to remember that these financial statements are only a subset of the total package of financial information presented by the company to users. Financial statements and other information are normally presented in the form of an annual report, which includes various types of discussion and analysis, supplemental information, and other types of schedules and financial data.

The auditor's report discussed throughout the previous chapter is intended to cover only the basic financial statements and footnotes accompanying those financial statements. However, users may erroneously assume that the auditor's report pertains to all information presented in the company's annual report. As a result, the auditor should perform certain procedures to determine the reasonableness of this information. The auditor's responsibility for information accompanying the financial statements varies depending on the nature of the information. This section discusses the auditor's responsibility for: (1) other information presented with the financial statements, (2) segment information, (3) supplementary information required by the FASB or GASB, and (4) information contained in auditor-submitted documents.

◘ Other Information Prepared by the Client[1]

Clients often publish other types of information along with the audited financial statements in their annual reports. Examples of this information include financial highlights, financial analyses made by management, the President's letter, and other financial data. Although the auditor does not have full audit responsibility for this information, the auditor should read this information to determine that it is consistent with the financial statements.

Assuming that the other information is consistent with the financial statements, the auditor does not report on this information. If, however, the other information is inconsistent with the information presented in the financial statements, the auditor should determine whether the financial statements, the auditor's opinion on the financial statements, or both, require revision. Assuming that the auditor feels that the financial statements are fairly stated and do not require revision, the client should be requested to revise the other information. If the client fails to do so, the following actions may be appropriate:

1. Revise the audit report to include an explanatory paragraph concerning the inconsistency of the other information with the financial statements.
2. Withhold the use of the audit report.
3. Withdraw from the engagement.

The auditor's actions with respect to other information accompanying the financial statements are summarized in Figure 18-1.

In discussing the auditor's actions when other information is inconsistent with the financial statements and the client refuses to revise this information, it is important to distinguish between modifications of the auditor's *report* and modifications of the auditor's *opinion*. For example, assume that Knick, CPA determines that an unqualified opinion on the financial statements of Ewing Company is appropriate. In reading the other information accompanying the financial statements, Knick determines that this information is inconsistent with the financial statements. If Ewing fails to revise this information, Knick would add a paragraph to the audit report discussing the inconsistency of the other information from the financial statements; however, Knick's opinion on the financial statements (unqualified) would not be affected.

---

[1] American Institute of Certified Public Accountants (AICPA), *Statement on Auditing Standards No. 8*, "Other Information in Documents Containing Audited Financial Statements" (New York: AICPA, 1976, AU 550).

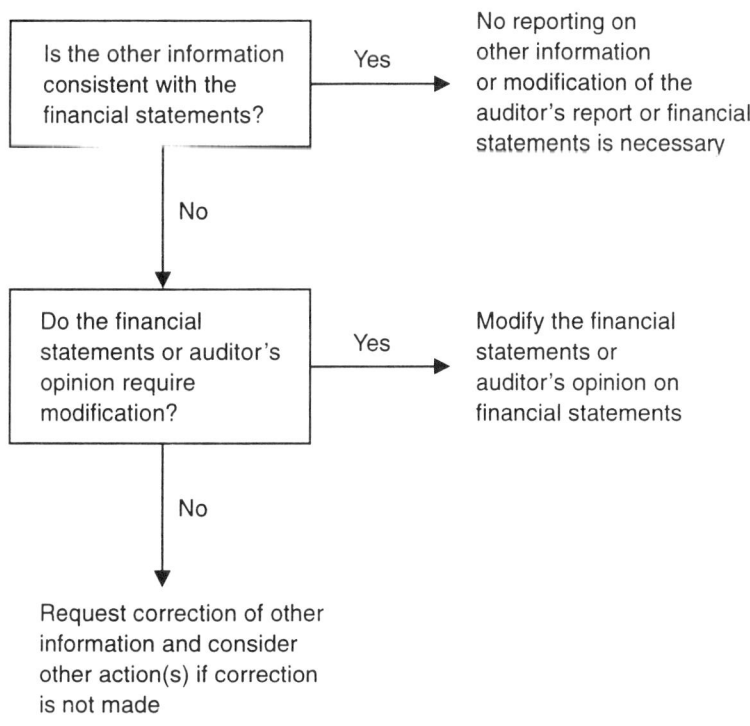

Figure 18-1: *Auditor's Actions for Other Information Prepared by the Client*

◘ Segment Information[2]

Under *Statement of Financial Accounting Standards No. 14 (SFAS No. 14)*,[3] companies are required to provide certain disclosures relating to identifiable industry segments. Because this information is a required part of the financial statements and footnotes accompanying these financial statements, the fairness of segment information is covered by the auditor's report on the company's financial statements.

It is important to note that the auditor has full audit responsibility for segment information. That is, the auditor must apply procedures and gather evidence relating to this information to determine that it is fairly stated. The auditor's reporting responsibility for segment information is **exception-based reporting**. In other words, the auditor's report does not mention segment information unless a problem

---

[2] American Institute of Certified Public Accountants (AICPA), *Statement on Auditing Standards No. 21*, "Segment Information" (New York: AICPA, 1977, AU 435).

[3] Financial Accounting Standards Board (FASB), *Statement of Financial Accounting Standards No. 14*, "Financial Reporting for Segments of a Business Enterprise" (Norwalk, CT: FASB, 1976).

is noted in the examination of this information. With respect to segment information, the following problems may be encountered in the auditor's examination:

- ▶ Segment information may be misstated or omitted.
- ▶ The auditor may encounter a scope limitation in examining segment information.

Misstatement or Omission. A misstatement in segment information that is material in relation to the financial statements taken as a whole should cause the auditor to modify his or her opinion on the financial statements due to a departure from GAAP. Because of the magnitude of segment information in relation to the financial statements taken as a whole, the auditor would not normally issue an adverse opinion for this type of GAAP departure. Instead, a qualified opinion would be issued in these cases. *SAS No. 21*[4] gives the following example of such a qualification:

SAMPLE AUDITOR'S REPORT
MISSTATEMENT IN SEGMENT INFORMATION: QUALIFIED OPINION

Independent Auditor's Report

[Same introductory and scope paragraphs as standard report]

With respect to the segment information in Note 3, $1.3 million of the operating expenses of Industry A were incurred jointly by Industries A and B. In our opinion, *Statement No. 14* **of the Financial Accounting Standards Board requires that those operating expenses be allocated between Industries A and B. The effect of the failure to allocate those operating expenses has been to understate the operating profit of Industry A and to overstate the operating profit of Industry B by an amount hat has not been determined.**

In our opinion, **except for the effects of not allocating certain common operating expenses between Industries A and B, as discussed in the preceding paragraph,** the financial statements referred to above present fairly ...

If the client does not include all or part of the required segment information, the auditor should modify his or her opinion due to inadequate disclosure. The auditor need not present the omitted information in the report, but should describe the omitted information. Once again, the magnitude of the effect of segment information on the financial statements taken as a whole would normally result in the issuance of a qualified opinion.

Scope Limitations. Two types of scope limitations may exist with respect to the auditor's ability to examine segment information. These limitations include: (1) the inability to determine whether the

---

[4] American Institute of Certified Public Accountants (AIPCA), *Statement on Auditing Standards No. 21*, "Segment Information" (New York: AICPA, 1977, AU 435.09).

client needs to present segment information, and (2) the inability to apply certain audit procedures to segment information presented by the client.

If an auditor is not able to conclude whether the client needs to disclose segments as required by *SFAS No. 14* and the client refuses to develop information that would be needed to reach such a conclusion, *SAS No. 21* notes that the auditor should treat this in a manner similar to a scope limitation. Thus, the scope and opinion paragraphs of the auditor's report are revised to refer to the scope limitation. In addition, an explanatory paragraph is added to identify the scope limitation. Similar to omission or departures from GAAP, the magnitude of segment information in relation to the financial statements taken as a whole would not ordinarily justify a disclaimer of opinion. Instead, the auditor would issue a qualified opinion, as shown below.

SAMPLE AUDITOR'S REPORT

SCOPE LIMITATION ON EXAMINATION OF SEGMENT INFORMATION: QUALIFIED OPINION

Independent Auditor's Report

[*Same introductory paragraph as standard report*]

Except as discussed in the following paragraph, we conducted our audit in conformity with generally accepted auditing standards ...

The Company has not developed the information we consider necessary to reach a conclusion as to whether the presentation of segment information concerning the Company's operations in different industries, its foreign operations and export sales, and its major customers is necessary to conform with *Statement No. 14* of the Financial Accounting Standards Board.

In our opinion, **except for the possible omission of segment information**, the financial statements referred to above present fairly ...

CHAPTER CHECKPOINTS

18-1. For what information is the auditor's report on the financial statements normally intended to provide assurance?

18-2. What is the auditor's responsibility for examining other information prepared by the client? For reporting on this information?

18-3. What actions may be taken by the auditor if he or she feels that other information prepared by the client is inconsistent with the financial statements and the financial statements are fairly stated?

18-4. What is the auditor's responsibility for examining segment information? For reporting on segment information?

18-5. What deficiencies in segment information may result in the auditor modifying his or her opinion on the financial statements?

◘ Reporting on Required Supplementary Information[5]

The FASB and Governmental Accounting Standards Board (GASB) require management to provide certain information other than the basic financial statements and footnotes accompanying those financial statements. In many cases, this supplementary information is industry specific, such as information on oil, gas, and mineral reserves for companies in the petroleum industry. In other cases, the information can pertain to companies in many industries, such as current cost and constant dollar information formerly required by the FASB under *Statement of Financial Accounting Standards No. 33*. Because of the unique nature of this information, it is specifically excluded from audit requirements by the FASB and SEC.

While no audit responsibility exists for supplementary information required by the FASB or GASB, the auditor should perform limited procedures with respect to this information. These limited procedures include:

1. Inquiring of management regarding whether information is prepared, measured, and presented according to FASB or GASB guidelines.
2. Comparing supplementary information required by the FASB to the financial statements for consistency.
3. Applying any other specific procedures felt to be appropriate in the circumstances.

SAS No. 52 notes that the auditor would not normally refer to the supplementary information in his or her report or the limited procedures applied to that information. The auditor's report should only be expanded in the following circumstances:

▶ The required supplementary information has been omitted.

▶ The measurement or presentation of the supplementary information provided by the client departs materially from FASB or GASB guidelines.

▶ The auditor has not been able to complete the prescribed procedures with respect to the supplementary information.

SAS No. 52 gives the following example of an additional paragraph that might be used by the auditor if the required supplementary information has been omitted by the client. It is important to note that this paragraph would be placed following the opinion paragraph and would not affect the auditor's overall opinion on the client's financial statements.

---

[5] American Institute of Certified Public Accountants (AICPA), *Statement on Auditing Standards No. 52*, "Omnibus Statement on Auditing Standards—1987" (New York: AICPA, 1988, AU 558).

> **SAMPLE EXPLANATORY PARAGRAPH**
> **SUPPLEMENTARY INFORMATION REQUIRED BY THE FASB**
>
> The Company has not presented *[describe the supplementary information required by the FASB in the circumstances]* that the Financial Accounting Standards Board has determined it is necessary to supplement, although not required to be, part of the basic financial statements.

◻ Reporting on Information Accompanying the Basic Financial Statements in Auditor-Submitted Documents[6]

In most cases, any financial or other information that is presented along with the basic financial statements is prepared by the client. As noted earlier in this chapter, the auditor's responsibility in these situations is to read the information to ensure that it is consistent with the content of the client's financial statements. Occasionally, independent auditors will include additional information along with the information prepared by the client that is intended to facilitate the interpretation of the basic financial statements. It is important to note that this information is derived from the basic financial statements and, therefore, is a representation of the client. However, because the auditor has included additional information along with the basic financial statements and information provided by the client, an additional reporting issue is introduced.

Situations where information is included by an auditor along with client-prepared information are referred to as **auditor-submitted documents**. It is important to distinguish between this situation and the other information described in a previous subsection. In this case, the auditor (and not the client) is preparing the document that includes the audit report, financial statements, and other information.

When the auditor submits information to clients or third parties, she or he must explicitly indicate the extent of responsibility assumed for all information included in the document. The auditor can do so by expanding the audit report on the financial statements or reporting on this information separately. Because this information was derived from the basic financial statements, the auditor's opinion on it will indicate whether the other information "... is fairly stated in all material respects in relation to the basic financial statements taken as a whole."

SAS No. 29 gives the following example of an unqualified opinion on the accompanying information. As noted above, this paragraph can be appended to the auditor's report on the financial statements or presented separately with the other information.

---

[6] This section is based on American Institute of Certified Public Accountants (AICPA), *Statement on Auditing Standards No. 29*, "Reporting on Information Accompanying the Basic Financial Statements in Auditor-Submitted Documents" (New York: AICPA, 1980, AU 551) as amended by *Statement on Auditing Standards No. 52*, "Omnibus Statement on Auditing Standards—1987" (New York: AICPA, 1988, AU 558).

> **SAMPLE AUDITOR'S REPORT**
> **OTHER INFORMATION IN AN AUDITOR-SUBMITTED DOCUMENT**
>
> Our examination was made for the purpose of forming an opinion on the basic financial statements taken as a whole. The [identify accompanying information] is presented for purposes of additional analysis and is not a required part of the basic financial statements. Such information has been subjected to the auditing procedures applied in the examination of the basic financial statements and, in our opinion, is fairly stated in all material respects in relation to the basic financial statements taken as a whole.

Alternatively, the auditor may choose to disclaim an opinion on all or part of the other information presented in an auditor-submitted document. Again, the disclaimer can be presented separately or appended to the auditor's report on the financial statements. Remember, the auditor must report (or disclaim an opinion) on all financial information contained in auditor-submitted documents.

◻ Summary: Other Reporting Responsibilities

Figure 18-2 provides a brief summary of the major aspects of the auditor's responsibility for financial information presented along with the client's financial statements. This summary includes both the audit responsibility and reporting responsibility for this information.

	Audit Responsibility	Reporting Responsibility	Other Comments
Other information	Limited	Exception-based	None
Segment information	Full audit	Exception-based	May affect opinion on financial statements
Supplemental information required by FASB	Limited	Exception-based	None
Other information in Auditor-Submitted Documents	Can vary from full audit to no responsibility	Explicit	May disclaim an opinion on all or part of this information

Figure 18-2: *Summary of Auditor Responsibility for Information Presented with Financial Statements*

Three important points are revealed by Figure 18-2. First, the auditor only has full audit responsibility for segment information. Because the remaining information is not considered as an integral part of the financial statements and footnotes, only limited auditing procedures are applied to that information. Second, with the exception of information contained in auditor-submitted documents, exception-based reporting is used for this information. That is, the auditor's report on the financial statements is not modified unless a problem is encountered with respect to the other information presented along with the financial statements. Finally, the auditor's opinion on the financial statements is only affected by problems associated with segment information. While other situations may require modifications of the auditor's *report* (by adding an explanatory paragraph), the *opinion* issued on the financial statements is unchanged.

CHAPTER CHECKPOINTS

18-6. What is supplementary information required by the FASB or GASB? Is the auditor required to audit this information?

18-7. What is an auditor-submitted document? What is the auditor's responsibility for examining information contained in an auditor-submitted document?

18-8. Must the auditor issue an opinion on information contained in an auditor-submitted document?

◉ SPECIAL REPORTS[7]

Statement on Auditing Standards No. 62[8] identifies several types of special reports. This section discusses reports issued on:

1. Financial statements prepared using a comprehensive basis of accounting other than GAAP (hereafter, basis other than GAAP).
2. Specified elements, accounts, or items in financial statements.
3. Company compliance with aspects of contractual or regulatory requirements.
4. Financial presentations intended to comply with contractual or regulatory requirements.
5. Financial information presented in prescribed forms or schedules that require a prescribed form of auditor's report.

These reports are referred to as **special reports** only because of their designation as such by *SAS No. 62*. They are discussed in detail in the following section.

---

[7] The reports illustrated in this section are based on *Statement on Auditing Standards No. 62*, "Special Reports" (New York: AICPA, 1989, AU 623) and *Statement on Auditing Standards No. 75*, "Applying Agreed-Upon Procedures to Specific Elements, Accounts, or Items of a Financial Statement" (New York: AICPA, 1995, AU 622).

[8] American Institute of Certified Public Accountants (AICPA), *Statement on Auditing Standards No. 62*, "Special Reports" (New York: AICPA, 1989, AU 623).

◘ Basis Other than GAAP

The purpose of an audit examination is to determine whether the company's financial statements and disclosures are prepared in conformity with established criteria. As noted earlier in this text, to comply with SEC reporting requirements, publicly-traded companies must prepare their financial statements in accordance with GAAP. However, these requirements do not exist for other (nonpublic) companies. For these companies, another basis of accounting is often more appropriate than GAAP. For example, nonpublic companies whose activities are subject to the review of external regulators are often required to file financial statements with those regulators. If the basis of accounting required by the regulatory body differs from GAAP, little is to be gained by having the auditor report on the conformity of these companies' financial statements with GAAP.

SAS No. 62 identifies the following bases of accounting other than GAAP that may be reported upon by the auditor:

- ▶ A basis of accounting used to comply with the reporting requirements of a governmental regulatory agency (for example, rules of the Federal Energy Regulatory Commission).
- ▶ The basis of accounting used by companies to file income tax returns.
- ▶ The cash receipts and cash disbursements basis of accounting and slight modifications of this basis.
- ▶ Any basis of accounting having substantial support that is applied to all material items in the company's financial statements. An example would be price-level adjusted accounting.

Shown below is the auditor's report on financial information prepared under the cash receipts and disbursements basis of accounting.

> **SAMPLE AUDITOR'S REPORT**
> **BASIS OTHER THAN GAAP:**
> **CASH RECEIPTS AND DISBURSEMENTS**
>
> ### Independent Auditor's Report
>
> We have audited the accompanying **statement of assets and liabilities arising from cash transactions** of XYZ Company as of December 31, 19X1, and the related **statement of revenue collected and expenses paid** for the year then ended. These financial statements are the responsibility of XYZ Company's management. Our responsibility is to express an opinion on these financial statements based on our audit.
>
> We conducted our audit in accordance with generally accepted auditing standards. Those standards require that we plan and perform the audit to obtain reasonable assurance about whether the financial statements are free of material misstatement. An audit includes examining, on a test basis, evidence supporting the amounts and disclosures in the financial statements. An audit also includes assessing the accounting principles used and significant estimates made by management, as well as evaluating the overall financial statement presentation. We believe that our audit provides a reasonable basis for our opinion.
>
> **As described in Note 4, the Company's policy is to prepare its financial statements on the basis of cash receipts and disbursements, which is a comprehensive basis of accounting other than generally accepted accounting principles.**
>
> In our opinion, the financial statements referred to above present fairly, in all material respects, **the assets and liabilities arising from cash transactions** of XYZ Company as of December 31, 19X1, and the **revenue collected and expenses paid** during the year then ended, on the **basis of accounting described in Note 4.**

Reviewing the above report reveals a great deal of similarity between it and the auditor's report on financial statements prepared in conformity with GAAP discussed in the preceding chapter. It is very important to emphasize that the only difference between the two engagements represented by these reports is the basis of accounting used by the company. No differences exist in the auditor's responsibility for the financial statements or the audit procedures performed during the engagement. Therefore, the scope paragraph will continue to indicate that a GAAS audit was performed and that this audit provides a reasonable basis for the opinion.

Two differences are evident between this report and the report on financial statements prepared in accordance with GAAP. First, because of differences in the basis of accounting, the names of the financial statements and information provided by these statements differ. For the cash basis of accounting, the terms "assets and liabilities arising from cash transactions" and "revenues collected and expenses paid" are the counterparts to the balance sheet and income statements prepared under GAAP. Therefore, the auditor should modify the introductory paragraph to indicate the names of the financial statements examined. In addition, these statements do not intend to present the financial position and results of operations as do GAAP financial statements, resulting in slight modifications to the opinion paragraph. The opinion paragraph will also be modified to indicate that these statements were in conformity with the basis of accounting used, and not GAAP.

The second major difference between this report and the report issued on financial statements prepared in conformity with GAAP is the addition of an explanatory paragraph. This paragraph indicates that the financial statements are prepared in accordance with a basis of accounting other than GAAP. The paragraph also refers to a footnote in the company's financial statements that explains the basis of accounting used and how that basis differs from GAAP. An example of such a footnote disclosure is shown below:

SAMPLE FOOTNOTE DISCLOSURE

BASIS OF ACCOUNTING OTHER THAN GAAP

The accompanying financial statements are presented on the cash basis, reflecting only cash received and disbursed. Therefore, receivables and payables, inventories, accrued revenues and expenses, and other assets and liabilities are not reflected in the statements. These statements do not intend to present the overall financial position or results of operations of the company in conformity with generally accepted accounting principles.

The above report is appropriate when the client prepares its financial statements using the cash basis of accounting. Reports using the remaining three allowable bases of accounting (basis required by a regulatory agency, tax basis, and any basis having substantial support) would be similar; only the names of the financial statements and the basis of accounting mentioned in the opinion paragraph would differ. However, if the auditor reports on a basis of accounting required by a regulatory agency, the report's distribution should be limited to the company being reported upon and the regulatory agency. The following paragraph would be added to the auditor's report:

SAMPLE EXPLANATORY PARAGRAPH

**BASIS OF ACCOUNTING REQUIRED
BY A REGULATORY AGENCY**

This report is intended solely for the information and use of the Board of Directors and management of XYZ Company and for filing with the Federal Energy Commission and should not be used for any other purpose.

> **CHAPTER CHECKPOINTS**
>
> **18-9.** What are the five major types of special reports identified by *SAS No. 62*?
>
> **18-10.** What is a comprehensive basis of accounting other than GAAP? Provide some examples of these bases of accounting.
>
> **18-11.** What major differences exist in the auditor's report on financial statements prepared under a comprehensive basis of accounting other than GAAP and the standard auditor's report issued on financial statements prepared under GAAP?
>
> **18-12.** What additional modifications should the accountant make to his or her report if financial statements are prepared on a basis of accounting required by a regulatory agency?

◻ Reports on Specific Elements, Accounts, or Items

In certain cases, the auditor may be engaged to report only on specific elements, accounts, or items contained in the company's financial statements. It is important to note that the auditor's engagement may still be conducted under GAAS; the only difference between this and a standard engagement is that the auditor is only examining (and reporting on) specific items presented in the company's financial statements. For example, assume that a company is applying for a loan from a bank and is intending to use its accounts receivable as collateral to secure the loan. As an alternative to a complete audit on the entire set of financial statements, the lender may request that the auditor examine the accounts receivable to determine whether they are presented in conformity with GAAP.

Audit Examination. If the auditor performs an audit examination of elements, accounts, or items of a financial statement, he or she can express an opinion on the fairness of these elements, accounts, or items. An example of an audit report on a client's accounts receivable is shown below.[9]

---

[9] American Institute of Certified Public Accountants (AICPA), *Statement on Auditing Standards No. 62*, "Special Reports" (New York: AICPA, 1989, AU 623.18).

> **SAMPLE AUDITOR'S REPORT**
> **AUDIT EXAMINATION OF ACCOUNTS RECEIVABLE**
>
> **Independent Auditor's Report**
>
> We have audited the **accompanying schedule of accounts receivable** of ABC Company as of December 31, 19X2. This schedule is the responsibility of the Company's management. Our responsibility is to express an opinion on this schedule based on our audit.
>
> We conducted our audit in accordance with generally accepted auditing standards. Those standards require that we plan and perform the audit to obtain reasonable assurance about whether the **schedule of accounts receivable** is free of material misstatement. An audit includes examining, on a test basis, evidence supporting the amounts and disclosures in the **schedule of accounts receivable**. An audit also includes assessing the accounting principles used and significant estimates made by management, as well as evaluating the overall **schedule presentation**. We believe that our audit provides a reasonable basis for our opinion.
>
> In our opinion, the **schedule of accounts receivable** referred to above presents fairly, in all material respects, the **accounts receivable** of ABC Company as of December 31, 19X2, in conformity with generally accepted accounting principles.

Note that the above report is quite similar to the auditor's standard report on the financial statements. The only differences are modifications to the report to indicate that the auditor's examination and opinion are limited to only a portion of the financial statements (in this case, accounts receivable). Also notice that, since a GAAS audit is performed, the auditor can still issue an opinion.

SAS No. 62 indicates that an auditor may express an opinion on elements, accounts, or items in financial statements as either a separate engagement or as part of an examination of the entire set of financial statements. However, in the latter instance, if an adverse opinion or disclaimer of opinion is given for the financial statements taken as a whole, the auditor should take care that the report on the specific elements, accounts, or items does not represent a **piecemeal opinion** on the financial statements. This is done by:

1. Ensuring that the elements, accounts, or items reported on do not encompass a major portion of the financial statements.
2. Not presenting the report on elements, accounts, or items along with the report on the entire set of financial statements.

Applying Agreed-Upon Procedures. The report shown in the previous section is based on a GAAS audit of specific elements, accounts, or items. Because a GAAS audit was conducted, the auditor was able to express an opinion on the element(s) examined. In some situations, the scope of the engagement can be reduced (because of cost, third-party requirements, or other considerations) to a level below that required by a GAAS audit. In many cases, third-party users may actually specify the scope of the engagement and types of procedures performed by the accountant. These types of engagements are referred to as **agreed-upon procedures engagements** and are the focus of *Statement on Auditing Standards No. 75 (SAS No. 75)*.[10]

SAS No. 75 notes that the accountant can apply agreed-upon procedures to elements, accounts, or items of a financial statement under the following circumstances:

1. The accountant is independent with respect to the client.
2. The accountant and specified users agree upon the procedures performed or to be performed.
3. The specified users take responsibility for the sufficiency of the agreed-upon procedures.
4. Use of the report is restricted to the specified users.

The actual scope of agreed-upon procedures engagements varies and may be as limited or extensive as the specified users desire. It is important to emphasize that the specified users must take responsibility for the scope of the accountant's engagement. However, *SAS No. 75* provides some guidelines to accountants for these engagements. For example, merely reading work performed by others to evaluate their findings or objectivity is not sufficient for performing an agreed-upon procedures engagement. In addition, *SAS No. 75* notes that the accountant should not agree to perform procedures that are overly subjective and, thus, are subject to varying interpretations. This includes the use of terms such as "general review," "limited review," "reconcile," "check," or "test" to describe procedures performed by the accountant.

Because an engagement to perform agreed-upon procedures is less in scope than a GAAS audit, the accountant is unable to express an opinion on the elements, accounts, or items examined. In addition, because these engagements are not comprised of standard procedures, standard levels of assurance cannot be provided. The accountant's report in an agreed-upon procedures engagement provides a summary of the procedures performed by the accountant and his or her findings. An example of such a report is shown below.[11]

---

[10] American Institute of Certified Public Accountants (AICPA), *Statement on Auditing Standards No. 75*, "Engagements to Apply Agreed-Upon Procedures to Elements, Accounts, or Items of a Financial Statement" (New York: AICPA, 1995, AU 622).

[11] American Institute of Certified Public Accountants (AICPA), *Statement on Auditing Standards No. 75*, "Engagements to Apply Agreed-Upon Procedures to Elements, Accounts, or Items of a Financial Statement" (New York: AICPA, 1995, AU 622.34).

> **SAMPLE ACCOUNTANT'S REPORT
> APPLYING AGREED-UPON PROCEDURES
> TO ELEMENTS, ACCOUNTS, OR ITEMS**
>
> **Independent Accountant's Report
> on Applying Agreed-Upon Procedures**
>
> We have performed the procedures enumerated below, which were agreed to by Third Bank, solely to assist you with respect to the accounts receivable of Allan Company. This engagement to apply agreed-upon procedures was performed in accordance with standards established by the American Institute of Certified Public Accountants. The sufficiency of the procedures is solely the responsibility of the specified users of the report. Consequently, we make no representation regarding the sufficiency of the procedures described below either for the purpose for which this report has been requested or for any other purpose.
>
> We confirmed all accounts receivable over $50,000 directly with customers using the positive request method. These accounts receivable totalled $3.2 million of the $4.0 million accounts receivable outstanding at year-end for Allan Company. The results of these confirmations, as well as follow-up of exceptions to these confirmations, indicated one customers' account was overstated by $400,000.
>
> We were not engaged to, and did not, perform an audit, the objective of which would be the expression of an opinion on the specified elements, accounts, or items. Accordingly, we do not express such an opinion. Had we performed additional procedures, other matters might have come to our attention that would have been reported to you.
>
> This report is intended solely for the use of the specified users listed above and should not be used by those who have not agreed to the procedures and taken responsibility for the sufficiency of the procedures for their purposes.

Agreed-upon procedures engagements are also a form of attestation engagement. These engagements are discussed in greater detail in Chapter 19.

◘ Compliance with Contractual Agreements

In addition to reporting on the fairness of the client's financial statements, the auditor is sometimes requested by third parties to provide assurances regarding whether the client is in compliance with contractual agreements or other regulatory provisions. For example, many lending agreements require companies to maintain key financial ratios (e.g., current ratio, debt-to-equity ratio) at minimum levels. When an accountant is asked to report on compliance with contractual agreements (such as a bond indenture, loan agreement, or regulatory requirement), this cannot be done unless the accountant has audited that company's financial statements. This requirement allows the accountant to have a reasonable basis for concluding that the company is in compliance with contractual agreements.

The accountant can report on compliance with contractual agreements either separately or as part of the report on the financial statements. In either case, **negative** (or **limited**) assurance will be provided concerning compliance. A sample report that provides negative assurance on a company's compliance with contractual provisions is shown below.[12]

SAMPLE AUDITOR'S REPORT

COMPLIANCE WITH CONTRACTUAL AGREEMENTS

We have audited, in accordance with generally accepted auditing standards, the balance sheet of XYZ Company as of December 31, 19X2, and the related statement of income, retained earnings, and cash flows for the year then ended, and have issued our report thereon dated February 16, 19X3.

In connection with our audit, nothing came to our attention that caused us to believe that the company was not in compliance with any of the terms or covenants of the loan agreement with First Bank. However, our audit was not directed primarily toward obtaining knowledge of such compliance.

This report is intended solely for the information and use of the Boards of Directors and management of XYZ Company and First Bank and should not be used for any other purpose.

Similar to an opinion on elements, accounts, or items, *SAS No. 62* notes that negative assurance on compliance with a contractual agreement should *not* be provided if an adverse opinion or disclaimer of opinion is issued on the company's financial statements.

◻ Financial Presentations Intended to Comply with Contractual or Regulatory Requirements

In some cases auditors may be asked to report on **special-purpose financial statements** that are prepared to comply with contractual agreements or regulatory provisions. In these engagements, the auditor is reporting on whether financial information requested by a third party is presented in conformity with some established criteria. While these financial statements may initially appear to be similar in nature to financial statements prepared under a comprehensive basis of accounting other than GAAP, they differ as follows:

▶ They represent a set of financial information less than a full set of financial statements.

▶ They are not prepared using one of the four bases of accounting that qualify as a comprehensive basis of accounting other than GAAP.

Because these statements are intended for parties who establish their form and content, the auditor may report on whether they are presented fairly. It is important to note that a GAAS audit is still conducted; thus, an opinion will be issued. The only difference in these engagements is that the financial

---

[12] American Institute of Certified Public Accountants (AICPA), *Statement on Auditing Standards No. 62*, "Special Reports" (New York: AICPA, 1989, AU 623.21).

information, basis of accounting, or both, may differ from a typical GAAS audit. The auditor's report on these financial statements should parallel the auditor's standard report on financial statements discussed in the preceding chapter. In addition, this report will also address the following items:

1. Indicate that the financial statements were prepared for the purpose of complying with contractual agreements or regulatory provisions.
2. Restrict its distribution to the client and third parties involved in the contractual agreement or regulatory provisions.

◻ Prescribed Forms

The final type of special report is issued in engagements where the financial statements are presented in a prescribed format or the auditor's report is preprinted using a certain format. These situations normally arise when reporting on the financial statements of companies subject to the oversight requirements of a regulatory agency. In either case, the auditor should consider whether the format required for either the financial statements or the auditor's opinion would force the auditor to make assertions that are unjustified. The auditor should revise the prescribed report (by inserting or deleting whatever language is considered necessary) or attach a separate report if the format of the report is not appropriate. If the prescribed form for the financial statements is considered inappropriate, the auditor should disclaim an opinion on the financial statements.

◻ Summary: Special Reports

A summary of the major aspects associated with the auditor's engagements and reports in special reporting situations (as defined by *SAS Nos. 62 and 75*) is presented in Figure 18-3. One important point can be observed by examining Figure 18-3: if the auditor conducts a GAAS audit, he or she can issue an opinion on the financial statements, regardless of the basis of accounting utilized or form of the financial statements.

	Item(s) Reported Upon	Extent of Procedures	Type of Opinion or Assurance
Other Basis of Accounting	Full Financial Statements	GAAS Audit	Audit Opinion
Audit of Specified Accounts, Elements, or Items	Limited Information	GAAS Audit	Audit Opinion
Applying Agreed-upon Procedures to Specified Accounts, Elements, or Items	Limited Information	Specified by client or third parties	Summary of findings
Compliance with Contractual Agreements	Compliance with Provisions or Agreements	GAAS Audit on Financial Statements	Negative Assurance on Compliance
Special-Purpose Financial Statements	Information Required by Agreements or Regulatory Agency (Limited Information)	GAAS Audit	Audit Opinion
Prescribed Forms	Full Financial Statements	GAAS Audit	May Disclaim an Opinion if Form of Financial Statements is Inappropriate

Figure 18-3: *Summary: Special Reports*

CHAPTER CHECKPOINTS

18-13. What two types of engagements can accountants perform on elements, accounts, and items of a financial statement?

18-14. Under what circumstances can an accountant perform an agreed-upon procedures engagement to elements, accounts, or items of a financial statement?

18-15. What type of assurance is expressed in an agreed-upon procedures engagement on elements, accounts, or items of a financial statement?

18-16. In what situations can the auditor report on compliance with contractual agreements? What type of assurance can he or she provide with respect to compliance with contractual agreements?

18-17. How do special-purpose financial statements differ from financial statements prepared under a comprehensive basis of accounting other than GAAP?

18-18. How should accountants report on engagements where the auditor's report is preprinted in a certain format and the accountant feels that this format would be misleading?

◙ OTHER TYPES OF REPORTS ISSUED IN CONJUNCTION WITH AUDITED FINANCIAL STATEMENTS

◘ Financial Statements Prepared for use in Other Countries

When a United States (U.S.) entity prepares financial statements for use outside the U.S., these statements may need to be prepared in conformity with accounting principles "generally accepted" for use in another country. According to *Statement on Auditing Standards No. 51 (SAS No. 51)*[13] the auditor should perform procedures that comply with the general and field work standards of U.S. GAAS; however, depending upon the GAAP in the other country, the auditing procedures performed under U.S. GAAS may need to be modified. For example, if another country's GAAP require assets to be restated to reflect the effect(s) of inflation, the auditor will need to perform procedures to test the revaluation adjustments made to reflect inflation. In these cases, the auditor is required to comply with the general standards and standards of field work in both the U.S. and the other country.

When reporting on financial statements prepared under another country's GAAP for use solely outside of the U.S., the auditor can either: (1) modify the U.S.-style report discussed in Chapter 17 to adapt it to the other country's GAAP, or (2) use the report form of the other country. An example of a U.S. report modified to adapt to accounting principles generally accepted in another country is shown below.[14]

---

[13] American Institute of Certified Public Accountants (AICPA), *Statement on Auditing Standards No. 51*, "Reporting on Financial Statements Prepared for Use in Other Countries" (New York: AICPA, 1986, AU 534).

[14] American Institute of Certified Public Accountants (AICPA), *Statement on Auditing Standards No. 51*, "Reporting on Financial Statements Prepared for Use in Other Countries" (New York: AICPA, 1986, AU 534.10).

> **SAMPLE AUDITOR'S REPORT**
> **FINANCIAL STATEMENTS PREPARED**
> **FOR USE IN OTHER COUNTRIES**
>
> **Independent Auditor's Report**
>
> We have audited the accompanying balance sheet of X Company as of December 31, 19X1, and the related statements of income, retained earnings, and cash flows for the year then ended, which have been prepared on the **basis of accounting principles generally accepted in Anywhere**. These financial statements are the responsibility of the Company's management. Our responsibility is to express an opinion on these financial statements based on our audit.
>
> We conducted our audit in accordance with auditing standards generally accepted in the United States **(and in Anywhere)**. U.S. standards require that we plan and perform the audit to obtain reasonable assurance about whether the financial statements are free of material misstatement. An audit includes examining, on a test basis, evidence supporting the amounts and disclosures in the financial statements. An audit also includes assessing the accounting principles used and significant estimates made by management, as well as evaluating the overall financial statement presentation. We believe that our audit provides a reasonable basis for our opinion.
>
> In our opinion, the financial statements referred to above present fairly, in all material respects, the financial position of X Company as of December 31, 19X1, and the results of its operations and its cash flows for the year then ended in conformity with **accounting principles generally accepted in Anywhere**.

If the auditor uses the report form of the other country, he or she should comply with the reporting standards of that country. If the auditor reports on financial statements that will be used in the U.S., and these financial statements are prepared in conformity with the accounting principles generally accepted in another country, the auditor should use the U.S. standard form of report. *SAS No. 51* notes that this report should be modified because of any departures from U.S. GAAP.

◘ Review of Interim Financial Information

As noted throughout this text, public companies are required by the Securities and Exchange Commission to have an annual audit of their financial statements. In addition to this requirement, these companies are also required to file interim financial information with the SEC. **Interim financial information** represents financial information for a period of time less than a full year or financial information for a full year ending on a date other than the company's fiscal year end. Interim financial information is normally filed on a quarterly basis with the SEC through the use of 10-Q reports. Unlike annual financial statements, the quarterly financial information filed with the SEC is not required to be audited or subjected to any other type of auditing procedures.[15]

---

[15] At least three of the "Big Six" accounting firms (Deloitte & Touche, LLP; Price Waterhouse, LLP; and Arthur Andersen & Co, LLP) have policies that require certain types of clients to have their quarterly financial statements reviewed. See "D&T Requires Timely Quarterly Reviews," *Public Accounting Report* (June 30, 1994), 5.

In addition to periodically filing interim financial information through the use of Form 10-Q, the SEC requires its registrants to include interim financial information as part of the footnotes accompanying their audited financial statements. While this information is specifically marked as "unaudited interim financial information", the accountant is required to perform certain types of procedures relating to this information. The procedures performed by the accountant with respect to interim financial information presented in the footnotes accompanying the financial statements are known as a **review**.

It is important to distinguish between the two types of interim information discussed above. To illustrate, assume that Ferotte Company is publicly-traded and, therefore, is require to file financial information with the SEC. Ferotte Company is required to file interim financial information (in the form of 10-Q reports) with the SEC within a certain period of time after each of its fiscal quarters (March 31, 19X1, June 30, 19X1, and September 30, 19X1 for a December 31, 19X1 year-end). This information is not required to be audited or reviewed. However, in preparing its annual financial statements, Ferotte Company is required to present a summary of the interim financial information *previously filed through the 10-Q reports* in a footnote accompanying the annual financial statements. It is this interim information that must be reviewed by the accountant.

Procedures in Reviewing Interim Financial Information. *Statement on Auditing Standards No. 71 (SAS No. 71)*[16] provides guidance for review engagements for public companies. Some of the major procedures performed in a review of interim financial information include:

1. Obtaining knowledge of the client's internal control policies related to the preparation of both annual and interim financial information.
2. Performing inquiry of client personnel concerning:
    a. The client's accounting system and changes in internal control.
    b. Changes in accounting principles.
    c. Subsequent events.
3. Reading minutes of meetings, reports prepared by other accountants (if any), and interim financial information.
4. Performing analytical procedures and evaluate current interim period information against:
    a. The preceding interim period.
    b. Anticipated results.
    c. Any relationships based on predictive patterns.

Note that many of the above procedures will be performed by the accountant as he or she audits the annual financial statements. It is also important to point out that the actual auditing procedures performed on the interim financial information are limited to inquiry and analytical procedures. As a result, the auditor cannot express an opinion on the fairness of the interim financial information.

---

[16] American Institute of Certified Public Accountants (AICPA), *Statement on Auditing Standards No. 71*, "Interim Financial Information" (New York: AICPA, 1992, AU 722).

Reporting on Interim Financial Information. Interim financial information may be presented: (1) separately from the audited financial statements, or (2) along with the audited financial statements as either supplementary information or in a footnote accompanying the financial statements. If presented along with the audited financial statements, the accountant's reporting responsibility is similar to that for "supplementary information" discussed earlier in this chapter. That is, the accountant does not issue a separate report on the interim financial information. In addition, the accountant would only modify his or her report on the audited financial statements if certain problems are encountered with respect to the interim financial information. Recall that this approach to reporting is known as **exception-based reporting**. Matters that would result in modifying the report on the audited financial statements because of the interim financial information include:

▶ Interim data required under GAAP are omitted.

▶ Interim data are not reviewed.

▶ Interim data are not marked as "unaudited."

▶ Interim data contain departures from GAAP.

The report on the audited financial statements would be modified by adding a paragraph discussing the matter related to the interim financial information. However, the accountant would not modify his or her opinion on the audited financial statements.

If interim financial information is presented separately from the audited financial statements, *SAS No. 71*[17] provides an example of the following report.

---

[17] American Institute of Certified Public Accountants (AICPA), *Statement on Auditing Standards No. 71*, "Interim Financial Information" (New York: AICPA, 1992, AU 722.28).

> **SAMPLE AUDITOR'S REPORT**
> **INTERIM FINANCIAL INFORMATION PRESENTED SEPARATELY**
> **FROM THE AUDITED FINANCIAL STATEMENTS**
>
> **Independent Accountant's Report**
>
> We have reviewed the balance sheet, income statement, and statement of cash flows of ABC Company and consolidated subsidiaries as of September 30, 19X1, and for the three-month and nine-month periods then ended. These financial statements are the responsibility of the company's management.
>
> We conducted our review in accordance with standards established by the American Institute of Certified Public Accountants. A review of interim financial information consists principally of applying analytical procedures to financial data and making inquiries of persons responsible for financial and accounting matters. It is substantially less in scope than an audit conducted in accordance with generally accepted auditing standards, the objective of which is the expression of an opinion regarding the financial statements taken as a whole. Accordingly, we do not express such an opinion.
>
> Based on our review, we are not aware of any material modifications that should be made to the accompanying financial statements for them to be in conformity with generally accepted accounting principles.

Communication with Audit Committees. Recently, the accountant's responsibility for communication with Audit Committees about matters noted during an interim review has been expanded. According to *SAS No. 71*, the accountant should communicate the following matters to management:

1. Departures from GAAP.
2. Any irregularities or illegal acts discovered during the review, unless they are clearly inconsequential.
3. Any matters related to the organization's internal control (*e.g.*, significant deficiencies in the design or operation of the internal control) coming to the accountant's attention.

◻ Letters for Underwriters and Other Third Parties

Chapter 3 describes the often complex process through which companies register securities for sale to the public under the Securities Act of 1933 (1933 Act). In offerings of this type, one or more underwriting firms are involved in handling the sale of securities. The 1933 Act indicates that any individual involved in the registration process (including underwriters) can be held liable to purchasers of securities if material false statements or misleading omissions are contained in information filed with the SEC. As a result, underwriters request accountants to provide them with assurance that the information contained in any registration statements, prospectuses, or other materials is accurate and complete. While the SEC requires audited annual financial statements, other information (such as selected financial data and supplementary financial information) is also included in the registration documents. In meeting the SEC requirement that underwriters perform a "reasonable investigation" of information in the registration statements, underwriters engage accountants to provide assurance in the form of a letter addressed to the underwriter, or a **"comfort letter"**.

Under the requirements of *Statement on Auditing Standards Nos. 72 and 76*,[18] letters to underwriters normally address the following subjects:

1. The independence of the accountants.
2. An opinion on the conformity of the financial statements and schedules in the registration statement with accounting requirements of the 1933 Act.
3. Negative assurance regarding changes in selected financial statement items since the last financial statement date.
4. Negative assurance relating to any other information (unaudited financial statements, interim information, forecasts) included in the registration statement.

If the accountant provides negative assurance in a comfort letter on unaudited interim financial information, he or she should perform a review of that information in accordance with *SAS No. 71*. The auditor's comfort letter normally concludes with a paragraph that limits the use of the comfort letter to the underwriters to whom this letter is addressed.

In addition to providing letters to underwriters, accountants can also provide assurance for individuals involved in financing transactions (such as debt or equity offerings or exchanges and guarantees of debt or other securities). Although individuals involved in financing transactions normally require accountant assurance through audited financial statements, they may request the accountant to provide assurance on information other than that contained in the audited financial statements. This information includes: (1) unaudited condensed financial statements, (2) capsule financial information, (3) *pro forma* financial information, (4) financial forecasts, and (5) changes in specified financial statement line items. For the above information, the accountant should perform a review on the specific information and issue a report providing negative assurance (under the guidance of *SAS No. 71*).

◻ Condensed Financial Statements and Selected Financial Data

In some instances, companies wish to present their financial results to users in an abridged form; these may be condensed financial statements with a level of detail less than GAAP (for example, a balance sheet showing only total current assets, long-term assets, etc.) or selected financial data drawn from a financial statement (for example, a schedule of current liabilities). If the complete set of financial statements from which the condensed financial statements or selected financial data have been drawn were audited, an issue that arises in this situation is whether the auditor's report on the full set of financial statements can be presented along with the condensed financial statements or selected financial data. By presenting the auditor's report along with these abridged data, users may mistakenly believe that these data provide all necessary disclosures required under GAAP. Therefore, the client

---

[18] American Institute of Certified Public Accountants (AICPA), *Statement on Auditing Standards No. 72*, "Letters for Underwriters and Certain Other Requesting Parties" (New York: AICPA, 1993, AU 634); *Statement on Auditing Standards No. 76*, "Amendments to *Statement on Auditing Standards No. 72*, 'Letters for Underwriters and Other Requesting Parties'" (New York: AICPA, 1995, AU 634).

is not permitted to present the auditor's report on the full set of financial statements alongside the condensed financial statements or selected financial data.

The auditor can, however, issue a separate opinion on the condensed financial statements or selected financial data. Since the auditor has examined the company's financial statements, he or she merely needs to verify that the condensed financial statements or selected financial data are correctly derived from the audited financial statements. It is important to note that the auditor is limited to reporting on information derived from the audited financial statements; if any additional information is presented along with the condensed financial statements or selected financial data (such as number of employees or square footage statistics), the auditor's report should clearly identify the data which are being reported upon.

The auditor's report on condensed financial statements derived from the company's audited financial statements is shown below:[19]

SAMPLE AUDITOR'S REPORT

CONDENSED FINANCIAL STATEMENTS

We have audited, in accordance with generally accepted auditing standards, the consolidated balance sheet of Jerome Company and subsidiaries as of December 31, 19X0, and the related consolidated statements of income, retained earnings, and cash flows for the year then ended (not presented herein); and in our report dated February 15, 19X1, we expressed an unqualified opinion on those consolidated financial statements.

In our opinion, the information set forth in the accompanying condensed financial statements is fairly stated, in all material respects, in relation to the consolidated financial statements from which it has been derived.

Two major points should be emphasized with respect to the above report. First, the report indicates that the auditor has examined the full set of financial statements and notes the type of opinion issued on those financial statements. Second, the auditor does *not* conclude that the condensed financial statements are prepared according to GAAP; this would not be appropriate, since the level of detail presented in these statements is less than GAAP. Instead, the auditor's conclusion is that these statements are fairly presented based on the full set of financial statements. The auditor's report on selected financial data would be similar to that shown above.

---

[19] American Institute of Certified Public Accountants (AICPA), *Statement on Auditing Standards No. 42*, "Condensed Financial Statements and Selected Financial Data" (New York: AICPA, 1982, AU 552.06).

> **CHAPTER CHECKPOINTS**
>
> 18-19. How is the auditor's examination influenced when accounting principles generally accepted in another country require auditing procedures beyond U.S. GAAS?
>
> 18-20. Define interim financial information. In what ways is interim financial information presented by the client?
>
> 18-21. What is the auditor's responsibility for interim financial information presented in the footnotes accompanying the client's financial statements?
>
> 18-22. How does the auditor report on interim financial information presented in the footnotes accompanying the client's financial statements? How does the auditor report on interim financial information presented separately from the audited financial statements?
>
> 18-23. What is a comfort letter? What information is normally included in a comfort letter?
>
> 18-24. How does the auditor report on condensed financial statements and selected financial data derived from a company's audited financial statements?

◉ SUMMARY OF KEY POINTS

1. The auditor's opinion on the client's financial statements applies to the financial statements themselves as well as the footnotes accompanying the financial statements. However, a great deal of other information is normally presented along with the client's financial statements and footnotes to the financial statements. This information includes: (1) other information prepared by the client, (2) segment information, (3) supplementary information required by the FASB or GASB, and (4) information contained in an auditor-submitted document.

2. Generally, the auditor has less than full audit responsibility for this other information. The exception is segment information; for segment information, the auditor has full audit responsibility to determine whether segment information is presented in accordance with GAAP.

3. In reporting on other information, the auditor normally uses exception-based reporting. Under exception-based reporting, the auditor does not mention other information unless some problem or deficiency is noted with respect to this information. However, the auditor is required to explicitly report on all information contained in an auditor-submitted document.

4. As defined by *SAS No. 62*, the five major types of special reports are reports on: (1) financial statements prepared using a comprehensive basis of accounting other than GAAP; (2) specified elements, accounts, or items in financial statements; (3) company compliance with contractual or regulatory requirements; (4) financial presentations intended to comply with contractual or regulatory requirements; and (5) financial information presented in prescribed forms or schedules that require a prescribed form of auditor's report.

5. In a report on financial statements prepared on a comprehensive basis other than GAAP, the auditor should include an explanatory paragraph that: (1) states the basis on which the statements are presented, (2) refers to a financial statement footnote that indicates how the basis differs from GAAP, and (3) states that the statements are not intended to be in conformity with GAAP.

6. Two types of engagements may be performed on specific elements, accounts, or items in financial statements. The accountant can either perform an audit examination in accordance with GAAS or an agreed-upon procedures engagement. In an agreed-upon procedures engagement, the accountant performs certain procedures requested by third-party users with respect to elements, accounts, or items in financial statements.

7. Other types of reports issued in conjunction with audited financial statements include reports on: (1) financial statements prepared for use in other countries, (2) interim financial information presented in the footnotes accompanying the audited financial statements, (3) letters to underwriters and other third parties, and (4) condensed financial statements and selected financial data.

8. Auditors are required to review interim financial information presented in the footnotes accompanying the financial statements. Common review procedures applied to this information include inquiries of client personnel and analytical procedures. If the interim financial information is presented along with the audited financial statements, the auditor would use exception-based reporting and modify the report on the audited financial statements for any problems noted with the interim financial information. If interim financial information is presented separately from the audited financial statements, the auditor would issue a report providing limited assurance on the interim financial information.

◉ GLOSSARY

Agreed-Upon Procedures Engagement. Engagements performed by accountants to apply specific procedures requested by third parties. The distribution of the accountant's report in an agreed-upon procedures engagement is limited to those parties who participated in establishing the scope of the engagement.

Auditor-Submitted Documents. Situations where an auditor includes information prepared by him or her along with client-prepared financial statements and other information. In these cases, the auditor must explicitly indicate the responsibility assumed for all information submitted by him or her that accompanies the financial statements.

Comfort Letter. A communication issued from the auditor to the underwriter in conjunction with an offering of securities under the 1933 Act. This letter provides a statement that the accountant is independent, an opinion on the fairness of the client's financial statements, and negative assurance regarding other information presented along with the client's financial statements.

Comprehensive Basis Other than GAAP. According to SAS No. 62, the following are comprehensive bases other than GAAP that can be used: (1) a basis used to comply with governmental regulatory agencies, (2) the income tax basis, (3) the cash basis and slight modifications of this basis, and (4) any other basis having substantial support.

Condensed Financial Statements. Financial statements that are presented in less detail than required under GAAP. Auditors can issue an opinion as to whether these financial statements are fairly presented in relation to the full set of audited financial statements from which they were derived.

Exception-Based Reporting. A method of reporting used with other information accompanying the financial statements and footnotes that only modifies the auditor's report if problems are encountered in the presentation or examination of this other information.

Interim Financial Information. Financial information for a period of time less than a full year or financial information for a full year ending on a date other than the company's fiscal year-end. The auditor is required to perform certain limited review procedures on a client's interim financial information.

Limited (or Negative) Assurance. A type of assurance provided when an engagement less in scope than an audit is conducted. Limited assurance states that nothing came to the auditor's attention to indicate that a violation (or departure) from some criteria was observed.

Other Financial Information. Information provided by clients in their annual reports along with the financial statements. The auditor is responsible for reading this information to determine that it is consistent with the client's financial statements.

Piecemeal Opinion. The act of issuing a report on elements, accounts, or items of financial statements when an adverse or disclaimer of opinion is issued on the full set of financial statements.

Segment Information. Information provided about the operating activities of separate industries (or "lines of business") in which the client participates. This information must be audited, as it is considered an essential part of the financial statements and footnotes accompanying those financial statements. In addition, the auditor may modify his or her opinion on the financial statements if necessary segment information is misstated or omitted.

Selected Financial Data. Financial data representing a presentation of the financial condition, results of operations, and/or cash flows in less detail than required by GAAP. Auditors can issue an opinion as to whether selected financial data are fairly presented in relation to the full set of audited financial statements from which they were drawn.

Special-Purpose Financial Statements. Financial statements prepared to comply with contractual agreements or regulatory requirements that are different from GAAP.

Special Reports. *SAS No. 62* identifies five types of special reports: (1) reports on a comprehensive basis of accounting other than GAAP; (2) reports on elements, accounts, or items in a financial statement; (3) reports on compliance with contractual or regulatory requirements; (4) reports on financial presentations intended to comply with contractual or regulatory requirements (special-purpose financial statements); and (5) financial information presented in prescribed forms or schedules that require a prescribed form of auditor's report.

Supplementary Information. Information required by the FASB or GASB that is ordinarily outside of the footnotes accompanying the financial statements. The auditor is required to perform limited review procedures to determine whether this information is prepared, measured, and presented according to FASB or GASB guidelines.

◉ SUMMARY OF PROFESSIONAL PRONOUNCEMENTS

Statement on Auditing Standards No. 8, "Other Information in Documents Containing Audited Financial Statements" (New York: AICPA, 1976, AU 550).

Statement on Auditing Standards No. 21, "Segment Information" (New York: AICPA, 1977, AU 435).

Statement on Auditing Standards No. 29, "Reporting on Information Accompanying the Basic Financial Statements in Auditor-Submitted Documents" (New York: AICPA, 1980, AU 551).

Statement on Auditing Standards No. 42, "Condensed Financial Statements and Selected Financial Data" (New York: AICPA, 1982, AU 552.06).

Statement on Auditing Standards No. 51, "Reporting on Financial Statements Prepared for Use in Other Countries" (New York: AICPA, 1986, AU 534).

Statement on Auditing Standards No. 52, "Omnibus Statement on Auditing Standards—1987" (New York: AICPA, 1988, AU 558).

Statement on Auditing Standards No. 62, "Special Reports" (New York: AICPA, 1989, AU 623).

Statement on Auditing Standards No. 71, "Interim Financial Information" (New York: AICPA, 1992, AU 722).

Statement on Auditing Standards No. 72, "Letters for Underwriters and Certain Other Requesting Parties" (New York: AICPA, 1993, AU 634).

Statement on Auditing Standards No. 75, "Applying Agreed-Upon Procedures to Specific Elements, Accounts, or Items of a Financial Statement" (New York: AICPA, 1995, AU 622).

Statement on Auditing Standards No. 76, "Amendments to *Statement on Auditing Standards No. 72*, 'Letters for Underwriters and Other Requesting Parties'" (New York: AICPA, 1995, AU 634).

⬤ QUESTIONS AND PROBLEMS

18-25. Select the **best** answer for each of the following items:

1. Whenever special reports, filed on a printed form designed by authorities, call upon the independent auditor to make an assertion that the auditor believes is **not** justified, the auditor should:

   a. Submit a standard report with explanations.
   b. Reword the form or attach a separate report.
   c. Submit the form with questionable items clearly omitted.
   d. Withdraw from the engagement.

2. An auditor's report would be designated as a special report when it is issued in connection with which of the following?

   a. Financial statements for an interim period that are subjected to a limited review.
   b. Financial statements prepared in accordance with a comprehensive basis of accounting other than GAAP.
   c. Financial statements that purport to be in accordance with GAAP but do not include a presentation of the statement of cash flows.
   d. Financial statements that are unaudited and are prepared from a client's accounting records.

3. In an engagement to examine financial statements prepared under a comprehensive basis of accounting other than GAAP, the auditor should:

   a. Issue either a qualified or adverse opinion because the financial statements are not prepared according to GAAP.
   b. Not accept the engagement because any report on this type of engagement would mislead users.
   c. Issue an opinion on the financial statements that describes differences between the basis of accounting used and GAAP.
   d. Issue an opinion on the financial statements that refers to a footnote describing differences between the basis of accounting used and GAAP.

4. A report to apply agreed-upon procedures should provide a(n) _____ on the elements, accounts, or items subjected to procedures by the accountant:

   a. Opinion.
   b. Limited Assurance.
   c. Summary of findings.
   d. Positive and negative assurance.

5. Which of the following is **not** a requirement in order for the accountant to perform agreed-upon procedures on elements, accounts, or items in a financial statement?

   a. The accountant must audit the entire set of financial statements from which the elements, accounts, or items are drawn.
   b. The accountant must be independent with respect to the client.
   c. The third-party user must participate in determining and take responsibility for the scope of the engagement.
   d. The distribution of the accountant's report should be limited to third-party users who participated in establishing the scope of the engagement.

6. Which of the following best describes the audit and reporting responsibility for other information provided by the client with the audited financial statements?

	Audit Responsibility	Reporting Responsibility
a.	Full	Explicit
b.	Full	Exception
c.	Limited	Explicit
d.	Limited	Exception

7. If the auditor determines that supplementary information required by the Financial Accounting Standards Board (FASB) is not presented in accordance with FASB guidelines, the auditor should:

   a. Withdraw from the engagement unless the client corrects the presentation of the information.
   b. Add an explanatory paragraph to his or her audit report.
   c. Issue a qualified or adverse opinion on the client's financial statements, depending upon the severity of the departure.
   d. Extend the scope of his or her examination of the supplementary information.

8. The auditor's report on compliance on contractual agreements will:

   a. Express an opinion on compliance with contractual agreements, and can be issued regardless of whether the auditor examined the client's financial statements.
   b. Express an opinion on compliance with contractual agreements, and can only be issued if the auditor examined the client's financial statements.
   c. Provide negative assurance on compliance with contractual agreements, and can be issued regardless of whether the auditor examined the client's financial statements.
   d. Provide negative assurance on compliance with contractual agreements, and can only be issued if the auditor examined the financial statements.

9. The primary procedures performed by the auditor in a review of interim financial information include:

   a. Reading the interim financial information to determine that it is consistent with the audited financial statements.
   b. Full audit procedures in accordance with GAAS.
   c. Procedures agreed-upon by specified third-party users.
   d. Inquiries and analytical procedures applied to the interim financial information.

10. When an auditor is requested to examine specific items included in the client's financial statements, the auditor should:

   a. Not accept the engagement unless she or he has audited the complete set of financial statements.
   b. Not accept the engagement because users may misunderstand the nature of the accountant's responsibility.
   c. Accept the engagement, provided that the distribution of the report is limited to the company's management.
   d. Accept the engagement, provided that a special report is issued.
   e. None of the above.

11. A report on financial statements prepared on a comprehensive basis of accounting other than GAAP should include all of the following except:

   a. An indication of the financial statements examined by the auditor.
   b. An opinion as to the fairness of the financial statements based on the method of accounting used by the client.
   c. An opinion as to the appropriateness of the basis of accounting selected by the client.
   d. A statement that the financial statements are not prepared using GAAP.
   e. A reference to a financial statement footnote that describes the basis of accounting used by the client.

12. Which of the following best describes the audit and reporting responsibility for segment information presented by the client along with the financial statements?

	Audit Responsibility	Reporting Responsibility
a.	Full	Explicit
b.	Full	Exception
c.	Limited	Explicit
d.	Limited	Exception

13. Which of the following is ordinarily not addressed in a comfort letter?

   a. The adequacy of the client's internal control.
   b. The independence of the accountant.
   c. The fairness of the client's financial statements.
   d. Negative assurance regarding changes in selected financial statement items since the last balance-sheet date.

14. Comfort letters are normally addressed to:

   a. The underwriter of the company's securities.
   b. The president of a company.
   c. The company's Audit Committee.
   d. Lending institutions that provide financing to the company.
   e. The Securities and Exchange Commission.

15. For which of the following types of information, other than the financial statements, does the auditor have the greatest responsibility?

   a. Information contained in an auditor-submitted document
   b. Other information prepared by the client.
   c. Segment information presented with the financial statements.
   d. Supplemental information required by the Financial Accounting Standards Board.
   e. A summary of financial highlights accompanying the financial statements.

(Items 1 through 2 in 18-25; AICPA Adapted)

18-26. *Statements on Auditing Standards No. 62* identifies five basic types of special reports: (1) reports on a comprehensive basis of accounting other than GAAP; (2) reports on specified accounts, elements, or items; (3) reports on compliance with contractual agreements; (4) reports on financial presentations intended to comply with contractual or regulatory requirements; and (5) reports prepared on prescribed forms. For each type of report, indicate the following type of information:

   a. The item(s) (financial statements, accounts, etc.) that are reported upon.
   b. The extent of audit procedures applied to the item(s) in (a) above.
   c. The type of opinion or assurance provided in the accountant's report.

18-27. Rose & Co., CPAs, has satisfactorily completed the examination of the financial statements of Bale & Booster, a partnership, for the year ended December 31, 19X1. The financial statements, which were prepared on the entity's income tax basis, include footnotes that indicate the partnership was involved in continuing litigation of material amounts relating to alleged infringement of a competitor's patent. The amount of damages, if any, resulting from this litigation could not be determined at the time of completion of the engagement. The prior-years' financial statements were not presented.

Required:

Based upon the information presented, prepare an auditor's report that includes appropriate explanatory disclosure of significant facts.

(AICPA Adapted)

18-28. To obtain information that is necessary to make informed decisions, management often calls upon the independent auditor for assistance. This may involve a request that the independent auditor apply certain audit procedures to specific accounts of a company that is a candidate for acquisition and report upon the results. In such an engagement, the agreed-upon procedures may constitute a scope limitation.

At the completion of an engagement performed at the request of Uclean Corporation, which was limited in scope as explained above, the following report was prepared by an audit assistant and was submitted to the auditor for review:

> To: Board of Directors of Ajax Corporation
>
> We have applied certain agreed-upon procedures, as discussed below, to accounting records of Ajax Corporation, as of December 31, 19X1, solely to assist Uclean Corporation in connection with the proposed acquisition of Ajax Corporation.
>
> We have examined the cash in banks and accounts receivable of Ajax Corporation as of December 31, 19X1, in accordance with generally accepted auditing standards and, accordingly, included such tests of the accounting records and such other auditing procedures as we considered necessary in the circumstances.

In our opinion, the cash and receivables referred to above are fairly presented as of December 31, 19X1, in conformity with generally accepted accounting principles. We therefore recommend that Uclean Corporation acquire Ajax Corporation pursuant to the proposed agreement.

(Signature)

Required:

Comment on the proposed report, describing those assertions that are:

a. Incorrect or should otherwise be deleted.
b. Missing and should be inserted.

(AICPA Adapted)

18-29. Young and Young, CPAs, completed an examination of the financial statements of XYZ Company, Inc., for the year ended June 30, 19X1, and issued a standard unqualified auditor's report dated August 15, 19X1. At the time of the engagement, the Board of Directors of XYZ requested a special report attesting to the adequacy of the provision for federal and state income taxes and the related accruals and deferred income taxes as presented in the June 30, 19X1, financial statements.

Young and Young submitted the appropriate special report on August 22, 19X1.

Required:

Prepare the special report that Young and Young should have submitted to XYZ Company, Inc.

(AICPA Adapted)

18-30. On March 12, 19X2, Brown & Brown, CPAs, completed the audit engagement of the financial statements of Modern Museum, Inc., for the year ended December 31, 19X1. Modern Museum presents comparative financial statements on a modified cash basis. Assets, liabilities, fund balances, support, revenues, and expenses are recognized when cash is received or disbursed, except that Modern includes a provision for depreciation of buildings and equipment. Brown & Brown believes that Modem's three financial statements—prepared in accordance with a comprehensive basis of accounting other than generally accepted accounting principles—are adequate for Modern's needs and wishes to issue an auditor's special report on the financial statements. Brown & Brown has gathered sufficient, competent evidential matter in order to be satisfied that the financial statements are fairly presented according to the modified cash basis. Brown & Brown audited Modern's 19X0 financial statements and issued the auditor's special report expressing an unqualified opinion.

Required:

Draft the auditors' report to accompany Modem's comparative financial statements.

Learning Objectives

Study of this chapter is designed to achieve several learning objectives. After studying this chapter, you should be able to:

1. Describe general characteristics of examination engagements, review engagements, agreed-upon procedures engagements, and compilation engagements.
2. Define an attest engagement and identify the various types of attest engagements.
3. Describe various types of engagements performed on a company's prospective financial information.
4. Describe the types of engagements performed as a part of providing accounting and review services.
5. Discuss the contents of compilation and review reports on nonpublic companies' financial statements.

19

Other Accountant Engagements and Reports

The focus of the text to this point has been on audit examinations conducted in accordance with GAAS. For a number of years, GAAS were the only guidance provided to accountants for reporting on the fairness of the client's financial statements and other information. Within the last twenty years, the AICPA has expanded the formal guidance provided to accountants for performing other types of engagements related to a client's financial statements as well as other written assertions made by management. Four major classifications of engagements are: (1) examination engagements, (2) review engagements, (3) agreed-upon procedures engagements, and (4) compilation engagements.[1] While the exact nature of these engagements will differ depending upon the type of information evaluated by the accountant, some general characteristics of these engagements are summarized below.

Examinations are engagements providing the highest level of assurance to users about the written assertion(s) of another party. An important characteristic of an examination is that it allows the accountant to express an **opinion** as to the reliability of another party's written assertion(s). A GAAS audit is an example of an examination engagement for historical financial statements; in this instance, the financial statements prepared by management are the written assertion(s) examined by the accountant. While the exact nature of examination engagements will differ depending upon the information being examined by the accountant, these engagements are of a relatively extensive scope. Since the result of an examination engagement is an opinion on another party's written assertion, the accountant is required to be independent to perform an examination.

A **review engagement** is one in which the accountant performs limited procedures to provide some level of assurance concerning the reliability of another party's written assertions. This level of assurance is less than that provided by an examination; however, it may be of use to third parties in certain

---

[1] A fifth type of engagements (assembly of financial statements for internal use) has been proposed by the AICPA. This type of engagement is discussed later in this chapter.

instances. Common review procedures include inquiries of client personnel and analytical procedures. Because a review is narrower in scope than an examination, an opinion cannot be issued. Instead, the accountant provides **limited (or negative) assurance** on the written assertions. This limited assurance will indicate that the accountant is not aware of any material modifications that should be made for the information to be presented in conformity with established criteria. However, since the accountant is providing some level of assurance to users on another party's written assertion(s), he or she is required to be independent to perform a review engagement.

In some types of engagements, the accountant performs and reports on procedures specifically requested by the client and/or third parties. These engagements are referred to as **agreed-upon procedures engagements** and were originally introduced in Chapter 18. Agreed-upon procedures engagements are characterized by the following:

1. Specified users must participate in establishing the scope of the engagement and take responsibility for the sufficiency of the procedures performed by the accountant.
2. The procedures applied by the accountant should result in findings that are capable of reasonably consistent estimation or measurement.
3. Evidential matter related to the subject matter being evaluated is expected to exist and provide a reasonable basis for the accountant's findings.
4. Use of the accountant's report is limited to the specified users who participated in developing the scope of the engagement.

Like a review engagement, because an examination has not been performed, the accountant cannot issue an opinion on the results of the engagement. Instead, the accountant's report provides a summary of the accountant's procedures and findings. However, because the accountant is providing some form of assurance (in the form of findings), he or she is required to be independent.

The final type of engagement performed by accountants is referred to as a **compilation engagement**. A compilation requires the accountant to assemble (or assist the client in assembling) the financial statements or other written assertion(s). The accountant will ordinarily read the financial statements or other information to determine that no "obvious" misstatements exist; however, no other procedures are performed to verify the accuracy of this information. In compilation engagements, the accountant does not provide an opinion or any form of assurance on the financial statements or written assertion(s). Because no opinion or assurance is provided, the accountant is not required to be independent to perform a compilation.

In addition to the type of assurance provided by the accountant, these engagements also differ in terms of the permitted distribution of the accountant's report. Examination, review, and compilation engagements have a standard scope and a consistent level of accountant procedures across engagements. As a result, the distribution of the accountant's reports is these engagements is not limited. This is referred to as **general use** of the report. In contrast, since the scope of agreed-upon procedures engagements is determined by the client and/or third party, the distribution of the accountant's report should be limited to individuals who participated in determining the scope of the engagement. This is referred to as a **limited use** report.

The attributes of the four major types of engagements are summarized in Figure 19-1. Three points become evident upon evaluating Figure 19-1. First, only examination engagements allow the accountant to issue an opinion. Second, the report resulting from all engagements other than agreed-upon procedures engagements are available for general use. Finally, if any assurance is provided by the accountant, he or she must be independent of the client.

Type of Engagement	Scope	Assurance Provided	Independence Required?	Distribution of Report
Examination	Extensive procedures that are standard across engagements	Opinion	Yes	General Use
Review	Inquiries of client personnel and analytical procedures	Limited Assurance	Yes	General Use
Agreed-Upon Procedures	Procedures specified by clients and third-party users	Summary of findings	Yes	Limited Use
Compilation	Assembling or assisting the client in assembling information	No assurance	No	General Use

Figure 19-1: *Characteristics of Types of Accountant Engagements*

The above engagements are performed by accountants performing two primary types of services: attestation services and accounting and review services. These services are discussed in the remainder of this chapter.

CHAPTER CHECKPOINTS

19-1. Define the following types of engagements:
   a. Examination engagement.
   b. Review engagement.
   c. Agreed-upon procedures engagement.
   d. Compilation engagement.

19-2. For each of the engagements in 19-1, indicate: (a) the type of assurance provided by the accountant, (b) whether the accountant is required to maintain independence from the client, and (c) the allowable distribution of the accountant's report.

ATTESTATION SERVICES

In 1986, the AICPA issued a series of standards for reporting on attest engagements referred to as *Attestation Standards*.[2] These standards have been periodically updated by *Statements on Standards for Attestation Engagements* (*SSAEs*). The actual attestation standards are presented in the appendix to this chapter. These standards define an **attest engagement** as:

> ...one in which a practitioner is engaged to issue or does issue a written communication that expresses a conclusion about the reliability of a written assertion that is the responsibility of another party.[3]

The above definition illustrates two important characteristics of an attest engagement.

1. Attest engagements require practitioners (accountants) to issue a written conclusion.
2. The written conclusion issued by the accountant is related to the reliability of a written assertion of another party.

Thus, an audit examination is a type of attest engagement, since the accountant issues an opinion (written conclusion) on the fairness of the financial statements (written assertion) that are the responsibility of another party (the client's management).

SSAEs extended the ability of accountants to provide written conclusions on assertions other than the company's financial statements. To date, accountants have been provided with guidance for evaluating written assertions regarding a company's: (1) internal control, (2) compliance with specified requirements, (3) prospective financial information, and (4) *pro forma* financial information. These types of engagements are discussed in the remainder of this section.

REPORTING ON MANAGEMENT'S ASSERTION ABOUT INTERNAL CONTROL

In some cases, management may wish to issue a written statement about the effectiveness of its internal control. While the exact form of the statement may vary, management will generally want to indicate that the organization's internal control is either designed or operating effectively. As with financial statements, any written statement by management about its internal control is considered more reliable if it is verified (or examined) by an independent accountant. Since the accountant is reporting on a written assertion (or statement) of management, this type of engagement is considered an attest engagement.

---

[2] American Institute of Certified Public Accountants (AICPA), "Attestation Standards" (New York: AICPA, 1986, AT 100).

[3] American Institute of Certified Public Accountants, "Attestation Standards" (New York: AICPA, 1986, AT 100.01).

Statement on Standards for Attestation Engagements No. 2 (SSAE No. 2)[4] indicates that an accountant can be engaged to examine and report on management's written assertion about:

- The design and operating effectiveness of an organization's internal control.
- The design and operating effectiveness of a segment of an organization's internal control.
- The suitability of design of an organization's internal control.
- The design and operating effectiveness of an organization's internal control based on criteria established by a regulatory agency.

It is important to note that the accountant's opinion in these engagements is on management's *written assertion* about its internal control and not the internal control itself. For example, management may issue a written statement (or assertion) that "Alpha Company maintained an effective internal control over financial reporting as of December 31, 19X1" or "Alpha Company's internal control over financial reporting is sufficient to meet the stated objectives of internal control." Management's written assertion can be presented: (1) in a separate report that will accompany the accountant's report, or (2) in a representation letter to the accountant.

◘ Management's Assertion about the Effectiveness of the Organization's Internal Control

Accountants can examine and report on management's assertion about the effectiveness of an organization's internal control if:

1. Management accepts responsibility for the effectiveness of its internal control.
2. Management evaluates the effectiveness of its internal control using reasonable criteria established by a recognized body. These criteria are known as **control criteria**.
3. The accountant can obtain sufficient evidential matter to support management's assertion.
4. Management bases its written assertion upon the control criteria noted in (2) above.

In general, the accountant's procedures in an engagement to examine and report on management's assertion about the effectiveness of internal control parallel the procedures employed in a GAAS audit for obtaining an understanding of internal control. For example, the accountant is required to obtain an understanding of the client's internal control in both types of engagements. In addition, the accountant performs tests of controls to examine the operating effectiveness of the internal control. The primary difference between the procedures in an engagement to report on management's assertion about its internal control and a GAAS audit is in the extent of the procedures performed by the

---

[4] American Institute of Certified Public Accountants (AICPA), *Statement on Standards for Attestation Engagements No. 2*, "Reporting on an Entity's Internal Control Over Financial Reporting" (New York: AICPA, 1993, AT 400). *SSAE No. 2* was later amended by *Statement on Standards for Attestation Engagements No. 6*, "Reporting on an Entity's Internal Control Over Financial Reporting: An Amendment to *Statement on Standards for Attestation Engagements No. 2* (New York: AICPA, 1995, AT 600).

accountant. In general, the accountant's consideration of internal control in a GAAS audit is more limited than that when the accountant is reporting on management's assertion about the operating effectiveness of its internal control.[5]

When reporting on management's assertion about the operating effectiveness of its internal control, the accountant should also obtain written representations from the client's management. These representations should:

- ▶ Acknowledge management's responsibility for establishing and maintaining an effective internal control.

- ▶ State that management has evaluated the effectiveness of its internal control.

- ▶ State that management's assertion is based on the control criteria and identify the criteria used by management in evaluating its internal control.

- ▶ Indicate that all deficiencies in internal control have been disclosed to the accountant.

- ▶ Indicate whether any changes in internal control have occurred since the date of management's assertion.

---

[5] The actual extent of the accountant's tests will depend upon the engagement and assertion made by management. For example, the number of controls tested to evaluate management's assertion that "our overall internal control is effective" would be greater than that tested to evaluate management's assertion that "our internal control over mathematical verification of Sales Invoices is effective."

The accountant's report on management's assertion about the effectiveness of the organization's internal control over financial reporting is presented below.

SAMPLE ACCOUNTANT'S REPORT
MANAGEMENT'S ASSERTION ABOUT THE EFFECTIVENESS
OF INTERNAL CONTROL OVER FINANCIAL REPORTING

Independent Accountant's Report

We have examined management's assertion that Alpha Company maintained an effective internal control over financial reporting as of December 31, 19X1 included in the accompanying "Reporting Highlights of Alpha Company."

Our examination was made in accordance with standards established by the American Institute of Certified Public Accountants and, accordingly, included obtaining an understanding of the internal control over financial reporting, testing and evaluating the design and operating effectiveness of the internal control, and such other procedures as we considered necessary in the circumstances. We believe that our examination provides a reasonable basis for our opinion.

Because of inherent limitations in any internal control, errors or irregularities may occur and not be detected. Also, projections of any evaluation of the internal control over financial reporting to future periods are subject to the risk that the internal control may become inadequate because of changes in conditions, or that the degree of compliance with the policies and procedures may deteriorate.

In our opinion, management's assertion that Alpha Company maintained an effective internal control over financial reporting as of December 31, 19X1 is fairly stated, in all material respects, based upon the criteria identified by *Statement on Auditing Standards No. 55*.

The above report represents an unqualified opinion about management's assertion. This opinion indicates that management's assertion regarding its internal control is fairly stated. In cases where a material weakness in internal control is noted, the accountant should modify his or her report on internal control to describe any material weaknesses noted in the engagement. If management's assertion does not acknowledge these weaknesses, an adverse opinion should be issued by the accountant.

◘ Management's Assertion about the Effectiveness of a Segment of the Organization's Internal Control

The report shown in the preceding section is appropriate when the accountant examines management's assertion about the effectiveness of its overall internal control. In some cases, management's assertion (and the accountant's engagement) may be limited to a particular segment of internal control. For example, the accountant may be asked to report on management's assertion about the effectiveness of its internal control over accounts receivable transactions. If so, the accountant's examination (and resulting report) are limited to the segment represented by management's assertion.

◘ Management's Assertion about the Suitability of the Design of the Organization's Internal Control

Management's assertion may be limited to the design of its internal control. An example of such an assertion is "Alpha Company's internal control is suitably designed to prevent or detect material misstatements in the financial statements on a timely basis as of December 31, 19X1." In this instance, management is providing no assertion about the **operating effectiveness** of its internal control; it only indicates that its internal control is **suitably designed**.

When examining and reporting on the above assertion, the accountant limits his or her procedures to obtaining an understanding of the elements of the organization's internal control. Tests of the operating effectiveness of the internal control are not considered necessary, since management's assertion does not address the operating effectiveness of the internal control. Accordingly, the accountant's report on management's assertion will be modified to:

▶ Omit references to testing the operating effectiveness of the organization's internal control.

▶ Limit the auditor's opinion to the suitability of the design of the internal control.

◘ Management's Assertion Based on Criteria Specified by a Regulatory Agency

When the organization is subject to regulation or supervision by a governmental or other agency, the agency may require management to provide an assertion that its internal control meets certain criteria established by that agency. In this case, the accountant's report expresses an opinion on whether management's assertion is fairly stated. The only difference in this engagement and previous engagements is that the control criteria are established by a regulatory or governmental agency.

The fact that the criteria are established by a regulatory or governmental agency (and not by a general standards-setting body) introduces additional issues for the accountant and management. If the criteria established by the regulatory agency are subjected to due process, the accountant's report would be similar to that issued for management's assertion about the operating effectiveness of the organization's internal control. However, if these criteria are not subjected to due process, the distribution of the accountant's report should be limited to the management of the client and the regulatory agency whose criteria are examined.

> **CHAPTER CHECKPOINTS**
>
> **19-3.** Define an attest engagement. Other than an audit of the financial statements, what types of assertions have accountants been provided with guidelines for examining through attest engagements?
>
> **19-4.** What are the major types of attest engagements that can be performed related to management's assertion about its internal control?
>
> **19-5.** What criteria are necessary before accountants can examine and report on management's assertion about the effectiveness of its internal control?
>
> **19-6.** What representations should be obtained by the accountant when reporting on management's assertion about the effectiveness of its internal control?
>
> **19-7.** What are the primary contents of the accountant's report on an examination of management's assertion about the effectiveness of its internal control?
>
> **19-8.** What additional issues are introduced if the accountant is reporting on management's assertion about the effectiveness of its internal control if the control criteria are specified by a regulatory agency?

REPORTING ON MANAGEMENT'S ASSERTION ABOUT COMPLIANCE WITH SPECIFIED REQUIREMENTS

In some cases, an accountant may be engaged to report on management's assertion related to the organization's compliance with the requirements of specified laws, regulations, rules, contracts, or grants.[6] For example, management may wish to include a statement such as the following in its annual report to shareholders: "In conducting our operations during the past year, we were in compliance with federal regulations regarding safe environmental practices."

Clearly, such a statement would have more validity if it has been examined and reported upon by an independent accountant. The need for accountants to provide services of this nature was highlighted by the Federal Deposit Insurance Corporation Improvement Act of 1991. This act required that certain depository institutions engage auditors to examine the compliance with laws about the safety and soundness of their financial statements. To provide accountants with guidance in performing these

---

[6] It is important to note that CPAs can also perform engagements related to the effectiveness of the organization's internal control over compliance with the requirements of laws, regulations, rules, contracts, or grants. Because of the similarity of the two types of engagements and reports on these engagements, our discussion focuses on engagements related to compliance with the requirements of laws, regulations, rules, contracts, or grants. This type of engagement will be referred to as "compliance with specified requirements" throughout the remainder of this section.

and other types of engagements, the AICPA issued *Statement on Standards for Attestation Engagements No. 3*[7] (*SSAE No. 3*).

Prior to performing engagements related to management's assertion about the organization's compliance with specified requirements, three conditions must be met. The organization's management must accept responsibility for compliance with the specified requirements. That is, management must indicate (normally in the form of a written representation provided to the accountant) that it is responsible for any noncompliance with laws and regulations. Any known instances of noncompliance should be disclosed to the accountant in these written representations. Therefore, the accountant should be aware of any known instances where the organization has not complied with specified requirements.

In addition to accepting responsibility for compliance with specified requirements, management must periodically evaluate the organization's compliance with specified requirements. The degree of organization compliance with specified requirements normally serves as the basis for management's assertion (i.e., "X Company complied with the requirements of its debt obligations with Z Bank"). When evaluating the organization's degree of compliance with specified requirements, management should:

▶ Identify the applicable specified requirements.

▶ Establish and maintain an effective internal control over compliance with specified requirements.

▶ Evaluate and monitor the degree of compliance with specified requirements.

▶ Specify and prepare any reports that satisfy legal, regulatory, or contractual requirements.

Finally, management must use reasonable criteria in evaluating the degree of organization compliance with specified requirements. These criteria should be established by a recognized body or stated in the presentation of management's assertion. To illustrate, if the accountant is asked to evaluate management's assertion about the organization's compliance with environmental regulations, assertions such as "our operations did not harm the environment" normally are not considered to be reasonable and, therefore, capable of evaluation. In contrast, a statement such as "our operations were in compliance with section X of regulation X" are normally capable of being evaluated by the accountant.

The basic form of the accountant's report on management's assertion regarding compliance with specified requirements is similar to that on management's written assertion about its internal control discussed in the preceding section. *SSAE No. 3* identifies two types of engagements related to management's assertion about compliance with specified requirements: agreed-upon procedures engagements

---

[7] American Institute of Certified Public Accountants (AICPA), *Statement on Standards for Attestation Engagements No. 3*, "Compliance Attestation" (New York: AICPA, 1993, AT 500).

and examination engagements. The accountant's report in these engagements provides the following conclusions.

Agreed-Upon Procedures: Summary of procedures performed and findings.

Examination: Opinion on compliance with specified requirements.

CHAPTER CHECKPOINTS

19-9. What conditions must be met prior to performing engagements related to management's assertion about the organization's compliance with specified requirements?

19-10. What types of engagements may be performed on management's assertion about compliance with specified requirements? What type of assurance is provided in these engagements?

◉ PROSPECTIVE FINANCIAL INFORMATION

To this point, our discussion of accountant involvement with financial statements or other financial data has focused on historical financial statements or data. The distinguishing characteristic of historical financial information is that the transactions and events reflected in that information have *already occurred*. Thus, the accountant could provide some form of assurance about the fairness of those statements. Recently, third-party users have increasingly requested entities to provide them with forecasted (or future) financial statements or information (hereafter referred to as **prospective financial information**) to assist them in making their decisions. As with historical financial information, this information is the representation of management. The same conflict of interest that resulted in accountant involvement with historical financial information gradually resulted in user demand for accountant involvement with prospective financial information.

An obvious limitation of prospective financial information from the accountant's standpoint is that the events and transactions have *not yet occurred;* accordingly, accountants cannot provide an opinion or any form of assurance on this information. However, accountants can evaluate the assumptions used to prepare the prospective financial information and determine whether this information is reasonable, based on those assumptions. For a number of years, the AICPA Code of Ethics (the predecessor to the Code of Professional Conduct) strictly forbade any accountant involvement with forecasted financial statements. In 1985, the AICPA issued *Statement on Standards for Accountant's Service on Prospective Financial Information—Financial Forecasts and Projections.* This statement initially provided guidelines for accountant involvement with prospective financial information and was later incorporated into the *Statements on Standards for Attestation Standards.*

◻ Types of Prospective Financial Information

The AICPA distinguishes between two types of prospective financial information. A **financial forecast** is defined as an estimate of future financial results based on assumptions reflecting *expected* courses of action and *expected* conditions. Therefore, a forecast represents the most likely estimate of the company's future financial condition, results of operations, and cash flows.

In contrast, a **financial projection** presents prospective financial results based on the occurrence of *one or more hypothetical events or assumptions*. That is, a projection provides prospective information on a "what if?" basis. Examples of hypothetical assumptions that may form the basis for a projection include:

- expanding operations into different product markets or geographic regions
- discontinuing a segment or line of business
- purchasing additional production equipment

Information Provided as Prospective Financial Information

In some cases, companies may choose to present prospective financial information as a complete set of financial statements, along with any relevant footnote disclosures. However, prospective financial information may also be presented in a summarized or condensed form. In order to qualify for designation as prospective financial information, certain items must be presented. These items are often referred to as **minimum presentation guidelines** and include the following (see AT 200.67 for a complete listing):[8]

1. Sales or gross revenues.
2. Gross profit or cost of sales.
3. Income from continuing operations and net income.
4. Primary and fully diluted earnings per share.
5. A summary of significant assumptions.
6. Significant changes in financial position.

A **partial presentation** is any presentation of prospective financial information that is less comprehensive than the requirements of minimum presentation guidelines. For example, in certain cases, a lender may only request companies to provide them with an estimate of future periods' sales; this would be an example of a partial presentation.

Use of Prospective Financial Information

In certain instances, the use of prospective financial information may be limited. This limitation should be distinguished from limitations placed on the distribution of the accountant's report. In the former case, we are referring to the individual(s) to whom the company can present the prospective financial information for their use in decisions related to the company. Similar to the distribution of the

---

[8] American Institute of Certified Public Accountants (AICPA), *Statement on Standards for Attestation Engagements No. 1*, "Financial Forecasts and Projections" (New York: AICPA, 1985, AT 200.67).

accountant's report discussed earlier in this chapter, two categories of use have emerged: general use and limited use.

General use allows the company to provide its prospective financial information to any individuals who could use this information. These users include person(s) who are negotiating directly with the company as well as others. In contrast, **limited use** means that the prospective financial information can only be distributed to individual(s) who are negotiating directly with the company.

The use of prospective financial information in influenced by: (1) the type of presentation (forecast vs. projection), and (2) the amount of information provided (minimum presentation vs. partial presentation). Because financial forecasts provide a more likely depiction of the company's prospective financial information, financial forecasts are available for general use. Projections, on the other hand, are only appropriate for individuals who are negotiating directly with the company, since these users should be familiar with the hypothetical event(s) that serve as the basis for the projection. In addition, only prospective financial information that meets minimum presentation guidelines can be distributed for general use.

The types of prospective financial information that are available for general and limited use are summarized below.

	General Use	Limited Use
Type of Information	Financial Forecast	Financial Projection
Extent of Information Provided	Minimum Presentation	Partial Presentation

---

CHAPTER CHECKPOINTS

19-11. Define a financial forecast and a financial projection.

19-12. What information is required to be presented in order to meet minimum presentation guidelines for prospective financial information?

19-13. Distinguish between general use and limited use of prospective financial information.

19-14. What types of prospective financial information are available for general use? What types are available for limited use?

◻ Engagements Related to Prospective Financial Information

The three types of accountant engagements on prospective financial information are compilations, examinations, and agreed-upon procedures. These engagements are discussed in the remainder of this section.

Compilation Engagements. A compilation of prospective financial information is a professional service that involves presenting a client's prospective financial information in the form of financial statements. As with other compilation engagements, the procedures performed in the accountant's compilation do not permit him or her to express an opinion or any form of assurance on the fairness of the prospective financial information.

Appropriate compilation procedures for prospective financial information include: (1) inquiring about the accounting procedures used in the preparing the information, (2) determining how the responsible party identified key factors and developed the assumptions, and (3) testing the mathematical accuracy of the computations used to determine the prospective financial information. The form of the accountant's standard report on the compilation of a financial forecast is shown below[9]:

SAMPLE ACCOUNTANT'S REPORT

COMPILATION OF PROSPECTIVE FINANCIAL INFORMATION

We have compiled the accompanying forecasted balance sheet, statements of income, retained earnings, and cash flows of XYZ Company as of December 31, 19X0, and for the year then ending, in accordance with standards established by the American Institute of Certified Public Accountants.

A compilation is limited to presenting in the form of a forecast information that is the representation of management and does not include evaluation of the support for the assumptions underlying the forecast. We have not examined the forecast and, accordingly, do not express an opinion or any other form of assurance on the accompanying statements or assumptions. Furthermore, there will usually be differences between the forecasted and actual results, because events and circumstances frequently do not occur as expected, and those differences may be material. We have no responsibility to update this report for events and circumstances occurring after the date of this report.

The above report provides three general statements regarding the compilation engagement and the assurances that are provided by this type of engagement:

1. A compilation of prospective financial information was performed.
2. A brief definition of a compilation engagement.
3. A disclaimer of opinion or any form of assurance on the compiled financial information.

---

[9] American Institute of Certified Public Accountants (AICPA), *Statement on Standards for Attestation Engagements No. 1*, "Financial Forecasts and Projections" (New York: AICPA, 1985, AT 200.17).

In addition to the standard information regarding the compilation engagement, the accountant's report provides two additional statements unique to prospective financial information.

1. Differences may occur between forecasted and actual results.
2. The accountant does not assume any responsibility to update his or her report for future events and circumstances.

When prospective financial information is presented in the form of a projection, a separate paragraph that describes the limitation on the usefulness of the presentation is included. In addition, reference should be made to the hypothetical assumptions made in developing the prospective financial information. This paragraph is placed between the first and second paragraphs of the above compilation report and is presented below.

SAMPLE EXPLANATORY PARAGRAPH

LIMITATION ON USE OF A FINANCIAL PROJECTION

The accompanying projection and this report were prepared for Third National Bank for the purposes of negotiating a loan to expand XYZ Company's plant and should not be used for any other purpose.

Examination Engagements. An examination of prospective financial information involves the following procedures:

1. Evaluating the preparation of the prospective financial information.
2. Evaluating the support underlying the assumptions used to prepare the prospective financial information.
3. Considering whether the prospective financial information is presented in conformity with AICPA presentation guidelines.

The standard report for an examination of a financial forecast is shown below:[10]

SAMPLE ACCOUNTANT'S REPORT
EXAMINATION OF PROSPECTIVE
FINANCIAL INFORMATION

We have examined the accompanying forecasted balance sheet, statements of income, retained earnings, and cash flows of XYZ Company as of December 31, 19X0, and for the year then ending. Our examination was made in accordance with standards for an examination of a forecast established by the American Institute of Certified Public Accountants and, accordingly, included such procedures as we considered necessary to evaluate both the assumptions used by management and the preparation and presentation of the forecast.

In our opinion, the accompanying forecast is presented in conformity with guidelines for presentation of a forecast established by the American Institute of Certified Public Accountants, and the underlying assumptions provide a reasonable basis for management's forecast. However, there will usually be differences between the forecasted and actual results, because events and circumstances frequently do not occur as expected, and those differences may be material. We have no responsibility to update this report for events and circumstances occurring after the date of this report.

Several important features of the above report should be mentioned. First, note that the report indicates an examination engagement has been performed and provides a brief description of an examination engagement. Second, note that the accountant expresses an opinion in an examination of prospective financial information. It is important to note that the accountant is *not* issuing an opinion on the fairness of the prospective financial information. Such an opinion would be inappropriate, since the underlying transactions and events have not occurred. Instead, the accountant provides an opinion on whether the:

1. Prospective financial information is presented in conformity with AICPA presentation guidelines.
2. Assumptions used to prepare the prospective financial information are reasonable.

Finally, note that the final paragraph of the report discusses the same limitations related to prospective financial information as the compilation report. That is: (1) differences may occur between forecasted and actual results, and (2) the accountant does not assume any responsibility to update his or her report for future events and circumstances.

If the accountant reports on the examination of a financial projection, he or she will express an opinion as to whether the hypothetical assumptions provide a reasonable basis for the projection. In addition, this report should include a separate paragraph (similar to that included in the compilation report) that describes the limitations on the usefulness of the presentation.

---

[10] American Institute of Certified Public Accountants (AICPA), *Statement on Standards for Attestation Engagements No. 1*, "Financial Forecasts and Projections" (New York: AICPA, 1985, AT 200.32).

Agreed-Upon Procedures Engagements. The final type of engagement related to prospective financial statements involves applying procedures requested by specific users to prospective financial information. As with other agreed-upon procedures engagements, for the accountant to perform this type of engagement, the specified users should participate in establishing the nature and scope of the engagement (i.e., the procedures to be applied by the accountant). The accountant is not required to perform any minimum level of procedures; however, the specified users of the report must be satisfied as to the adequacy of these procedures.

The accountant's report on applying agreed-upon procedures is not presented, but it is similar in nature to the report required by *SAS No. 75*[11] for applying agreed-upon procedures to elements, accounts, and items in historical financial statements (see Chapter 18). *Statement on Standards for Attestation Engagements No. 4 (SSAE No. 4)*[12] indicates that the accountant's report should include:

1. A listing of the procedures actually performed by the accountant.
2. A disclaimer concerning whether the prospective financial information is presented in conformity with AICPA guidelines.
3. A summary of findings regarding the items examined.
4. A statement that actual results may differ from forecasted results.
5. A statement that the accountant has no update responsibility for events after the date of the report.
6. A statement limiting distribution of the report to users who participated in determining the scope of the engagement.

◉ *PRO FORMA* FINANCIAL INFORMATION

A final type of written assertion that can be the subject of an accountant engagement is *pro forma* financial information. *SSAE No. 1*[13] defines ***pro forma* financial information** as a summary of the client's historical financial information adjusted to reflect either: (1) a proposed transaction or event, or (2) the occurrence of an actual transaction or event at an earlier date. Transactions or events that serve as the basis for preparing *pro forma* financial information are:

▶ Business combinations.
▶ Changes in capitalization.
▶ Disposals of a significant portion or line of a business.

---

[11] American Institute of Certified Public Accountants (AICPA), *Statement on Auditing Standards No. 75*, "Engagements to Apply Agreed-Upon Procedures to Specified Elements, Accounts, or Items of a Financial Statement" (New York: AICPA, 1995, AU 622).

[12] American Institute of Certified Public Accountants (AICPA), *Statements on Standards for Attestation Engagements No. 4*, "Agreed-Upon Procedures Engagements" (New York: AICPA, 1995, AT 600).

[13] American Institute of Certified Public Accountants (AICPA), *Statements on Standards for Attestation Engagements No. 1*, "Reporting on Pro Forma Financial Information" (New York: AICPA, 1988, AT 300).

- ▶ Changes in the form of business organization.
- ▶ Proposed sale of securities and use of the proceeds.

Essentially, the process of preparing *pro forma* financial information is as follows:

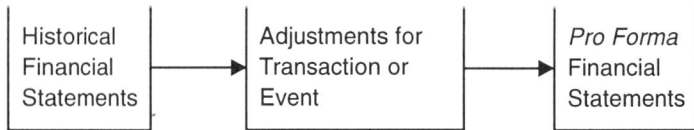

It is important to distinguish between *pro forma* financial information and prospective financial information. Unlike prospective financial information, *pro forma* financial information does not entirely reflect future conditions or events. Instead, this information represents historical financial information adjusted to reflect a single (or a few) transactions or events. In some cases, *pro forma* financial information adjusts earlier historical financial information for the effect(s) of a transaction that actually occurred at a later date.

In order to report on *pro forma* financial information, the document containing the *pro forma* information must also include (or incorporate by reference) the historical financial statements of the entity. In cases where the *pro forma* financial information is prepared to reflect the effect(s) of a business combination, the historical information of all entities involved in the business combination (known as **constituent groups**) must be presented or referenced. In addition, the historical financial statements that serve as the basis for the *pro forma* financial information must have been audited or reviewed, with the accountant's report included or incorporated by reference. Finally, if the *pro forma* financial information is based on a business combination, the accountant should have knowledge of the accounting and reporting practices of each constituent group.

Accountants can either examine or review *pro forma* financial information. The accountant's report on *pro forma* financial information will express an opinion (examination engagement) or limited assurance (review engagement) on whether:

1. Management's assumptions provide a reasonable basis for presenting the effect(s) of the underlying transaction or event.
2. The *pro forma* adjustments made to the historical financial statements are consistent with management's assumptions.
3. The *pro forma* amounts reflect the proper adjustments made to the historical financial statements.

A sample report of an accountant's examination of *pro forma* financial information reflecting the acquisition of a new entity is shown below.[14]

SAMPLE ACCOUNTANT'S REPORT

**EXAMINATION OF *PRO FORMA*
FINANCIAL INFORMATION**

We have examined the *pro forma* adjustments reflecting the acquisition transaction described in Note 1 and the application of those adjustments to the historical amounts in the accompanying *pro forma* balance sheet of X Company as of December 31, 19X1, and the *pro forma* condensed statement of income for the year then ended. The historical condensed financial statements are derived from the historical financial statements of X Company, which were audited by us, and of Y Company, which were audited by other accountants whose report is presented herein. Such *pro forma* adjustments are based on management's assumptions described in Note 2. Our examination was made in accordance with standards established by the American Institute of Certified Public Accountants and, accordingly, included such procedures as we considered necessary in the circumstances.

The objective of this *pro forma* financial information is to show what the significant effects on the historical financial information might have been had the acquisition occurred at an earlier date. However, the *pro forma* condensed financial statements are not necessarily indicative of the results of operations or related effects on financial position that would have been attained had the above-mentioned acquisition actually occurred earlier.

In our opinion, management's assumptions provide a reasonable basis for presenting the significant effects directly attributable to the above-mentioned acquisition described in Note 1, the related *pro forma* adjustments give appropriate effect to those assumptions, and the *pro forma* column reflects the proper application of those adjustments to the historical financial statement amounts in the *pro forma* condensed balance sheet as of December 31, 19X1, and the *pro forma* condensed statement of income for the year then ended.

---

[14] American Institute of Certified Public Accountants (AICPA), *Statements on Standards for Attestation Engagements No. 1*, "Reporting on Pro Forma Financial Information" (New York: AICPA, 1988, AT 300.16).

> **CHAPTER CHECKPOINTS**
>
> **19-15.** What are three types of engagements that can be performed on prospective financial information?
>
> **19-16.** What procedures are ordinarily performed in a compilation of prospective financial information?
>
> **19-17.** What are the major statements in the accountant's report on a compilation of prospective financial information? What type of assurance does the accountant provide in this type of engagement?
>
> **19-18.** What are the major procedures performed in an examination of prospective financial information? What are the contents of the accountant's report in this type of engagement?
>
> **19-19.** How is an accountant's report on a compilation or examination of prospective financial information affected if the information is a financial projection and not a financial forecast?
>
> **19-20.** What are the major contents in the accountant's report in an agreed-upon procedures engagement for prospective financial information?
>
> **19-21.** What are *pro forma* financial statements? What types of engagements can be performed on *pro forma* financial statements?
>
> **19-22.** On what matters should accountants express an opinion or provide assurance on *pro forma* financial statements?

ACCOUNTING AND REVIEW SERVICES

To this point, the discussion in this text regarding accounting services for historical financial statements has focused on services performed by accountants for public companies and the reports associated with those services. A distinguishing feature of a public company is that it is required to have its annual financial statements audited by an independent accountant. No such requirement exists for nonpublic companies. *Statement on Standards for Accounting and Review Services No. 2 (SSARS No. 2)*[15] 16 defines a nonpublic company as any company or subsidiary of a company:

---

[15] American Institute of Certified Public Accountants (AICPA), *Statement on Standards for Accounting and Review Services No. 2*, "Reporting on Comparative Financial Statements" (New York: AICPA, 1979, AR 200).

- With securities that are *not* traded in a public market (either on a stock exchange or over-the-counter) or
- Which does *not* make a filing with a regulatory agency to sell its securities in a public market.

Although no audit requirement currently exists for nonpublic companies, potential creditors and investors are often interested in obtaining assurance from an independent third party regarding the fairness of these companies' financial statements. Thus, nonpublic companies may undergo audit examinations similar to those discussed throughout this text. However, in certain cases, third parties are willing to accept a lower level of assurance than that provided by an audit, primarily because of the higher cost of an audit examination. In addition, some nonpublic companies may only require assistance in preparing their financial statements and do not desire any accountant assurance on these statements. Services of this nature provided for nonpublic companies are often referred to as **limited assurance engagements** because they provide a lesser amount of assurance than that provided by an audit engagement. The guidelines for these engagements are provided by the issuance of *Statements on Standards for Accounting and Review Services* (or *SSARS*).

It is important to emphasize that these engagements are not alternatives to an audit examination for public companies. Recall that public companies are required to have an audit engagement conducted in accordance with GAAS. However, for nonpublic companies, the lack of an audit requirement allows limited assurance engagements to be performed as alternatives to audit examinations. In practice, the preferences of third parties will normally dictate the type of engagement performed for nonpublic companies.

Three services discussed in this section are: (1) assemblies of financial statements for internal use, (2) compilations, and (3) reviews.

▢ Assembly of Financial Statement for Internal Use[16]

An assembly of financial statements is defined as:

> Providing various manual or automated bookkeeping or data processing services the output of which is in the form of financial statements intended for internal use only. The function of assembling financial statements may include preparing a working trial balance, assisting in adjusting the books of account, and consulting on accounting matters. Assembly does not refer to the mere typing or reproduction of client-prepared financial statements.[17]

This definition reveals the distinguishing feature of this engagement: the financial statements are intended only for use within the organization requesting the accountant's service.

When performing an assembly of financial statements, the accountant should obtain a written understanding with the client (in the form of an engagement letter) that the financial statements are

---

[16] Currently, the guidance for these types of engagements is in proposed form. This section is based on the AICPA's Exposure Draft "Assembly of Financial Statements for Internal Use Only" (September 6, 1995).

[17] American Institute of Certified Public Accountants (AICPA), *Proposed Statement on Standards for Accounting and Review Services*, "Assembly of Financial Statements for Internal Use Only" (New York: AICPA, September 6, 1995).

to be used for internal purposes only. In addition, the accountant may wish to include a reference on each page of the financial statements to limit the use of these financial statements, such as "Restricted to Internal Use Only—See Engagement Letter Dated November 10, 19X2."

Because the financial statements are intended only for internal use, the accountant will not prepare a report for third parties. However, in order to prevent any misunderstandings regarding the accountant's engagement or assurance, a transmittal letter may be included along with the financial statements. A sample of the form of this transmittal letter is shown below:[18]

SAMPLE ACCOUNTANT'S TRANSMITTAL LETTER

FINANCIAL STATEMENTS ASSEMBLED

FOR INTERNAL USE ONLY

To: Art Vandalay, President of Vandalay Industries

Enclosed are financial statements for Vandalay Industries as of December 31, 19X2. These statements have been assembled for internal use only, pursuant to the terms of our engagement letter dated November 10, 19X2 to provide accounting services.

Please call us at your convenience to discuss any questions or comments you may have.

While the above letter clearly limits the use of the financial statements to internal purposes, situations may arise where the accountant becomes aware that these financial statements have been distributed to third parties. If so, the accountant should advise the client and/or notify third-party users about the limitations of the accountant's involvement and assurance with respect to these financial statements.

◻ Compilation Engagements

Statement on Standards for Accounting and Review Services No. 1 (SSARS No. 1) defines a compilation as:

Presenting in the form of financial statements information that is the representation of management (owners) without undertaking to express any assurance on the statements.[19]

Therefore, in a compilation, the accountant assembles (or assists the entity in assembling) financial statements. In its simplest form, consider a compilation as an engagement where the company's management provides the accountant with account balances and asks the accountant to prepare

---

[18] American Institute of Certified Public Accountants (AICPA), *Proposed Statement on Standards for Accounting and Review Services*, "Assembly of Financial Statements for Internal Use Only" (New York: AICPA, September 6, 1995).

[19] American Institute of Certified Public Accountants, *Statement on Standards for Accounting and Review Services No. 1*, "Compilation and Review of Financial Statements" (New York: AICPA, 1978, AR 100.04).

financial statements from these balances. As noted at the beginning of this chapter, no assurance is provided in a compilation; as a result, the accountant does not need to be independent with respect to the company in order to perform a compilation engagement.

Compilation Procedures. At first glance, a compilation may seem to mirror an assembly engagement. However, it is important to note that the financial statements resulting from a compilation will be used by external parties. As a result, the accountant is required to perform additional procedures beyond assembling the financial statements (as is done in an assembly engagement). These procedures include:

1. Obtaining knowledge about the accounting principles and practices in the client's industry.
2. Obtaining knowledge and an understanding of the nature of the client's business transactions, form of its accounting records, the accounting basis on which the statements are to be presented, and the form and content of the financial statements.
3. Assembling, or assisting the client in assembling, the financial statements.
4. Reading the compiled financial statements to determine that they are in the appropriate form and are free from obvious material errors.

A few points should be discussed regarding the above procedures. First, and most obvious, note that the accountant does not make inquiries or perform other procedures to corroborate or verify any of the information presented in the company's financial statements. As a result, the accountant cannot issue an opinion or provide any other form of assurance regarding the compiled financial statements. Also, the accountant does not need to possess knowledge of the client's industry or business prior to beginning the compilation engagement. Such knowledge can be obtained during the engagement, through reference to AICPA industry guides and publications, financial statements of other entities in the client's industry, and other individuals possessing industry expertise.

Compilation Reports. The report prepared by an accountant to accompany compiled financial statements is presented below. This report should be dated as of the completion of the compilation engagement. In addition, each page of the financial statements should be marked "See Accountant's Compilation Report" to remind the readers that these statements were compiled and not audited or reviewed.[20]

---

[20] American Institute of Certified Public Accountants, *Statement on Standards for Accounting and Review Services No. 1*, "Compilation and Review of Financial Statements" (New York: AICPA, 1978, AR 100.17).

> **SAMPLE ACCOUNTANT'S REPORT**
> **COMPILATION OF HISTORICAL**
> **FINANCIAL STATEMENTS**
>
> I (we) have compiled the accompanying balance sheet of XYZ Company as of December 31, 19X1, and the related statement of income, retained earnings, and cash flows for the year then ended in accordance with Statements on Standards for Accounting and Review Services issued by the American Institute of Certified Public Accountants.
>
> A compilation is limited to presenting in the form of financial statements information that is the representation of management (owners). I (we) have not audited or reviewed the accompanying financial statements and, accordingly, do not express an opinion or any other form of assurance on them.

Similar to the compilation report on prospective financial statements (see the previous section), the accountant's compilation report on historical financial statements addresses the following three major issues:

1. A compilation engagement was performed (in accordance with *SSARS*).
2. A description of a compilation engagement.
3. A disclaimer of opinion or assurance on the compiled financial statements.

Financial Statements that Omit Substantially all Disclosures. A special form of compilation is an engagement in which the accountant is asked to compile financial statements that omit substantially all disclosures required by GAAP. The omitted disclosures can include both supplemental disclosures as well as information that appears in the body of the financial statements. Thus, in this type of engagement, the accountant is compiling financial information that does not represent a complete set of financial statements. An example would be compiling an income statement (without the remaining financial statements or corresponding footnote disclosures) for a nonpublic company.

The accountant is not precluded from accepting such an engagement, provided that she or he does not believe that disclosures have intentionally been omitted by management to mislead financial statement users. The following paragraph would be added to the accountant's standard compilation report in such an engagement. Note that this paragraph: (1) informs users that substantially all disclosures required by GAAP are omitted, and (2) warns users that the compiled financial statements may not be appropriate for use unless the users are informed about the omitted disclosures.[21]

---

[21] American Institute of Certified Public Accountants, *Statement on Standards for Accounting and Review Services No. 1*, "Compilation and Review of Financial Statements" (New York: AICPA, 1978, AR 100.21).

> **SAMPLE EXPLANATORY PARAGRAPH**
>
> **COMPILATION OF FINANCIAL STATEMENTS THAT OMIT SUBSTANTIALLY ALL DISCLOSURES**
>
> Management has elected to omit substantially all of the disclosures required by generally accepted accounting principles. If the omitted disclosures were included in the financial statements, they might influence the user's conclusions about the company's financial position, results of operations, and cash flows. Accordingly, these financial statements are not designed for those who are not informed about such matters.

Lack of Independence. Because the accountant is not issuing an opinion or providing any form of assurance on the entity's financial statements in a compilation, he or she is not required to be independent with respect to the client. However, in cases where the accountant is not independent, the compilation report should be modified to disclose this lack of independence. The reason for the lack of independence is *not* disclosed. SSARS No. 1 (AU 100) suggests the following statement: "I am (we are) not independent with respect to XYZ Company."

Departures from GAAP. In some instances, the accountant's limited procedures may reveal that the financial statements contain a departure from GAAP. If so, the standard compilation report should be modified to add a separate paragraph describing the departure and its financial statement effect(s), if known. Because a compilation only requires the auditor to present information provided by management, the auditor may not be able to determine the financial statement effect(s) of GAAP departures. In this case, the accountant's report should indicate that such a determination has not been made.

Reports on Financial Statements in Prescribed Forms. Similar to our discussion about audited financial statements presented in prescribed forms (see Chapter 18), some nonpublic companies may need to provide information to others (industry trade associations, credit agencies, banks, and other regulatory bodies) in certain formats. SSARS No. 3[22] notes that problems arise for the accountant when this format specifies an accounting treatment or measurement principle that is not in conformity with GAAP.

Although this is technically a GAAP departure, it is assumed that the party requesting the financial information is aware of differences between their accounting requirements and GAAP. In these situations, the accountant adds a paragraph to the standard compilation report that indicates: (1) the financial statements are presented in accordance with the requirements of a given party, (2) the requirements of this party differ from GAAP, and (3) the financial statements are not designed for individuals not aware of differences between the party's accounting requirements and GAAP.

---

[22] American Institute of Certified Public Accountants (AICPA), *Statement on Standards for Accounting and Review Services No. 3*, "Compilation Reports on Financial Statements included in Certain Prescribed Forms" (New York: AICPA, 1981, AR 300).

> **CHAPTER CHECKPOINTS**
>
> **19-23.** Describe an engagement to assemble financial statements for internal use. What type of communication is ordinarily issued by the accountant in this type of engagement?
>
> **19-24.** Define a compilation. What are the primary types of compilation procedures performed by the accountant?
>
> **19-25.** List the major contents of the accountant's standard compilation report.
>
> **19-26.** Are accountants permitted to compile financial statements that omit "substantially all disclosures"? What special precautions must be taken in this type of engagement?

◻ Review Engagements

A review of unaudited financial statements is similar in nature to the review of interim financial information for public companies discussed in Chapter 18. Like a compilation, the accountant should possess a level of understanding of the accounting principles and practices in the client's industry. In addition, the accountant should have an understanding of the client's business and the nature of the client's transactions. However, in a review of unaudited financial statements, the accountant is attempting to provide limited assurance about the fairness of the company's financial statements. Two procedures performed by the accountant in a review engagement beyond those required in a compilation are inquiries of client personnel and analytical procedures. The subjects of inquiries normally made in a review engagement include:

1. The client's accounting principles and practices.
2. The client's procedures for recording, classifying, and summarizing transactions and accumulating information for disclosure in the financial statements.
3. Actions taken at meetings of stockholders and Board of Directors that may affect the financial statements.
4. Whether the statements are prepared in conformity with GAAP and whether any subsequent events may materially affect the financial statements.

The inquiries made to client personnel involving accounting principles and the client's recording of transactions (items 1 and 2 above) will vary, depending on the account(s) involved. Figure 19-2 illustrates sample inquiries for the cash, accounts receivable, and inventory accounts that may be appropriate in a review engagement. *SSARS No. 7*[23] requires the accountant to obtain written representations to confirm any information received during inquiries of client personnel.

---

[23] American Institute of Certified Public Accountants (AICPA), *Statement on Standards for Accounting and Review Services No. 7*, "Omnibus SSARS—1992" (New York: AICPA, 1992).

Cash

- Have bank balances been reconciled with book balances?
- Are there any restrictions on the availability of cash balances?
- Has a proper cutoff of cash transactions been made?

Accounts Receivable

- Has an adequate allowance been made for doubtful accounts?
- Have receivables considered to be uncollectible been written off?
- Are there any receivables from employees and related parties?

Inventories

- Have inventories been physically counted?
- If physical inventories are taken at a date other than the balance-sheet date, what procedures were used to record changes in inventory between the physical inventory date and the balance-sheet date?
- What is the basis of inventory valuation?
- Have write-downs for obsolescence or cost in excess of net realizable value been made?

Source: American Institute of Certified Public Accountants (AICPA), *Statement on Standards for Accounting and Review Services No. 1*, "Compilation and Review of Financial Statements" (New York AICPA, 1978, AR 100.52).

Figure 19-2: *Sample Inquiries Made in a Review Engagement*

In addition to inquiries, the auditor performs analytical procedures involving the client's financial information. These analytical procedures will normally consist of comparing components of the financial statements with: (1) the components of the financial statements for comparable prior period(s); and (2) anticipated results, such as budgets and forecasts. Also, the accountant may examine relationships among financial statement elements (for example, the relationship between sales and accounts receivable).

Reports on Reviewed Financial Statements. Upon completion of the above procedures, the accountant prepares a review report similar in nature to that prepared for a review of interim information of public companies. Similar to the compilation report, *SSARS No. 1* notes that the financial statements should be accompanied by a report that is dated as of the completion of the accountant's inquiry and analytical procedures. In addition, each page of the financial statements should include a notation such as "See Accountant's Review Report." The following standard report is suggested by SSARS No. 1:[24]

SAMPLE ACCOUNTANT'S REPORT

REVIEW OF HISTORICAL FINANCIAL STATEMENTS

I (we) have reviewed the accompanying balance sheet of XYZ Company as of December 31, 19X1, and the related statements of income, retained earnings, and cash flows for the year then ended, in accordance with Statements on Standards for Accounting and Review Services issued by the American Institute of Certified Public Accountants. All information included in these financial statements is the representation of the management (owners) of XYZ Company.

A review consists principally of inquires of company personnel and analytical procedures applied to financial data. It is substantially less in scope than an examination in accordance with generally accepted auditing standards, the objective of which is the expression of an opinion regarding the financial statements taken as a whole. Accordingly, I (we) do not express such an opinion.

Based on my (our) review, I am (we are) not aware of any material modifications that should be made to the accompanying financial statements in order for them to be in conformity with generally accepted accounting principles.

The above report includes the following major statements:

1. A statement that a review engagement was performed in accordance with SSARS.
2. A brief description of a review engagement.
3. A disclaimer of opinion.
4. An indication of limited assurance.

Note that the final paragraph of the accountant's review report indicates that "we are not aware of any material modifications that should be made ... for them to be in conformity with GAAP." As discussed earlier, this is a statement of **limited (or negative) assurance**. Contrast this statement to an opinion on financial statements that indicates that "the financial statements ... present fairly ... in conformity with GAAP." Clearly, a statement of limited assurance is not as strong as an opinion on financial statements, which can only be issued as a result of a GAAS audit.

Independence. Although limited assurance is clearly a lower level of assurance than an opinion, the accountant is still providing some small level of assurance on the entity's financial statements. Accordingly, the accountant must be independent when performing a review engagement. Recall that,

---

[24] American Institute of Certified Public Accountants, *Statement on Standards for Accounting and Review Services No. 1*, "Compilation and Review of Financial Statements" (New York: AICPA, 1978, AR 100.35).

because a compilation did not provide either an opinion or limited assurance on the client's financial statements, no independence requirement existed for this engagement.

Departures from GAAP. As with a compilation, the accountant's report should be modified when a departure from GAAP is noted. The report would be modified by adding a paragraph to the standard review report illustrated above. This paragraph should indicate the nature of the departure from GAAP.

CHAPTER CHECKPOINTS

19-27. What procedures are ordinarily performed in a review engagement?

19-28. List the major contents of the accountant's standard review report.

19-29. How is the accountant's report in a review engagement modified if a departure from GAAP is noted?

◻ Comparative Reporting Involving Accounting and Review Services

In Chapter 17, the auditor's responsibility for examining and reporting on comparative financial statements was discussed. Because users may assume that all information has been examined by the auditor, an opinion (or disclaimer of opinion) on the financial statements of all comparative periods presented is required. The same basic rationale exists when an accountant provides accounting and review services for nonpublic companies. That is, if the accountant issues a review report on the 19X3 financial statements but has not reviewed nor compiled the 19X1 and 19X2 statements presented in comparative form with the 19X3 statements, readers may incorrectly assume that all three years of financial information were reviewed. Accordingly, the accountant must comment on all periods presented in comparative form. The guidance for comparative reporting is provided by *SSARS No. 2*.[25]

Continuing Accountant. A continuing accountant is one who has compiled, reviewed, or audited the financial statements of the current period and one or more periods prior to the current period. In cases where the same or a higher level of service is provided in the current period (for example, a compilation in 19X1 and a review in 19X2), the continuing accountant should update the report on previous years' financial statements. In **updating** the report, the continuing accountant should consider whether information obtained in the current year's engagement affects her or his report on previous financial statements.

When the level of assurance provided in a previous year *exceeds* that provided in the current year, the accountant should **reissue** the report on the previous year's financial statements. A reissued report

---

[25] American Institute of Certified Public Accountants (AICPA), *Statement on Standards for Accounting and Review Services No. 2*, "Reporting on Comparative Financial Statements" (New York: AICPA, 1979, AR 200).

is a report issued on one or more previous years' financial statements that contains the same date of the original report. In contrast to updating the report, the accountant does not perform additional procedures to determine whether the report on previous financial statements is still appropriate.

Predecessor Accountant. In some cases, financial statements presented in comparative form with current-period financial statements were compiled or reviewed by a different (predecessor) accountant. Similar to the reporting options when financial statements of one or more prior years were audited by a predecessor auditor, two options are available. First, the predecessor accountant could reissue the compilation or review report on prior years' financial statements. If the predecessor does so, the following procedures must be performed:

1. Read the financial statements of the current period and the successor accountant's report on those statements.
2. Compare the financial statements previously examined with those presented in comparative form in the current period.
3. Obtain a letter from the successor accountant to determine whether any information is known that may affect the financial statements reported upon by the predecessor accountant.

These procedures are intended to identify any changes or subsequent events that may affect the appropriateness of the report previously issued by the predecessor accountant.

When the predecessor does not agree to reissue her or his report, the successor accountant modifies the report on the current financial statements by indicating: (1) that a predecessor compiled or reviewed comparative statements, (2) the date of their report and a description of the standard disclaimer or limited assurance, and (3) any modifications made by the predecessor to the standard compilation or review report.

◘ Other Issues Involving Accounting and Review Services

Communication between Accountants. *SSARS No. 4*[26] notes that a successor accountant (an accountant who has been asked to make a proposal or has accepted an engagement) in either a compilation or a review engagement is not required to communicate with the predecessor accountant, but at his or her option may do so. Examples of circumstances that may encourage such contact include:

1. When the client or prospective client has a history of frequently changing accountants.
2. When the time period between the end of the year and the change of accountants is relatively long.

---

[26] American Institute of Certified Public Accountants (AICPA), *Statement on Standards for Accounting and Review Services No. 4*, "Communications Between Predecessor and Successor Accountants" (New York: AICPA, 1981, AR 400).

3. When the successor accountant feels that more information is needed about the client or prospective client and its management.

As we have previously noted, a CPA must treat information regarding a client or former client as confidential. Consequently, the successor accountant should request the client to: (1) permit contact with the predecessor accountant, and (2) authorize the predecessor accountant to answer the successor accountant's inquiries. The refusal to give such authorization should be given consideration by the successor accountant in determining whether to accept the engagement.

Association with Financial Statements of Nonpublic Companies. *SSARS No. 1* notes that users should be able to identify the degree of responsibility (if any) assumed by the accountant for the financial statements of nonpublic companies. In order to avoid any misperceptions on the part of users, accountants should not allow their names to be used in a document or written communication containing unaudited financial statements of a nonpublic entity unless: (1) the accountant has compiled or reviewed these statements and prepared a corresponding report, or (2) the accountant clearly indicates that he or she has not compiled or reviewed the financial statements and assumes no responsibility for them (by issuing a disclaimer of opinion). Also, accountants should not submit financial statements to clients or others unless, at a minimum, they perform procedures commensurate with a compilation engagement. "Submitting" financial statements includes:

1. Generating the financial statements for clients, either manually or through computer software.
2. Modifying client financial statements by changing account classification, amounts, or disclosures on the face of the financial statements.

Other Matters Affecting Accounting and Review Service Engagements. Another potential reporting issue arises when the accountant performs more than one service (for example, a compilation and a review) in a given year. In these cases, the accountant should issue the report that is appropriate for the service providing the highest level of assurance.

Finally, situations may arise when an accountant was originally engaged to perform an audit examination or a review engagement but has been requested to perform an engagement providing lower levels of assurance (*i.e.*, a compilation). For example, assume that a client engages the accountant to perform an audit examination to satisfy a third-party lender as to the fairness of their financial statements. Subsequently, the third party indicated a willingness to accept the assurances provided by a review engagement. The accountant may normally comply with the client's request and provide the lower level of assurance. In considering this request, the accountant should consider:

1. The reason given for the request.
2. The additional effort required to complete the engagement having a higher level of assurance.
3. The estimated additional cost required to complete the engagement having a higher level of assurance.

In particular, the accountant should evaluate the reason given for the request. Changes in circumstances (such as a third-party user's willingness to accept the assurances provided by the new engagement or a misunderstanding concerning the scope of the original engagement) are normally considered to be a reasonable basis for the client's request. However, if the reason for the client's request is a scope limitation (for example, the refusal to furnish a client representation letter), the client's request would not normally be considered reasonable. In these cases, the accountant should evaluate the possibility that the information related to the scope limitation may be incorrect, incomplete, or unsatisfactory.

◘ Summary: Accounting and Review Services for Nonpublic Companies

Some of the major characteristics of engagements and reports associated with assembly, compilation, and review engagements are summarized in Figure 19-3.

	Assembly	Compilation	Review
Does the accountant obtain knowledge about accounting practices in the client's industry?	No	Yes	Yes
Does the accountant obtain an understanding of the nature of the client's transactions?	No	Yes	Yes
Does the accountant perform limited inquiries and analytical procedures?	No	No	Yes
Is the accountant required to be independent of the client?	No	No	Yes
Is an opinion provided on the fairness of the client's financial statements?	No	No	No
Is limited assurance provided on the fairness of the client's financial statements?	No	No	Yes
Is the accountant required to obtain an engagement letter from the client?	Yes	No	No

Figure 19-3: *Characteristics of Engagements and Reports Involving Nonpublic Companies*

CHAPTER CHECKPOINTS

19-30. Distinguish between updating a report versus reissuing a report. When would each course of action be chosen when a continuing accountant provides accounting and review services?

19-31. What options are available if a predecessor accountant compiled or reviewed financial statements that are presented in comparative form with current-period financial statements?

19-32. What type of report should be issued by an accountant if he or she is associated with financial statements but did not compile or review these statements?

Appendix

Attestation Standards

General Standards

1. The engagement is to be performed by a practitioner having adequate technical training and proficiency in the attest function.
2. The engagement is to be performed by a practitioner or practitioners having adequate knowledge in the subject matter of the assertion.
3. The practitioner shall perform an engagement only if he or she has reason to believe that the following two conditions exist:
    a. The assertion is capable of evaluation against reasonable criteria that either have been established by a recognized body or are stated in the presentation of the assertion in a sufficiently clear and comprehensive manner for a knowledgeable reader to be able to understand them
    b. The assertion is capable of reasonably consistent estimation or measurement using such criteria.
4. In all matters relating to the engagement, an independence in mental attitude shall be maintained by the practitioner or practitioners.
5. Due professional care shall be exercised in the performance of the engagement.

Standards of Field Work

1. The work shall be adequately planned and assistants, if any, shall be properly supervised.
2. Sufficient evidence shall be obtained to provide a reasonable basis for the conclusion that is expressed in the report.

Standards of Reporting

1. The report shall identify the assertion being reported on and state the character of the engagement.
2. The report shall state the practitioner's conclusion about whether the assertion is presented in conformity with the established or stated criteria against which it was measured.
3. The report shall state all of the practitioner's significant reservations about the engagement and the presentation of the assertion.

4. The report on an engagement to evaluate an assertion that has been properly performed in conformity with agreed-upon criteria or on an engagement to apply agreed-upon procedures should contain a statement limiting its use to the parties who have agreed upon such criteria or procedures.

SUMMARY OF KEY POINTS

1. Accountants can perform four general types of engagements related to an entity's financial statements and other written information. These engagements include examination engagements, review engagements, agreed-upon procedures engagements, and compilation engagements. These engagements differ in terms of the scope of the engagement, the assurance provided by the accountant, the need for the accountant to maintain independence from the client, and the allowable use of the accountant's report.

2. An attest engagement is an engagement in which the accountant issues a written communication that expresses a conclusion concerning the reliability of an assertion of another party. Four types of attest engagements are engagements to report on: (1) management's assertion about internal control, (2) management's assertion about compliance with specified requirements, (3) prospective financial information, and (4) *pro forma* financial information.

3. Accountants may report on management's assertion about either the design or operating effectiveness of the organization's internal control. In this type of engagement, the accountant's procedures with respect to internal control are ordinarily more extensive than those in a GAAS audit.

4. Two types of prospective financial information are financial forecasts and financial projections. A financial forecast is an estimate of the company's future financial position, results of operations, and cash flows based on assumptions reflecting expected conditions and expected entity courses of action. In contrast, a financial projection presents prospective financial information based on assumptions reflecting expected conditions and courses of action given the occurrence of one or more hypothetical events.

5. Prospective financial information can be available for either general or limited use. General use allows the company to provide its prospective financial information to any individuals who could use this information. In contrast, limited use means that the prospective financial information can only be distributed to individual(s) who are negotiating directly with the company. Financial forecasts are available for general use; financial projections are only available for limited use.

6. There are three levels of accountant services related to prospective financial statements: compilation engagements, examination engagements, and agreed-upon procedures engagements. While the nature of the accountant's conclusion will differ depending upon the engagement performed by him or her, the accountant's report on prospective financial information will indicate that: (1) differences may occur between prospective and actual results, and (2) the accountant does not assume any responsibility to update the report for future events and circumstances.

7. Accounting and review services are available for the financial statements of nonpublic companies. Three types of engagements on nonpublic companies' financial statements other than audits are assembly of financial statements for internal use, compilations, and reviews.

8. An assembly of financial statements for internal use is an engagement where the accountant provides bookkeeping services that produce financial statements. In this type of engagement, the accountant does not prepare a report for third-party use; instead, a letter of transmittal is provided to the client along with the financial statements.

9. A compilation of financial statements involves presenting information that is the representation of management in the form of financial statements. In addition, the accountant is required to obtain an understanding of the accounting practices in the client's industry. The accountant does not undertake to express any assurance on financial statements during a compilation.

10. In a review of financial statements, the accountant performs limited procedures to provide reasonable assurance that there are no material modifications that should be made in order for the statements to conform to GAAP. The primary procedures performed in a review are inquiry and analytical procedures. The accountant's report provides limited assurance (or negative assurance) to third parties.

GLOSSARY

Agreed-Upon Procedures Engagement. A type of attest engagement in which an accountant applies procedures that are identified by specified third-party users. The distribution of the accountant's report is generally limited to those users participating in establishing the scope of the engagement.

Assembly of Financial Statements. An engagement in which the accountant provides bookkeeping services to produce financial statements for a client. The distinguishing feature of this type of engagement is that a report is not prepared by the accountant for third-party use.

Attest Engagement. An engagement in which an accountant issues a written communication regarding the reliability of a written assertion that is the responsibility of another party. Attest engagements are performed on management assertions about its internal control, management assertions about compliance with specified requirements, prospective financial information, and *pro forma* financial information.

Attestation Standards. Standards that provide guidance and develop a framework for the accountant performing an attest engagement.

Compilation Engagement. An engagement in which the accountant obtains an understanding of the accounting practices in the client's industry and assists the client in assembling its financial statements. Independence is not required in a compilation engagement because the accountant does not provide any assurance about the fairness of the client's financial statements.

Examination Engagement. A type of attest engagement having the greatest scope. In an examination, the accountant issues an opinion on the written assertion provided by the client.

Financial Forecast. Estimates of future financial results based on assumptions reflecting expected conditions and expected courses of action by the entity.

Financial Projection. Estimates of future financial results based on assumptions reflecting expected conditions and courses of action, given the occurrence of one or more hypothetical events.

General Use. A situation where prospective financial information or an accountant's report can be provided to any individuals who could use this information.

Limited (or Negative) Assurance. A conclusion provided in review engagements. When providing limited assurance, the accountant indicates that no information came to his or her attention that the identified financial information was not presented in conformity with some established criteria.

Limited Use. A situation where prospective financial information or an accountant's report can only be provided to individual(s) who are negotiating with the company.

Prospective Financial Information. Financial information that is estimated for a period of time in the future. Financial forecasts and financial projections are two types of prospective financial information.

Review Engagement. An engagement in which the accountant performs limited inquiry of client personnel and analytical procedures to financial information. This type of engagement provides limited assurance to users.

Statements on Standards for Accounting and Review Services (SSARS). Standards issued by the AICPA's Accounting and Review Services Committee to provide guidance in performing engagements on unaudited financial statements or unaudited financial information of nonpublic entities.

Statements on Standards for Attestation Engagements (SSAEs). Standards issued by the AICPA's Auditing Standards Board, Accounting and Review Services Committee, and the Management Advisory Services Executive Committee that govern attest engagements.

SUMMARY OF PROFESSIONAL PRONOUNCEMENTS

Statement on Standards for Accounting and Review Services No. 1, "Compilation and Review of Financial Statements" (New York: AICPA, 1978, AR 100).

Statement on Standards for Accounting and Review Services No. 2, "Reporting on Comparative Financial Statements" (New York: AICPA, 1979, AR 200).

Statement on Standards for Accounting and Review Services No. 3, "Compilation Reports on Financial Statements Included in Certain Prescribed Forms" (New York: AICPA, 1981, AR 300).

Statement on Standards for Accounting and Review Services No. 4, "Communications Between Predecessor and Successor Accountants" (New York: AICPA, 1981, AR 400).

Statement on Standards for Accounting and Review Services No. 7, "Omnibus Statement on Standards for Accounting and Review Services—1992" (New York: AICPA, 1992).

Statement on Standards for Attestation Engagements No. 1, "Codification of Statements on Standards for Attestation Engagements" (New York: AICPA, 1993, AT 100-300).

Statement on Standards for Attestation Engagements No. 2, "Reporting on an Entity's Internal Control Over Financial Reporting" (New York: AICPA, 1993, AT 400).

Statement on Standards for Attestation Engagements No. 3, "Compliance Attestation" (New York: AICPA, 1993, AT 500).

Statement on Standards for Attestation Engagements No. 4, "Agreed-Upon Procedures Engagements" (New York: AICPA, 1995, AT 600).

Statement on Standards for Attestation Engagements No. 5, "Amendment to *Statement on Standards for Attestation Engagements No. 1*, 'Attestation Standards'" (New York: AICPA, 1995, AU 100.71-100.75).

Statement on Standards for Attestation Engagements No. 6, "Reporting on an Entity's Internal Control Over Financial Reporting: An Amendment to *Statement on Standards for Attestation Engagements No. 2*" (New York: AICPA, 1995, AT 400).

Proposed Statement on Standards for Accounting and Review Services, "Assembly of Financial Statements for Internal Use Only" (New York: AICPA, September 6, 1995).

QUESTIONS AND PROBLEMS

19-33. Select the **best** answer for each of the following items:

1. When an independent CPA is associated with the financial statements of a publicly-held entity but has not audited or reviewed such statements, the appropriate form of report to be issued must include a (an):

   a. Negative assurance.
   b. Compilation opinion.
   c. Disclaimer of opinion.
   d. Explanatory paragraph.

2. Which of the following would **not** be included in a CPA's report based upon a review of the financial statements of a nonpublic entity?

   a. A statement that the review was in accordance with generally accepted auditing standards.
   b. A statement that all information included in the financial statements are the representations of management.
   c. A statement describing the principal procedures performed.
   d. A statement describing the auditor's conclusions based upon the results of the review.

3. Which of the following procedures is **not** included in a review engagement of a nonpublic entity?

   a. Inquiries of management.
   b. Inquiries regarding events subsequent to the balance-sheet date.
   c. Any procedures designed to identify relationships among data that appear to be unusual.
   d. A study and evaluation of internal control.

4. Which of the following types of attest engagements is of the greatest scope?

   a. Application of agreed-upon procedures.
   b. Compilation.
   c. Examination.
   d. Review.

5. An auditor who is not independent with respect to the client:

   a. May not perform a compilation engagement.
   b. May perform a compilation engagement, but need not disclose the lack of independence in her or his report.
   c. May perform a compilation engagement and must disclose both the lack of independence and the reason for the lack of independence in his or her report.
   d. May perform a compilation engagement and must disclose the lack of independence, but not the reason for the lack of independence, in the report.
   e. None of the above.

6. In which of the following types of prospective financial statements and engagements related to prospective financial statements would the distribution of the accountant's report or financial information be limited?

	Financial Forecast	Application of Agreed-Upon Procedures
a.	Yes	Yes
b.	Yes	No
c.	No	Yes
d.	No	No

7. Accepting an engagement to examine a financial projection for a publicly-held company would be least appropriate when the projection (and accountant's report) were to be distributed to:

   a. A regulatory agency that is familiar with the company and its operations.
   b. The Board of Directors of the company.
   c. All stockholders of the company.
   d. A lender with whom the company has been directly negotiating regarding potential financing.
   e. A labor union that is currently negotiating wage rates with the company.

8. Which of the following statements would not be included in a standard compilation report?

   a. The financial statements were compiled in accordance with standards established by the AICPA.
   b. A brief definition of a compilation engagement.
   c. A disclaimer of opinion on the financial statements.
   d. Limited assurance on the fairness of the financial statements.
   e. All of the above would be included in a standard compilation report.

9. An estimate of an entity's future financial results based on expected conditions and expected courses of action is known as a(n):

   a. Attest engagement.
   b. Financial forecast.
   c. Financial projection.
   d. *Pro forma* financial statements.

10. In which of the following types of engagements is the accountant required to maintain his or her independence from the client?

    a. Assembly of financial statements for internal use.
    b. Compilation engagement.
    c. Review engagement.
    d. a and c above.
    e. All of the above.

11. Performing analytical procedures and inquiries of client personnel is most descriptive of a(n):

    a. Agreed-upon procedures engagement.
    b. Assembly of financial statements for internal use.
    c. Compilation engagement.
    d. Review engagement.

12. The accountant's report on an examination of prospective financial statements would include each of the following except:

    a. An engagement was performed in accordance with AICPA standards.
    b. A brief description of an examination engagement.
    c. The auditor's opinion as to the fairness of the financial statements.
    d. A statement that differences may exist between prospective and actual results.
    e. All of the above would be included in the accountant's report.

13. Which of the following is indicative of performing an agreed-upon procedures engagement for a financial forecast?

	Independence Required?	Provide Limited Assurance?
a.	Yes	Yes
b.	Yes	No
c.	No	Yes
d.	No	No

14. Which of the following types of accountant's reports would be available for general use?

    a. An agreed-upon procedures engagement performed on a financial forecast.
    b. An examination engagement performed on a financial projection.
    c. An assembly of financial statements for internal use.
    d. A compilation engagement for a nonpublic company's financial statements.

15. Which of the following procedures is ordinarily **not** performed during a compilation engagement?

    a. Obtaining an understanding of the nature of the client's business transactions.
    b. Obtaining an understanding of the client's internal control.
    c. Obtaining an understanding of the accounting principles and practices in the client's industry.
    d. Reading the compiled financial statements to determine that they are free from obvious material errors.

(Items 1 through 4 in 19-33; AICPA Adapted)

19-34. The AICPA has recently provided standards for attestation engagements. These standards reflect the wide variety of assurances and services provided by CPAs.

Required:

a. Define an attest engagement.
b. What are the three types of attest engagements identified by the AICPA?
c. Provide examples of each type of attest engagement in (b) above.
d. For each class of attest engagement, indicate: (1) the scope of the engagement, (2) the type of assurance provided by the CPA, and (3) the distribution of the CPA's report.

19-35. Companies are more frequently preparing financial statements based on expected future results to provide users with additional information. These statements are referred to as prospective financial statements. Like historical financial statements, users desire accountant involvement with this prospective financial information to enhance the reliability of these statements.

Required:

a. Define a financial forecast and a financial projection. What is the difference in the individuals to whom these two types of prospective financial statements can be shown?
b. What are the three types of engagements that accountants may perform for prospective financial statements? What are the major procedures performed in each of these engagements?
c. Does the accountant's report on prospective financial statements address whether forecast results will be achieved? If so, how?
d. What are the major components of the accountant's report on each of the three types of engagements related to prospective financial statements? (Do not write the reports.)
e. Which of the three engagements related to prospective financial statements are appropriate for general use of the prospective financial statements? Which are only appropriate for limited use of the prospective financial statements?

19-36. An alternative to an audit examination for companies that are not publicly-held are compilation and review engagements.

Required:

a. What procedures are performed by the accountant in compilation and review engagements?
b. Indicate the major components of the accountant's compilation and review reports.
c. How would the standard compilation and review report be modified if a departure from GAAP was observed during the engagement?
d. Assume that the auditor was originally engaged to perform an audit examination. After discussion with the client, the auditor realizes that a review engagement would more efficiently meet the client's needs. Can the auditor perform a review engagement? If so, are there any restrictions on their engagement or modifications to the accountant's review report?

19-37. CPA J is employed to compile the financial statements of the Reach Corporation for the year ended December 31, 19X1. On each page, the financial statements include the notation "Compilation." The compilation report prepared by J read as follows:

> The accompanying balance sheet of Reach Corporation as of December 31, 19X1, and the related statement of income, retained earnings, and cash flows for the year then ended have been compiled by us. We have not audited the accompanying financial statements and accordingly do not express an opinion on them.

Required:

Cite any deficiencies that exist in CPA J's work.

19-38. Sloppy Rubbish, Inc., is a nonpublic corporation that has been in business for two years. The company collects trash for residential homes in Jenktowne, Pennsylvania. The company was founded two years ago by its current president, I. M. Sloppy. Until this year, the corporation has relied on the capital supplied by the original stockholder for financing. This year, however, the president decided that a fleet of 10 new trash trucks is needed. Thus, the president decided to apply to a bank for a loan. The president is in a hurry to get a loan because he feels that if he acts within the next three days he can get a 20 percent discount on the trucks. At the country club, one of his golf partners told him that banks no longer require an audit. The president heard that there is a "new thing" called a compilation, which is as good as an audit, cheaper than an audit, and can be obtained immediately from a CPA.

Required:

a. Comment on the accuracy of what the president heard at the country club.
b. Assume you are a CPA and the president asks you to do a compilation for the current year for the corporation. The condition he places on the engagement is that it must be accomplished within the next 24 hours so he can use the report to obtain a loan. Should you honor his request?

19-39. CPA K reviewed the financial statements for the year ended December 31, 19X1, for his client, Gear, Inc., a nonpublic corporation. The following report was submitted to the client along with the financial statements:

> I have examined the accompanying balance sheet of Gear, Inc., as of December 31, 19X1, and the related statements of income, retained earnings, and cash flows for the year then ended, in accordance with generally accepted review standards. All information included in the financial statements is the representation of the management of Gear, Inc.
>
> A review consists principally of inquires of company personnel and audit procedures applied to financial data. It is substantially lesser in scope than an examination in accordance with generally accepted auditing standards, the objective of which is to compile financial statements. Accordingly, I do not express such an opinion.
>
> Based on my review, I am not aware of any material modifications that should be made to the accompanying financial statements for them to be in conformity with generally accepted auditing standards.

Required:

Cite any deficiencies in CPA K's report.

19 10. BRN Corporation is a closely-held corporation that is owned entirely by the Brian family. BRN's accounting department has satisfied the corporate management's internal reporting needs and the limited needs for information to support borrowing requests.

Mark Brian, BRN's longtime president, is now retiring. Brian's children will assume the management of the corporation, and they intend to obtain additional capital from other, unrelated investors. The children do not now intend to "go public," but they recognize that there will be a different reporting responsibility to the new, unrelated investors than existed previously.

Donna Brian, the corporation's new president, is investigating the types of reports that an external auditor may issue on a corporation's financial statements. In a recent interview with a representative of a local CPA firm, Brian heard a description of the CPA firm's services with respect to a compilation, a review, and an audit.

Required:

a. Discuss the level of assurance the certified public accountant gives in a(n):
   1. Compilation.
   2. Review.
   3. Audit.

b. Explain what factors the management of BRN Corporation should consider before deciding which one of the three types of external accountant's reports (compilation, review, audit) to accept.

c. Explain the implications that management's plans to "go public" with its stock within five years might have on BRN's selection of the type of report it accepts.

(CMA Adapted)

V

Other Types of Audits

Learning Objectives

Study of this chapter is designed to achieve several learning objectives. After studying this chapter, you should be able to:

1. Define compliance, internal, and operational auditing and distinguish these types of audit engagements from a financial statement audit.
2. Understand how laws and regulations affect the financial statements of governmental entities and how these laws and regulations influence the auditor's examination of the entity's financial statements.
3. Understand the audit and reporting requirements for governmental entities under Government Auditing Standards.
4. Understand the audit and reporting requirements for audits conducted under the Single Audit Act.
5. Identify the various types of activities performed by internal auditors and classify these activities based on the type of audit function involved.
6. Identify the IIA's *Standards for the Professional Practice of Internal Auditing* and compare these to the 10 generally accepted auditing standards.
7. Identify the major steps performed in an operational audit.

20

Compliance, Internal, and Operational Auditing

To this point, the discussion of audit examinations has focused on the auditor's examination of an entity's financial statements to determine whether these financial statements are prepared in conformity with GAAP. This type of examination is known as a **financial statement audit**. In Chapter 1, three other types of audits were identified: compliance audits, operational audits, and internal audits. These audits differ from financial statement audits in terms of the objectives of the engagement, the users who rely on the auditor's work, and the types of conclusions reached by the auditor.

This chapter provides a brief overview of compliance auditing, operational auditing, and internal auditing. These topics are very detailed and entire textbooks are devoted to them, but this overview should allow the student to identify the major characteristics associated with each of these types of audits and how they differ from the financial statement audit described in the majority of the text.

◉ COMPLIANCE AUDITING[1]

In a **compliance audit**, the auditor attempts to obtain and evaluate information to determine whether certain financial, operating, or other activities of an entity are in conformity with specified criteria, policies, or regulations. There are many instances where compliance is of interest. For example, as noted in Chapter 18, third-party creditors are often interested in whether entities are in compliance with debt covenants related to bonds or notes held by those entities. Also, the entity's management may be interested in ascertaining the degree to which its employees follow prescribed internal control

---

[1] Much of the discussion in this section is based on *Statement on Auditing Standards No. 74*, "Compliance Auditing Applicable to Governmental Entities and Other Recipients of Governmental Financial Assistance" (New York: AICPA, 1995, AU 801).

policies and procedures in performing their day-to-day activities. Thus, both independent (external) auditors and internal auditors perform compliance audits. Compliance auditing by external auditors was introduced in Chapter 18. Later in this chapter, compliance auditing in an internal audit environment is discussed in more detail.

Although it is important to remember that compliance auditing is important in a corporate environment, compliance auditing assumes increased importance for governmental entities. Various aspects of compliance with laws and regulations have a tremendous effect on both the financial statements and operations of governmental entities. A unique aspect of governmental entities' financial statements is that they are affected by various laws and regulations. For example, governmental entities must frequently contribute their own funds toward carrying out activities funded by grants received from other agencies. In cases where requirements of this nature exist, governmental entities cannot recognize revenues relating to funds received until the matching requirements are met.

A second distinguishing feature of state and local governmental entities is that they receive grants from the federal government. In many cases, these funds must be utilized for purposes specified by the requirements of the federal program granting the funds. For example, funds received from a federal housing program are usually restricted to the construction of housing for individuals meeting certain eligibility requirements. In addition to receiving funds from federal programs, state and local governmental entities also receive funds from such sources as bond issuances, tax levies, and other assessments. Like funds received from federal governmental agencies, these funds normally have restrictions placed on their use. For example, proceeds from a bond issuance are required to be used for the purpose to which the issuance relates. Also, funds raised by a gasoline tax are usually restricted to use for highway repair and improvement. In any case, it is important that funds received from the federal government, bond issuances, tax levies, and other types of assessments be utilized in the manner specified by these sources.

In short, laws and regulations affect both the financial statements of governmental entities as well as the types of activities that these entities may conduct. A major purpose of compliance auditing is to allow the auditor to determine whether governmental entities are operating in compliance with: (1) all applicable laws and regulations; and (2) the operating requirements of federal financial assistance programs, bond issuances, tax levies, or other assessments. The audit of governmental entities introduces the following issues:

1. Compliance auditing in a financial statement audit conducted in accordance with GAAS.
2. Audits conducted in accordance with Government Auditing Standards.
3. Audits conducted in accordance with the Single Audit Act, OMB Circular A-128, and OMB Circular A-133.

These issues are discussed in the remainder of this section.

◘ Compliance Auditing in a GAAS Audit

The purpose of a GAAS audit is to allow the auditor to determine whether the entity's financial statements are prepared in conformity with GAAP. In doing so, the auditor considers the effect of errors, irregularities, and illegal acts on the entity's financial statements. As noted earlier in Chapter

4, *Statement on Auditing Standards No. 53 (SAS No. 53)*[2] requires the auditor to plan the audit to detect errors and irregularities material to the client's financial statements. In addition, *SAS No. 54*[3] indicates that the audit should be planned to detect illegal acts that have a direct and material effect on the financial statements. It is important to note that an auditor's responsibility for detecting illegal acts in a GAAS audit is not based on identifying the extent of the entity's compliance with laws and regulations. Rather, the auditor's concern is that the lack of compliance with laws and regulations will result in materially misstated financial statements.

A unique characteristic of governmental entities is that their activities are usually subject to a wide variety of laws and regulations, which are of such a nature that noncompliance with them affects their financial statements. Two examples are:

1. **Legal requirements for accounting for revenues resulting from specific sources**. Governmental entities must account for their revenues arising from various sources in identified funds. These funds can be established by constitutional provisions, local charters, ordinances, or governing-body orders. Therefore, it is important that the entity account for revenues using the proper fund. For example, if a state constitutional amendment requires revenues from a state gasoline tax to be accounted for in a designated fund, the financial statements would be considered to be misstated if these revenues were accounted for in another fund.

2. **Matching requirements for recognizing revenues**. In many cases, grants provided to governmental entities require the receiving entity to contribute its own funds in carrying out the activities specified by the grant. This contribution is often referred to as matching. Under the provisions of the Government Accounting Standards Board's (GASB's) *Codification of Governmental Accounting and Reporting Standards (Codification)*,[4] any matching requirements must be satisfied before funds received from grants can be recognized as revenue. Thus, recognition of these funds as revenues prior to meeting the specified matching requirements would result in misstated financial statements.

These types of laws and regulations are unique to governmental entities. Accordingly, the auditor must consider these in addition to other laws and regulations normally associated with public corporations.

Obtaining an Understanding of the Effects of Laws and Regulations.
In the audit of a governmental entity, the auditor first identifies laws and regulations that may affect the entity's financial statements. The auditor then obtains an understanding of the possible financial statement effects of these laws and regulations on that entity's financial statements. Once again, note that the emphasis in a GAAS audit is not compliance with these laws and regulations per se, but the potential impact of noncompliance with laws and regulations on the governmental entity's financial statements. *SAS No. 74* (AU 801.07) notes that procedures used by the auditor to identify laws and regulations

---

[2] American Institute of Certified Public Accountants (AICPA), *Statement on Auditing Standards No. 53*, "The Auditor's Responsibility to Detect and Report Errors and Irregularities" (New York: AICPA, 1988, AU 316).

[3] American Institute of Certified Public Accountants (AICPA), *Statement on Auditing Standards No. 54*, "Illegal Acts by Clients" (New York: AICPA, 1988, AU 317).

[4] Government Accounting Standards Board (GASB), *Codification of Accounting and Financial Reporting Standards* (Norwalk, CT: GASB, 1990).

and obtain an understanding of the effect of these laws and regulations on the entity's financial statements include:

1. Consider knowledge obtained about laws and regulations from prior years' audits.
2. Discuss the possible impact of laws and regulations on the entity's financial statements with client personnel.
3. Review minutes of meetings of the legislative body of the entity being audited.
4. Review portions of any directly-related grant or loan agreements.
5. Inquire of others (grant administrators, audit oversight organizations) about the laws and regulations for which governmental entities in their jurisdictions are responsible.

Once the auditor has identified the types of laws and regulations that may materially affect the entity's financial statements, the audit must be planned to provide reasonable assurance of detecting noncompliance with these laws and regulations. As in all GAAS audits, the auditor evaluates internal control to determine its effectiveness in detecting and/or preventing misstatements. However, in audits of governmental entities, internal control policies and procedures related to compliance with laws and regulations assume additional importance. For example, the auditor should evaluate management's awareness of the laws and regulations confronting the governmental entity as he or she obtains an overall understanding of the entity's internal control.

At this point, it may be helpful to contrast the procedures performed with respect to the effect of compliance with laws and regulations on the financial statements of governmental entities with those performed for nongovernmental entities. The sole difference is that the auditor is required to consider and obtain an understanding of how an additional set of laws and regulations may affect the entity's financial statements. Because many of these laws and regulations are not applicable to nongovernmental entities, this understanding is not necessary in these types of audits.

Substantive Tests. At this point, the auditor has: (1) identified the potential impact of laws and regulations on the entity's financial statements, and (2) evaluated the entity's internal control to determine its effectiveness in preventing and detecting misstatements arising from noncompliance with these laws and regulations. The auditor now performs substantive tests similar to those in other GAAS audits discussed in this text. The primary difference in the audit of a governmental entity is that the auditor has planned the audit to detect instances where noncompliance with a unique set of laws and regulations results in materially misstated financial statements. The substantive testing procedures performed in this regard are slightly different from those previously illustrated. For example, to determine whether GASB matching requirements have been met for revenues recognized by governmental entities, the auditor should examine some form of evidence (cash disbursements or transfers by the entity) that contributions have been made by the entity.

At the conclusion of the audit, as part of the written representations obtained from management, the auditor will obtain additional representations regarding the governmental entity's compliance with laws and regulations. These representations include statements that: (1) management is responsible for the governmental entity's compliance with laws and regulations, and (2) all laws and regulations having a direct and material effect on the financial statements have been identified and disclosed to the auditor.

Reporting Requirements. At the conclusion of an audit of a governmental entity's financial statements conducted under GAAS, the auditor issues an opinion as to whether these financial statements were prepared according to GAAP. This report is identical to that discussed in Chapter 17. The auditor does not issue a special report on the entity's compliance with laws and regulations as a result of a GAAS audit; however, this type of report is issued in engagements conducted under *Government Auditing Standards* (described in the following section).

Figure 20-1 summarizes the differences introduced during various stages of the audit when the financial statements of a governmental entity are examined.

Planning	Understand the effect of laws and regulations on the governmental entity's financial statements.
	Plan the audit to provide reasonable assurance of detecting noncompliance with laws and regulations having a material effect on the entity's financial statements.
Study and Evaluation of Internal Control	Evaluate internal control policies and procedures designed to prevent or detect instances of noncompliance with laws and regulations having a material effect on the financial statements.
Substantive Tests	Test compliance with laws and regulations having a material effect on the financial statements. Obtain representations from management regarding laws and regulations that materially affect the financial statements.

Figure 20-1: *Procedures Performed in a GAAS Audit of a Governmental Entity's Financial Statements*

> **CHAPTER CHECKPOINTS**
>
> **20-1.** Define compliance auditing. Why is compliance auditing particularly important for governmental entities?
>
> **20-2.** What three issues are introduced related to compliance auditing in the examination of a governmental entity?
>
> **20-3.** What is the auditor's responsibility for examining compliance with laws and regulations in the financial statement audit of a governmental entity under GAAS? What is the responsibility for reporting on internal control in this type of audit?
>
> **20-4.** What procedures can be used by the auditor to identify laws and regulations related to a governmental entity and determine the effect of these laws and regulations on that entity's financial statements?
>
> **20-5.** How do laws and regulations faced by governmental entities affect the auditor's planning procedures and study and evaluation of internal control in a GAAS audit?

◻ Government Auditing Standards (The Yellow Book)

As noted above, in a GAAS audit, the auditor considers compliance with laws and regulations solely in terms of how they impact the fairness of the entity's financial statements. Although a GAAS audit may be sufficient for many governmental entities, in some cases additional audit requirements are necessary to satisfy legal, regulatory, or contractual requirements. For example, certain regulatory agencies require reports on the governmental entity's compliance with laws and regulations. Also, as noted in the next major section, entities receiving federal financial assistance of certain amounts are required to have audits performed in accordance with the Single Audit Act of 1984. These additional requirements introduce additional issues and may require the auditor to perform additional audit procedures and/or issue additional audit reports.

In this section, audits conducted in accordance with *Government Auditing Standards*[5] (also known as a *Yellow Book audit*) are discussed. These audits are often referred to as generally accepted governmental auditing standards (GAGAS) audits. In a GAGAS audit, the procedures performed by the auditor with respect to compliance with laws and regulations[6] are identical to those in a GAAS audit. The sole difference is that the auditor has expanded reporting responsibility for: (1) compliance

---

[5] U.S. General Accounting Office, *Government Auditing Standards*, "Standards for the Audit of Governmental Organizations, Programs, Activities, and Functions" (Washington, DC: U.S. Government Printing Office, 1994).

[6] It is important to note that Government Auditing Standards identify three main types of audits: (1) financial and financial-related audits; (2) economy and efficiency audits; and (3) program audits. In terms of compliance auditing, the applicable guidance is provided by the standards for financial and financial-related audits. The remaining types of audits are discussed later in this chapter under "Operational Auditing."

with laws and regulations, and (2) internal control. This expanded reporting responsibility is described below.

Compliance with Laws and Regulations. In order to report on an entity's compliance with laws and regulations, the auditor must perform procedures to test the extent of entity compliance. These tests of compliance are identical to those performed in a GAAS audit—that is, the auditor identifies laws and regulations that may have a material effect on the entity's financial statements. Then the auditor designs the audit to provide reasonable assurance of detecting instances of noncompliance that are material to the financial statements. In designing the audit in this fashion, compliance with various laws and regulations is tested by the auditor. Therefore, no procedures beyond those in a GAAS audit are performed in a GAGAS audit.

The auditor is required to specifically report on compliance with laws and regulations as a part of a GAGAS audit. This report is prepared in addition to the auditor's report on the fairness of an entity's statements. In the report on compliance with laws and regulations, the auditor should:

1. Refer to both GAAS and GAGAS.
2. Disclaim an opinion on compliance.
3. Mention any material instances of noncompliance or indicate that no material instances were discovered.

Figure 20-2 illustrates a sample report prepared by the auditor on a governmental entity's compliance with laws and regulations. As shown therein, the fourth paragraph provides the auditor's conclusion with respect to compliance; in this case, no instances of noncompliance were noted by the auditor.

If material noncompliance with laws and regulations is noted by the auditor, the report shown in Figure 20-2 should be modified to report any detected instances of noncompliance. In addition, *Government Auditing Standards* require the auditor to communicate any discovered illegal acts to the entity, unless these acts are clearly inconsequential. If immaterial noncompliance is noted by the auditor, the report shown in Figure 20-2 is not modified to describe the actual instances of noncompliance noted. These matters are normally communicated separately to management, preferably in writing. This separate communication would be referenced in the auditor's report on compliance with laws and regulations shown in Figure 20-2.

Reporting on Internal Control. In addition to reporting on a governmental entity's compliance with laws and regulations, a GAGAS audit also requires additional reporting responsibilities with respect to the entity's internal control. Similar to laws and regulations, this reporting responsibility *does not* entail additional procedures on the part of the auditor. That is, the auditor performs the same procedures with respect to an entity's internal control as in a GAAS audit. The only difference in a GAGAS audit is that a report on the entity's internal control is required in all examinations.

We have audited the financial statements of the city of Bryan College, Texas as of and for the year ended June 30, 19X1, and have issued our report thereon dated August 15, 19X1.

We conducted our audit in accordance with generally accepted auditing standards and *Government Auditing Standards*, issued by the Comptroller General of the United States. Those standards require that we plan and perform the audit to obtain reasonable assurance about whether the financial statements are free of material misstatement.

Compliance with laws, regulations, contracts, and grants applicable to the city of Bryan College, Texas is the responsibility of the city of Bryan College, Texas' management. As part of obtaining reasonable assurance about whether the financial statements are free of material misstatement, we performed tests of the city of Bryan College, Texas' compliance with certain provisions of laws, regulations, contracts, and grants. However, the objective of our audit of the financial statements was not to provide an opinion on overall compliance with such provisions. Accordingly, we do not express such an opinion.

The results of our tests disclosed no instances of noncompliance that are required to be reported herein under *Government Auditing Standards*.

This report is intended for the information of the audit committee, management, and the city council. This is not intended to limit the distribution of this report, which is a matter of public record.

[*Signature*]
[*Date*]

Figure 20-2: *Report on Entity Compliance with Laws and Regulations Made in a GAGAS Audit*

Three types of deficiencies that are communicated by the auditor in a GAGAS audit are reportable conditions, material weaknesses, and nonreportable conditions. These deficiencies are summarized below:

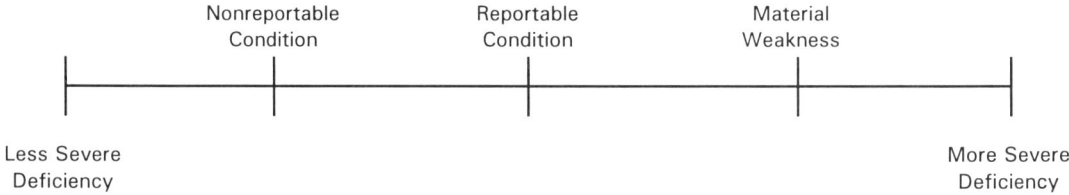

A **material weakness** is an internal control deficiency that has a high probability of resulting in a material financial statement error that would not be detected by employees performing their assigned functions. Thus, a material weakness has the potential to result in materially misstated financial statements. In contrast, a **reportable condition** is a deficiency that is less serious than a material weakness. Generally, a reportable condition is not expected to result in material financial statement errors. A **nonreportable condition** would be any deficiency that is considered to be less significant than a reportable condition.

The auditor's responsibility for reporting on internal control in a GAGAS audit differs markedly from that in a GAAS audit. Recall from the discussion of internal control in Chapter 5 that, under the provisions of *SAS No. 60*,[7] the auditor is only required to communicate information about an internal control when reportable conditions or material weaknesses are noted. In addition, this communication can either be oral or written. In a GAGAS audit, a written report is required in all audits, regardless of whether any deficiencies are noted. Other reporting differences are as follows:

1. The auditor is required to communicate internal control deficiencies of a less serious nature (nonreportable conditions) in a GAGAS audit.
2. In a GAGAS audit, material weaknesses are clearly distinguished from reportable conditions. Auditors may distinguish between these deficiencies in the SAS No. 60 communication, but this distinction is not required.
3. The auditor describes the scope of the procedures performed to obtain an understanding of internal control and assess control risk in a GAGAS audit. No such description is made by the auditor in the communication required for GAAS audits under SAS No. 60.

The Auditor's Report on Internal Control. Figure 20-3 illustrates the auditor's report on internal control prepared in a GAGAS audit. Several of the more important statements contained in this report include:

1. The fact that the auditor has audited the governmental entity's financial statements and a reference to the report on those statements.
2. The auditor considered the entity's internal control to determine audit procedures for the purpose of expressing an opinion on the entity's financial statements and not to provide assurance on the internal control.
3. A description of the scope of the auditor's examination of internal control.
4. A definition of a reportable condition and a description of any reportable conditions noted.
5. A definition of a material weakness and a description of any material weaknesses noted.
6. Reference to a separate communication of any nonreportable conditions made to the entity. Note that these conditions are not normally communicated in the auditor's report on internal control in a GAGAS audit.

---

[7] American Institute of Certified Public Accountants (AICPA), *Statement on Auditing Standards No. 60*, "Communication of Internal Control Structure Related Matters Noted in an Audit" (New York: AICPA, 1988, AU 325).

We have audited the financial statements of the city of Bryan College, Texas as of and for the year ended June 30, 19X1, and have issued our report thereon dated August 15, 19X1.

We conducted our audit in accordance with generally accepted auditing standards and *Government Auditing Standards*, issued by the Comptroller General of the United States. Those standards require that we plan and perform the audit to obtain reasonable assurance about whether the financial statements are free of material misstatement.

The management of the city of Bryan College, Texas is responsible for establishing and maintaining internal control. In fulfilling this responsibility, estimates and judgments by management are required to assess the expected benefits and related costs of internal control policies and procedures. The objectives of an internal control are to provide management with reasonable, but not absolute, assurance that assets are safeguarded against loss from unauthorized use or disposition and that transactions are executed in accordance with management's authorization and recorded properly to permit the preparation of financial statements in accordance with generally accepted accounting principles. Because of inherent limitations in any internal control, errors or irregularities may nevertheless occur and not be detected. Also, projection of any evaluation of the internal control to future periods is subject to the risk that procedures may become inadequate because of changes in conditions or that the effectiveness of the design and operation of policies and procedures may deteriorate.

In planning and performing our audit of the financial statements of the city of Bryan College, Texas for the year ended June 30, 19X1, we obtained an understanding of the internal control. With respect to the internal control, we obtained an understanding of the design of relevant policies and procedures and whether they have been placed in operation, and we assessed control risk to determine our auditing procedures for the purpose of expressing our opinion on the financial statements and not to provide an opinion on the internal control. Accordingly, we do not express such an opinion.

We noted certain matters involving the internal control and its operation that we consider to be reportable conditions under standards established by the American Institute of Certified Public Accountants. Reportable conditions involve matters coming to our attention relating to significant deficiencies in the design or operation of the internal control that, in our judgment, could adversely affect the entity's ability to record, process, summarize, and report financial data consistent with the assertions of management in the financial statements.

[*Include paragraphs to describe the reportable conditions noted.*]

A material weakness is a reportable condition in which the design or operation of one or more of the internal control elements does not reduce to a relatively low level the risk that errors or irregularities in amounts that would be material in relation to the financial statements being audited may occur and not be detected within a timely period by employees in the normal course of performing their assigned functions.

Figure 20-3: *Report on Internal Control Prepared in a GAGAS Audit*

Our consideration of the internal control would not necessarily disclose all matters in the internal control that might be reportable conditions and, accordingly, would not necessarily disclose all reportable conditions that are also considered to be material weaknesses as defined above. However, we believe none of the reportable conditions described above is a material weakness.

We also noted other matters involving the internal control and its operation that we have reported to the management of the city of Bryan College, Texas in a separate letter dated August 15, 19X1.

This report is intended for the information of the audit committee, management, and the city council. This is not intended to limit the distribution of this report, which is a matter of public record.

Figure 20-3: *(concluded)*

CHAPTER CHECKPOINTS

20-6. How does the auditor's examination under *Government Auditing Standards* differ from an examination in a GAAS audit?

20-7. What type of conclusion is provided by the auditor when he or she examines compliance with laws and regulations?

20-8. In an audit conducted under *Government Auditing Standards*, how is the auditor's report on compliance with laws and regulations modified for material instances of noncompliance? Immaterial instances of noncompliance?

20-9. How does the auditor's reporting responsibility for internal control in an audit conducted under *Government Auditing Standards* differ from that in a GAAS audit?

◻ The Single Audit Act

An important consideration for state and local governmental entities receiving financial assistance from the federal government is that the funds received must be used for specified purposes. To ensure that they are operating in compliance with the requirements of federal financial assistance programs, governmental entities are required to have an audit conducted under the provisions of the Single Audit Act of 1984.[8] The audit requirements for state and local governments depend on the amount of assistance received from federal programs. These requirements are summarized below:

---

[8] To provide assistance to auditors performing audits under the Single Audit Act, the Office of Management and Budget (OMB) has issued *Circular A-128* "Audits of State and Local Governments" and *Circular A-133* "Audits of Institutions of Higher Education and Other Nonprofit Institutions." The following discussion is based on the requirements of the Single Audit Act, *OMB Circular A-123*, and *OMB Circular A-133*.

1. Federal assistance greater than $100,000: state and local entities are required to have audits conducted under the Single Audit Act.
2. Federal assistance between $25,000 and $100,000: state and local entities are required to have: (a) audits conducted under the Single Audit Act, or (b) audits performed in accordance with federal laws and regulations governing the programs in which the entity participates.
3. Federal assistance less than $25,000: no audit requirements.

It is important to note that the above audit requirements relate solely to compliance with the requirements of federal financial assistance programs providing funds to state and local governmental entities. The requirements of the Single Audit Act also include financial statement audits as in a GAAS or GAGAS audit.

Reports Required under the Single Audit Act. The Single Audit Act requires auditors to perform the same procedures and prepare the reports applicable to the GAAS and GAGAS audits described previously. Thus, in an audit performed under the Single Audit Act, the auditor will: (1) express an opinion on the fairness of the governmental entity's financial statements, (2) provide a summary of findings on the entity's compliance with laws and regulations, and (3) identify any reportable conditions and material weaknesses noted in the entity's internal control. In preparing these reports, it is important to note that no additional procedures beyond those in the GAAS and GAGAS audits are performed. Therefore, the auditor only tests compliance with laws and regulations that materially affect the entity's financial statements. In addition, the governmental entity's internal control is examined to obtain an overall understanding of the internal control and to assess control risk.

In addition to performing the above procedures and issuing the related reports, the auditor must perform additional procedures in an audit conducted under the Single Audit Act. These procedures relate to the state and local entity's compliance with the provisions of federal assistance programs. Based on these procedures, the reports presented in Figure 20-4 are issued in addition to those prepared in a GAGAS audit (opinion on the financial statements, report on compliance with laws and regulations, and report on internal control). The procedures performed and reports prepared by the auditor for federal assistance programs are discussed in the following sections.

---

1. Compliance with specific requirements of major federal financial assistance programs.
2. Compliance with specific requirements of nonmajor federal financial assistance programs.
3. Compliance with general requirements of major and nonmajor federal financial assistance programs.
4. Schedule of findings and questioned costs.

Figure 20-4: *Reports Prepared under the Single Audit Act*

Specific Requirements: Major Federal Financial Assistance Programs. A major federal financial assistance program (major program) is defined as a program for which expenditures made by the governmental entity constitute a large portion of that entity's expenditures for all programs. The Single Audit Act provides very explicit guidance as to the necessary magnitude of expenditures for a federal assistance program to be classified as a major program. Some examples are shown below:

Total Expenditures for all Programs	Expenditures for a Major Program
Greater than $7 billion	$20 million
Between $3 and $4 billion	$10 million
Between $1 and $2 billion	$ 4 million
*	*
*	*
*	*
Between $100 million and $100,000	Larger of $300,000 or 3 percent of total expenditures for all programs

In any case, the distinguishing feature of a major program is that expenditures for these programs account for a large proportion of the total expenditures made by the governmental entity for all of its programs.

Audit Requirements of Major Programs. For each major federal financial assistance program identified, the auditor is required to test compliance with specific requirements of the programs. **Specific requirements** represent limitations on the use of funds or types of operations and activities that can be conducted with funds received from the federal government. Specific requirements are closely related to the federal assistance programs and vary from one program to another. The specific requirements identified by the Single Audit Act are:

1. The types of goods and services that may be purchased with funds received from the federal financial assistance programs.
2. The eligibility of individuals for receiving federal assistance.
3. Any matching, level of effort, or earmarking of funds by the state and local governmental entity toward projects funded by federal financial assistance programs.
4. Reporting requirements for the federal financial assistance program.
5. Other provisions required for projects funded by the federal government, such as requiring a hearing on the proposed use of federal assistance.

The auditor is required to plan the audit to detect instances of material noncompliance with specific requirements. In doing so, both the inherent risk and control risk associated with each federal financial assistance program are considered. In considering inherent risk, factors such as the newness of the program, lack of previous auditor experience with the program, and the extent to which the program is conducted through subrecipients may result in a higher probability of noncompliance. Recall that, in a financial statement audit, inherent risk relates to the susceptibility of an account balance or class of transactions to misstatement. In an audit conducted to determine the extent of entity compliance with specific requirements, the inherent risk is related to the susceptibility of a program to noncompliance with specific requirements.

As previously noted, under the Single Audit Act the auditor must issue a report on the effectiveness of the entity's internal control. In doing so, the auditor obtains an overall understanding of the internal control and assesses control risk based on the effectiveness of the internal control in preventing or detecting material noncompliance with specific requirements. Based on the assessed level of inherent risk and control risk, the auditor then plans compliance tests to examine each major program for compliance with these requirements.

An additional point should be mentioned at this time. When auditors tested for entity compliance with laws and regulations in a GAAS (or GAGAS) audit, they were concerned with laws and regulations that have a material effect on the financial statements taken as a whole. Under the Single Audit Act, auditors are concerned with noncompliance with laws and regulations that have a material effect on the **major program** examined. This introduces two issues. First, each major program will differ in magnitude. As a result, materiality is expected to differ between programs. Second, in most cases, materiality levels for major programs are expected to be lower than those for the financial statements taken as a whole. As a result, the extent of compliance testing performed by the auditor is usually greater in an audit conducted under the Single Audit Act than either a GAAS or GAGAS audit.

Instances of Noncompliance. Once the audit has been planned, the auditor selects a sample of items for examination. For most of the specific requirements identified earlier, the auditor examines expenditures made by the governmental entity and any related records to determine whether they were made in compliance with the requirements of the federal assistance program. To illustrate, expenditures can be reviewed to determine that they are only made for goods and services stipulated by the federal program. In addition, the auditor can verify that any individual(s) on whose behalf the expenditures were made were actually eligible to receive federal assistance.

After examining expenditures, the auditor may detect situations where the entity was not in compliance with specific requirements of the federal assistance program. In evaluating whether the noncompliance could materially affect the federal financial assistance program, the auditor should consider both the frequency of noncompliance and whether the noncompliance resulted in a **questioned cost**. The following are examples of types of questioned costs for specific program requirements:

1. Costs not allowed under the requirements of the program (**unallowable costs**).
2. Costs for which documentation does not exist to allow the auditor to determine whether the expenditure was made for appropriate goods and services or eligible individual(s) (**undocumented costs**).
3. Costs for which the auditor cannot find specific approval by appropriate personnel of the entity (**unapproved costs**).
4. Costs that are not reasonable given the circumstances (**unreasonable costs**).

> **QUESTIONED COSTS**[9]
>
> An audit conducted by the Office of the State Auditor for the State of Texas found that nursing homes and health care companies who received financial assistance from the state of Texas spent $1 million dollars on some highly questionable activities. These activities included: (1) providing jobs for relatives who were not actually working for the facilities; (2) paying for Texas Ranger baseball tickets, automobiles and automobile window tinting and employee parties; and (3) leasing an airplane from an employee. The auditor concluded that the monies spent on these questionable activities could have been used to provide 6,115 additional days of nursing home care and 40,471 hours of the most expensive level of in-home care.

For any questioned costs discovered in the tests of compliance, the auditor considers the likely amount of questioned cost for the federal financial assistance program. The total questioned costs include both actual questioned costs discovered as well as projected questioned costs. Based on the total amount of likely questioned costs, the auditor may issue an unqualified opinion, qualified opinion, or adverse opinion on compliance with specific requirements. Regardless of the auditor's opinion on compliance with specific requirements, any questioned costs identified during the audit must be reported. Thus, even when only minor amounts of questioned costs are noted by the auditor, they are reported along with the auditor's opinion on compliance (discussed in the following subsection).

Reports on Compliance with Specific Requirements. The auditor's report on compliance with specific requirements of federal financial assistance programs is illustrated in Figure 20-5. This report is an example of an unqualified opinion. The more important statements in this report are:

1. The auditor has examined compliance with specific requirements and a list of the requirements examined.
2. An indication that the auditor's procedures to determine compliance with specific requirements are similar to those used in a GAAS audit. That is, the auditor is required to plan and perform the audit to obtain reasonable assurance about whether any material noncompliance with specific requirements occurred.
3. A summary of any immaterial instances of noncompliance noted during the audit (if no immaterial instances are noted, this statement is omitted).
4. The auditor's opinion on compliance with specific requirements.

Note that the auditor's report on compliance with specific requirements includes a reference to a "schedule of findings and questioned costs" that summarizes instances of noncompliance that are considered to be immaterial to the federal assistance program. If the auditor identifies material instances of noncompliance, a qualified or adverse opinion should be issued. The material instances of noncompliance would be specifically mentioned in the auditor's report shown in Figure 20-5.

---

[9] "State Audit Questions Nursing Home Spending," *Houston Chronicle* (September 25, 1996), 19A.

We have audited the financial statements of the city of Bryan College, Texas as of and for the year ended June 30, 19X1, and have issued our report thereon dated August 15, 19X1.

We also have audited the city of Bryan College, Texas' compliance with the requirements governing the eligibility of individuals receiving assistance that are applicable to each of its major federal financial assistance programs, which are identified in the accompanying schedule of federal financial assistance, for the year ended June 30, 19X1. The management of the city of Bryan College, Texas is responsible for their compliance with those requirements. Our responsibility is to express an opinion on compliance with those requirements based on our audit.

We conducted our audit of compliance with those requirements in accordance with generally accepted auditing standards, *Government Auditing Standards*, issued by the Comptroller General of the United States, and *OMB Circular A-128*, "Audits of State and Local Governments." Those standards and *OMB Circular A-128* require that we plan and perform the audit to obtain reasonable assurance about whether material noncompliance with the requirements referred to above occurred. An audit includes examining, on a test basis, evidence about the city of Bryan College, Texas' compliance with those requirements. We believe that our audit provides a reasonable basis for our opinion.

The results of our audit procedures disclosed immaterial instances of noncompliance with the requirements referred to above, which are described in the accompanying schedule of findings and questioned costs. We considered these instances of noncompliance in forming our opinion on compliance, which is expressed in the following paragraph.

In our opinion, the city of Bryan College, Texas complied, in all material respects, with the requirements governing the eligibility of individuals receiving assistance that are applicable to each of its major federal financial assistance programs for the year ended June 30, 19X1.

This report is intended for the information of the audit committee, management, and the city council. This is not intended to limit the distribution of this report, which is a matter of public record.

[*Signature*]
[*Date*]

Figure 20-5: *Report on Compliance with Specific Requirements of Major Programs under the Single Audit Act*

Specific Requirements: Nonmajor Programs. The auditor's responsibility for testing compliance with the specific requirements pertaining to nonmajor programs is much more limited than that discussed above for major programs. Recall that a **nonmajor program** is one that accounts for a relatively lower percentage of entity expenditures for all programs. For these programs, the auditor is *not* required to select expenditures for these programs for the purpose of testing compliance with program requirements. The auditor is only required to test transactions that were selected as a result of the financial statement audit or study and evaluation of internal control over federal financial assistance programs. In general, the auditor only tests compliance with the allowability of program expenditures and eligibility of individuals or groups to whom the entity provides financial assistance.

After testing compliance with the requirements of nonmajor programs, the auditor issues a report that provides positive assurance on items tested and negative assurance on those not tested.

Figure 20-6 illustrates a sample report prepared by the auditor on compliance with requirements of nonmajor programs. Figure 20-6 clearly indicates the difference between the auditor's responsibility for major programs and nonmajor programs. Recall that, for these former programs, the auditor specifically examined entity compliance with specific and general requirements having a material effect on the federal financial assistance program. Accordingly, an opinion on compliance with these requirements is provided. In contrast, the report on compliance with nonmajor programs clearly indicates that the requirements were tested in connection with the audit of the financial statements and study and evaluation of internal control. As a result, only positive and negative assurance can be provided in this situation.

We have audited the financial statements of the city of Bryan College, Texas as of and for the year ended June 30, 19X1, and have issued our report thereon dated August 15, 19X1.

In connection with our audit of the financial statements of the city of Bryan College, Texas and our consideration of the city of Bryan College, Texas' internal control used to administer federal financial assistance programs, as required by the *OMB Circular A-128*, we selected certain transactions applicable to certain nonmajor federal financial assistance programs for the year ended June 30, 19X1. As required by *OMB Circular A-128*, we performed auditing procedures to test for compliance with the requirements governing types of services allowed or unallowed and eligibility that are applicable to those transactions. Our procedures were substantially less in scope than an audit, the objective of which is the expression of an opinion on the city of Bryan College, Texas' compliance with these requirements. Accordingly, we do not express such an opinion.

With respect to the items tested, the results of these procedures disclosed no material instances of noncompliance with the requirements listed in the preceding section. With respect to items not tested, nothing came to our attention that caused us to believe that the city of Bryan College, Texas had not complied, in all material respects, with those requirements. However, the results of our procedures disclosed immaterial instances of noncompliance with those requirements, which are described in the accompanying schedule of findings and questioned costs.

This report is intended for the use of the audit committee, management, and city council. However, this report is a matter of public record and its distribution is not limited.

[Signature]
[Date]

Figure 20-6: *Report on Compliance with Specific Requirements of Nonmajor Programs under the Single Audit Act*

One other matter that should be addressed is a situation where no transactions are selected by the auditor from nonmajor programs as part of the financial statement audit or study and evaluation of internal control. In these cases, the auditor should not prepare a report on compliance with the requirements of nonmajor programs.

General Requirements. In addition to the specific requirements noted above, the Single Audit Act requires the auditor to examine and report on entity compliance with general requirements. **General requirements** are those requirements identified by OMB Circular A-128 as having significant national policy implications. These requirements are identical for each federal financial assistance program. The general requirements are summarized in Figure 20-7.

---

1. The use of funds for partisan political activity is prohibited.
2. Laborers working on federally funded projects must be paid at rates at least equal to prevailing regional wage rates established by the Secretary of Labor (Davis-Bacon Act).
3. The use of funds in such a manner as to violate another party's civil rights is prohibited.
4. Recipients should minimize the time elapsed between receipt and disbursement of funds.
5. Recipients should observe preestablished procedures for acquiring real property and assisting in the relocation of individuals affected by acquisitions of real property.
6. Recipients must file prescribed financial reports.
7. Recipients should only receive reimbursement for specified direct and indirect costs.
8. Recipients must certify that they provide a drug-free workplace to their employees.
9. Recipients must follow certain administrative requirements (Common Rule).

Source: *Compliance Supplement for Single Audits of State and Local Governments* (Washington, DC: Office of Management and Budget, revised September 1990).

Figure 20-7: *General Requirements*

Although the Single Audit Act requires auditors to examine compliance with general requirements for both major and nonmajor programs, little professional guidance is provided. While the *Compliance Supplement*[10] provides the authoritative guidance for the procedures that are to be performed in examining compliance with general requirements, there is no guidance for the extent of these procedures. Examples of procedures identified by the *Compliance Supplement* for examining compliance with general requirements include:

1. Testing state and local governmental entity expenditures for evidence of lobbying activities or other attempts to influence legislation.
2. Reviewing selected construction contracts and determining whether they contain provisions for paying "prevailing" wage rates.
3. Examining the number of complaints filed with state or local agencies for discrimination.
4. Identifying the dates and amounts of expenditures and receipts of federal funds and evaluating the size of cash balances maintained by the entity.

The auditor's report on compliance with general requirements provides positive assurance on items examined and negative assurance on those not examined. A single report is prepared to describe

---

[10] *Compliance Supplement for Single Audits of State and Local Governments* (Washington, DC: Office of Management and Budget, revised September 1990).

compliance with general requirements for all of a state and local entity's federal financial assistance programs (both major and nonmajor programs). Contrast this report with that for specific requirements for major programs, which provided an opinion on the entity's compliance with specific requirements. An opinion cannot be issued in the former type of engagement because the scope of the auditor's tests of compliance were less extensive than those conducted in a GAAS audit.

Summary: Procedures and Reports for Major and Nonmajor Programs. Figure 20-8 summarizes the auditor's responsibilities and reports for major and nonmajor federal financial assistance programs. These reports are only a subset of those issued under the Single Audit Act. The auditor is also required to issue reports on the entity's financial statements, compliance with laws and regulations, and internal control, as in a GAGAS audit.

	Major Programs	Nonmajor Programs
Auditor Responsibility	Detect noncompliance having a material effect on the major program being examined.	No responsibility beyond a financial statement audit or study and evaluation of internal control.
Transactions Examined	Transactions material to the program being examined.	Transactions selected as part of a financial statement audit or study and evaluation of internal control.
Reporting on General Requirements	Positive and negative assurance.	Positive and negative assurance.
Reporting on Specific Requirements	Opinion on compliance.	Positive and negative assurance.

Figure 20-8: *Audit Responsibilities and Reports for Major and Nonmajor Programs under the Single Audit Act*

◘ Summary: Compliance Auditing

Figure 20-9 summarizes the responsibilities of the auditor for compliance with laws and regulations, internal control, and program requirements for examining and reporting relating to state and local governmental entities in financial statement audits, GAGAS audits, and audits conducted under the Single Audit Act. An examination of this summary reveals that each type of engagement "builds" on the previous engagement(s)—that is, all of the procedures performed and reports issued in a GAAS audit also apply to GAGAS audits. Similarly, all of the procedures performed and reports issued in GAGAS audits are applicable to audits conducted under the Single Audit Act. These audit procedures and reports served as the focus of the preceding discussion.

	Audit Responsibility	Reporting Responsibility
Financial Statement Audit	Plan the audit to detect instances of noncompliance with laws and regulations having a material effect on the entity's financial statements.	Opinion on financial statements.
Government Auditing Standards	Same audit responsibilities as a financial statement audit.	Opinion on financial statements.
		Report on compliance with laws and regulations.
		Report on internal control.
Single Audit Act	Same audit responsibilities as a financial statement audit.	Opinion on financial statements.
		Report on compliance with laws and regulations.
		Report on internal control.
	Tests of compliance with specific requirements of major programs.	Report on compliance with specific requirements of major programs.
		Schedule of findings and questioned costs for major programs.
	For nonmajor programs, tests of compliance with specific requirements selected as part of the financial statement audit.	Report on compliance with specific requirements of nonmajor programs.
	Tests of compliance with general requirements of major and nonmajor programs.	Report on compliance with general requirements of major and nonmajor programs.

Figure 20-9: *Auditor Responsibilities in a Financial Statement Audit, GAGAS Audit, and Audit Conducted under the Single Audit Act*

> **CHAPTER CHECKPOINTS**
>
> **20-10.** What entities are required to have audits conducted under the provisions of the Single Audit Act?
>
> **20-11.** What reports are required under the Single Audit Act?
>
> **20-12.** Distinguish between major programs and nonmajor programs. What are the audit requirements for each of these types of programs? What types of reports are issued on each of these programs?
>
> **20-13.** Define general requirements. What are the nine general requirements?
>
> **20-14.** Define specific requirements. Provide some examples of specific requirements.
>
> **20-15.** Identify and provide an example of the four major types of questioned costs that may be detected in an audit of compliance with specific requirements of major programs.

INTERNAL AUDITING

Internal auditing is defined by the Institute of Internal Auditors (IIA) as:

> an independent appraisal activity established within an organization to examine and evaluate its activities as a service to the organization. The objective of internal auditing is to assist members in the organization in the effective discharge of their duties.[11]

From the above definition, two aspects of internal auditing are clear. First, internal auditors are employed by and provide service to the organization they audit. Second, the primary function performed by internal auditors is to provide service to the organization (primarily management and the board of directors). These services are discussed throughout this section.

The importance of internal auditing in the organization is evidenced by the explosive growth in the membership of the Institute of Internal Auditors (IIA), the professional organization of internal auditors. The growth of the internal audit profession (both past growth as well as expected future growth) can be attributed to two main events. In 1977, the Foreign Corrupt Practices Act (FCPA) was promulgated. As noted in Chapter 5, this Act required publicly-traded corporations to establish and maintain effective internal control. Because an internal audit department acts as a very high level of internal control within the organization, the FCPA resulted in a growth in both the number and quality of internal audit departments established by United States corporations. More recently, the *Report of*

---

[11] Institute of Internal Auditors (IIA), *Codification of Standards for the Professional Practice of Internal Auditing* (Altamonte Springs, FL: IIA, 1989), 1.

the National Commission on Fraudulent Financial Reporting[12] (Treadway Report) suggested that all public companies establish internal audit departments.

This section provides a brief overview of internal auditing and the role of the internal auditor in the organization. It is important to emphasize that the role of internal auditing is expanding and will continue to expand in the future. A conclusion that the student should reach after reading this section is that internal auditors are extensively involved in all areas of the organization's operations.

The Role of Internal Auditing in the Organization

Internal auditors assist other members of the organization in fulfilling their obligations by providing them with reports, analyses, and advice with respect to various matters. The *Statement of Responsibilities of Internal Auditors* indicates that the scope of internal auditing encompasses several activities. These activities, along with the classification of the activities, are summarized in Figure 20-10.

Activity	Classification
1. Reviewing the reliability and integrity of financial information.	Financial statement auditing.
2. Reviewing the systems established to ensure compliance with policies, plans, procedures, laws, and regulations that could have a significant impact on operations and reports, and determining whether the organization is in compliance with these matters.	Compliance auditing.
3. Reviewing the means used by the organization to safeguard assets.	Studying and evaluating internal control.
4. Appraising the economy and efficiency with which resources are utilized by the organization.	Operational auditing.
5. Reviewing organization operations or programs to determine whether results are consistent with organizational objectives and goals.	Operational auditing.

Source: Institute of Internal Auditors (IIA), *Codification of Standards for the Practice of Internal Auditing* (Altamonte Springs, FL: IIA, 1989).

Figure 20-10: *Activities of Internal Audit Departments*

---

[12] *Report of the National Commission on Fraudulent Financial Reporting* (Washington, DC: National Commission on Fraudulent Financial Reporting, 1987).

The activities summarized in Figure 20-10 reflect the extensive range of responsibilities accorded to an organization's internal audit department. As shown therein, their duties include procedures performed in financial statement audits, compliance audits, evaluations of internal control, and operational audits. A common theme embodied in each of these duties is that they provide benefits to the organization.

As noted in Figure 20-10, internal auditors' responsibilities may overlap somewhat with the responsibilities of the external auditor in the financial statement audit—that is, the internal auditor may perform certain procedures to evaluate the recording and processing of transactions. An example is the periodic confirmation of accounts receivable to detect possible instances of lapping or delays in recording sales made to customers on account. Also, internal auditors may perform procedures to evaluate the effectiveness of the organization's internal control. As noted in Chapter 4, *Statement on Auditing Standards No. 65 (SAS No. 65)*[13] provides the external auditor with guidance as to how the work of the internal auditors may be used in the external audit examination.

Compliance audits were discussed earlier in this chapter. The focus in that discussion was on compliance auditing for governmental entities, but it is important to note that corporations are also subject to laws and regulations in conducting their operations. An effective internal audit department provides assurance to the corporation's management that these laws and regulations are being complied with by the organization. In addition, internal auditors can also examine the extent of organization compliance with established internal control policies and procedures. This type of work is closely related to the role of the internal auditor in the organization's internal control.

Operational auditing provides benefits to the organization by improving the efficiency, economy, and effectiveness of its operations. When performing operational audits, internal auditors evaluate some function or division of the organization with the intention of enabling that function or division to improve its operations. Examples of the types of improvements that have resulted from internal auditor recommendations are illustrated in the following section.

In summary, the duties and responsibilities of internal auditors span the following major areas of auditing discussed in this text:

1. Financial statement auditing, through evaluating the reliability of the organization's methods of recording financial information and the organization's internal control.

2. Compliance auditing, through evaluating the organization's compliance with laws and regulations and established internal control policies and procedures.

3. Operational auditing, through providing recommendations to improve the efficiency, economy, and effectiveness of the organization's operations.

◘ Differences Between Internal Auditing and External Auditing

Although their responsibilities overlap, several important differences between internal and external auditors can be highlighted at this point. The previous subsection reveals the extensive variety of tasks performed by internal auditors. These same tasks can also be performed by external auditors and CPAs

---

[13] American Institute of Certified Public Accountants (AICPA), *Statement on Auditing Standards No. 65*, "The Auditor's Consideration of the internal Audit Function in an Audit of Financial Statements" (New York: AICPA, 1991, AU 322).

serving the organization in a consulting capacity. However, internal auditors continuously perform these tasks as part of their ordinary duties.

In addition to the wider range of activities generally performed by internal auditors, other differences between internal auditors and external auditors deserve mention. First, and most apparent, internal auditors are employed by the company for whom they perform their work. As a result, they cannot be expected to refrain from some of the relationships (for example, employment and decision-making relationships) required of external auditors for independence. However, it is important to note that the IIA Standards for the Practice of Internal Auditing[14] (discussed later in this section) recognize that certain factors influence the ability of the internal auditor to freely report findings to the organization. Therefore, independence is still very important to internal auditors, despite the fact that they will probably never achieve the appearance of independence accorded to external auditors.

The second major difference between internal and external auditors are the subjects and recipients of their reports. As noted in Chapters 17 and 18, external auditors issue reports on the fairness of the entity's financial statements. These reports are included with the entity's financial statements and are used by external third parties in making decisions with respect to the entity. In contrast, the reports of internal auditors are provided to persons within the organization and rarely circulate outside it. Some of the topics addressed in the reports of internal auditors include:

1. Observed weaknesses in the organization's internal control.
2. The degree of organization compliance with established policies, procedures, plans, laws, and regulations.
3. Evaluations of the economy and efficiency of various operating departments and functions.
4. The extent to which the results of operating departments and functions are consistent with the organization's objectives.

An important feature of the reports and analyses prepared by internal auditors is that, in addition to presenting the internal auditor's conclusions, recommendations are provided. For example, reports prepared by internal auditors on an organization's internal control should indicate both observed weaknesses in internal control and deviations from established internal control policies and procedures and recommendations for improving these deficiencies.

◻ Code of Ethics

As noted in Chapter 2, in order to increase the public confidence in the accounting profession, the AICPA has established a Code of Professional Conduct that must be observed by all of its member firms. Similarly, the IIA has established a Code of Ethics for its members. This Code of Ethics provides basic principles related to the practice of internal auditing. Like the AICPA's Code of Conduct, it consists of a series of standards that describe allowable and unallowable behavior. The basic components of the IIA's Code of Ethics are summarized in Figure 20-11.

---

[14] Institute of Internal Auditors (IIA), *Codification of Standards for the Professional Practice of Internal Auditing* (Altamonte Springs, FL: IIA, 1989).

1. Members shall exercise honesty, objectivity and diligence in performing their duties.
2. While members should exhibit loyalty to those for whom they are rendering services, they shall not knowingly participate in any illegal or improper activities.
3. Members should not engage in acts discreditable to the profession of internal auditing or their organization.
4. Members should refrain from activities that may be in conflict with the interest of their organization or prejudice their ability to objectively discharge their duties.
5. Members shall not accept anything of value from individuals in their organization that may impair their professional judgment.
6. Members should only undertake services they can complete with professional competence.
7. Members shall comply with *Standards for the Professional Practice of Internal Auditing.*
8. Members shall not use confidential information for personal gain or in any manner contrary to the welfare of their organization.
9. Members shall reveal all material facts known to them when reporting on their work.
10. Members shall strive for improvement in their proficiency and the effectiveness of their services.
11. Members shall maintain the high standards of competence, morality, and dignity promulgated by the IIA and abide by the *Bylaws* of the IIA.

Source: Institute of Internal Auditors (IIA), *Code of Ethics* (Altamonte Springs, FL: IIA, 1992).

Figure 20-11: *IIA Code of Ethics*

Note that several aspects of the IIA's Code of Ethics parallel matters contained in the AICPA's Code of Professional Conduct. Common elements in the Codes are issues related to objectivity, integrity, acts discreditable, competence, performing in accordance with professional standards, and confidential information. A notable difference in the IIA's Code of Ethics is discussion related to loyalty to the employing organization. This reflects the unique auditor/auditee relationship held by internal auditors.

◘ Standards of Internal Auditing[15]

Similar to GAAS, the IIA has promulgated a series of standards that govern the practice of internal auditing. Known as the *Standards for the Professional Practice of Internal Auditing* (or *Standards*), these Standards were established to:

1. Impart an understanding of the role and responsibilities of internal auditing to all levels of management, boards of directors, public bodies, external auditors, and related professional organizations.

---

[15] This subsection is based on *Codification of Standards for the Professional Practice of Internal Auditing* (Altamonte Springs, FL: IIA, 1989).

2. Establish the basis for the guidance and measurement of internal auditing performance.
3. Improve the practice of internal auditing.[16]

The IIA standards can be roughly categorized into five groups. Like GAAS, which are updated and interpreted periodically by *Statements on Auditing Standards*, the IIA Standards are updated and interpreted by *Statements on Internal Auditing Standards (SIAS)*. The IIA *Standards* are summarized in Figure 20-12 and discussed in the remainder of this section. The complete standards are presented in the appendix to this chapter.

---

100 **INDEPENDENCE**: Internal auditors should be independent of the activities they audit.

200 **PROFESSIONAL PROFICIENCY**: Internal audits should be performed with proficiency and due professional care.

300 **SCOPE OF WORK**: The scope of the internal audit should encompass the examination of internal control and the quality of performance in carrying out assigned responsibilities.

400 **PERFORMANCE OF AUDIT WORK**: Audit work should include planning the audit, examining and evaluating information, communicating results, and following up on work performed.

500 **MANAGEMENT OF THE INTERNAL AUDIT DEPARTMENT**: The director of internal auditing should properly manage the internal audit department.

Figure 20-12: *IIA Standards*

Independence. Earlier in this chapter, it was noted that internal auditors were employed by the organization for which they provided services. Although this relationship may appear to preclude the need for any form of independence, this is clearly not appropriate. Independence is important in an internal audit setting because internal auditors should be able to examine the operations of any division within the organization. In addition, internal auditors should report their findings to a level high enough in the organization to allow their recommendations to be implemented.

The Standards recognize two matters that enhance the independence of internal auditors: the organizational status of the internal auditing department and their objectivity. In terms of organizational status, the internal auditor should have support from upper management and the Board of Directors so that they can perform their work with the cooperation of auditees within the organization. This support is normally provided by having the director of the internal audit department communicate regularly with the organization's Board of Directors. This communication helps enhance the independence of the internal audit department and allows both parties to be informed about matters of interest.

Objectivity is an independent mental attitude that should be held by internal auditors. To ensure internal auditor objectivity, the following guidelines are suggested:

1. Staff assignments should be made to avoid potential conflicts of interest or biases.
2. Staff assignments should be rotated periodically.

---

[16] *Codification of Standards for the Professional Practice of Internal Auditing* (Altamonte Springs, FL: IIA, 1989).

3. Persons transferred to the internal audit department should not examine activities they performed in another department within the organization until a reasonable period of time has elapsed.

Professional Proficiency. In addressing professional proficiency, the *Standards* discuss issues related to this matter at two levels: the internal auditing department and the individual internal auditor. Professional proficiency provides the internal auditor with reasonable assurance of performing work in an effective manner. To enhance professional proficiency, internal auditing departments should be properly staffed and have the knowledge, skills, and discipline necessary to carry out their audit responsibilities. In addition, it is important that the work of internal auditors be properly supervised. According to the standards, supervision includes:

1. Providing instructions to subordinates at the outset of the audit.
2. Approving the audit program.
3. Determining that workpapers adequately support the findings and conclusions of the internal auditor.
4. Determining that audit objectives are currently being met.

On an individual basis, the *Standards* require that internal auditors comply with the Code of Ethics, have the necessary knowledge, skills, and discipline to perform their work, maintain technical competence through continuing professional education, and exhibit due professional care. Similar to GAAS, due professional care is defined as the level of care and skill expected of a reasonably prudent and competent professional. It is important to emphasize that due care means using reasonable skill and judgment and does not imply levels of extraordinary performance.

Scope of the Work. This standard is perhaps the most comprehensive and has the greatest impact on the internal auditors' work. The scope of the internal auditors' work includes: (1) reviewing the reliability and integrity of financial information; (2) evaluating organization compliance with policies, procedures, plans, laws, and regulations; (3) reviewing the means used to safeguard assets; (4) appraising the economy and efficiency with which the organization uses resources; and (5) ascertaining whether the organization is achieving its objectives. As noted earlier, these activities include those performed in a financial statement audit, study and evaluation of internal control, compliance audit, and operational audit. These activities were summarized earlier in Figure 20-10.

Performance of Audit Work. The fourth standard deals with performing the audit work. The audit work is separated into four steps. First, the internal audit should be properly planned. **Planning activities** include establishing audit objectives, obtaining background information, writing the audit program, and obtaining approval of the audit work plan. Next, the auditor should examine and evaluate information. Similar to the requirements under GAAS, the information should be sufficient, competent, relevant, and useful and provide a basis for audit findings and recommendations. Once this information has been gathered, audit workpapers should be prepared to record the information obtained during the audit and support the findings and recommendations reported by the internal auditors. These workpapers are subsequently reviewed by management of the internal auditing department.

Following the gathering of evidence, the auditor should **communicate the results** of the examination. The results are ordinarily communicated in writing through the preparation of a report. The reports prepared by internal auditors should present the results of their examination and, where appropriate, an expression of the auditor's opinion. In addition, reports often contain recommendations for improvements noted as a result of the audit examination. Finally, internal auditors should **follow up** on recommendations made in their reports to determine whether corrective action has been taken on reported audit findings.

The chronological order of the audit work can be summarized as shown below.

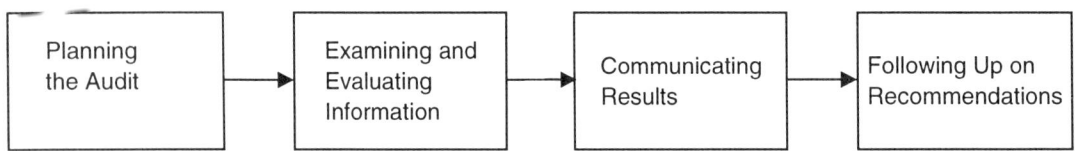

With the exception of following up on reported audit findings, these procedures are performed in a financial statement audit. However, the type of evidence gathered and report issued will obviously differ in GAAS and internal audits.

Management of the Internal Audit Department. The final internal audit standard addresses the responsibilities of the management of the internal audit department. Three general responsibilities identified by this standard include taking necessary steps to ensure that:

1. Audit work corresponds to the purposes approved by management and is accepted by the Board of Directors.
2. Resources of the internal audit department are utilized efficiently and effectively.
3. Audit work conforms with the *Standards*.

These objectives can be attained through proper planning, devising written policies and procedures, establishing programs for personnel management and development, coordinating internal and external audit relationships, and establishing and maintaining a quality review program. A **quality review program** is similar in nature to the peer review programs discussed in Chapter 2 for member firms of the AICPA. That is, a quality review program is intended to provide internal audit departments with reasonable assurance that the work they perform is conducted in accordance with the Standards. According to this standard, a quality review program consists of:

1. Supervision of the work of internal auditors.
2. Internal reviews by members of the internal audit staff.
3. External reviews by qualified persons independent of the organization.

Summary: Internal Audit Standards. The overall nature of the IIA Standards is similar to the nature of the 10 GAAS for financial statement audits. Both sets of standards are measures of the quality of the auditor's performance that do not change from one engagement to another. Throughout the preceding discussion, similarities between the IIA Standards with the 10 GAAS are apparent. Figure 20-13 compares the IIA *Standards* with the GAAS described throughout the text. As shown therein, a great deal of similarity does exist in these standards, despite the differences in the types of procedures performed and reports issued by internal and external auditors.

Internal Audit Standard		GAAS
100	Independence	Independence
200	Professional Proficiency	Training and Proficiency Supervision of Assistants Due Professional Care
300	Scope of Work	Internal Control
400	Performance of Work	Planning Sufficient, Competent Evidence Reporting Standards
500	Management of the Internal Auditing Department	No Similar GAAS

Figure 20-13: *Comparison of Internal Audit Standards and GAAS*

CHAPTER CHECKPOINTS

20-16. Define internal auditing. What are some common activities performed by internal auditors?

20-17. How do internal auditors' activities relate to financial statement auditing, compliance auditing, and operational auditing?

20-18. What are some of the major topics addressed in the reports prepared by internal auditors?

20-19. What are the *Standards for the Professional Practice of Internal Auditing*? List the five categories of these Standards.

20-20. According to the *Standards for the Professional Practice of Internal Auditing* what are the four major steps in performing audit work?

20-21. Briefly compare the categories of the *Standards for the Professional Practice of Internal Auditing* with the 10 GAAS.

OPERATIONAL AUDITING

The AICPA has defined **operational auditing** as:

> a systematic review of an organization's activities ... in relation to specified objectives. The purpose of the engagement may be: *(a)* to assess performance, *(b)* to identify opportunities for improvement, and *(c)* to develop recommendations for improvements or further action.[17]

Operational audits focus on the **efficiency**, **economy**, and **effectiveness** of an entity's operations. In an operational audit, the auditor evaluates the operations of a division or department of an entity and recommends opportunities for improvement. In doing so, the operations of the department evaluated are compared against some established criteria. For example, in evaluating the efficiency of production operations, auditors can compare actual performance (units produced, hours worked, or materials used) to performance standards or budgeted levels. To evaluate the effectiveness of this production process, the auditor can determine the number of spoiled or defective units emerging from the process and compare that to some allowable measure established by the organization. In any case, operational audits require the auditor to evaluate performance (whether the efficiency or effectiveness) against some predetermined measure.

Who Performs Operational Audits?

Operational audits may be performed by external auditors, internal auditors, or governmental auditors. In conducting an audit in accordance with GAAS, external auditors acquire a great deal of information about the client and its operations. This information may be beneficial to the client in allowing it to identify certain deficiencies and improve upon those areas. As noted in Chapter 5, a secondary purpose of the auditor's study and evaluation of internal control is to provide management with constructive suggestions that enable them to improve the effectiveness of their internal controls. Consistent with these suggestions, *SAS No. 60*[18] requires the auditor to communicate certain types of deficiencies noted during the study and evaluation of internal control (referred to as reportable conditions and material weaknesses) to their clients. As these communications identify deficiencies noted during the audit, they can be viewed as a form of operational auditing.

External CPAs may also perform operational auditing during consulting (or management advisory services) engagements. In these cases, CPAs evaluate some aspect of an entity's operations and provide suggestions for improving those operations. For example, CPAs can evaluate the computer systems used by their clients to determine whether redundant storage of data results in excessive costs to the company. The recent growth in consulting services provided by CPAs and the emergence of the

---

[17] *Operational Audit Engagements* (New York: AICPA, 1982), 2.

[18] American Institute of Certified Public Accountants (AICPA), *Statement on Auditing Standards No. 60*, "Communication of Internal Control Structure Related Matters Noted in an Audit" (New York: AICPA, 1988, AU 319).

consulting divisions of large CPA firms indicate that these services are being increasingly provided by external CPAs.[19]

As noted in the preceding section, some of the activities performed by internal auditors fall into the category of operational audits. Recall that duties identified by the Standards included: (1) appraising the economy and efficiency with which resources are applied, and (2) reviewing operations or programs to ascertain whether results are consistent with established objectives. Both types of duties involve operational auditing. In these cases, the management of the organization may request that the internal audit division evaluate the operations of some area of the company.

Finally, governmental auditors may perform operational audits. According to Government Auditing Standards[20] (the *Yellow Book*), the following types of audits are performed by governmental auditors:

1. **Financial and financial-related audits**. These audits determine whether the governmental entity's financial statements are prepared according to GAAP and whether the entity has complied with laws and regulations having a material effect on the entity's financial statements.
2. **Economy and efficiency audits**. Economy and efficiency audits *(a)* determine whether entities are managing their resources economically and efficiently, *(b)* identify the causes of any inefficiencies, and *(c)* determine whether the entity has complied with laws and regulations concerning matters of economy and efficiency.
3. **Program results audits**. This type of audit determines whether the desired results of a given program are being achieved and if the agency has considered alternatives that may achieve these results at a lower cost.

Financial and financial-related audits were described earlier in this chapter as part of the discussion of compliance auditing. These types of audits are performed by external auditors in conjunction with the examination of the governmental entity's financial statements. However, both economy and efficiency audits and program results audits are clearly operational in nature. These types of audits are normally performed by governmental auditors employed by the General Accounting Office (GAO). A distinguishing aspect of operational audits for governmental entities is that results are often not evaluated in financial terms, but in nonquantitative terms (such as the improvement in environmental conditions).

◘ Steps in Performing an Operational Audit

The AICPA's report *Operational Audit Engagements* notes that, although a given operational audit may differ in terms of the details, the following activities are commonly performed in all operational audits:

1. Planning, control, and supervision.
2. Fact finding, analysis, and documentation.

---

[19] See, for example, "Arthur Andersen Weighs Restructuring To Make Consulting Practice Separate," *The Wall Street Journal* (September 27, 1989).

[20] *Standards for Audit of Governmental Organizations, Programs, Activities, and Functions* (Washington, DC: U.S. General Accounting Office, 1994), 3.

3. Recommendations.
4. Reporting.

Each of these types of activities is briefly discussed in the remainder of this section.

Planning, Control, and Supervision. In planning an operational audit, the auditor performs some of the same procedures and faces many of the same issues as those confronting auditors in a financial statement audit. For example, the auditor should become familiar with the organizational unit being examined, define the purpose and scope of the engagement, identify the nature of the report to be issued, and decide on the type of procedures to be performed. The end result of these activities will be an audit program that will be used to gather evidence and, ultimately, make recommendations to the entity.

A significant difference between an operational audit and a financial statement audit that affects the auditor's planning is the diversity of activities performed in the former type of engagement. Financial statement audits are defined by GAAS; in planning, the main issues faced by the auditor relate to the nature, timing, and extent of substantive testing procedures to be performed. In contrast, an operational audit differs widely from one organizational unit to another. Therefore, the types of procedures performed by the auditor are tailored to each specific engagement. In planning operational audits, it is critical that the auditor focus on the objectives in designing the procedures to be performed.

Once the operational audit has been planned, it is important that any staff assigned to the engagement be properly supervised. The importance of proper supervision in all audits is evidenced by the inclusion of this requirement in both GAAS and the IIA *Standards*; however, supervision takes on additional importance in operational audits. Once again, the diverse nature of these engagements increases the importance of properly supervising staff to ensure that the audit is conducted in such a manner as to achieve the objectives identified during the planning stages.

Fact Finding, Analysis, and Documentation. The majority of the operational audit is conducted within the fact finding, analysis, and documentation stage. This stage of the audit is comprised of the tests performed by the auditor to gather evidence concerning the effectiveness, economy, and efficiency of operations. In performing these tests, many of the evidence-gathering procedures described in detail throughout this text are utilized. For example, auditors can select and examine deposit slips (documentary evidence) and compare these deposits to cash receipts records. Doing so may reveal delays in depositing cash receipts, a situation that results in an opportunity loss to the organization through lower interest earned on cash held on deposit.

Also, operational audits often entail a great deal of physical observation and inquiry about matters being investigated. Although production and cost accounting records may reveal inefficiencies in the organization's production process, inquiry and observation may allow the auditor to identify the actual cause of these inefficiencies. To illustrate, based on variance analysis, the auditor may initially conclude that an unfavorable direct labor efficiency variance reflects inefficiencies on the part of the organization's production staff. However, based on further inquiry, the auditor may determine that increased quality requirements for the organization's products render existing production standards obsolete. Thus, a situation initially thought to represent poor performance may instead reflect adequate performance.

Once evidence has been gathered regarding the operations of the department under examination, the auditor must analyze the information using some established criteria. Actual performance can be compared to budgets or standards established by the organization. Alternatively, the performance of one organizational unit can be evaluated against the performance of similar organizational units. Any inefficiencies or ineffective performance should be investigated further and discussed with the supervisor of the organizational unit whose operations are examined. The auditor should document the evidence and results of his or her analysis because these procedures will provide the basis for recommendations made in a report.

Recommendations and Reporting. After the evidence has been gathered and the analysis conducted by the auditor, the findings, conclusions, and recommendations resulting from the engagement are summarized in a report. Unlike audits conducted in accordance with GAAS, there is no standardized form for the report. The diversity of operational audits requires that the report be tailored to the engagement performed by the auditor. The lack of a standardized report makes it essential that the auditor's report clearly communicates the evidence gathered, analysis performed, conclusions reached, and recommendations made from the operational audit.

A second major difference in reporting for operational audits is the need for the auditor to conduct postaudit procedures (or "follow-up") with the auditee. Following up on reported recommendations is necessary to allow the auditor to ensure that the recommendations made in the report are understood by the entity. In addition, these procedures allow the auditor to determine the extent to which they have been incorporated by the auditee.

SUMMARY: CLASSIFICATIONS OF AUDITING

Figure 20-14 summarizes the various types of audit engagements and compares them to financial statement auditing, the area that has been the focus of this text. It is important to note that, while some similarities exist, major differences between the types of auditing engagements are present. These differences are highlighted in Figure 20-14.

	Performed by	Objective(s) of Audit	Recipient(s) of Reports
Financial Statement Auditing	Independent CPAs	Determine whether financial statements are prepared in conformity with GAAP	Third-party users (investors and creditors)
Compliance Auditing	Independent CPAs Internal auditors Governmental auditors	Determine the extent of entity compliance with laws, regulations, policies, plans, and procedures*	Entity management Administrator of governmental programs
Internal Auditing	Internal auditors	Evaluate financial statement reliability	Entity management
		Determine entity compliance with laws, regulations, policies, plans, and procedures	
		Evaluate the organization's internal control	
		Appraise the economy, efficiency, and effectiveness of the use of resources	
		Review programs for consistency of results with organization objectives	
Operational Auditing	Independent CPAs Internal auditors Governmental auditors	Evaluate the economy, efficiency, and effectiveness of the use of resources	Entity management

*For governmental entities, these audits are often performed in conjunction with the financial statement audit.

Figure 20-14: *Types of Audit Engagements*

CHAPTER CHECKPOINTS

20-22. Define operational auditing. What individuals perform operational audits?

20-23. What three types of audits are performed under *Government Auditing Standards*? Which of these types of audits would be considered operational audits?

20-24. What are the major steps in operational auditing? Briefly describe each step.

20-25. In performing an operational audit the auditor analyzes information gathered against established criteria. What are some of the criteria used in this regard?

Appendix

◉ INTERNAL AUDITING STANDARDS

◻ IIA Standards

100: Independence: Internal auditors should be independent of the activities they audit

    110 Organizational status
    120 Objectivity

200: Professional proficiency: Internal audits should be performed with proficiency and due professional care

Standards Related to the Internal Audit Department

    210 Staffing
    220 Knowledge, skills, and discipline
    230 Supervision

Standards Related to the Internal Auditor

    240 Compliance with standards of conduct
    250 Knowledge, skills, and discipline
    260 Human relations and communication
    270 Continuing education
    280 Due professional care

300   Scope of work: The scope of the internal audit should encompass the examination of internal control and the quality of performance in carrying out assigned responsibilities

    310 Reliability and integrity of information
    320 Compliance with policies, plans, procedures, laws, and regulations
    330 Safeguarding of assets
    340 Economical and efficient use of resources
    350 Accomplishment of established objectives and goals for operations or programs

400 Performance of audit work: Audit work should include planning the audit, examining and evaluating information, communicating results, and following up

    410 Planning the audit
    420 Examining and evaluating information
    430 Communicating results
    440 Following up

500 Management of the internal audit department: The director of internal auditing should properly manage the internal audit department

    510 Purpose, authority, and responsibility
    520 Planning
    530 Policies and procedures
    540 Personnel management and development
    550 External auditors
    560 Quality assurance

Source: Institute of Internal Auditors (IIA), *Codification of the Standards for the Professional Practice of Internal Auditing* (Altamonte Springs, FL: IIA, 1993).

◉ SUMMARY OF KEY POINTS

1. Compliance auditing allows the auditor to determine whether organizations are operating in conformity with established laws, regulations, or other criteria. Because the financial statements of governmental entities are affected by a large number of laws and regulations, compliance auditing is especially important in the examination of those entities' financial statements.

2. In a GAAS audit of a governmental entity, the auditor has the responsibility to plan the audit to detect situations of noncompliance with laws and regulations that may materially affect the entity's financial statements. This responsibility requires the auditor to: (1) understand the effect of laws and regulations on the entity's financial statements, (2) evaluate internal control policies and procedures designed to detect or prevent noncompliance with laws and regulations, and (3) perform tests to determine instances of noncompliance with laws and regulations having a material effect on the entity's financial statements.

3. When conducting an audit under *Government Auditing Standards* (the *Yellow Book*), the auditor assumes additional reporting responsibility for the entity's: (1) compliance with laws and regulations, and (2) internal control beyond those assumed in a GAAS audit. It is important to note that the auditor does not perform additional audit procedures in an audit conducted under Government Auditing Standards beyond those performed in a GAAS audit.

4. When state and local governmental entities receive specified dollar amounts of federal financial assistance, they are required to have an audit conducted under the provisions of the Single Audit Act. The Single Audit Act requires auditors to perform all of the procedures and prepare all of the reports prepared under an audit conducted under *Government Auditing Standards*. In addition, the auditor is required to report on compliance with the requirements of individual federal financial assistance programs.

5. A major program constitutes a large proportion of the total expenditures made by the state and local governmental unit. For major programs, the auditor is required to examine and report on compliance with specific requirements. Specific requirements differ from program to program and include such matters as the types of goods and services that can be purchased, the eligibility of individuals for receiving federal assistance, and any matching or earmarking requirements. For major programs, the auditor selects transactions material to the program and examines the related expenditures for compliance with specific program requirements.

6. Nonmajor programs are those programs that represent a relatively minor proportion of the total expenditures of state and local governmental entities. The auditor is not specifically required to select and test expenditures made under nonmajor programs for compliance with specific requirements. For these programs, any transactions selected during the financial statement audit or study and evaluation of internal control will be examined by the auditor for compliance with specific requirements.

7. General requirements are requirements representing federal policy and do not vary from one program to another. General requirements include such matters as not using funds for partisan political activities and providing a drug-free workplace. Under the Single Audit Act, auditors are required to test compliance with general requirements for both major and nonmajor programs.

8. Internal auditing is an appraisal function established within the organization to assist others in fulfilling their responsibilities. The duties performed by internal auditors can be classified into many categories, including financial statement auditing, compliance auditing, studying and evaluating internal control, and operational auditing.

9. Similar to CPAs, internal auditors also have a Code of Ethics and *Standards for the Professional Practice of Internal Auditing*. The IIA *Standards* are grouped into five main categories: independence, professional proficiency, scope of work, performance of audit work, and management of the internal audit department.

10. Operational auditing is the systematic review of an organization's activities to assess performance, identify opportunities for improvement, and develop recommendations for improvements or further action. Operational auditing is performed by external CPAs, internal auditors, and governmental auditors.

11. The four major steps performed in operational audits are: (1) planning, supervision and control; (2) fact finding, analysis, and documentation; (3) developing recommendations; and (4) reporting.

◉ GLOSSARY

Compliance Auditing. The purpose of compliance auditing is to determine whether the organization is operating in conformity with laws, regulations, policies, procedures, or other established criteria.

General Requirements. Requirements identified by *OMB Circular A-128* as having major national policy implications. These requirements do not vary from one program to another and include: (1) prohibiting the use of funds for partisan political activity, (2) paying workers at rates at least equal to the prevailing regional wage rates, (3) prohibiting the use of funds to violate another individual's civil rights, and (4) minimizing the time elapsing between receipt and disbursement of funds.

Government Auditing Standards. Also known as the Yellow Book. A set of standards that are applicable to the audit of governmental entities. In addition to the report on the fairness of the entity's financial statements, the auditor is required to issue reports on: (1) the entity's compliance with laws and regulations, and (2) the entity's internal control in audits conducted under *Government Auditing Standards*.

Institute of Internal Auditors (IIA). The professional organization of internal auditors. The IIA has established both a Code of Ethics and *Standards for the Professional Practice of Internal Auditing* to provide guidance for the practice of internal auditing.

Internal Auditing. An independent appraisal activity established within an organization as a service to the organization. The activities performed by internal auditors relate to financial statement auditing, operational auditing, compliance auditing, and studying and evaluating internal control.

Major Program. A program that accounts for a relatively large portion of the total expenditures made by a state and local governmental entity. The auditor is required to examine compliance with the specific requirements of major programs.

Nonmajor Program. A program that does not account for a large portion of the total expenditures made by a state and local governmental entity. In evaluating compliance with the specific requirements of nonmajor programs, the auditor only examines transactions selected as part of the financial statement audit or study and evaluation of internal control.

Operational Auditing. The systematic review of an organization's activities to assess performance, identify opportunities for improvement, and develop recommendations for improvements or further action. Operational auditing is performed by external CPAs, internal auditors, and governmental auditors.

Single Audit Act. This act specifies the audit requirements for state and local governmental entities receiving financial assistance from the federal government. Under the Single Audit Act, the auditor is required to issue the same reports as in a *Government Auditing Standards* audit (reports on financial statements, compliance with laws and regulations, and internal control). In addition, the auditor is required to report on the entity's compliance with provisions of the federal programs from whom assistance has been received.

Specific Requirements. Limitations on the use of funds and types of operations and activities that can be conducted with funds received from the federal government. These requirements vary from one program to another and include such matters as the types of services and goods that may be purchased, the eligibility of individuals for receiving federal assistance, and any matching or other requirements of the state or local entity.

Standards for the Practice of Internal Auditing. These standards, established by the IIA, provide guidelines for the planning, performance, and reporting of internal audit engagements. The five major issues addressed by the *Standards* include independence, professional proficiency, scope of work, performance of audit work, and management of the internal audit department.

◉ SUMMARY OF PROFESSIONAL PRONOUNCEMENTS

Codification of Standards for the Professional Practice of Internal Auditing (Altamonte Springs, FL: IIA, 1993).

Statement on Auditing Standards No. 53, "The Auditor's Responsibility to Detect and Report Errors and Irregularities" (New York: AICPA, 1988, AU 316).

Statement on Auditing Standards No. 54, "Illegal Acts by Clients" (New York: AICPA, 1988, AU 317).

Statement on Auditing Standards No. 60, "Communication of Internal Control Structure Related Matters Noted in an Audit" (New York: AICPA, 1988, AU 325).

Statement on Auditing Standards No. 65, "The Auditor's Consideration of the Internal Audit Function in an Audit of Financial Statements" (New York: AICPA, 1991, AU 322).

Statement on Auditing Standards No. 74, "Compliance Auditing Applicable to Governmental Entities and Other Recipients of Governmental Financial Assistance" (New York: AICPA, 1995, AU 801).

QUESTIONS AND PROBLEMS

20-26. Select the **best** answer for each of the following items:

1. Which of the following statements is not true with respect to the auditor's responsibility under *Government Auditing Standards*?

   a. The auditor has the same responsibility for examining the entity's compliance with laws and regulations as in a GAAS audit.
   b. The auditor has a lesser responsibility for examining the entity's compliance with laws and regulations than under the Single Audit Act.
   c. The auditor has a greater reporting responsibility for the entity's internal control than under the Single Audit Act.
   d. The auditor has a greater reporting responsibility for the entity's compliance with laws and regulations than in a GAAS audit.

2. Which of the following would not be considered a general requirement under the Single Audit Act?

   a. Compliance with the Davis-Bacon Act.
   b. Minimizing the time elapsing between receipt and disbursement of funds received from the federal government.
   c. Prohibiting the use of funds for partisan political activities.
   d. Ensuring that recipients of federal assistance meet eligibility requirements specified by the program.

3. In which of the following cases would the auditor provide an opinion in a report resulting from the audit of a governmental entity?

   a. Compliance with specific requirements of major programs.
   b. Compliance with general requirements of major programs.
   c. Compliance with specific requirements of nonmajor programs.
   d. (a) and (b) above.
   e. All of the above.

4. Which of the following best describes the auditor's reporting responsibility for internal control under *Government Auditing Standards* and the Single Audit Act?

	Government Auditing Standards	Single Audit Act
a.	Required	Exception
b.	Exception	Exception
c.	Exception	Required
d.	Required	Required

5. Which of the following statements is true with respect to the auditor's responsibility for examining and reporting on compliance with laws and regulations in a GAAS audit of a governmental entity?

   a. The auditor is primarily concerned with laws and regulations that affect the governmental entity's compliance with federal assistance programs as opposed to their financial statements.
   b. The auditor must issue a separate report on compliance with laws and regulations in a GAAS audit.
   c. The auditor is primarily concerned with the effect of laws and regulations on the entity's financial statements.
   d. The auditor is required to plan the audit to detect all material and immaterial instances of noncompliance with laws and regulations.

6. Which of the following types of reports is not issued in an audit conducted under the Single Audit Act?

   a. An opinion on compliance with specific requirements of major programs.
   b. An opinion on the fairness of the entity's financial statements.
   c. Positive and negative assurance on compliance with general requirements of major and nonmajor programs.
   d. Positive and negative assurance on compliance with specific requirements of nonmajor programs.
   e. All of the above are issued in an audit conducted under the Single Audit Act.

7. Which of the following procedures would normally not be performed in the GAAS audit of a governmental entity?

   a. Obtaining an understanding of the effects of laws and regulations on the governmental entity's financial statements.
   b. Testing compliance with laws and regulations having a material effect on federal financial assistance programs providing funds to the entity.
   c. Obtaining representations from management regarding laws and regulations that materially affect the financial statements.
   d. Providing written communication regarding reportable conditions and material weaknesses noted during the study and evaluation of the entity's internal control.
   e. All of the above are performed in a GAAS audit.

8. Which of the following reporting actions is followed when compliance with laws and regulations is not examined in an audit conducted under *Government Auditing Standards*?

   a. The auditor should issue a disclaimer of opinion on compliance with laws and regulations.
   b. The auditor should not issue any type of report on compliance with laws and regulations.
   c. This situation is not possible because the auditor must examine compliance with laws and regulations in all examinations conducted under Government Auditing Standards.
   d. The auditor should provide negative assurance on compliance with laws and regulations.

9. How is compliance with laws and regulations reported on in an audit conducted under Government Auditing Standards?

   a. A report is not issued unless instances of noncompliance are identified by the auditor.
   b. The auditor issues an opinion on the entity's compliance with laws and regulations.
   c. The auditor issues positive and negative assurance on the entity's compliance with laws and regulations.
   d. The auditor provides a summary of procedures performed and findings with respect to compliance with laws and regulations.

10. When examining major federal financial assistance programs under the Single Audit Act, the auditor examines specific requirements _____ and provides _____ on the entity's compliance with those requirements.

    a. material to the program being examined; an opinion
    b. material to the program being examined; positive and negative assurance
    c. material to the financial statements; an opinion
    d. material to the financial statements; positive and negative assurance

11. In terms of the number of reports that must be prepared by the auditor, which of the following best depicts the relationship between a GAAS audit (1), an audit conducted under *Government Auditing Standards* (2), and an audit conducted under the Single Audit Act (3)?

    a. The greatest number of reports are issued in (1), followed by (2), then (3).
    b. The greatest number of reports are issued in (2), followed by (1), then (3).
    c. The greatest number of reports are issued in (3), followed by (1), then (2).
    d. The greatest number of reports are issued in (3), followed by (2), then (1).

12. Which of the following statements is not included in the auditor's report on internal control prepared under *Government Auditing Standards*?

    a. The auditor has examined the entity's financial statements in accordance with GAAS and *Government Auditing Standards*.
    b. The auditor considered internal control in such a manner as to provide assurance on the organization's internal control.
    c. Identification of all reportable conditions and material weaknesses noted during the examination.
    d. A disclaimer indicating that the consideration of internal control would not necessarily identify all material weaknesses.
    e. All of the above are contained in this report.

13. Which of the following statements is not contained in the auditor's report on compliance with specific requirements of major programs under the Single Audit Act?

    a. The audit was conducted in accordance with GAAS, *Government Auditing Standards*, and OMB Circular A-128.
    b. Management is responsible for compliance with the specific requirements of major programs.
    c. A listing of all material and immaterial instances of noncompliance noted during the examination.
    d. An opinion on the entity's compliance with specific requirements of major programs.
    e. All of the above are contained in this report.

14. For which of the following matters does the auditor have additional audit or reporting responsibility under the Single Audit Act compared to *Government Auditing Standards*?

	Internal Control	Laws and Regulations Affecting Specific Programs
a.	Yes	Yes
b.	No	Yes
c.	No	No
d.	No	Yes

15. Which of the following types of activities are not performed by internal auditors?

    a. Reviewing the reliability and integrity of financial information.
    b. Reviewing systems established by the organization to ensure compliance with policies procedures plans laws and regulations.
    c. Issuing an opinion on the fairness of the entity's financial statements.
    d. Appraising the economy and efficiency with which resources are utilized by the organization.
    e. All of the above are performed by internal auditors.

16. Which of the following procedures is not performed by the auditor in a *Government Auditing Standards* audit?

    a. Planning the audit to provide reasonable assurance that noncompliance with laws and regulations material to the financial statements is detected.
    b. Examining internal control for the purpose of providing assurance on that internal control.
    c. Reporting on the entity's compliance with laws and regulations.
    d. Reporting on the entity's internal control.

17. Which of the following parties would most likely utilize the reports prepared by internal auditors?

    a. The independent auditor.
    b. Third parties external to the organization.
    c. Parties administering federal government programs.
    d. Management of the organization.

18. Which of the following is not one of the major categories of the IIA's *Standards for the Professional Practice of Internal Auditing*?

    a. Independence.
    b. Internal control.
    c. Management of the internal audit department.
    d. Performance of audit work.
    e. Scope of the audit work.

19. Which of the following statements is true with respect to the IIA *Standards*?

    a. Because internal auditors are employed by the organization they examine, independence is not an issue of concern.
    b. Supervision is normally limited to providing instructions to staff auditors at the outset of the examination.
    c. A quality review program requires review of the internal audit department's work by individuals both internal and external to the organization.
    d. The internal auditor must express an opinion on the division being examined or indicate that an opinion cannot be expressed.

20. Audits that focus on the efficiency, economy, and effectiveness of an organization's operations are referred to as:

    a. Compliance audits.
    b. Financial statement audits.
    c. Governmental audits.
    d. Operational audits.
    e. Audits conducted under the Single Audit Act.

20-27. When performing the audit of a governmental entity, the auditor must consider the effect of laws and regulations on that entity's financial statements in various stages of the audit examination.

Required:

Indicate how the auditor considers the effect of laws and regulations in planning the audit, conducting the examination, and reporting on the financial statements of a governmental entity.

20-28. Respond to each of the following statements overheard during the examination of Bart, a state and local governmental entity:

   a. "These governmental audits are much more difficult than audits of a regular corporation. In order to follow GAAS, we have additional responsibilities to detect noncompliance with laws and regulations."
   b. "*Government Auditing Standards* really do not affect the audit too much. All we have to do is issue additional reports without performing any audit procedures beyond a GAAS audit."
   c. "I can see why we need to do extensive testing for nonmajor federal assistance programs. It's important that we be able to support our opinion on compliance with specific and general requirements."
   d. "I don't see why compliance auditing for governmental entities is such a major issue. Governmental entities are not too different from our corporate audit clients."

20-29. One of the major reports required in an audit conducted under *Government Auditing Standards* is a report on the entity's internal control.

Required:

a. What are the three types of deficiencies that may be noted by the auditor in an examination of the entity's internal control? Define each type of deficiency.
b. How are each of the above types of deficiencies reported to the entity?
c. What are some of the more important components of the auditor's report on internal control in an audit conducted under *Government Auditing Standards*?
d. How do the reporting requirements of *Government Auditing Standards* differ from those of GAAS?

20-30. Under the Single Audit Act, the auditor is required to examine and report on various requirements of federal financial assistance programs.

Required:

a. Distinguish between major and nonmajor programs. What are the criteria for classification of a program into these categories?
b. What is the audit responsibility for each type of program? How are transactions selected for examination by the auditor for each type of program?
c. Distinguish between general and specific requirements. Give examples of each.
d. What is the auditor's reporting responsibility for general and specific requirements? Answer this question separately for major and nonmajor programs.

20-31. In audits of governmental entities, additional audit and reporting responsibilities emerge with respect to: (1) laws and regulations affecting the fairness of the entity's financial statements, (2) the organization's internal control, and (3) laws and regulations affecting federal financial assistance programs.

Required:

For each type of audit examination shown below, indicate the appropriate level of audit responsibility and reporting responsibility. Organize your answer in the following format:

GAAS Audit	Audit Responsibility	Reporting Responsibility
1. Laws and regulations affecting the entity's financial statements.		
2. Internal control.		
3. Laws and regulations affecting federal financial assistance programs.		

Audit under Government Auditing Standards

1.
2.
3.

Audit under the Single Audit Act

1.
2.
3.

20-32. Internal auditors provide a wide variety of services to their organizations. In many cases, their functions overlap with duties traditionally performed by external auditors.

Required:

a. Define internal auditing.
b. What types of activities are commonly performed by internal auditors? Classify each of these activities based on the type of auditing it represents.
c. What factors distinguish internal auditors from external auditors?
d. How can the work of internal auditors be used in the financial statement audit by external auditors?

20-33. Respond to the following comments overheard during a discussion of the organization's internal audit function at a divisional manager's meeting.

   a. "I don't know why the internal audit staff insists on examining my area of responsibility. We're about to be audited by our independent CPA firm. It seems like a big waste of time to me."
   b. "How can the internal auditors be independent? They work for the company."
   c. "I'll tell the Chief Financial Officer about that internal auditor snooping around in my area. I know what I'm doing is illegal, but the internal auditor owes this company loyalty. He's just going to have to overlook this particular matter."
   d. "Well, it looks like my dealings with the internal audit department are over. They've given me a list of recommendations. Who's ever going to know whether I actually follow any of these recommendations?"
   e. "It sure would be nice to have outside parties examine our internal audit function, but I just don't think we have the money to do it now."

20-34. Compare compliance auditing, internal auditing, and operational auditing with financial statement auditing. In making this comparison, consider: (1) what individual(s) may perform the examination, (2) the objective(s) of the audit, and (3) the recipients of the auditor's report(s).

Index

-A-

Acceptance of clients, 4-4/5
   and quality control, 2-25
Access controls (computer), 9-14
Account Adjustments Department, 10-13
Accounting and Review Services
   assembly of financial statements, 19-21/22
   comparative reporting, 19-29/30
   compilation engagement, 19-22/25
   downgrading an engagement, 19-31/32
   review engagement, 19-26/29
Accounting changes, 17-17/18
Accounting data, 6-3
Accounting principles
   and Code of Conduct, 2-14
   Interpretations of, 2-30
Accounting Principles Board Opinions
   No. 16, 15-10
   No. 17, 15-10
   No. 18, 15-10
Accounting Research Bulletin No. 43, 15-34, 13-16
Accounting system, 5-17
   Conversion cycle, 14-21; 14-25/27
   Investing and Financing cycle, 15-8
   Purchases and Disbursements cycle, 12-19/20
   Revenue cycle, 10-25; 10-38/40
Accounts payable
   analytical procedures, 13-25
   audit approach, 13-18/19
   computerized processing, 12-22/26; 12-28/29
   control risk, 13-18
   financial statement presentation, 13-25
   inherent risk, 13-18
   Listing of, 13-20/22
   searching for unrecorded, 13-24/26
   substantive tests, 13-18/26
   verifying, 13-22/23
Accounts Payable Department, 12-8/9; 12-24/26
Accounts receivable
   Aged Listing, 11-6
   analytical procedures, 11-14/15

   computerized processing, 10-31/39
   confirmation of, 11-6/11
   control risk, 11-3
   evaluating uncollectible, 11-12/14
   financial statement presentation, 11-15
   inherent risk, 11-3
   substantive tests, 11-4/15
Accrued payables, 13-27/28
Acts discreditable, 2-16/17
   interpretations of, 2-30/31
Adequate documents and records, 5-14
Adjusting journal entries, 6-34/35
Adjustment Request, 10-13
Adverse opinion, 1-21; 17-5
Advertising, 2-17/18
   interpretations of, 2-31
Aged Listing of Accounts Receivable, 11-6
Aggregate error, 16-10
Agreed-upon procedure engagements
   defined, 19-2
   on elements, accounts, or items, 18-14/16
   on prospective financial information, 19-17
Aiding-and-abetting, 3-33
Allowance for sampling risk, 7-5
   incremental, 8-30/31
American Institute of Certified Public Accountants (AICPA), 1-13/14
Analytical procedures
   accounts payable, 13-25
   accounts receivable, 11-14/15
   cash, 11-26
   cost of goods sold, 13-28
   final review, 16-8
   interest-bearing liabilities, 15-28
   inventory, 13-15
   investments, 15-15
   payroll, 14-31
   preliminary, 4-30/32
   property, plant and equipment, 15-23
   purchases, 13-28
   sales, 11-31
   stockholders' equity, 15-34/35

substantive tests, 6-24/26
Application controls, 5-13; 9/17-22
    input, 9-18/20
    master file, 9-22
    output, 9-21/22
    processing, 9-21
    testing, 9-26/29
Application development and maintenance controls, 9-13
Application and Programming Function, 9-12
Assembly engagements, 19-21/22
Assembly Sheets, 6-32
Assertions (management), 4-17/20
    and detection risk, 6-16/18
Assigning authority and responsibility, 5-8/9
Attestation engagements
    compliance with specified requirements, 19-9/11
    defined, 1-5; 19-4
    internal control, 19-4/8
    pro forma financial information, 19-17/19
    prospective financial information, 19-11/17
    standards for, 19-33/34
"Attestation Standards," 19-4; 19-33/34
Attorney letter, 16-5/6
Attribute sampling
    defined, 7-7
    deviations, 7-11
    discovery, 7-30
    evaluating results, 7-22/28
    overview of, 7-7/8
    population, 7-12
    risks associated with, 7-8/10
    sample selection, 7-12
    sample size, 7-15/20
    sampling plan, 7-21/22
    sequential, 7-30/33
Audit Committee, 4-3; 5-7
    communication with after audit, 16-18/20
    communication with during review, 18-24
Audit program, 1-18; 4-32
Audit reports (see Reports)
Audit risk, 4-22
Audit risk model, 4-20/25, 6-1/2
Audit Memoranda, 6-34
Audit sampling (see sampling)
Audit Schedules, 6-32/34
Audit strategy, 5-26; 5-28/29
Audit team, 4-32
Audited account balance, 8-1
Auditing
    around the computer, 9-26
    compliance, 1-9; 20-1/20
    definition, 1-2/3
    internal, 1-8/9; 20-21/29
    operational, 1-8/9; 20-30/32
    overview of, 4-1/2
    purpose of, 1-1/2
    through the computer, 9-26
    types of, 1-8/9

Auditing procedures, 1-22
Auditing standards, 1-15/22
Auditors, 1-9/10
Auditor-submitted document, 18-7/8
Authorization of transactions, 5-14
Available-for-sale securities, 15-9

-B-

Bank Reconciliation, 11-19/24
BarChris case, 3-28/29
Basic precision, 8-30
Basis other than GAAP, 18-10/13
Batch processing, 9-2/4
Batch totals, 9-19
Bates et al. v. State Bar of Arizona, 2-17
Bill of Lading, 10-9
Billing Department, 10-10
Block sampling, 7-15
Board of Directors, 5-7
Board of Directors' Minutes, 15-5
Boards of Accountancy, 1-14
Bonds payable (see interest-bearing liabilities)
Bookkeeping services, 1-12
    and independence, 2-10
Breach of contract, 3-10/11; 3-13
British rule, 3-34
Broker's Advice, 15-13

-C-

Capital expenditure, 15-22
Cascade International, 15-33
Cash
    analytical procedures, 11-26
    Bank Reconciliation, 11-19/24
    computerized processing, 10-36/39; 12-28/29
    control risk, 11-16
    counting, 11-29
    financial statement presentation, 11-30
    inherent risk, 11-16
    kiting, 11-24
    lapping, 11-28
    Proof of Cash, 11-26/28
    Schedule of Interbank Transfers, 11-24/26
    substantive tests, 11-18/30
Cash Disbursements Department, 12-15; 14-7/8
Cash Disbursements Exception Report, 12-26
Cash Disbursements subcycle, 12-15/18; 12-28/29
Cash Receipts subcycle, 10-20/24; 10-26/27; 10-36/39
Cashier, 10-22
Causation defense, 3-15
Ceneco Incorporated v. Seidman and Seidman, 3-41
Central Bank of Denver v. First Interstate Bank of Denver, 3-33
Certified Public Accounting (CPA) Firms, 1-7
Check, 12-15; 14-7
Check digit, 9-18
Check Summary, 12-16; 14-7

CIT v. Glover, 3-17
City of Miami, 1-5
Classical variables sampling
    difference estimation, 8-21/22
    mean-per-unit, 8-9/21
    overview of, 8-4/8
    ratio estimation, 8-22/23
    versus PPS, 8-32/33
Clients, liability to
    cases, 3-37/38
    common law liability, 3-13/16
    overview of, 3-10/11
    tort liability, 3-15/16
Client
    acceptance, 4-4/5
    contact, 4-3/4
    continuance, 4-3/4
    knowledge, 4-8/9
    representations, 6-29; 16-6/8
Code of Conduct, 2-1/31
    enforcement of, 2-23/24
    Ethics Rulings, 2-4/5
    Interpretations, 2-4/5; 2-28/31
    Principles, 2-2/3
    Rules of Conduct, 2-2; 2-6/23
    structure of, 2-2/5
Code of Ethics (IIA), 20-24/25
College Bound, Inc., 11-26
Collusion, 5-24
Comfort letter, 3-25, 18-25
Commissions, 2-19/20
Committee of Sponsoring Organizations (COSO), 5-2/3
Common law liability
    cases, 3-37/38
    to clients and subrogees, 3-13/16
    to third parties, 3-16/22
Comparative financial statements, 17-22/30
Comparisons, 6-28
Compensating balance, 11-30
Competence of evidence, 6-4/5
Compilation engagement
    defined, 19-2; 19-22
    on historical financial information, 19-22/25
    on prospective financial information, 19-14/15
Completeness assertion, 4-19
Compliance
    with contractual agreements, 18-16/17
    with general requirements, 20-17/19
    with laws and regulations, 20-7/8
    with specific requirements, 20-12/17
    with specified requirements, 19-9/11
Compliance auditing
    definition, 20-1
    GAAS audit, 20-2/5
    GAS audit, 20-6/11
    Single Audit Act, 20-11/19
Compliance objective of internal control, 5-4
Components of internal control, 5-5/21

documenting, 5/34/38
    obtaining an understanding of, 5-29/32
Computer Department, organization of, 9-10/13
Computer Operations, 9-13
Computer processing
    assessing control risk, 9-23/32
    computer controls, 9-10/22
    computerized systems, 9-2/6
    Conversion cycle, 14-34/41
    Purchases and Disbursements cycle, 12-22/29
    Revenue cycle, 10-31/39
    versus manual, 9-7/9
Condensed financial information, 18-25/26
Confirmation, 6-23/24
    accounts receivable, 11-6/11
    blank, 11-9
    cash, 11-19/22
    factors affecting, 11-9
    interest-bearing liabilities, 15-27
    inventory, 13-13
    investments, 15-13/14
    negative, 11-8/9
    positive, 11-6; 11-8
    property, plant and equipment, 15-22
    stockholders' equity, 15-33/34
Confidential client information
    definition of, 2-14/15
    Interpretations of, 2-30
    legal liability and, 3-10; 3-14/15
Consistency, 17-18/19
Consolidata Services, Inc. v. Alexander Grant and Company, 3-14
Consulting services, 1-11
    independence and, 2-10/11
Continental Vending case, 3-40
Contingent fees
    definition of, 2-16
    Interpretations of, 2-30
Contingent liabilities, 15-29
Continuance of clients, 4-4/5
    and quality control, 2-25
Continued existence, 17-20/21
Contributory negligence defense, 3-15
Control activities, 5-11/16
    Cash Disbursements subcycle, 12-15/18
    Cash Receipts subcycle, 10-20/24; 10-26/27
    Credit Sales subcycle, 10-5/12; 10-13/14
    Investing and Financing cycle, 15-5/7
    Payroll subcycle, 14-3/10; 14-12/13
    Production subcycle, 14-11; 14-14/24
    Purchases subcycle, 12-3/10; 12-12/13
    Sales Adjustments subcycle, 10-13; 10-16/20
Control environment, 5-6/9
    Conversion cycle, 14-2/3
    Investing and Financing cycle, 15-5
    Purchases and Disbursements cycle, 12-2
    Revenue cycle, 10-4
Control risk
    accounts payable, 13-18

accounts receivable, 11-3
    assessing, 5-35/40
    assessing in computerized environment, 9-23/32
    cash, 11-16
    computerized processing, 9-23/32
    definition of, 4-23/24
    documenting assessments of, 5-46
    final assessments of, 5-45
    inventory, 13-2
    Investing and Financing cycle, 15-1/4
    obtaining an additional reduction of, 5-40/44
    payroll, 14-29
Controls
    application, 5-13/14; 9-17/22
    computer, 9-10/22
    general, 5-12/13; 9-10/16
    information processing, 5-12/14
    performance review, 5-12
    physical, 5-14/15
    segregation of duties, 5-15
    service bureau, 9-29/31
    tests of, 5-31; 5-41/44; 9-26/29
Control total, 9-18/19
Conversion cycle
    computerized processing, 14-34/41
    internal control, 14-1/27
    Payroll subcycle, 14-3/10; 14-12/13
    Production subcycle, 14-11; 14-14/24
    substantive tests, 14-38/33
Corroborating information, 6-3
Cost Accounting Department, 14-18/19
Cost of Goods Sold, 13-28/29
Cost Summary, 14-19
Credit Alliance Corporation and Leasing Services Corporation v. Arthur Andersen & Co., 3-19
Credit Department, 10-8/9
Credit Memorandum, 10-13
Credit sales subcycle, 10-5/12; 10-14/15; 10-31/36
Credit Summary, 10-13
Current file (workpapers), 6-35/36
Customer Order, 10-8
Customer Master File, 10-34
Cutoff Bank Statement, 11-23/24
Cutoff tests
    purchase, 13-29
    sales, 11-31/33

-D-

Dantzler Lumber and Export Co. v. Columbia Casualty Company, 3-15/16
Data or procedural controls, 9-15
Data Control Group, 9-13
Deep-pockets theory, 3-11
Deferred liabilities, 13-27/28
Departure from GAAP, 17-14/18
Departure from promulgated principle, 17-18
Deposit slip, 10-22
Depreciation, 15-22

Detection risk (see also substantive tests)
    accounts payable, 13-18/26
    accounts receivable, 11-4/15
    cash, 11-17/29
    definition of, 4-24
    determining, 5-46/47; 6-10/13
    factors affecting, 6-13/16
    inventory, 13-2/17
    Investing and Financing cycle, 15-1/4
    management assertions and, 6-16/18
    payroll, 14-30/33
Deviation, 5-41; 7-8; 7-11
Deviation rate, 5-45
    population, 7-8
    sample, 7-22
    tolerable, 7-6
Difference estimation sampling, 8-21/22
Disclaimer of opinion, 1-21; 17-5
Discovery sampling, 7/30
Division of responsibility, 17-10/14
Documents, 5-14; 6-20/22
    tests of controls, 5-42
Documenting understanding of internal control, 5-34/38
Dual-date, 16-13/14
Dual-purpose tests, 5-42; 6-22
Due diligence, 3-25; 3-27
Due professional care, 1-17

-E-

Earnings Record, 14-7
Echo check, 9-14
EDP Manager, 9-12
EDP processing (see computer processing)
Elements, accounts, or items, 18-13/16
1136 Tenants' Corporation case, 3-38
Emphasis of a matter, 17-21
Engagement acceptance, 2-25; 4-4/5
Engagement letter, 3-14; 4-5/7
Engagement performance, 2-25
Equity Funding case, 3-40
Ernst & Ernst v. Hochfelder, 3-31/32
Error, 4-9/12
    known, 16-10
    likely, 16-10
    projected, 8-30; 16-10
Error correction routine, 9-20
Escott v. BarChris Construction Company, 3-27/28
Estimates, 6-27/28
Ethical values, 5-7
Ethics Rulings, of Code of Conduct, 2-4/5
Evidence (see substantive tests), 1-19; 6-3/6
Examination engagement
    defined, 19-1
    on prospective financial information, 19-15/16
Exception, 5-41; 7-8
Exception-based reporting, 18-13
Exception rate, 5-45

Existence and occurrence assertion, 4-18
Extent of substantive tests, 6-16
Exxon *Valdez*, 10-10

-F-

Fidelity and Deposit Company of Maryland v. Atherton, 3-16
Field work, standards of, 1-17/18; 6-2
Financial accounting, 1-1/2
Financial forecast, 19-11/12
Financial objective of internal control, 5-3
Financial projection, 19-12
Financial statement presentation, evaluating
    accounts payable, 13-25
    accounts receivable, 11-15
    cash, 11-30
    interest-bearing liabilities, 15-29
    inventory, 13-17
    investments, 15-16
    property, plant and equipment, 15-23/24
    stockholders' equity, 15-35
Financial statements
    basis other than GAAP, 18-10/13
    comparative, 17-22/30
    prepared in conformity with contractual agreements, 18-17/18
    prepared for use in other countries, 18-20/21
    special-purpose, 18-17/18
Flowchart, 5-34/36; 5-38
Foreign Corrupt Practices Act, 5-22/23
Foreseeable third parties, 3-20
Foreseen third parties, 3-20
Form of practice and name, 2-21/23
    Interpretations of, 2/31
Fraud
    accountant liability for, 3-12
    communicating, 4-40
    definition of (auditor), 3-12
    definition of (client), 4-36
    effect on substantive tests, 4-39/40
    factors affecting, 4-37/39
Fraudulent financial reporting, 4-36; 4-37/38
Full and fair disclosure, 3-23
Fund of Funds Limited v. Arthur Andersen & Co., 3-15

-G-

General controls, 5-12/13; 9-10/16
    access controls, 9-14
    application development and maintenance controls, 9-13
    data or procedural controls, 9-15
    hardware controls, 9-14
    organization of the Computer Department, 9-10/13
    testing, 9-25/26
General Function
    Cash Disbursements subcycle, 12-16
    Cash Receipts subcycle, 10-22
    Credit Sales subcycle, 10-11
    Payroll subcycle, 14-7
    Production subcycle, 14-19
    Purchases subcycle, 12-9
General standards, 1-16/17
    Interpretations, 2-30
    Rule 201, 2-12
General requirements, 20-17/19
General use, 19-2; 19-13
Generalized Audit Software, 7-32/36
Generally Accepted Accounting Principles (GAAP), 1-3
    basis other than, 18-10/13
    reporting for departures under, 17-14/18
Generally Accepted Auditing Standards
    definition, 1-15; 1-21
    general standards, 1-16/17
    reporting standards, 1-19/21; 17-4/5
    standards of field work, 1-18/19
Good faith defense, 3-31
Government Accounting Standards Board, 20-3
Government Auditing Standards, 20-6/11
Government entity
    GAAS audit of, 20-2/6
    GAS audit of, 20-6/11
    Single Audit Act and, 20-11/19
Grandfather-father-son, 9-15
Gross negligence, 3-12

-H-

Haphazard sampling, 7-15
Hardware controls, 9-14
Hash totals, 9-19
Held-to-maturity securities, 15-9
Hochfelder case, 3-31/32
Hollinger v. Titan Capital Corp., 3-32
Human error, 5-24
Human resource policies and practices, 5-9

-I-

Illegal acts, 4-12
Inadequate disclosures, reporting, 17-16/17
Incorrect acceptance, risk of, 8-2/4; 8-36/37
Incorrect rejection, risk of, 8-2/4; 8-34/35
Incremental allowance for sampling risk, 8-30/31
Independence, 1-17
    bookkeeping services and, 2-10
    consulting services and, 2-10/11
    family relationships and, 2-8/9
    in appearance, 2-6
    in fact, 2-6
    loans and, 2-9/10
    member and member's firm and, 2-7/8
    other issues and, 2-11
    quality control, 2-25

reporting, 17-21
Rule 101, 2-6/11
Independent checks on performance, 5-14
Information and communication, 5-17/18
    Conversion cycle, 14-21; 14-25/27
    Investing and Financing cycle, 15-8
    Purchases and Disbursements cycle, 12-19/20
    Revenue cycle, 10-25; 10-38/30
Information processing controls, 5-12/14
    Cash Disbursements subcycle, 12-15/16
    Cash Receipts subcycle, 10-20/23
    Credit Sales subcycle, 10-8/11
    Investing and Financing cycle, 15-5/6
    Payroll subcycle, 14-3/8
    Production subcycle, 14-11;14-14/19
    Purchases subcycle, 12-3/10
Information system, 5-17
Inherent risk
    accounts payable, 13-18
    accounts receivable, 14-29
    cash, 11-16
    definition, 4-22/23
    interest-bearing liabilities, 15-24
    inventory, 13-2
    investments, 15-10
    payroll, 14-29
    property, plant and equipment, 15-17/18
    stockholders' equity, 15-30
Input controls, 9-18/20
Inquiry (oral), 6-28/29
    as test of controls, 5-42
Inspecting
    cash, 11-29
    interest-bearing liabilities, 15-27
    investments, 15-13/14
    property, plant and equipment, 15-21/22
    stockholders' equity, 15-33/34
Institute of Internal Auditors (IIA), 20-21
Integrated Test Facility (ITF), 9-28
Integrity, 2-11; 5-17
    Interpretations, 2-29/30
    quality control, 2-25
Interactive processing, 9-4/6
Interest-bearing liabilities
    analytical procedures, 15-28
    audit approach, 15-24
    confirming, 15-27
    financial statement presentation, 15-29
    inspecting, 15-27
    interest expense, 15-28
    Listing of Interest-Bearing Liabilities, 15-24/26
    substantive tests, 15-24/29
    unrecorded liabilities, 15-28
    verifying transactions, 15-27
Interest expense, 15-28
Interim financial information, 18-21/24
Interim tests, 5-43
Internal auditing
    Code of Ethics, 20-24/25
    definition of, 20-21/22
    effect on audit examination, 4-28/30
    role in organization, 20-22/23
    standards, 20-25/29
    versus external auditing, 20-23/24
Internal control
    auditor responsibility for, 5-21/23
    components of, 5-5/21
    Conversion cycle, 14-1/27; 14-34/41
    COSO and, 5-2/3
    deficiencies, 5-47; 5-49; 16-16/19; 20-8
    definition of, 1-18; 5-3
    effect on substantive tests
        accounts payable, 13-19
        accounts receivable, 11-4
        cash, 11-17
        inventory, 13-3; 14-28
        Investing and Financing cycle, 15-1/4
        payroll, 14-30
    example of, 5-24/25
    Foreign Corrupt Practices Act, 5-22/23
    Investing and Financing cycle, 15-4/9
    limitations of, 5-24
    management's responsibility for, 5-23
    objectives of, 5-3/4
    Purchases and Disbursements cycle, 12-1/29
    reporting on, 5-49/50; 19-4/8
    reporting on, in GAS audit, 20-7/10
    Revenue cycle, 5-2/39
    service bureau, 9-29/31
    studying, 5-26/47
Internal control questionnaire, 5-34/35; 5-37
Interpretations of Code of Conduct, 2-4/5; 2-28/29
Introductory paragraph, 1-19; 17-2
Inventory
    analytical procedures, 13-15
    computerized processing, 10-31/36; 12-22/26; 14-34/41
    confirming, 13-13
    consigned, 13-15/16
    control risk, 13-2
    financial statement presentation, 13-17
    inherent risk, 13-2
    Inventory Listing, 13-5
    lower of cost or market and, 13-16/17
    observing physical counts, 13-5/12
    price tests, 13-13/15
    substantive tests, 13-5/17; 14-28/29
Inventory Department, 10-9/10; 12-3; 12-6; 14-16/18
Inventory Observation Memorandum, 13-11
Investing and Financing cycle
    audit approach, 15-1/4
    interest-bearing liabilities, 15-24/29
    internal control, 15-4/9
    investments, 15-9/16
    property, plant and equipment, 15-16/24
    stockholders' equity, 15-30/35
    substantive tests, 15-9/35

Investments
    analytical procedures, 15-15
    audit approach, 15-9/10
    confirming, 15-13/14
    financial statement presentation, 15-16
    inspecting, 15-13/14
    Listing of Securities, 15-10/12
    market values, 15-14/15
    revenue accounts, 15-15
    substantive tests, 15-9/16
    verifying transactions, 15-13
Invoicing Program, 10-35
Irregularities, 4-9/12

-J-

Job Cost Sheet, 14-17
Joint-and-several liability, 3-34

-K-

Kiting, 11-24
Knowledge of clients, 4-8/9
Known error, 16-10
Kroger Co., 12-8

-L-

Labor Distribution Report, 14-6
Landell v. Lybrand, 3-17
Lapping, 11-28
Laribee Wire Manufacturing Company, 13-12
Lead Schedules, 6-32
    of Cash Balances, 11-19
Legal liability
    common law, 6-13/22
    overview of, 3-10/12
    statutory liability, 3-23/31
Letter of inquiry, 16-5/6
Likely error, 16-10
Limitations of internal control, 5-24
Limited assurance, 19-2; 19-21
Limited use, 19-2; 19-13
Limited liability partnership, 2-22; 3-34
Limits or reasonableness tests, 9-19
Listing
    of accounts payable, 13-20/22
    of accounts receivable, 11-6
    of interest-bearing liabilities, 15-24/26
    of inventory, 13-5
    of property, plant and equipment, 15-18/19
    of securities, 15-10; 15-12
Long-term liabilities (see interest-bearing liabilities)
Lower of cost or market, 13-16/17

-M-

Mailroom, 10-20
Major program, 20-12
Management assertions, 4-17/20

    detection risk and, 6-16/18
Management letter, 16-20/24
Management override, 5-24
Management philosophy and operating style, 5-7/8
Management representations (see client representations)
Manager, 1-7/8
Maryland Casualty Co. v. Jonathan Cook, 3-14
Master file, 9-4; 9/22
Material weakness, 5-4; 16-17; 20-8
Materiality, 4-14/16
Materials Requisition, 14-11
McKesson and Robbins case, 3-39
McLean v. Alexander, 3-40/41
Mean-per-unit estimation, 8-9/21
Member and member's firm, 2-7/8
Miniscribe, 11-14; 11-33; 13-17
Misappropriation of assets, 4-37; 4-38/39
Monitoring, 5-18; 5-20
    Conversion cycle, 14-27
    Investing and Financing cycle, 15-8/9
    Purchases and Disbursements cycle, 12-20
    quality control and, 2-25
    Revenue cycle, 10-30

-N-

Narrative, 5-34; 5-37
National Commission on Fraudulent Financial Reporting, 5-2/3; 20-12
National Student Marketing case, 3-39
National Surety Corporation v. Lybrand, 3-37
Nature of substantive tests, 6-14
Niagara Mowhawk Power Corporation, 9-9
Nonmajor programs, 20-16/17
Nonreportable conditions, 20-8
Nonpublic companies, 1-4
Nonsampling risk, 7-3
Nonstatistical sampling, 7-3/4; 7-29/30; 8-38/40
Normal distribution, 8-4/6
Notes payable (see interest-bearing liabilities)

-O-

Objectivity, 2-11
    Interpretations of, 2-29/30
Observation, 6-19/20
    cash, 11-29
    interest-bearing liabilities, 15-27
    inventory, 13-5/12
    investments, 15-1314
    property, plant and equipment, 15-21/22
    stockholders' equity, 15-33/34
    substantive tests, 6-19/20
    test of controls, 5-42
Off-site peer review, 2-26
OMB Circular A-128, 20-11
OMB Circular A-133, 20-11
Omitted procedures, 16-14/16

O'Neil v. Atlas Automobile Finance Corporation, 3-37
On-site peer review, 2-26
Operating cycles
    Conversion cycle, 14-1/40
    definition, 10-1/2
    Investing and Financing cycle, 15-1/35
    Purchases and Disbursements cycle, 12-1/29
    Revenue cycle, 10-1/39
Operating objective of internal control, 5-4
Operational auditing, 1-8/9; 20-30/32
Opinion paragraph, 1-20; 17-2
Opinion shopping, 4-3
Opinions, types of, 1-20/21; 17-5
Oral inquiry, 6-28/29
Order Department, 10-8/9
Ordinary negligence, 3-11
Organization of the Computer Department, 9-10/13
Organization structure, 5-8
Output controls, 9-21/22
Overhead Ticket, 14-18
Overreliance, risk of, 7-8/10

-P-

Parallel simulation, 9-28
Parity check, 9-14
Partner, 1-7
Payment agency, 15-30
Payroll Check, 14-7
Payroll Department, 14-5/7
Payroll Exception Report, 14-36
Payroll Register, 14-6
    substantive tests, 14-29/33
Payroll subcycle, 14-3/10; 14-12/13; 14-34/37
Peer review, 1-13; 2-25/27; 16-14
Performance reviews, 5-12
    Cash Disbursements subcycle, 12-17/18
    Cash Receipts subcycle, 10-24
    Credit Sales subcycle, 10-12
    Investing and Financing cycle, 15-7
    Payroll subcycle, 14-9
    Production subcycle, 14-20
    Purchases subcycle, 12-10/11
Permanent file (workpapers), 6-37
Personnel Authorization Form, 14-3
Personnel Department, 14-3/5
Personnel management, 2-25
Phar-Mor, Inc., 1-23; 13-12
Physical controls, 5-14/15
    Cash Disbursements subcycle, 12-16/17
    Cash Receipts subcycle, 10-23/24
    Credit Sales subcycle, 10-11/12
    Investing and Financing cycle, 15-6/7
    Payroll subcycle, 14-8/9
    Production subcycle, 14-20
    Purchases subcycle, 12-10
Physical observation, 6-19/20 (see observation)
Planning, 1-18; 4-8/35

Population deviation rate, 7-8
Precision, 7-5
Precision interval, 7-4
Predecessor auditor, 4-5
Preengagement procedures, 4-3/7
Preliminary audit strategy, 5-26; 5-28/29
Prescribed forms, 18-18
Presentation and disclosure assertion, 4-20
Price tests for inventory, 13-13/15
Primary beneficiary, 3-16/17
Principal auditor, 17-10
Private Companies Practice Section, 1-14
Privity, 3-11; 3-14
Probabilistic selection techniques, 7-3
Probability-Proportional-to-Size Sampling (PPS)
    defined, 8-25
    evaluating results, 8-29/32
    sample size, 8-26/27
    selecting sample, 8-27/29
    versus classical variables sampling, 8-32/33
Processing controls, 9-21
Production Department, 14-16/18
Production Order, 14-11
Production Planning Department, 14-11; 14-16
Production Report, 14-17
Production subcycle, 14-11/24; 14-37/41
Professional corporation, 2-21/22
Pro forma financial information, 19-17/19
Program (audit), 4-32
Projected error, 8-30; 16-10
Proof of Cash, 11-26/28
Property, plant and equipment
    analytical procedures, 15-23
    audit approach, 15-17/18
    depreciation, 15-22
    financial statement presentation, 15-23/24
    inspecting, 15-21/22
    Listing of PPE, 15-18
    subsequent expenditures, 15-22
    substantive tests, 15-17/24
    verifying transactions, 15-18/21
Proportionate liability, 3-34
Prospective financial information, 19-11/17
Prospectus, 3-24
Public accounting, 1-7/12
Public companies, 1-4
Public practice, 2-6
Purchase cutoff tests, 13-29
Purchases, substantive tests, 13-28/29
Purchases and Disbursements cycle
    accounts payable, 13-18/26
    accrued payables/deferred assets, 13-27/28
    audit approach, 13-1/2
    Cash Disbursements subcycle, 12-11; 12-14/18
    computerized processing in, 12-22/29
    cost of goods sold/purchases, 13-28/29
    internal control, 12-1/28
    inventory, 13-18/26

Purchases subcycle, 12-3/10; 12-12/13
   substantive tests, 13-5/29
Purchase Order, 12-6
Purchase Requisition, 12-6
Purchases subcycle, 12-3/10; 12-12/13; 12-22/26
Purchasing Department, 12-6; 12-22/23
Purchasing Exception Report, 12-23

-Q-

Qualified opinion, 1-20; 17-5
Questioned cost, 20-14
Questionnaire (internal control), 5-34/35; 5-37

-R-

Racketeer Influenced and Corrupt Organization Act (RICO), 3-33
Random number table, 7-12/13
Random sampling, 7-12/13
Ratio estimation, 8-22/23
Raw Materials Inventory Department, 14-16
Reasonable assurance, 5-9/10
Recalculation, 6-27/28
Receiving Department, 12-7/8; 12-23/24
Receiving Exception Report, 12-23
Receiving Report, 10-13; 12-8
Record count, 9-18/19
Registrar, 15-30
Registration of securities, 3-24/25
Registration statement, 3-24/25
Reissuing a report, 17-27
Related parties, 4-25/27
Relevance of evidence, 6-5
Reliability, 7-5
Reliance approach, 5-28/29
Remittance Advice, 10-20
Remittance Listing, 10-20
Reperformance, 5-42
Reportable conditions, 5-49; 16-17; 20-8
Reporting standards, 1-19/21; 17-4/5
Reports
   assembly of financial statements, 19-11/17
   auditor-submitted documents, 18-7/8
   comfort letters, 18-25
   comparative financial statements, 17-22/30
   compliance with specified requirements, 19-9/11
   compilation, 19-22/25
   condensed financial information, 18-25/26
   consistency, 17-18/19
   departure from GAAP, 17-14/18
   departure from promulgated principles, 17-18
   division of responsibility, 17-10/14
   dual-dating, 16-13/14
   emphasis of a matter, 17-21
   financial statements used in other countries, 18-20/21
   Government Auditing Standards audit, 20-12/19
   independence, 17-21
   information prepared by the client, 18-2/3
   interim financial information, 18-21/24
   internal control, 5-49/50; 19-4/8
   opinions, 17-5
   pro forma financial information, 19-17/19
   prospective financial information, 19-11/17
   review, 19-26/29
   scope limitations, 17-6/10
   segment information, 18-3/5
   selected financial data, 18-25/26
   special-purpose financial statements, 18-17/18
   special reports, 18-10/18
   standard report, 1-19/20; 17-2/3
   supplementary information, 18-6/7
   uncertainties, 17-19/21
Restatement of Torts, 3-19/20
Retained earnings, 15-34
Revenue cycle
   accounts receivable, 11-3/15
   audit approach, 11-1/3
   cash, 11-15/30
   Cash Receipts subcycle, 10-20/24; 10-26/27
   computerized processing in, 10-31/39
   Credit Sales subcycle, 10-5/12; 10-14/15
   internal control, 10-2/39
   sales, 11-30/33
   Sales Adjustments subcycle, 10-13; 10-16/20
   substantive tests, 11-3/33
Revenue expenditures, 15-22
Review engagement
   definition of, 19-1/2
   historical financial information, 19-26/29
   interim financial information, 18-21/24
Review of workpapers, 6-38; 16-9/10
Rhode Island Hospital Trust National Bank v. Swartz, 3-37
Rights and obligations assertion, 4-18/19
Risk
   of assessing control risk too high, 7-8/10
   of assessing control risk too low, 7-8/10
   of incorrect acceptance, 8-2/4; 8-36/37
   of incorrect rejection, 8-2/4; 8-34/35
   of overreliance, 7-8/10
   of underreliance, 7-8/10
Risk assessment, 5-9/10
   Cash Disbursements subcycle, 12-15/18
   Cash Receipts subcycle, 10-20/24; 10-26/27
   Credit Sales subcycle, 10-5/12; 10-13/14
   Investing and Financing cycle, 15-5/7
   Payroll subcycle, 14-3/10; 14-12/13
   Production subcycle, 14-11; 14-14/24
   Purchases subcycle, 12-3/10; 12-12/13
   Sales Adjustments subcycle, 10-13; 10-16/20
Rosenblum v. Adler, 3-20
Rule 10b-5, 3-31
Rules of Conduct, 2-2; 2-6/23
   Interpretations of, 2-28/31
   Rule 101 (Independence), 2-6/11
   Rule 102 (Integrity and Objectivity), 2-11/12

Rule 201 (General Standards), 2-12
Rule 202 (Compliance with Standards), 2-12/13
Rule 203 (Accounting Principles), 2-14; 17-18
Rule 301 (Confidential Client Information), 2-14/15
Rule 302 (Contingent Fees), 2-16
Rule 501 (Acts Discreditable), 2-16/17
Rule 502 (Advertising), 2-17/18
Rule 503 (Commissions), 2-19/20
Rule 505 (Form of Practice and Name), 2-21/23
Rusch Factors, Inc. v. Levin, 3-19

-S-

Sales, substantive tests, 11-30/33
Sales Adjustments subcycle, 10-13; 10-16/20; 10-36/39
Sales Cutoff tests, 11-31/33
Sales Invoice, 10-10
Sales Order, 10-8
Sales Order Exception Report, 10-34
Sales Register, 11-30/31
Sales Summary, 10-10
Sample deviation rate, 7-22
Sample selection
 attribute, 7-12/15
 block, 7-15
 classical variables, 8-17
 haphazard, 7-15
 PPS, 8-27/29
 stratified, 8-17
 systematic, 7-14/15
 unrestricted random, 7-12/13
Sample size
 in attribute sampling, 7-15/20
 in classical variables sampling, 8-10/16
 in PPS sampling, 8-26/27
Sampling
 attribute, 7-7/29
 classical variables, 8-4/24
 defined, 7/2
 difference estimation, 8-21/22
 discovery, 7-30
 mean-per-unit, 8-9/21
 nonstatistical, 7-3/4; 7-29/30; 8-38/40
 PPS, 8-24/33
 ratio, 8-22/23
 sequential, 7-30/33
 statistical, 7-3/4
 stratified, 8-17
 variables, 8-1/40
Sampling risk
 attribute, 7-8/10
 controlling, 8-34/37
 defined, 7-3; 8-2
 variables, 8-2/4
Schedule of Changes in Stockholders' Equity, 15-31/32
Schedule of Interbank Transfers, 11-24/26

Scienter, 3-32
Scope limitation, 17-6/10
Scope paragraph, 1-19; 17-2
Second-partner review, 1-13; 16-10
Securities Act of 1933, 3-24/25; 3-27/29; 18-24/25
Securities and Exchange Commission, 1-14/15; 3-23/24
Securities and Exchange Commission Practice Section, 1-13/14
Securities Exchange Act of 1934, 3-26; 3-30/32
Segment information, 18-3/5
Segregation of duties, 5-15
 Cash Disbursements subcycle, 12-16
 Cash Receipts subcycle, 10-23
 Credit Sales subcycle, 10-11
 Investing and Financing cycle, 15-6
 Payroll subcycle, 14-8
 Production subcycle, 14-19
 Purchases subcycle, 12-10
 Sales Adjustments subcycle, 10-17
Senior accountants, 1-8
Sequential sampling, 7-30/33
Service auditor, 9-29
Service bureau, 9-29
Shipping Department, 10-9/10
Shipping Document, 10-9
Shipping Exception Report, 10-34
Single Audit Act, 20-12/19
Sirota (Howard) v. Solitron Devices, Inc., 3-41
Skip interval, 7-14
Smith v. London Assurance Corp., 3-37
Solicitation, 2-17
 Interpretations of, 2-31
Specialists, 4-27/28
Special-purpose financial statements, 18-17/18
Special reports
 basis other than GAAP, 18-10/13
 compliance with contractual agreements, 18-16/17
 elements, accounts, or items, 18-13/16
 financial statements prepared in conformity with contractual requirements, 18-17/18
 prescribed forms, 18-18
Specific requirements, 20-12/17
Staff accountants, 1-8
Staffing, 4-33/34
Standard deviation, 8-7
Standards of field work, 1-17/18
Standards of internal auditing, 20-25/28
Standards of reporting, 1-19/21
State societies of CPAs, 1-14
Statement of Financial Accounting Standards
 Code of Conduct and, 2-13
 SFAS No. 5, 15-29; 17-19
 SFAS No. 14, 18-3
 SFAS No. 47, 15-29
 SFAS No. 57, 4-25/27
 SFAS No. 105, 15-29
 SFAS No. 121, 15-23

Statement of Quality Control Standards
    SQCS No. 2, 2-25; 4-4
Statement on Auditing Standards
    Code of Conduct and, 2-13
    defined, 1-21
    SAS No. 1, 1-4; 1-16; 4-4; 13-5; 5-21
    SAS No. 8, 18-2
    SAS No. 12, 16-5
    SAS No. 19, 6-29, 16-6
    SAS No. 21, 18-3/4
    SAS No. 22, 4-8/9
    SAS No. 26, 17-4
    SAS No. 29, 18-7
    SAS No. 31, 6-3; 6-16
    SAS No. 32, 17-7
    SAS No. 39, 7-2
    SAS No. 41, 6-31
    SAS No. 42, 18-26
    SAS No. 43, 13-13
    SAS No. 45, 6-15
    SAS No. 46, 16-15
    SAS No. 47, 4-14; 4-20/25; 8-13; 16-10
    SAS No. 48, 9-1; 9-10
    SAS No. 51, 18-20
    SAS No. 52, 18-6, 18-7
    SAS No. 53, 4-9; 20-3
    SAS No. 54, 4-12; 20-3
    SAS No. 55, 5-35; 5-43
    SAS No. 56, 4-30/32; 6-24/26; 16-8
    SAS No. 57, 6-27/28; 11/14
    SAS No. 58, 17-6; 17-22
    SAS No. 59, 17-20
    SAS No. 60, 5-20; 5-48; 16-17; 20-9; 20-30
    SAS No. 61, 4-4; 16-18
    SAS No. 62, 18-9; 18-13; 18-17
    SAS No. 65, 4-28/30
    SAS No. 67, 6-23; 11-6
    SAS No. 70, 7-29
    SAS No. 71, 18-22/23
    SAS No. 72, 18-25
    SAS No. 73, 4-27/28; 13-7
    SAS No. 74, 20-1
    SAS No. 75, 18-9; 18-15; 19-17
    SAS No. 76, 3-25; 18-25
    SAS No. 77, 4-32; 17-21
    SAS No. 78, 5-3; 5-6; 5-9; 5-11; 5-17/18
    SAS No. 79, 17-20
Statements on Standards for Accounting and Review Services (SSARS)
    SSARS No. 1, 19-22/24; 19-28
    SSARS No. 2, 19-20; 19-29
    SSARS No. 3, 19-25
    SSARS No. 4, 19-30
    SSARS No. 7, 19-26
Statements on Standards for Attestation Engagements (SSAE)
    defined, 19-4
    SSAE No. 1, 1-4; 16-9; 19-12; 19-14; 19-16/17; 19-19

SSAE No. 2, 19-5
SSAE No. 3, 19-10
SSAE No. 4, 19-17
SSAE No. 6, 19-5
State Street Trust Co. v. Ernst, 3-18
Statistical sampling, 7-3/4
Statutory liability, 3-23/33; 3-39/41
Stockholders' equity
    analytical procedures, 15-34/35
    audit approach, 15-30
    confirmation, 15-33/34
    financial statement presentation, 15-35
    inspecting, 15-33/34
    retained earnings, 15-34
    Schedule of Changes in Stockholders' Equity, 15-31/32
    substantive tests, 15-30/35
    verifying transactions, 15-32/33
Stop-and-go sampling, 7-30/33
Stratified sampling, 8-17
Studying internal control
    determining detection risk, 5-46/47
    documenting control risk assessments, 5-46
    documenting understanding of internal control, 5-34/38
    making a final assessment of control risk, 5/45
    making an initial assessment of control risk, 5-35/40
    obtaining an additional reduction of control risk, 5-40/44
    selecting a preliminary audit strategy, 5-26/29
    understanding the internal control, 5-29/32
Submitting financial statements, 19-31
Subrogee, 3-13
    liability to, 3-13/16
Subsequent discovery of facts, 16-13/14
Subsequent event, 16-1/5
Substantive approach, 5-26; 5-27/29
Substantive tests
    accounts
        accounts payable, 13-18/26
        accounts receivable, 11-4/15
        cash, 11-18/30
        interest-bearing liabilities, 15-24/29
        inventory, 13-5/17; 14-28/29
        investments, 15-9/16
        payroll, 14-29/33
        property, plant and equipment, 15-17/24
        sales, 11-30/32
        stockholders' equity, 15-30/35
    defined, 5-21
    detection risk and, 6-10/18
    extent of, 6-16
    general approaches to, 6-7/10
    governmental audit, 20-4
    nature of, 6-14
    overview, 6-2/6
    procedures, 6-18/30
    timing of, 6-15/16

workpapers, 6-30/38
Successor auditor, 4-5
Sundstrand Corp. v. Sun Chemical Corp., 3-32
Sufficiency of evidence, 6-4/5
Supervision, 4-33/34
Supervisor, 1-7/8
Supplemental information, 18-6/7
Systematic sampling, 7-14/15

-T-

Tagging, 9-29
Tax services, 1-10
Test data, 9-26/28
Test of balances, 6-7/8
    accounts payable, 13-18/19
    accounts receivable, 11-4
    cash, 11-16/17
    inventory, 13-1/2
Test of transactions, 6-8/10
    interest-bearing liabilities, 15-27
    Investing and Financing cycle, 15-3/4
    investments, 15-13
    property, plant and equipment, 15-18; 15-21
    purchases, 13-28
    sales, 11-30/31
    stockholders' equity, 15-32/33
Tests of controls, 5-31; 5-41/44
Third parties, liability to
    common law, 3-16/22; 3-38
    overview, 3-10/11
    statutory liability, 3-23/33; 3-39/41
Timekeeping Department, 14-5/6
Time Sheets, 14-5
Timing of substantive tests, 6-15/16
Tolerable deviation rate, 7-6
Tolerable error, 8-1
Tort liability, 3-11
    cases involving, 3-37/41
    to clients and subrogees, 3-15/16
    to third parties under common law, 3-16/22; 3-38
    to third parties under statutory liability, 3-23/33; 3-39/41
Tracing, 6-21
Trading securities, 15-9
Training and proficiency, 1-17
Transfer Agent, 15-30
Transfer Ticket, 14-17
Treadway Commission, 5-2/3
Treasurer, 12-15; 14-7/8

-U-

Ultramares, 3-17/18
Unaudited financial statements, 1-11
Uncertainties, 17-19/21
Uncollectible accounts, 11-12/14
Underlying accounting data, 6-3

Underreliance, risk of, 7-8/10
Understanding of internal control components, 5-29/32
Underwriters, 18-24/25
Unqualified opinion, 1-20; 17-5
Unrecorded liabilities
    accounts payable, 13-24/26
    accrued liabilities, 13-27/28
    interest-bearing liabilities, 15-28
Unrestricted random sampling, 7-12/13
Updating a report, 17-24; 17-27
Upper precision limit, 7-6; 7-22/26
User auditor, 9-29
User Department, 9-11

-V-

Valid character check, 9-14
Validity checks, 9-20
Validity of evidence, 6-5
Valuation and allocation assertion, 4-19/20
Variables sampling
    classical variables, 8-4/24
    definition, 8-1
    difference estimation, 8-21/22
    evaluating results, 8-18
    mean-per-unit, 8-9/21
    nonstatistical, 8-38/40
    ratio estimation, 8-22/23
    sample selection, 8-17
    sample size, 8-10/16
    sampling plan, 8-18
    sampling risks, 8-2/4; 8-34/37
    sampling technique, 8-10
Vendor Invoice, 12-8
Voucher, 12-9
Voucher Exception Report, 12-25
Voucher Register
    substantive tests, 13-28
Vouching, 6-21

-W-

Walk-through, 5-31
Working Trial Balance, 6-32
Workpapers
    definition, 6-30/31
    filing of, 6-35, 6-37
    ownership and custody of, 6-37/38
    review of, 6-38; 16-9/10
    types of, 6-31/35
Written representations (see client representations)

-XYZ-

Yale Express case, 3-40
Yellow Book, 20-6/11